Fodor's 2016

ENGLAND

ABOUT OUR WRITERS

Longtime contributor **Robert Andrews** loves warm beer and soggy moors, but hates scavenging seagulls and the sort of weather when you're not sure if it's raining—all of which he found in abundance while updating the West Country chapter. He writes and revises other guidebooks and has penned his own guide to Devon and Cornwall.

Jo Caird is a travel and arts journalist who writes on theater, visual arts, film, literature, and food and drink, as well as cycling and scuba diving. For this edition, she updated the Nightlife and Performing Arts section of the London chapter, as well as several neighborhoods.

A leading family travel expert, Manchester-based writer **Rhonda Carrier** writes for publications like National Geographic Traveller, The Guardian, and CondéNast Traveller, as well as serving as comissioning editor for TaketheFamily.com. She updated the Manchester, Liverpool, and the Peak District chapter this edition.

Julius Honnor lives in London, but his Fodor's beat included rural spots in the Lake District, where he has observed chic new hotels and restaurants popping up alongside more traditional places. His work for other guidebooks has taken him around the globe.

Writer and editor **Kate Hughes** acquired a liking for the big city when she studied classical literature in Liverpool. Having since indulged her penchant for the country and landed gentry by getting a master's in garden history, she feels qualified to pass judgment on matters both urban and rural. She is responsible for the Experience England and Bath and the Cotswolds chapters, as well as the sections on Stratford-upon-Avon and Shakespeare Country.

A Londoner since public transportation was cheap, **Jack Jewers** has directed films for the BBC and reviewed pubs for *Time Out;* he also makes independent films. He updated the Southeast, Thames Valley, East Anglia, Northeast, and Wales chapters, as well as the non-Stratford portions of the Stratford-upon-Avon and the Heart of England chapter. Jack is also responsible for the Where to Stay section of London and several London neighborhoods.

James O'Neill loves London and—as his work updating several neighborhood sections for this edition proves—loves rediscovering it, too. Although originally from Ireland, he's lived in London for almost 20 years—and still loves it just as much now as he did back then.

Ellin Stein has written for publications on both sides of the Atlantic, including the *New York Times*, the *Times of London*, and *InStyle*. Her book *That's Not Funny, That's Sick: The* National Lampoon *and the Comedy Insurgents Who Captured the Mainstream*, was published by W. W. Norton & Co. in 2013. She has lived in London for two decades and is married to a native. For this edition, Ellin updated the South and Yorkshire chapters as well as Travel Smart England. Her territory also included London shopping and several London neighborhoods.

London restaurant maven **Alex Wijeratna** is always amazed by the capital's rocket-fueled restaurant scene. He has written for publications including *The Times, Guardian,* and *Independent.* Alex updated the Where to Eat section of London.

MAYOR OF LONDON

tfl.gov.uk

24 hour travel information 0343 222 1234*

*Service and network charges may apply. See tfl.gov.uk/terms for details.

Sign up for email updates tfl.gov.uk/emailupdates

@TfLTravelAlerts

UNDERGROUND

TRANSPORT FOR LONDON

EVERY JOURNEY MATTERS

 Reg. user No. 15/2827/P Version C 12.2014

Improvement works may affect your journey, please check before you travel

Correct at time of going to print

WELCOME TO ENGLAND

From medieval cathedrals to postmodern towers, from prehistoric stones to one-pub villages, England is a spectacular tribute to the strength—and flexibility—of tradition. In the capital city of London and beyond, you can explore grand manors and royal castles steeped in history, and also discover cutting-edge art, innovative cultural scenes, and trendy shops. Quintessentially English treasures like the Georgian town of Bath, academic Oxford, and eccentric Brighton remain vibrant, and silvery lakes and green hills provide enduring grace notes.

TOP REASONS TO GO

★ **London:** Landmarks, top theater, museums, village-like neighborhoods—it's all here.

★ **Idyllic Towns:** The Cotswolds' stone cottages, Cornwall's seaside charmers, and more.

★ **Pubs:** For a pint or a chat, a visit to one of "England's living rooms" is essential.

★ **History:** Sights from Stonehenge to Windsor Castle bring the country's past to life.

★ **Great Walks:** Classic trails await in the Lake District and Yorkshire's dales and moors.

★ **Gardens:** Roses, flower borders, and sculpted landscapes flaunt a national talent.

Fodor's ENGLAND 2016

Publisher: Amanda D'Acierno, *Senior Vice President*

Editorial: Arabella Bowen, *Editor in Chief*; Linda Cabasin, *Editorial Director*

Design: Tina Malaney, *Associate Art Director*; Chie Ushio, *Senior Designer*

Photography: Jennifer Arnow, *Senior Photo Editor*; Mary Robnett, *Photo Researcher*

Production: Linda Schmidt, *Managing Editor*; Evangelos Vasilakis, *Associate Managing Editor*; Angela L. McLean, *Senior Production Manager*

Maps: Rebecca Baer, *Senior Map Editor*; David Lindroth, Mark Stroud (Moon Street Cartography), *Cartographers*

Sales: Jacqueline Lebow, *Sales Director*

Marketing & Publicity: Heather Dalton, *Marketing Director*; Katherine Punia, *Publicity Director*

Business & Operations: Susan Livingston, *Vice President, Strategic Business Planning*; Sue Daulton, *Vice President, Operations*

Fodors.com: Megan Bell, *Executive Director, Revenue & Business Development*; Yasmin Marinaro, *Senior Director, Marketing & Partnerships*

Writers: Robert Andrews, Jo Caird, Rhonda Carrier, Julius Honnor, Kate Hughes, Jack Jewers, James O'Neill, Ellin Stein, and Alex Wijeratna

Editors: Amanda Sadlowski (lead editor), Bethany Beckerlegge, Mike Dunphy, Denise Leto

Production Editor: Carrie Parker

ISBN 978-1-101-87848-4

ISSN 1558-870X

SPECIAL SALES

This book is available at special discounts for bulk purchases for sales promotions or premiums. For more information, e-mail specialmarkets@penguinrandomhouse.com.

PRINTED IN THE UNITED STATES OF AMERICA

10 9 8 7 6 5 4 3 2 1

CONTENTS

Fodor's Features

CONTENTS

CONTENTS

MAPS

CONTENTS

ABOUT THIS GUIDE

Fodor's Recommendations

Everything in this guide is worth doing—we don't cover what isn't—but exceptional sights, hotels, and restaurants are recognized with additional accolades. **Fodor's Choice★** indicates our top recommendations, and **Best Bets** call attention to notable hotels and restaurants in various categories. Care to nominate a new place? Visit Fodors.com/contact-us.

Trip Costs

We list prices wherever possible to help you budget well. Hotel and restaurant price categories from **$** to **$$$$** are noted alongside each recommendation. For hotels, we include the lowest cost of a standard double room in high season. For restaurants, we cite the average price of a main course at dinner or, if dinner isn't served, at lunch. For attractions, we always list adult admission fees; discounts are usually available for children, students, and senior citizens.

Hotels

Our local writers vet every hotel to recommend the best overnights in each price category, from budget to expensive. Unless otherwise specified, you can expect private bath, phone, and TV in your room. *For expanded hotel reviews, facilities, and deals visit Fodors.com.*

Top Picks
★ Fodor's Choice

Listings
- Address
- Branch address
- Telephone
- Fax
- Website
- E-mail
- Admission fee
- Open/closed times
- Subway
- Directions or Map coordinates

Hotels & Restaurants
- Hotel
- Number of rooms
- Meal plans
- Restaurant
- Reservations
- Dress code
- No credit cards
- Price

Other
- See also
- Take note
- Golf facilities

Restaurants

Unless we state otherwise, restaurants are open for lunch and dinner daily. We mention dress code only when there's a specific requirement and reservations only when they're essential or not accepted. *To make restaurant reservations, visit Fodors.com.*

Credit Cards

The hotels and restaurants in this guide typically accept credit cards. If not, we'll say so.

EUGENE FODOR

Hungarian-born Eugene Fodor (1905–91) began his travel career as an interpreter on a French cruise ship. The experience inspired him to write *On the Continent* (1936), the first guidebook to receive annual updates and discuss a country's way of life as well as its sights. Fodor later joined the U.S. Army and worked for the OSS in World War II. After the war, he kept up his intelligence work while expanding his guidebook series. During the Cold War, many guides were written by fellow agents who understood the value of insider information. Today's guides continue Fodor's legacy by providing travelers with timely coverage, insider tips, and cultural context.

EXPERIENCE ENGLAND

ENGLAND TODAY

England is the biggest region in the United Kingdom (or U.K.), the nation that also includes Scotland, Wales, Northern Ireland, and the Channel Islands (Guernsey and Jersey). England, Scotland, and Wales form what is referred to as Great Britain (or just Britain). Despite being given the opportunity in a 2014 referendum to be independent, Scottish voters chose to remain part of the U.K. It's worth noting that, while England, Scotland, and Wales are all part of Britain and the U.K., Wales and Scotland aren't part of England, and vice versa. Get that one wrong at your peril—you haven't seen angry until you've seen a Welshman referred to as English.

Although it's about the size of Louisiana, England has a population 12 times as large: 54 million people find space to live on its green rolling hills and in its shallow valleys and crowded cities.

Politics

Contrary to insider expectations and many opinion polls, the Conservative Party, led by prime minister David Cameron, won the general election on May 7, 2015 by a majority of 16 seats, giving the Party government control for the next five years. Both the Liberal Democrats, who had been in coalition with the Conservatives since 2010, and the Labour Party suffered major defeats. The most surprising result however was the landslide victory of the Scottish National Party, led by Nicola Sturgeon, which gained 56 out of 59 seats in Scotland. Despite growing support for the UKIP (UK Independence Party), it only managed to win one single seat. David Cameron has promised to "govern as a party of one nation," but faces challenges not only from the SNP, but from increasing immigration numbers and the referendum on the U.K.'s membership in the European Union, scheduled to take place by the end of 2017.

The Royal Family

How things have changed for the Windsor family. Essentially a figurehead monarchy but with a symbolic political role, the Royal Family has teetered on the brink of obsolescence. After the death of Princess Diana in 1997 and the royal scandals and divorces that littered the late 20th century, the idea of ending the monarchy's political role—and its government subsidy—was discussed publicly. Maintaining the Royal Family costs taxpayers almost £38 million (more than $55 million) each year, and that amount was increasingly difficult to justify as the popularity of the family—aside from the beloved Queen—plummeted.

It's not surprising, then, that some in the media maintain that when Prince William married the appealing Catherine Middleton, he saved the monarchy. The young couple's popularity is enormous, particularly after the birth of their son, George, Prince of Cambridge, and their daughter, Charlotte, Princess of Cambridge, so much so that, together with Prince Harry, they have formed a company to prevent the misuse of their image. The Queen, who will celebrate her 90th birthday in 2016 and has no thoughts of retiring, is scaling down her public engagements, gradually transferring them to her son, Prince Charles, his wife the Duchess of Cornwall (who steadily rises higher in the public's esteem), and other members of the Royal Family.

Fashion

Known for their quirky, creative, and bold style, British fashion designers have been influential on the global stage for decades. Whether it's from top of the line companies like Burberry and Mulberry or from individual designers such as Paul Smith, Stella McCartney, Victoria Beckham, and the late Alexander McQueen, clothes made by British designers are sought after. London Fashion Week takes place twice a year, taking an estimated £100 million each season.

Catherine, the Duchess of Cambridge, still holds sway as chief ambassador for British fashion. The "Kate effect," first fired by her wedding dress, has not diminished, nor has constant analysis of her attire. Even the Queen takes note; Kate was reportedly advised by her grandmother-in-law to adopt lower hemlines for her 2014 tour of Australia and New Zealand. She mixes high fashion with moderately priced high street clothing, causing such chains as Reiss, LK Bennett, Hobbs, Zara, and Whistles to sell out the moment she dons their garments, and keeps designers such as Jenny Packham, Alice Temperley, and Jimmy Choo in the spotlight.

Housing and Development

As one of the most crowded countries in Europe and faced with an ever-expanding population, England has a growing housing crisis on its hands. The government's call for the building of 200,000 houses a year, along with its relaxation in planning policies, has caused contention. Building developers now find it much easier to place housing in the countryside that surrounds rural towns and villages, often referred to as the "green belt." This has caused opposition from organizations such as the National Trust, the Campaign to Protect Rural England (CPRE), and *Country Life* magazine as well as local residents. The argument is that enough land in cities and postindustrial areas has already been granted planning permission and that these "brown field" sites are enough to meet housing demands. Even archaeological monuments have not been immune: in February 2015, hundreds took part in a Hillfort Hug, which successfully stopped a housing development bordering a Shropshire Iron Age fort.

Drinking Culture

According to published studies, Britain is only the 16th-heaviest drinking nation in Europe, but on a Friday night in any town center that rating can be hard to believe. The British refer to some busy towns as "no-go areas" after 11 pm, because they're packed with raucous, drunken young people stumbling out of pubs. Even normally staid towns, such as Harrogate in Yorkshire and Rochester in Kent, can take on a Spring Break atmosphere after the pubs close on a Friday night. Seaside towns tend to have the most problems, including Bristol, Newquay, and Hastings.

The main cause, experts say, is a binge-drinking culture, particularly among the young. Recent surveys indicate that the British are a nation of closet drinkers, and reluctant to admit the true extent of their drinking habits. But it seems that the under 25s have no such inhibitions and flaunt their excesses in public, despite rises in the price of alcohol and campaigns from medics and the government alike.

WHAT'S WHERE

The following numbers refer to chapters.

2 London. Not only Britain's financial and governmental center but also one of the world's great cities, London has mammoth museums, posh palaces, double-decker buses, and iconic sights such as Big Ben. Intriguing villagelike neighborhoods from Notting Hill to Bloomsbury call out to be explored. When you need a break, pop into a pub or relax in one of the city's sprawling parks.

3 The Southeast. This compact green and pleasant region within day-trip distance of London takes in Canterbury and its cathedral, funky seaside Brighton, the appealing towns of Rye and Lewes, Dover's white cliffs, and castles such as Bodiam, Leeds, and Hever. Noted gardens as different as smaller, romantic Sissinghurst and large-scale Wisley add to the mix.

4 The South. Hampshire, Dorset, and Wiltshire have quintessential English countryside, with gentle hills and green pastures. Explore the stone circles at Stonehenge and Avebury, take in Winchester (Jane Austen country) and Salisbury, and discover Highclere Castle and Lyme Regis.

5 The West Country. Somerset, Devon, and Cornwall are sunnier and warmer than the rest of the country, with sandy beaches. Cornwall has lush gardens and a stunning coast. Of the cities, Bristol is the largest and most vibrant, while Wells and Exeter are attractive and compact. Take in the brooding heaths and moors of Exmoor, Dartmoor, and Bodmin Moor, too.

6 The Thames Valley. London's commuter belt takes in Windsor, where the Queen spends time, and Eton. Then there are the spires of Oxford and peaceful river towns such as Henley and Marlow; in all of these you have the opportunity for some relaxing river excursions. Among the stately homes not to be missed are over-the-top Blenheim Palace and Waddesdon Manor.

7 Bath and the Cotswolds. The grand Georgian town of Bath is one of England's highlights, with the Roman Baths and golden-stone 18th- and 19th-century architecture. Nearby, pretty as a picture, the Cotswolds region is justly famous for tranquil, stone-built villages, such as Chipping Campden, Stow-on-the-Wold, and Tetbury. Notable gardens include those at Hidcote Manor and Sudeley Castle.

Hartlepool
Keswick
Penrith
Darlington
Middlesbrough
ENGLAND
Wales
Kendal
Barrow-in-Furness
Scarborough
Lancaster
York
Leeds
Blackpool
Bradford
Kingston upon Hull
Grimsby
Liverpool
Manchester
Sheffield
Chester
Skegness
Stoke on-Trent
Boston
The Wash
Newcastle
Nottingham
Grantham
Shrewsbury
King's Lynn
Norwich
WALES
Leicester
Wolverhampton
Birmingham
Peterborough
Lowestoft
Coventry
Stratford-upon Avon
Ipswich
Worcester
Chipping Campden
ENGLAND
Colchester
Harwich
Cheltenham
Luton
Oxford
Gloucester
2
Southend-on-Sea
Swansea
7
Marlow
Cardiff
Henley
Reading
6
Bristol
LONDON
Windsor
Canterbury
Bath
Channel
Wells
Royal Tunbridge Wells
Dover
Salisbury
Winchester
Calais
Lewes
Rye
Southampton
4
3
Exeter
Bournemouth
Portsmouth
Brighton
Isle of Wight
Lyme Regis
Weymouth
English Channel
50°N
Dieppe
FRANCE
0°
Cherbourg
Le Havre
Rouen

WHAT'S WHERE

8 Stratford-upon-Avon and the Heart of England. One hundred miles northwest of London, Stratford-upon-Avon is the place to see Shakespeare's birthplace and watch his plays, and Warwickshire has Warwick and Kenilworth castles, too. Nearby Birmingham offers a modern urban experience. You can explore the Industrial Revolution museums of Ironbridge Gorge, Ludlow's half-timber buildings, medieval Shrewsbury, and popular Chester with its centuries-old walls.

9 Manchester and Liverpool. Liverpool rides the Beatles' coattails but, like Manchester, has transformed its warehouses and docks into sleek hotels, restaurants, and shops. Buzzing nightlife and excellent museums are highlights in both cities. The surrounding Peak District has great opportunities for walking and visiting stately homes such as Chatsworth and Haddon Hall.

10 The Lake District. A popular national park, this is a startlingly beautiful area of craggy hills, wild moorland, stone cottages, and glittering silvery lakes. Nature lovers and hikers crowd the area in summer. Among the literary high points are the homes of Wordsworth and Beatrix Potter.

11 East Anglia. The biggest lure in this green, flat, low-key region is Cambridge, with its medieval halls of learning. The countryside is dominated by the cathedrals of Ely and Norwich, and by time-warp towns such as Lavenham. Coastal spots such as Aldeburgh add a salty flavor.

12 Yorkshire. This wilder part of England has great appeal for lovers of the outdoors, but ancient walled York is also a center of attention. To York's west are the moors and dales that inspired the Brontës, and in east Yorkshire the moors collide with the sea at towns such as Whitby. Leeds is a vibrant urban center.

13 The Northeast. Here travelers can walk in the footsteps of Roman soldiers along Hadrian's Wall. Bamburgh and Dunstanburgh castles guard the coast; Alnwick Castle has stunning gardens. The small city of Durham is a medieval gem, a contrast to modern Newcastle.

14 Wales. Clinging to the western edge of England, Wales is green and ruggedly beautiful, with mountains and magnificent coastline. Except for Cardiff and Swansea, this is a rural country, with three national parks. Wales is also known for its castles.

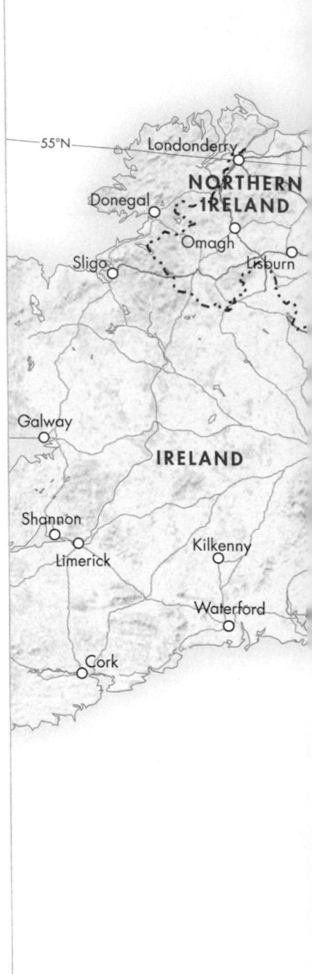

ENGLAND
Wales
SCOTLAND
WALES
ENGLAND
FRANCE
North Sea
Irish Sea
Bristol Channel
English Channel
The Wash
Isle of Man
Isle of Anglesey
Isle of Wight
BELFAST
DUBLIN
LONDON
Perth
Dundee
Greenock
Glasgow
Edinburgh
Berwick-upon-Tweed
Ayr
Dumfries
Newcastle
Sunderland
Carlisle
Durham
Penrith
Keswick
Darlington
Middlesbrough
Whitby
Scarborough
Kendal
Barrow-in-Furness
Douglas
Dundalk
Lancaster
York
Leeds
Drogheda
Blackpool
Bradford
Kingston upon Hull
Manchester
Liverpool
Grimsby
Holyhead
Sheffield
Chester
Skegness
Caernarfon
Stoke-on-Trent
Boston
Wells-next-the-Sea
Newcastle
Nottingham
Grantham
King's Lynn
Shrewsbury
Norwich
Leicester
Wolverhampton
Birmingham
Peterborough
Lowestoft
Aberystwyth
Coventry
Ely
Aldeburgh
Stratford upon Avon
Ludlow
Worcester
Cambridge
Lavenham
Colchester
Harwich
Luton
Cheltenham
Oxford
Gloucester
Swansea
Southend-on-Sea
Cardiff
Reading
Bristol
Bath
Canterbury
Dover
Barnstaple
Calais
Southampton
Rye
Exeter
Bournemouth
Portsmouth
Brighton
Lyme Regis
Weymouth
Plymouth
Penzance
Falmouth
Dieppe
5°W
0°
Cherbourg
Le Havre
Rouen
10
13
12
9
14
8
11

NEED TO KNOW

AT A GLANCE

Capital: London

Population: 5,400,000

Currency: Pound

Money: ATMs common; credit cards widely accepted

Language: English

Country Code: 44

Emergencies: 999 or 112

Driving: On the left

Electricity: 230v/50 cycles; plugs have three rectangular blades

Time: Five hours ahead of New York

Documents: Up to six months with valid passport

Mobile Phones: GSM (900, 1800 and 2100 bands)

Major Mobile Companies: O2, EE, Vodaphone

WEBSITES

Visit Britain: 🌐 *www.visitbritain.com*

Visit England: 🌐 *www.visitengland.com*

Visit London: 🌐 *www.visitlondon.com*

GETTING AROUND

✈ **Air Travel:** Major airports are Heathrow, Gatwick, Manchester, and Stansted.

🚌 **Bus Travel:** The comprehensive short-haul bus and long-distance coach network is cheaper than train travel, but can take longer.

🚗 **Car Travel:** Cars aren't recommended for London, but can be good for countryside travel. Traffic flows on the left, and most rentals have manual transmissions. Gas is expensive, but roads are generally in great condition.

🚆 **Train Travel:** England's train network is extensive, with all major cities and towns served.

PLAN YOUR BUDGET

	HOTEL ROOM	MEAL	ATTRACTIONS
Low Budget	£100	£12	National Portrait Gallery, free
Mid Budget	£225	£30	London Eye ticket, £19.20
High Budget	£500	£120	Shakespeare's Globe performance, £60

WAYS TO SAVE

Eat ethnic. Some of London's cheapest good eats can be found at Vietnamese, Indian, Korean, and Middle Eastern restaurants, just to name a few.

Stay in university housing. In addition to London's many hostels, several central city universities rent out rooms at rates much lower than at hotels.

Use an Oyster card. London's public transit system is pricey, but with an Oyster card your daily travels are capped at the same rate you'd pay for a one-day Travelcard within the same zones.

Fill up on museums. Not only does London have some of the best museums in the world, but many are free.

PLAN YOUR TIME

Hassle Factor	Low. Numerous airlines offer frequent direct flights from North America, and transport within the country is easy.
3 days	Dive into exploring the many sights of London, and take a half-day trip out to see The Queen's preferred residence at Windsor Castle.
1 week	Spend an extra day in London, then head northwest to see some of the best the country has to offer with stops in Oxford, Shakespeare's home of Stratford-upon-Avon, the musical mecca of Manchester, and The Beatles' old stomping grounds at Liverpool.
2 weeks	With an additional week you can also see the highlights of the southwest: the rolling Cotswolds district, the old Roman city of Bath, King Arthur's legendary retreat at Glastonbury Abbey, and historic Salisbury and nearby Stonehenge. Round things out with a stop at Brighton on the southern coast.

WHEN TO GO

High Season: The summer months of June, July, and August give the best chance of good weather, although the crowds are most intense. The start of August can be very busy, and hot weather makes Tube travel a nightmare.

Low Season: November to March is when you'll find England's best flight and hotel deals. Winter, while not generally frigid, can be dismal; the sun sets at 4 and it's pitch dark by 5.

Value Season: Late spring is the time to see the countryside and the royal parks and gardens at their freshest, while fall brings autumnal beauty and fewer people. Temperatures are usually mild at both times.

BIG EVENTS

May: One of the UK's top annual arts events, Brighton Festival features an international roster of theater, music, dance and more.

June: Born as a hippie festival in the 1970s, Glastonbury is now one of England's largest and most beloved contemporary music and performance fests.

August: Among the world's largest street fests, London's colorful three-day Notting Hill Carnival attracts a million people annually.

November: All across England, Guy Fawkes Night on November 5 is celebrated with bonfires and fireworks.

READ THIS

- ***The Picture of Dorian Gray,*** Oscar Wilde. A young 19th-century narcissist becomes obsessed with hedonism.
- ***Mrs Dalloway,*** Virginia Woolf. A day in the life of a post–World War I high-society woman.
- ***Night Haunts,*** Sukhdev Sandhu. Poetic profiles of a diverse array of nocturnal workers in contemporary London.

WATCH THIS

- ***The Queen.*** The royal family faces public scrutiny after the death of Princess Diana.
- ***This is England.*** A troubled working-class youth encounters skinhead culture in 1983.
- ***Hope and Glory.*** The World War II bombings of The Blitz as seen through the eyes of a 10-year-old London boy.

EAT THIS

- ***Fish-and-chips***: battered and fried fish (usually cod or haddock) with French-fried potatoes
- ***Yorkshire pudding***: airy popover side dish made from baked batter of flour, eggs, and milk, usually served with gravy
- ***Black pudding***: side dish of pork blood blended with oatmeal, onions, and pork fat

ENGLAND TOP ATTRACTIONS

London

(A) Packed with treasures and pleasures, London entices with superb museums, royal pageantry, and exciting theater, shopping, and nightlife. Its iconic sights include the Houses of Parliament, Westminster Abbey, the Tower of London, and the British Museum, but parks and pubs offer memorable diversions as well.

Yorkshire Dales

(B) Shaped by ice and sliced by rivers, the dales (valleys) are bounded either by wild, rocky formations and crags or soft-rounded hills. Cascades of waterfalls, drystone walls, and enchanting cottage gardens invite hikes, which can be as easy or challenging as you please.

Stonehenge and Avebury

(C) Prehistoric monuments dot England's landscape, silent but tantalizing reminders of the distant past. Of these, the great circle of stones at Stonehenge is one of the country's icons. Nearby, the Avebury Stone Circles surround part of a village and are also deeply intriguing.

Brighton and Its Seafront

(D) England is more than stately homes and pretty towns. This longtime seaside resort lives it up with classic seaside fun as well as the eccentric Royal Pavilion. Good shopping and restaurants, plus energetic nightlife, keep the action going nonstop.

Bath

(E) Exquisitely preserved but entertaining, this Georgian town still centers on the hot mineral springs that made it a fashionable spa for the wealthy in the 18th and early 19th centuries. Streets lined with Palladian buildings made of golden limestone, an ancient abbey, boutiques, and the ruined Roman baths give Bath real character.

Hadrian's Wall

(F) Begun in AD 122, the thick stone wall built by the Emperor Hadrian across the rugged far north of the country is a

remarkable survivor from Roman Britain, where it protected Roman soldiers from invading tribes. Biking, hiking, and horseback riding are wonderful ways to explore.

Oxford and Cambridge

(G) It's hard to choose a favorite between these two ancient university towns. Oxford is larger and more cosmopolitan, but lovely with its fairy-tale cityscape of steeples and towers. In Cambridge you can stroll through the colleges, visit the university's museums, and relax in the city's pubs.

Coastal Cornwall

(H) The coasts of Cornwall, in the far southwest, are beloved by many (too many, in summer) for different reasons. The rugged northern coast has cliffs that drop to tiny coves and beaches; ruined, cliff-top Tintagel Castle and Padstow with its lively harbor are here. The south coast has resort towns such as Penzance and arty St. Ives.

Cotswold Villages

(I) Marked by rolling uplands, green fields, and mellow limestone cottages with prim flower beds, the Cotswolds, 100 miles west of London, make a peaceful getaway. There's little to do in idyllic villages, but that's exactly the point. Exquisite gardens and stately homes add further charm.

Lake District

(J) Sprawling across northwest England, this area of 16 major lakes and jagged mountains inspired Romantic poets. You can hike the trails or view the mountains from a boat, or visit the retreats of Wordsworth and Beatrix Potter.

QUINTESSENTIAL ENGLAND

Pints and Pubs

Pop in for a pint at a pub to encounter what has been the center—literally the "public house"—of English social life for centuries. The basic pub recipe calls for a variety of beers on draft—dark creamy stouts like Guinness; bitter, including brews such as Tetley's and Bass; and lager, the blondest and blandest of the trio—a dartboard, oak paneling, and paisley carpets. Throw in a bunch of young suits in London, a generous dash of undergrads in places such as Oxford or Cambridge, and, in rural areas, a healthy helping of blokes around the television and ladies in the corner sipping their *halves* (half pints) and having a *natter* (gossip). In smaller pubs, listen in and enjoy the banter among the regulars—you may even be privy to the occasional *barney* (harmless argument). Join in if you care to, but remember not to take anything too seriously—a severe breach of pub etiquette.

Daily Rags

To blend in with the English, stash your smart phone and slide a newspaper under your arm. If you're on the move, pick up free copies of the *Evening Standard* (in London) and *Metro* (in London and on local trains and buses in various other cities), or head for a park bench or café and lose yourself in one of the national dailies for insight into Britain's worldview. The ramifications of the Leveson Inquiry into the role and relationships of the media in 2012 still rumble on in the press from the tabloid *Sun,* the biggest-selling daily (though the days of the topless model on Page 3 look numbered), to the *i,* the cheapest and shortest of the dailies, and the Sunday papers, such as the *Observer* and the more conservative *Sunday Telegraph*. For a more satirical view, the fortnightly *Private Eye,* with its hallmark cartoons and parodies, offers British wit at its best.

If you want to get a sense of contemporary English culture, and indulge in some of its pleasures, start by familiarizing yourself with the rituals of daily life. Here are a few highlights—things you can take part in with relative ease.

A Nice Cuppa Tea

For almost four centuries the English and tea have been immersed in a love affair passionate enough to survive revolutions, rations, tariffs, and lattes, but also soothing, as "putting the kettle on" heralds moments of quiet comfort in public places and in homes and offices across the nation. The ritual known as "afternoon tea" had its beginnings in the early 19th century, in the private chambers of the duchess of Bedford, where she and her "ladies of leisure" indulged in afternoons of pastries and fragrant blends. Department stores, hotels, and tearooms offer everything from simple tea and biscuits to shockingly overpriced spreads with sandwiches and cakes that would impress even the duchess herself. Some restaurants are now even offering a different tea with each course of the meal. But, if tea isn't your cup of tea, coffee is fine, too.

Sports Fever

Whoever says England isn't an overtly religious country hasn't considered the sports mania that's descended here, and not merely because of the effects of the 2012 Olympic Games in London or Andy Murray winning Wimbledon in 2013. Whether water events (such as Henley, Cowes, and the Head of the River Race) or a land competition (the Crabbie's Grand National steeplechase, the Virgin Money London Marathon, a good football match), most bring people to the edge of their seats—or more often the living room couch. To partake in the rite, you'll need Pimm's (the drink for swank spectators of the Henley Royal Regatta) or beer (the drink for most everything else). You may experience the exhilaration yourself—which, you'll probably sense, is not for the love of *a* sport, but for the love of *sport* itself.

IF YOU LIKE

Castles and Stately Homes

Exploring the diversity and magnificence of England's castles and stately homes can occupy most of a blissful vacation. You'll find clusters in the southeast, west of Salisbury, in the Cotswolds, and on the remote northeastern coast. Note that most stately homes are open only from spring through fall. If your itinerary extends to Wales, look for Edward I's "iron ring" of castles, including Caernarfon and Conwy.

Blenheim Palace, Thames Valley. This baroque extravaganza is touted as England's only rival to Versailles.

Buckingham Palace, London. Glimpse royal life in the magnificent staterooms, open in August and September.

Hever Castle, Southeast. The childhood home of Anne Boleyn is the archetypal castle with battlements, turrets, and moat.

Holkham Hall, East Anglia. The splendid 60-foot-tall Marble Hall and salons filled with old masters distinguish this Palladian house.

Knole, Southeast. Within the seven courtyards of this 16th-century family home are silver furniture and a golden bed.

Petworth House, the Southeast. One of the National Trust's glories, it's known for art by J.M.W. Turner.

Stourhead, the South. A visit here brings you what is considered by many the most beautiful house and landscape garden in Europe.

Wilton House, the South. The Double Cube room designed by Inigo Jones is one of the country's best interior designs.

Windsor Castle, Thames Valley. The Queen's favorite residence has a fabulous art collection.

Idyllic Towns and Villages

Year after year, armies of tourists with images of green meadows, thatched roofs, and colorful flower beds flock to England's countryside. Most will find their way to famously adorable towns along the Thames, timeless seaside resorts in the West Country, and a smattering of fairy-tale hamlets in the Cotswolds. But don't dismiss the pastoral flatlands and historic villages of East Anglia beyond Cambridge, the Norfolk coast, or the mountainside hamlets and sleepy seaside resorts of Wales.

Clovelly, Southwest. A steep cobbled street threads between flower-bedecked cottages down to the tiny harbor on the south Devon coast.

Henley-on-Thames, Thames Valley. Famous for its Regatta, the affluent town has a lovely position on the Thames and is ideal for strolling.

Lavenham, East Anglia. This village is full of Tudor buildings, the former houses of wool merchants and weavers.

Ludlow, Stratford-upon-Avon and the Heart of England. Medieval and Georgian buildings cluster below a castle in this town, whose restaurants have made it a foodie favorite.

Rye, Southeast. Writers and artists have always been drawn to the cobbled streets and timber houses of this historic little town.

Whitby, Yorkshire. A ruined abbey and a cliff-lined harbor combine with a rich fishing and whaling legacy to enhance this coastal gem.

Winchcombe, Bath and the Cotswolds. Cottages of honey-color stone line the streets of this quintessential Cotswold town.

Glorious Gardens

Despite being cursed with impertinent weather and short summers, English gardeners need no encouragement to grab their gardening tools. A pilgrimage to a garden is an essential part of any spring or summer trip. Green havens thrive all over England, but perhaps the most fertile hunting grounds are in Oxfordshire, Gloucestershire (including the Cotswolds), and Kent (the "Garden of England").

Eden Project, Southwest. Much ingenious thought and inspiration has gone into presenting the world's plants from three climate zones in huge geodesic domes in Cornwall.

Hidcote Manor, Bath and the Cotswolds. A masterful example of the Arts and Crafts garden, it is divided into garden rooms and contains the stunning Red Border.

Kew Gardens, London. A treetop walk, huge 19th-century greenhouses, and a pagoda, as well as swaths of colorful flower beds, adorn this center of academic research.

Sissinghurst Castle Garden, Southeast. Vita Sackville-West's masterpiece, set within the remains of a Tudor castle, is busy in summer and spectacular in autumn.

Stourhead, South. One of the country's most impressive house-and-garden combinations is an artful 18th-century sanctuary with a tranquil lake, colorful shrubs, and grottoes.

Wisley, Southeast. The Royal Horticultural Society's garden splendidly blends the pretty and the practical in its inspirational displays and glasshouses.

Urban Excitement

London has everything a world capital should have—rich culture and history, thrilling art and theater scenes, world-class restaurants, and sensational shopping—along with crowds, traffic, and high prices. It's not to be missed, but if you appreciate modern cities, spend time in some of England's reviving urban centers, including those in its former industrial heartland. Here blossoming multiculturalism has paved the way for a unique vibe.

Birmingham, Heart of England. Interlaced with canals, the country's second-largest city is a vibrant center for culture and cuisine and has a unique Jewellery Quarter.

Brighton, Southeast. Bold, bright, and boisterous are the words to describe a seaside charmer that has everything from the dazzling Royal Pavilion to the trendy shops of the Lanes.

Bristol, West Country. With its lively waterfront and music and food culture, this youthful city has vibrant nightlife as well as a long history.

Leeds, Yorkshire. A former industrial city now polishing its Victorian buildings, Leeds is known for its shopping arcades and a spirited music scene.

Liverpool. Dramatic regeneration, a historic waterfront, Beatles sites, and the stellar museums of the Albert Dock are stars of this city.

Manchester. Much more than football, the city offers chic urban shopping, bars and clubs, and fabulous museums, reflective of its industrial heritage.

Ancient Mysteries

Stone circles as well as ancient stone and earthen forts and mounds offer intriguing hints about Britain's mysterious prehistoric inhabitants. The country's southwestern landscape, particularly the Salisbury Plain, Dorset, and the eastern side of Cornwall, has a notably rich concentration of these sites, perplexing mysteries that human nature compels us to try to solve.

Avebury Stone Circles, South. Large and marvelously evocative, these circles surround part of the village of Avebury. You can walk right up to these stones.

Castlerigg Stone Circle, Lake District. The setting of this Neolithic creation, surrounded by brooding peaks, is as awesome as the surviving remains.

Maiden Castle, South. The largest Iron Age hill fort in England has impressive rings of ramparts and ditches that fire your sense of history.

Stanton Drew Circles, West Country. Take in the vast size of the two avenues of standing stones, three rings, and burial chamber that now lie in a field.

Stonehenge, South. The stone circle begun 5,000 years ago stands on the wide Salisbury Plain. Hypotheses about its purpose range from the scientific (ancient calendar) to the fantastic (a gift from extinct giants).

Vale of the White Horse, Thames Valley. The gigantic horse here was actually carved into the chalky hillside around 1750 BC.

Wonderful Walks

England seems to be designed with walking in mind—footpaths wind through the contours of the landscape, and popular routes are well endowed with cozy bed-and-breakfasts and pubs. You can walk the whole or small chunks of the many long-distance trails or ramble through one of England's national parks. Famous walking spots are in the Lake District (congested in summer) and Yorkshire's dales and moors. Wherever you hike, always be prepared for storms or fog. Check out 🌐 *www.nationaltrail.co.uk* for inspiration and advice.

Borrowdale, Lake District. Have a color-pencil kit handy to capture the beauty of the dramatically verdant valleys and jagged peaks.

Brecon Beacons, Wales. The windswept uplands here are crossed with easy paths and are uncrowded.

Cotswolds Way, Bath and the Cotswolds. Hike the Cotswold Way and combine open grassland, pretty villages, and sweeping views to the Malvern Hills and Severn Valley.

Peak District, Manchester and Liverpool. Its rocky outcrops and vaulting meadows make some people say this is the country's most beautiful national park.

Snowdonia, Wales. Ferocious peaks in this national park promise challenging hikes.

South West Coast Path, West Country. Spectacular is the word for the 630-mile trail that winds from Minehead in Somerset to Poole Harbour in Dorset.

Thames Path, Thames Valley. Follow the Thames from its source through water meadows and riverside villages to the heart of London.

Thrilling Theater

There's no better antidote to an overdose of stately homes and well-groomed gardens than a face-to-face encounter with another British specialty, the theater. London is the heart and soul of the action: here companies consistently turn out superb productions. Still, be sure to sample theater outside London. Stratford-upon-Avon may be the Bard's hometown, but festivals all over the country celebrate Shakespeare's work—among the best is London's Globe Theatre. Or even try a university production.

Chichester Festival Theatre, Southeast. This modernist building is known for its innovative performances.

Harrogate International Festival, Yorkshire. See street theater at northern England's best arts festival.

Minack Theatre, West Country. The open-air theater in coastal Cornwall, near Land's End, nuzzles the slope of a sandy cliff.

Royal Shakespeare Company, Stratford-upon-Avon and the Heart of England. Seeing any Shakespeare play is a treat in the home of the Bard.

Stephen Joseph Theater, Scarborough, Yorkshire. Alan Ayckbourn's plays are performed here.

Theatre Royal, Bath, Bath and the Cotswolds. Pre- or post-London tours often visit this Regency-era theater.

Theatre Royal, York, Yorkshire. Traditional pantomime—with dames (men dressed as ladies), slapstick, and music—takes place in December and January.

Yvonne Arnaud Theatre, Guildford, the Southeast. The productions at this theater on an island often travel to London.

Country-House Hotels

In all their luxurious glory, country-house hotels are an essential part of the English landscape, particularly in the southern part of the country. Some hotels are traditional, but there's a newer modern breed as well, and many will have spas, pools, and sports available. If you can't spend a night, consider dinner or afternoon tea. The Cotswolds and the Thames Valley are prime ground for these retreats. One tip: Ask if a wedding party will be using the hotel during your stay; these can take over a smaller establishment.

Calcot Manor, Bath and the Cotswolds. Luxury and opulence join with family-friendly amenities here where traditional and modern mix.

Cliveden House, Thames Valley. This very grand stately pile, once the Astors' home, offers champagne boat trips on the River Thames.

Coworth Park, Thames Valley. It's 18th century on the outside but very 21st century within: this retreat combines playful luxury with spacious grounds.

Gidleigh Park, West Country. Beautiful grounds in a wooded valley on edge of Dartmoor are the backdrop for superb food and antiques-filled rooms.

Lime Wood, South. This woodland hideaway in a Regency house has the added treat of a fabulous spa.

Miller Howe, Lake District. Stunning views of Windermere, Arts and Crafts touches, and superior service are the appeal here.

Thornbury Castle, West Country. A stay in this 16th-century castle with a royal pedigree connects you to history but also includes plenty of modern pampering.

FLAVORS OF ENGLAND

The New Food Scene

England has never lacked a treasure store of nature's bounty: green pastures, fruitful orchards, and the encompassing sea. Over the past few decades, dowdy images of English cooking have been sloughed off. A new focus on the land and a culinary confidence and expertise are exemplified by the popularity and influence of celebrity chefs such as Rick Stein, Heston Blumenthal, Gordon Ramsay, Jamie Oliver, and Mary Berry. The chefs are only one indicator of change: all over the country, artisanal food producers and talented cooks are indulging their passion for high-quality, locally sourced ingredients. And television programs on home baking have proved phenomenally popular.

Food festivals, farmers' markets, and farm shops have sprung up in more cities and towns. Alongside the infiltration of supermarkets, much opposed by some people, comes a more discriminating attitude to food supplies. Outdoors-reared cows, sheep, and pigs; freshly caught fish; and seasonal fruits and vegetables provide a bedrock upon which traditional recipes are tempered with cosmopolitan influences. The contemporary English menu takes the best of Mediterranean and Asian cuisines and reinterprets them.

Natural Bounty

Cask ales. The interest in the provenance of food extends to beer, encouraging microbreweries to develop real or cask ales: beer that's unfiltered and unpasteurized, and that contains live brewer's yeast. The ales can be from kegs, bottles, or casks, and they range from pale amber to full-bodied. The Casque Mark outside pubs signals their availability.

Dairy produce. The stalwart Cheddar, Cheshire, Double Gloucester, and Stilton cheeses are complemented by traditional and experimental cheeses from small, local makers. Some cheeses come wrapped in nettles or vine leaves, others stuffed with apricots, cranberries, or herbs. Dairies are producing more sheep and goat cheeses, yogurts, and ice creams.

Game. In the fall and winter, pheasant, grouse, partridge, and venison are prominent on restaurant menus, served either roasted, in rich casseroles, or in pies. Duck (particularly the Gressingham and Aylesbury breeds) and rabbit are available all year-round.

Meat. Peacefully grazing cattle, including Aberdeen Angus, Herefordshire, and Welsh Black varieties, are an iconic symbol of the countryside. When hung and dry-aged for up to 28 days, English beef is at its most flavorsome. Spring lamb is succulent, and salt-marsh lamb from Wales and the Lake District, fed on wild grasses and herbs, makes for a unique taste. Outdoors-reared and rare breeds of pig, such as Gloucester Old Spot, often provide the breakfast bacon.

Preserved foods. Marmalade is a fixed item on the breakfast menu, and a wide variety of jams, including the less usual quince, find their place on the tea-shop table. Chutneys made from apples or tomatoes mixed with onions and spices are served with cheese at the end of a meal or as part of a pub lunch.

Seafood. The traditional trio of cod, haddock, and plaice is still in evidence, but declining fishing stocks have brought other varieties to prominence. Hake, bream, freshwater trout, wild salmon, sardines, pilchards, and mackerel are on the restaurant table, along with crab, mussels, and oysters. The east and Cornish coasts are favored fishing grounds.

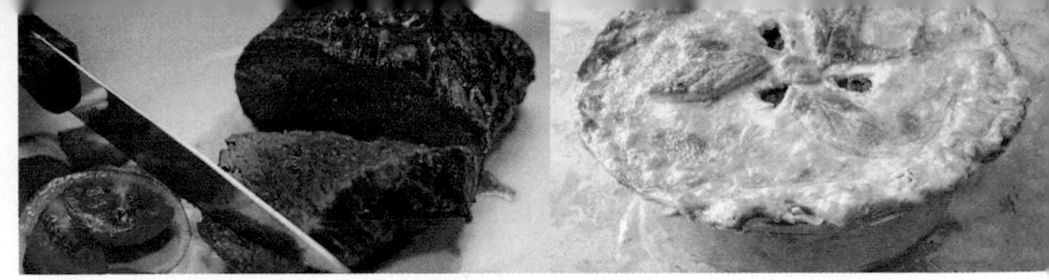

Traditional Dishes

Good international fare is available, and you shouldn't miss the Indian food in England. But do try some classics.

Black pudding. In this dish, associated with Lancashire, Yorkshire, and the Midlands, onions, pork fat, oatmeal, herbs, and spices are blended with the blood from a pig. At its best this dish has a delicate, crumbly texture and can be served at breakfast or as a starter to a meal.

Fish-and-chips. This number-one seaside favorite not only turns up in every seaside resort, but in fish-and-chip shops and restaurants throughout the land. Fish, usually cod, haddock, or plaice, is deep-fried in a crispy batter and served with thick french fries (chips) and, if eaten out, wrapped up in paper. The liberal sprinkling of salt and vinegar as well as "mushy" (processed) peas are optional.

Meat pies and pasties. Pies and pastics make a filling lunch. Perhaps the most popular is steak-and-kidney pie, combining chunks of lean beef and kidneys mixed with braised onions and mushrooms in a thick gravy, topped with a light puff- or short-pastry crust. Other combinations are chicken with mushrooms or leek and beef slow-cooked in ale (often Guinness). Cornish pasties are filled with beef, potato, rutabaga, and onions, all enveloped in a circle of pastry folded in half.

Sausages. "Bangers and mash" are sausages, commonly made with pork, beef, or lamb, served with mashed potatoes and onion gravy. Lincolnshire sausage consists of pork flavored with sage. Cumberland sausage comes in a long coil and has a peppery taste.

Shepherd's and cottage pie. These classic pub dishes have a lightly browned mashed-potato topping over stewed minced meat and onions in a rich gravy. Shepherd's pie uses lamb, cottage pie beef.

Meals Not to Be Missed

Full English breakfast. The "full English" is a three-course affair. Starting with orange juice, cereals, porridge, yogurt, or stewed fruit, it's followed by any combination of sausages, eggs, bacon, tomatoes, mushrooms, black pudding, baked beans, and fried bread. The feast finishes with toast and marmalade and tea or coffee. Alternatives to the fry-up are kippers, smoked haddock, or boiled or poached eggs. Some cafés serve an all-day breakfast.

Ploughman's lunch. Crusty bread, English cheese (perhaps farmhouse Cheddar, blue Stilton, crumbly Cheshire, or waxy red Leicester), and tangy pickles with a side-salad garnish make up a delicious light lunch, found in almost every pub.

Roast dinners. On Sunday, the traditional roast dinner is still popular. The meat, either beef, pork, lamb, or chicken, is served with roast potatoes, carrots, seasonal green vegetables, and Yorkshire pudding, a savory batter baked in the oven until crisp, and then topped with a rich, dark, meaty gravy. Horseradish sauce and English mustard are on hand for beef; a mint sauce accompanies lamb; and an apple sauce enhances pork.

Tea in the afternoon. Tea, ideally served in a country garden on a summer afternoon, ranks high on the list of England's must-do experiences. You may simply have a scone with your tea, or you can opt for a more ample feast: dainty sandwiches with the crusts cut off; scones with jam and clotted cream; and an array of homemade cakes. You can also choose from a variety of teas; Earl Grey is an afternoon favorite that you can take with either milk or lemon.

ENGLAND LODGING PRIMER

If your England dreams involve staying in a cozy cottage with a lovely garden, here's some good news: you won't have to break the bank. Throughout the country you'll find stylish lodging options—from good-value hotels and intimate bed-and-breakfasts to chic apartments and unique historic houses—in all price ranges.

⇨ *For resources and contacts, and information on hotel grading and booking, see Travel Smart England.*

Apartments and House Rentals

For a home base with cooking facilities that's roomy enough for a family, consider serviced apartments (available for short stays). These are popular in cities and towns throughout the country and can save you money. They also provide more privacy than a hotel or B&B.

Cottages and other houses are available for weekly rental in all areas. These vary from quaint older homes to brand-new buildings in scenic surroundings. For families and large groups they offer the best value-for-money accommodations, but because they're often in isolated locations, a car is vital. Living Architecture offers stays in one-of-a-kind architect-designed country houses. Lists of rental properties are available free of charge from VisitBritain. You may find discounts of up to 50% on rentals during the off-season (October through March).

Bed-and-Breakfasts

A special English tradition, and the backbone of budget travel, B&Bs are usually in a family home. Typical prices (outside London) range from £55 to £100 a night. They vary in style and grace, but these days most have private bathrooms. B&Bs range from the ordinary to the truly elegant. The line between B&Bs and guesthouses is growing increasingly blurred, but the latter are often larger.

Some Tourist Information Centres in cities and towns can help you find and book a B&B even on the day you show up in town. Many private services also deal with B&Bs.

Farmhouses

Over the years farmhouses have become popular; their special appeal is the rural experience, whether in Cornwall or Yorkshire. Consider this option only if you are touring by car, because farmhouses may be in remote locations. Prices are generally reasonable. Ask VisitBritain for the booklet "Stay on a Farm" or contact Farm Stay UK. Regional tourist boards may have information as well.

Historic Buildings

Looking for a unique experience and want to spend your vacation in a Gothic banqueting house, an old lighthouse, or maybe in an apartment at Hampton Court Palace? Several organizations, such as the Landmark Trust, National Trust, English Heritage, and Vivat Trust, have specially adapted historic buildings to rent. Many of these have kitchens, and some may require minimum stays.

Hotels

England is a popular vacation destination, so be sure to reserve hotel rooms weeks (months for London) in advance. The country has everything from budget chain hotels to luxurious retreats in converted country houses. In many towns and cities you'll find old inns that are former coaching inns; these served travelers as they journeyed around the country in horse-drawn carriages and stagecoaches.

GREAT ITINERARIES

HIGHLIGHTS OF ENGLAND: UNFORGETTABLE IMAGES

12 days

London

Day 1. The capital is just the jumping-off point for this trip, so choose a few highlights that grab your interest. If it's the Changing of the Guard at Buckingham Palace, check the time to be sure you catch the pageantry. If Westminster Abbey appeals to your sense of history, arrive as early as you can. Pick a museum (many are free, so you needn't linger if you don't want to), whether it's the National Gallery in Trafalgar Square, the British Museum in Bloomsbury, or a smaller gem like the Queen's Gallery. Stroll Hyde Park or take a boat ride on the Thames before you find a pub or Indian restaurant for dinner. End with a play; the experience of theatergoing may be as interesting as whatever work you see.

Windsor

Day 2. Resplendent with centuries of treasures, Windsor Castle is favored by the Queen, and has been by rulers for centuries. Tour it to appreciate the history and wealth of the monarchy. The State Apartments are open if the Queen isn't in residence, and 10 kings and queens are buried in magnificent St. George's Chapel. Time permitting, take a walk in the adjacent Great Park. If you can splurge for a luxurious stay (versus making Windsor a day trip from London), head up the valley to Cliveden, the Thames Valley's most spectacular hotel.

Logistics: Trains from Paddington and Waterloo stations leave about twice hourly and take less than one hour. Green Line buses depart from the Colonnades opposite London's Victoria Coach Station.

Salisbury and Stourhead

Day 3. Visible for miles around, Salisbury Cathedral's soaring spire is an unforgettable image of rural England. See the Magna Carta in the cathedral's Chapter House as you explore this marvel of medieval engineering, and walk the town path to get the view John Constable painted. Pay an afternoon visit to Stourhead to experience the finest example of the naturalistic 18th-century landscaping for which England is famous; the grand Palladian mansion here is a bonus.

Logistics: For trains to Salisbury from Windsor and Eton Riverside, head back to London's Waterloo to catch a train on the West of England line.

Bath and Stonehenge

Day 4. Bath's immaculately preserved, golden-stone Georgian architecture helps you recapture the late 18th century. Take time to stroll; don't miss the Royal Crescent (you can explore the period interior of No. 1), and sip the Pump Room's some say vile-tasting water as Jane Austen's characters might have. The Roman Baths are an amazing remnant of the ancient empire, complete with curses left by soldiers. Today you can do as the Romans did as you relax in the warm mineral waters at the Thermae Bath Spa. There's plenty to do in Bath (museums, shopping, theater), but you might make an excursion to Stonehenge (by car or tour bus). Go early or late to avoid the worst crowds at Stonehenge, and use your imagination—and the good audio guide—to appreciate this enigma.

Logistics: Trains and buses leave hourly from Salisbury to Bath.

The Cotswolds

Day 5. Antiques-shop in fairy-tale Stow-on-the-Wold and feed the ducks at the brook in Lower Slaughter for a taste of the mellow stone villages and dreamy green landscapes for which the area is beloved. Choose a rainy or off-season day to visit Broadway or risk jams of tourist traffic. Another great experience is a walk on the Cotswold Way or any local path.

Logistics: Drive to make the best of the beautiful scenery. Alternatively, opt for a guided tour bus.

Oxford and Blenheim Palace

Day 6. Join a guided tour of Oxford's glorious quadrangles, chapels, and gardens to get the best access to these centuries-old academic treasures. This leaves time for a jaunt to Blenheim, a unique combination of baroque opulence (inside and out) and naturalistic parkland, the work of the great 18th-century landscape designer Capability Brown. For classic Oxford experiences, rent a punt or join students and go pub-crawling around town.

Logistics: Hourly trains depart from Bath for Oxford. Buses frequently depart from Oxford's Gloucester Green for Blenheim Palace.

Stratford-upon-Avon

Day 7. Skip this stop if you don't care about you-know-who. Fans of Shakespeare can see his birthplace and Anne Hathaway's Cottage (walking there is a delight), and then finish with a memorable performance at the Royal Shakespeare Company's magnificently renovated main stage. Start the day early and be prepared for crowds.

Logistics: From Oxford there are direct trains and a less frequent Stagecoach bus service.

Shrewsbury to Chester

Day 8. Head north to see the half-timber buildings of Shrewsbury, one of the best preserved of England's Tudor towns. Strolling is the best way to experience it. In Chester the architecture is more or less the same (though not always authentic), but the Rows, a series of two-story shops with medieval crypts beneath, and the fine city walls are sights you can't pass by. You can walk part or all of the city walls for views of the town and surrounding area.

Logistics: For Shrewsbury, change trains at Birmingham. The train ride to Chester is less than an hour.

The Lake District

Days 9 and 10. In the area extending north beyond Kendal and Windermere, explore the English lakes and beautiful surrounding mountains on foot in the Lake District

National Park. This area is jam-packed with hikers in summer and on weekends, so rent a car to seek out the more isolated routes. Take a cruise on Windermere or Coniston Water, or rent a boat for another classic Lakeland experience. If you have time for one Wordsworth-linked site, head to Dove Cottage; you can even have afternoon tea there.

Logistics: Train to Oxenholme with a change at Warrington Bank Quay. At Oxenholme you can switch to Windermere.

York

Day 11. This historic cathedral city is crammed with 15th- and 16th-century buildings, but don't miss York Minster, with its stunning stained glass, and the medieval streets of the Shambles. Take your pick of the city's museums or go shopping; have tea at Betty's or unwind at a pub. A walk along the top of the city walls is fun, too.

Logistics: By train from Oxenholme, switch at Manchester Piccadilly, or from Carlisle change at Newcastle.

Cambridge

Day 12. Spend the afternoon touring King's College Chapel and the Backs—gardens and sprawling meadows—and refining your punting skills on the River Cam. The excellent Fitzwilliam Museum, full of art and antiquities, is another option, as is the Polar Museum. To relax, join the students for a pint at a pub.

Logistics: For train service, switch at Peterborough. Trains leave Cambridge for London frequently.

TIPS

■ Train travelers should keep in mind that regional "Rovers" and "Rangers" offer unlimited train travel in one-day, three-day, or weeklong increments. See 🌐 *www.nationalrail.co.uk* for details. Also check out BritRail passes, which must be purchased before your trip.

■ Buses are time-consuming, but more scenic and cheaper than train travel. National Express offers discounts including fun fares—fares to and from London to various cities (including Cambridge) for as low as £5 if booked more than 24 hours in advance. Or check out low-cost Megabus.

■ To cut the tour short, consider skipping Chester and Shrewsbury and proceed to the Lake District from Stratford-upon-Avon on day eight. Likewise, you can consider passing up a visit to Cambridge if you opt for Oxford. You can add the time to your London stay or another place you want to linger.

■ It's easy to visit Stonehenge from Salisbury, as well as from Bath, whether you have a car or want a guided excursion.

■ Buy theater tickets well in advance for Stratford-upon-Avon.

GREAT ITINERARIES

STATELY HOMES AND LANDSCAPES TOUR

11 days

Hampton Court Palace

Day 1. Start your trip royally at this palace a half hour from London by train. It's two treasures in one: a Tudor palace with magnificent baroque additions by Christopher Wren. As you walk through cobbled courtyards, Henry VIII's State Apartments, and the enormous kitchens, you may feel as if you've been whisked back to the days of the Tudors and William and Mary. A quiet stroll through the 60 acres of immaculate gardens—the sculpted yews look like huge green gumdrops—is recommended. Be sure to get lost in the 18th-century maze—if it's open (diligent maintenance leads to occasional closures). It's easy to spend a whole day here, so start early.

Logistics: Tube to Richmond, then Bus R68; or catch the train from Waterloo to Hampton Court Station.

Knole and Ightham Mote

Days 2 and 3. Clustered around Royal Tunbridge Wells south of London is the highest concentration of stately homes in England, and, as if that weren't enough, the surrounding fields and colorful orchards are often wrapped in clouds of mist, creating a picture-perfect scene. We've picked two very different homes to visit, leaving you plenty of time to tour at a leisurely pace. Knole, Vita Sackville-West's sprawling childhood home, has dark, baroque rooms and a famous set of silver furniture. Ightham Mote, a smaller, moated house, is a vision from the Middle Ages. Its rooms are an ideal guide to style changes from the Tudor to Victorian eras. Spend the evening at one of the many good restaurants in Royal Tunbridge Wells.

Logistics: Take the train from London's Charing Cross to Sevenoaks, from which it's a 20-minute walk to Knole. There's no public transportation to Ightham Mote.

Petworth House

Day 4. Priceless paintings by Gainsborough, Reynolds, and Turner (19 by Turner alone) embellish the august rooms of Petworth House, present-day home to Lord and Lady Egremont and one of the National Trust's treasures. Check out Capability Brown's 700-acre deer park or the Victorian kitchens, and for the perfect lunch peruse the offerings in the winding lanes of Petworth town. Head to Chichester for the evening, along a route passing through the rolling grasslands and deep valleys of the South Downs.

Logistics: Train to Chichester, switching in Redhill, then bus to Petworth.

Wilton House

Day 5. Base yourself in Salisbury for two days, taking time to see the famous cathedral with its impressively tall spire and to walk the town path from the Long Bridge for the best view of it. Visit neoclassical Wilton House (in nearby Wilton) first, where the exquisite Double Cube Room contains a spectacular family portrait by Van Dyck and gilded furniture that accommodated Eisenhower when he contemplated the Normandy invasion here. On your way back make a detour to Stonehenge to view the wide-open Salisbury Plain and ponder the enigmatic stones.

Logistics: Take a train from Chichester to Salisbury, with a switch in Cosham or Southampton; then bus it to Wilton House.

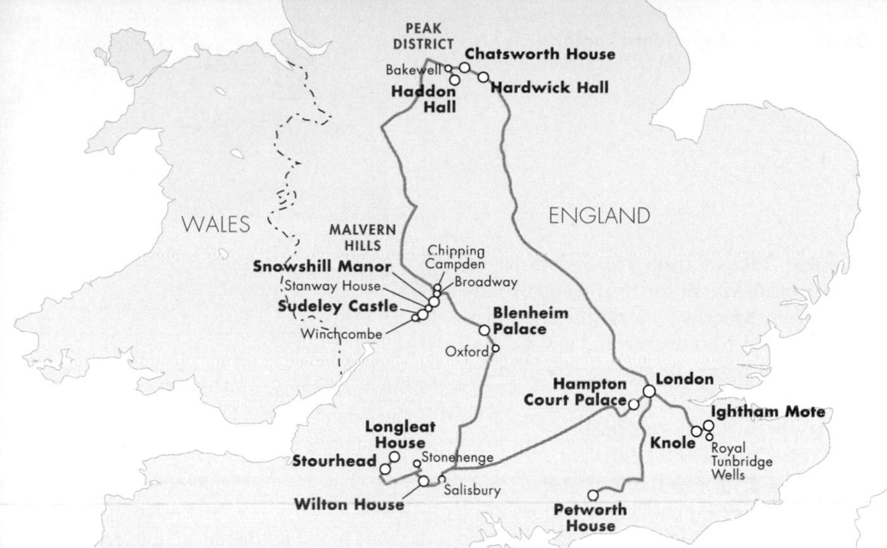

Stourhead to Longleat House

Day 6. Day-trip west from Salisbury to Stourhead to experience perhaps the most stunning house-garden combination in the country, and either spend the day here (climb Alfred's Tower for a grand view of the house) or leave some time for nearby Longleat House—a vast, treasure-stuffed Italian Renaissance palace complete with safari park and a devilish maze. If you want to see the safari park, you'll need plenty of time here. Once back in Salisbury, relax in one of New Street's many cafés.

Logistics: Bus to Warminster and then a taxi for the 5-mile journey to Longleat; for Stourhead, take the train to Gillingham from Salisbury, followed by a short cab ride.

Blenheim Palace

Day 7. Home of the dukes of Marlborough and birthplace of Winston Churchill, Blenheim Palace uniquely combines exquisitely designed parklands (save time to walk) and one of the most ornate baroque structures in the world. After your visit, have afternoon tea at Blenheim Tea Rooms in the adorable village of Woodstock. Overnight in Oxford; do your own pub crawl.

Logistics: From Salisbury by train, change at Basingstoke for Oxford, then catch a bus to Blenheim.

Snowshill Manor and Sudeley Castle

Days 8 and 9. Here you can take in the idyllic Cotswold landscape, a magical mix of greenery and mellow stone cottages and ancient churches (built with wool-trade money), along with some famous buildings. Spend the first night in Broadway to explore nearby Snowshill Manor—with its delightfully eccentric collection of Tibetan scrolls, Persian lamps, and samurai armor—in the unspoiled village of Snowshill. If you have a car, don't linger in busy Broadway. Instead, head to Chipping Campden, one of the best-preserved Cotswolds villages, which nestles in a secluded valley. Move to another charming town, Winchcombe, on the second day. Take a stroll past honey-color stone cottages and impeccably well-kept gardens. Visit Sudeley Castle, once home to Catherine Parr (Henry VIII's last wife), a Tudor-era palace with romantic gardens (only a few rooms are now open to the public). Another option near Winchcombe is Stanway House, a Jacobean manor owned by Lord Neidpath; hours are limited, but this timeworn home and its gabled gatehouse are typically English.

Logistics: Take a train from Oxford to Moreton-in-Marsh for the bus to Broadway; from Broadway, walk the 2½ miles to Snowshill Manor; for Sudeley Castle, take a bus from Broadway to Winchcombe, then walk.

Chatsworth House, Haddon Hall, and Hardwick Hall

Days 10 and 11. For the final stops, head north, east of Manchester, to a more dramatic landscape. In or near the craggy Peak District, where the gentle slopes of the Pennine Hills begin their ascent to Scotland, are three of England's most renowned historic homes. Base yourself in Bakewell, and spend your first day taking in the art treasures amassed by the dukes of Devonshire at Chatsworth House. The gardens, grounds, shops, and farmyard exhibits make it easy to spend a day here. If you have any time left over, get out of Bakewell and take a walk in the hills of the Peak District National Park (maps are available at the town's tourist information center).

On the second day, devote the morning to the crenellations and boxy roofs of medieval Haddon Hall, a quintessentially English house. Give your afternoon to Hardwick Hall, an Elizabethan stone mansion with a facade that's "more glass than wall"—a truly innovative idea in the 16th century. Its collections of period tapestries and embroideries are remarkable reminders of the splendor of the age.

Logistics: Take a train back to Oxford and then up to Manchester for the connection to Buxton; then catch a bus to Bakewell.

TIPS

■ All stately homes in this itinerary, with the exception of Hampton Court Palace and Longleat House, are closed for winter, though gardens may remain open. Even homes open April through October may not be open every day. It's best to confirm all hours before visiting.

■ A car is best for this itinerary, as some houses are remote. Use a GPS or get good maps.

■ Country roads around the Peak District are hard to negotiate; be especially careful when driving to Chatsworth House, Haddon Hall, and Hardwick Hall. Drives will take longer than you expect.

■ Look into discount passes, such as those from the National Trust or English Heritage (⇨ *See Sightseeing Passes in Essentials in Travel Smart England*), which provide significant savings on visits to multiple sites. Memberships are also available.

2

LONDON

Visit Fodors.com for advice, updates, and bookings

WELCOME TO LONDON

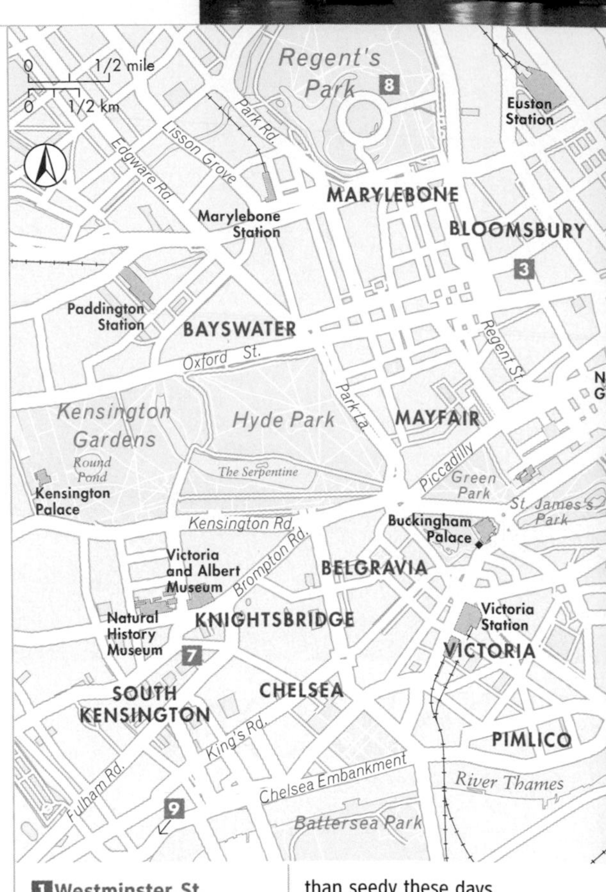

TOP REASONS TO GO

★ **The abbey and the cathedral:** That Gothic splendor, Westminster Abbey, soars above the final resting place of several of Britain's most distinguished figures. To the east is St. Paul's, the beautiful English Baroque cathedral.

★ **Buckingham Palace:** Although not the prettiest royal residence, this is the public face of the monarchy and the place to watch the culmination of the Changing the Guard ceremony.

★ **Tower of London:** Parts of this complex date back 11 centuries. The tower has been a prison, an armory, and a mint—now it houses the Crown Jewels.

★ **Majestic museums:** Discover the old masters at the National Gallery, the cutting-edge works at Tate Modern, and the historical artifacts of the British Museum.

★ **A city of villages:** Each of London's dozens of neighborhoods has its own personality. Parks, shops, pubs: walk around and discover them for yourself.

1 Westminster, St. James's, and Royal London. Embrace your inner tourist. Take pictures of the mounted Horse Guards, and drink in the Old Masters at the National Gallery. It's well worth braving the crowds to visit historic Westminster Abbey.

2 Soho and Covent Garden. More sophisticated than seedy these days, the heart of London puts Theatreland, strip joints, Chinatown, and notable restaurants side by side.

3 Bloomsbury and Holborn. The University of London dominates the city's historical intellectual center, Bloomsbury. Allow for long visits to the incomparable British Museum.

2

GETTING ORIENTED

London grew from a wooden bridge built over the Thames in the year AD 43 to its current 600 square miles and 8.3 million inhabitants in haphazard fashion, expanding from two centers of power: Westminster, seat of government and royalty, to the west, and the City, site of finance and commerce, to the east. The patchwork of urban villages is ever evolving, though the great parks, described by Lord Chatham as "the lungs of London," and the River Thames remain constants.

4 The City. London's Wall Street might be the oldest part of the capital, but thanks to the futuristic skyscrapers and a sleek Millennium Bridge, it looks like the newest. There's plenty for period architecture buffs as well: St. Paul's Cathedral, Westminster Abbey, and the Tower of London.

5 East End. Once known for its slums immortalized by Charles Dickens and Jack the Ripper, today the area is home to London's contemporary art scene, along with Brick Lane's curry houses and Spitalfields Market.

6 The South Bank. The National Theatre, Old Vic, Royal Festival Hall, BFI Southbank, Shakespeare's Globe, and Tate Modern make this area a cultural hub. Get a bird's-eye view of the whole city from the Shard or the London Eye.

7 Kensington, Knightsbridge, and Mayfair. Kensington's museums are filled with treasures, with the Science Museum and the Natural History Museum offering the most fun for children. Shopaholics should head for Bond Street and Sloane Street.

8 Regent's Park and Hampstead. London becomes noticeably calmer and greener as you head north from Euston Road. Come here to experience just how laid-back moneyed Londoners can be.

9 Up and Down the Thames. Maritime Greenwich boasts masterpieces by Wren and Inigo Jones. Other river excursions take you to Kew Gardens and Hampton Court Palace.

Updated by
Jo Caird,
Jack Jewers,
James O'Neill,
Ellin Stein,
And Alex
Wijeratna

If London's only attraction were its famous landmarks, it would still be unmissable. But London is so much more. Though its long history is evident at every turn, it's also one of the world's most modern and vibrant cities.

London beckons with great museums, royal pageantry, and historically significant buildings. Unique Georgian terraces perch next to cutting-edge modern skyscrapers, and parks and squares provide unexpected oases of greenery amid the dense urban landscape. Modern central London still largely follows its winding medieval street pattern. Even Londoners armed with the indispensable *London A–Z* street finder or equivalent app can get lost in their own city.

As well as visiting landmarks like St. Paul's Cathedral and the Tower of London, set aside time for random wandering; the city repays every moment spent exploring its backstreets and mews on foot. Go to lesser-known but thoroughly rewarding sites such as Kensington Palace and the unique home of 19th-century architect Sir John Soane, which houses his outstanding collection of antiquities and art.

Today the city's art, style, fashion, and restaurant scenes make headlines around the world. London's chefs have become internationally influential, its fashion designers and art stars set global trends, its nightlife continues to produce exciting new acts, and its theater remains celebrated for superb classical and innovative productions.

Then there's that greatest living link with the past—the Royal Family. Don't let fear of looking like a tourist stop you from enjoying the pageantry of the Changing the Guard at Buckingham Palace, one of the greatest free shows in the world.

As the eminent 18th-century man of letters Samuel Johnson said, "When a man is tired of London, he is tired of life, for there is in London all that life can afford." Armed with energy and curiosity, you can discover its riches.

LONDON PLANNER

WHEN TO GO

The heaviest tourist season runs from mid-April through mid-October, with another peak around Christmas—though the tide never really ebbs. Spring is the time to see the royal London parks and gardens at their freshest, fall to enjoy near-ideal exploring conditions. In late summer, be warned: air-conditioning is rarely found in places other than department stores, modern restaurants, hotels, and cinemas, although it's really needed for only a few days. Winter can be rather dismal, but all the theaters, concerts, and exhibitions go full speed ahead.

Avoid the February and October "half-terms" when schools in the capital take a break for a week and children flood nearly all the attractions. The start of August can be a very busy time, and the weather makes Tube travel a nightmare. Shopping in central London the week before Christmas is an idea best left only to desperate Londoners who have forgotten to buy presents.

GETTING HERE AND AROUND

ADDRESSES

Central London and its surrounding inner suburbs are divided into 32 boroughs—33, counting the City of London. More useful for finding your way around, however, are the subdivisions of London into postal districts. The first one or two letters give the location: N means north, NW means northwest, and so on.

AIR TRAVEL

For information about airports and airport transfers, see Getting Here and Around in Travel Smart England.

BUS TRAVEL

In central London, Transport for London (TfL) buses are traditionally bright red double- and single-deckers. Not all buses run the full length of their route at all times, so check with the driver. In central London you must purchase tickets from machines at bus stops along the routes before you board. The main bus stops have a red TfL symbol on a white background. When the word "Request" is written across the sign, you must flag the bus down. Buses are a good way to see the town, but don't take one if you're in a hurry.

All journeys cost £2.40, and there are no transfers. If you plan to make a number of journeys in one day, consider buying a Day Travelcard, good for both Tube and bus travel. Weekly Travelcards are also available. Prepaid Oyster cards can offer a considerable saving, with single journeys costing £1.45. Visitor Oyster cards cost £10 and can be topped up. They are available from the Gatwick Express desks at Gatwick airport and Victoria Station, or in advance through VisitBritain (🌐 *www.visitbritainshop.com*). Traveling without a valid ticket makes you liable for a fine (£20).

Night buses, denoted by an "N" before their route numbers, run from midnight to 5 am on a more restricted route than day buses. However, some night bus routes should be approached with caution and the top deck avoided. All night buses run by request stop, so flag them down if you're waiting, or push the button if you want to alight.

Buses, or "coaches," as privately operated bus services are known here, operate mainly from London's Victoria Coach Station to more than 1,200 major towns and cities. *For information, see Getting Here and Around in Travel Smart England.*

Contact Transport for London. ☎ *0343/222–1234* 🌐 *www.tfl.gov.uk.*

CAR TRAVEL

The major approach roads to London are six-lane motorways. Motorways (from Heathrow, M4; from Gatwick, M23 to M25, then M3; Stansted, M11) are usually the faster option for getting in and out of town, although rush-hour traffic is horrendous. Stay tuned to local radio stations for updates.

The simple advice about driving in London is: don't. If you must drive, remember to drive on the left and stick to the speed limit (30 mph on some city streets, in the process of changing to 20 mph in several boroughs).

To encourage public-transit use and reduce traffic congestion, the city charges drivers of most vehicles entering central London £10 on weekdays from 7 am to 6 pm (excluding public holidays). Traffic signs designate the entrance to congestion-charge zones, and cameras read car license plates and send the information to a database. Drivers who don't pay up by midnight of the next charging day are penalized £120 (reduced to £60 if paid within 14 days).

TAXI TRAVEL

Taxis are expensive, but if you're with several people they can be practical. Hotels and main tourist areas have taxi ranks; you can also hail taxis on the street. If the yellow "For Hire" sign is lighted on top, the taxi is available. Fares start at £2.20, and there are per-minute charges—a journey of a mile that takes five minutes will cost £4.90, one that takes 12 minutes will cost £8.60. Taxi fares increase between 10 pm and 6 am, and a £2 surcharge is applied to telephone bookings. You don't have to tip taxi drivers, but it's advised; 10% of the fare is the norm, and most passengers round up to the nearest pound.

TRAIN TRAVEL

London has eight major train stations, each serving a different area of the country, and all are accessible by Underground or bus. Various private companies operate trains, but National Rail Enquiries acts as a central rail information number. *For further information on train travel, see Getting Here and Around in Travel Smart England.*

Contact National Rail Enquiries. ☎ *0845/748–4950* 🌐 *www.nationalrail.co.uk.*

UNDERGROUND (TUBE) TRAVEL

London's extensive Underground (Tube) system has color-coded routes, clear signs, and far-reaching connections. Trains run out into the suburbs, and all stations are marked with the London Underground circular symbol. (In Britain, subway means "pedestrian underpass.") Some lines have branches (Central, District, Northern, Metropolitan, and Piccadilly), so be sure to note which branch is needed for your destination.

Electronic platform signs indicate the final stop and route of the next train and how many minutes until it arrives. The London Overground now travels in a loop around Zone 2, calling at Shepherd's Bush in the west, Hampstead Heath in the North, Shoreditch High Street in the east, and Clapham Junction in the south, plus stations in between.

London is divided into six concentric zones (ask at Underground ticket booths for a map and booklet, which give details of the ticket options). For one-way fares paid in cash, a flat £4.70 price per journey applies between Zones 1 and 3, whether you're traveling for one stop or 12. If you're planning several trips in one day, it's much cheaper to buy a Visitor Oyster card or Day Travelcard, which is good for unrestricted travel on the Tube, buses, and Overground trains. The off-peak Oyster-card fare for Zones 1 and 2, for example, is £2.20. A one-day Travelcard for Zones 1 and 2 costs £9 if purchased before 9:30 am, and £8.90 if bought after 9:30 am. The more zones included in your travel, the more the Travelcard will cost.

Daily except Sunday, trains begin running just after 5 am; the last services leave central London between midnight and 12:30 am. On Sunday, trains start two hours later and finish about an hour earlier. The frequency of trains depends on the route and the time of day, but normally you won't have to wait more than 10 minutes in central areas.

DISCOUNTS AND DEALS

All national collections (such as the Natural History Museum, Science Museum, Victoria & Albert Museum) are free, a real bargain for museumgoers. *For other discounts, see Sightseeing Passes in Essentials in Travel Smart England.*

TOUR OPTIONS

BIKE TOURS

A 24-hour cycle-for-hire scheme, the Barclays Cycle Hire, introduced in 2010 to enable Londoners to pick up a bicycle at one of more than 570 docking stations and return it at another, has proved very popular. The first 30 minutes are free. After that, charges rise incrementally from £1 for one hour up to £50 for 24 hours. There is also a £2 per-day access charge. Fees are payable online, by phone, and at docking stations, by credit or debit card only—cash is not accepted. But whether you join the scheme or just rent a bike from a shop, remember that London is still a busy metropolis: the best way to see it on two wheels is probably to contact one of the excellent cycle tour companies.

Tour Operators Barclays Cycle Hire. ☎ *0343/222–6666 within U.K., 208/216–6666 from outside U.K.* 🌐 *https://web.barclayscyclehire.tfl.gov.uk/maps.* **Cycle Tours of London.** ☎ *07788/994430* 🌐 *www.biketoursoflondon.com.* **Fat Tire Bike Tours.** ☎ *07882/338779* 🌐 *www.fattirebiketours.com.* **London Bicycle Tour Company.** ☎ *020/7928–6838* 🌐 *www.londonbicycle.com.*

BOAT TOURS

Year-round, but more frequently from April to October, tour boats cruise the Thames, offering a singular view of the London skyline. Most leave from Westminster Pier, Charing Cross Pier, and Tower Pier. Boats on downstream routes pass by the Tower of London, Greenwich, and the Thames Barrier. Upstream destinations include Kew, Richmond, and Hampton Court (mainly in summer). Depending upon the destination, river trips may last from one to four hours.

London's tranquil side can be experienced on narrow boats that cruise the city's two canals, the Grand Union and the Regent's Canal; most vessels operate on the latter, which runs between Little Venice in the west (nearest Tube: Warwick Avenue, on the Bakerloo Line) and Camden Lock (about 200 yards north of the Camden Town Tube station). Fares start at £9 for 1½-hour round-trip cruises.

Contacts Bateaux London. ☎ *020/7695–1800* 🌐 *www.bateauxlondon.com.* **Canal Cruises.** ☎ *020/8440–8962* 🌐 *www.londoncanalcruises.com.* **Jason's Trip.** 🌐 *www.jasons.co.uk.* **London Duck Tours.** ☎ *020/7928–3132* 🌐 *www.londonducktours.co.uk.* **Thames Cruises.** ☎ *020/7928–9009* 🌐 *www.thamescruises.com.* **Thames River Boats.** ☎ *020/7930–2062* 🌐 *www.wpsa.co.uk.* **Thames River Services.** ☎ *020/7930–4097* 🌐 *www.thamesriverservices.co.uk.*

BUS TOURS

Guided sightseeing tours on hop-on, hop-off double-decker buses—open-top in summer—cover the main central sights. Many companies run daily bus tours that depart, usually between 8:30 and 9 am, from central points. Best Value and other outfits conduct guided tours in traditional coach buses. Tickets can be bought from the driver and are good all day. Prices vary according to the type of tour, although £25 is the benchmark. Other guided bus tours, such as those offered by Golden, take place on enclosed (and more expensive) coach buses and are not hop-on, hop-off excursions.

Contacts Best Value Tours. ☎ *0870/803–1316* 🌐 *www.bestvaluetours.co.uk.* **Big Bus Tours.** ☎ *020/7808–6753* 🌐 *www.bigbustours.com.* **Black Taxi Tour of London.** ☎ *020/7935–9363* 🌐 *www.blacktaxitours.co.uk.* **Golden Tours.** ☎ *020/7630–2028 in U.K., 800/509–2507 in U.S.* 🌐 *www.goldentours.co.uk.* **Original London Sightseeing Tour.** ☎ *020/8877–1722* 🌐 *www.theoriginaltour.com.* **Premium Tours.** ☎ *020/7713–1311, 800/815–4003 in U.S.* 🌐 *www.premiumtours.co.uk.*

WALKING TOURS

One of the best ways to get to know London is on foot, and there are many guided and themed walking tours, which cover everything from Jack the Ripper's East End to Dickens's West End. Context London's expert docents lead small groups on walks with art, architecture, and similar themes. The London Walks Company hosts more than 100 walks every week.

Contacts Blood and Tears Walk. ☎ *07905/746–733* 🌐 *www.shockinglondon.com.* **Blue Badge.** ☎ *020/7403–1115* 🌐 *www.britainsbestguides.org.* **Context London.** ☎ *020/3514–1780, 800/691–6036 in U.S.* 🌐 *www.contexttravel.com/london.* **London Walks.** ☎ *020/7624–3978* 🌐 *www.walks.com.* **Richard Jones's London Walking Tours.** ☎ *020/8530–8443* 🌐 *www.londondiscoverytours.co.uk.* **Shakespeare City Walk.** ☎ *07905/746–733* 🌐 *www.shakespeareguide.com.*

A classic photo op: don't miss the cavalry from the Queen's Life Guard at Buckingham Palace.

VISITOR INFORMATION

You can get good information at the Travel Information Centres at Victoria Station and St. Pancras International train station. These are helpful if you're looking for brochures for London sights and if you need a hotel. Travel Information Centres can also be found at the Euston and Liverpool Street train stations, Heathrow Airport, St. Paul's Cathedral churchyard, and Piccadilly Circus, as well as in Greenwich and some other Outer London locations.

Information Visit London. 🌐 *www.visitlondon.com.*

EXPLORING LONDON

Westminster and the City contain many of Britain's most historically significant buildings: the Tower of London, St. Paul's Cathedral, Westminster Abbey, the Houses of Parliament, and Buckingham Palace. Within a few-minutes' walk of Buckingham Palace lie St. James's and Mayfair, neighboring quarters of elegant town houses built for the nobility during the 17th and early 18th centuries and now notable for shopping opportunities.

Hyde Park and Kensington Gardens, originally Henry VIII's hunting ground, create an oasis of greenery in congested west London. Just south of the parks is South Kensington's museum district, with the Natural History Museum, the Science Museum, and the Victoria & Albert Museum. Another cultural center is the South Bank and Southwark: the concert halls of the South Bank Centre, the National Theatre, Tate Modern, and the reconstructed Shakespeare's Globe. Farther downstream is Maritime Greenwich, home of the meridian and a World Heritage Site, with its gorgeous Wren and Inigo Jones landmarks.

WESTMINSTER, ST. JAMES'S, AND ROYAL LONDON

This is postcard London at its best. Crammed with historic churches, grand state buildings, and major art collections, the area unites politics, high culture, and religion. (Oh, and the Queen lives here, too.) World-class monuments such as Buckingham Palace, the Houses of Parliament, Westminster Abbey, and the National Gallery sit alongside lesser-known but lovingly curated museums redolent of British history. If you only have time to visit one part of London, this is it. This is concentrated sightseeing, so pace yourself. For much of the year a large portion of Royal London is floodlighted at night, adding to the theatricality of the experience.

GETTING HERE

Trafalgar Square—easy to access and in the center of the action—is a good place to start. Take the Tube to Embankment (District, Circle, Bakerloo, and Northern lines) and walk north until you cross the Strand, or alight at Charing Cross (Bakerloo, Jubilee, and Northern lines), where the Northumberland Avenue exit deposits you on the southeast corner of the Square.

PLANNING YOUR TIME

A lifetime of exploring may still be insufficient to cover this historically rich part of London, but two to three days can take in the highlights: Begin with Buckingham Palace then move on to Westminster Abbey and the Houses of Parliament to the south, or east to the art of the National Gallery.

TOP ATTRACTIONS

Fodor's Choice ★ **Buckingham Palace.** The doors of the monarch's official residence are only open to the public in August and September, when the Queen heads off to Scotland on her annual summer holiday. (Want to know if the Queen's at home? If she's in residence the Royal Standard flies above the palace; if not, it's the more famous red, white, and blue Union Flag.) The standard tour covers the palace's 19 State Rooms, with their fabulous gilt moldings and walls adorned with old masters.

The **Grand Hall,** followed by the **Grand Staircase** and **Guard Room,** are visions in marble and gold leaf, filled with massive, twinkling chandeliers. Don't miss the theatrical **Throne Room,** with the original 1953 coronation throne, or the sword in **the Ballroom,** used by the Queen to bestow knighthoods and other honors with a touch on the recipient's shoulders. Royal portraits line the **State Dining Room,** and the **Blue Drawing Room** is dazzling in its splendor. The bow-shape **Music Room** features lapis lazuli columns between arched floor-to-ceiling windows, and the alabaster-and-gold plasterwork of the **White Drawing Room** is a dramatic statement of wealth and power.

Changing of the Guard remains one of London's best free shows and culminates in front of the palace. Marching to live military bands, the old guard proceeds up the Mall from St. James's Palace to Buckingham

Palace. Shortly afterward, the new guard approaches from Wellington Barracks. Then within the forecourt, the captains of the old and new guards symbolically transfer the keys to the palace. **■TIP→ Get there by 10:30 to grab a spot in the best viewing section for the Changing the Guard (www.changing-the-guard.com), daily at 11:30 from May until the end of July (varies according to troop deployment requirements) and on alternate days for the rest of the year, weather permitting.** ✉ *Buckingham Palace Rd., St. James's* ☎ *020/7766–7300* 🌐 *www.royalcollection.org.uk/visit* 🎫 *£20.50; joint ticket with Queen's Gallery and Royal Mews £35.60* ⏲ *Aug., daily 9:30–7:30 (last admission 5:15); Sept., daily 9:30–6:30 (last admission 4:15). Times subject to change; check website* Ⓜ *Victoria, St. James's Park, Green Park.*

2

FAMILY Fodor's Choice ★ **Churchill War Rooms.** It was from this small warren of underground rooms—beneath the vast government buildings of the Treasury—that Winston Churchill and his team directed troops in World War II. Designed to be bombproof, the whole complex has been preserved almost exactly as it was when the last light was turned off at the end of the war. Every clock shows almost 5 pm, and the furniture, fittings, and paraphernalia of a busy, round-the-clock war office are in situ, down to the colored map pins.

During air raids, the leading government ministers met here, and the Cabinet Room is still arranged as if a meeting were about to convene. In the Map Room, the Allied campaign is charted on wall-to-wall maps with a rash of pinholes showing the movements of convoys. In the hub of the room, a bank of differently colored phones known as the "Beauty Chorus" linked the War Rooms to control rooms around the nation. The Prime Minister's Room holds the desk from which Churchill made his morale-boosting broadcasts; the Telephone Room (a converted broom cupboard) has his hotline to FDR. You can also see the restored rooms that the PM used for dining and sleeping. Telephonists (switchboard operators) and clerks who worked 16-hour shifts slept in lesser quarters in unenviable conditions.

A great addition to the War Rooms is the Churchill Museum, a tribute to the great wartime leader himself. ✉ *Clive Steps, King Charles St., Westminster* ☎ *020/7930–6961* 🌐 *www.iwm.org.uk* 🎫 *£18* ⏲ *Daily 9:30–6; last admission 5* Ⓜ *Westminster.*

FAMILY **Horse Guards Parade.** Once the tiltyard for jousting tournaments, Horse Guards Parade is best known for the annual Trooping the Colour ceremony, in which the Queen takes the salute on her official birthday tribute, on the second Saturday in June. (Though it's called a birthday it's actually the anniversary of her coronation—the current Queen's real birthday is April 21.) It's a must-see if you're around, with marching bands and throngs of onlookers. Throughout the rest of the year the changing of two mounted sentries known as the **Queen's Life Guard** at the Whitehall facade of Horse Guards provides what may be London's most popular photo opportunity. The ceremony lasts about half an hour. At 4 pm daily is the dismounting ceremony, aka the 4 O'Clock Parade, during which sentries are posted and horses returned to their stables. ✉ *Whitehall* ☎ *020/7930–4832* ⏲ *Changing of the Guard*

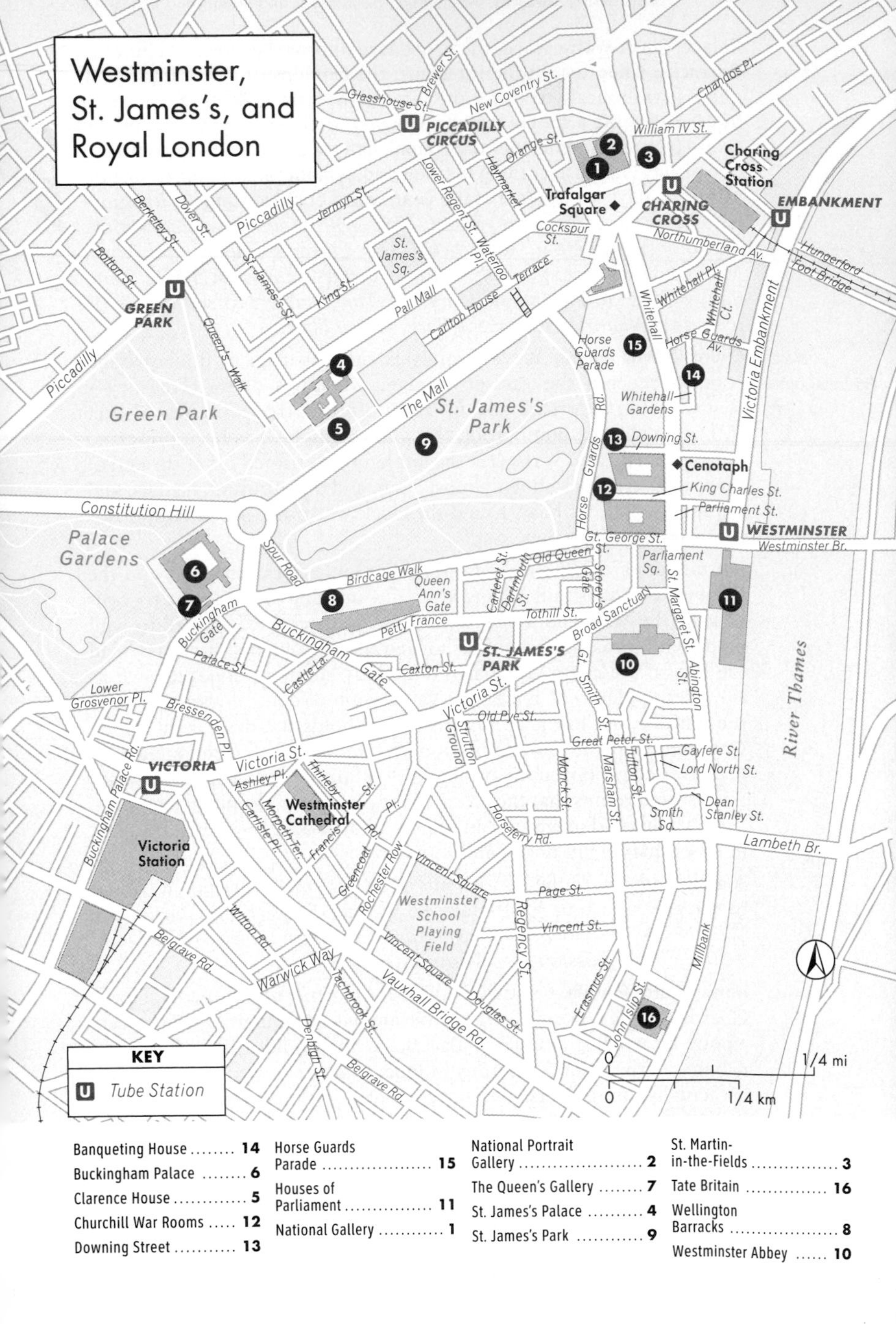

Banqueting House **14**
Buckingham Palace **6**
Clarence House **5**
Churchill War Rooms **12**
Downing Street **13**
Horse Guards Parade **15**
Houses of Parliament **11**
National Gallery **1**
National Portrait Gallery **2**
The Queen's Gallery **7**
St. James's Palace **4**
St. James's Park **9**
St. Martin-in-the-Fields **3**
Tate Britain **16**
Wellington Barracks **8**
Westminster Abbey **10**

11 am Mon.–Sat., 10 am Sun.; dismounting ceremony daily at 4 pm Ⓜ *Westminster.*

Fodor'sChoice ★ **Houses of Parliament.** The Palace of Westminster, as the complex is called, was first established on this site by Edward the Confessor in the 11th century. William II started building a new palace in 1087, and this became the seat of English power. Fire destroyed most of the palace in 1834, and the current complex dates largely from the mid-19th century.

The **Visitors' Galleries** of the House of Commons provide a view of democracy in action when the benches are filled by opposing MPs (members of Parliament). Debates are formal but raucous, especially during the **Prime Minister's Questions** (PMQs), when any MP can put a question to the nation's leader. Tickets to PMQs are free but highly sought after, so the only way for non–U.K. citizens to gain access is by lining up on the day and hoping for returns or no-shows. The action starts at 1 pm every Wednesday when Parliament is sitting, and the whole shebang is broadcast live on television. There are also Visitors Galleries for The House of Lords.

Westminster Hall, with its remarkable hammer-beam roof, was the work of William the Conqueror's son William Rufus. It's one of the largest remaining Norman halls in Europe, and its dramatic interior was the scene of the trial of Charles I.

After the 1834 fire, the Clock Tower—renamed **Elizabeth Tower** in 2012, in honor of the Queen's Diamond Jubilee—was completed in 1858, and contains the 13-ton bell known as **Big Ben.** At the southwest end of the main Parliament building is the 323-foot-high Victoria Tower. ✉ *St. Stephen's Entrance, St. Margaret St., Westminster* ☎ *020/7219–4272 information and tours, 0161/425–8677 public tours (from overseas), 0207/219–4114 public tours* 🌐 *www.parliament.uk/visiting* 💷 *Free; tours £16.50 (booking ahead)* ⏲ *Tour times and hrs for Visitor's Gallery vary wk to wk* Ⓜ *Westminster.*

FAMILY Fodor'sChoice ★ **National Gallery.** Standing proudly on the north side of Trafalgar Square, this is truly one of the world's supreme art museums, with more than 2,300 masterpieces on show. Michelangelo, Leonardo, Turner, Monet, van Gogh, Picasso, and more—all for free. Watch out for outstanding temporary exhibitions, too.

This brief selection is your jumping-off point, but there are hundreds of other paintings to see, enough to fill a full day. In chronological order: (1) **Van Eyck** (c. 1395–1441), *The Arnolfini Portrait*—a solemn couple holds hands, the fish-eye mirror behind them mysteriously illuminating what can't be seen from the front view. (2) **Holbein** (1497–1543), *The Ambassadors*—two wealthy visitors from France stand surrounded by what were considered luxury goods at the time. Note the elongated skull at the bottom of the painting, which takes shape only when viewed from an angle. (3) **Da Vinci** (1452–1519), *The Virgin and Child*—this exquisite black-chalk "Burlington Cartoon" depicts the master's most haunting Mary. (4) **Velázquez** (1599–1660), *Christ in the House of Martha and Mary*—in this enigmatic masterpiece the Spaniard plays with perspective and the role of the viewer. (5) **Turner** (1775–1851), *Rain, Steam and Speed: The Great Western Railway*, the whirl of rain, mist, steam, and locomotion is nothing short of astonishing (spot the hare). (6) **Caravaggio** (1573–1610), *The Supper at Emmaus*—a freshly resurrected Christ blesses bread in an astonishingly domestic vision from the master of chiaroscuro. (7) **Van Gogh** (1853–90), *Sunflowers*—painted during his sojourn with Gauguin in Arles, this is quintessential Van Gogh. (8) **Seurat** (1859–91), *Bathers at Asnières*—this summer day's idyll is one of the master pointillist's extraordinaire's best-known works. ✉ *Trafalgar Sq., Westminster* ☎ *020/7747–2885* 🌐 *www.nationalgallery.org.uk* 🎟 *Free; charge for special exhibitions; audio guide £4* ⏲ *Sun.–Thurs. 10–6, Fri. 10–9* Ⓜ *Charing Cross, Embankment, Leicester Sq.*

FAMILY
Fodor's Choice ★

National Portrait Gallery. The National Portrait Gallery was founded in 1856 with a single aim: to gather together portraits of famous (and infamous) Britons throughout history. More than 150 years and 160,000 portraits later, it is an essential stop for all history and literature buffs. If you visit with kids, ask at the desk about the excellent Family Trails, which make exploring the galleries with children much more fun. **■ TIP→ On the top floor, the Portrait Restaurant has one of the best views in London—a panoramic vista of Nelson's Column and the backdrop along Whitehall to the Houses of Parliament.**

Galleries are arranged clearly and chronologically, from Tudor times to contemporary Britain. A Holbein miniature of Henry VIII is among the most famous image in the Tudor Gallery, although the enormous portrait of Elizabeth I—bejeweled and literally astride the world in a powerful display of Imperial intent—may be the most impressive. The huge permanent collections include portraits of Shakespeare, the Brontë sisters, and Jane Austen. Look for the four Andy Warhol *Queen Elizabeth II* silkscreens from 1985 and Maggi Hambling's surreal self-portrait. Contemporary portraits range from the iconic (*Julian with T-shirt*—an LCD screen on a continuous loop—by Julian Opie) to the extreme (Marc Quinn's *Self*, a realization of the artist's head done in frozen blood). Temporary exhibitions can be explored on the first three floors, particularly in the Wolfson and Porter galleries, on the ground floor. ✉ *St. Martin's Pl., Westminster* ☎ *020/7306–0055, 020/7312–2463 information line* 🌐 *www.npg.org.uk* 🎟 *Free; charge for special exhibitions; audiovisual guide £3; family audio guides £6 for 5 people, £4 for 2 people* ⏲ *Mon.–Wed. and weekends 10–6, Thurs. and Fri. 10–9; last admission 10 min before closing* Ⓜ *Charing Cross, Leicester Sq.*

The Queen's Gallery. Technically speaking, the sovereign doesn't "own" the rare and exquisite works of art in the Royal Collection, she merely holds them in trust for the nation—and what a collection it is! Only a selection is on view at any one time, presented in themed exhibitions. Let the excellent (free) audio guide take you through the elegant galleries filled with some of the world's greatest artworks.

A rough time line of the major royal collectors starts with Charles I (who also commissioned Rubens to paint the Banqueting House ceiling). An avid art enthusiast, Charles established the basis of the Royal Collection, purchasing works by Raphael, Titian, Caravaggio, and Dürer. During the Civil War and in the aftermath of Charles's execution, many masterpieces were sold abroad and subsequently repatriated

CLOSE UP

Where to See the Royals

The Queen and the Royal Family attend hundreds of functions a year, and if you want to know what they are doing on any given date, turn to the Court Circular, printed in the major London dailies, or check out the Royal Family website, *www.royal.gov.uk*, for the latest events on the Royal Diary. Trooping the Colour is usually held on the second Saturday in June, to celebrate the Queen's official birthday. This spectacular parade begins when she leaves Buckingham Palace in her carriage and rides down the Mall to arrive at Horse Guards Parade at 11 exactly. Just turn up along the Mall with your binoculars.

You can also view the Queen in full regalia when she and the Duke of Edinburgh ride in state to open the Houses of Parliament. The black and gilt-trimmed Irish State Coach travels from Buckingham Palace—ideally on a clear day, as this ceremony takes place in late October or early November. The fairy-tale Gold State Coach is used for coronations and jubilees only. You can also see the Queen riding in an open carriage with foreign heads of state during official visits.

Perhaps the most relaxed, least formal time to see the Queen is during Royal Ascot, held at the racetrack near Windsor Castle—a short train ride out of London—usually during the third week of June (Tuesday–Friday). The Queen may walk down to the paddock on a special path, greeting race goers along the way. If you meet her, remember to address her as "Your Majesty."

by Charles II. George III, who bought Buckingham House, scooped up a notable collection of Venetian (including Canaletto), Renaissance (Bellini and Raphael), and Dutch (Vermeer) art, and a large number of baroque drawings, in addition to patronizing English contemporary artists such as Gainsborough and Beechey. The Prince Regent, later George IV, had a particularly good eye for Rembrandt, equestrian works by Stubbs, and lavish portraits by Lawrence. Queen Victoria had a penchant for Landseer animals and landscapes, and Frith's contemporary scenes. Later, Edward VII indulged Queen Alexandra's love of Fabergé, and many royal tours around the empire produced gifts of gorgeous caliber, such as the Cullinan diamond from South Africa and an emerald-studded belt from India. ✉ *Buckingham Palace, Buckingham Palace Rd., St. James's* ☎ *020/7766–7301* 🌐 *www.royalcollection.org.uk* 🎫 *£9.75; joint ticket with Royal Mews £16.75; joint ticket with Mews and Buckingham Palace £35.60* 🕓 *Daily 10–5:30; last admission 1 hr before closing. Closed for 2 wks in Oct./early Nov.* Ⓜ *Victoria, St. James's Park, Green Park.*

FAMILY Fodor's Choice ★ **St. James's Park.** In a city of royal parks, this one—bordered by three palaces (the Palace of Westminster, St. James's Palace, and Buckingham Palace)—is the most regal of them all. It's not only London's oldest park, but also its smallest and most ornate. Once marshy meadows, the land was acquired by Henry VIII in 1532 as royal deer-hunting grounds (with dueling and sword fights strictly forbidden). Later, James I drained the land and installed an aviary and zoo (complete with crocodiles, camels,

Historic Westminster Abbey is a beautiful setting for any choral performance.

and an elephant). When Charles II returned from exile in France, where he had been hugely impressed by the splendor of the gardens at the Palace of Versailles, he transformed the park into formal gardens, with avenues, fruit orchards, and a canal. Lawns were grazed by goats, sheep, and deer, and in the 18th century the park became a different kind of hunting ground, for wealthy lotharios looking to pick up nighttime escorts. A century later, John Nash redesigned the landscape in a more naturalistic, romantic style, and if you gaze down the lake toward Buckingham Palace, you could easily believe yourself to be on a country estate.

A large population of waterfowl—including pelicans, geese, ducks, and swans (which belong to the Queen)—breed on and around Duck Island at the east end of the lake. From April to September, the deck chairs (charge levied) come out, crammed with office workers at midday, eating lunch while being serenaded by music from the bandstands. One of the best times to stroll the leafy walkways is after dark, with Westminster Abbey and the Houses of Parliament rising above the floodlit lake. The popular Inn the Park restaurant is a wood-and-glass pavilion with a turf roof that blends in beautifully with the surrounding landscape; it's an excellent stopping place for a meal or a snack on a nice day. ✉ *The Mall or Horse Guards approach or Birdcage Walk, St. James's* 🌐 *www.royalparks.org.uk* ⏲ *Daily 5 am–midnight* Ⓜ *St. James's Park, Westminster.*

FAMILY Fodor's Choice ★ **Tate Britain.** First opened in 1897, and funded by the sugar magnate Sir Henry Tate, this stately neoclassical institution may not be as ambitious as its sibling Tate Modern on the South Bank, but its bright galleries lure only a fraction of the Modern's overwhelming crowds and are a great place to explore British art from 1500 to the present. The museum includes the Linbury Galleries on the lower floors, which stage temporary exhibitions, and a permanent collection on the upper floors. And what a collection it is—classic works by John Constable, Thomas Gainsborough, David Wilkie, Francis Bacon, Duncan Grant, Barbara Hepworth, and Ben Nicholson, and an outstanding display from J. M. W. Turner in the Clore Gallery, including many later vaporous and light-infused works such as *Sunrise with Sea Monsters*. Sumptuous Pre-Raphaelite pieces are a major draw, while the Contemporary British Art galleries bring you face to face with Damien Hirst's *Away from the Flock* and other recent conceptions. The Tate Britain also hosts the annual Turner Prize exhibition, with its accompanying furor over the state of contemporary art, from about October to January each year. There's a good little café, and the excellent Rex Whistler Restaurant has been something of an institution since it first opened in 1927. It's open daily for lunch, and for dinner on semiregular **Late at Tate** Friday evening events, when the gallery is open late for talks or performances—check the website for details.

■ TIP→ Craving more art? Head down the river on the Tate to Tate boat (£6.80 one-way) to the Tate Modern, running between the two museums every 40 minutes. A River Roamer ticket (£16.50) permits a day's travel, with stops including the London Eye and the Tower of London. You get a discount of roughly a third if you have a Travelcard. ✉ *Millbank, Westminster* ☎ *020/7887–8888* 🌐 *www.tate.org.uk/britain* 🎫 *Free, special exhibitions extra* ⏲ *Daily 10–6; last ticket sold and special exhibitions close 5:15* Ⓜ *Pimlico.*

Fodor's Choice ★

Westminster Abbey. Steeped in millennia of rich and often bloody history, Westminster Abbey is one of England's most iconic buildings. An abbey has stood here since the 7th century, although the current building dates mostly from the 1240s. About 3,300 people, from kings and queens to artists and writers, are buried or memorialized here. It has hosted 38 coronations—beginning in 1066 with William the Conqueror—and no fewer than 16 royal weddings, the latest being that of Prince William and Kate Middleton in 2011.

But be warned: there's only one way around the abbey, and as a million visitors flock through its doors each year, you'll need to be alert to catch the highlights. Enter by the north door then turn around and look up to see the **painted-glass rose window**, the largest of its kind. Step into the small Chapel of St. Michael, where a tomb effigy of Joseph Gascoigne Nightingale fights off a sheet-draped figure of death. Next enter the adjacent Tomb of St. John the Baptist past a lovely statue of the Virgin Mary and child.

As you walk east toward the apse you'll see the **Coronation Chair** at the foot of the Henry VII Chapel, which has been briefly graced by nearly every regal posterior since Edward I had it made in 1301. Farther along, the exquisite confection of the Henry VII's Lady Chapel is topped by a magnificent fan-vaulted ceiling. The wooden seats (or "stalls") carry the heraldic banners of knights. The tomb of Henry

VII lies behind the altar; his queen, Elizabeth of York, is also here, as are, it is believed, the bodies of the so-called Princes in the Tower, the 13-year-old King Edward V and nine-year-old Richard, Duke of York (murdered, it is commonly supposed, by the man who would become Richard III). Elizabeth I is buried above her sister "Bloody" Mary I in the tomb just to the north, while her arch enemy, Mary Queen of Scots, rests in the tomb to the south. In front of the **High Altar**, which was used for the funerals of Princess Diana and the Queen Mother, is a black-and-white marble pavement laid in 1268. The intricate Italian Cosmati work contains three Latin inscriptions, one of which states that the world will last for 19,683 years.

Continue through the South Ambulatory to the **Chapel of St. Edward the Confessor**, which contains the shrine to the pre-Norman king. Because of its great age, you must join the vergers' tours to be admitted to the chapel (£3; book at the admission desk), or attend Holy Communion within the shrine on Tuesdays at 8 am. To the left, you'll find **Poets' Corner**. Geoffrey Chaucer was the first poet to be buried here in 1400, and other statues and memorials include those to William Shakespeare, D. H. Lawrence, T. S. Eliot, and Oscar Wilde as well as nonpoets, Laurence Olivier and George Frederick Handel among them; look out for the 700-year-old frescoes. A door from the south transept and south choir aisle leads to the calm of the **Great Cloisters,** filled in part with the headstones of 26 monks who died during the Black Death. A café is nicely tucked into the cloisters.

The medieval Chapter House is adorned with 14th-century frescoes and a magnificent 13th-century tiled floor, one of the finest in the country. The King's Council met here between 1257 and 1547. Near the entrance is Britain's oldest door, dating from the 1050s. Take a left out of the Chapter House to visit the **Abbey Museum**, which houses a collection of macabre effigies made from the death masks and actual clothing of Charles II and Admiral Lord Nelson (complete with eye patch). Past the museum, the **Little Cloister** is a quiet haven, and just beyond, the **College Garden** is a pleasant diversion. Filled with medicinal herbs, it has been tended by monks for more than 900 years. On the west side of the abbey, the **Dean's Yard** is the best spot for a fine view of the massive flying buttresses above.

Continue back to the nave of the abbey. In the choir screen, north of the entrance to the choir, is a marble **monument to Sir Isaac Newton.** If you walk toward the West Entrance, you'll see **a plaque to Franklin D. Roosevelt**—one of the Abbey's very few tributes to a foreigner. The poppy-wreathed **Grave of the Unknown Warrior** commemorates soldiers who lost their lives in both world wars.

Exact hours for the various parts of the abbey are frustratingly long and complicated, and can change daily, so it's important to check before setting out, particularly if you're visiting early or late in the day, or during off-season. The full list of times is posted online daily (or you can call).

Arrive early if possible, but be prepared to wait in line to tour the abbey. ✉ *Broad Sanctuary, Westminster* ☎ *020/7222–5152* 🌐 *www.westminster-abbey.org* 🎫 *Abbey and museum £18; annual pass £40;*

audio tour free ⏲ Abbey, Mon., Tues., Thurs., and Fri. 9:30–4:30; Wed. 9:30–7; Sat. 9:30–2.30; last admission 1 hr before closing time; Sun. open for worship only. Museum, Mon.–Sat. 10:30–4. Cloisters daily 8–6. College Garden, Apr.–Sept., Tues.–Thurs. 10–6; Oct.–Mar., Tues.–Thurs. 10–4. Chapter House, daily 10:30–4. Verger tours: Apr.–Sept., weekdays 10, 10:30, 11, 2, and 2:30; Sat. 10, 10:30, and 11. Oct.–Mar., weekdays 10:30, 11, 2, and 2:30; Sat. 10:30 and 11. Times do vary, so always call ahead Ⓜ *Westminster, St. James's Park.*

WORTH NOTING

Banqueting House. James I commissioned Inigo Jones, one of England's great architects, to undertake a grand building on the site of the original Tudor Palace of Whitehall, which was (according to one foreign visitor) "ill-built, and nothing but a heap of houses." Jones's Banqueting House, finished in 1622 and the first building in England to be completed in the neoclassical style, bears all the hallmarks of the Palladian sophistication and purity which so influenced Jones during his time in Italy. James's son, Charles I, enhanced the interior by employing the Flemish painter Peter Paul Rubens to glorify his father and himself (naturally) in a series of vibrant painted ceiling panels called "The Apotheosis of James I." As it turned out, these allegorical paintings, depicting a wise monarch being received into heaven, were the last thing Charles saw before stepped through the open first-floor window onto the scaffold, which had been erected directly outside for his execution by Cromwell's Parliamentarians in 1649. Twenty years later his son, Charles II, would celebrate the restoration of the monarchy in the exact same place. ✉ *Whitehall, Westminster* ☎ *084/4482–7777* 🌐 *www.hrp.org.uk* 🎟 *£6.60* ⏲ *Daily 10–5; last admission 45 min before closing. May close at short notice for events; call ahead* Ⓜ *Charing Cross, Embankment, Westminster.*

Clarence House. The London home of the Queen Mother for nearly 50 years until her death in 2002, Clarence House is now the residence of Prince Charles, the Prince of Wales; his wife, Camilla, the Duchess of Cornwall; and Prince Harry. The Regency mansion was built by John Nash for the Duke of Clarence (later to become William IV) who considered next-door St. James's Palace to be too cramped for his liking, although postwar renovation work means that little remains of Nash's original. Since then it has remained a royal home for princesses, dukes, and duchesses, including the present monarch, Queen Elizabeth, as a newlywed before her coronation. The rooms have been sensitively preserved to reflect the Queen Mother's taste, with the addition of many works of art from the Royal Collection, including works by Winterhalter, Augustus John, and Sickert. Clarence House is usually open only for the month of August and tickets must be booked in advance. ✉ *St. James's Palace, The Mall, St. James's* ☎ *020/7766–7300* 🌐 *www.royalcollection.org.uk* 🎟 *£9.50; exclusive guided tour £35* ⏲ *Aug. weekdays 10–4:30; weekend 10–5:30; last admission 1 hr before closing* Ⓜ *Green Park.*

Downing Street. Looking like an unassuming alley but for the iron gates (and armed guards) that block the entrance, this is the location of the famous **No. 10,** London's modest equivalent of the White House. The

Georgian entrance to the mid-17th century mansion is deceptive; it's actually a huge complex of discreetly linked buildings. Since 1732 it has been the official home and office of the prime minister—the last private resident was the magnificently named Mr. Chicken—although the current prime minister actually lives in the private apartments above No. 11, because those in No. 10 are too small to house a family. (No. 11 is traditionally the residence of the chancellor of the exchequer, the head of the treasury.) There are no public tours, and you can't get past the wrought-iron gates into Downing Street itself, but the famous black front door to No. 10 is clearly visible from Whitehall. Just south of Downing Street, in the middle of Whitehall, is the **Cenotaph,** a stark white monolith built to commemorate the 1918 armistice. On Remembrance Day (the Sunday nearest November 11) it's strewn with red poppy wreaths to honor the dead of both world wars and all British and Commonwealth soldiers killed in action since; the first wreath is traditionally laid by the Queen. ✉ *Whitehall* 🌐 *www.number10.gov.uk* Ⓜ *Westminster.*

St. James's Palace. Commissioned by Henry VIII, this Tudor brick palace was the residence of kings and queens for more than 300 years; indeed, while all monarchs have actually lived at Buckingham Palace since Queen Victoria's day, it is still the official residence of the Sovereign. (Foreign ambassadors, for instance, are received by the "Court of St. James.") Today it contains various royal apartments and offices, including the working office of Prince Charles. The palace is not open to the public but the surprisingly low-key Tudor exterior is well worth the short detour from the Mall to see. Friary Court out front is a splendid setting for Trooping the Colour, part of the Queen's official birthday celebrations. Everyone loves to take a snapshot of the scarlet-coated guardsman standing sentry outside the imposing Tudor gateway. Note that the Changing the Guard ceremony at St. James's Palace occurs only on days when the guard at Buckingham Palace is changed. If you're approaching from St. James Street, take a quick peek at the delightfully old-looking **Berry Bros. & Rudd** wine store at No. 3, near the back entrance to the palace; it's been trading here continuously since 1698. ✉ *Friary Ct., St. James's* 🌐 *www.royal.gov.uk* Ⓜ *Green Park.*

FAMILY **St. Martin-in-the-Fields.** One of London's best-loved and most welcoming of churches is more than just a place of worship. Named after St. Martin of Tours, known for the help he gave to beggars, this parish has long been a welcome sight for the homeless, who have been given soup and shelter at the church since 1914. The church is also a haven for music lovers; the internationally known Academy of St. Martin-in-the-Fields was founded here, and a popular program of concerts continues today. (Although the interior is a wonderful setting for a recital, beware the hard wooden benches!) The crypt is a hive of activity, with a popular café and shop. Here you can also make your own life-size souvenir knight, lady, or monarch from replica tomb brasses, with metallic waxes, paper, and instructions (about £5). ✉ *Trafalgar Sq., Westminster* ☎ *020/7766–1100* 🌐 *www.smitf.org* 🎟 *Free; concerts £7–£30* 🕙 *Open all day for worship; sightseeing: Mon., Tues., and Fri.*

8:30–1 and 2–6; Wed. 8:30–1:15 and 2–5; Thurs. 8:30–1 and 2–6; Sat. 9:30–6; Sun. 3:30–5 Ⓜ *Charing Cross, Leicester Sq.*

FAMILY **Wellington Barracks and the Guards Museum.** These are the headquarters of the Guards Division, the Queen's five regiments of elite foot guards (Grenadier, Coldstream, Scots, Irish, and Welsh), who protect the sovereign and, dressed in tunics of gold-purled scarlet and tall bearskin caps, patrol her palaces. Guardsmen alternate these ceremonial postings with serving in current conflicts, for which they wear more practical uniforms. If you want to learn more about the guards, visit the **Guards Museum,** which has displays on all aspects of a guardsman's life in conflicts dating back to 1642; the entrance is next to the Guards Chapel. Next door is the **Guards Toy Soldier Centre,** a great place for a souvenir. ✉ *Birdcage Walk, Westminster* ☎ *020/7414–3428* 🌐 *www.theguardsmuseum.com* 🎫 *£5* ⏲ *Daily 10–4; last admission 3:30* Ⓜ *St. James's Park, Green Park.*

SOHO AND COVENT GARDEN

Soho has long been the media and nightlife center of London, its narrow, winding streets unabashedly devoted to pleasure. Wardour Street bisects the neighborhood. Many interesting boutiques and some of London's best-value restaurants can be found to the west, especially around Foubert's Place and on Brewer and Lexington streets. Nightlife central lies to the east—including London's gay mecca and Old Compton Street. Beyond that is the city's densest collection of theaters, on Shaftesbury Avenue, with London's compact Chinatown just past it. A bit of erudition surfaces to the east on Charing Cross Road, still with a couple of the secondhand bookshops it was once known for, and on tiny Cecil Court, a pedestrianized passage lined with small antiquarian booksellers.

To the east of Charing Cross Road you'll find Covent Garden, once a wholesale fruit and vegetable market and now more of a shopping mall. Although boutiques and outposts of high-end chains line the surrounding streets, many Londoners come to Covent Garden for two notable arts venues: the Royal Opera House and the Donmar Warehouse, one of London's best and most innovative theaters. To the south, the Strand leads to the huge, stately piazza of Somerset House, home to the many masterpieces on view at the Courtauld Gallery, a fine small art museum.

GETTING HERE

Almost all Tube lines cross the Covent Garden and Soho areas, so it's easy to hop off for a dinner or show in this lively part of London. For Soho, take any train to Piccadilly Circus, or Leicester Square, Oxford Circus, or Tottenham Court Road. For Covent Garden, get off at the Covent Garden station on the Piccadilly Line. It might be easier to exit the Tube at Leicester Square or Holborn and walk. Thirty buses connect to the Covent Garden area from all over London.

PLANNING YOUR TIME

You can comfortably tour all the sights in Covent Garden in a day. Visit the small but perfect Courtauld Gallery on Monday before 2 pm, when it's free. That leaves plenty of time to visit the market, watch the street entertainers, do a bit of shopping, and have energy left over for a night on the town in Soho.

TOP ATTRACTIONS

Fodor's Choice ★ **The Courtauld Gallery.** One of London's most beloved art collections, the Courtauld is to your right as you pass through the archway into the grounds of the beautifully restored, grand 18th-century neoclassical **Somerset House.** Founded in 1931 by the textile magnate Samuel Courtauld to house his remarkable private collection, this is one of the world's finest Impressionist and post-Impressionist galleries, with artists ranging from Bonnard to van Gogh. A déjà-vu moment with Cézanne, Degas, Seurat, or Monet awaits on every wall (Manet's *Bar at the Folies-Bergère* and *Le Déjeuner sur L'Herbe* are two of the stars). Botticelli, Bruegel, Tiepolo, and Rubens are also represented, thanks to the exquisite bequest of Count Antoine Seilern's Princes Gate collection. German Renaissance paintings, bequeathed in 1947, include the colorful and sensual *Adam and Eve* by Lucas Cranach the Elder. The second floor has a more provocative, experimental feel, with masterpieces such as Modigliani's iconic *Female Nude*. Don't miss the little café downstairs—a perfect place for a spot of tea. ✉ *Somerset House, Strand, Covent Garden* ☎ *020/7848–2526* 🌐 *www.courtauld.ac.uk* 🎫 *£6* ⏲ *Daily 10–6; last admission 5:30* Ⓜ *Temple, Covent Garden.*

Covent Garden Piazza. Once home to London's main flower market, where *My Fair Lady's* Eliza Doolittle peddled her blooms, the square around which Covent Garden pivots is known as the Piazza. In the center, the fine old market building now houses stalls and shops selling expensive clothing, plus several restaurants and cafés, and knickknack stores that are good for gifts. One particular gem is Benjamin Pollock's Toyshop at No. 44 in the market. Established in the 1880s, it sells delightful toy theaters. The superior **Apple Market** has good crafts stalls on most days, too. On the south side of the Piazza, the indoor **Jubilee Market,** with its stalls of clothing, army-surplus gear, and more crafts and knickknacks, feels a bit like a flea market. In summer it may seem that everyone in the huge crowds around you in the Piazza is a fellow tourist, but there's still plenty of office life in the area. Londoners who shop here tend to head for Neal Street and the area to the north of Covent Garden Tube station rather than the market itself. In the Piazza, street performers—from global musicians to jugglers and mimes—play to the crowds, as they have done since the first English Punch and Judy Show, staged here in the 17th century. ✉ *Covent Garden* 🌐 *www.coventgardenlondonuk.com* Ⓜ *Covent Garden.*

FAMILY **London Transport Museum.** Housed in the old flower market at the southeast corner of Covent Garden, this stimulating museum is filled with impressive vehicle, poster, and photograph collections. As you watch the crowds drive a Tube-train simulation and gawk at the horse-drawn trams (and the piles of detritus that remained behind) and steam locomotives, it's unclear who's enjoying it more, children or adults. Best of all, the kid-friendly museum (under 17 admitted free) has a multilevel approach to education, including information for the youngest visitor to the most advanced transit aficionado. Food and drink are available at the Upper Deck café and the shop has lots of good options for

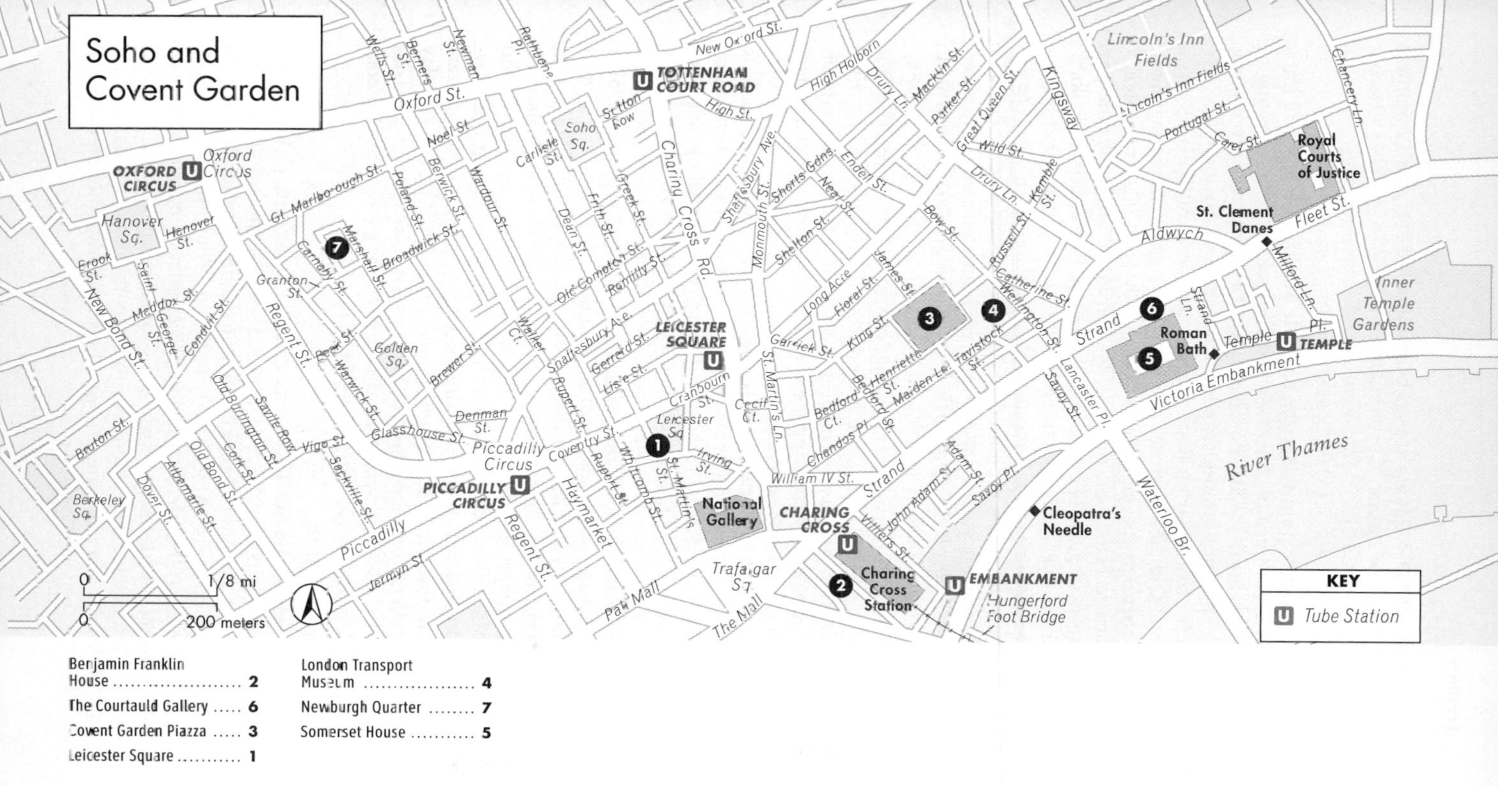

Benjamin Franklin House 2
The Courtauld Gallery 6
Covent Garden Piazza 3
Leicester Square 1
London Transport Museum 4
Newburgh Quarter 7
Somerset House 5

2

gift-buying. ■ **TIP→ Tickets are valid for unlimited entry for 12 months.** ✉ *Covent Garden Piazza, Covent Garden* ☎ *020/7379–6344* 🌐 *www.ltmuseum.co.uk* 🎫 *£15* ⏲ *Sat.–Thurs. 10–6 (last admission 5:15), Fri. 11–6 (last admission 5:15)* Ⓜ *Covent Garden, Leicester Sq.*

Fodor's Choice ★ **Newburgh Quarter.** Want to see the hip style of today's London? Find it one block east of Carnaby Street—where the look of the '60s "Swinging London" was born—in an adorable warren of cobblestone streets now lined with specialty boutiques, edgy stores, and young indie upstarts. Here, not far from roaring Regent Street, the future of England's fashion is being incubated in stores like Lucy in Disguise and Flying Horse Jeans. A check of the ingredients reveals one part '60s London, one part Futuristic Fetishism, one part Dickensian charm, and one part British street swagger. The Nouveau Boho look best flourishes in shops like Peckham Rye, a tiny boutique crowded with rockers and fashion plates who adore its grunge-meets– *Brideshead Revisited* vibe. Quality independent coffee shops abound—take a break at Speakeasy Espresso & Brew Bar, where you can also browse for home coffee-making equipment. ✉ *Newburgh St., Foubert's Pl., Ganton St., and Carnaby St., Soho* 🌐 *carnaby.co.uk.*

FAMILY Fodor's Choice ★ **Somerset House.** In recent years this huge complex—the work of Sir William Chambers (1723–96), and built during the reign of George III to house offices of the Navy—has been transformed from dusty government offices to one of the capital's most buzzing centers of culture and the arts, often hosting several interesting exhibitions at one time. The cobblestone Italianate courtyard, where Admiral Nelson used to walk, makes a great setting for 55 playful fountains and is transformed into a romantic ice rink in winter; the grand space is the venue for music and outdoor movie screenings in summer. The **Courtauld Gallery** occupies most of the north building, facing the busy Strand. Across the courtyard are the Embankment Galleries, with a vibrant calendar of design, fashion, architecture, and photography exhibitions. Creative activities for children are a regular feature (the website has details). The East Wing has another fine exhibition space and events are sometimes also held in the atmospherically gloomy cellars below the Fountain Court. Tom's Kitchen offers fine dining and the Deli has mouthwatering cakes and pastries. In summer eating and drinking spills out onto the large terrace next to the Thames. ✉ *Strand, Covent Garden* ☎ *020/7845–4600* 🌐 *www.somersethouse.org.uk* 🎫 *Embankment Galleries price varies, Courtauld Gallery £7, other areas free* ⏲ *Daily 10–6; last admission 5:15* Ⓜ *Charing Cross, Waterloo, Blackfriars.*

WORTH NOTING

Benjamin Franklin House. This architecturally significant 1730 house is the only surviving residence of American statesman, scientist, writer, and inventor Benjamin Franklin, who lived and worked here for 16 years preceding the American Revolution. The restored Georgian town house has been left unfurnished, the better to show off the original features—18th-century paneling, stoves, beams, bricks, and windows. Visitors are led around the house by the costumed character of Polly Hewson, the daughter of Franklin's landlady, who interacts with engaging video projections and recorded voices. On Monday you can take a guided tour focusing on the architectural details of the building. ✉ *36 Craven St., Covent Garden* ☎ *020/7839–2006, 020/7925–1405 booking line* 🌐 *www.benjaminfranklinhouse.org* 🎫 *Historical Experience £7; architectural tour £3.50* 🕙 *Historical Experience Wed.–Sun. noon, 1, 2, 3:15, and 4:15; architectural tour Mon. noon, 1, 2, 3:15, and 4:15.*

Leicester Square. Looking at the neon of the major movie houses, the fast-food outlets, and the disco entrances, you'd never guess that this square (pronounced *Lester*) was a model of formality and refinement when it was first laid out around 1630. By the 19th century the square was already bustling and disreputable, and although it's not a threatening place, you should still be on your guard, especially at night—any space so full of people is bound to attract pickpockets, and Leicester Square certainly does. Although there's a bit of residual glamour (red-carpet film premieres) Londoners generally tend to avoid the place, though it's worth a visit for its hustle and bustle, its mime artists, and the pleasant modern fountain at its center. Also in the middle is a statue of a sulking Shakespeare, perhaps remembering the days when the movie houses were live theaters—burlesque houses, but live all the same. On the northeast corner, in Leicester Place, stands the church of **Notre Dame de France**, with a wonderful mural by Jean Cocteau in one of its side chapels. For more in the way of atmosphere, head north and west from here, through Chinatown and the narrow streets of Soho. ✉ *Covent Garden* Ⓜ *Leicester Sq.*

BLOOMSBURY AND HOLBORN

The character of London can change visibly from one area to the next. There's a distinct difference between fun-loving Soho and intellectual Bloomsbury, a mere 100 yards to the northeast, or between the diversions of Covent Garden and the sober businesslike Holborn (pronounced *hoe*-bun) on the other side of Kingsway.

The British Museum, the British Library, and the University of London anchor the neighborhood that lent its name to the Bloomsbury Group, the clique who personified early-20th-century literary bohemia. The circle's mainstays included the writers Virginia Woolf, E.M. Forster, and Lytton Strachey and the painter Vanessa Bell.

Originally a notorious red-light district, these days Holborn is legal London's center. Because the neighborhood's buildings were among the few structures spared during the Great Fire of 1666, its serpentine alleys, cobbled courtyards, and the Inns of Court, where most British trial lawyers still have offices, ooze history.

GETTING HERE

You can easily get to where you need to be on foot in Bloomsbury, and the Russell Square Tube stop on the Piccadilly Line leaves you right at the corner of Russell Square. The best Tube stops for Holborn are on the Central and Piccadilly lines and Chancery Lane on the Central Line. Tottenham Court Road on the Northern and Central lines and Russell Square (Piccadilly Line) are best for the British Museum.

PLANNING YOUR TIME

Bloomsbury can be seen in a day, or in half a day, depending on your interests. If you plan to visit the Inns of Court as well as the British Museum, and you'd like to walk through the quiet, leafy squares, then you might want to devote an entire day to Bloomsbury and Holborn.

TOP ATTRACTIONS

FAMILY **British Library.** Once a part of the British Museum, the 18-million-volume collection of the British Library has had its own state-of-the-art home since 1997. The library's greatest treasures are on view to the general public: the Magna Carta, the Codex Sinaiticus (an ancient bible containing the oldest complete copy of the New Testament), Jane Austen's writings, and Shakespeare's First Folio. Musical manuscripts by G.F. Handel as well as Sir Paul McCartney are on display in the Sir John Ritblat Gallery. ✉ *96 Euston Rd., Bloomsbury* ☎ *0330/333–1144* 🌐 *www.bl.uk* 🎫 *Free, donations appreciated; charge for special exhibitions* ⏲ *Mon.–Thurs. 9:30–8, Fri. 9:30–6, Sat. 9:30–5, Sun. and public holidays 11–5* Ⓜ *Euston, Euston Sq., King's Cross St. Pancras.*

Fodor's Choice ★ **British Museum.** With a facade like a great temple, this celebrated treasure house, filled with plunder of incalculable value and beauty from around the globe, occupies an imposing neoclassical building in the heart of Bloomsbury. Inside are some of the greatest relics of humankind: the Parthenon Sculptures (Elgin Marbles), the Rosetta Stone, the Sutton Hoo Treasure—almost everything, it seems, but the original Ten Commandments. The three rooms that comprise the **Sainsbury African Galleries** are a must-see in the Lower Gallery—together they present 200,000 objects, highlighting such ancient kingdoms as the Benin and Asante. The museum's focal point is the **Great Court**, a brilliant modern design with a vast glass roof atop the museum's covered courtyard. The revered **Reading Room** has a blue-and-gold dome and hosts temporary exhibitions. If you want to navigate the highlights of the almost 100 galleries, join a free **eyeOpener** 30- or 40-minute tour by a museum guide (details at the information desk), or hire a multimedia guide for £5 (available from the Multimedia Guide desk in the Great Court). There's plenty to keep kids interested here, by way of activities, games, and videos (check website for details), and the exhibits themselves, of course.

The collection began when Sir Hans Sloane, physician to Queen Anne and George II, bequeathed his personal collection of antiquities to the nation. It grew quickly, thanks to enthusiastic kleptomaniacs after the Napoleonic Wars—most notoriously the seventh Earl of Elgin, who acquired the marbles from the Parthenon and Erechtheion in Athens during his term as British ambassador in Constantinople. Here follows a highly edited résumé (in order of encounter) of the British Museum's greatest hits: close to the entrance hall, in Room 4, is the **Rosetta Stone,** found by French soldiers in 1799, and carved in 196 BC by decree of Ptolemy V in Egyptian hieroglyphics, demotic (a cursive script developed in Egypt), and Greek. This inscription provided the French Egyptologist Jean-François Champollion with the key to deciphering hieroglyphics. Also in Room 4 is the Colossal statue of Ramesses II, a 7-ton likeness of this member of the 19th dynasty's (circa 1270 BC) upper half. Maybe the **Parthenon Sculptures** should be back in Greece,

The massive, glass-roofed Great Court in the British Museum has a couple of cafés.

but while the debate rages on, you can steal your own moment with the **Elgin Marbles** in Room 18. Carved in about 400 BC, these graceful decorations are displayed along with a high-tech exhibit of the Acropolis. Be sure to stop in the Enlightenment Gallery in Room 1 to explore the great age of discovery through the thousands of objects on display. Also in the West Wing is one of the Seven Wonders of the Ancient World—in fragment form—in Room 21: the **Mausoleum of Halikarnassos.** The **JP Morgan Chase North American Gallery** (Room 26) has one of the largest collections of native culture outside North America, going back to the earliest hunters 10,000 years ago. Next door, the **Mexican Gallery** holds such alluring pieces as the 15th-century turquoise mask of Xiuhtecuhtli, the Mexican Fire God and Turquoise Lord. The Living and Dying displays in Room 24 include **Cradle to the Grave**, an installation by a collective of artists and a doctor displaying more than 14,000 drugs (the number estimated to be prescribed to every person in the United Kingdom in his lifetime) in a colorful tapestry of pills and tablets.

Upstairs are some of the most popular galleries, especially beloved by children. Rooms 62–63 are where the **Egyptian mummies** live. Nearby are the glittering 4th-century **Mildenhall Treasure** and the equally splendid 8th-century Anglo-Saxon **Sutton Hoo Treasure** (with magnificent helmets and jewelry). Next along is the **Lindow Man**, a ritually slain chap from the 1st century who lay perfectly pickled in a Cheshire bog until he was unearthed by archaeologists in 1984. The **Korean Foundation Gallery** (Room 67) delves into the art and archaeology of the country, including a reconstruction of a *sarangbang*, a traditional scholar's study. ✉ *Great Russell St., Bloomsbury* ☎ *020/7323–8299*

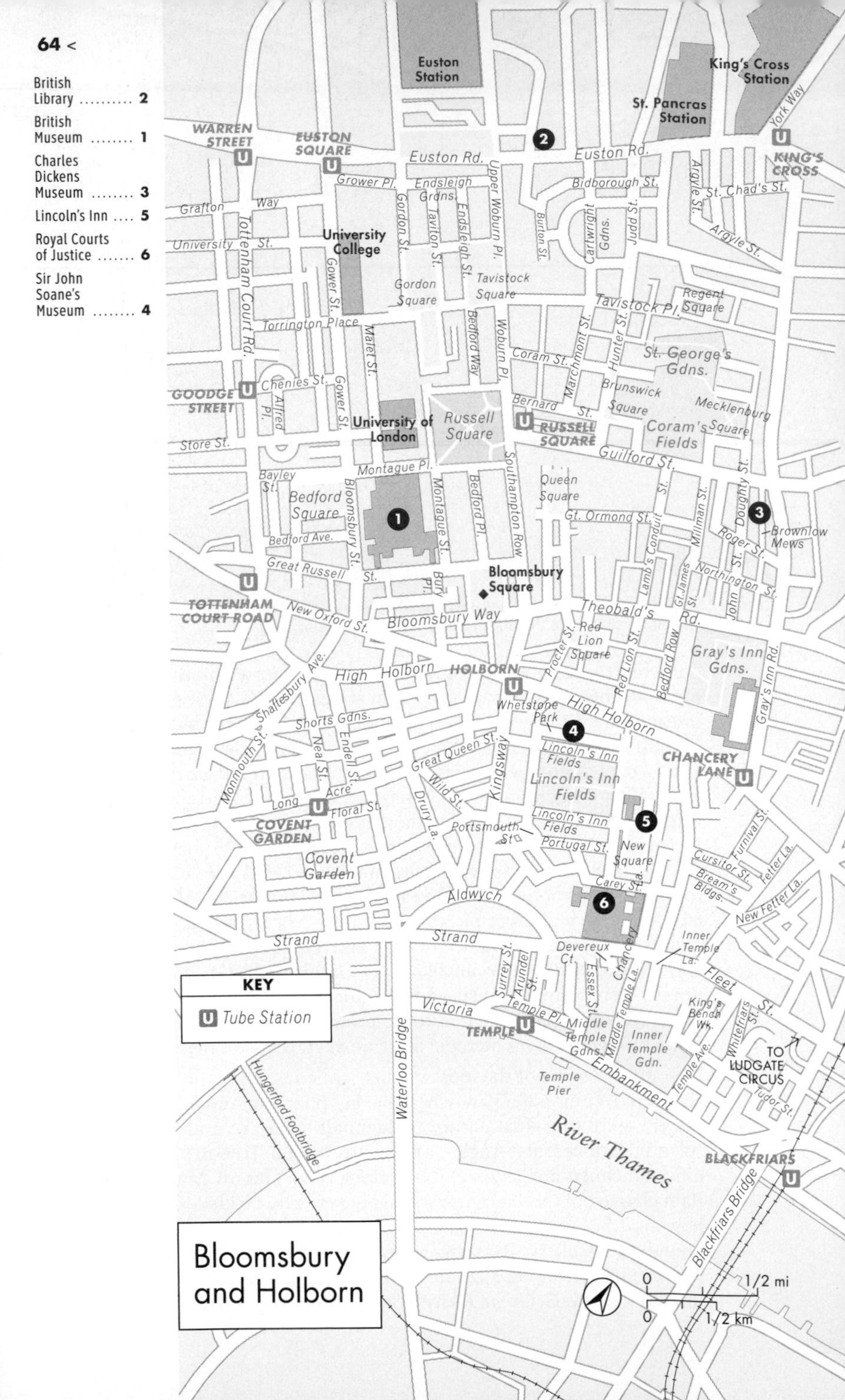
British Library 2
British Museum 1
Charles Dickens Museum 3
Lincoln's Inn 5
Royal Courts of Justice 6
Sir John Soane's Museum 4
Bloomsbury and Holborn
KEY
Tube Station
Euston Station
King's Cross Station
St. Pancras Station
York Way
WARREN STREET
EUSTON SQUARE
KING'S CROSS
Euston Rd.
Grower Pl.
Endsleigh Gdns.
Upper Woburn Pl.
Bidborough St.
Argyle St.
St. Chad's St.
Grafton Way
University St.
Tottenham Court Rd.
Gordon St.
Taviton St.
Endsleigh St.
Burton St.
Cartwright Gdns.
Judd St.
University College
Gower St.
Gordon Square
Tavistock Square
Tavistock Pl.
Regent Square
Torrington Place
Malet St.
Bedford Way
Woburn Pl.
Coram St.
Marchmont St.
Hunter St.
St. George's Gdns.
GOODGE STREET
Chenies St.
Alfred Pl.
Brunswick Square
Bernard St.
Mecklenburg Square
University of London
Russell Square
RUSSELL SQUARE
Coram's Fields
Store St.
Guilford St.
Montague Pl.
Bayley St.
Queen Square
Bedford Square
Bloomsbury St.
Montague St.
Bedford Pl.
Southampton Row
Gt. Ormond St.
Lamb's Conduit St.
Millman St.
Doughty St.
Brownlow Mews
Roger St.
Bedford Ave.
Great Russell St.
Bury Pl.
Bloomsbury Square
Gt. James St.
Northington St.
John St.
TOTTENHAM COURT ROAD
New Oxford St.
Bloomsbury Way
Theobald's Rd.
Red Lion Square
Procter St.
Red Lion St.
Bedford Row
Gray's Inn Gdns.
Gray's Inn Rd.
Shaftesbury Ave.
High Holborn
HOLBORN
Whetstone Park
Shorts Gdns.
Monmouth St.
Neal St.
Endell St.
Great Queen St.
Kingsway
Lincoln's Inn Fields
CHANCERY LANE
Long Acre
Floral St.
Wild St.
Drury La.
COVENT GARDEN
Covent Garden
Portsmouth St.
Portugal St.
New Square
Furnival St.
Cursitor St.
Fetter La.
Bream's Bldgs.
Carey St.
Aldwych
New Fetter La.
Strand
Devereux Ct.
Chancery La.
Inner Temple La.
Fleet St.
Surrey St.
Arundel St.
Essex St.
Middle Temple La.
Victoria Embankment
Temple Pl.
TEMPLE
Middle Temple Gdns.
Inner Temple Gdn.
King's Bench Wk.
Whitefriars St.
Temple Ave.
TO LUDGATE CIRCUS
Tudor St.
Temple Pier
Hungerford Footbridge
Waterloo Bridge
River Thames
BLACKFRIARS
Blackfriars Bridge
0
1/2 mi
0
1/2 km

www.britishmuseum.org *Free; donations encouraged* *Galleries Sat.–Thurs. 10–5:30, Fri. 10–8:30. Great Court Sat.–Thurs. 9–6, Fri. 9–8:30* *Russell Sq., Holborn, Tottenham Court Rd.*

Charles Dickens Museum. This is one of the few London houses Charles Dickens (1812–70) inhabited that is still standing, and it's the place where the master wrote *Oliver Twist* and *Nicholas Nickleby* and finished *Pickwick Papers*. The house looks exactly as it would have in Dickens's day, complete with first editions, letters, and a tall clerk's desk (Dickens wrote standing up). The museum also houses a shop and café. *48 Doughty St., Bloomsbury* *020/7405–2127* *www.dickensmuseum.com* *£8* *Daily 10–5 (last admission 4)* *Chancery La., Russell Sq.*

Fodor's Choice ★ **Sir John Soane's Museum.** Sir John (1753–1837), architect of the Bank of England, bequeathed his eccentric house to the nation on one condition: nothing be changed. It's a house full of surprises. In the Picture Room, two of Hogarth's famous *Rake's Progress*paintings swing away to reveal secret gallery recesses where you can find works by Canaletto and Turner. Everywhere, mirrors play tricks with light and space, and split-level floors worthy of a fairground funhouse disorient you. Ongoing restoration work, due to be completed by 2016, will see Soane's private apartments finally opened up to the public, as well as the catacombs in the basement. *13 Lincoln's Inn Fields, Bloomsbury* *020/7405–2107* *www.soane.org* *Free; tours £10* *Tues.–Sat. 10–5; also 6–9 on 1st Tues. of month* *Holborn.*

WORTH NOTING

Lincoln's Inn. There's plenty to see at one of the oldest, best preserved, and most attractive of the Inns of Court—from the Chancery Lane Tudor brick gatehouse to the wide-open, tree-lined, atmospheric Lincoln's Inn Fields and the 15th century chapel remodeled by Inigo Jones in 1620. The chapel and the gardens are open to the public, but to see more you must prebook a place on one of the official tours. But be warned: they tend to prefer group bookings of 15 or more, so it's best to check the website or call for details and note that there are no tours at weekends or in August. *Chancery La., Bloomsbury* *020/7405–1393* *www.lincolnsinn.org.uk* *Free* *Gardens weekdays 7–7; chapel weekdays 9–5* *Chancery La.*

Royal Courts of Justice. Here is the vast Victorian Gothic pile of 35 million bricks containing the nation's principal law courts, with 1,000-odd rooms running off 3½ miles of corridors. This is where the most important civil law cases—that's everything from divorce to fraud, with libel in between—are heard. You can sit in the viewing gallery to watch any trial you like, for a live version of Court TV. The more dramatic criminal cases are heard at the Old Bailey. Other sights are the 238-foot-long main hall and the compact exhibition of judges' robes. Guided tours must be booked in advance. *The Strand, Bloomsbury* *020/7947–6000, 07789/751–248 tour reservations* *www.hmcourts-service.gov.uk (search for Royal Courts of Justice in A–Z option)* *Free; tours £12* *Weekdays 9–4:30* *Temple, Holborn, Chancery La.*

THE CITY

The City, as opposed to the city, is the capital's economic engine room. But the "Square Mile" captures attention for more than its role as London's Wall Street. Wren's masterpiece, the English Baroque St. Paul's Cathedral, still stuns, as does the medieval Tower of London (full name: Her Majesty's Royal Palace and Fortress), which has served many functions during its more than 1,000-year history. Off the main roads, The City's winding lanes and courtyards are rich in historic churches and pubs.

The City has twice nearly been destroyed, first by the Great Fire of 1666—after which Sir Christopher Wren was put in charge of a total reconstruction that resulted in St. Paul's Cathedral and 49 lovely parish churches—and later by German bombing raids during World War II. Following the raids the area was rebuilt over time, but with no grand plan. Consequently, the City is a mishmash of the old, the new, the innovative, the distinguished, and the flagrantly awful. A walk across the Millennium Bridge from Tate Modern to St. Paul's offers a superb view of the river and the cathedral that presides over it.

GETTING HERE

The Underground serves the City at several stops. St Paul's and Bank, on the Central Line, and Mansion House, Cannon Street, and Monument, on the District and Circle lines, deliver visitors to its center. Liverpool Street and Aldgate border the City's eastern edge, and Chancery Lane and Farringdon lie to the west. Barbican and Moorgate provide easy access to the theaters and galleries of the Barbican, and Blackfriars, to the south, leads to Ludgate Circus and Fleet Street.

PLANNING YOUR TIME

The City is compact, making it ideal for an afternoon's exploration. For full immersion in the Tower of London, set aside half a day, especially if seeing the Crown Jewels is a priority. Allow an hour minimum each for the Museum of London and St. Paul's Cathedral. Weekdays are best, since on weekends the City is nearly deserted, with shops and restaurants closed. At the same time, this is when the major attractions are at their busiest.

TOP ATTRACTIONS

FAMILY **Monument.** Commemorating the "dreadful visitation" of the Great Fire of London, in 1666, this huge stone column stands both 202 feet tall and exactly 202 feet from Farrier's baking house in Pudding Lane, where the fire started. (Note the gilded orb of fire at the column's pinnacle.) It was designed by Sir Christopher Wren and Dr. Robert Hooke, who were asked to erect it "on or as neere unto the place where the said Fire soe unhappily began as conveniently may be." The view of The City from the viewing platform at the top is spectacular, but if climbing the 311 steps seems too arduous, you can watch a live view relayed on a screen at the entrance. ✉ *Monument St., The City* ☎ *020/7626–2717* 🌐 *www.themonument.info* 🎟 *£4; combined ticket with Tower Bridge £10.50* ⏲ *Apr.–Sept., daily 9:30–6; Oct.–Mar., daily 9:30–5:30; last admission 30 min before closing* Ⓜ *Monument.*

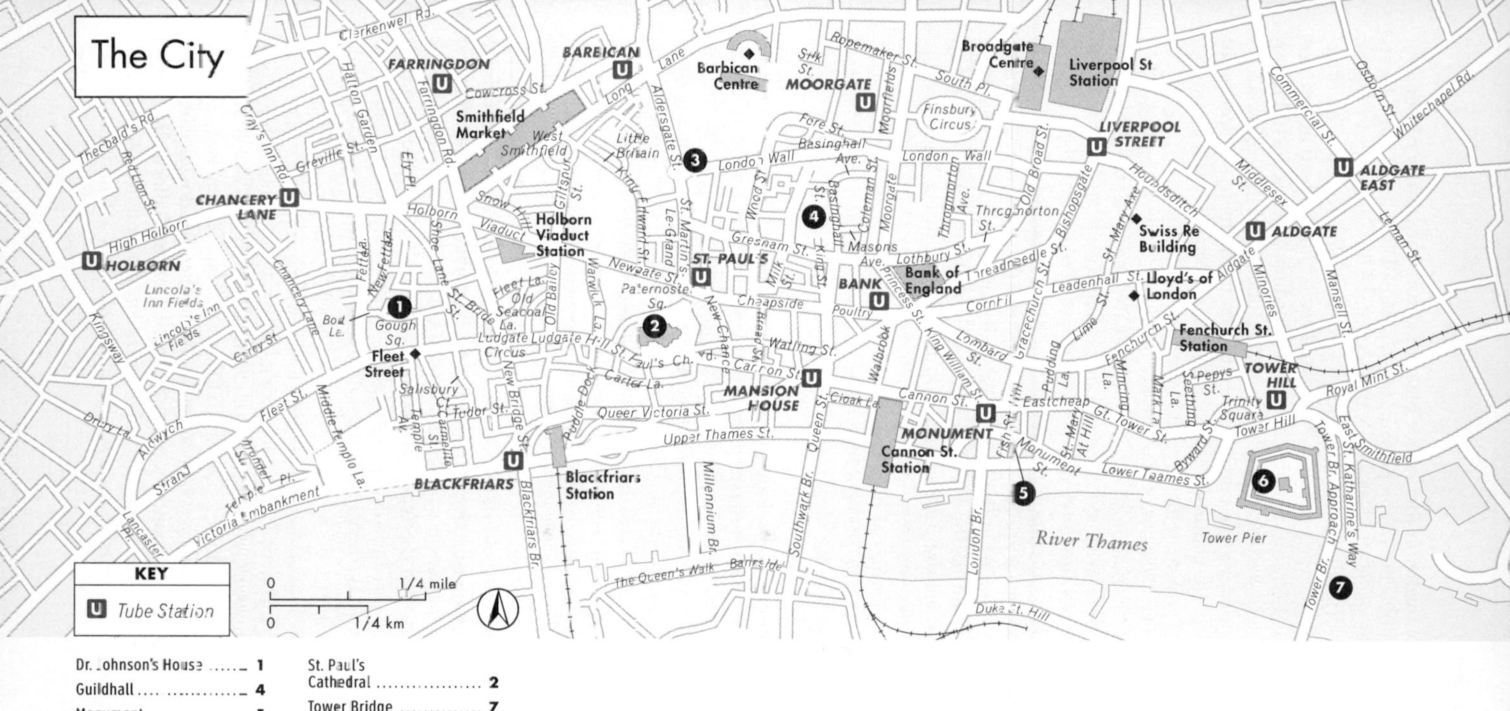

Dr. Johnson's House	1
Guildhall	4
Monument	5
Museum of London	3
St. Paul's Cathedral	2
Tower Bridge	7
Tower of London	6

FAMILY Fodor's Choice ★ **Museum of London.** If there's one place to absorb the history of London, from 450,000 BC to the present day, it's here. There are 7,000 objects to wonder at in all, including Oliver Cromwell's death mask, Queen Victoria's crinoline gowns, Selfridges's art-deco elevators, and an original door from the infamous Newgate Prison. The collection devoted to Roman London contains some extraordinary gems, including an astonishingly well-preserved floor mosaic uncovered just a few streets away. (Appropriately enough the museum itself shelters a section of the 2nd- to 4th-century London wall, which you can view through a window.) Permanent displays highlight prehistoric, medieval, and Tudor London. The Galleries of Modern London are equally enthralling: experience the "Expanding City," "People's City," and "World City," each gallery dealing with a section of London's history from 1666 until the 21st century. Innovative interactive displays abound, and there's also a fine schedule of temporary exhibitions. Meanwhile, locals are waiting with bated breath for the display of an extraordinary hoard of artifacts, including some from the Bronze Age and Roman periods, which were uncovered during the building of the Crossrail Underground railway. Check the website for details about the fantastic **Street Museum** app, which allows you to hold up your phone in many London streets and be shown pictures of how things looked in the past. ✉ *London Wall, The City* ☎ *020/7001–9844* 🌐 *www.museumoflondon.org.uk* 🎫 *Free* ⏲ *Daily 10–6; last admission 5:30; galleries start to close 5:40* Ⓜ *Barbican, St. Paul's.*

Fodor's Choice ★ **St. Paul's Cathedral.** St. Paul's is simply breathtaking. The structure is Sir Christopher Wren's masterpiece, completed in 1710 after 35 years of building, and, much later, miraculously spared (mostly) by World War II bombs. Wren's first plan, known as the New Model, did not make it past the drawing board. The second, known as the Great Model, got as far as a 20-foot oak rendering—now displayed in the Trophy Room—before it also was rejected.

The third plan was accepted, with the fortunate proviso that the architect be allowed to make changes as he saw fit. Without that, there would be no dome, because the approved design had a steeple—and St. Paul's simply would not be St. Paul's as we know it without the dome (the third largest in the world). Even so, from inside the vast cathedral the dome may seem smaller than you'd expect—the inner dome is 60 feet lower than the lead-covered outer dome. Beneath the lantern is Wren's famous and succinct epitaph, which his son composed and had set into the pavement: "Lector, si monumentum requiris, circumspice" ("Reader, if you seek his monument, look around you"). The epitaph also appears on Wren's memorial in the Crypt.

Up 163 spiral steps is the **Whispering Gallery,** with its incredible acoustic phenomenon; you whisper something to the wall on one side, and a second later it transmits clearly to the other side, 107 feet away. Ascend to the **Stone Gallery,** which encircles the base of the dome. Farther up (280 feet from ground level) is the small **Golden Gallery,** the dome's highest point. From both these galleries (if you have a head for heights) you can walk outside for a spectacular panorama of London.

The remains of the poet John Donne, who was Dean of St. Paul's for his final 10 years (he died in 1631), are in the south choir aisle. The vivacious choir-stall carvings nearby are the work of Grinling Gibbons, as are those on the **great organ**, which Wren designed. Behind the high altar is the **American Memorial Chapel,** dedicated to the 28,000 GIs stationed in the United Kingdom who lost their lives in World War II. Among the famous figures whose remains lie in the **Crypt** are the Duke of Wellington and Admiral Lord Nelson. Free, 90-minute guided tours take place Monday to Saturday at 10, 11, 1, and 2; book a place at the welcome desk (on the day of only). A tour of the Triforium (upper galleries) can be taken on Monday, Tuesday, or Friday by groups of five for £8 per person, but you have to book a week in advance; call or see the website for details. ✉ *St. Paul's Churchyard, The City* ☎ *020/7246–8350, 020/7246–8357 Triforium tours* 🌐 *www.stpauls.co.uk* 🎟 *£17 (includes multimedia guides and guided tours); £2 less if bought online* 🕒 *Mon.–Sat. 8:30–4:30 (last ticket sold at 4); open Sun. for services only* Ⓜ *St. Paul's.*

FAMILY Fodor's Choice ★ **Tower Bridge.** Despite its medieval, fairy-tale appearance, Britain's most iconic bridge was actually built at the tail end of the Victorian age, first opening to traffic in 1894. Constructed of steel, then clothed in Portland stone, the Horace Jones masterpiece was built in the Gothic style that was highly popular at the time (and it nicely complements the Tower of London, next door). The bridge is famous for its enormous bascules—the 1,200-ton "arms" that open to allow large ships to glide beneath. This still happens a few times per month (the website lists upcoming times), but when river traffic was dense, the bascules were raised about five times a day.

The **Tower Bridge Exhibition** is a family-friendly tour where you can discover how the bridge actually works before heading out onto the walkways for wonderful city views. First, take in the romance of the panoramas from the east and west walkways between those grand turrets. On the east are the modern superstructures of the Docklands, and on the west is the Tower of London, St. Paul's, the Monument, and the misshapen steel-and-glass egg that is Greater London Assembly's City Hall (memorably described as "a glass testicle" by former mayor Ken Livingstone). Then it's back down to explore the Victorian engine rooms and discover the inner workings, which you learn about through hands-on displays and films. ✉ *Tower Bridge Rd., The City* ☎ *020/7403–3761* 🌐 *www.towerbridge.org.uk* 🎟 *£9* 🕒 *Apr.–Sept., daily 10–5:30; Oct.–Mar., daily 9:30; last admission 30 min before closing* Ⓜ *Tower Hill.*

FAMILY Fodor's Choice ★ **Tower of London.** *See the highlighted feature in this section for more information.* ✉ *Tower Hill, The City* ☎ *0844/482–777* 🌐 *www.hrp.org.uk* 🎟 *£22* 🕒 *Mar.–Oct. Tues.–Sat. 9–5:30, Sun. and Mon. 10–5:30; Nov.–Feb. Tues.–Sat. 9–4:30, Sun. and Mon. 10–4:30.*

WORTH NOTING

Dr. Johnson's House. Built in 1700, this elegant Georgian residence, with its paneled rooms and period furniture, is where Samuel Johnson lived between 1748 and 1759. The Great Bear (as he was affectionately known) compiled *A Dictionary of the English Language* in the attic as his health deteriorated. Two early editions are on view, among other mementos of Johnson and his friend, diarist, and later, his biographer, James Boswell. After soaking up the atmosphere, repair around the corner in Wine Office Court to the famed **Ye Olde Cheshire Cheese** pub, once Johnson and Boswell's favorite watering hole. ✉ *17 Gough Sq., The City* ☎ *020/7353–3745* 🌐 *www.drjohnsonshouse.org* 🎫 *£4.75* ⏲ *May–Sept., Mon.–Sat. 11–5:30; Oct.–Apr., Mon.–Sat. 11–5* Ⓜ *Holborn, Chancery La., Temple.*

Guildhall. The Corporation of London, which oversees The City, has ceremonially elected and installed its Lord Mayor here for the last 800 years. The Guildhall was built in 1411, and though it failed to avoid the conflagrations of either 1666 or 1940, its core survived. The Great Hall is a psychedelic patchwork of coats of arms and banners of the City Livery Companies, which inherited the mantle of the medieval trade guilds. Tradesmen couldn't even run a shop without kowtowing to these prototypical unions, and their grand banqueting halls, the plushest private dining venues in The City, are testimony to the wealth they amassed. Inside the hall, Gog and Magog, the pair of mythical giants who founded ancient Albion and the city of New Troy, which London was said to have been built on, glower down from their west-gallery grandstand in 9-foot-high painted lime wood. The hall was also the site of famous trials, including that of Lady Jane Grey in 1553, before her execution at the Tower of London. To the right of Guildhall Yard is the **Guildhall Art Gallery,** which includes portraits of the great and the good, cityscapes, famous battles, and a slightly cloying pre-Raphaelite section. The construction of the gallery in the 1980s led to the exciting discovery of London's only **Roman amphitheater,** which had lain underneath Guildhall Yard undisturbed for more than 1,800 years. It was excavated and now visitors can walk among the remains, although most of the relics are now at the Museum of London. ✉ *Aldermanbury, The City* ☎ *020/7606–3030, 020/7332–3700 gallery* 🌐 *www.cityoflondon.gov.uk* 🎫 *Free (fee for some gallery exhibitions)* ⏲ *Hall Mon.–Sat. 10–4:30 (also Sun. 10–4:30 1st weekend in May to last weekend in Sept.). Last admission 30 mins before closing. Sometimes closed for events; call to check* Ⓜ *St. Paul's, Moorgate, Bank, Mansion House.*

EAST END

Made famous by Dickens and infamous by Jack the Ripper, East London is one of London's most enduringly evocative neighborhoods, rich in popular history, architectural gems, and artists' studios. Since the early 1990s, hip gallerists, designers, and new-media entrepreneurs have colonized its handsome Georgian buildings and converted industrial lofts. Today, the collection of neighborhoods that makes up East London lays claim to being the city's most trendsetting neighborhoods.

The British equivalent of Brooklyn, East London is a patchwork of districts encompassing struggling artists, ethnic enclaves, upscale professionals, and the digerati, occasionally teetering, like its New York equivalent, on the edge of self-parody. The vast area ranges from gentrified districts like Spitalfields—where bankers and successful artists

Continued on page 78

THE TOWER OF LONDON

The Tower is a microcosm of the city itself—a sprawling, organic hodgepodge of buildings that inspires reverence and terror in equal measure. See the block on which Anne Boleyn was beheaded, marvel at the Crown Jewels, and pay homage to the ravens who keep the monarchy safe.

An architectural patchwork of time, the oldest building of the complex is the fairytale White Tower, conceived by William the Conqueror in 1078 as both a royal residence and a show of power to the troublesome Anglo-Saxons he had subdued at the Battle of Hastings. Today's Tower has seen everything, as a palace, barracks, a mint for producing coins, an armoury, and the Royal menagerie (home of the country's first elephant). The big draw is the stunning opulence of the Crown Jewels, kept on-site in the heavily fortified Jewel House. Most of all, though, the Tower is known for death: it's been a place of imprisonment, torture, and execution for the realm's most notorious traitors as well as its martyrs. These days, unless you count the killer admission fees, there are far less morbid activities taking place in the Tower, but it still breathes London's history and pageantry from its every brick and offers hours of exploration.

TOURING THE TOWER

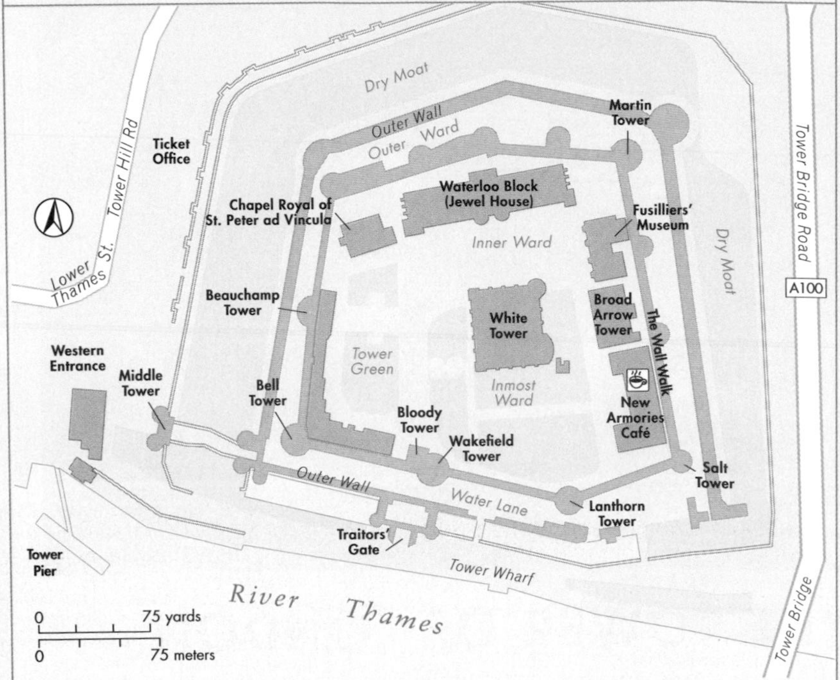

Entry to the Tower is via the **Western Entrance** and the **Middle Tower,** which feed into the outermost ring of the Tower's defenses.

Water Lane leads past the dread-inducing **Traitors' Gate,** the final point of entry for many Tower prisoners.

Toward the end of Water Lane, the **Lanthorn Tower** houses by night the ravens rumored to keep the kingdom safe, and by day a timely high-tech reconstruction of the Catholic Guy Fawkes's plot to blow up the Houses of Parliament in 1605.

The **Bloody Tower** earned its name as the apocryphal site of the murder of two young princes, Edward and Richard, who disappeared from the Tower after being put there in 1483 by their uncle, Richard III. Two little skeletons (now in Westminster Abbey) were found buried close to the White Tower in 1674 and are thought to be theirs.

The **Beauchamp Tower** housed upper-class miscreants: Latin graffiti about Lady Jane Grey can be glimpsed today on its walls.

Like a prize gem set at the head of a royal crown, the **White Tower** is the centerpiece of the complex. Its four towers dominate the Inner Ward, a fitting and forbidding reminder of Norman strength at the time of the conquest of England.

Once inside the White Tower, head upstairs for the **Armouries,** where the biggest attraction, quite literally,

GOLD DIGGER?

Keep your eyes peeled as you tour the Tower: according to one story, Sir John Barkstead, goldsmith and Lieutenant of the Tower under Cromwell, hid £20,000 in gold coins here before his arrest and execution at the Restoration of Charles II.

Jewel House, Waterloo Barracks

ROYAL BLING

The Crown of Queen Elizabeth, the Queen Mother, from 1937, contains the exotic 105-carat Koh-i-Noor (mountain of light) diamond.

TIME KILLERS

Some prisoners managed to keep themselves plenty amused: Sir Walter Raleigh grew tobacco on Tower Green, and in 1561 suspected sorcerer Hugh Draper carved an intricate astronomical clock on the walls of his Salt Tower cell.

is the suit of armor worn by a well-endowed Henry VIII. There is a matching outfit for his horse.

Other fascinating exhibits include the set of Samurai armor presented to James I in 1613 by the emperor of Japan, and the tiny set of armor worn by Henry VIII's young son Edward.

The **Jewel House** in **Waterloo Block** is the Tower's biggest draw, perfect for playing pick-your-favorite-crown from the wrong side of bulletproof glass. Not only are these crowns, staffs, and orbs encrusted with heavy-duty gems, they are invested with the authority of monarchical power in England, dating back to the 1300s.

Outside, pause at **Tower Green,** permanent departure point for those of noble birth. The hoi polloi were dispatched at nearby Tower Hill. The Tower's most famous female victims—Anne Boleyn, Margaret Countess of Salisbury, Catherine Howard, and Lady Jane Grey—all went this "priviledged" way.

Behind a well-kept square of grass stands the **Chapel Royal of St. Peter ad Vincula,** a delightful Tudor church and final resting place of six beheaded Tudor bodies. ■**TIP→ Visitors are welcome for services and can also enter after 4:30 pm daily.**

The **Salt Tower,** reputedly the most haunted corner of the complex, marks the start of the **Wall Walk,** a bracing promenade along the stone spiral steps and battlements of the Tower that looks down on the trucks, taxis, and shimmering high-rises of modern London.

The Wall Walk ends at the **Martin Tower,** former home of the Crown Jewels and now host to the crowns and diamonds exhibition that explains the art of fashioning royal headwear and tells the story of some of the most famous stones.

On leaving the Tower, browse the **gift shop**, and wander the wharf that overlooks the Thames, leading to a picture-postcard view of Tower Bridge.

WHO ARE THE BEEFEATERS?

First of all, they're Yeoman Warders, but probably got the nickname "beefeater" from their position as Royal Bodyguards which entitled them to eat as much beef as they liked. Part of the "Yeoman of the Guard," started in the reign of Edmund IV, the warders have formed the Royal Bodyguard as far back as 1509 when Henry VIII left a dozen of the Yeoman of the Guard at the Tower to protect it.

Originally, the Yeoman Warders also served as jailers of the Tower, doubling as torturers when necessary. (So it would have been a Beefeater tightening the thumb screws, or ratchetting the rack another notch on some unfortunate prisoner. Smile nicely.) Today 36 Yeoman Warders (men and women since 2007), along with the Chief Yeoman Warder and the Yeoman Gaoler, live within the walls of the Tower with their families, in accommodations in the Outer Ward. They stand guard over the Tower, conduct tours, and lock up at 9:53 pm every night with the Ceremony of the Keys.

■ TIP→ Free tickets to the Ceremony of the Keys are available by writing several months in advance; check the Tower Web site for details.

HARK THE RAVENS!

Legend has it that should the hulking black ravens ever leave, the White Tower will crumble and the kingdom fall. Charles II, no doubt jumpy after his father's execution and the monarchy's short-term fall from grace, made a royal decree in 1662 that there should be at least six of the carrion-eating nasties present at all times. There have been some close calls. During World War II, numbers dropped to one, echoing the precarious fate of the war-wracked country. In 2005, two (of eight) died over Christmas when Thor—the most intelligent but also the largest bully of the bunch—killed new recruit Gundolf, named after the Tower's 1070 designer. Pneumonia put an end to Bran, leaving lifelong partner Branwen without her mate.

■ DID YOU KNOW? In 1981 a raven named Grog, perhaps seduced by his alcoholic moniker, escaped after 21 years at the Tower. Others have been banished for "conduct unbecoming."

The six that remain, each one identified by a colored band around a claw, are much loved for their fidelity (they mate for life) and their cheek (capable of 440 noises, they are witty and scolding mimics). It's not only the diet of blood-soaked biscuits, rabbit, and scraps from the mess kitchen that keeps them coming back. Their lifting feathers on one wing are trimmed, meaning they can manage the equivalent of a lop-sided air-bound hobble but not much more. For the first half of 2006 the ravens were moved indoors full-time as a preventive measure against avian flu but have since been allowed out and about again. In situ they are a territorial lot, sticking to Tower Green and the White Tower, and lodging nightly by Wakefield Tower. They've had free front-row seats at all the most grisly moments in Tower history—Anne Boleyn's execution included.

■ TIP→ Don't get too close to the ravens: they are prone to pecking and not particularly fond of humans, unless you are the Tower's Raven Master.

And *WHAT* are they wearing?

Anyone who refers to this as a costume will be lucky to leave the Tower with head still attached to body: this is the ceremonial uniform of the Yeoman Warders, and it comes at a cool £13,000 a throw.

A **pike** (or halberd), also known as a partisan, is the Yeoman Warder's weapon of choice. The Chief Warder carries a staff topped with a miniature silver model of the White Tower.

The black Tudor **bonnet** is made of velvet; the blue undress consists of a felt top hat, with a single Tudor rose in the middle.

This **Tudor-style ruff** helps date the ceremonial uniform, which was first worn in 1552.

Insignia on a Yeoman Warder's upper right arm denote the rank he carried in the military.

The **medals** on a Yeoman Warder's chest are more than mere show: all of the men and women have served for at least 22 years in the armed forces.

This version of the **royal livery** bears the insignia of the current Queen ("E" for Elizabeth) but originally dates from Tudor times. The first letter changes according to the reigning monarch's Christian name; the second letter is always an "R" for *rex* (king) or *regina* (queen).

Slits in the **tunic** date from the times when Beefeaters were expected to ride a horse.

Red socks and **black patent shoes** are worn on special occasions. Visitors are more likely to see the regular blue undress, introduced in 1858 as the regular working dress of the Yeoman Warders.

The **red lines down the trousers** are a sign of the blood from the swords of the Yeoman Warders in their defense of the realm.

(IN)FAMOUS PRISONERS OF THE TOWER

Anne Boleyn Lady Jane Grey Sir Walter Raleigh

Sir Thomas More. A Catholic and Henry VIII's friend and chancellor, Sir Thomas refused to attend the coronation of Anne Boleyn (Henry VIII's second wife) or to recognize the multi-marrying king as head of the Church. Sent to the Tower for treason, in 1535 More was beheaded.

Anne Boleyn. The first of Henry VIII's wives to be beheaded, Anne, who failed to provide the king with a son, was accused of sleeping with five men, including her own brother. All six got the chop in 1536. Her severed head was held up to the crowd, and her lips were said to be mouthing prayer.

Margaret, Countess of Salisbury. Not the best-known prisoner in her lifetime, she has a reputation today for haunting the Tower. And no wonder: the elderly 70-year-old was condemned by Henry VIII in 1541 for a potentially treacherous bloodline (she was the last Plantagenet princess) and hacked to death by the executioner after she refused to put her head on the block like a common traitor and attempted to run away.

Queen Catherine Howard. Henry VIII's fifth wife was locked up for high treason and infidelity and beheaded in 1542 at age 20. Ever eager to please, she spent her final night practicing how to lay her head on the block.

Lady Jane Grey. The nine-days-queen lost her head in 1554 at age 16. Her death was the result of sibling rivalry gone seriously wrong, when Protestant Edward VI slighted his Catholic sister Mary in favor of Lady Jane as heir, and Mary decided to have none of it.

Guy Fawkes. The Roman Catholic soldier who tried to blow up the Houses of Parliament and kill the king in the 1605 Gunpowder plot was first incarcerated in the chambers of the Tower, where King James I requested he be tortured in ever-worsening ways. Perhaps unsurprisingly, he confessed. He met his seriously grisly end in the Old Palace Yard at Westminster, where he was hung, drawn, and quartered in 1607.

Sir Walter Raleigh. Once a favorite of Elizabeth I, he offended her by secretly marrying her Maid of Honor and was chucked in the Tower. Later, as a conspirator against James I, he paid with his life. A frequent visitor to the Tower (he spent 13 years there in three stints), he managed to get the Bloody Tower enlarged on account of his wife and growing family. He was finally executed in 1618 in Old Palace Yard, Westminster.

Josef Jakobs. The last man to be executed in the Tower was caught as a spy when parachuting in from Germany and executed by firing squad in 1941. The chair he sat in when he was shot is preserved in the Royal Armouries' artifacts store.

FOR FURTHER EVIDENCE . . .

A trio of buildings in the Inner Ward, the **Bloody Tower, Beauchamp Tower,** and **Queen's House,** all with excellent views of the execution scaffold in Tower Green, are the heart of the Tower's prison accommodations and home to a permanent exhibition about notable inmates.

TACKLING THE TOWER (without losing your head)

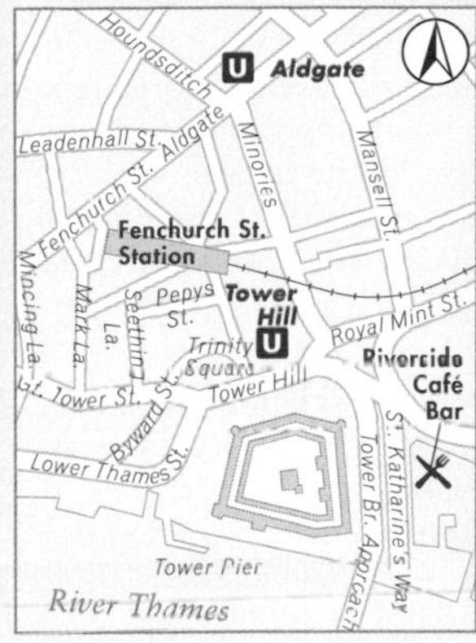

✉ H.M. Tower of London, Tower Hill ☎ 0844/482–7777/7799 🌐 www.hrp.org.uk 🎫 Adult: £22, children under 16: £11, Family tickets (2 adults, 2 children): £58, children under 5, free. ⏱ Mar.–Oct., Tues.–Sat. 9–5:30, Sun. and Mon. 10–5:30; last admission at 5. Nov.–Feb., Tues.–Sat. 9–4:30, Sun. and Mon. 10–4:30; last admission at 4 Ⓤ Tower Hill

■ **TIP→ You can buy tickets from automatic kiosks on arrival, or up to seven days in advance at any Tube station. Avoid lines completely by booking by telephone (0844 482 7777/7799 weekdays 9–5), or online.**

MAKING THE MOST OF YOUR TIME: Without doubt, the Tower is worth two to three hours. A full hour of that would be well spent by joining one of the Yeoman Warders' tours (included in admission). It's hard to better their insight, vitality, and humor—they are knights of the realm living their very own fairytale castle existence.

The Crown Jewels are worth the wait, the White Tower is essential, and the Medieval Palace and Bloody Tower should at least be breezed through.

■ **TIP→ It's best to visit on weekdays, when the crowds are smaller.**

WITH KIDS: The Tower's centuries-old cobblestones are not exactly stroller-friendly, but strollers are permitted inside most of the buildings. If you do bring one, be prepared to leave it temporarily unsupervised (the stroller, that is—not your child) outside the White Tower, which has no access. There are baby-changing facilities in the Brick Tower restrooms behind the Jewel House. Look for regular free children's events such as the Knight's school where children can have a go at jousting, sword-fighting, and archery.

■ **TIP→ Tell your child to find one of the Yeoman Warders if he or she should get lost; they will in turn lead him or her to the Byward Tower, which is where you should meet.**

IN A HURRY? If you have less than an hour, head down Wall Walk, through a succession of towers, which eventually spit you out at the Martin Tower. The view over modern London is quite a contrast.

TOURS: Tours given by a Yeoman Warder leave from the main entrance near Middle Tower every half-hour from 10–4, and last about an hour. Beefeaters give occasional 30-minute talks in the Lanthorn Tower about their daily lives. Both tours are free. Check website for talks and workshops live in desirable renovated Georgian town houses—to parts of Hackney where seemingly derelict, graffiti-covered industrial buildings are hives of exciting creative activity. As with all neighborhoods in transition, it can be a little rough around the edges, so stick to busier streets at night.

At the start of the new millennium, Hoxton, an enclave of Shoreditch, became the glossy hub of London's buzzing contemporary art scene, which accelerated the gentrification process. Some artists, such as Tracey Emin and Gilbert & George, long-term residents of Spitalfields' handsome Georgian terraces (and successful enough to still afford the area), have remained.

GETTING HERE

The London Overground, with stops at Shoreditch High Street, Hoxton, Whitechapel, Dalston Kingsland, and Hackney Central, is the easiest way to reach East London. Alternatively, the best Tube stations to use are Old Street on the Northern line, Bethnal Green on the Central line, and Liverpool Street on the Metropolitan and Circle lines.

PLANNING YOUR TIME

To experience East London at its most lively, visit on the weekend. Spitalfields Market bustles all weekend, while Brick Lane and Columbia Road are best on a Sunday morning. If you're planning to explore East London's art galleries, pick up a free map at the Whitechapel Art Gallery. As for the area's booming nightlife scene, there's no time limit.

TOP ATTRACTIONS

FAMILY Fodor's Choice ★ **Columbia Road Flower Market.** On Sunday morning this largely built-up area is transformed into a riot of color and scent as the Columbia Road Flower Market. There's everything from bedding plants to banana trees, including herbs, cut flowers, and bouquets at very reasonable prices. The vendors' patter is part of the fun. Columbia Road itself is lined with some 60 independent shops, so you can pick up some art, antiques, handcrafted jewelry, or, of course, garden accessories to go with your greenery. To avoid the crowds, get here the earlier the better. ✉ *Columbia Rd., Hackney* ☎ *020/7613–0876* 🌐 *www.columbiaroad.info* ⏲ *Sun. 8–3* Ⓜ *Old St., Northern Line.*

Fodor's Choice ★ **Whitechapel Art Gallery.** Founded in 1901, this internationally renowned gallery mounts shows that rediscover overlooked masters and exhibits tomorrow's legends. Painter and leading exponent of abstract expressionism, Jackson Pollock was exhibited here in the 1950s as was pop artist Robert Rauschenberg in the 1960s; the 1970s saw a young David Hockney's first solo show. The exhibitions continue to be on the cutting edge of contemporary art. The gallery also hosts talks, film screenings, workshops, and other events. Pick up a free East London art map to help you plan your visit to the area. ✉ *77–82 Whitechapel High St., Whitechapel* ☎ *020/7522–7888* 🌐 *www.whitechapelgallery.org* 🎫 *Free, charge for some special exhibits* ⏲ *Tues., Wed., and Fri.–Sun. 11–6;Thurs. 11–9* Ⓜ *Aldgate East.*

WORTH NOTING

The Ten Bells. Although the number of bells in its name has varied between 8 and 12 (depending on how many bells were used by neighboring Christ Church Spitalfields), this pub retains its authentic mid-Victorian interior and original tiles, including a frieze depicting the area's weaving tradition on the north wall and particularly fine floral tiling on two others. Legend has it the Ripper's third victim, Annie Chapman, had a drink here before meeting her gory end—the pub is depicted in Alan Moore's acclaimed graphic novel *From Hell.* ✉ *84 Commercial St., Spitalfields* ☎ *07530/492986* 🌐 *tenbells.com* Ⓜ *Overground: Shoreditch High St.*

THE SOUTH BANK

Culture, history, markets—the South Bank has them all. Installed in a converted 1930s power station, Tate Modern is the star attraction, with the eye-catching Millennium Bridge connecting it to the City across the river. Near the National Theatre and the concert halls of the South Bank Centre, the London Eye observation wheel gives you a bird's-eye view of the city.

Traditionally, Southwark was a rough area known for its inns, prisons, bear-baiting arenas, and theaters. The Globe, which housed the company Shakespeare wrote for and performed with, was one of several here. It has been reconstructed on the original site, so you can experience watching the Bard's plays as the Elizabethans would have. Be sure to take a stroll along Queen's Walk, the embankment along the Thames from Southwark to Blackfriars Bridge, taking in Tate Modern along the way.

GETTING HERE

For the South Bank, use Embankment on the District, Circle, Northern, and Bakerloo lines. From here you can walk across the Queens Jubilee footbridges. Another option is Waterloo—on the Northern, Jubilee, and Bakerloo lines—from where it's a five-minute walk to the Royal Festival Hall (slightly longer from the Jubilee Line station). London Bridge on the Northern and Jubilee lines is a five-minute walk from Borough Market and Southwark Cathedral.

PLANNING YOUR TIME

Don't attempt to explore the area south of the Thames all in one go. Not only will you exhaust yourself, but you'll also miss out on the varied delights that it has to offer. Tate Modern alone deserves a whole morning or afternoon, especially if you want to do justice to both the temporary exhibitions and the permanent collection. The Globe requires about two hours for the exhibition theater tour and two to three hours for a performance.

TOP ATTRACTIONS

FAMILY
Fodor's Choice ★

IWM London. Despite its name, the cultural venue formerly known as the Imperial War Museum (one of five IWM branches around the country) does not glorify either Empire or bloodshed but emphasizes understanding through conveying the impact of 20th- and 21st-century warfare on citizens and soldiers alike. After a major renovation, a dramatic six-story atrium at the main entrance encloses an impressive amount of hardware—including a Battle of Britain Spitfire, a German V2 rocket, tanks, guns, and submarines—along with accompanying interactive material and a café. The "Trench Experiences" in the World War I

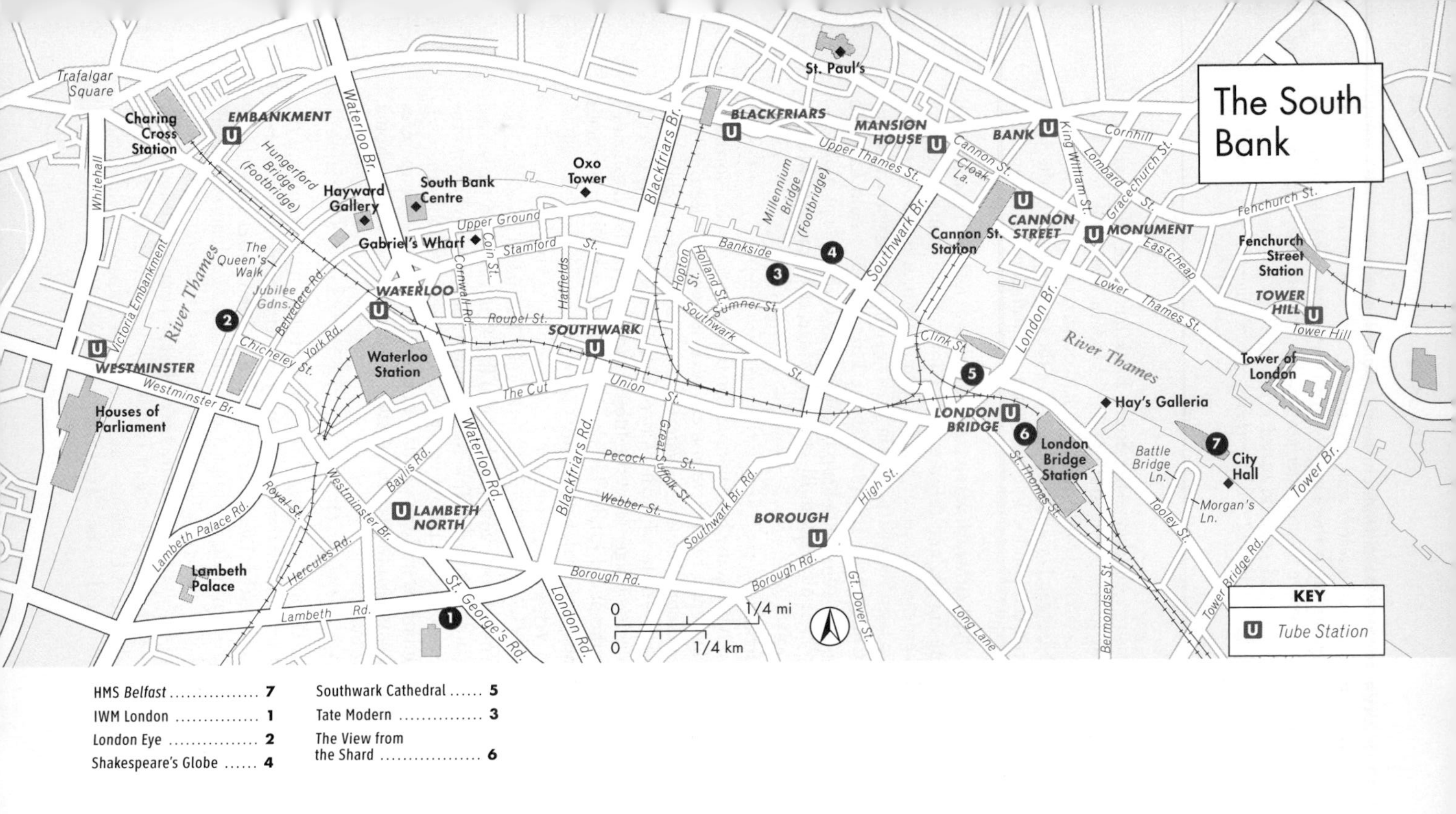
The South Bank
KEY
Tube Station
Trafalgar Square
Charing Cross Station
EMBANKMENT
Hungerford Bridge (Footbridge)
Whitehall
Victoria Embankment
River Thames
The Queen's Walk
Jubilee Gdns.
Belvedere Rd.
WESTMINSTER
Westminster Br.
Houses of Parliament
Chicheley St.
York Rd.
Waterloo Br.
Hayward Gallery
South Bank Centre
Gabriel's Wharf
Upper Ground
Coin St.
Cornwall Rd.
Stamford St.
Hatfields
Oxo Tower
WATERLOO
Waterloo Station
Roupel St.
The Cut
SOUTHWARK
Union St.
Waterloo Rd.
Baylis Rd.
LAMBETH NORTH
Westminster Br.
Royal St.
Lambeth Palace Rd.
Lambeth Palace
Hercules Rd.
Lambeth Rd.
St. George's Rd.
London Rd.
Blackfriars Rd.
Blackfriars Br.
BLACKFRIARS
St. Paul's
Upper Thames St.
MANSION HOUSE
Millennium Bridge (Footbridge)
Bankside
Hopton St.
Holland St.
Sumner St.
Southwark St.
Pecock St.
Great Suffolk St.
Webber St.
Southwark Br. Rd.
Borough Rd.
BOROUGH
Gt. Dover St.
Long Lane
High St.
Southwark Br.
Cannon St.
Cloak La.
BANK
King William St.
Cornhill
Lombard St.
Gracechurch St.
Cannon St. Station
CANNON STREET
MONUMENT
Eastcheap
Fenchurch St.
Fenchurch Street Station
TOWER HILL
Tower Hill
Lower Thames St.
London Br.
Clink St.
LONDON BRIDGE
London Bridge Station
St. Thomas St.
Hay's Galleria
Tower of London
Battle Bridge Ln.
Morgan's Ln.
City Hall
Tooley St.
Tower Br.
Tower Bridge Rd.
Bermondsey St.
0
1/4 mi
0
1/4 km
1
2
3
4
5
6
7
HMS *Belfast* 7
IWM London 1
London Eye 2
Shakespeare's Globe 4
Southwark Cathedral 5
Tate Modern 3
The View from the Shard 6

Galleries uses sights, sounds, and smells to re-create the grimness of life in No Man's Land, while an equally effective "Blitz Experience" in the revamped World War II galleries provides a 10-minute glimpse of an air raid, putting you on a "street" filled with acrid smoke as sirens wail and searchlights glare. Also in the World War II galleries is an extensive and haunting Holocaust Exhibition, while "Conflict Since 1945" documents the fact that there has been fighting somewhere in the world almost continuously since the end of World War II. Other galleries are devoted to works relating to conflicts from World War I to the present day by painters, poets, documentary filmmakers, and photographers (a new exhibition about pioneering female war correspondent Lee Miller opens in late 2015). James Bond fans won't want to miss the intriguing Secret War Gallery, which charts the work of secret agents. ✉ *Lambeth Rd., South Bank* ☎ *020/7416–5000* 🌐 *www.iwm.org.uk* 🎟 *Free (charge for special exhibitions)* ⏲ *Daily 10–6; last admission 5:30* Ⓜ *Lambeth North.*

FAMILY Fodor's Choice ★ **London Eye.** To mark the start of the new millennium, architects David Marks and Julia Barfield devised an instant icon that allows Londoners and visitors alike to see the city from a completely new perspective. The giant Ferris wheel was the largest cantilevered observation wheel ever built at the time, and it's one of the city's tallest structures. The 25-minute slow-motion ride inside one of the enclosed passenger capsules is so smooth you'd hardly know you were suspended over the Thames. On a clear day you can see up to 25 miles, with a bird's-eye view of London's most famous landmarks as you circle 360 degrees. If you're looking for a special place to celebrate, Champagne and canapés can be arranged ahead of time. ■ **TIP→ Buy your ticket online to avoid the long lines and get a 10% discount.** For an extra £8.55, you can save even more time with a Fast Track flight (check in 15 minutes before your "departure"). You can buy a combination ticket for the Eye and other London attractions—check online for details—and board the London Eye River Cruise here for a 40-minute sightseeing voyage on the Thames. In December, there's a scenic ice rink just below the wheel. ✉ *Jubilee Gardens, South Bank* ☎ *0871/781–3000* 🌐 *www.londoneye.com* 🎟 *£20.95; cruise £13 (£11.70 online)* ⏲ *Varies; see website.* ⏲ *Closed Jan. 7–14* Ⓜ *Waterloo.*

FAMILY Fodor's Choice ★ **Shakespeare's Globe.** This spectacular theater is a replica of Shakespeare's open-roof, wood-and-thatch Globe Playhouse (built in 1599 and burned down in 1613), where most of the Bard's greatest works premiered. American actor and director Sam Wanamaker worked ceaselessly for several decades to raise funds for the theater's reconstruction 200 yards from its original site, using authentic materials and techniques, a dream that was realized in 1997. "Groundlings"—patrons with £5 standing-only tickets—are not allowed to sit during the performance. Fortunately, you can reserve an actual seat on any one of the theater's three levels, but you will want to rent a cushion for £1 (or bring your own) to soften the backless wooden benches. The show must go on, rain or shine, warm or chilly, so come prepared for anything. Umbrellas are banned, but you can bring a raincoat or buy a cheap Globe rain poncho, which doubles as a great souvenir. In the winter months, the Sam Wanamaker Playhouse, a 350-seat re-creation of an indoor Jacobean theater lit by candles, offers plays and concerts in a less exposed though still atmospheric setting.

Shakespeare's Globe Exhibition, a museum under the theater (the entry is adjacent), provides background material on the Elizabethan theater and the construction of the modern-day Globe. Admission to the museum also includes a tour of the theater. On matinee days in summer (there are no winter matinees), the tour visits either the archaeological site of the nearby (and older) Rose Theatre or the Wanamaker. ✉ *21 New Globe Walk, Bankside* ☎ *020/7902–1400 general information, 020/7401–9919 box office* 🌐 *www.shakespearesglobe.com* 🎫 *Exhibition and Globe Theatre tour £13.50 (£2 reduction with valid performance ticket); ticket prices for plays vary; Globe £5–£42, Wanamaker £10–£60* ⏲ *Exhibition: daily 9–5:30; Globe: mid-Apr.–mid-Oct.; Wanamaker: mid-Oct.–mid-Apr. Call or check website for performance schedules* Ⓜ *London Bridge; Mansion House, then cross Southwark Bridge.*

Fodor's Choice ★ **Tate Modern.** This spectacular renovation of a mid-20th-century power station is one of the most-visited museums of modern art in the world. Its great permanent collection, which starts in 1900 and ranges from Modern masters like Matisse to the most cutting-edge contemporary artists, is arranged thematically—Landscape, Still Life, and the Nude. Its blockbuster temporary exhibitions showcase the work of individual artists like Gaugin, Roy Lichtenstein, and Gerhard Richter. The vast **Turbine Hall** is a dramatic entrance point used to showcase big, audacious installations that tend to generate a lot of publicity. Past highlights include Olafur Eliasson's massive glowing sun and Carsten Holler's huge metal slides.

The museum is in the process of rearranging its galleries prior to the opening of an ambitious new extension in 2016, so check the website ahead of time. Not to be missed is the new collection of Rothko murals, originally created for the Seagram building in New York, and displays devoted to Cy Twombley and the video pioneer Nam June Paik (both on Level 4).

Head to the Restaurant on Level 6 or the Espresso Bar on Level 3 for stunning vistas of the Thames. The view of St. Paul's from the Espresso Bar's balcony is one of the best in London. ✉ *Bankside* ☎ *020/7887–8888* 🌐 *www.tate.org.uk/modern* 🎫 *Free, charge for special exhibitions* ⏲ *Sun.–Thurs. 10–6, Fri. and Sat. 10–10 (last admission to exhibitions 45 min before closing)* Ⓜ *Southwark, Mansion House, St. Paul's.*

WORTH NOTING

FAMILY **HMS *Belfast*.** At 613.5 feet, this is one of the last remaining big-gun armored warships from World War II, in which it played an important role in protecting the Arctic convoys and supporting the D-Day landings in Normandy; the ship later saw action during the Korean War. The *Belfast* has been moored in the Thames as a maritime branch of the **IWM London** since 1971. A tour of all nine decks—which include the admiral's quarters, mess decks, bakery, punishment cells, operations room, engine room, and more—gives a vivid picture of life on board the ship, while the riveting interactive gun-turret experience puts you in the middle of a World War II naval battle. ✉ *The Queen's Walk, Borough* ☎ *020/7940–6300* 🌐 *www.iwm.org.uk* 🎟 *£15.50* ⏲ *Mar.–Oct., daily 10–6; Nov.–Feb., daily 10–5; last admission 1 hr before closing* Ⓜ *London Bridge.*

Southwark Cathedral. Pronounced "Suth-uck," this is the oldest Gothic church in London, with parts dating back to the 12th century. It remains off the beaten track, despite being the site of some remarkable memorials and a concert program that offers regular organ recitals at lunchtime on Monday (except in August and December) and classical music at 3:15 on Tuesday (except in December). Originally the priory church of St. Mary Overie (as in "over the water"—on the South Bank), it became a palace church under Henry VIII and was only promoted to cathedral status in 1905. Look for the gaudily renovated 1408 tomb of John Gower, a poet who was a friend of Chaucer's, and for the Harvard Chapel, where John Harvard, a local butcher's son who went on to found the American university, was baptized. Another notable buried here is Edmund Shakespeare, brother of William. The Refectory serves full English breakfasts, light lunches, and teas 9–6 weekdays, 10–6 weekends. ✉ *London Bridge, Bankside* ☎ *020/7367–6700* 🌐 *cathedral.southwark.anglican.org* 🎟 *Free, suggested donation £4* ⏲ *Daily 8–6* Ⓜ *London Bridge.*

The View from the Shard. At 800 feet, this 2013 addition to the London skyline currently offers the highest vantage point in Western Europe. Designed by the noted architect Renzo Piano, it has attracted both admiration and disdain. While the building itself is generally highly regarded, many felt it would have been better sited in Canary Wharf (or perhaps Dubai), as it spoils views of St. Paul's Cathedral from traditional vantage points such as Hampstead's Parliament Hill. No matter how you feel about the building, there's no denying that it offers spectacular 360-degree views over London (extending to 40 miles on a clear day) from viewing platforms on floors 68, 69, and 72—almost twice as high as any other viewpoint in the city. Digital telescopes provide information about 200 points of interest. If you find the price as eye-wateringly high as the viewing platforms, there's a less dramatic but still very impressive—and free—view from the lobby of the Shangri-La hotel on floor 35, or, in the evenings, the hotel's chic Gong bar on floor 52 (over-18s only). ✉ *32 London Bridge St., Borough* ☎ *0344/499–7222* 🌐 *www.theviewfromtheshard.com* 🎟 *From £24.95* ⏲ *Apr.–Oct., daily 10–10; Nov.–Mar., Sun.–Wed. 10–7, Thurs.–Sat. 10–10; admission by timed ticket only. Last admission 90 min before closing. May be closed for special events, check website* Ⓜ *London Bridge.*

KENSINGTON, KNIGHTSBRIDGE, AND MAYFAIR

The Royal Borough of Kensington & Chelsea (or "K&C" as the locals call it) is London at its richest, and not just in the moneyed sense. South Kensington has a concentration of great museums near Cromwell Road, while within Kensington Gardens is historic Kensington Palace, home to royal family members including Queen Victoria, Princess Diana, and now Prince William, Duke of Cambridge and Catherine, Duchess of Cambridge (plus baby George). Knightsbridge has become a playground for the international wealthy.

Hyde Park and Kensington Gardens together form by far the biggest of central London's royal parks. As the property of the Crown, which still owns them, they were spared from being devoured by London's inexorable westward development that began in the late 18th century.

With world-famous department stores, boutiques selling the biggest names in international luxury, and expensive jewelers, London's wealthiest enclave reflects the taste of those who can afford the best and are prepared to pay for it.

Around the borders of Hyde Park are several of London's most elegant and upscale neighborhoods. South of the park and a short carriage ride from Buckingham Palace are the cream-stucco terraces of Belgravia, one of the most impressive set-pieces of 19th-century urban planning, in this case by the developer Thomas Cubitt. On the eastern border of Hyde Park lies the most fashionable shopping area in London, Mayfair, which gives Belgravia a run for its money as London's wealthiest district.

GETTING HERE

Several useful Tube stations are nearby: Knightsbridge and Hyde Park Corner on the Piccadilly Line will take you to Knightsbridge, Belgravia, and Hyde Park; South Kensington and Gloucester Road on the District, Circle, and Piccadilly lines are convenient stops for the South Kensington museums and Kensington Palace; Bond Street (Central Line) and Green Park (Piccadilly and Victoria lines), both on the Jubilee Line, serve Mayfair.

PLANNING YOUR TIME

The best way to approach these neighborhoods is to treat Knightsbridge shopping and the South Kensington museums as separate days out, although the three vast museums may be too much to take in at once. The parks are best when the leaves are out and during fall, when the foliage is turning. On the rare hot day, you may want to brave a dip in the waters of Hyde Park's Serpentine. Otherwise, explore by rented pedalo.

TOP ATTRACTIONS

FAMILY Fodor's Choice ★ **Hyde Park.** Along with the smaller St. James's and Green parks to the east, the 350-acre Hyde Park started as Henry VIII's hunting grounds. Along its south side runs Rotten Row, once Henry's royal path to the hunt—the name is a corruption of *Route du Roi* (route of the king). It's still used by the Household Cavalry, who live at the Hyde Park Barracks—a high-rise and a low, ugly, red block, now up for sale—to the left. You can see the Guardsmen in full regalia leaving on horseback for guard duty at Buckingham Palace at about 10:30, or come at noon when they return. Hyde Park is wonderful for strolling, cycling, or just relaxing by the Serpentine, the long body of water near its southern border. On the south side, by the 1930s **Serpentine Lido**, is the site of the **Diana Princess of Wales Memorial Fountain**, which opened in 2003 and is a good spot to refuel at a café. On Sunday close to Marble Arch you'll find the uniquely British tribute to free speech, Speakers' Corner.

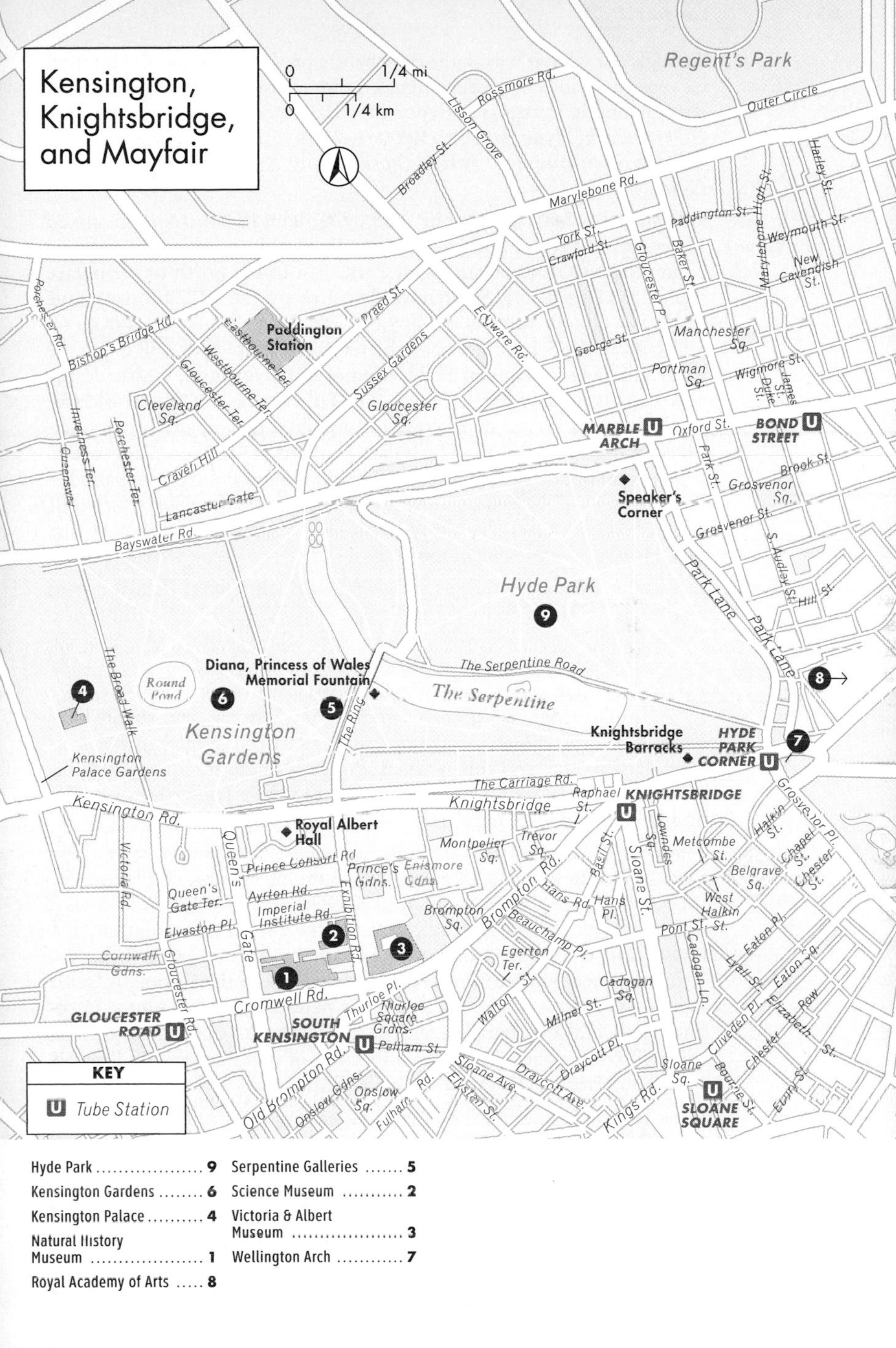

- Hyde Park 9
- Kensington Gardens 6
- Kensington Palace 4
- Natural History Museum 1
- Royal Academy of Arts 8
- Serpentine Galleries 5
- Science Museum 2
- Victoria & Albert Museum 3
- Wellington Arch 7

Though not what it was in the days before people could use the Internet to vent their spleen, it still offers a unique assortment of passionate, if occasionally irrational, advocates literally getting up on soapboxes. ✉ *Hyde Park, Hyde Park* ☎ *030/0061–2000* 🌐 *www.royalparks.org.uk* ⏲ *Daily 5 am–midnight* Ⓜ *Hyde Park Corner, Knightsbridge, Lancaster Gate, Marble Arch.*

FAMILY Fodor's Choice ★ **Kensington Gardens.** Laid out in 1689 by William III, who commissioned Christopher Wren to build Kensington Palace, the gardens are a formal counterpart to neighboring Hyde Park. Just to the north of the palace itself is the Dutch-style **Sunken Garden**. Nearby, the 1912 bronze statue *Peter Pan* commemorates the boy in J. M. Barrie's story who lived on an island in the Serpentine and who never grew up. Kids will enjoy the magical **Diana Princess of Wales Memorial Playground,** whose design was also inspired by Barrie's book. The **Elfin Oak** is a 900-year-old tree trunk that was carved with scores of tiny elves, fairies, and other fanciful creations in the 1920s. The **Italian Gardens** (1860) comprise several ornamental ponds and fountains, while the **Round Pond** attracts model-boat enthusiasts. ✉ *Kensington* ☎ *030/0061–2000* 🌐 *www.royalparks.org.uk* ⏲ *Daily 6 am–dusk* Ⓜ *High Street Kensington, Lancaster Gate, Queensway, South Kensington.*

FAMILY **Kensington Palace.** Neither as imposing as Buckingham Palace nor as charming as Hampton Court, Kensington Palace is something of a Royal Family commune, with various close relatives of the Queen occupying large apartments in the private part of the palace. Bought in 1689 by Queen Mary and King William III, it was converted into a palace by Sir Christopher Wren and Nicholas Hawksmoor, and royals have been in residence ever since. Princess Diana lived here with her sons after her divorce, and this is where Prince William now lives with his wife, Catherine, Duchess of Cambridge and their young son, George, and baby daughter, Charlotte.

The State Apartments are open to the public. One permanent exhibition, "Victoria Revealed," is devoted to the private life of Queen Victoria, who was born and grew up at KP. The Queen's State Apartments are given over to William and Mary and the Glorious Revolution. The lavish King's State Apartments, originally build for George I, have a semipermanent exhibit that explores the world of the Georgian Court through the story of George II and his politically active queen, Caroline. There is also a changing temporary exhibition. Through late 2015, this will be "Fashion Rules," a collection of gowns worn by Princess Margaret, Princess Diana, and Queen Elizabeth.

Look for the King's Staircase, with its panoramic trompe l'oeil painting, and the King's Gallery, with royal artworks surrounded by rich red damask walls, intricate gilding, and a beautiful painted ceiling. Outside, the grounds are almost as lovely as the palace itself. ✉ *The Broad Walk, Kensington Gardens, Kensington* ☎ *0844/482–7799 advance booking, 0844/482–7777 information, 0203/166–6000 from outside U.K.* 🌐 *www.hrp.org.uk* 🎟 *£16.50* ⏲ *Mar.–Sept., daily 10–6; Oct.–Feb., daily 10–5; last admission 1 hr before closing* Ⓜ *Queensway, High Street Kensington.*

These ice-skaters outside the Natural History Museum in South Kensington are making the best of London's winter.

FAMILY
Fodor's Choice ★

Natural History Museum. The ornate terra-cotta facade of this enormous Victorian museum is embellished with relief panels depicting living creatures to the left of the entrance and extinct ones to the right (although some species have subsequently changed categories). Most are represented inside the museum, which contains more than 70 million different specimens. Only a small percentage is on public display, but you could still spend a day here and not come close to seeing everything.

A giant diplodocus skeleton dominates the vaulted, cathedral-like entrance hall, affording you perhaps the most irresistible photo opportunity in the building. It's just a cast, but the **Dinosaur Gallery** (Gallery 21) contains plenty of real-life dino bones, fossils, and some extremely long teeth. You'll also come face-to-face with velociraptors and a giant animatronic *Tyrannosaurus rex* that's programmed to sense when human prey is near and "respond" in character. When he does, you can hear the shrieks of fear and delight all the way across the room.

An escalator takes you into a giant globe in the **Earth Galleries,** where there's a choice of levels to explore. Don't leave without checking out the earthquake simulation in the **Volcanoes and Earthquake Gallery.**

The **Darwin Centre** houses some of the millions of items the museum itself doesn't have room to display, including "Archie," a 28-foot giant squid. If you want to see Archie and some of the other thousands of specimens on the shelves, you'll need to book one of the free behind-the-scenes Spirit Collection tours. These can be booked on the day, but space is limited, so come early. The Centre's **Cocoon Experience** is a 45-minute tour during which you can see specimens from plant and insect collections previously in storage. ✉ *Cromwell Rd., South*

Kensington ☎ *0207/942–5000* 🌐 *www.nhm.ac.uk* 🎫 *Free (some fees for special exhibitions)* ⏲ *Daily 10–5:50, last admission at 5:30* Ⓜ *South Kensington.*

Fodor's Choice ★ **Royal Academy of Arts.** Burlington House was built in 1664, with later Palladian additions for the 3rd Earl of Burlington in 1720. The piazza in front dates from 1873, when the Renaissance-style buildings around the courtyard were designed by Banks and Barry to house a gaggle of noble scientific societies, including the Royal Society of Chemistry and the Royal Astronomical Society.

The house itself is home to the Royal Academy of Arts. In a city with many major public galleries, the Royal Academy more than holds its own. The statue of the academy's first president, Sir Joshua Reynolds, palette in hand, is prominent in the piazza, while within the house are statues of the major painters J. W. M. Turner and Thomas Gainsborough. Free tours show off part of the collection and the excellent temporary exhibitions. Every June, the RA puts on its Summer Exhibition, a huge and eclectic collection of art by living Royal Academicians and many other contemporary artists. ✉ *Burlington House, Piccadilly, Mayfair* ☎ *020/7300–8000, 020/7300–5839 lectures and family programs* 🌐 *www.royalacademy.org.uk* 🎫 *Prices vary with exhibition, £8–£16* ⏲ *Sat.–Thurs. 10–6, Fri. 10–10; tours Tues. and Wed. 1, Thurs. and Fri. 3, Sat. 11:30* Ⓜ *Piccadilly Circus, Green Park.*

FAMILY Fodor's Choice ★ **Science Museum.** This, one of the three great South Kensington museums, stands next to the Natural History Museum in a far plainer building. It has lots of hands-on painlessly educational exhibits, but don't dismiss the Science Museum as just for kids. Highlights include the Launch Pad gallery, which demonstrates basic laws of physics; *Puffing Billy,* the oldest steam locomotive in the world; and the actual *Apollo 10* capsule. The six floors are devoted to subjects as diverse as the history of flight, space exploration, the large Hadron collider, 3-D printing, and a sublime exhibition on science in the 18th century. The Information Age gallery, devoted to communication networks, including telegraph, television, mobile phones, and Internet, was opened in 2014 by Queen Elizabeth, who marked the occasion by sending her first tweet. The architecturally imaginative Mathematics gallery opens in 2016. Overshadowed by a three-story blue-glass wall, the Wellcome Wing is an annex to the rear of the museum, devoted to contemporary science and technology. It contains a 450-seat IMAX theater and the Legend of Apollo—an advanced motion simulator that combines seat vibration with other technical gizmos to re-create the experience of a moon landing. If you're a family of at least five, you might be able to get a place on one of the popular Science Night sleepovers by booking well in advance. Aimed at kids seven years old, these nighttime science workshops offer the chance to camp out in one of the galleries, and include a free IMAX show the next morning. Check the website for details. ✉ *Exhibition Rd., South Kensington* ☎ *0870/870–4868* 🌐 *www.sciencemuseum.org.uk* 🎫 *Free; charge for special exhibitions, IMAX, and simulator rides* ⏲ *Daily 10–6; last admission 5:15* Ⓜ *South Kensington.*

FAMILY Fodor's Choice ★ **Victoria & Albert Museum.** Known to all as the V&A, this huge museum is devoted to the applied arts of all disciplines, all periods, and all nationalities. First opened as the South Kensington Museum in 1857, it was renamed in 1899 in honor of Queen Victoria's late husband and has since grown to become one of the country's best-loved cultural institutions.

Many collections at the V&A are presented not by period but by category—textiles, sculpture, jewelry, and so on. Nowhere is the benefit of this more apparent than in the **Fashion Gallery** (Room 40), where formal 18th-century court dresses are displayed alongside the haute couture styles of contemporary designers. The Fashion Gallery has become known for high-profile temporary exhibitions devoted to icons such as David Bowie and Alexander McQueen.

The **British Galleries** (rooms 52–58 and 118–125), devoted to art and design from 1500 to 1900, are full of beautiful diversions—among them the Great Bed of Ware (immortalized in Shakespeare's *Twelfth Night*). Here, a series of actual rooms have been painstakingly reconstructed piece by piece. These include an ornate music room and the Henrietta St. Room, a breathtakingly serene parlor dating from 1722.

The **Asian Galleries** (rooms 44–47) are full of treasures, but among the most striking items on display is a remarkable collection of ornate samurai armor in the **Japanese Gallery** (Room 44). There are also galleries devoted to China, Korea, and the Islamic Middle East. More recently installed areas include the Ceramics gallery and the Medieval and Renaissance galleries, which have the largest collection of works from the period outside of Italy. The Europe Gallery (rooms 1–7), opened after an extensive refurbishment, brings together more than 1,100 objects from 1600 to 1800. ✉ *Cromwell Rd., South Kensington* ☎ *020/7942–2000* 🌐 *www.vam.ac.uk* 🎫 *Free; charge for some special exhibitions (from £5)* ⏲ *Sat.–Thurs. 10–5:45, Fri. 10–10* Ⓜ *South Kensington.*

WORTH NOTING

Serpentine Galleries. Built in 1934 as a tea pavilion in Kensington Gardens, the Serpentine has an international reputation for exhibitions of modern and contemporary art. Henry Moore, Andy Warhol, Bridget Riley, Damien Hirst, and Rachel Whiteread are a few of the artists who have exhibited here. It's a seven-minute walk across the park from the main gallery. The annual summer Pavilion, a striking temporary structure designed by a different leading architect every year, is always worth catching. ✉ *Kensington Gardens, Kensington* ☎ *020/7402–6075* 🌐 *www.serpentinegalleries.org* 🎫 *Free* ⏲ *Tues.–Sun. 10–6* Ⓜ *Lancaster Gate, Knightsbridge, South Kensington.*

Wellington Arch. Opposite the Duke of Wellington's mansion, Apsley House, this majestic stone arch surveys the traffic rushing around Hyde Park Corner. Designed by Decimus Burton and completed in 1828, it was created as a grand entrance to the west side of London and echoes the design of that other landmark gate, Marble Arch. Both were triumphal arches commemorating Britain's victory against France in the Napoleonic Wars. Atop the building, the Angel of Peace descends on the quadriga, or four-horse chariot of war. This replaced the Duke of Wellington on his horse, which was considered too large and moved to an army barracks in Aldershot. Inside the arch, three floors of permanent and temporary exhibits reveal the monument's history. ✉ *Hyde Park Corner, Mayfair* ☎ *020/7930–2726* 🌐 *www.english-heritage.org.uk* 🎫 *£4.20* 🕘 *Daily 10–4, but platform sometimes closed for exhibition installations* Ⓜ *Hyde Park Corner.*

REGENT'S PARK AND HAMPSTEAD

Regent's Park, Primrose Hill, and Hampstead are three of London's prettiest and most civilized neighborhoods. The city becomes noticeably peaceable as you wind your way up from Marylebone Road through Regent's Park, with its elegant Nash terraces, to the well-tended lawns of Primrose Hill and the handsome Georgian streets of Hampstead.

GETTING HERE

To get to Hampstead by Tube, take the Northern Line (make sure you get on the Edgware branch, not High Barnet) to Hampstead station, or take the London Overground to Hampstead Heath station. To get to Regent's Park, take the Bakerloo Line to Regent's Park Tube station or, for the Zoo, the Camden Town stop on the Northern Line. St. John's Wood has its own stop on the Jubilee Line.

PLANNING YOUR TIME

Depending on your pace and inclination, Regent's Park and Hampstead can realistically be covered in a day. It might be best to spend the morning in Hampstead, then head south toward Regent's Park in the afternoon so that you're closer to central London come nightfall, if that is where your hotel is located.

TOP ATTRACTIONS

FAMILY Fodor's Choice ★ **Hampstead Heath.** For generations, Londoners have headed to Hampstead Heath to escape the dirt and noise of the city. A unique expanse of *rus in urbe* ("country in the city"), its 791 acres encompass a variety of wildlife as well as habitats: grassy meadows, woodland, scrub, wetlands, and some of Europe's most venerable oak forests. Be aware that, aside from the southern slope of Parliament Hill and Golders Hill Park, it is more like countryside than a park, with signs and facilities in short supply. Pick up a map at Kenwood House, or the **Education Centre** near the Lido off Gordon House Road, where you can also get details about the history of the Heath and the flora and fauna growing there. An excellent alfresco café near the Athletics Field serves Italian food.

Today the Heath is popular with walkers, dog walkers, and swimmers. It has inspired artists from John Constable, who painted views several times, to contemporary author Zadie Smith, to C.S. Lewis, whose *The Lion, The Witch and The Wardrobe* was supposedly inspired by a walk through the Heath's winter landscape. Coming onto the Heath from the South End Green entrance, walk east past a well-equipped children's adventure **Playground** and **Paddling Pool,** turn left, and head to the top of **Parliament Hill.** At 321 feet above sea level, it's one of the highest points in London. You'll find a stunning panorama over the city. On

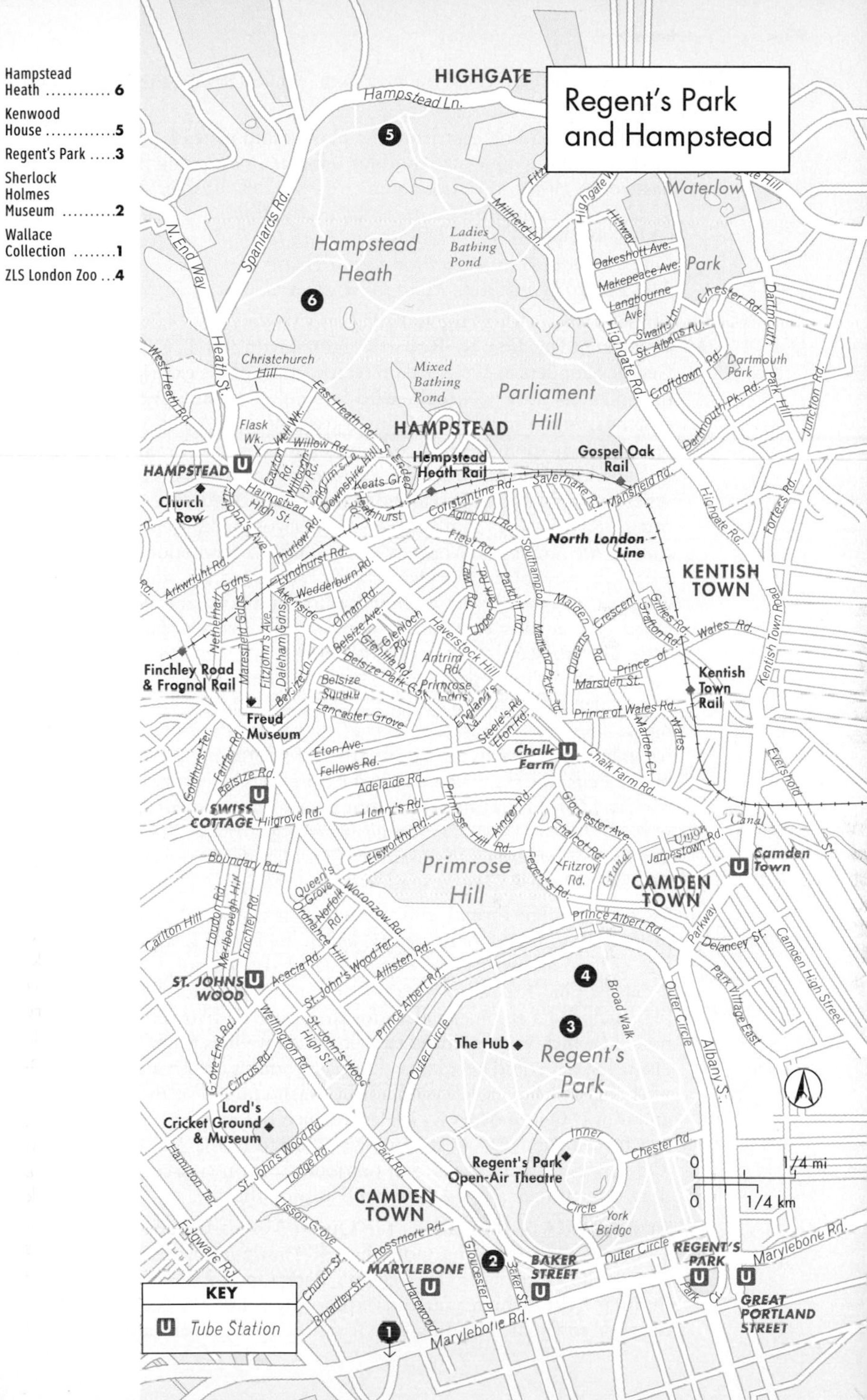

Regent's Park and Hampstead
Hampstead Heath 6
Kenwood House 5
Regent's Park 3
Sherlock Holmes Museum 2
Wallace Collection 1
ZLS London Zoo ...4
HIGHGATE
Hampstead Ln.
Hampstead Heath
Ladies Bathing Pond
Mixed Bathing Pond
Parliament Hill
Waterlow Park
HAMPSTEAD
Hempstead Heath Rail
Gospel Oak Rail
North London Line
KENTISH TOWN
Kentish Town Rail
Church Row
Finchley Road & Frognal Rail
Freud Museum
Chalk Farm
SWISS COTTAGE
Primrose Hill
CAMDEN TOWN
Camden Town
ST. JOHNS WOOD
The Hub
Regent's Park
Lord's Cricket Ground & Museum
Regent's Park Open-Air Theatre
CAMDEN TOWN
MARYLEBONE
BAKER STREET
REGENT'S PARK
GREAT PORTLAND STREET
Marylebone Rd.
KEY
Tube Station
0 1/4 mi
0 1/4 km

clear days you can see all the way to the South Downs, the hills beyond southern London.

If you keep heading east from the playground instead, you'll come to the **Lido,** an Olympic-size outdoor unheated swimming pool that gets packed on all-too-rare hot summer days. ✉ *Hampstead* ☎ *020/7332–3322 Heath Education Centre* 🌐 *www.cityoflondon.gov.uk/hampstead* 🎫 *Free* Ⓜ *Overground: Hampstead Heath for south of Heath or Gospel Oak for Lido; Hampstead for east of Heath; Golders Green, then Bus 210, 268 to Whitestone Pond for north and west of Heath.*

Fodor's Choice ★ **Kenwood House.** This largely Palladian villa was first built in 1616 and later extended, first by Robert Adam starting in 1767 and later by George Saunders in 1795. Adam refaced most of the exterior and added the splendid library, which, with its vaulted ceiling and Corinthian columns, is the highlight of the house's design. A major renovation restored four rooms to reflect Adam's intentions as closely as possible, incorporating the furniture he designed for them and his original color schemes. Kenwood is also home to the **Iveagh Bequest,** a superb collection of 63 paintings that includes masterworks like Rembrandt's *Portrait of the Artist* and Vermeer's *The Guitar Player,* along with major works by Reynolds, Van Dyck, Hals, Gainsborough, and Turner. The grounds, designed by Humphrey Repton and bordered by Hampstead Heath, are equally elegant and serene, with lawns sloping down to a little lake crossed by a trompe-l'oeil bridge. All in all, the perfect home for an 18th-century gentleman. In summer the grounds host a series of popular and classical concerts, culminating in fireworks on the last night. The Brew House café, occupying part of the old coach house, has outdoor tables in the courtyard and a terraced garden. The 2014 movie *Belle*, the story of Kenwood House's 18th-century resident Lord Mansfield and his family, was shot here. ✉ *Hampstead La., Highgate* ☎ *0870/333–1181* 🌐 *www.english-heritage.org.uk* 🎫 *Free* ⏲ *House daily 10–5; gardens daily 8–dusk* Ⓜ *Golders Green or Archway, then Bus 210. London Overground: Gospel Oak.*

FAMILY Fodor's Choice ★ **Regent's Park.** The formal, cultivated Regent's Park, more country house grounds than municipal amenity, began life in 1812, when John Nash was commissioned by the Prince Regent (later George IV) to create a master plan for the former royal hunting ground. Nash's original plan included a summer palace for the prince and 56 villas for friends, none of which were realized except for eight villas (only two survive). However, the grand neoclassical terraced houses on the south, east, and west edges of the park were built by Nash and reflect the scope of his ambitions. Queen Mary's Gardens, which has some 30,000 roses and is a favorite spot for weddings, was created in the 1930s. Today the 395-acre park, with the largest outdoor sports area in central London, draws the athletically inclined from around the city.

At the center of the park is the **Queen Mary's Gardens**, a fragrant 17-acre circle containing more than 400 varieties of roses. Just to the east of the Gardens is the **Regent's Park Open-Air Theatre** and the **Boating Lake,** which you can explore by renting a pedalo (paddleboat) or rowboat. Heading east from the rose gardens along Chester

Road past the **Broad Walk** will bring you to Nash's iconic white-stucco **Cumberland Terrace,** with its central Ionic columns surmounted by a triangular Wedgwood-blue pediment. At the north end of the Broad Walk you'll find the **London Zoo,** while to the northwest of the central circle is **The Hub** (☎ *0300/061–2323*), a state-of-the-art community sports center that has changing rooms, exercise classes, and a café with 360-degree views of the surrounding sports fields, used for soccer, rugby, cricket, field hockey, and softball contests. There are also tennis courts toward the park's southeast (Baker Street) entrance, and the park is a favorite north–south route for cyclists. ✉ *Chester Rd., Regent's Park* ☎ *0300/061–2300* 🌐 *www.royalparks.org.uk* 🎟 *Free* Ⓜ *Baker St., Regent's Park, Great Portland St.*

FAMILY Fodor's Choice ★ **Wallace Collection.** With its Great Gallery stunningly refurbished in 2014, there's even more reason to visit this exquisite gem of an art gallery—although housing one of the world's finest collections of old master paintings is reason enough. This glorious collection and the 18th-century mansion in which it's located were bequeathed to the nation by the widow of Sir Richard Wallace (1818–90). Wallace's father, the 4th Marquess of Hertford, took a house in Paris after the French Revolution and set about snapping up paintings by what were then dangerously unpopular artists, for a song. Frans Hals's *Laughing Cavalier* is probably the most famous painting here, or perhaps Jean-Honoré Fragonard's *The Swing*. The full list of painters in the collection reads like a who's-who of classical European art: from Rubens, Rembrandt, and Van Dyck to Canaletto, Titian, and Velázquez. English works include paintings by Gainsborough and Turner. There are also fine collections of furniture, porcelain, Renaissance gold, and majolica (15th- and 16th-century Italian tin-glazed pottery). The conditions of the bequest mean that no part of the collection can leave the building; this is the only place in the world you'll ever be able to see these works. ✉ *Hertford House, Manchester Sq., Marylebone* ☎ *020/7563–9500* 🌐 *www.wallacecollection.org* 🎟 *Free* ⏱ *Daily 10–5 (except Dec. 24–26)* Ⓜ *Bond St.*

FAMILY Fodor's Choice ★ **ZSL London Zoo.** Operated by the nonprofit Zoological Society of London, the zoo was begun with the royal animals collection, moved here from the Tower of London in 1828. The zoo itself did not open to the public until 1847. A recent modernization program has seen the introduction of several big attractions, with a focus on education, wildlife conservation, and the breeding of endangered species. The huge **B.U.G.S.** pavilion (Biodiversity Underpinning Global Survival) is a self-sustaining, contained ecosystem for 140 less cuddly species, including invertebrates such as spiders and millipedes, plus some reptiles and fish. At **Gorilla Kingdom,** a walk-through re-creation of the habitat of the Western Lowland Gorilla, you can watch the four residents at close range. **Rainforest Life** is an indoor tropical rain forest (complete with humidity) inhabited by the likes of armadillos, monkeys, and sloths. A special nighttime section offers glimpses of nocturnal creatures like slow lorises and bats. The **Animal Adventures** Children's Zoo allows kids to get up close to animals including mongooses and llamas, as well as feeding and grooming sheep and goats. Two of the most popular attractions are **Penguin Beach,** especially at feeding time (1:30) and

A TRIP TO ABBEY ROAD

The black-and-white crossroads (known as a "zebra crossing") near the Abbey Road Studios at No. 3 is a place of pilgrimage for Beatles' fans from around the world, many of them teenagers born long after the band split up. They converge here to re-create the cover of the Beatles' 1969 *Abbey Road* album, posing on the crossing despite the onrushing traffic. ■ **TIP→ Be careful if you're going to attempt this. Abbey Road is a dangerous intersection.** The studio is where the Beatles recorded their entire output, from "Love Me Do" onward. One of the best—and safer—ways to explore landmarks in the Beatles' story is to take one of the excellent walking tours offered by **Original London Walks** (*020/7624–3978* ⊕ *www.walks.com*). Try **The Beatles In-My-Life Walk** (11:20 am outside Marylebone Underground on Saturday and Tuesday) or **The Beatles Magical Mystery Tour** (Wednesday at 2 pm, February to November, and Thursday and Sunday at 11 am, year-round, at Underground Exit 3, Tottenham Court Road).

Meerkat Manor, where you can see the sociable animals keeping watch over their own sandy territory. If you're feeling flush, try to nab one of the six daily "Meet the Penguins" VIP tickets (2 pm) that offer a 20-minute guided close encounter with the locals (£45 weekdays, £60 weekends). There are similar VIP encounters with giraffes, lions, owls, meerkats, kangaroos, and aardvarks. Other zoo highlights include **Butterfly Paradise**; the **Blackburn Pavilion,** with its hundreds of tropical bird species; the **Big Cats** enclosure, home to a pride of Asian lions; and **Tiger Territory,** an enclosure for five beautiful endangered Sumatran tigers (including three cubs born at the zoo). For a more grown-up experience, check out Zoo Lates, where comedy, cabaret, and a wine bar are offered to over-18s (in addition to all the usual zoo attractions). These are held on Friday evenings (6–10 pm) in summer. Check the website or the information board out front for free events, including creature close encounters and "ask the keeper" sessions. ✉ *Outer Circle, Regent's Park* ☎ *0844/225–1826* ⊕ *www.zsl.org* 🎫 *£19–£22* ⏲ *Mid-Nov.–Feb., daily 10–4; Mar.–early Sept., daily 10–6; early-Sept.–Oct., daily 10–5:30; early–mid-Nov., daily 10–4:30; last admission 1 hr before closing* Ⓜ *Camden Town, then Bus 274.*

WORTH NOTING

Sherlock Holmes Museum. Outside Baker Street station, by the Marylebone Road exit, is a 9-foot-high bronze statue of Arthur Conan Doyle's celebrated detective, who "lived" around the corner at number 221B Baker Street—now a museum to all things Sherlock. Inside, Mrs. Hudson, Holmes's housekeeper, guides you into a series of Victorian rooms where the great man lived, worked, and played the violin. It's all carried off with such genuine enthusiasm and attention to detail that you could be forgiven for thinking that Mr. Holmes actually *did* exist. ✉ *221B Baker St., Regent's Park* ☎ *020/7224–3688* ⊕ *www.sherlock-holmes.co.uk* 🎫 *£10* ⏲ *Daily 9:30–6* Ⓜ *Baker St.*

UP AND DOWN THE THAMES

Downstream—meaning seaward, or east—from central London, Greenwich will require a day to explore, especially if you have any interest in maritime history or technology. Upstream to the west, are the royal palaces and grand houses that were built as country residences with easy access to London by river. Hampton Court Palace, with its famous maze, is the most notable.

GREENWICH

8 miles east of central London.

Greenwich makes an ideal day out from central London. Maritime Greenwich is a UNESCO World Heritage Site and includes Inigo Jones's Queens House, the first Palladian building in England; the Old Royal Observatory, home of the Greenwich Meridian that is the baseline for the world's time zones and the dividing line between the two hemispheres (you can stand astride it with one foot in either one); and the National Maritime Museum, which tells the story of how Britain came to rule the waves. Landlubbers, meanwhile, can explore the surrounding Royal Park, laid out in the 1660s and thus the oldest of the royal parks, or central Greenwich with its attractive 19th-century houses.

The monorail-like Docklands Light Railway (DLR) will take you to Cutty Sark station from Canary Wharf and Bank Tube stations in the City. Or take the DLR to Island Gardens and walk the old Victorian Foot Tunnel under the river. However, the most appropriate way to travel is—time and weather permitting—by water via River Bus.

Fodor's Choice ★ ***Cutty Sark.*** This sleek, romantic clipper was built in 1869, one among a vast fleet of tall-masted wooden ships that plied the oceanic highways of the 19th century, trading in exotic commodities—in this case, tea. *Cutty Sark* (named after a racy witch in a Robert Burns poem) was the fastest, sailing the London–China route in 1871 in only 107 days. The clipper has been preserved in dry docks as a museum ship since the 1950s, but was severely damaged in a devastating fire in 2007. But up from the ashes, as the song goes, grow the roses of success—after a major restoration project the visitor facilities are now better than ever. Not only can you tour the ship in its entirety, but the glittering visitor center (which the ship now rests directly above, in an enormous gold mount) allows you to view the hull from below. (And as luck would have it, roughly half the ship had been dismantled and taken away for cleaning at the time of the fire, so the full extent of the damage was much less than it might have been.) There's plenty to see here, and the cramped quarters form a fantastic time capsule to walk around in—this boat was never too comfortable for the 28-strong crew (as you'll see). And don't forget to take in the amusing collection of figureheads. ✉ *King William Walk, Greenwich* ☎ *020/8858–4422* 🌐 *www.rmg.co.uk* 🎫 *£13.50 (£18.50 with Royal Observatory attractions)* ⏲ *Daily 10–5; last admission 4* Ⓜ *DLR: Cutty Sark.*

Fodor's Choice ★ **National Maritime Museum.** From the time of Henry VIII until the 1940s Britain was the world's preeminent naval power, and the collections here trace half a millennia of that seafaring history. The story is as

Among the botanical splendors of Kew Gardens is the Waterlily House.

much about trade as it is warfare; the "Atlantic: Slavery, Trade and Empire" gallery explores how trade in goods—and people—irrevocably changed the world, while "Voyagers: Britons and the Sea" focuses on stories of the ordinary people who took to the waves over the centuries. One gallery is devoted to Admiral Lord Nelson, Britain's most famous naval commander, and among the exhibits is the uniform he was wearing, complete with bloodstains, when he died at the Battle of Trafalgar in 1805. Temporary exhibitions here are usually fascinating; those in recent years have included the Arctic convoys of World War II and how the race to measure longitude (east–west position) at sea opened the door to global exploration on an unprecedented scale. The museum has a good café with views over Greenwich Park. The adjacent **Queen's House** is home to the museum's art collection, the largest collection of maritime art in the world, including works by William Hogarth, Canaletto, and Joshua Reynolds. Permission for its construction was granted by Queen Anne only on condition that the river vista from the house be preserved, and there are few more majestic views in London than Inigo Jones's awe-inspiring symmetry. Completed around 1638, the Tulip Stair, named for the fleur-de-lis-style pattern on the balustrade, is especially fine, spiraling up without a central support to the Great Hall. The Great Hall itself is a perfect cube, exactly 40 feet in all three dimensions, decorated with paintings of the Muses and the Virtues. ✉ *Romney Rd., Greenwich* ☎ *020/8858–4422* 🌐 *www.rmg.co.uk/national-maritime-museum* 🎫 *Free* 🕘 *Daily 10–5; last admission 4:30* Ⓜ *DLR: Greenwich.*

QUICK BITES

Trafalgar Tavern. With its excellent vista of the Thames, there is no more handsomely situated pub in Greenwich than the Trafalgar Tavern. Featured in Charles Dickens's *Our Mutual Friend*, it's still as grand a place to have a pint and some (upscale) pub grub as it ever was. ✉ *Park Row, Greenwich* ☎ *020/8858–2909* 🌐 *www.trafalgartavern.co.uk.*

Fodor's Choice ★ **Old Royal Naval College.** Begun by Christopher Wren in 1694 as a rest home for ancient mariners, the college became a school in 1873. It's still used for classes by the University of Greenwich and the Trinity College of Music, although you're more likely to recognize it as a film location—recent blockbusters to have made use of its elegant interiors include *Skyfall*, *Les Misérables*, and *The King's Speech*. Architecturally, you'll notice how the structures part to reveal the **Queen's House** across the central lawns. Behind the college are two more buildings you can visit. The **Painted Hall**, the college's dining hall, which derives its name from the baroque murals of William and Mary (reigned jointly 1689–95; William alone 1695–1702) and assorted allegorical figures. James Thornhill's frescoes, depicting scenes of naval grandeur with a suitably pro-British note, were painstakingly completed 1708–12 and 1718–26, and were good enough to earn him a knighthood. In the opposite building stands the **College Chapel**, which was rebuilt after a fire in 1779 in an altogether more restrained, neo-Grecian style. Check the website for an outstanding program of special events, including talks, tours, and concerts—many of them free. ✉ *King William Walk, Greenwich* ☎ *020/8269–4747* 🌐 *www.ornc.org* 🎫 *Free, guided tours £6* ⏲ *Painted Hall and chapel daily 10–5 (Sun. chapel from 12:30); grounds 8–6* Ⓜ *DLR: Greenwich*.

FAMILY **Royal Observatory.** Greenwich is on the prime meridian at 0° longitude, and the ultimate standard for time around the world has been set here since 1884, when Britain was the world's maritime superpower.

The observatory is actually split into two sites, a short walk apart—one devoted to astronomy, the other to the study of time. The enchanting **Peter Harrison Planetarium** is London's only planetarium, its bronze-clad turret glinting in the sun. Shows on black holes and how to interpret the night sky are enthralling and enlightening. Even better for kids are the high-technology rooms of the **Astronomy Centre,** where space exploration is brought to life through cutting-edge interactive programs and fascinating exhibits—including the chance to touch a 4.5-billion-year-old meteorite.

Across the way is **Flamsteed House,** designed by Christopher Wren in 1675 for John Flamsteed, the first Royal Astronomer. A climb to the top of the house reveals a **28-inch telescope,** built in 1893 and now housed inside an onion-shape fiberglass dome. It doesn't compare with the range of modern optical telescopes, but it's still the largest in the United Kingdom. Regular viewing evenings reveal startlingly detailed views of the lunar surface. In the **Time Galleries,** linger over the superb workmanship of John Harrison (1693–1776), whose famous **Maritime Clocks** won him the Longitude Prize for solving the problem of accurate timekeeping at sea, which paved the way for modern navigation. ✉ *Romney Rd., Greenwich* ☎ *020/8858–4422* 🌐 *www.rmg.co.uk/royal-observatory* 🎫 *Astronomy Centre free; Flamsteed House and Meridian Line courtyard £8.50; planetarium shows £6.50; combined ticket £12.50; combined ticket with Cutty Sark £18.50* ⏲ *Daily 10–5 (May–Aug., Meridian courtyard until 6); last entry 30 min before closing; last planetarium show 4:15. Planetarium closed 1st Tues. of every month except Aug. and during Easter* ⏲ *Closed first Tues. of every month except Aug.* Ⓜ *DLR: Greenwich.*

HAMPTON COURT PALACE

20 miles southwest of central London.

FAMILY Fodor's Choice ★ **Hampton Court Palace.** The beloved seat of Henry VIII's court, sprawled elegantly beside the languid waters of the Thames, Hampton Court is steeped in more history than virtually any other royal building in England. The Tudor mansion, begun in 1514 by Cardinal Wolsey to curry favor with the young Henry, actually conceals a larger 17th-century baroque building, which was partly designed by Christopher Wren. The earliest dwellings on this site belonged to a religious order founded in the 11th century and were expanded over the years by its many subsequent residents, until George II moved the royal household closer to London in the early 18th century.

Wander through the **State Apartments**, decorated in the Tudor style, and on to the wood-beamed magnificence of **Henry's Great Hall**, before taking in the strikingly azure ceiling of the **Chapel Royal.** Well-handled reconstructions of Tudor life take place all year, from live appearances by "Henry VIII" to cook-historians preparing authentic Tudor feasts in the 15th-century **Henry's Kitchens**. Watch out for the ghost of Henry VIII's doomed fifth wife, Catherine Howard, who lost her head yet is said to scream her way along the **Haunted Gallery.** Latter-day masters of the palace, the joint rulers William and Mary (reigned 1689–1702), were responsible for the beautiful **King's and Queen's Apartments** and the elaborate baroque of the **Georgian Rooms.**

Don't miss the famous **maze** (the oldest hedge maze in the world), its half mile of pathways among clipped hedgerows still fiendish to negotiate. There's a trick, but we won't give it away here: It's much more fun just to go and lose yourself.

The **Lower Orangery Exotic Garden** shows off thousands of exotic species that William and Mary, avid plant collectors, gathered from around the globe. ✉ *Hampton Court Rd., East Molesley* ☎ *0844/482–7799 tickets, 0844/482–7777 information (24 hrs), 20/3166–6000 from outside U.K.* 🌐 *www.hrp.org.uk/hamptoncourtpalace* 🎫 *Palace, maze, and gardens £18.70; maze only £4.80; gardens only £6.40* ⏲ *Apr.–late Oct., daily 10–6; late Oct.–Mar., daily 10–4:30; last admission 1 hr before closing; last entry to maze 45 min before closing). Formal Gardens daily: 10–6 summer, 10–4:30 winter. Informal Gardens daily: 7–8 summer, 7–6 winter* Ⓜ *Richmond, then Bus R68. National Rail: Hampton Court Station, 35 min from Waterloo (most trains require change at Surbiton).*

KEW GARDENS

6 miles southwest of central London.

FAMILY Fodor's Choice ★ **Kew Gardens.** Enter the Royal Botanic Gardens, as Kew Gardens are officially known, and you are enveloped by blazes of color, extraordinary blooms, hidden trails, and lovely old follies. Beautiful though it all is, Kew's charms are secondary to its true purpose as a major center for serious research. Academics are hard at work on more than 300 scientific projects across as many acres, analyzing everything from the cacti of eastern Brazil to the yams of Madagascar. First opened to the public in 1840, Kew has been supported by royalty and nurtured by landscapers, botanists, and architects since the 1720s. Today the gardens, now a UNESCO World Heritage Site, hold more than 30,000 species of plants, from every corner of the globe. Although the plant houses make Kew worth visiting even in the depths of winter (there's also a seasonal garden), the flower beds are, of course, best enjoyed in the fullness of spring and summer.

Architect Sir William Chambers built a series of temples and follies, of which the crazy 10-story **Pagoda,** visible for miles around, is the star. The Princess of Wales conservatory houses 10 climate zones, and the Rhizotron and Xstrata Treetop Walkway takes you 59 feet up into the air. Two great 19th-century greenhouses—the **Palm House** and the **Temperate House**—are filled with exotic blooms, and many of the plants have been there since the final glass panel was fixed into place. Unfortunately the enormous Temperate House is closed for maintenance until 2018, so until then you won't be able to gawk at the largest greenhouse plant in the world, a Chilean wine palm planted in 1846 (and so big that you have to climb the spiral staircase to the roof to get a proper view of it). ✉ *Kew Rd. at Lichfield Rd., for Victoria Gate entrance, Kew* ☎ *020/8332–5655* 🌐 *www.kew.org* 🎟 *£15* 🕓 *Mid-Feb.–Mar., daily 9:30–5:30; Apr.–late Aug., weekdays 9:30–6:30, weekends and holiday Mon. 9:30–7:30; late Aug.–late Oct., daily 9:30–6; late Oct.–mid-Feb., daily 9:30–4:15. Last admission to park, greenhouses, galleries, and treetop walkway 30 min before closing* Ⓜ *Kew Gardens. National Rail: Kew Gardens, Kew Bridge.*

Fodor's Choice ★ **Kew Palace and Queen Charlotte's Cottage.** The elegant redbrick exterior of the smallest of Britain's royal palaces seems almost humble when compared with the grandeur of, say, Buckingham or Kensington palaces. Yet inside is a fascinating glimpse into life at the uppermost end of society from the 17th to 19th century. This is actually the third of several palaces that stood here; once known as Dutch House, it was one of the havens to which George III retired when insanity forced him to withdraw from public life. Queen Charlotte had an *orné*—a rustic-style cottage retreat—added in the late 18th century. In a marvelously regal flight of fancy, she kept kangaroos in the paddock outside. The main house and gardens are maintained in the 18th-century style. Entry to the palace itself is free, but it lies within the grounds of Kew Gardens, and you must buy a ticket to that to get here. ✉ *Kew Gardens, Kew Rd. at Lichfield Rd., Kew* ☎ *0844/482–7777 (only in U.K.), 020/3166–6000* 🌐 *www.hrp.org.uk* 🎟 *Free with entry to Kew Gardens* 🕓 *Palace*

Apr.–Sept., daily 10:30–5:30 (last admission 5); Queen Charlotte's Cottage late Mar.–Sept., weekends 10–4 Ⓜ *Kew Gardens.*

QUICK BITES

The Original Maids of Honour. This most traditional of Old English tearooms is named for a type of jam tart invented here and still baked by hand on the premises. Legend has it that Henry VIII loved them so much he had the recipe kept under armed guard. Full afternoon tea is served daily 2:30–6, and lunch in two sittings at 12:30 and 1:45. Or opt to take out food for a picnic at Kew Gardens or on Kew Green. (While you do, keep an eye out for their 1930s-era delivery van, which still makes the rounds daily.) ✉ *288 Kew Rd., Kew* ☎ *020/8940–2752* 🌐 *www.theoriginalmaidsofhonour.co.uk* ⏲ *Daily 8:30–6.*

WHERE TO EAT

Use the coordinate (✣ B2) at the end of each listing to locate a site on the corresponding map.

For many years English food was a joke, especially to England's near neighbors, the French. But the days of steamed suet puddings and overboiled brussels sprouts are long gone. For a good two decades London's restaurant scene has been booming, with world-class chefs—Jamie Oliver, Gordon Ramsay, Heston Blumenthal, and Jason Atherton among them—pioneering concepts that quickly spread overseas. Whether you're looking for bistros that rival their Parisian counterparts, five-star fine dining establishments, fantastic fried-chicken and burger joints (American diner food is a current trend), gastro-pubs serving "Modern British," or places serving Peruvian–Japanese fusion, gourmet Indian, or nouveau greasy spoon, you'll be spoiled for choice. And that's just as well because you'll be spending, on average, 25% of your travel budget on dining out.

The British now take pride in the best of authentic homegrown food—local, seasonal, regional, and foraged are the buzzwords of the day. But beyond reinterpretations of native dishes, London's dining revolution is built on its incredible ethnic diversity, with virtually every international cuisine represented.

PRICES AND SAVING MONEY

In pricey London a modest meal for two can easily cost £40, and the £110-a-head meal is not unknown. Damage-control strategies include making lunch your main meal—the top places have bargain midday menus—going for early- or late-evening deals, or sharing an à la carte entrée and ordering an extra appetizer. Seek out fixed-price menus, and watch for hidden extras on the menu—that is, bread or vegetables charged separately.

TIPPING AND TAXES

Do not tip bar staff in pubs and bars—though you can always offer to buy them a drink. In restaurants, tip 12.5% of the check for full meals if service is not already included; tip a small token if you're just having coffee or tea. If paying by credit card, double-check that a tip (aka "service charge") has not already been included in the bill. If you leave cash it's more likely to go to the server rather than into a pool.

	WHAT IT COSTS IN POUNDS			
	$	$$	$$$	$$$$
At Dinner	under £16	£17–£23	£24–£32	over £32

Prices are the average cost of a main course at dinner or, if dinner is not served, at lunch.

2

WESTMINSTER, ST. JAMES'S, AND ROYAL LONDON

ST. JAMES'S

$$$ MODERN EUROPEAN FAMILY

Le Caprice. Celebville grande dame Le Caprice commands the deepest loyalty of any restaurant in London. Why? Because it gets practically everything right—*every* time. It's the 35-odd-year celebrity history—think Liz Taylor, Joan Collins, and Lady Di—the sparkling monochrome decor, the giddy David Bailey '60s black-and-white pics, charming Bolivian-born Jesus Adorno as the veteran maître'd, the pitch-perfect service, and the long-standing menu that sits somewhere between Euro peasant and trendy fashion plate. Sit at the raised counter or at a coveted corner table and enjoy calves' liver with crispy pancetta, roast pheasant with caramelized quince, yellowfin tuna with borlotti beans, and signature Scandinavian iced berries with a swirl of hot white chocolate sauce. Note the weekend live jazz sessions. *Average main: £24 Arlington House, Arlington St., St. James's 020/7629–2239 www.le-caprice.co.uk Reservations essential Green Park D4.*

$$$$ BRITISH

Wiltons. Aristos, Euro princes, and captains of industry blow the family bank at this old-fashioned bastion of English fine dining on Jermyn Street (the place first opened on the Haymarket as a shellfish stall in 1742). Invariably fresh from a little snooze in their nearby St. James's gentlemen's clubs, male diners are requested to wear long-sleeved shirts and no sportswear or open-toed shoes at this linen-covered clubby time capsule and *frightfully* snooty ode to all things English. Armigerous signet ring–wearing posh patrons like to take half a dozen Beau Brummell oysters, followed by grilled Dover sole on the bone or fabulous native game in season, such as roast grouse, partridge, or teal. There are antediluvian savories like soft herring roe on toast, plus desserts like sherry trifle or bread-and-butter pudding. The use of mobile phones is prohibited, the wine's weighed heavily toward Bordeaux claret, and service, naturally, would put Jeeves to shame. *Average main: £34 55 Jermyn St., St. James's 020/7629–9955 www.wiltons.co.uk Closed Sun. No lunch Sat. Reservations essential Jacket required Green Park D3.*

$$ AUSTRIAN FAMILY

The Wolseley. A glitzy procession of stars come for the spectacle, swish service, and soaring elegance at this bustling Viennese-style grand café on Piccadilly. Framed with 1920s black lacquerware in a former Wolseley luxury car showroom, this all-day brasserie begins its long decadent days with breakfasts at 7 am and serves highly adorable Dual Monarchy delights until midnight. Don't be shy to turn up on spec (they welcome

Where to Eat in London
A
B
C
D
1
2
3
4
5
6
Regent's Park
Inner Circle
Chester Rd.
Outer Circle
Albany St.
EUSTON STATION
Prince Albert Rd.
Park Rd.
Edgware Rd.
St. John's Wood Rd.
Lisson Grove
Rossmore Rd.
Balcombe St.
Broadley St.
Dorset Square
MARYLEBONE STATION
Bloomfield Rd.
Harrow Rd.
Marylebone Flyover
Marylebone Rd.
Euston Rd.
Tottenham Court Rd.
Gt. Portland St.
Portland Pl.
Cleveland St.
Whitfield St.
Weymouth St.
Wimpole St.
Gloucester Pl.
Baker St.
Chiltern St.
Seymour Pl.
Riding House Café
Dabbous
Berners Tavern
Goodge St.
Berners St.
New Cavendish St.
Chiltern Firehouse
Golden Hind
Mortimer St.
The Ledbury
PADDINGTON STATION
Praed St.
Sussex Gdns.
Bishop's Bridge Rd.
Queensway
Zoilo
Manchester Square
Marylebone High St.
Wigmore St.
Cavendish Square
Oxford Circus
Social Eating House
Wardour St.
Hereford Road
BAYSWATER
Duke St.
Bond St.
La Petite Maison
Pollen Street Social
Goodman
Poland St.
Craven Hill
Oxford St.
Grosvenor Square
Brook St.
Grosvenor St.
Conduit St.
Regent St.
Flat Iron
Andrew Edmunds
Bayswater Rd.
N. Carriage Dr.
Le Gavroche
Hélène Darroze at the Connaught
SOHO
Cecconi's
34
Scott's
Berkeley Square
CUT at 45 Park Lane
Gymkhana
Wiltons
Kensington Gardens
Hyde Park
Park Lane
Sth. Audley St.
MAYFAIR
Kitty Fisher's
Jermyn St.
The Wolseley
King St.
Curzon St.
Ritz Restaurant
Le Caprice
Pall Mall
Dr.
The Serpentine
Piccadilly
KENSINGTON PALACE
W. Carriage
Green Park
The Mall
Dinner by Heston Blumenthal
S. Carriage Rd.
Knightsbridge
Constitution Hill
Kensington Rd.
Kensington Gore
Bar Boulud
Grosvenor Cres.
Halkin St.
Grosvenor Pl.
BUCKINGHAM PALACE
Birdcage
Yashin
Mari Vanna
Ametza with Arzak Instruction
Buckingham Gate
Prince Consort Rd.
KNIGHTSBRIDGE
Belgrave Square
Upper Belgrave St.
Palace St.
Palace Gate
Belgrave Pl.
Hobart Pl.
Victoria St.
KENSINGTON
Exhibition Rd.
V&A MUSEUM
Brompton Rd.
Beauchamp Pl.
Pont St.
Cadogan Pl.
Eaton Square
Ebury St.
Buckingham Palace Rd.
VICTORIA STATION
Rochester Row
Gloucester Rd.
Queen's Gate
Sloane St.
Wilton Rd.
Cromwell Rd.
Vauxhall Br. Rd.
Vincent Square
Pelham St.
Draycott Ave.
Sloane Ave.
Sloane Sq.
Eccleston St.
Old Brompton Rd.
Fulham Rd.
Warwick Way
Belgrave Rd.
Pimlico Rd.
CHELSEA
Royal Hospital Rd.
Chelsea Br. Rd.
PIMLICO
SOUTH KENSINGTON
Sydney St.
Old Church St.
King's Rd.
Lupus St.
The Harwood
Redcliffe Gdns
Finborough Rd.
Fulham Rd.
Chelsea Embankment
Grosvenor Rd.
Chelsea Br.
Beaufort St.
Cheyne Walk
Thames
Battersea Park
Oakley St.
Nine Elms

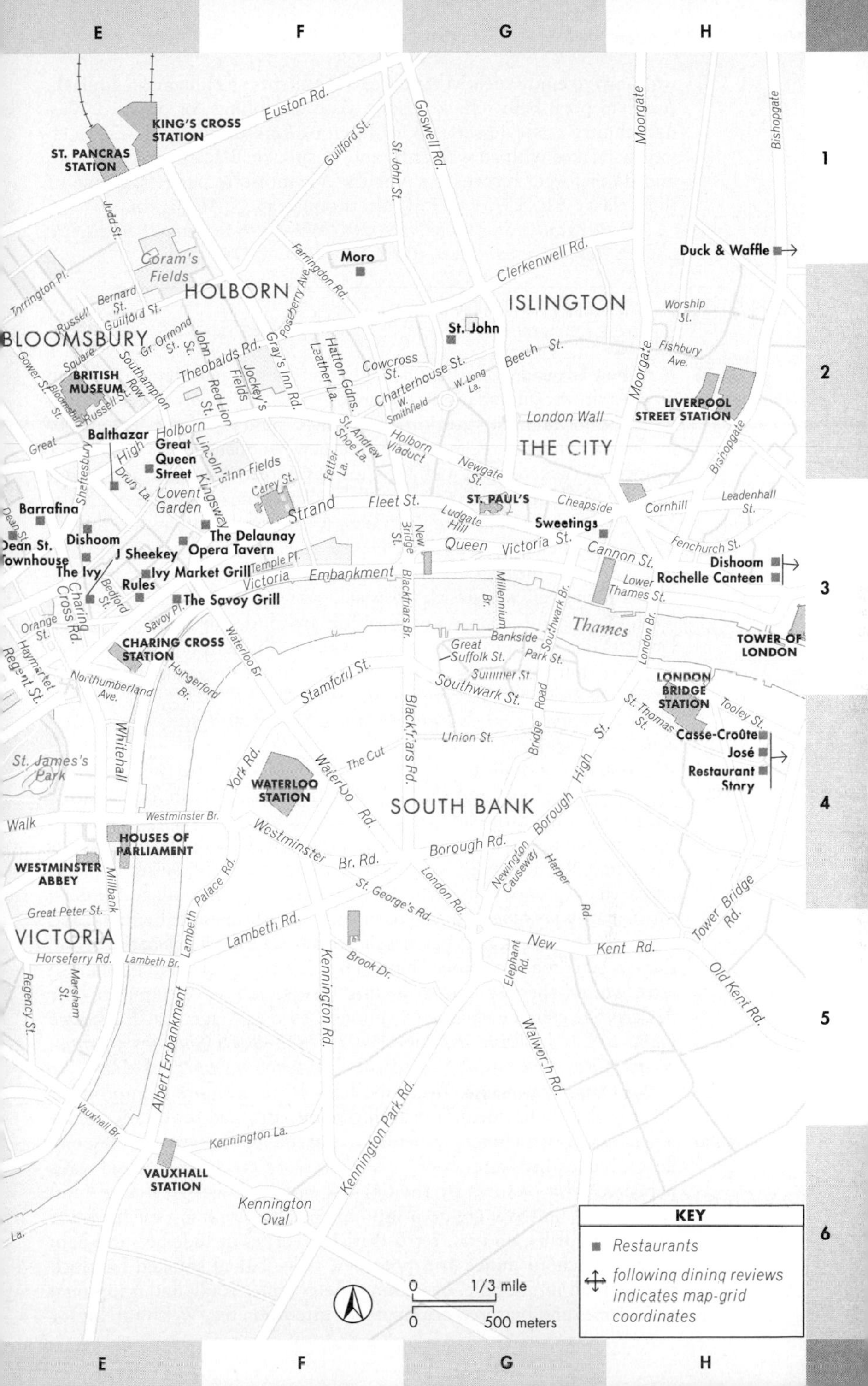
E
F
G
H
1
2
3
4
5
6
KING'S CROSS STATION
ST. PANCRAS STATION
Euston Rd.
Moro
St. John
Duck & Waffle
HOLBORN
ISLINGTON
BLOOMSBURY
BRITISH MUSEUM
LIVERPOOL STREET STATION
Balthazar
Great Queen Street
THE CITY
Barrafina
Dishoom
Dean St. Townhouse
J Sheekey
The Delaunay
Opera Tavern
The Ivy
Ivy Market Grill
Rules
The Savoy Grill
ST. PAUL'S
Sweetings
Dishoom
Rochelle Canteen
Thames
TOWER OF LONDON
CHARING CROSS STATION
LONDON BRIDGE STATION
Casse-Croûte
José
Restaurant Story
WATERLOO STATION
SOUTH BANK
HOUSES OF PARLIAMENT
WESTMINSTER ABBEY
VICTORIA
VAUXHALL STATION
Kennington Oval
KEY
Restaurants
following dining reviews indicates map-grid coordinates
0 1/3 mile
0 500 meters

walk-ins) to enjoy such Mitteleuropa highlights as Hungarian goulash, Austrian pork belly, chicken soup with dumplings, or breaded Wiener schnitzel . For dessert, go for luscious *Kaiserschmarren*—caramelized pancakes with stewed fruit and raisins, or Black Forest gâteaux, and don't forget return to savor the Viennoiserie pastries at one of their classy £10.75 to £33.50 afternoon teas. *Average main: £18 ⊠ 160 Piccadilly, St. James's ☎ 020/7499–6996 www.thewolseley.com Reservations essential Ⓜ Green Park ✢ D4.*

SOHO AND COVENT GARDEN

SOHO

$$ MEDITERRANEAN **Andrew Edmunds.** Candlelit at night and with a haunting Dickensian vibe, Andrew Edmunds is a permanently packed, deeply romantic old-world Soho dining institution—though it could be larger, less creaky underfoot, and the reclaimed church-pew wooden bench seats more forgiving. Tucked away behind Carnaby Street in a dark and atmospheric 18th-century Soho town house, it's a cozy favorite with the boho-chic Soho media elite that come for the foolscap hand-scribbled, fixed-price lunch menus and the historic vibe. Keenly priced starters and mains draw on the tastes of Ireland, the Med, and Middle East. Harissa-spiced mackerel, woodcock on toast, seafood paella, and Herdwick lamb shanks with champ and broccoli are all deeply hale and hearty. Desserts like warm treacle tart or bread-and-butter pudding offer few surprises, but the wine's superb and the markups reasonable. *Average main: £17 ⊠ 46 Lexington St., Soho ☎ 020/7437–5708 www.andrewedmunds.com Reservations essential Ⓜ Oxford Circus, Piccadilly Circus ✢ D3.*

$ TAPAS **Barrafina.** London's top Spanish tapas bar is modeled on Cal Pep in old-town Barcelona, and similarly has only a few—23 in total—raised bar stools at the three-sided counter. It's no-reservations—so expect to stand in queue—but the tapas is well worth the wait. Their motto is "Sourcing Not Saucing," so get ready to nosh on brilliant small plates prepared in front of you: garlic prawns, ham *croquetas,* salt cod fritters, rare Galician *percebes* ("goose barnacles") crustaceans, baby squid, and octopus with capers, plus classics like Spanish *torilla*, spicy chorizo, and thin-sliced cured Montanera ham. There's a crack selection of Spanish reds, whites, sherries, and sparkling Cavas, and leave room for cute desserts like *crèma Catalana* or almond-based Santiago tart. *Average main: £13 ⊠ 54 Frith St., Soho ☎ 020/7813–8016 www.barrafina.co.uk Reservations not accepted Ⓜ Tottenham Court Rd. ✢ E3.*

$$ BRITISH FAMILY **Dean Street Townhouse.** Everyone feels 10 times more glamorous at this candlelit Soho media mustering point, attached to the *swellegant* 39-room Georgian hotel of the same name. Simpatico lighting, dark oak floors, red leather banquettes, raised bar seats, crack service, and walls peppered with pictures by the likes of Brit-pack artists Tracey Emin and Mat Collinshaw create a hip hangout for London's media *haute monde*. No frills, no fuss, retro-British favorites include pea-and-ham soup, old-school mince and potatoes, twice-baked smoked haddock soufflé, toad-in-the-hole, or yummy sherry trifle. You'll find traditional fruit scones and buttered crumpets for afternoon tea, Welsh rarebit for

high tea, and a smattering of vaguely familiar-looking celebs Tweeting around on their iPhones. *Average main: £20* ✉ *69–71 Dean St., Soho* ☎ *020/7434–1775* *www.deanstreettownhouse.com* *Reservations essential* Ⓜ *Oxford Circus, Tottenham Court Rd.* ⊕ *D3.*

$ STEAKHOUSE FAMILY

Flat Iron. Premium steaks priced at £10 are the only mains on the printed menu at this bustling hipster canteen on Beak Street in Soho. The char grilled "flat iron" shoulder cuts of beef arrive already sliced on wooden blocks with watercress and mini–meat cleavers. This three-story, no-reservations steak den and craft-beer basement bar is decked out in exposed brick walls, enamel lights, and bump-'n'-grind shared wooden tables. Sides include beef-dripping chips, creamed spinach, and roast eggplant with Parmesan, while sauces range from béarnaise to French horseradish cream. Shared seating is first-come, first-served, and at peak times you'll need to leave a number and hang downstairs sipping a heritage cocktail or rare small-batch beer while you wait. Check Twitter for daily specials like 12-hour braised Highland heifer steaks, a bone-in rib eye from Thirsk, or a Brazilian-style "Picanha" steak from mini grass fed Dexter cows. *Average main: £10* ✉ *17 Beak St., Soho* *flatironsteak.co.uk* *Reservations not accepted* *No phone* Ⓜ *Oxford Circus, Piccadilly Circus* ⊕ *D3.*

$$ FRENCH Fodor's Choice ★

Social Eating House. Decidedly upmarket "boil-in-the-bag" aromatic wild mushrooms on toast, which are snipped open and served steaming at the table, are just one of many excellent dishes found at this lighthearted but technically brilliant neo-French "bistronomy" Soho hangout. Chef/patron Paul Hood casts aside uptight haute cuisine, and makes merry with witty, pretty, and winning dishes like smoked duck's "ham" (made with smoked and cured duck's breast), and Scotch egg and chips, and pulls everyone's leg with his no-bread CLT, consisting of white crabmeat, lettuce (castelfranco radiccio leaf), and roast heritage tomato. A buzzed-up Soho foodie crowd enjoy jars of shrimps and grits and perfect mains of Kentish salt-marsh lamb with mint yogurt in a rollicking, moodily lit bare-brick salon, tricked out with dark parquet floors, antique mirrored ceilings, and red-leather banquettes. Class-act hipster staff sport beards, braces, and Brylcreemed 'tashes, the first-floor copper-ceilinged speakeasy, the Blind Pig, is *most*bodacious, and the Monday-to-Saturday £19 two-course set lunch is seriously worth investigating. *Average main: £18* ✉ *58 Poland St., Soho* ☎ *0207/993–3251* *www.socialeatinghouse.com* *Closed Sun.* *Reservations essential* Ⓜ *Oxford Circus, Tottenham Court Rd.* ⊕ *D3.*

COVENT GARDEN

$$$ BRASSERIE

Balthazar. Brit restauranteur Keith McNally re-creates his famed New York all-day faux Parisian brasserie at a winning spot right off the piazza in Covent Garden. The decor of brass-studded red leather banquettes, distressed vintage mirrors, illuminated columns, pewter bar tops, a seafood bar, and intricate mosaic floors creates a sparkly, soft patina, and enchanting backdrop in which to enjoy a classic all-day French brasserie menu of few surprises. Breakfast, brunch, lunch, afternoon tea, dinner, and pre- and post-theater meals are all well catered for at this bustling and notably well-serviced 175-seat venue. Pick out flavor-packed dishes like macaroni and Gruyère cheese, duck shepherd's pie, or ox cheek bourguignonne , and kick back and linger over the diverting all-French wine list, which carries everything from a modest Chablis Colombier 2012 (£11.50 per glass) to a grand Margaux Château Palmer '71 from Bordeaux, at £540 a pop. *Average main: £24 4–7 Russell St., Covent Garden 020/3301–1155 www.balthazarlondon.com Reservations essential Covent Garden, Charing Cross E3.*

$$$ AUSTRIAN FAMILY Fodor's Choice ★

The Delaunay. It's all fin de siècle Vienna and *The Radetsky March*at this magnificent art deco–style take on an all-day Viennese grand café and coffeehouse on the Aldwych. Dine like Emperor Franz Joseph I on a majestic 60-item menu that would do the dual-monarchy and Austro-Hungarian Empire proud. Dishes are von Trapp fabulous—think Wiener schnitzels , Hungarian goulash, and *würstchen* frankfurters and hot dogs, served with sauerkraut and onions. There are other goodies like borscht and beef Stroganoff, kedgeree, and sour lamb shank *sauerbraten*. Desserts delight, too, including *apfelstrudel* and an evocative three-peaked Salzburg soufflé, while the innocuous "Kinder" ice cream coupe is a blowout knickerbocker bursting with meringue, marshmallows, and whipped cream. Classy Viennese breakfast, brunch, Viennoiserie *konditorei*pastries, and afternoon teas are also served, and be sure to discover the hidden café within the café to reminisce about times past. *Average main: £24 55 Aldwych, Holborn 020/7499–8558 www.thedelaunay.com Reservations essential Covent Garden, Holborn F3.*

$ MODERN INDIAN FAMILY Fodor's Choice ★

Dishoom. Whirring ceiling fans, Indian film posters, checkerboard tiles, oak panels, and vintage Indian cola bottles create an evocative Bombay backdrop for this inexpensive all-day Indian café off Covent Garden. Modeled after the Persian-run Irani cafés of Victorian Bombay, try the *naan* bread with keema minced lamb and peas, or classic chili jam spiked and handkerchief-thin spicy charred chicken tikka *roomali* roti rolls (£6.90). A succulent lamb *raan* bun comes on a wooden block with slow-cooked pulled lamb in a sourdough bun with pomegranate slaw, *sali* chips, and fried green chilies, while gorgeous creamy black dahl is simmered in spices for 24 hours. Drinks and tipples range from a Bollybellini to Limca lemonade or a mango-and-fennel-rich lassi. *Average main: £8 12 Upper St. Martin's La., Covent Garden 020/7420–9320 www.dishoom.com Reservations essential Leicester Sq. E3.*

$$ MODERN BRITISH

Great Queen Street. Expect a boisterous best-of-British foodie crowd at one of Covent Garden's leading gastro-pubs, and proud doyenne of hearty retro-British dishes. Not far from the Royal Opera House, the ground-floor open kitchen eatery is done up with simple cardamom-color walls and bare-oak floors and tables. Unadulterated wine-fueled diners dive into nostalgic offerings like pressed tongue, pickled herrings, pigs' cheeks, and cockles or smoked mackerel with rhubarb. You'll find stacks of other unpretentious vintage British fare, like brown crab on toast, brawn, rabbit livers, or Swaledale beef mince pie, plus hunking great roasts for the table—think seven-hour shoulder of lamb with dauphinoise potatoes. Salads and veggies follow the same theme, from sweet heritage carrots to forgotten Roseval potatoes. *Average main:*

£16 ✉ 32 Great Queen St., Covent Garden ☎ 020/7242–0622 ⊙ No dinner Sun. ✍ Reservations essential Ⓜ Covent Garden, Holborn ✥ E3.

$$$ BRITISH FAMILY ✕ **The Ivy.** The triple-A-list spurns The Ivy for its upstairs private members' club (and other luxe spots like Scott's, 34, and Chiltern Firehouse) but, nonetheless, this venerable luvvies landmark still receives a thousand calls a day! A mesmerizing mix of daytime TV stars, gawkers, day-trippers, and out-of-towners dine on salt-beef hash, squash risotto, Thai-baked sea bass, salmon fish cakes, eggs Benedict, and good ol' English classics like shepherd's pie or kedgeree (curried rice with smoked haddock, boiled egg, and parsley) in a handsome mullioned stained-glass and oak-paneled dining salon. Desserts are standards like Baked Alaska or sticky toffee pudding, service is unfailingly professional, and for low- to mid-range West End star-spotting this is still a happy hunting ground. If you can't snag a table by phone or online, try walking in on spec—it's been known to work. *$ Average main: £25 ✉ 1–5 West St., Covent Garden ☎ 020/7836–4751 🌐 www.the-ivy.co.uk ✍ Reservations essential Ⓜ Covent Garden ✥ E3.*

$$$ BRITISH Fodor's Choice ★ ✕ **Ivy Market Grill.** Scrub up like Eliza Doolittle and perch at the pewter bar sipping a dreamy My Fair Lady (with Ivy-made gin, Belle de Brillet, and orange blossom) at this Covent Garden piazza all-dayer and laid-back lil' sister to the famed Ivy restaurant. Radiant mottled-green leather banquettes, minibooths, dark timber tables, and hexagonal floor mosaics are stunningly set off by late-19-century antique brass lamps and chandeliers, distressed painted walls, and a glazed tiled dado panel in shades of orange, green, and teal. If a mini "Three Martini Lunch" ain't your thing, there's bargains galore on the lengthy, comfort-laden all-day menu—from five-spice warm crispy duck salad or poached lobster cocktail with Marie Rose sauce to brioche-crumbed chicken Milanese and classic shepherd's pie. Monogrammed cutlery and shiny copper serving pans proliferate, and be sure to try the chocolate bombe—a spherical chocolatey mush of milk foam, vanilla ice cream, and sticky hot salted caramel sauce. *$ Average main: £25 ✉ 1 Henrietta St., Covent Garden ☎ 207/307–5903 🌐 www.theivymarketgrill.com Ⓜ Covent Garden ✥ E3.*

$$$ SEAFOOD ✕ **J Sheekey.** The A-list sneaks into this classy 1896 side-alley seafood haven, a discreet alternative to the more overtly celeb-central Scott's, 34, or Chiltern Firehouse. Umbilically linked with the surrounding Theatreland district, J Sheekey is one of Londoners' all-time favorite West End haunts. Beautifully orchestrated by longtime maître'd John Andrews, Sheekey charms with warm wood paneling, vintage showbiz black and white portraits, a warren of alcoves, and twinkly lava-rock bar tops. Opt for snappingly fresh Atlantic prawns, pickled Arctic herrings, scallop, shrimp, and salmon burgers, or famous Sheekey fish pie. Better still, sip Gaston Chiquet Champagne and slide down half a dozen Jersey rock oysters at the old mirrored oyster bar for the ultimate in true romance. Alternatively, enjoy the £26.50 weekend three-course set-lunch deals. *$ Average main: £26 ✉ 28–35 St. Martin's Ct., Covent Garden ☎ 020/7240–2565 🌐 www.j-sheekey.co.uk ✍ Reservations essential Ⓜ Leicester Sq. ✥ E3.*

$$$ BRITISH Fodor's Choice ★ **Rules.** Come, escape the 21st century. Opened in 1798, London's oldest restaurant is, according to some, still London's most beautiful. The main dining salons are, indeed, an old-world wonderland, what Maxim's is to Paris. The decor begins with plush red banquettes, lacquered yellow walls, and spectacular etched-glass skylights. Then, in High Victorian fashion, every cranny is covered with vintage needlepoint, Regency oil paintings, figurines, antlers, antique clocks, stuffed pheasants, and endless framed prints and etchings. Little wonder Rules has been a stage across which everyone from Charles Dickens to Sir Laurence Olivier has pranced. Be sure to ask for a table in one of the "glass house" skylight rooms, the bar area, or the Margaret Thatcher corner, then dig into the menu's historic British puddings and pies, like jugged hare, steak-and-kidney pie, or roast beef and Yorkshire pudding. For a taste of the 18th century, you can choose game specials from the restaurant's High Pennines Lartington estate, including roast grouse, partridge, woodcock, snipe, and ptarmigan. *Average main: £29* *35 Maiden La., Covent Garden* *020/7836–5314* *www.rules.co.uk* *Reservations essential* *Jacket required* *Covent Garden* *E3.*

$$$ BRITISH FAMILY **The Savoy Grill.** You can *feel* the history in the room at this glamorous 1889 art deco hotel-dining powerhouse, which has hosted everyone from Oscar Wilde and Frank Sinatra to Liz Taylor and Marilyn Monroe. Nowadays—buffed up with Swarovski chandeliers, velvet coverings, gold leaf–backed tortoiseshell walls, and vintage mirror and black-and-white pics—it caters to bulky business barons, top-end tourists, and nostalgia freaks who come for the Grill's famed table-side trolley, which might trundle up laden with hulking great roasts like beef Wellington, rack of pork, or saddle of lamb. Savoy legends like omelet Arnold Bennett (with smoked haddock, Parmesan, and cream) or baked egg cocotte with smoked bacon, wild mushrooms, and red wine sauce are to the fore, plus there's timeless standbys like T-bone and Chateaubriand steaks, alongside Carlingford oysters and lobster thermidor. For dessert, you can't top the Baked Alaska. *Average main: £32* *The Savoy, 100 The Strand, Covent Garden* *020/7592–1600 for reservations only* *www.gordonramsay.com/thesavoygrill* *Reservations essential* *Smart casual* *Charing Cross, Covent Garden* *E3.*

BLOOMSBURY AND HOLBORN

BLOOMSBURY

$$ MODERN BRITISH FAMILY Fodor's Choice ★ **Berners Tavern.** All the cool cats swing by this *wowy!*grand brasserie at Ian Schrager's trendy London Edition hotel. It's hard not to feel like a million *dollah* as you enter the 18-foot triple-height all-day dining salon, crammed with 1835 ornate stucco plasterwork, Grand Central Station–style bronze chandeliers, church candles, and 150-odd stately home-style paintings. Bag a half-moon chestnut mohair-and-leather banquette and start the day with an impeccable £14 full English breakfast (with herb sausage and Stornaway black pudding) and return for a light lunch of crispy rock shrimp roll or ironbark pumpkin risotto. Reemerge refreshed for dinner, and swoon over a deep-fried duck egg, Cumbrian-ham-and-pea-puree appetizer, and then it's a toss-up between Creedy

caver duck, Cornish cod, or Buccleuch Estate bavette. You'll find stunning dishes to share—like *sous vide* Romney Marsh lamb or whole Irish ox, tongue, and cheek—and battered cod, chips, and mushy peas on Fish Fridays. 💲 *Average main: £17* ✉ *The London Edition, 10 Berners St., Fitzrovia* ☎ *020/7908–7979* 🌐 *www.bernerstavern.com* ✍ *Reservations essential* Ⓜ *Oxford Circus, Tottenham Court Rd.* ✣ *D2.*

$ BURGER FAMILY

✕ The Riding House Café. Hirsute and hipster-chic London diners flock to this NYC-style small-plates and luxe-burgers all-day brasserie behind Oxford Circus in NOHO (North of Soho). Everything's appropriately salvaged, reclaimed, or bespoke here so you'll find stuffed squirrels, birds, and other taxidermy dotted around, reclaimed blue leather theater seats at the long bar, bright orange leather banquettes, or old snooker table legs holding up your dining table. Opt for bargain £6.50 small plates of spicy crayfish tails with lemongrass or superfood salads, and then head for poached egg chorizo hash browns, salt marsh lamb broth, 28-day hormone-free cheeseburger with chips—a steal at £12.50—or their famed lobster lasagna (£25). Service is private-members' club friendly, and you'll find neat all-day breakfasts, plus milk shakes, cocktails, and sundaes. 💲 *Average main: £14* ✉ *43–51 Great Titchfield St., Noho* ☎ *020/7927–0840* 🌐 *www.ridinghousecafe.co.uk* ✍ *Reservations essential* Ⓜ *Oxford Circus* ✣ *D2.*

FITZROVIA

$$ MODERN EUROPEAN Fodor's Choice ★

✕ Dabbous. It's a triumph of taste over technology at wunderkind Ollie Dabbous's extraordinary game changer off Charlotte Street in Fitzrovia. Startlingly minimalist, pure, inventive, and seasonally based new wave dishes elicit *Oohs! Aahhs!* and *Oh-my-Goshes!* in a flummery-free hard-edged NYC–industrial–chic setting of exposed concrete, overhead ducting, and heavy metal screens and cages. Phenomenal flavors abound. Ingredient-led dishes like a peas-and-mint appetizer ping your taste buds with frozen mint tea, edible violets, and broad bean flowers, and a famed coddled hen's egg with smoked butter and woodland mushrooms sits handsomely in a rustic-chic bowl of hay. Palette-popping barbecued Ibèrico pork with acorn praline, halibut with coastal herbs (sea aster and oyster leaf), and brittle chocolate ganache with green basil moss are instant classics, and set Dabbous apart as one of London's most dazzling talents. Book far in advance. 💲 *Average main: £23* ✉ *39 Whitfield St., Fitzrovia* ☎ *020/7323–1544* 🌐 *www.dabbous.co.uk* ⏲ *Closed Sun. and Mon.* ✍ *Reservations essential* Ⓜ *Goodge St.* ✣ *D2.*

THE CITY AND ENVIRONS

THE CITY

$ MODERN BRITISH FAMILY Fodor's Choice ★

✕ Duck & Waffle. Zoom up to the 40th floor of the Heron Tower near Liverpool Street, and head straight for the cult signature dish of crispy confit duck leg, fried duck egg, Belgium waffle, and grain mustard maple syrup for a taste of awesomeness from supernova young Brit chef Dan Doherty. Eclectic flourishes abound amid spectacular panoramas that take in the Tower of London, Tower Bridge, the Thames, and the Gherkin. A wax-sealed brown paper bag contains spiced pigs ears, and ox cheek doughnuts with apricot jam and smoked paprika sugar are as big as mini cannonballs. Handily open 24/7and often showcasing live music, you might satisfy the munchies with an all-day foie gras breakfast, with streaky bacon and homemade Nutella, a "Full Elvis" PBJ waffle with banana brûlée, or later share tender octopus with lemon and capers, bacon-wrapped dates, or flavor-packed baked Cornish pollock "meatballs" with lobster cream. A stunning vanilla ice-cream Baked Alaska with strawberry and mint oil is the ultimate finale. *Average main: £8 ✉ Heron Tower, 110 Bishopsgate, The City 🌐 www.duckandwaffle.com ✍ Reservations essential Ⓜ Liverpool St. ✣ H1.*

$$ SEAFOOD **✕ Sweetings.** Sweetings was established in 1889 and little seems to have changed at this time warp since the height of the British Empire. There are some things Sweetings *doesn't* do: dinner, reservations, coffee, or weekends. It does, mercifully, do seafood—and rather well. Not far from St. Paul's Cathedral, and kitted out with arcane Victoriana, sporting and Colonel Blimp cartoons, the restaurant is patronized by pinstriped and covert coated City gents who down pewter tankards of Black Velvet (Guinness and Champagne) and simply love to eat potted shrimps, soft roe on toast, Dover sole, and skate wings with black butter sauce, all this while perched on high stools at white linen–covered raised wooden counters. West Mersea oysters are fresh and plump, and desserts like spotted dick or baked jam roll are timeless public schoolboy favorites. The long-serving waitstaff wear funereal black and white and are naturally acquainted with all the regulars. *Average main: £23 ✉ 39 Queen Victoria St., The City ☎ 020/7248–3062 🌐 www.sweetingsrestaurant.com ⏲ Closed weekends. No dinner ✍ Reservations not accepted Ⓜ Mansion House ✣ G3.*

CLERKENWELL

$$ MEDITERRANEAN FAMILY **✕ Moro.** Up from The City, near Clerkenwell and Sadler's Wells contemporary dance theater, is Exmouth Market, a cluster of cute indie shops, bookstores, vinyl stores, artisan bakeries, an Italian Catholic church, and more fine indie-spirited restaurants like Moro. Lovingly nurtured for over a decade by husband-and-wife chefs Sam and Sam Clark, the menu includes an expansive mélange of Spanish, Moroccan, and Moorish North African flavors. Flavor-packed and rustic tapas—like baba ganoush eggplant dip, Syrian lentils, baby squid with *harissa*, or ox heart tabouleh—compete with spiced meats, Serrano ham, salt cod, and seared char-grilled offerings. Wood-fired sea bass with hispi cabbage, grilled lamb with aubergine, or sea bream with chickpea salad are among the standout mains. Sidle up to the long zinc bar, or squeeze into a tiny table and lean in—it's noisy here, but then again that's all part of the buzz. *Average main: £19 ✉ 34–36 Exmouth Market, Clerkenwell ☎ 020/7833–8336 🌐 www.moro.co.uk ⏲ No dinner Sun. ✍ Reservations essential Ⓜ Farringdon, Angel ✣ F2.*

$$ MODERN BRITISH **✕ St. John.** Purists and gastronauts travel the globe for pioneering Brit-chef Fergus Henderson's nose-to-tail cuisine at this puritan stark-white converted former ham-and-bacon smokehouse near historic Smithfield Market. Henderson famously uses *all* scraps of a carcass, and his waste-not, want-not chutzpah chimes increasingly the age: one appetizer is pig's skin and others like ox heart, rolled pig's spleen, or calves' brain and chicory are marginally less extreme. Open since 1994,

long-standing St. John signatures like bone marrow and parsley salad, chitterlings with dandelion, or pheasant and pig's-trotter pie appear stark on the plate, but arrive with aplomb. Look out for a metropolitan art world–and–designer crowd, who enjoy feasting meals for the table, like whole roast suckling pig or braised venison with red wine sauce. Finish with Eccles cakes and Lancashire cheese tapioca and crab apple jelly or half a dozen Madeleines. *Average main: £18 ✉ 26 St. John St., Clerkenwell ☎ 020/7251–0848 🌐 www.stjohnrestaurant.com ⏲ No dinner Sun. ✍ Reservations essential Ⓜ Farringdon, Barbican ✣ G2.*

THE EAST END

$ INDIAN ✕ **Dishoom.** The humble curry is England's surrogate national dish and in London you'll find some of the best around. Dark-wood and memorabilia-adorned Dishoom is modeled on the all-day Irani cafés of Victorian-era Bombay and it expertly churns out mesmerizing street food, from *naan* breads and handkerchief-thin *roomali* roti wraps, to masala prawns, black dhal, lamb biryani, and yogurt-and-milk-based sweet *lassi* drinks. Average price of dinner for two: £40. *Average main: £12 ✉ 7 Boundary St., Shoreditch ☎ 020/7420–9324 🌐 www.dishoom.com ✍ Reservations essential Ⓜ Shoreditch High St., Liverpool St. ✣ H3.*

$$ BRITISH FAMILY ✕ **Rochelle Canteen.** You feel quite the foodie insider once you finally track down the quirky Rochelle Canteen—it's set in an old former bike shed at the restored Victorian-era Rochelle School (off Arnold Circus in Shoreditch, not far from Liverpool Street and the trendy boutiques of Redchurch Street). Ring a buzzer next to a pale blue door, go in through the "Boys" entrance (passing a former playground), and enter chef Margot Henderson's long white, austere canteen, which has an open kitchen and two long Formica tables, Ercol chairs, and Shaker coat pegs on the wall. Gloriously understated British fare arrives at a leisurely pace, from simple deviled kidneys on toast to a retro plate of Yorkshire ham and parsley sauce. Bump along with the Frieze London art and design crowd, and enjoy seasonal guinea fowl with bacon, or skate and capers, and finish with lemon posset or quince jelly. Note it's BYO (£5 corkage), and only open 9 am to 4:30 pm weekdays for breakfast, elevenses, lunch, and tea. *Average main: £16 ✉ Rochelle School, Arnold Circus, Shoreditch ☎ 020/7729–5677 for reservations only 🌐 www.arnoldandhenderson.com ⏲ Closed weekends. No dinner ✍ Reservations essential Ⓜ Liverpool St. ✣ H3.*

THE SOUTH BANK

$$ BISTRO Fodor's Choice ★ ✕ **Casse-Croûte.** French radio plays in the background and a chubby Michelin Man perches benignly over the *'Allo 'Allo!* bar at this jaunty Parisian style local mini-French bistro on Bermondsey Street near The Shard. Run by three friendly French guys—Alex, Hervé, and Sylvain—and minuscule with 19 tightly packed seats and six counter stools, the daily changing blackboard offers a highly restricted three-option/course menu of exceptional Gallic bistro riffs and classics. Sip Ricard pastis or an electro-green crème de menthe before lopping off two *ouefs à la coque* (boiled eggs with asparagus soldiers) or untangling your way

BRITISH TO A "T": TOP TEAS IN TOWN

So, what is Afternoon Tea, exactly? Well, it means real loose-leaf tea—Earl Grey, English Breakfast, Ceylon, Darjeeling, or Assam—brewed in a fine bone china or porcelain pot, and served with fine bone cups and saucers, milk or lemon, and silver spoons, taken between noon and 6 pm. Tea goers dress smartly (though not ostentatiously), and conversation by tradition should avoid politics and religion. Here are some top places in town to head:

Hands-down, the super-glam **Savoy** on the Strand offers one of the most beautiful settings for tea. The Thames Foyer, a symphony of grays and golds centered around a winter garden wrought-iron gazebo, is just the place for the house pianist to accompany you as you enjoy the award-winning house teas along with finger sandwiches, homemade scones, and *yumptious* pastries.

Setting the standard in its English Tea Room for some of London's best-known traditional teas, **Brown's Hotel**, at 33 Albermarle Street—charmingly set in a classic Mayfair town house—offers Afternoon Tea for £41 or, if you wish to splash out, Champagne Tea for £51.

If you seek timeless chic, the sumptuous 1920s dining room at the **Wolseley** Viennese grand café on Piccadilly remains a fashionable hangout for London's top luvvies. The silver service teas here—light Afternoon Tea is £10.75 and Champagne Tea £33.50—are among the best in town.

Moving west, you can sit looking out onto fab lawns amid mini potted orange trees at **The Orangery** in Prince William and Kate's London pad, Kensington Palace, inside resplendent Kensington Gardens. Afternoon Tea is £22.65 and a suitably Royal Afternoon Tea (with a glass of Laurent-Perrier) is £32.50.

Alternatively, add spice to your Afternoon Tea by trying a popular Moroccan-style Afternoon Tea (£22) at the souk-chic tearoom at **Momo** off Regent Street, where you'll enjoy sweet mint tea in colorful glass cups plus scones with fig jam, Maghrebian pastries, Moroccan chicken wraps, and honey-and-nut-rich Berber-style crêpes.

Bea's of Bloomsbury (motto: "Life is short. Eat More Cake") is one of the best Afternoon Tea and cupcake stops around. With its on-site bakery, Bea's churns out freshly baked delights like blackberry cupcakes or heavenly chocolate fudge cupcakes with fudge icing. Cheery Afternoon Tea services (noon–7 pm daily) with loose-leaf Jing tea, cupcakes, scones with jam and clotted cream, mini meringues, marshmallows, and Valrhona brownies is £16 weekdays, and £19 on weekends.

Finally, for frilly trompe l'oeil grandeur, few can compete with Afternoon Tea at **The Ritz** on Piccadilly. It's served in the impressive Palm Court, replete with marble tables, Louis XVI chaises, resplendent bouquets, and musical accompaniment: a true taste of Edwardian London in the 21st century. Afternoon Tea is £47 and Champagne Tea £59. Reserve a few months ahead and remember to wear a jacket and tie.

through a blue cheese salad or perfectly constructed *gratinée à l'oignon* (French onion soup). With mains reasonable at £15–£18, it's elbows in as you slice into a generous *bonette* steak with pepper sauce or sublime turbot with Noilly Prat sauce. The £6 desserts like Paris-Brest choux pastry and cream will instantly transport you back to Montmartre or the Left Bank. *Average main: £16* *109 Bermondsey St., Bermondsey* *020/7407–2140* *www.cassecroute.co.uk* *No dinner Sun.* *Reservations essential* *London Bridge* *H4.*

2

$ TAPAS **José.** Revered Spanish chef José Pizarro packs 'em in like so many slices of *jamón jamón* at this tiny tapas-and-sherry treasure trove on hot gastro-trail Bermondsey Street, just south of the Shard. With only 30 seats and no reservations, you'll be hard-pressed to find a spot at the open-kitchen tapas bar or a perch at an upturned sherry barrel after 6 pm, but stick with it, *hombre*—the Spanish tapas dishes are superb. Quaff a glass of Amontillado sherry and keep those delicately handcrafted small plates a comin': *patatas bravas . . . croquetas* . . . meatballs . . . pisto and crispy duck eggs . . . hake and aioli . . . razor clams with chorizo . . . *pluma* Ibérico pork loin fillets. Everything's impeccably sourced—from the peppery Marques de Valdueza olive oil to the rare Manuel Maldonado chorizo. Service is decidedly *excellente!*, but you'll either love or hate the *in-yer-face* crowds. *Average main: £9* *104 Bermondsey St., Southwark* *020/7403–4902* *www.josetapasbar.com* *Reservations not accepted* *Borough, London Bridge* *H4.*

$$$ MODERN BRITISH Fodor's Choice ★ **Restaurant Story.** Ambitious young Brit hotshot Tom Sellers storms the ramparts at this sell-out gastro-mecca, with his conceptual take on intensively flavored ingredient-led New British and New Nordic cuisine. Housed in a modishly Scandinavian-inspired dining space, expect touches like edible nasturtium flowers, "trash cooking"–inspired roast cod skin, or eel mousse Oreos to kick things off. The real fun, however, begins with a surprise tallow beef dripping candle that melts into an Ebenezer Scrooge–like silver candle holder, which you mop up with own-baked bread throughout the meal. Genius dishes like pureed Désirée heritage potatoes with dandelion beurre blanc, coal oil, and barley grass, or meadowsweet-pickled scallops with dill ash and horseradish cream pop up throughout the no-choice 3-, 6-, or 10-course set menus. Standout desserts include Earl Grey–soaked prunes with lovage ice cream, edible twig, and a smudge of milk skin. Reservations are taken a month in advance. *Average main: £28* *199 Tooley St., Bermondsey* *020/7183–2117* *www.restaurantstory.co.uk* *Closed Sun. and Mon.* *Reservations essential* *London Bridge* *H4.*

KENSINGTON, KNIGHTSBRIDGE, AND MAYFAIR

KENSINGTON

$$$ JAPANESE Fodor's Choice ★ **Yashin.** "*Without Soy Sauce . . . but if you want to*" proclaims the neon sign on the wall behind the sushi counter at this top London sushi bar off Kensington High Street. Take their advice, bag a ringside seat, and watch Japanese head chef and cofounder Yasuhiro Mineno tease, slice, tweak, and blowtorch his way to the most awesome, fresh, funky, spunky, colorful, and exquisite sushi, sashimi, salads, and carpaccios that you're likely to find this side of the East China Sea. Tofu-topped

miso cappuccino comes in a Victorian cup and saucer, and softshell blue crab salad is a tangle of *mizuna* (Japanese greens). Delectable 5-, 11-, or 15-piece sushi spreads (£15–£60) might mesmerize with ponzu-spiked salmon, Japanese sea bream with rice cracker dust, salted Wagyu beef, or Japanese prawns. The bargain £12.50 five-piece salmon *nigiri* set lunch, with hot miso and bracing raw salad, is a smashing way to sample Yashin's below-the-radar brilliance. *Average main: £25* *1A Argyll Rd., Kensington* *020/7938–1536* *yashinsushi.com* *Reservations essential* *High Street Kensington* *A4.*

CHELSEA

$$$ MODERN BRITISH FAMILY Fodor's Choice ★

The Harwood. British game doesn't get much better than at this forest-floor and game-lover's paradise and London's only Michelin-starred gastro-pub off Fulham Broadway. Co-owned by game-shooting enthusiast and two-starred Aussie chef Brett Graham, you'll find a catalog of awesome game-based dishes like haunch of Berkshire roe deer with pickled mushrooms or Muggleswick grouse with potato and malt to keep you tickled. Tuck into game pie with Somerset cider jelly, Irish Sika deer with smoked bone marrow, or Herdwick lamb with rosemary curd in a relaxed 1840s comfy-sofas-and-Sunday-newspapers home-away-from-home Sloaney pub setting. You'll find thoughtful openers like treacle-cured smoked salmon with spelt are served on a gnarled slab of wood, and there are popular carve-your-own whole-roast lamb, pork, or beef joints for the table—and yes, you *can* ask for doggy bags on the way out! *Average main: £24* *27 Walham Grove, Fulham* *020/7386–1847* *www.harwoodarms.com* *Reservations essential* *Fulham Broadway* *A6.*

KNIGHTSBRIDGE

$$$ SPANISH Fodor's Choice ★

Ametsa with Arzak Instruction. Cool hunters and Hispanophiles bask in a fantasia of New Basque cuisine at this modernist romp at the Halkin off Belgrave Square. The father-and-daughter team of Juan Mari and Elena Arzak behind the eponymous three-Michelin-star restaurant in San Sebastián break out triumphantly at their first European venue outside Spain. You'll love or loath the sparkling ceiling feature which undulates in a wave of 7,000 test tubes filled with golden-hue spices, and look beyond the austere stark white-gray, boxy setting. Instead, enjoy the ultrapro and passionate service, and marvel at high-spec riffs on traditional Basque dishes, such as slow-cooked hens eggs flecked with paprika-rich Chistorra cured sausage with dabs of wild cep mushrooms, pancetta, and chorizo. Lobster is updated with a white cassava powder, and seared venison appears on a black plate with pickled red chilies and an electric green mint and sea hawthorn mojo. Flawless desserts range from clove custard to an extraordinary science experiment—like hydromel mead "Fractal" surprise. *Average main: £27* *Halkin Hotel, 5 Halkin St., Knightsbridge* *0207/333–1234* *www.comohotels.com/thehalkin/dining/ametsa* *No lunch Mon., no dinner Sun.* *Reservations essential* *Hyde Park Corner, Knightsbridge* *C4.*

2

$$ BRASSERIE FAMILY **Bar Boulud.** U.S.-based French superchef Daniel Boulud combines the best of French high-end brasserie fare with a winning dash of superior Yankee gourmet burgers and fries at this popular street-level, all-day hangout at the Mandarin Oriental in Knightsbridge. Lilliputian-size platters of the most delicate Gilles Verot charcuterie, heartier coq au vin, or white pork sausages with truffle mash compete with palm-size Yankee, Frenchie, Piggie, or signature "BB" foie gras–beef burgers and fries in black onion or sesame-seed buns. The knockout grazing menu has something for everyone, and professional but informal waitstaff make for a convivial vibe in this handy spot opposite Harvey Nichols department store. Note the £19 three-course noon–7 pm prix-fixe deals. [$] *Average main: £21* ✉ *Mandarin Oriental Hyde Park, 66 Knightsbridge, Knightsbridge* ☎ *020/7201–3899 for reservations only* 🌐 *www.barboulud.com/london* *Reservations essential* [M] *Knightsbridge* ✣ *C4.*

$$$$ BRITISH FAMILY Fodor's Choice ★ **Dinner by Heston Blumenthal.** Splendidly revived old English dishes executed with ultramodern precision in an open kitchen is the big schtick at Ashley Palmer-Watts' award winner at the Mandarin Oriental. (Palmer-Watts is a protégée of TV chef Heston Blumenthal, who's closely involved.) As you take in views of Hyde Park, you simply must slice into a chilled Meat Fruit appetizer (circa 1500), deceptively shaped like a mandarin, but encasing the smoothest foie gras and chicken liver parfait on the planet. A plate of Rice and Flesh (circa 1390) is a picture of yellow saffron rice with calf's tails and red wine, and grilled octopus Frumenty (circa 1390) is a lively dish of cracked wheat cooked with lovage in a smoked sea broth from the court of Richard II. Marvel at beef royale (circa 1720) cooked sous vide for 72 hours at 56°C, plus cod in cider (circa 1940), or Spiced Pigeon (circa 1780) with ale and artichokes. Head off with resplendent spit-roast pineapple Tipsy cake (circa 1810)—an homage to English spit-roasting from centuries past. [$] *Average main: £34* ✉ *Mandarin Oriental Hyde Park, 66 Knightsbridge, Knightsbridge* ☎ *020/7201–3833* 🌐 *www.dinnerbyheston.com* *Reservations essential* [M] *Knightsbridge* ✣ *C4.*

$$$ RUSSIAN **Mari Vanna.** All of London's Russian molls, dolls, and porcelain-skinned babushkas squeeze into this kitsch White Russian fantasy dining salon in Knightsbridge, which overflows with a maximalist decor of vintage chandeliers, books, pics, knickknacks, Tiffany lamps, tchotchkes, gilt mirrors, Cheburashkas, and a Russian *pechka* stove. Note the crochet- and linen-covered tables tended by chirpy staff (some in dirndls) and dishes proffered with what feels like great aunt Vanna's old family silver and jumbled crockery. Then snap into character with a horseradish vodka shot or two, and carb-up on pierogi sea bass savories, clear Siberian Pelmeni dumpling soup, or feather-light smoked salmon blinis. There's good borscht and creamy beef Stroganoff with mash and wild mushrooms, and lest we forget the sweet crepes with condensed milk. But it's the nostalgic dacha-like antebellum home-away-from-home setting that makes you feel like you're participating in some kind of *Anna Karenina*–esque historical reenactment. [$] *Average main: £28* ✉ *The Wellington Court, 116 Knightsbridge, Knightsbridge* ☎ *020/7225–3122* 🌐 *www.marivanna.ru/london* *Reservations essential* [M] *Knightsbridge* ✣ *C4.*

MAYFAIR

$$$ INTERNATIONAL **34.** Megawatt celebs from Sandra Bullock to Stella McCartney head straight for 34 in Mayfair because . . . *all* the other stars go there, too! It must be the plush English Edwardian and art deco–inspired dining salon, the swank artwork and burnt-orange banquettes, the nightly live jazz, the interesting fish, game, steak, and seafood grill-focused menu, the copious starched white table linens, and the smooth Upper Manhattan–style service. Appetizers like salt-baked beetroot with soft burrata cheese or Dorset crab and gazpacho jelly square off against chunkier delights from the Argentinian *parrilla* charcoal grill—think 28-day Scottish Red Angus sirloin steaks, Creekstone T-bones, and Australian Wagyu flank steak. Top crowd pleasers include meatball spaghetti, cod and shallots, or Cornish lamb with pumpkin pesto, while game goes down well, too, with roast wood pigeon and damsons standing out. *Average main: £28 34 Grosvenor Sq., Mayfair 020/3350–3434 www.34-restaurant.co.uk Reservations essential Entrance on South Audley St. Marble Arch C3.*

$$$ MODERN ITALIAN **Cecconi's.** Spot the odd glossy A-lister and wallow in glamorous all-day Mayfair buzz at this upscale Italian brasserie wedged strategically between Old Bond Street, Cork Street, and Savile Row, and across from the 1768 Royal Academy of Arts. The G5 jet set and fine art world connoisseurs spill out onto pavement tables for breakfast, brunch, and *cicchetti* (Italian tapas), and return later in the day for something more substantial. À la mode English designer Ilse Crawford's luxe green-and-brown interior is a tony backdrop for well-loved classics like sea bream carpaccio, veal Milanese, and *pappardelle*pasta with Chianti ragù, and not forgetting a flavorsome pick-me-up tiramisu. It's perfect for a *what-the-hell!* pit stop during a kamikaze West End shopping spree or after old masters art buying at the nearby Mayfair auction houses, art galleries, and salons. *Average main: £24 5A Burlington Gardens, Mayfair 020/7434–1500 www.cecconis.co.uk No dinner Sun. Reservations essential Green Park, Piccadilly Circus D3.*

$$$$ STEAKHOUSE FAMILY **CUT at 45 Park Lane.** U.S.–based Austrian *übernuber* star chef Wolfgang Puck amps up the steak stakes at this ultraexpensive, superprime steak emporium on Park Lane. Against a mid-1990s luxe backdrop of Damien Hirst kaleidoscope paintings, globe lights, and a 1980s sound track of T'Pau and Bon Jovi, an army of hedge fund and private equity knuckleheads go gangbusters for perfectly seared prime cuts from England, Japan, and the United States. Grilled over charcoal and hardwood, and finished under a 650°C broiler, there's awesome 35-day Arkansas Creekstone filet mignon for £36, USDA Black Angus New York sirloins for £58, and a wet-aged 8-ounce rib eye of A5 100% Wagyu Omi beef from Shiga in Japan for a top whack £140. Add bone marrow, french fries, white truffles, chimichurri, or creamed spinach with a fried egg on top for the whole nine yards. *Average main: £41 45 Park La., Mayfair 020/7439–4545 for reservations only www.dorchestercollection.com Reservations essential Marble Arch, Hyde Park Corner C3.*

$$$$ STEAKHOUSE **Goodman.** This Manhattan-themed, Russian-owned, Mayfair-based swanky steak house, named after Chicago jazz legend Benny Goodman,

has everyone in agreement—these are some of the best steaks in town. USDA-certified, 150-day corn-fed and on-site dry-aged Black Angus T-bones, rib eye, Porterhouse, and New York sirloins compete for taste and tenderness with heavily marbled grass-fed prime cuts from Scotland and the Lake District. There's token Russian sweet herring, lobster bisque, beef carpaccio, and Caesar salad, but everyone at this sultry and rollicking dark-wood mecca seems to have only one big thing on their minds: the sizzling 250-gram–400-gram Josper char-grilled steaks, which come with lobster tails or panfried foie gras, truffle chips, and creamed spinach, plus béarnaise pepper or Stilton sauce. $ *Average main: £34* ✉ *24–26 Maddox St., Mayfair* ☎ *020/7499–3776* 🌐 *www.goodmanrestaurants.com* ⏲ *Closed Sun.* ✍ *Reservations essential* Ⓜ *Oxford Circus, Piccadilly Circus* ✢ *D3.*

$$$ MODERN INDIAN FAMILY Fodor's Choice ★ ✕ **Gymkhana.** Indian curry king Karam Sethi invokes the last days of the Raj at London's finest top-end curry emporium in Mayfair. Inspired by the Colonial-era Anglo-Indian gymkhana sporting clubs and high-society mustering points of yesteryear, you'll be charmed by the ceiling fans, rattan chairs, lacquered oak floors, and dark chocolate leather banquettes. Chuckle at the grand old Punch sketches, cricket memorabilia, and hunting trophies from the Maharajah of Jodhpur before exploring the exceptional menu. Choices include all-India delights such as a golden pancakelike *dosa* with fennel-rich Chettinad duck and coconut chutney, egg-white-soaked *kasoori* chicken tikka with *moong*beans, or wild Muntjac deer *biryani* with pomegranate and mint *raita*. There's fine tandoori broccoli and suckling pig vindaloo and oodles of well-spiced game—like *achari* wild roe deer or partridge pepper fry—while the saffron pistachio *kulfi falooda* (a sort of sundae) with wild basil seeds is equally sublime. $ *Average main: £27* ✉ *42 Albemarle St., Mayfair* ☎ *020/3011–5900* 🌐 *www.gymkhanalondon.com* ⏲ *Closed Sun.* ✍ *Reservations essential* Ⓜ *Green Park* ✢ *D3.*

$$$$ FRENCH FAMILY ✕ **Hélène Darroze at the Connaught.** London's crème de la crème flock to French virtuoso Hélène Darroze's restaurant at the Connaught for her dazzling regional French haute cuisine, served up in a sexy Edwardian dark-wood-paneled dining salon tricked out by Parisian It-designer India Mahdavi with geometric carpets and high-backed comfy chairs. Taking inspiration from Les Landes in southwestern France, Darroze sallies forth with a procession of *magnifique* dishes, like local Robert Dupérier foie gras with cardamom and sorrel or Limousin sweetbreads with girolles and Jerusalem artichokes. Spit-roasted and flambéed Racan pigeon is served gloriously pink and Pyrenean lamb is served *en rognonade* (with its kidneys). To finish, choose poached yellow peach from Provence with gingerbread cream. Darroze is perfect for a splurge, but beware the high prices: £38 for lunch, £55 for brunch, and £92–£155 for set dinner. $ *Average main: £37* ✉ *The Connaught, Carlos Pl., Mayfair* ☎ *020/3147–7200 for reservations only* 🌐 *www.the-connaught.co.uk* ⏲ *Closed Sun. and Mon.* ✍ *Reservations essential* 👔 *Jacket required* ☞ *No trainers or sportswear* Ⓜ *Green Park* ✢ *C3.*

$$ BRITISH ✕ **Kitty Fisher's.** Named after a racy 18th-century courtesan who once ate a thousand-guinea note on a slice of bread and butter, Kitty Fisher's is situated in a classy, dark, and creaky Georgian town house in Mayfair's

Dickensian Shepherd Market square. Come and be seduced here in the basement by some of the finest modern British grill and smokehouse fare around. The famed set-piece wood-grilled 12-year-old Galician beef sirloin is a singed and seared yet pink and oozing carved column of meat, accompanied by a heap of grilled onions, pickled walnuts, and barbecued pink fir potatoes with soft white Tunworth cheese. Look for the beef tartar with nasturtium, and roast leeks or charred lamb cutlets with mint and parsley. It's tony but tiny, with only 40 seats, and filled with vintage 18th-century prints and paintings, historic cast-iron wall ovens, and decadent antique silver candelabras. *Average main: £21 ✉ 10 Shepherd Market, Mayfair ☎ 020/3302–1661 www.kittyfishers.com Closed Sun. and Mon. No lunch Sat. No credit cards Ⓜ Green Park ✥ D3.*

$$$ FRENCH FAMILY

La Petite Maison. With the legend *"Tous Célèbres Ici"* boldly etched on the frosted glass front doors, the light-filled and delightful La Petite Maison boasts an impressively well-sourced French Mediterranean, Côte d'Azur, Liguria, and Provençale menu. Try figure-friendly broad bean and Pecorino salad, soft burrata cheese with sweet Datterini-tomato-and-basil spread, or aromatic baked turbot with artichokes, chorizo, five spices, and gloppy white wine sauce. Based on the Riviera style of the original La Petite Maison in Nice in the south of France, dishes come to the table as soon as they're ready, and the chirpy, *très jolie*, and informal waitstaff make for a convivial Gucci Gucci party vibe. More rosé, anyone? *Average main: £27 ✉ 53–54 Brook's Mews, Mayfair ☎ 020/7495–4774 www.lpmlondon.co.uk Reservations essential Ⓜ Bond St., Oxford Circus ✥ D3.*

$$$$ FRENCH Fodor's Choice ★

Le Gavroche. Famed masterchef Michel Roux Jr. works the floor and glad-hands all comers in the old-fashioned proprietorial way at this clubby Mayfair basement institution—established by his father and uncle in 1967—and which many still rate to this day as the *best* formal dining in London. Resplendent with magnificent shiny silver domes and unpriced ladies' menus, Roux's mastery of classical French haute cuisine hypnotizes all comers with signatures like foie gras with cinnamon-scented crispy duck pancake, soufflé Suissesse, roast venison with red wine *jus*, or saddle of rabbit with a crust of Parmesan cheese. Desserts like Roux's delectable chocolate omelet soufflé or upside-down apple tart are unswervingly accomplished. Notable three-course set lunches (£55) are the sanest way to experience such unashamed, overwrought flummery—with half a bottle of wine, water, coffee, and petits fours thrown in. *Average main: £41 ✉ 43 Upper Brook St., Mayfair ☎ 020/7408–0881 www.le-gavroche.co.uk Closed Sun. and bank holiday Mon. Reservations essential Jacket required Ⓜ Marble Arch, Bond St. ✥ C3.*

$$$ MODERN EUROPEAN Fodor's Choice ★

Pollen Street Social. Unstoppable gastro god Jason Atherton knocks the London dining scene for a loop at his smash-hit flagship found in a cute alleyway off Regent Street. Braying fans enjoy refined small and large dishes ranging from a full "English breakfast" appetizer—a miniature of poached egg on tomato compote, with parsley-flecked bacon, morels, and croutons—to sublime Scottish ox cheek with 50-day Black Angus rib-eye beef, or Devon red mullet with pears and parsley. Diners can opt to get up from their tables to sit and perch at the dessert bar to watch staff as they chop, slice, squeeze, and fiddle away to prepare immaculate Eton Mess with wild strawberries and basil-ash meringue or sashimi-like pressed watermelon with an unlikely basil sorbet. Look out for Atherton, who's often around, and note the £28.50 set lunch. *Average main: £30* *8–10 Pollen St., Mayfair* *020/7290–7600* *www.pollenstreetsocial.com* *Reservations essential* *Oxford Circus, Piccadilly Circus* *D3.*

2

$$$$ BRITISH FAMILY **The Ritz Restaurant.** London's's most flamboyantly ornate dining room at The Ritz would moisten the eye of Marie Antoinette with its sumptuous Belle Époque–inspired trompe-d'oeil , rococo garlanded gilt chandeliers, fairy-tale silk drapery, marble statuette, and double-height mirrored wall. A cavalcade of liveried waiters glide across the carpeted salon, and gentlemen diners are expected to wear a jacket and tie at all times. Sit at the late Baroness Thatcher's favorite seat overlooking Green Park (Table 1) and enjoy unreconstructed "Palace style" British haute cuisine. A Bresse chicken with black Périgord truffle stuffed under its skin arrives in a pig's bladder and is carved table-side and served with *sauce suprême*. Set and surprise menus at steep prices (£95, or £185 with fine wine) might captivate with exquisite turbot with cep and brown butter sauce or Anjou pigeon with *pomme Anna*, and don't miss the famous *crêpes Suzette,* which are flambéed table-side by the unflappable maître d'. *Average main: £38* *The Ritz London, 150 Piccadilly, St. James's* *020/7300–2370 for reservations only* *www.theritzlondon.com* *Reservations essential* *Jacket and tie* *Green Park* *D3.*

$$$ SEAFOOD **Scott's.** Bowler-hatted doormen greet the A-list with a discreet nod at this ever-fashionable seafood haven on fashion-central Mount Street in Mayfair. Originally founded in 1851, and a former haunt of James Bond author Ian Fleming (he liked the potted shrimps, apparently), these days you're more likely to see Bill Clinton in one corner, Kate Winslet in another, and former hell-raiser Brit-pack artists Damien Hirst or Tracey Emin joshing around on a burgundy banquette nearby. Scott's draws London's top-tier 1% movers and shakers who enjoy day-boat-fresh Lindisfarne oysters, baked crab, whole salt-baked turbot, cod cheeks, and scrummy shrimp burgers. Glorious standouts like sautéed razor clams with wild boar sausages or sole Colbert are similarly divine. Prices could make a Saudi sheikh blanch, but fear not: this really is the *hottest* joint in town. *Average main: £32* *20 Mount St., Mayfair* *020/7495–7309* *www.scotts-restaurant.com* *Reservations essential* *Bond St., Green Park* *C3.*

MARYLEBONE

$$$ ECLECTIC FAMILY Fodor's Choice ★ **Chiltern Firehouse.** There may be a waiting list for the waiting list to get into the red hot pap-central Chiltern Firehouse, but if you do snag a table, you're in for a treat. Set beside a luxury bespoke 26-room hotel of the same name opened by überchic hotelier André Balazs's in the sensationally converted 1888 Grade II–listed redbrick fire station, the Chiltern Firehouse sets the bar for glamor-chic dining. Once escorted through a courtyard wildflower garden and past a pantheon of prettier-than-thou front-of-house staff, sit at the raised open kitchen counter

and watch Portuguese maestro Nuno Mendes plate up, while taking in the buzzy buttermilk-hued surrounds—part mid-1970s Parisian brasserie, and part industrial-heritage chic splendor (think huge firehouse doors, riveted iron beams, tracery, carvings, and a fireman's pole). Pick winners from a spanking menu—like slider-style crab meat "donuts," charred octopus with cep mushrooms, or red prawns in almond milk—and get down to the business of major-league celeb spotting. *Average main: £24* *Chiltern Firehouse, 1 Chiltern St.* *00207/073–7676 for restaurant reservations only* *www.chilternfirehouse.com* *Reservations essential* *Baker St.* *C2.*

$ SEAFOOD FAMILY **The Golden Hind.** You'll land some of the best fish-and-chips in town at this great British "chippy" in a cheery retro 1914 art-deco café off Marylebone High Street. Gaggles of satisfied tourists and chirpy Marylebone village locals and workers alike hunker down for the homemade cod fishcakes, skate wings, feta cheese fritters, and breaded scampi tails at simple dark-wood tables, but it's the neatly prepared and decidedly nongreasy deep-fried or steamed battered cod, haddock, and plaice from Grimsby (£9.10), the classic hand-cut Maris Piper chips, and the traditional mushy peas that are the big draw. It's BYO (£1 corkage) and takeaway, but note there's no lunch Saturday and it's closed Sunday. *Average main: £9* *73 Marylebone La., Marylebone* *020/7486–3644* *Closed Sun. No lunch Sat.* *Reservations not accepted* *Bond St.* *C2.*

NOTTING HILL AND BAYSWATER

NOTTING HILL

$$$$ MODERN FRENCH FAMILY Fodor's Choice ★ **The Ledbury.** Acclaimed Aussie chef Brett Graham wins hearts, minds—and *serious* global accolades—at this no-diary, no-carbs high-ceilinged modern French (with Pacific and British hints) dining landmark in deepest Notting Hill. In a handsome four-square salon full of drapes, mirrored walls, and plush cream leather seats, you won't find a more inventive vegetable dish than Graham's ash-baked celeriac with hazelnut and wood sorrel, and it's impossible to best his pretty and complex mains like roast quail with walnut cream, roe deer with bone marrow, or Cornish turbot with Riesling, cockles, and sea lettuce. Besides his obsessive interest in all things British game, Graham's also famed for wicked desserts, so why not finish with thinly sliced figs with honey, olives, and sourdough ice cream? The assured service and sommelier round out this peerless proposition. *Average main: £34* *127 Ledbury Rd., Notting Hill* *0207/7792–9090* *www.theledbury.com* *No lunch Mon. or Tues.* *Reservations essential* *Westbourne Park, Ladbroke Grove* *A2.*

BAYSWATER

$ MODERN BRITISH FAMILY **Hereford Road.** Bespeckled chef and co-owner Tom Pemberton mans the busy front-of-house grill station at this Bayswater favorite, renowned for its pared-down, pomp-free, and ingredient-driven seasonal British fare. With an accent on well-sourced honest-to-goodness seasonal and regional British produce, many dishes are as unfussy as you'll find. Slide into side booths, and work your way though pure and uncluttered combos like steamed mussels with cider and thyme, lemon sole with sea dulse, duck breast with old-fashioned pickled walnuts, or warm and soothing English rice pudding with strawberry jam. Expect to brush past the entire Tory party leadership and the rest of the well-heeled Notting Hill set on the way out. Note the £9.50 to £15.50 set lunches are arguably the *best* high-quality weekday set lunch deals, bar none. $ *Average main: £14* ✉ *3 Hereford Rd., Bayswater* ☎ *020/7727–1144* 🌐 *www.herefordroad.org* ✍ *Reservations essential* Ⓜ *Bayswater, Queensway* ✥ *A3.*

PUBS

The city's public houses, more popularly known as pubs or "locals," dispense beer, good cheer, and simple food in structures that range from atmospheric old ones with authentic low wood-beamed ceilings and Victorian spots with ornate etched glass to modern shabby-chic hangouts and sticky-carpeted dens. Following the repeal in 2003 of some antiquated licensing laws and the prohibition on smoking that went into effect four years later, a surge in gastro-pubs occurred. The emphasis shifted as much toward eating as drinking, with alternatives such as Moroccan chicken replacing the usually mediocre "ploughman's lunch." But whatever you order, don't neglect the beer. American-style beer is called "lager" in Britain, whereas the real British brew is "bitter" and usually served at cellar temperature, which is cooler than room temperature but not actually chilled. Beer comes in two sizes—pints or half-pints. Some London pubs also sell "real ale," which is less gassy than bitter and, many would argue, has a better flavor.

The list below offers a few pubs selected for their central location, historical interest, pleasant garden, music, or good food, but you might just as happily adopt your own temporary local.

SOHO AND COVENT GARDEN

Harp. This is the sort of friendly little local you might find on some out-of-the-way backstreet, except that it's right in the middle of town, between Trafalgar Square and Covent Garden. As a result, the Harp can get crowded, especially because it was named British pub of the year by the Campaign for Real Ale, but the squeeze is worth it for the excellent beer (there are usually 10 carefully chosen ales, often including a London microbrew) and a no-frills menu of high-quality British sausages, cooked behind the bar. ✉ *47 Chandos Pl., Covent Garden* ☎ *020/7836–0291* 🌐 *www.harpcoventgarden.com* Ⓜ *Charing Cross.*

Lamb & Flag. This refreshingly ungentrified 17th-century pub was once known as the Bucket of Blood because the upstairs room was used as a ring for bare-knuckle boxing. Now it's a friendly—and bloodless—place, serving food and real ale. It's on the edge of Covent Garden, up a hidden alley off Garrick Street. ✉ *33 Rose St., Covent Garden* ☎ *020/7497–9504* 🌐 *www.lambandflagcoventgarden.co.uk* Ⓜ *Covent Garden.*

BLOOMSBURY AND HOLBORN

The Lamb. Charles Dickens and his contemporaries drank here, but today's enthusiastic clientele make sure this intimate and eternally popular pub avoids the pitfalls of feeling too old-timey. For private chats at the bar, you can close a delicate etched-glass "snob screen" to the bar staff, opening it only when you fancy another pint. ✉ *94 Lamb's Conduit St., Bloomsbury* ☎ *020/7405–0713* 🌐 *www.youngs.co.uk* Ⓜ *Russell Sq.*

Fodor's Choice ★ **Princess Louise.** This fine, popular pub is an exquisite museum piece of a Victorian interior, with glazed tiles and intricately engraved glass screens that divide the bar area into cozy little annexes. It's not all show, either. There's a good selection of excellent-value Yorkshire real ales from the Samuel Smith's brewery. ✉ *208 High Holborn, Holborn* ☎ *020/7405–8816* Ⓜ *Holborn.*

THE CITY

Fodor's Choice ★ **The Blackfriar.** A step from Blackfriars Tube station, this spectacular pub has an Arts and Crafts interior that is entertainingly, satirically ecclesiastical, with inlaid mother-of-pearl, wood carvings, stained glass, and marble pillars all over the place. Under finely lettered temperance tracts on view just below the reliefs of monks, fairies, and friars, there is a nice group of ales on tap from independent brewers. The 20th-century poet Sir John Betjeman once led a successful campaign to save the pub from demolition. ✉ *174 Queen Victoria St., The City* ☎ *020/7236–5474* 🌐 *www.nicholsonspubs.co.uk/theblackfriarblackfriarslondon* Ⓜ *Blackfriars.*

Fodor's Choice ★ **Jerusalem Tavern.** Owned by the well-respected St. Peter's Brewery from Suffolk, the Jerusalem Tavern is one-of-a-kind: small, and endearingly eccentric. Ancient Delft-style tiles meld with wood and concrete in a converted watchmaker and jeweler's shop dating back to the 18th century. The beer, both bottled and on tap, is some of the best available anywhere in London. It's loved by Londoners and is often busy, especially after work. ✉ *55 Britton St., Clerkenwell* ☎ *020/7490–4281* 🌐 *www.stpetersbrewery.co.uk/london-pub* Ⓜ *Farringdon.*

Ye Olde Cheshire Cheese. Yes, this extremely historic pub (it dates from 1667, the year after the Great Fire of London) is full of tourists, but it deserves a visit for its sawdust-covered floors, low wood-beam ceilings, and the 14th-century crypt of Whitefriars' monastery under the cellar bar. This was the most regular of Dr. Johnson's and Dickens's many locals. Food is served. ✉ *145 Fleet St., The City* ☎ *020/7353–6170* ⏲ *Closed Sun.* Ⓜ *Blackfriars.*

SOUTH BANK

Anchor & Hope. One of London's most popular gastro-pubs, the Anchor & Hope doesn't take reservations (except for the three-course prix-fixe Sunday lunch that begins at 12:30 pm). Would-be diners snake around the red-walled, wooden-floored pub, kept happy by some good real ales and a fine wine list as they wait for at least 45 minutes for a table. The excellent, meaty food is old-fashioned English—for instance, salt cod, tripe, and chips (fries)—with a few modern twists. ✉ *36 The Cut, South Bank* ☎ *020/7928–9898* 🌐 *www.charleswells.co.uk* Ⓜ *Southwark.*

2

KENSINGTON, KNIGHTSBRIDGE, AND MAYFAIR

Fodor's Choice ★ **The Nag's Head.** The landlord of this idiosyncratic little mews pub in Belgravia runs a tight ship, and no mobile phones are allowed. The lovingly collected artifacts (including antique penny arcade games) that decorate every inch of the place, high-quality beer, and old-fashioned pub grub should provide more than enough distraction. ✉ *53 Kinnerton St., Belgravia* ☎ *020/7235–1135* Ⓜ *Knightsbridge, Hyde Park Corner.*

REGENT'S PARK AND HAMPSTEAD

The Holly Bush. A short walk up the hill from Hampstead Tube station, the friendly Holly Bush was a country pub before London spread this far north. It retains something of a rural feel, with stripped wooden floors and an open fire, and is an intimate place to enjoy great ales and organic and free-range pub food. Try the homemade pork scratchings (rinds) and pickled eggs. ✉ *22 Holly Mount, Hampstead* ☎ *020/7435–2892* 🌐 *www.hollybushhampstead.co.uk* Ⓜ *Hampstead.*

WHERE TO STAY

Use the coordinate at the end of each listing to locate a site on the corresponding map.

Her Majesty hasn't offered you a bed? No matter. London's grande-dame hotels are the next best thing—and possibly better. If your budget won't stretch to five-star luxury, don't worry. There are plenty of comfortable, clean, friendly options available for a relatively reasonable price. The key word is relatively. In recent years London has seen a welcome growth in the value-for-money sector, but overall, accommodations here still remain on the costly side.

If money is no object, London has some of the world's most luxurious hotels, ranging from blingtastic newcomers such as the Corinthia to the quirkily charming Firmdale Hotels, run by Tim and Kit Kemp. Even these high-end places have deals, and you can sometimes find a bargain, particularly during January and February. Other worthy recent arrivals in this sector include the gorgeous remodeled Victorian landmark, St. Pancras Renaissance.

Meanwhile, several mid-range hotels have dropped their average prices, which has made some desirable options such as Hazlitt's more affordable. As well, large business-oriented hotels frequently offer weekend packages. Those on a budget should check out the stylish and super-cheap hotels that have shaken up the lodging scene of late. The downside is that these places tend to be a little out of the way, but you may find this a price worth paying. Another attractive alternative includes hotels in the Premier and Millennium chains, which offer sleek, modern rooms, many up-to-date conveniences, and discount prices that sometimes fall below £100 a night.

You should confirm *exactly* what your room costs before checking in. The usual practice in all but the less expensive hotels is for quoted prices to cover room alone; breakfast, whether Continental or "full English" (i.e. cooked), costs extra. Also check whether the quoted rate includes V.A.T. (sales tax), which is a hefty 20%. Most expensive hotels include it in the initial quote, but some middle-of-the-range and budget places may not. *Hotel reviews have been shortened. For full information, visit Fodors.com.*

WHAT IT COSTS IN POUNDS

	$	$$	$$$	$$$$
For Two People	under £100	£101–£200	£201–£300	over £300

Hotel prices are the lowest cost of a standard double room in high season, including 20% V.A.T.

WESTMINSTER, ST. JAMES'S, AND ROYAL LONDON

WESTMINSTER

$$$$ HOTEL Fodor's Choice ★ **The Corinthia.** The London outpost of the exclusive Corinthia chain is design heaven-on-earth, with levels of service that make anyone feel like a VIP. **Pros:** so much luxury and elegance you'll feel like royalty. **Cons:** prices jump to the stratosphere once the cheapest rooms sell out. *Rooms from: £426* ✉ *Whitehall Pl., Westminster* ☎ *020/7930–8181* 🌐 *www.corinthia.com* *294 rooms* *Breakfast* Ⓜ *Embankment* ✣ *G4.*

$$$ HOTEL FAMILY **DoubleTree by Hilton Hotel London Westminster.** Spectacular views of the river, Big Ben, and the London Eye fill the floor-to-ceiling windows in this rather stark, steel-and-glass building steps from the Tate Britain, and a plethora of techy perks await inside. **Pros:** amazing views; flat screens and other high-tech gadgetry. **Cons:** small bedrooms; tiny bathrooms; TV has to be operated through a computer (confusing if you're not used to it). *Rooms from:* ✉ *30 John Islip St., Westminster* ☎ *020/7630–1000* 🌐 *www.doubletreewestminsterhotel.com* *444 rooms, 16 suites* *Some meals* Ⓜ *Westminster, Pimlico* ✣ *F5.*

$$$$ HOTEL Fodor's Choice ★ **Hotel 41.** Faultless service; sumptuous designer furnishings and a sense of fun to boot—this impeccable hotel breathes new life into the cliché "thinks of everything." Yet the epithet is really quite apt. **Pros:** impeccable service; beautiful and stylish; Buckingham Palace is on your doorstep. **Cons:** unusual design is not for everyone. *Rooms from:* ✉ *41 Buckingham Palace Rd., Victoria* ☎ *020/7300–0041* 🌐 *www.41hotel.com* *26 rooms, 4 suites, 2 apartments* *Breakfast* Ⓜ *Victoria* ✣ *E5.*

$$ HOTEL **Lime Tree Hotel.** In a central neighborhood where hotels veer from wildly overpriced at one extreme to grimy boltholes at the other, the Lime Tree gets the boutique style just about right—and at a surprisingly reasonable cost for the neighborhood. **Pros:** lovely and helpful hosts; great location; rooms are decent size. **Cons:** cheaper rooms are small; some are up several flights of stairs and there's no elevator; two-night minimum on weekends. *Rooms from: £165* ✉ *135–137 Ebury St., Victoria* ☎ *020/7730–8191* 🌐 *www.limetreehotel.co.uk* *25 rooms* *Breakfast* Ⓜ *Victoria, Sloane Sq.* ✣ *D5.*

WHERE SHOULD I STAY?

	NEIGHBORHOOD VIBE	PROS	CONS
Westminster, St. James's, and Royal London	This historic section, aka "Royal London," is home to major tourist attractions like Buckingham Palace.	Central area near tourist sites; easy Tube access; considered a safe area to stay.	Mostly expensive lodging options; few restaurants and entertainment venues nearby.
Soho and Covent Garden	A tourist hub with endless entertainment on the streets and in theaters and clubs—it's party central for young adults.	Buzzing area with plenty to see and do; late-night entertainment abounds; wonderful shopping district.	The area tends to be noisy at night; few budget hotels; keep your wits about you at night, and watch out for pickpockets.
Bloomsbury, Holborn, Hampstead, and Islington	Diverse area that is part bustling business center and part tranquil respite with tree-lined streets and squares.	Easy access to Tube, and 15 minutes to city center; major sights, like British Museum are here.	Busy streets filled with honking trucks and roving students; the area around King's Cross can be sketchy—particularly at night.
The City and South Bank	London's financial district, where most of the city's banks and businesses are headquartered.	Central location with easy transportation access; great hotel deals in South Bank; many major sights nearby.	It can be as quiet as a tomb after 8 pm; many nearby restaurants and shops close over the weekend.
East End	Hipster central, with great art, restaurant, and nightlife scenes.	Great for art lovers, shoppers, and business execs with meetings in Canary Wharf.	Still a transitional area around the edges, parts of Hackney can be a bit dodgy at night; 20-minute Tube ride from central London.
Kensington, Knightsbridge, and Mayfair	This is one of London's most upscale neighborhoods, with designer boutiques and five-star hotels designed to appeal to those who can afford the best.	Diverse hotel selection; great area for meandering walks; superb shopping district; London's capital of high-end shopping.	Depending on where you are, the nearest Tube might be a hike; residential area might be too quiet for some. Few budget hotel or restaurant options.
Notting Hill and Bayswater	This is an upscale, trendy area favored by locals, with plenty of good hotels.	Hotel deals abound in Bayswater if you know where to look; gorgeous greenery in Hyde Park; great independent boutiques.	Choose the wrong place and you may end up in a flea pit; residential areas may be too quiet at night for some.
Regent's Park and Hampstead	Village-like enclaves where successful actors and intellectuals go to settle down.	Good access to central London; bucolic charm.	Some distance from center; lack of hotel and dining options.

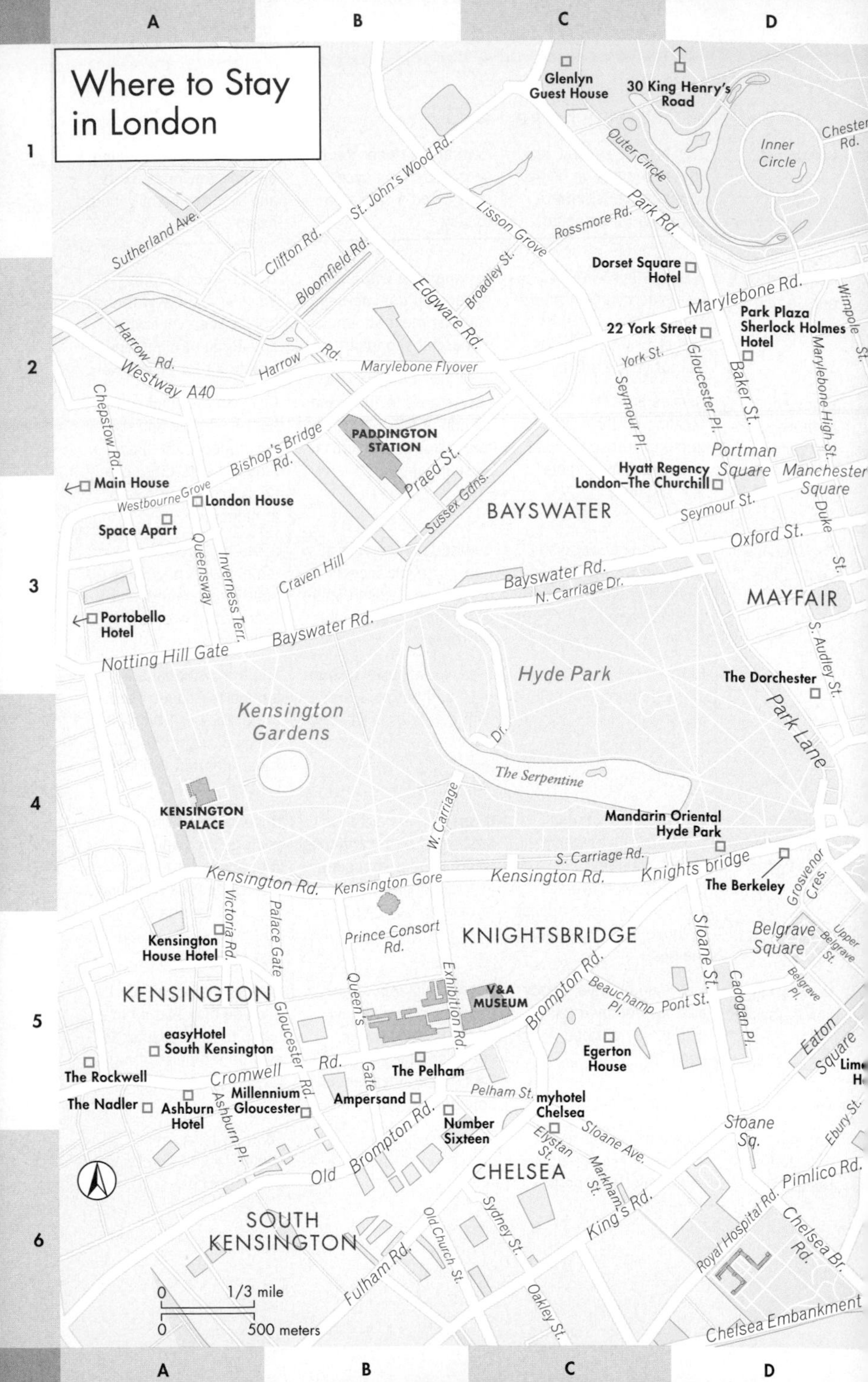

Where to Stay in London
A
B
C
D
1
2
3
4
5
6
Glenlyn Guest House
30 King Henry's Road
Outer Circle
Inner Circle
Chester Rd.
St. John's Wood Rd.
Lisson Grove
Rossmore Rd.
Park Rd.
Sutherland Ave.
Clifton Rd.
Bloomfield Rd.
Broadley St.
Edgware Rd.
Dorset Square Hotel
Marylebone Rd.
Wimpole St.
22 York Street
Park Plaza Sherlock Holmes Hotel
Harrow Rd.
Westway A40
Harrow Rd.
Marylebone Flyover
York St.
Gloucester Pl.
Baker St.
Marylebone High St.
Seymour Pl.
Chepstow Rd.
Bishop's Bridge Rd.
PADDINGTON STATION
Praed St.
Portman Square
Manchester Square
Hyatt Regency London–The Churchill
Main House
Westbourne Grove
London House
Sussex Gdns.
BAYSWATER
Seymour St.
Space Apart
Duke St.
Oxford St.
Queensway
Inverness Terr.
Craven Hill
Bayswater Rd.
N. Carriage Dr.
MAYFAIR
Portobello Hotel
Bayswater Rd.
S. Audley St.
Notting Hill Gate
Hyde Park
The Dorchester
Kensington Gardens
Park Lane
Dr.
The Serpentine
W. Carriage
KENSINGTON PALACE
Mandarin Oriental Hyde Park
S. Carriage Rd.
Kensington Rd.
Kensington Gore
Kensington Rd.
Knights bridge
The Berkeley
Grosvenor Cres.
Victoria Rd.
Palace Gate
Prince Consort Rd.
KNIGHTSBRIDGE
Sloane St.
Belgrave Square
Upper Belgrave St.
Kensington House Hotel
Brompton Rd.
Beauchamp Pl.
Cadogan Pl.
Belgrave Pl.
KENSINGTON
Gloucester Rd.
Queen's Gate
Exhibition Rd.
V&A MUSEUM
Pont St.
easyHotel South Kensington
Egerton House
Eaton Square
The Rockwell
Cromwell Rd.
The Pelham
The Nadler
Ashburn Hotel
Millennium Gloucester
Ashburn Pl.
Ampersand
Pelham St.
myhotel Chelsea
Number Sixteen
Sloane Ave.
Elystan St.
Stoane Sq.
Ebury St.
Old Brompton Rd.
CHELSEA
Markham St.
Pimlico Rd.
King's Rd.
Royal Hospital Rd.
SOUTH KENSINGTON
Old Church St.
Sydney St.
Chelsea Br. Rd.
Fulham Rd.
0
1/3 mile
0
500 meters
Oakley St.
Chelsea Embankment

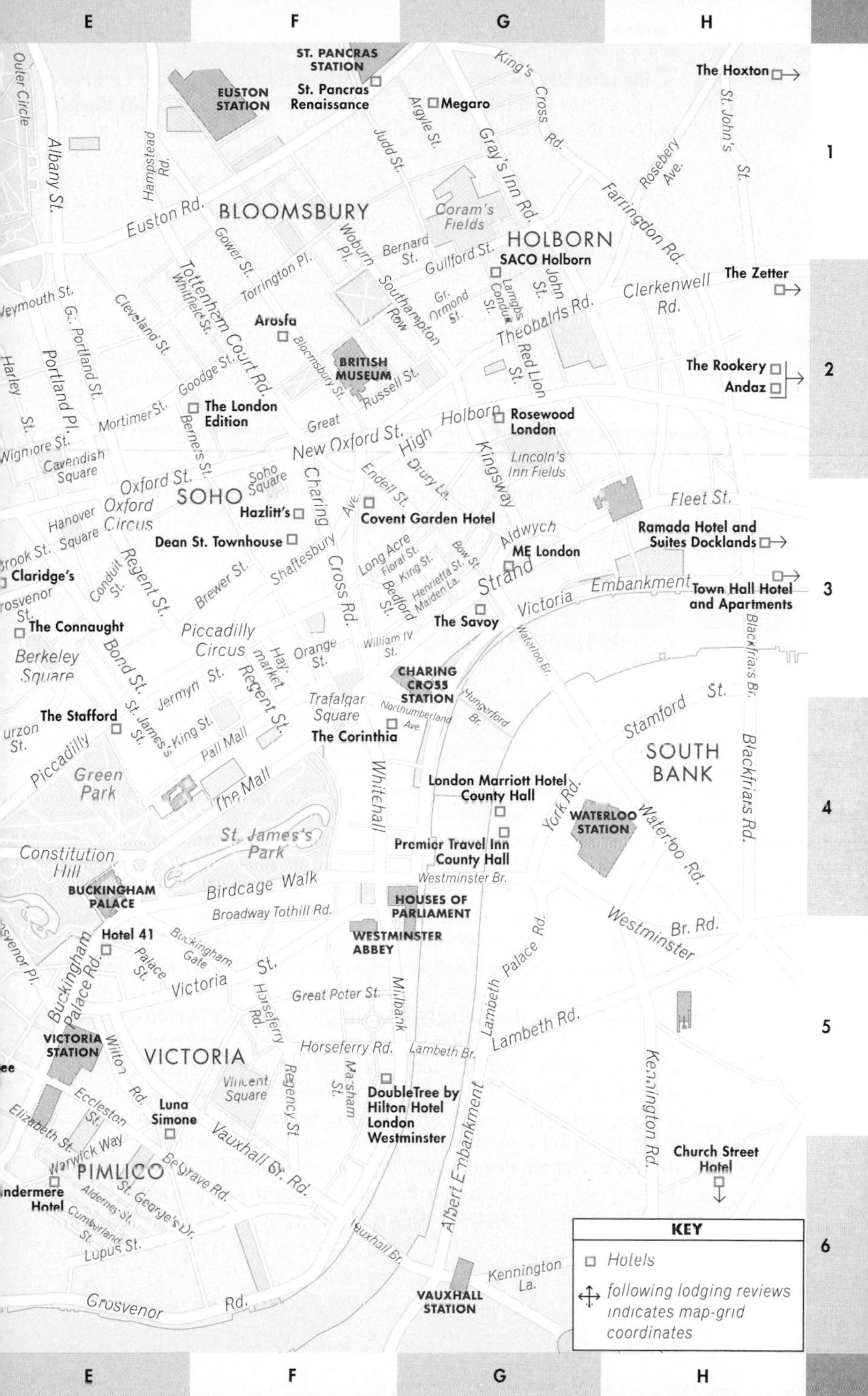
E
F
G
H
1
2
3
4
5
6
ST. PANCRAS STATION
EUSTON STATION
St. Pancras Renaissance
Megaro
The Hoxton
BLOOMSBURY
HOLBORN
SACO Holborn
The Zetter
Arosfa
BRITISH MUSEUM
The Rookery
Andaz
The London Edition
Rosewood London
SOHO
Hazlitt's
Covent Garden Hotel
Dean St. Townhouse
ME London
Ramada Hotel and Suites Docklands
Town Hall Hotel and Apartments
Claridge's
The Connaught
The Savoy
CHARING CROSS STATION
The Stafford
The Corinthia
SOUTH BANK
London Marriott Hotel County Hall
WATERLOO STATION
Premier Travel Inn County Hall
BUCKINGHAM PALACE
HOUSES OF PARLIAMENT
WESTMINSTER ABBEY
Hotel 41
VICTORIA STATION
VICTORIA
DoubleTree by Hilton Hotel London Westminster
Luna Simone
PIMLICO
Windermere Hotel
Church Street Hotel
VAUXHALL STATION
Outer Circle
Albany St.
Hampstead Rd.
Euston Rd.
King's Cross Rd.
Argyle St.
Judd St.
Gray's Inn Rd.
Rosebery Ave.
St. John's St.
Farringdon Rd.
Coram's Fields
Gower St.
Woburn Pl.
Bernard St.
Guilford St.
Torrington Pl.
Tottenham Court Rd.
Whitfield St.
Southampton Row
Gr. Ormond St.
Lambs Conduit St.
John St.
Theobalds Rd.
Clerkenwell Rd.
Weymouth St.
Gt. Portland St.
Cleveland St.
Harley St.
Portland Pl.
Goodge St.
Bloomsbury St.
Russell St.
Red Lion St.
Mortimer St.
Berners St.
Great Russell St.
High Holborn
New Oxford St.
Wigmore St.
Cavendish Square
Oxford St.
Soho Square
Charing Cross Rd.
Endell St.
Drury La.
Kingsway
Lincoln's Inn Fields
Fleet St.
Hanover Square
Oxford Circus
Shaftesbury Ave.
Long Acre
Floral St.
King St.
Bow St.
Aldwych
Brook St.
Conduit St.
Regent St.
Brewer St.
Bedford St.
Henrietta St.
Maiden La.
Strand
Embankment
Victoria
Grosvenor St.
Piccadilly Circus
Orange St.
William IV St.
Waterloo Br.
Blackfriars Br.
Berkeley Square
Bond St.
Jermyn St.
Haymarket
Trafalgar Square
Northumberland Ave.
Hungerford Br.
Stamford St.
Curzon St.
St. James's St.
King St.
Pall Mall
Piccadilly
Green Park
The Mall
Whitehall
York Rd.
Blackfriars Rd.
St. James's Park
Constitution Hill
Waterloo Rd.
Birdcage Walk
Westminster Br.
Broadway
Tothill Rd.
Westminster Br. Rd.
Grosvenor Pl.
Buckingham Gate
Palace St.
Buckingham Palace Rd.
Victoria St.
Horseferry Rd.
Great Peter St.
Millbank
Lambeth Palace Rd.
Lambeth Rd.
Lambeth Br.
Wilton Rd.
Vincent Square
Regency St.
Marsham St.
Kennington Rd.
Eccleston St.
Elizabeth St.
Warwick Way
Vauxhall Br. Rd.
Belgrave Rd.
St. George's Dr.
Alderney St.
Cumberland St.
Albert Embankment
Lupus St.
Vauxhall Br.
Kennington La.
Grosvenor Rd.
KEY
Hotels
following lodging reviews indicates map-grid coordinates

$$ HOTEL **The Luna Simone Hotel.** This delightful and friendly little family-run hotel, a short stroll from Buckingham Palace, is a real find for the price in central London. **Pros:** friendly and well run; family rooms are outstanding value; superb location. **Cons:** tiny bathrooms; thin walls; no elevator or air-conditioning. *Rooms from: £134* *47–49 Belgrave Rd., Pimlico* *020/7834–5897* *www.lunasimonehotel.com* *36 rooms* *Breakfast* *Pimlico, Victoria* *E6.*

$$ HOTEL **Windermere Hotel.** This sweet and rather elegant old hotel, on the premises of London's first B&B (in 1881), is a decent, well-located option. **Pros:** good location close to Victoria Station; free Wi-Fi; good amenities for an old hotel of this size, including air-conditioning and an elevator. **Cons:** rooms and bathrooms are tiny. *Rooms from: £148* *142–144 Warwick Way, Victoria* *020/7834–5163* *www.windermere-hotel.co.uk* *19 rooms* *Breakfast* *Victoria* *E6.*

ST. JAMES'S

$$$$ HOTEL Fodor's Choice ★ **The Stafford London.** This is a rare find: a posh hotel that's equal parts elegance and friendliness, and located in one of the few peaceful spots in the area, down a small lane behind Piccadilly. **Pros:** great staff; big, luxurious rooms; quiet location. **Cons:** traditional style is not to all tastes; perks in the more expensive rooms could be more generous (free airport transfer, but only one-way; free clothes pressing, only one item per day). *Rooms from: £365* *St. James's Pl., St. James's* *020/7493–0111* *www.thestaffordlondon.com* *81 rooms* *Breakfast* *Green Park* *E4.*

SOHO AND COVENT GARDEN

SOHO

$$$ HOTEL Fodor's Choice ★ **Dean Street Townhouse.** Discreet and unpretentious, but oh-so-stylish—and right in the heart of Soho—this place has a bohemian vibe and an excellent modern British restaurant, hung with pieces by renowned artists like Peter Blake and Tracy Emin. **Pros:** übercool; resembles an upper-class pied-à-terre. **Cons:** some rooms are extremely small; rooms at the front of the building can be noisy, especially on weekends. *Rooms from: £260* *69–71 Dean St., Soho* *020/7434–1775* *www.deanstreettownhouse.com* *39 rooms* *Breakfast* *Leicester Sq., Tottenham Court Rd.* *F3.*

$$$ HOTEL **Hazlitt's.** This disarmingly friendly place, full of personality, robust antiques, and claw-foot tubs, occupies three connected early-18th-century houses, one of which was the last home of essayist William Hazlitt (1778–1830). **Pros:** great for lovers of art and antiques; historic atmosphere with lots of small sitting rooms and wooden staircases; truly beautiful and relaxed. **Cons:** no in-house restaurant; breakfast is £12 extra; no elevators. *Rooms from: £225* *6 Frith St., Soho* *020/7434–1771* *www.hazlittshotel.com* *20 rooms, 3 suites* *No meals* *Tottenham Court Rd.* *F3.*

COVENT GARDEN

$$$$ HOTEL Fodor'sChoice ★ **Covent Garden Hotel.** It's little wonder this is now the London home-away-from-home for off-duty celebrities, actors, and style mavens, with its Covent Garden location and guest rooms that are design-magazine stylish. **Pros:** great for star-spotting; supertrendy. **Cons:** you can feel you don't matter if you're not famous; location in Covent Garden can be a bit boisterous. *Rooms from: £384 ✉ 10 Monmouth St., Covent Garden ☎ 020/7806–1000, 800/553–6674 in U.S. www.firmdale.com 55 rooms, 3 suites Some meals M Covent Garden ✣ F3.*

$$$$ HOTEL Fodor'sChoice ★ **ME London.** One can only imagine the endless concept meetings that went into this shiny fortress of luxury that brought a splash of modern cool to a rather stuffy patch of the Strand when it opened in 2013—and the result is almost achingly on-trend. **Pros:** sleek and fashionable; full of high-tech comforts; excellent service; stunning views from rooftop bar. **Cons:** design can sometimes verge on form over function; very small closets and in-room storage areas; ludicrously high average price tag. *Rooms from: £510 ✉ 336 The Strand, Covent Garden ☎ 0808/234–1953 www.melia.com 141 rooms, 16 suites Breakfast M Covent Garden ✣ G3.*

$$$$ HOTEL Fodor'sChoice ★ **The Savoy.** One of London's most iconic hotels maintains its status at the top with winning attributes of impeccable service, stunning decor, and a desirable Covent Garden location. **Pros:** one of the top hotels in Europe; iconic pedigree; Thames-side location. **Cons:** everything comes with a price tag; guest rooms can be noisy, particularly on lower floors; right off the super-busy Strand. *Rooms from: £354 ✉ The Strand, Covent Garden ☎ 020/7836–4343, 800/257 7544 in U.S. www.fairmont.com/savoy-london 206 rooms, 62 suites Breakfast M Covent Garden, Charing Cross ✣ G3.*

BLOOMSBURY AND HOLBORN

BLOOMSBURY

$$ B&B/INN **Arosfa.** Simple, friendly, and pleasantly quirky, this little B&B, once the home of Pre-Raphaelite painter Sir John Everett Millais, is on an elegant Georgian street within walking distance of the West End and the British Museum. **Pros:** friendly staff; check-in from 7 am; good location for museums and theaters; free Wi-Fi. **Cons:** some rooms are very small; bathrooms have showers only; few services. *Rooms from: £138 ✉ 83 Gower St., Bloomsbury ☎ 020/7636–2115 www.arosfalondon.com 16 rooms Breakfast M Goodge St., Euston Sq. ✣ F2.*

$$ HOTEL **Megaro.** Directly across the street from St Pancras International station (for the Eurostar), the snazzy, well-designed, modern bedrooms here surround guests with startlingly contemporary style and amenities that include powerful showers and espresso machines. **Pros:** comfortable beds; great location for Eurostar; short hop on Tube to city center. **Cons:** neighborhood isn't great; standard rooms are small; interiors may be a bit stark for some. *Rooms from: £170 ✉ Belgrove St., King's Cross ☎ 020/7843–2222 www.hotelmegaro.co.uk 49 rooms Breakfast M Kings Cross, St. Pancras ✣ G1.*

$$$ HOTEL Fodor's Choice ★ **St. Pancras Renaissance.** Reopened in 2011 after nearly a century of dereliction, this stunningly restored Victorian landmark—replete with gingerbread turrets and castlelike ornaments—started as a love letter to the golden age of railways; now it's one of London's most sophisticated places to stay. **Pros:** unique and beautiful; faultless service; just an elevator ride to the Eurostar. **Cons:** very popular bar and restaurant; streets outside are busy 24 hours. *Rooms from: £219 Euston Rd., King's Cross 020/7841–3540 www.marriott.com 207 rooms, 38 suites Breakfast Kings Cross, St. Pancras. National Rail: Kings Cross, St. Pancras F1.*

HOLBORN

$$$$ HOTEL **Rosewood London.** So striking it was featured in the movie *Howards End,* this landmark structure (built by the Pearl Assurance Company in 1914) now houses a beautiful hotel with a clubby atmosphere. **Pros:** gorgeous, romantic space; excellent restaurant; great spa; friendly service. **Cons:** luxury comes at a price; area is a ghost town at night and on weekends. *Rooms from: £380 252 High Holborn, Holborn 020/7781–8888, 888/767–3966 in U.S. www.rosewoodhotels.com/en/london 294 rooms, 12 suites Some meals Holborn G2.*

$$$ RENTAL **SACO Holborn.** Down a quiet backstreet, a 10-minute walk from the British Museum, these serviced apartments are spacious, modern, and extremely well equipped, including a kitchen with dishwasher and washing machine. **Pros:** more independence than hotels; pleasant and spacious accommodations; on-site parking. **Cons:** exterior is dated; you must provide own bedding for baby cots. *Rooms from: £246 82 Lamb's Conduit St., Holborn 0845/122–0405 www.sacoapartments.co.uk 30 apartments (mixture of studios, 1-, 2-, and 3-bed) No meals Russell Sq. G2.*

$$$ HOTEL Fodor's Choice ★ **The Zetter.** The five-story atrium, art-deco staircase, and slick European restaurant hint at the delights to come in this converted warehouse—a breath of fresh air with its playful color schemes, elegant wallpapers, and wonderful views of The City from the higher floors. **Pros:** huge amounts of character; big rooms; free Wi-Fi; award-winning restaurant. **Cons:** rooms with good views cost more. *Rooms from: £205 86–88 Clerkenwell Rd., Clerkenwell 020/7324–4444 www.thezetter.com 59 rooms Breakfast Farringdon H2.*

FITZROVIA

$$$$ HOTEL Fodor's Choice ★ **The London Edition.** A solidly bohemian air permeates this handsome new hotel in the heart of Fitzrovia, which opened to much fanfare in the fall of 2013. **Pros:** very fashionable; great bars; beautifully designed bedrooms. **Cons:** rooms may feel small to some; lobby can get crowded with trendsetters descending upon the bars and nightclub. *Rooms from: £345 10 Berners St., Fitzrovia 020/7781–0000 editionhotels.marriott.com/london 173 rooms Breakfast Oxford Circus F2.*

THE CITY

$$ HOTEL Fodor's Choice ★ **The Rookery.** An absolutely unique and beautiful 1725 town house, the Rookery is the kind of place where you want to allow quality time to enjoy and soak up the atmosphere. **Pros:** helpful staff; free Wi-Fi; good deals in the off-season. **Cons:** breakfast costs extra; Tube ride to tourist sites. *Rooms from: £165 ✉ 12 Peter's La., at Cowcross St., The City ☎ 020/7336–0931 🌐 www.rookeryhotel.com 30 rooms, 3 suites No meals Ⓜ Farringdon ⊕ H2.*

THE EAST END

$$ HOTEL **Andaz.** Swanky and upscale, this hotel sports a modern, masculine design, and novel check-in procedure—instead of standing at a desk, guests sit in a lounge while a staff member with a handheld computer takes their information. **Pros:** nice attention to detail; guests can borrow an iPod from the front desk; no standing in line to check in; "healthy minibars" are stocked with nuts, fruit, and yogurt. **Cons:** sparse interior design is not for all; rates rise significantly for midweek stays. *Rooms from: £155 ✉ 40 Liverpool St., East End ☎ 020/7961–1234, 800/492–8804 in U.S. 🌐 www.andaz.hyatt.com 267 rooms Breakfast Ⓜ Liverpool St. ⊕ H2.*

$ HOTEL Fodor's Choice ★ **The Hoxton Hotel.** The design throughout this trendy East London lodging is contemporary—but not so modern as to be absurd—and in keeping with a claim to combine a country-lodge lifestyle with true urban living, a fire crackles in the lobby. **Pros:** cool vibe; neighborhood known for funky galleries and boutiques; huge weekend discounts; way-cool restaurant; one hour of free international calls. **Cons:** price rockets during the week; away from tourist sights. *Rooms from: £69 ✉ 81 Great Eastern St., East End ☎ 020/7550–1000 🌐 www.hoxtonhotels.com 205 rooms Breakfast Ⓜ Shoreditch High St. ⊕ H1.*

$ HOTEL **Ramada Hotel and Suites Docklands.** Many of the sleek and modern rooms at this hotel, dramatically set at the edge of the river in the rejuvenated Docklands area of East London, have water views, while others have views of the city. **Pros:** waterfront views; free Wi-Fi; great value weekend rates. **Cons:** lacks character; area is tumbleweed quiet on weekends; about a 20-minute Tube ride to central London. *Rooms from: £96 ✉ ExCel, 2 Festoon Way, Royal Victoria Dock, East End ☎ 020/7540–4820 🌐 www.ramadadocklands.co.uk 224 rooms Breakfast Ⓜ Old St. ⊕ H3.*

$$ HOTEL **Town Hall Hotel and Apartments.** An art-deco town hall, abandoned in the early 1980s and turned into a chic hotel in 2010, is now a lively and stylish place, with the best of the building's elegant original features intact. **Pros:** beautifully designed; lovely staff; big discounts on weekends. **Cons:** though touted as "cool" and "cutting edge," this is not a great part of town; a 15-minute Tube ride from Central London. *Rooms from: £148 ✉ Patriot Sq., Bethnal Green, East End ☎ 020/7657–8080 🌐 www.townhallhotel.com 98 rooms, 86 suites Breakfast Ⓜ Bethnal Green ⊕ H3.*

RENTALS AND HOME EXCHANGES

APARTMENT RENTALS

For a home base that's roomy enough for a family and that comes with cooking facilities, consider renting furnished "flats" (the British word for apartments).

INTERNATIONAL AGENTS

Hideaways International. This company offers boutique hotels, tours, and cruises. ✉ *767 Islington St., Portsmouth* ☎ *603/430–4433, 800/843–4433* 🌐 *www.hideaways.com.*

LOCAL AGENTS

The Apartment Service. This agency specializes in executive apartments for business travelers, so prices are high, but so is the quality. ✉ *5 Francis Grove, Wimbledon* ☎ *020/8944–1444* 🌐 *www.apartmentservice.com.*

At Home in London. Rooms in private homes in Knightsbridge, Kensington, Mayfair, Chelsea, and West London are handled by this agency. ✉ *70 Black Lion La., Hammersmith* ☎ *020/8748–2701* 🌐 *www.athomeinlondon.co.uk.*

The Bed and Breakfast Club. Contact this company for delightful little London apartments, in Kensington, Chelsea, and Knightsbridge, costing from around £50–£140 per night with full English breakfasts. ✉ *405 Kings Rd., Suite 192, Chelsea* ☎ *01243/370–692* 🌐 *www.thebedandbreakfastclub.co.uk*
☞ *There's a 2.5% fee for using a credit card; debit cards incur no fees; the full price of room must be paid in advance. Check cancellation policies carefully.*

Landmark Trust. Specializing in unusual and historic buildings, this agency has London apartments starting at around £650 for a four-night-minimum stay. ✉ *Shottesbrooke, Maidenhead* ☎ *01628/825–925* 🌐 *www.landmarktrust.org.uk.*

HOME EXCHANGES

If you would like to exchange your home for someone else's, join a home-exchange organization, which will send you its updated listings of available exchanges for a year.

Intervac U.S. It costs from $99 per year for a listing and online access with this company. ☎ *866/884–7567* 🌐 *us.intervac-homeexchange.com.*

THE SOUTH BANK

$ HOTEL Fodor's Choice ★

Church Street Hotel. Like rays of sunshine in gritty South London, these rooms above a popular tapas restaurant are individually decorated in rich, bold tones and authentic Central American touches—elaborately painted crucifixes; tiles handmade in Guadalajara; homemade iron bed frames. **Pros:** unique and arty; great breakfasts; lovely staff; closer to central London than it might appear. **Cons:** a trendy but not great part of town (stay out of neighboring Elephant and Castle); would suit adventurous young things more than families; a mile from a Tube station (though bus connections are handier); some rooms have shared bathrooms. *$ Rooms from: £90* ✉ *29–33 Camberwell Church St., Camberwell, South East* ☎ *020/7703–5984* 🌐 *www.churchstreethotel.com* *31 rooms* *Breakfast* Ⓜ *Oval St.* ✥ *H6.*

$$$ HOTEL **London Marriott Hotel County Hall.** This grand hotel on the Thames enjoys perhaps the most iconic view in the city—right next door is the London Eye, and directly across the River Thames are the Houses of Parliament and Big Ben. Until the 1980s this building was the seat of London's government, and the public areas are suitably grand, full of pedimented archways, bronze doors, and acres of polished mahogany. **Pros:** handy for South Bank arts scene, London Eye, and Westminster; great gym; good weekend discounts. **Cons:** interior design can be overdone for some tastes; breakfasts are pricey; rooms facing the river cost extra. *Rooms from: £255 County Hall, Westminster Bridge Rd., South Bank 020/7928–5200, 888/236–2427 in U.S. www.marriott.com 186 rooms, 14 suites Breakfast Westminster, Waterloo. National Rail: Waterloo G4.*

$ HOTEL FAMILY **Premier Travel Inn County Hall.** The small but nicely decorated rooms at this budget choice share the same County Hall complex as the fancier London Marriott Hotel County Hall, and though it has none of the spectacular river views, and the facilities are more basic, the selling point is the same convenient location at a fraction of the price. **Pros:** fantastic location for the South Bank; bargains to be had if you book in advance; kids (sharing with adults) stay free. **Cons:** no river views; limited services; cookie-cutter chain hotel atmosphere; on a busy road. *Rooms from: £90 Belvedere Rd., South Bank 0871/527–8648 www.premierinn.com 313 rooms Breakfast Westminster, Waterloo. National Rail: Waterloo G4.*

KENSINGTON, KNIGHTSBRIDGE, AND MAYFAIR

KENSINGTON

$$$ HOTEL **Ampersand.** A sense of style emanates from every surface of this sumptuous hotel in the heart of Kensington—but the playful, vintage vibe lends the property a refreshingly down-to-earth feel in a neighborhood that often feels cooler-than-thou. **Pros:** flawless design; great service; good restaurant. **Cons:** ground-floor rooms can be noisy. *Rooms from: £216 10 Harrington Rd., Kensington www.ampersandhotel.com 106 rooms, 5 suites Breakfast Gloucester Rd. B5.*

$$ HOTEL **Ashburn Hotel.** A short walk from Gloucester Road Tube station and within walking distance of Harrods and the Kensington museums, the Ashburn is one of the better "boutique" hotels in this part of town. **Pros:** friendly atmosphere; free Wi-Fi; turndown gift (different every night). **Cons:** summer prices sometimes hike the cost. *Rooms from: £179 111 Cromwell Rd., Kensington 020/7938–5930 reservations, 020/7244–1999 www.ashburn-hotel.co.uk 55 rooms, 3 suites Breakfast Gloucester Rd. A5.*

$ HOTEL **easyHotel South Kensington.** London's original "pod hotel" has tiny rooms with a double bed, private shower room, and little else—each brightly decorated in the easyGroup's trademark orange and white (to match their budget airline easyJet). **Pros:** amazing price; safe and decent enough space. **Cons:** not for the claustrophobic—rooms are truly tiny and most have no windows; six floors and no elevator; basic as basic can be; inquiries are via the website only—they don't even have a phone.

Rooms from: £47 ✉ 14 Lexham Gardens, Kensington 🌐 www.easyhotel.com 34 rooms No meals Ⓜ Gloucester Rd. ⊕ A5.

$$ HOTEL **Kensington House Hotel.** A short stroll from High Street Kensington and Kensington Gardens, this refurbished 19th-century town house has streamlined, contemporary rooms with large windows letting in plenty of light, comfortable beds with luxurious fabrics and soft comforters. **Pros:** attractive design; relaxing setting; free Wi-Fi. **Cons:** rooms are small; bathrooms are minuscule; the elevator is Lilliputian. *Rooms from: £132 ✉ 15–16 Prince of Wales Terr., Kensington ☎ 020/7937–2345 🌐 www.kenhouse.com 39 rooms, 2 suites Breakfast Ⓜ High Street Kensington ⊕ A5.*

$ HOTEL **Millennium Gloucester.** With a Tube station opposite and Kensington's many attractions nearby, this hotel is both convenient and alluring, its sleek and opulent lobby, with polished wood columns, a warming fireplace, and glittering chandeliers giving way to guest rooms with a traditionally masculine look. **Pros:** good deals available if you book in advance. **Cons:** lighting in some bedrooms is a bit too subtle; bathrooms are relatively small. *Rooms from: £91 ✉ 4–18 Harrington Gardens, Kensington ☎ 020/7373–6030 🌐 www.millenniumhotels.co.uk 610 rooms Breakfast Ⓜ Gloucester Rd. ⊕ B5.*

$$ HOTEL **The Nadler.** This newly refurbished "aparthotel" in a creamy white Georgian town house offers a useful compromise between full-service hotel and the freedom of self-catering in the form of comfortable rooms with a stylish, modern look and tiny kitchenettes. **Pros:** great alternative to hotel; handy mini-kitchens; free Wi-Fi; 24-hour reception. **Cons:** basic rooms are small; movies in entertainment system are pay-per-view; 15-minute Tube ride to central London. *Rooms from: £142 ✉ 25 Courtfield Gardens, South Kensington ☎ 020/7244–2255 🌐 www.thenadler.com 65 rooms No meals Ⓜ Earls Ct. ⊕ A5.*

$$$ HOTEL **Number Sixteen.** Guest rooms at this lovely luxury guesthouse, just around the corner from the Victoria & Albert Museum, look like they come from the pages of *Architectural Digest*, and the delightful garden is an added bonus. **Pros:** just the right level of helpful service; interiors are gorgeous. **Cons:** no restaurant; small elevator. *Rooms from: £294 ✉ 16 Sumner Pl., South Kensington ☎ 020/7589–5232, 888/559–5508 in U.S. 🌐 www.firmdale.com 42 rooms Breakfast Ⓜ South Kensington ⊕ B5.*

$$ HOTEL **The Pelham Hotel.** One of the first and most stylish of London's famed "boutique" hotels, this still-chic choice is but a short stroll away from the Natural History, Science, and V&A museums. **Pros:** great location for museum-hopping; gorgeous marble bathrooms; soigné interior design; lovely staff; good package deals for online booking. **Cons:** taller guests will find themselves cursing the top-floor rooms with sloping ceilings. *Rooms from: £187 ✉ 15 Cromwell Pl., South Kensington ☎ 020/7589–8288, 888/757–5587 in U.S. 🌐 www.pelhamhotel.co.uk 47 rooms, 4 suites Breakfast Ⓜ South Kensington ⊕ B5.*

$$ HOTEL **The Rockwell.** Despite being on the notoriously traffic-clogged Cromwell Road, this excellent little place is one of the best boutique hotels in this part of London—and windows have good soundproofing. **Pros:** large bedrooms; stylish surroundings; helpful staff; advance booking

can drop the price below £100. **Cons:** on a busy road; 20-minute Tube ride to central London. *Rooms from: £127* ✉ *181 Cromwell Rd., South Kensington* ☎ *020/7244–2000* *www.therockwell.com* *38 rooms, 2 suites* *Breakfast* Ⓜ *Earls Court* ✣ *A5.*

2

CHELSEA

$$ HOTEL **myhotel chelsea.** Rooms at this small, chic charmer—tucked away down a side street in an upscale neighborhood—are bijou tiny but sophisticated, with mauve satin throws atop crisp white down comforters. **Pros:** stylish rooms made for relaxation; good neighborhood. **Cons:** price a bit high for what you get; tiny rooms; no restaurant. *Rooms from: £144* ✉ *35 Ixworth Pl., Chelsea* ☎ *020/7225–7500* *www.myhotels.com* *45 rooms, 9 suites* *Breakfast* Ⓜ *South Kensington* ✣ *C5.*

KNIGHTSBRIDGE

$$$$ HOTEL **The Berkeley.** Convenient for Knightsbridge shopping, the very elegant Berkeley is known for its renowned restaurants and luxuries that culminate—literally—in a splendid penthouse swimming pool. **Pros:** lavish and elegant; attentive service; prices aren't quite as stratospheric as some high-end places. **Cons:** you'll need your best designer clothes to fit in. *Rooms from: £480* ✉ *Wilton Pl., Knightsbridge* ☎ *020/7235–6000, 800/637–2869 in U.S.* *www.the-berkeley.co.uk* *103 rooms, 55 suites* *Breakfast* Ⓜ *Knightsbridge* ✣ *D4.*

$$$$ HOTEL **Egerton House.** Sensationally soigné, chicly decorated, and feeling like your own private London home, this hotel has some truly luxuriant design touches, including guest rooms lavishly decorated with rich fabrics and a knockout white-on-gold dining room. **Pros:** lovely staff; magnificent interiors; striking art; seniors discounts available. **Cons:** some style touches a little too froufrou—even if Toulouse-Lautrec would have approved. *Rooms from: £315* ✉ *17–19 Egerton Terr., Knightsbridge* ☎ *020/7589–2412, 877/955–1515 in U.S.* *www.redcarnationhotels.com* *23 rooms, 6 suites* *Breakfast* Ⓜ *Knightsbridge, South Kensington* ✣ *C5.*

$$$$ HOTEL Fodor'sChoice ★ **Mandarin Oriental Hyde Park.** Built in 1880, the Mandarin Oriental welcomes you with one of the most exuberantly Victorian facades in town, then fast-forwards you to high-trend modern London, thanks to striking and luxurious guest rooms filled with high-tech gadgets. **Pros:** great shopping at your doorstep; amazing views of Hyde Park; excellent service. **Cons:** nothing comes cheap; you must dress for dinner (and lunch and breakfast). *Rooms from: £462* ✉ *66 Knightsbridge, Knightsbridge* ☎ *020/7235–2000* *www.mandarinoriental.com/london* *177 rooms, 23 suites* *Breakfast* Ⓜ *Knightsbridge* ✣ *D4.*

MAYFAIR

$$ B&B/INN **22 York Street.** This Georgian town house has a cozy, family feel, with polished pine floors and fetching antiques decorating the homey, individually furnished guest rooms. **Pros:** good location for shoppers; friendly hosts; nicely flexible check-in times; entirely no-smoking. **Cons:** if you take away the great location, you're paying a lot for a B&B; not everyone enjoys socializing with strangers over breakfast. *Rooms from:*

£150 ✉ 22 York St., Mayfair ☎ 020/7224–2990 ⊕ www.22yorkstreet.co.uk ⇆ 10 rooms 🍴 Breakfast Ⓜ Baker St. ✣ D2.

$$$$ HOTEL FAMILY Fodor's Choice ★ **Claridge's.** The well-heeled have been meeting—and eating—at Claridge's for generations, and the tradition continues in the original art-deco public spaces of this super-glamorous London institution. **Pros:** see-and-be-seen dining and drinking; serious luxury everywhere—this is an old-money hotel; comics, books, and DVDs to help keep kids amused. **Cons:** better pack your designer wardrobe if you want to fit in with the locals. $ *Rooms from: £480 ✉ Brook St., Mayfair ☎ 020/7629–8860, 866/599–6991 in U.S. ⊕ www.claridges.co.uk ⇆ 136 rooms, 678 suites 🍴 Breakfast Ⓜ Bond St. ✣ E3.*

$$$$ HOTEL FAMILY Fodor's Choice ★ **The Connaught.** A huge favorite of the "we wouldn't dream of staying anywhere else" monied set since its opening in 1917, the Connaught has many dazzlingly modern compliments to its famously historic delights. **Pros:** legendary hotel; great for star-spotting. **Cons:** history comes at a price; bathrooms are small. $ *Rooms from: £540 ✉ Carlos Pl., Mayfair ☎ 020/7499–7070, 866/599–6991 in U.S. ⊕ www.the-connaught.co.uk ⇆ 87 rooms, 34 suites 🍴 Breakfast Ⓜ Bond St. ✣ E3.*

$$$$ HOTEL **The Dorchester.** Few hotels this opulent manage to be as personable as the Dorchester, which opened in 1939 and boasts a prime Park Lane location with unparalleled glamour—gold leaf and marble adorn the public spaces, and guest quarters are awash in English country house–meets–art deco style. **Pros:** historic luxury in 1930s building; lovely views of Hyde Park; top-notch star-spotting; excellent spa; Michelin-starred dining from Alain Ducasse. **Cons:** traditional look is not to all tastes; prices are high; some rooms are rather small. $ *Rooms from: £505 ✉ Park La., Mayfair ☎ 020/7629–8888 ⊕ www.thedorchester.com ⇆ 195 rooms, 55 suites 🍴 Breakfast Ⓜ Marble Arch, Hyde Park Corner ✣ D4.*

MARYLEBONE

$$$ HOTEL Fodor's Choice ★ **Dorset Square Hotel.** Reopened in June 2012 after extensive updates and refurbishment, this boutique hotel, in one of London's most fashionable neighborhoods, occupies a charming town house. **Pros:** ideal location; lovely design; welcoming vibe. **Cons:** some rooms are small; no bathtub in some rooms; fee for Wi-Fi. $ *Rooms from: £300 ✉ 39 Dorset Sq., Marylebone ☎ 020/7723–7874 ⊕ www.firmdalehotels.com ⇆ 35 rooms, 3 suites 🍴 Breakfast Ⓜ Baker St. ✣ D2.*

$$$ HOTEL **Hyatt Regency London—The Churchill.** Even though it's one of London's largest hotels, the Churchill is always abuzz with guests smiling at the purring perfection they find here, including warmly personalized service and calmly alluring guest rooms. **Pros:** comfortable and stylish; efficient service; up to three can stay in one room. **Cons:** feels more geared to business than leisure travelers. $ *Rooms from: £232 ✉ 30 Portman Sq., Marylebone ☎ 020/7486–5800 ⊕ www.london.churchill.hyatt.com ⇆ 389 rooms, 45 suites 🍴 Breakfast Ⓜ Marble Arch ✣ D3.*

$$ HOTEL **Park Plaza Sherlock Holmes Hotel.** Named in honor of the fictional detective who had his home on Baker Street, rooms here have a masculine edge with lots of earth tones and pinstripe sheets (along with hyper-modern bathrooms stocked with fluffy bathrobes). **Pros:** nicely decorated; international electrical outlets, including those that work

with American equipment. **Cons:** have to walk through the bar to get to reception; not well soundproofed from the noisy street. *Rooms from: £168 108 Baker St., Marylebone 020/7486–6161 www.sherlockholmeshotel.com 99 rooms, 20 suites Breakfast Baker St. D2.*

NOTTING HILL AND BAYSWATER

NOTTING HILL

$$ B&B/INN Fodor's Choice ★ **The Main House.** A stay in this delightfully welcoming B&B feels more like sleeping over at a friend's house than in a hotel—albeit a particularly wealthy and well-connected friend. **Pros:** unique and unusual place; charming and helpful owners. **Cons:** three-night-minimum stay is restrictive; few in-house services. *Rooms from: £110 6 Colvile Rd., Notting Hill 020/7221–9691 www.themainhouse.com 4 rooms Breakfast Notting Hill Gate A3.*

$$ HOTEL **The Portobello Hotel.** One of London's quirkiest hotels, the little Portobello (formed from two adjoining Victorian houses) has attracted scores of celebrities to its small but stylish rooms over the years, and the decor reflects these hip credentials with joyous abandon. **Pros:** stylish and unique; celebrity vibe; guests have use of nearby gym and pool. **Cons:** all but the priciest rooms are quite small; may be too eccentric for some. *Rooms from: £195 22 Stanley Gardens, Notting Hill 020/7727–2777 www.portobello-hotel.co.uk Closed 10 days at Christmas 21 rooms Breakfast Notting Hill Gate A3.*

BAYSWATER

$$ HOTEL **London House Hotel.** Set in a row of white Georgian town houses, this excellent budget option in hit-or-miss Bayswater is friendly, well run, and spotlessly clean. **Pros:** friendly and efficient; emphasis on value for money; good location. **Cons:** some public areas feel a bit too clinical; smallest rooms are tiny. *Rooms from: £100 81 Kensington Garden Sq., Bayswater 020/7243–1810 www.londonhousehotels.com 100 rooms Breakfast Queensway, Bayswater A3.*

$$ RENTAL **Space Apart Hotel.** These studio apartments near Hyde Park are done in soothing tones of white and gray, with polished wood floors and attractive modern kitchenettes equipped with all you need to make small meals. **Pros:** especially good value for the money; the larger suites have space for four people; handy location. **Cons:** no in-house restaurant or bar; minimum two-night stay required. *Rooms from: £140 32–37 Kensington Gardens Sq., Bayswater 020/7908–1340 www.aparthotel-london.co.uk 30 rooms No meals Bayswater A3.*

REGENT'S PARK AND HAMPSTEAD

$ B&B/INN **Glenlyn Guest House.** An excellent option for travelers who don't mind being a long Tube ride away from the action, this converted Victorian town house offers a high standard of accommodation a few miles north of Hampstead. **Pros:** comfortable and friendly; you get more for your money than you would in central London; adjoining rooms can be converted to family suites; five-minute walk to Tube station. **Cons:** you have to factor in the cost and inconvenience of a ½-hour Tube ride to central London; no restaurant. *Rooms from: £90* ✉ *6 Woodside Park Rd., North Finchley* ☎ *020/8445–0440* 🌐 *www.glenlynhotel.com* *27 rooms, 2 apartments* *Breakfast* Ⓜ *Woodside Park* ✢ *C1.*

$$ B&B/INN Fodor's Choice ★ **30 King Henry's Road.** Floor-to-ceiling books and a wealth of art decorate this lovely little B&B in Primrose Hill, the perennially trendy "village" neighborhood north of Regent's Park. **Pros:** unique, homey atmosphere; lovely hosts; great neighborhood. **Cons:** no extras; not very central; smaller rooms share a bathroom. *Rooms from: £130* ✉ *30 King Henry's Rd., Primrose Hill* ☎ *020/7483–2871* *5 rooms* *Breakfast* Ⓜ *Chalk Farm* ✢ *D1.*

NIGHTLIFE AND PERFORMING ARTS

London is a must-go destination for both nightlife enthusiasts and culture vultures. Whether you prefer a refined evening at the opera or ballet, funky rhythm and blues in a Soho club, hardcore techno in East London, a pint and gourmet pizza at a local gastro-pub, or cocktails and sushi at a chic Mayfair bar, Great Britain's capital has entertainment to suit all tastes. Admission prices are not always low, but when you consider how much a London hotel room costs, the city's arts and nightlife diversions seem like a bargain.

NIGHTLIFE

There isn't *one* London nightlife scene—there are many. As long as there are audiences for obscure indie bands, cabaret comedy, or the latest trend in dance music, someone will create a venue to satisfy the need. The result? London is more than ever party central.

WESTMINSTER, ST. JAMES'S, AND ROYAL LONDON

BARS

Fodor's Choice ★ **American Bar.** Festooned with a chin-dropping array of club ties, signed celebrity photographs, sporting mementos, and baseball caps, this sensational hotel cocktail bar has superb martinis. The name dates from the 1930s, when hotel bars in London started to cater to growing numbers of Americans crossing the Atlantic in ocean liners, but it wasn't until the 1970s, when a customer left a small carved wooden eagle, that the collection of paraphernalia was started. ✉ *Stafford Hotel, 16–18 St. James's Pl., St. James's* ☎ *020/7493–0111* 🌐 *www.thestaffordhotel.co.uk* ⏲ *Daily 11:30 am–11 pm* Ⓜ *Green Park.*

Bedford and Strand. The wine bar enjoyed something of a renaissance in the first decade of the 21st century in London, and this is one of the best of a new generation. You'll find it down below the streets of Covent Garden, with dark wood and hanging shades; the wine list is short but well chosen, the service is faultless, and the bistro food is created with plenty of care. ✉ *1A Bedford St., Charing Cross* ☎ *020/7836–3033* 🌐 *www.bedford-strand.com* ⏲ *Weekdays noon–midnight, Sat. 5 pm–midnight* Ⓜ *Charing Cross.*

SOHO AND COVENT GARDEN

BARS

Fodor's Choice ★ **Gordon's Wine Bar.** Nab a rickety table in the atmospheric, vaulted interior of what claims to be the oldest wine bar in London, or fight for standing room in the long pedestrian-only alley that runs alongside it. Either way, the mood is always cheery as a diverse crowd sips on more than 60 different wines, ports, and sherries. Tempting cheese and meat plates are great for sharing. ✉ *47 Villiers St., Westminster* ☎ *020/7930–1408* 🌐 *www.gordonswinebar.com* ⏲ *Mon.–Sat. 11–11, Sun. noon–10* Ⓜ *Charing Cross, Embankment.*

2

Fodor's Choice ★ **Sketch.** One seat never looks like the next at this downright extraordinary collection of esoteric living-room bars. The exclusive Parlour, a patisserie during the day, exudes plenty of rarefied charm; the intimate East Bar at the back is reminiscent of a sci-fi film set; and in the Glade it's permanently sunset in a forest. The restrooms are surely London's quirkiest. ✉ *9 Conduit St., Mayfair* ☎ *020/7659–4500* 🌐 *www.sketch.london* ⏲ *Parlour weekdays 8 am–2 am, Sat. 10 am–2 am, Sun. 10 am–midnight; the Glade Mon.–Thurs. 1 pm–2 am, Fri. and Sat. noon–2 am, Sun. noon–midnight; East Bar daily 6:30 pm–2 am* Ⓜ *Oxford Circus.*

COMEDY AND CABARET

Comedy Store. Before heading off to prime time, some of the United Kingdom's funniest stand-ups cut their teeth here, at what's considered the birthplace of alternative comedy. Comedy Store Players, a team with six comedians doing improvisation with audience suggestions, entertain on Wednesday and Sunday; the Cutting Edge steps in every Tuesday. Thursday, Friday, and Saturday have the best stand-up acts. There's also a bar with food. You must be over 18 to go here. ✉ *1A Oxendon St., Soho* ☎ *0844/871–7699 ticket and booking line* 🌐 *www.thecomedystore.co.uk* 🎫 *£14–£26* ⏲ *Shows daily 7:30 or 8 pm, with extra shows Fri. and Sat. at 11 pm* Ⓜ *Piccadilly Circus, Leicester Sq.*

JAZZ AND BLUES

Fodor's Choice ★ **Pizza Express Jazz Club Soho.** One of the United Kingdom's most ubiquitous pizza chains also runs a leading Soho jazz venue. The dimly lighted restaurant hosts top-quality international jazz acts every night. The Italian-style thin-crust pizzas are about what you'd expect from a major chain. ✉ *10 Dean St., Soho* ☎ *0845/602–7017 club, 020/7437–9595 restaurant* 🌐 *www.pizzaexpresslive.com* 🎫 *£10–£30* ⏲ *Mon.–Sat. 11:30 am–midnight, Sun. 11:30 am–11:30 pm for food; music after 7:30 pm (times vary)* Ⓜ *Tottenham Court Rd.*

ECLECTIC MUSIC

Fodor's Choice ★ **Cafe Oto.** A relaxed café by day, and London's leading venue for experimental music by night, Cafe Oto is a Dalston institution. Its programming of free jazz, avant-garde electronica, and much more is enough of a draw that it regularly sells out, with music fans steaming up the windows and spilling out onto the pavement and road outside to smoke in the breaks. Healthy Japanese food is served in the daytime, before customers are kicked out at 5:30 pm to make way for sound checks. It's open as a bar (with no admission charge) on nights when no concerts are taking place. ✉ *18–22 Ashwin St., Dalston* 🎫 *Café free; concerts*

£8–£18 ⏲ Café weekdays 8:30 am–5:30 pm, Sat. 9:30 am–5:30 pm, Sun. 10:30 am–5:30 pm; concerts daily 8 pm–12:30 am Ⓜ Dalston Junction.

THE GAY SCENE

Fodor's Choice ★ **Friendly Society.** An unremarkable-looking door in a Soho alleyway leads down some dingy steps into one of the most fun joints in the neighborhood. Hopping with activity almost any night of the week, the place is known for being gay but also with a friendly place for women. The decor alone—including garden gnome stools and a ceiling covered in Barbie dolls and disco balls—is enough to lift the spirits. ✉ *79 Wardour St., Soho* ⏲ *Mon.–Thurs. 4 pm–11:30 pm, Fri. and Sat. 4 pm–midnight, Sun. 4 pm–10:30 pm* Ⓜ *Leicester Sq.*

Fodor's Choice ★ **Heaven.** With the best light show on any London dance floor, Heaven is unpretentious, loud, and huge, with a labyrinth of rooms, bars, and live-music parlors. Friday and Saturday nights there's a gay comedy night (£13–£15, 7–10 pm). Check in advance about live performances—they can take place any night of the week. If you go to just one gay club in London, Heaven should be it. ✉ *The Arches, Villiers St., Covent Garden* ☎ *020/7930–2020* 🌐 *www.heavennightclub-london.com* 🎫 *£4–£12* ⏲ *Mon. 11 pm–5:30 am, Tues.–Fri. 11 pm–4 am, Sat. 10:30 pm–5 am* Ⓜ *Charing Cross, Embankment.*

The Yard. A corridor of kitsch leads to a surprisingly laid-back bar and spacious terrace at The Yard. This oasis of calm in the middle of Soho attracts a mixed, friendly crowd. ✉ *57 Rupert St., Soho* ☎ *020/7437–2652* 🌐 *www.yardbar.co.uk* ⏲ *Mon.–Wed. 4 pm–11:30 pm, Thurs. 3 pm–11:30 pm, Fri. and Sat. 2 pm–midnight, Sun. 2 pm–10:30 pm* Ⓜ *Piccadilly Circus.*

BLOOMSBURY AND HOLBORN

BARS

Booking Office. Taking full advantage of the soaring Victorian redbrick vaults and arches of the restored St. Pancras Renaissance Hotel, Booking Office is closer in feel to a cathedral than a traditional station bar. Seasonal cocktails using traditional English ingredients are high on flavor and low on mixers, and there's also a restaurant and live music Thursday through Saturday evenings. ✉ *St. Pancras Renaissance Hotel, Euston Rd., King's Cross* ☎ *020/7841–3566* 🌐 *www.bookingofficerestaurant.com* ⏲ *Mon.–Wed. 6:30 am–2 am, Thurs.–Sat. 6:30 am–3 am, Sun. 6:30 am–1 am* Ⓜ *Kings Cross St Pancras.*

THE EAST END

DANCE CLUBS

Cargo. Housed under a series of old railroad arches, this spacious brick-wall bar, restaurant, dance floor, and live-music venue pulls a young, international crowd with its hip vibe and diverse selection of music. Long tables bring people together, as does the food, which draws on global influences and is served tapas-style. Drinks are expensive. ✉ *83 Rivington St., Shoreditch* ☎ *020/7739–3440* 🌐 *www.cargo-london.com* 🎫 *Free–£20* ⏲ *Mon.–Thurs. noon–1 am, Fri. and Sat. noon–3 am, Sun. noon–midnight* Ⓜ *Old St.*

SOUTH OF THE THAMES

BARS

Aqua Shard. This classy bar on level 31 of the Shard, London's new skyscraper and the tallest building in Western Europe, is worth a visit for the phenomenal views alone. The cocktail list is pretty special, too, with ranges inspired by teas and botanicals, as well as all the usual classics. No reservations are taken in the bar, so be prepared to wait during busy periods. ✉ *Level 31, The Shard, 31 St. Thomas St., London Bridge* ☎ *020/3011–1256* 🌐 *www.aquashard.co.uk* 🕐 *Daily noon–1 am* Ⓜ *London Bridge.*

Fodor's Choice ★ **Three Eight Four.** Epitomizing a new breed of Brixton bar, Three Eight Four mixes up inventive cocktails. Don't miss whatever's being cooked up at the flambé station at the end of the bar—perhaps the peach-theme Mr. Flambastic, for instance. Bare light bulbs and brick walls seem to be the decor of choice for lots of cool London bars these days, but this place manages it with particular panache. A delectable selection of small dishes is also available. ✉ *384 Coldharbour La., Brixton* ☎ *02/3417 7309* 🌐 *www.threeeightfour.com* 🕐 *Mon.–Wed. 5 pm–midnight, Thurs. and Fri. 5 pm–2 am, Sat. 11 am–2 am, Sun. 11 am–midnight* Ⓜ *Brixton.*

DANCE CLUBS

Ministry of Sound. This is more of an industry than a club, with its own record label, online radio station, and international DJs. Though it's too much a part of the establishment these days to be at the forefront of cool, the stripped-down warehouse-style club has a super sound system and still pulls in the world's most legendary names in dance. There are chill-out rooms, four bars, four dance floors, and a spacious smoking area with its own snack bar. ✉ *103 Gaunt St., Borough* ☎ *0870/060–0010* 🌐 *www.ministryofsound.com* 🎫 *£15–£25* 🕐 *Fri. 10:30 pm–6 am (last entry 4 am), Sat. 11 pm–7 am (last entry 5 am)* Ⓜ *Elephant & Castle.*

ECLECTIC MUSIC

Fodor's Choice ★ **O2 Academy Brixton.** This legendary Brixton venue has seen it all—mods and rockers, hippies and punks—and it remains one of the city's top indie and rock venues. Despite a capacity for almost 5,000, this refurbished Victorian hall with original art-deco fixtures retains a clublike charm; it has plenty of bars and upstairs seating. ✉ *211 Stockwell Rd., Brixton* ☎ *0844/477–2000 box office* 🌐 *www.o2academybrixton.co.uk* 🎫 *£15–£50* 🕐 *Hrs vary* Ⓜ *Brixton.*

KENSINGTON, KNIGHTSBRIDGE, AND MAYFAIR

BARS

The Blue Bar at the Berkeley Hotel. With low-slung dusty-blue walls, this hotel bar is ever so slightly sexy. Immaculate service, an excellent seasonal cocktail list and a trendy David Collins design make this an ideal spot for a romantic tête-à-tête, complete with jazzy music in the background. ✉ *Wilton Pl., Knightsbridge* ☎ *020/7235–6000* 🌐 *the-berkeley.co.uk* 🕐 *Mon.–Sat. 9 am–1 am, Sun. 9 am–11 pm* Ⓜ *Knightsbridge.*

JAZZ AND BLUES

606 Club. This Chelsea jazz club has been doing things speakeasy-style since long before it became a nightlife trend in London. Buzz the door and you'll find a basement venue showcasing mainstream and contemporary jazz by well-known British-based musicians. You must eat a meal in order to consume alcohol, so allow for an extra £30. Reservations are advisable. Sunday lunchtime jazz takes place on selected Sundays; call ahead. ✉ *90 Lots Rd., Chelsea* ☎ *020/7352–5953* 🌐 *www.606club.co.uk* 🎫 *£10–£12 music charge added to bill* ⏲ *Mon.–Thurs. 7 pm–11:15 pm, Fri. and Sat. 8 pm–12:45 am, Sun. 12:30 pm–3:30 pm and 7 pm–11:15 pm* Ⓜ *Earl's Ct., Fulham Broadway.*

NOTTING HILL

BARS

Beach Blanket Babylon. In a Georgian house close to Portobello Market, this always-packed bar is distinguishable by its eclectic indoor-outdoor spaces with Gaudí-esque curves and snug corner spaces—like a fairy-tale grotto or a medieval dungeon. A sister restaurant-bar-gallery offers a slightly more modern take on similar themes in an ex-warehouse in Shoreditch (*19–23 Bethnal Green Rd.; 020/7749–3540*). ✉ *45 Ledbury Rd., Notting Hill* ☎ *020/7229–2907* 🌐 *www.beachblanket.co.uk* ⏲ *Mon. 6–midnight, Tues.–Fri. noon–midnight, weekends 10 am–midnight* Ⓜ *Notting Hill Gate.*

DANCE CLUBS

Notting Hill Arts Club. Rock stars like Liam Gallagher and Courtney Love have been seen at this small basement club-bar. What the place lacks in looks it makes up for in mood, and an alternative crowd swills beer to eclectic music that spans Asian underground, hip-hop, Latin-inspired funk, deep house, and jazzy grooves. ✉ *21 Notting Hill Gate, Notting Hill* ☎ *020/7460–4459* 🌐 *www.nottinghillartsclub.com* 🎫 *Free–£8* ⏲ *Tues.–Sat. 7 pm–2 am, alternate Sun. 6 pm–1 am* Ⓜ *Notting Hill Gate.*

REGENT'S PARK AND HAMPSTEAD

DANCE CLUBS

KOKO. This Victorian theater has seen acts from Charlie Chaplin to Madonna, and genres from punk to rave. Furnished with lush reds that make it not unlike a cockney Moulin Rouge, this is still one of London's most stunning venues. Sounds of live indie rock, cabaret, funky house, and club classics keep the big dance floor moving, even when it's not heaving. ✉ *1A Camden High St., Camden Town* ☎ *0870/432–5527* 🌐 *www.koko.uk.com* 🎫 *£5–£30* ⏲ *Hrs vary, depending on shows and club nights* Ⓜ *Mornington Crescent.*

JAZZ AND BLUES

Jazz Café. A palace of cool in bohemian Camden, this remains an essential hangout for fans of both the mainstream end of the jazz repertoire and hip-hop, funk, world music, and Latin fusion. It's also the unlikely venue for "I Love the 80s Vs I Love the 90s" on Saturday nights. Book ahead if you want a prime table in the balcony restaurant overlooking the stage. ✉ *5 Parkway, Camden Town* ☎ *020/7485–6834 venue info, 0844/847–2514 tickets (Ticketmaster)* 🌐 *mamacolive.com/thejazzcafe*

£6–£35 Sun.–Thurs. 7 pm–10:30 pm, Fri. and Sat. 7 pm–3 am M Camden Town.

ROCK

Roundhouse. This former steam-engine repair shed hosts some of the most atmospheric medium-scale rock and pop gigs in the capital, plus a varied program of circus, theater, dance, and the occasional art installation. There's a good restaurant on the first floor, and in the summer the terrace bar is transformed into an "urban beach," complete with sand. *Chalk Farm Rd., Camden 0844/482–8008 box office, 020/7424–9991 enquiries www.roundhouse.org.uk Free–£40 Daily 9:30–5 (later when performances are taking place; times vary) M Chalk Farm.*

PERFORMING ARTS

Whether you prefer your art classical or contemporary, you'll find that London's vibrant cultural scene has as much to offer as any in the world. The Royal Opera House hosts world-class productions of opera and ballet, the reconstructed Shakespeare's Globe re-creates seeing the Bard's work as its original audience would have, and the National Theatre, the Royal Court, and several other subsidized theaters produce challenging new plays and reimagined classics.

To find out what's showing now, the free weekly magazine *Time Out* (issued every Tuesday in print and online at *www.timeout.com*) is invaluable. The free *Evening Standard* carries listings, many of which are also available online at *www.thisislondon.co.uk*. *Metro*, London's other widely available free newspaper, is also worth checking out . You can pick up the free fortnightly *London Theatre Guide* from hotels and tourist-information centers.

MAIN PERFORMING ARTS CENTERS

FAMILY **Barbican Centre.** Opened in 1982, The Barbican is an enormous Brutalist concrete maze that Londoners either love or hate—but its importance to the cultural life of the capital is beyond dispute. At the largest performing arts center in Europe, you could listen to Elgar, see 1960s photography, and catch German animation with live accompaniment. The main theater, known for its acoustics, is most famous as the home of the London Symphony Orchestra. The Barbican is also a frequent host of the BBC Symphony Orchestra. *Silk St., The City 020/7638–8891 box office www.barbican.org.uk Mon.–Sat. 9 am–11 pm, Sun. 10 am–11 pm M Barbican.*

Southbank Centre. The Royal Festival Hall is one of London's best spaces for large-scale choral and orchestral works and is home to the Philharmonia and London Philharmonic orchestras. The Queen Elizabeth Hall is a popular venue for top-tier soloists, and the Purcell Room is known for chamber music recitals. Free events take place in foyer spaces around the complex. Southbank hosts everything from the London International Mime festival to large-scale dance performances, plus highly regarded pop, rock and jazz acts. Also part of the complex is the **Hayward Gallery** (*Monday noon–6; Tuesday, Wednesday, and weekends 11–7; Thursday and Friday 11–8*), a landmark 1960s building and one of London's best contemporary art venues. ✉ *Belvedere Rd., South Bank* ☎ *020/7960–4200,* 🌐 *www.southbankcentre.co.uk* Ⓜ *Waterloo, Embankment.*

CLASSICAL MUSIC

Whether it's a concert by cellist Yo-Yo Ma or Mozart's Requiem by candlelight, it's possible to hear first-rate musicians in world-class venues almost every day of the year. If you can't book in advance, arrive at the hall an hour before the performance for a chance at returns.

■ **TIP→ Lunchtime concerts take place all over the city in smaller concert halls, the big arts-center foyers, and churches; they usually cost less than £5 or are free, and feature string quartets, singers, jazz ensembles, or gospel choirs.** St. John's, Smith Square, and St. Martin-in-the-Fields are popular locations. Performances usually begin about 1 pm and last one hour.

A great British tradition since 1895, the **Henry Wood Promenade Concerts** (more commonly known as the "Proms" 🌐 *www.bbc.co.uk/proms*) run eight weeks, from July to September, at the Royal Albert Hall. Despite an extraordinary quantity of high-quality concerts, it's renowned for its (atypical) last night: a madly patriotic display of singing "Land of Hope and Glory," and Union Jack–waving. For regular Proms, tickets run from £5 to £90, with hundreds of standing tickets for £5 available at the hall on the night of the concert. ■ **TIP→ The last night is broadcast in Hyde Park on a jumbo screen, but even a seat on the grass requires a paid ticket (around £25).**

Fodor's Choice ★ **Royal Albert Hall.** Opened in 1871, this splendid iron-and-glass–dome auditorium hosts everything from pop and classical headliners to Cirque du Soleil, awards ceremonies, and sumo wrestling championships, but is best known for the annual July–September BBC Promenade Concerts. Bargain-price standing (or promenading, or sitting-on-the-floor) tickets for "the Proms" are sold on the night of the concert. The domed, circular 5,272-seat auditorium has a terra-cotta exterior surmounted by a mosaic frieze depicting figures engaged in cultural pursuits. The hall is open daily for daytime guided tours (£12.25) and, Wednesday–Sunday, afternoon tea (£10.50–£33). ✉ *Kensington Gore, Kensington* ☎ *0845/401–5034 box office* 🌐 *www.royalalberthall.com* Ⓜ *South Kensington.*

St. Martin-in-the-Fields Concerts. Popular lunchtime concerts (£3.50 donation suggested) are held in this lovely 1726 church, as are regular evening concerts. Stop for a snack at the Café in the Crypt. ✉ *Trafalgar Sq., Westminster* ☎ *020/7766–1100* 🌐 *www.stmartin-in-the-fields.org* Ⓜ *Charing Cross.*

Fodor's Choice ★ **Wigmore Hall.** Hear chamber music and song recitals in this charming hall with near-perfect acoustics. Don't miss the Sunday morning concerts (11:30 am). ✉ *36 Wigmore St., Marylebone* ☎ *020/7935–2141* 🌐 *www.wigmore-hall.org.uk* Ⓜ *Bond St.*

2

DANCE

Dance aficionados in London can enjoy the classicism of the world-renowned Royal Ballet, innovative works by the Rambert Dance Company, Matthew Bourne's New Adventures, the Wheeldon Company, and other groups, and the latest pieces by scores of independent choreographers. The English National Ballet and visiting international companies perform at the Coliseum and at Sadler's Wells, which also hosts various other ballet companies and dance troupes. Encompassing the refurbished Royal Festival Hall, the Southbank Centre has a seriously good contemporary dance program that hosts top international companies and important U.K. choreographers, as well as multicultural offerings ranging from Japanese Butoh and Indian Kathak to hip hop. The Place and the Lilian Bayliss Theatre at Sadler's Wells are where you'll find the most daring, cutting-edge performances. Also check ⊕ *www.londondance.com* for performances and fringe venues.

The Place. The Robin Howard Dance Theatre at The Place is London's only theater dedicated to contemporary dance, and with tickets often under £15 (tickets to performances by student dancers cost just £5) it's good value, too. "Resolution!" is the United Kingdom's biggest platform event for new choreographers. ✉ *17 Duke's Rd., Bloomsbury* ☎ *020/7121–1100* ⊕ *www.theplace.org.uk* Ⓜ *Euston.*

FAMILY Fodor's Choice ★ **Sadler's Wells.** This gleaming building opened in 1998, the seventh on the site in its 300-year history. Head here to see performances by leading classical and contemporary dance companies. The Random Dance Company is in residence, and the little Lilian Baylis Theatre hosts avant-garde work. ✉ *Rosebery Ave., Islington* ☎ *0844/412–4300 tickets* ⊕ *www.sadlerswells.com* Ⓜ *Angel.*

FILM

There are many lovely movie theaters in London and several that are committed to non-mainstream cinema, notably the BFI Southbank and the Curzon and Everyman mini-chains. Most of the big cinemas, such as the Odeon Leicester Square and the Empire, are in the Leicester Square–Piccadilly Circus area, where tickets average £15. Tickets on Monday and for matinees are often cheaper (from £6 to £10), and there are fewer crowds.

FAMILY **BFI Southbank.** With the best repertory programming in London, the three movie theaters and studio here are effectively a national film center run by the British Film Institute. More than 1,000 titles are screened each year, with art-house, foreign, silent, overlooked, classic, noir, and short films favored over recent Hollywood blockbusters. The center also has a gallery, bookshop, and "mediatheque" where visitors can watch film and television from the National Archive for free (closed Monday). This is one of the venues for the BFI London Film Festival; throughout the year there are minifestivals, seminars, and guest speakers. ✉ *Belvedere Rd., South Bank* ☎ *020/7928–3232 box office* ⊕ *www.bfi.org.uk* Ⓜ *Waterloo.*

Curzon Soho. This popular, comfortable movie theater runs a vibrant and artsy program of mixed repertoire and mainstream films, with a good calendar of director talks and other events, too. The bar is great

The Proms at Royal Albert Hall have standing tickets for £5 on the night of the concerts.

for a quiet drink, even when Soho is crawling with people. There are branches in Mayfair, Bloomsbury, Victoria, Chelsea, and Richmond. ✉ *99 Shaftesbury Ave., Soho* ☎ *0330/500–1331* 🌐 *www.curzoncinemas.com* Ⓜ *Piccadilly Circus, Leicester Sq.*

OPERA

The two key players in London's opera scene are the Royal Opera House (which ranks with the Metropolitan Opera House in New York) and the more innovative English National Opera (ENO), which presents English-language productions at the London Coliseum. Only the Theatre Royal, Drury Lane, has a longer theatrical history than the Royal Opera House—the third theater to be built on the site since 1858.

Despite occasional performances by the likes of Björk, the Royal Opera House struggles to shrug off its reputation for elitism and ticket prices that can rise to £800. It is, however, more accessible than it used to be—the cheapest tickets cost less than £10. Prices for the ENO range from around £20 to £95.

In summer, the increasingly adventurous Opera Holland Park presents the usual chestnuts, along with some obscure works, under a canopy in leafy Holland Park. International touring companies often perform at Sadler's Wells, the Barbican, the Southbank Centre, and Wigmore Hall, so check the weekly listings for details.

The London Coliseum. A veritable architectural extravaganza of Edwardian exoticism, the baroque-style theater has a magnificent auditorium and a rooftop glass dome with a bar and great views. As one of the city's most venerable theaters, the Coliseum functions mainly as the home of the English National Opera which continues to produce innovative opera, sung in English, for lower prices than the Royal Opera House. During opera's off-season, the house hosts the English National Ballet (*www.ballet.org.uk*). Guided tours (every other Saturday at 11:30 am, when productions are scheduled) cost £10. ✉ *St. Martin's La., Covent Garden* ☎ *020/7845–9300 box office, 020/7836–0111 inquiries* 🌐 *www.eno.org* Ⓜ *Leicester Sq.*

2

FAMILY **Opera Holland Park.** In summer, well-loved operas and imaginative productions of lesser-known works are presented under a spectacular canopy against the remains of Holland House, one of the first great houses built in Kensington. The company has successfully branched out into opera for families in recent years, too. Ticket prices range from £10 to £75, with around 1,000 tickets offered free to young people ages 9–18 every season. Tickets go on sale in March. ✉ *Holland Park, Kensington High St., Kensington* ☎ *0300/999–1000 box office (opens Mar.), 020/7361–3570 inquiries* 🌐 *www.operahollandpark.com* Ⓜ *High Street Kensington, Holland Park.*

Fodor's Choice ★ **Royal Opera House.** Along with Milan's La Scala, New York's Metropolitan, and the Palais Garnier in Paris, this is one of the world's greatest opera houses. The resident troupe has mounted spectacular productions in the past, though recent productions have tended toward more contemporary operas. Whatever the style of the performance, the extravagant theater—also home to the famed Royal Ballet—delivers a full dose of opulence. Tickets range in price from £3 to £235. The box office opens at 10 am, but lines for popular productions start as early as 7 am; unsold tickets are offered at half price four hours before a performance. If you wish to see the hall but are not able to procure a ticket, you can join a backstage tour (£12) or one of the infrequent tours of the auditorium (£9.50). ✉ *Bow St., Covent Garden* ☎ *020/7304–4000* 🌐 *www.roh.org.uk* ⏲ *Public areas generally 10–3:30; backstage tours weekdays 10:30, 12:30, and 2:30, Sat. 10:30, 11:30, 12:30, and 1:30 (check in advance)* Ⓜ *Covent Garden.*

THEATER

The London theater scene encompasses long-running popular musicals, the most recent work from leading contemporary playwrights, imaginative physical theater from experimental companies, lavish Disney spectacles, and small fringe productions above pubs. Glitzy West End jukebox musicals and star-studded revivals of warhorses continue to pull in the audiences, but more challenging productions do so as well—only in London will a Tuesday matinee of the Royal Shakespeare Company's *Henry IV* sell out a 1,200-seat theater. In London, the words "radical" and "quality," or "classical" and "experimental," are not mutually exclusive. The Royal Shakespeare Company (🌐 *www.rsc.org.uk*) and the National Theatre (🌐 *www.nationaltheatre.org.uk*) often stage contemporary interpretations of the classics. The Almeida, Battersea Arts Centre (BAC), Donmar Warehouse, Royal Court Theatre, Soho Theatre, and Old Vic attract famous actors and have excellent reputations for showcasing new writing and innovative theatrical approaches. These are the venues where you'll see an original production before it becomes a hit in the West End or on Broadway (and for a fraction of the cost). During the summer you can take in an open-air production of

Shakespeare at the Globe Theatre or under the stars in Regent's Park's Open Air Theatre.

Though less pricey than Broadway, theatergoing here isn't cheap. Tickets under £15 are a rarity, although designated productions at the National Theatre have seats at this price. At the commercial theaters you should expect to pay from £15 for a seat in the upper balcony to at least £25 for a good one in the stalls (orchestra) or dress circle (mezzanine). However, last-minute returns available on the night may provide some good deals. Tickets may be booked through ticket agents, at individual theater box offices, or over the phone by credit card. Be sure to inquire about any extra fees—prices can vary enormously, but agents are legally obliged to reveal the face value of the ticket if you ask. All the larger hotels offer theater bookings, but they tack on a hefty service charge. ■ **TIP→ Be very wary of ticket touts (scalpers) and unscrupulous ticket agents outside theaters.**

Ticketmaster (*0844/277–4321* 🌐 *www.ticketmaster.co.uk*) sells tickets to a number of different theaters, although it charges a booking fee. For discount tickets, **Society of London Theatre** (*020/7557–6700* 🌐 *www.tkts.co.uk*) operates "tkts," a half-price ticket booth on the southwest corner of Leicester Square, and sells the best available seats to performances at about 25 theaters. It's open daily from 9 to 7 except Sunday (10:30 to 4:30). A £3 service charge is included in the price. Major credit cards are accepted.

THEATERS

Almeida Theatre. This Off–West End venue, helmed by director Rupert Goold, premiers excellent new plays and exciting twists on the classics, often featuring high-profile actors. There's a good café and a licensed bar that serves "sharing dishes" as well as tasty main courses. ✉ *Almeida St., Islington* ☎ *020/7359–4404* 🌐 *www.almeida.co.uk* Ⓜ *Angel, Highbury & Islington.*

BAC. Battersea Arts Centre has a reputation for producing innovative new work, as well as hosting top alternative stand-up comics. Performances take place in quirky spaces all over this atmospheric former town hall. Check out Scratch events, low-tech theater where the audience provides feedback on works-in-progress. Entry for Scratch events is on a pay-what-you-can basis (minimum £1). There's also a fun bar that serves good food. ✉ *176 Lavender Hill, Battersea* ☎ *020/7223–2223* 🌐 *www.bac.org.uk* Ⓜ *National Rail: Clapham Junction.*

Donmar Warehouse. Hollywood stars often perform in this not-for-profit theater in diverse and daring new works, bold interpretations of the classics, and small-scale musicals. Nicole Kidman, Gwyneth Paltrow, and Ewan McGregor have all been featured. ✉ *41 Earlham St., Seven Dials, Covent Garden* ☎ *0844/871–7624* 🌐 *www.donmarwarehouse.com* Ⓜ *Covent Garden.*

FAMILY **Little Angel Theatre.** Innovative puppetry performances for children and adults have been taking place in this adorable former temperance hall since 1961. The theater runs a number of festivals a year, including the biennial Suspense festival, with puppetry for adults.

✉ 14 Dagmar Passage, Islington ☎ 020/7226–1787 box office 🌐 www.littleangeltheatre.com Ⓜ Angel, Highbury & Islington.

FAMILY
Fodor's Choice ★
National Theatre. When this theater designed by Sir Denys Lasdun opened in 1976, Londoners weren't all so keen on the low-slung Brutalist block. Prince Charles described it as "a clever way of building a nuclear power station in the middle of London without anyone objecting." But whatever its merits or demerits, the National Theatre's interior spaces are worth a visit. Interspersed with the three theaters—the 1,150-seat Olivier, the 890-seat Lyttelton, and the 450-seat Dorfman—is a multilayered foyer with exhibitions, bars, restaurants, and free entertainment. Musicals, classics, and plays are performed by top-flight professionals. The Clore Learning Centre offers courses and events on all aspects of theater making, and you can watch staff at work in the backstage workshops from the Sherling High-Level Walkway. *✉ Belvedere Rd., South Bank ☎ 020/7452–3000 🌐 www.nationaltheatre.org.uk 🎫 Tour £8.50 ⏲ Foyer Mon.–Sat. 9:30 am–11 pm, selected Sun. noon–6 pm; 75-min tour backstage, times vary Ⓜ Waterloo.*

FAMILY
Fodor's Choice ★
Open Air Theatre. On a warm summer evening, open-air theater in the pastoral Regent's Park is hard to beat. Enjoy a supper before the performance, a bite during the intermission on the lawn, or drinks in the bar. The only downside is that warm summer nights in London are not always reliable—a raincoat is advisable. *✉ Inner Circle, Regent's Park ☎ 0844/826–4242 🌐 openairtheatre.com Ⓜ Baker St., Regent's Park.*

Royal Court Theatre. Britain's undisputed epicenter of new theatrical works, the Court continues to produce gritty British and international drama. Don't miss the best deal in town—four 10-pence standing tickets go on sale one hour before each performance, and £10 tickets are available on Monday. *✉ Sloane Sq., Chelsea ☎ 020/7565–5000 🌐 www.royalcourttheatre.com Ⓜ Sloane Sq.*

Fodor's Choice ★
Soho Theatre. This sleek theater in the heart of Soho is devoted to fostering new work and is a prolific presenter of plays by emerging writers, comedy performances, cabaret shows, and other entertainment. The bar is always buzzing. *✉ 21 Dean St., Soho ☎ 020/7478–0100 🌐 www.sohotheatre.com Ⓜ Tottenham Court Rd.*

FAMILY
Fodor's Choice ★
Unicorn Theatre. Dedicated to innovative work for young audiences, this modern theater programs plays, musicals, and interactive theater for everyone from babies on up. Inclusivity is a major focus, with performances for those with visual and hearing and other impairments taking place regularly. *✉ 147 Tooley St., Borough ☎ 020/7645–0560 box office, 020/7645–0500 inquiries 🌐 www.unicorntheatre.com Ⓜ London Bridge.*

Fodor's Choice ★
Young Vic. In a home near Waterloo, big names perform alongside young talent, often in daring, innovative productions of classic plays that appeal to a more diverse audience than is traditionally found in London theaters. Good food is served at the bustling bar. *✉ 66 The Cut, Waterloo, South Bank ☎ 020/7922–2922 box office 🌐 www.youngvic.org Ⓜ Southwark, Waterloo.*

LONDON'S SPECTATOR SPORTS

Sport in the capital comes into its own when it's watched, rather than participated in. You'll most easily witness London's fervent sporting passions in front of a screen in a pub with a pint in hand. And those passions run deep.

FOOTBALL

London's top teams—Chelsea, Arsenal, Tottenham Hotspur—are world-class (especially the first two) and often progress in the European Champions League. It's unlikely you'll be able to get tickets for anything except the least popular Premier League games during the August–May season, despite absurdly high ticket prices—as much as £41 for a standard, walk-up, match-day seat at Chelsea, and a whopping £126 for the match-day tickets at Arsenal!

TENNIS

Wimbledon Lawn Tennis Championships. The All England Club's Wimbledon Lawn Tennis Championships are famous for Centre Court, rain, strawberries and cream, and an old-school insistence on players wearing white. Thankfully, the rain has been banished on Centre Court by the retractable roof, but whether you can get tickets for Centre Court all comes down to the luck of the draw—there's a ballot system for advance purchase. See *www.wimbledon.com* for details. ✉ *The All England Lawn Tennis Club, Church Rd.* ☎ *020/8944–1066 for general inquries* 🌐 *www.wimbledon.com.*

SHOPPING

The keyword of London shopping has always been "individuality," whether expressed in the superb custom tailoring of Savile Row, the nonconformist punk roots of quintessential British designer Vivienne Westwood, or the unique small stores that purvey the owner's private passion, whether paper theaters, toy soldiers, or buttons. This tradition is under threat from the influx of chains—global luxury, domestic mid-market, and international youth—but the distinctively British mix of quality and originality, tradition and character, remains.

You can try on underwear fit for a queen at Her Majesty's lingerie supplier, track down a leather-bound Brontë classic at an antiquarian bookseller, or find a bargain antique on Portobello Road. Whether you're just browsing or on a fashion-seeking mission, London shopping offers something for all tastes and budgets.

Although it's impossible to pin down one particular look that defines the city, London style tends to fall into two camps: one is the quirky, individualistic, somewhat romantic look exemplified by homegrown designers such as Vivienne Westwood. The other reflects Britain's celebrated tradition of classic knitwear and suiting, with labels such as Oswald Boateng and Paul Smith taking tradition and giving it a very modern twist. If your budget can't stretch to the custom-made shirts and suits of Jermyn Street and Savile Row or the classic handbags at Mulberry, Asprey, and Anya Hindmarch, no problem; the Topshop chain, aimed at the younger end of the market, is an excellent place to pick up designs copied straight from the catwalk at a fraction of the price, and mid-market chains such as Reiss and Jigsaw offer smart design and better quality for the more sophisticated shopper.

If there's anything that unites London's designers, it's a commitment to creativity and originality, underpinned by a strong sense of heritage. This combination of posh and rock-n-roll sensibilities is exemplified by designers like Sarah Burton—the late Alexander McQueen's successor at his eponymous label and designer of the Duchess of Cambridge's wedding dress—Stella McCartney, the creative milliner Philip Treacy, and the imaginative shoemakers United Nude. If anything, London is even better known for its vibrant street fashion found at the stalls at Portobello, Camden, and Spitalfields markets.

London's shopping districts are spread all over the city, so pace yourself and take in only one or two areas in a day. Or visit one of the grand department stores such as Selfridges, Liberty, or Harvey Nichols, where you can find a wide assortment of designers, from mass to class, all under one roof.

WESTMINSTER, ST. JAMES'S, AND ROYAL LONDON

BEAUTY

Floris. What do Queen Victoria and Marilyn Monroe have in common? They both used fragrances from Floris, one of the most beautiful shops in London, with gleaming glass-and-Spanish-mahogany showcases salvaged from the Great Exhibition of 1851. In addition to scents for both men and women, Floris makes its own shaving products, reflecting its origins as a barbershop. Other gift possibilities include goose-down powder puffs, a famous rose-scented mouthwash, and beautifully packaged soaps and bath essences. There's another branch in Belgravia. ✉ *89 Jermyn St., St. James's* ☎ *0845/702–3239* 🌐 *www.florislondon.com* 🕓 *Closed Sun.* Ⓜ *Piccadilly Circus, Green Park.*

BOOKS AND STATIONERY

Fodor's Choice ★ **Hatchards.** This is the United Kingdom's oldest bookshop, open since 1797 and beloved by writers themselves (customers have included Oscar Wilde, Rudyard Kipling, and Lord Byron). Despite its wood-paneled, "gentleman's library" atmosphere, and eclectic selection of books, Hatchards is owned by the large Waterstone's chain. Nevertheless, the shop still retains its period charm, aided by the staff's old-fashioned helpfulness and expertise. Look for the substantial number of books signed by notable contemporary authors on the well-stocked shelves. ✉ *187 Piccadilly, St. James's* ☎ *020/7439–9921* 🌐 *www.hatchards.co.uk* Ⓜ *Piccadilly Circus.*

CLOTHING: MENSWEAR

Turnbull & Asser. The Jermyn Street store sells luxurious jackets, cashmere sweaters, suits, ties, pajamas, ready-to-wear shirts, and accessories perfect for the billionaire who has everything. The brand is best known for its superb custom made shirts—worn by Prince Charles, Woody Allen, and every filmic James Bond to name a few. These can be ordered at the nearby Bury Street branch. At least 15 separate measurements are taken, and the cloth, woven to the company's specifications, comes in 1,000 different patterns—the cottons feel as good as silk. The first order must be for a minimum of six shirts, which start from £195 each. There's another branch in The City. ✉ *71–72 Jermyn St., St. James's* ☎ *020/7808–3000* 🌐 *www.turnbullandasser.com* ⏲ *Closed Sun.* Ⓜ *Green Park.*

FOOD

Fodor's Choice ★ **Berry Bros. & Rudd.** Nothing matches Berry Bros. & Rudd for rare offerings and a unique shopping experience. A family-run wine business since 1698, BBR stores its vintage bottles and casks in vaulted cellars that are more than 300 years old. The in-house wine school offers educational tasting sessions, while the dedicated whisky room also has an excellent selection. The shop has a quirky charm and the staff is extremely knowledgeable—and not snooty if you're on a budget. ✉ *3 St. James's St., St. James's* ☎ *800/280–2440* 🌐 *www.bbr.com* ⏲ *Closed Sun.* Ⓜ *Green Park.*

Fodor's Choice ★ **Fortnum & Mason.** Although F&M is jokingly known as "the Queen's grocer," and the impeccably mannered staff still wear traditional tailcoats, its celebrated food hall stocks gifts for all budgets, including irresistibly packaged luxury foods stamped with the gold "By Appointment" crest for under £5. Try the teas, preserves (including the unusual rose-petal jelly), condiments, or Gentleman's Relish (anchovy paste). The store's famous hampers are always a welcome gift. The gleaming food hall spans two floors and incorporates a sleek wine bar, with the rest of the store devoted to upscale housewares, men and women's accessories and toiletries, a dedicated candle room, a jewelry department featuring exclusive designs by breakthrough talent, and clothing and toys for children. If you start to flag, break for afternoon tea at the juice bar or one of the four other restaurants (one's an indulgent ice-cream parlor)—or a treatment in the Beauty Rooms. There's another branch at St. Pancras International. ✉ *181 Piccadilly, St. James's* ☎ *020/7734–8040* 🌐 *www.fortnumandmason.com* Ⓜ *Green Park.*

TOYS

The Armoury of St. James's. The fine toy soldiers and military models in stock here are collectors' items. Painted and mounted knights only 6 inches high can cost up to £1,200 (though figures start at a mere £7.50 for a toy soldier). Besides lead and tin soldiers, the shop has regimental brooches, historic orders and medals, and military antiques. ✉ *17 Piccadilly Arcade, St. James's* ☎ *020/7493–5082* 🌐 *www.armoury.co.uk* ⏲ *Closed Sun.* Ⓜ *Piccadilly Circus.*

SOHO AND COVENT GARDEN

ACCESSORIES

Fodor's Choice ★ **Peckham Rye.** On the small cobblestone streets leading off Carnaby Street you'll find small specialty shops like the family-run Peckham Rye, which sells heritage-style men's accessories—handmade silk and twill ties, bow ties, and scarves, all using traditional patterns drawn from the archives going back to 1799. More Ralph Lauren than Ralph Lauren, the socks, striped shirts, and handkerchiefs attract modern-day

CAMDEN TOWN
cheap second-hand and club gear
CLERKENWELL
a historical hot spot for crafts and design
HOXTON & SHOREDITCH
edgy young designers
MARYLEBONE
small shops in village-like setting
NOTTING HILL
antiques, vintage clothing, and boho boutiques
OXFORD CIRCUS
global flagships, department stores, and street style on Carnaby
SOHO
books abound on Charing Cross Road
COVENT GARDEN
an urban-wear mecca around Seven Dials
MAYFAIR
catwalk names on Bond St., trad tailors on Savile Row
ST JAMES'S
old-fashioned specialists, from hatters to shirtmakers
KNIGHTSBRIDGE
luxe labels and, of course, Harrods
CHELSEA
the King's Rd. spans fashion to furniture
REGENT'S PARK
Albany Rd.
Park Rd.
Albany St.
Euston Rd.
Grays Inn Rd.
BLOOMSBURY
Marylebone Rd.
Gt. Portland St.
Tottenham Court Rd.
Baker St.
New Oxford St.
Holborn
Kingsway
Wigmore St.
Charing Cross Rd.
Edgware Rd.
BAYSWATER
Oxford St.
Bayswater Rd.
Aldwych
Strand
Shaftesbury Ave.
New Bond St.
Regent St.
Waterloo Br.
Pall Mall
HYDE PARK
Piccadilly
Green Park
Whitehall
Victoria Embankment
Thames
St. James's Park
The Mall
Knightsbridge
Constitution Hill
Kensington Rd.
Birdcage Walk
Westminster Br.
WESTMINSTER
River
Brompton Rd.
BELGRAVIA
Lambeth Palace Rd.
Victoria St.
Buckingham Palace Rd.
Horseferry Rd.
Lambeth Br.
Wilton Rd.
LAMBETH
Sloane St.
Vauxhall Br. Rd.
Millbank
Albert Embankment
VICTORIA
Pimlico Rd.
King's Rd.
0
1/2 mile
0
1/2 km

Choices, choices: there are plenty of prints—and much else—at the Portobello Road Market.

dandies such as Mark Ronson and David Beckham. ✉ *11 Newburgh St., Soho* ☎ *0207/734–5181* 🌐 *www.peckhamrye.com* Ⓜ *Oxford St.*

BOOKS AND PRINTS

Fodor's Choice ★ **Foyles.** Founded in 1903 by the Foyle brothers after they failed the Civil Service exam, this family-owned bookstore is in a 1930s art-deco building, once the home of the legendary art college Central Saint Martins. Foyles carries almost every title imaginable on its 4 miles of bookshelves. One of London's best sources for textbooks and the United Kingdom's largest retailer of foreign language titles, Foyles also stocks everything from popular fiction to military history, sheet music, medical tomes, graphic novels, and handsome illustrated fine arts books. It also offers the store-within-a-store Ray's Jazz (one of London's better outlets for music) and a cool café. Foyles has branches in the Southbank Centre, St. Pancras International train station (the Eurostar's U.K. terminus), Waterloo station, and the Westfield shopping centers in Shepherd's Bush and Stratford. ✉ *107 Charing Cross Rd., Soho* ☎ *020/7437–5660* 🌐 *www.foyles.co.uk* Ⓜ *Tottenham Court Rd.*

CLOTHING

Paul Smith. British classics with an irreverent twist define Paul Smith's collections for women, men, and children. Beautifully tailored suits for men and women take hallmarks of traditional British style and turn them on their heads with humor and color, combining exceptional fabrics with flamboyant linings or unusual detailing. Gift ideas abound—wallets, scarves, diaries, spectacles, even a soccer ball—all in Smith's signature rainbow stripes. There are several branches throughout London, in Notting Hill, Soho, Canary Wharf, and Borough Market, plus a Mayfair shop that includes vintage furniture and a shoes-and-accessories shop on Marylebone High Street. ✉ *40–44 Floral St., Covent Garden* ☎ *020/7379–7133* 🌐 *www.paulsmith.co.uk* Ⓜ *Covent Garden.*

CLOTHING: WOMEN'S WEAR

Topshop. A hot spot for straight-from-the-runway affordable fashion, Topshop is destination shopping for teenagers and fashion editors alike. Clothes and accessories are geared to the youthful end of the market, although women who are young at heart and girlish of figure can find plenty of wearable items here. However, you will need a high tolerance for loud music and busy dressing rooms. The store also features collections designed by a rotating roster of high-end designers as well as offering its own premium designer line called Topshop Unique. Topman brings the same fast-fashion approach to clothing for men. If the crowds become too much, head to one of the smaller Topshops in Kensington High Street, Knightsbridge, Victoria, Marble Arch, The City, or Holborn. ✉ *214 Oxford St., Fitzrovia* ☎ *0844/848–7487* 🌐 *www.topshop.com* Ⓜ *Oxford Circus.*

DEPARTMENT STORES

Fodor's Choice ★ **Liberty.** The wonderful black-and-white mock-Tudor facade, created from the timbers of two Royal Navy ships, reflects this store's origins in the late-19th-century Arts and Crafts movement. Leading designers were recruited to create the classic art nouveau Liberty prints that are still a centerpiece of the brand, gracing everything from cushions and silk kimonos to embossed leather bags and photo albums. Inside, Liberty is a labyrinth of nooks and crannies stuffed with thoughtfully chosen merchandise. Clothes for both men and women focus on high quality and high fashion with labels like Helmut Lang and Roland Mouret. The store regularly commissions new prints from contemporary designers, and sells both these and its classic patterns by the yard. If you're not so handy with a needle, an interior design service will create soft furnishings for you. ✉ *Regent St., Soho* ☎ *020/7734–1234* 🌐 *www.liberty.co.uk* Ⓜ *Oxford Circus.*

TOYS

FAMILY Fodor's Choice ★ **Benjamin Pollock's Toyshop.** This landmark shop still carries on the tradition of its founder, who sold miniature theater stages made from richly detailed paper from the late 19th century until his death in 1937. Among his admirers was Robert Louis Stevenson, who wrote, "If you love art, folly, or the bright eyes of children, speed to Pollock's." Today the antique model theaters are expensive, but there are plenty of magical reproductions for less than £10. There's also an extensive selection of new but nostalgic puppets, marionettes, teddy bears, spinning tops, jack-in-the-boxes, and similar traditional children's toys from the days before batteries were required (or even possible). ✉ *44 The Market Bldg., Covent Garden* ☎ *020/7379–7866* 🌐 *www.pollocks-coventgarden.co.uk* Ⓜ *Covent Garden.*

BLOOMSBURY AND HOLBORN

ACCESSORIES

Fodor's Choice ★ **James Smith & Sons Ltd.** This has to be the world's ultimate umbrella shop, and a must for anyone interested in real Victorian London. The family-owned shop has been in this location on a corner of New Oxford Street since 1857, and sells every kind of umbrella, cane, and walking stick imaginable. The interior is unchanged since the 19th century; you will feel as if you have stepped back in time. Umbrellas range from about £60 for a folding umbrella to more than £250 for a classic man's umbrella with a carved handle. If the umbrellas seem too high, James Smith also sells smaller accessories and handmade wooden bowls. ✉ *Hazelwood House, 53 New Oxford St., Bloomsbury* ☎ *020/7836–4731* 🌐 *www.james-smith.co.uk* ⏲ *Closed Sun.* Ⓜ *Tottenham Court Rd., Holborn.*

ANTIQUES

London Silver Vaults. Housed in a basement vault, this extraordinary space holds stalls from more than 30 silver dealers. Products range from the spectacularly over-the-top costing thousands to smaller items—like teaspoons, candlesticks, or a set of Victorian cake forks—starting at £25. Most of the silver merchants actually trade out of room-size, underground vaults, which were originally rented out to London's upper crust to store their valuables. ✉ *53–64 Chancery La., Holborn* ☎ *020/7242–3844* 🌐 *www.thesilvervaults.com* ⏲ *Closed Sat. after 1 and Sun.* Ⓜ *Chancery La.*

THE EAST END

HOUSEHOLD

Fodor's Choice ★ **Labour & Wait.** Although mundane items like colanders and clothespins may not sound like ideal souvenirs, this shop (selling both new and vintage) will make you reconsider. The owners are on a mission to revive retro, functional British household goods, such as enamel kitchenware, genuine feather dusters, bread bins, and traditional Welsh blankets. ✉ *85 Redchurch St., Shoreditch* ☎ *020/7729–6253* 🌐 *www.labourandwait.co.uk* ⏲ *Closed Mon.* Ⓜ *London Overground: Shoreditch High St.*

MUSIC

Rough Trade East. Although many London record stores are struggling, this veteran indie-music specialist in the Old Truman Brewery seems to have gotten the formula right. The spacious surroundings are as much a hangout as a shop, complete with a stage for live gigs, a café, and Internet access. There's another branch on Portobello Road in Notting Hill. ✉ *Dray Walk, Old Truman Brewery, 91 Brick La., Spitalfields* ☎ *020/7392–7788* Ⓜ *Liverpool St. London Overground: Shoreditch High St.*

STREET MARKETS

Old Spitalfields Market. Once the East End's wholesale fruit and vegetable market and now restored to its original splendor, this fine example of a Victorian market hall is at the center of the area's gentrified revival.

The original building is largely occupied by shops, with traders' stalls in the courtyard. A modern shopping precinct under a Norman Foster–designed glass canopy adjoins the old building and holds many more traders' stalls. You may have to wade through a certain number of stalls selling cheap imports to find the good stuff, which includes crafts, vintage and new clothing, handmade rugs, jewelry, hand-carved toy trains, unique baby clothes, rare vinyl, and cakes. Thursday is particularly good for antiques; Friday for fashion, art, and a biweekly record fair; and Saturday for produce and handmade crafts. The food outlets (mostly small, upscale chains but some indies as well) sell Spanish tapas, Thai satays, and many other dishes from all over. ✉ *16 Horner Sq., Brushfield St., Spitalfields* ☎ *020/7375–2963* 🌐 *www.oldspitalfieldsmarket.com* 🕓 *Stalls Mon.–Wed. 10–5, Thurs. and Sun. 9–5, Fri. 10–4, Sat. 11–5; restaurants weekdays 11–11, Sun. 9–11 am; retail shops daily 10–7* Ⓜ *Liverpool St. London Overground: Shoreditch High St.*

THE SOUTH BANK

STREET MARKETS

Fodor's Choice ★ **Borough Market.** There's been a market in Borough since Roman times. This latest incarnation, spread under the arches and railroad tracks leading to London Bridge station, is where some of the city's best food sellers set up stalls. Fresh coffees, gorgeous cheeses, olives, and baked goods complement the organically farmed meats, fresh fish, fruits, and vegetables.

Don't make any other lunch plans for the day; this is where celebrity chef Jamie Oliver's scallop man cooks them up fresh at Shell Seekers, and The Ginger Pig's rare-breed sausages sizzle on grills, while for the sweets lover there are chocolates, preserves, and Whirld's artisanal confectionery, as well as 18 restaurants and cafés, most above average. The Market Hall hosts workshops, tastings, and demonstrations and also acts as a greenhouse (even hops are being grown here).

Seven of the original Borough Market traders, including the celebrated Kappacasein Swiss raclette stand that serves heaping plates of melted Ogleshield cheese, have established a separate market on nearby Maltby Street. This opens on Saturday morning from 9 am. ✉ *8 Southwark St., Borough* ☎ *020/7402–1002* 🌐 *www.boroughmarket.org.uk* 🕓 *Mon. and Tues. 10–5 (lunch stalls only), Wed. and Thurs. 10–5, Fri. 10–6, Sat. 8–5* Ⓜ *London Bridge.*

KENSINGTON, KNIGHTSBRIDGE, AND MAYFAIR

ANTIQUES

Alfie's Antique Market. This four-story, bohemian-chic labyrinth is London's largest indoor antiques market, housing over 75 dealers specializing in art, lighting, glassware, textiles, jewelry, furniture, and collectibles, with a particular strength in vintage clothing and 20th-century design. Come here to pick up vintage (1900–70) clothing, accessories, and luggage from Tin Tin Collectables, art-deco items (lamps, small furnishings, and mirrors) at Andrew Martin, or a spectacular mid-20th-century

Italian lighting fixture at Vincenzo Caffarrella. There's also a rooftop restaurant if you need a coffee break. In addition to the market, this end of Church Street is lined with excellent antiques shops. ✉ *13–25 Church St., Marylebone* ☎ *020/7723–6066* 🌐 *www.alfiesantiques.com* ⊗ *Closed Sun. and Mon.* Ⓜ *Marylebone.*

Rupert Cavendish. Having cornered the Biedermeier market, this most high-end of Chelsea dealers has now expanded into art deco, with pieces that are often museum quality. Look out for Frank Lloyd Wright–designed carpets and other 20th-century classics. ✉ *1 Penywern Rd., Kensington* ☎ *020/7731–7041* 🌐 *www.rupertcavendish.co.uk* Ⓜ *Earls Court.*

ACCESSORIES

Fodor's Choice ★ **Lulu Guinness.** Famous for her flamboyantly themed bags (think the satin "bucket" topped with roses or the elaborately beaded red "lips" clutch), Guinness also showcases vintage-inspired luggage and beauty accessories in this frilly little shop, which is just as whimsical as her designs. There are other branches in Mayfair, and The City. ✉ *3 Ellis St., Belgravia* ☎ *020/7823–4828* 🌐 *www.luluguinness.com* ⊗ *Closed Sun.* Ⓜ *Sloane Sq.*

Mulberry. Staying true to its roots in rural Somerset, this luxury goods company epitomizes *le style Anglais*, a sophisticated take on the earth tones and practicality of English country style. Best known for highly desirable luxury handbags, such as those in the Cara Delevigne line and the Bayswater, the company also produces gorgeous leather accessories, from wallets to luggage, as well as shoes and clothing for men and women. Aside from the New Bond Street flagship, there are branches in Knightsbridge and Covent Garden, and Mulberry concessions in most of the major department stores. The small store on St. Christopher's Place in Marylebone stocks accessories only. ✉ *50 New Bond St., Mayfair* ☎ *020/7491–3900* 🌐 *www.mulberry.com* Ⓜ *Bond St.*

Fodor's Choice ★ **Philip Treacy.** Magnificent hats by Treacy are annual showstoppers on Ladies Day at the Royal Ascot races and regularly grace the glossy magazines' society pages. Part Mad Hatter, part Cecil Beaton, Treacy's creations always guarantee a grand entrance (remember Princess Beatrice's eye-catching headdress at the Royal Wedding?). In addition to the extravagant, haute couture hats handmade in the atelier, ready-to-wear hats are also for sale, as are some bags. ✉ *69 Elizabeth St., Belgravia* ☎ *020/7730–3992* 🌐 *www.philiptreacy.co.uk* ⊗ *Closed Sun.* Ⓜ *Sloane Sq.*

Fodor's Choice ★ **Swaine Adeney Brigg.** Providing practical supplies for country pursuits since 1750, Swaine Adeney Brigg carries beautifully crafted umbrellas, walking sticks, and hip flasks, or ingenious combinations, such as the umbrella with a slim tipple-holding flask secreted inside the stem. The same level of quality and craftsmanship applies to the store's leather goods, which include attaché cases (you can buy the "Q Branch" model that James Bond carried in *From Russia with Love*) and wallets. You'll find scarves, caps, and the Herbert Johnson "Poet Hat," the iconic headgear (stocked since 1890) worn by Harrison Ford in every Indiana Jones

Bring your appetite to Borough Market on the South Bank; it's a foodie favorite.

film. ✉ *7 Piccadilly Arcade, St. James's* ☎ *020/7409–7277* 🌐 *www.swaineadeney.co.uk* ⏲ *Closed Sun.* Ⓜ *Green Park.*

BOOKS AND STATIONERY

Smythson of Bond Street. No hostess of any standing would consider having a leather-bound guest book made by anyone other than this elegant stationer, and the shop's social stationery and distinctive diaries, with pale-blue pages, are the epitome of British good taste. Diaries, stationery, and small leather goods can be personalized. Smythson also produces a small line of leather handbags and purses. You'll find other branches in Chelsea, Notting Hill, and The City. ✉ *40 New Bond St., Mayfair* ☎ *020/7629–8558* 🌐 *www.smythson.com* Ⓜ *Bond St., Oxford Circus.*

Waterstone's. At this mega-bookshop (Europe's largest) located in a former art deco department store near Piccadilly Circus, browse through your latest purchase or admire the view with a glass of wine or a snack at the 5th View Bar and Grill, which is open until 9. Waterstone's is the country's leading book chain, and they've pulled out all the stops to make their flagship as comfortable and welcoming as a bookstore can be. There are several smaller branches throughout the city. ✉ *203–206 Piccadilly, Mayfair* ☎ *0207/851–2400* 🌐 *www.waterstones.com* Ⓜ *Piccadilly Circus.*

CLOTHING

Fodor's Choice ★ **Dover Street Market.** With its creative displays and eclectic, well-chosen mix of merchandise, this six-floor emporium is as much art installation as store. The merchandise and its configuration change every six months, so you never know what you will find, which is half the fun.

The creation of Comme des Garçons' Rei Kawakubo, Dover Street Market showcases all of the label's collections for men and women alongside a changing roster of other designers, including Erdem, Alexander Wang, and Givenchy—all of whom have their own customized mini-boutiques—plus avant-garde art books, vintage couture, and curiosities, such as antique plaster anatomy models. An outpost of the Rose Bakery on the top floor makes for a good break. ✉ *17–18 Dover St., Mayfair* ☎ *020/7518–0680* 🌐 *www.doverstreetmarket.com* Ⓜ *Green Park.*

Jack Wills. Jack Wills specializes in heritage and country sports-inspired styles, giving them a fresh, sexy edge. This means crowds of lithe young things who don't mind the pumping music while browsing for slim-line Fair Isle sweaters, fitted plaid shirts, and short floral sundresses for the girls, plus sweatshirts, blazers, skinny cords, and rugby shirts for the boys. The store also carries Union Jack carry-on bags, bobble hats galore, knitted jackets for hot-water bottles, and other traditional-with-irony items. Other branches are in Notting Hill, Covent Garden, Islington, Soho, and Shoreditch. ✉ *72 Kings Rd., Chelsea* ☎ *020/7581–0347* 🌐 *www.jackwills.com* Ⓜ *Sloane Sq.*

CLOTHING: MENSWEAR

Ozwald Boateng. The dapper menswear by Ozwald Boateng (pronounced Bwa-teng) combines contemporary funky style with traditional Savile Row quality. His made-to-measure suits have been worn by trendsetters such as Jamie Foxx, Mick Jagger, and Laurence Fishburne, who appreciate the sharp cuts, luxurious fabrics, and occasionally vibrant colors (even the more conservative choices sport jacket linings in bright silk). ✉ *30 Savile Row, Mayfair* ☎ *020/7437–2030* 🌐 *www.ozwaldboateng.co.uk* ⏲ *Closed Sun.* Ⓜ *Piccadilly Circus.*

CLOTHING: WOMEN'S WEAR

Alexander McQueen. Since McQueen's untimely death in 2010, his right-hand woman Sarah Burton has been at the helm, receiving raves for continuing his tradition of theatrical, darkly romantic, and beautifully cut clothes incorporating corsetry, lace, embroidery, and hourglass silhouettes, all of which were exemplified in Burton's celebrated wedding dress for Kate Middleton. Can't afford a gala gown? Go home with a skull-printed scarf. ✉ *4–5 Old Bond St., Mayfair* ☎ *020/7355–0088* 🌐 *www.alexandermcqueen.com* Ⓜ *Bond St.*

Browns. This shop—actually a collection of small shops—was a pioneer designer boutique in the 1970s and continues to talent-spot the newest and best around. You may find the windows showcasing the work of top graduates from this year's student shows or displaying well-established designers such as Christopher Kane, Valentino, or Balenciaga. The men's store at No. 23 has a similar designer selection, while Browns Focus at No. 24 showcases youthful, hip designs and denim. There is a smaller boutique on Sloane Street, too. If you're about to go down the aisle, check out the two bridal boutiques, one at 12 Hinde Street, which stocks various designers, and another at 59 Brook Street, devoted to Vera Wang gowns exclusive to Browns in the United Kingdom. ✉ *24–27 S. Molton St., Mayfair* ☎ *020/7514–0016* 🌐 *www.brownsfashion.com* ⏲ *Closed Sun.* Ⓜ *Bond St.*

Jigsaw. Jigsaw specializes in clothes that are classic yet trendy, ladylike without being dull. The style is epitomized by the former Kate Middleton, who was a buyer for the company before her marriage. The quality of fabrics and detailing belie the reasonable prices, and the cuts are kind to the womanly figure. Although there are numerous branches across London, no two stores are the same. Preteens have their own line, Jigsaw Junior. ✉ *The Chapel, 6 Duke of York Sq., Chelsea* ☎ *020/730–4404* 🌐 *www.jigsawonline.com* Ⓜ *Sloane Sq.*

Rigby & Peller. Lovers of luxury lingerie shop here for brands like Prima Donna and Aubade, as well as R&P's own line. If the right fit eludes you, the made-to-measure service starts at around £300. Many of London's most affluent women shop here, not only because this is the Queen's favored underwear supplier but also because the quality is excellent and the service impeccably knowledgeable while being much friendlier than you might expect. There are also branches in Mayfair, Chelsea, and The City. ✉ *2 Hans Rd., Knightsbridge* ☎ *020/7225–4760* 🌐 *www.rigbyandpeller.com* Ⓜ *Knightsbridge.*

Stella McCartney. It's not easy emerging from the shadow of a Beatle father, but Stella McCartney has become a major force in fashion in her own right. Her signature jumpsuits and tuxedo pantsuits embody her design philosophy, combining minimalist tailoring with femininity and sophistication with ease of wear. Her love of functionality and clean lines has led to her branching off into sportswear, designing a line for Adidas and dressing Team GB for the London Olympics. A vegetarian like her parents, she refuses to use fur or leather, making her a favorite with similarly minded fashionistas. There's another boutique in South Kensington. ✉ *30 Bruton St., Mayfair* ☎ *020/7518–3100* 🌐 *www.stellamccartney.com* Ⓜ *Bond St.*

Vivienne Westwood. From beginnings as the most shocking and outré designer around, Westwood (now Dame Vivienne) has become a standard bearer for high-style British couture. From the boutique in Chelsea she first sold the lavish corseted ball gowns, the dandyfied nipped-waist jackets, and the tartan with a punk edge that formed the core of her signature look. Here you can still buy ready-to-wear, mainly the more casual Anglomania diffusion line and the exclusive Worlds End label, based on the archives. The small Davies Street boutique sells only the more expensive Gold Label and Couture collections (plus bridal), while the flagship Conduit Street store carries all of the above. ✉ *44 Conduit St., Mayfair* ☎ *020/7439–1109* 🌐 *www.viviennewestwood.co.uk* ⊙ *Closed Sun.* Ⓜ *Oxford Circus.*

DEPARTMENT STORES

Harrods. With an encyclopedic assortment of luxury brands, this Knightsbridge institution, now owned by the State of Qatar, has more than 300 departments and 20 restaurants, all spread over 1 million square feet on a 5-acre site. If you approach Harrods as a blingtastic tourist attraction rather than as a center of elegant sophistication, you won't be disappointed. Focus on the spectacular food halls, the huge ground-floor perfumery, the revamped toy and technology departments, the excellent Urban Retreat spa, and the Vegas-like Egyptian Room.

Nevertheless, standards of taste are enforced with a customer dress code (no shorts, ripped jeans, or flip-flops). Be prepared to brave the crowds, especially on weekends. ✉ *87–135 Brompton Rd., Knightsbridge* ☎ *020/7730–1234* 🌐 *www.harrods.com* Ⓜ *Knightsbridge.*

Fodor's Choice ★ **Harvey Nichols.** While visiting tourists flock to Harrods, fashionistas shop at Harvey Nichols, aka "Harvey Nicks." The womenswear and accessories departments are outstanding, featuring top designers like McQueen, Alexander Wang, Lanvin, Louboutin, and just about every trendy name you can think of. The furniture and housewares are equally gorgeous (and pricey), though they become somewhat more affordable during the twice-annual sales in January and July. The Fifth Floor restaurant is the place to see and be seen, but if you're just after a quick bite, there's also a more informal café on the same floor or sushi-to-go from Yo! Sushi. To keep you looking as fresh as the fashion, there's also a MediSpa, an Elemis spa, and a hair salon, plus nail and brow bars. ✉ *109–125 Knightsbridge, Knightsbridge* ☎ *020/7235–5000* 🌐 *www.harveynichols.com* Ⓜ *Knightsbridge.*

Marks & Spencer. You'd be hard-pressed to find a Brit who doesn't have something in the closet from Marks & Spencer (or "M&S," as it's popularly known). This major chain is famed for its classic, dependable clothing for men, women, and children—affordable cashmere and lambswool sweaters are particularly good buys—and occasionally scores a fashion hit. The food department at M&S is consistently good, especially for frozen food, and a great place to pick up a sandwich or premade salad on the go (look for M&S Simply Food stores all over town). The flagship branch at Marble Arch and the Pantheon location at 173 Oxford Street have extensive fashion departments. ✉ *458 Oxford St., Marylebone* ☎ *020/7935–7954* 🌐 *www.marksandspencer.com* Ⓜ *Marble Arch.*

Fodor's Choice ★ **Selfridges.** This giant, bustling store (the second largest in the United Kingdom after Harrods) gives Harvey Nichols a run for its money as London's most fashionable department store. Packed to the rafters with clothes ranging from mid-price lines to the latest catwalk names, the store continues to break ground with its innovative retail schemes, especially the ground-floor Wonder Room (for extravagant jewelry and luxury gifts), the self-contained Louis Vuitton "town house," a dedicated Denim Studio, an array of pop-up shops, and the Concept Store, used for a rotating series of themed displays There are so many zones that merge into one another—from youth-oriented Miss Selfridge to audio equipment to the large, comprehensive cosmetics department—that you practically need a map. Don't miss the Shoe Galleries, the world's largest shoe department, which is filled with more than 5,000 pairs from 120 brands, displayed like works of art under spotlights. Take a break with a glass of wine at the rooftop restaurant or pick up some tea in the Food Hall as a gift. At the Everyman movie theater in the basement, you can watch first-run art-house movies. ✉ *400 Oxford St., Marylebone* ☎ *0800/123400* 🌐 *www.selfridges.com* Ⓜ *Bond St.*

2

HOUSEHOLD

The Conran Shop. This is the brainchild of Sir Terence Conran, who has been a major influence on British taste since he opened Habitat in the 1960s. Although he is no longer associated with Habitat, his Conran Shops remain bastions of similarly clean, unfussy modernist design. Housewares from furniture to stemware and textiles—both handmade and mass-produced, by famous names and emerging designers—are housed in a building that is a modernist design landmark in its own right. Both the flagship store and the branch on Marylebone High Street are bursting with great gift ideas. ✉ *Michelin House, 81 Fulham Rd., South Kensington* ☎ *020/7589–7401* 🌐 *www.conranshop.co.uk* Ⓜ *South Kensington.*

JEWELRY

Asprey. Refurbished a decade ago by architect Norman Foster and interior designer David Mlinaric (some 155 years after Asprey first moved in), this "global flagship" store displays exquisite jewelry—as well as silver and leather goods, watches, china, and crystal—in a discreet, very British setting that oozes quality, expensive good taste, and hushed comfort. If you're in the market for an immaculate 1930s cigarette case, a silver cocktail shaker, a pair of pavé diamond and sapphire earrings, or a ladylike handbag, you won't be disappointed. And, for the really well-heeled, there's a custom-made jewelry service available as well. ✉ *167 New Bond St., Mayfair* ☎ *020/7493–6767* 🌐 *www.asprey.com* ⏲ *Closed Sun.* Ⓜ *Green Park.*

Butler & Wilson. Specialists in bold costume jewelry and affordable glamor, Butler & Wilson have added semiprecious stones to their foundation diamanté, colored rhinestone, and crystal collections. Flamboyant skull brooches or dainty floral earrings make perfect gifts. ✉ *189 Fulham Rd., South Kensington* ☎ *020/7352–3045* 🌐 *www.butlerandwilson.co.uk* Ⓜ *South Kensington.*

Kabiri. A carefully curated array of exciting contemporary jewelry by emerging and established designers from around the world is packed into this small shop. There is something to suit most budgets and tastes, from flamboyant statement pieces to subtle, delicate adornment. Look out for British talent Johanne Mills, among many others. There's another branch in Chelsea. ✉ *37 Marylebone High St., Marylebone* ☎ *020/7317–2150* 🌐 *www.kabiri.co.uk* Ⓜ *Baker St.*

NOTTING HILL

BOOKS

Fodor's Choice ★ **Books for Cooks.** It may seem odd to describe a bookshop as delicious-smelling, but the aromas wafting out of the tiny test kitchen—which serves daily-changing lunch dishes drawn from recipes in the 8,000 cookbooks on the shelves, as well as cakes and culinary experiments—will whet your appetite even before you've opened one of the books. Just about every world cuisine is represented, along with a complete lineup of works by celebrity chefs. Before you come to London, visit the shop's website to sign up for a cooking class. ✉ *4 Blenheim Crescent,*

Notting Hill ☎ 020/7221–1992 🌐 www.booksforcooks.com ⏲ Closed Sun. and Mon. Ⓜ Notting Hill Gate, Ladbroke Grove.

MUSIC

Music & Video Exchange. This store is a music collector's treasure trove, with a constantly changing stock refreshed by customers selling and exchanging as well as buying. The main store focuses on rock, pop, soul, and dance, both mainstream and obscure, in a variety of formats ranging from vinyl to CD, cassette, and even mini-disk. Don't miss the discounts in the basement and the rarities upstairs. Classical music is at No. 40, comics and books on nearby Pembridge Road, and there are branches in Soho and Greenwich. ✉ *38 Notting Hill Gate, Notting Hill ☎ 020/7243–8573 🌐 www.mgeshops.com Ⓜ Notting Hill Gate.*

STREET MARKETS

Portobello Market. Still considered the best all-round market in town by many fans, and certainly the most famous, Portobello Market stretches almost 2 miles, from fashionable Notting Hill to the lively cultural melting pot of North Kensington, changing character as it goes.

The southern end, starting at Chepstow Villas and going to Elgin Crescent, is lined with shops, stalls, and arcades selling antiques, silver, and bric-a-brac on Saturday. The middle, from Elgin Crescent to Talbot, is devoted to fruit and vegetables, interspersed with excellent hot food stalls. On Friday and Saturday, the area between Talbot Road and the elevated highway (called the Westway) becomes more of a flea market specializing in new household and mass-produced goods sold at a discount. North of the Westway up to Goldborne Road are more stalls selling even cheaper secondhand household goods and bric-a-brac. Scattered throughout but mostly concentrated under the Westway are clothing stalls selling vintage pieces and items from emerging designers, custom T-shirts, and supercool baby clothes, plus jewelry. New and established designers are also found in the boutiques of the Portobello Green Arcade.

Some say Portobello Road has become a tourist trap, but if you acknowledge that it's a circus and get into the spirit, it's a lot of fun. Perhaps you won't find many bargains, but this is such a fascinating part of town that just hanging out is a good enough excuse to come. There are some food and flower stalls throughout the week (try the Hummingbird Bakery for delicious cupcakes) but Saturday is when the market in full swing. Serious shoppers avoid the crowds and go on Friday morning. Bring cash (several vendors don't take credit cards), but also be sure to keep an eye on it. ✉ *Portobello Rd., Notting Hill 🌐 www.portobelloroad.co.uk ⏲ Mon.–Wed. 9–6, Thurs. 9–1, Fri. and Sat. 9–7 Ⓜ Notting Hill Gate.*

THE SOUTHEAST

WELCOME TO THE SOUTHEAST

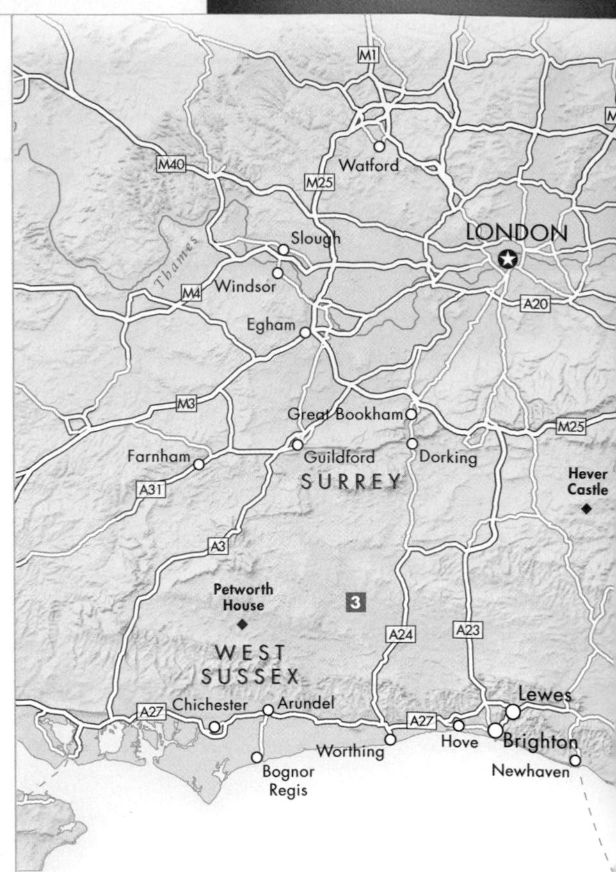

TOP REASONS TO GO

★ **Bodiam, Dover, Hever, and Herstmonceux castles:** Take your pick from the most evocative castles in a region filled with them, and let these fortresses dazzle you with their fortitude and fascinate you with their histories.

★ **Brighton:** With its nightclubs, sunbathing, and funky atmosphere, this is the quintessential modern English seaside city.

★ **Canterbury Cathedral:** This massive building, a textbook of medieval architecture, inspires awe with its soaring towers and flagstone corridors.

★ **Treasure houses:** Here is one of England's richest concentrations of historic homes: among the superlatives are Petworth House, Knole, Ightham Mote, and Chartwell.

★ **Amazing gardens:** Gardens of all kinds are an English specialty, and at Sissinghurst and Wisley, as well as in the gardens of Hever Castle and Chartwell, you can easily spend an entire afternoon wandering through acres of floral exotica.

1 Canterbury and Dover. Dover's distinctive chalk-white cliffs plunging hundreds of feet into the sea are just a part of this region's dramatic coastal scenery. Don't miss Canterbury's medieval town center, dominated by its massive cathedral.

2 Rye and Lewes. Medieval villages dot the hills along this stretch of Sussex coastline. The centerpiece is Rye, a pretty hill town of cobbled streets lined with timbered homes. Lewes, with its crumbling castle, is another gem.

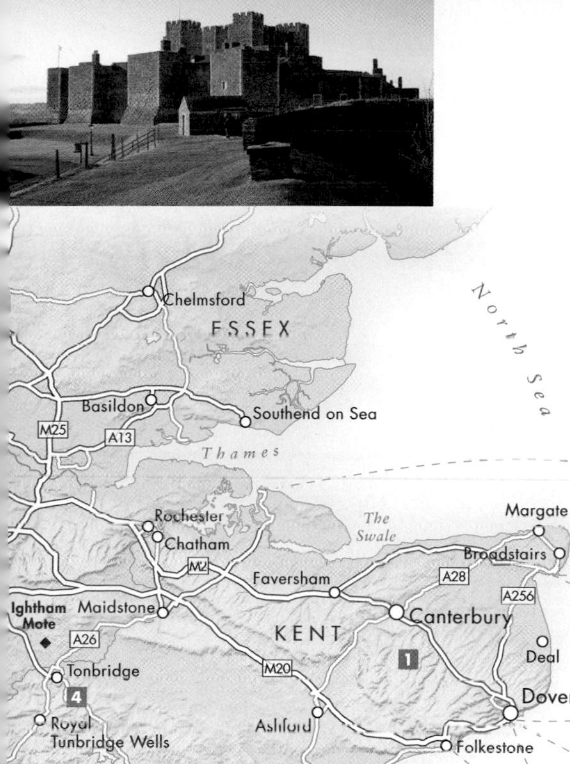

GETTING ORIENTED

For sightseeing purposes, the Southeast can be divided into four sections. The eastern part of the region takes in the cathedral town of Canterbury, as well as the port city of Dover. The next section stretches along the southern coast from the medieval hill town of Rye to picturesque Lewes. A third area reaches from the coastal city of Brighton inward to Chichester and to sprawling Guildford. The fourth section takes in the spa town of Royal Tunbridge Wells and western Kent, where stately homes and castles dot the farmland. Larger towns in the area can be easily reached by train or bus from London for a day trip. To visit most castles, grand country homes, or quiet villages, though, you need to rent a car or join a tour.

3 Brighton, the Sussex Coast, and Surrey. Funky, lively Brighton perfectly melds Victorian architecture with a modern vibe that includes the best shopping and dining on the coast. Outside town are beautiful old homes such as Petworth House and even a Roman villa.

4 Tunbridge Wells and Around. From Anne Boleyn's regal childhood abode at Hever Castle to the medieval manor at Ightham Mote, this area is rich with grand houses. Spend a couple of days exploring them; Tunbridge Wells is a comfortable base.

TEA TIME IN ENGLAND

Tea is often called the national drink, and for good reason. Most people start their day with "a cuppa," have tea breaks in the afternoon, and a cup after dinner. Join in by lifting a cup, or try a cream tea with a scone or a fancier formal afternoon tea.

(*above*) Relaxing with tea and a scone with clotted cream and jam is a civilized pastime; (*top right*) Cucumber sandwiches at afternoon tea; (*right, bottom*) Tea store

It's hard to imagine a time when tea wasn't part of English culture. But there was no tea in Europe until the 1600s, when it was first brought by Portuguese and Dutch traders. Charles II and his wife, Catherine of Braganza, were tea drinkers. When coffeehouses in London began serving the drink in the mid-17th century, it was seen as an expensive curiosity. By the early 18th century tea was sold in coffeehouses all over the country, and consumed by all classes. The duchess of Bedford is credited with popularizing formal afternoon tea in the early 1800s. Dinner in those days was often not served until after 8 pm, so a light meal in late afternoon was welcome. The tradition faded when more people began working in offices in the 20th century—though the love of tea remains.

WHICH TEA?

England's most popular tea is English Breakfast tea, a full-bodied blend of black teas. Second in line is Earl Grey: oil of bergamot orange creates an elegant perfume, but it's an acquired taste. Assam is one of the major teas blended into English Breakfast, and it tastes similar, if a bit more brisk. By contrast, Darjeeling is light and delicate; it's perfect for afternoons.

CREAM TEA

In popular tourist areas in Britain, signs everywhere advertise "cream tea." This is the national shorthand for "tea and scones." The "cream" part is delectable clotted cream—a cream so thick it has a texture like whipped butter. Some scones are fruity and have raisins or dried fruit; others are more like a cross between American biscuits and shortbread. Along with the cream, you'll usually be offered jam. It's customary to put both jam and cream on the scone, treating the cream like butter.

Cream teas are widely offered in areas favored by travelers, such as Stratford-upon-Avon, the Cotswolds, Devon, and Canterbury. In those regions you'll see it advertised in pubs, restaurants, and dedicated tea shops. Cream tea is a casual afternoon affair: think of it as a coffee break, with tea. Your tea will likely be a teabag rather than loose tea. The cost is usually from £3 to £7.

AFTERNOON TEA

A pricey treat reserved for vacations and special occasions, afternoon tea (called "high tea" in America, but not in England, where that term referred to a meal between 5 and 7 pm) is served in upscale hotels in London, but also in Oxford, Cambridge, and Brighton, or anywhere popular with travelers. Along with tea—and you can choose from a variety of teas—you'll be served finger

sandwiches (usually cucumber, egg, ham, and smoked salmon) and scones, as well as tiny cakes and pastries. These will usually be brought on tiered plate stands, with sweet options higher up and savory on the lower level. Tea will be brewed in a china pot and served with china cups and saucers; milk and lemon are accompaniments.

Afternoon tea is generally offered between 3 and 5:30 pm and can last for hours. It's generally quite formal, and most people dress up for the occasion. Expect to spend from £17 to £50.

TEA IN THE SOUTHEAST

Michael Caines. In Canterbury, afternoon tea in this restaurant at the ABode hotel has all the requisite teas, finger sandwiches, cakes, and scones. ✉ *ABode Canterbury, 30–33 High St., Canterbury* ☎ *01227/766266* 🌐 *www.michaelcaines.com.*

Very good cream teas are served in the tearooms at all National Trust–run houses and gardens, as well as at most other historic estates open to the public.

Victoria Lounge at the Grand Brighton. Afternoon tea at this elegant hotel is a local tradition. Dress up to fit in. ✉ *Grand Brighton Hotel, 97–99 Kings Rd., Brighton* ☎ *01273/224300* 🌐 *www.grandbrighton.co.uk.*

Updated by Jack Jewers

Surrey, Kent, and Sussex form the breadbasket of England, where bucolic farmland stretches as far as the eye can see. Once a favorite destination of English nobility, this region is rich with history, visible in the great castles and stately homes that dot the countryside. Its cities are similarly historic, especially ancient Canterbury, with its spectacular cathedral and medieval streets. Along the coast, funky seaside towns have a more relaxed attitude, especially artsy Brighton, where artists and musicians use the sea as inspiration for their work.

Although it's close to London (both Surrey and Kent reach all the way to London's suburbs) and is one of the most densely populated areas of Britain, the Southeast feels far away from the big city. In Kent, acres of orchards burst into a mass of pink-and-white blossoms in spring, while Dover's white cliffs and brooding castle have become symbols of Britain. Historic mansions, such as Petworth House and Knole, are major draws for travelers, and lush gardens such as Vita Sackville-West's Sissinghurst and the Royal Horticultural Society's Wisley attract thousands to their vivid floral displays.

Because the English Channel is at its narrowest here, a great deal of British history has been forged in the Southeast. The Romans landed in this area and stayed to rule Britain for four centuries. So did the Saxons—*Sussex* means "the land of the South Saxons." The biggest invasion of them all took place here when William ("the Conqueror") of Normandy defeated the Saxons at a battle near Hastings in 1066, changing the island forever.

SOUTHEAST PLANNER

WHEN TO GO

It's best to visit in spring, summer, or early fall. Many privately owned castles and mansions are open only between April and September or October. Failing that, the parks surrounding the stately houses are often open all year. If crowds tend to spoil your fun, avoid August, Sunday, and national holidays, particularly in Canterbury and the seaside towns.

PLANNING YOUR TIME

With the exception of Brighton, you can easily see the highlights of each of the towns in less than a day. Brighton has more to offer, and you should allot at least two days to take it all in. Consider basing yourself in one town while exploring a region. For example, you could stay in Brighton and take in Lewes on a day trip. Base yourself in Rye for a couple of days while exploring Winchelsea, Battle, Hastings, and Herstmonceux Castle. Tunbridge Wells is a great place to overnight if you plan on exploring the many stately homes and castles nearby.

GETTING HERE AND AROUND

AIR TRAVEL

Heathrow is convenient for Surrey, but Gatwick Airport is a more convenient gateway for Kent. The rail station inside Gatwick has trains to Brighton and other major towns, and you can take a taxi from Heathrow to Guildford for around £50.

BUS TRAVEL

National Express buses serve the region from London's Victoria Coach Station. Trips to Brighton and Canterbury take two hours; to Chichester, three hours. Megabus runs buses at budget prices from Victoria Coach Station to many of the same destinations as National Express and can be cheaper, although luggage limits are strict.

Bus service between towns can be useful but is often intermittent. Out in the country, don't expect buses more often than once every half hour or hour. Sometimes trains are a better option; sometimes they're much worse. Traveline is the best central place to call for bus information, and local tourist information centers can be a big help.

Contacts Megabus. ☎ *0900/160–0900* 🌐 *www.megabus.co.uk.* **National Express.** ☎ *0871/781–8178* 🌐 *www.nationalexpress.com.* **Traveline.** ☎ *0871/200–2233* 🌐 *www.traveline.org.uk.*

CAR TRAVEL

Traveling by car is the best way to get to the stately homes and castles in the region. Having a car in Canterbury or Brighton, however, is a nuisance; you'll need to park and walk. Major routes radiating outward from London to the Southeast are, from west to east, M23/A23 to Brighton (52 miles); A21, passing by Royal Tunbridge Wells to Hastings (65 miles); A20/M20 to Folkestone (58 miles); and A2/M2 via Canterbury (56 miles) to Dover (71 miles).

TRAIN TRAVEL

Trains are the fastest and most efficient way to travel to major cities in the region, but they don't stop in many small towns. From London, Southeastern trains serve Sussex and Kent from Victoria and Charing Cross stations, and South West trains travel to Surrey from Waterloo Station. Getting to Brighton takes about 1 hour, to Canterbury about 1½ hours, and to Dover between 1½ and 2 hours. A Network Railcard costing £30, valid throughout the southern and southeastern regions for a year, entitles you and three companions to one-third off many off-peak fares.

Contacts National Rail Enquiries. ☎ *0845/748–4950* 🌐 *www.nationalrail.co.uk.* **Network Railcard.** ☎ *0345/300–0250* 🌐 *www.railcard.co.uk.*

RESTAURANTS

If you're in a seaside town, look for that great British staple, fish-and-chips. Perhaps "look" isn't the word—just follow your nose. On the coast, seafood, much of it locally caught, is a specialty. Try local smoked fish (haddock and mackerel) or the succulent local oysters. Inland, sample fresh local lamb and beef. In cities such as Brighton and Tunbridge Wells there are numerous restaurants and cafés, but out in the countryside the best options are often pubs.

HOTELS

All around the coast, resort towns stretch along beaches, their hotels standing cheek by jowl. Of the smaller hotels and guesthouses not all remain open year-round; many do business only from mid-April to September or October. Some hotels have all-inclusive rates for a week's stay. Prices rise in July and August, when the seaside resorts can get solidly booked, especially Brighton. (On the other hand, hotels may drop rates by up to 40% off season.) Places in Brighton may not take a booking for a single night in summer or on weekends. *Hotel reviews have been shortened. For full information, visit Fodors.com.*

WHAT IT COSTS IN POUNDS

	$	$$	$$$	$$$$
Restaurants	under £15	£15–£19	£20–£25	over £25
Hotels	under £100	£100–£160	£161–£220	over £220

Restaurant prices are per person for a main course at dinner, or if dinner is not served, at lunch. Hotels prices are the lowest cost of a standard double room in high season, including 20% V.A.T.

VISITOR INFORMATION

Tourist boards in the main towns can help with information, and many will also book local accommodations.

Contacts Southeast England Tourist Board. 🌐 *www.visitsoutheastengland.com.*

CANTERBURY AND DOVER

The cathedral city of Canterbury is an ancient place that has attracted travelers since the 12th century. Its magnificent cathedral, the Mother Church of England, remains a powerful draw. Even in prehistoric times, this part of England was relatively well settled. Saxon settlers, Norman conquerors, and the folk who lived here in late-medieval times all left their mark. From Canterbury there's rewarding wandering to be done in the gentle Kentish countryside between the city and the busy port of Dover. Here the landscape ravishes the eye in spring with apple blossoms, and in autumn with lush fields ready for harvest. It's a county of orchards, market gardens, and round oast houses with their tilted, pointed roofs; they were once used for drying hops, but now many are expensive homes.

CANTERBURY

56 miles southeast of London.

Just mention Canterbury and most people are taken back to memories of high-school English classes and Geoffrey Chaucer's *Canterbury Tales,* about medieval pilgrims making their way to Canterbury Cathedral. Judging from the tales, however, in those days Canterbury was as much a party town as it was a spiritual center.

The city has been the seat of the Primate of All England, the archbishop of Canterbury, since Pope Gregory the Great dispatched St. Augustine to convert the pagan hordes of Britain in 597. The height of Canterbury's popularity came in the 12th century, when thousands of pilgrims flocked here to see the shrine of the murdered archbishop St. Thomas à Becket. This southeastern town became one of the most visited in England, if not Europe. Buildings that served as pilgrims' inns (and that survived World War II bombing of the city) still dominate the streets of Canterbury's center, though it's tourists, not pilgrims, who flock to this city of about 40,000 people today.

Prices at city museums are higher than average, so if you plan to see more than one, ask at the tourist office if a combination ticket might be cheaper.

GETTING HERE AND AROUND

The fastest way to reach Canterbury from London is by train. Southeastern trains to Canterbury run every half hour in peak times from London's Charing Cross Station. The journey takes between 1 and 1½ hours. Canterbury has two centrally located train stations, Canterbury East Station (a five-minute walk from the cathedral square) and Canterbury West Station (a 10-minute walk from the cathedral).

National Express and Megabus buses bound for Canterbury depart several times a day from London's Victoria Coach Station. Trips to Canterbury take around two hours, and drop passengers near the train stations. If you're driving, take the A2/M2 to Canterbury from London (56 miles). Park in one of the signposted parking lots at the edge of the town center.

Canterbury has a small, walkable town center. Although the town has good local bus service, you're unlikely to need it. Most major tourist sites are on one street that changes name three times—beginning as St. George's Street and then becoming High Street and St. Peter's Street.

TIMING

The town tends to get crowded around religious holidays—particularly Easter weekend—and on other national holiday weekends. If you'd rather avoid the tour buses, try visiting midweek.

ESSENTIALS

Visitor Information Canterbury Visitor Centre. ✉ *The Beaney House of Art & Knowledge, 18 High St.* ☎ *01227/862162* 🌐 *www.canterbury.co.uk.*

TOURS

Canterbury Guided Tours. Expert guides lead walking tours at 11 am daily, with an additional tour at 2 pm from April to October. ✉ *Arnett House, Hawks La.* ☎ *01227/459779* 🌐 *www.canterburyguidedtours.com* 🎫 *From £7.*

EXPLORING

TOP ATTRACTIONS

Beaney House of Art and Knowledge. This excellent museum contains a small but impressive collection of art and artifacts relating to Kentish rural life. Permanent galleries include rooms devoted to the work of local painter Thomas Sidney Cooper (1803–1902), known for his scenes of Kentish rural life; a museum of Anglo-Saxon jewelry and other objects from the region, including a 6th-century glass beaker; and an eclectic cabinet of curiosities dating from the 18th century. Handily enough, the tourism office is also located here. ✉ *18 High St.* ☎ *01227/862162* 🌐 *www.canterbury.co.uk/beaney* 🎫 *Free* ⏲ *Mon.–Wed., Fri., and Sat. 9–5, Thurs. 9–7, Sun. 10–5.*

Fodor's Choice ★ **Canterbury Cathedral.** The focal point of the city was the first of England's great Norman cathedrals. Nucleus of worldwide Anglicanism, the Cathedral Church of Christ Canterbury (its formal name) is a living textbook of medieval architecture. The building was begun in 1070, demolished, begun anew in 1096, and then systematically expanded over the next three centuries. When the original choir section burned to the ground in 1174, another replaced it, designed in the new Gothic style, with tall, pointed arches.

The cathedral was only a century old, and still relatively small, when Thomas Becket, the archbishop of Canterbury, was murdered here in 1170. Becket, as head of the church, had been engaged in a political struggle with his old friend Henry II. Four knights supposedly overheard Henry scream "will no one will rid me of this troublesome priest?" although there is no evidence that those were his actual words—the only contemporary record has his saying "what miserable drones and traitors have I nourished and brought up in my household, who let their lord be treated with such shameful contempt by a low-born cleric?"

Thinking they were carrying out the king's wishes, the knights went immediately to Canterbury and hacked Becket to pieces in one of the side chapels. Henry, racked with guilt, went into deep mourning. Becket was canonized and Canterbury's position as the center of English Christianity was assured.

For almost 400 years Becket's tomb was one of the most extravagent shrines in Christendom, until it was destroyed by Henry VIII's troops during the Reformation. In **Trinity Chapel,** which held the shrine, you can still see a series of 13th-century stained-glass windows illustrating Becket's miracles. (The actual site of Becket's murder is down a flight of steps just to the left of the nave.) Nearby is the tomb of Edward, the Black Prince (1330–76), warrior son of Edward III and a national hero. In the corner of Trinity Chapel, a second flight of steps leads down to the enormous Norman **undercroft,** or vaulted cellar, built in the early 12th century. A row of squat pillars engraved with dancing beasts (mythical and otherwise) supports the roof.

To the north of the Cathedral are the **cloisters** and a small compound of monastic buildings. The 12th-century octagonal water tower is still part of the cathedral's water supply. The Norman staircase in the northwest corner of the Green Court dates from 1167 and is a unique example of the architecture of the times. **■TIP→ The cathedral is popular, so arrive early or late in the day to avoid the crowds.** ✉ *Cathedral Precincts* ☎ *01227/762862* 🌐 *www.canterbury-cathedral.org* 🎫 *£10.50; free for services and ½ hr before closing; £5 tour; £4 audio guide* ⏲ *Cathedral Easter–Oct., Mon.–Sat. 9–5:30, Sun. 12:30–2:30; Nov–Easter, Mon.–Sat. 9–5, Sun. 12:30–2:30. Crypt Mon.–Sat. 10–5:30 (5 in winter). Last entry ½ hr before closing. Restricted access during services. Tours weekdays 10:30 (except Jan.), noon, and 2 (2:30 summer), Sat. 10:30, noon, and 1.*

QUICK BITES

The Custard Tart. A short walk from the cathedral, the Custard Tart serves freshly made sandwiches, pies, tarts, and cakes, along with steaming cups of tea and coffee. You can take your selection upstairs to the seating area. Arrive early, as it's not open for dinner. ✉ ***35A St. Margaret's St.*** ☎ ***01227/785178.***

Canterbury Roman Museum. Below ground, at the level of the remnants of Roman Canterbury, this museum features colorful mosaic Roman pavement and a hypocaust—the Roman version of central heating. Displays of excavated objects (some of which you can hold in the **Touch the Past** area) and computer-generated reconstructions of Roman buildings and the marketplace help re-create the past. **■TIP→ Up to four kids get in free with an adult.** ✉ *Butchery La.* ☎ *01227/785575* 🌐 *www.canterbury.co.uk/museums* 🎫 *£8; combined ticket with Canterbury Heritage Museum £10* ⏲ *Daily 10–5; last admission 45 min before closing.*

Medieval City Walls. For an essential Canterbury experience, follow the circuit of the 13th- and 14th-century walls, built on the line of the Roman walls. Roughly half survive; those to the east are intact, towering some 20 feet high and offering a sweeping view of the town. You can access these from a number of places, including Castle Street and Broad Street. ✉ *Canterbury.*

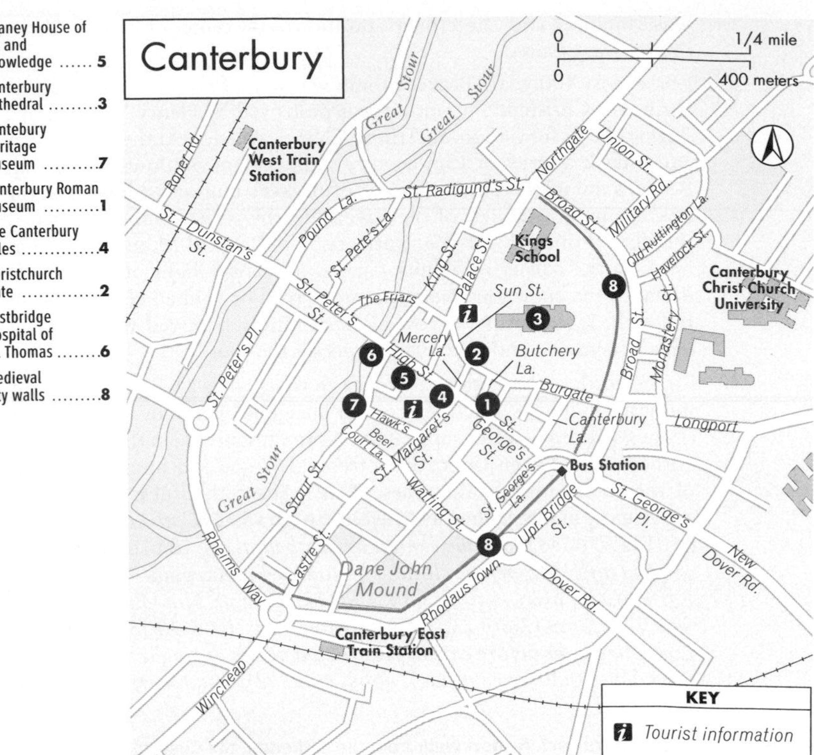

WORTH NOTING

FAMILY **Canterbury Heritage Museum.** The medieval Poor Priests' Hospital is the site of this quirky local museum, where exhibits provide an overview of the city's history and architecture from Roman times to World War II. It covers everything and everyone associated with the town, including the Blitz, the mysterious death of the 16th-century writer Christopher Marlowe, and the British children's book and TV characters Rupert the Bear and Bagpuss. Kids get in free with their parents. ✉ *20 Stour St.* ☎ *01227/475202* 🌐 *www.canterbury.co.uk/museums* 🎫 *£8; combined ticket with Canterbury Roman Museum £10* ⏱ *Late Mar.–Sept., Wed.–Sun. 11–5; also 1 wk in late Oct/early Nov. and late Dec./early Jan., daily 11–5.*

FAMILY **The Canterbury Tales.** Take an audiovisual tour of the sights and sounds (and smells) of 14th-century England at this cheesy but popular attraction. You'll "meet" Chaucer's pilgrims and view tableaux illustrating five of his tales. In summer, costumed actors perform scenes from the town's history. ✉ *St. Margaret's St.* ☎ *01227/479227* 🌐 *www.canterburytales.org.uk* 🎫 *£9* ⏱ *Jan.–Feb., and Nov.–Dec., daily 10–4:30; Mar.–June, Sept., and Oct., daily 10–5; July and Aug., daily 9:30–5.*

Christchurch Gate. This immense gate, built in 1517, leads into the cathedral close. As you pass through, look up at the sculpted heads of two

Impressive both inside and out, ancient Canterbury Cathedral dominates the town.

young figures: Prince Arthur, elder brother of Henry VIII, and the young Catherine of Aragon, to whom Arthur was betrothed. After Arthur's death, Catherine married Henry. Her failure to produce a male heir after 25 years of marriage led to Henry's decision to divorce her, creating an irrevocable breach with the Roman Catholic Church and altering the course of English history. ✉ *Cathedral Close.*

Eastbridge Hospital of St. Thomas. The 12th-century building (which would now be called a hostel) lodged pilgrims who came to pray at the tomb of Thomas Becket. It's a tiny place, fascinating in its simplicity. The refectory, the chapel, and the crypt are open to the public. ✉ *25 High St.* ☎ *01227/471668* 🌐 *www.eastbridgehospital.org.uk* 🎟 *£3* 🕓 *Mon.–Sat. 10–5; last admission 4:30.*

WHERE TO EAT

$ BRITISH **✕ City Fish Bar.** Long lines and lots of satisfied finger-licking attest to the deserved popularity of this excellent fish-and-chip shop in the center of town. Everything is freshly fried, the batter crisp, and the fish tasty; the fried mushrooms are also surprisingly good. There's no seating, so your fish is wrapped up in paper and you eat it where you want, perhaps in the park. This place closes at 7. $ *Average main: £7* ✉ *30 St. Margaret's St.* ☎ *01227/760873.*

$$ BRITISH **✕ The Goods Shed.** Next to Canterbury West Station, this vaulted wooden space with stone-and-brick walls was a storage shed in Victorian times. Now it's a farmers' market with a restaurant that has wooden tables and huge arched windows overlooking the market and a butchers' stall. It's well known for offering fresh, seasonal Kentish food—think locally caught fish and smoked meats, local cider, and freshly baked bread.

Whatever is freshest that day appears on the menu, whether it's John Dory with garlic, or steak with blue cheese butter. *Average main: £19* *Station Rd. W.* *01227/459153* *www.thegoodsshed.co.uk* *Closed Mon. No dinner Sun.*

$$ MODERN FRENCH Fodor's Choice ★ **Michael Caines at ABode.** Canterbury's most sought-after tables are at Michael Caines (not the actor—an eminent British chef with a similar name). Occupying a light-filled corner of the trendy ABode Canterbury, with its pine tables, white walls, and sophisticated country style, this place is hugely popular with local foodies. The modern European cuisine is excellent; dishes change weekly but could include roast partridge with toasted walnuts or Kentish pork with pumpkin puree that's spiced with smoked paprika. Leave room for a dessert of chocolate fondant with salted peanuts or apple mousse served with green apple sorbet. The seven-course tasting menu (£55, or £85 with matching wine) is great for special occasions. **■TIP→ True aficionados will want to reserve the chef's table in the kitchen to watch the staff in action.** *Average main: £19* *ABode Canterbury, 30–33 High St.* *01227/766266* *www.abodecanterbury.co.uk/michael-caines-dining/michael-caines-restaurants* *Reservations essential.*

$ BRITISH **Old Brewery Tavern.** Although it's part of a hotel, this pub has a separate entrance leading to a room with polished floors, wooden tables, and whitewashed stone. The menu and kitchen are overseen by top chef Michael Caines, so it's a good place to try his food at a much more reasonable price. The atmosphere is relaxed and casual, except on weekend nights when the music gets turned up for the party crowd. Expect reliably good comfort food—juicy burgers, crispy fish-and-chips, or sirloin steak grilled to order. The courtyard is perfect for alfresco dining. *Average main: £11* *ABode Canterbury, 30–33 High St.* *01227/766266* *www.abodecanterbury.co.uk/eat-drink/old-brewery-tavern-canterbury.*

$ BRITISH **Old Buttermarket.** A colorful, friendly old pub near the cathedral, the Buttermarket is a great place to grab a hearty lunch and sample some traditional English fare with a modern inflection. You can indulge in a fresh English ale from the changing selection while sampling some chicken and mushroom pie with Chantenay carrots, or perhaps a wild boar chorizo burger if you're feeling more adventurous. There's been a pub on this site for more than 500 years; historical records show that there were once secret tunnels connecting it to Canterbury Cathedral. *Average main: £11* *39 Burgate* *01227/462170* *www.nicholsonspubs.co.uk/theoldbuttermarketcanterbury* *No credit cards.*

WHERE TO STAY

$$ HOTEL **ABode Canterbury.** This glossy boutique hotel inside the old city walls offers up-to-date style in traditional Canterbury, with good-size rooms—modern but not minimal—classed as Comfortable, Desirable, and Enviable. **Pros:** central location; luxurious handmade beds; great restaurants and bars. **Cons:** one of the priciest hotels in town; bar gets quite crowded; breakfast is extra. *Rooms from: £130* *30–33 High St.* *01227/766266* *www.abodecanterbury.co.uk* *73 rooms* *No meals.*

$$ HOTEL **Canterbury Cathedral Lodge.** Small and modern, this hotel tucked away within the grounds of the cathedral has quiet, soothingly decorated rooms with creamy white walls and exposed oak trim. **Pros:** outstanding location; incredible views; free entry to the cathedral (worth £10.50). **Cons:** no restaurant; few services. *Rooms from: £115* *The Precincts* *01227/865350* *www.canterburycathedrallodge.org* *35 rooms* *Breakfast.*

$$ HOTEL **Ebury Hotel.** Family-run, this hotel earns raves for its laid-back attitude and comfortable accommodations inside two big Victorian buildings. **Pros:** cozy lounge; free Wi-Fi; three- and four-bed rooms good value for families. **Cons:** a bit of a walk to the town center; no elevator. *Rooms from: £120* *65–67 New Dover Rd.* *01227/768433* *www.ebury-hotel.co.uk* *15 rooms* *Breakfast.*

$ B&B/INN **Magnolia House.** A converted Georgian house with a walled garden, this lovely B&B with a traditional air is a 10-minute walk from the center of town. **Pros:** adorable house; friendly atmosphere; free Wi-Fi. **Cons:** a bit of a walk to the town center; some rooms are small; no elevator. *Rooms from: £105* *36 St. Dunstan's Terr.* *01227/765121* *www.magnoliahousecanterbury.co.uk* *7 rooms* *Breakfast.*

$$ B&B/INN **The White House.** Reputed to have been the place in which Queen Victoria's head coachman came to live upon retirement, this handsome Regency building sits on a quiet road off St. Peter's Street. **Pros:** historic house; spacious rooms; family-friendly atmosphere. **Cons:** a bit outside the center; no restaurant; no elevator. *Rooms from: £100* *6 St. Peter's La.* *01227/761836* *www.whitehousecanterbury.co.uk* *7 rooms* *Breakfast.*

NIGHTLIFE AND PERFORMING ARTS

NIGHTLIFE

Canterbury is home to a popular university, and the town's many pubs and bars are busy, often crowded with college-age folks.

Alberry's Wine Bar. With late-night jazz and hip-hop and a trendy crowd, Alberry's Wine Bar is one of Canterbury's coolest nightspots. At lunchtime they serve a fine burger, too. *St. Margaret's St.* *01227/452378* *www.alberrys.co.uk.*

Parrot. Built in 1370, the Parrot is an atmospheric old pub known for its real ale. They also do good food; Sunday lunch here is popular. *1–9 Church La.* *01227/454170* *www.theparrotonline.com.*

Thomas Becket. A traditional English pub, with bunches of hops hanging from the ceiling and a fire crackling in the hearth on a cold winter's day, the Thomas Becket is a convivial kind of place. The staff serves food, though it can be inconsistent; most people just come for the atmosphere. *21 Best La.* *01227/464384.*

PERFORMING ARTS

Canterbury Festival. The two-week-long Canterbury Festival fills the town with music, dance, theater, and other colorful events every October. *Canterbury* *01227/787787* *www.canterburyfestival.co.uk.*

Gulbenkian Theatre. Outside the town center, the Gulbenkian Theatre mounts all kinds of plays, particularly experimental works, and is a venue for dance performances, concerts, comedy shows, and films. ✉ *University of Kent, Giles La.* ☎ *01227/769075* 🌐 *www.thegulbenkian.co.uk*.

The Marlowe Theatre. Check out this excellent performance for theater, music, dance, and comedy. It is also a venue for popular touring shows. ✉ *The Friars, off King St.* ☎ *01227/787787* 🌐 *www.marlowetheatre.com*.

SHOPPING

Canterbury's medieval streets are lined with shops, perfect for an afternoon of rummaging. The best are in the district just around the cathedral. The King's Mile, which stretches past the cathedral and down Palace Street and Northgate, is a good place to start.

925. This shop has a great selection of handmade silver jewelry. ✉ *57 Palace St.* ☎ *01227/785699* 🌐 *www.925-silver.co.uk*.

Burgate Antiques. This rambling shop is full of fine British and French antiques, mostly Georgian and Victorian, with both high-end and less expensive selections. It's a great place to nose around on a rainy day. ✉ *23a Palace St.* ☎ *01227/456500*.

Crowthers of Canterbury. Behind the delightfully old-style red shop-front, Crowthers of Canterbury carries an extensive selection of musical instruments, gifts, and other souvenirs for music lovers. ✉ *1 The Borough* ☎ *01227/763965* 🌐 *www.crowthersofcanterbury.co.uk*.

BROADSTAIRS

17 miles east of Canterbury.

Like other Victorian seaside towns such as Margate and Ramsgate, Broadstairs was once the playground of vacationing Londoners, and grand 19th-century houses line the waterfront. In the off-season Broadstairs is peaceful, but day-trippers pack the town in July and August.

Park your car in one of the town lots, and strike out for the crescent beach or wander down the residential Victorian streets. Make your way down to the amusement pier and try your hand in one of the game arcades. You can grab fish-and-chips to go and dine on the beach.

Charles Dickens spent many summers in Broadstairs between 1837 and 1851 and wrote glowingly of its bracing freshness.

GETTING HERE AND AROUND

By car, Broadstairs is about a two-hour drive (78 miles) from London, off A256 on the southeast tip of England. Trains run from London's St. Pancras and Victoria stations to Broadstairs up to four times an hour; it's a one-and-a-half- to two-hour trip and sometimes involves a change in Rochester. Broadstairs Station is off Broadway in the town center. National Express buses travel to Broadstairs from London several times a day; the journey takes about three hours.

EXPLORING

Dickens House Museum. This house was originally the home of Mary Pearson Strong, on whom Dickens based the character of Betsey Trotwood, David Copperfield's aunt. Dickens lived here from 1837 to 1839 while writing *The Pickwick Papers* and *Oliver Twist*. Some rooms have been decorated to look as they would have in Dickens's day, and there's a reconstruction of Miss Trotwood's room as described by Dickens. ✉ *2 Victoria Parade* ☎ *01843/861232* *£4.50* ⊙ *Apr.–mid-June and mid-Sept.–Oct., daily 1–4:30; mid-June–mid-Sept., daily 10–4:30; Nov, weekends 1–4.*

DEAL

18 miles south of Broadstairs.

3

The large seaside town of Deal, known for its castle, is famous in history books as the place where Caesar's legions landed in 55 BC, and it was from here that William Penn set sail in 1682 on his first journey to the American colony he founded, Pennsylvania.

GETTING HERE AND AROUND

Southeastern trains travel to Deal twice an hour from London's St. Pancras Station, and once an hour from London's Charing Cross. The journey takes about two hours. You can also get a National Express bus from London's Victoria Coach Station, but there are only two buses a day (both late afternoon) and the trip takes between three and four hours.

ESSENTIALS

Visitor Information Deal Tourist Information Centre. ✉ *Town Hall, High St.* ☎ *01304/369576* 🌐 *www.deal.gov.uk.*

EXPLORING

Deal Castle. Erected in 1540 and intricately built to the shape of a Tudor rose, Deal Castle is the largest of the coastal defenses constructed by Henry VIII. A moat surrounds its gloomy passages and austere walls. The castle museum has exhibits about prehistoric, Roman, and Saxon Britain. ✉ *Victoria Rd.* ☎ *01304/372762* 🌐 *www.english-heritage.org.uk* *£5.50* ⊙ *Apr.–Oct., daily 10–6; Nov.–Mar., weekends 10–4.*

Walmer Castle and Gardens. Another of Henry VIII's coastal fortifications, this castle was converted in 1708 into a residence for the Lord Warden of the Cinque Ports, a ceremonial honor dating back to the early Middle Ages. Made up of four round towers around a circular keep, the castle has sprawling lavender gardens with gorgeous ocean views. Among its famous lord wardens were William Pitt the Younger (1759–1806) and the Duke of Wellington (1769–1852), hero of the Battle of Waterloo, who lived here from 1829 until his death. A small museum, renovated in 2015, tells the story of his victory at Waterloo and contains a rather random selection of memorabilia, including an original pair of Wellington boots, which the duke is credited with inventing. Later wardens of the castle included Sir Winston Churchill. The drawing and dining rooms are open to the public except when the lord warden is in residence. The castle is about a mile south of Deal. ✉ *A258* ☎ *01304/364288* 🌐 *www.english-heritage.org.uk* *£8.20* ⊙ *Mar., weekends 10–4; Apr.–Sept., daily 10–4; Oct.–early Nov., Wed.–Sun. 10–4. Closed mid Nov.–Feb.*

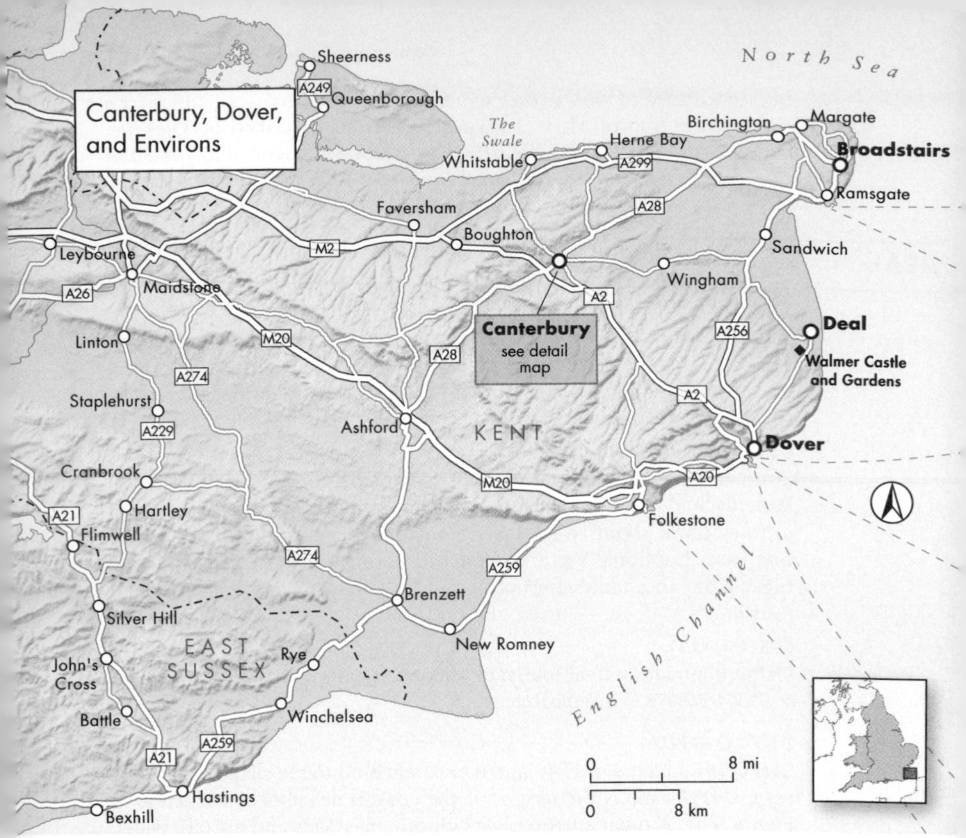

DOVER

8 miles south of Deal, 78 miles east of London.

The busy passenger port of Dover has for centuries been Britain's gateway to Europe and is known for the famous white cliffs. You may find the town itself disappointing; the savage bombardments of World War II and the shortsightedness of postwar developers left the city center an unattractive place. Roman legacies include a lighthouse adjoining a stout Anglo-Saxon church.

GETTING HERE AND AROUND

National Express buses depart from London's Victoria Coach Station for Dover about every 90 minutes. The journey takes between 2½ and 3 hours. Drivers from London take the M20, which makes a straight line south to Dover. The journey should take around two hours. Southeastern trains leave London's Charing Cross, Victoria, and St. Pancras stations about every 30 minutes for Dover Priory Station in Dover. The trip is between one and two hours; some services require changes in Ashford.

For the best views of the cliffs, you need a car or taxi; it's a long way to walk from town.

ESSENTIALS

Visitor Information Dover Visitor Information Centre. ✉ *Dover Museum, Market Sq.* ☎ *01304/201066* 🌐 *www.whitecliffscountry.org.uk.*

EXPLORING

FAMILY Fodor's Choice ★ **Dover Castle.** Spectacular and with plenty to explore, Dover Castle, towering high above the ramparts of the white cliffs, is a mighty medieval castle that has served as an important strategic center over the centuries. Most of the castle, including the keep, dates to Norman times. It was begun by Henry II in 1181 but incorporates additions from almost every succeeding century. The **Great Tower** recreates how the opulent castle would have looked in Henry's time, complete with sound effects, interactive displays, and courtly characters in medieval costume. History jumps forward the better part of a millennium (and becomes rather more sober in the telling) as you venture down into the recently opened **Secret Wartime Tunnels**. Dover Castle played a surprisingly dramatic role in World War II, and these well-thought-out interactive galleries tell the complete story. The tunnels themselves, originally built during the Napoleonic Wars, were used as a top-secret nerve center in the fight against Hitler. ✉ *Castle Rd.* ☎ *01304/211067* 🌐 *www.english-heritage.org.uk* 🎫 *£17.50* ⏲ *Apr.–July and Sept., daily 10–6; Aug., daily 9:30–6; Oct.–early Nov., daily 10–5; mid-Nov.–Mar., weekends 10–4.*

Roman Painted House. Believed to have been a hotel, the remains of this nearly 2,000-year-old structure were excavated in the 1970s. It includes some Roman wall paintings (mostly dedicated to Bacchus, the god of revelry), along with the remnants of an ingenious heating system. ✉ *New St.* ☎ *01304/203279* 🌐 *www.theromanpaintedhouse.co.uk* 🎫 *£3* ⏲ *Early–mid-Apr., Tues.–Sat. 10–5, Sun. 1–5; late Apr.–May, Tues. and Sat. 10–5; June–late Sept., daily 10–5, Sun. 1–5; last admission 30 min before closing. Closed late Sept.–Mar.*

Fodor's Choice ★ **White Cliffs.** Plunging hundreds of feet into the sea, Dover's chalk-white cliffs are an inspirational site and considered an iconic symbol of England. They stay white because of the natural process of erosion. Because of this, you must be cautious when walking along the cliffs—experts recommend staying at least 20 feet from the edge. The best places to see the cliffs are at Samphire Hoe, St. Margaret's Bay, or East Cliff and Warren Country Park. Signs will direct you from the roads to scenic spots. **■ TIP → The visitor center at Langdon Cliffs has 5 miles of walking trails with some spectacular views.** ✉ *Dover.*

WHERE TO EAT AND STAY

$$ BRITISH Fodor's Choice ★ ✕ **The Allotment.** This charming and slightly quirky restaurant in the center of Dover doesn't look like much from the outside, but don't be fooled—delicious, creative modern British meals are served within. The unusual name comes from an old-fashioned British tradition of communal gardens for city dwellers; the "allotment" being a small strip of land allocated to a family with no garden who wants to grow its own vegetables. It's appropriate then that plenty of local and regional ingredients find their way onto the menu; try the Dungeness mackerel to start, followed by roast Canterbury lamb or perhaps a rich sweet potato and coconut curry. For dessert, the lemon posset is a great choice—it's

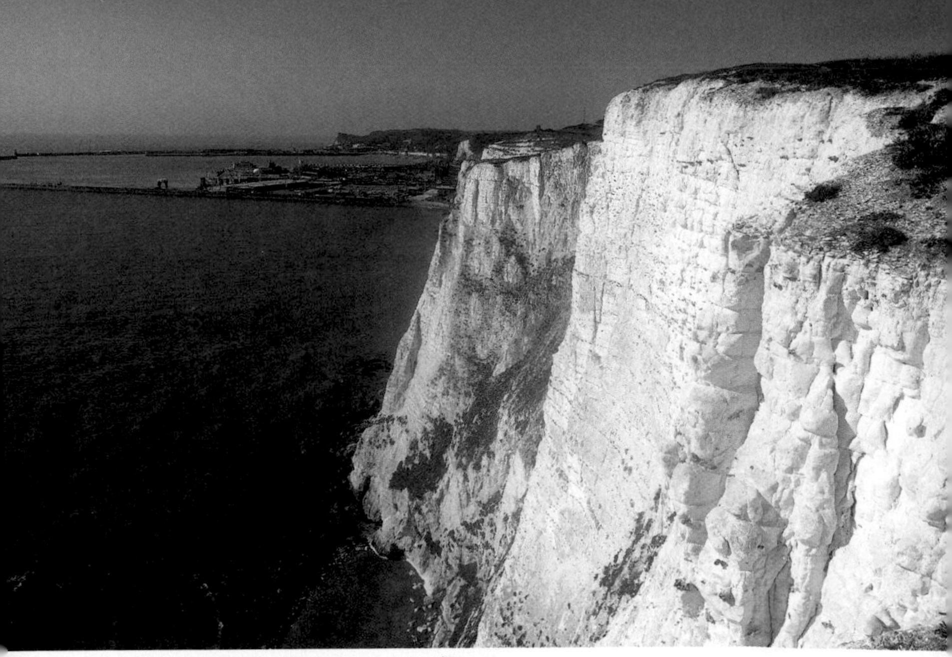

The majestic White Cliffs of Dover are a national icon.

a type of pudding that has been served since medieval times. *Average main: £14* *9 High St.* *www.theallotmentdover.co.uk.*

$ SICILIAN **La Scala.** This cheerful Italian restaurant in the center of Dover is much favored by locals looking for an authentic, inexpensive Italian meal without feeling the need to sit up too straight. The menu is mostly Sicilian-influenced; you might start with a simple salad of fresh tomatoes with mozzarella and basil, before moving on to some homemade pasta with swordfish in a tomato and white wine sauce, or lamb cooked with garlic and rosemary. It gets busy on weekends, so try and book. *Average main: £11* *19 High St.* *01304/208044* *www.lascalarestaurant.org.uk.*

$$ B&B/INN **White Cliffs Hotel.** Literally in the shadow of the famous White Cliffs of Dover, this colorful little hotel is attached to a high-end housewares store and a good restaurant. **Pros:** bags of character; beautiful location; dinner just £25 for residents; guests can use the spa at another local hotel. **Cons:** far from central Dover; difficult to get here without a car. *Rooms from: £129* *High St., St. Margaret's-at-Cliffe* *01304/852229* *www.thewhitecliffs.com* *15 rooms* *Breakfast.*

RYE AND LEWES

From Dover the coast road winds west through Folkestone (a genteel resort, small port, and Channel Tunnel terminal), across Romney Marsh (famous for its sheep and, at one time, its ruthless smugglers), and on to the delightful medieval town of Rye. The region along the coast is noted for Winchelsea, the history-rich sites of Hastings, Herstmonceux, and Bodiam, and the Glyndebourne Opera House festival, based outside Lewes, a town celebrated for its architectural heritage. One of the three steam railroads in the Southeast services part of the area: the Romney, Hythe, and Dymchurch Railway.

RYE

68 miles southeast of London, 34 miles southwest of Dover.

Fodor's Choice ★ With cobbled streets and ancient timbered dwellings, Rye is an artist's dream. It was an important port town until the harbor silted up and the waters retreated more than 150 years ago; now the nearest harbor is two miles away. Virtually every building in the little town center is intriguingly historic. Rye is known for its many antiques stores and also for its sheer pleasantness. This place can be easily walked without a map, but the local tourist office has an interesting audio tour of the town as well as maps.

GETTING HERE AND AROUND

If you're driving to Rye, take the M20 to A2070. Trains from London's St. Pancras leave once an hour and take just over an hour, with a change in Ashford.

ESSENTIALS

Visitor Information Rye Tourist Information Centre. ✉ *4 Lion St.* ☎ *01797/229049* 🌐 *www.ryesussex.co.uk.*

EXPLORING

TOP ATTRACTIONS

FAMILY **Bodiam Castle.** Immortalized in paintings, photographs, and films, Bodiam Castle (pronounced Boe-dee-um) rises out of the distance like a piece of medieval legend. From the outside it's one of Britain's most impressive castles, with turrets, battlements, a glassy moat (one of the very few still in use), and 2-foot-thick walls. However, once you cross the drawbridge to the interior there's little to see but ruins, albeit on an impressive scale. Built in 1385 to withstand a threatened French invasion, it was partly demolished during the English Civil War of 1642–46 and has been uninhabited ever since. Still, you can climb the intact towers to take in sweeping countryside views, and kids love running around the keep. The castle, 12 miles west of Rye, schedules organized activities for kids during school holidays. ✉ *Off B2244, Bodiam* ☎ *01580/830196* 🌐 *www.nationaltrust.org.uk* 🎫 *£7.80* ⏲ *Daily 10–5; last admission 1 hr before closing.*

Church of St. Mary the Virgin. At the top of the hill at the center of Rye, this classic English village church is more than 900 years old and encompasses a number of architectural styles. The turret clock dates to 1561 and still keeps excellent time. Its huge pendulum swings inside the church nave. ■ **TIP→ Climb the tower for amazing views of the surrounding area.** ✉ *Church Sq.* ☎ *01797/222318* 🌐 *www.ryeparishchurch.org.uk* 🎫 *Free* ⏲ *Apr.–Sept., daily 9:15–5:30; Oct.–Mar., daily 9:15–4:30; last admission 15 min before closing.*

Great Dixter House and Gardens. Combining a large timber-frame hall with a cottage garden on a grand scale, this place will get your green thumbs twitching. The house dates to 1464 (you can tour a few rooms) and was restored in 1910 by architect Edwin Lutyens, who also designed the garden. From these beginnings, the late horticulturist and writer Christopher Lloyd, whose home this was, developed a series of creative, colorful "garden rooms" and a dazzling herbaceous Long Border. The house is 9 miles northwest of Rye. ✉ *Off A28, Northiam* ☎ *01797/252878* 🌐 *www.greatdixter.co.uk* 🎫 *£11; gardens only £9* ⏲ *Apr.–Oct., Tues.–Sun. and public holidays 11–5 (house 2–5).*

Mermaid Street. One of the town's original cobbled streets, and perhaps its most quintissential view, heads steeply from the top of the hill to the former harbor. Its name supposedly came from the night a drunken sailor swore he heard a mermaid call him down to the sea (back when Rye was still a seaside town). The houses here date from between the Medieval and Georgian periods; a much-photographed pair have the delightfully fanciful names "The House With Two Front Doors" and "The House Opposite." ⚠ **Be careful on your feet—the cobbles are very uneven.** ✉ *Rye.*

Ypres Tower. Down the hill past Church Square, Ypres Tower (pronounced "Wipers" by locals) was originally built as part of the town's fortifications (now all but disappeared) in 1249; it later served as a prison. A recent refurbishment has added an interesting exhibition on life here during the 1830s as a female prisoner in the "women's tower"; otherwise its local history museum holds a rather random collection of items, from smuggling bric-a-brac to shipbuilding mementos. A row of defensive cannons are fixed to the rampart overlooking the (disappointingly industrial) edge of Rye and several miles of flatland beyond. When they were installed, however, the canons pointed directly out to sea. ✉ *Gungarden* ☎ *01797/226728* 🌐 *www.ryemuseum.co.uk* 🎫 *£3* ⏲ *Apr.–Oct., daily 10:30–5; Nov.–Mar., daily 10–3:30; last admission 30 min before closing.*

WORTH NOTING

Bodiam Boating Station. By far the prettiest way to approach Bodiam Castle is on a 45-minute river cruise through Sussex countryside. Boats leave from the riverbank by the old stone road bridge on the outskirts of Newenden (it's easy to find—the village is minuscule). ✉ *Riverside Cottage, Rye Rd., Newenden* ☎ *01797/253838* 🌐 *www.bodiamboatingstation.co.uk* 🎫 *£12* ⏲ *Days of operation: early Apr.–late May, June–late July, and Sept., Wed. and weekends; late July–Aug. daily. Sailing times from Boating Station: 10:30, 12:45, and 3. Sailing times from Bodiam Castle: 11:30, 1:45, and 4.*

Chapel Down Winery. After decades as little more than the butt of jokes, the English wine industry is slowly beginning to be taken more seriously—and one of Britain's leading wine producers is a few miles north of Rye. You can visit the wine shop and explore the herb gardens for free. You can also take an hour-long guided tour of the rest of the grounds (call to book). ✉ *Off B2082, Small Hythe, Tenterton* ☎ *01580/766111* 🌐 *www.chapeldown.com* 🎫 *Tours £10* ⏲ *Daily 10–5; guided tours Apr.–Nov.*

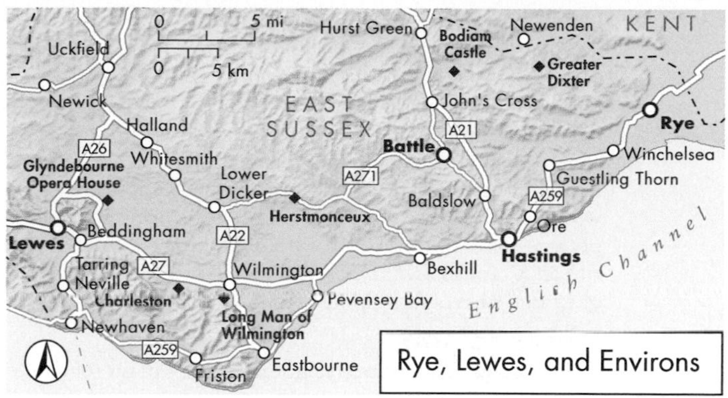

Rye, Lewes, and Environs

Lamb House. Something about Lamb House, an early 18th-century dwelling, attracts writers. The novelist Henry James lived here from 1898 to 1916. E. F. Benson, onetime mayor of Rye and author of the witty *Lucia* novels (written in the 1920s and 1930s), was a later resident. The ground-floor rooms contain some of James's furniture and personal belongings. ✉ *West St.* ☎ *01580/762334* 🌐 *www.nationaltrust.org.uk/lamb-house* 🎟 *£5.60* ⏲ *Apr.–Oct., Tues., Fri., and Sat. 11–5; last admission 30 min before closing.*

Rye Castle Museum. The diminutive Rye Castle Museum, below the remains of the castle wall on East Street, displays watercolors and examples of Rye pottery, for which the town was famous. One of the most curious pieces of local memorabilia is the town's original fire engine, which was built in 1745 and kept in service for 120 years. ✉ *3 East St.* ☎ *01797/226728* 🌐 *www.ryemuseum.co.uk* 🎟 *£1.50* ⏲ *Apr.–Sept., daily 10:30–5; last admission 30 min before closing.*

Winchelsea. Like Rye, Winchelsea perches prettily atop its own small hill amid rolling farmland. Look for the splendid (though damaged) church built in the 14th century with stone from Normandy. Winchelsea was built on a grid system devised in 1283. This was once a walled town, and some original town gates still stand. Beneath the narrow streets are at least 56 medieval cellars; a few are accessible by guided tour (£5) on various dates from April to October. The tour, which is run by somewhat overenthusiastic volunteers, is interesting but long. See the town website, email tours@winchelsea.net, or call 01797/224446 for recorded information. The town is 2 miles southwest of Rye. ✉ *Winchelsea* 🌐 *www.winchelsea.net.*

WHERE TO EAT

$ ITALIAN ✕ **Simply Italian.** In a prime location near the marina, this popular Italian eatery packs in the crowds on weekend nights with its inexpensive classic pasta-and-pizza dishes. The atmosphere is cheerful and bright, and the food is straightforward and unfussy. Try tagliatelle with salmon in a creamy sauce, or grilled lemon sole with white wine sauce. Good pizza picks are the *quarto stagioni,* with mushrooms, salami, and peppers on a crisp crust, and pizza *reale* with red peppers, spinach, goat cheese, and red onion. [$] *Average main: £9* ✉ *The Strand* ☎ *01797/226024* 🌐 *www.simplyitalian.co.uk.*

$$ SEAFOOD Fodor's Choice ★ ✕ **Webbes at the Fish Café.** One of Rye's most popular restaurants occupies a brick building that dates to 1907, but the interior has been redone in a sleek, modern style. The ground-floor café has a relaxed atmosphere, and upstairs is a more formal dining room. Most of the seafood here is caught nearby, so it's very fresh. Sample the chargrilled squid with chili and ginger, or the scallops with vermouth sauce and creamed potato. Reservations are recommended for dinner. [$] *Average main: £15* ✉ *17 Tower St.* ☎ *01797/222226* 🌐 *www.webbesrestaurants.co.uk* ⊗ *Closed Mon. Oct.–Apr. No dinner Sun.*

WHERE TO STAY

$$ HOTEL **The George.** This attractive hotel on Rye's main road takes a boutique approach, cleverly mixing modern pieces with antiques in a sprawling Georgian building. **Pros:** elegant room design; very central. **Cons:** weddings are popular here—they can happen weekly in summer, take over public areas, and stay noisy until late. [$] *Rooms from: £125* ✉ *98 High St.* ☎ *01797/222114* 🌐 *www.thegeorgeinrye.com* *24 rooms* *Breakfast.*

$$ B&B/INN Fodor's Choice ★ **Jeake's House.** Antiques fill the cozy bedrooms of this rambling 1689 house, where the snug, painted-and-paneled parlor has a wood-burning stove for cold days. **Pros:** pleasant atmosphere; delicious breakfasts; winter discounts. **Cons:** Mermaid Street is steep and cobbled; cheapest room has bathroom across the hall. [$] *Rooms from: £115* ✉ *Mermaid St.* ☎ *01797/222828* 🌐 *www.jeakeshouse.com* *No credit cards* *11 rooms, 10 with bath* *Breakfast.*

$$ HOTEL Fodor's Choice ★ **The Mermaid.** Steeped in a history of smuggling, the Mermaid is Rye's most historic inn, and one of the oldest in the country—it's been in business for 600 years. **Pros:** dripping in atmosphere; good restaurant; 24-hour room service. **Cons:** price is high for what's on offer; allegedly haunted. [$] *Rooms from: £150* ✉ *Mermaid St.* ☎ *01797/223065* 🌐 *www.mermaidinn.com* *31 rooms* *Breakfast; Some meals.*

$$ B&B/INN **White Vine House Hotel.** Occupying a building from the late 1500s, this small hotel embraces tradition with features such as wood-paneled lounges with warming fireplaces. **Pros:** beautiful building; excellent restaurant. **Cons:** main street location can be a bit noisy; few services. [$] *Rooms from: £130* ✉ *24 High St.* ☎ *01797/224748* 🌐 *www.whitevinehouse.co.uk* *7 rooms* *Breakfast.*

SHOPPING

Rye has great antiques shops, perfect for an afternoon of rummaging, with the biggest cluster at the foot of the hill near the tourist information center.

Britcher & Rivers. This traditional candy store is like something out of a bygone age. Choose from row upon row of tall jars packed with every imaginable type of candy, measured out into little paper bags. ✉ *89 High St.* ☎ *01797/227152.*

David Sharp Pottery. Like the distinctive ceramic name plaques that are a feature of the town? They are on offer at this sweet little shop. ✉ *55 The Mint* ☎ *01797/222620.*

Glass Etc. A glorious collection of quality antique glass can be found in this colorful, friendly shop by the train station. ✉ *18–22 Rope Walk* ☎ *01797/226600* 🌐 *www.decanterman.com.*

HASTINGS

12 miles southwest of Rye, 68 miles southeast of London.

In the 19th century Hastings became one of England's most popular spa resorts. Tall Victorian row houses painted in lemony hues still cover the cliffs around the deep blue sea, and the views from the hilltops are extraordinary. The pretty Old Town, on the east side of the city, offers a glimpse into the city's 16th-century past. Hastings has been through difficult times in recent decades, and the town developed a reputation as a rough place. It's currently trying hard to reinvent itself—a clutch of trendy new boutique bed-and-breakfasts have opened, also an important new art gallery—but the town center can still be quite rowdy after dark. Expect a handsome but tattered town, with a mix of traditional English seaside amusements: miniature golf, shops selling junk, fish-and-chip stands, and a rocky beach that stretches for miles.

GETTING HERE AND AROUND

If you're driving to Hastings from London, take A21. Trains travel to Hastings three or four times an hour from London's Victoria and St. Pancras stations. The journey takes between 1½ and 2 hours; some trains involve a change in Brighton or Ashford. The station, Hastings Warrior Square, is in the town center, within easy walking distance of most sights. National Express buses travel from London to Hastings about twice a day in around 3½ hours.

ESSENTIALS

Visitor Information Hastings Old Town Tourist Information Centre. ✉ *Old Town Hall Museum, High St.* ☎ *01424/451111* 🌐 *www.visit1066country.com.*

EXPLORING

FAMILY **Hastings Castle.** Take a thrilling ride up the West Hill Cliff Railway from George Street precinct to the atmospheric ruins of the thousand-year-old fortress now known as Hastings Castle. It was built by William the Conqueror in 1066, before he had even won the Battle of Hastings and conquered England—making it the first Norman castle in the country. All that remains are mere fragments of the fortifications, some ancient walls, and a number of gloomy dungeons. Nevertheless, you get an excellent view of the chalky cliffs, the rocky coast, and the town below. You can buy a joint ticket that covers admission to Smuggler's Adventure and a nearby aquarium for £18 (£14 children). ✉ *West Hill* ☎ *01424/422964* 🎫 *£4.50* ⏲ *Easter–Oct., daily 10–5; last admission 1 hr before closing.*

Fodor's Choice ★ **The Jerwood Gallery.** A symbol of Hastings's slow but growing regeneration after decades of neglect, this new exhibition space in the Old Town became one of the most talked about new galleries outside London when it opened in 2012. The permanent collection includes works by Augustus John, Walter Sickert, and Stephen Lowry, and temporary exhibitions change every couple of months. The glazed tile building on the seafront was designed to reflect the row of distinctive old, blackened fishing sheds it sits alongside. ✉ *Rock-a-Nore Rd.* ☎ *01424/728377* 🌐 *www.jerwoodgallery.org* 🎟 *£8* ⏲ *Tues.–Sun. and holiday Mon. 11–5.*

FAMILY **Smuggler's Adventure.** The history of smuggling on the south coast is told through waxworks and other exhibits inside this labyrinth of caves underneath the West Hill, a 15-minute walk from Hastings Castle. ✉ *St. Clement Caves* ☎ *01424/422964* 🌐 *www.smugglersadventure.co.uk* 🎟 *£8* ⏲ *Easter–Sept., daily 10–5:30; Oct.–early Nov. and Feb.–Easter, daily 10–4:30; last admission 30 min before closing. Closed mid-Nov.–Feb.*

WHERE TO EAT

$ SEAFOOD ✕ **Blue Dolphin.** The crowds line up all day to make their way into this small fish-and-chips shop just off the seafront, down near the fish shacks. Although the decor is humble, reviewers consistently rank the battered fish and huge plates of double-cooked chips (chunky fries) as among the best in the country. Everything is steaming fresh, and it's all cheaper if you get it to take out (the beach is just a few steps away). $ *Average main: £6* ✉ *61 High St.* ☎ *01424/425778* ⏲ *No dinner.*

WHERE TO STAY

$ B&B/INN **The Cloudesley.** No TVs and a general Zen vibe at this boutique B&B in the quieter St. Leonard's district of Hastings make it a thoroughly relaxing place to stay. **Pros:** oasis of calm; great spa treatments; impeccable eco credentials. **Cons:** super-chill vibe won't be for everyone; two-night minimum at certain times. $ *Rooms from: £80* ✉ *7 Cloudesley Rd., St. Leonards-on-Sea* ☎ *01424/722759, 07507/000148* 🌐 *www.thecloudesley.co.uk* *5 rooms* 🍽 *Breakfast.*

$ HOTEL **Hastings House.** In Warrior Square at the edge of Hastings near St. Leonards-on-Sea, this renovated boutique guesthouse in a Victorian house takes a funky, modern approach. **Pros:** spacious rooms; stylish and modern decor; near the sea. **Cons:** no restaurant; few services; area can be noisy at night. $ *Rooms from: £80* ✉ *9 Warrior Sq., St. Leonards-on-Sea* ☎ *01424/422709* 🌐 *www.hastingshouse.co.uk* *9 rooms* 🍽 *Breakfast.*

$$ B&B/INN Fodor's Choice ★ **Swan House.** Originally a bakery, this extraordinary 15th-century building has been beautifully converted into an elegant and welcoming B&B. **Pros:** beautiful, historic building; welcoming hosts; delicious breakfasts. **Cons:** some bathrooms have shower only; two-night minimum on summer weekends. $ *Rooms from: £120* ✉ *1 Hill St.* ☎ *01424/430014* 🌐 *www.swanhousehastings.co.uk* *27 rooms* 🍽 *Breakfast.*

$$ HOTEL **Zanzibar Hotel.** This spacious, light-filled hotel overlooking the sea has guest rooms designed as a playful, yet restrained homage to exotic destinations. **Pros:** great facilities for a small hotel; sea views; champagne is served with breakfast. **Cons:** a bit over-the-top for some tastes; pricey for Hastings; nonrefundable deposit; two-night minimum on summer weekends. $ *Rooms from: £125* ✉ *9 Everfield Pl., St. Leonards-on-Sea* ☎ *01424/460109* 🌐 *www.zanzibarhotel.co.uk* *9 rooms* 🍽 *Breakfast.*

BATTLE

7 miles northwest of Hastings, 61 miles southeast of London.

Battle is the actual site of the crucial Battle of Hastings, at which, on October 14, 1066, William of Normandy and his army trounced King Harold's Anglo-Saxon army. Today it's a sweet, quiet town and a favorite of history buffs.

GETTING HERE AND AROUND

Southeastern trains arrive from London's Charing Cross station every half hour. The journey takes between 1½ and 2 hours. National Express buses travel once daily in the early evening from London's Victoria Coach Station. The trip takes around 2½ hours.

ESSENTIALS

Visitor Information Battle Information Point. ✉ *Yesterdays World, 89–90 High St.* ☎ *01797/229049* 🌐 *www.visit1066country.com.*

EXPLORING

Battle Abbey. This great Benedictine abbey was erected by William the Conqueror on the site of the Battle of Hastings—one of the most decisive turning points in English history and the last time the country was successfully invaded. A memorial stone marks the high altar, which in turn was supposedly laid on the spot where Harold II, the last Saxon king, was killed. All of this meant little to Henry VIII, who didn't spare the building from his violent dissolution of the monasteries. Today the abbey is just a ruin, but films and interactive exhibits help bring it all to life. You can also take the mile-long walk around the edge of the battlefield and see the remains of the abbey's former outbuildings. ✉ *High St.* ☎ *01424/775705* 🌐 *www.english-heritage.org.uk* 🎫 *£8* ⏲ *Apr.–Sept., daily 10–6; Oct.–early Nov., daily 10–4; early Nov.–Mar., weekends 10–4.*

FAMILY Fodor's Choice ★ **Herstmonceux.** A banner waving from one tower and a glassy moat crossed by what was once a drawbridge—this fairy-tale castle has everything except knights in shining armor. The redbrick structure was originally built by Sir Roger Fiennes (ancestor of actor Ralph Fiennes) in 1444, although it was altered in the Elizabethan age and again early in the 20th century after it had largely fallen to ruin. Canadian Queen's University owns the castle, so only part of it is open for guided tours once or twice a day, except Saturday; call in advance to book. Highlights include the magnificent ballroom, a medieval room, and the stunning Elizabethan-era staircase. Explore the formal walled garden, lily-covered lakes, and miles of woodland—the perfect place for a picnic on a sunny afternoon. There's a hands-on science center for kids. When school isn't in session, the castle rents out its small, plain guest rooms from £40 per night. On the last weekend of August, the castle hosts a large **Medieval Festival**, complete with jousting, falconry shows, and around 100 craft stalls; visit www.englandsmedievalfestival.com for more details. The castle is 8 miles southwest of Battle. ✉ *Wartling Rd., Hailsham* ☎ *01323/833816* 🌐 *www.herstmonceux-castle.com* 🎫 *Castle, grounds, and science center £13; grounds only £6.50; castle* *tours £3 ⏲ Apr.–Sept., daily 10–6; Oct., daily 10–5; last admission 1 hr before closing.*

WHERE TO EAT

$$$$ MODERN FRENCH ✕ **The Sundial.** This 17th-century brick farmhouse with views of the South Downs is home to a popular Modern French restaurant. Wood-beamed rooms and white tablecloths provide a backdrop for the imaginative three-course set menus, which may include rack of lamb with rosemary cream sauce, or roulade of sole with cockles and mussels in Vermouth sauce. Dessert may be pineapple carpaccio marinated in Malibu and star anise, or perhaps marscapone mousse with plum compote. The Sundial is near the castle in Herstmonceux, 8 miles southwest of Battle. [$] *Average main: £42* ✉ *Gardner St., Herstmonceux* ☎ *01323/832217* 🌐 *www.sundialrestaurant.co.uk* ⏲ *Closed Mon. No dinner Sun.*

EN ROUTE **Long Man of Wilmington.** Wilmington, 9 miles southwest of Herstmonceux Castle on A27, has a famous landmark that people drive for miles to see. High on the downs to the south of the village (signposted off A27), a 226-foot-tall white figure with a staff in each hand, known as the Long Man of Wilmington, is carved into the chalk. His age is a subject of great debate; some researchers think he might have been created as far back as Roman, or even Neolithic times, but recent soil analysis places the figure closer to the 16th century. ✉ *Wilmington.*

LEWES

24 miles east of Battle, 8 miles northeast of Brighton, 54 miles south of London.

Fodor's Choice ★ The town nearest to the celebrated Glyndebourne Opera House, Lewes is so rich in history that the Council for British Archaeology has named it one of the 50 most important English towns. A walk is the best way to appreciate its steep streets and appealing jumble of building styles and materials—flint, stone, brick, tile—and the secret lanes (called "twittens") behind the castle, with their huge beeches. Here and there are smart antiques shops, good eateries, and secondhand-book dealers. Most of the buildings in the center date to the 18th and 19th centuries.

Something about this town has always attracted rebels. It was once the home of Thomas Paine (1737–1809), whose pamphlet *Common Sense* advocated that the American colonies break with Britain. It was also favored by Virginia Woolf and the Bloomsbury Group, early 20th-century countercultural artistic innovators.

Today Lewes's beauty and proximity to London mean that the counterculture crew can't really afford to live here anymore, but its rebel soul still peeks through, particularly on Guy Fawkes Night (November 5), the anniversary of Fawkes's foiled attempt to blow up the Houses of Parliament in 1605. Flaming tar barrels are rolled down High Street and into the River Ouse; costumed processions fill the streets.

BONFIRE NIGHT IN LEWES

In 1605 a group of Catholic rebels attempted to blow up Parliament in the most famous failed coup in English history. Known as the Gunpowder Plot, it's still commemorated with fireworks every year on the Saturday closest to the anniversary on November 5. As befitting a 400-year-old custom, it's a night rich with tradition—nowhere more spectacularly than in Lewes. Thousands parade through the town with flaming torches; many wear elaborate costumes and play instruments. Huge pyres are lit ("bonfires"), effigies of the plotters and other, more modern bogeymen are burned (recent examples include North Korean leader Kim Jong Un, depicted as a giant baby in a stroller) and the fireworks carry on well into the night. Admittedly it may be too much for some visitors—anti-Catholic chants and the burning of a Papal effigy are genuinely in the spirit of historical tradition and bone-dry humor, rather than actual anti-Catholic sentiment—but it's a unique event with a carnival atmosphere. Similar, though smaller parades happen in Rye and Hastings, usually on different weeks. For more details see *www.lewesbonfirecelebrations.com* or check the town websites.

GETTING HERE AND AROUND

If you're driving to Lewes from London, take the M23 south. The journey takes around an hour and 45 minutes. Southern trains run direct to Lewes from Victoria Station about three times an hour; the journey takes an hour. There's no easy way to get to Lewes by bus; you need to take a National Express or Megabus to Brighton and change to a regional bus line.

ESSENTIALS

Visitor Information Lewes Tourist Information Centre. *187 High St. 01273/483448 www.lewes.gov.uk.*

EXPLORING

FAMILY **Anne of Cleves House.** This 16th-century structure, a fragile-looking, timber-frame building, holds a small collection of Sussex ironwork and other items of local interest, such as Sussex pottery. The house was part of Anne of Cleves's divorce settlement from Henry VIII, although she never lived in it. There are medieval dress-up clothes for kids. To get to the house, walk down steep, cobbled Keere Street, past lovely Grange Gardens, to Southover High Street. *52 Southover High St. 01273/474610 www.sussexpast.co.uk/anneofcleves £5.50; combined ticket with Lewes Castle £11.50 Feb. and Nov.–mid-Dec., Mon.–Sat. 10–4, Sun. 11–4; Mar.–Oct., Mon.–Sat. 10–5, Sun. 11–4. Last admission 30 min before closing.*

Fodor's Choice ★ **Charleston.** Art and life mixed at Charleston, the farmhouse Vanessa Bell—sister of Virginia Woolf—bought in 1916 and fancifully decorated, along with Duncan Grant (who lived here until 1978). The house became a refuge for the writers and artists of the Bloomsbury Group. On display are colorful ceramics and textiles of the Omega Workshop—in which Bell and Grant participated—and paintings by Picasso and Renoir, as well as by Bell and Grant themselves. You view the house

A mixture of architectural styles and good shops make Lewes a wonderful town for a stroll.

on a guided tour except on Sunday, when you can wander freely. On a handful of dates there's a special 80-minute themed tour (£13.50) that focuses on a different aspect of Charleston's history, such as the great influence French culture had on the Bloomsbury Group. They also have 30-minute family tours on certain dates. (Schedules are listed on the website.) The house isn't suitable for those with mobility problems, although reduced-price ground-floor-only tickets are available. ✉ *Off A27, 7 miles east of Lewes, Firle* ☎ *01323/811626* 🌐 *www.charleston.org.uk* 🎫 *£11; ground floor only £6; gardens only £4.50* ⏲ *Late Mar.–June and Sept.–late Oct., Wed.–Sat. 1–6, Sun. 1–5:30; July and Aug., Wed.–Sat. noon–6, Sun. 1–5:30. Last admission 1 hr before closing.*

Lewes Castle. High above the valley of the River Ouse stand the majestic ruins of Lewes Castle, begun in 1100 by one of the country's Norman conquerors and completed 300 years later. The castle's barbican holds a small museum with archaeology collections, a changing temporary exhibition gallery, and a bookshop. There are panoramic views of the town and countryside. ✉ *169 High St.* ☎ *01273/486290* 🌐 *www.sussexpast.co.uk/properties-to-discover/lewes-castle* 🎫 *£7.50; combined ticket with Anne of Cleves House £11.50* ⏲ *Mar.–Oct., Mon.–Sat. 10–5:30, Sun. 11–5:30; Nov., Dec., and Feb., Mon.–Sat. 10–4:30, Sun. 11–4:30; Jan., Tues–Sat. 10:30–4:30, Sun. 11–4:30.*

WHERE TO EAT

$ POLISH ✕ **Baltica.** This popular café is a happy mishmash in more ways than one—drop in for British teatime treats, tasty Polish meals, or just to shop at the boutique selling delightful artisan pottery. You could settle for a cup of coffee and a cupcake or have a serving of steaming hot *bigos* (a traditional stew made with meat and sauerkraut, served with salad and a hunk of bread). $ *Average main: £8* ✉ *145 High St.* ☎ *01273/483449* 🌐 *www.baltictrader.co.uk* ⏲ *No dinner.*

$$ BRITISH ✕ **The Limetree Kitchen.** Elegant, imaginative menus and a commitment to locally sourced produce is at the heart of this popular restaurant in the center of Lewes. The menus, which change weekly, are heavily influenced by what's in season, with just a few menu options—shoulder of marsh lamb, for instance, or locally caught sea bream with saffron and vanilla cream. For dessert, try the delicious gin-and-tonic ice cream. The fixed-price menus are terrific value—five courses for £33, or £29 for the vegetarian version. $ *Average main: £17* ✉ *14 Station St.* ☎ *01273 /478636* 🌐 *www.limetreekitchen.co.uk* ⏲ *Closed Mon. and Tues.*

$ CAFÉ ✕ **Robson's of Lewes.** Good coffee, fresh produce, and delicious pastries make this coffee shop one of the best places in Lewes to drop by for an afternoon pick-me-up. A light-filled space with wood floors and simple tables creates a pleasant, casual spot to enjoy a cup of coffee with breakfast, a scone, or a light sandwich or salad lunch. You can also order to go. $ *Average main: £6* ✉ *22A High St.* ☎ *01273/480654* 🌐 *www.robsonsoflewes.co.uk* ⏲ *No dinner.*

WHERE TO STAY

$$ HOTEL **Crossways Hotel.** Near the Long Man of Wilmington, this small "restaurant with rooms" in a whitewashed house with 2 acres of gardens is decorated in warm, upbeat colors that contrast with the lovely antique furniture. **Pros:** lovely location near Glyndebourne; spacious bedrooms. **Cons:** few frills. $ *Rooms from: £145* ✉ *Lewes Rd., Polegate* ☎ *01323/482455* 🌐 *www.crosswayshotel.co.uk* *7 rooms, 1 cottage* *Breakfast.*

$$$ B&B/INN **Horsted Place.** On 1,100 acres, this luxurious Victorian manor house was built as a private home in 1850; it was owned by a friend of the current queen until the 1980s, and she was a regular visitor. **Pros:** historic building; amazing architecture; lovely gardens. **Cons:** too formal for some; creaky floors bother light sleepers. $ *Rooms from: £190* ✉ *Horsted Pond La., Off A26, Little Horsted* ☎ *01825/750581* 🌐 *www.horstedplace.co.uk* *15 rooms, 5 suites* *Breakfast.*

$ B&B/INN **The Ram Inn.** Roaring fires, cozy rooms, and friendly locals give this 500-year-old inn its wonderful feeling of old-world authenticity. **Pros:** proper village pub atmosphere; good food; cozy, well-designed rooms. **Cons:** you need a car to get here from Lewes. $ *Rooms from: £90* ✉ *The Street, West Firle* ☎ *01273/858222* 🌐 *www.raminn.co.uk* *4 rooms* *Breakfast.*

$$ B&B/INN **The Shelleys.** The lounge and dining room in this 17th-century building are on the grand scale, furnished with antiques that set the tone for the rest of the lovely building. **Pros:** historic atmosphere; good, French influenced cuisine. **Cons:** service a bit spotty; securing a table at the restaurant can be tough. $ *Rooms from: £150* ✉ *High St.* ☎ *01273/472361* 🌐 *www.the-shelleys.co.uk* *19 rooms* *Breakfast.*

3

NIGHTLIFE AND PERFORMING ARTS

NIGHTLIFE

Lewes has a relatively young population and a nightlife scene to match; there are also many lovely old pubs.

Brewers' Arms. On High Street, this is a good pub with a friendly crowd. The half-timbered building dates from 1906, but a pub has stood on this spot since the 16th century. ✉ *91 High St.* ☎ *01273/475524* 🌐 *www.brewersarmslewes.co.uk.*

King's Head. A traditional pub, the King's Head has a good menu with locally sourced fish and meat dishes. ✉ *9 Southover High St.* ☎ *01273/474628* 🌐 *www.thekingsheadlewes.co.uk.*

PERFORMING ARTS

Fodor's Choice ★ **Glyndebourne Opera House.** Nestled beneath the Downs, this world-famous opera house combines first-class productions, a state-of-the-art auditorium, and a beautiful setting. Seats are *very* expensive (the cheapest are around £85, though for many productions they start at twice that, rising to around £250) and you have to book months in advance, but it's worth every penny to aficionados, who traditionally wear evening dress and bring a hamper to picnic in the gardens. The main season runs from mid-May to the end of August. ■ **TIP→ If you can't afford a seat, there are other ways to see the show: standing room tickets cost £10, and a handful of performances every year are broadcast live to U.K. cinemas.** The Glyndebourne Touring Company performs here in October, when seats are cheaper. Glyndebourne is 3 miles east of Lewes off B2192. ✉ *New Rd., off A26, Ringmer* ☎ *01273/813813* 🌐 *www.glyndebourne.com.*

SHOPPING

Antiques shops offer temptation along the busy High Street. Lewes also has plenty of tiny boutiques and independent clothing stores vying for your pounds.

Cliffe Antiques Centre. This shop carries a fine mix of vintage English prints, estate jewelry, and art at reasonable prices. ✉ *47 Cliffe High St.* ☎ *01273/473266* 🌐 *www.cliffeantiquescentre.co.uk.*

The Fifteenth Century Bookshop. A wide collection of rare and vintage books can be found at this ancient, timber-framed building in the center of Lewes. Antique children's books are a specialty. ✉ *99–100 High St.* ☎ *01273/474160* 🌐 *www.oldenyoungbooks.co.uk.*

Louis Potts & Co. From frivolous knickknacks to full-on formal dining sets, Louis Potts specializes in stylish bone china and glassware. ✉ *43 Cliffe High St.* ☎ *01273/472240* 🌐 *www.louispotts.com.*

BRIGHTON, THE SUSSEX COAST, AND SURREY

The self-proclaimed belle of the coast, Brighton is upbeat, funky, and endlessly entertaining. Outside town the soft green downs of Sussex and Surrey hold stately homes you can visit, including Arundel Castle and Petworth House. Along the way, you'll discover the largest Roman villa in Britain, the bustling city of Guildford, and Chichester, whose cathedral is a poem in stone.

BRIGHTON

9 miles southwest of Lewes, 54 miles south of London.

Fodor's Choice ★ For more than 200 years, Brighton has been England's most interesting seaside city, and today it's more vibrant, eccentric, and cosmopolitan than ever. A rich cultural mix—Regency architecture, specialty shops, sidewalk cafés, lively arts, and a flourishing gay scene—makes it unique and unpredictable.

3

In 1750 physician Richard Russell published a book recommending seawater treatment for glandular diseases. The fashionable world flocked to Brighton to take Dr. Russell's "cure," and sea bathing became a popular pastime. Few places in the south of England were better for it, since Brighton's broad beach of smooth pebbles stretches as far as the eye can see. It's been popular with sunbathers ever since.

The next windfall for the town was the arrival of the Prince of Wales (later George IV). "Prinny," as he was called, created the Royal Pavilion, a mock-Asian pleasure palace that attracted London society. This triggered a wave of villa building, and today the elegant terraces of Regency houses are among the town's greatest attractions. The coming of the railway set the seal on Brighton's popularity: the *Brighton Belle* brought Londoners to the coast in an hour.

Londoners still flock to Brighton. Add them to the many local university students, and you have a trendy, young, laid-back city that does, occasionally, burst at its own seams. Property values have skyrocketed, but all visitors may notice is the good shopping and restaurants, attractive (if pebbly) beach, and wild nightlife. Brighton is also the place to go if you're looking for hotels with offbeat design and party nights.

GETTING HERE AND AROUND

Southeastern trains leave from London's Victoria and London Bridge stations several times an hour. The journey takes about an hour, and the trains stop at Gatwick Airport. Brighton-bound National Express and Megabus buses depart from London's Victoria Coach Station every half hour. The trip takes between 2½ and 3 hours. By car from London, head to Brighton on the M23/A23. The journey should take about 1½ hours.

Brighton (and the adjacent Hove) sprawls in all directions, but the part of interest to travelers is fairly compact. None of the sights is more than a 10-minute walk from the train station. You can pick up a town map at the station. City Sightseeing has a hop-on, hop-off tour bus that leaves Brighton Pier every 20 to 30 minutes. It operates May through mid-September (plus weekends, March and April) and costs £11.

TIMING

On summer weekends the town is packed with Londoners looking for a day by the sea. Oceanfront bars can be rowdy, especially on national holidays when concerts and events bring in crowds. But summer is also when Brighton looks its best, and revelers pack the shops, restaurants,

Brighton Beach .. 8
Brighton Museum and Art Gallery 1
Brighton Pier 5
Brighton Wheel.............4
The Lanes 3
Royal Pavilion 2
Sea Life Centre 6
Volk's Electric Railway 7

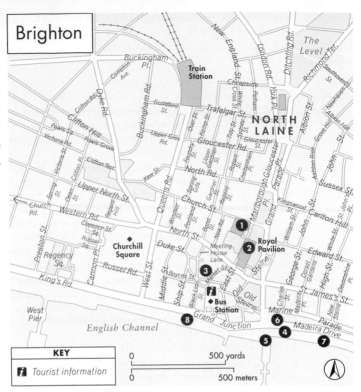

and bars. At other times, it's much quieter. The Brighton Festival in May fills the town with music and other performances.

ESSENTIALS

Visitor and Tour Information **Brighton Visitor Information Centre.** ✉ *The Brighton Centre, King's Rd.* ☎ *01273/290337* 🌐 *www.visitbrighton.com.* **City Sightseeing.** ☎ *01273/886200* 🌐 *www.city-sightseeing.com.*

EXPLORING

TOP ATTRACTIONS

Brighton Beach. Brighton's most iconic landmark is its famous beach, which sweeps smoothly from one end of town to the other. In summer sunbathers, swimmers, and hawkers selling ice cream and toys pack the shore; in winter people stroll at the water's stormy edge, walking their dogs and searching for seashells. The water is bracingly cold, and the beach is covered in a thick blanket of large, smooth pebbles (615 billion of them, according to the tourism office). ■ **TIP→ Bring a pair of rubber swimming shoes if you're taking a dip—the stones are hard on bare feet.** **Amenities:** food and drink; lifeguards; toilets; parking (fee); water sports. **Best for:** partiers; sunset; swimming. ✉ *Marine Parade.*

Brighton Museum and Art Gallery. The grounds of the Royal Pavilion contain this museum, in a former stable block designed for the Prince Regent (1762–1830), son of George III. The museum has particularly interesting art nouveau and art deco collections. Look out for a tiny replica of Salvador Dalí's famous sofa in the shape of Mae West's lips. The Fashion & Style Gallery has clothes from the Regency period to the present day, and the Performance gallery has a collection of masks, puppets, and other theatrical curiosities. ✉ *Royal Pavilion, Church St.* ☎ *0300/029–0900* 🌐 *www.brightonmuseums.org.uk/brighton* 🎟 *Free* ⏲ *Tues.–Sun. (and holiday Mon.) 10–5.*

3

FAMILY **Brighton Pier.** Opened in 1899, the pier is an amusement park set above the sea. In the early 20th century it had a music hall and entertainment; today it has roller coasters and other carnival rides, as well as game arcades, clairvoyants, candy stores, and greasy-food stalls. In summer it's packed with children by day and teenagers by night. The skeletal shadow of a pier you can see off in the water is all that's left of the old West Pier. A gleaming new 162-meter (531-foot) observation tower, **i360**, is due to open next to the pier by 2016. However, the controversial structure has been beset by delays and scandal for years, so the opening date should be considered tentative. ✉ *Madeira Dr.* ☎ *01273/609361* 🌐 *www.brightonpier.co.uk* ⏲ *Daily 10–10; individual attractions vary (most close by 7 or 8 pm).*

The Lanes. This maze of tiny alleys and passageways was once the home of fishermen and their families. Closed to vehicular traffic, the area's narrow cobbled streets are filled with interesting restaurants, boutiques, and antiques shops. Fish and seafood restaurants line the heart of the Lanes, at Market Street and Market Square. ✉ *Bordered by West, North, East, and Prince Albert Sts.*

Fodor'sChoice ★ **Royal Pavilion.** The city's most remarkable building is this delightfully over-the-top domed and pinnacled fantasy. Built as a simple seaside villa in the fashionable classical style of 1787 by architect Henry Holland, the Pavilion was rebuilt between 1815 and 1822 by John Nash for the Prince Regent (later George IV). The result was an exotic, foppish Eastern design with opulent Chinese interiors. The two great set pieces are the **Music Room,** styled in the form of a Chinese pavilion, and the **Banqueting Room,** with its enormous flying-dragon "gasolier," or gaslight chandelier, a revolutionary invention in the early 19th century. The gardens, too, have been restored to Regency splendor, following John Nash's naturalistic design of 1826. For an elegant time-out, a tearoom serves snacks and light meals. ✉ *Old Steine* ☎ *03000/290900* 🌐 *www.brightonmuseums.org.uk/royalpavilion* 🎟 *£12* ⏲ *Oct.–Mar., daily 10–5:15; Apr.–Sept., daily 9:30–5:45; last admission 45 min before closing.*

QUICK BITES

Mock Turtle. Less than a five-minute walk from the Royal Pavilion, the Mock Turtle is a great old-fashioned, homey café. Alongside a decent selection of teas and coffees are four types of rarebit, soups, and scones, as well as cakes and enormous doughnuts. ✉ ***4 Pool Valley*** ☎ ***01273/327380.***

WORTH NOTING

Brighton Wheel. Brighton's answer to the London Eye, this 50-meter (164-foot) Ferris wheel gives you a spectacular panorama of the town and the sea, from air-conditioned capsules. VIP tickets, including

George IV loved the sea at Brighton and built the flamboyant Royal Pavilion as a seaside escape.

rides where wine or champagne is served, cost from £20 per couple to £60 per group of four. There's a 10% discount on all tickets if you book online. ✉ *Daltons Bastion, Madeira Dr.* ☎ *01273/722822* 🌐 *www.brightonwheel.com* 🎫 *£8* 🕑 *Sun.–Thurs. 10–9, Fri. and Sat. 10 am–11 pm.*

FAMILY **Sea Life Centre.** Near Brighton Pier, this aquarium has many sea-dwelling creatures—from sharks to sea horses—in more than 30 marine habitats. A recent renovation added an octopus garden, a jellyfish disco (yes, really), and a rain-forest enclosure featuring a 7-foot-long anaconda. You can pay extra for a ticket that includes a glass-bottomed boat ride in the turtle enclosure (£4 extra per person). Book online at least a day in advance for more than 30% off the ticket price. ✉ *Marine Parade* ☎ *0871/423–2110 booking, 01273/604234 inquiries* 🌐 *www.visitsealife.com/brighton* 🎫 *£17.70* 🕑 *Late Feb.–Apr. and mid-Sept.–mid-Feb, daily 10–5 (10–6 on certain days; full weekly schedule on website); May–early Sept., daily 10–6. Last admission 1 hr before closing.*

FAMILY **Volk's Electric Railway.** Built by inventor Magnus Volk in 1883, this was the first public electric railroad in Britain. In summer you can take the 1¼-mile trip along Marine Parade. ✉ *Marine Parade* ☎ *01273/292718* 🌐 *www.volkselectricrailway.co.uk* 🎫 *£4 round-trip* 🕑 *Easter–Sept., Mon. and Fri. 11:15–5, Tues.–Thurs. 10:15–5, weekends and holidays 10:15–6.*

WHERE TO EAT

$ CAFÉ ✕ **Bill's.** Even groceries seem attractive at this casual, pleasant coffee shop–restaurant–deli. On tall shelves all around the light-filled dining room, bottles of olive oil and vinegars glisten alongside stacks of fresh

CLOSE UP

Brighton and the Regent

The term "Regency" comes from the last 10 years of the reign of George III (1811–20), who was deemed unfit to rule because of his mental problems. Real power was officially given to the Prince of Wales, also known as the Prince Regent, who became King George IV and ruled until his death in 1830.

Throughout his regency, George spent grand sums indulging his flamboyant tastes in architecture and interior decorating—while failing in affairs of state.

The distinctive architecture of the Royal Pavilion is a prime, if extreme, example of the Regency style, popularized by architect John Nash (1752–1835) in the early part of the 19th century. The style is characterized by a diversity of influences—French, Greek, Italian, Persian, Japanese, Chinese, Roman, Indian—you name it. Nash was George IV's favorite architect, beloved for his interest in Indian and Asian art and for his neoclassical designs, as evidenced in his other most famous work—Regent's Park and its terraces in London.

fruit, vegetables, baskets, and flowers. Blackboards near the counter list the day's specials; these usually include a variety of salads, sandwiches (your choice of fresh breads), in addition to full, posh diner-style lunch and dinner menus. Try the amazing *halloumi* (a salty Middle Eastern cheese) burger or Bill's fish pie. Breakfast is popular here, too. $ *Average main: £12* ✉ *The Depot, 100 North Rd.* ☎ *01273/692894* 🌐 *www.bills-website.co.uk*.

$ CAFÉ FAMILY Fodor's Choice ★ ✕ **Gelato Gusto.** No seaside town would be complete without an ice cream store, and the delicious, homemade, artisan gelato on sale here is a real treat. Everything is made fresh daily; try the lemon meringue pie flavor, or maybe a scoop of the delicious sea salt caramel. They also serve a full menu of desserts, including the "gelato burger" (sandwiched between brioche with chocolate sauce); the magnificent, old-school British concotion known as the knickerbocker glory (a tall glass filled with a mixture of ice cream, whipped cream, fruit, and nuts); and waffles. Alternatively, if you have Shaolin levels of self control, you could just have coffee. $ *Average main: £6* ✉ *2 Gardner St.* ☎ *01273/673402* 🌐 *www.gelatogusto.com* *Reservations not accepted.*

$ VEGETARIAN ✕ **Iydea.** This popular café-restaurant is a must for visiting vegetarians, though even the most ardent carnivores are likely to leave satisfied. The food is laid out canteen style, so you choose your meal based on choices of main, side, and toppings. You could go for some harissa couscous or pea-and–goat cheese *arancini* (breaded and fried rice balls), maybe with some Cajun spiced potato wedges or beet, chili, and ginger coleslaw. The restaurant also does a very popular vegetarian breakfast. A second branch, at 105 Western Road, stays open until 10 pm. $ *Average main: £6.50* ✉ *17 Kensington Gardens* ☎ *01273/667992* 🌐 *www.iydea.co.uk* *Reservations not accepted.*

$ MIDDLE EASTERN Fodor's Choice ★ **Pomegranate.** A contemporary Kurdish restaurant, Pomegranate takes a lighthearted, fun approach to Middle Eastern cuisine. Its small dining area spreads over two floors and has large windows and exposed brick walls. The sprawling menu includes lamb stuffed with apricot and nuts, or chicken kebabs served with a yogurt sauce. The lunch menu (£12.50 for three courses) is a particularly good value. *Average main: £13 10 Manchester St. 01273/628386 www.eatpomegranates.com.*

$$ SEAFOOD Fodor's Choice ★ **Riddle and Finns.** White tiles, bare metal tables, and sparkling chandeliers set the tone as soon as you walk through the door of this casually elegant restaurant. The house specialty is oysters, fresh and sustainably sourced, served with or without a tankard of black velvet (champagne and Guinness) on the side. Other options include wild sea bass served with aubergine caviar and red pepper coulis, or local cod with squid ink risotto. Come before 7:15 on weekdays for the outstandingly good value set menu (two courses for just £13). It's also open weekends for breakfast—and, yes, they serve oysters and champagne. The restaurant doesn't take bookings, so come early or be prepared to wait. However, you can reserve a table at their new sister restaurnt, **Riddle & Finns 2** (*139 King's Arches, 01273/821218*), overlooking the sea. The menu is largely the same, with a few meaty options thrown in, too. *Average main: £19 12B Meeting House La. 01273/323008 www.riddleandfinns.co.uk Reservations not accepted.*

$$ VEGETARIAN **Terre à Terre.** This inspiring vegetarian restaurant is incredibly popular, so come early for a light lunch or later for a more sophisticated evening meal. Dishes have a pan-Asian influence, so you may have some cauliflower and ginger *bhaji* (an Indian dish made with deep-fried onions and chickpeas), or a tasty dish of croquettes made from Yarg (a Cornish cheese) with buttered samphire, mushrooms, and garlic. There's also an excellent collection of wines from around the globe. *Average main: £15 71 East St. 01273/729051 www.terreaterre.co.uk.*

WHERE TO STAY

$ B&B/INN Fodor's Choice ★ **Brightonwave.** Chic and sleek, this hotel off the seafront but near Brighton Pier is all about relaxation. **Pros:** big, comfy beds; soothing decor. **Cons:** rooms on the small side; few extras. *Rooms from: £90 10 Madeira Pl. 01273/676794 www.brightonwave.com 8 rooms Breakfast.*

$$ HOTEL Fodor's Choice ★ **Drakes.** It's easy to miss the low-key sign for this elegant, modern hotel tucked away amid the frilly houses on Marine Parade; it's worth the trouble, because everything is cool, calm, and sleekly designed. **Pros:** attention to detail; well-designed bathrooms; excellent restaurant. **Cons:** two-night minimum on weekends; breakfast is extra. *Rooms from: £120 43–44 Marine Parade 01273/696934 www.drakesofbrighton.com 20 rooms No meals.*

$$$ HOTEL **Grand Brighton.** The city's most famous hotel, this seafront landmark is a huge, creamy Victorian wedding cake of a building dating from 1864. **Pros:** as grand as its name; lovely sea views. **Cons:** a bit impersonal; prices can rise sharply at weekends. *Rooms from: £209 97–99 Kings Rd. 01273/224300 www.grandbrighton.co.uk 200 rooms, 3 suites Breakfast.*

$ HOTEL **Granville Hotel.** Three grand Victorian buildings facing the sea make up this hotel where the guest quarters include the pink-and-white Brighton Rock Room and the art-deco Noël Coward Room. **Pros:** creative design; friendly staff; rambunctious atmosphere. **Cons:** some may find the rooms too quirky; sea-facing rooms can be noisy. *Rooms from: £80 124 King's Rd. 01273/326302 www.granvillehotel.co.uk 24 rooms Breakfast.*

$$ HOTEL **Hotel du Vin.** In the Lanes area, this outpost of a snazzy boutique chain has chic modern rooms. **Pros:** gorgeous rooms; comfortable beds; excellent restaurant. **Cons:** bar can get crowded; big price fluctuations in summer. *Rooms from: £145 Ship St. 0844/364–251 www.hotelduvin.com 40 rooms, 3 suites No meals.*

$$ HOTEL **Hotel Pelirocco.** Here the imaginations of designers have been given free rein, and the result is a vicarious romp through pop culture and rock and roll. **Pros:** quirky design; laid-back atmosphere; near the beach. **Cons:** design is often form-over-function; no restaurant. *Rooms from: £109 10 Regency Sq. 01273/327055 www.hotelpelirocco.co.uk 18 rooms, 1 suite Breakfast.*

$ B&B/INN **Nineteen Brighton.** A calm oasis, this guesthouse is filled with contemporary art and designer accessories. **Pros:** relaxing rooms; innovative design; three nights for the price of two. **Cons:** not on the nicest street; two-night minimum on weekends. *Rooms from: £95 19 Broad St. 01273/675529 www.nineteenbrighton.com 7 rooms Breakfast.*

$ HOTEL **Oriental Brighton.** With a casual elegance that typifies Brighton, this Regency-era hotel sits close to the seafront. **Pros:** close to the beach; beautiful rooms. **Cons:** no restaurant; busy bar; minimum stay on weekends. *Rooms from: £85 9 Oriental Pl. 01273/205050 www.orientalbrighton.co.uk 9 rooms Breakfast.*

NIGHTLIFE AND PERFORMING ARTS

NIGHTLIFE

Brighton is a techno hub, largely because so many DJs have moved here from London. Clubs and bars present live music most nights, and on weekends the entire place can be a bit too raucous for some tastes. There's a large and enthusiastic gay scene.

The Jazz Lounge at the Bohemia Grand Café. Every Thursday from 9 pm the best local jazz acts take over this upscale café-bar. It's arranged like a traditional jazz club, with table service and an old-school vibe. *54 Meeting House La. 01273/777770 www.bohemiabrighton.co.uk.*

Patterns. One of Brighton's foremost venues, in an art-deco building east of Brighton Pier, Patterns is the latest incarnation of a string of popular nightclubs that have occupied this spot. Expect to hear live acts during the week (including a regular local slot—this being Brighton, the quality is generally quite high) and techno and house on the weekend. *10 Marine Parade 01273/606906.*

The Plotting Parlour. There's something of the glamorous speakeasy about this ultra-hip nightclub on Stein Street. Cocktails are a specialty, and the bar staff certainly know what they're doing (try the fierce chili Martini). It's extremely popular with the cooler brand of local partygoer, and magnificently good fun to boot. ✉ *6 Steine St.* ☎ *01273/621238* 🌐 *brighton.shooshh.com.*

Proud Cabaret. A mixture of vintage and avante-garde cabaret and burlesque is on offer at this stylish nightclub, which also serves a 1920s-style three-course dinner from Thursday to Saturday. Booking is advisable. ✉ *83 St. Georges Rd.* ☎ *01273/605789* 🌐 *www.brightoncabaret.com.*

PERFORMING ARTS

Brighton Dome. West of the Royal Pavilion, the Brighton Dome was converted from the Prince Regent's stables in the 1930s. It includes a theater and a concert hall that stage pantomime (a traditional British children's play with songs and dance, usually featuring low-rent TV stars), and classical and pop concerts. ✉ *Church St.* ☎ *01273/709709* 🌐 *www.brightondome.org.*

Brighton Festival. The three-week-long Brighton Festival, one of England's biggest and liveliest arts festivals, takes place every May in venues around town. The more than 600 events include drama, music, dance, and visual arts. ✉ *Brighton* ☎ *01273/709709* 🌐 *www.brightonfestival.org.*

Duke of York's Picture House. The elegant 1910 Duke of York's Picture House, a 10-minute walk north of the main train station, shows art-house movies. ✉ *Preston Circus* ☎ *0871/902–5728* 🌐 *www.picturehouses.co.uk.*

Theatre Royal. Close to the Royal Pavilion, the Theatre Royal has a gem of an auditorium that's a favorite venue for shows on their way to or fresh from London's West End. For tickets visit *www.atgtickets.com/venues/theatre-royal-brighton.* ✉ *35 Bond St.* ☎ *01273/764400.*

SHOPPING

Brighton Lanes Antique Centre. Although this shop specializes in gold and jewelry, it also has a good selection of furniture and ornaments. ✉ *2 Brighton Sq., The Lanes* ☎ *01273/321183* 🌐 *www.brightonlanesantiques.co.uk.*

Colin Page Antiquarian Books. At the western edge of the Lanes, Colin Page stocks a wealth of antiquarian and secondhand books at all prices. ✉ *36 Duke St., The Lanes* ☎ *01273/325954.*

Cologne & Cotton. This lovely little bed-and-bath emporium sells vintage bed linens, blankets, bath products, and tableware. ✉ *13 Pavilion Bldgs.* ☎ *01273/729666* 🌐 *www.cologneandcotton.com.*

Curiouser & Curiouser. This shop made several pieces of jewelry for the Harry Potter movies. It is filled with unique handmade pieces, mostly sterling silver with semiprecious stones. ✉ *2 Sydney St.* ☎ *01273/673120* 🌐 *www.curiousersilverjewellery.co.uk.*

The Lanes. Brighton's main shopping area is the Lanes, especially for antiques or jewelry. It also has clothing boutiques, coffee shops, and pubs. ✉ *Brighton.*

Lavender Room. This relaxing boutique tempts with scented calendars, glittery handmade jewelry, and little things you just can't live without. ✉ *16 Bond St.* ☎ *01273/220380* 🌐 *www.lavender-room.co.uk.*

North Laine. Across North Street from the Lanes lies the North Laine, a network of narrow streets full of little stores. They're less glossy than those in the Lanes, but are fun, funky, and exotic. ✉ *Brighton.*

Pecksniff's Bespoke Perfumery. The delightfully old-fashioned Pecksniff's Bespoke Perfumery mixes and matches ingredients to suit your wishes. ✉ *45–46 Meeting House La.* ☎ *01273/723292* 🌐 *www.pecksniffs.com.*

Royal Pavilion Shop. Next door to the Royal Pavilion, this shop carries well-designed toys, trinkets, books, and cards, all with a loose Regency theme. There are also high-quality fabrics, wallpapers, and ceramics based on material in the pavilion itself. ✉ *4–5 Pavilion Bldgs.* ☎ *01273/292798.*

3

ARUNDEL

23 miles west of Brighton, 60 miles south of London.

The little hilltop town of Arundel is dominated by its great castle, the much-restored home of the dukes of Norfolk for more than 700 years, and an imposing neo-Gothic Roman Catholic cathedral (the duke is Britain's leading Catholic peer). The town itself is full of interesting old buildings and well worth a stroll.

GETTING HERE AND AROUND

Arundel is on the A27, about a two-hour drive south of central London. Trains from London's Victoria Station leave every half hour and take 1½ hours. No direct buses run from London, but you can take a National Express bus to Worthing or Chichester and change to a local bus to Arundel, though that journey could easily take five hours.

ESSENTIALS

Visitor Information Arundel Visitor Information Centre. ✉ *Crown Yard, River Rd.* ☎ *01903/737838* 🌐 *www.sussexbythesea.com.*

EXPLORING

FAMILY Fodor's Choice ★ **Arundel Castle.** You've probably already seen Arundel Castle without knowing it—the striking resemblence to Windsor means that it's frequently used as a stand-in for its more famous cousin in movies and television. Begun in the 11th century, this vast castle remains rich with the history of the Fitzalan and Howard families and with paintings by Van Dyck, Gainsborough, and Reynolds. During the 18th century and in the Victorian era it was reconstructed in the fashionable Gothic style—although the keep, rising from its conical mound, is as old as the original castle (climb its 130 steps for great views of the River Arun), and the barbican and the Barons' Hall date from the 13th century. Among the treasures are the rosary beads and prayer book used by Mary, Queen of Scots, in preparing for her execution. The newly redesigned formal garden is a triumph of order and beauty. Although the castle's ceremonial entrance is at the top of High Street, you enter at the bottom, close to the parking lot. ✉ *Mill Rd.* ☎ *01903/882173* 🌐 *www.arundelcastle.org* 🎫 *Castle and grounds £18; castle and grounds excluding bedrooms £16; castle (keep only) and grounds £11; chapel and grounds only £9* ⏲ *Easter–early Nov., Tues.–Sun. and holidays 10–5 (main castle rooms open at noon; keep closes at 4:30). Last admission 1 hr before closing.*

Brighton, the Sussex Coast, and Surrey

WHERE TO EAT AND STAY

$ CAFÉ ✕ **Berties of Arundel.** This place is a real little charmer. A lovely, old-school café in the center of Arundel, Berties serves delicious sandwiches, panini, light lunches, and homemade cakes. Tea is served in colorful ceramic pots in a dining room bedecked with bunting. The staff is delightfully friendly, too. *Average main: £6 ✉ 31 Tarrant St. ☎ 01903/882110.*

$$$$ BRITISH ✕ **The Town House.** This small but elegant restaurant in a beautifully converted Regency town house (look above you—the dining room ceiling is quite something) serves top-notch British and European cuisine. The fixed-price lunch and dinner menus change regularly, but could include honey roast pork with seasonal vegetables, or wild sea bass with basil mashed potato. If you want to see more of the place, they also do bed-and-breakfast accommodations from £105 per night. *Average main: £29.50 ✉ 65 High St. ☎ 01903/883847 🌐 www.thetownhouse.co.uk.*

$$$ HOTEL Fodor's Choice ★ **Amberley Castle.** Enter under the portcullis of this genuine medieval castle, where across the moat, present-day luxury dominates. **Pros:** sleep in a real castle; lovely gardens and grounds. **Cons:** you have to dress up for dinner. *Rooms from: £195 ✉ Bury Hill, Off B2139, Amberley ☎ 01798/831992 🌐 www.amberleycastle.co.uk 19 rooms 🍴 Breakfast.*

$ HOTEL **Norfolk Arms Hotel.** Like the cathedral and the castle in Arundel, this 18th-century coaching inn on the main street was built by one of the dukes of Norfolk. **Pros:** charming building; historic setting. **Cons:** older rooms on the small side; a little old-fashioned. *Rooms from: £99* ✉ *22 High St.* ☎ *0844/855–9101* 🌐 *www.norfolkarmshotel.com* *34 rooms* *Breakfast.*

NIGHTLIFE AND PERFORMING ARTS

Arundel Festival. The popular Arundel Festival presents dramatic productions, classical and pop concerts, and a few more locally centered fun and games, such as a rubber duck race. Most events take place in and around the castle grounds for 10 days in late August. The full schedule is published on the website. ✉ *Arundel* ☎ *01903/883690* 🌐 *www.arundelfestival.co.uk.*

3

CHICHESTER

10 miles west of Arundel, 66 miles southwest of London.

The Romans founded Chichester, the capital city of West Sussex, on the low-lying plains between the wooded South Downs and the sea. The city walls and major streets follow the original Roman plan. This cathedral town, a good base for exploring the area, is a well-respected theatrical hub, with a reputation for attracting good acting talent during its summer repertory season. North of town is Petworth House, one of the region's finest stately homes.

GETTING HERE AND AROUND

From London, take A3 south and follow exit signs for Chichester. The journey takes slightly more than two hours; much of it is on smaller highways. Southern trains run to Chichester four times an hour from Victoria Station, with a travel time of between 1½ and 2 hours. Half involve a train from Brighton. Buses leave from London's Victoria Coach Station a handful of times per day and take between 3½ and 4 hours.

ESSENTIALS

Visitor Information Chichester Tourist Information Centre. ✉ *The Novium, Tower St.* ☎ *01243/775888* 🌐 *www.visitchichester.org.*

EXPLORING

Chichester Cathedral. Standing on Roman foundations, 900-year-old Chichester Cathedral has a glass panel that reveals Roman mosaics uncovered during restorations. Other treasures include the wonderful Saxon limestone reliefs of the raising of Lazarus and Christ arriving in Bethany, both in the choir area. Among the outstanding contemporary artworks are a stained-glass window by Marc Chagall and a colorful tapestry by John Piper. Free guided tours begin every day except Sunday at 11:15 and 2:30. You can also prebook tours that concentrate on subjects including the English Civil War and the cathedral's art collection; call or go online for details. ✉ *West St.* ☎ *01243/782595* 🌐 *www.chichestercathedral.org.uk* *Free; £4.50 suggested donation* *Easter–Sept., daily 7:15–7; Oct.–Easter, daily 7:15–6.*

Fodor's Choice ★ **Fishbourne Roman Palace.** In 1960, workers digging a water-main ditch uncovered a Roman wall; so began nine years of archaeological excavation of this site, the remains of the largest, grandest Roman villa in Britain. Intricate mosaics (including Cupid riding a dolphin) and painted walls lavishly decorate what is left of many of the 100 rooms of the palace, built in AD 1st century, possibly for local chieftain Tiberius Claudius Togidubnus. You can explore the sophisticated bathing and heating systems, along with the only example of a Roman garden in northern Europe. An expansion has added many modern attributes, including a video reconstruction of how the palace might have looked. The site is ½ mile west of Chichester. ✉ *Salthill Rd., Fishbourne* ☎ *01243/785859* 🌐 *www.sussexpast.co.uk* 🎫 *£8.90* ⏲ *Feb. and Nov.–mid-Dec., daily 10–4; Mar.–Oct., daily 10–5. Closed Jan.*

Fodor's Choice ★ **Pallant House Gallery.** This small but important collection of mostly modern British art includes work by Henry Moore and Graham Sutherland. It's in a modern extension to Pallant House, a mansion built for a wealthy wine merchant in 1712, and considered one of the finest surviving examples of Chichcester's Georgian past. At that time its state-of-the-art design showed the latest in complicated brickwork and superb wood carving. Appropriate antiques and porcelains furnish the faithfully restored rooms. Temporary and special exhibitions (usually around three at once) invariably find new and interesting angles to cover. ✉ *9 N. Pallant* ☎ *01243/774557* 🌐 *www.pallant.org.uk* 🎫 *Ground floor galleries free; rest of museum £9* ⏲ *Tues., Wed., Fri., and Sat. 10–5, Thurs. 10–8, Sun. and holiday Mon. 11–5.*

Fodor's Choice ★ **Petworth House.** One of the National Trust's greatest treasures, Petworth is the imposing 17th-century home of Lord and Lady Egremont and holds an outstanding collection of English paintings by Gainsborough, Reynolds, and Van Dyck, as well as 19 oil paintings by J. M. W. Turner, the great proponent of romanticism who often visited Petworth and immortalized it in luminous drawings. A 13th-century chapel is all that remains of the original manor house. The celebrated landscape architect Capability Brown (1716–83) added a 700-acre deer park. Other highlights include Greek and Roman sculpture and Grinling Gibbons wood carvings, such as those in the spectacular Carved Room. Six rooms in the servants' quarters, among them the old kitchen, are also open to the public. A restaurant serves light lunches. You can reach the house off A283; Petworth House is 13 miles northeast of Chichester and 54 miles south of London. ✉ *A283, Petworth* ☎ *01798/342207* 🌐 *www.nationaltrust.org.uk* 🎫 *£12.50* ⏲ *Mid-Mar.–early Nov., Sat.–Wed. 11–5. Also partial opening and special tours, Thurs. and Fri. Last admission 1 hr before closing. Grounds year-round, daily 10–5 or until dusk if earlier.*

FAMILY **Weald and Downland Open Air Museum.** On the outskirts of Singleton, a secluded village 5 miles north of Chichester, is this excellent museum, a sanctuary for historical buildings dating from the 13th to 19th centuries. Among the 45 structures moved to 50 acres of wooded meadows are a cluster of medieval houses, a water mill, a Tudor market hall, and an ancient blacksmith's shop. ✉ *Town La., off A286, Singleton* ☎ *01243/811363* 🌐 *www.wealddown.co.uk* 🎫 *£12.50* ⏲ *Mid-Mar.–late*

Oct., daily 10:30–6; late Mar.–late Dec., daily 10:30–4; late Dec.–Jan 1, daily 10:30–4; Jan.–Feb., Wed., Sat., and Sun. 10:30–4. Last admission 1 hr before closing.

WHERE TO EAT AND STAY

$$ BISTRO **Woodies Wine Bar & Brasserie.** This upbeat restaurant in the center of Chichester gets it just right—top-notch bistro cooking, not overcomplicated, at completely reasonable prices. You might start with some phyllo-wrapped prawns with chili-and-tomato mayo, following it with a sea-bass fillet with squid-ink noodles, or duck confit served with parsnip tatin. The fixed-price lunch menu is a particularly good value at £14 for two courses, including a glass of wine. *Average main: £15* *10–13 St. Pancras* *01243/779895* *www.woodiesbrasserie.com* *No credit cards* *Closed Sun.*

$$ HOTEL **Ship Hotel.** Originally the home of Admiral George Murray, one of Admiral Nelson's right-hand men, this architecturally interesting hotel is known for its flying (partially freestanding) staircase and colonnade. **Pros:** well-restored building; good location. **Cons:** rooms are small; not many amenities. *Rooms from: £125* *North St.* *01243/778000* *www.theshiphotel.net* *36 rooms* *Some meals.*

NIGHTLIFE AND PERFORMING ARTS

Chichester Festival Theatre. The modernist Chichester Festival Theatre presents classics and modern plays from May through September and is a venue for touring companies the rest of the year. Built in 1962, it has an international reputation for innovative performances and attracts theatergoers from across the country. *Oaklands Park, Broyle Rd.* *01243/781312* *www.cft.org.uk.*

GUILDFORD

22 miles north of Petworth House, 35 miles north of Chichester, 28 miles southwest of London.

Guildford, the largest town in Surrey and the county's capital, has a lovely historic center with charming original storefronts. Gabled merchants' houses line the steep, pleasantly provincial High Street, where the remains of a Norman castle are tucked away in a peaceful garden, and the iconic clock on the old guildhall dates from 1683. The area around the train station is rather seedy and crowded, but once you make your way to the center it's a much nicer town. Guildford is a good place to base yourself if you're planning to visit nearby attractions such as the Royal Horticultural Society gardens in Wisley or the ruins of Waverley Abbey.

GETTING HERE AND AROUND

From London, take A3 south and then exit onto the A31, following signs for Guildford. The 28-mile journey takes about an hour in traffic. Southwest trains run to Guildford several times an hour from London's Waterloo Station; the trip takes between 30 minutes and 1¼ hours. Guildford Station is extremely busy and surrounded by traffic, but fortunately the center is a five-minute walk; just follow the signs for High

Street. National Express buses travel from London to Guildford every couple of hours; the trip takes an hour.

ESSENTIALS

Visitor Information **Guildford Tourist Information Centre.** ✉ *155 High St.* ☎ *01483/444333* 🌐 *www.guildford.gov.uk/visitguildford.*

EXPLORING

TOP ATTRACTIONS

Fodor's Choice ★ **Polesden Lacey.** This gorgeous, creamy-yellow Regency mansion, built in 1824, contains impressive collections of furniture, paintings, porcelain, and silver gathered in the early part of the 20th century. Edwardian society hostess Mrs. Ronald Greville was responsible for the lavish interiors; the future King George VI stayed here for part of his honeymoon in 1923. On summer days you can wander its vast landscaped gardens or rent croquet equipment from the house and take advantage of its smooth lawns. The house is in Great Bookham, 8 miles from Guildford. ✉ *Off A246, Great Bookham* ☎ *01372/452048* 🌐 *www.nationaltrust.org.uk/polesden-lacey* 🎟 *£12.70; gardens only £7.90* ⏲ *House Mar.–Oct., daily 11–5 (guided tours weekdays 11–12:30 and weekends in winter). Grounds year-round, daily 10–5 or until dusk if earlier.*

Fodor's Choice ★ **Watts Gallery and Memorial Chapel.** An extraordinary small museum that's often overlooked, Watts Gallery was built in tiny Compton in 1904 by the late-19th-century artist George Frederic Watts (1817–1904) to display his work. After a major renovation to the gallery, Watts' romantic, mystical paintings are beautifully displayed. His sculptures are astonishing both for their size and the near-obsessive attention to detail. Even more of a draw, however, is the extraordinary **Watts Memorial Chapel**, less than ½ mile from the museum in the village cemetery. Designed by his wife, Mary—virtually unknown as an artist, then and now, but arguably the superior talent—the tiny chapel is a true masterpiece in art nouveau style, from the intricately carved brick exterior to the stunning painted interior. The museum is 3 miles south of Guildford. ✉ *Down La., Compton* ☎ *01483/810235* 🌐 *www.wattsgallery.org.uk* 🎟 *Museum £7.50; chapel free* ⏲ *Museum Tues.–Sun. and holiday Mon. 11–5. Chapel weekdays 8–5, weekends 10–5:30.*

Waverley Abbey. One of the oldest Cistercian abbeys in England, this was an important center of monastic power from 1128 until Henry VIII's dissolution of the monastries. What remains is a strikingly picturesque ruin surrounded by open countryside. Roofed sections of the undercroft and monks' dormitory survive, as does the refrectory tunnel and a magnificent yew tree in the former churchyard, thought to be around 700 years old. A more unexpected historical footnote sits on the banks of the abbey stream: moss-covered tank traps, overlooked from across a field by a pillbox (sniper station). They were placed here during World War II after British generals role-played a Nazi invasion and decided this was the route they'd choose to attack London. Unused plans later found in Berlin showed they were precisely right. The abbey is off the B3001, 9 miles southwest of Guildford. ✉ *Waverley La., Farnham* 🌐 *www.english-heritage.org.uk* 🎟 *Free* ⏲ *Daily dawn–dusk.*

Fodor's Choice ★ **Wisley.** In a nation of gardeners and garden goers, Wisley is the Royal Horticultural Society's innovative and inspirational 240-acre showpiece. Both an ornamental and scientific center, it claims to have greater horticultural diversity than any other garden in the world. The flower borders and displays in the central area, the rock garden and alpine meadow in spring, and the large, modern conservatories are just a few highlights, along with an impressive bookstore and a garden center that sells more than 10,000 types of plants. The garden is 10 miles northeast of Guildford. ✉ *Off A3, Woking* ☎ *0845/260–9000* 🌐 *www.rhs.org.uk/gardens/wisley* 🎟 *£12* 🕒 *Mar.–Oct., weekdays 10–6, weekends and holiday Mon. 9–6; Nov.–mid-Mar., weekdays 10–4:30, weekends and holiday Mon. 9–4:30. Last admission 1 hr before closing.*

WORTH NOTING

Guildford Museum. In the old castle building, this museum has exhibits on local history and archaeology, as well as memorabilia of Charles Dodgson, better known as Lewis Carroll, author of *Alice in Wonderland.* They run a couple of special exhibitions per year; recently these have included the history of the area during the First World War (when it was bombed in Zeppelin raids). Dodgson spent his last years in a house on nearby Castle Hill and is buried in the Mount Cemetery, up the hill on High Street. Castle Arch, all that remains of the entrance of the old castle, displays a slot for a portcullis. ✉ *Quarry St.* ☎ *01483/444751* 🌐 *www.guildford.gov.uk/museum* 🎟 *Free* 🕒 *Mon.–Sat. 11–5.*

FAMILY **Sculpture Park at Churt.** Set in a forested park 8 miles outside Guildford, this is a wild, fanciful place where giant steel spiders climb trees, bronze horses charge up hillsides, and metal girls and boys dance on lakes. You follow signposted paths across the parkland, spotting tiny sculptures up trees, in bushes, and walking through the legs of other more gigantic creations. You can also follow the footpath beside the little car park outside up to the **Devil's Jumps,** a ruggedly beautiful spot with views over the South Downs. The name derives from a piece of local folklore: one night the devil stole a cauldron from a witch who lived near Waverley Abbey. She gave chase on her broomstick, so with each leap the devil kicked up huge clods of earth, which in turn became hills—hence "jumps." The park is off the A287 between Guildford and Farnham. ✉ *Jumps Rd., Churt* ☎ *01428/605453* 🌐 *www.thesculpturepark.com* 🎟 *£6* 🕒 *Daily 10–5.*

WHERE TO EAT

$ CAFÉ ✕ **Glutton and Glee.** With a name like Glutton and Glee it's hard not to be intrigued, and this popular, independent little coffee shop in the center of Guildford has plenty of fans. The sandwiches are excellent—try the cheddar cheese and pear on sourdough, with date and ale chutney—along with savory tarts, salads, and other light lunchtime nibbles. Breakfasts here are a real specialty, served until a deliciously lazy noon (1 pm on Sundays). $ *Average main: £6* ✉ *6 Tunsgate* ☎ *01483/452931* 🌐 *www.gluttonandglee.co.uk.*

$ AMERICAN ✕ **Gourmet Burger Kitchen.** This very popular place does what it says on the label—good burgers and not a lot else. You wait for a table, then order at the counter. All the burgers are excellent: try the Camemburger, with Camembert cheese, hash browns, and onion jam; the Habanero,

HIKING IN THE SOUTHEAST

For those who prefer to travel on their own two feet, the Southeast offers long sweeps of open terrain that makes walking a pleasure. Ardent walkers can explore all or part of the **North Downs Way** (153 miles) and the **South Downs Way** (106 miles), following ancient paths along the tops of the downs—the undulating treeless uplands typical of the area. Both trails are now part of the **South Downs National Park** (🌐 *www.southdowns.gov.uk*), but each maintains its separate identity.

TRAILS ON THE DOWNS

The North Downs Way starts outside Guildford, in the town of Farnham, alongside the A31. You can park at the train station, about ½ mile away. The path starts with absolutely no fanfare, on a traffic-choked bypass. A better way to reach it from the station is to take the footpath next to the Tasty House Chinese takeout, almost opposite the entrance; turn left at the top and walk along this quiet street for about 10 minutes until you come to another footpath on the left. Official markers start at the bottom of this path.

The North Downs Way passes along the White Cliffs of Dover and ends in the Dover town square. It follows part of the old Pilgrim's Way to Canterbury that so fascinated Chaucer.

The South Downs Way starts in Winchester, at Water Lane. It ends on the promenade in the seaside town of Eastbourne. Along the way it crosses the chalk landscape of Sussex Downs, with parts of the route going through deep woodland. Charming little villages serve the walkers cool ale in inns that have been doing precisely that for centuries.

The 30-mile **Downs Link** joins the two routes. Along the Kent coast, the **Saxon Shore Way**, stretching 143 miles from Gravesend to Rye, passes four Roman forts.

RESOURCES

Guides to these walks are available from the excellent website for **National Trails** (🌐 *www.nationaltrail.co.uk*). Tourist information offices throughout the region also have good information.

with spicy salsa; or the Wellington, with mushrooms and horseradish sauce. The enormous milk shakes are tasty diet-busters. One order of fries will be enough for two. $ *Average main: £9* ✉ *10 Friary St.* ☎ *01483/572464* 🌐 *www.gbk.co.uk* ▭ *No credit cards.*

$ BRITISH ✕ **The Mill.** A short hop down the road from Waverley Abbey, this unusually handsome pub is in an old watermill (which is still working—you can see it in the lobby). The menu nicely balances British pub classics and more contemporary tastes; expect to find cottage pie (ground beef and vegetables topped with mashed potato), and some excellent fish-and-chips, alongside clementine, lentil, and feta salad, or crispy gnocchi with artichokes. The huge beer garden—overlooking the mill stream and usually patrolled by a flock of ducks who are very well practiced at begging for crumbs—is an extremely popular spot in summer. The pub is on the B3001, 9 miles southwest of Guildford. $ *Average main: £13* ✉ *Farnham Rd.* ☎ *01252/703333* 🌐 *www.millelstead.co.uk.*

$ THAI **Rumwong.** With an incredibly long menu, Rumwong has dozens of choices from all over Thailand. Tasty dishes include the fisherman's soup, a spicy mass of delicious saltwater fish in a clear broth, or *yam pla muek,* a hot salad with squid. The owners also run an Asian supermarket next door. *Average main: £10 18–20 London Rd. 01483/536092 www.rumwong.co.uk No credit cards.*

WHERE TO STAY

$$ HOTEL **Angel Posting House and Livery.** Guildford was once famous for its coaching inns, and this handsome 500-year-old hotel is the last to survive. **Pros:** historic building; central location. **Cons:** some rooms suffer from poor ventilation and get very hot in summer; could do with a face-lift; location can be noisy. *Rooms from: £109 91 High St. 01483/564555 www.angelpostinghouse.com 21 rooms No meals.*

$$ HOTEL **Radisson Blu Edwardian Guildford.** The Guildford branch of the Radisson chain is mostly aimed at business travellers, which makes it a good, reliable place to stay in town. **Pros:** central location; free Wi-Fi. **Cons:** lacks character; parking is expensive (£12 per 24 hours). *Rooms from: £135 3 Alexandra Terr., off High St. 01483/792300 www.radissonblu-edwardian.com 183 Breakfast.*

3

TUNBRIDGE WELLS AND AROUND

England is famous for its magnificent stately homes and castles, but many of them are scattered across the country, presenting a challenge for travelers. Within a 15-mile radius of Tunbridge Wells, however, in that area of hills and hidden dells known as the Weald, lies a wealth of architectural wonder in historic homes, castles, and gardens: Penshurst Place, Hever Castle, Chartwell, Knole, Ightham Mote, Leeds Castle, and lovely Sissinghurst Castle Garden.

ROYAL TUNBRIDGE WELLS

39 miles southeast of London.

Nobody much bothers with the "Royal" anymore, but Tunbridge Wells is no less regal because of it. Because of its wealth and political conservatism, this historic bedroom community has been the subject of (somewhat envious) British humor for years. Its restaurants and lodgings make it a convenient base for exploring the many homes and gardens nearby.

The city owes its prosperity to the 17th- and 18th-century passion for spas and mineral baths. In 1606 a mineral-water spring was discovered here, drawing legions of royal visitors looking for eternal health. Tunbridge Wells reached its zenith in the mid-18th century, when Richard "Beau" Nash presided over its social life. The buildings at the lower end of High Street are mostly 18th century, but as the street climbs the hill north, changing its name to Mount Pleasant Road, structures become more modern.

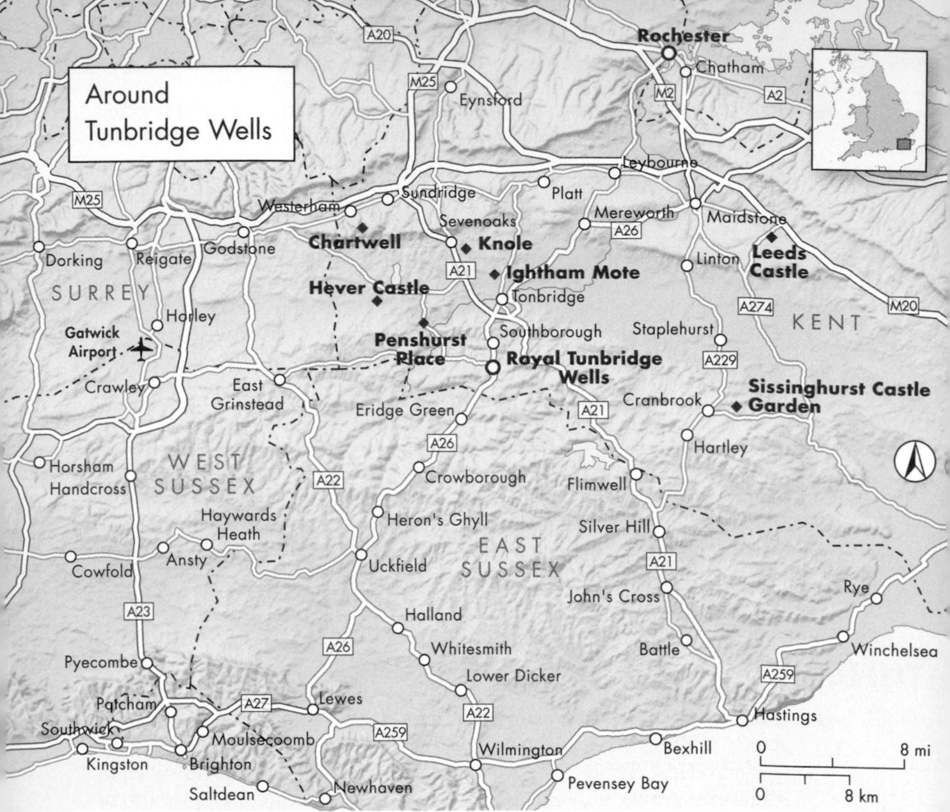

GETTING HERE AND AROUND

Southeastern trains leave from London's Charing Cross Station every 15 minutes. The journey to Tunbridge Wells takes just under an hour. If you're traveling by car from London, head here on the A21; travel time is about an hour.

Tunbridge Wells sprawls in all directions, but the historic center is compact. None of the sights is more than a 10-minute walk from the main train station. You can pick up a town map at the station.

ESSENTIALS

Visitor Information Royal Tunbridge Wells Tourist Information Centre. ✉ *Unit 2, The Corn Exchange, The Pantiles* ☎ *01892/515675* 🌐 *www.visittunbridgewells.com.*

EXPLORING

All Saints Church. This modest 13th-century church holds one of the glories of 20th-century church art. The building is awash with the luminous yellows and blues of 12 windows by Marc Chagall (1887–1985), commissioned as a tribute by the family of a young girl who was drowned in a sailing accident in 1963. The church is 4 miles north of Tunbridge Wells; turn off A26 before the confusingly similar-sounding town of Tonbridge and continue a mile or so east along B2017. ✉ *B2017, Tudeley* ☎ *01732/833241* 🎫 *Free; £2.50 donation requested* ⏲ *Daily 9–6.*

Church of King Charles the Martyr. Across the road from the Pantiles, this church dates from 1678, when it was dedicated to Charles I, who had been executed by Parliament in 1649. Its plain exterior belies its splendid interior, with a particularly beautiful plastered baroque ceiling. ✉ *Chapel Pl.* ☎ *01892/511745* 🌐 *www.kcmtw.org* 🎫 *Free* ⏲ *Mon.–Sat. 11–3.*

Pantiles. A good place to begin a visit is at the Pantiles, a famous promenade with colonnaded shops near the spring on one side of town. Its odd name derives from the Dutch "pan tiles" that originally paved the area. Now sandwiched between two busy main roads, the Pantiles remains an elegant, tranquil oasis, and the site of the actual well. ■ **TIP→ You can still drink the waters when a "dipper" (the traditional water dispenser) is in attendance, from Easter through September.** ✉ *Royal Tunbridge Wells.*

3

WHERE TO EAT

$ ASIAN

✕ **Himalayan Gurkha.** It's not what you might expect to find in the cozy confines of Tunbridge Wells, but the Nepalese cuisine at this friendly spot is popular with locals. The spicy mountain cuisine is similar to Indian food, with distinctive touches. Meats and fish are cooked with care in traditional clay ovens or barbecued on flaming charcoal. Try the spicy *thulo jhinge tarkari* (a spicy curry made with king prawns) or *kukhara bjojan* (tender marinated chicken, cooked with deep-fried cabbage). The vegetarian options are appealing, too. Ⓢ *Average main: £8* ✉ *31 Church Rd.* ☎ *01892/527834* 🌐 *www.himalayangurkha.com.*

$ JAPANESE Fodor's Choice ★

✕ **Kitsu.** Good Japanese food is often difficult to come by in England, so this tiny, unassuming restaurant seems an unlikely venue for the best sushi you're likely to find for miles. Everything is fresh and delicious, from the fragrant miso soup to the light tempura to the sushi platters that are big enough to share. For something heartier, try a bowl of steaming fried noodles or a katsu curry. There are only two drawbacks: the place doesn't take credit cards and doesn't serve alcohol, although you're welcome to bring your own. Ⓢ *Average main: £13* ✉ *82a Victoria Rd.* ☎ *01892/515510* 🌐 *www.kitsu.co.uk.*

$$$$ FRENCH Fodor's Choice ★

✕ **Thackeray's House.** Once the home of Victorian novelist William Makepeace Thackeray, this mid-17th-century tile-hung house is now an elegant restaurant known for creative French cuisine. The menu changes daily, but often lists such dishes as beef bourguignonne with watercress, or halibut with marinated fennel and broccoli puree. If you really want to splurge, try the 10-course tasting menu (£98 per person, or £148 with accompanying wines; whole tables only). Ⓢ *Average main: £28* ✉ *85 London Rd.* ☎ *01892/511921* 🌐 *www.thackerays-restaurant.co.uk* ⏲ *Closed Mon. and last wk in Dec. No dinner Sun.*

WHERE TO STAY

$$ HOTEL

🏨 **Hotel du Vin.** An elegant sandstone house dating from 1762 has been transformed into a chic boutique hotel with polished wood floors and luxurious furnishings. **Pros:** historic building; luxurious linens. **Cons:** restaurant can get booked up; bar can be crowded. Ⓢ *Rooms from: £125* ✉ *Crescent Rd., near Mount Pleasant Rd.* ☎ *01892/526455* 🌐 *www.hotelduvin.com/locations/tunbridge-wells* 🛏 *34 rooms* 🍽 *Breakfast.*

$ HOTEL **Smart & Simple Hotel.** This lodging near the train station takes a contemporary approach with rooms that are small but nicely decorated. **Pros:** handy location; free Wi-Fi. **Cons:** few services; no frills at all; no parking (must use nearby lots). *Rooms from: £75 ⊠ 54–57 London Rd. ☎ 01892/552700 ⊕ www.smartandsimple.co.uk 40 rooms Some meals.*

$$$ HOTEL **Spa Hotel.** Carefully chosen furnishings and period-perfect details help maintain the country-house flavor of this 1766 Georgian mansion. **Pros:** lap-of-luxury feel; gorgeous views. **Cons:** breakfast is extra; very formal atmosphere; can be a bit stuffy. *Rooms from: £130 ⊠ Mount Ephraim ☎ 01892/520331 ⊕ www.spahotel.co.uk 70 rooms No meals.*

PENSHURST PLACE

7 miles northwest of Royal Tunbridge Wells, 33 miles southeast of London.

One of the best preserved of the great medieval houses in Britain, and surrounded by stunning landscaped gardens, Penshurst Place is like an Elizabethan time machine.

GETTING HERE AND AROUND

To get to Penshurst, take the A26 north to Penshurst Road. The drive from Tunbridge Wells takes about 12 minutes. Buses 231, 233, and 237 run from Tunbridge Wells to Penshurst (no buses on Sunday).

EXPLORING

Fodor's Choice ★ **Penshurst Place.** At the center of the adorable hamlet of Penshurst stands this fine medieval manor house, hidden behind tall trees and walls. Although it has a 14th-century hall, Penshurst is mainly Elizabethan and has been the family home of the Sidneys since 1552. The most famous Sidney is the Elizabethan poet Sir Philip, author of *Arcadia*. The **Baron's Hall,** topped with a chestnut roof, is the oldest and one of the grandest halls to survive from the early Middle Ages. Family portraits, furniture, tapestries, and armor help tell the story of the house, which was first inhabited in 1341 by Sir John de Pulteney, the very wealthy four-time London mayor. On the grounds are a toy museum, a gift shop, and the enchanting 11-acre walled Italian Garden, which displays tulips and daffodils in spring and roses in summer. Take time to study the village's late-15th-century half-timber structures adorned with soaring brick chimneys. To get here from Tunbridge Wells, take the A26 and B2176. *⊠ Rogues Hill, off Leicester Square, Penshurst ☎ 01892/870307 ⊕ www.penshurstplace.com £10.50; grounds only £8.50 House and toy museum Mar.–Oct., daily noon–4. Grounds Apr.–Oct., daily 10:30–6. Last admission 1 hr before closing.*

WHERE TO EAT

$ BRITISH **The Spotted Dog.** This pub first opened its doors in 1520 and in many ways hardly appears to have changed. Its big inglenook fireplace and heavy beams give it character, the views from the hilltop are lovely, and the good food and friendly crowd make it a pleasure to relax inside. It's a mixture of traditional pub grub and slightly more sophisticated fare—so you might have a homemade beef burger, or maybe some sea-bass in garlic butter—but it's all done very well and many ingredients are locally sourced, as is the ale. There's seating in the sunny garden in the summertime. The pub, which sells locally made ales, is a mile from Penshurst via the narrow B2188. Ⓢ *Average main: £12* ✉ *Smarts Hill, Penshurst* ☎ *01892/870253* 🌐 *www.spotteddogpub.co.uk.*

HEVER CASTLE

3 miles west of Penshurst, 10 miles northwest of Royal Tunbridge Wells, 30 miles southeast of London.

A fairy-tale medieval castle on the outside, and a Tudor mansion within, Hever contains layer on layer of history. It's one of the most unusual and romantic of the great English castles.

GETTING HERE AND AROUND

Hever Castle is best reached via the narrow, often one-lane B2026. From Tunbridge Wells, take A264 east then follow signs directing you north toward Hever.

EXPLORING

Fodor'sChoice ★ **Hever Castle.** For some, 13th-century Hever Castle ticks every box for how a *real* castle should look: all turrets and battlements, the whole encircled by a water lily–bound moat. (There are even fabulous beasts swimming in its waters, too, in the form of enormous Japanese koi carp.) Here, at her childhood home, the unfortunate Anne Boleyn, second wife of Henry VIII and mother of Elizabeth I, was courted and won by Henry. He loved her dearly for a time but had her beheaded in 1536 after she failed to give birth to a son. He then gave Boleyn's home to his fourth wife, Anne of Cleves, as a present. Famous though it was, the castle fell into disrepair in the 19th century. When American millionaire William Waldorf Astor acquired it in 1903, he needed somewhere to house his staff. His novel solution was to build a replica Tudor village, using only methods, materials, and even tools appropriate to the era. The result is more or less completely indistinguishable from the genuine Tudor parts. (Today it is mostly used for private functions.) Astor also created the stunning gardens, which today include an excellent yew maze, ponds, playgrounds, tea shops, gift shops, plant shops—you get the picture. There's a notable collection of Tudor portraits, and in summer activities are nonstop here, with jousting, falconry exhibitions, and country fairs, making this one of southern England's most rewarding castles to visit. In one of the Victorian wings, B&B rooms go for upwards of £160 per night. ✉ *Off B2026, Hever* ☎ *01732/865224* 🌐 *www.hevercastle.co.uk* 🎟 *£16; grounds only £13.50* ⏲ *Castle late Mar.–late Oct., daily noon–6; late Oct.–early Nov., daily noon–4:30; early Nov.–late Mar., Wed.–Sun. noon–4:30. Grounds open 90 min before castle. Last admission 90 min before closing.*

CHARTWELL

9 miles north of Hever Castle, 12 miles northwest of Royal Tunbridge Wells, 28 miles southeast of London.

Beloved of Winston Churchill, Chartwell retains a homely warmth despite its size and grandeur. Almost as lovely are the grounds, with a rose garden and magnificent views across rolling Kentish hills.

GETTING HERE AND AROUND

From Tunbridge Wells, take A21 north toward Sevenoaks, then turn east onto A25 and follow signs from there. You can travel to Chartwell by bus from the town of Sevenoaks. Take Go Coach 401, but check with the driver to make sure the bus passes near the mansion.

EXPLORING

Chartwell. A grand Victorian mansion with views over the Weald, Chartwell was the home of Sir Winston Churchill from 1924 until his death in 1965. Virtually everything has been kept as it was when he lived here, with his pictures, books, photos, and maps. There's even a half-smoked cigar that the World War II prime minister never finished. Churchill was an amateur artist, and his paintings show a softer side of the stiff-upper-lipped statesman. Admission to the house is by timed ticket available only the day of your visit. ■ **TIP→ Be sure to explore the rose gardens and take one of the walks in the nearby countryside.** ✉ *Mapleton Rd., Westerham* ☎ *01732/868381* ⊕ *www.nationaltrust.org.uk/chartwell* 🎫 *£13; garden only £6.50* ⏲ *House Mar.–Oct., daily 11–5 (or dusk if earlier). Grounds year-round 10–5 (or dusk if earlier). Last admission 1 hr before closing.*

KNOLE

8 miles east of Chartwell, 11 miles north of Royal Tunbridge Wells, 27 miles southeast of London.

Perhaps the quintessential Tudor mansion, Knole is as famous for its literary connections and impressive collection of furniture and tapestries as it is for its elegant 15th- and 16th-century architecture.

GETTING HERE AND AROUND

To get to the town of Sevenoaks from Chartwell, drive north to Westerham, then pick up A25 and head east for 8 miles to A225. The route is well signposted. Southeastern trains travel from London's Charing Cross Station to Sevenoaks every few minutes and take about half an hour. Knole is a 20-minute walk from the train station.

EXPLORING

Fodor's Choice ★ **Knole.** The town of Sevenoaks lies in London's commuter belt, a world away from the baronial air of its premier attraction, the grand, beloved home of the Sackville family since the 16th century. Begun in the 15th century and enlarged in 1603 by Thomas Sackville, Knole, with its sprawling complex of courtyards and outbuildings, resembles a small town. You'll need most of an afternoon to explore it thoroughly. The house is noted for its wonderful tapestries, embroidered furnishings, and an extraordinary set of 17th-century silver furniture. Most of the salons are in the pre-baroque mode, rather dark and armorial. The magnificently florid staircase was a novelty in its Elizabethan heyday. Vita Sackville-West grew up here and used it as the setting for her novel *The Edwardians,* a witty account of life among the gilded set. The gardens are beautiful to wander through (but you can only do so on Tuesdays). Encircled by a 1,000-acre park where herds of deer roam free, the house lies in the center of Sevenoaks; the incongruously low-key entrance is opposite St. Nicholas Church. ✉ *Knole La., off A225, Sevenoaks* ☎ *01732/462100* 🌐 *www.nationaltrust.org.uk/knole* 🎫 *House £10.90; parking £4* ⏲ *House mid-Mar.–Oct., Tues.–Sun. 11–4. Gardens mid-Apr.–Sept., Tues. only 11–4. Last admission 30 min before closing.*

IGHTHAM MOTE

7 miles southeast of Knole, 10 miles north of Royal Tunbridge Wells, 31 miles southeast of London.

Almost unique among medieval manor houses in that it still has a moat (although that has nothing to do with the name) Ightham is a captivating, unreal-looking place reached down a warren of winding country lanes.

GETTING HERE AND AROUND

The house sits 6 miles south of Sevenoaks. From Sevenoaks, follow A25 east to A227 and then follow the signs. At the village of Ivy Hatch follow signs to tiny Mote Road, which winds its way to the house. The 404 bus from Sevenoaks stops here on Thursday and Friday only; otherwise you'll have to get off in Ivy Hatch and walk just under a mile from there. The 308 bus from Sevenoaks to Ivy Hatch runs hourly from Monday to Saturday, as does the 222 (although that may not run every day).

EXPLORING

Fodor's Choice ★ **Ightham Mote.** This wonderful, higgledy-piggledy timber-framed Medieval manor house looks like something out of a fairy tale. Even its name is a bit of an enigma—"Igtham" is pronounced "Item" (we can't quite figure that out either) and "Mote" doesn't refer to the kind of moat you get in a castle, but an old English word for meeting place. Perhaps it's somewhat fitting, then, that finding the place takes careful navigation down tiny, winding country lanes, and then even to reach the front door you must first cross a narrow stone bridge over a dry moat (yes, it has one of those, too). But it's all worth the effort to see a vision right out of the Middle Ages. Built nearly 700 years ago, Ightham's magical exterior has hardly changed since the 14th century, but within you'll find that it encompasses styles of several periods, Tudor to Victorian. The Great Hall, Tudor chapel, and drawing room are all highlights. ✉ *Mote Rd., off A227, Sevenoaks* ☎ *01732/810378* 🌐 *www.nationaltrust.org.uk/ightham-mote* 🎫 *£11 Apr.–Oct.; £5.50 Nov.–Mar.* ⏲ *Mar.–Oct., daily 11–5; Nov.–Feb., daily 11–3. Last admission 30 min before closing.*

THE SOUTHEAST'S BEST HISTORIC HOUSES

Touring the Southeast's historic houses isn't just a procession of beautiful photo ops; it's a living history lesson. From modest manor houses to the sprawling stately homes of the aristocracy, each building has something to tell about private life or the history of the nation, and often the story is presented in an entertaining way.

(above) Penshurst Place gracefully evokes the Elizabethan era; (*right, top*) Bodiam Castle has a moat; (*right, bottom*) Hever Castle claims Tudor connections.

Historic houses reveal the evolution of the country, from medieval fortresses planned for defense to architectural wonders that displayed the owner's power. In time, gardens and grounds became another way to display status. Times, however, changed. And the aristocratic rewards of owning tracts of countryside, art, and family treasures encountered reality in the 20th century, as cash flow and death taxes presented huge challenges. Private owners opened homes to the public for a fee, some with marketing flair. Hundreds of other homes and castles are now owned by the National Trust or English Heritage, organizations that raise part of the money needed to maintain them through entrance fees.

BEYOND THE HOUSE

The idea of exploring historic houses may inspire joy—or, frankly, boredom. If the latter, please don't give up: many houses have gardens and extensive grounds that make a great day out for garden lovers or walkers. You may be able to purchase a ticket that includes only the grounds. Some houses have so many activities aimed at kids that the whole family will find something to do.

CHOOSING A HOUSE

We admit it: there are almost too many houses to visit in the Southeast, but they're conveniently close to each other. Here are the prime characteristics of some top spots to help you decide.

Arundel Castle: Still a family home for the duke of Norfolk, Arundel has its Norman-era keep and Barons' Hall, as well as magnificent examples of Gothic-style domestic remodeling by the Victorians.

Bodiam Castle: This place is what most of us picture when we think of a medieval castle, complete with turrets and an exquisite moat. However, the inside is mostly a ruin.

Chartwell: The National Trust owns this Victorian mansion, the former home of Winston Churchill. There's plenty of memorabilia, plus good woodland walks. Tours are by timed ticket.

Herstmonceux Castle: This romantic, moated 15th-century brick castle was saved by a 20th-century rehab. Only a few rooms are open (it's now a school), but they and the extensive gardens and grounds are evocative.

Hever Castle: Turrets, battlements, and a moat set the mood: Hever dates to the 13th century but has a Tudor link as the childhood home of Anne Boleyn, Henry VIII's second wife. The American Astors restored it after 1903. Gardens and activities—jousting, fairs—keep things entertaining.

Ightham Mote: Ideal for lovers of romantic antiquity, this 14th-century manor house also has a moat. The Great Hall is ancient, but there are Tudor and Victorian sections, too.

Knole: Home of the Sackvilles and now a National Trust property, this sprawling Tudor house resembles a village. Furnishings are dark and florid, and include a set of 17th-century silver furniture. Writer Vita Sackville-West grew up here.

Leeds Castle: The setting of this castle on two islands on a lake is amazing. The inside reflects a 20th-century refurbishing by the last owner, and family activities are plentiful. You can eat and spend the night here, too, at themed events.

Penshurst Place: For more than 500 years this medieval manor house has been the family home of the Sidneys. The medieval hall is famous, and the interior is Elizabethan. An 11-acre Italian garden and a toy museum are other interests.

Petworth House: Art lovers, take note: This sprawling 17th-century mansion has the National Trust's richest collection of paintings, including treasures by J. M. W. Turner, who visited here. Capability Brown's park is also a big draw.

Polesden Lacey: This National Trust property dates to the early 19th century but is famous for its lavish early 20th-century interiors.

3

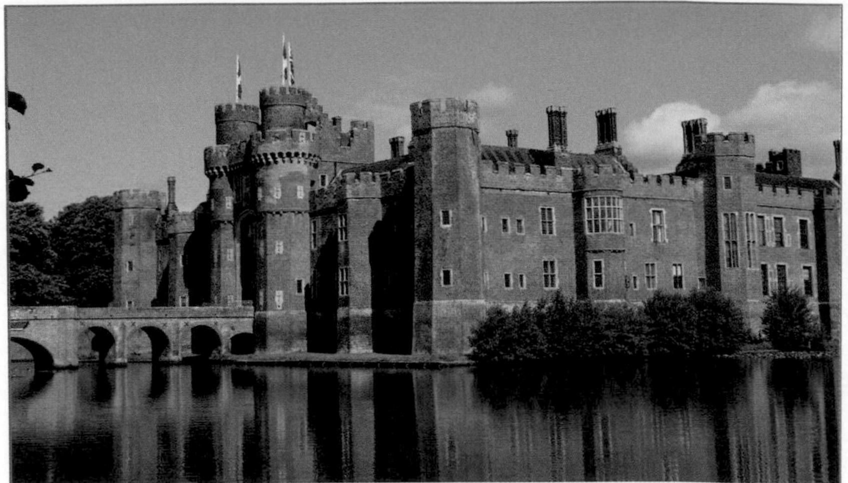

TIPS FOR VISITING

Keep in mind that houses and castles are unique. You may be free to wander at will, or you may be organized into groups like prisoners behind enemy lines. Sometimes the exterior of a building may be spectacular, but the interior dull. And the gardens and grounds may be just as interesting as (or more so than) the house. Our individual reviews alert you to these instances, but you should study websites. You can often pay separately for the house and grounds.

Consider the kids. Some houses have activities or special events aimed at kids, especially in summer; some even have playgrounds.

Look into money-saving passes. If you plan to see lots of historic houses and castles, it might be cheaper to buy a pass, such as the ones from the National Trust or English Heritage, or to join an organization such as the National Trust and thus get free entry. Check entrance fees against your itinerary to be sure what you'll save.

Check seasonal opening hours. Hours can change abruptly, so call the day before or check online. Many houses are open only from April to October, and they may have unpredictable hours. In other cases the houses have celebrated parks and gardens that are open much of the year. Consider a trip in shoulder seasons if you can't take the crowds that pack the most popular houses. Some places are open during December.

Plan your transportation. Some places are very hard to reach without a car. Plan your transportation in advance—and remember that rural bus and train services can finish early!

Consider a stay at a property. You can rent a cottage from the **National Trust** (🌐 *www.nationaltrustcottages.co.uk*) or **English Heritage** (🌐 *www.english-heritage.org.uk/holidaycottages*). The **Landmark Trust** (🌐 *www.landmarktrust.org.uk*) and **Vivat Trust** (🌐 *www.vivat-trust.org*) also have properties for rent.

DID YOU KNOW

Visits to England's historic houses aren't just about looking at rooms from behind velvet ropes. Some places, including Hever Castle, offer plenty of family fun and activities including fairs and jousting displays.

One of England's most notable stately homes, sprawling Knole displayed the power of the Sackvilles.

ROCHESTER

15 miles north of Ightham Mote, 28 miles southeast of London.

Positioned near the confluence of the Thames and the River Medway, this posh town has a history of Roman, Saxon, and Norman occupation, all of which have left architectural remains, including the vast castle at the town center. Novelist Charles Dickens called Rochester home for more than a decade, until his death in 1870, and would sometimes walk here all the way from London. You can take things at a much easier pace by strolling through the gardens of the Swiss-style chalet where he wrote. Every December the city hosts the Dickensian Christmas Festival.

Across the river from Rochester is Chatham, with a noted maritime museum and the Dickens World theme park.

GETTING HERE AND AROUND

To drive to Rochester, take the M2, turning off on the A2. The journey from London should take about 45 minutes. Southeastern trains run from several London stations, including St. Pancras, Victoria, and Charing Cross. The journey takes between 40 minutes and 1¼ hours.

ESSENTIALS

Visitor Information Rochester Visitor Information Centre. ✉ *95 High St.* ☎ *01634/338141* 🌐 *www.visitmedway.org.*

EXPLORING

FAMILY **Dickens World.** Filling an aluminum-clad hangar in a giant shopping center, Dickens World is a literary theme park. Inside is a beautifully designed Victorian London scene where you can walk down an alley and enter re-created shops and houses from the period. Entry is by 90-minute guided tour only, led by costumed actors. The tours give you an overview of both Dickens's work and the Victorian age in which he lived, complete with authentic-seeming sights, sounds, and smells. In December the park is taken over by a Christmas market. This place is very popular with families with young kids, and it's sometimes closed for private events, so it's essential to call ahead to check opening times. **■ TIP→ Tickets for the 3:30 pm tours are always a couple of pounds cheaper than the regular entry price. Kids under three get in free all day.** ✉ *Leviathan Way, Chatham* ☎ *01634/890421* 🌐 *www.dickensworld.co.uk* 🎫 *£7.50* ⏲ *Weekends 10–3:30. Opening times vary and certain dates are restricted to schools only; call ahead.*

3

FAMILY **Historic Dockyard.** The buildings and 47 retired ships at the 80-acre dockyard across the River Medway from Rochester constitute the country's most complete Georgian-to-early-Victorian dockyard. Fans of maritime history could easily spend a day at the exhibits and structures. The dockyard's origins go back to the time of Henry VIII; some 400 ships were built here over the centuries. Highlights include Maritime Treasures, a museum of naval artifacts including some remarkable 18th-century scale models; the Victorian Ropery, where costumed guides take you on a tour of an old rope factory, including its impressive ¼-mile-long rope walk, where ropes are still made using old methods; and the Courtyard, part of the old Smithery (blacksmith), where special events are sometimes held, including pirate-themed fun days for kids in summer. There's also a guided tour of the submarine HMS *Ocelot*, the last warship to be built for the Royal Navy at Chatham. **■ TIP→ Save your ticket, as it's good for a year.** ✉ *Main Gate Rd., Chatham* ☎ *01634/823800* 🌐 *www.thedockyard.co.uk* 🎫 *£19* ⏲ *Mid-Feb.–Mar. and late Oct.–Nov., daily 10–4; Apr.–late Oct., daily 10–6. Closed Dec.–mid-Feb. Last admission 45 min before closing.*

Rochester Castle. The impressive ruins of Rochester Castle are a superb example of Norman military architecture. The keep, built in the 1100s using the old Roman city wall as a foundation, is the tallest in England. It's been shored up but left without floors, so that from the bottom you can see to the open roof and study the complex structure. At the shop you can pick up well-researched guides to the building. ✉ *Boley Hill* ☎ *01634/335882* 🌐 *www.english-heritage.org.uk* 🎫 *£6* ⏲ *Apr.–Sept., daily 10–6; Oct.–Mar., daily 10–4; last admission 30 min before closing.*

Rochester Cathedral. Augustine of Canterbury ordained the first English bishop in a small cathedral that stood on this site in the year 604. The current cathedral, England's second oldest, is a jumble of architectural styles. Much of the original Norman building from 1077 remains, including the striking west front, the highly carved portal, and the tympanum above the doorway. Some medieval art survives, including a 13th-century Wheel of Fortune on the choir walls; it's a reminder of how difficult medieval life was. Informative tours (£4) are available all day, but must be booked in advance. ✉ *Boley Hill* ☎ *01634/843366* 🌐 *www.rochestercathedral.org* 🎫 *Free* ⏲ *Sun.–Fri. 7:30–6, Sat. 7:30–5. Tours Sun.–Fri. 10–4:30, Sat. 10–2.*

WHERE TO EAT AND STAY

$ ITALIAN **Don Vincenzo.** This lively Italian trattoria in the center of Rochester specializes in delicious pizza. One of the best is the simple *capriana*, topped with mozarella, goat cheese, tomato, and arugula. If that's just not enough to satisfy your appetite, try a hearty calzone stuffed with two types of Italian cheeses, tomatoes, and salami. There's also a good range of pasta, fish, and meat dishes. Best of all, the prices are reasonable. *Average main: £10 108 High St. 01634/408373 www.donvincenzo.co.uk.*

$ B&B/INN **Orchard Cottage.** Longtime Rochester locals Kevin and Sue Farrelly run this sweet little B&B overlooking the Kent countryside. **Pros:** free Wi-Fi; you feel more like a houseguest than a customer; family rooms just £15 extra; good value. **Cons:** few frills; building isn't very interesting. *Rooms from: £80 11 View Rd. 01634/222780 www.orchardcottagekent.co.uk 5 rooms Breakfast.*

NIGHTLIFE AND PERFORMING ARTS

Fodor's Choice ★ **Dickensian Christmas Festival.** Rochester sponsors a Dickensian Christmas Festival on the first weekend in December. Thousands of people in period dress participate in reenactments of scenes from *A Christmas Carol*. A candlelight procession, mulled wine and roasted chestnuts, and Christmas carols at the cathedral add to the celebration. There's also a summer festival that takes place in early June. Two other important Dickens festivals take place in Broadstairs, 40 miles east, every June and December. *Rochester 01634/306000 www.visitmedway.org/events/rochester-dickensian-christmas-festival.*

LEEDS CASTLE

12 miles south of Rochester, 19 miles northwest of Royal Tunbridge Wells, 40 miles southeast of London.

Every inch the grand medieval castle, Leeds is like a storybook illustration of what an English castle should look like—from the fortresslike exterior to the breathtaking rooms within.

GETTING HERE AND AROUND

Just off the M20 motorway, signs direct you to Leeds Castle from every road in the area, so it's hard to miss. The nearest train station is in Bearsted, 3.7 miles away; trains from London's Victoria station arrive here twice an hour and on most days there's a shuttle bus to the castle. Otherwise you may be able to catch a taxi from the station, but they're not always easy to come by. The smaller Hollinbourne station is slightly closer; walking to the castle from here takes just under an hour. Trains to Hollingbourne leave London's Victoria and St. Pancras stations once an hour.

EXPLORING

Fodor's Choice ★ **Leeds Castle.** One of England's finest castles, this storybook medieval stronghold commands two small islands on a peaceful lake. Dating to the 9th century and rebuilt by the Normans in 1119, Leeds (not to be confused with the city in the north of England) became a favorite home of many medieval English queens. Henry VIII liked it so much he had it converted from a fortress into a grand palace. The interior doesn't match the glories of the much-photographed exterior, although there are fine paintings and furniture, including many pieces from the 20th-century refurbishment by the castle's last private owner, Lady Baillie. The outside attractions are more impressive and include a maze, a grotto, two adventure playgrounds, an aviary of native and exotic birds, and woodland gardens. The castle is 5 miles east of Maidstone. ■**TIP→ All tickets are valid for a year and there's a 10% discount if you buy them online.** ✉ *A20, Maidstone* ☎ *01622/765400* 🌐 *www.leeds-castle.com* 🎫 *£25* 🕙 *Apr.–Sept., daily 10:30–6 (last admission to grounds 4:30; last admission to castle 4); Oct.–Mar., daily 10:30–5 (last admission to grounds 3; last admission to castle 2:30). Grounds open 30 min before castle.*

SISSINGHURST CASTLE GARDEN

10 miles south of Leeds Castle, 53 miles southeast of London.

Impeccable literary credentials go hand in hand with enchanting grounds, magnificent countryside views, and even a working kitchen garden at this beautiful home in the Sussex countryside.

GETTING HERE AND AROUND

For those without a car, take a train from London's Charing Cross Station and transfer to a bus in Staplehurst. Direct buses operate on Tuesday, Friday, and Sunday between May and August; at other times, take the bus to Sissinghurst village and walk the remaining 1¼ miles. From Leeds Castle, make your way south on B2163 and A274 through Headcorn, and then follow signs.

EXPLORING

Fodor's Choice ★ **Sissinghurst Castle Garden.** One of the most famous gardens in the world, unpretentiously beautiful and quintessentially English, Sissinghurst rests deep in the Kentish countryside. The gardens, with 10 themed "rooms," were laid out in the 1930s around the remains of part of a moated Tudor castle by writer Vita Sackville-West (one of the Sackvilles of Knole, her childhood home) and her husband, diplomat Harold Nicolson. ■**TIP→ Climb the tower to see Sackville-West's study and to get wonderful views of the garden and surrounding fields. The view is best in June and July, when the roses are in bloom.** The beautiful White Garden is filled with snow-color flowers and silver-gray foliage, while the herb and cottage gardens reveal Sackville-West's encyclopedic knowledge of plants. There are woodland and lake walks, too, making it easy to spend a half day or more here. Stop by the big tea shop for lunch made with the farm's fruits and vegetables. If you'd like to linger, the National Trust rents the Priest's House on the property for a minimum stay of three nights; prices start at £650 and rise to around £1,500 in midsummer. ✉ *A262, Cranbrook* ☎ *01580/710700* 🌐 *www.nationaltrust.org.uk/sissinghurst-castle* 🎫 *£12* 🕙 *Garden mid-Mar.–Oct., daily 11–5:30; Nov.–Dec., daily 11–4; last admission 1 hr before closing. Estate daily dawn–dusk.*

WHERE TO STAY

$ B&B/INN **Bishopsdale Oast.** This converted 18th-century double-kiln oast house (used for drying hops) makes an atmospheric place to stay in tiny Biddenden, near Sissinghurst. **Pros:** quiet and restful setting; owner is a chef so breakfasts are great; nice garden. **Cons:** some rooms are small; car needed to get around. *Rooms from: £75* *Off Tenterden Rd., Biddenden* *01580/291027* *www.bishopsdaleoast.co.uk* *5 rooms* *Breakfast.*

$$ B&B/INN Fodor's Choice ★ **Sissinghurst Castle Farmhouse.** On the grounds of Sissinghurst Castle, this beautiful 1885 farmhouse was lovingly restored by the National Trust in 2009; bedrooms are simple but quite spacious, decorated in historical color schemes, and boast sumptuous views across the estate. **Pros:** beautiful location on the grounds of a historic home; lovely hosts; elevator makes building more accessible than most older B&Bs; discounts for two or more nights. **Cons:** few amenities; need a car to get here. *Rooms from: £150* *The Street, Sissinghurst* *01580/720992* *www.sissinghurstcastlefarmhouse.com* *No credit cards* *7 rooms* *Breakfast.*

4

THE SOUTH

WELCOME TO THE SOUTH

TOP REASONS TO GO

★ **Salisbury Cathedral:** Crowned with England's tallest church spire, this impressive cathedral looks out to spectacular views of the surrounding countryside from the roof and spire, accessible by daily tours.

★ **Stonehenge:** The power and mystery of this Neolithic stone circle on Salisbury Plain is still spellbinding.

★ **House and garden at Stourhead:** The cultivated English landscape at its finest, with an 18th-century Palladian stately home and beautiful gardens adorned with neoclassical temples.

★ **The New Forest:** Get away from it all in the South's most extensive woodland, crisscrossed by myriad trails ideal for horseback riding, hiking, and biking.

★ **Literary trails:** Jane Austen, Thomas Hardy, John Fowles, and Ian McEwan have made this area essential for book buffs, with a concentration of sights in Chawton, Dorchester, Chesil Beach, and Lyme Regis.

1 Winchester, Portsmouth, and Southampton. One of the region's most culturally and historically significant towns, Winchester lies a short distance from the genteel village of Chawton, home to Jane Austen, and the great south-coast ports of Portsmouth and Southampton.

2 Isle of Wight. Osborne House, near Cowes, and Carisbrooke Castle, outside Newport, provide historic interest, while beach lovers and sailors head for the charming east-coast resorts of Ryde and Ventnor or the island's iconic Needles landmark, on the western tip.

GETTING ORIENTED

In the south of England, Salisbury Plain, part of the inland county of Wiltshire, presents a sharp contrast to the sheltered villages of coastal Hampshire and Dorset, and the bustle of the port cities of Southampton and Portsmouth. Spend your nights in the more culturally compelling towns of Salisbury and Winchester instead of these cities. Salisbury puts you within easy reach of Stonehenge and the equally ancient stone circles at Avebury. From there you can swing south to the New Forest. The southern coast of Dorset has a couple of popular vacation resorts, Bournemouth and Weymouth, and some historic sites: Corfe Castle, Maiden Castle, and the Cerne Abbas Giant. Lyme Regis is the gateway to the Jurassic Coast, a fossil-filled World Heritage Site.

3 Salisbury, Stonehenge, and Salisbury Plain. Wiltshire's great cathedral city of Salisbury is close to the prehistoric monuments of Stonehenge and Avebury, as well as Wilton, a Palladian estate. Farther afield are more great estates, Stourhead and Longleat.

4 New Forest, Dorset, and the South Coast. The rustic, although not sparsely populated by U.S. standards, New Forest parkland stretches between Southampton and Bournemouth. The route west passes Wimborne Minster, dominated by its church, and ruined Corfe Castle. Also worth a stop are Sherborne, with its beautiful abbey; Dorchester, the heart of "Hardy Country"; and coastal Weymouth and Lyme Regis.

FOSSIL HUNTING ON THE JURASSIC COAST

Besides the dramatic beauty of its jagged cliffs and hidden coves, the lure of the Jurassic Coast for visitors is fossils and fossil hunting. The varied and dramatic coastline is a World Heritage Site encompassing 200 million years of geological history, and constant erosion makes finding fossils a distinct possibility.

(above) Scenery can distract you from fossil hunting on the beautiful Jurassic Coast; (right, top) Intriguing fossil finds; (right, bottom) The coast near Charmouth

A 65-million-year geological journey through time forming an almost complete record of the Mesozoic Era, the Jurassic Coast stretches for 95 miles between the younger, Cretaceous chalk stacks known as "Old Harry Rocks" at Studland Bay in Dorset in the east to the older, striking red Triassic cliffs at Exmouth (Devon) in the west. The earliest Jurassic cliffs of West Dorset formed in a tropical sea that flooded a vast desert. After the sea level dropped 140 million years ago, forest, swampland, and dinosaurs thrived, before the rising sea flooded the area once again. Fossils are continually uncovered, and both amateurs and professionals have made many important finds here.

MARY ANNING

In 1811 a local child named Mary Anning (1799–1847) dug out an ichthyosaur skeleton near Lyme Regis; it's now on display in London's Natural History Museum. Anning's obsession with Jurassic remains left her labeled locally as the "fossil woman." Throughout her life she made many valuable discoveries that were sought after by museums and collectors in Britain, Europe, and beyond.

WHEN TO GO

If you're intent on collecting fossils, consider visiting in winter, when storms and rough seas encourage cliff erosion that sweeps fossils onto the beaches below. Search at low tide if you want the very best chance of making discoveries. Winter is less crowded, too. In summer the seas are calmer and the weather is more reliable. Although summer has more visitor traffic, the days are longer and buses more frequent—a plus if you're exploring the coastal path.

WHAT TO LOOK FOR

Fossil hunters should stick to the area around Charmouth (the beach below Stonebarrow Hill, east of Charmouth, is especially fruitful) and Lyme Regis. The rock here is rich in fossils of the creatures that lived in the Jurassic oceans and especially prone to rapid erosion. You're free to pick and chip at the rocks; no permit is needed.

Keep your eyes peeled on the shore at low tide for ammonites. These chambered cephalopods from the Jurassic era, related to today's nautilus, are usually preserved in either calcite or iron pyrite ("fool's gold"); shinier, more fragile specimens may be found in aragonite. Visit the museums in Lyme Regis and Dorchester to remind you what to look for: the lustrous spirals are similar in heft and size to a brass coin, most smaller than a 10p piece. Other common

fossils include sea urchins, white oyster shells, and coiled worm tubes. Look out for belemnites, an extinct cephalopod.

SEEING THE COAST

The South West Coast Path National Trail, more than 600 miles long, passes through the area and is a great way to get closer to the Jurassic Coast. The Jurassic Coaster X53 bus travels along the Jurassic Coast from Poole to Weymouth and Exeter, and allows you to walk a section of the path and return by bus.

You can join a pro: information on guided walks is available from local tourist offices and the Lyme Regis Museum. Operators run boat trips from gateway towns, an easy way to appreciate the coastline. See the boards at harbors, or ask at information centers. Fossil collector **Brandon Lennon** (*07944/664757* 🌐 *www.lymeregisfossilsforsale.co.uk* *£8*) runs fossil-hunting expeditions with geologist Ian Lennon. A mile east of Lyme Regis, the **Charmouth Heritage Coast Centre** (*01297/560772* 🌐 *www.charmouth.org* *£7.50 walks*) organizes two-hour walks, kids' events, and has a permanent exhibit. Late March through November, **Harry May** (*07974/753287* 🌐 *www.mackerelfishinglymeregis.com* *£9*) operates mackerel fishing and sightseeing boat trips on the *Marie F* and the *Sunbeam* from the Cobb in Lyme Regis.

4

Updated by Ellin Stein

Cathedrals, stately homes, stone circles—the South, made up of Hampshire, Dorset, and Wiltshire counties—contains a variety of notable attractions as well as several quieter pleasures. Two important cathedrals, Winchester and Salisbury (pronounced *sawls*-bree), are here, as are classic stately homes such as Longleat, Stourhead, and Wilton House—and remarkable prehistoric sites, two of which, Avebury and Stonehenge, are of world-class significance.

These are just the tourist-brochure highlights. Anyone spending time in these parts should rent a bike or a car and set out to discover the back-road villages and larger market towns. Close to London, the green fields of Hampshire divide the cliffs and coves of the West Country from the sprawl of the suburbs. Even if you have a coastal destination in mind, hit the brakes—there's plenty to see. Originally a Roman town, historic Winchester was made capital of the ancient kingdom of Wessex in the 9th century by Alfred the Great, a pioneer in establishing the rule of law and considered to be the first king of a united England. The city is dominated by its imposing cathedral, the final resting place of notables ranging from Saxon kings to the son of William the Conqueror to Jane Austen. It's a good base for visiting the villages associated with several of England's literary greats, for example Chawton, home to Jane Austen.

North of Hampshire and the New Forest lies the somewhat harsher terrain of Salisbury Plain, part of it owned by the British army and used for training and weapons testing. Two monuments, millennia apart, dominate the plain. One is the 404-foot-tall stone spire of Salisbury Cathedral, the subject of one of John Constable's finest paintings. Not far away is the most imposing and dramatic prehistoric structure in Europe: Stonehenge. The many theories about its construction and purpose only add to its otherworldly allure.

Other subregions have their own appeal, and many are of literary or historical interest. The Dorset countryside of grass-covered chalk hills—the downs—wooded valleys, meandering rivers, and meadows, immortalized in the novels of Thomas Hardy, is interspersed with unspoiled market towns and villages. Busy beach resorts such as Lyme Regis perch next to hidden coves on the fossil-rich Jurassic Coast. Just off Hampshire is the Isle of Wight—Queen Victoria's favorite getaway—where colorful flags flutter from the many sailboats anchored at Cowes, home of the famous regatta.

The South has been quietly integral to England's history for well over 4,000 years, occupied successively by prehistoric man, the Celts, the Romans, the Saxons, the Normans, and the modern British. Though short on historic buildings due to wartime bombing, the port cities of Southampton and Portsmouth are rich in history itself; the Mayflower departed from the former, and the latter is home to the oldest dry dock in the world—Henry VIII's navy built its ships here. Portsmouth was also the departure point for Nelson to the Battle of Trafalgar, Allied forces to Normandy on D-Day, and British forces to the Falklands.

SOUTH PLANNER

WHEN TO GO

In summer the coastal resorts of Bournemouth and Weymouth are crowded; it may be difficult to find the accommodations you want. The Isle of Wight gets its fair share of summer visitors, too, especially during the weeklong Cowes Regatta in late July or early August. Because ferries fill up to capacity, you may have to wait for the next one. The New Forest is most alluring in spring and early summer (for the foaling season) and fall (for the colorful foliage), whereas summer can be busy with walkers and campers. In all seasons, take waterproof boots for the mud and puddles. Major attractions such as Stonehenge and Longleat House attract plenty of people at all times; bypass such sights on weekends, public holidays, or school vacations. Don't plan to visit the cathedrals of Salisbury and Winchester on a Sunday, when your visit will be restricted, or during services, when it won't be appreciated by worshippers.

PLANNING YOUR TIME

The South has no obvious hub, though many people base themselves in one or both of the cathedral cities of Winchester and Salisbury and make excursions to nearby destinations. The coastal cities of Portsmouth and Southampton have their charms, but neither of these large urban centers is particularly attractive as an overnight stop. Busy Bournemouth, whose major sight is a Victorian-era museum, has quieter areas that are more conducive to relaxation. To escape the bustle, the New Forest, southwest of Southampton, has space and semi wilderness. It's easy to take a morning or afternoon break to enjoy the available activities, whether on foot, bike, or horseback. The Isle of Wight needs more time and is worth exploring at leisure over at least a couple of days.

GETTING HERE AND AROUND

BUS TRAVEL

National Express buses at London's Victoria Coach Station on Buckingham Palace Road depart every 60–90 minutes for Bournemouth (2½ hours), Southampton (2¼ hours), and Portsmouth (1¾ hours), and every two hours for Winchester (1¾ hours). There are five buses daily to Salisbury (about 3 hours). Bluestar operates a comprehensive service in the Southampton and Winchester areas, as well as buses to the New Forest. Stagecoach South has service in Portsmouth and around Hampshire. Salisbury Reds serves Salisbury; More travels to Bournemouth and Poole; First serves Portsmouth, Southampton, Weymouth, and Dorchester; and Southern Vectis covers the Isle of Wight. More, Bluestar, Salisbury reds, and Southern Vectis sell one-day (and two-day from Southern Vectis) passes as well as seven-, 30-, and 90-day passes for all routes. Ask about the Megarider tickets sold by Stagecoach South. Contact Traveline for all information on routes and tickets. During the school summer holidays (late July and August), the hop-on, hop-off Beach Bus runs from the Hythe Pier in Southampton to Lymington in the New Forest. Tickets are £6.

Bus Contacts Beach Bus. ☎ *01590/ 646600* 🌐 *www.thebeachbus.info.* **Bluestar.** ☎ *01202/338421* 🌐 *www.bluestarbus.co.uk.* **First.** ☎ *0333/014–3490* 🌐 *www.firstgroup.com.* **More.** ☎ *01202/338420* 🌐 *www.morebus.co.uk.* **National Express.** ☎ *0871/781–8181* 🌐 *www.nationalexpress.com.* **Salisbury reds.** ☎ *01202/338420* 🌐 *www.salisburyreds.co.uk.* **Southern Vectis.** ☎ *01983/827000* 🌐 *www.islandbuses.info.* **Stagecoach South.** ☎ *0345/121–0190* 🌐 *www.stagecoachbus.com.* **Traveline.** ☎ *0871/200–2233* 🌐 *www.traveline.info.*

CAR TRAVEL

On the whole, the region is easily negotiable using public transportation. But for rural spots, especially the grand country estates, a car is useful. The well-developed road network includes M3 to Winchester (70 miles from London) and Southampton (77 miles); A3 to Portsmouth (77 miles); and M27 along the coast, from the New Forest and Southampton to Portsmouth. For Salisbury, take M3 to A303, then A30. A35 connects Bournemouth to Dorchester and Lyme Regis, and A350 runs north to Dorset's inland destinations.

TRAIN TRAVEL

South West Trains serves the South from London's Waterloo Station. Travel times average 1 hour to Winchester, 1¼ hours to Southampton, 1¾ hours to Bournemouth, and 2¾ hours to Weymouth. The trip to Salisbury takes 1½ hours, and Portsmouth about 1¾ hours. A yearlong Network Railcard, valid throughout the South and Southeast, entitles you and up to three accompanying adults to one-third off most train fares, and up to four accompanying children ages 5–15 to a 60% discount off each child fare. It costs £30. Weekend First tickets, available on weekends and public holidays, let you upgrade to First Class for £5.

Train Contacts National Rail Enquiries. ☎ *0845/748–4950* 🌐 *www.nationalrail.co.uk.* **South West Trains.** ☎ *0345/600–0650* 🌐 *www.southwesttrains.co.uk.*

TOURS

Guild of Registered Tourist Guides. This organization maintains a directory of qualified Blue Badge guides who can meet you anywhere in the region for private tours. Tours are tailored to your particular interests or needs and generally start around £240 per full day, £149 per half day. ☎ *020/7403–1115* 🌐 *www.britainsbestguides.org* 🎫 *From £145.*

RESTAURANTS

In summer, and especially on summer weekends, visitors can overrun the restaurants in small villages, so either book a table in advance or prepare to wait. The more popular or upscale the restaurant, the more critical a reservation is. For local specialties, try fresh-grilled river trout or sea bass poached in brine, or dine like a king on New Forest's renowned venison. Hampshire is noted for its pig and sheep farming, and you might zero in on pork and lamb dishes on local restaurant menus. The region places a strong emphasis on seasonal produce, so venison, for example, is best between September and February.

4

HOTELS

Modern hotel chains are well represented, and in rural areas you can choose between elegant country-house hotels, traditional coaching inns (updated to different degrees), and modest guesthouses. Some seaside hotels don't accept one-night bookings in summer. If you plan to visit Cowes on the Isle of Wight during Cowes Week, the annual yachting jamboree in late July or early August, book well in advance. *Hotel reviews have been shortened. For full information, visit Fodors.com.*

WHAT IT COSTS IN POUNDS

	$	$$	$$$	$$$$
Restaurants	under £15	£15–£19	£20–£25	over £25
Hotels	under £100	£100–£160	£161–£220	over £220

Restaurant prices are the average cost of a main course at dinner, or if dinner is not served, at lunch. Hotels prices are the lowest cost of a standard double room in high season, including 20% V.A.T.

VISITOR INFORMATION

Contacts Tourism South East. ☎ *023/8062–5400* 🌐 *www.tourismsoutheast.com.* **Visit South West England.** ☎ *01172/323036 (Visit Wiltshire)* 🌐 *www.visitsouthwest.co.uk.*

WINCHESTER, PORTSMOUTH, AND SOUTHAMPTON

From the cathedral city of Winchester, 70 miles southwest of London, you can meander southward to the coast, stopping at the bustling ports of Southampton and Portsmouth to explore their maritime heritage. From either port you can strike out for the restful shores of the Isle of Wight, vacation destination of Queen Victoria and thousands of modern-day Britons.

WINCHESTER

70 miles southwest of London, 12 miles northeast of Southampton.

Winchester is among the most historic of English cities, and as you walk the graceful streets and wander the many public gardens, a sense of the past envelops you. Although it's now merely the county seat of Hampshire, for more than four centuries Winchester served first as the capital of the ancient kingdom of Wessex and then of England. The first king of England, Egbert, was crowned here in AD 827, and the court of his successor Alfred the Great was based here until Alfred's death in 899. After the Norman Conquest in 1066, William I ("the Conqueror") had himself crowned in London, but took the precaution of repeating the ceremony in Winchester. William also commissioned the local monastery to produce the Domesday Book, a land survey begun in 1085. The city remained the center of ecclesiastical, commercial, and political power until the 13th century, when that power shifted to London. Despite its deep roots in the past, Winchester is also a thriving market town living firmly in the present, with numerous shops and restaurants on High Street.

GETTING HERE AND AROUND

On a main train line and on the M3 motorway, Winchester is easily accessible from London. The train station is a short walk from the sights; the bus station is in the center, opposite the tourist office. The one-way streets are notoriously confusing, so find a parking lot as soon as possible. The city center is very walkable, and most of the High Street is closed to vehicular traffic. A walk down High Street and Broadway brings you to St. Giles Hill, which has a panoramic view of the city.

TIMING

The city is busier than usual during the farmers' market, the largest in the country, held on the second and last Sunday of each month.

TOUR INFORMATION

Winchester Tourist Guides. A 90-minute "City Highlights" walking tour (which takes in central Winchester) departs from the tourist information center on weekdays at 11 am in April and October; Saturdays in January, February, and early November; and Sundays at 11:30 from May to September, with additional noon tours (except Sunday) in August. The "Discover Upper Winchester" tour adds the cathedral and the Great Hall and leaves at 11 am on Saturdays in March, April, and October, and every day but Sunday from May to September. "Discover Lower Winchester" tour, which includes the center, Jane Austen's House, and Winchester College, follows the same schedule as the Upper Winchester tour, except it leaves at 2:30; check the website for more information. ☎ *01962 /840500* 🌐 *www.winchestertouristguides.com* 🎫 *From £5.*

ESSENTIALS

Visitor Information **Winchester Tourist Information Centre.** ✉ *Winchester Guildhall, High Street* ☎ *01962/840500* 🌐 *www.visitwinchester.co.uk.*

EXPLORING

TOP ATTRACTIONS

FAMILY **City Museum.** This museum reflects Winchester's history from the Iron Age to the present through displays of Anglo-Saxon pottery, jewelry, and coins, agricultural tools from the Middle Ages, reconstructed Victorian shop fronts, and scale models of the city over the past 1,500 years. It's an imaginative, well-presented collection that appeals to children and adults alike. Check out the history detective quiz and costumes for kids of every period starting with the Romans. On the top floor are some well-restored Roman mosaics. Pick up an audio guide at the entrance (£2) to get the most out of the museum. ✉ *The Square, next to cathedral* ☎ *01962/863064* 🌐 *www.winchester.gov.uk* 🎫 *Free* ⏲ *Nov.–Mar., Tues.–Sat. 10–4, Sun. noon–4; Apr.–Oct., Mon.–Sat. 10–5, Sun. noon–5.*

4

Fodor's Choice ★ **The Great Hall.** A short walk west of the cathedral, this outstanding example of early English gothic architecture, and one of Britain's finest surviving 13th-century halls, is all that remains of the city's original Norman castle (razed by Oliver Cromwell). It's also the site of numerous historically significant events: the English Parliament is thought to have had one of its first meetings here in 1246; Sir Walter Raleigh was tried for conspiracy against King James I in 1603; and Dame Alice Lisle was sentenced to death by the brutal Judge Jeffreys for sheltering fugitives after Monmouth's Rebellion in 1685. Hanging on the west wall is the hall's greatest artifact, a huge oak table, which, legend has it, was King Arthur's original Round Table. In fact, it was probably created around 1290 at the beginning of the reign of Edward I for a tournament. It is not clear when the green and white stripes that divide the table into 24 places, each with the name of a knight of the mythical Round Table, were added, but it is certain that the Tudor Rose in the center surmounted by a portrait of King Arthur was commissioned by Henry VIII. Take time to wander through the garden—a re-creation of a medieval shady retreat, named for two queens: Eleanor of Provence and Eleanor of Castile. ✉ *Castle Avenue* ☎ *01962/846476* 🌐 *www3.hants.gov.uk/greathall* 🎫 *Free; suggested donation £3* ⏲ *Daily 10–5* ☞ *May be closed for events—check website.*

Gurkha Museum. This unique museum tells the story of the Gurkha brigade, whose Nepalese soldiers have fought alongside the British since the early 19th century, through tableaux, dioramas, uniforms, weapons, artifacts, and interactive touch-screen displays. A program of lectures includes a curry lunch. ✉ *Peninsula Barracks, Romsey Road* ☎ *01962/842832* 🌐 *www.thegurkhamuseum.co.uk* 🎫 *£3* ⏲ *Mon.–Sat., 10–5; last admission 30 min before closing.*

Highclere Castle. Set in 1,000 acres of parkland designed by Capability Brown, this is the historic home of the actual earls of Carnarvon—as opposed to the imaginary earls of Grantham in television drama *Downton Abbey*. Much of which is shot here owes its appearance to Sir Charles Barry, architect of the Houses of Parliament. Commissioned by the third earl to transform a simpler Georgian mansion, Barry used golden Bath stone to create this fantasy castle bristling with "gothic" turrets. Like its fictional counterpart, it served as a hospital during

City Mill 7
City Museum 8
The Great Hall 5
Gurkha Museum 6
Highclere Castle 9
King's Gate/ St. Swithun's Church 2
Watercress Line 10
Westgate 4
Winchester Cathedral 1
Winchester College 3

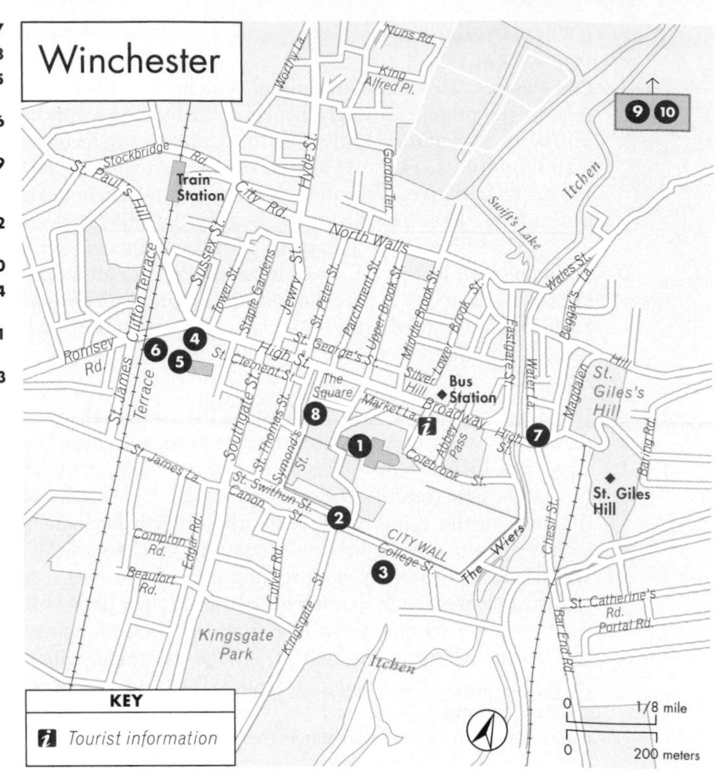

World War I. Highlights of the State Rooms include Van Dyke's equestrian portrait of Charles I in the Dining Room and the imposing library (Lord Grantham's retreat). There's also an exhibit of Egyptian antiquities collected by the 5th earl, known for his pivotal role in the 1920s excavation of ancient Egyptian tombs, notably Tutankhamun's. Find pleasant views of the house and countryside by walking the gardens and grounds. The house is 25 miles north of Winchester and 5 miles south of Newbury; there's train service from London and Winchester to Newbury, and taxis can take you the 5 miles to Highclere. ✉ *Highclere Castle, Highclere Park, Highclere Park* ✣ *off A34* ☎ *01635/253204* 🌐 *www.highclerecastle.co.uk* 🎫 *£20 castle, exhibition, and gardens; £13 castle and gardens or exhibition; £5 gardens only* ⏲ *Mid-July–mid-Sept., castle Sun.–Thurs. 10:30–5; gardens 10:30–6; last admission at 4. Additional days in May and during Easter school vacation.* ☞ *Castle tour at 10:30 am and 1 pm only. Tickets can only be prebooked through website.*

King's Gate. One of two surviving gateways in the city's original ancient walls, this structure to the south of the Close is thought to date back to the 14th century. The tiny medieval church of **St. Swithun-upon-Kingsgate** is on the upper floor. Near St. Swithun's Church at King's Gate, 8 College Street, is the house where Jane Austen died on July 18, 1817,

The historic city of Winchester, with its graceful cathedral, is well worth exploring.

three days after writing a comic poem about the legend of St. Swithun's Day (copies are usually available in the cathedral). ✉ *St. Swithun St.*

Fodor's Choice ★ **Winchester Cathedral.** The imposing Norman exterior of the city's greatest monument, begun in 1079 and consecrated in 1093, makes the Gothic lightness within even more breathtaking. Throughout the structure are outstanding examples of every major architectural style from the 11th to 16th century: the transepts and crypt are 11th-century Romanesque; the great nave, the longest in Europe, is 14th- and 15th century Perpendicular Gothic, and the presbytery (behind the choir, holding the high altar) is 14th-century Decorated Gothic. Other notable features include the richly carved 14th-century choir stalls, the ornate 15th-century stone screen behind the high altar, and the largest surviving spread of 13th-century floor tiles in England. Little of the original stained glass has survived, except in the large window over the entrance. When Cromwell's troops ransacked the cathedral in the 17th century, locals hid away bits of stained glass they found on the ground so that it could later be replaced. Free tours are run year-round. ■ **TIP→ The Library and Triforium Gallery, which contains the Winchester Bible, one of the finest remaining 12th-century illuminated manuscripts, is being renovated and will reopen in August 2016.**

Among the well-known people buried here are William the Conqueror's son, William II ("Rufus"), mysteriously murdered in the New Forest in 1100; Izaak Walton (1593–1683), author of *The Compleat Angler,* whose memorial window in the "Fishermen's Chapel" was paid for by "the fishermen of England and America"; and Jane Austen, whose grave lies in the north aisle of the nave. The tombstone makes no mention of Austen's literary status, though a brass plaque in the wall, dating from 80 years after her death, celebrates her achievements, and modern panels provide an overview of her life and work. Firmly in the 20th century, Antony Gormley's evocative statue *Sound II* (1986) looms in the crypt, often standing in water (as it was designed to do), because of seasonal flooding. You can also explore the tower—with far-reaching views in fair weather—and other recesses of the building on a tour. Special services or ceremonies may mean the cathedral is closed to visits, so call ahead. Outside the cathedral, explore the Close, the area to the south of the cathedral with neat lawns, the Deanery, Dome Alley, and Cheyney Court. ✉ *The Close, Cathedral Precincts* ☎ *01962/857200* 🌐 *www.winchester-cathedral.org.uk* 🎫 *Cathedral £7.50, tour included; tower tour £6* ⏲ *Cathedral, crypt, and treasury Mon.–Sat. 9:30–5, Sun. 12:30–3. Cathedral tours hourly 10–3. Crypt tours Mon.–Sat. 10:30, 12:30, and 2:30. Tower tours Jan.–Apr. and Oct.–Nov., Wed. 2:15, Sat. 11:30 and 2:15; additional 2:15 tours on all weekdays May–Sept.*

WORTH NOTING

City Mill. Set over the River Itchen, this rare surviving example of an 18th-century urban water mill, complete with small island garden, is at the east end of the High Street. The medieval corn mill on the site was rebuilt in 1743 and remained in use until the early 20th century. Restored by the National Trust in 2004, it still operates as a working mill on weekends, and you can purchase stone-ground flour produced here in the gift shop. ✉ *Bridge St.* ☎ *01962/870057* 🌐 *www.nationaltrust.org.uk* 🎫 *£4* ⏲ *Jan.–mid-Feb., daily 10–4; mid-Feb.–Nov., daily 10–5; early Dec.–Christmas, daily 10–4.*

FAMILY **Watercress Line.** Alresford, 8 miles northeast of Winchester by A31 and B3046, is the starting point of the Watercress Line, a 10-mile-long railroad reserved for steam locomotives that run to Alton. The line (named for the area's watercress beds) travels on a scenic route, taking in the highest station in southern England and locomotive restoration workshops. Alresford, crossed by the River Alre, has some antiques shops and Georgian houses. ✉ *The Railway Station, Station Rd., New Alresford* ☎ *01962/733810* 🌐 *www.watercressline.co.uk* 🎫 *£16* ⏲ *Mar., weekends only; Apr., call for schedule; May–July and Sept., Tues.–Thurs. and weekends; Aug., daily; Dec., weekends and national holidays; times vary.*

FAMILY **Westgate.** This atmospheric fortified medieval gateway, with a stunning Tudor ceiling, was a debtor's prison for 150 years and now holds a motley assortment of items relating to Tudor and Stuart times, displayed among 16th-century graffiti by former prisoners. Child-size replicas of authentic 16th-century armor that can be tried on, as well as the opportunity to make brass rubbings, make it popular with kids. You can take in a view of Winchester from the roof. ✉ *High St.* ☎ *01962/869864* 🌐 *www.winchester.gov.uk* 🎫 *Free* ⏲ *Apr.–Oct., Sat. 10–5, Sun. noon–5; mid-Feb.–Mar., Sat. 10–4, Sun. noon–4.*

Winchester College. This prestigious "public" (meaning private) school—the oldest continuously run one in the country, with several buildings still in use after six centuries—was founded in 1382 by Bishop William of Wykeham, whose alabaster tomb sits in a chapel dedicated to him in Winchester Cathedral. The wooden ceiling of the school's own 14th-century chapel is notable for its delicate fan vaulting. The boys wearing monk-style cassocks are "scholars"—students holding academic scholarships. Tours are sometimes canceled due to college events, so call ahead. ✉ *College St.* ☎ *01962/621209* 🌐 *www.winchestercollege.org/guided-tours* 🎫 *£7* ⏲ *1-hr tours Sept.–Mar., Mon., Wed., Fri., and Sat. 10:15, 11:30, and 2:15; Tues. and Thurs. 10:15 and 11:30; Sun. 2:15 and 3:30. Apr.–Aug., additional tours Mon., Wed., Fri., and Sat. at 3:30* ☞ *Admission by guided tour only.*

WHERE TO EAT

$$ MODERN FRENCH ✕ **The Bistro at Hotel du Vin.** Classic French bistro cuisine, like escargots, a Comté cheese soufflé, and steak frites, is served at this stylish restaurant converted from a redbrick Georgian town house and paneled in light wood. The wine list is extensive and eclectic. In summer, meals are served on a terrace and in a walled garden. The hotel's crisply modern rooms are richly furnished and stylish. $ *Average main: £18* ✉ *Hotel du Vin, 14 Southgate St.* ☎ *084474/89267* 🌐 *www.hotelduvin.com.*

$$ MODERN BRITISH ✕ **Chesil Rectory.** The timbered and gabled building may be Old English—it dates back to the mid-15th century—but the cuisine is Modern British, using locally sourced ingredients. Dishes might include venison with wild mushrooms and cavolo nero cabbage or roasted and spiced monkfish. Good-value fixed-price lunches and early-evening dinners are available. Service and the heritage charm of the surroundings enhance the quality of the food. $ *Average main: £18* ✉ *1 Chesil St.* ☎ *01962/851555* 🌐 *www.chesilrectory.co.uk.*

$ CAFÉ ✕ **Ginger Two for Tea.** This bright and airy corner café is the place to come for a relaxed afternoon tea. White walls and wooden furniture lend it a modern, rustic feel. The kitchen serves simple homemade lunches like crepes, wraps, salads, soups, and sandwiches, plus locally baked pastries and a variety of teas. The cakes and coffees are acclaimed, the service less so. You'll find this place on a quiet road off the High Street. $ *Average main: £6* ✉ *29 St. Thomas St.* ☎ *01962/877733* 🌐 *www.gingertwofortea.co.uk* ⏲ *No dinner.*

$ BRITISH ✕ **Green's Wine Bar.** Reasonably priced comfort food is served cafeteria style at this local favorite, including dishes like chicken and leek pie, lamb stew with dumplings, and paninis. The space is small, but sidewalk seating means there's plenty of space in good weather. In the evening, the place transforms into a busy bar with DJs and dancing on weekends. Despite the name, the atmosphere and beverage selection make the place more like a lively pub than a sophisticated wine bar. $ *Average main: £10* ✉ *4 Jewry St.* ☎ *01962/869630.*

$$$ SEAFOOD ✕ **Rick Stein, Winchester.** Renowned as Britain's finest seafood chef, Rick Stein chose Winchester for his first venture away from the Cornish coast. The airy room embodies tasteful nautical chic, but the restaurant's popularity means it can be noisy when busy. The focused menu leans towards simply but confidently prepared classics like turbot hollandaise or Dover sole meunière, plus a few exotic choices like brilliantly fresh sashimi or spicy Indonesian curry with prawn and squid. A set lunch at £20 (two courses) or £25 (three courses) is good value.

$ *Average main: £24* ✉ *7 High St.* ☎ *01962/353535* 🌐 *www.rickstein.com* ✍ *Reservations essential.*

WHERE TO STAY

$$$ HOTEL Fodor's Choice ★ **Lainston House.** The 63 acres surrounding this elegant 17th-century country house retain many original features, including the walls of the kitchen garden (still in use), the apple trees in the former orchard, and a mile-long avenue of Linden trees, the longest in Europe. **Pros:** beautiful setting; atmospheric guest rooms. **Cons:** lower-priced modern rooms small; country house "shabby chic" not to everyone's taste. $ *Rooms from: £165* ✉ *Woodman La., off B3049, Sparsholt* ☎ *01962/776088* 🌐 *www.lainstonhouse.com* *25 rooms, 25 suites or Jr. suites* *Some meals.*

$$ B&B/INN **Old Vine.** Blessed with an ideal location opposite the cathedral, this 18th-century inn, now a gastro-pub with rooms, has received a smart, modern makeover without losing any of its character. **Pros:** elegant rooms; delicious food; attentive service. **Cons:** rooms over bar may be noisy on weekends. $ *Rooms from: £120* ✉ *8 Great Minster St.* ☎ *01962/854616* 🌐 *www.oldvinewinchester.com* *4 rooms, 1 suite, 1 apartment* *Breakfast.*

$$ B&B/INN **Wykeham Arms.** A watering hole since 1755, this pub with rooms near the cathedral and the college wears its Britishness proudly, with photos of national heroes like Nelson and Churchill, military artifacts, and an assortment of pewter mugs hanging from the ceiling. **Pros:** quirky charm; lively bar; good food. **Cons:** rooms above bar can be noisy; no kids under 14; small portions at restaurant. $ *Rooms from: £156* ✉ *75 Kingsgate St.* ☎ *01962/853834* 🌐 *wykehamarmswinchester.co.uk* *13 rooms, 1 suite* *Breakfast.*

SHOPPING

Kingsgate Books and Prints. This is a good stop for a selection of secondhand books, maps, and prints. ✉ *1 Kingsgate St.* ☎ *01962/864710* 🌐 *www.kingsgatebooksandprints.co.uk.*

King's Walk Antique Market. Off Friarsgate, this long-established antiques market in a Victorian market building has a number of stalls selling furniture, silver, jewelry, and collectibles. ✉ *Kings Walk* 🌐 *www.kingswalksantiquemarket.co.uk.*

P&G Wells. The oldest bookshop in the country, P&G Wells has numerous books by and about Jane Austen, who had an account here and in 1817 died almost next door. It also has the region's largest selection of children's books. ✉ *11 College St.* ☎ *01962/852016* 🌐 *bookwells.co.uk.*

CHAWTON

16 miles northeast of Winchester.

In Chawton you can visit the home of Jane Austen (1775–1817), who lived the last eight years of her life in the village, moving to Winchester only during her final illness. The site has always drawn literary pilgrims, but with the ongoing release of successful films based on her novels, the town's popularity among visitors has grown enormously.

OPEN-AIR MARKETS

Among the best markets is the Winchester Farmers' Market held in Winchester's Middle Brook Street on the second and last Sunday (and some Saturdays) of each month. The largest in the UK, it specializes in local produce. Also worth a look are Salisbury's traditional Charter Market (Tuesday and Saturday), Southampton's Bargate Market for artisanal foods and local produce (Friday), typical market stall wares (Saturday), and arts and crafts (Sunday); and Dorchester's large produce and flea market (Wednesday) and Farmers' Market (fourth Saturday). The largest of all is outside Wimborne Minster (Friday, Saturday, and Sunday).

GETTING HERE AND AROUND

Hourly Stagecoach bus X64 service connects Winchester and Alresford with Chawton. It's a 10-minute walk from the bus stop to Jane Austen's House. By car, take A31. Alternatively, take a 40-minute stroll along the footpath from Alton.

EXPLORING

Chawton House Library. Located in a Elizabethan country house on 275-acre estate (part of the South Downs National Park), this library specializes in works by English women writers from 1600 to 1830—including Mary Shelley, Mary Wollstonecraft, and Frances Burney. It also houses the Knight Collection, the library created by the family who previously owned the house for generations. Jane Austen's brother Edward eventually inherited the property and the library and added the walled kitchen garden, shrubberies, and parkland. The property's original stable block also offers one charming and airy bedroom with a four-poster bed and conservatory dining area, if you'd like to stay the night. ✉ *Chawton* ☎ *01420/541010* 🌐 *www.chawtonhouse.org* 🎫 *Library and gardens £6; gardens only £3.50* 🕐 *House: Late Mar.–Oct., Tues.–Fri., 2–4:30; gardens: late Mar.–Oct., Tues.–Fri., 1–4:30. Last admission at 4.*

Fodor's Choice ★ **Jane Austen's House Museum.** Here, in an unassuming redbrick house, Jane Austen wrote *Emma, Persuasion,* and *Mansfield Park,* and revised *Sense and Sensibility, Northanger Abbey,* and *Pride and Prejudice.* Now a museum, the house retains the modest but genteel atmosphere suitable to the unmarried daughter of a clergyman. In the drawing room, there's a piano similar to the one Jane would play every morning before repairing to a small writing table in the family dining parlor—leaving her sister, Cassandra, to do the household chores ("I find composition impossible with my head full of joints of mutton and doses of rhubarb," Jane wrote). In the early 19th century the road near the house was a bustling thoroughfare, and one traveler reported that a window view proved that the Misses Austen were "looking very comfortable at breakfast." Jane was famous for working through interruptions, but one protection against the outside world was the famous door that creaked. She asked that its hinges remain unattended to because they gave her warning that someone was coming. ■ **TIP→ It's often closed**

IN SEARCH OF JANE AUSTEN

Jane Austen country—verdant countryside interspersed with relatively unspoiled villages—still bears traces of the decorous early-19th-century life she described with wry wit in novels such as *Emma, Persuasion, Sense and Sensibility,* and *Pride and Prejudice.* You can almost hear the clink of teacups raised by the likes of Elinor Dashwood and Mr. Darcy. Serious Janeites will want to retrace her life in Bath (⇨ *see Chapter 7*), Chawton, Winchester, and Lyme Regis.

BATH

Bath provided the elegant backdrop for the society Austen observed with such razor sharpness. She lived in Bath between 1801 and 1806, and although she wrote relatively little while she was here, she used it as a setting for *Northanger Abbey* and *Persuasion.* Bath's Jane Austen Centre explores her relationship to the city.

CHAWTON

About 83 miles southeast of Bath is this tiny Hampshire village, the heart of Jane Austen country. Here you find the tastefully understated house, a former bailiff's cottage on her brother's estate, where Austen worked on three of her novels. It's now a museum that sensitively evokes her life there.

WINCHESTER

Driving southwest from Chawton, take the A31 for about 15 miles to Winchester, where you can visit Austen's austere grave within the cathedral and view an exhibit about her life; then see the commemorative plaque on No. 8 College Street, where her battle with Addison's disease ended in her death on July 18, 1817.

LYME REGIS

Lyme Regis, 110 miles southwest of Winchester, is the 18th-century seaside resort on the Devon border where Austen spent the summers of 1804 and 1805. Here you find the Cobb, the stone jetty that juts into Lyme Bay, where poor Louisa Musgrove jumps off the steps known as Granny's Teeth—a turning point in *Persuasion.*

for special events, so call ahead. ✉ *Winchester Rd., signed off A31/A32 roundabout* ☎ *01420/83262* 🌐 *www.jane-austens-house-museum.org.uk* 🎫 *£8* 🕒 *Jan.–mid-Feb., weekends 10:30–4:30; mid-Feb.–May and Sept.–Dec., daily 10:30–4:30; June–Aug., daily 10–5; last admission 30 min before closing.*

WHERE TO STAY

$$$$ HOTEL Fodor's Choice ★ **Four Seasons Hotel Hampshire.** Although deep in the peaceful British countryside, this country-house hotel on a 500-acre estate is only a half hour from Heathrow. **Pros:** peaceful location; great spa; plenty of activities. **Cons:** pricey; not in the center of any action. $ *Rooms from: £500* ✉ *Dogmersfield Park, Chalky La., Hook* ☎ *01252/853000* 🌐 *www.fourseasons.com/hampshire* 🛏 *111 rooms, 22 suites* 🍴 *No meals.*

PORTSMOUTH

24 miles south of Chawton, 77 miles southwest of London.

In addition to a historic harbor and revitalized waterfront, Portsmouth has the energy of a working port. At Gunwharf Quays is the soaring Spinnaker Tower, as well as shops, restaurants, bars, and a contemporary art gallery. The main attractions for many visitors are the HMS Victory, the well-preserved flagship from which Nelson won the Battle of Trafalgar, on view at the Portsmouth Historic Dockyard; the extraordinary record of seafaring history at the National Museum of the Royal Navy; and the D-Day Museum (Operation Overlord embarked from Portsmouth). For others, Portsmouth is primarily of interest for the ferries that set off from here to the Isle of Wight and more distant destinations.

GETTING HERE AND AROUND

The M27 motorway from Southampton and the A3 from London take you to Portsmouth. There are also frequent buses and trains that drop you off at the Hard, the main transport terminus. It's only a few steps from the Historic Dockyard and Gunwharf Quays. Regular passenger ferries cross Portsmouth Harbour from the Hard for Gosport's Royal Navy Submarine Museum. Attractions in the nearby town of Southsea are best reached by car or by buses departing from the Hard.

ESSENTIALS

Visitor Information Portsmouth Visitor Information Centre. ✉ *D-Day Museum, Clarence Esplanade* ☎ *023/9282–6722* 🌐 *www.visitportsmouth.co.uk.*

EXPLORING

TOP ATTRACTIONS

FAMILY **D-Day Museum.** The absorbing D-Day Museum in the Southsea district tells the story of the D-Day landings of June 6, 1944, and the invasion's planning and preparation, through an eclectic range of exhibits. The museum's centerpiece is the Overlord Embroidery ("Overlord" was the invasion's code name), a 272-foot-long embroidered cloth with 34 panels illustrating the history of the operation, from the Battle of Britain in 1940 to victory in Normandy in 1944. ✉ *Clarence Esplanade* ☎ *023/9282–7261* 🌐 *www.ddaymuseum.co.uk* 🎫 *£6.80* ⏲ *Apr.–Sept., daily 10–5:30; Oct.–Mar., daily 10–5; last admission 30 min before closing.*

FAMILY Fodor's Choice ★ **Portsmouth Historic Dockyard.** The city's most impressive attraction includes an unrivaled collection of historic ships. The dockyard's youngest ship, HMS *Warrior* (1860), was England's first ironclad battleship. The flagship of British naval hero Vice Admiral Lord Horatio Nelson, HMS *Victory,* is in the process of being painstakingly restored to appear as it did at the Battle of Trafalgar (1805). You can inspect the cramped gun decks, visit the cabin where Nelson met his officers, and stand on the spot where he was mortally wounded by a French sniper. Another museum houses the *Mary Rose,* the former flagship of Henry VIII's navy. Built in this very dockyard more than 500 years ago, the boat sank in the harbor in 1545 before being raised in 1982. Described in the 16th century as "the flower of all the ships that ever sailed," it's berthed

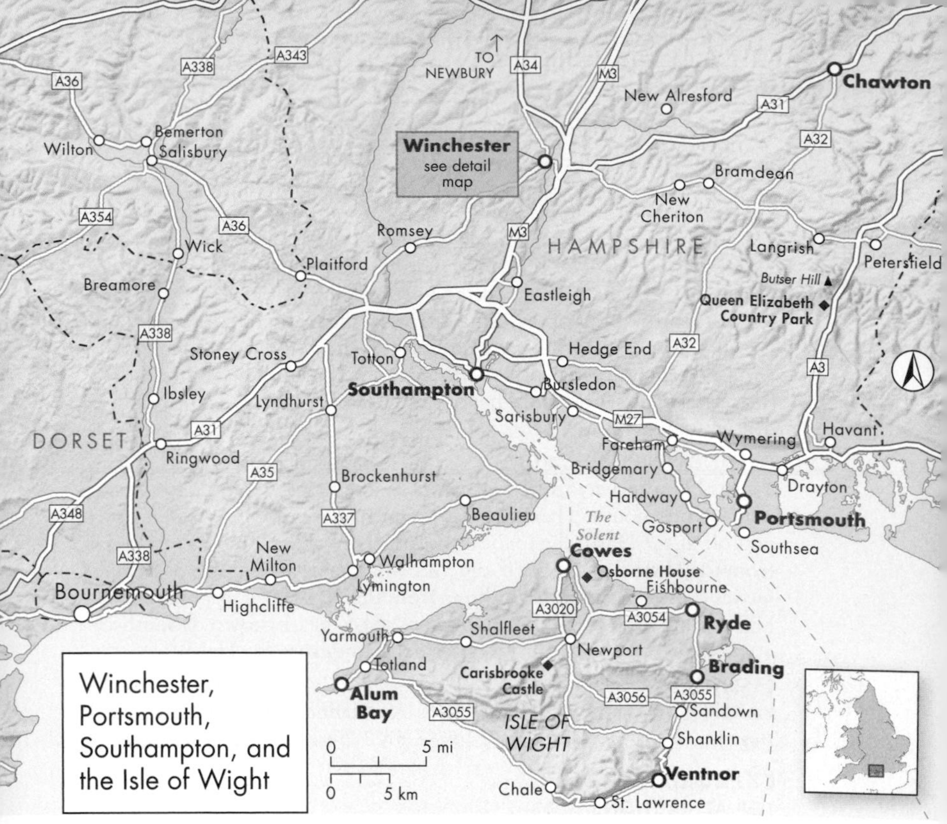

in a special enclosure where water continuously sprays the timbers to prevent them from drying out and breaking up.

The **National Museum of the Royal Navy** has extensive exhibits about Nelson and the Battle of Trafalgar, a fine collection of painted figureheads, and galleries of paintings and mementos recalling naval history from King Alfred to the present. **Action Stations,** an interactive attraction, gives insight into life in the modern Royal Navy and tests your sea legs with tasks such as piloting boats through gales. **Dockyard Apprentice** showcases the skills of the shipbuilders and craftsmen who constructed and maintained the naval vessels, with illustrations of rope making, sail making, caulking, signals, and knots. You should allow one or two days to tour all the attractions in the Historic Dockyard. The entrance fee includes a boat ride around the harbor, and the all-attractions ticket is valid for one year. ✉ *Victory Gate, HM Naval Base* ☎ *023/9283–9766* 🌐 *www.historicdockyard.co.uk* 🎫 *£18 each HMS Victory, The Mary Rose, HMS Warrior, Action Stations; £13 Museum of the Royal Navy; £32 includes all on-site attractions plus Explosion! and Royal Marines Museum* ⏲ *Apr.–Oct., daily 10–5:30; Nov.–Mar., daily 10–5; last admission 1 hr before closing. Specific attractions may close earlier in winter–check website* ☞ *Nov.–late Mar., access to HMS Victory by 50-min guided tour only.*

Spinnaker Tower. The focal point of the lively Gunwharf Quays development of shops and bars, the Spinnaker Tower is a striking addition to Portsmouth's skyline. The slender structure evokes a mast with a billowing sail, and rises to a height of 558 feet. An elevator whisks you to three viewing platforms 330 feet high for thrilling all-around views of the harbor and up to 23 miles beyond. ✉ *Gunwharf Quays* ☎ *023/9285–7520* 🌐 *www.spinnakertower.co.uk* 🎫 *£9.50* ⏲ *Viewing decks: Sept.–July, daily 10–6; Aug., daily 9:30–6:30; last admission 30 min before closing.*

WORTH NOTING

FAMILY **Explosion! The Museum of Naval Firepower** This museum located in a Georgian building used by the Royal Navy since 1771 to store weapons and ammunition explores the history of warfare at sea with interactive touch-screen exhibits on naval armaments, from cannonballs to mines, missiles, torpedoes, and even a decommissioned nuclear bomb. Reached by waterbus from the Historic Dockyard, the museum also tells the story of the local people who manufactured the weapons. ✉ *Priddy's Hard, Gosport* ☎ *023/9250–5600* 🌐 *www.explosion.org.uk* 🎫 *£10* ⏲ *Apr.–Oct., daily 10–5; Nov.–Mar., weekends 10–4; last admission 1 hr before closing.*

Portchester Castle. Incorporating what is believed to be the most complete set of Roman walls in northern Europe, this fort was originally built more than 1,700 years ago. Inside the impressive fortifications are the remains of royal apartments added by Richard II in the 1390s. From the keep's central tower you can take in sweeping views of the harbor and coastline. ✉ *Church Road, Portchester* ✥ *Off A27 near Fareham* ☎ *02392/378291* 🌐 *www.english-heritage.org.uk* 🎫 *£5.40* ⏲ *Apr.–Sept., daily 10–6; Oct., daily 10–5; Nov.–Mar., weekends 10–4.*

FAMILY **Royal Navy Submarine Museum.** The highlight here is a tour of the newly restored World War II submarine HMS *Alliance* from the cramped quarters to the engine room. Here you can learn about submarine history and the rigors of life below the waves. There are three actual subs spread around the large site, including Holland 1, the first Royal Navy sub built in 1901. From Portsmouth Harbour, take the ferry to Gosport and walk along Millennium Promenade past the huge sundial clock. From April to October, an hourly waterbus runs from the Historic Dockyard. ✉ *Halsar Jetty Rd., Gosport* ☎ *023/9251–0354* 🌐 *www.submarine-museum.co.uk* 🎫 *£14* ⏲ *Apr.–Oct., daily 10–5:30; Nov.–Mar., Wed.–Sun. 10–4:30; last tour 1 hr before closing.*

WHERE TO EAT AND STAY

$ MODERN BRITISH ✕ **Abarbistro.** A relaxed, modern bistro midway between Old Portsmouth and Gunwharf Quays, this place is ideal for a snack, meal, or glass of vino from the thoughtfully chosen wine list. The changing Modern British menu specializes in seafood dishes like *moules marinière*, fish cakes, or beer-battered fish-and-chips, mostly sourced from Portsmouth's fish market directly opposite. Alternatively, opt for the pork sirloin steak with apple puree, or a grilled Mediterranean vegetable salad. You can sit indoors, in a garden at the back, or at Continental-style

You can tour Admiral Nelson's famous flagship, the HMS *Victory*, at Portsmouth's Historic Dockyard.

tables on the pavement. *Average main: £12 58 White Hart Rd. 023/9281–1585 www.abarbistro.co.uk No credit cards.*

$$$$ BRITISH **Montparnasse.** Modern art on taupe walls add a contemporary touch to this relaxed restaurant, a local favorite for 30 years. The fixed-price menus (£35 and £41) add a twist to British classics, like slow-cooked pork belly with braised sweetbreads, or a sea bass fillet with a red pepper sauce and hazelnuts. Ingredients come from local suppliers wherever possible. Service is discreet but attentive and knowledgeable. *Average main: £35 103 Palmerston Rd. 023/9281–6754 www.bistromontparnasse.co.uk Closed Sun. and Mon.*

$ B&B/INN **Fortitude Cottage.** With sleek modern bedrooms done in white and neutral colors, this friendly B&B provides top-class waterside accommodation in two buildings in the center of Old Portsmouth, within walking distance of the Historic Dockyard via the Millennium Promenade just across the street. **Pros:** central but quiet location; immaculate, modern rooms; great view from penthouse. **Cons:** stairs; some rooms have poor view. *Rooms from: £99 51 Broad St. 023/9282–3748 www.fortitudecottage.co.uk 6 rooms Breakfast.*

SPORTS AND THE OUTDOORS

FAMILY **Queen Elizabeth Country Park.** Designated an Area of Outstanding Natural Beauty, this park has more than 2,000 acres of woodland and rolling hills, including 20 miles of scenic trails for hikers, cyclists, and horse riders. You can climb to the top of 888-foot-tall Butser Hill to take in a panoramic view of the coast. Part of the South Downs National Park, it lies 15 miles north of Portsmouth and 4 miles south of the Georgian market town of Petersfield. A visitor center has a theater, café, and shop. ✉ *Gravel Hill, Horndean ⊕ Park has its own signed sliproads off the A3.* ☎ *023/9259–5040* 🌐 *www3.hants.gov.uk/countryside/qecp* 🎫 *Free* ⏲ *Park open 24 hrs; visitor center Mar.–Oct., daily 10–5:30; Nov.–Feb., daily 10–4:30.*

SOUTHAMPTON

17 miles northwest of Portsmouth, 24 miles southeast of Salisbury, 77 miles southwest of London.

Southampton is England's leading passenger port. It is rich in historic embarkations, from Henry V's fleet bound for France and the battle of Agincourt to the *Mayflower*, the ill-fated *Titanic*, and the maiden voyages of the great ocean liners of the 20th century such as the *Queen Mary* and the *Queen Elizabeth 2*. Parts of the town center can seem mundane, having been hastily rebuilt after World War II bombing, but bits of the city's history emerge from between modern buildings. The Old Town retains its medieval feel, and some remnants of the old castellated town walls remain. Other attractions include a decent art gallery, extensive parks, and a couple of good museums. The Southampton Boat Show, a 10-day event in mid-September, draws huge crowds.

GETTING HERE AND AROUND

Located on the M3 motorway from London and Winchester, and on the M27 from Portsmouth, Southampton is also easily accessed by bus or train from these cities. The bus and train stations are a few minutes' walk from the tourist office, and the main sights can be reached by foot.

EXPLORING

Broadlands. This 60-room Palladian mansion located on 6,000 acres near the town of Romsey was the home of 19th-century British Prime Minister Lord Palmerston and later of Earl Mountbatten of Burma (1900–79), uncle of Prince Philip and mentor to Prince Charles, who, as the last viceroy of India, was in charge of that country's transition to independence before being killed by the IRA. One of the grandest houses in Hampshire, Broadlands dates back to the 18th century and holds a large collection of antiques, Greek and Roman marbles, and Old Master paintings, including three Van Dycks. Landscape designer Capability Brown laid out the grounds, which include wide lawns sweeping down to the banks of the River Test. ✉ *Broadlands Park, Romsey* ⊕ *Off A3090 Romsey Bypass* ☎ *01794/529750* 🌐 *www.broadlandsestates.co.uk* 🎫 *£10* ⏲ *Late June–early Sept., weekdays 1–5:30; last admission at 4* ☞ *Open by guided tour (1 hr) only.*

Mayflower Park and the Pilgrim Fathers' Memorial. This memorial was built to commemorate the departure of 102 passengers on the North America–bound *Mayflower* from Southampton on August 15, 1620. A plaque also honors the 2 million U.S. troops who embarked from Southampton during World War II. ✉ *Western Esplanade.*

SeaCity Museum. Devoted to Southampton's venerable maritime history, this museum brings together artifacts from Roman and Saxon days to the present and uses audiovisual installations to tell the story of the traders and travelers who've come and gone through the port. Boat buffs relish the collections devoted to the Merchant Navy, the great clippers, and cruise ships—most notably the Titanic. A special gallery displays a wealth of footage, photos, crew lists, and so on relating to the ill-fated vessel that sailed from here. ✉ *Havelock Rd.* ☎ *023/8083–3007* 🌐 *www.seacitymuseum.co.uk* 🎫 *£9.50* ⏲ *Daily 10–5; last admission at 4.*

WHERE TO EAT AND STAY

$$ BRASSERIE ✕ **Oxford Brasserie.** Close to the docks, this informal place gets lively in the evening but it's calmer at lunchtime. Fresh fish is always available (the fixed-price lunch menus are a particularly good value), along with regional Italian dishes. The restaurant has a tile floor and taupe walls enlivened with funky sections of brightly painted wood doors for a color-block effect. 💲 *Average main: £17* ✉ *33–34 Oxford St.* ☎ *023/8063–5043* 🌐 *www.theoxfordbrasserie.co.uk.*

$$ B&B/INN **The Pig In The Wall.** On a quiet street across from Mayflower Park, this snug hotel in two converted town houses has guest rooms with a funky but chic aesthetic, with goose-down bedding and monsoon showers. **Pros:** stylish rooms; lovely common areas; limited but good menu. **Cons:** breakfast not included; very steep stairs to top-floor room; wood floors mean some overhead noise. 💲 *Rooms from: £150* ✉ *8 Western Esplanade* ☎ *0845/077–9494* 🌐 *www.thepiginthewall.com* *12 rooms* 🍽 *No meals.*

$$$ HOTEL Fodor's Choice ★ **TerraVina Hotel.** This comfortable boutique hotel in a converted Victorian house on the edge of the New Forest is renowned for its professionalism and high standards, be it the chic design of the public rooms; the spacious, contemporary guest rooms with rain showers; or the restaurant. **Pros:** high quality furnishings; fantastic food; good showers. **Cons:** some rooms small; a little remote from Southampton. 💲 *Rooms from: £195* ✉ *174 Woodlands Rd., Woodlands, Netley Marsh* ☎ *023/8029–3784* 🌐 *www.hotelterravina.co.uk* *11 rooms* 🍽 *No meals.*

ISLE OF WIGHT

Drawn by the island's slightly old-fashioned and unspoiled feel, throngs of visitors flock to the 23-mile-long Isle of Wight (pronounced white) in summer. It became a fashionable holiday destination during the reign of Queen Victoria, who spent her own vacations here at her favorite residence, Osborne House, where she ultimately died. The island attracted the cream of Victorian society, including Darwin, Thackeray, and Tennyson, with the latter living here until tourist harassment drove him away. Perhaps understandably, islanders have a love-hate relationship with the crowds of tourists who disembark from the ferries and hydrofoils that connect the island with Southampton, Portsmouth, Southsea, and Lymington. The attractions include its seaside resorts—Ryde, Bembridge, Ventnor, and Freshwater (stay away from rather tacky Sandown and Shanklin)—and its green interior landscape, narrow lanes, curving bays, sandy beaches, and walking paths. Although the revitalizing ocean air is, to quote Tennyson, "worth sixpence a pint," the island offers more than sailing and the sea. There are splendid scenic roads to explore in Brading Down, Ashley Down, Mersely Down, and along

Military Road, and historic holiday getaways to visit, notably Osborne House itself.

GETTING HERE AND AROUND

Wightlink operates a car ferry between the mainland and the Isle of Wight. The crossing takes about 40 minutes from Lymington to Yarmouth and 45 minutes from Portsmouth to Fishbourne. The company also operates a catamaran service between Portsmouth and Ryde (22 minutes). Red Funnel runs a car ferry (one hour) between Southampton and East Cowes and a hydrofoil service (25 minutes) to West Cowes. Hovertravel runs a hovercraft shuttle between Southsea (Portsmouth) and Ryde (15 minutes). The island is covered by a good network of roads, and you can rely on a regular local bus service. Southern Vectis, the local bus company, operates hop on-hop-off open-top tours. The "Needles Breezer" goes to Dimbola Lodge, the Needles, and Alum Bay between mid-March and early November, while the Downs Breezer, which goes to Sandown and Brading, runs from late May through August. You can board and disembark at different points for £10, and the fare includes unlimited access to all Southern Vectis services for 24 hours.

TIMING

Summer traffic slows things down considerably. Try to avoid Cowes Week in late July or early August, the Garlic Festival in mid-August, and the two major rock festivals that take place in mid-June and mid-September.

ESSENTIALS

Ferry Information Hovertravel. ☎ *08434/878887* 🌐 *www.hovertravel.co.uk.* **Red Funnel.** ☎ *0844/844–9988 in U.K., 0845/155–2442 from U.S.* 🌐 *www.redfunnel.co.uk.* **Wightlink.** ☎ *0333/999–7333, 023/9285–5230 from U.S.* 🌐 *www.wightlink.co.uk.*

Visitor Information Isle of Wight Tourism. ☎ *01983/813813* 🌐 *www.visitisleofwight.co.uk.*

COWES

7 miles northwest of Ryde.

If you embark from Southampton, your ferry crosses the Solent channel and docks at Cowes, near Queen Victoria's Osborne House. Cowes is a magic name in the sailing world because of the internationally known Cowes Week yachting festival (🌐 *www.aamcowesweek.co.uk*), held each July or August. At the north end of the high street, on the Parade, a tablet commemorates the two ships that sailed from here in 1633 carrying the English settlers who founded what later became Maryland.

GETTING HERE AND AROUND

A car ferry and a hydrofoil shuttle passengers from Southampton. Southern Vectis runs numerous buses connecting Cowes with other destinations on the island.

4

EXPLORING

Carisbrooke Castle. This castle, built more than a thousand years ago by the Normans, was remodeled extensively during the Middle Ages and surrounded by a mile of artillery fortifications in 1600 to defend against the threat of the Spanish Armada. During the English Civil War Carisbrooke served as a prison for Royalists, most notably King Charles I, who also tried (unsuccessfully) to escape through a tiny window in the north curtain wall, which you can still see. (The small museum has memorabilia relating to the imprisoned King.) The castle was restored during Victoria's reign and served as the residence of her daughter Princess Beatrice, who has a namesake Edwardian-style garden here. There are excellent views from the top of the Norman keep and battlements. Children love meeting the donkeys who still pull the wheel that draws water from the castle well. The castle is about a mile southwest of the Isle of Wight's capital, Newport. From Cowes, take Bus 1 or 5 (1 from West Cowes, near Holmwood Hotel; 5 from East Cowes, near Osborne House) to Newport, from where it's a 30-minute walk or a short ride on Bus 6, 7, or 38 to The Mall in Carisbrooke, ¼ mile away. ✉ *Castle Hill* ✥ *Off B3401* ☎ *01983/522107* 🌐 *www.english-heritage.org.uk* 🎫 *£9.20* ⏲ *Apr.–Sept., daily 10–6; Oct., daily 10–5; Nov.–Mar., weekends 10–4.*

Fodor's Choice ★ **Osborne House.** This palazzo-style Italianate house, much of it designed by Prince Albert in collaboration with Thomas Cubitt, was the royal family's private retreat and Queen Victoria's favorite residence. The house reveals Albert's interest in engineering through clever innovations like an early form of central heating, as well as Victoria's determination to give her children a normal but disciplined upbringing. After Albert's death in 1861, the queen retreated to Osborne to mourn her loss in relative seclusion, and the antiques-filled rooms have scarcely been altered since she died here in 1901. The house and extensive grounds (also designed by Albert)—which can be quite crowded during July and August—were used as a location for the 1998 movie *Mrs. Brown.* During the summer, a minibus takes you to what used to be Victoria's private beach, now open to the public, where you can see her personal bathing machine. Another minibus goes to the Swiss Cottage, a replica Alpine chalet built as a playhouse for Victoria and Albert's nine children. **■TIP→ Book ahead for guided tours of the house and gardens.** Buses 4 (from Ryde) and 5 (from Cowes and Newport) stop outside. ✉ *York Ave.* ✥ *Off A3021* ☎ *01983/200022* 🌐 *www.english-heritage.org.uk* 🎫 *£14.30 house and grounds; £11.70 house (ground floor only) and grounds (in winter)* ⏲ *Apr.–Sept., daily 10–6; Oct., daily 10–5; Nov.–Mar., weekends (house by prebooked guided tour only) 10–4.*

WHERE TO STAY

$$ HOTEL **Best Western New Holmwood Hotel.** The rooms may be unremarkable and basic, but the staff is friendly, and the views are special from the hotel's unrivaled location above the western end of the Esplanade—ideal for watching yachters in the Solent. **Pros:** good sea views; friendly staff; within walking distance of passenger ferry. **Cons:** bathrooms and design somewhat dated. [$] *Rooms from: £120* ✉ *65 Queens Rd., Egypt*

Pt. ☎ 01983/292508 🌐 www.newholmwoodhotel.co.uk 24 rooms, 2 suites 🍴 Breakfast.

$$$$ RENTAL **No.1 and No. 2 Sovereign's Gate.** English Heritage has created two new cottages out of what was the ceremonial entrance to the Osborne estate (it's still the entrance the royal family uses when they visit the property). **Pros:** unusual location; out-of-hours access to Osborne House grounds. **Cons:** limited booking options; no staff services. *$ Rooms from: £414 ✉ Royal Entrance, York Ave., Cowes ☎ 0370/333–1187 🌐 www.english-heritage.org.uk 2 lodges 🍴 No meals.*

RYDE

4

7 miles southeast of Cowes.

The town of Ryde has long been one of the Isle of Wight's most popular summer resorts with several family attractions. After the construction of Ryde Pier in 1814, elegant town houses sprang up along the seafront and on the slopes behind, commanding fine views of the harbor. In addition to its long, sandy beach, Ryde has a large lake (you can rent rowboats and pedal boats) and playgrounds.

GETTING HERE AND AROUND

From Portsmouth, catamaran service takes about 20 minutes; from Southsea a hovercraft gets you to Ryde in 10 minutes. If you're driving from Cowes, take the A3021 to the A3054.

WHERE TO EAT AND STAY

$$$$ SEAFOOD **✕ Seaview.** A strong maritime flavor defines this outstanding restaurant in the heart of a harbor village just outside Ryde. Choose between the two main dining areas, one a smaller Victorian room, the other bright and modern, with tables spilling out into a conservatory. The kitchen specializes in seafood and fresh island produce, much of it from the Seaview's own farm. You might start with the local crab ravioli in a shellfish jus, then move on to roast cod or pan-fried skate in a butter sauce with duxelle mushrooms. The restaurant menu is available as a three-course £28 prix-fixe only, but simple pub food can be ordered à la carte in the two congenial bars—one modern and one traditional. Luxurious fabrics characterize the chic guest rooms in the adjoining hotel. *$ Average main: £28 ✉ Seaview Hotel, The High St., Seaview ☎ 01983/612711 🌐 www.seaviewhotel.co.uk.*

$$ HOTEL **Lakeside Park Hotel.** Halfway between Cowes and Ryde in the tiny town of Wootton Bridge, this waterfront hotel on a 20-acre tidal lake is perfectly located for exploring the northern part of the island. **Pros:** scenic location; pretty views; comfortable rooms. **Cons:** air-conditioning can be noisy; somewhat characterless. *$ Rooms from: £160 ✉ High St., Wootton Bridge ☎ 01983/882266 🌐 www.lakesideparkhotel.com 44 bedrooms, 3 suites 🍴 Breakfast.*

$$$ HOTEL Fodor's Choice ★ **Priory Bay Hotel.** This country-house hotel has architectural flourishes that date back to Tudor times, 60 acres of grounds, and its own private sandy beach. **Pros:** quirky character; beautiful setting; restful atmosphere. **Cons:** sometimes more shabby than chic; not much to do in vicinity; minimum stay required. *$ Rooms from: £200 ✉ Priory*

Dr., Seaview ☎ 01983/613146 🌐 www.priorybay.com 🛏 16 rooms, 2 suites, 2 barns, 8 self-catering cottages, 2 self-catering houses, 3 yurts 🍴 Breakfast ☞ Breakfast not included in self-catering units.

BRADING

3 miles south of Ryde on A3055.

The Anglo-Norman St. Mary's Church in Brading dates back to 1180. It contains the tombs of the Oglanders, a local family whose Norman ancestor is thought to have fought under William the Conqueror at the Battle of Hastings in 1066. You can still see the old lockup, dating from 1750, complete with stocks and whipping post at the Hall.

GETTING HERE AND AROUND

To get here from Ryde, take the Island Line trains or local bus services.

ESSENTIALS

Contacts Island Line. ☎ *0845/600–0650* 🌐 *www.southwesttrains.co.uk.*

EXPLORING

Brading Roman Villa. Housed within a striking wooden-walled, glass-roofed building 1 mile south of Brading are the remains of this substantial 3rd-century Roman villa, with original walls, splendid mosaic floors, and a well-preserved heating system. The mosaics, depicting peacocks (symbolizing eternal life), gods, gladiators, sea beasts, and reclining nymphs, are a rare example of this type of floor preserved in situ in a domestic building. A new space hosts related temporary exhibitions, and there's also a café at the site. ✉ *Morton Old Rd.* ✣ *Off A3055* ☎ *01983/406223* 🌐 *www.bradingromanvilla.org.uk* 🎟 *£9.50* 🕒 *Daily 10–5; last entry at 4.*

VENTNOR

11 miles south of Ryde.

The south-coast resorts are the sunniest and most sheltered on the Isle of Wight. Handsome Ventnor rises from such a steep slope that the ground floors of some of its houses are level with the roofs of those across the road.

GETTING HERE AND AROUND

Local bus service connects Ventnor with the rest of the island.

EXPLORING

Ventnor Botanic Garden. Laid out over 22 acres, these gardens contain more than 3,500 species of trees, plants, and shrubs. Thanks to a unique microclimate there are outdoor gardens devoted to flora from the Mediterranean, Antipodes, and South Africa. The impressive greenhouse includes banana trees and a waterfall; a visitor center, with a gift shop that sells plants and seeds, puts the gardens into context. Admission includes a guided tour. There is a two-bedroom self-catering cottage in the garden itself, available for short-term rentals at £135 a night. ✉ *Undercliff Dr.* ☎ *01983/855397* 🌐 *www.botanic.co.uk* 🎟 *£7.50* 🕒 *Oct.–Mar., daily 10–4; Apr.–Sept., daily 10–dusk* ☞ *1/3 off if purchased with Red Funnel ferry ticket.*

WHERE TO EAT

$$ MODERN BRITISH ✕ **The Pond Café.** Overlooking a secluded, elongated pond in the hamlet of Bonchurch, a mile north of Ventnor, this quiet, understated restaurant is a good place to gently unwind. The simply furnished interior is compact and contemporary in style, and there are a few outdoor tables for eating alfresco when the weather permits. The cafe specializes in rustic, Italian-influenced cuisine. Light pastas, homemade pizzas, and antipasti are served at lunch, while an à la carte menu in the evenings features dishes like duck leg confit with sweet potato, wild mushrooms, and spinach, or locally caught sea bass with crab mayonnaise. Bread and cakes are baked on-site. *Average main: £15 ✉ Bonchurch Village Rd., Bonchurch ☎ 01983/855666 🌐 www.thehambrough.com.*

4

ALUM BAY AND THE NEEDLES

19 miles northwest of Ventnor, 18 miles southwest of Cowes.

At the western tip of the Isle of Wight is the island's most famous natural landmark, the **Needles,** a long line of jagged chalk stacks jutting out of the sea like giant teeth, with a lighthouse at the end. It's part of the Needles Pleasure Park, which has mostly child-oriented attractions. Adjacent is **Alum Bay,** accessed from the Needles by chairlift. Here you can catch a good view of the "colored sand" in the cliff strata or take a boat to view the lighthouse. **Yarmouth,** a charming fishing village, is a 10-minute drive from Alum Bay.

GETTING HERE AND AROUND

Wightlink car and passenger ferries from Lymington dock at nearby Yarmouth. The spectacular A3055 runs along the southwest coast from Ventnor to Freshwater, the nearest town. From there you can follow the coast road to Alum Bay. Local bus services connect Freshwater with the rest of the island.

EXPLORING

Dimbola. This was the home of Julia Margaret Cameron (1815–79), the eminent Victorian portrait photographer and friend of Lord Tennyson. A gallery includes more than 60 examples of her work, including striking images of Carlyle, Tennyson, and Browning. There's also a room devoted to the various Isle of Wight rock festivals, most famously the five-day event in 1970 that featured the Who, the Doors, Joni Mitchell, and Jimi Hendrix. On the ground floor is a shop and a good Alice in Wonderland–themed tearoom for snacks, hot lunches, and a traditional cream tea. *✉ Terrace La., Freshwater Bay ✢ Off Gate La. ☎ 01983/756814 🌐 www.dimbola.co.uk 🎫 £4.50 ⏲ Apr.–Sept., daily 10–5 (last admission 4:30); Nov., Dec., Feb., and Mar., Tues.–Sun. 10–4; Jan., Fri.–Sun. 10–4.*

SALISBURY, STONEHENGE, AND SALISBURY PLAIN

Filled with sites of cultural and historical interest, this area includes the handsome city of Salisbury, renowned for its spectacular cathedral, and the iconic prehistoric stone circles at Stonehenge and Avebury. A trio of nearby stately homes displays the ambitions and wealth of their original aristocratic inhabitants—Wilton House with its Inigo Jones–designed staterooms, Stourhead and its exquisite neoclassical gardens, and the Elizabethan splendor of Longleat. Your own transportation is essential to get to anything beyond Salisbury, other than Stonehenge or Avebury.

SALISBURY

24 miles northwest of Southampton, 44 miles southeast of Bristol, 79 miles southwest of London.

The silhouette of Salisbury Cathedral's majestic spire signals your approach to this historic city long before you arrive. Although the cathedral is the principal focus of interest here, and its Cathedral Close is one of the country's most atmospheric spots (especially on a foggy night), Salisbury has much more to see, not least its largely unspoiled—and relatively traffic-free—old center. Here are stone shops and houses that over the centuries grew up in the shadow of the great church. You're never far from any of the five rivers that meet here, or from the bucolic water meadows that stretch out to the west of the cathedral and provide the best views of it. Salisbury didn't become important until the early 13th century, when the seat of the diocese was transferred here from Old Sarum, the original settlement 2 miles to the north, of which only ruins remain. In the 19th century, novelist Anthony Trollope based his tales of ecclesiastical life, notably *Barchester Towers,* on life here, although his fictional city of Barchester is really an amalgam of Salisbury and Winchester. The local tourist office organizes walks—of differing lengths for varying stamina—to guide you to the must-sees. And speaking of must-sees, prehistoric Stonehenge is less than 10 miles away and easily visited from the city.

GETTING HERE AND AROUND

Salisbury is on main bus and train routes from London and Southampton; regular buses also connect Salisbury with Winchester. The bus station is centrally located on Endless Street. Trains stop west of the center. After negotiating a ring-road system, drivers will want to park as soon as possible. The largest of the central parking lots is by Salisbury Playhouse. The city center is compact, so you won't need to use local buses for most sights. For Wilton House, take Bus Red 3 or Red 8 from Salisbury town center.

TIMING

Market Place hosts general markets every Tuesday and Saturday and farmers' markets on the first and third Wednesday of the month. It's also the venue for other fairs and festivals, notably the one-day Food & Drink Festival in mid-September and the three-day Charter Fair in

October. The city gets busy during the arts festival in May and June, when accommodations may be scarce.

TOURS

Salisbury City Guides. Blue Badge guides lead 90-minute city tours from the tourist information center at 11 every morning from April through October and on weekends the rest of the year. Tickets are £5. ☎ *07873/212941* 🌐 *www.salisburycityguides.co.uk* 🎫 *From £5.*

Stonehenge Tour. Hop-on, hop-off open-top buses leave once or twice an hour all year from the train station and the bus station, and the route includes Old Sarum and Salisbury Cathedral as well as Stonehenge. Tickets for a tour of all three attractions are £33; an Old Sarum and Stonehenge tour is £27; and bus only without a tour is £14. ☎ *0845/072–7093* 🌐 *www.thestonehengetour.co.uk* 🎫 *From £14.*

ESSENTIALS

Visitor Information Salisbury Information Centre. ✉ *Fish Row, off Market Pl.* ☎ *01722/342860* 🌐 *www.visitwiltshire.co.uk/explore/salisbury.*

4

EXPLORING

TOP ATTRACTIONS

Cathedral Close. Eighty acres of rolling lawns and splendid period architecture provide one of Britain's finest settings for a cathedral. The Close, the largest in the country, contains two museums: historic Mompesson House and the Chapter House, which houses the Magna Carta. ✉ *65 The Close* ✣ *Bounded by West Walk, North Walk, and Exeter St.* 🌐 *www.salisburycathedral.org.uk.*

Mompesson House. A perfect example of Queen Anne architecture, this family home, built in 1701, sits on the north side of Cathedral Close. It's notable for magnificent plasterwork, an exceptionally carved oak staircase, fine period furniture, and a collection of 18th century drinking glasses. Tea and refreshments are served in a walled garden. ✉ *The Close* ☎ *01722/420980* 🌐 *www.nationaltrust.org.uk* 🎫 *£6.50* ⏲ *Mid-Mar.–Oct., Sat.–Wed. 11–5; last admission at 4:30.*

Old Sarum. Massive earthwork ramparts on a bare sweep of Wiltshire countryside are all that remain of this impressive Iron Age hill fort, which was successively taken over by Romans, Saxons, and Normans (who built a castle and cathedral within the earthworks). The site was still fortified in Tudor times, though the population had mostly decamped in the 13th century to New Sarum, or Salisbury. You can clamber over the huge banks and take in the far-reaching views to Salisbury Cathedral. Family days on selected weekends give youngsters the chance to take part in a 12th-century "siege." ✉ *Castle Rd.* ✣ *Off A345* ☎ *01722/335398* 🌐 *www.english-heritage.org.uk* 🎫 *£4.20* ⏲ *Mar.– Sept., daily 10–6; Oct., daily 10–5; Nov.–Mar., daily 10–4.*

Salisbury and South Wiltshire Museum. Opposite the cathedral's west front, this excellent museum is in the King's House, parts of which date to the 15th century (James I stayed here in 1610 and 1613). The history of the area from prehistoric times through the 12th century is explored in the Wessex gallery, where Stonehenge-related models and exhibits provide helpful background information for a visit to the famous megaliths.

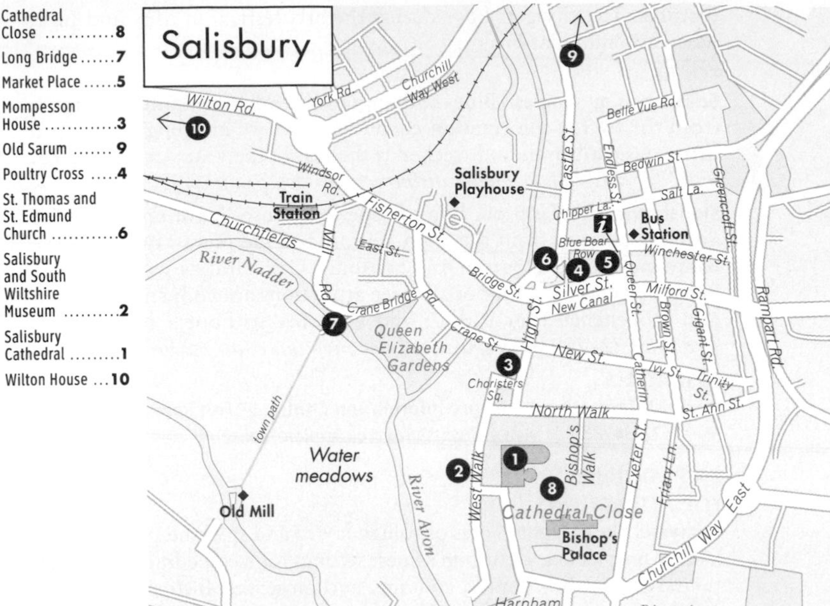

Also on view are collections of costumes, embroidery, Wedgwood pottery, and Turner watercolors, all dwarfed by the 12-foot Salisbury Giant, a 13-century pageant figure, and his companion hobbyhorse, Hob Nob. A cozy café (closed Sunday) is in one of the oldest sections of the building. ✉ *The King's House, 65 The Close* ☎ *01722/332151* 🌐 *www.salisburymuseum.org.uk* 🎫 *£8* ⏲ *June–Sept., Mon.–Sat. 10–5, Sun. noon–5; Oct.–May, Mon.–Sat. 10–5* ☞ *Tickets good for a year.*

Fodor's Choice ★ **Salisbury Cathedral.** Salisbury is dominated by the towering cathedral, a soaring hymn in stone. It is unique among cathedrals in that it was conceived and built as a whole in the amazingly short span of 38 years (1220–58). The spire, added in 1320, is the tallest in England and a miraculous feat of medieval engineering—even though the point, 404 feet above the ground, is 2½ feet off vertical. For a fictional, keenly imaginative reconstruction of the drama underlying such an achievement, read William Golding's novel *The Spire*. The excellent model of the cathedral in the north nave aisle, directly in front of you as you enter, shows the building about 20 years into construction, and makes clear the ambition of Salisbury's medieval builders. For all their sophistication, the height and immense weight of the great spire have always posed structural problems. In the late 17th century Sir Christopher Wren was summoned from London to strengthen the spire, and

Salisbury Cathedral has a towering spire—the tallest in England—that you can tour.

in the mid-19th century Sir George Gilbert Scott, a leading Victorian Gothicist, undertook a major program of restoration. He also initiated a clearing out of the interior and removed some less-than-sympathetic 18th-century alterations, returning a more authentically Gothic feel. Despite this, the interior seems spartan and a little gloomy, but check out the remarkable lancet windows and sculpted tombs of crusaders and other medieval notables. Next to the cathedral model in the north aisle is a medieval clock—probably the oldest working mechanism in Europe, if not the world—made in 1386.

The **cloisters** are the largest in England, and the octagonal **Chapter House** contains a marvelous 13th-century frieze showing scenes from the Old Testament. Here you can also see one of the four original copies of the **Magna Carta,** the charter of rights the English barons forced King John to accept in 1215; it was sent here for safekeeping in the 13th century. A new interactive exhibition opened in 2015 to mark the document's 800th anniversary. ■ **TIP→ Join a free 45-minute tour of the church, leaving two or more times a day. There are also tours of the roof and spire that leave hourly April–September, and every two hours October–March between 11:15 and 3:15, except on Sundays, when there's one tour at 1:15—check website.** For a peaceful break, the café in the cloister serves freshly baked cakes and pastries, plus hot lunches. ✉ *Cathedral Close* ☎ *01722/555150* 🌐 *www.salisburycathedral.org.uk* 🎫 *Cathedral and Chapter House free, suggested donation £7.50; tower tour £12.50* ⏲ *Cathedral Mon.–Sat. 9–5, Sun. noon–4; Chapter House Apr.–Oct., Mon.–Sat. 9:30–4:30, Sun. noon–3:45; Nov.–Mar., Mon.–Sat. 10–4:30, Sun. noon–3:45.*

With its art and gilded furniture, the Double Cube Room at Wilton House may well be one of England's most beautiful interiors.

Fodor's Choice ★ **Wilton House.** This is considered to be one of the loveliest stately homes in England and, along with its grounds, a fine example of the English Palladian style. The seat of the earls of Pembroke since Tudor times, the south wing of the current building was rebuilt in the early 17th century by Isaac de Caus, with input from Inigo Jones, Ben Jonson's stage designer and the architect of London's Banqueting House. It was completed by James Webb, again with input from Jones, Webb's uncle-by-marriage, after the recently finished south wing was ravaged by fire in 1647. Most noteworthy are the seven state rooms in the south wing, among them the Single Cube Room (built as a perfect 30-foot cube) and one of the most extravagantly beautiful rooms in the history of interior decoration, the aptly named Double Cube Room. The name refers to its proportions (60 feet long by 30 feet wide and 30 feet high), evidence of Jones's classically inspired belief that beauty in architecture derives from harmony and balance. The room's headliner is the spectacular Van Dyck portrait of the Pembroke family. Elsewhere at Wilton House, the art collection includes several other old master paintings, including works by Rembrandt and members of the Brueghel family. Another exhibition is devoted to Cecil Beaton's photo portraits of 20th-century notables and the current Lord Pembroke's collection of classic cars. Also of note are the lovely grounds, which have sweeping lawns dotted with towering oaks; the gardens; and the Palladian bridge crossing the small River Nadder, designed by the 9th earl after the Rialto Bridge in Venice. Some public rooms may be closed on some open days—check website for more information. ■**TIP→ Be sure to explore the extensive gardens; children appreciate the large playground.** The town of Wilton is 3 miles west of Salisbury. Buses 2, 13, 25, 26, 27, and Red

3 from Salisbury depart every 10 to 15 minutes and stop outside Wilton House. ✉ *Off A36, Wilton* ☎ *01722/746714* 🌐 *www.wiltonhouse.co.uk* 🎫 *£16; grounds only £6.50* ⏲ *House Easter and May–Aug., Sun.–Thurs. and holiday Saturdays 11:30–5. Grounds late Mar.–mid-Apr. and May–mid-Sept., Sun.–Thurs. and holiday Saturdays 11–5:30* ☞ *On "quieter days," admission to house by 40-min guided tour only.*

WORTH NOTING

Long Bridge. For a classic view of Salisbury, head to Long Bridge and Town Path. From the main street, walk west to Mill Road, which leads you across Queen Elizabeth Gardens. Cross the bridge and continue on Town Path through the water meadows, from which you can see the vista that inspired John Constable's 1831 *Salisbury Cathedral from the Meadows,* one of Britain's most iconic paintings, which is now in London's Tate Britain. ✉ *Salisbury.*

4

Market Place. One of southern England's most popular markets fills this square on Tuesday and Saturday. Permission to hold an annual fair here was granted in 1221, and that right is still exercised for three days every October, when the Charter Fair takes place. A narrow side street links Poultry Cross to Market Place. ✉ *Salisbury.*

Poultry Cross. One of Salisbury's best-known landmarks, the hexagonal Poultry Cross is the last remaining of the four original medieval market crosses that gave shelter to market traders (other crosses indicated the dairy, wool, and livestock markets). A cross on the site was first mentioned in 1307, though the current structure dates from the late 15th century. The canopy and flying buttresses were added in 1852. ✉ *Silver St.*

St. Thomas and St. Edmund Church. This church, which dates back to 1229, contains a rare medieval Doom painting of Judgment Day, considered to be one of the best preserved and most complete of the few such works left in Britain. Created around 1470 and covering the chancel arch, the scenes of heaven and hell served to instill the fear of damnation into the congregation. ■ **TIP→ It's best seen on a spring or summer evening when the light through the west window illuminates the details.** ✉ *St. Thomas's Sq., Beckets* ☎ *01722/322537* 🌐 *www.stthomassalisbury.co.uk* 🎫 *Free* ⏲ *Mon.–Sat. 8:30–dusk, Sun. noon–dusk.*

WHERE TO EAT

$$ INDIAN Fodor's Choice ★

✕ **Anokaa.** For a refreshingly modern take on Indian cuisine, try this bustling restaurant a few minutes from the center. Classic recipes are taken as starting points for the artistically presented dishes, which include tandoori-seared rack of lamb, cinnamon-glazed duck breast stuffed with garlicky spinach, and black tiger prawns in a sauce of curry leaves and coconut oil. At lunchtime, choose from the buffet. The setting is contemporary and cosmopolitan, and service by staff in traditional dress is friendly and prompt. $ *Average main: £16* ✉ *60 Fisherton St.* ☎ *01722/414142* 🌐 *www.anokaa.com.*

$ CAFÉ FAMILY

✕ **Boston Tea Party.** Specializing in quick, nourishing meals, this relaxed and child-friendly café in a 14th-century building serves hot and cold breakfasts, lunches, and afternoon snacks. Choices include cheeseburgers served with bacon jam, a veggie version with portobello mushroom, pulled-pork buns, or a huge vegan super salad with mango and avocado. Freshly roasted coffee and a wide selection of teas are a nice complement to the freshly baked cakes. You can eat upstairs in the spectacular Tudor great hall or the quieter side room. *Average main: £8* *Old George Inn, 13 High St.* *01722/330731* *www.bostonteaparty.co.uk* *No dinner.*

$$ BRITISH **Charter 1227.** Casual and friendly but upscale, with red carpets and taupe leather seats, this second-floor restaurant enjoys a prime position overlooking Market Place. The menu blends traditional British and Mediterranean dishes, such as crisp suckling pig belly with black pudding croquettes, or roast fillet of sole with a brioche crust. There are good-value, fixed-price, early-bird dinners. *Average main: £19* *6/7 Ox Row, Market Pl.* *01722/333118* *www.charter1227.co.uk* *Closed Mon. No dinner Sun.*

$$$$ MODERN BRITISH Fodor's Choice ★ **Howard's House.** If you're after complete tranquillity, head for this early 17th-century house on 2 acres of grounds in the Nadder Valley. The style is traditional and smart, and a terrace provides alfresco dining overlooking the tidy lawns in summer. The excellent restaurant has fixed-price menus specializing in contemporary English cooking using local and seasonal ingredients, such as a fillet of wild turbot with crab bisque, or roast loin of local Sika deer. Ten comfortable guest rooms may tempt you into forgoing the 10-mile drive back to Salisbury. *Average main: £32.50* *Teffont Evias, Teffont Evias* *Off B3089* *01722/716392* *www.howardshousehotel.co.uk.*

WHERE TO STAY

$ B&B/INN **Cricket Field House.** Located halfway between Wilton and Salisbury, this comfortable ex-gamekeeper's cottage overlooks a cricket ground and has a large, peaceful garden of its own. **Pros:** efficient, helpful management; well-maintained rooms; good breakfasts. **Cons:** dated design; on a busy road; lacks charm. *Rooms from: £95* *Wilton Rd.* *01722/322595* *www.cricketfieldhouse.co.uk* *18 rooms* *Breakfast.*

$$ HOTEL **Mercure Salisbury White Hart Hotel.** Behind the pillared portico and imposing 17th-century classical facade of this city center hotel (part of the Mercure chain) are modern bedrooms (of various sizes) with a muted cream-and-brown color scheme. **Pros:** polite staff; cozy public areas; rooms are comfortable. **Cons:** some rooms are small; impersonal, corporate feel; some tired design. *Rooms from: £130* *1 St. John St.* *01722/312801* *www.mercure.com* *67 rooms, 1 suite* *Breakfast.*

$ B&B/INN **Rokeby Guest House.** Easy to find on the east side of town, this four-story Edwardian B&B represents good value for your money with its spic-and-span, tastefully decorated interiors and a large, landscaped garden with a summerhouse. **Pros:** comfortable rooms, relaxed atmosphere; helpful hosts; abundant and tasty breakfasts. **Cons:** not central; no children under 12. *Rooms from: £65* *3 Wain-a-Long Rd.* *01722/329800* *www.rokebyguesthouse.co.uk* *10 rooms* *Breakfast.*

$ B&B/INN **Wyndham Park Lodge.** This simple Victorian house in a quiet part of town (off Castle Street) provides an excellent place to rest and a delicious breakfast, as well as a garden. **Pros:** efficient and hospitable owners; convenient location; good breakfast; handy parking. **Cons:** spotty Wi-Fi. $ *Rooms from: £60* ✉ *51 Wyndham Rd.* ☎ *01722/416517* 🌐 *www.wyndhamparklodge.co.uk* *3 rooms* *Breakfast.*

NIGHTLIFE AND PERFORMING ARTS

Salisbury International Arts Festival. Held from late May through early June, the festival has outstanding classical recitals, plays, author talks, international cinema, dance, comedy, and family events. ✉ *87 Crane St.* ☎ *01722/332241* 🌐 *www.salisburyfestival.co.uk.*

Salisbury Playhouse. The playhouse presents high-caliber drama all year and is the main venue for the Salisbury Arts Festival. ✉ *Malthouse La.* ☎ *01722/320117* 🌐 *www.salisburyplayhouse.com.*

4

SHOPPING

Most of the shops are gathered around Market Place, venue for twice-weekly markets and the annual Charter Fair, and along the High Street, where chain stores predominate.

Dauwalders of Salisbury. This shop specializes in stamps, coins, medals, and die-cast models, including some quirky gift ideas. ✉ *42 Fisherton St.* ☎ *01722/412100.*

National Trust Shop. There's a large range of traditional gifts here, from pottery and books to bags, soaps, jam, biscuits, honey, and garden-inspired accessories. ✉ *House of Steps, 41 High St.* ☎ *01722/331884* 🌐 *www.nationaltrust.org.uk.*

SPORTS AND THE OUTDOORS

Hayball Cyclesport. Bike rentals here cost about £15 per day or £70 per week, with a £25 cash deposit. ✉ *26–30 Winchester St.* ☎ *01722/411378* 🌐 *www.hayballcyclesport.co.uk* ⏲ *Closed Sun.*

STONEHENGE

8 miles north of Salisbury, 20 miles south of Avebury.

Almost five millennia after their construction, these stone circles on the Salisbury Plain continue to pose fascinating questions. How were the giant stones, some weighing as much as 45 tons, brought here, possibly from as far away as Wales? What was the site used for? Why were the stones aligned with the midsummer sunrise and the midwinter sunset? But Stonehenge is more than just the megaliths; the surrounding landscape is dotted with ancient earthworks, remains of Neolithic settlements, and processional pathways, creating a complex of ceremonial structures that testifies to the sophisticated belief system of these early Britons.

GETTING HERE AND AROUND

Stonehenge Tour buses leave from Salisbury's train and bus stations every half hour from 9:30 to 2:30, and then hourly from 3 to 5, from early June to August and hourly from 10 to 4 from late March to early June. Tickets cost £14, or £27 (includes Stonehenge and a visit to Old Sarum). Other options are a taxi or a custom tour. Drivers can find the monument near the junction of A303 with A344.

ESSENTIALS

Visitor Information Amesbury Community and Visitor Centre. ✉ *5 Stonehenge Walk, Unit 4, Amesbury* ☎ *01980/622525* 🌐 *www.visitwiltshire.co.uk.*

EXPLORING

Fodor's Choice ★ **Stonehenge.** *See the highlighted feature in this chapter for more information.* ✉ *Junction of A360 and Airman's Corner* ☎ *0870/333–1181* 🌐 *www.english-heritage.org.uk* 🎫 *£14.50* 🕓 *Mid-Mar.–May and Sept.–mid-Oct., daily 9:30–7; June–Aug., daily 9–8; mid-Oct.–mid-Mar., daily 9:30–5; last admission 2 hrs before closing.*

AVEBURY

24 miles north of Stonehenge, 34 miles north of Salisbury, 25 miles northeast of Longleat, 27 miles east of Bath.

The village of Avebury was built much later than its famous stone circles; it has an informative museum with an outstanding collection of Bronze Age artifacts from the area around here and Stonehenge. You can also explore a cluster of other prehistoric sites nearby.

GETTING HERE AND AROUND

From Salisbury, follow A345 north to Upavon and take the A342 to Devizes; then continue 7 miles northeast on the A361. You can also take the hourly Stagecoach bus No. 49 from Swindon to Avebury (30 minutes).

EXPLORING

TOP ATTRACTIONS

Alexander Keiller Museum. The Avebury Stone Circles are put into context by this collection of Neolithic and Bronze Age artifacts from the site, one of the most important prehistoric archeological collections in Britain. The museum contains charts, photos, models, and home movies taken by its namesake, archaeologist Alexander Keiller. It's suggested that Keiller, responsible for the excavation of Avebury in the 1930s, may have adapted the site's layout to highlight presentation more than authenticity. The exhibits are divided between the 17th-century **Stables Gallery,** which displays finds from Keiller's excavations, the child-friendly **Barn Gallery**, where you find interactive exhibits about the history of Avebury, and an activity area where kids can dress up in Bronze Age clothes. You can also visit the **Manor House**, where Keiller lived, and its surrounding gardens. The Tudor-era building received several subsequent (Queen Anne, Regency, and art deco) additions, and the rooms have been filled with acquired or commissioned period-appropriate furniture to illustrate how previous occupants lived. ✉ *High St.* ✣ *Off A4361* ☎ *01672/539250* 🌐 *www.nationaltrust.org.uk* 🎫 *Museum £4.40; manor house and gardens £9* 🕑 *Museum Apr.–Oct., daily 10–6; Nov.–Mar., daily 10–4. Manor house mid-Feb.–Mar., daily 11–4; Nov.–Dec., Thurs.–Sun. 11–4; Apr.–Oct., daily 11–5; closed Jan.–mid-Feb. Gardens Mar., daily 11–4; Apr.–Oct., daily 11–5; closed Nov.–Feb. Last entry 1 hr before closing.*

Fodor's Choice ★ **Avebury Stone Circles.** Surrounding part of Avebury village, the Avebury Stone Circles, the largest in the world, are one of England's most evocative prehistoric monuments—not so famous as Stonehenge, but all the more powerful for their lack of commercial exploitation. The stones were erected around 2600 BC, about the same time the better-known monument. As with Stonehenge, the purpose of this stone circle has never been ascertained, although it most likely was used for similar ritual purposes. Unlike Stonehenge, however, there are no certain astronomical alignments at Avebury, at least none that have survived. The main site consists of a wide, circular ditch and bank, about 1,400 feet across and more than half a mile around. Entrances break the perimeter at roughly the four points of the compass, and inside stand the remains of three stone circles. The largest one originally had 98 stones, although only 27 remain. Many stones on the site were destroyed centuries ago, especially in the 14th century when they were buried for unclear reasons, possibly religious fanaticism. Others were later pillaged in the 18th century to build the thatched cottages you see flanking the fields. You can walk around the circles, a World Heritage Site, at any time; early morning and early evening are recommended. As with Stonehenge, the summer solstice tends to draw the crowds. ✉ *Avebury* ✣ *1 mile north of A4* ☎ *01672/539-250* 🌐 *www.english-heritage.org.uk* 🎫 *Free* 🕑 *Daily dawn–dusk.*

Continued on page 275

MYSTERIOUS
STONEHENGE

A circle of giant stones sitting on the wide sweep of Salisbury Plain, Stonehenge is one of the most famous prehistoric sites in England. It still has the capacity to fascinate and move those who view it, but Stonehenge can also be perplexing. The site seems to pose more questions than it answers about its 5,000-year-long history, and its meaning and purpose are continually reevaluated and debated. With some context, you can experience Stonehenge as it once was: deeply mystical and awe-inspiring.

The ineffable mystery of Stonehenge—the name derives from the Anglo-Saxon term for "hanging stones"—remains despite the presence of a busy road nearby and close to a million visitors a year. With an improved visitor center 1.5 miles away scheduled to be completed before 2014 and traffic re-routed as of mid-2014, the experience of seeing Stonehenge promises to be hugely improved. But timing your visit and taking advantage of what the site offers—including a good audio guide—are important.

It also helps to sort through the theories, and to look at the landscape. Stonehenge was created in, broadly speaking, three stages: the earliest stage around 3000 BC, the stone settings around 2500 BC, and the rearrangement of the stones around 2300 BC. It was built on Salisbury Plain, an area devoid of trees since the last ice age—but it does not stand in isolation. The Stonehenge part of the UNESCO World Heritage Site of Stonehenge and Avebury (a nearby stone circle) covers almost 6,500 acres containing more than 350 burial mounds and prehistoric monuments. Archaeologists continue to rewrite the site's history as they uncover more evidence about Stonehenge and the surrounding ancient structures.

—by Ellin Stein

Opposite: Theories about the sun and its alignment with Stonehenge continue to invite debate. Above: An aerial view provides perspective on the great stone circle.

VIEWING STONEHENGE TODAY

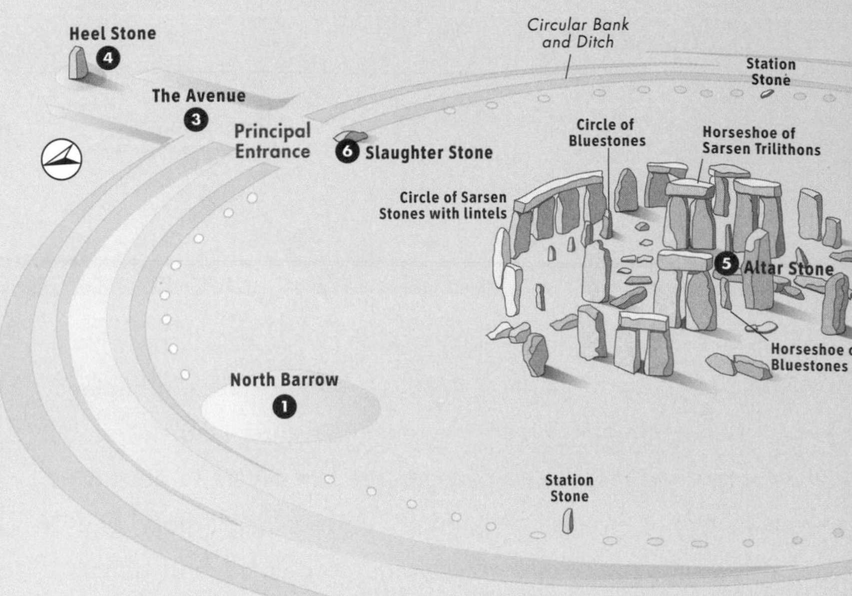

LAYOUT OF THE CIRCLE

Stonehenge today has an **outer circle of sarsen stones**, sandstone blocks from nearby Marlborough Downs. It is the only stone circle in the world with lintels. The huge stones are around 13 feet high, 7 feet wide, and weigh about 25 tons each. This sarsen circle surrounds a smaller **circle of bluestones**, a dolerite stone that appears blue when wet. Bluestones were possibly the first stones at the site, brought from the Preseli Hills in West Wales 150 miles away.

Sarsen stones form the **trilithons**, the tall (over 20 feet) pairs of upright stones with lintels across the top, in the center of the circle, part of an **inner horseshoe of sarsen stones and bluestones.** The sandstone **Altar Stone** is also in the center. The horseshoe's open end and central upright stones face midsummer sunrise and midwinter sunset.

The word "henge" refers to another feature of the site: a henge is a **circular earthwork bank with an internal ditch** surrounding flattened ground. Stonehenge is unusual in that the ditch is outside the earthwork bank.

OVER THE CENTURIES

Circular ditch with interior bank constructed

2850 BC Construction of nearby Avebury stone circles begins

2500 BC Large sarsen stones brought to Stonehenge; first bluestones brought from Wales

3000 BC 2800 BC 2500 BC 240

Heel Stone

South Barrow

Secondary Entrance

Aubrey Holes

1 North Barrow. The outer ditch and bank intersect with the largely unexcavated North Barrow, thought to have been used for burials. The barrow may predate Stonehenge.

2 Aubrey Holes. These 56 pits inside the outer bank, now with concrete markers, are named after John Aubrey, the antiquarian who identified them in 1666. Evidence suggests they may once have contained bluestone or timber uprights and were later used for cremated remains.

3 The Avenue. The Avenue's parallel ditches and banks stretch over 2.8 km (1.7 miles) to the bank of the River Avon. It was discovered in 2009, but little remains. Periglacial stripes, a natural geographic feature, run parallel to the banks of the Avenue and align in place with the solstice axis.

4 Heel Stone. This sarsen block stands at the entrance to the Avenue, on the edge of the current site. At midsummer solstice, the sun rises over the Heel Stone.

5 Altar Stone. Now recumbent, the great sandstone Altar Stone stood nearly 6 feet tall at the center of Stonehenge. Unlike the sarsen stones, it probably came from Milford Haven in Wales. Despite the name, its purpose remains unknown. Today the stone is the centerpiece for rituals around the summer and winter solstice.

6 Slaughter Stone. This stone, originally upright, now lies within the northeast entrance, and may have formed part of a portal. It is stained a rusty red by rainwater acting on the iron in the stone, rather than by the blood of human sacrifice, as 18th-century legend says.

Trilithon standing stones

HOW MANY STONES?

Many of the site's original stones have been lost over the years to builders of roads and houses and souvenir hunters, and some have fallen down. However, out of the original 30 large sarsen uprights, 17 remain, with 3 of the 5 trilithons still standing. Forty-three bluestones are left from the original 80 or so, and other major stones remain at the site.

MOVING THE STONES

The first 80 bluestones were brought by sea and river over 150 miles from Wales around 2500 BC. People probably used rafts to transport the bluestones over water. The heavier sarsen stones were dragged about 25 miles over land from the Marlborough Downs, and tipped into pits dug in the chalk plain. It is possible that people used wooden rollers for transporting the stones.

00 BC The Avenue nstructed, leading to ›st Amesbury Henge the River Avon

2300 BC Final rearrangement of bluestones into interior circle

1600 BC Concentric circles of Y and Z holes dug

2300 BC | 2000 BC | 1800 BC | 1600 BC

LEGENDS, MYTHS, and CURRENT THEORIES

Above: Many stones have fallen, but Stonehenge is still a powerful sight.

LEGENDARY STONEHENGE

Because of its prominence, Stonehenge has become steeped in myths assigning it any number of religious, mystical, and spiritual functions: it was built by the legendary Arthurian wizard Merlin, by the devil, giants, even aliens. The rebel queen Boudicca, who fought against the Romans, was said to have been buried at Stonehenge after the Romans fought the Druids, giving rise to the myth that the Druids built the stone circle to mark her tomb. One thing is certain: the Druids had nothing to do with the construction of Stonehenge, which had already stood for 2,000 years when they appeared.

WHO BUILT STONEHENGE?

The Neolithic and Bronze Age people who built Stonehenge, beginning around the time that the great pyramids in Egypt were built, had only hand tools for shaping the stones and their own manpower for moving them. No other stone circle contains such carefully shaped and meticulously placed stones. Some stones also show carvings of daggers and axes.

The first Neolithic people at what is now the World Heritage Site were semi-nomadic farmers who buried their dead in large, east-west facing barrows. Later, between 2500 and 2200 BC, the "Beaker People" started to use the site. Their name comes from their tradition of burying their dead with pottery (seen in displays at the Salisbury and South Wiltshire Museum), and they may have been sun worshipers. The final group was the Wessex people, around 1600 BC, who probably made the carvings in the stones and finalized Stonehenge's structure.

NEW THEORIES

Recent excavations have put forward two major new theories about its purpose. Evidence from the Stonehenge Riverside Project, a major ongoing archaeological study running since 2003, indicates that it was a domain of the dead: both a burial ground and a memorial. Numerous burials have been found all over the site and the surrounding area. Stonehenge is joined to Durrington Walls, the world's largest known henge and a nearby ancient settlement, by the River Avon and the Avenue. The journey along the river to Stonehenge may have been a ritual passage from life to death.

Another theory is that Stonehenge was a place of healing, accounting for the number of burials with physical injury and disease found in the tombs here as well as the unusual number of people who were not native to the area. That the bluestones were brought from so far away suggests that they were thought to harbor great powers.

STONEHENGE AND THE SUN

Stonehenge's design offers an intriguing clue as to its purpose, although there are no definitive answers. The horseshoe of trilithons and other stone settings align on the solstitial (midsummer sunrise and midwinter sunset) axis. This has led to much speculation and a variety of ideas. The centuries-old theory persists that Stonehenge was an astronomical observatory, a calendar, or a sun temple. It is fairly certain that it was a religious site, and worship here may have involved cycles of the sun.

On Summer Solstice (June 21), thousands gather to watch the sun rise over the Heel Stone. But the discovery of a neighboring stone to the Heel Stone questions even this, suggesting it may not itself have been a marker of sunrise, but part of a "solar corridor" that framed the sunrise.

Ongoing archaeological research, not to mention speculation, continues to revise the story of Stonehenge.

NEAR STONEHENGE

Hundreds of Neolithic monuments and barrows dot the landscape around Stonehenge. Excavations at **Durrington Walls**, a couple of miles northeast of Stonehenge off A345, have unearthed a substantial settlement dating from around 2500 BC, probably occupied by Stonehenge's builders. Although there is little left of most Neolithic sites today, concrete posts mark nearby **Woodhenge** (also off A345), which dates from around 2300 BC. Its long axis is aligned to the midsummer sunrise and the midwinter sunset. Admission and parking are free at both these sites.

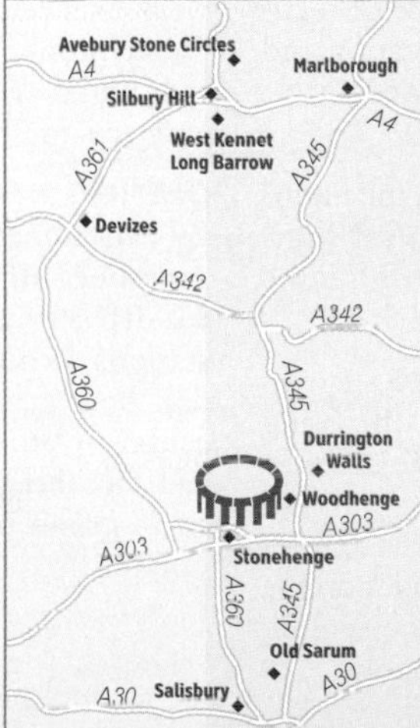

AVEBURY AND ENVIRONS

Twenty-four miles to the north lie Avebury and the **Avebury Stone Circles,** the largest stone circles in the world (dating to around 2850 BC). You can walk freely among the stones—a major attraction for those who prefer the site to Stonehenge.

Silbury Hill, the last of the great monuments, and **West Kennet Long Barrow**, a tomb, are close by.

Above, Silbury Hill

MAKING THE MOST OF YOUR VISIT

Avebury, Wiltshire

WHEN TO VISIT

Come early before the crowds arrive, or in the evening when the light is low and skies darkening. Summer weekends and school holidays can be especially crowded. Stonehenge is packed at Summer Solstice, when visitors stay all night to watch the sun rise.

English Heritage, which manages the site, can arrange access to the inner circle (not a guided tour) outside of regular hours. This requires application and a fee well in advance, as Stone Circle Access visits are popular.

The visitor center is located a mile-and-a-half from the stones. Frequent shuttles take you to the circles, a 10-minute trip. You can also walk.

TIPS AND WHAT TO BRING

Since the stones are roped off, bring binoculars to see the Broze Age carvings on them. Spend a few hours: walk all around the site to get that perfect photo and to observe the changing light on the plain. The free audio guide is essential, and the shop sells plenty of books.

MAKING A DAY OF IT

The Salisbury and South Wiltshire Museum in Salisbury has models and burial reconstructions that help put Stonehenge into perspective. The smaller Alexander Keiller Museum in Avebury has finds from the area.

It's an easy drive between nearby prehistoric sites. Stonehenge is set in 1,500 acres of National Trust land with excellent walks. The 36.5 mile Great Stone Way is a walking route that links Avebury with Stonehenge and runs to Old Sarum, near Salisbury.

GETTING HERE

By car, Stonehenge is 2 miles west of Amesbury off A36. The **Stonehenge Tour Bus** departs from Salisbury rail and bus stations frequently; buses leave every half hour or hour. Other options are a taxi or an organized tour. **Salisbury and Stonehenge Guided Tours** operates small-group tours from Salisbury and London.

Fodor's Choice ★ **West Kennet Long Barrow.** One of the largest Neolithic chambered tombs in Britain, West Kennet Long Barrow was built around 3400 BC. You can explore all around the site and also enter the tomb, which was used for more than 1,000 years before the main passage was blocked and the entrance closed, around 2000 BC. More than 300 feet long, it has an elevated position with a great view of Silbury Hill and the surrounding countryside. It's about 1 mile east of Avebury. ✉ *Avebury* ✢ *¾ mile southwest of West Kennett, along footpath off A4* ☎ *01672/539250* 🌐 *www.english-heritage.org.uk* 🎫 *Free.*

WORTH NOTING

Cherhill Down. Four miles west of Avebury, Cherhill Down is a prominent hill carved with a vivid white horse and topped with a towering obelisk. The horse is one of a number of hillside etchings in Wiltshire, all but two of which date back no further than the late 18th century. This one was put there in 1780 to indicate the highest point of the downs between London and Bath. The views from the top are well worth the half-hour climb. The best view of the horse is from A4, on the approach from Calne. ✉ *Avebury* ✢ *A4 south of Cherhill village, near Calne* ☎ *01672/539167* 🌐 *www.nationaltrust.org.uk.*

Silbury Hill. Rising 130 feet and comparable in height and volume to the roughly contemporary pyramids in Egypt, this largest man-made mound in Europe dates from about 2400 BC. Though there have been periodic excavations of the mound since the 17th century, its original purpose remains unknown. The viewing area, less than 1 mile east of Avebury, is open only during daylight hours, but there's no direct access to the mound itself ✉ *Avebury* ✢ *A4, 1 mile west of West Kennett* 🌐 *www.english-heritage.org.uk.*

West Kennet Avenue. Lined with what remains of the original 100 standing stones, spaced 80 feet apart, this 1½-mile path was once a prehistoric processional way leading to the stone circles at Avebury. Only the half mile nearest the main monument survives intact. The lost stones are marked with concrete obelisks. ✉ *Avebury* ✢ *Off B4003, south of Avebury* ☎ *01672/539250* 🌐 *www.english-heritage.org.uk* 🎫 *Free* ⏲ *Dawn–dusk.*

WHERE TO EAT AND STAY

$ BRITISH ✕ **Waggon and Horses.** A 17th-century thatched-roof building with foundations made from sarsen stones, this traditional inn and pub is a two-minute drive from the Avebury stone circle (the beer garden has views of Silbury Hill). Dickens mentioned the building in the *Pickwick Papers.* Excellent lunches and dinners are served beside a fire; homemade dishes include duck leg in a port, blackberry, and thyme sauce; wild boar, with apple and sage sausages; and a butternut squash, sage, and blue cheese risotto. In high season it's something of a tourist hub. [$] *Average main: £11* ✉ *Beckhampton* ✢ *A4, 300 feet east of junction with A361* ☎ *01672/539418* 🌐 *www.waggonandhorsesbeckhampton.co.uk.*

$$$ B&B/INN **The Lodge.** With their eclectic design, rare prints, and antique furnishings, the two spacious guest rooms of this charming B&B are full of character. **Pros:** unique location and views; comfortable rooms; friendly host. **Cons:** can book up; expensive. [$] *Rooms from: £175* ✉ *Rawlings Park* ✢ *Off A4361* ☎ *01672/539023* 🌐 *www.aveburylodge.co.uk* 2 *rooms* 🍽 *Breakfast.*

LONGLEAT HOUSE

31 miles southwest of Avebury, 6 miles north of Stourhead, 19 miles south of Bath, 27 miles northwest of Salisbury.

With its popular safari park and a richly decorated High Elizabethan house to explore, Longleat can provide a day of diversions.

GETTING HERE AND AROUND

Longleat House is off A36 between Bath and Salisbury. The nearest train station is Warminster, about 5 miles away. Your best option is to take a taxi from there.

ESSENTIALS

Visitor Information Warminster Information Centre. ✉ *Central car park, off Station Rd., Warminster* ☎ *01985/218548* 🌐 *warminsterinfocentre.co.uk.*

EXPLORING

FAMILY Fodor's Choice ★ **Longleat House.** Home of the Marquess of Bath, Longleat House is one of southern England's most famous private estates, and possibly the most ambitiously, even eccentrically, commercialized, as evidenced by the presence of a drive-through safari park (open since 1966) with giraffes, zebras, monkeys, rhinos, and lions. The house, considered to be one of the finest remaining examples of High Elizabethan, was largely completed in 1580 for more than £8,000, an astronomical sum at the time. It contains outstanding tapestries, paintings, porcelain, furniture, and one of the largest private collections of books in England (more than 40,000 volumes housed in seven libraries). Notable period features include Victorian kitchens, an Elizabethan minstrels' gallery, painted ceilings, and a great hall with massive wooden beams. In addition to 900 acres of parkland designed by Capability Brown and the safari park, the property has a butterfly garden, a miniature railway, an extensive (and fairly fiendish) hedge maze, and an "adventure castle," all of which make it extremely popular, particularly in summer and during school vacations. ■ **TIP→ You can easily spend a whole day here. Visit the house in the morning, when tours are more relaxed, and the safari park in the afternoon.** A first-come, first-served safari bus service is available (£5) for those arriving without their own transport. ✉ *Warminster* ✣ *Off A362* ☎ *01985/844400* 🌐 *www.longleat.co.uk* 🎫 *£32.95; house and grounds only £17.50* ⏲ *Feb., daily; early–mid-Mar., Fri.–Mon.; mid-Mar.–Nov., daily; mid-Nov.–early Dec., Fri.–Sun. Opens at 10, closing times vary between 5–7 (check website); last admission to Safari Park 1 hr before closing, to house 30 min before closing* ☞ *10% discount with online booking.*

WHERE TO STAY

$$ HOTEL **Bishopstrow House.** This ivy-covered Regency manor house set in 27 acres has been converted into a relaxed country-house hotel that combines well-chosen antiques with modern amenities. **Pros:** country-house ambience; impressive suites; friendly staff. **Cons:** expensive extras; lackluster spa. 💲 *Rooms from: £135* ✉ *Boreham Rd., Warminster* ☎ *01985/212312* 🌐 *www.bishopstrow.co.uk* *29 rooms, 3 suites* 🍽 *Breakfast.*

STOURHEAD

9 miles southwest of Longleat, 15 miles northeast of Sherborne, 30 miles west of Salisbury.

England has many memorable gardens, but Stourhead is one of the most glorious. Its centerpiece is a magnificent artificial lake surrounded by neoclassical temples, atmospheric grottos, and rare trees. The Palladian stately home is also worth a look.

GETTING HERE AND AROUND

By car, you can reach Stourhead via B3092. It's signposted off the main road. From London, board a train to Gillingham and take a five-minute cab ride to Stourton.

4

EXPLORING

Fodor's Choice ★ **Stourhead.** Close to the village of Stourton lies one of Wiltshire's most breathtaking sights—Stourhead, a country-house-and-garden combination that has few parallels for beauty anywhere in Europe. Most of Stourhead was built between 1721 and 1725 by the wealthy banker Henry Hoare, more colorfully known as Henry the Magnificent. A fire gutted the center of the house in 1902, but it was reconstructed with only a few differences. Many rooms in the Palladian mansion contain Chinese and French porcelain, and some have furniture by Chippendale. The elegant Regency library and picture gallery were built for the cultural enrichment of this cultivated family. Still, the house takes second place to the adjacent gardens designed by Henry Hoare II, which are the most celebrated example of the English 18th-century taste for "natural" landscaping. Temples, grottoes, follies, and bridges have been placed among shrubs, trees, and flowers to make the grounds look like a three-dimensional oil painting. A walk around the artificial lake (1½ miles) reveals changing vistas that conjure up the 17th-century landscapes of Claude Lorrain and Nicolas Poussin; walk counterclockwise for the best views. **■ TIP→ The best time to visit is early summer, when the massive banks of rhododendrons are in full bloom, or mid-October for autumn color, but the gardens are beautiful at any time of year.** You can get a fine view of the surrounding area from Alfred's Tower, a 1772 folly (a structure built for picturesque effect). A restaurant and plant shop are on the grounds. All in all, it's easy to spend half a day here. To tie in with the WWI centennial commemorations, a new property-wide exhibit tells "Harry's Story," about the son of the last private owner, one of the many soldiers who died in the conflict. ✉ *Stourton* ✣ *Off B3092, near Mere* ☎ *01747/841152* 🌐 *www.nationaltrust.org.uk* 🎫 *House £13.70; gardens £8.30; Alfred's Tower £3.40* 🕒 *House Feb.–late Oct., daily 11–4:30; late Oct.–Dec., 11–3:30. Gardens Apr.–Sept., daily 9–6; Oct.–Mar., daily 9–5. Alfred's Tower Aug.–Oct, weekends noon–4; last entry 30 min before closing.*

WHERE TO STAY

$$ B&B/INN **The Spread Eagle.** You can't stay at Stourhead, but you can stay at this popular inn built at the beginning of the 19th century just inside the main entrance. **Pros:** period character; lovely rooms; free access to Stourhead. **Cons:** needs some modernization; food can be disappointing and service brusque. 💲 *Rooms from: £120* ✉ *Church Lawn, near*

Warminster, Stourton ☎ *01747/840587* 🌐 *www.spreadeagleinn.com* ⇨ *5 rooms* 🍽 *Breakfast.*

NEW FOREST, DORSET, AND THE SOUTH COAST

The New Forest, a woodland southwest of Southampton, was once a hunting preserve of William the Conqueror, so he could pursue his favorite sport close to the royal seat at Winchester. Thus protected from the worst of the deforestation that has befallen most of southern England's other forests, this relatively undeveloped, scenic national park has great possibilities for walking, riding, and biking. West of here stretches the largely unspoiled county of Dorset, which encompasses the beaches, coves, rolling hills, and lush fields that were the setting for most of Thomas Hardy's books, including *Far from the Madding Crowd*, and other classic Victorian-era novels. "I am convinced that it is better for a writer to know a little bit of the world remarkably well than to know a great part of the world remarkably little," Hardy wrote, and the bit he chose to know was the towns, villages, and countryside of this rural area, not least the county capital, Dorchester, an ancient agricultural center. North of here is the picturesque market town of Sherborne, with its impressive abbey. Other places of historic interest, such as Maiden Castle and the Cerne Abbas giant, are close to the bustling seaside resorts of Bournemouth and Weymouth. You may find Lyme Regis (associated with 20th-century novelist John Fowles) and the villages along the route closer to your ideal of coastal England. Fossil enthusiasts should head for the Jurassic Coast.

LYNDHURST

26 miles southeast of Stonehenge, 18 miles southeast of Salisbury, 9 miles west of Southampton.

Lyndhurst is famous as the capital of the New Forest. Although some popular spots can get crowded in summer, there are ample parking lots, picnic areas, and campgrounds. Miles of trails crisscross the region.

GETTING HERE AND AROUND

From Salisbury, follow A36, B3079, and continue along A337 another 4 miles or so. To explore the New Forest, take A35 out of Lyndhurst (the road continues southwest to Bournemouth) or A337 south. The New Forest Tour is a hop-on, hop-off open-top bus. Regular bus services are operated by Bluestar and Wilts & Dorset. Many parts of the New Forest are readily accessible by train from London via the centrally located Brockenhurst Station.

TOUR INFORMATION

New Forest Tour. The bus runs three circular routes with hourly departures through the New Forest daily between July and mid-September; all-day hop on-hop off tickets, beginning at £14, are purchased onboard. 🌐 *www.thenewforesttour.info.*

New Forest, Dorset, and the South Coast

ESSENTIALS

Visitor Information Lyndhurst Visitor Information Centre. ✉ *Main Car Park, High St.* ☎ *023/8028–2269* 🌐 *www.thenewforest.co.uk.*

EXPLORING

Fodor's Choice ★ **New Forest.** This national park, still largely owned by the Crown, consists of 150 square miles of woodland, heaths, grassland, bogs, and the remains of coppices and timber plantations established in the 17th–19th centuries. Residents have had grazing rights since the 12th century, and you can still encounter free-roaming cattle, and, most famously, the hardy New Forest ponies. An extensive network of trails makes it a wonderful place for biking, walking, and horseback riding. ✉ *Lyndhurst* 🌐 *www.thenewforest.co.uk* 🎫 *Free.*

FAMILY **New Forest Centre Museum.** This visitor complex contains displays and activities related to the area's geology, history, wildlife, and culture. Quizzes and other interactive elements keep children engaged. ✉ *Main car park, High St.* ☎ *023/8028–3444* 🌐 *www.newforestcentre.org.uk* 🎫 *£4* 🕒 *Daily 10–5; last entry at 4.*

St. Michael and All Angels. Lyndhurst's High Street is dominated by this imposing redbrick, a Victorian gothic church, notable for its stained glass windows designed by Pre-Raphaelites William Morris and Edward Burne-Jones, as well as a large fresco of the Parable of the Wise and

Foolish Virgins by Frederick Leighton. Fans of Lewis Carroll's *Alice in Wonderland* should note that Alice Hargreaves (née Liddell), the inspiration for the fictional Alice, is buried in the churchyard. ✉ *High St.* ☎ *023/8028–3175* 🌐 *www.newforestparishes.com.*

WHERE TO EAT AND STAY

$$ MODERN BRITISH ✕ **The Pig.** Funkier sister of glamorous Lime Wood, this New Forest "restaurant with rooms" puts the emphasis on localism and seasonality and is a local favorite. Lunch and dinner are served in a large Victorian greenhouse overlooking lawns, and 95% of the ingredients come from the premises or other sources within 25 miles. The frequently changing menu may include dishes like a pulled-pork croquette and blackberry salad, or roast-wood pigeon breasts with foraged oyster mushrooms. As the name suggests, porcine dishes feature prominently. You may accompany the "staff forager" on expeditions to find shellfish or edible flora like wild garlic and berries. Overnight in one of the 26 comfortable rooms in the main building (an 18th-century former royal hunting lodge) or the converted stable block. All combine a slightly retro, shabby-chic style with modern bathrooms. $ *Average main: £16* ✉ *Beaulieu Rd., Brockenhurst* ☎ *01590/622354* 🌐 *www.thepighotel.com.*

$$$$ HOTEL Fodor's Choice ★ **Chewton Glen Hotel and Spa.** This grand early-19th-century country-house hotel and spa on extensive manicured grounds ranks among Britain's most acclaimed—and most expensive—lodgings. **Pros:** classic English luxury; top-notch leisure facilities; high staff-to-guest ratio. **Cons:** expensive rates; breakfast not included in basic rate. $ *Rooms from: £415* ✉ *Christchurch Rd., New Milton* ☎ *01425/275341, 800/344–5087 in U.S.* 🌐 *www.chewtonglen.com* *35 rooms, 23 suites, 12 treehouse suites* 🍽 *Some meals.*

$$$$ HOTEL Fodor's Choice ★ **Lime Wood.** If you're looking for a discreet, luxurious hideaway in a woodland setting with uninterrupted views and an excellent spa, this hugely relaxing country-house hotel is hard to beat. **Pros:** great location; stylish yet comfortable design; friendly staff. **Cons:** hard to reach without a car; breakfast not included; pricey. $ *Rooms from: £295* ✉ *Beaulieu Rd.* ☎ *023/8028–7177* 🌐 *www.limewoodhotel.co.uk* *14 rooms, 15 suites* 🍽 *No meals.*

$ B&B/INN **Rufus House.** Personal service and easy access to the New Forest are the draws at this turreted Victorian house close to Lyndhurst run by a Japanese-Italian couple. **Pros:** friendly owners; delicious breakfasts; great location. **Cons:** traffic noise in front rooms; some rooms and beds are small; weak pressure in some showers. $ *Rooms from: £80* ✉ *Southampton Rd.* ☎ *023/8028–2930* 🌐 *www.rufushouse.co.uk* *8 rooms* 🍽 *Breakfast.*

SPORTS AND THE OUTDOORS

Largely unspoiled and undeveloped, yet accessible even to those not normally given to long walks or bike rides, the New Forest provides numerous opportunities to explore the outdoors. Bike rental and horseback riding are widely available. Numerous trails lead through thickly wooded country, across open heaths, and through the occasional bog. With very few hills, it's fairly easy terrain, and rich with wildlife. You're almost guaranteed to see wild ponies and deer, and occasionally free-roaming cattle and pigs.

BIKING

Cycle Experience. Bike rentals from £17 per day allow you to explore a range of trails weaving through the New Forest, one of Britain's best terrains for off-road biking. ✉ *2 Brookley Rd., Brockenhurst* ☎ *01590/624204* 🌐 *www.cyclex.co.uk.*

HORSEBACK RIDING

FAMILY **Burley Manor Riding Stables.** There are rides for all levels at Burley Manor Riding Stables. Hour-long rides are £35. ✉ *Burley Manor Hotel, 1 Ringwood Rd., Burley* ☎ *01425/403489* 🌐 *www.burleymanorridingstables.com.*

WALKING

New Forest walks. The area is crisscrossed with short, easy trails, as well as longer hikes. For an easy walk (about 4 miles), start from Lyndhurst and head directly south for Brockenhurst, a commuter village. The path goes through woods, pastureland, and heath—and you'll see plenty of New Forest ponies. ✉ *Lyndhurst.*

4

BEAULIEU

7 miles southeast of Lyndhurst.

The unspoiled village of Beaulieu (pronounced *byoo*-lee) has three major attractions in one at Beaulieu Abbey and is near the museum village of Buckler's Hard.

GETTING HERE AND AROUND

Beaulieu is best reached by car on B3056 from Lyndhurst or B3054 from Lymington. It's signposted off A326 from Southampton. Bus 112 has a limited service (twice daily on Tuesday and Thursday, once on Saturday) between Beaulieu and Lymington and Hythe, except during August, when it becomes the "Beach Bus" and runs daily. During the summer, the New Forest Tour bus extends to Beaulieu.

EXPLORING

FAMILY **Beaulieu.** With a ruined 13th-century abbey, a stately home, and an automobile museum, Beaulieu appeals to several different interests. **Beaulieu Abbey** was founded in 1204 by Cistercian monks on land given to them by King John (the name means "beautiful place" in French.) You can still see the ruins of the cloister and the herb garden, as well as two remaining buildings, one containing an exhibition re-creating daily life in the monastery. **Palace House** incorporates the abbey's original 14th-century gatehouse and has been the home of the Montagu family since they purchased it in 1538, after the dissolution of the monasteries, when the abbey was badly damaged. You can explore the drawing rooms, dining halls, fine family portraits, and the beautiful grounds. The present Lord Montagu established the **National Motor Museum,** which traces the history of British motoring. The collection contains more than 250 classic cars and motorcycles, from late 19th-century vehicles to futuristic F1 racing cars, plus galleries devoted to popular British TV show *Top Gear* (complete with test track) and famous film cars like

Mr. Bean's Mini. Other museum attractions include interactive experiences, audiovisual displays, and rides in vehicles ranging from a monorail to a 1912 London bus. ✉ *Beaulieu* ✥ *Off B3056* ☎ *01590/612345* 🌐 *www.beaulieu.co.uk* 🎫 *Abbey, Palace House, and Motor Museum £24* ⏲ *Late May–late Sept., daily 10–6; late Sept.–late May, daily 10–5.*

FAMILY **Buckler's Hard.** This restored 18th-century shipbuilding village, 2 miles south of Beaulieu, is home to a re-created Shipwright's Cottage and a Shipwright's School in a replica 18th-century timber workshop, where courses are given in traditional shipbuilding techniques. There's also a fascinating **Maritime Museum**, which traces the village's role in British history, including the building of Nelson's warships (the New Forest lost many of its trees from the 16th to 18th centuries, when it served as the principal source of timber for British Navy ships). April through October, you can take a cruise on the privately owned Beaulieu River. The **Master Builder's House Hotel** has a bar and restaurant. ✉ *Off B3056* ☎ *01590/616203* 🌐 *www.bucklershard.co.uk* 🎫 *£6.50; river cruise £5* ⏲ *Easter.–Sept., daily 10–5; Oct.–Easter., daily 10–4:30; last entry 30 min before closing.*

EN ROUTE From Beaulieu, take any of the minor roads leading west through wide-open heathland to Lymington and pick up A337 for the popular seaside resort of Bournemouth, a journey of about 18 miles.

BOURNEMOUTH

26 miles southwest of Southampton, 26 miles south of Salisbury, 24 miles east of Dorchester.

Bournemouth has 7 miles of beaches, and the waters are said to be some of southern England's most pristine. The resort was founded in 1810 by Lewis Tregonwell, an ex-army officer. He settled near what is now the Square and planted the first pine trees in the distinctive steep little valleys—or chines—cutting through the cliffs to the Bournemouth sands. The scent of fir trees was said to be healing for consumption (tuberculosis) sufferers, and the town grew steadily.

Today the city has expanded to swallow up neighboring settlements, making it a somewhat amorphous sprawl on first view. Its stodgier, more traditional side is kept in check by the presence of a lively student population—partly made up of foreign-language students from abroad. Gardens laid out with trees and lawns link the Square and the beach. This is an excellent spot to relax and listen to music wafting from the Pine Walk bandstand. Regular musical programs take place at the Pavilion.

GETTING HERE AND AROUND

From the New Forest, take A35 or A31/A338 southwest to Bournemouth. The center of town is best explored on foot, but to reach East Cliff or Boscombe you need to drive or hop aboard the frequent local buses. Fast trains from London take about two hours.

ESSENTIALS

Visitor Information Bournemouth Tourist Information Centre. ✉ *Westover Rd., near bandstand* ☎ *0845/051–1700* 🌐 *www.bournemouth.co.uk.*

EXPLORING

FAMILY **Bournemouth Beach.** With 7 miles of clean sandy beaches tucked beneath its cliffs, Bournemouth is said to enjoy some of the country's warmest sea temperatures. You can descend to the seafront either by taking the zigzag paths through the public gardens near Bournemouth Pier (where there's a family-friendly amusement arcade) or by taking the three outdoor elevators from the cliffs. If you're not tempted to swim, you can stroll along the nearby promenade. Book well in advance, you can hire a beach hut (from £12–45 per day, £40–180 per week) or innovative beach pod with kitchenette on Boscombe Beach (from £70–315 per week) to provide a restful viewing spot or shelter from the changeable English weather. Europe's first artificial **surf reef** attracts surf fans as well as creating an area of calm water that's perfect for children—surfers, however, have reported that the reef is more suitable for bodyboarding than standing up. Windsurfing, sailing, and other water sports are also big here. **Amenities**: food and drink; lifeguards; parking (from £1 an hour); water sports. **Best for:** walking. ✉ *Westover Rd.* ☎ *0845/051–1700.*

4

Russell-Cotes Art Gallery and Museum. Perched on East Cliff, this lavish late-Victorian villa overflows with sculpture, paintings, and artifacts, including cases of butterflies and an exquisite suit of Japanese armor—just a few of the treasures collected from around the world by Russell-Cotes, a widely traveled Victorian couple. The house, a combination of Italian Renaissance and Scottish Baronial, with added Moorish-, Japanese-, and French-themed rooms, was designed to showcase the collection. There's also a small landscaped garden and café. The museum hosts temporary exhibitions, as well, such as ones devoted to female artists, or to art-nouveau master Alphonse Mucha. ✉ *East Cliff* ☎ *01202/451800* 🌐 *www.russell-cotes.bournemouth.gov.uk* *Oct.–Mar. free; Apr.–Sept. £5* ⏰ *Tues.–Sun. and holiday Mon. 10–5.*

St. Peter's Church. This parish church is easily recognizable by its 200-foot-high tower and spire. Lewis Tregonwell, founder and developer of Bournemouth, is buried in the churchyard. Here, too, is the elaborate tombstone of Mary Shelley, author of *Frankenstein* and wife of the great Romantic poet Percy Bysshe Shelley, whose heart is buried with her. ✉ *Hinton Rd.* ☎ *01202/290986* 🌐 *btcp.org.uk.*

WHERE TO EAT AND STAY

$$ SEAFOOD ✕ **WestBeach.** Superbly positioned on the marine promenade, close to Bournemouth Pier, this fish restaurant serves the best seafood in town, whether grilled, baked, or in fish pies and stews. The menu usually lists haddock, wild locally caught sea bass, plaice, and shellfish (local oysters, crab, mussels, clams, lobster). Non-fish dishes may include beef fillet steak or a Mediterranean vegetable risotto. Simple wooden tables and a large glass front lend a modern, minimalist feel, and there's a narrow deck and terrace for open-air dining and excellent views over sea and sand. In summer, pick up ice cream and snacks from the adjacent stand. [$] *Average main: £18* ✉ *Pier Approach* ☎ *01202/587785* 🌐 *www.west-beach.co.uk.*

$$ HOTEL **The Urban Beach.** A short walk from the seafront and a 10-minute drive from Bournemouth's center, this funky boutique hotel

provides the contemporary style and energy so needed by the town. **Pros:** designer decor; friendly staff; great food. **Cons:** not central; rooms over bar can be noisy. *Rooms from: £130 ✉ 23 Argyll Rd., Boscombe ☎ 01202/301509 🌐 www.urbanbeachhotel.co.uk 12 rooms 🍴 Breakfast.*

$ B&B/INN **Wood Lodge Hotel.** Small and sedate, this family-run hotel in an Edwardian building near the shore is good value. **Pros:** welcoming staff; close to beach; reasonable rates. **Cons:** some bathrooms need improving; upper-floor shower water pressure may be weak. *Rooms from: £85 ✉ 10 Manor Rd., East Cliff ☎ 01202/290891 🌐 www.woodlodgehotel.co.uk 15 rooms 🍴 Breakfast.*

WIMBORNE MINSTER

7 miles northwest of Bournemouth.

The impressive minster of this quiet market town makes it seem like a miniature cathedral city. The town is exceptionally quiet on Sunday.

GETTING HERE AND AROUND

To reach Wimborne Minster from central Bournemouth, take any main road heading west, following signs for A341 or A349, or take advantage of the regular bus service.

ESSENTIALS

Visitor Information Wimborne Minster Tourist Information Centre. *✉ 29 High St. ☎ 01202/886116 🌐 www.visit-dorset.com/tourist-information.*

EXPLORING

Kingston Lacy. Sir Charles Barry, co-architect of the Houses of Parliament in London, created this grand 19th-century country house built to resemble a 17th-century Italian palazzo. It contains notable paintings by Titian, Rubens, Van Dyck, and Velásquez, as well as a fabulous Spanish Room lined with gilded leather and topped by an ornate Venetian ceiling. There's also a fine collection of Egyptian artifacts. Formal gardens (including a Japanese garden with a tea house) and extensive parkland with walking paths surround the house. *✉ Wimborne Minster ✢ Off B3082, 1½ miles northwest of Wimborne Minster ☎ 01202/883402 🌐 www.nationaltrust.org.uk £13; grounds and garden only £7.25 ⏲ House Mar.–Oct., Wed.–Sun. 11–5; last admission at 4; Mon.–Tues., 11–3:40, admission by guided tour only (every 20 min); Nov., daily 11–3. Dec. until Christmas, daily 11–6. Garden and grounds Mar.–Oct., daily 10:30–6; Nov., Jan., and Feb., daily 10:30–4; Dec., daily 10:30–7.*

Priest's House Museum & Garden. With an emphasis on local archeological finds (largely Roman and Iron Age), costume, and history, this museum in an Elizabethan town house charts the development of the East Dorset area. You can see how residents might have lived in the house through rooms furnished in several period styles, including a 17th-century hall and working Victorian kitchen. In the garden are displays of agricultural and horticultural tools plus a tearoom. *✉ 23–27*

High St. ☎ 01202/882533 🌐 www.priest-house.co.uk 🎫 £5.50 ⏲ Apr.–Oct., Mon.–Sat. 10–4:30; Nov.–Christmas, Feb., and Mar., Mon.–Sat. 10:30–3.

Wimborne Minster. Although there has been a church here since the 8th century, the current building, with its crenellated and pinnacled twin towers, was built between 1120 and 1180. The nave reflects the Norman influence in its zigzag molding interspersed with carved heads. Several Gothic components were added later, as were fine Victorian geometric tiles and stained glass windows. Don't miss the late 17th-century chained library, one of the first public libraries in Britain and still the second largest. Its collection includes a 14th-century manuscript and a 1522 book with a title page designed by Hans Holbein. Also look out for the pre-Copernican astronomical clock, which dates to before the 15th century. It's on the inside wall of the west tower. ✉ *High St.* ☎ *01202/884753* 🌐 *www.wimborneminster.org.uk* ⏲ *Church Mar.–Christmas., Mon.–Sat. 9:30–5:30, Sun. 2:30–5:30; Jan. and Feb., Mon.–Sat. 9:30–4, Sun. 2:30–5:30. Chained library Easter–Oct., weekdays 10:30–12:30 and 2–4, Sat. 10–12:30; Nov.–Easter, Sat. 10–12:30 or by arrangement.*

WHERE TO STAY

$$ B&B/INN Fodor's Choice ★ **Museum Inn.** It's worth seeking out this characterful inn, located 10 miles north of Wimborne Minster, in an Area of Outstanding Natural Beauty. **Pros:** pretty village location; great food. **Cons:** car required. [$] *Rooms from: £130* ✉ *Farnham* ✣ *Off A354, near Blandford Forum* ☎ *01725/516261* 🌐 *www.museuminn.co.uk* *8 rooms* *Breakfast.*

CORFE CASTLE

25 miles south of Wimborne Minster, 15 miles south of Poole, 5 miles southeast of Wareham.

The village of Corfe Castle is best known for the ancient, ruined castle that overlooks it.

ESSENTIALS

Visitor Information Discover Purbeck Information Centre. ✉ *Wareham Library, South St., Corfe* ☎ *01929/552740* 🌐 *www.visit-dorset.com.*

EXPLORING

Corfe Castle. One of the most dramatic ruins in Britain, Corfe Castle overlooks the picturesque gray limestone village of the same name. The present ruins are of the castle built in 1086, when the great central keep was erected by William the Conqueror to guard the principal route through the surrounding Purbeck Hills. The outer walls and towers were added in the 1270s. Cromwell's soldiers blew up the castle in 1646 during the Civil War, after a long siege during which its Royalist chatelaine, Lady Bankes, led its defense. ✉ *A351, Corfe* ✣ *Off A351, in Corfe Castle* ☎ *01929/481294* 🌐 *www.nationaltrust.org.uk* 🎫 *£7.72 (£8.18 weekends and during school vacations and national holidays* ⏲ *Mar. and Oct., daily 10–5; Apr.–Sept., daily 10–6; Nov.–Feb., daily 10–4.*

4

OFF THE BEATEN PATH

Clouds Hill. This brick-and-tile cottage served as the retreat of T.E. Lawrence (Lawrence of Arabia) before he was killed in a motorcycle accident on the road from Bovington in 1935. The house remains very much as he left it, with photos and memorabilia from his time in the Middle East. It's particularly atmospheric on a gloomy day, as there's no electric light. Clouds Hill is 8 miles northwest of Corfe. ✉ *King George V Rd., Morton* ☎ *01929/405616* 🌐 *www.nationaltrust.org.uk* 🎫 *£6.50* ⏲ *Mid-Mar.–Oct., Wed.–Sun. and holiday Mon. 11–5; last admission 4:30 or dusk.*

FAMILY **Swanage Railway.** Train enthusiasts love this largely volunteer-run railroad that makes 25-minute, 6-mile scenic trips, with steam (and some diesel) locomotives pulling vintage train carriages across the Isle of Purbeck—actually a peninsula. Trips begin from Norden in the center and go to the seaside town of Swanage via Corfe Castle. Small, pretty stations with flower baskets, painted signs, and water bowls for dogs add to the excursion's charm. Trains leave approximately every 80 minutes in low season, and every 40 minutes in high season. ✉ *Station House, Springfield Rd., Swanage* ☎ *01929/425800* 🌐 *www.swanagerailway.co.uk* 🎫 *£2.50–£12.50* ⏲ *Late Mar.–Oct., school holidays, daily 10–5:20; Nov.–late Mar., weekends 10–4.*

WHERE TO EAT AND STAY

$ BRITISH ✕ **Castle Inn.** This family-run traditional pub has flagstones, bare stone walls, an inglenook fireplace, an open fire in winter, and a beer garden in the summer. The homemade food leans towards the traditional, with superior versions of old favorites like steak-and-ale pie, along with local specialties like fresh crab, pan-fried sea bass, and oysters, plus local Purbeck-brand salted caramel ice cream for dessert. The Sunday roast lunch aims to source everything within 3 miles and be organic. The beer selection is highly regarded. The inn also has 11 rooms for guests who want to stay the night. $ *Average main: £12* ✉ *63 East St.* ☎ *01929/480208* 🌐 *www.castleinncorfe.com.*

$$$ HOTEL Fodor's Choice ★ **The Pig at the Beach.** This latest outpost of the Hampshire luxury mini-chain is in a former Victorian Gothic private residence in an unspoiled village on the scenic, peaceful Studland Peninsula. **Pros:** beautiful location; comfortable bedrooms and welcoming public rooms; excellent restaurant. **Cons:** not many bad-weather activities; breakfast not included. $ *Rooms from: £165* ✉ *Manor House, Manor Rd.* ☎ *01929/450288* 🌐 *www.thepighotel.com/on-the-beach* *23 rooms, 2 cottages, 1 hut* 🍽 *No meals.*

DORCHESTER

21 miles west of Corfe, 30 miles west of Bournemouth, 43 miles southwest of Salisbury.

The traditional market town of Dorchester was immortalized as Casterbridge by Thomas Hardy in his 19th-century novel *The Mayor of Casterbridge*. In fact, the whole area around here, including a number of villages tucked away in the rolling hills of Dorset, has become known as "Hardy country" because of its connection with the author. Hardy was born in a cottage in the hamlet of Higher Bockhampton, about

The ruins of Corfe Castle, destroyed during the 17th-century English Civil War, are evocative after a snowfall.

3 miles northeast of the town, and his bronze statue looks westward from a bank on Colliton Walk. Two important historical sites, as well as the author's birthplace and a former residence, are a short drive from Dorchester.

Dorchester has many reminders of its Roman heritage. A stroll along Bowling Alley Walk, West Walk, and Colliton Walk follows the approximate line of the original Roman town walls, part of a city plan laid out around AD 70. On the north side of Colliton Park is an excavated Roman villa with a marvelously preserved mosaic floor. While the high street in the center of town can be busy with vehicular traffic, the tourist office has walking itineraries that cover the main points of interest along quieter routes and help you appreciate the character of Dorchester today.

GETTING HERE AND AROUND

Dorchester can be reached from Corfe Castle via A351 and A352. From Salisbury take A354. Park wherever you can (pay parking lots are scattered around the center) and explore the town on foot.

ESSENTIALS

Visitor Information Dorchester Tourist Information Centre. ✉ *11 Antelope Walk* ☎ *01305/267992* 🌐 *www.visit-dorset.com.*

EXPLORING

TOP ATTRACTIONS

Athelhampton House and Gardens. This outstandingly well-preserved example of 15th-century domestic Tudor architecture (with 16th- and 20th-century additions) turns up as Athelhall in some of Thomas

Hardy's writings (Hardy was a frequent visitor and his father, a stonemason, worked on the house). Don't miss the Great Hall, built in 1485, still with its original linenfold paneling, heraldic stained glass, and vaulted timber roof. The paneled Library contains more than 3,000 books. Outside, 20 acres of grounds include eight formal walled gardens created in the 19th century and 12 yew pyramids, each 30 feet high. ✉ *Dorchester* ✣ *A35, 5 miles east of Dorchester* ☎ *01305/848363* 🌐 *www.athelhampton.co.uk* 🎫 *£13* ⏲ *Mar.–Oct., Sun.–Thurs. 10:30–5; Nov.–Feb., Sun. 11–dusk.*

Dorset County Museum. This labyrinthine museum contains eclectic collections devoted to nearby Roman and Celtic archeological finds, Jurassic Coast geology, social history (especially rural crafts and agriculture), decorative arts, regional costumes, and local literary luminaries, primarily Hardy but also T.E. Lawrence and others. ✉ *High West St.* ☎ *01305/262735* 🌐 *www.dorsetcountymuseum.org* 🎫 *£6.35* ⏲ *Apr.–Oct., Mon.–Sat. 10–5; Nov.–Mar., Mon.–Sat. 10–4.*

QUICK BITES

Potters Café Bistro. Drop into Potters Café, in a 17th-century cottage, for cream teas and delicious cakes and pastries, as well as homemade soups and panini. The lunch specials, such as smoked haddock fishcakes or cassoulet, are excellent, and the pleasant courtyard garden provides outdoor seating, weather permitting. ✉ ***19 Durngate St.*** ☎ ***01305/260312.***

Maiden Castle. Although called a castle, this is actually one of the most important pre-Roman archaeological sites in England and the largest, most complex Iron Age hill fort in Europe, made of stone and earth with ramparts that enclose about 45 acres. England's Neolithic inhabitants built the fort some 4,000 years ago, and many centuries later it was a Celtic stronghold. In AD 43 invading Romans, under the general (later emperor) Vespasian, stormed the fort. Finds from the site are on display in the Dorset County Museum in Dorchester. To experience an uncanny silence and sense of mystery, climb Maiden Castle early in the day. Leave your car in the lot at the end of Maiden Castle Way, a 1½-mile lane. ✉ *Winterborne Monkton* ✣ *Off A354, 2 miles southwest of Dorchester* ☎ *0370/333-1181* 🌐 *www.english-heritage.org.uk* ⏲ *Daily during daylight hours.*

WORTH NOTING

FAMILY **Dinosaur Museum.** This popular family-oriented museum engages children with fossils, skeletons, life-size dinosaur reconstructions, multimedia displays, and interactive exhibits. ✉ *Icen Way* ✣ *Off High East St.* ☎ *01305/269880* 🌐 *www.thedinosaurmuseum.com* 🎫 *£6.99* ⏲ *Apr.–Sept., daily 10–5; Oct.–Mar., daily 10–4. Closed mid–late Dec.*

Hardy's Cottage. Thomas Hardy's grandfather built this small thatch-and-cob cottage, where the writer was born in 1840, and little has changed since the family left. Here Hardy grew up and wrote many of his early works, including *Far from the Madding Crowd*, at a desk you can still see. Access is by foot only, via a walk through woodland or down a country lane from the parking lot. There's a new visitor center with information about the surrounding landscape and trails that let you follow in Hardy's footsteps. ✉ *Brockhampton La., Higher*

CLOSE UP

Hardy's Dorset

Among this region's proudest claims is its connection with Thomas Hardy (1840–1928), one of England's most celebrated novelists. If you read some of Hardy's novels before visiting Dorset—evoked as Hardy's part-fact, part-fiction county of Wessex—you may well recognize some places immediately from his descriptions. The tranquil countryside surrounding Dorchester is lovingly described in *Far from the Madding Crowd*, and Casterbridge, in *The Mayor of Casterbridge*, stands in for Dorchester itself. Any pilgrimage to Hardy's Wessex begins at the author's birthplace in Higher Bockhampton, 3 miles east of Dorchester. Salisbury makes an appearance as "Melchester" in *Jude the Obscure*. North of Dorchester, walk in the footsteps of Jude Fawley by visiting the village of Shaftesbury—"Shaston" and its steep Gold Hill, a street lined with cottages. It is still possible get a sense of the landscapes and streetscapes that inspired the writer, and any trip will give his books a greater resonance for readers.

4

Bockhampton ✢ *½ mile south of Blandford Rd.* ☎ *01305/262366* 🌐 *www.nationaltrust.org.uk* 🎫 *£6* ⏲ *Mid-Mar.–Oct., Wed.–Sun. and holiday Mon. 11–5; last admission 4:30.*

Maumbury Rings. This large Neolithic henge, 278 feet in diameter, is the oldest monument in Dorchester. It's survived by adapting. In the 1st century AD it became a Roman amphitheater, one of the largest in Britain, and the site of gladiatorial contests and executions. In the Middle Ages it was used for jousting tournaments, while during the English Civil War it was converted into an artillery fort. After the Restoration, it once again became a place of public execution, notoriously that of 80 rebels ordered by the infamous Judge Jeffreys. Vividly evoked in Hardy's *Mayor of Casterbridge*, it's now used for public events such as the Dorset Arts Festival. ✉ *Maumbury Rd.* ✢ *Off Weymouth Ave.* 🌐 *www.visit-dorchester.co.uk.*

Max Gate. Thomas Hardy lived in Max Gate from 1885 until his death in 1928. An architect by profession, Hardy designed the house himself, and visitors can now see the study where he wrote *Tess of the d'Urbevilles, The Mayor of Casterbridge,* and *Jude the Obscure.* The dining room, the drawing room, and the garden are open to the public. ✉ *Off Syward Rd.* ✢ *1 mile east of Dorchester* ☎ *01305/262538* 🌐 *www.nationaltrust.org.uk* 🎫 *£6* ⏲ *Mar.–Oct., Wed.–Sun. and holiday Mon. 11–5; last entry at 4:30.*

OFF THE BEATEN PATH

Poundbury. Owned by the Duchy of Cornwall and under the aegis of the Prince of Wales, this development in a traditional vernacular style showcases Prince Charles's vision of urban planning and community living. The emphasis is on conservation and energy efficiency; private houses coexist with shops, offices, small-scale factories, and leisure facilities. Central Pummery Square is dominated by the colonnaded Brownsword Hall. Dorchester's Farmers' Market is held in the Queen

Mother's Square the first Saturday of the month. Poundbury, a mile west of Dorchester on the B3150, has attracted the ire of modernist architects, but any properties for sale are quickly snapped up. ✉ *Poundbury* 🌐 *www.duchyofcornwall/poundbury.*

WHERE TO EAT AND STAY

$$ BRASSERIE ✕ **No. 6.** Just behind the County Museum, this pleasant neighborhood brasserie makes an ideal stop for a relaxed lunch or evening meal. Fresh fish comes in twice a day, so the weekly-changing menu may list locally caught sea bass in olive oil and herbs, monkfish, langoustines, or Portland crab, while for carnivores there's locally sourced game such as pheasant, hare, or venison marinated in thyme and port. The atmosphere is intimate without being chichi, and the tiled floor and sidewalk tables lend a Continental air. [$] *Average main: £18* ✉ *6 North Sq.* ☎ *01305/267679* 🌐 *www.no6-restaurant.co.uk* ⏲ *Closed Sun. and Mon.*

$$$ MODERN FRENCH ✕ **Yalbury Cottage.** Oak-beamed ceilings, exposed stone walls, and inglenook fireplaces add to the charm of this restaurant in 300-year-old cottage. It specializes in superior Modern French cooking using locally sourced produce, with dishes like seared Lyme Bay scallops, pork tenderloin in a sauce of local Blue Vinny cheese, and pan-fried Dorset Coast sea bass. A fixed-price dinner menu with two (£32) or three (£37.50) courses gives good value. Eight comfortable bedrooms are available in an extension overlooking gardens or fields. Lower Bockhampton is signposted off the A35, 1½ miles east of Dorchester. [$] *Average main: £24* ✉ *Bockhampton La., Lower Bockhampton* ☎ *01305/262382* 🌐 *www.yalburycottage.com* ⏲ *No dinner Sun. or Mon.*

$$ B&B/INN 🏨 **The Casterbridge.** Small but full of character, this family-owned inn in a Georgian building dating from 1790 is elegantly decorated with period antiques. **Pros:** central location; period setting; good breakfasts. **Cons:** traffic noise in front rooms; annex rooms are small and lack character; limited parking. [$] *Rooms from: £110* ✉ *49 High East St.* ☎ *01305/264043* 🌐 *www.thecasterbridge.co.uk* 🛏 *11 rooms* 🍽 *Breakfast.*

SHOPPING

Wednesday Market. This large traditional market sells organic local produce and Dorset delicacies such as Blue Vinny cheese (which some connoisseurs prefer to Blue Stilton), plus antiques. ✉ *Fairfield parking lot, off Weymouth Ave.* ⏲ *Wed. 8–3.*

SPORTS AND THE OUTDOORS

Thomas Hardy Society. From April through October, the Thomas Hardy Society organizes guided walks that follow in the steps of Hardy's novels. Readings and discussions accompany the walks, which range from a couple of hours to most of a day. ✉ *66 High West St.* ☎ *01305/251501* 🌐 *www.hardysociety.org.*

SHERBORNE

12 miles north of Cerne Abbas, 20 miles north of Dorchester, 15 miles west of Shaftesbury, 40 miles west of Wilton, 43 miles west of Salisbury.

Originally the capital of Wessex (the actual Saxon kingdom, not Hardy's retro conceit), this unspoiled market town is populated with medieval buildings built using the local honey-colored stone. The focal point of the winding streets is Sherborne Abbey, where King Alfred's older brothers are buried. Also worth visiting are the ruins of the 12th-century Old Castle and Sherborne Castle, a Tudor mansion originally built by Sir Walter Raleigh, and its Capability Brown–designed gardens.

GETTING HERE AND AROUND

Hourly trains from Salisbury take 45 minutes to reach Sherborne. The station is at the bottom of Digby Road, near the abbey. Drivers should take A30, passing through Shaftesbury.

ESSENTIALS

Visitor Information Sherborne Tourist Information Centre. ✉ *3 Tilton Ct., Digby Rd.* ☎ *01935/815341* 🌐 *www.visit-dorset.com.*

EXPLORING

Shaftesbury. The model for the town of Shaston in Thomas Hardy's *Jude the Obscure* is still a small market town. It sits on a ridge overlooking Blackmore Vale—you can catch a sweeping view of the surrounding countryside from the top of Gold Hill, a steep street lined with cottages so picturesque it was used in an iconic TV commercial to evoke the quintessential British village of yore. Shaftesbury is 20 miles west of Salisbury and 15 miles east of Sherborne. ✉ *Sherborne* ✣ *Intersection of A30 and A350* 🌐 *www.shaftesburytourism.co.uk.*

Sherborne Abbey. As much as the golden hamstone exterior, majestic tower, and fine flying buttresses impress, the glory of Sherbourne Abbey is the delicate 15th-century fan vaulting that extends the length of the soaring nave and choir. ("I would pit Sherborne's roof against any contemporary work of the Italian Renaissance," enthused Simon Jenkins in his *England's Thousand Best Churches.*) Some features from the original 8th-century cathedral, like the Saxon doorway in the northwest corner, still remain. If you're lucky, you might hear "Great Tom," one of the heaviest bells in the world, pealing out from the bell tower. Guided tours are run from April through September on Tuesday (10:30) and Friday (2:30), or by prior arrangement. ✉ *3 Abbey Close* ☎ *01935/812452* 🌐 *www.sherborneabbey.com* ⏲ *Apr.–Sept., daily 8–6; Oct.–Mar., daily 8–4.*

Fodor's Choice ★ **Sherborne Castle.** Built by Sir Walter Raleigh in 1594, this castle remained his home for 10 years before it passed to the custodianship of the Digby family. The castle has interiors from a variety of periods, including Tudor, Jacobean, and Georgian. The Victorian Gothic rooms are notable for their splendid plaster moldings on the ceiling. After admiring the extensive collections of Meissen and Asian porcelain, stroll around the lake and landscaped grounds (a designated English Heritage Grade I site), the work of Capability Brown. The house is less than a mile southeast of town. ✉ *New Rd.* ☎ *01935/812072* 🌐 *www.sherbornecastle.*

com ✉ *£11; gardens only £6* ⏲ *Apr.–Oct., Tues.–Thurs., holiday Mon., and weekends 11–5; last admission at 4:30.*

WHERE TO STAY

$ B&B/INN **The Alders.** This homey B&B, a secluded stone house set in an old walled garden opposite a 13th-century church, is in a quiet, unspoiled village 3 miles north of Sherborne. **Pros:** peaceful setting; hospitable owners. **Cons:** a bit remote; nothing to do in evening. $ *Rooms from: £70* ✉ *Sandford Orcas* ✣ *Off B3145* ☎ *01963/220666* 🌐 *www.thealdersbb.com* *3 rooms* *Breakfast.*

WEYMOUTH

8 miles south of Dorchester, 28 miles south of Sherbourne.

West Dorset's main coastal resort, Weymouth, is known for its sandy and pebble beaches and its royal connections. King George III began seawater bathing here for his health in 1789, setting a trend among the wealthy and fashionable of the day. The legacy of this popularity is Weymouth's many fine buildings, including the Georgian row houses lining the Esplanade. Striking historical details command attention: a wall on Maiden Street holds a cannonball that was embedded in it during the English Civil War, while a nearby column commemorates the embarkation of U.S. forces from Weymouth on D-Day.

Weymouth and its lively harbor provide the full bucket-and-spade seaside experience: donkey rides, sand castles, and plenty of fish-and-chips. Weymouth and Portland hosted the 2012 Olympic sailing events.

GETTING HERE AND AROUND

You can reach Weymouth on frequent local buses and trains from Dorchester, or on less frequent services from Bournemouth. The bus and train stations are close to each other near King's Statue, on the Esplanade. If you're driving, take A354 from Dorchester and park on or near the Esplanade—an easy walk from the center—or in a lot near the harbor.

EXPLORING

Fodor's Choice ★ **Chesil Beach.** The unique geological curiosity known as Chesil Beach is in fact not a beach but a tombolo, a thin strip of sand and shingle that joins two bits of land together. Part of the Jurassic Coast World Heritage Site, Chesil, 18 miles long, is remarkable for its pebbles that decrease in size from east to west. It's also known as the setting for Ian McEwan's novel *On Chesil Beach*. You can access the eastern section leading to the Isle of Portland (a peninsula) and the western section beyond Abbotsbury all year round. However, access to the central section is restricted, with its environmentally sensitive eastern side facing the shallow saltwater Fleet lagoon entirely off-limits and its western side closed April to August to protect nesting birds. The entire beach is better suited to walking and fossil hunting than sunbathing and swimming since powerful undertow makes the water dangerous (plus it's cold). There are walking and cycle trails along the rugged coastline. **Amenities:** parking (at five access points, £6.50 per day); toilets (at five access points). **Best for:** walking;

windsurfing. ✉ *Portland Beach Rd., Portland* ☎ *01305/206191* 🌐 *www.chesilbeach.org* 🎫 *£0.50–£8 parking.*

WHERE TO EAT

$ BRITISH ✕ **Old Rooms Inn.** This recently refurbished popular pub has great views over the harbor. The extensive menu ranges from wraps and salads to grilled steaks, curries, burgers, and comfort food. At lunch, there's a fixed-price menu (two courses £6.95, three courses £8.95). There are two separate dining areas and tables outside, or you can mix with the locals at the bar. 💲 *Average main: £8* ✉ *2 Cove Row* ☎ *01305/771130* 🌐 *www.oldroomsinnweymouth.co.uk.*

$ BISTRO ✕ **Time for Tea.** Tucked away from the busy harbor, this French-owned local favorite serves classic Gallic dishes and superlative baked goods. The onion soup, eggs Benedict, and croque monsieur are favorites. If you're looking for an afternoon pit stop, try the substantial, and very English, cream tea selection with homemade cakes and scones. A fixed-price dinner (£20 for two courses, £25 for three) is served on the third Friday and Saturday of each month only. 💲 *Average main: £8* ✉ *8 Cove St.* ☎ *01305/777500* 💳 *No credit cards* 🕒 *No dinner.*

4

ABBOTSBURY

10 miles northwest of Weymouth.

Pretty Abbotsbury is at the western end of Chesil Beach and has a swannery. In other parts of the village, you can also visit a children's farm, housed in an impressive medieval barn, and subtropical gardens.

GETTING HERE AND AROUND

By car, take B3157 from Weymouth, or the steep and very minor road passing through Martinstown off A35 from Dorchester; the latter route has marvelous views of the coast.

ESSENTIALS

Visitor Information Abbotsbury Tourism. ✉ *West Yard Barns, West St.* ☎ *01305/871130* 🌐 *www.abbotsbury.co.uk.*

EXPLORING

FAMILY **Abbotsbury Swannery.** This lagoon outside the village, a famous breeding ground for the birds, is the only managed colony of nesting mute swans in the world. Originally tended by Benedictine monks as a source of meat in winter, the swans have remained for centuries, drawn by the lagoon's soft, moist eelgrass—a favorite food—and fresh water. They now build nests in reeds provided by the swannery. Cygnets hatch between mid-May and late June. Try to visit during feeding time, at noon and 4 pm. ✉ *New Barn Rd.* ☎ *01305/871858* 🌐 *www.abbotsbury-tourism.co.uk/swannery* 🎫 *£11.50, £16 including subtropical gardens* 🕒 *Mid-Mar.–Oct., daily 10–5; last admission 1 hr before closing*

WHERE TO EAT

$$ MODERN BRITISH ✕ **The Seaside Boarding House.** Perched on a bluff overlooking sandy Burton beach, this airy restaurant in a hamlet at the western end of Chesil beach specializes in freshly caught seafood, and locally raised meat and produce. The small but focused menu includes dishes like pan-fried cod with samphire, smoked duck salad with spring onions,

Sunrise is lovely at the Cobb, the harbor wall built by Edward I in Lyme Regis.

and crab cakes, plus excellent cocktails. The restaurant is in a Victorian villa remodeled to evoke a chic '20s feel, and the tables outside on the '70s-built terrace have fabulous views across Lyme Bay. A fixed-price lunch (£14 for two courses, £17 for three) is good value. Service is genial but a bit spotty. There are also eight light-filled bedrooms with views upstairs. $ *Average main: £16* ✉ *Cliff Rd.* ☎ *01308/897205* 🌐 *www.theseasideboardinghouse.com.*

LYME REGIS

19 miles west of Abbotsbury.

Fodor's Choice ★

"A very strange stranger it must be, who does not see the charms of the immediate environs of Lyme, to make him wish to know it better," wrote Jane Austen in *Persuasion*. Judging from the summer crowds, many people agree with her. The scenic seaside town of Lyme Regis and the so-called Jurassic Coast are highlights of southwest Dorset. The crumbling Channel-facing cliffs in this area are especially fossil rich.

GETTING HERE AND AROUND

Lyme Regis is off the A35, extending west from Bournemouth and Dorchester. Drivers should park as soon as possible—there are lots at the top of town—and explore the town on foot. First buses run here from Dorchester and Axminster, 6 miles northwest; the latter town is on the main rail route from London Waterloo and Salisbury, as is Exeter, from which you can take the X53 bus.

ESSENTIALS

Visitor Information Lyme Regis Tourist Information Centre. ✉ *Guildhall Cottage, Church St.* ☎ *01297/442138* 🌐 *www.lymeregis.org.*

EXPLORING

Cobb. Lyme Regis is famous for its curving stone harbor breakwater, the Cobb, built by King Edward I in the 13th century to improve the harbor. The duke of Monmouth landed here in 1685 during his ill-fated attempt to overthrow his uncle James II, and the Cobb figured prominently in the movie of John Fowles's novel *The French Lieutenant's Woman*, as well as in the film version of Jane Austen's *Persuasion*. There's a sweeping coastal view to Chesil Beach to the east. ✉ *Lyme Regis.*

4

FAMILY **Dinosaurland Fossil Museum.** Located in a former church, this compact private museum run by a paleontologist has an excellent collection of local fossils with more than 10,000 specimens. It also provides information on regional geology, how fossils develop, and guided fossil-hunting walks. There are more fossils for sale in the shop on the ground floor along with minerals. ✉ *Coombe St.* ☎ *01297/443541* 🌐 *home.btconnect.com/dinosaurland.co.uk* 🎫 *£5* ⏲ *Mid-Feb.–mid-Oct., daily 10–5; mid-Oct.–mid-Feb., hrs vary.*

Lyme Regis Museum. A gabled and turreted Edwardian building on the site of fossilist Mary Anning's former home, this lively museum is devoted to the town's maritime and domestic history, geology, local artists, writers (John Fowles was an honorary curator for a decade), and, of course, fossils. The museum also leads fossil-hunting and local history walks throughout the year. ✉ *Bridge St.* ☎ *01297/443370* 🌐 *www.lymeregismuseum.co.uk* 🎫 *£3.95* ⏲ *Easter–Oct., Mon.–Sat. 10–5, Sun. 11–5; Nov.–Easter, Wed.–Sun. 11–4.*

FAMILY **Marine Aquarium.** This small but child-friendly aquarium has the usual up-close look at maritime creatures, from spider crabs to fish found in nearby Lyme Bay. Children love hand-feeding the gray mullets. ✉ *The Cobb Lower Walkway* ☎ *01297/444230* 🌐 *www.lymeregismarineaquarium.co.uk* 🎫 *£6* ⏲ *Mar.–Oct., daily 10–5; Nov.–Feb., weekends 10:30–3* ☞ *May be closed in bad weather in winter.*

WHERE TO EAT AND STAY

$ BRITISH ✕ **The Bell Cliff Restaurant and Tea Rooms.** This cozy, welcoming, child-friendly place in a 17th-century building at the bottom of Lyme Regis's main street makes a great spot for a light lunch or a cream tea with views over the bay, although it can get noisy and cramped. Apart from hot drinks and sandwiches, you can order seafood, including salmon and hollandaise, crab salad, battered cod, a gammon steak (a thick slice of cured ham), or vegetarian lasagna. Dogs are welcome. $ *Average main: £10* ✉ *5–6 Broad St.* ☎ *01297/442459* ⏲ *No dinner Nov.–Mar.*

$$ SEAFOOD Fodor's Choice ★ ✕ **Hix Oyster & Fish House.** This coastal outpost of one of London's trendiest restaurants combines stunning views overlooking the Cobb with the celebrity chef's trademark high standards and originality. Simply cooked and beautifully presented seafood rules here, including Torbay lemon sole grilled on the bone or Portland crab. As the name suggests, the local oysters are a particular specialty. Non-fish-eaters have limited choices, but the dessert menu is extensive, including cider-brandy chocolate

truffles and buttermilk pudding. A selection of three appetizers (like smoked salmon with soda bread) is a good value at £12, though it's only available Friday afternoons from 3 until 5. Book well ahead to sit by the floor-to-ceiling windows, on the small terrace, or at the Kitchen Table where you can watch the chefs at work. *Average main: £17* *Cobb Rd.* *01297/446910* *www.hixoysterandfishhouse.co.uk* *No dinner Sun. and closed Mon., Nov.–Feb.* *Reservations essential.*

$$$ HOTEL **Alexandra.** Magnificently sited above the Cobb, this family-owned boutique hotel combines contemporary design with the genteel charm of yesteryear. **Pros:** great garden; deck overlooking the Cobb and bay; central location. **Cons:** cheaper rooms have no sea views; small bathrooms; restricted parking. *Rooms from: £180* *Pound St.* *01297/442010* *www.hotelalexandra.co.uk* *Closed Jan.* *24 rooms, 2 cottages* *Breakfast.*

$ B&B/INN **Coombe House.** In a stone house tucked away on one of the oldest (14th century) lanes in Lyme, and one minute from the seafront, this uncluttered, stylish B&B has genial hosts and airy, modern guest rooms decorated in maritime blue and white. **Pros:** friendly owners; pleasant rooms; central location; Wi-Fi access. **Cons:** only three rooms. *Rooms from: £72* *41 Coombe St.* *01297/443849* *www.coombe-house.co.uk* *3 rooms* *Breakfast.*

SPORTS AND THE OUTDOORS

Dorset Coast Path. This 95-mile path—a section of the 630-mile-long Southwest Coast Path National Trail—runs east from Lyme Regis to Old Harry Rocks near Studland, bypassing Weymouth and taking in the quiet bays, shingle beaches, and low chalk cliffs of the coast. Some highlights are Golden Cap, the highest point on the south coast; the Swannery at Abbotsbury; Chesil Beach; Durdle Door; and Lulworth Cove (between Weymouth and Corfe Castle). Villages and isolated pubs dot the route, as do many rural B&Bs. *Lyme Regis* *01392/383560* *www.southwestcoastpath.com.*

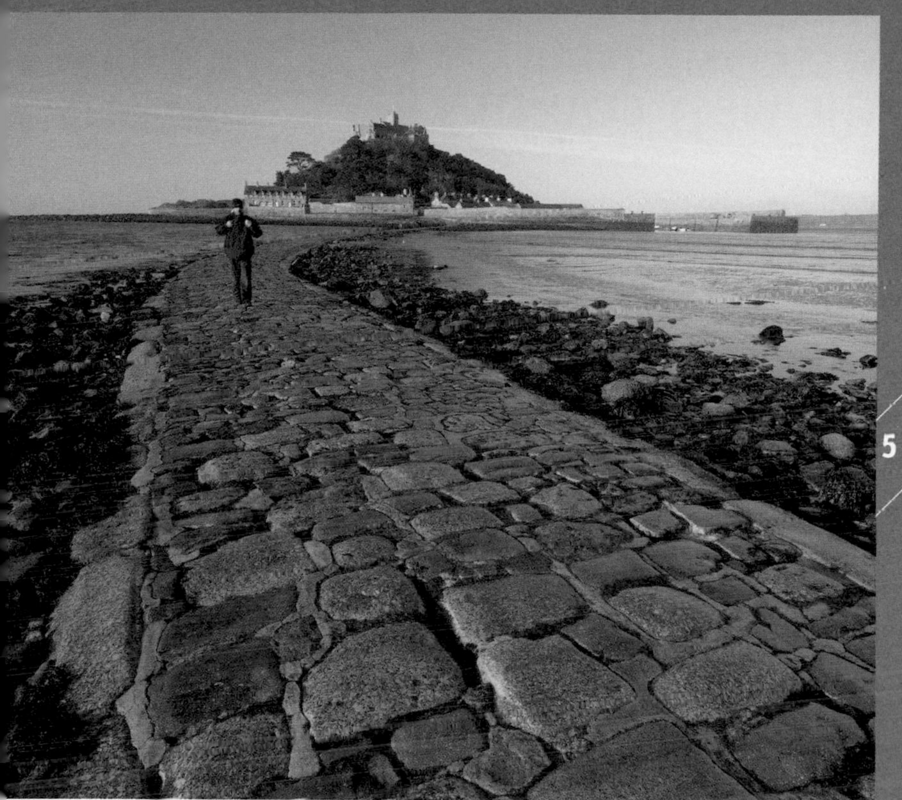

5

THE WEST COUNTRY

WELCOME TO THE WEST COUNTRY

TOP REASONS TO GO

★ **Coastal walks:** For high, dramatic cliff scenery, choose the Exmoor coast around Lynmouth or the coast around Tintagel. The South West Coast Path is 630 miles long.

★ **Riding or hiking on Dartmoor:** Escape to southern England's greatest wilderness—a treeless expanse dotted with rocky outcrops; there are many organized walks and pony-trekking operations.

★ **Tate St. Ives:** There's nowhere better to absorb the local arts scene than this offshoot of London's Tate in the pretty seaside town of St. Ives. A rooftop café claims views over Porthmeor Beach.

★ **A visit to Eden:** It's worth the journey west for Cornwall's Eden Project alone—a wonderland of plant life in a former clay pit. Two gigantic geodesic "biomes" are filled with flora.

★ **Wells Cathedral:** A perfect example of medieval craftsmanship, the building is a stunning spectacle.

1 Bristol, Wells, and North Devon. Bristol is filled with remnants of its long history, but you need to explore small towns like Wells and Glastonbury to get the full flavor of the region. West of here, Exmoor National Park has an unfettered, romantic appeal, with some entrancing coastline.

2 Cornwall. You're never more than 20 miles from the sea in this western outpost of Britain, and the maritime flavor imbues such port towns as Padstow and Falmouth. A string of good beaches and resort towns such as St. Ives pull in the summer crowds.

GETTING ORIENTED

Going from east to west, the counties of Somerset, Devon, and Cornwall make up the West Country. A circular tour of the West Country peninsula covers stark contrasts, from the bustling city of Bristol in the east to the remote and rocky headlands of Devon and Cornwall to the west. On the whole, the northern coast is more rugged, the cliffs dropping dramatically to tiny coves and beaches, whereas the south coast shelters many more resorts and wider expanses of sand. The crowds gravitate to the southern shore, but there are many remote inlets and estuaries, and you don't need to go far to find a degree of seclusion. The national parks of Exmoor on the northern part of the peninsula and Dartmoor, with their wilder landscapes, add even more variety.

3 Plymouth and Dartmoor. Though modern in appearance, Plymouth has some important historical sights. To the northeast, the open heath and wild moorland of Dartmoor National Park invite walking and horseback riding; towns such as Chagford make a good base for exploring.

4 Exeter, Torbay, Totnes, and Dartmouth. Exeter's sturdy cathedral dominates the historic city, from which you can make an easy foray to Topsham. South of Exeter, relaxed Totnes and bustling Dartmouth lie close to the English Riviera resorts of Torquay and Brixham.

5

GREAT COASTAL DRIVES

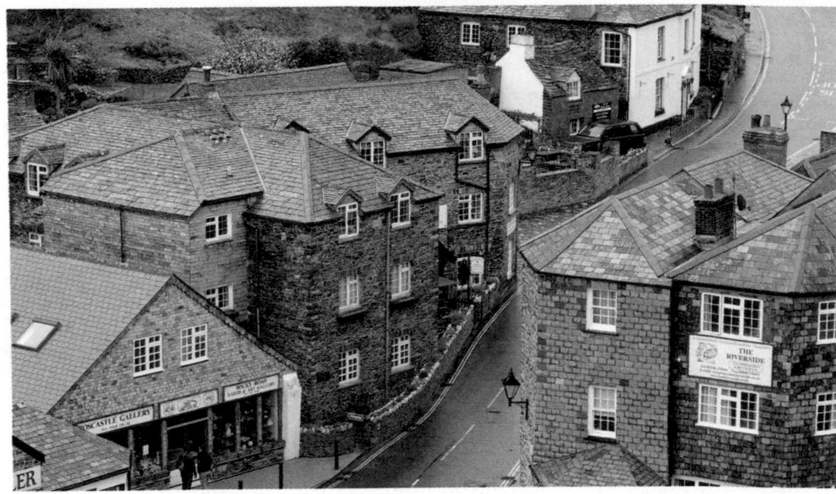

(above) Exploring coastal towns such as Tintagel is a West Country pleasure; (right, top) Romantic sunset at Tintagel; (right, below) Coastal view in Cornwall

The best way to explore the West Country is by car. The coast and countryside here are wondrously varied, but the area isn't well traversed by buses or trains. A drive can take you from spectacular ocean views to mysterious moors in an hour, and the routes are nearly endless.

Choose your ideal coastal tour based on the scenery that appeals to you. For plunging cliffs and crashing seas, you'll want the north Devon and Cornwall coast. For sheltered white beaches carved out of rocky shores, southern Cornwall is the place for you. You can combine your driving route with breaks for sightseeing or for bike riding, walking on the South West Coast Path, or even surfing. If you prefer a more relaxed option, stop at a café for a cup of tea and a scone; treat yourself to the clotted cream. Stretch your coastal tour out over days, or pack it all into one busy afternoon: your route can fit your own plans. Either way, you're bound to see something beautiful along the way.

BE PREPARED

Gas stations (called petrol stations here) are fairly frequent on major roads but rare on rural lanes. Don't let your tank get low if you're spending your time on small country roads. Coastal roads will be more crowded on summer weekends than weekdays, as you might expect. Heavy traffic is generally limited to the most popular towns and beaches. Outside towns, there are few lights at night—it gets very dark.

THE ATLANTIC HIGHWAY

Length and driving time: 55 miles one-way; about 5 hours with stops, 2 hours without stops

Difficulty: Moderate, with some steep, narrow roads

Running from the top of Devon down to the tip of Cornwall, A39, known as the Atlantic Highway, takes a handy route along the peninsula's northern coast, and you can hop off and on it to see the sights. Starting at the charming hillside town of Clovelly, you can explore the steep streets and adorable cottages before driving south on A39 to Boscastle (30 miles; turn off on B3266 and follow signs), a stone-built village at the foot of a steep, forested ravine. Stop for tea and spend some time browsing Boscastle's pottery shops before driving 4 miles (on B3263) to Tintagel with its cliff-top castle ruins (linked to King Arthur). The ocean views are breathtaking. Back on A39, drive 20 miles to the beachfront town of Padstow, a perfect place to stop for the day, and perhaps indulge in a meal at one of Rick Stein's famous seafood restaurants.

ST. IVES TO CAPE CORNWALL, VIA PENZANCE

Length and driving time: 44 miles; about 4 hours with stops, 1½ hours without stops

Difficulty: Moderate, with narrow, winding roads

You can spend hours in St. Ives looking through its art galleries and relaxing on the beach, but when you're ready to explore, strike out for Penzance, 8 miles south on B3311. Park in the lots by the sea and take in the shops and cafés of Chapel Street before heading to Mousehole, 3 miles away along the seafront. In this tiny village, the Lilliputian cottages are scattered around the harbor.

From Mousehole, the winding B3315 road will take you the 10 miles to Land's End, the tip of Cornwall: you can either join in the tourist fest of the amusement park there, or strike out on foot along the coastal path for some stunning scenery.

It's less than 8 miles from Land's End to Cape Cornwall on B3306, but the road twists and turns. It can take time to get there, particularly if you're lured by awesome coastal views along the way. Cape Cornwall is a promontory where Atlantic currents split, heading south to the English Channel or north toward Bristol. The dramatic, rocky shoreline has spectacular views and makes a great picnic spot; there's plenty of well-marked parking.

From Cape Cornwall, you're only 14 miles from St. Ives on B3306, completing your coastal loop.

5

Updated by Robert Andrews

England's West Country is a land of granite promontories, windswept moors, hideaway hamlets, and—above all—the sea. Leafy, narrow country roads lead through miles of buttercup meadows and cider-apple orchards to heathery heights and mellow villages. With their secluded beaches and dreamy backwaters, Somerset, Devon, and Cornwall can be some of England's most relaxing regions to visit.

The counties of the West Country each have their own distinct flavor, and each comes with a regionalism that borders on patriotism. Somerset is noted for its rolling green countryside; Devon's wild and dramatic moors—bare, boggy, upland heath dominated by heathers and gorse—contrast with the restfulness of its many sandy beaches and coves; and Cornwall has managed to retain a touch of its old insularity, despite the annual invasion of thousands of people lured by the Atlantic waves or the ripples of the English Channel.

The historic port of Bristol is where you come across the first unmistakable burrs of the western brogue. Its Georgian architecture and a dramatic gorge create a backdrop to what has become one of Britain's most dynamic cities. To the south lie the cathedral city of Wells and Glastonbury, with its ruined abbey and Arthurian associations. Abutting the north coast is heather-covered Exmoor National Park.

There's more wild moorland in Devon, where Dartmoor is famed for its ponies roaming amid an assortment of strange tors: rocky outcroppings eroded into weird shapes. Devon's coastal towns are as interesting for their cultural and historical appeal—many were smuggler havens—as for their scenic beauty. Parts of south Devon resemble some balmy Mediterranean shore—hence its soubriquet, the English Riviera.

Cornwall, England's westernmost county, has always regarded itself as separate from the rest of Britain, and the Arthurian legends really took root here, not least at Tintagel Castle, the legendary birthplace of Arthur. The south coast is filled with sandy beaches, delightful coves, and popular resorts.

WEST COUNTRY PLANNER

WHEN TO GO

In July and August, traffic chokes the roads leading into the West Country. Somehow the region squeezes in all the "grockles," or tourists, and the chances of finding a remote oasis of peace and quiet are severely curtailed. The beaches and resort towns are either bubbling with zest or unbearably tacky, depending on your point of view. In summer your best option is to find a secluded hotel and make brief excursions from there. Avoid traveling on Saturday, when weekly rentals start and finish and the roads are jammed. Most properties that don't accept business year-round open for Easter and close in late September or October. Those that remain open have reduced hours. Winter has its own appeal: the Atlantic waves crash dramatically against the coast, and the austere Cornish cliffs are at their most spectacular.

The most notable festivals are Padstow's Obby Oss, a traditional celebration of the arrival of summer that takes place around May 1; the Cornish-themed Golowan Festival in Penzance in late June; and the St. Ives September Festival of music and art in mid-September. In addition, many West Country maritime towns host regattas over summer weekends. The best times to visit Devon are late summer and early fall, during the end-of-summer festivals, especially popular in the coastal towns of east Devon.

PLANNING YOUR TIME

The elongated shape of Britain's southwestern peninsula means that you may well spend more time traveling than seeing the sights. The key is to base yourself in one or two places and make day trips to the surrounding region. The cities of Bristol, Exeter, and Plymouth make handy bases from which to explore the region, but they can also swallow up a lot of time, at the expense of smaller, less demanding places. The same is true of the resorts of Torquay, Newquay, and Falmouth, which can get very busy. Choose instead towns and villages such as Wells, Lynmouth, Port Isaac, St. Mawes, and Fowey to soak up local atmosphere. If you stick to just a few towns in Somerset and Devon (Bristol, Wells, and Exeter) you could get a taste of the area in four or five days. If you intend to cover Cornwall, at the end of the peninsula, you'll need at least a week. Allow time for aimless rambling—the best way to explore the moors and the coast—and leave enough free time for doing nothing at all.

GETTING HERE AND AROUND

AIR TRAVEL

Bristol International Airport, a few miles southwest of the city, has frequent flights from London, as well as from Dublin, Amsterdam, and other international cities. Exeter International Airport is 5 miles east of the city. Newquay Cornwall Airport, 5 miles northeast of town, has daily flights to London Gatwick.

Airport Information Bristol International Airport. ✉ *A38, Lulsgate Bottom* ☎ *0871/334–4344* 🌐 *www.bristolairport.co.uk.* **Exeter International Airport.** ✉ *A30, Clyst Honiton* ☎ *01392/367433* 🌐 *www.exeter-airport.co.uk.* **Newquay Cornwall Airport.** ✉ *Off A3059, St. Mawgan* ☎ *01637/860600* 🌐 *www.newquaycornwallairport.com.*

BUS TRAVEL

National Express buses leave London's Victoria Coach Station for Bristol (2½ hours), Exeter (4–5 hours), Plymouth (5–6 hours), and Penzance (8–10 hours). Megabus (book online to avoid premium-line costs) offers cheap service to Bristol, Exeter, Plymouth, Newquay, and Penzance. There's also a good network of regional bus services. First buses serve Somerset, Devon, and Cornwall, and Stagecoach South West covers mainly south Devon and the north Devon coast. Dartline Coaches has a small network around Dartmoor and mid-Devon. Western Greyhound operates mostly in Cornwall. First, Stagecoach South West, and Western Greyhound offer money-saving one- or seven-day passes good for unlimited bus travel. Traveline can help you plan your trip.

Bus Contacts Dartline Coaches. ☎ *01392/872900* 🌐 *www.dartline-coaches.co.uk.* **First.** ☎ *01823/211180 for services in Somerset, 01752/967800 for services in Devon, 01872/305950 for services in Cornwall* 🌐 *www.firstgroup.com.* **Megabus.** ☎ *0900/160–0900 for booking, 0141/352–4444 for general inquiries* 🌐 *www.megabus.com.* **National Express.** ☎ *0871/781–8178* 🌐 *www.nationalexpress.com.* **Stagecoach South West.** ☎ *01392/427711* 🌐 *www.stagecoachbus.com.* **Traveline.** ☎ *0871/200–2233* 🌐 *www.travelinesw.com.* **Western Greyhound.** ☎ *01637/871871* 🌐 *www.westerngreyhound.com.*

CAR TRAVEL

Unless you confine yourself to a few towns—for example, Exeter, Penzance, and Plymouth—you'll be at a huge disadvantage without your own transportation. The region has a few main arteries, but you should take minor roads whenever possible, if only to see the real West Country at a leisurely pace.

The fastest route from London to the West Country is via the M4 and M5 motorways. Allow at least two hours to drive to Bristol, three to Exeter. The main roads heading west are the A30 (burrowing through the center of Devon and Cornwall all the way to the tip of Cornwall), the A39 (near the northern shore), and the A38 (near the southern shore, south of Dartmoor and taking in Plymouth).

TRAIN TRAVEL

Rail travelers can make use of a fast service connecting Exeter, Plymouth, and Penzance. First Great Western and South West Trains serve the region from London's Paddington and Waterloo stations. Average travel time to Exeter is 2¾ hours, to Plymouth 3½ hours, and to Penzance about 5½ hours. Once you've arrived, however, you'll find trains to be of limited use in the West Country, as only a few branch lines leave the main line between Exeter and Penzance.

Freedom of the South West tickets provide three days of unlimited travel throughout the West Country in any seven-day period, or eight days in any 15-day period; localized Ranger passes cover Devon or Cornwall.

Train Contacts National Rail Enquiries. ☎ *0845/748–4950* 🌐 *www.nationalrail.co.uk.*

RESTAURANTS

The last several years have seen a food renaissance in England's West Country. In the top restaurants the accent is firmly on local and seasonal products. Seafood is the number one choice along the coasts, from Atlantic pollock to Helford River oysters, and it's available in places from haute restaurants to harborside fish shacks. Celebrity chefs have marked their pitch all over the region, including Michael Caines in Exeter and Dartmoor, the Tanner brothers in Plymouth, Rick Stein in Padstow and Falmouth, Mitch Tonks in Dartmouth, and Jamie Oliver in Newquay. Better-known establishments are often completely booked on Friday or Saturday, so reserve well in advance.

HOTELS

Accommodations include national hotel chains, represented in all of the region's principal centers, as well as ancient inns and ubiquitous bed-and-breakfast places. Availability can be limited on the coasts during August and during the weekend everywhere, so book well ahead. Many farmhouses also rent out rooms—offering tranquil rural surroundings—but these lodgings are often difficult to reach without a car. If you have a car, though, renting a house or cottage with a kitchen may be ideal. It's worth finding out about weekend and winter deals that many hotels offer. *Hotel reviews have been shortened. For full information, visit Fodors.com.*

WHAT IT COSTS IN POUNDS

	$	$$	$$$	$$$$
Restaurants	under £15	£15–£19	£20–£25	over £25
Hotels	under £100	£100–£160	£161–£220	over £220

Restaurant prices are the average cost of a main course at dinner, or if dinner is not served, at lunch. Hotels prices are the lowest cost of a standard double room in high season, including 20% V.A.T.

Visitor Information Contacts Visit Cornwall. ✉ *Pydar House, Pydar St., Truro* ☎ *01872/322900* 🌐 *www.visitcornwall.com.* **Visit Devon.** 🌐 *www.visitdevon.co.uk.* **Visit Somerset.** ✉ *Roadchef Services, M5 S, Axbridge* ☎ *01823/750833* 🌐 *www.visitsomerset.co.uk.*

BRISTOL, WELLS, AND NORTH DEVON

On the eastern side of this region is the vibrant city of Bristol. From here you might head south to the pretty cathedral city of Wells and continue on via Glastonbury, which just might be the Avalon of Arthurian legend. Proceed west along the Somerset coast into Devon, skirting the moorlands of Exmoor and tracing the northern shore via Clovelly.

BRISTOL

120 miles west of London, 46 miles south of Birmingham, 45 miles east of Cardiff, 13 miles northwest of Bath.

The West Country's biggest city (population 430,000), Bristol has in recent years become one of the country's most vibrant centers, with a thriving cultural scene encompassing some of the best contemporary art, theater, and music. Buzzing bars, cafés, and restaurants, and a largely youthful population make it an attractive place to spend time.

Now that the city's industries no longer rely on the docks, the historic harbor along the River Avon has been given over to recreation. Arts and entertainment complexes, museums, and galleries fill the quayside. The pubs and clubs here draw the under-25 set and make the area fairly boisterous (and best avoided) on Friday and Saturday night.

Bristol also trails a great deal of history in its wake. It can be called the "birthplace of America" with some confidence, for John Cabot and his son Sebastian sailed from the old city docks in 1497 to touch down on the North American mainland, which he claimed for the English crown. The city had been a major center since medieval times, but in the 17th and 18th centuries it became the foremost port for trade with North America, and played a leading role in the Caribbean slave trade. Bristol was the home of William Penn, developer of Pennsylvania, and a haven for John Wesley, whose Methodist movement played an important role in colonial Georgia.

GETTING HERE AND AROUND

Bristol has good connections by bus and train to most cities in the country. From London, calculate about 2½ hours by bus or 1¾ hours by train. From Cardiff it's about 50 minutes by bus or train. By train, make sure you get tickets for Bristol Temple Meads Station (not Bristol Parkway), which is a short bus, taxi, or river-bus ride from the center. The bus station is more central, near the Broadmead shopping center. Most sights can be visited on foot, though a bus or a taxi is necessary to reach the Clifton neighborhood.

ESSENTIALS

Visitor Information Bristol Tourist Information Centre. ✉ *E Shed, Canon's Rd.* ☎ *0906/711–2191* 🌐 *www.visitbristol.co.uk.*

EXPLORING

TOP ATTRACTIONS

FAMILY Fodor's Choice ★ **At-Bristol.** One of the country's top family-friendly science centers, this multimedia attraction provides a "hands-on, minds-on" exploration of science and technology in more than 300 interactive exhibits and displays. "All About Us" is dedicated to the inner workings of the human body. Another section allows you to create your own animations. A planetarium in a gleaming stainless-steel sphere takes you on a 25-minute voyage through the galaxy. There are up to 10 shows a day, bookable when you buy your ticket. A popular exhibit lets kids test their skills at creating animations. Allow at least three hours to see it all. ✉ *Anchor Rd., Harbourside* ☎ *0845/345–1235* 🌐 *www.at-bristol.org.uk* 🎫 *£12.60* 🕑 *Weekdays 10–5; weekends, holiday Mon., and school vacations 10–6.*

QUICK BITES

Watershed. The excellent café-restaurant upstairs at Watershed overlooks part of the harbor side. Sandwiches and hot snacks are served during the day, along with coffees and cakes. ✉ ***1 Canon's Rd., Harbourside*** ☎ ***0117/927–5101*** 🌐 ***www.watershed.co.uk.***

OFF THE BEATEN PATH

Berkeley Castle. In the sleepy village of Berkeley (pronounced *bark*-ley), this castle is perfectly preserved, down to its medieval turrets, and full of family treasures. It witnessed the murder of King Edward II in 1327—the cell in which it occurred can still be seen. Edward was betrayed by his French consort, Queen Isabella, and her paramour, the earl of Mortimer. Roger De Berkeley, a Norman knight, began work on the castle in 1153, and it has remained in the family ever since. Magnificent furniture, tapestries, and pictures fill the state apartments, but even the ancient buttery and kitchen are interesting. Guided tours and entry to the Butterfly House (May–September) are included in the ticket price. The castle is 20 miles north of Bristol, accessed from M5. ✉ *Off A38, Berkeley* ☎ *01453/810303* 🌐 *www.berkeley-castle.com* 🎫 *£10* 🕑 *Apr.–Oct., Sun.–Wed. 11–5; last admission at 4, last tour at 3:30.*

Church of St. Mary Redcliffe. Built by Bristol merchants who wanted a place in which to pray for the safe (and profitable) voyages of their ships, the rib-vaulted, 14th-century church was called "the fairest in England" by Queen Elizabeth I. High up on the nave wall hang the arms and armor of Sir William Penn, father of the founder of Pennsylvania. The church is a five-minute walk from Temple Meads train station toward the docks. ✉ *Redcliffe Way* ☎ *0117/929–1487* 🌐 *www.stmaryredcliffe.co.uk* 🎫 *Free* 🕑 *Mon.–Sat. 8:30–5, Sun. 8–8.*

FAMILY **Clifton Suspension Bridge.** A monument to Victorian engineering, this 702-foot-long bridge spans the Avon Gorge. Work began on Isambard Kingdom Brunel's design in 1831, but the bridge wasn't completed until 1864. Free hour-long guided tours usually take place at 3 on weekends between Easter and October, departing from the tollbooth at the Clifton end of the bridge. At the far end of the bridge, the **Clifton Suspension Bridge Visitor Centre** has a small exhibition on the bridge and its construction, including a range of videos and hands-on experiences. Near

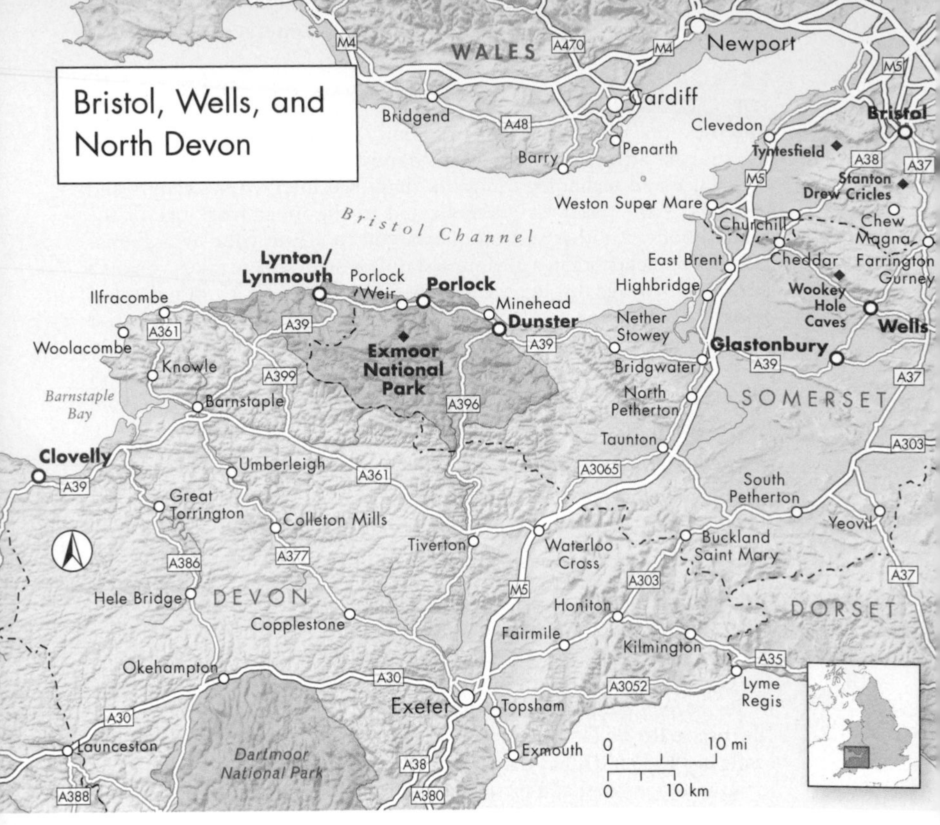

the bridge lies **Clifton Village,** studded with boutiques, antiques shops, and smart crafts shops in its lanes and squares. Bus number 8 from Bristol Temple Meads Station and the city center stops in Clifton Village. ✉ *Bridge Rd., Leigh Woods* ☎ *0117/974–4664* 🌐 *www.cliftonbridge.org.uk* 🎫 *Free* 🕒 *Daily 10–5.*

FAMILY
Fodor's Choice ★

M Shed. In a refurbished transit shed on the harbor side, this museum is dedicated to the city's history. The collection comprises three main galleries—Bristol People, Bristol Places, and Bristol Life—that focus on everything from the slave trade to scientific inventions to recent cultural innovations associated with the city. Check out the artifacts, photos, and sound and video recordings of and by Bristolians, all jazzed up with the latest interactive technology. ✉ *Princes Wharf, Wapping Rd.* ☎ *0117/352–6600* 🌐 *www.mshed.org* 🎫 *Free* 🕒 *Tues.–Fri. 10–5, weekends and holiday Mon. 10–6.*

Fodor's Choice ★

SS Great Britain. On view in the harbor is the first iron ship to cross the Atlantic. Built by the great English engineer Isambard Kingdom Brunel in 1843, it remained in service until 1970, first as a transatlantic liner and ultimately as a coal storage hulk. Everything from the bakery to the officers' quarters comes complete with sounds and smells of the time, and there are even shadowy glimpses of rats in the galley. You can climb the ship's rigging, try on typical garments of the time, and descend into the ship's dry dock for a view of the hull and propeller. Your ticket also admits you to an absorbing exhibit on the ship's history. A replica of the *Matthew,* the tiny craft that carried John Cabot to North America in 1497, is occasionally moored alongside (when it's not sailing on the high seas). ✉ *Great Western Dockyard, Gas Ferry Rd.* ☎ *0117/926–0680* 🌐 *www.ssgreatbritain.org* 🎟 *£14* 🕒 *Mar.–Oct., daily 10–5:30; Nov.–Feb., daily 10–4:30; last entry 1 hr before closing.*

Fodor's Choice ★ **Tyntesfield.** This extravagant, 35-bedroom Victorian–Gothic Revival mansion has been magnificently restored to reveal a showcase of the decorative arts where every ornate detail compels attention. Besides magnificent woodwork, stained glass, tiles, and original furniture and fabrics, the house contains the modern conveniences of the 1860s, such as a heated billiards table, and the servants' quarters are equally absorbing. There's a restaurant and family play area, too. You can see the house, garden, and chapel at your own pace, or join a free garden tour. ■ **TIP→ Arrive early in the day to avoid the crowds competing for timed tickets—Monday and Tuesday are the quietest days.** A food and craft market takes place in the grounds on the first Sunday of the month from April through November. Tyntesfield is 7 miles southwest of Bristol; the daily bus service X6 is the most convenient public transport from the city (present your ticket for a 20% discount on admission charges). The house is a 15-minute walk from the bus stop. ✉ *B3128, Wraxall* ☎ *0344/800–4966* 🌐 *www.nationaltrust.org.uk* 🎟 *£13.90; gardens only £8.55* 🕒 *House early Mar.–Oct., daily 11–5; Nov.–early Mar., daily 11–3; last entry 1 hr 15 min before closing. Gardens early Mar.–Oct., daily 10–6; Nov.–early Mar., daily 10–5 or dusk.*

WORTH NOTING

FAMILY **Bristol Zoo Gardens.** Alongside the leafy expanse of Clifton Down is one of the country's most famous zoos. More than 400 animal species live in 12 acres of gardens; the Seal and Penguin coasts, with underwater viewing, are rival attractions for Gorilla Island, Bug World, and Twilight World. Take Bus 8 or 9 from Temple Meads Station or the city center; a Zoo Safari ticket available from any First bus gives you discounted bus travel and zoo entry. ✉ *Clifton Down* ☎ *0117/974–7399* 🌐 *www.bristolzoo.org.uk* 🎟 *£14.50* 🕒 *Apr.–Oct., daily 9–5:30; Nov.–Mar., daily 9–5; last entry 1 hr before closing.*

New Room. John Wesley and Charles Wesley were among the Dissenters from the Church of England who found a home in Bristol, and in 1739 they built the New Room, a meeting place that became the first Methodist chapel. Its simplicity contrasts with the style of Anglican churches and with the modern shopping center hemming it in. Upstairs you can visit the Preachers' Rooms, now containing a small museum. ✉ *36 The Horsefair* ☎ *0117/926–4740* 🌐 *www.newroombristol.org.uk* 🎟 *Free* 🕒 *Mon.–Sat. 10–4.*

OFF THE BEATEN PATH

Stanton Drew Circles. Three rings, two avenues of standing stones, and a burial chamber make up the Stanton Drew Circles, one of the largest and most mysterious monuments in Britain, dating from 3000 to 2000 BC. It's far less well known than Stonehenge and other circles, however. The size of the circles suggests that the site was once as important as

EATING WELL IN THE WEST COUNTRY

From cider to cream teas, many specialties tempt your palate in the West Country. Lamb, venison, and, in Devon and Cornwall, seafood, are favored in restaurants, which have risen to heights of gastronomic excellence, notably through the influence of Rick Stein's seafood-based culinary empire in Padstow, in Cornwall. Seafood is celebrated at fishy frolics that include the Newlyn Fish Festival (late August) and Falmouth's Oyster Festival (early or mid-October).

WHAT TO EAT

Cheddar. Somerset is the home of Britain's most famous cheese—the ubiquitous cheddar, originally from the Mendip Hills village of the same name. Make certain that you sample a real farmhouse cheddar, made in the traditional barrel shape known as a truckle.

Cream teas. Devon's caloric cream teas consist of a pot of tea, homemade scones, and lots of strawberry jam and thickened clotted cream (a regional specialty, which is sometimes called Devonshire cream).

Pasties. Cornwall's specialty is the pasty, a pastry shell filled with chopped meat, onions, and potatoes. The pasty was devised as a handy way for miners to carry their dinner to work; today's versions are generally pale imitations of the original, though you can still find delicious home-cooked pasties if you're willing to search a little.

Seafood. In many towns in Devon and Cornwall, the day's catch is unloaded from the harbor and transported directly to eateries. The catch varies by season, but lobster is available year-round, as is crab, stuffed into sandwiches at quayside stalls and in pubs.

WHAT TO DRINK

Perry. This is similar to cider but made from pears.

Scrumpy. For liquid refreshment, try scrumpy, a homemade dry cider that's refreshing but carries a surprising kick.

Wine and mead. English wine, similar to German wine, is made in all three counties (you may see it on local menus), and in Devon and Cornwall you can find a variant of age-old mead made from local honey.

Stonehenge for its ceremonial functions, although little of great visual impact remains. English Heritage supervises the stones, which stand on private land. Access is given at any reasonable time, and a small admission fee or donation may be requested. **■ TIP→ You have to walk through a farmyard to reach the field where the site lies, so wear sturdy shoes.** To get here from Bristol, head south on the A37 and turn right after about 5 miles onto the B3130, marked Stanton Drew. The circles are just east of the village, where more of the stones may be seen in the garden of the Druid's Arms pub. ✉ *Off B3130, Stanton Drew* ☎ *0117/975–0700* 🌐 *www.english-heritage.org.uk.*

WHERE TO EAT

$$ MEDITERRANEAN ✕ **Bell's Diner & Bar Rooms.** A local institution, this bistro in a former grocery shop concentrates on delectable Mediterranean-style tapas using locally sourced ingredients. Choices include fennel and pomegranate salad with buffalo mozzarella, seared mackerel fillet, and charcoal-grilled pigeon breast; many of the dishes are available in small or main-course sizes. The ambience is youthful and lively, though the decor in the three small rooms has a retro feel, with wood floors, pale gray walls, and an old record-player and other curios on display. Bell's is rather hard to find—take A38 north, then turn right on Ashley Road and immediately left at Picton Street, which leads to York Road. Alternatively, from the city center, board any bus heading up Stokes Croft. *Average main: £15* ✉ *1 York Rd., Montpelier* ☎ *0117/924–0357* 🌐 *www.bellsdiner.com* ⏲ *Closed Sun. No lunch Mon.*

$ MODERN BRITISH FAMILY ✕ **Bordeaux Quay.** This converted riverside warehouse is dedicated to food, incorporating a delicatessen, a wine bar, a brasserie, a formal restaurant, and a cookery school. The lively street-level brasserie (open daily) is recommended for breakfasts of buttermilk pancakes or eggs Florentine and dinners centered on locally sourced mussels, duck leg confit, or sirloin steak. With its large skylight and harbor views, the upstairs dining room (open weekends only) offers more sophisticated dining, including such dishes as rolled pork belly and Cornish sea bass fillet with chestnut gnocchi, and desserts like pear tarte tatin with star anise and molasses parfait. *Average main: £12* ✉ *V-Shed, Canon's Way, Harbourside* ☎ *0117/943–1200* 🌐 *www.bordeaux-quay.co.uk* ⏲ *Restaurant closed weekdays. No lunch Sat. No dinner Sun.*

$ BRITISH ✕ **Boston Tea Party.** Despite the name, this laid-back and vaguely eccentric place is quintessentially English, and ideal for a relaxed lunch away from the nearby rigors of the Park Street shopping scene. Tasty sandwiches can be taken out or eaten in the terraced backyard or the upstairs sofa salon, a comfy spot for a cup of tea with orange and almond cake. Generous salads, soups, and burgers are also available. Get here early, as the restaurant closes at 8 (7 on Sunday). *Average main: £7* ✉ *75 Park St.* ☎ *0117/929–8601* 🌐 *www.bostonteaparty.co.uk.*

$$ MODERN BRITISH ✕ **Riverstation.** Occupying a former police station, this modern, clean-lined restaurant affords serene views over the passing swans and boats. Book early for a window seat. Upstairs, the more formal restaurant serves such delicately cooked dishes as grilled Iberico pork with *morcilla* (Spanish blood sausage) and pan-fried sea bass, and some irresistible desserts, including chocolate fondant pudding and vanilla crème brûlée with poached rhubarb, pistachio, and cardamom shortbread. The bar has a more rough-and-ready menu that includes warm savory tarts and chargrilled steak. With its terrace seating, this place also makes a great spot for breakfast, afternoon coffee, or evening drinks. *Average main: £17* ✉ *The Grove, Harbourside* ☎ *0117/914–4434* 🌐 *www.riverstation.co.uk* ⏲ *No dinner Sun.*

$ MODERN BRITISH ✕ **Source Food Hall.** In the heart of the old city, this trendy eatery benefits from its location in the St. Nicholas Market by offering a range of fresh seasonal produce, either to eat in or take out from the deli, meat, or fish counters. The wholesome lunch menu might feature Italian cold meats, Goan fish curry, or beef burgers. The breakfasts and coffees are energizing, making this an ideal place to kick off a sightseeing excursion or take a pause en route. The attractive Bath-stone building has an airy, high-ceilinged interior. *Average main: £11 St. Nicholas Market, 1–3 Exchange Ave. 0117/927–2998 www.source-food.co.uk Closed Sun. (except first Sun. of month). No dinner.*

WHERE TO STAY

$ B&B/INN Fodor's Choice ★ **9 Prince's Buildings.** With Clifton Suspension Bridge at the end of the street and the Avon Gorge directly below, this elegant Georgian B&B offers classic views of Bristol from its windows. **Pros:** beautiful house in a historic neighborhood; friendly hosts. **Cons:** no elevator; no credit cards. *Rooms from: £95 9 Prince's Buildings, Clifton 0117/973–4615 www.9princesbuildings.co.uk No credit cards 4 rooms Breakfast.*

$$ HOTEL **Hotel du Vin.** This hip chain has brought high-tech flair to six former sugar-refining warehouses, built in 1728 when the River Frome ran outside the front door. **Pros:** tastefully restored old building; great bathrooms; excellent bar and bistro. **Cons:** traffic-dominated location; dim lighting in rooms; limited parking. *Rooms from: £139 The Sugar House, Narrow Lewins Mead 0844/736–4252 www.hotelduvin.com 36 rooms, 4 suites No meals.*

$$$ HOTEL Fodor's Choice ★ **Thornbury Castle.** An impressive lodging, Thornbury has everything a genuine 16th-century Tudor castle needs: huge fireplaces, moody paintings, mullioned windows, and a large garden. **Pros:** grand medieval surroundings; sumptuous rooms; doting service. **Cons:** many steps to climb; some rooms are relatively small. *Rooms from: £195 Castle St., off A38, Thornbury 01454/281182 www.thornburycastle.co.uk 23 rooms, 4 suites Breakfast.*

$ HOTEL **Victoria Square Hotel.** In two mellow Victorian buildings overlooking one of Clifton's leafiest squares, this Best Western hotel makes an excellent base for exploring this part of Bristol. **Pros:** good advance-booking deals; pleasant location; friendly staff. **Cons:** numerous steps; some rooms need sprucing up; limited parking. *Rooms from: £75 Victoria Sq., Clifton 0117/973–9058 www.victoriasquarehotel.co.uk 41 rooms No meals.*

NIGHTLIFE AND PERFORMING ARTS

Arnolfini. In a converted warehouse on the harbor, the Arnolfini is one of the country's most prestigious contemporary-art venues, known for uncovering innovative yet accessible art. There are galleries, a cinema, a bookshop, and a lively bar and bistro. *16 Narrow Quay 0117/917–2300 www.arnolfini.org.uk.*

St. George's. A church built in the 18th century, St. George's now serves as one of the country's leading venues for classical, jazz, and world music. Stop by for lunchtime concerts. *Great George St., off Park St. 0845/402–4001 www.stgeorgesbristol.co.uk.*

Watershed. A contemporary arts center by the harbor, the Watershed also has a movie theater that screens excellent international films. *1 Canon's Rd., Harbourside 0117/927–5100 www.watershed.co.uk.*

Harmonious and stately, Wells Cathedral has a monumental west front decorated with medieval statues of kings and saints.

WELLS

22 miles south of Bristol, 132 miles west of London.

England's smallest cathedral city, with a population of 10,000, lies at the foot of the Mendip Hills. Although set in what feels like a quiet country town, the great cathedral is a masterpiece of Gothic architecture—the first to be built in the Early English style. The city's name refers to the underground streams that bubble up into St. Andrew's Well within the grounds of the Bishop's Palace. Spring water has run through High Street since the 15th century. Seventeenth-century buildings surround the ancient marketplace, which hosts market days on Wednesday and Saturday.

GETTING HERE AND AROUND

Regular First buses from Bristol take one hour to reach Wells; the bus station is a few minutes south of the cathedral. Drivers should take A37, and park outside the compact and eminently walkable center.

ESSENTIALS

Visitor Information Wells Visitor Information Service. ✉ *Wells Museum, 8 Cathedral Green* ☎ *01749/671770* 🌐 *www.wellssomerset.com.*

EXPLORING

Bishop's Palace. The Bishop's Eye gate leading from Market Place takes you to the magnificent, moat-ringed Bishop's Palace, which retains parts of the original 13th-century residence. The peaceful grounds command the most attention, including the gatehouse, the ramparts, and the impressive remains of a late-13th-century great hall which fell into ruin after the lead in its roof was sold in the 16th century. Most rooms of the palace are closed to the public, but you can see the undercroft, the private chapel, and the sumptuously decorated Long Gallery. ✉ *Market Pl.* ☎ *01749/988111* 🌐 *www.bishopspalacewells.co.uk* 🎫 *£7.20* ⏲ *Mid-Feb.–Mar. and late Oct.–late Dec., daily 10–4; Apr.–late Oct., daily 10–6; last admission 30 min before closing.*

Wells Cathedral. The great west towers of the Cathedral Church of St. Andrew, the oldest surviving English Gothic church, can be seen for miles. Dating from the 12th century, Wells Cathedral (as it's more commonly known) derives its beauty from the perfect harmony of all of its parts, the glowing colors of its original stained-glass windows, and its peaceful setting among stately trees and majestic lawns. To appreciate the elaborate west-front facade, approach the building from the cathedral green, accessible from Market Place through a great medieval gate called "penniless porch" (named after the beggars who once waited here to collect alms from worshippers). The cathedral's west front is twice as wide as it is high, and some 300 statues of kings and saints adorn it. Inside, vast inverted arches—known as scissor arches—were added in 1338 to stop the central tower from sinking to one side.

The cathedral has a rare and beautiful medieval clock, the second-oldest working clock in the world, consisting of the seated figure of a man called Jack Blandifer, who strikes a bell on the quarter hour while mounted knights circle in a joust. Near the clock is the entrance to the Chapter House—a small wooden door opening onto a great sweep of stairs worn down on one side by the tread of pilgrims over the centuries. Free guided tours lasting up to an hour begin at the back of the cathedral. A cloister restaurant serves snacks and teas. ✉ *Cathedral Green* ☎ *01749/674483* 🌐 *www.wellscathedral.org.uk* 🎫 *£6 suggested donation* ⏲ *Apr.–Sept., daily 7–7; Oct.–Mar., daily 7–6. Tours Apr.–Oct., Mon.–Sat. at 10, 11, 1, 2, and 3; Nov.–Mar., Mon.–Sat. at 11, noon, and 2.*

QUICK BITES

Sadler Street Café. This little café and patisserie near the cathedral serves exquisite cakes and pastries, chocolate concoctions, and excellent coffee. Soups, sandwiches, and light meals are also available, and Mediterranean-style country dishes are served Wednesday to Saturday evening. ✉ ***5 Sadler St.*** ☎ ***01749/673866*** 🌐 ***www.goodfellowswells.co.uk/sadler_street_cafe.htm.***

Vicar's Close. To the north of the cathedral, the cobbled Vicar's Close, one of Europe's oldest streets, has terraces of handsome 14th-century houses with strange, tall chimneys. A tiny medieval chapel here is still in use. ✉ *Wells.*

OFF THE BEATEN PATH

Wookey Hole Caves. These limestone caves in the Mendip Hills, 2 miles northwest of Wells, may have been the home of Iron Age people. Here, according to ancient legend, the Witch of Wookey turned to stone. You can tour the caves, dip your fingers in an underground river (artful lighting keeps things lively), and visit a museum, a penny arcade full of Victorian amusement machines, and a working paper mill that once supplied banknotes for the Confederate States of America. ✉ *Off High St., Wookey Hole* ☎ *01749/672243* 🌐 *www.wookey.co.uk* 🎫 *£18* ⏲ *Apr.–Oct., daily 10–6; Nov., Feb., and Mar., daily 10–5; Dec. and Jan., weekends and school vacation 10–5; last tour 1 hr before closing.*

WHERE TO EAT AND STAY

$$ MEDITERRANEAN ✕ **The Old Spot.** For relaxed but top-notch dining in the heart of Wells, this sociable bistro with wood paneling and creamy white walls hits all the right notes. The modern British and Mediterranean dinner menu varies seasonally, but might include a starter of steamed mussels with cider, thyme, and cream, followed by a main course of roast guinea fowl, cauliflower puree, and Madeira sauce. Set-price two-course lunches are £18.50. Arrive early for a table at the back, where there are views of the cathedral's west front. [$] *Average main: £18* ✉ *12 Sadler St.* ☎ *01749/689099* 🌐 *www.theoldspot.co.uk* ⏲ *Closed Mon. and Tues. No dinner Sun.*

$$ B&B/INN **Ancient Gate House.** This venerable hostelry makes a convenient and atmospheric base for exploring the area. **Pros:** historic character; cathedral views; handy base. **Cons:** steps to climb; cramped rooms; some street noise in front rooms. [$] *Rooms from: £110* ✉ *20 Sadler St.* ☎ *01749/672029* 🌐 *www.ancientgatehouse.com* *9 rooms* 🍴 *Breakfast.*

$$ HOTEL **Swan Hotel.** A former coaching inn built in the 15th century, the Swan has an ideal spot facing the cathedral. **Pros:** professional service; some great views; good restaurant. **Cons:** some rooms are small; occasional noise issues; parking lot tricky to negotiate. [$] *Rooms from: £147* ✉ *11 Sadler St.* ☎ *01749/836300* 🌐 *www.swanhotelwells.co.uk* *49 rooms, 1 suite* 🍴 *Breakfast.*

GLASTONBURY

5 miles southwest of Wells, 27 miles south of Bristol, 27 miles southwest of Bath.

Fodor's Choice ★ A town steeped in history, myth, and legend, Glastonbury lies in the lea of Glastonbury Tor, a grassy hill rising 520 feet above the drained marshes known as the Somerset Levels. The Tor is supposedly the site of crossing ley lines (hypothetical alignments of significant places), and, in legend, Glastonbury is identified with Avalon, the paradise into which King Arthur was reborn after his death.

Partly because of these associations but also because of its world-class rock-music festival, the town has acquired renown as a New Age center, mixing crystal gazers with druids, yogis, and hippies, variously in search of Arthur, Merlin, Jesus—and even Elvis. **TIP→ Between April and September, a shuttle bus runs every half hour between all of Glastonbury's major sights. Tickets are £3.50, and are valid all day.**

GETTING HERE AND AROUND

Frequent buses link Glastonbury to Wells and Bristol, pulling in close to the abbey. Drivers should take the A39. You can walk to all the sights or take the shuttle bus, though you'll need a stock of energy for ascending the tor.

5

DID YOU KNOW?

There's no gain without pain: the steep walk up 520-foot-high Glastonbury Tor gives you sweeping views of the Vale of Avalon. The ruined tower at the top of the hill is all that remains of St. Michael's Church.

ESSENTIALS

Visitor Information Glastonbury Tourist Information Centre. ✉ *The Tribunal, 9 High St.* ☎ *01458/832954* 🌐 *www.glastonburytic.co.uk.*

EXPLORING

Glastonbury Abbey. The ruins of this great abbey, in the center of town, are on the site where, according to legend, Joseph of Arimathea built a church in the 1st century. A monastery had certainly been erected here by the 9th century, and the site drew many pilgrims. The ruins are those of the abbey completed in 1524 and destroyed in 1539, during Henry VIII's dissolution of the monasteries. A sign south of the Lady Chapel marks the sites where Arthur and Guinevere were supposedly buried. Between April and October, guides in period costumes are on hand to point out some of the abbey's most interesting features. The visitor center has a scale model of the abbey as well as carvings and decorations salvaged from the ruins. ✉ *Magdalene St.* ☎ *01458/832267* 🌐 *www.glastonburyabbey.com* 💷 *£6.90* ⏲ *Mar.–May, Sept. and Oct., daily 9–6; June–Aug., daily 9–8; Nov.–Feb., daily 9–4; last admission 30 min before closing.*

Glastonbury Tor. At the foot of Glastonbury Tor is **Chalice Well,** the legendary burial place of the Grail. It's a stiff climb up the tor, but your reward is the fabulous view across the Vale of Avalon. At the top stands a ruined tower, all that remains of **St. Michael's Church,** which collapsed after a landslide in 1271. Take the Glastonbury Tor bus to the base of the hill. ✉ *Glastonbury.*

TALE OF THE GRAIL

According to tradition, Glastonbury was where Joseph of Arimathea brought the Holy Grail, the chalice used by Jesus at the Last Supper. Centuries later, the Grail was said to be the objective of the quests of King Arthur and the Knights of the Round Table. When monks claimed to have found the bones of Arthur and Guinevere at Glastonbury in 1191, the popular association of the town with the mythical Avalon was sealed. Arthur and Guinevere's presumed remains were lost to history after Glastonbury Abbey was plundered for its riches in 1539.

WHERE TO EAT AND STAY

$ BRITISH ✕ **Who'd a Thought It.** As an antidote to the natural-food cafés of Glastonbury's High Street, try this traditional backstreet inn for some more down-to-earth fare that doesn't compromise on quality. Bar classics such as fish pie and Somerset sausages appear alongside chicken or vegetable curries and sizzling steaks. The beers and ciders are local, and the pub's quirky decor—including ancient radios, a red telephone box, and a bicycle on the ceiling—has a definite entertainment quotient. [$] *Average main: £12* ✉ *17 Northload St.* ☎ *01458/834460* 🌐 *www.whodathoughtit.co.uk* 💳 *No credit cards.*

$ B&B/INN **The Glastonbury White House.** You'll receive warm hospitality from the owner of this eco-friendly B&B a few minutes from High Street. **Pros:** friendly host; lots of period details; flexible breakfasts. **Cons:** not great for families. [$] *Rooms from: £65* ✉ *21 Manor House Rd.* ☎ *01458/830886* 🌐 *www.theglastonburywhitehouse.com* 💳 *No credit cards* 🛏 *2 rooms* 🍽 *No meals.*

The hugely popular Glastonbury Festival attracts music lovers and free spirits from all over the world.

$ B&B/INN **Magdalene House.** Formerly a convent, this Georgian B&B sits directly opposite the Abbey grounds, with views over the walls. **Pros:** central location; convenient for anyone with mobility issues. **Cons:** slightly over-decorated; no one under seven allowed to stay. *Rooms from: £90* ✉ *Magdalene St.* ☎ *01458/830202* 🌐 *www.magdalenehouseglastonbury.com* *3 rooms* *Breakfast.*

NIGHTLIFE AND PERFORMING ARTS

Glastonbury Festival. Held a few miles away in Pilton, the Glastonbury Festival is England's biggest and perhaps best annual rock festival. For five days over the last weekend in June, it hosts hundreds of bands—established and up-and-coming—on three main stages and myriad smaller venues. Tickets are steeply priced—around £225—and sell out months in advance; they include entertainment, a camping area, and service facilities. ✉ *Pilton* 🌐 *www.glastonburyfestivals.co.uk.*

DUNSTER

35 miles west of Glastonbury, 43 miles north of Exeter.

Lying between the Somerset coast and the edge of Exmoor National Park, Dunster is a picture-book village with a broad main street. The eight-sided yarn-market building on High Street dates from 1589.

GETTING HERE AND AROUND

To reach Dunster by car, follow the A39. By bus, there are frequent departures from nearby Minehead and Taunton. Dunster Castle is a brief walk from the village center. In the village is the Exmoor National

Park Visitor Centre, which can give you plenty of information about local activities.

ESSENTIALS

Visitor Information Exmoor National Park Visitor Centre. ✉ *Dunster Steep* ☎ *01643/821835* 🌐 *www.exmoor-nationalpark.gov.uk.*

EXPLORING

Fodor's Choice ★ **Dunster Castle.** A 13th-century fortress remodeled in 1868, Dunster Castle dominates the village from its site on a hill. Parkland and unusual gardens with subtropical plants surround the building, which has fine plaster ceilings, stacks of family portraits (including one by Joshua Reynolds), 17th-century Dutch leather hangings, and a magnificent 17th-century oak staircase. The climb to the castle from the parking lot is steep. ✉ *Off A39* ☎ *01643/821314* 🌐 *www.nationaltrust.org.uk* 🎫 *£10; gardens only, £6.80* ⏲ *Castle early Mar.–Oct., daily 11–5. Gardens early Mar.–Oct., daily 10–5; Nov.–Dec., daily 11–4.*

SOUTH WEST COAST PATH

Britain's longest national trail, the South West Coast Path, wraps around the coast of the peninsula for 630 miles from Minehead (near Dunster, Somerset) to South Haven Point, near Poole (Dorset). To complete the trail takes 50 to 60 days. An annual guide to hiking in the region is published by the South West Coast Path Association (🌐 *www.southwestcoastpath.org.uk*).

WHERE TO STAY

$$ B&B/INN **Luttrell Arms.** In style and atmosphere, this classic inn harmonizes perfectly with Dunster village and castle; it was used as a guesthouse by the abbots of Cleeve in the 14th century. **Pros:** central location; historic trappings; good dining options. **Cons:** some standard rooms are small and viewless; no parking. $ *Rooms from: £140* ✉ *High St.* ☎ *01643/821555* 🌐 *www.luttrellarms.co.uk* *28 rooms* 🍽 *Breakfast.*

EXMOOR NATIONAL PARK

16 miles southwest of Dunster.

When you're headed to Exmoor National Park, stop by the visitor information centers at Dulverton, Dunster, and Lynmouth for information and maps. Guided walks, many of which have themes (archaeology, for example), cost £3 to £5. If you're walking on your own, check the weather, take water and a map, and tell someone where you're going.

GETTING HERE AND AROUND

A car is usually necessary for getting around the inner reaches of Exmoor. Bus 300, run by Quantock Heritage, traces the coast between Minehead and Lynmouth. Bus 398, operated by Beacon Bus, runs from Minehead to Dunster and inland to Dulverton.

ESSENTIALS

Bus Contacts Beacon Bus. ☎ *01805/804240* 🌐 *www.beaconbus.co.uk.* **Quantock Heritage.** ☎ *01984/624906* 🌐 *www.quantockheritage.com.*

Visitor Information Dulverton National Park Centre. ✉ *7–9 Fore St., Dulverton* ☎ *01398/323841* 🌐 *www.exmoor-nationalpark.gov.uk/visiting/*

5

national-park-centres/dulverton. **Lynmouth National Park Centre.** ✉ *The Pavilion, The Esplanade, Lynmouth* ☎ *01598/752509* 🌐 *www.exmoor-nationalpark.gov.uk/visiting/national-park-centres/lynmouth.*

EXPLORING

Exmoor National Park. Less wild and forbidding than Dartmoor to its south, 267-square-mile Exmoor National Park is no less majestic for its bare heath and lofty views. The park extends right up to the coast and straddles the county border between Somerset and Devon. Some walks offer spectacular views over the Bristol Channel. Taking one of the more than 700 miles of paths and bridle ways through the bracken and heather (at its best in fall), you might glimpse the ponies and red deer for which the region is noted. Be careful: the proximity of the coast means that mists and squalls can descend with alarming suddenness. ✉ *Exmoor National Park Authority, Exmoor House, Dulverton* ☎ *01398/323665* 🌐 *www.exmoor-nationalpark.gov.uk.*

PORLOCK

6 miles west of Dunster, 45 miles north of Exeter.

Buried at the bottom of a valley, with the slopes of Exmoor all about, the small, unspoiled town of Porlock lies near "Doone Country," the setting for R. D. Blackmore's swashbuckling saga *Lorna Doone.* Porlock had already achieved a place in literary history by the late 1790s, when Samuel Taylor Coleridge declared it was a "man from Porlock" who interrupted his opium trance while the poet was composing "Kubla Khan."

GETTING HERE AND AROUND

Porlock is best reached via the A39 coastal route. WebberBus operates several buses between Porlock and Minehead. The village can be easily explored by foot.

ESSENTIALS

Bus Contacts WebberBus. ☎ *0800/096–3039 toll-free, 01278/452086* 🌐 *www.webberbus.com.*

Visitor Information Porlock Visitor Centre. ✉ *The Old School, High St.* ☎ *01643/863150* 🌐 *www.porlock.co.uk.*

EXPLORING

Coleridge Way. The 36-mile Coleridge Way passes through the northern fringes of the Quantock Hills, the isolated villages of the Brendon Hills, and parts of Exmoor National Park between Nether Stowey (site of Coleridge's home) and Porlock. ✉ *Porlock* 🌐 *www.coleridgeway.co.uk.*

Porlock Hill. As you're heading west from Porlock to Lynton, the coast road A39 mounts Porlock Hill, an incline so steep that signs encourage drivers to "keep going." The views across Exmoor and north to the Bristol Channel and Wales are worth it. Less steep but quieter and equally scenic routes, up the hill on toll roads, can be accessed from Porlock and Porlock Weir. ✉ *Porlock.*

Porlock Weir. Two miles west of Porlock, this tiny harbor is the starting point for an undemanding 2-mile walk along the coast through chestnut and walnut trees to **Culbone Church,** reputedly the smallest and most isolated church in England. Saxon in origin, it has a small Victorian spire and is lighted by candles, making it hard to find a more enchanting spot. ✉ *Porlock.*

WHERE TO EAT

$ MODERN BRITISH ✕ **The Café Porlock Weir.** Don't be put off by its unassuming name, because this self-styled "café-with-rooms" in a sea-facing Georgian building is pure, relaxed, English country house. Run by a husband-and-wife team, it offers top-quality food and accommodations. You can settle down in its spacious dining room for a cream tea with warm scones, or opt for a light lunch or more ambitious fare at dinner, including a seafood tasting menu with crab cakes, seafood terrine, and grilled mackerel. The five reasonably priced guest rooms are done in restful hues. $ *Average main: £12* ✉ *Dunster Steep, Porlock Weir* ☎ *01643/863300* 🌐 *www.thecafeporlockweir.co.uk* ⏲ *Closed Mon. and Tues. Mar.–Oct. and Mon.–Thurs. Nov.–Feb.*

5

LYNTON AND LYNMOUTH

13 miles west of Porlock, 60 miles northwest of Exeter.

A steep hill separates this pretty pair of Devonshire villages, which are linked by a Victorian cliff railway you can still ride. Lynmouth, a fishing village at the bottom of the hill, crouches below 1,000-foot-high cliffs at the mouths of the East and West Lyn rivers; Lynton is higher up. The poet Percy Bysshe Shelley visited Lynmouth in 1812, in the company of his 16-year-old bride, Harriet Westbrook. During their nine-week sojourn, the poet found time to write his polemical *Queen Mab.* The grand landscape of Exmoor lies all about, with walks to local beauty spots: Watersmeet, the Valley of Rocks, or Hollerday Hill, where rare feral goats graze.

GETTING HERE AND AROUND

These towns are best reached via the A39. Lynton is a stop on Quantock Heritage Bus 300, which runs Monday through Saturday from Minehead. It's a steep and winding ascent to Lynton from Lynmouth; take the cliff railway to travel between them.

ESSENTIALS

Visitor Information Lynton and Lymouth Tourist Information Centre. ✉ *Lee Rd., Lynton* ☎ *0845/458–3775* 🌐 *www.lynton-lynmouth-tourism.co.uk.*

EXPLORING

Lynton and Lynmouth Cliff Railway. Water and a cable system power the 862-foot cliff railway that connects these two towns. As they ascend a rocky cliff, you are treated to fine views over the harbor. Inaugurated in 1890, it was the gift of publisher George Newnes, who also donated Lynton's imposing town hall, near the top station on Lee Road. ✉ *The Esplanade, Lynmouth* ☎ *01598/753908* 🌐 *www.cliffrailwaylynton.co.uk* 🎫 *£3.70 round-trip* ⏲ *Mid-Feb.–early Apr. and early Oct.–late Oct., daily 10–5; mid-Apr.–late May and mid-Sept.–early Oct., daily 10–6; Easter week, late May–late July, and early Sept.–mid-Sept., daily 10–7; Aug., daily 10–9; early Nov., daily 10–4.*

Clovelly may have it all: cobbled streets, quaint houses, and the endless blue sea.

WHERE TO EAT AND STAY

$$ **MODERN BRITISH** ✕ **Rising Sun.** A 14th-century inn and a row of thatched cottages make up this pub-restaurant with great views over the Bristol Channel. The kitchen specializes in local cuisine with European influences, so expect such dishes as a smoked haddock tartlet, or duck confit with tomato and olive ragout. There's fresh seafood all year round, and a superb game menu January through March. In the attached hotel, corridors and creaking staircases lead to cozy guest rooms decorated in stylish print or solid fabrics. *Average main: £18* ✉ *Riverside Rd., Lynmouth* ☎ *01598/753223* 🌐 *www.risingsunlynmouth.co.uk.*

$$ **B&B/INN** **Shelley's Hotel.** Centrally located, this well-maintained hotel has bright and spacious rooms with generous windows and excellent views. **Pros:** harbor views from most rooms; great breakfasts; hospitable owners. **Cons:** some rooms overlook public car park; no restaurant; no kids under 12. *Rooms from: £130* ✉ *8 Watersmeet Rd., Lynmouth* ☎ *01598/753219* 🌐 *www.shelleyshotel.co.uk* ⊙ *Closed Dec.–Feb.* *11 rooms* *Breakfast.*

SPORTS AND THE OUTDOORS

BEACHES

West of Lynton, the Atlantic-facing beaches of Saunton Sands, Croyde Bay, and Woolacombe Bay are much beloved by surfers, with plenty of outlets renting equipment and offering lessons. Croyde Bay and Woolacombe Bay are more family-friendly.

Woolacombe Bay. One of the most famous beaches in the country, North Devon's Woolacombe is popular with surfers for its waves and with families for its soft sand and tidal pools that are great for kids to explore. This beach has all you could need for a dreamy day by the sea: cafés, chairs, and surfing equipment to rent, lifeguards, ice cream—you name it. But if you're not looking for crowds and kids, you may want to go elsewhere. The beach is 17 miles west of Lynton: to get here, take A361 and follow signs. **Amenities:** food and drink; lifeguard; parking (fee), toilets; water sports. **Best for:** surfing; swimming. ✉ *Woolacombe.*

BOATING

Exmoor Coast Boat Cruises. Cruise around the dramatic Devon coast on these boats that depart from Lynmouth Harbour. The round-trip journey to Lee Bay costs £10 and takes 45 minutes; the 75-minute excursion to Woody Bay and beyond, costing £15, lets you experience the clamorous birdlife on the cliffs. ✉ *Lynmouth Harbour, Watersmeet Rd., Lynmouth* ☎ *01598/753207.*

DONKEYS AT WORK

Donkey stables, donkey rides for kids, and abundant donkey souvenirs in Clovelly recall the days when these animals played an essential role in town life, carrying food, packages, and more up and down the village streets. Even in the 1990s, donkeys helped carry bags from the hotels. Today sleds do the work, but the animals' labor is remembered.

5

CLOVELLY

40 miles southwest of Lynton, 60 miles northwest of Exeter.

Fodor's Choice ★

Lovely Clovelly always seems to have the sun shining on its flower lined cottages and stepped and cobbled streets. Alas, its beauty is well-known, and day-trippers can overrun the village in summer. Perched precariously among cliffs, a steep, cobbled road—tumbling down at such an angle that it's closed to cars—leads to the toylike harbor with its 14th century quay. Allow about two hours (more if you stop for a drink or a meal) to take in the village. Hobby Drive, a 3-mile cliff-top carriageway laid out in 1829 through thick woods, gives scintillating views over the village and coast.

GETTING HERE AND AROUND

To get to Clovelly by bus, take Stagecoach service 319 from Barnstaple or Bideford. If you're driving, take the A39 and park at the Clovelly Visitor Centre for £6.95. The center of town is steep and cobbled. The climb from the harbor to the parking lot can be exhausting, but from April through early November a reasonably priced shuttle service brings you back.

EXPLORING

Clovelly Visitor Centre. Here you'll see a 20-minute film that puts Clovelly into context. In the village you can visit a 1930s-style fisherman's cottage and an exhibition about Victorian writer Charles Kingsley, who lived here as a child. The admission fee includes parking. To avoid the worst crowds, arrive early or late in the day. ✉ *Off A39* ☎ *01237/431781* 🌐 *www.clovelly.co.uk* 💰 *£6.95* ⏲ *Apr.–Oct., daily 9:30–5; Nov.–Mar., daily 10–4.*

WHERE TO STAY

$$$ HOTEL **Red Lion Hotel.** You can soak up the tranquillity of Clovelly after the day-trippers have gone at the 18th-century Red Lion, located right on the harbor in this coastal village. **Pros:** superb location; clean and comfortable. **Cons:** some rooms are small; food is inconsistent. *Rooms from: £180 The Quay 01237/431237 www.clovelly.co.uk 11 rooms Breakfast.*

CORNWALL

Cornwall stretches west into the sea, with plenty of magnificent coastline to explore, along with tranquil towns and some bustling resorts. One way to discover it all is to travel southwest from Boscastle and the cliff-top ruins of Tintagel Castle, the legendary birthplace of Arthur, along the north Cornish coast to Land's End. This predominantly cliff-lined coast, interspersed with broad expanses of sand, has many tempting places to stop, including Padstow (for a seafood feast), Newquay (a surfing and tourist center), or St. Ives (a delightful artists' colony).

From Land's End, the westernmost tip of Britain, known for its savage land- and seascapes and panoramic views, return to the popular seaside resort of Penzance, the harbor town of Falmouth, and the river port of Fowey. The Channel coast is less rugged than the northern coast, with more sheltered beaches. Leave time to visit the excellent Eden Project, with its surrealistic-looking conservatories in an abandoned clay pit, and to explore the boggy, heath-covered expanse of Bodmin Moor.

BOSCASTLE

15 miles north of Bodmin, 30 miles south of Clovelly.

In tranquil Boscastle, some of the stone-and-slate cottages at the foot of the steep valley date from the 1300s. A good place to relax and walk, the town is centered on a little harbor and set snug within towering cliffs. Nearby, 2 miles up the Valency valley, is St. Juliot's, the "Endelstow" referred to in Thomas Hardy's *A Pair of Blue Eyes*—the young author was involved with the restoration of this church while he was working as an architect.

5

GETTING HERE AND AROUND

Drivers can reach Boscastle along A39 and B3263. There are regular Western Greyhound buses from Bodmin Parkway, the nearest rail connection. The village is easily explored on foot.

ESSENTIALS

Visitor Information **Boscastle Visitor Centre.** ✉ *The Harbour* ☎ *01840/250010* 🌐 *www.visitboscastleandtintagel.com.*

WHERE TO STAY

$ B&B/INN Fodor's Choice ★ **The Old Rectory.** While restoring St. Juliot's Church, Thomas Hardy stayed in the building that now holds this delightful B&B. **Pros:** secluded setting; romantic ambience; helpful hosts. **Cons:** a little hard to find; two-night minimum stay in summer; no kids under 10. *$ Rooms from: £95* ✉ *Off B3263, St. Juliot* ☎ *01840/250225* 🌐 *www.stjuliot.com* *4 rooms* *Breakfast.*

TINTAGEL

3 miles southwest of Boscastle.

The romance of Arthurian legend thrives around Tintagel's ruined castle on the coast. Ever since the somewhat unreliable 12th-century chronicler Geoffrey of Monmouth identified Tintagel as the home of Arthur, son of Uther Pendragon and Ygrayne, devotees of the legend cycle have revered the site. In the 19th century Alfred, Lord Tennyson described Tintagel's Arthurian connection in *The Idylls of the King*. Today the village has its share of tourist junk—including Excaliburgers—but the headland around Tintagel is still splendidly scenic.

GETTING HERE AND AROUND

To drive to Tintagel, take the A39 to the B3263. Numerous parking lots are found in the village center. There's a bus stop near the tourist office for Western Greyhound buses from Bodmin Parkway, the nearest train station. Between April and October a shuttle service brings mobility-impaired passengers to the castle.

CLOSE UP

All About King Arthur

Legends about King Arthur have resonated through the centuries, enthusiastically taken up by writers and poets, from 7th-century Welsh and Breton troubadours to Tennyson and Mark Twain in the 19th century and T. H. White in the 20th century.

WHO WAS ARTHUR?

The historical Arthur was probably a Christian Celtic chieftain battling against the Saxons in the 6th century, although most of the tales surrounding him have a much later setting, thanks to the vivid but somewhat fanciful chronicles of his exploits by medieval scholars.

The virtuous warrior-hero of popular myth has always been treated with generous helpings of nostalgia for a golden age. For Sir Thomas Malory (circa 1408–71), author of *Le Morte d'Arthur,* the finest medieval prose collection of Arthurian romance, Arthur represented a lost era of chivalry and noble romance before the loosening of the traditional bonds of feudal society and the gradual collapse of the medieval social order.

FINDING KING ARTHUR

Places associated with Arthur and his consort, Guinevere, the wizard Merlin, the knights of the Round Table, and the related legends of Tristan and Isolde (or Iseult) can be found all over Europe, but the West Country claims the closest association. Arthur was said to have had his court of Camelot at Cadbury Castle (17 miles south of Wells) and to have been buried at Glastonbury.

Cornwall holds the greatest concentration of Arthurian links, notably his supposed birthplace, Tintagel, and the site of his last battle, on Bodmin Moor. However tenuous the links—and, barring the odd, somewhat ambiguous inscription, there's nothing in the way of hard evidence of Arthur's existence—the Cornish have taken the Once and Future King to their hearts, and his spirit is said to reside in the now-rare bird, the Cornish chough.

ESSENTIALS

Visitor Information Tintagel Visitor Centre. ✉ *Bossiney Rd.* ☎ *01840/779084* 🌐 *www.tintagelparishcouncil.gov.uk.*

EXPLORING

Old Post Office. This gorgeous 14th-century stone manor house with yard-thick walls, smoke-blackened beams, and an undulating slate-tile roof has been furnished with items from the 17th and 18th centuries. The walls are hung with "samplers"—embroidered poems and prayers usually produced by young girls. One room originally served as a post office and has been restored to its Victorian appearance. ✉ *Fore St.* ☎ *01840/770024* 🌐 *www.nationaltrust.org.uk* 🎫 *£3.80* ⏲ *Early Mar.–late Mar. and Oct., daily 11–4; late Mar.–Sept., daily 10:30–5:30.*

Fodor's Choice ★ **Tintagel Castle.** Although all that remains of the ruined cliff-top Tintagel Castle, legendary birthplace of King Arthur, is the outline of its walls, moats, and towers, it requires only a bit of imagination to conjure up a picture of Sir Lancelot and Sir Galahad riding out in search of the Holy Grail over the narrow causeway above the seething breakers.

The coast near Tintagel Castle has lovely views.

Archaeological evidence, however, suggests that the castle dates from much later—about 1150, when it was the stronghold of the earls of Cornwall. Long before that, Romans may have occupied the site. The earliest identified remains here are of Celtic (AD 5th century) origin, and these may have some connection with the legendary Arthur. Legends aside, nothing can detract from the castle ruins, dramatically set off by the wild, windswept Cornish coast, on an island joined to the mainland by a narrow isthmus. Paths lead down to the pebble beach and a cavern known as **Merlin's Cave.** Exploring Tintagel Castle involves some arduous climbing on steep steps, but even on a summer's day, when people swarm over the battlements and a westerly Atlantic wind sweeps through Tintagel, you can feel the proximity of the distant past. ✉ *Castle Rd., ½ mile west of the village* ☎ *01840/770328* 🌐 *www.english-heritage.org.uk* 🎫 *£7.20* ⏲ *Apr.–Sept., daily 10–6; Oct., daily 10–5; Nov.–late Mar., weekends 10–4.*

PORT ISAAC

6 miles southwest of Tintagel.

A mixture of granite, slate, and whitewashed cottages tumbles precipitously down the cliff to the tiny harbor at Port Isaac, still dedicated to the crab-and-lobster trade. Low tide reveals a pebbly beach and rock pools. Relatively unscathed by tourists, it makes for a peaceful and secluded stay. For an extra slice of authentic Cornwall life, you can hear the local choir sing shanties at the harborside on Friday nights in summer.

GETTING HERE AND AROUND

If you're driving, Port Isaac is reached via the A39, then the B3314. Park at the lot at the top of the village rather than attempting to drive into the center. By bus, take Western Greyhound service 555 from the train station at Bodmin Parkway, changing to 584 at Wadebridge. The bus services run every day but Sunday.

WHERE TO STAY

$$ HOTEL **The Old School Hotel and Restaurant.** Perched on the cliffs above Port Isaac's minuscule harbor, this idiosyncratic lodging was a Victorian schoolhouse until the 1980s, and nostalgically retains many of the features of its previous role. **Pros:** lots of character; great views. **Cons:** old building and in need of renovation; some rooms are tiny. *Rooms from: £115 Fore St. 01208/880721 www.theoldschoolhotel.co.uk 12 rooms Breakfast.*

PADSTOW

10 miles southwest of Port Isaac.

A small fishing port at the mouth of the River Camel, Padstow attracts attention and visitors as a center of culinary excellence, largely because of the presence here since 1975 of pioneering seafood chef Rick Stein. Stein's empire includes two restaurants, a café, a fish-and-chips joint, a delicatessen, a patisserie, and a cooking school where classes fill up months in advance.

Even if seafood isn't your favorite fare, Padstow is worth visiting. The cries of seagulls fill its lively harbor, a string of fine beaches lies within a short ride—including some choice strands highly prized by surfers—and two scenic walking routes await: the Saints Way across the peninsula to Fowey, and the Camel Trail, a footpath and cycling path that follows the river as far as Bodmin Moor. If you can avoid peak visiting times—summer weekends—so much the better.

GETTING HERE AND AROUND

Regular buses connect Padstow with Bodmin, the main transportation hub hereabouts, and on the main Plymouth–Penzance train line. To get here from Port Isaac, change buses at Wadebridge. Alternatively, take the bus to Rock and the passenger ferry across the river. There are numerous direct buses on the Newquay–Padstow route. Drivers should take A39/A389 and park in the waterside parking lot before reaching the harbor.

ESSENTIALS

Ferry Contacts Padstow Rock Ferry. *Padstow 01841/532239 www.padstow-harbour.co.uk.*

Visitor Information Padstow Tourist Information Centre. *North Quay 01841/533449 www.padstowlive.com.*

WHERE TO EAT AND STAY

$$$$ MODERN BRITISH Fodor's Choice ★ **Paul Ainsworth at Number 6.** There is more to Padstow's culinary scene than Rick Stein, as this intimate bistro persuasively demonstrates. Diners seated in a series of small, stylish rooms can feast on ingeniously concocted dishes that make the most of local and seasonal produce. Try the blow-torched mackerel with celeriac and ham for starters, and cod with grilled leeks and crab, Cornish venison, or roast Galloway beef for the main course, leaving space for some astounding desserts. Set-price lunches are a particularly good value. The atmosphere is warm and lively, with swift, amiable service. *Average main: £30* *6 Middle St.* *01841/532093* *www.number6inpadstow.co.uk* *Closed Sun and Mon.*

$$$$ SEAFOOD Fodor's Choice ★ **The Seafood Restaurant.** Just across from where the lobster boats and trawlers unload their catches, Rick Stein's flagship restaurant has built its reputation on the freshest fish and the highest culinary artistry. The exclusively fish and shellfish menu includes everything from grilled Padstow lobster with herbs to stir-fried Singapore chilli crab. Choose between sitting formally at a table or grabbing a stool at the Seafood Bar in the center of the modern, airy restaurant (no reservations for bar). Don't want to move after your meal? Book one of the sunny, individually designed guest rooms overlooking the harbor. *Average main: £30* *Riverside* *01841/532700* *www.rickstein.com* *Reservations essential.*

$$$ FRENCH **St. Petroc's Bistro.** Part of chef Rick Stein's empire, this bistro with contemporary art adorning its walls has a secluded feel. In fine weather you can dine in the sunny walled garden. The French-inspired menu features such dishes as hot Toulouse sausage and Chateaubriand. If you want to stay, the spacious bedrooms are individually decorated with stylish modern pieces. *Average main: £21* *4 New St.* *01841/532700* *www.rickstein.com* *No lunch Mon.–Wed., Nov.–Feb.*

$$$$ B&B/INN **St. Edmund's House.** The most luxurious Rick Stein venture has a sophisticated minimalist style. **Pros:** stylish bedrooms; top-notch service; central but secluded. **Cons:** short walk to breakfast; extravagant prices; not all rooms have a sea view. *Rooms from: £295* *St. Edmund's La.* *01841/532700* *www.rickstein.com* *6 rooms* *Breakfast.*

SPORTS AND THE OUTDOORS

BIKING

Trail Bike Hire. Bikes of all shapes and sizes can be rented at Trail Bike Hire, at the start of the Camel Trail. *South Quay* *01841/532594* *www.trailbikehire.co.uk.*

SURFING

Harlyn Surf School. This school can arrange two-hour to four-day surfing courses at its base in Harlyn Bay, 3 miles west of Padstow. *Harlyn Bay Beach* *01841/533076* *www.harlynsurfschool.co.uk.*

WALKING

Saints Way. This 30-mile inland path takes you between Padstow and the Camel Estuary on Cornwall's north coast to Fowey on the south coast. It follows a Bronze Age trading route, later used by Celtic pilgrims to

5

cross the peninsula. Several relics of such times can be seen along the way. ✉ *Padstow.*

NEWQUAY

14 miles southwest of Padstow, 30 miles southwest of Tintagel.

The biggest, most developed resort on the north Cornwall coast is a fairly large town established in 1439. It was once the center of the trade in pilchards (a small herringlike fish), and on the headland you can still see a white hut where a lookout known as a "huer" watched for pilchard schools and directed the boats to the fishing grounds. Newquay has become Britain's surfing capital, and in summer young California-dreamin' devotees can pack the wide, cliff-backed beaches.

GETTING HERE AND AROUND

A branch line links Newquay with the main Plymouth–Penzance train line at Par, and there are regular buses from Padstow, Bodmin, and St. Austell. Train and bus stations are both in the center of town. Newquay has good road connections with the rest of the peninsula via the A30 and A39. The best beaches are a long walk or a short bus ride from the center.

ESSENTIALS

Visitor Information Newquay Tourist Information Centre. ✉ *Marcus Hill* ☎ *01637/854020* 🌐 *www.visitnewquay.org.*

WHERE TO EAT

$$$$ ITALIAN Fodor's Choice ★

✕ **Fifteen Cornwall.** Bright and capacious, this modern Italian restaurant has won plaudits both for its fabulous food and for its fine location overlooking magnificent Watergate Bay, a broad beach much beloved of water-sports enthusiasts. One of Britain's culinary heroes, Cockney chef Jamie Oliver, helped to set up the enterprise, which has the aim of training local young people for careers in catering. To provide the staff with the widest possible repertoire, the £60 tasting menu changes frequently and lists five courses that might include a starter of gnocchi with wild mushrooms and hazelnuts, followed by scallops or duck breast for a main course and *affogato al caffè* (ice cream soaked in black coffee) to finish. You can also order à la carte, and there are usually moderately priced fixed-menu lunch options available. Watergate Bay lies 3 miles east of Newquay. [$] *Average main: £26* ✉ *Watergate Rd., Watergate Bay* ☎ *01637/861000* 🌐 *www.fifteencornwall.co.uk.*

SPORTS AND THE OUTDOORS

Surfing is Newquay's raison d'être for many of the enthusiasts who flock here throughout the year. Great Western and Tolcarne beaches are most suitable for beginners, while Fistral Beach is better for those with more experience. There are dozens of surf schools around town, many offering accommodation packages, and rental outlets are also ubiquitous.

BEACHES

Fistral Bay. This favorite of serious surfers is a long stretch of flat, soft sand, renowned for its powerful tides and strong currents. Surf shops rent equipment and offer lessons on the beach, or you can just check out the scene. Lifeguards watch the water in summer, and there are cafés and shops selling beach supplies. The beach is at the western edge of

Newquay. **Amenities:** food and drink; lifeguard; parking (fee); toilets; water sports. **Best for:** partiers; surfing; swimming. ✉ *Off Headland Rd.*

SURFING

Extreme Academy. One of the West Country's water-sports specialists, Extreme Academy offers courses in wave-skiing, kite-surfing, kite-buggying, paddle-surfing, and just plain old surfing, as well as equipment for hire. ✉ *Trevarrian Hill, Watergate Bay* ☎ *01637/860840* 🌐 *www.extremeacademy.co.uk*.

ST. IVES

25 miles southwest of Newquay, 10 miles north of Penzance.

Fodor's Choice ★ James McNeill Whistler came here to paint his landscapes, Barbara Hepworth to fashion her modernist sculptures, and Virginia Woolf to write her novels. Today sand, sun, and superb art continue to attract thousands of vacationers to the fishing village of St. Ives, named after Saint Ia, a 5th-century female Irish missionary said to have arrived on a floating leaf. Many come to St. Ives for the sheltered beaches; the best are Porthmeor, on the northern side of town, and, facing east, Porthminster—the choice for those seeking more space to spread out.

5

GETTING HERE AND AROUND

St. Ives has good bus and train connections with Bristol, Exeter, and Penzance. Train journeys usually involve a change at St. Erth (the brief St. Erth–St. Ives stretch is one of the West Country's most scenic train routes). The adjacent bus and train stations are within a few minutes' walk of the center. Drivers should avoid the center—parking lots are well marked in the higher parts of town.

ESSENTIALS

Visitor Information Visit St. Ives Information Centre. ✉ *The Guildhall, Street-an-Pol* ☎ *0905/252-2250* 🌐 *www.visitstives.org.uk.*

EXPLORING

Barbara Hepworth Museum and Sculpture Garden. The studio and garden of Dame Barbara Hepworth (1903–75), who pioneered abstract sculpture in England, are now a museum and sculpture garden, managed by the Tate St. Ives. The artist lived here for 26 years. ✉ *Trewyn Studio, Barnoon Hill* ☎ *01736/796226* 🌐 *www.tate.org.uk* 🎟 *£6, £10 combined ticket with Tate St. Ives* ⏲ *Mar.–Oct., daily 10–5:20; Nov.–Feb., Tues.–Sun. 10–4:20.*

FAMILY **Geevor Tin Mine.** The winding B3306 coastal road southwest from St. Ives passes through some of Cornwall's starkest yet most beautiful countryside. Barren hills crisscrossed by low stone walls drop abruptly to granite cliffs and wide bays. Evidence of the ancient tin-mining industry is everywhere. Now a fascinating mining heritage center, the early-20th-century Geevor Tin Mine employed 400 men, but in 1985 the collapse of the world tin market wiped Cornwall from the mining map. Wear sturdy footwear for the surface and underground tours. A museum, shop, and café are at the site. ✉ *B3306, Pendeen* ☎ *01736/788662* 🌐 *www.geevor.com* 🎟 *£12* ⏲ *Apr.–Oct., Sun.–Fri. 9–5; Nov.–Mar., Sun.–Fri. 9–4; last admission 1 hr before closing.*

SURFERS WELCOME

The four-story Tate St. Ives, at the base of a cliff fronted by Porthmeor Beach, may be the only art museum with special storage space for visitors' surfboards.

St. Ives Society of Artists Gallery. Local artists display selections of their current work for sale at this gallery in the former Mariners' Church. The Crypt Gallery in the basement is used for private exhibitions. ✉ *Norway Sq.* ☎ *01736/795582* 🌐 *www.stisa.co.uk* ⏲ *Mar.–Easter and mid-Oct.–early Jan., Mon.–Sat. 10:30–5:30; Easter–mid-Oct., Mon.–Sat. 10:30–5:30, Sun. 2–5.*

Tate St. Ives. The spectacular sister of the renowned London gallery displays the work of artists who lived and worked in St. Ives, mostly from 1925 to 1975. There are also frequent exhibitions of contemporary art connected to West Cornwall. The collection occupies a modernist building—a fantasia of seaside art deco–period architecture with a panoramic view of rippling ocean. The rooftop café is excellent for the food and views. Work to refurbish and extend the gallery, due to be completed in 2017, may affect opening times—see the website or call ahead to check. ✉ *Porthmeor Beach* ☎ *01736/796226* 🌐 *www.tate.org.uk* 🎟 *£7, £10 combined ticket with Barbara Hepworth Museum and Sculpture Garden* ⏲ *Mar.–Oct., daily 10–5:20; Nov.–Feb., Tues.–Sun. 10–4:20.*

QUICK BITES

Sloop Inn. One of Cornwall's oldest pubs, the 1312 Sloop Inn serves simple lunches as well as evening meals in wood-beam rooms that display the work of local artists. If the weather's good, you can eat at the tables outside and watch the harbor. ✉ ***The Wharf*** ☎ ***01736/796584*** 🌐 ***www.sloop-inn.co.uk.***

WHERE TO EAT

$$ MODERN BRITISH

✕ **The Garrack.** This elegant restaurant is known for the panoramic sea views from its hilltop location and for relaxed and undemanding fine dining. The à la carte menu may include pan-fried scallops and roast fillet of hake, as well as duck, partridge, and belly pork. Breads are made on the premises, and desserts include local ice cream and homemade sorbets. Some rooms at the attached hotel are furnished in traditional style; others are more modern. $ *Average main: £18* ✉ *Burthallan La.* ☎ *01736/796199* 🌐 *www.garrack.com* ⏲ *No lunch Mon.–Sat.*

$$ MODERN BRITISH

✕ **Gurnard's Head.** This pub with bright, homey furnishings and a relaxed ambience looks past green fields to the ocean beyond. The frequently changing menu features fresh, inventively prepared meat and seafood dishes; look for pork tenderloin with squash risotto, or roasted brill with new potatoes, leeks, mussels, and herb mustard. Seven smallish rooms provide guest accommodations. The inn sits near the curvy coast road 6 miles west of St. Ives. $ *Average main: £16* ✉ *B3306 , near Zennor, Treen* ☎ *01736/796928* 🌐 *www.gurnardshead.co.uk* ✍ *Reservations essential.*

$$$ SEAFOOD

✕ **Porthminster Café.** Unbeatable for its location alone—on the broad, golden sands of Porthminster Beach—this sleek, modern eatery prepares imaginative breakfasts, lunches, teas, and evening meals that you can savor while you take in the marvelous vista across the bay. The accent is on Mediterranean and Asian flavors, and typical choices include wild sea-bass fillet with crab fritters, monkfish curry, and Iberico pork rib. The sister Porthgwidden Beach Café, in the Downalong neighborhood, has a smaller and cheaper menu that's equally strong on seafood. *Average main: £21 ✉ Porthminster Beach ☎ 01736/795352 ⊕ www.porthminstercafe.co.uk ⊗ Closed Mon. Nov.–mid-Mar. No dinner Sun., Tue. and Wed. Nov.–mid-Mar.*

WHERE TO STAY

$ B&B/INN Fodor's Choice ★ **Cornerways.** Everything in St. Ives seems squeezed into the tiniest of spaces, and this cottage B&B in the quiet Downalong quarter is no exception. **Pros:** friendly owners; tasteful decor; excellent breakfast choices. **Cons:** rooms are mostly small; narrow stairways to climb; very limited parking. *Rooms from: £95 ✉ 1 Bethesda Pl. ☎ 01736/796706 ⊕ www.cornerwaysstives.com ▭ No credit cards ⇨ 6 rooms ⚲ Breakfast.*

$$ HOTEL **Primrose Valley Hotel.** Blending the elegance of an Edwardian villa with clean-lined modern style, this friendly hotel has the best of both worlds. **Pros:** close to beach and train and bus stations; friendly atmosphere; attention to detail. **Cons:** some rooms are small and lack views; tricky access to car park; stairs to climb; no kids under 8. *Rooms from: £122 ✉ Porthminster Beach ☎ 01736/794939 ⊕ www.primroseonline.co.uk ⇨ 8 rooms, 1 suite ⚲ Breakfast.*

LAND'S END

17 miles southwest of St. Ives, 9 miles southwest of Penzance.

The coastal road, B3306, ends at the western tip of Britain at what is, quite literally, Land's End.

GETTING HERE AND AROUND

Frequent buses serve Land's End from Penzance (around one hour). There is no direct service from St. Ives in winter, but in summer an open-top double-decker tracks the coast between St. Ives and Penzance, taking in Land's End en route.

EXPLORING

Land's End. The sea crashes against the rocks at Land's End and lashes ships battling their way around the point. **■ TIP→ Approach from one of the coastal footpaths for the best panoramic view.** Over the years, sightseers have caused some erosion of the paths, but new ones are constantly being built, and Cornish "hedges" (granite walls covered with turf) have been planted to prevent erosion. The scenic grandeur of Land's End remains undiminished. The Land's End Hotel here is undistinguished, though the restaurant has good views.

SPORTS AND THE OUTDOORS

Porthcurno Beach. A protected, blue bay in South Cornwall, Porthcurno has a crescent moon of white sand (from crushed shells) at the foot of imposing dark, blocklike granite cliffs. The extraordinary Minack Theatre—carved from solid rock—is on one side, and there are pubs and cafés nearby. A steep slope can make swimming a challenge at

5

times, but one area near a stream is good for families. The town and beach are signed off B3315, and the coastal path is nearby. **Amenities:** food and drink; lifeguard; parking (fee); toilets. **Best for:** swimming; walking. ✉ *3 miles east of Land's End, Porthcurno.*

Sennen Cove. Located in the aptly named Whitesand Bay, Sennen Cove is a gorgeous expanse of creamy soft sand on the western tip of Cornwall. When the tide is coming in, the waves attract legions of surfers. When the tide's out, kids paddle in the tidal pools and the sand stretches as far as you can see. Cafés are nearby, and surfing equipment is for rent on the beach. Sennen is off A30 less than 2 miles north of Land's End, and can be reached on foot on the South West Coast Path. **Amenities:** food and drink; lifeguard; parking (fee); toilets; water sports. **Best for:** sunset; surfing; swimming; walking. ✉ *Off A30, Whitesand Bay.*

MOUSEHOLE

7 miles east of Land's End, 3 miles south of Penzance.

Fodor's Choice ★ Between Land's End and Penzance, Mousehole (pronounced *mow*-zel, the first syllable rhyming with "cow") merits a stop—and plenty of people do stop—to see this archetypal Cornish fishing village of tiny stone cottages. It was the home of Dolly Pentreath, supposedly the last person to speak solely in Cornish, who died in 1777.

GETTING HERE AND AROUND

Frequent buses take 20 minutes to travel from Penzance to Mousehole. From Land's End, change buses at Newlyn. Drivers should take the B3315 coastal route and park in one of the seaside lots before entering the village.

WHERE TO EAT AND STAY

$$ MODERN BRITISH ✕ **2 Fore Street.** Within view of Mousehole's tiny harbor, you can dine on the freshest seafood in this popular bistro. The seasonal, Mediterranean-inspired menu takes in everything from crab soup with Parmesan croutons to roasted gurnard fillets with mussels, chili, coconut, ginger, and jasmine rice. Meat eaters are also well catered to with dishes like beef bourguignonne and chargrilled rib-eye steak. The bright, white-walled dining room has a fresh, modern feel, and there are tables in the sheltered back garden. $ *Average main: £15* ✉ *2 Fore St.* ☎ *01736/731164* 🌐 *www.2forestreet.co.uk* ⏲ *Closed Jan. and early Feb.*

$$ HOTEL **Old Coastguard.** The best views of Mousehole can be enjoyed from the bedrooms of this lodging; some rooms have balconies and four-poster beds, and all come with proper coffee with fresh milk and Cornish tea. **Pros:** panoramic views; walking paths; cheerful staff. **Cons:** unprepossessing exterior; could do with a scrub-up in places; food sometimes disappoints. $ *Rooms from: £130* ✉ *The Parade* ☎ *01736/731222* 🌐 *www.oldcoastguardhotel.co.uk* *13 rooms, 1 suite* *Breakfast.*

EN ROUTE

About 2 miles north of Mousehole on B3315, **Newlyn** has long been Cornwall's most important fishing port. The annual Fish Festival takes over the town at the end of August. Newlyn became the magnet for artists at the end of the 19th century, and a few of the fishermen's cottages that first attracted them remain. Today the village has a good gallery of contemporary art.

PENZANCE

3 miles north of Mousehole, 1½ miles north of Newlyn, 10 miles south of St. Ives.

Superb views over Mount's Bay are one lure of this popular, unpretentious seaside resort. Even though it does get very crowded in summer, Penzance makes a good base for exploring the area. The town's isolated position has always made it vulnerable to attack from the sea. During the 16th century, Spanish raiders destroyed most of the original town, and the majority of old buildings date from as late as the 18th century. The main street is Market Jew Street, a folk mistranslation of the Cornish expression Marghas Yow, which means "Thursday Market." Where Market Jew Street meets Causeway Head is Market House, an impressive, domed granite building constructed in 1837, with a statue of locally born chemist Humphry Davy in front.

In contrast to artsy St. Ives, Penzance is a no-nonsense working town. Though lacking the traffic-free lanes and quaint cottages of St. Ives, Penzance preserves pockets of handsome Georgian architecture.

GETTING HERE AND AROUND

The main train line from Plymouth terminates at Penzance, which is also served by National Express buses. Bus and train stations are next to each other at the east end of town. A car is an encumbrance here, so use one of the parking lots near the tourist office or the bus and train stations.

ESSENTIALS

Visitor Information Penzance Welcome Centre. ✉ *Station Approach* ☎ *01736/335530* 🌐 *www.westcornwall.org.uk.*

EXPLORING

Chapel Street. One of the prettiest thoroughfares in Penzance, Chapel Street winds down from Market House to the harbor. Its predominantly Georgian and Regency houses suddenly give way to the extraordinary **Egyptian House**, whose facade recalls the Middle East. Built around 1830 as a geological museum, today it houses vacation apartments. Across Chapel Street is the 17th-century **Union Hotel,** where in 1805 the death of Lord Nelson and the victory of Trafalgar were first announced. Near the Union Hotel on Chapel Street is the **Turk's Head,** an inn said to date from the 13th century. ✉ *Penzance.*

OFF THE BEATEN PATH

Isles of Scilly. Fondly regarded in folklore as the lost land of Lyonesse, this compact group of more than 100 islands 30 miles southwest of Land's End is equally famed for the warm summer climate and ferocious winter storms. In fair weather you can find peace, flowers—wild, cultivated, and subtropical—swarms of seabirds, and unspoiled beaches galore. There's a 2¾-hour ferry service from Penzance and a plane service from Land's End airport and other mainland airports. Planes and ferries both arrive at the largest of the five inhabited islands, St. Mary's, which has the bulk of the lodgings, though the most palatial retreats are on the islands of Tresco and St Martin's. ✉ *Penzance.*

Penlee House Gallery and Museum. A small collection in this gracious Victorian house in Penlee Park focuses on paintings by members of the so-called Newlyn School from about 1880 to 1930. These works evoke the life of the inhabitants of Newlyn, mostly fisherfolk. The museum also covers 5,000 years of West Cornwall history through archaeology, decorative arts, costume, and photography exhibits. ✉ *Morrab Rd.* ☎ *01736/363625* 🌐 *www.penleehouse.org.uk* 🎫 *£4.50* 🕘 *Apr.–Sept., Mon.–Sat. 10–5; Oct.–Mar., Mon.–Sat. 10–4:30; last admission 30 min before closing.*

St. Michael's Mount. Rising out of Mount's Bay just off the coast, this spectacular granite-and-slate island is one of Cornwall's greatest natural attractions. The 14th-century castle perched at the highest point—200 feet above the sea—was built on the site of a Benedictine chapel founded by Edward the Confessor. In its time, the island has served as a church (Brittany's island abbey of Mont St. Michel was an inspiration), a fortress, and a private residence. The castle rooms you can tour include the Chevy Chase Room—a name probably associated with the Cheviot Hills or the French word *chevaux* (horses), after the hunting frieze that decorates the walls of this former monks' refectory. Family portraits include works by Reynolds and Gainsborough. Don't miss the wonderful views from the castle battlements. Around the base of the rock are buildings from medieval to Victorian times, but they appear harmonious. Fascinating gardens surround the Mount, and many kinds of plants flourish in its microclimate.

To get to the island, walk the cobbled causeway from the village of Marazion or, when the tide is in during summer, take the £2 ferry. There are pubs and restaurants in the village, but the island also has a café and restaurant. **■ TIP→ Wear stout shoes for your visit, which requires a steep climb.** Visits may be canceled in severe weather. ✉ *A394, 3 miles east of Penzance, Marazion* ☎ *01736/710507* 🌐 *www.stmichaelsmount.co.uk* 🎫 *£11.50; castle only £8.50; garden only £5.50* 🕘 *Castle mid-Mar.–June and Sept.–Oct., Sun.–Fri. 10:30–5; July and Aug., Sun.–Fri. 10:30–5:30; Nov.–mid-Mar., tours Tues. and Fri. 11 and 2 (call first to check weather conditions). Garden mid-Apr.–June, weekdays 10:30–5; July and Aug., Thurs. and Fri. 10:30–5:30; Sept., Thurs. and Fri. 10:30–5; last admission 45 min before closing.*

WHERE TO EAT

$ BRITISH

✕ **Admiral Benbow.** One of the town's most famous inns, the 17th-century Admiral Benbow was once a smugglers' pub—look for the figure of a smuggler on the roof. Seafaring memorabilia, a brass cannon, model ships, and figureheads fill the place. In the family-friendly dining room, decorated to resemble a ship's galley, you can enjoy seafood or a steak-and-ale pie. $ *Average main: £11* ✉ *46 Chapel St.* ☎ *01736/363448.*

$$$ MODERN BRITISH

✕ **Harris's.** Seafood is the main event in the two small, pink-toned rooms of this restaurant off Market Jew Street. The menu showcases whatever the boats bring, though crab Florentine, grilled on a bed of spinach with a cheese sauce, is usually available. Meat dishes might include noisettes of Cornish lamb with fennel puree and rosemary sauce in spring and summer or breast of pheasant in winter. The semiformal style is intimate, elegant, and traditional. $ *Average main: £20* ✉ *46 New St.* ☎ *01736/364408* 🌐 *www.harrissrestaurant.co.uk* 🕘 *Closed Nov. and Feb. Closed Sun. year-round and Mon. Dec.–June.*

The stunning ocean setting of the open-air Minack Theatre near Penzance may distract you from the onstage drama.

WHERE TO STAY

$$ B&B/INN **Artist Residence.** A classic Georgian building has been converted with flair and wit to create a contemporary guesthouse with a strong artistic bent. **Pros:** idiosyncratic style; central location; generous breakfasts. **Cons:** street noise in front rooms; no parking; no elevator. *Rooms from: £110* *20 Chapel St.* *01736/365664* *www.artistresidencecornwall.co.uk* *18 rooms* *Breakfast.*

$ B&B/INN **Camilla House.** This flower-bedecked Georgian house close to the harbor has smartly decorated guest rooms with sea views from those at the front—top-floor rooms have all-round views but have low ceilings. **Pros:** friendly and helpful management; quiet location near seafront. **Cons:** some rooms are small; lengthy walk from bus and train stations. *Rooms from: £87* *12 Regent Terr.* *01736/363771* *www.camillahouse.co.uk* *Closed Dec.–Feb.* *8 rooms* *Breakfast.*

$ HOTEL **Union Hotel.** Strong on historical atmosphere, this central lodging housed the town's assembly rooms, where news of Admiral Nelson's victory at Trafalgar and of the death of Nelson himself were first announced from the minstrels' gallery in 1805. **Pros:** historic character; central location; good value. **Cons:** dowdy in places; sparse staff; no elevator. *Rooms from: £77* *Chapel St.* *01736/362319* *www.unionhotel.co.uk* *28 rooms* *Breakfast.*

NIGHTLIFE AND PERFORMING ARTS

Minack Theatre. The open-air Minack Theatre perches high above a beach 3 miles southeast of Land's End and about 6 miles southwest of Penzance. The slope of the cliff forms a natural amphitheater, with bench seats on the terraces and the sea as a magnificent backdrop. Different companies present everything from classic dramas to modern comedies, as well as operas and concerts, on afternoons and evenings between Easter and late September. An exhibition center tells the story of the theater's creation. ✉ *Off B3315, Porthcurno* ☎ *01736/810181* 🌐 *www.minack.com* 🎫 *Exhibition center £4.50, performances £9–£11.50* ⏲ *Apr.–Sept., daily 9:30–5:30 (9:30–11:30 am on afternoon performance days); Oct.–Mar., daily 10–4.*

SPORTS AND THE OUTDOORS

Many ships have foundered on Cornwall's rocky coastline, resulting in an estimated 3,600 shipwrecks. The area around Land's End has some of the best diving in Europe, in part because the convergence of the Atlantic and the Gulf Stream here results in impressive visibility and unusual subtropical marine life.

Cornwall Divers. This small company offers year-round dive excursions in the waters around West Cornwall. ✉ *Marine Crescent, Bar Rd., Falmouth* ☎ *01326/311265, 07785/232555* 🌐 *www.cornwalldivers.co.uk.*

LIZARD PENINSULA

23 miles southeast of Penzance.

Fodor's Choice ★ The southernmost point on mainland Britain, this peninsula is a government-designated Area of Outstanding Natural Beauty, named so for the rocky, dramatic coast rather than the flat and boring interior. The huge, eerily rotating dish antennae of the Goonhilly Satellite Earth Station are visible from the road as it crosses Goonhilly Downs, the backbone of the peninsula. There's no coast road, unlike Land's End, but the coastal path offers marvelous opportunities to explore on foot—and is often the only way to reach the best beaches. With no large town (Helston at the northern end is the biggest, but isn't a tourist center), it's far less busy than the Land's End peninsula.

GETTING HERE AND AROUND

If you're driving, take A394 to reach Helston, gateway town to the Lizard Peninsula. From Helston, A3083 heads straight down to Lizard Point. Helston is the main public transport hub, but bus service to the villages is infrequent.

EXPLORING

Kynance Cove. A path close to the tip of the peninsula plunges down 200-foot cliffs to this tiny cove dotted with a handful of pint-size islands. The sands here are reachable only during the 2½ hours before and after low tide. The peninsula's cliffs are made of greenish serpentine rock, interspersed with granite; souvenirs of the area are carved out of the stone. ✉ *The Lizard.*

FALMOUTH

8 miles northeast of Lizard Peninsula.

The bustle of this resort town's fishing harbor, yachting center, and commercial port only adds to its charm. In the 18th century Falmouth was the main mail-boat port for North America, and in Flushing, a village across the inlet, you can see the slate-covered houses built by prosperous mail-boat captains. A ferry service now links the two towns. On Custom House Quay, off Arwenack Street, is the King's Pipe, an oven in which seized contraband was burned.

GETTING HERE AND AROUND

Falmouth can be reached from Truro on a branch rail line or by frequent bus service, and is also served by local and National Express buses from other towns. Running parallel to the seafront, the long, partly pedestrianized main drag links the town's main sights. Visitors to Pendennis Castle traveling by train should use Falmouth Docks Station, from which it's a short walk. Alternatively, drive or take a local bus to the castle to save legwork.

ESSENTIALS

Visitor Information Fal River Visitor Information Centre. ✉ *Prince of Wales Pier, 11 Market Strand* ☎ *01326/741194* 🌐 *www.falmouth.co.uk.*

5

EXPLORING

FAMILY **National Maritime Museum Cornwall.** The granite-and-oak-clad structure by the harbor is an excellent place to come to grips with Cornish maritime heritage, weather lore, and navigational science. You can view approximately 30 of the collection of 140 or so boats, examine the tools associated with Cornish boatbuilders, and gaze down from the lighthouselike lookout, which is equipped with maps, telescopes, and binoculars. In the glass-fronted Tidal Zone below sea level, you come face-to-face with the sea itself. ✉ *Discovery Quay* ☎ *01326/313388* 🌐 *www.nmmc.co.uk* 🎫 *£12* 🕒 *Daily 10–5.*

FAMILY Fodor's Choice ★ **Pendennis Castle.** At the end of its own peninsula stands this formidable castle, built by Henry VIII in the 1540s and improved by his daughter Elizabeth I. You can explore the defenses developed over the centuries. In the Royal Artillery Barracks, the Pendennis Unlocked exhibit explores the castle's history and its connection to Cornwall and England. The castle has sweeping views over the English Channel and across to St. Mawes Castle, designed as a companion fortress to guard the roads. There are free tours of the Half Moon Battery and regular performances, historical reenactments, and shows for kids. ✉ *Pendennis Head* ☎ *01326/316594* 🌐 *www.english-heritage.org.uk* 🎫 *£7.50* 🕒 *Apr.–Sept., daily 10–6; Oct., daily 10–5; Nov–Mar., weekends 10–4; last entry 1 hr before closing.*

WHERE TO EAT AND STAY

$$ MODERN BRITISH ✕ **Gylly Beach.** For views and location, this beachside eatery with a crisp, modern interior and deck seating can't be beat. By day, it's a breezy café offering burgers, salads, and sandwiches, while the evening menu presents a judicious balance of meat, seafood, and vegetarian dishes, from "seafood taster" of freshly caught fish to pork belly or wild mushroom goulash. There are barbecues in summer, and live music on Sunday evening. 💲 *Average main: £16* ✉ *Gyllyngvase Beach, Cliff Rd.* ☎ *01326/312884* 🌐 *www.gyllybeach.com* 🕒 *No dinner Mon.–Wed., Nov.–Easter.*

$ BRITISH **Pandora Inn.** This thatched pub on a creek 4 miles north of Falmouth is a great retreat, with both a patio and a moored pontoon for summer dining. Maritime memorabilia and fresh flowers provide decoration, and there's a blazing fire in winter. You can eat in the bar, in the oak-beamed room upstairs, or outside. The menu highlight is fresh seafood—try the fish pie in a shallot and Pernod cream sauce. *Average main: £13 Restronguet Creek, Mylor Bridge, Mylor Bridge 01326/372678 www.pandorainn.com.*

$ SEAFOOD **Rick Stein's Fish.** Celebrity chef Rick Stein has expanded his seafood empire to Falmouth, where this no-frills takeaway and restaurant opposite the National Maritime Museum makes a welcome addition to the local dining scene. The hake, plaice, and haddock are grilled, fried to a golden hue, or charcoal-roasted and served with salad. Local mussels, oysters, and rump steak are also on the menu in the white-tiled dining room, and there are fixed-price deals for lunch and dinner. Across the square, Stein's Deli stocks all the fixings for a picnic. *Average main: £13 Discovery Quay 01841/532700 www.rickstein.com Closed Sun. and Mon. Oct.–Easter Reservations not accepted.*

$$$ HOTEL **St. Michael's Hotel.** A cool, contemporary ambience pervades this seaside hotel overlooking Falmouth Bay and fronted by a lush, subtropical garden. **Pros:** excellent facilities; good restaurant; attentive and amiable staff. **Cons:** spa facilities can be busy; cheapest rooms are small and viewless; some rooms are noisy. *Rooms from: £204 Gyllyngvase Beach 01326/312707 www.stmichaelshotel.co.uk 58 rooms, 3 suites Breakfast.*

TRELISSICK

6 miles northeast of Falmouth.

Trelissick is known for the colorful Trelissick Garden, owned by the National Trust.

GETTING HERE AND AROUND

Between Easter and October, the most rewarding way to arrive at Trelissick is by ferry from Falmouth or St. Mawes. There are also frequent year-round buses from these towns. By car, it's on B3289, between A39 and A3078.

EXPLORING

King Harry Ferry. A chain-drawn car ferry, the King Harry runs to the scenically splendid Roseland Peninsula each day three times an hour. From its decks you can see up and down the Fal, a deep, narrow river with steep, wooded banks. The river's great depth provides mooring for old ships waiting to be sold; these mammoth shapes often lend a surreal touch to the riverscape. On very rare occasions, you may even spot deer swimming across. *B3289 01872/862312 www.falriver.co.uk £6 Apr.–Sept., Mon.–Sat. 7:20 am–9:20 pm, Sun. 9 am–9:20 pm; Oct.–Mar., Mon.–Sat. 7:20 am–7:20 pm, Sun. 9 am–7:20 pm.*

Trelissick Garden. Cornwall's mild climate has endowed it with some of the country's most spectacular gardens, among which is Trelissick Garden on the banks of the Rivre Fal. Famous for its camellias, hydrangeas, magnolias, and rhododendrons, the terraced garden is set within 375 acres of wooded parkland, offering wonderful panoramic views and making this a paradise for walkers. There are also tranquil views from the porticoed Trelissick House and exhibitions of contemporary Cornish art in the gallery. ✉ *B3289, Feock* ☎ *01872/862090* 🌐 *www.nationaltrust.org.uk* 🎫 *£8.60* ⏲ *Garden Jan.–mid-Feb., daily 10:30–4:30 or dusk; mid-Feb.–Oct., daily 10:30–5:30 or dusk; Nov. and Dec., daily 10:30–4:30 or dusk; House Mar.–Oct., Wed.–Sun. 10:30–5:30; last admission 30 min before closing.*

RENT A COTTAGE

You can experience rural peace in a rented cottage in the West Country, but book early for summer.

Classic Cottages. ☎ *01326/555555* 🌐 *www.classic.co.uk.*

Cornish Cottage Holidays. ☎ *01326/573808* 🌐 *www.cornishcottageholidays.co.uk.*

Cornish Traditional Cottages. ☎ *01208/821666* 🌐 *www.corncott.com.*

Helpful Holidays. ☎ *01647/433593* 🌐 *www.helpfulholidays.com.*

ST. MAWES

6 miles south of Trelissick, 16 miles east of Falmouth.

Fodor's Choice ★ At the tip of the Roseland Peninsula is the quiet, unspoiled village of St. Mawes, where subtropical plants thrive. The peninsula itself is a lovely backwater with old churches, a lighthouse, and good coast walking. One or two sailing and boating options are available in summer, but most companies operate from Falmouth.

GETTING HERE AND AROUND

By road, St. Mawes lies at the end of A3078. You could drive from Falmouth, but it's easier to hop on a ferry crossing the estuary. Shuttling passengers between the ports in Falmouth and St. Mawes, the St. Mawes Ferry passes by two atmospheric castles along the way. It runs all year from Falmouth's Prince of Wales Pier and, between April and October, the Custom House Quay.

ESSENTIALS

Ferry Contacts St. Mawes Ferry. ☎ *01326/741194* 🌐 *www.falriver.co.uk/smf.*

EXPLORING

St. Just in Roseland. North of St. Mawes on the A3078 is St. Just in Roseland, one of the most beautiful spots in the West Country. The tiny hamlet has a 13th-century church set within a subtropical garden, often abloom with magnolias and rhododendrons, as well as a holy well and a graveyard on the banks of a secluded creek. ✉ *Roseland.*

5

St. Mawes Castle. Outside the village, the well-preserved Tudor-era St. Mawes Castle has a cloverleaf shape that makes it seemingly impregnable, yet during the Civil War its Royalist commander surrendered without firing a shot. (In contrast, Pendennis Castle in Falmouth held out at this time for 23 weeks before submitting to a siege.) Outdoor theater productions occasionally take place here in summer. ✉ *Castle Dr.* ☎ *01326/270526* 🌐 *www.english-heritage.org.uk* 🎫 *£4.70* ⏲ *Apr.–Sept., daily 10–6; Oct., daily 10–5; Nov.–Mar., weekends 10–4.*

WHERE TO STAY

$$ HOTEL **Lugger Hotel.** It's worth the winding drive on some of Cornwall's narrowest roads to get to this waterfront hideaway in a tiny fishing village. **Pros:** unforgettable setting; attention to detail; quality cuisine. **Cons:** location is remote; some rooms are cramped with limited views; could pose mobility issues. $ *Rooms from: £128* ✉ *Portloe* ☎ *0843/178 7155* 🌐 *www.bespokehotels.com/thelugger* 22 *rooms* 🍽 *Breakfast.*

$$$$ HOTEL Fodor's Choice ★ **Tresanton Hotel.** It's the Cornish Riviera, Italian style: this former yachtsman's club, owned by hotelier Olga Polizzi, makes for a luxuriously relaxed stay. **Pros:** relaxed but professional service; terrific views; stylishly luxurious setting. **Cons:** steps to climb; some rooms are small. $ *Rooms from: £270* ✉ *Lower Castle Rd.* ☎ *01326/270055* 🌐 *www.tresanton.com* *26 rooms, 4 suites* 🍽 *Breakfast.*

FOWEY

25 miles northeast of St. Mawes.

Fodor's Choice ★ Nestled in the mouth of a wooded estuary, Fowey (pronounced Foy) is still very much a working china-clay port as well as a focal point for the sailing fraternity. Increasingly, it's also a favored home of the rich and famous. Good and varied dining and lodging options abound; these are most in demand during Regatta Week in mid- to late August and the annual Fowey Festival of Words and Music in mid-May. The Bodinnick and Polruan ferries take cars as well as foot passengers across the river for the coast road on to Looe.

A few miles west of Fowey are a pair of very different gardens: the Eden Project, a futuristic display of plants from around the world, and the Lost Gardens of Heligan, a revitalized reminder of the Victorian age.

GETTING HERE AND AROUND

Fowey isn't on any train line, but the town is served by frequent buses from St. Austell. Don't attempt to drive into the steep and narrow-lane town center, which is ideal for strolling around. Parking lots are signposted on the approach roads.

ESSENTIALS

Visitor Information **Fowey Tourist Information Centre.** ✉ *Daphne du Maurier Literary Centre, 5 South St.* ☎ *01726/833616* 🌐 *www.fowey.co.uk.*

EXPLORING

FAMILY Fodor's Choice ★ **Eden Project.** Spectacularly set in a former china-clay pit, this garden presents the world's major plant systems in microcosm. The crater contains more than 70,000 plants—many of them rare or endangered species—from three climate zones. Plants from the temperate zone are outdoors, and those from other zones are housed in hexagonally paneled geodesic domes. In the Mediterranean Biome, olive and citrus groves mix with cacti and other plants indigenous to warmer climates. The Rainforest Biome steams with heat, resounds to the gushing of a waterfall, and blooms with exotic flora; the elevated Canopy Walkway enables you to experience a monkey's-eye view of all of it. The emphasis is on conservation and ecology, but is free of any editorializing. A free shuttle helps the footsore, and well-informed guides provide information. An entertaining exhibition in the visitor center gives you the lowdown on the project, and the Core, an education center, provides amusement and instruction for children—if you can drag them away from the zipwire and giant swing. There are open-air concerts in summer and an ice-skating rink in winter. The Eden Project is 3 miles northeast of Charleston and 5 miles northwest of Fowey. There's frequent bus service from Fowey to St. Austell. ✉ *Bodelva Rd., off A30, A390, and A391, St. Austell* ☎ *01726/811911* 🌐 *www.edenproject.com* 🎫 *£23.50, £19.50 if arriving by bike, on foot, or on public transport* ⏲ *Apr.–Oct., daily 9:30–6; Nov.–Mar., daily 10–4; last admission 90 min before closing.*

5

Lost Gardens of Heligan. These sprawling grounds have something for all garden lovers, as well as an intriguing history. Begun by the Tremayne family in the late 18th century, they were rediscovered and spruced up in the early 1990s by former rock music producer Tim Smit (the force behind the Eden Project). In Victorian times the gardens displayed plants from around the British Empire. The Jungle area contains surviving plants from this era, including a lone Monterey pine, as well as giant redwood and clumps of bamboo. The Italian Garden and walled Flower Gardens are delightful, but don't overlook the fruit and vegetable gardens or Flora's Green, bordered by a ravine. It's easy to spend half a day here. Guided tours can be arranged for groups. ■ **TIP→ Travel via St. Austell to avoid confusing country lanes, then follow signs to Mevagissey.** ✉ *B3273, Pentewan* ☎ *01726/845100* 🌐 *www.heligan.com* 🎫 *£12.50* ⏲ *Apr.–Sept., daily 10–6; Oct.–Mar., daily 10–5; last entry 1½ hrs before closing.*

WHERE TO EAT AND STAY

$ AMERICAN ✕ **Sam's.** This small and buzzing bistro has a rock-and-roll flavor, thanks to the walls adorned with posters of music icons. Diners squeeze onto benches and into booths to savor dishes made with local seafood, including a majestic bouillabaisse, or just a simple "Samburger." You may have to wait for a table, but there's a slinky lounge-bar upstairs for a preprandial drink. $ *Average main: £12* ✉ *20 Fore St.* ☎ *01726/832273* 🌐 *www.samsfowey.co.uk* ✍ *Reservations not accepted.*

$$$$ HOTEL FAMILY 🏨 **Fowey Hall.** A showy Victorian edifice, all turrets and elaborate plasterwork, this hotel with 5 acres of gardens, a spa, and a pool was the original inspiration for Toad Hall in *The Wind in the Willows*. **Pros:** grand manorial setting; family-friendly rates. **Cons:** dated in parts; not ideal for anyone seeking an adult ambience. $ *Rooms from: £240* ✉ *Hanson Dr.* ☎ *01726/833866* 🌐 *www.foweyhallhotel.co.uk* 🛏 *24 rooms, 12 suites* 🍽 *Breakfast.*

SPORTS AND THE OUTDOORS

Fowey River Expeditions. Between late May and mid-September, Fowey River Expeditions runs daily canoe trips up the tranquil River Fowey, the best way to observe the abundant wildlife. Kayaks are also available to rent. ✉ *17 Passage St.* ☎ *01726/833019* 🌐 *www.foweyexpeditions.co.uk.*

BODMIN

12 miles north of Fowey.

Bodmin was the only Cornish town recorded in the 11th-century Domesday Book, William the Conqueror's census. During World War I, the Domesday Book and the Crown Jewels were sent to Bodmin Prison for safekeeping. From the Gilbert Memorial on Beacon Hill you can see both of Cornwall's coasts. Lanhydrock, a stately home, is also near Bodmin.

GETTING HERE AND AROUND

At the junction of A38 and A30, Bodmin is a major transport hub for north Cornwall. Trains stop at Bodmin Parkway, 3 miles southeast of the center. A car is your best bet for touring Bodmin Moor and visiting Lanhydrock.

ESSENTIALS

Visitor Information Bodmin Visitor Information Centre. ✉ *The Shire Hall, Mount Folly* ☎ *01208/76616* 🌐 *www.bodminlive.com.*

EXPLORING

Dozmary Pool. For a taste of Arthurian legend, follow A30 northeast out of Bodmin across the boggy, heather-clad granite plateau of Bodmin Moor. After about 10 miles, turn right at Bolventor to get to Dozmary Pool. A lake rather than a pool, it was here that King Arthur's legendary magic sword, Excalibur, was supposedly returned to the Lady of the Lake after Arthur's final battle. ✉ *Bodmin.*

Fodor's Choice ★ **Lanhydrock.** One of Cornwall's greatest country piles, Lanhydrock gives a look into the lives of the upper classes in the 19th century. The former home of the powerful, wealthy Robartes family was originally constructed in the 17th century but was totally rebuilt after a fire in 1881. Its granite exterior remains true to the house's original form, however, and the long picture gallery in the north wing, with its barrel-vaulted plaster ceiling depicting 24 biblical scenes, survived the devastation. A small museum shows photographs and letters relating to the family. The house's endless pantries, sculleries, dairies, nurseries, and linen cupboards bear witness to the immense amount of work involved in maintaining this lifestyle. About 900 acres of wooded parkland border the River Fowey, and in spring the gardens present an exquisite ensemble of magnolias, azaleas, and rhododendrons. Allow two hours to see the house and more time to stroll the grounds. The house is 3 miles southeast of Bodmin. ✉ *Off A30, A38, and B3268* ☎ *01208/265950* 🌐 *www.nationaltrust.org.uk* 🎫 *£11.70; grounds only, £7.20* ⏲ *House Mar.–Oct., daily 11–5:30; Nov., weekends 11–4; Dec., daily 11–4;*

Upstairs, downstairs: at Lanhydrock you can tour both the elegant picture gallery and the vast kitchens, pantries, and sculleries.

garden mid-Feb.–Dec., daily 10–6; park daily dawn–dusk; last admission 30 min before closing.

PLYMOUTH AND DARTMOOR

Just over the border from Cornwall is Plymouth, an unprepossessing city but one with a historic old core and splendid harbor that recall a rich maritime heritage. North of Plymouth, you can explore the vast, boggy reaches of hilly Dartmoor, the setting for the Sherlock Holmes classic *The Hound of the Baskervilles*. This national park is a great place to hike or go horseback riding away from the crowds.

PLYMOUTH

48 miles southwest of Exeter, 124 miles southwest of Bristol, 240 miles southwest of London.

Devon's largest city has long been linked with England's commercial and maritime history. The Pilgrims sailed from here to the New World in the *Mayflower* in 1620. Although much of the city center was destroyed by air raids in World War II and has been rebuilt in an uninspiring style, there are worthwhile sights. A harbor tour is also a good way to see the city.

The Barbican 5
Elizabethan House 4
Hoe 1
Mayflower Steps/Plymouth Boat Trips 6
Merchant's House 9
National Marine Aquarium 8
Plymouth Mayflower Exhibition 7
Royal Citadel 3
Saltram 10
Smeaton's Tower 2

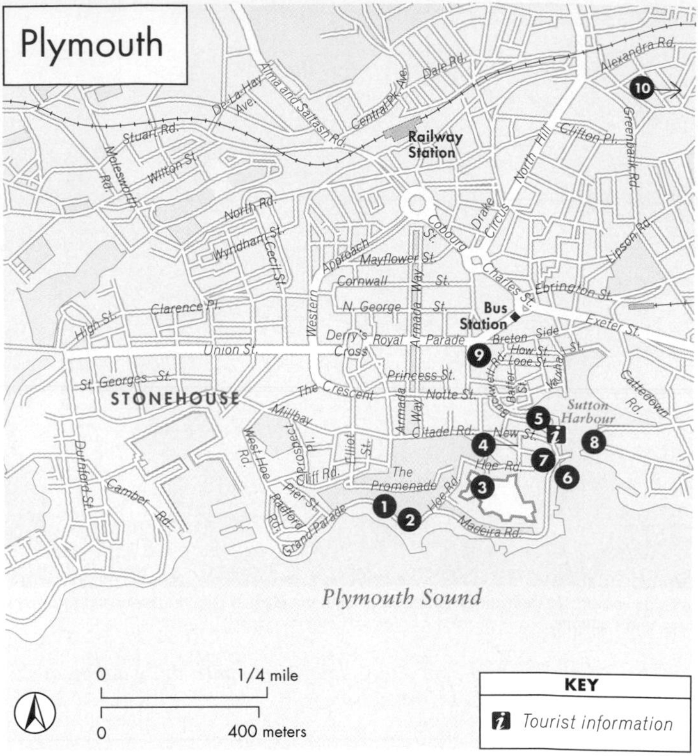

Plymouth

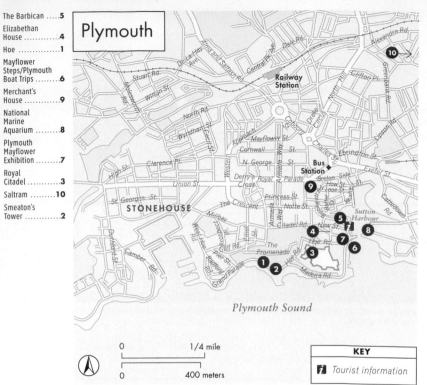

KEY
Tourist information

GETTING HERE AND AROUND

Frequent trains arrive from Bodmin, Penzance, and Exeter. From London Paddington, trains take three to four hours; Megabus and National Express buses from London's Victoria Coach Station take five or six hours. The train station is 1 mile north of the seafront, connected by frequent buses. Long-distance buses stop at the centrally located bus station off Royal Parade. Drivers can leave their cars in one of the numerous parking lots, including a couple right by the harbor. The seafront and central city areas are best explored on foot.

ESSENTIALS

Visitor Information **Plymouth Tourism Information Centre.** ✉ *Plymouth Mayflower, 3–5 The Barbican* ☎ *01752/306330* 🌐 *www.visitplymouth.co.uk.*

EXPLORING

TOP ATTRACTIONS

The Barbican. East of the Royal Citadel is The Barbican, the oldest surviving section of Plymouth. Here Tudor houses and warehouses rise from a maze of narrow streets leading down to the fishing harbor and marina. Many of these buildings have become antiques shops, art shops, and cafés. It's well worth a stroll for the atmosphere. ✉ *Plymouth.*

Elizabethan House. In the heart of the Barbican section, this former sea captain's home offers a fascinating insight into how well-to-do

Plymothians lived during the city's golden age. The three floors of the timber-frame house are filled with 16th- and 17th-century furnishings, and there's a reconstructed kitchen and a spiral staircase built around a ship's mast. ✉ *32 New St.* ☎ *01752/304774* 🌐 *www.plymouthmuseum.gov.uk* 🎫 *£2.80* ⏲ *Apr.–Sept., Tues.–Sat. 10–noon and 1–5.*

Hoe. From the Hoe, a wide, grassy esplanade with crisscrossing walkways high above the city, you can take in a magnificent view of the inlets, bays, and harbors that make up Plymouth Sound. ✉ *Plymouth.*

FAMILY **National Marine Aquarium.** This excellent aquarium on the harbor presents aqueous environments, from a freshwater stream to a seawater wave tank to a huge "shark theater." Not to be missed is the extensive collection of sea horses, part of an important breeding program, and the chance to walk under sharks in the Mediterranean tank. Feeding times are fun for the kids, and Waves café, with its harbor views, makes a good spot for a rest and refreshment. ✉ *Rope Walk, Coxside* ☎ *0844/893–7938* 🌐 *www.national-aquarium.co.uk* 🎫 *£14.75* ⏲ *Daily 10–5; last admission 1 hr before closing.*

5

FAMILY **Plymouth Mayflower Exhibition.** On three floors, this interactive exhibition narrates the story of Plymouth, from its beginnings as a fishing and trading port to the modern industrial city it is today. Along the way, you'll take in the stories of various expeditions that embarked from here to the New World, including the *Mayflower* itself. The city's tourist office is also in this building. ✉ *3–5 The Barbican* ☎ *01752/306330* 🌐 *www.visitplymouth.co.uk* 🎫 *£2* ⏲ *Apr.–Oct., Mon.–Sat. 9–5, Sun. 10–4; Nov.–Mar., weekdays 9:30–5, Sat. 10:30–4; last entry 1 hr before closing.*

Saltram. An exquisite 18th-century home with many of its original furnishings, Saltram was built around the remains of a late-Tudor mansion. Its jewel is one of Britain's grandest neoclassical rooms—a vast, double-cube salon designed by Robert Adam and hung with paintings by Sir Joshua Reynolds, first president of the Royal Academy of Arts, who was born nearby in 1723. Fine plasterwork adorns many rooms and three have original Chinese wallpaper. The outstanding garden includes rare trees and shrubs, and there's a restaurant and a cafeteria. Saltram is 3½ miles east of Plymouth city center. ✉ *South of A38, Plympton* ☎ *01752/333500* 🌐 *www.nationaltrust.org.uk* 🎫 *£10.30; garden only £5.30* ⏲ *House Mar.–Oct., daily 11–4:30; Nov.–Dec., daily 11–3:30; last admission 45 min before closing. Garden Mar.–Oct., daily 10–5; Nov.–Feb., daily 10–4. Park daily dawn–dusk.*

WORTH NOTING

Mayflower Steps. By the harbor you can visit the Mayflower Steps, where the Pilgrims embarked in 1620; the **Mayflower Stone** marks the exact spot. They had sailed from Southampton but had to stop in Plymouth because of damage from a storm. ✉ *The Barbican.*

Merchant's House. Near the Barbican, just off the Royal Parade, this largely 17th-century house is a museum of local history. ✉ *33 St. Andrew's St.* ☎ *01752/304774* 🌐 *www.plymouthmuseum.gov.uk* 🎫 *£2.80* ⏲ *Apr.–Sept., Tues.–Sat. 10–noon and 1–5.*

Plymouth Boat Trips. Harbor cruises leave from the Mayflower Steps and Cremyll Quay all year, while longer scenic trips on the rivers Tamar and Yealm operate between April and October. Check the website for daily times. ✉ *Mayflower Steps, 2–5 Commercial Wharf* ☎ *01752/253153* 🌐 *www.plymouthboattrips.co.uk.*

Royal Citadel. This huge citadel was built by Charles II in 1666 and still operates as a military center. Book ahead with Armada Tours or just turn up at the main entrance for the daily tour; you are only able to see the citadel while on a tour. Note that photography is not permitted. ✉ *End of the Hoe* ☎ *07933/429604 Armada Tours* 🌐 *www.english-heritage.org.uk* 🎫 *£5* ⏲ *May–Sept., Tues., Thurs., and Sun. 1¼-hr guided tours at 2:30.*

Smeaton's Tower. This lighthouse, transferred here at the end of the 19th century from its original site 14 miles out to sea, provides a sweeping vista over Plymouth Sound and the city as far as Dartmoor. Brace yourself for the 93 steps to the top. ✉ *Hoe Rd.* ☎ *01752/304774* 🌐 *www.plymouthmuseum.gov.uk* 🎫 *£2.80* ⏲ *Feb. and Mar., Tues.–Sat. 10–4; Apr.–Sept., Mon.–Fri. 10–5, weekends 10–6; Oct. and Nov., Tues.–Sat. 10–3; Dec. and Jan., Sat. 10–3.*

WHERE TO EAT AND STAY

$$ MODERN BRITISH

✕ **Quay 33.** Fresh seafood landed at the nearby quays, such as sea-bass and cod, features high on the menu at this Barbican eatery, but you will also find pastas, risottos, steaks, and slow-cooked pork belly. Exmouth mussels or grilled scallops make an ideal light lunch, while puddings include panna cotta and homemade cheesecake. The modern decor in the two dining areas—upstairs and downstairs—is crisply white, the service is enthusiastic, and the atmosphere is lively. 💲 *Average main: £16* ✉ *33 Southside St.* ☎ *01752/229345* 🌐 *www.quay33.co.uk.*

$$ MODERN BRITISH

✕ **River Cottage Canteen & Deli.** Renowned chef and food campaigner Hugh Fearnley-Whittingstall has set up an outpost of his culinary chain in the old naval depot in Plymouth's newly fashionable Stonehouse neighborhood. The menu offers tapas-size dishes, such as gravad max with rye breadcrumbs and grilled radicchio with buffalo mozzarella, and mains that might include roast gurnard with Jerusalem artichokes or venison ragu. Sit indoors in the buzzy, open-plan dining area, or at tables outside where you can take in views over a yacht marina and across to wooded slopes. From the deli counter, you can choose from an enticing range of locally produced ham, bread, pasties, cheese, cider, and wine. 💲 *Average main: £15* ✉ *Royal William Yard, Stonehouse* ☎ *01752/252702* 🌐 *www.rivercottage.net* ⏲ *Closed Mon. Oct.–Mar. No dinner Sun.*

$$ HOTEL

🏨 **Holiday Inn.** Grandly sited in a tall block overlooking Plymouth Hoe, this modern chain hotel has a businesslike tone but doesn't skimp on comforts. **Pros:** excellent location; large rooms; lofty views. **Cons:** impersonal feel; overhaul overdue; tight parking. 💲 *Rooms from: £105* ✉ *Armada Way* ☎ *01752/639988, 0871/423–4896* 🌐 *www.ihg.com* 🛏 *211 rooms* 🍽 *Breakfast.*

$$ HOTEL

🏨 **Langdon Court Hotel.** Situated in peaceful grounds 8 miles outside Plymouth, this venerable country house hotel was once the property of Catherine Parr—last wife of Henry VIII—and later hosted

Pony trekking in Dartmoor National Park lets you get off the beaten path.

such distinguished guests as the future Edward VII and his mistress Lilie Langtry. **Pros:** tranquil rural setting; attentive staff; great food. **Cons:** few leisure facilities; some rooms are small; poor soundproofing in some rooms. *Rooms from: £129* *Adam's Lane, Wembury* *01752/862358* *www.langdoncourt.com* *15 rooms, 2 suites* *Breakfast.*

NIGHTLIFE AND PERFORMING ARTS

Theatre Royal. Plymouth's Theatre Royal presents ballet, musicals, and plays by some of Britain's best companies. *Royal Parade* *01752/267222* *www.theatreroyal.com.*

SHOPPING

Black Friars Distillery. At the Black Friars Distillery, Plymouth's most famous export, gin, has been distilled since 1793. You can purchase bottles of sloe gin, damson liqueur, fruit cup, or the fiery "Navy Strength" gin that traditionally was issued to the Royal Navy. Learn the full story on walking tours around the distillery, ending with a sampling in the wood-paneled Refectory Bar. The building originally housed a friary and was where the Pilgrims spent their last night on English soil in 1620. *60 Southside St.* *01752/665292* *www.plymouthgin.com.*

EN ROUTE

From Plymouth you have a choice of routes northeast to Exeter. If rugged, desolate, moorland scenery appeals to you, take A386 and B3212 northeast across Dartmoor. There's plenty to stir the imagination.

DARTMOOR NATIONAL PARK

10 miles north of Plymouth, 13 miles west of Exeter.

Devon presents no greater contrast to the country's quaint and picturesque image than the bleak, deserted expanses of Dartmoor. Southern England's greatest natural wilderness is largely a treeless landscape of sometimes alarming emptiness though it also harbors surprises in the form of hidden lakes, abandoned quarries, and the dramatically wind-sculpted tors, or craggy peaks, that puncture the horizon in every direction. Sudden mists and above-average rainfall levels add to the simultaneously inhospitable and alluring scene.

GETTING HERE AND AROUND

Public transport services are extremely sparse on Dartmoor, making a car indispensable for anywhere off the beaten track. The peripheral towns of Okehampton and Tavistock are well served by bus from Exeter and Plymouth, and Chagford also has direct connections to Exeter, but central Princetown has only sporadic links with the outside world.

EXPLORING

Dartmoor National Park. Even on a summer's day, the brooding hills of this sprawling wilderness appear a likely haunt for such monsters as the hound of the Baskervilles, and it seems entirely fitting that Sir

Arthur Conan Doyle set his Sherlock Holmes thriller in this landscape. Sometimes the wet, peaty wasteland of Dartmoor National Park vanishes in rain and mist, although in clear weather you can see north to Exmoor, south over the English Channel, and west far into Cornwall. Much of Dartmoor consists of open heath and moorland, unspoiled by roads—wonderful walking and horseback-riding territory but an easy place to lose your bearings. Dartmoor's earliest inhabitants left behind stone monuments and burial mounds that help you envision prehistoric man roaming these pastures. Ponies, sheep, and birds are the main animals to be seen.

Several villages scattered along the borders of this 368-square-mile reserve—one-third of which is owned by Prince Charles—make useful bases for hiking excursions. Accommodations include simple inns and some elegant havens. **Okehampton** is a main gateway, and **Chagford** is a good base for exploring north Dartmoor. Other scenic spots include **Buckland-in-the-Moor,** a hamlet with thatch-roof cottages; **Widecombe-in-the-Moor,** whose church is known as the Cathedral of the Moor; and **Grimspound,** the Bronze Age site featured in Conan Doyle's most famous tale. Transmoor Link buses connect many of Dartmoor's towns and villages. The **National Park Visitor Centre** in Princetown is a good place to start your trip, as are centers in Postbridge and Haytor. You can also pick up information in Ivybridge, Okehampton, Moretonhampstead, Tavistock, and Buckfastleigh. ✉ *National Park Visitor Centre, Tavistock Rd., Princetown* ☎ *01822/890414* 🌐 *www.dartmoor-npa.gov.uk.*

SPORTS AND THE OUTDOORS

Hiking is extremely popular in Dartmoor National Park. The areas around Widgery Cross, Becky Falls, and the Bovey Valley, as well as the short but dramatic walk along Lydford Gorge, have wide appeal, as do the many valleys around the southern edge of the moors. Guided hikes, typically costing £3 to £8, are available through the park's visitor information centers. Reservations are usually not necessary. Longer hikes in the bleak, less-populated regions—for example, the tors south of Okehampton—are appropriate only for most experienced walkers. Dartmoor is a great area for horseback riding; many towns have stables for guided rides.

TAVISTOCK AND AROUND

13 miles north of Plymouth.

On the River Tavy, the ancient town of Tavistock historically owed its importance to its Benedictine abbey (dissolved by Henry VIII in the 16th century) and to its status as a stannary town, where tin was weighed, stamped, and assessed. Today the town of 11,000 preserves a prosperous, predominantly Victorian appearance, especially at the bustling indoor Pannier Market off central Bedford Square. Tavistock makes a useful base for exploring a scattering of nearby sights—Buckland Abbey, Cotehele House, and Morwellham Quay—and for touring Dartmoor's western reaches.

GETTING HERE AND AROUND

Tavistock, on A386 and A390, is easily accessed via the frequent buses from Plymouth, which take about an hour. You'll need your own transportation to visit the attractions scattered around it, however.

EXPLORING

Buckland Abbey. A 13th-century Cistercian monastery, Buckland Abbey became the home of Sir Francis Drake in 1581. Today it's filled with mementos of Drake and the Spanish Armada, but the highlight is a beautifully expressive self-portrait by Rembrandt, displayed in its own gallery. Part of a bequest, the painting was only identified, painstakingly restored, and revealed to the public in 2014. The house, which has a restaurant, is 6 miles south of Tavistock; to get here, take A386 south to Crapstone and then head west. ✉ *Off A386, Yelverton* ☎ *01822/853607* 🌐 *www.nationaltrust.org.uk* 🎟 *£10; grounds only £5* ⏲ *Mid Feb.–early Mar. and early Dec.–late Dec., daily 11–4; early Mar.–Oct., daily 10:30–5:30; early Nov.–late Nov., weekends 11–4; early Dec.–late Dec., daily 11–4.*

Cotehele House and Quay. About 4 miles west of Buckland Abbey and 9 miles southwest of Tavistock, Cotehele House and Quay was formerly a busy port on the River Tamar, but it is now usually visited for the well-preserved, atmospheric late-medieval manor, home of the Edgcumbe family for centuries. The house has original furniture, tapestries, embroideries, and armor, and you can also visit the impressive gardens, a quay museum, and a restored mill (usually in operation on Sunday and Thursday—call for other days). A limited number of visitors are allowed per day, so arrive early and be prepared to wait during busy periods. Choose a bright day, because the rooms have no electric light. Shops, crafts studios, a gallery, and a restaurant provide other diversions. **■ TIP→ Take advantage of the shuttle bus that runs every half hour between the house, quay, and mill.** ✉ *Off A390, St. Dominick* ☎ *01579/351346* 🌐 *www.nationaltrust.org.uk* 🎟 *£9.50; gardens and mill only £6* ⏲ *House mid-Mar.–Dec., daily 11–4 (limited access in Nov. and Dec.). Mill mid-Mar.–Sept., daily 11–5; Oct., daily 11–4:30. Gardens daily dawn–dusk.*

FAMILY **Morwellham Quay.** In the 19th century, Morwellham (pronounced More-*wel*-ham) was England's main copper-exporting port, and it has been carefully restored as a working museum, with quay workers and coachmen in costume. Visitors can board a special train that goes along the River Tamar and into the George and Charlotte Copper Mine. Fairs and other special events take place throughout the year. The site lies 2 miles east of Cotehele House and 5 miles southwest of Tavistock. ✉ *Off B3257, Morwellham* ☎ *01822/832766* 🌐 *www.morwellham-quay.co.uk* 🎟 *£8.95, mine train £3.50* ⏲ *Mar.–May and Sept.–Oct., daily 10–5; June–Aug., daily 10–5:30; Nov.–Feb., daily 10–4.*

WHERE TO EAT AND STAY

$$$$ MODERN BRITISH Fodor's Choice ★

✕ The Horn of Plenty. The restaurant within this Georgian house has magnificent views across the wooded, rhododendron-filled Tamar Valley and a sophisticated menu favoring local and seasonal ingredients. A typical starter and main course might be pan-fried scallops with celeriac fondant followed by roast squab pigeon with orange braised chicory and hazelnuts, while desserts include rhubarb meringue tart with gingerbread ice cream. There are several fixed-price menus (lunch £19.50 and £24.50, dinner £49.50); the best value is Monday evening's potluck menu (£29). A converted coach house and the main house contain 16 sumptuously furnished guest rooms. It's 3 miles west of Tavistock. *Average main: £50 ✉ A390, Gulworthy ☎ 01822/832528 ⊕ www.thehornofplenty.co.uk.*

STAY ON A FARM

One way to experience the authentic rural life in Somerset, Devon, and Cornwall is to stay on a farm. **Cartwheel Holidays** (⊕ *www.cartwheelholidays.co.uk*) has details about working farms that supply accommodations—including bed-and-breakfasts and house rentals—throughout the region. Other reference points are **Devon Farms** (⊕ *www.devonfarms.co.uk*), for farms in Devon, and **Cornish Farm Holidays** (⊕ *www.cornishfarmholidays.co.uk*), for Cornwall.

$$ HOTEL **Bedford Hotel.** This grand, castellated hotel in the center of town harks back to its Victorian heyday, with lounge areas furnished with comfy armchairs, warmed by open fires, and dotted with old artifacts and local photos. **Pros:** old-fashioned charisma; staff are smart and friendly. **Cons:** some noise in street-facing rooms; a little frayed in places. *Rooms from: £140 ✉ 1 Plymouth Rd., Tavistock ☎ 01822/613221 ⊕ www.bedford-hotel.co.uk 32 rooms Breakfast.*

$$$$ HOTEL **Hotel Endsleigh.** Under the auspices of hotelier Olga Polizzi, the Endsleigh has risen to be one of the country's best-loved hotels, nestled in a fold of the Tamar valley with the river itself rolling serenely by at the bottom of the garden. **Pros:** beautiful rural setting; discreet but ever-present staff. **Cons:** remote location; some bathrooms lack showers. *Rooms from: £265 ✉ Milton Abbot ☎ 01822/870000 ⊕ www.hotelendsleigh.com 13 rooms, 4 suites Breakfast.*

LYDFORD

7 miles north of Tavistock, 24 miles north of Plymouth.

The sequestered hamlet of Lydford packs a lot into a small area: there's the dramatic scenery of the gorge just outside the village, the remains of a medieval castle, and some attractive options for eating and sleeping. The Granite Way cycle track, much of it running along a disused railway route, connects Lydford with Okehampton.

GETTING HERE AND AROUND

The gorge is easily accessed on Plymouth Citybus buses from Plymouth (which stop in Tavistock) and Okehampton (connected to Exeter). By car, take A386 between Tavistock and Okehampton.

EXPLORING

Fodor's Choice ★ **Lydford Gorge.** The River Lyd carved a spectacular 1½-mile-long chasm through the rock at Lydford Gorge, outside the pretty village of Lydford, midway between Okehampton and Tavistock. Two paths follow the gorge past gurgling whirlpools and waterfalls with evocative names such as the Devil's Cauldron and the White Lady Waterfall. ■ **TIP→ Sturdy footwear is recommended.** Although the walk can be quite challenging, the paths can still get congested during busy periods. Two tea-rooms are open early March through late December. In winter, access is restricted to the waterfall and the top of the gorge. ✉ *Off A386, Lydford* ☎ *01822/820320* 🌐 *www.nationaltrust.org.uk* *£7.20; £3.50 or free in winter* ⏲ *Early Mar.–early Oct., daily 10–5; early Oct.–early Mar., short walk always open.*

WHERE TO EAT AND STAY

$$ MODERN BRITISH

✕ **Dartmoor Inn.** Locals and visitors alike make a beeline for this gastropub in a 16th-century building with a number of small dining spaces done in spare, contemporary country style. The elegantly presented dishes may include roasted rump of lamb, pan-fried skate wing with olives and bacon, or slow-cooked duck leg confit with vanilla apple puree and red wine sauce. Set-price menus may be available, and there's a separate, reasonably priced bar menu. Four spacious guest rooms make it possible to linger. $ *Average main: £18* ✉ *Moorside, on A386, Lydford* ☎ *01822/820221* 🌐 *www.dartmoorinn.com* ⏲ *No dinner Sun. Closed Mon.*

$ B&B/INN

Castle Inn. In the heart of Lydford village, this 16th-century inn sits next to Lydford Castle. **Pros:** antique character; peaceful rural setting. **Cons:** shabby in places; some small rooms. $ *Rooms from: £70* ✉ *School Rd., off A386, Lydford* ☎ *01822/820241* 🌐 *www.castleinndartmoor.co.uk* *8 rooms* *Breakfast.*

$$$ HOTEL Fodor's Choice ★

Lewtrenchard Manor. Paneled rooms, stone fireplaces, leaded-glass windows, and handsome gardens outfit this spacious 1620 manor house on the northwestern edge of Dartmoor. **Pros:** beautiful Jacobean setting; conscientious service; outstanding food. **Cons:** creaking doors and floors in main building; rooms in outbuildings have less atmosphere; not very child-friendly. $ *Rooms from: £175* ✉ *Off A30, Lewdown* ☎ *01566/783222* 🌐 *www.lewtrenchard.co.uk* *10 rooms, 4 suites* *Breakfast.*

SPORTS AND THE OUTDOORS

Cholwell Riding Stables. Cholwell Riding Stables. One- and two-hour horseback rides through some of Dartmoor's wilder tracts are available with Cholwell Riding Stables. Riders of all abilities are escorted, and equipment is provided. The stables are about 2 miles south of Lydford. ✉ *Off A386, Mary Tavy* ☎ *01822/810526* 🌐 *www.cholwellridingstables.co.uk.*

OKEHAMPTON

8 miles northeast of Lydford Gorge, 28 miles north of Plymouth, 23 miles west of Exeter.

This town at the confluence of the rivers East and West Okement is a good base for exploring north Dartmoor. It has a fascinating museum dedicated to the moor, as well as a helpful tourist office.

A walk in Lydford Gorge takes you through lush forest.

GETTING HERE AND AROUND

There's good bus service to Okehampton from Plymouth, Tavistock, and Exeter, and on summer Sundays you can travel by train from Exeter. If you're driving, the town is on A30 and A386; parking is easy in the center of town.

EXPLORING

FAMILY **Museum of Dartmoor Life.** The three floors of this informative museum contain historical artifacts, domestic knickknacks, traditional agricultural and mining tools, and fascinating insights into the lives of ordinary folk living on the moor. The museum also provides tourist information for the Okehampton area. ✉ *Museum Courtyard, 3 West St.* ☎ *01837/52295* 🌐 *www.museumofdartmoorlife.org.uk* 🎫 *£2.50* 🕒 *Apr.–late Nov., weekdays 10:15–4:15, Sat. 10:15–1.*

Okehampton Castle. On the riverbank a mile southwest of the town center, the jagged ruins of this Norman castle occupy a verdant site with a picnic area and woodland walks. ✉ *Castle Lodge, off B3260* ☎ *01837/52844* 🌐 *www.english-heritage.org.uk* 🎫 *£4.20* 🕒 *Apr.–June and Sept.–Oct., daily 10–5; July and Aug., daily 10–6.*

SPORTS AND THE OUTDOORS

Eastlake Riding Stables. A couple of miles outside Okehampton, Eastlake Riding Stables arranges horseback rides throughout the year. Trips last 30 minutes, one or two hours, or a full day. ✉ *Off A30, Belstone* ☎ *01837/52513* 🌐 *www.eastlakeridingstables.co.uk.*

CHAGFORD

9 miles southeast of Okehampton, 30 miles northeast of Plymouth.

Once a tin-weighing station, Chagford was an area of fierce fighting between the Roundheads and the Cavaliers during the English Civil War. Although officially a "town" since 1305, Chagford is more of a village, with taverns grouped around a seasoned old church and a curious "pepper-pot" market house on the site of the old Stannary Court. With a handful of cafés and shops to browse around, it makes a convenient base from which to explore north Dartmoor.

GETTING HERE AND AROUND

Infrequent local buses connect Chagford with Okehampton and Exeter (except on Sunday, when there's no service). The village is off A382; a car or bicycle is the best way to see its far-flung sights.

EXPLORING

Castle Drogo. Northeast of Chagford, this castle looks like a stout medieval fortress, complete with battlements, but construction actually took place between 1910 and 1930. Designed by noted architect Sir Edwin Lutyens for Julius Drewe, a wealthy grocer, the castle is only half finished (funds ran out). Inside, this magisterial pile combines medieval grandeur and early-20th-century comforts, and there are awesome views over Dartmoor's Teign Valley. The grounds are well worth a prolonged wander, with paths leading down to the river at Fingle Bridge. ⚠ **Major renovation work will be ongoing until 2018, which means that many parts of the castle are hidden behind scaffolding and some rooms are closed to visitors. However, new rooms have been opened, the main exhibits relocated, and a viewing platform constructed outside to see the work in progress.** Turn off the A30 Exeter–Okehampton road at Whiddon Down to reach the castle. ✉ *Off A30 and A382, Drewsteignton* ☎ *01647/433306* 🌐 *www.nationaltrust.org.uk* 🎫 *£8.70; grounds only £5.50* ⏲ *Castle early Mar.–Oct., daily 11–5; early Nov.–late Dec., weekends 11–4. Grounds daily dawn–dusk.*

Devon Guild of Craftsmen. The southwest's most important contemporary arts-and-crafts center, the Devon Guild is in a converted 19th-century coach house in the village of Bovey Tracey, 10 miles southeast of Chagford and 14 miles southwest of Exeter. The center has excellent exhibitions of local, national, and international crafts, as well as a shop and café. ✉ *Riverside Mill, Fore St., Bovey Tracey* ☎ *01626/832223* 🌐 *www.crafts.org.uk* 🎫 *Free* ⏲ *Daily 10–5:30.*

QUICK BITES

The Old Cottage Tea Shop. This is the real deal, perfect for a light lunch or, even better, a cream tea served on bone china. Warm scones come in baskets, with black currant and other homemade jams and plenty of clotted cream. It's closed every afternoon and all day Sunday. ✉ *20 Fore St., Bovey Tracey* ☎ *01626/833430.*

WHERE TO EAT AND STAY

$$$$ MODERN BRITISH Fodor'sChoice ★ **Gidleigh Park.** One of England's foremost country-house hotels, Gidleigh Park occupies an enclave of landscaped gardens and streams. It's reached via a lengthy, winding country lane and private drive at the edge of Dartmoor. The extremely pricey contemporary restaurant, directed by chef Michael Caines, has been showered with culinary awards. You may see why when you dig into the Cornish salt cod with crab, chorizo, and lemon puree, one of the choices often on the prix-fixe menus (£38.50 for two courses at lunch, £118 for a three-course banquet at dinner). The wine list is formidable, and the locally pumped spring water is like no other. Antiques fill the long, half-timber building, built in 1928 in Tudor style; there are also 24 luxurious guest rooms. *Average main: £118 ✉ Gidleigh Park ☎ 01647/432367 ⊕ www.gidleigh.com ✍ Reservations essential.*

$$$$ HOTEL FAMILY Fodor'sChoice ★ **Bovey Castle.** With the grandeur of a country estate and the amenities of a modern hotel, Bovey Castle, built in 1906 for Viscount Hambledon, has it all. **Pros:** baronial splendor; range of activities. **Cons:** service can be slow; overpriced food and extras. *Rooms from: £249 ✉ Off B3212, North Bovey ☎ 0844/474–0077, 1647/445000 from outside the U.K. ⊕ www.boveycastle.com 64 rooms, 14 lodges No meals.*

$ B&B/INN **Easton Court.** Discerning travelers such as C.P. Snow, Margaret Mead, John Steinbeck, and Evelyn Waugh—who completed *Brideshead Revisited* here—made this their Dartmoor home-away-from-home. **Pros:** helpful hosts; peaceful ambience. **Cons:** rooms upstairs accessed by exterior stairs; a drive from the village. *Rooms from: £75 ✉ Easton Cross ☎ 01647/433469 ⊕ www.easton.co.uk 5 rooms Breakfast.*

EXETER AND SOUTH DEVON

The ancient city of Exeter, Devon's county seat, has preserved some of its historical character despite wartime bombing. From Exeter you can explore southeast to the estuary village of Topsham. Sheltered by the high mass of Dartmoor to the west, the coastal resort area of Torbay, known as the English Riviera, enjoys a mild, warm climate that allows for subtropical vegetation, including palm trees. Between the two, on the banks of the River Dart, is the pretty market town of Totnes, while the well-to-do yachting center of Dartmouth lies south of Torbay at the river's estuary.

EXETER

18 miles east of Chagford, 48 miles northeast of Plymouth, 85 miles southwest of Bristol, 205 miles southwest of London.

Exeter has been the capital of the region since the Romans established a fortress here 2,000 years ago and evidence of the Roman occupation remains in the city walls. Although it was heavily bombed in 1942, Exeter retains much of its medieval character, as well as examples of the gracious architecture of the 18th and 19th centuries. It's convenient to both Torquay and Dartmoor.

GETTING HERE AND AROUND

Once- or twice-hourly train service from London Paddington takes about two hours and 45 minutes; the cheaper Megatrain service takes 3 hours and 20 minutes and leaves London Waterloo up to five times daily. From London's Victoria Coach Station, National Express buses leave every two hours and Megabus has four daily departures, all taking between 4¼ and 5 hours. Exeter is a major transportation hub for Devon. Trains from Bristol, Salisbury, and Plymouth stop at Exeter St. David's, and connect to the center by frequent buses. Some trains also stop at the more useful Exeter Central. The bus station is off Paris Street near the tourist office. Cars are unnecessary in town, so park yours as soon as possible—all the sights are within an easy walk.

TOURS

Red Coat Guided Tours. Free 90-minute walking tours of Exeter by Red Coat Guided Tours take place daily all year, focusing on different aspects of the city. See the website for details, or contact the tourist office. You can also pick up a leaflet on self-guided walks from here. ✉ *Exeter* ☎ *01392/265203* 🌐 *www.exeter.gov.uk/guidedtours.*

ESSENTIALS

Visitor Information Exeter Visitor Information and Tickets. ✉ *Dix's Field* ☎ *01392/665700* 🌐 *www.heartofdevon.com.*

EXPLORING

TOP ATTRACTIONS

Fodor's Choice ★ **Cathedral of St. Peter.** At the heart of Exeter, the great Gothic cathedral was begun in 1275 and completed almost a century later. Its twin towers are even older survivors of an earlier Norman cathedral. Rising from a forest of ribbed columns, the nave's 300-foot stretch of unbroken Gothic vaulting is the longest in the world. Myriad statues, tombs, and memorial plaques adorn the interior. In the minstrels' gallery, high up on the left of the nave, stands a group of carved figures singing and playing musical instruments, including bagpipes. Outside in Cathedral Close, don't miss the 400-year-old door to No. 10, the bishop of Crediton's house, ornately carved with angels' and lions' heads. ✉ *Cathedral Close* ☎ *01392/255573* 🌐 *www.exeter-cathedral.org.uk* 🎫 *£6* ⏲ *Mon.–Sat. 9–5:30, Sun. 11:15–5:30. Guided tours weekdays at 11, 12:30, and 2:30, Sat. at 11 and 12:30. Access is restricted during services.*

OFF THE BEATEN PATH

Powderham Castle. Seat of the earls of Devon, this notable stately home 8 miles south of Exeter is famed for its staircase hall, a soaring fantasia of white stuccowork on a turquoise background, constructed in 1739–69. Other sumptuous rooms, adorned with family portraits by Sir Godfrey Kneller and Sir Joshua Reynolds, were used in the Merchant-Ivory film *Remains of the Day.* A tower built in 1400 by Sir Philip Courtenay, ancestor of the current owners, stands in the deer park. "Safari" rides (a tractor pulling a trailer) to see the 600-odd fallow deer depart daily during school vacations, and October sees daily "Deer Rut Safaris." There are also falconry displays in summer. The restaurant serves light lunches, and there's a children's play area, a pets' corner, a farm shop, and a plant center. ✉ *A379, Kenton* ☎ *01626/890243*

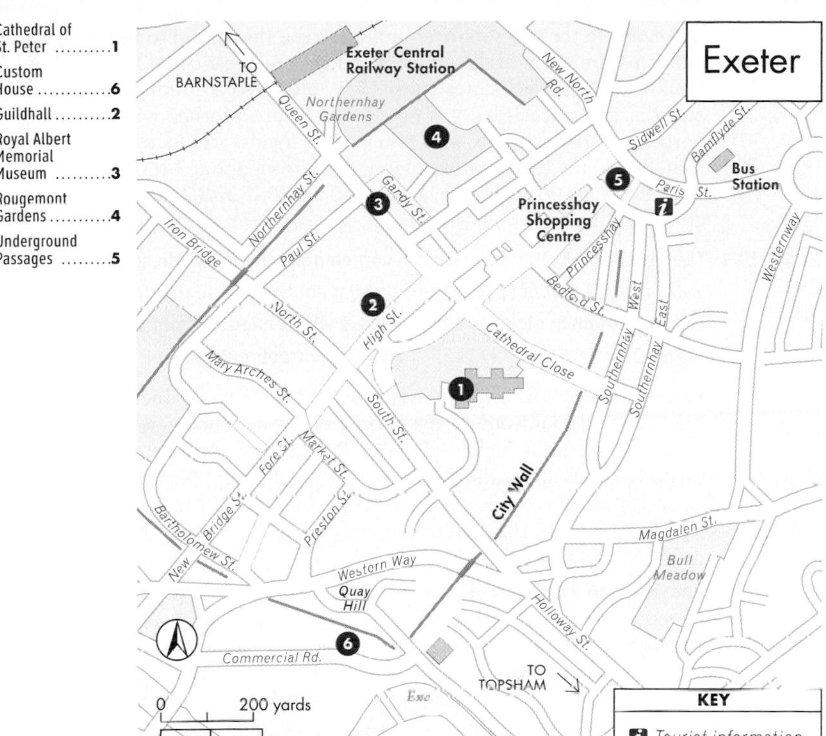

www.powderham.co.uk £9.50–£12.50 (according to season), deer park £2.50 Apr.–late July, Sept., and Oct., Sun.–Fri. 11–4:30; late July–Aug., daily 11–5:30; last tour 1 hr before closing (but Fri. last tour at 2:30).

FAMILY **Fodor's Choice** ★ **Royal Albert Memorial Museum.** This family-friendly museum is housed in a recently refurbished Victorian building. The centerpiece is the extensive Making History gallery, a giddy mix of objects imaginatively illustrating the city's history and covering everything from Roman pottery to memorabilia from World War II. The geology section is thrillingly enhanced by the latest video technology, and there are also excellent ethnography and archaeological collections, natural-history displays, and works by West Country artists. *Queen St. 01392/265858 www.rammuseum.org.uk Free Tues.–Sun. 10–5.*

WORTH NOTING

Custom House. Exeter's historic waterfront on the River Exe was the center of the city's medieval wool industry, and the Custom House, built in 1682, attests to the city's prosperity. The city's earliest surviving brick building is now flanked by Victorian warehouses and houses a visitor center where you can view documents on the city's maritime history and an audiovisual display. *The Quay.*

Guildhall. On the city's main shopping street, this is said to be the oldest municipal building in the country still in use. The current hall, with its Renaissance portico, dates from 1330, although a guildhall has occupied this site since at least 1160. The walls are adorned with imposing portraits of royal figures and noteworthy locals, and its timber-braced roof, one of the earliest in England, dates from about 1460. ✉ *High St.* ☎ *01392/665500* 🎫 *Free* ⏲ *Weekdays 10:30–1 and 2–4, Sat. 10:30–1* ☞ *Closed during functions.*

QUICK BITES

The Prospect. At this pub you can contemplate the quayside comings and goings over a pint of real ale and a hot or cold meal. The nautical theme comes through in pictures and the ship's wheel hanging from the ceiling. ✉ ***The Quay*** ☎ ***01392/273152*** 🌐 ***www.heavitreebrewery.co.uk.***

Rougemont Gardens. These gardens behind the Royal Albert Memorial Museum were laid out at the end of the 18th century. The land was once part of the defensive ditch of Rougemont Castle, built in 1068 by decree of William the Conqueror. The adjoining Northernhay Gardens contain the original Norman gatehouse and the remains of the Roman city wall, the latter forming part of the ancient castle's outer wall. ✉ *Off Queen St.*

FAMILY **Underground Passages.** Exeter's Underground Passages, which once served as conduits for fresh water, are the only medieval vaulted passages open to the public in Britain. They date to the mid-14th century, although some were enlarged by the Victorians. An exhibition and video precede the 25-minute guided tour. Many of the passages are narrow and low: be prepared to stoop. The tours often sell out during school vacations, so come early. Children under five are not permitted in the tunnels. ✉ *2 Paris St.* ☎ *01392/665887* 🌐 *www.exeter.gov.uk* 🎫 *£6* ⏲ *June–Sept. and school vacations, Mon.–Sat. 9:30–5:30, Sun. 10:30–4; Oct.–May, Tues.–Fri. 11:30–5:30, Sat. 9:30–5:30, Sun. 11:30–4; last tours 1 hr before closing.*

WHERE TO EAT

$ ITALIAN ✕ **Ask.** This outpost of an Italian chain has secured an enviable site in a part-medieval, part-Georgian building opposite the cathedral. With three dining areas, it has windows with superb views across the Close, as well as a courtyard that is perfect for warm days. Although the food is unadventurous and of varying quality, there are good antipasti and salads and a generous selection of pizzas and pastas. [$] *Average main: £12* ✉ *5 Cathedral Close* ☎ *01392/427127* 🌐 *www.askitalian.co.uk.*

$ VEGETARIAN ✕ **Herbie's.** A mellow stop, this friendly vegetarian bistro with wood floors and simple tables is ideal for unwinding over leisurely conversation. You can snack on pita bread with hummus and salad, or tackle the Mediterranean platter, Moroccan tagine, Indonesian salad, or Greek vegetable pie. The puddings are scrumptious, and all the beers and wines are organic. [$] *Average main: £10* ✉ *15 North St.* ☎ *01392/258473* ⏲ *Closed Sun. No dinner Mon.*

$$ MODERN BRITISH Fodor's Choice ★ **Michael Caines Restaurant.** Perfectly located within the Cathedral Close, this ultrachic restaurant is in the centuries-old building that is now the ABode Exeter. Master chef Michael Caines oversees the kitchen, which serves eclectic contemporary fare like roast venison with braised pork belly and chestnut puree, or roast hake with scallops and leek fondue. Fixed-price lunch and evening menus are also available. Alternatively, the more relaxed (and moderately priced) Café-Bar & Grill next door, under the same ownership, serves meals all day, including good fixed-price lunches. *Average main: £16 ABode Exeter, Cathedral Yard 01392/223638 www.abodeexeter.co.uk Closed Sun.*

$ BRITISH **Ship Inn.** Here you can lift a tankard of stout in the very rooms where Sir Francis Drake and Sir Walter Raleigh enjoyed their ale. Drake, in fact, once wrote, "Next to mine own shippe, I do most love that old 'Shippe' in Exon." The pub dishes out casual bar fare, from sandwiches to grills and beef and ale pie, either in the bar or in the beamed and paneled upstairs restaurant. *Average main: £8 1–3 St. Martin's La. 01392/272040 www.gkpubs.co.uk.*

5

WHERE TO STAY

$$ HOTEL **ABode Exeter.** Claimed to be the first inn in England to be described as a "hotel," the 1769 Royal Clarence (the old name still appears outside) has been transformed into a strikingly modern boutique hotel. **Pros:** superb central location; wonderful views from front; friendly young staff. **Cons:** some rooms are small and viewless; occasional noise disturbance from outside; no parking. *Rooms from: £104 Cathedral Close 01392/319955 www.abodeexeter.co.uk 53 rooms No meals.*

$$$ HOTEL Fodor's Choice ★ **Combe House.** Rolling parkland surrounds this luxurious Elizabethan manor house 16 miles east of Exeter. **Pros:** beautiful rural surroundings; relaxed ambience; attentive but informal staff. **Cons:** rather remote; decor a bit tired in places; no Wi-Fi in bedrooms. *Rooms from: £220 Off A30, Gittisham 01404/540400 www.combehousedevon.com 13 rooms, 2 suites, 1 cottage Breakfast.*

$$ HOTEL Fodor's Choice ★ **The Magdalen Chapter.** This former hospital has been reimagined as a modish hotel with a zippy, happening vibe, and add-ons that include a heated indoor-outdoor pool, a fitness room, and spa treatments. **Pros:** contemporary style; great food; health facilities. **Cons:** rooms on the small side; not for technophobes; limited parking. *Rooms from: £155 Magdalen St. 01392/288171 www.themagdalenchapter.com 59 rooms Breakfast.*

$ B&B/INN Fodor's Choice ★ **Raffles.** A 10-minute walk from the center, this quirky B&B in a quiet neighborhood makes an ideal base for a night or two in town. **Pros:** peaceful location; plenty of character. **Cons:** single room is small; parking costs £5. *Rooms from: £78 11 Blackall Rd. 01392/270200 www.raffles-exeter.co.uk 6 rooms Breakfast.*

$ HOTEL **White Hart.** Guests have been welcomed to this inn since the 15th century, and it is said that Oliver Cromwell stabled his horses here. **Pros:** close to center; historic building; on-site parking. **Cons:** can be noisy; drab in parts. *Rooms from: £94 66 South St. 01392/279897 www.whitehartpubexeter.co.uk 55 rooms Breakfast.*

NIGHTLIFE AND PERFORMING ARTS

Exeter Festival of South West Food and Drink. This festival, which showcases local producers, chefs, and their gastronomic specialties, takes place in Rougemont Gardens and Northernhay Gardens over three days in April or May. Live music is offered in the evenings. ✉ *Exeter* 🌐 *www.exeterfoodanddrinkfestival.co.uk.*

Northcott Theatre. Some of the country's most innovative companies stage plays and dance performances at the Northcott Theatre. ✉ *Stocker Rd.* ☎ *01392/493493* 🌐 *www.exeternorthcott.co.uk.*

SHOPPING

Many of Exeter's most interesting shops are along Gandy Street, off the main High Street drag, with several good food and clothes outlets. Exeter was the silver-assay office for the West Country, and the earliest example of Exeter silver (now a museum piece) dates from 1218; Victorian pieces are still sold. The Exeter assay mark is three castles.

Exeter Quay Antiques Centre. Twenty dealers display their diverse wares in Exeter's former fish market, including everything from silverware and ceramics to "royalty thimbles." The Centre includes a quayside café. ✉ *The Quay* ☎ *01392/493501* 🌐 *www.exeterquayantiques.co.uk* 🕒 *Open daily 10–5.*

SPORTS AND THE OUTDOORS

Saddles and Paddles. Renting out bikes, kayaks, and canoes, this shop is handily placed for a 7-mile trip along the scenic Exeter Canal Trail, which follows the River Exe and the Exeter Ship Canal. ✉ *4 Kings Wharf* ☎ *01392/424241* 🌐 *www.sadpad.com.*

TOPSHAM

4 miles southeast of Exeter on B3182.

This small town, full of narrow streets and hidden courtyards, was once a bustling river port, and it remains rich in 18th-century houses and inns.

GETTING HERE AND AROUND

Frequent bus service connects Topsham with Exeter; the village is also a stop for twice-hourly trains running between Exmouth and Exeter. Topsham is best negotiated on foot.

EXPLORING

A la Ronde. The 16-sided, nearly circular A la Ronde was built in 1798 by two cousins inspired by the Church of San Vitale in Ravenna, Italy. Among the 18th- and 19th-century curiosities here is an elaborate display of feathers and shells. The house is 5 miles south of Topsham. ✉ *Summer La.* ☎ *01395/265514* 🌐 *www.nationaltrust.org.uk* 🎫 *£8* 🕒 *Feb.–Oct., daily 11–5.*

Topsham Museum. Occupying a 17th-century Dutch-style merchant's house beside the river, this museum has period-furnished rooms and displays on local and maritime history. One room has memorabilia belonging to the late actress Vivien Leigh, who spent much time in the region. ✉ *25 The Strand* ☎ *01392/873244* 🌐 *www.devonmuseums.*

net/topsham-museum/devon-museums 🎫 *Free* ⏲ *Apr.–July, Sept., and Oct., Mon., Wed., Thurs., and weekends 2–5; Aug., Mon.–Thurs. and weekends 2–5.*

EN ROUTE

The **Jurassic Coast** (🌐 *www.jurassiccoast.org*), from Exmouth to Studland Bay in Dorset, 95 miles to the east, has been designated a World Heritage Site because of the rich geological record of ancient rocks and fossils exposed here. The reddish, grass-topped cliffs of the region are punctuated by quiet seaside resorts such as Budleigh Salterton, Sidmouth, and Seaton. ⇨ *For more information, see Chapter 4, The South.*

TORQUAY

26 miles south of Topsham, 23 miles south of Exeter.

The most important resort area in South Devon, Torquay envisions itself as the center of the "English Riviera." Since 1968 the towns of Paignton and Torquay (pronounced tor- *kee*) have been amalgamated under the common moniker of Torbay. Torquay is the supposed site of the hotel in the popular British television comedy *Fawlty Towers* and was the home of mystery writer Agatha Christie. Fans should check out the exhibit devoted to Christie at the town museum, and visit Greenway, her holiday home on the River Dart. Torquay's tourist office has leaflets outlining an Agatha Christie Trail that takes in all the Christie-related places in town.

The town has shed some of its old-fashioned image in recent years with modern hotels, luxury villas, and apartments that climb the hillsides above the harbor. Still, Torquay is more like Brighton's maiden aunt in terms of energy and fizz, though a pubs-and-clubs culture makes an appearance on Friday and Saturday nights. Palm trees and other semitropical plants (a benefit of being near the warming Gulf Stream) flourish in the seafront gardens; the sea is a clear and intense blue.

GETTING HERE AND AROUND

Buses arrive near Torquay's harbor and the tourist office. The train station is close to Torre Abbey, but other points in town are best reached on local buses or by taxi. Drivers should take A38 and A380 from Exeter.

ESSENTIALS

Visitor Information English Riviera Visitor Information Centre. ✉ *5 Vaughan Parade, Torbay* ☎ *01803/211211* 🌐 *www.englishriviera.co.uk.*

EXPLORING

Cockington. Just a mile outside the heart of Torbay by bus or car lies this chocolate-box village with thatched cottages, a 14th-century forge, and the square-tower Church of St. George and St. Mary. Repair to the Old Mill for a café lunch or head to the Drum Inn, designed by Sir Edwin Lutyens to be an archetypal pub. On the village outskirts lies Cockington Court—a grand estate with crafts studios, shops, and an eatery. Cockington has, however, more than a touch of the faux: cottages that don't sell anything put up signs to this effect. ✉ *Torbay.*

5

FAMILY Fodor's Choice ★ **Torre Abbey.** For lovers of fine things, Torquay's chief attraction is Torre Abbey, surrounded by parkland but close to the seafront. The abbey itself, founded in 1196, was razed in 1539, though you can still see traces of the old construction. The mansion that now occupies the site was the home of the Cary family for nearly 300 years, and it was later converted into a museum and art gallery. Artistic riches lie within the main building: marine paintings, Victorian sculptures, Pre-Raphaelite window designs, and drawings by William Blake. There are plenty of family-friendly activities, including brass-rubbing. *King's Dr., Torbay 01803/293593 www.torre-abbey.org.uk £7.50 Mar.–Dec., Wed.–Sun. and holiday Mon. 10–5, school vacations daily 10–5; last admission at 4.*

FAWLTY TOWERS

John Cleese was inspired to write the TV series *Fawlty Towers* after he and the Monty Python team stayed at a hotel in Torquay while filming the series *Monty Python's Flying Circus* in the early 1970s. The "wonderfully rude" owner became the model for Basil Fawlty, the exasperated, accident-prone manager in the series. The owner died in 1981, but his hotel, the Gleneagles, is still going strong—though happily nothing like the chaotic Fawlty Towers.

WHERE TO EAT AND STAY

$$ MODERN BRITISH **The Elephant.** Set back from Torquay's harbor, this elegant eatery offers sophisticated but relaxed dining, either in the dining room upstairs with views over Torbay or in the less formal street-level brasserie. In the latter, you can tuck into such dishes as braised pig's cheek, breast of Crediton duck with pumpkin puree, and warm chocolate fondant with clementine sorbet. The upstairs dining room, with its high-back chairs, antique lighting fixtures, and polished floorboards, has more innovative concoctions available on a fixed-price tasting menu, which may include Brixham crab with turnip, samphire, and lovage as a starter, and fallow deer with beetroots, blueberries, and truffle for a main course. *Average main: £18 3–4 Beacon Terr., Torbay 01803/200044 www.elephantrestaurant.co.uk Closed Sun., Mon., and 2 wks early Jan; upstairs restaurant closed Oct.–early Apr. No lunch in upstairs restaurant.*

$$ SEAFOOD Fodor's Choice ★ **Number 7 Fish Bistro.** Seafood fans can indulge their passion at this unpretentious, convivial spot near the harbor; wood floors and an array of maritime knickknacks set the mood. Fresh, locally caught fish is brought to your table for inspection before being simply but imaginatively prepared. The extensive menu offers dishes ranging from humble—but abundant and beautifully cooked—fish-and-chips to lobster and crab grilled with garlic and brandy. *Average main: £18 7 Beacon Terr., Torbay 01803/295055 www.no7-fish.com Closed Sun. Oct.–June, Mon. Nov.–May. No lunch Sun.–Tues. Closed 3 wks Feb. and 1st wk Nov. Reservations essential.*

$ HOTEL **The Imperial Hotel Torquay.** This enormous pile perched above the sea exudes slightly faded Victorian splendor. **Pros:** grand setting; great views; good online rates. **Cons:** renovation overdue; back rooms face parking lot; expensive parking. *Rooms from: £84 Park Hill Rd.,*

Torbay ☎ *01803/294301* 🌐 *www.thehotelcollection.co.uk* 🛏 *139 rooms, 13 suites* 🍴 *No meals.*

$$ B&B/INN **Lanscombe House.** Located in the postcard-pretty village of Cockington, this family-run Victorian guesthouse offers spacious bedrooms with floral wallpaper and period furnishings, and a walled garden where you can try your hand at croquet. **Pros:** quiet atmosphere; great breakfasts; helpful hosts. **Cons:** touristy environment; car necessary for local sights; no guests under 16. 💲 *Rooms from: £105* ✉ *Cockington La., Cockington* ☎ *01803/606938* 🌐 *www.lanscombehouse.co.uk* 🕓 *Closed mid-Oct.–Easter* 🛏 *7 rooms* 🍴 *Breakfast.*

SPORTS AND THE OUTDOORS

Torbay's beaches, a mixture of sand and coarse gravel, have won awards for their water quality and facilities, and can get crowded in summer. Apart from the central Torre Abbey Sands, they're mainly to the north of town, often separated by the crumbly red cliffs characteristic of the area. To sun and swim, head for Anstey's Cove, a favorite spot for scuba divers, with more beaches farther along at neighboring Babbacombe.

5

TOTNES

8 miles west of Torquay, 28 miles southwest of Exeter.

This busy market town on the banks of the River Dart preserves plenty of its medieval past, and on summer Tuesdays vendors dress in period costume for the Elizabethan Market. Market days are Friday and Saturday, when the town's status as a center of alternative medicine and culture becomes especially clear, and on the third Sunday of the month, when there's a local produce market on Civic Square. The historic buildings include a guildhall and St. Mary's Church.

GETTING HERE AND AROUND

Totnes is on a regular fast bus route between Plymouth and Torbay, and is a stop for main-line trains between Plymouth and Exeter. Buses pull into the center, and the train station is a few minutes' walk north of the center. Drivers should take A38 and A385 from Plymouth or A385 from Torbay.

ESSENTIALS

Visitor Information Totnes Tourist Information Centre. ✉ *The Town Mill, Coronation Rd.* ☎ *01803/863168* 🌐 *www.totnesinformation.co.uk.*

EXPLORING

Brixham. At the southern point of Tor Bay, Brixham has kept much of its original charm, partly because it still has an active fishing harbor. Much of the catch goes straight to restaurants as far away as London. Sample fish-and-chips on the quayside, where there's a (surprisingly petite) full-scale reproduction of the vessel on which Sir Francis Drake circumnavigated the world. The village is 10 miles southeast of Totnes by A385 and A3022. ✉ *Brixham.*

FAMILY **South Devon Railway.** Steam trains of this railway run through 7 miles of the wooded Dart Valley between Totnes and Buckfastleigh, on the edge of Dartmoor. Call about special trips around Christmas. ✉ *Dart Bridge*

Rd., Buckfastleigh ☎ *01364/644370* 🌐 *www.southdevonrailway.co.uk* 🎫 *£14 round-trip* ⏲ *Mid-Feb., late Mar.–Oct., and mid-Dec.–early Jan., daily; see website or call for hrs.*

Totnes Castle. You can climb up the hill in town to the ruins of this castle—a fine Norman motte and bailey design—for a wonderful view of Totnes and the River Dart. ✉ *Castle St.* ☎ *01803/864406* 🌐 *www.english-heritage.org.uk* 🎫 *£3.80* ⏲ *Late Mar.–Sept., daily 10–6; Oct., daily 10–5; Nov.–late Mar., weekends 10–4.*

WHERE TO STAY

$$ HOTEL **Royal Seven Stars Hotel.** Conveniently located at the bottom of the main street, this centuries-old coaching inn has counted Daniel Defoe and Edward VII among its former guests. **Pros:** central location; friendly staff; spotless rooms. **Cons:** some accommodations are small; rooms over bars can be noisy; busy public areas. $ *Rooms from: £119* ✉ *The Plains* ☎ *01803/862125* 🌐 *www.royalsevenstars.co.uk* *21 rooms* 🍴 *Breakfast.*

NIGHTLIFE AND PERFORMING ARTS

Dartington Hall. One of the foremost arts centers of the West Country, Dartington Hall lies 2 miles northwest of Totnes. There are concerts, film screenings, and exhibitions. The gardens, free year-round, are the setting for outdoor performances of Shakespeare in summer. There's a café, and you can stay overnight in rooms in the hall. ✉ *Off A384 and A385, Dartington* ☎ *01803/847070* 🌐 *www.dartington.org/arts.*

SHOPPING

Shops at Dartington. Near Dartington Hall, 15 stores and two restaurants in and around an old cider press make up the Shops at Dartington. Open daily, it's a good place to find handmade Dartington crystal glassware, kitchenware, crafts, books, and toys. The farm shop sells fudge, ice cream, and cider, and Cranks is an excellent vegetarian restaurant. ✉ *Shinners Bridge, Dartington* ☎ *01803/847500* 🌐 *www.dartington.org/shops.*

DARTMOUTH

13 miles southeast of Totnes, 35 miles east of Plymouth, 35 miles south of Exeter, 5 miles southwest of Brixham.

An important port in the Middle Ages, Dartmouth is today a favorite haunt of yacht owners. Traces of its past include the old houses in Bayard's Cove at the bottom of Lower Street, where the *Mayflower* made a stop in 1620, the 16th-century covered Butterwalk, and the two castles guarding the entrance to the River Dart. The Royal Naval College, built in 1905, dominates the heights above the town. A few miles south of Dartmouth on Start Bay there are a number of pretty beaches including Blackpool Sands, popular with families.

GETTING HERE AND AROUND

Frequent buses connect Dartmouth with Plymouth and Totnes. Drivers coming from the west should follow A381 and A3122. Approaching from the Torbay area via A3022 and A379, you can save mileage by using the passenger and car ferries crossing the Dart. Travelers on foot can take advantage of a vintage steam train service operating between Paignton and Kingswear, where there are ferry connections with Dartmouth. River ferries also link Dartmouth with Totnes.

ESSENTIALS

Visitor Information Dartmouth Tourist Information Centre. ✉ *The Engine House, Mayors Ave.* ☎ *01803/834224* 🌐 *www.discoverdartmouth.com.*

EXPLORING

FAMILY **Dartmouth Steam Railway.** These lovingly restored trains chug along on tracks beside the River Dart between Paignton and Kingswear (across the river from Dartmouth). You can combine a train ride with a river excursion between Dartmouth and Totnes and a bus between Totnes and Paignton on a £25 Round Robin ticket. ✉ *5 Lower St.* ☎ *01803/555872* 🌐 *www.dartmouthrailriver.co.uk* 🎫 *£15* 🕑 *Mid-Feb.–Oct., with some dates in Nov. and Dec.; check website or call for departure times.*

5

Greenway. A rewarding way to experience the River Dart is to join a cruise from Dartmouth's quay to visit Greenway, the 16th century riverside home of the Gilbert family (Sir Humphrey Gilbert claimed Newfoundland on behalf of Elizabeth I), more famous today for its association with the crime writer Agatha Christie. Mrs. Mallowan (Christie's married name) made it her holiday home beginning in 1938, and the house displays collections of archaeological finds, china, and silver. The gorgeous gardens are thickly planted with magnolias, camellias, and rare shrubs, and richly endowed with panoramic views. Beware, however, that the grounds are steeply laid out, and those arriving by boat face a daunting uphill climb. Allow three hours to see everything; timed tickets for the house are given on arrival. Parking spaces here are restricted and must be booked in advance. Alternatively, ask at the tourist office about walking and cycling routes to reach the house, as well as a vintage bus service from Torquay and Brixham. A round-trip ticket between Dartmouth and Greenway costs £8.50 on Greenway Ferry Pleasure Cruises (🌐 *www.greenwayferry.co.uk*), which also operates a vintage bus service to Greenway from Torquay, Paignton, and Brixham. ✉ *Greenway Rd., Galmpton* ☎ *01803/842382* 🌐 *www.nationaltrust.org.uk* 🎫 *£9.90* 🕑 *Early Mar.–late July, and early Sept.–Oct., Wed.–Sun. 10:30–5; late July–early Sept., Tues.–Sun. 10:30–5; early Dec.–late Dec. weekends 11–4.*

WHERE TO EAT AND STAY

$$$ SEAFOOD Fodor's Choice ★ ✕ **The Seahorse.** In a prime riverside location, this seafood restaurant epitomizes the region's ongoing food revolution. The knowledgeable staff will guide you through the Italian-inspired menu, which primarily depends on the day's catch: look for scallops with garlic and white port, grilled monkfish, and *fritto misto*—a platter of fried seafood with aioli. The meat dishes are equally enticing, while the formidable desserts are well worth leaving space for. The restaurant is usually packed, with a relaxed and convivial atmosphere. Set-price lunch and early evening menus are often available. The owner, celebrity chef Mitch Tonks, also runs a much more basic fish-and-chips restaurant a few doors along

called RockFish, open daily. [$] *Average main: £25* ✉ *5 S. Embankment* ☎ *01803/835147* 🌐 *www.seahorserestaurant.co.uk* ⏲ *Closed Sun. and Mon.*

$$$ HOTEL Fodor's Choice ★ **Royal Castle Hotel.** Part of Dartmouth's historic waterfront (and consequently a hub of activity), this hotel has truly earned the name "Royal"—several monarchs have slept here. **Pros:** historical resonance; superb central location; professional staff. **Cons:** some cheaper rooms are nondescript; no elevator. [$] *Rooms from: £175* ✉ *11 The Quay* ☎ *01803/833033* 🌐 *www.royalcastle.co.uk* *25 rooms* *Breakfast.*

SPORTS AND THE OUTDOORS

Blackpool Sands. Located on Start Bay, this privately managed beach sits at the edge of an extraordinary natural setting of meadows and forest. It's favored for its clear water and long, wide stretch of shingle. Popular with families, the beach is big enough that you can always find a quiet stretch. Take A379 south of Dartmouth and look for signs. **Amenities:** food and drink; lifeguards; parking (fee); showers, toilets; water sports. **Best for:** swimming. ✉ *3 miles south of Dartmouth* ☎ *01803/771800* 🌐 *www.blackpoolsands.co.uk.*

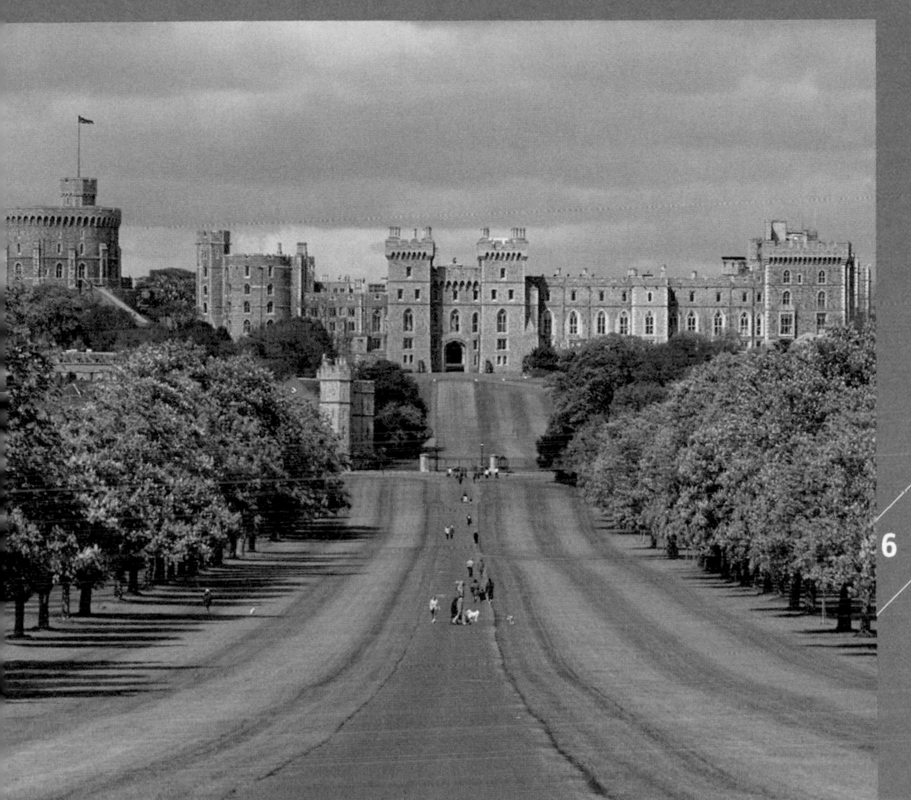

6

THE THAMES VALLEY

WELCOME TO THE THAMES VALLEY

TOP REASONS TO GO

★ **Oxford:** While scholars' noses are buried in their books, you get to sightsee among Oxford University's ancient stone buildings and memorable museums.

★ **Windsor Castle:** The mystique of eight successive royal houses of the British monarchy permeates Windsor and its famous castle, where a fraction of the current Queen's vast wealth is displayed.

★ **Blenheim Palace:** The only British historic home to be named a World Heritage Site has magnificent baroque architecture, stunning parkland, and remembrances of Winston Churchill.

★ **Boating on the Thames:** Life is slower on the river, and renting a boat or taking a cruise is an ideal way to see verdant riverside pastures and villages. Windsor, Marlow, Henley, and Oxford are good options.

★ **Mapledurham House:** This is the house that inspired Toad Hall from *The Wind in the Willows*; you can picnic here on the grounds and drink in the views.

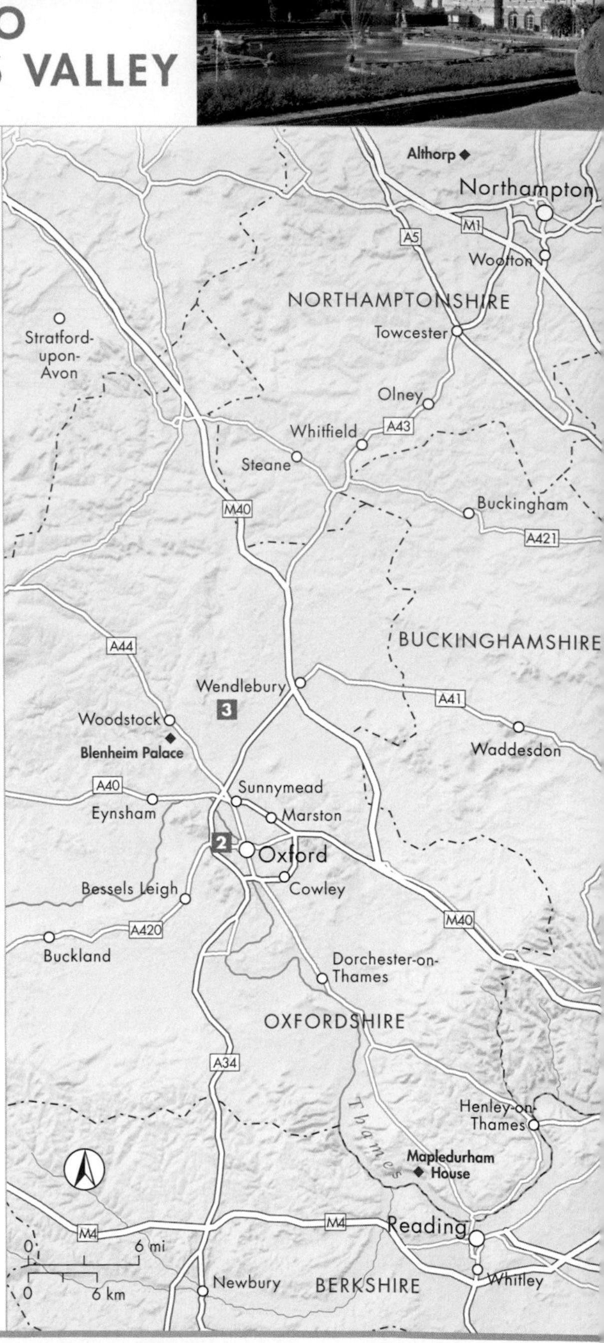

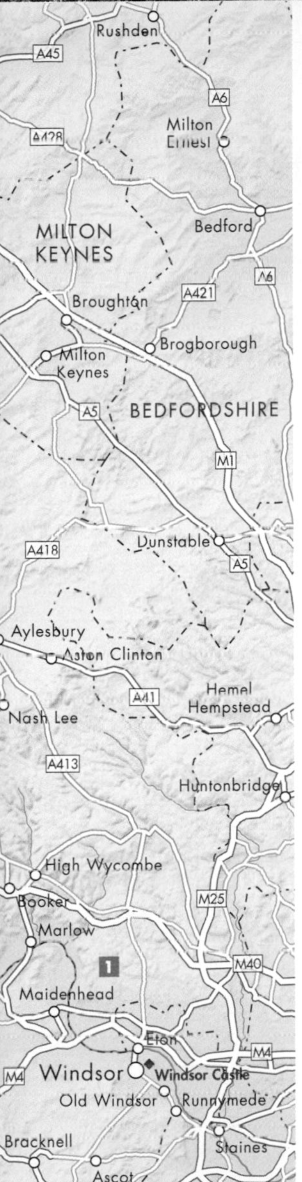

1 Windsor, Marlow, and Nearby. Gorgeous Windsor has its imposing and battlemented castle, stone cottages, and tea shops, and nearby Eton is also charming. The meadows and villages around Marlow and Henley are lovely in summer when the flowers are in bloom. Mapledurham House near Henley-on-Thames is an idyllic stop; you can take a boat here.

2 Oxford. Wonderfully walkable, this university town has handsome, golden-stone buildings and museum after museum to explore. Take a punt on the local waterways for a break. Oxford's good bars, pubs, and restaurants keep you going late at night as well.

3 Oxfordshire. So many grand manor houses, so little time: around the Thames Valley are many intriguing stops. Blenheim is a vast, ornate, extraordinary place that takes the better part of a day to see. Althorp House, home of the late Princess Diana, seems almost small by comparison, although it's actually enormous.

GETTING ORIENTED

An ideal place to begin any exploration of the Thames Valley is the town of Windsor, about an hour's drive west of central London. From there you can follow the river to Marlow and to Henley-on-Thames, site of the famous regatta, and then make a counterclockwise sweep west to the area around Henley-on-Thames. To the north is Oxford, with its pubs, colleges, and museums; it can make a good base for exploring some of the area's charming towns and notable stately homes. If you're extending your itinerary, west of the region but still nearby are the Cotswolds and Stratford-upon-Avon.

BOATING ON THE THAMES

Whether you're drifting lazily along in your own boat or taking a sightseeing cruise past crucial points of English history, you'll see the River Thames from a new and delightful vantage point out on the water.

(above) Views of tranquil countryside are one pleasure of boating on the Thames; (right, top) Riverside towns add interest; (right, bottom) Colorful boats in Henley

"There is nothing—absolutely nothing—half so much worth doing as simply messing about in boats." So says the Water Rat in Kenneth Grahame's timeless children's novel *The Wind in the Willows*. So take Ratty's advice: it's hard to beat gliding peacefully on the river, water meadows on either side of you, and then tying up for a picnic or lunch at a riverside pub. You can just putter about in a rowboat for an hour or so, or hire a boat and organize your own itinerary for a few days. If this doesn't appeal, go on a romantic lunch cruise or take one of the many organized trips. There are 125 miles of navigable water to explore, quieter nearer the source of the Thames in the Cotswolds, perhaps most picturesque between Pangbourne and Marlow, and busiest nearer London. Wherever you go, your pace of life will slow right down: boats aren't allowed to travel above 5 mph.

CHOOSE A BOAT

Most boats rented by the hour accommodate four people. Motorboats are noisy, but you can opt for electric canoes or launches that have the benefit of canopies. Punts (flat-bottom wooden boats) require a strong arm so you can maneuver the long wooden pole and push the boat along. Narrowboats carried freight on canals but are now well equipped for pleasure trips.

MESS ABOUT ON THE RIVER

The main hubs for hiring self-drive boats on the Thames are at Windsor, Henley-on-Thames, Oxford, and Lechlade. The cost varies from £15 an hour for a rowboat, £25 for an electric boat, £60 for half a day with a punt, to £175 a day for a motor cruiser. A short trip for four on a narrowboat from Oxfordshire Narrowboats ranges from around £160 to £1,000.

Cotswold Boat Hire. ✉ *Buscot Mill, Brandy Island* ☎ *01793/727083* 🌐 *www.cotswoldboat.co.uk.*

Hobbs of Henley. ✉ *Station Rd., Henley-on-Thames* ☎ *01491/572035* 🌐 *www.hobbsofhenley.com.*

John Logie Motorboats. ✉ *The Promenade, Barry Ave., Windsor* ☎ *07774/983809* 🌐 *www.johnlogiemotorboats.com.*

Oxfordshire Narrowboats. ✉ *Heyford Wharf, Station Rd., Lower Heyford* ☎ *01869/340348* 🌐 *www.oxfordshire-narrowboats.co.uk.*

PUSH THE BOAT OUT IN STYLE

Hire an Edwardian electric launch with your own skipper (around £90 per hour) from the Compleat Angler in Marlow; take a vintage boat (from £185 per hour) or champagne cruise (£49) from Cliveden; or climb aboard the gleaming Victorian steam launch *Nuneham* for a short summertime afternoon tea (£39) or Sunday lunch cruise (£36) from Windsor with the French Brothers.

Cliveden. ✉ *Off 404, near Maidenhead, Taplow* ☎ *01628/668561* 🌐 *www.clivedenhouse.co.uk.*

Compleat Angler. ✉ *Marlow Bridge, Bisham Rd., Marlow* ☎ *0844/879–9128* 🌐 *www.macdonaldhotels.co.uk/compleatangler.*

French Brothers. ✉ *The Promenade, Barry Ave., Windsor* ☎ *01753/851900* 🌐 *www.frenchbrothers.co.uk.*

PICK AN ORGANIZED CRUISE

Windsor Castle, Runnymede, Henley (where you can stop for the River and Rowing Museum), and Mapledurham all lie on the banks of the Thames. Thames River Cruise has outings to Mapledurham from Caversham on weekends. Salter's Steamers runs short round-trips out of Windsor, Henley, Oxford, and Marlow, and French Brothers *(see above)* runs round-trips from Windsor.

Salter's Steamers. ✉ *Folly Bridge, Oxford* ☎ *01865/243421* 🌐 *www.salterssteamers.co.uk.*

Thames River Cruise. ✉ *Bridge St., Reading* ☎ *0118/948–1088* 🌐 *www.thamesrivercruise.co.uk.*

Updated by Jack Jewers

Easy proximity to London made the Thames Valley enormously popular with the rich and powerful throughout the country's history. They built the lavish country estates and castles, including Windsor, that form the area's most popular tourist attractions today. Some of these, as well as Oxford and its university, are easy day trips from London. Consider exploring this stretch of the River Thames by boat, either jumping aboard a cruiser or getting behind the oars. Windsor, Henley, and Marlow all make good starting points.

Once an aquatic highway connecting London to the rest of England and the world, the Thames was critical to the power of the city when the sun never set on the British Empire. By the 18th century the Thames was one of the world's busiest water systems, declining in commercial importance only when the 20th century brought other means of transportation to the forefront. Traditionally, the area west of London is known as the Thames Valley, and the area to the east is called the Thames Gateway.

Anyone who wants to understand the mystique of the British monarchy should visit Windsor, home to the medieval and massive Windsor Castle. Farther upstream, the green quadrangles and graceful spires of Oxford are the hallmarks of one of the world's most famous universities. Within 10 miles of Oxford the storybook village of Woodstock and gracious Blenheim Palace, one of the grandest houses in England, are both well worth your time.

The railroads and motorways carrying traffic to and from London have turned much of this area into commuter territory, but you can still find timeless villages and miles of relaxing countryside. The stretches of the Thames near Marlow and Henley-on-Thames are lovely, with rowing clubs, piers, and sturdy waterside cottages and villas. It all conspires to make the Thames Valley a wonderful find, even for experienced travelers.

THAMES VALLEY PLANNER

WHEN TO GO

High summer is lovely, but droves of visitors have the same effect on some travelers as bad weather. Consider visiting in late spring or early fall, when the weather isn't too bad and the crowds have headed home. Book tickets and accommodations well in advance for Henley's Royal Regatta at the cusp of June and July and Ascot's Royal Meeting in mid-June. Visiting Eton and the Oxford colleges is much more restricted during term time (generally September to late March and late April to mid-July). Most stately homes are open March through September or October only—call in advance if you're planning an itinerary. Avoid any driving in the London area during morning and afternoon rush hours.

PLANNING YOUR TIME

The major towns of the Thames Valley are easy to visit on a day trip from London. A train to Windsor, for example, takes about an hour, and you can fully explore Windsor and its environs in a day. Base yourself in Oxford for a couple of days, though, if you want to make a thorough exploration of the town and the surrounding countryside. To visit the great houses and the rural castles you need to either rent a car or join an organized tour. Blenheim Palace and Waddesdon Manor require at least half a day to do them justice, as do Stowe Landscape Gardens and Woburn Abbey.

6

GETTING HERE AND AROUND

BUS TRAVEL

Oxford and the area's main towns are convenient by bus from London, as is Windsor (although trains are faster), but St. Albans is best reached by train.

You can travel between the major towns by local bus, but it's complicated and can require changing more than once. For information, contact Traveline. If you want to see more than one town in this area in a day, it's best to rent a car or join a tour.

Contacts Arriva. ☎ *0871/200–2233* 🌐 *www.arrivabus.co.uk.* **First.** ☎ *01344/782222* 🌐 *www.firstgroup.com.* **Megabus.** ☎ *0900/160–0900 booking line, calls cost £0.60 per minute* 🌐 *www.megabus.co.uk.* **Oxford Bus Company.** ☎ *01865/785400* 🌐 *www.oxfordbus.co.uk.* **Reading Buses.** ☎ *0118/959–4000* 🌐 *www.reading-buses.co.uk.* **Stagecoach Oxford Tube.** ☎ *01865/772250* 🌐 *www.oxfordtube.com.* **Traveline.** ☎ *0871/200–2233* 🌐 *www.traveline.org.uk.*

CAR TRAVEL

Most towns in this area are within a one- or two-hour drive of central London—except during rush hour, of course. Although the roads are good, this wealthy section of the commuter belt has heavy traffic, even on the secondary roads. Parking in towns can be a problem, so take advantage of public parking lots near the outskirts of town centers.

TRAIN TRAVEL

Trains to Oxford (one hour) and the region depart from London's Paddington Station. Trains bound for Ascot (50 minutes) leave from Waterloo every 30 minutes. Trains to St. Albans (20 minutes) leave from St.

Pancras Station. A number of lines, including Chiltern and First Great Western, serve the area; National Rail Enquiries has information.

Contacts National Rail Enquiries. ☎ *0845/748–4950* 🌐 *www.nationalrail.co.uk.*

RESTAURANTS

Londoners weekend here, and where they go, stellar restaurants follow. Bray (near Windsor), Marlow, and Great Milton (near Oxford) claim some excellent tables; you need to book months ahead for these. Simple pub food, as well as classic French cuisine, can be enjoyed in waterside settings at many restaurants beside the Thames. Even in towns away from the river, well-heeled commuters and Oxford professors support top-flight establishments. Reservations are often not required but are strongly recommended, especially on weekends.

HOTELS

From converted country houses to refurbished Elizabethan inns, the region's accommodations are rich in history and distinctive in appeal. Many hotels cultivate traditional gardens and retain a sense of the past with impressive collections of antiques. Book ahead, particularly in summer; you're competing for rooms with many Londoners in search of a getaway. ⇨ *Hotel reviews have been shortened. For full information, visit Fodors.com.*

	WHAT IT COSTS IN POUNDS			
	$	$$	$$$	$$$$
Restaurants	under £15	£15–£19	£20–£25	over £25
Hotels	under £100	£100–£160	£161–£220	over £220

Restaurant prices are the average cost of a main course at dinner, or if dinner is not served, at lunch. Hotels prices are the lowest cost of a standard double room in high season, including 20% V.A.T.

VISITOR INFORMATION

Contacts Tourism Southeast. 🌐 *www.visitsoutheastengland.com.* **Visit Thames.** 🌐 *www.visitthames.co.uk.*

WINDSOR, MARLOW, AND NEARBY

Windsor Castle is one of the jewels of the area known as Royal Windsor, but a journey around this section of the Thames has other pleasures. The town of Eton holds the eponymous private school, Ascot has its famous racecourse, and Cliveden is a stately home turned into a grand hotel.

The stretch of the Thames Valley from Marlow to Henley-on-Thames is enchanting. Walking through its fields and along its waterways, it's easy to see how it inspired Kenneth Grahame's classic 1908 children's book *The Wind in the Willows*. Whether by boat or on foot, you can discover some of the region's most delightful scenery. On each bank are fine wooded hills with spacious homes, greenhouses, flower gardens, and neat lawns that stretch to the water's edge. Grahame wrote his book in Pangbourne, and his illustrator, E. H. Shepard, used the great house at Mapledurham as the model for Toad Hall. It all still has the power to inspire.

WINDSOR

21 miles west of London.

Only a small part of old Windsor—the settlement that grew up around the town's famous castle in the Middle Ages—has survived. The town isn't what it was in the time of Sir John Falstaff and the *Merry Wives of Windsor,* when it was famous for its convivial inns—in 1650, it had about 70 of them. Only a handful remain today, with the others replaced, it seems, by endless cafés. Windsor can feel overrun by tourists in summer, but even so, romantics appreciate cobbled Church Lane and noble Queen Charlotte Street, opposite the castle entrance.

GETTING HERE AND AROUND

Fast Green Line buses leave from the Colonnades opposite London's Victoria Coach Station every half hour for the 70-minute trip to Windsor. First Group has frequent services from Heathrow Airport's Terminal 5; the journey takes less than an hour. First Group also runs regional bus services to small towns and villages near Windsor.

6

Trains travel from London Waterloo every 30 minutes, or you can catch a more frequent train from Paddington and change at Slough. The trip takes less than an hour from Waterloo and around 30 minutes from Paddington. If you're driving, the M4 from London takes around an hour. Park in one of the public lots near the edge of the town center.

TIMING

Windsor is at its best in winter and fall when it's not as crowded with tour groups. In summer it can be uncomfortably packed. Queen Elizabeth is in residence when her banner flies above the palace—everybody perks up a bit when that happens.

TOURS

Ascot Carriages. Year-round carriage rides depart from the Savill Garden Visitor Centre, 4 miles south of the castle (£45 for 30 minutes, £7.50 per person, or £100 per hour). You can combine a ride with a vintage afternoon tea (£8.25 per person) in the Savill Garden Gallery Cafe. ✉ *Savill Garden, Wick La., Englefield Green* ☎ *07811/543019* 🌐 *www.ascotcarriages.co.uk.*

City Sightseeing. Hop on, hop-off tours of Windsor and Eton are offered by City Sightseeing, though it's easy to explore the compact Windsor on foot. ☎ *020/444102* 🌐 *www.city-sightseeing.com* 🎫 *From £12.*

ESSENTIALS

Bus Contacts First Group. ☎ *0175/352–4144* 🌐 *www.firstgroup.com.* **Green Line.** ☎ *0844/801 7261* 🌐 *www.greenline.co.uk.*

Visitor Information Royal Windsor Information Centre. ✉ *Old Booking Hall, Windsor Royal Station, Thames St.* ☎ *01753/743900, 01753/743907 for accommodations* 🌐 *www.windsor.gov.uk.*

Windsor, Marlow, and Nearby

EXPLORING

Savill Garden. The main horticultural delight of Windsor Great Park, the exquisite Savill Garden is about 4 miles from Windsor Castle. The 35 acres of ornamental gardens contain an impressive display of 2,500 rose bushes and a tremendous diversity of trees and shrubs. The Savill Building, easily recognizable by its undulating roof in the shape of a leaf, holds a visitor center, restaurant, and terrace where you can dine overlooking the garden, as well as a large shopping area with plenty of gifts, cards, and original art work. ✉ *Wick Rd., Egham* ☎ *01784/435544* 🌐 *www.theroyallandscape.co.uk* 🎫 *£9.75 Mar.–Nov., free Dec.–Feb.; parking charge* ⏲ *Mar.–Oct., daily 10–6; Nov.–Feb., daily 10–4:30; last admission 30 min before closing.*

Fodor's Choice ★ **Windsor Castle.** From William the Conqueror to Queen Victoria, the kings and queens of England added towers and wings to this brooding, imposing castle, visible for miles and now the largest inhabited castle in the world. Despite the multiplicity of hands involved in its design, the palace manages to have a unity of style and character. The most impressive view of Windsor Castle is from the A332 road, coming into town from the south. Admission includes an audio guide and, if you wish, a guided tour of the castle precincts. Entrance lines can be long in season, and you're likely to spend at least half a day here, so come early.

William the Conqueror began work on the castle in the 11th century, and Edward III modified and extended it in the mid-1300s. One of Edward's largest contributions was the enormous and distinctive **Round Tower.** Later, between 1824 and 1837, George IV transformed the still essentially medieval castle into the fortified royal palace you see today. Most of England's kings and queens have demonstrated their undying attachment to the castle, the only royal residence in continuous use by the Royal Family since the Middle Ages.

As you enter the castle, **Henry VIII's gateway** leads uphill into the wide castle precincts, where you're free to wander. Across from the entrance is the exquisite **St. George's Chapel** (closed Sunday). Here lie 10 of the kings of England, including Henry VI, Charles I, and Henry VIII (Jane Seymour is the only one of his six wives buried here). One of the noblest buildings in England, the chapel was built in the Perpendicular style popular in the 15th and 16th centuries, with elegant stained-glass windows; a high, vaulted ceiling; and intricately carved choir stalls. The colorful heraldic banners of the Knights of the Garter—the oldest British Order of Chivalry, founded by Edward III in 1348—hang in the choir. The ceremony in which the knights are installed as members of the order has been held here with much pageantry for more than five centuries. The elaborate **Albert Memorial Chapel** was created by Queen Victoria in memory of her husband.

6

The **North Terrace** provides especially good views across the Thames to Eton College, perhaps the most famous of Britain's exclusive public schools (confusingly, "public schools" in Britain are highly traditional, top-tier private schools). From the terrace, you enter the **State Apartments,** which are open to the public most days. On display to the left of the entrance to the State Apartments in Windsor Castle, **Queen Mary's Dolls' House** is a perfect miniature Georgian palace-within-a-palace, created in 1923. Electric lights glow, the doors all have tiny keys, and a miniature library holds Lilliputian-size books written especially for the young queen by famous authors of the 1920s. Five cars, including a Daimler and Rolls-Royce, stand at the ready. In the adjacent corridor are exquisite French couturier–designed costumes made for the two Jumeau dolls presented to the Princesses Elizabeth and Margaret by France in 1938.

Although a fire in 1992 gutted some of the State Apartments, hardly any works of art were lost. Phenomenal repair work brought to new life the **Grand Reception Room,** the **Green and Crimson Drawing Rooms,** and the **State and Octagonal Dining Rooms.** A green oak hammer-beam (a short horizontal beam that projects from the tops of walls for support) roof looms magnificently over the 600-year-old **St. George's Hall,** where the Queen gives state banquets. The State Apartments contain priceless furniture, including a magnificent Louis XVI bed and Gobelin tapestries; carvings by Grinling Gibbons; and paintings by Canaletto, Rubens, Van Dyck, Holbein, Dürer, and Bruegel. The tour's high points are the **Throne Room** and the **Waterloo Chamber,** where Sir Thomas Lawrence's portraits of Napoléon's victorious foes line the walls. You can also see arms and armor—look out for Henry VIII's ample suit. A visit between October and March also includes the Semi-State rooms, the private apartments of George IV, resplendent with gilded ceilings.

To see the castle come magnificently alive, check out the Changing of the Guard, which takes place daily at 11 am from April through July and on alternate days at the same time from August through March. Confirm the exact schedule before traveling to Windsor. ✉ *Castle Hill* ☎ *020/7766–7304 tickets, 01753/831118 recorded information* 🌐 *www.royalcollection.org.uk* 🎫 *£19.50 for Precincts, State Apartments, Gallery, St. George's Chapel, and Queen Mary's Dolls' House; £10.50 when State Apartments are closed* 🕒 *Mar.–Oct., daily 9:45–5:15; Nov.–Feb., daily 9:45–4:15; last admission 1 hr 15 min before closing.*

QUICK BITES

Crooked House of Windsor. With two tiny rooms in a 300-year-old house, the Crooked House of Windsor is a traditional favorite for tea and plates of cakes and scones for £10. It's open daily until 5:30 (5 in winter). ✉ ***51 High St.*** ☎ ***01753/857534*** 🌐 ***www.crooked-house.com.***

Fodor's Choice ★

Windsor Great Park. The remains of an ancient royal hunting forest, this park stretches for some 5,000 acres south of Windsor Castle. Much of it is open to the public and can be explored by car or on foot. Its chief attractions are clustered around the southeastern section, known (or at least marketed) as the **Royal Landscape**. These include **Virginia Water,** a 2-mile-long lake that forms the park's main geographical focal point. More than anything, however, the Royal Landscape is defined by its two beautiful gardens. **Valley Gardens**, located on the north shore of Virginia Water, is particularly vibrant in April and May, when the dazzling multicolored azaleas are in full bloom.

If you're feeling fit, the romantic **Long Walk** is one of England's most photographed footpaths—the 3-mile-long route, designed by Charles II, starts in the Great Park and leads all the way to Windsor Castle.

Divided from the Great Park by the busy A308 highway, the smaller **Windsor Home Park**, on the eastern side of Windsor Castle, is the private property of the Royal Family. It contains **Frogmore House**, a lavish royal residence. Completed in 1684, Frogmore was bought by George III as a gift for his wife, Queen Charlotte. The sprawling white mansion later became a beloved retreat of Queen Victoria. Today it's mainly used for official functions, but you can visit by guided tour (£9.80) on a handful of days in July and August; see 🌐 *www.royalcollection.org.uk*, or call *020/7766–7321* for more information. ✉ *Entrances on A329, A332, B383, and Wick La.* ☎ *01784/435544* 🌐 *www.theroyallandscape.co.uk* 🎫 *Free; Saville Garden £9.75 Mar.–Nov., free Dec.–Feb.* 🕒 *Daily dawn–dusk. Last admission 30 min before closing.*

WHERE TO EAT

Bray, a tiny village 6 miles outside Windsor, is known for its restaurants more than anything else.

$$$$ MODERN BRITISH Fodor's Choice ★

✕ **Fat Duck.** One of the top restaurants in the country, and ranked by many food writers among the best in the world, this extraordinary place packs in fans of hypercreative, hyperexpensive cuisine. "Culinary alchemist" Heston Blumenthal is famed for bizarre taste combinations—scrambled-egg-and-bacon ice cream, for example—and his laboratory-like kitchen, where this advocate of molecular gastronomy creates his dishes. There's just one sitting per night, which is just as well, as the 14-course tasting menu takes around 4½ hours to get through. It's impossible to say exactly where the culinary flights of fancy may take you. A tray of oak moss with truffle toast is brought to life with liquid nitrogen, poured like gravy (it smells like a forest after a rainstorm); at one point you're given headphones, which play the sounds of the sea from conch shells, while you munch edible sand and seaweed. It's as much theater as it is food, and the very definition of "not for everyone." However, those with a taste for adventure (and deep pockets) find it a magical experience. The Fat Duck is a discreet building in the small village of Bray, look for the duck-inspired implements hanging outside. You must reserve a table two months in advance, and the booking process is strict; call or see the website for details. *Average main: £225 ✉ High St., Bray-on-Thames ☎ 01628/580333 ⊕ www.fatduck.co.uk ⏲ Closed Sun. and Mon. ✍ Reservations essential.*

$$$ MODERN BRITISH **Hinds Head.** Fat Duck's esteemed chef Heston Blumenthal owns this Michelin-starred pub across the road, where he sells less extreme dishes at more reasonable prices. The atmosphere and dress code are relaxed, and the look of the place is historic, with exposed beams, polished wood-panel walls, and brick fireplaces. A brilliant modern take on traditional English cuisine, the menu includes hash of snails as a starter, followed by sea bream with crab and mussel broth, or Hereford rib-eye steak with bone-marrow sauce and triple-cooked fries. There's also a menu for kids. It gets busy, so book ahead if you can. *Average main: £24 ✉ High St., Bray-on-Thames ☎ 01628/626151 ⊕ www.hindsheadbray.com ⏲ No dinner Sun.*

$$ BRITISH **Two Brewers.** Locals congregate in a pair of low-ceiling rooms at this tiny 17th-century establishment by the gates of Windsor Great Park. Those under 18 aren't allowed inside the pub (though they can be served at a few outdoor tables), but adults find a suitable collection of wine, espresso, and local beer, plus an excellent menu with such dishes as sausages with mash and pea gravy, fish cakes, and a good selection of hot and cold sandwiches. On Sunday the pub serves a traditional, hearty lunchtime roast. *Average main: £15 ✉ 34 Park St. ☎ 01753/855426 ⊕ www.twobrewerswindsor.co.uk ⏲ No dinner Fri.–Sun. ✍ Reservations essential.*

WHERE TO STAY

$$ B&B/INN FAMILY **Langton House.** A former residence for representatives of the crown, this Victorian mansion on a quiet, leafy road is a 10-minute walk from Windsor Castle. **Pros:** soothing decor; family-friendly environment. **Cons:** not for those who prefer privacy; a little out of town. *Rooms from: £100 ✉ 46 Alma Rd. ☎ 01753/858299 ⊕ www.langtonhouse.co.uk ⇆ 5 rooms 🍽 Breakfast.*

$$$ HOTEL **MGallery Windsor Castle Hotel.** You're treated to an exceptional view of Windsor Castle's changing of the guard ceremony from this former coaching inn, parts of which date back to the 16th century. **Pros:** excellent location; wonderful afternoon tea. **Cons:** older rooms are small; furniture is faux antique. *Rooms from: £175 ✉ 18 High*

No T-shirts here: at Eton College, students wear the school's traditional shirts, coats, and pinstripe pants.

St. ☎ *01753/252800* 🌐 *www.mercure.com* *108 rooms, 4 suites* 🍽 *Breakfast.*

$$ HOTEL **Oakley Court.** A romantic getaway on the Thames, this Victorian-era mansion stands on landscaped grounds 3 miles west of Windsor. **Pros:** stunning mansion; lots of pampering; friendly staff. **Cons:** bedrooms could do with an update; river views cost more; noisy parakeets on grounds. $ *Rooms from: £130* ✉ *Windsor Rd., Water Oakley* ☎ *01753/609988* 🌐 *www.theoakleycourthotel.co.uk* *108 rooms, 10 suites* 🍽 *Breakfast.*

$$ B&B/INN **Rainworth House.** Ducks come knocking at the door of this country house with an expansive green lawn 2 miles from Windsor. **Pros:** peaceful setting; lovely garden. **Cons:** out of town; no online booking. $ *Rooms from: £105* ✉ *Oakley Green Rd.* ☎ *01753/856749* 🌐 *www.rainworthhouse.com* *7 rooms* 🍽 *Breakfast.*

$$$ HOTEL Fodor's Choice ★ **Stoke Park.** On a 350-acre estate, Stoke Park's neoclassical grandeur can make Windsor Castle, visible in the distance, seem almost humble in comparison. **Pros:** luxurious rooms; sweeping grounds; wonderful for antiques lovers. **Cons:** not for those lukewarm about golf. $ *Rooms from: £220* ✉ *Park Rd., Stoke Poges* ☎ *01753/717171* 🌐 *www.stokeparkclub.com* *77 rooms* 🍽 *Breakfast.*

NIGHTLIFE AND PERFORMING ARTS

FAMILY **Firestation Arts Centre.** Windsor's former fire station has a whole new lease of life as a contemporary arts venue, presenting films, theater, music, dance, and comedy, with plenty of events for kids. ✉ *The Old Court, St. Leonard's Rd.* ☎ *01753/866865* 🌐 *www.firestationartscentre.com.*

Theatre Royal. Windsor's Theatre Royal, where productions have been staged since 1910, is one of Britain's leading provincial theaters. It puts on plays and musicals year-round, including a pantomime for five weeks around Christmas. ✉ *Thames St.* ☎ *01753/853888* 🌐 *www.theatreroyalwindsor.co.uk.*

Windsor Festival. Concerts, poetry readings, and children's events highlight the two-week Windsor Festival, held over the last two weeks in September, with events occasionally taking place in the castle. The festival also runs a smaller program in March, with a focus on classical music events. ☎ *01753/743585* 🌐 *www.windsorfestival.com.*

SHOPPING

Check out Peascod Street, opposite the castle, for a good selection of independent stores selling gifts, jewelry, toiletries, chocolates, and more.

Windsor Royal Station. A Victorian-era train station, Windsor Royal Station is now home to fashion outlets like Jaeger, Viyella, Hobbs, and Whistles. ✉ *5 Goswell Hill* ☎ *01753/797070* 🌐 *www.windsorroyalshopping.co.uk.*

SPORTS AND THE OUTDOORS

John Logie Motorboats. From Easter to September, John Logie Motorboats rents motorboats and rowboats, starting at £25 for a half hour. ✉ *Barry Ave.* ☎ *07774/983809* 🌐 *www.johnlogiemotorboats.com.*

6

ETON

23 miles west of London.

Some observers may find it symbolic that almost opposite Windsor Castle—which embodies the continuity of the royal tradition—stands Eton, a school that for centuries has educated many leaders of the country. With High Street, its single main street, leading from the river to the famous school, the old-fashioned town of Eton is much quieter than Windsor.

GETTING HERE AND AROUND

Eton is linked to Windsor by a footbridge across the Thames. Most visitors barely notice passing from one to the other.

EXPLORING

Fodor's Choice ★ **Eton College.** Signs warn drivers of "Boys Crossing" as you approach the splendid Tudor-style buildings of Eton College, the distinguished boarding school for boys ages 13 through 18 founded in 1440 by King Henry VI. It's all terrifically photogenic, because during the college semester students still dress in pin-striped trousers, swallow-tailed coats, and stiff collars. Rivaling St. George's at Windsor in terms of size, the Gothic **Chapel** contains superb 15th-century grisaille wall paintings juxtaposed against modern stained glass by John Piper. Beyond the cloisters are the school's playing fields where, according to the Duke of Wellington, the Battle of Waterloo was really won, since so many of his officers had learned discipline and strategy during their school days. Among the country's prime ministers to be educated here is David Cameron. The **Museum of Eton Life** has displays on the school's history and vignettes of school life. The school gives public tours, although as of this writing they were suspended due to construction. They are set to resume again by early 2016, but call ahead for more information. ✉ *Brewhouse Yard* ☎ *01753/370100* 🌐 *www.etoncollege.com.*

WHERE TO EAT AND STAY

$$ MODERN BRITISH **Gilbey's Eton.** Just over the bridge from Windsor, this restaurant at the center of Eton's Antiques Row serves a changing menu of imaginative fare, from potted ham hock and rhubarb with sweet onion and mustard seed to crayfish and dill hot-smoked trout fishcakes. The £21 two-course set menu—served at lunch and dinners most days of the week—is a good deal. Well-priced wines, both French and from the restaurant's own English vineyard, are a specialty, as are the savories—meat, fish, and vegetarian pâtés. Scrumptious cakes are served with afternoon tea on weekends. The conservatory, with its colorful scattering of cushions, is a pleasant place to sit, as is the courtyard garden. [$] *Average main: £18* ✉ *82–83 High St.* ☎ *01753/854921* 🌐 *www.gilbeygroup.com/restaurants/gilbeys-eton.*

$$ HOTEL **Christopher Hotel.** This former coaching inn on the village's main shopping street has spacious rooms in the handsome main building as well as in the courtyard mews. **Pros:** a nice mix of modern and historic; good restaurant. **Cons:** steep stairs; courtyard rooms can be noisy. [$] *Rooms from: £110* ✉ *110 High St.* ☎ *01753/852359* 🌐 *www.thechristopher.co.uk* *34 rooms* *No meals.*

SHOPPING

Jam. This shop has a lovely selection of ceramic and jewelry pieces by contemporary artists. ✉ *81 High St.* ☎ *01753/622333* 🌐 *www.jam-eton.co.uk.*

ASCOT

8 miles southwest of Windsor, 28 miles southwest of London.

The posh town of Ascot (pronounced *as*-cut) has for centuries been famous for horse racing and for style. Queen Anne chose to have a racecourse here, and the first race meeting took place in 1711. The impressive show of millinery for which the Royal Meeting, or Royal Ascot, as it is also known, was immortalized in *My Fair Lady,* in which a hat with osprey feathers and black-and-white silk roses transformed Eliza Doolittle into a grand lady. Betting on the races at England's most prestigious course is as important as dressing up; it's all part of the fun.

GETTING HERE AND AROUND

If you're driving, leave M4 at Junction 6 and take A332. Trains from London leave Waterloo Station every half hour, and the journey takes 50 minutes. The racecourse is a seven-minute walk from the train station.

EXPLORING

Ascot Racecourse. The races run regularly throughout the year, and Royal Ascot takes place annually in mid-June. **■ TIP→ Tickets for Royal Ascot generally go on sale in November, so buy them well in advance.** Prices range from £15 for standing room on the heath to around £80 for seats in the stands. Car parking costs £25. ✉ *A329* ☎ *0844/346–3000* 🌐 *www.ascot.co.uk.*

The horses at Royal Ascot are beautiful and so is the formal attire of the memorably dressed spectators.

WHERE TO STAY

$$$$ HOTEL FAMILY Fodor's Choice ★ **Coworth Park.** Much imagination and thoughtful renovation has transformed this 18th-century mansion, set in 240 acres of parkland, into a playful and contemporary lodging. **Pros:** country-house atmosphere; attentive and friendly service; free activities for kids. **Cons:** not for traditionalists; eye-wateringly expensive. *Rooms from: £302* ✉ *Blacknest Rd.* ☎ *01344/876600* 🌐 *www.dorchestercollection.com/en/ascot/coworth-park* *55 rooms, 15 suites* *Breakfast.*

CLIVEDEN

8 miles northwest of Windsor, 16 miles north of Ascot, 26 miles west of London.

This grand stately home, designed by Charles Barry, the architect of the Houses of Parliament, and the setting of the notorious Profumo affair in the 1960s, has spectacular gardens and sweeping views to the Thames.

GETTING HERE AND AROUND

If you're driving, take the M4 to the A4, where brown signs lead you to the entrance off the A4094.

EXPLORING

Cliveden. Described by Queen Victoria as a "bijou of taste," Cliveden (pronounced *Cliv*-dn) is a magnificent country mansion that for more than 300 years has lived up to its Georgian heritage as a bastion of aesthetic delights. The house, set in 376 acres of gardens and parkland above the River Thames, was rebuilt in 1851; but it was the rich and powerful Astor family, who purchased it in 1893, that made Cliveden famous. In the 1920s and 1930s this was the meeting place for the influential salon known as the "Cliveden Set"—a group of strongly conservative thinkers who many accused of being Nazi sympathizers. Its doyenne was Nancy Astor, an American by birth, who became the first woman to sit in the British Parliament. The ground-floor rooms of the house are open, as well as the Octagon Chapel, with its beautiful gilt-painted ceiling and wall panels. You can wander the beautiful grounds, which include a water garden, miles of woodland and riverbank paths, a kids' play area, and a yew-tree maze. Book your timed ticket for the house beforehand or early on the day. Boat hire and trips are available daily in July and August. ✉ *Cliveden Rd., Taplow* ✣ *Near Maidenhead* ☎ *01628/605069, 01494/755562 recorded information* 🌐 *www.nationaltrust.org.uk/cliveden* 🎫 *Garden and woodland £9.75, house £2* ⏲ *House Apr.–late Oct., Thurs. and Sun. 3–5. Grounds daily 10–5:30 or dusk if earlier (gardens closed Jan.–mid-Feb., but woodland remains open). Last admission 30 min before closing.*

WHERE TO STAY

$$$$ HOTEL Fodor's Choice ★

Cliveden House. If you've ever wondered what it would feel like to be an Edwardian grandee, then sweep up the drive to this stately home, one of Britain's grandest hotels. **Pros:** like stepping back in time; outstanding sense of luxury; beautiful grounds. **Cons:** airplanes fly overhead; two-night minimum on weekends; you'll need deep pockets. $ *Rooms from: £445* ✉ *Cliveden Rd., Taplow* ☎ *01628/668561* 🌐 *www.clivedenhouse.co.uk* 🛏 *22 rooms, 16 suites, 1 cottage* 🍽 *Breakfast.*

SPORTS AND THE OUTDOORS

Cliveden Boathouse. Here you can rent two vintage boats and an electric canoe that ply the Thames. The 45-minute champagne sunset cruise is the most affordable at £50 per person. They sail most days April through August at 5 and 6 pm, and an hour earlier in September and October. ✉ *Cliveden, Cliveden Rd., Taplow* ☎ *01628/668561* 🌐 *www.clivedenhouse.co.uk/boat-trips.*

MARLOW

7 miles west of Cliveden, 15 miles northwest of Windsor.

Just inside the Buckinghamshire border, Marlow and the surrounding area overflow with Thames-side prettiness. The unusual suspension bridge was built in the 1830s by William Tierney Clark, architect of the bridge in Hungary linking Buda and Pest. Marlow has a number of striking old buildings, particularly the privately owned Georgian houses along Peter and West streets. In 1817 the Romantic poet Percy Bysshe Shelley stayed with friends at 67 West Street and then bought **Albion House** on the same street. His second wife, Mary, completed her Gothic novel *Frankenstein* here. Ornate **Marlow Place,** on Station Road, dating from 1721, is reputedly the finest building.

Marlow hosts its own one-day regatta in mid-June. The town is a good base from which to join the **Thames Path** to Henley-on-Thames. On summer weekends tourism can often overwhelm the town.

GETTING HERE AND AROUND

Trains leave London from Paddington every half hour and involve a change at Maidenhead; the journey takes an hour. By car, leave M4 at Junction 8/9, following A404 and then A4155. From M40, join A404 at Junction 4.

ESSENTIALS

Visitor Information Marlow Tourist Information Centre. ✉ *55a High St.* ☎ *01628/483597* 🌐 *www.visitbuckinghamshire.org.*

EXPLORING

Swan-Upping. This traditional event, which dates back 800 years, takes place in Marlow during the third week of July. By bizarre ancient laws, the Queen owns every single one of the country's swans, so each year swan-markers in skiffs start from Sunbury-on-Thames, catching the new cygnets and marking their beaks to establish ownership. The Queen's Swan Marker, dressed in scarlet livery, presides over this colorful ceremony. ✉ *Marlow* ☎ *01628/523030* 🌐 *www.royal.gov.uk.*

WHERE TO EAT AND STAY

$$$$ FRENCH **Vanilla Pod.** Discreet and intimate, this restaurant is a showcase for the French-inspired cuisine of Chef Michael Macdonald, who, as the restaurant's name implies, holds vanilla in high esteem. The fixed-price menu borrows the flavor of a French bistro and shakes it up a bit, so you might have filet mignon with polenta, or lamb rump with bean cassoulet, or something more adventurous, such as fennel escabeche with mackerel and vanilla. The three-course lunch menu is a fantastic bargain at £19.50, and the seven-course *menu gourmand* for £60 is a tour de force. *$ Average main: £45* ✉ *31 West St.* ☎ *01628/898101* 🌐 *www.thevanillapod.co.uk* ⏲ *Closed Sun. and Mon.* *Reservations essential.*

$$ HOTEL **Macdonald Compleat Angler.** Although fishing aficionados consider this luxurious 17th-century Thames-side inn the ideal place to stay, the place is stylish enough to attract those with no interest in casting a line. **Pros:** gorgeous rooms; great views of the Thames. **Cons:** river views cost more, except Rooms 9 and 10; need a car to get around. *$ Rooms from: £117* ✉ *Marlow Bridge, Bisham Rd.* ☎ *0844/879–9128, 01628/484444 international* 🌐 *www.macdonaldhotels.co.uk/compleatangler* *61 rooms, 3 suites* *Breakfast.*

HENLEY-ON-THAMES

7 miles southwest of Marlow, 8 miles north of Reading, 36 miles west of central London.

Fodor's Choice ★ Henley's fame is based on one thing: rowing. The Henley Royal Regatta, held at the cusp of June and July on a long, straight stretch of the River Thames, has made the little riverside town famous throughout the world. Townspeople launched the Henley Regatta in 1839, initiating the Grand Challenge Cup, the most famous of its many trophies. The best amateur oarsmen from around the globe compete in crews of eight, four, or two, or as single scullers. For many spectators, the event is on par with Royal Ascot and Wimbledon.

The town is set in a broad valley between gentle hillsides. Henley's historic buildings, including half-timber Georgian cottages and inns (as well as one of Britain's oldest theaters, the Kenton), are all within a few minutes' walk. The river near Henley is alive with boats of every shape and size, from luxury cabin cruisers to tiny rowboats.

GETTING HERE AND AROUND

Frequent First Great Western trains depart for Henley from London Paddington; the journey time is around an hour. If you're driving from London or from the west, leave M4 at Junction 8/9 and follow A404(M) and then A4130 to Henley Bridge. From Marlow, Henley is a 7-mile drive southwest on A4155.

ESSENTIALS

Visitor Information Henley Visitor Information Centre. ✉ *Henley Town Hall, Market Pl., Henley* ☎ *01491/578034* 🌐 *www.henleytowncouncil.gov.uk/information-centre-including-tourism.aspx.*

EXPLORING

Mapledurham House. This section of the Thames inspired Kenneth Grahame's 1908 *The Wind in the Willows*, which began as a bedtime story for Grahame's son Alastair while the family lived at Pangbourne. Some of E.F. Shepard's illustrations are of specific sites along the river—none more fabled than this redbrick Elizabethan mansion, bristling with tall chimneys, mullioned windows, and battlements. It became the inspiration for Shepard's vision of Toad Hall. Family portraits, magnificent oak staircases, wood paneling, and plasterwork ceilings abound. Look out for the life-size deer guarding the fireplace in the entrance hall. There's also a 15th-century working grain mill on the river. The house is 10 miles southwest of Henley-on-Thames. ✉ *Off A074, Mapledurham* ☎ *0118/972–3350* 🌐 *www.mapledurham.co.uk* 🎟 *£9.50* ⏲ *Easter–Sept., weekends and holiday Mon. 2–5:30; Oct., Sun. 2–5:30; last admission 30 min before closing.*

FAMILY **River & Rowing Museum.** Focusing on the history and sport of rowing, this absorbing museum built on stilts includes exhibits devoted to actual vessels, from a Saxon log boat to an elegant Victorian steam launch to Olympic boats. One gallery tells the story of the Thames as it flows from its source to the ocean, while another explores the history of the town and its famed regatta. A charming *Wind in the Willows* walk-through exhibit evokes the settings of the famous children's book. ✉ *Mill Meadows, Henley* ☎ *01491/415600* 🌐 *www.rrm.co.uk* 🎟 *£9.50* ⏲ *Daily 10–5.*

St. Mary's Church. With a 16th-century "checkerboard" tower, St. Mary's is a stone's throw from the bridge over the Thames. The adjacent, yellow-washed **Chantry House,** built in 1420, is one of England's few remaining merchant houses from the period. It's an unspoiled example of the rare timber-frame design, with upper floors jutting out. You can enjoy tea here on Sunday afternoons in summer. ✉ *Hart St., Henley* ☎ *01491/577340* 🌐 *www.stmaryshenley.org.uk* 🎟 *Free* ⏲ *Church daily 9–5.*

The rowing competitions at the Henley Royal Regatta draw spectators all along the river.

WHERE TO EAT AND STAY

$$ MODERN BRITISH **Crooked Billet.** It's worth negotiating the maze of lanes leading to this cozy 17th-century country pub 6 miles west of Henley-on-Thames. Choices could include John Dory with anchovy beignet, and duck breast with bubble and squeak (a dish made with fried mashed potato and cabbage). British cheeses and filling desserts round out the meal. There's a garden for open-air dining and live music on many evenings. Fixed-price lunches are a good deal. The restaurant is popular, so book ahead. *Average main: £18* *Newlands La., Stoke Row* *01491/681048* *www.thecrookedbillet.co.uk.*

$ MODERN BRITISH **The Three Tuns.** Walk past the cozy bar in this traditional 17th-century pub to eat in the snug dining room with the clutch of locals who come nightly for the traditional British comfort food. Plates such as beer-battered fish-and-chips or local butcher's sausages and mashed potato are easy crowd pleasers, as are the waist-expanding tarts and crumbles for dessert. The two-course deal (turn your £13 main course into £15 for dessert as well) is a steal. They also do a popular traditional roast on Sundays at lunchtime. *Average main: £13* *5 Market Pl.* *01491/410138* *www.threetunshenley.co.uk* *No dinner Sun.*

$$ HOTEL **Hotel du Vin.** A sprawling brick brewery near the river has been transformed into a distinctive modern architectural showplace. **Pros:** very chic; lovely river views from upper floors; good for oenophiles. **Cons:** won't thrill traditionalists; a charge for parking; steps inside are tricky to navigate. *Rooms from: £135* *New St., Henley* *01491/848400* *www.hotelduvin.com* *41 rooms, 2 suites* *Breakfast.*

$ B&B/INN **The Row Barge.** This historic, 15th-century pub certainly looks the part, with low-beamed ceilings and a fire crackling in the grate. **Pros:**

historic inn with lots of character; friendly owners; good food. **Cons:** entrance to guestrooms through bar and up a staircase with very low ceiling; room No. 1 has no door to the bathroom. *Rooms from: £95 ✉ West St. ☎ 01491/572649 🌐 www.therowbarge.com 5 🍴 Breakfast.*

NIGHTLIFE AND PERFORMING ARTS

Henley Festival. A floating stage and spectacular musical events from classical to folk draw a dress-code-abiding crowd to the upscale Henley Festival during the week after the regatta in July. Book well ahead. *✉ Henley ☎ 01491/843404 🌐 www.henley-festival.co.uk.*

SPORTS AND THE OUTDOORS

Henley Royal Regatta. A series of rowing competitions attracting participants from many countries, the annual Henley Royal Regatta takes place over five days in late June and early July. Large tents are erected along both sides of a straight stretch of the river known as Henley Reach, and every surrounding field becomes a parking lot. There's plenty of space on the public towpath from which to watch the early stages of the races. **■ TIP→ If you want to attend, book a room months in advance. After all, 500,000 people turn out for the event.** *✉ Henley ☎ 01491/571900 for ticket line, 01491/572153 for inquiries 🌐 www.hrr.co.uk.*

OXFORD

Fodor's Choice ★ With arguably the most famous university in the world, Oxford has been a center of learning since 1167, with only the Sorbonne preceding it. It doesn't take more than a day or two to explore its winding medieval streets, photograph its ivy-covered stone buildings and ancient churches and libraries, and even take a punt down one of its placid waterways. The town center is compact and walkable, and at its heart is Oxford University. Alumni of this prestigious institution include 48 Nobel Prize winners, 26 British prime ministers (including David Cameron), and 28 foreign presidents (including Bill Clinton), along with poets, authors, and artists such as Percy Bysshe Shelley, Oscar Wilde, and W. H. Auden.

Oxford is 55 miles northwest of London, at the junction of the rivers Thames and Cherwell. The city is more interesting and more cosmopolitan than Cambridge, and although it's also bigger, its suburbs aren't remotely interesting to visitors. The charm is all at the center, where the old town curls around the grand stone buildings, good restaurants, and historic pubs. Victorian writer Matthew Arnold described Oxford's "dreaming spires," a phrase that has become famous. Students rush past you on the sidewalks on the way to their exams, clad with marvelous antiquarian style in their requisite mortar caps, flowing dark gowns, stiff collars, and crisp white bow ties. **■ TIP→ Watch your back when crossing roads, as bikes are everywhere.**

GETTING HERE AND AROUND

Megabus, Oxford Bus Company, and Stagecoach Oxford Tube all have buses traveling from London 24 hours a day; the trip takes between 1 hour 40 minutes and 2 hours. In London, Megabus departs from Victoria Coach Station while Oxford Bus Company and Stagecoach Oxford Tube have pickup points on Buckingham Palace Road, Victoria; Oxford Tube also picks up from the Marble Arch underground station. Oxford Bus Company runs round-trip shuttle service from Gatwick (£37) every hour and Heathrow (£29) every half hour. Most of the companies have multiple stops in Oxford, with Gloucester Green, the final stop, being the most convenient for travelers. You can easily traverse the town center on foot, but the Oxford Bus Company has a one-day ticket (£4) for unlimited travel in and around Oxford.

Trains to Oxford depart from London's Paddington Station for the one-hour trip. Oxford Station is at the western edge of the historic town center on Botley Road.

To drive, take the M40 northwest from London. It's an hour's drive, except during rush hour, when it can take twice as long. In-town parking is notoriously difficult, so use one of the five free park-and-ride lots and pay for the bus to the city. The Thornhill Park and Ride and the St. Clement's parking lot before the roundabout that leads to Magdalen Bridge are convenient for the M40.

6

TIMING

You can explore major sights in town in a day or so, but it takes longer than that to spend an hour in each of the key museums and absorb the scene at the colleges. Some colleges are open only in the afternoons during university terms. When the undergraduates are in residence, access is often restricted to the chapels, dining rooms, and libraries, too, and you're requested to refrain from picnicking in the quadrangles. All are closed certain days during exams, usually from mid-April to late June.

ESSENTIALS

Bus Contacts Megabus. ☎ *0871/266–3333 for inquiries, 0900/1600–900 booking line, calls cost £0.60 per minute* 🌐 *www.megabus.com.* **Oxford Bus Company.** ☎ *01865/785400* 🌐 *www.oxfordbus.co.uk.* **Stagecoach Oxford Tube.** ☎ *01865/772250* 🌐 *www.oxfordtube.com.*

VISITOR AND TOUR INFORMATION

City Sightseeing. This company runs hop-on, hop-off bus tours with 19 stops around Oxford; your ticket, purchased from the driver, is good for 24 hours. ☎ *01865/790522* 🌐 *www.citysightseeingoxford.com* 🎫 *From £14.*

Oxford Tourist Information Centre. You can find information here on the many guided walks of the city. The best way of gaining access to the collegiate buildings is to take the two-hour university and city tour, which leaves the Tourist Information Centre at 10:45 and 1 daily, 1 and 2 on Saturdays. You can book in advance. ✉ *15/16 Broad St.* ☎ *01865/252200* 🌐 *www.visitoxfordandoxfordshire.com* 🎫 *From £9.*

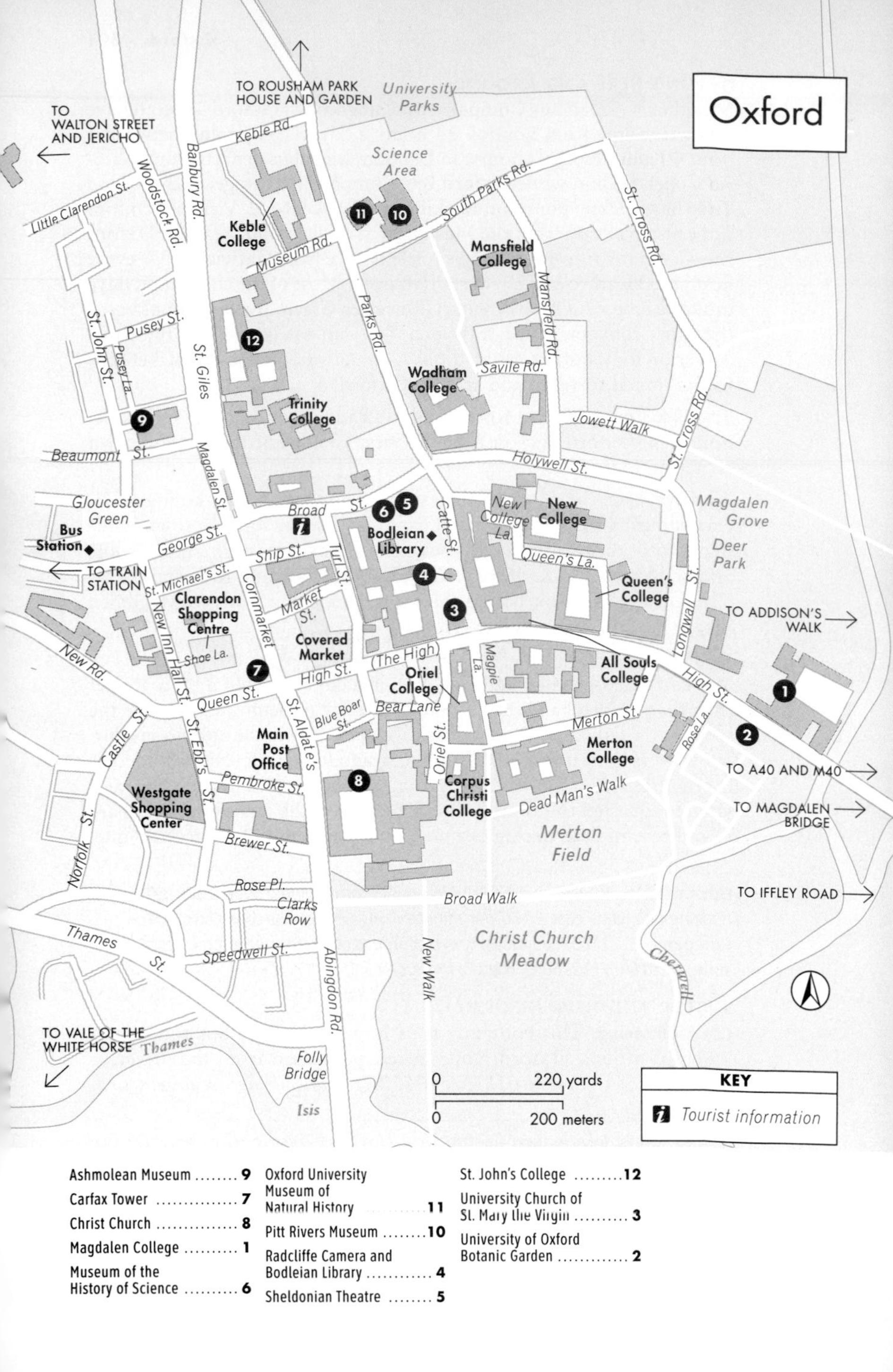
Oxford
TO ROUSHAM PARK HOUSE AND GARDEN
University Parks
TO WALTON STREET AND JERICHO
Keble Rd.
Science Area
South Parks Rd.
St. Cross Rd.
Little Clarendon St.
Woodstock Rd.
Banbury Rd.
Keble College
Museum Rd.
Mansfield College
Parks Rd.
Mansfield Rd.
St. John St.
Pusey St.
Pusey La.
St. Giles
Wadham College
Savile Rd.
Trinity College
Jowett Walk
Beaumont St.
Magdalen St.
Holywell St.
Gloucester Green
Broad St.
Catte St.
New College La.
New College
Magdalen Grove
Bus Station
George St.
Bodleian Library
Deer Park
TO TRAIN STATION
Ship St.
Turl St.
Queen's La.
St. Michael's St.
Queen's College
Clarendon Shopping Centre
Cornmarket
Market St.
Longwall St.
TO ADDISON'S WALK
New Inn Hall St.
Covered Market
Shoe La.
New Rd.
(The High)
High St.
Magpie La.
All Souls College
Oriel College
Queen St.
Blue Boar St.
Bear Lane
High St.
Castle St.
St. Ebb's St.
St. Aldate's
Merton St.
Rose La.
Main Post Office
Oriel St.
Merton College
Westgate Shopping Center
Pembroke St.
Corpus Christi College
TO A40 AND M40
Dead Man's Walk
TO MAGDALEN BRIDGE
Norfolk St.
Brewer St.
Merton Field
Rose Pl.
Broad Walk
TO IFFLEY ROAD
Clarks Row
Thames St.
Speedwell St.
Christ Church Meadow
Abingdon Rd.
New Walk
Cherwell
TO VALE OF THE WHITE HORSE
Thames
Folly Bridge
Isis
0 220 yards
0 200 meters
KEY
Tourist information
Ashmolean Museum 9
Carfax Tower 7
Christ Church 8
Magdalen College 1
Museum of the History of Science 6
Oxford University Museum of Natural History 11
Pitt Rivers Museum 10
Radcliffe Camera and Bodleian Library 4
Sheldonian Theatre 5
St. John's College 12
University Church of St. Mary the Virgin 3
University of Oxford Botanic Garden 2

EXPLORING

Oxford University isn't one easily identifiable campus, but a sprawling mixture of 38 colleges scattered around the city center, each with its own distinctive identity and focus. Oxford students live and study at their own college, and also use the centralized resources of the overarching university. The individual colleges are deeply competitive. Most of the grounds and magnificent dining halls and chapels are open to visitors, though the opening times (displayed at the entrance gates) vary greatly.

The **city center** of Oxford is bordered by High Street, St. Giles, and Longwall Street. Most of Oxford University's most famous buildings are within this area. **Jericho,** the neighborhood where many students live, is west of St. Giles, just outside the city center. Its narrow streets are lined with lovely cottages. The area north of the center around Banbury and Marston Ferry Roads is called **Summertown,** and the area east of the center, along St. Clement's Street, is known as **St. Clement's.**

TOP ATTRACTIONS

Fodor's Choice ★ **Ashmolean Museum.** Britain's oldest public museum displays its rich and varied collections from the Neolithic to the present day over five floors. Innovative and spacious galleries on the theme of "Crossing Cultures, Crossing Time" explore connections between the priceless Greek, Roman, and Indian artifacts, as well as the Egyptian and Chinese objects, all of which are among the best in the country. In regards to the superb art collection, not to be missed are drawings by Raphael, the shell-encrusted mantle of Powhatan (father of Pocahontas), the lantern belonging to Guy Fawkes, and the Alfred Jewel, set in gold, which dates from the reign of King Alfred the Great (ruled 871–899). There's too much to see in one visit, but the free admission makes return trips easy. The rooftop Ashmolean Dining Room is a good spot for refreshments. ✉ *Beaumont St.* ☎ *01865/278002* 🌐 *www.ashmolean.org* 🎫 *Free* ⏲ *Tues.–Sun. and holiday Mon. 10–5.*

Christ Church. Built in 1546, the college of Christ Church is referred to by its members as "The House." This is the site of Oxford's largest quadrangle, Tom Quad, named after the huge bell (6¼ tons) that hangs in the Christopher Wren–designed gate tower and rings 101 times at five past nine every evening in honor of the original number of Christ Church scholars. The vaulted, 800-year-old chapel in one corner has been Oxford's cathedral since the time of Henry VIII. The college's medieval dining hall contains portraits of many famous alumni, including 13 of Britain's prime ministers, but you'll recognize it from its recurring role in the Harry Potter movies (although they didn't actually film here, the room was painstakingly re-created in a film studio). ■ **TIP→ Plan carefully, as the dining hall is only open weekdays 10:30–11:40 and 2:30–4:30, and weekends 2:30–4:30.** Lewis Carroll, author of *Alice in Wonderland,* was a teacher of mathematics here for many years; a shop opposite the meadows on St. Aldate's sells Alice paraphernalia. ✉ *St. Aldate's* ☎ *01865/276492* 🌐 *www.chch.ox.ac.uk* 🎫 *£8; £9 in July and Aug.* ⏲ *Mon.–Sat. 10–5, Sun. 2–5; last admission 45 min before closing. Sometimes closed for events; call to confirm.*

6

Christ Church Picture Gallery. This connoisseur's delight in Canterbury Quadrangle exhibits works by the Italian masters as well as Hals, Rubens, and Van Dyck. Drawings in the 2,000-strong collection are shown on a changing basis. ✉ *Oriel Sq.* ☎ *01865/276172* 🌐 *www.chch.ox.ac.uk/gallery* 🎫 *£4* ⏲ *June, Mon. and Wed.–Sat. 10:30–5, Sun. 2–5; July–Sept., Mon.–Sat. 10:30–5, Sun. 2–5; Oct.–May, Mon. and Wed.–Sat. 10:30–1 and 2–4:30, Sun. 2–4:30.*

Fodor's Choice ★ **Magdalen College.** Founded in 1458, with a handsome main quadrangle and a supremely monastic air, Magdalen (pronounced *maud*-lin) is one of the most impressive of Oxford's colleges and attracts its most artistic students. Alumni include such diverse people as P.G. Wodehouse, Oscar Wilde, and John Betjeman. The school's large, square tower is a famous local landmark. ■ **TIP→ To enhance your visit, take a stroll around the Deer Park and along Addison's Walk; then have tea in the Old Kitchen, which overlooks the river.** ✉ *High St.* ☎ *01865/276000* 🌐 *www.magd.ox.ac.uk* 🎫 *£5* ⏲ *July–Sept., daily noon–7 or dusk; Oct.–June, daily 1–6 or dusk.*

FAMILY **Oxford University Museum of Natural History.** This highly decorative Victorian Gothic creation of cast iron and glass, more a cathedral than a museum, is worth a visit for its architecture alone. Among the eclectic collections of entomology, geology, mineralogy, and zoology are the towering skeleton of a *Tyrannosaurus rex* and casts of a dodo's foot and head. There's plenty for children to explore and touch. ✉ *Parks Rd.* ☎ *01865/272950* 🌐 *www.oum.ox.ac.uk* 🎫 *Free* ⏲ *Daily 10–5.*

FAMILY Fodor's Choice ★ **Pitt Rivers Museum.** More than half a million intriguing archaeological and anthropological items from around the globe, based on the collection bequeathed by Lieutenant-General Augustus Henry Lane Fox Pitt Rivers in 1884, are crammed into a multitude of glass cases and drawers. Items are organized thematically rather than geographically, an eccentric approach that's surprisingly thought-provoking. Labels are handwritten, and children are given flashlights to explore the farthest corners and spot the world's smallest dolly. Give yourself plenty of time to wander through the displays of shrunken heads, Hawaiian feather cloaks, and fearsome masks. Children will have a field day. ✉ *S. Parks Rd.* ☎ *01865/270927* 🌐 *www.prm.ox.ac.uk* 🎫 *Free, suggested donation £3* ⏲ *Mon. noon–4:30, Tues.–Sun. and holiday Mon. 10–4:30.*

Radcliffe Camera and Bodleian Library. A vast library, the domed Radcliffe Camera is Oxford's most spectacular building, built in 1737–49 by James Gibbs in Italian Baroque style. It's usually surrounded by tourists with cameras trained at its golden-stone walls. The Camera contains part of the Bodleian Library's enormous collection, begun in 1602 and one of six "copyright libraries" in the U.K. Like the Library of Congress in the United States, this means it must by law contain a copy of every book printed in Great Britain. The shelves are therefore very crowded—the collection grows by about 5,000 items a week. It also contains valuable treasures such as a Gutenberg Bible and a Shakespeare First Folio. Tours reveal the magnificent Duke Humfrey's Library, which was the original chained library and completed in 1488. (The ancient tomes are dusted once a decade.) Guides can show you the spots used for Hogwarts School in the Harry Potter films. **TIP→ Arrive early to secure tickets for the two to six daily tours. 10:30 am tours can be prebooked, as can the extended tours on Wednesday and Saturday. Otherwise tours are first-come, first-served.** Audio tours, the only tours open to kids under 11, don't require reservations. Call ahead to confirm times, as tours don't run on days when private events are booked at the library. *Broad St. 01865/287400 www.bodleian.ox.ac.uk Audio tour £2.50, minitour £5, standard tour £7, extended tour £13 Bodleian and Divinity School weekdays 9–5, Sat. 9–4:30, Sun. 11–5; sometimes closed for events, call to confirm.*

Sheldonian Theatre. This fabulously ornate theater is where Oxford's impressive graduation ceremonies are held, conducted almost entirely in Latin. Dating to 1663, it was the first building designed by Sir Christopher Wren when he served as professor of astronomy. The D-shaped auditorium has pillars, balconies, and an elaborately painted ceiling. The stone pillars outside are topped by 18 massive stone heads. Climb the stairs to the cupola for the best view of the city's "dreaming spires." Guided tours take place a few times per week between late April and early October; call or email tours@sheldon.ox.ac.uk to book a place in advance (or you can buy a ticket from the box office on the day if there's space). *Broad St. 01865/277299 www.sheldon.ox.ac.uk £3.50; tours £8 Feb.–Apr. and Oct.–Nov., Mon.–Sat. 10–4:30; May–Sept., Mon.–Sat. 10–4:30, Sun. 10:30–4:30; last admission 30 min before closing. Times may vary if events are planned; check website for full schedule.*

St. John's College. One of Oxford's most attractive campuses, St. John's has seven quiet quadrangles surrounded by elaborately carved buildings. You enter the first through a low wooden door. This college dates to 1555, when Sir Thomas White, a merchant, founded it. His heart is buried in the chapel (it's a tradition for students to curse as they walk over it). The Canterbury Quad represented the first example of Italian Renaissance architecture in Oxford, and the Front Quad includes the buildings of the old St. Bernard's Monastery. *St. Giles 01865/277300 www.sjc.ox.ac.uk Free Daily 1–5 or dusk.*

QUICK BITES

Eagle and Child. Close to St. John's College, this pub is a favorite not only for its good ales (try the local Old Hooky) and sense of history, but also for its literary associations. From the 1930s to the 1960s this was the meeting place of C.S. Lewis, J.R.R. Tolkien, and their circle of literary friends who called themselves the "Inklings." ***49 St. Giles 01865/302925 www.nicholsonspubs.co.uk/theeagleandchildoxford.***

WORTH NOTING

Carfax Tower. Passing through Carfax, the center of Oxford and where four roads meet, you can spot this tower. It's all that remains of **St. Martin's Church,** where Shakespeare stood as godfather for William Davenant, who himself became a playwright. Every 15 minutes, little mechanical "quarter boys" mark the passage of time on the tower front. Climb up the 99 steps of the dark stairwell for a good view of the town center. ✉ *Queen St. and Cornmarket* ☎ *01865/792653* 🎫 *£2.50* ⏲ *Apr.–Sept., daily 10–5:30; Oct.–Mar., daily 10–dusk.*

Museum of the History of Science. The Ashmolean, the world's oldest public museum, was originally housed in this 1683 building, which now holds scientific and mathematical instruments, from astrolabes to quadrants. Among the gems are a wonderful collection of 18th- and 19th-century models of the solar system and the chalkboard Einstein used in a lecture on the Theory of Relativity. There are guided tours on Thursday (2:30 and 3:15) and Saturday (12:30 and 1:15). ✉ *Broad St.* ☎ *01865/277280* 🌐 *www.mhs.ox.ac.uk* 🎫 *Free; suggested donation £2* ⏲ *Tues.–Sun., noon–5.*

University Church of St. Mary the Virgin. Seven hundred years' worth of funeral monuments crowd this galleried and spacious church, including the tombstone on the altar steps of Amy Robsart, the wife of Robert Dudley, Elizabeth I's favorite. One pillar marks the site where Thomas Cranmer, author of the *Anglican Book of Common Prayer*, was brought to trial and executed for heresy by Queen Mary I (Cranmer had been a key player in the Protestant reforms). The top of the 14th-century tower has a panoramic view of the city's skyline. It's worth the 127 steps. The Vaults and Garden Café, part of the church accessible from Radcliffe Square, serves breakfasts and cream teas as well as good lunches. ✉ *High St.* ☎ *01865/279111* 🌐 *www.university-church.ox.ac.uk* 🎫 *Church free, tower £4* ⏲ *Sept.–June, daily 9–5; July–Aug., daily 9–6; last admission 30 min before closing.*

University of Oxford Botanic Garden. Founded in 1621 as a healing garden, this is the oldest of its kind in the British Isles. Set on the river, the diverse garden displays 6,000 species ranging from lilies to citrus trees. There is a spacious walled garden, six luxuriant glass houses, including insectivorous and lily houses, and interesting medicinal, rock, and bog gardens to explore. Picnics are allowed, but you must bring your own food and drinks, as there's nowhere to buy them inside. ✉ *Rose La.* ☎ *01865/286690* 🌐 *www.botanic-garden.ox.ac.uk* 🎫 *£5* ⏲ *Mar., Apr., Sept., and Oct., daily 9–5; May–Aug., daily 9–6; Nov.–Feb., daily 9–4; last admission 45 min before closing.*

OFF THE BEATEN PATH

Vale of the White Horse. Stretching up into the foothills of the Berkshire Downs between Swindon and Oxford is a wide fertile plain known as the Vale of the White Horse. Here, off B4507, cut into the turf of the hillside to expose the underlying chalk, is the 374-foot-long, 110-foot-high **figure of a white horse,** an important prehistoric site. Some historians believed that the figure might have been carved to commemorate King Alfred's victory over the Danes in 871, whereas others date it to the Iron Age, around 750 BC. More current research suggests that it's at least 1,000 years older, created at the beginning of the second millennium BC. **Uffington Castle,** above the horse, is a prehistoric fort. English Heritage maintains these sites. To reach the Vale of the White Horse from Oxford (about 20 miles), follow A420, then B4508 to the village of Uffington.

WHERE TO EAT

$$ FRENCH ✕ **Brasserie Blanc.** Raymond Blanc's sophisticated brasserie in the Jericho neighborhood is the more affordable chain restaurant cousin of Le Manoir aux Quat'Saisons in Great Milton. Wood floors, pale walls, and large windows keep the restaurant open and airy. The changing menu always lists innovative adaptations of bourgeois French fare, sometimes with Mediterranean or Asian influences. Try the cod fillet marinated in lemon or the chicken served with mousseline potato. There's a good selection of steaks as well. The £12 fixed-price lunch is a good value, and kids have their own menu. [$] *Average main: £16* ✉ *71–72 Walton St.* ☎ *01865/510999* 🌐 *www.brasserieblanc.com.*

$$ FRENCH ✕ **Coto.** This reliably good brasserie serves decent French-influenced cooking in a contemporary setting. Start with an order of excellent calamari, fried in breadcrumb with a subtle infusion of garlic, before moving on to a main of fish parmentier (pie with a potato topping), or a classic steak in peppercorn sauce served with French fries. Desserts are rich and tempting, although the simple French cheeseboard, taken with the last of the excellent bottle of red you had with dinner, can make for an unexpectedly fine finish. Reservations are recommended, especially on weekends. [$] *Average main: £12* ✉ *41–47 George St.* ☎ *01865/251992* 🌐 *www.cote-restaurants.co.uk.*

$ SEAFOOD ✕ **Fishers.** The clue's in the name here—this popular local restaurant specializes in fresh, upmarket seafood. Dishes are prepared with a European touch and frequently come with butter, cream, and other sauces, such as sardines served with lemon and parsley butter. Hot and cold shellfish platters are popular, as are the mussels in white wine and oysters in red wine shallot vinegar. The interior has a casual nautical theme with wooden floors and tables, porthole windows, and red sails overhead. Lunches are a very good value. [$] *Average main: £14* ✉ *36–37 St. Clement's St.* ☎ *01865/243003* 🌐 *www.fishers-restaurant.com.*

$$ MODERN BRITISH ✕ **Gee's.** With its glass-and-steel framework, this former florist's shop just north of the town center makes a charming conservatory dining room, full of plants and twinkling with lights in the evening. The menu concentrates on the best of Oxfordshire produce. You could start with a roasted squash and sage soup and continue with such dishes as pollock with pink fir potatoes, wild rocket and speck pizzetta, or pork, venison, and lamb chops from the charcoal grill. Prune and sherry ice cream and a blood orange tart make fine desserts. There's an affordable lunch and early supper menu, too. [$] *Average main: £16* ✉ *61 Banbury Rd.* ☎ *01865/553540* 🌐 *www.gees-restaurant.co.uk.*

$ ITALIAN ✕ **Jamie's Italian.** One of Chef Jamie Oliver's missions is to re-create the best rustic Italian fare all over the country, and it's no different at this big and buzzing eatery. There's a diverse range of starters, pastas, and mains such as truffle tagliatelle with Parmesan and nutmeg or British lamb lollipops with toasted nuts and lemon yogurt. Desserts are light and refreshing—tutti frutti lemon meringue pie and granola crumble, for example—and the lively crowd appreciates it all. [$] *Average main: £14* ✉ *24–26 George St.* ☎ *01865/838383* 🌐 *www.jamieoliver.com.*

6

$$$$ FRENCH Fodor'sChoice ★ ✕ **Le Manoir aux Quat' Saisons.** One of the original gastronomy-focused hotels, Le Manoir was opened in 1984 by Chef Raymond Blanc, whose culinary talents have earned the hotel's restaurant two Michelin stars—now held for an incredible 29 years and running. You can dine à la carte, but if money is no object you might like to try one of the fixed-price menus ranging from £125 to £160; the five-course set-price lunch at £84 (Monday to Friday) is marginally easier on the wallet. Decide from among such innovative French creations as spiced cauliflower velouté with langoustines, beef fillet with braised Jacob's ladder, or Dover sole with brown butter and rosemary. There is a separate vegetarian menu as well. With more than 1,000 wines in stock, mostly French, you'll find the perfect glass to accompany your meal. You need to book up to three months ahead in summer. A stroll through the hotel's kitchen and Japanese tea gardens is de rigueur. Elegant guest rooms are available, but at upwards of £530 for even a standard double, you could just as well get a taxi back to almost anywhere south of Scotland. The pretty town of Great Milton is 7 miles southeast of Oxford. *$ Average main: £52 ✉ Church Rd., Great Milton ☎ 01844/278881 🌐 www.manoir.com ✍ Reservations essential.*

WHERE TO STAY

$ B&B/INN **Brown's Guest House.** At the southern edge of central Oxford, this redbrick Victorian house is a good bet in a town that has precious few affordable guesthouses. **Pros:** comfortable rooms; friendly owners. **Cons:** a long walk to the center; single rooms lack private bathroom. *$ Rooms from: £90 ✉ 281 Iffley Rd. ☎ 01865/246822 🌐 www.brownsguesthouse.co.uk 🛏 11 rooms, 7 with bath 🍴 Breakfast.*

$$ B&B/INN **Coach and Horses.** Everything is new in this airy and spacious lodging, but it doesn't mean the place lacks atmosphere or charm. **Pros:** lovely modern design; friendly; central location. **Cons:** limited parking; gets booked up quickly. *$ Rooms from: £135 ✉ 62 St. Clements St. ☎ 01865/200017 🌐 www.oxfordcoachandhorses.co.uk 🛏 8 rooms 🍴 Breakfast.*

$$$$ HOTEL FAMILY Fodor'sChoice ★ **Le Manoir aux Quat'Saisons.** Standards are high at this 15th-century stone manor house, the ultimate place for a gourmet getaway, where master Chef Raymond Blanc's epicurean touch shows at every turn, including one of the country's finest kitchens. **Pros:** one of the top Michelin-starred restaurants in Britain; attentive service; design is plush, but not stuffy; perfect for romance, but also accommodates kids; famous on-site cooking school. **Cons:** every room is different, so if you have specific requirements, let them know when booking; tough on the waistline and even tougher on the wallet. *$ Rooms from: £530 ✉ Church Rd., Great Milton ☎ 01844/278881 🌐 www.manoir.com 🛏 32 rooms, 16 suites 🍴 Breakfast.*

$$$ HOTEL **Macdonald Randolph.** A 19th-century neogothic landmark, this hotel is ideally situated near the Ashmolean Museum. **Pros:** handy location; grand building. **Cons:** on a busy street; some small bathrooms; formality can be a bit daunting. *$ Rooms from: £215 ✉ Beaumont St. ☎ 01865/256400 🌐 www.macdonaldhotels.co.uk/randolph 🛏 151 rooms, 15 suites 🍴 Breakfast.*

$$ HOTEL **Malmaison Oxford Castle.** Housed in what was a 19th-century prison, this high-concept boutique hotel remains true to its unusual history by showing off the original metal doors and exposed-brick walls. **Pros:** modern luxury in a beautifully converted building; you can't get more unique a setting; great bar and restaurant. **Cons:** no matter how comfortable they make it, the prison thing is just weird; expensive parking; no elevator and lots of stairs. *Rooms from: £155 ✉ 3 Oxford Castle ☎ 01865/268400 🌐 www.malmaison.com/locations/oxford ➪ 86 rooms, 8 suites 🍴 Breakfast.*

$$ B&B/INN **Newton House.** This handsome Victorian mansion, a five-minute walk from all of Oxford's action, is a sprawling, friendly place on three floors. **Pros:** great breakfasts; handy parking lot. **Cons:** on a main road; no elevator. *Rooms from: £104 ✉ 82 Abingdon Rd. ☎ 01865/240561 🌐 www.oxfordcity.co.uk/accom/newton ➪ 14 rooms, 13 with bath 🍴 Breakfast.*

$$ HOTEL **Old Bank Hotel.** From the impressive collection of modern artwork throughout the hotel to the sleek furnishings in the guest rooms, this stately converted bank building displays contemporary style in a city that favors the traditional. **Pros:** excellent location; interesting artwork at every turn. **Cons:** standard rooms can be small; breakfast costs extra. *Rooms from: £145 ✉ 91–94 High St. ☎ 01865/799599 🌐 www.oldbank-hotel.co.uk ➪ 42 rooms 🍴 Breakfast.*

$$$ HOTEL **Old Parsonage.** A 17th-century gabled stone house in a small garden next to St. Giles Church, the Old Parsonage is a dignified retreat. **Pros:** beautiful vine-covered building; complimentary walking tours; free parking. **Cons:** pricey; some guest rooms are small. *Rooms from: £219 ✉ 1 Banbury Rd. ☎ 01865/310210 🌐 www.oldparsonage-hotel.co.uk ➪ 31 rooms, 4 suites 🍴 Breakfast.*

$$ HOTEL **Royal Oxford Hotel.** This efficiently run hotel, a few steps from the train station, has bright, modern rooms with simple contemporary furniture. **Pros:** comfortable rooms; free Wi-Fi. **Cons:** not many amenities; outward facing rooms can get traffic noise from the busy instersection. *Rooms from: £132 ✉ 17 Park End St. ☎ 01865/248432 🌐 www.royaloxfordhotel.co.uk ➪ 26 rooms 🍴 Breakfast.*

$ B&B/INN **Tilbury Lodge.** What this modern house on the city's western outskirts lacks in history, it makes up for in hospitality; the homemade tea and scones that greet you on arrival set the right tone. **Pros:** quiet location; free Wi-Fi; short walk to city center. **Cons:** far from attractions; not good for families with young kids. *Rooms from: £95 ✉ 5 Tilbury La., Botley ☎ 01865/862138 🌐 www.tilburylodge.com ➪ 9 rooms 🍴 Breakfast.*

6

NIGHTLIFE AND PERFORMING ARTS

NIGHTLIFE

Head of the River. Near Folly Bridge, the terrace at the Head of the River is the perfect place to watch life on the water. You can also enjoy a pint in the clubby interior. *✉ St Aldate's ☎ 01865/721600 🌐 www.headoftheriveroxford.co.uk.*

Kings Arms. The capacious Kings Arms, popular with students and fairly quiet during the day, carries excellent local brews as well as inexpensive pub food. ✉ *40 Holywell St.* ☎ *01865/242369* 🌐 *www.kingsarmsoxford.co.uk.*

Fodor's Choice ★ **Raoul's.** This trendy cocktail bar is located in the equally trendy Jericho neighborhood. It was named one of the 100 best cocktail bars in the world by the Times of London, and the bartenders can prove it with their mixology, encyclopedic knowledge, and creative flair. The crowd is generally as bright and young as you'd expect. ✉ *32 Walton St.* ☎ *01865/553732* 🌐 *www.raoulsbar.com.*

Turf Tavern. Off Holywell Street, the Turf Tavern has a higgledy-piggledy collection of little rooms and outdoor spaces where you can enjoy a quiet drink and inexpensive pub food. ✉ *Bath Pl.* ☎ *01865/243235* 🌐 *www.turftavern-oxford.co.uk.*

White Horse. The cozy White Horse, one of the city's oldest pubs, serves real ales and traditional food all day. ✉ *52 Broad St.* ☎ *01865/204801* 🌐 *www.whitehorseoxford.co.uk.*

PERFORMING ARTS

CONCERTS

Music at Oxford. This acclaimed series of weekend classical concerts takes place October through June in such esteemed venues as Christ Church Cathedral and the Sheldonian Theatre. ☎ *01865/244806 for box office* 🌐 *www.musicatoxford.com.*

Oxford Coffee Concerts. This program of Sunday-morning chamber concerts, string quartets, piano trios, and soloists presents baroque and classical pieces in a 1748 hall. Tickets cost £12. ✉ *Holywell Music Room, Holywell Rd.* ☎ *01865/305305* 🌐 *www.coffeeconcerts.co.uk.*

FESTIVALS

Fodor's Choice ★ **Oxford Literary Festival.** The festival takes place during the last week of March at Christ Church College, the Sheldonian, and other university venues. Leading authors come to give lectures and interviews, and there's plenty to entertain children. ✉ *Christ Church College, St Aldate's* ☎ *0870/343–1001* 🌐 *www.oxfordliteraryfestival.org.*

THEATER

New Theatre. Oxford's main performance space, the New Theatre stages popular shows, comedy acts, and musicals. ✉ *George St.* ☎ *0844/871–3020* 🌐 *www.atgtickets.com/venues/new-theatre-oxford.*

Oxford Playhouse. This theater presents classic and modern dramas as well as dance and music performances. ✉ *Beaumont St.* ☎ *01865/305305* 🌐 *www.oxfordplayhouse.com.*

SHOPPING

Alice's Shop. This store sells all manner of *Alice in Wonderland* paraphernalia. ✉ *83 St. Aldate's* ☎ *01865/723793* 🌐 *www.aliceinwonderlandshop.com.*

Blackwell's. Family-owned and family-run since 1879, Blackwell's stocks an excellent selection of books. Inquire about the literary and

Continued on page 406

SEE YOU AT THE PUB

Pubs have been called "England's living rooms": more than just a bar or a place to drink, they are gathering places, conversation zones. A trip to a pub ranks high on most visitors' list of things to do, and that's not surprising: in many ways, pubs *are* England. You simply haven't experienced the country properly until you've been to one.

Pubs started appearing in the late 15th century, when whole communities would gather at the pub to meet and swap news. The very name—pub is short for "public house"—sums up their role. As towns grew into cities, the humble pub came to be seen as an antidote to the anonymity of modern life. "The local," as Brits call it, is a place to relax and socialize. It's not all about drinking. Pubs can be good places for lunch as well, and during the day they're often family environments, before giving way to a lively, adults-only crowd at night.

While numbers are going down, pubs are still a mainstay in both cities and small towns. Visit a town's pub and you're getting a true taste of the place.

—by Jack Jewers

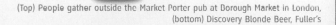

(Top) People gather outside the Market Porter pub at Borough Market in London, (bottom) Discovery Blonde Beer, Fuller's

CHOOSING A PUB

Pubs vary enormously, and that's a wonderful thing: in cities you may find splendid Victorian survivors; in the country there are Tudor pubs with atmospheric wood beams and warm fires. Or perhaps a simple pub with a sincere welcome is all you need.

To find a pub, ask the locals: everyone knows the good ones. Otherwise, if a pub looks attractive and well kept, check it out. Telltale signs that it's probably not the best include banners advertising lagers and "2-for-1" deals, or TV sports channels. Some basic definitions are useful:

A **freehouse** is a pub that is not tied to a single brewery, which means it can sell as many varieties of beer and wine as it likes. **Chain pubs** affiliated with particular breweries are middle-of-the-road, inexpensive franchises that serve decent food and drink. Bass, Wetherspoons, Courage, Whitbread, and Young's are chains; you will see their names on the pub's sign. The **gastropub** serves very high-quality food, but a pub with good food isn't necessarily a gastropub: the name implies culinary aspirations, and some expense. Another useful term is **"the local,"** shorthand for a favorite pub in your town. Everybody has a "local"—but the term is also used generally to refer to any pub that's good for cozy, convivial conversation.

CAN I TAKE MY KIDS TO THE PUB?

As pubs emphasize what's coming out of the kitchen rather than what's flowing out of the tap, whether to bring the kids has become a question. By law, patrons must be 18 in order to drink alcohol in a pub. Children 14 to 17 may enter a pub, but, children under 14 are not permitted in the bar area of a pub unless it has a "children's certficate" and they are accompanied by an adult. In general, however, some pubs have a section set aside for families—especially during the day. Check with the bartender. Some pubs actively encourage families and have play areas and a kid-friendly menu.

(Left) The Flask, Hampstead, London, (Right) Lamb and Flag pub, Covent Garden, London

PUB ETIQUETTE AND BASICS

Ordering: You order drinks from the bartender, known in England as the "barman" or "barmaid"—and pay up front. Don't be put off by a crowd at the bar. Never be impatient; wait as close to the bar as possible and they'll get to you. At most pubs you also order food from the bar and it is brought to you. Credit cards are common but likely require a minimum of £10.

Tipping: If you're only buying drinks, don't tip.

The round: If you're with friends, generally everyone takes turns buying drinks for the group. This is called a "round."

Smoking: Sorry, no: smoking has been banned since 2007.

Hours: In small towns, most pubs stick to the traditional hours of 11 am–11 pm (10:30 pm on Sunday), with the exception of Friday and Saturday nights. In large towns and cities, a few stay open past midnight, sometimes as late as 2 am. A handful are open 24 hours, but they are invariably dives.

Music: Some pubs have live music, usually local bands that vary in quality; but even big stars started out like this. You're not usually expected to pay.

Conversation: People don't generally get involved in a stranger's discussions, but for the best chance to chat with locals, hang out at the bar.

"Last orders please!": This is the traditional call of a landlord 20 minutes before closing, usually accompanied by a bell and a rush to buy drinks. When 20 minutes is up, they'll yell "Time please!" Then you have a few minutes to finish up.

DO I HAVE TO DRINK?

It's fine to go to a pub and not drink alcohol. They're social places first, watering holes second. All pubs serve soft drinks and most have tea and coffee. Other popular alternatives include lime and soda water; orange juice and lemonade; and a St. Clement's, a mixture of orange and bitter lemon (like lemonade, only more sour).

WHEN TO GO?

The English take their drink seriously, and pubs are where people go to hang out and, sometimes, drink heavily. Unless you're checking a place out on recommendation (a good idea), you may want to pick a midweek night for your first pub experience. On Friday and Saturday nights, rowdy young drinkers can take over some pubs.

KNOW YOUR BEER

Whether you're ordering a pint (the usual quantity), or a "half" (for half-pint), you have plenty of options, including imported beers. You can discuss your choice with the barman and then turn to your neighbor, raise your glass, and utter that amiable toast, "Cheers!"

Adnams Broadside

ALE. The most quintessentially English type of beer is brewed from barley and hops and usually served at cellar (cooler than room, but not chilled) temperature. The term *real ale* distinguishes the traditionally made product, containing only authentic ingredients and no carbonation, from mass-produced alternatives; real ales have a devoted following. The flavor of ales varies greatly, from nutty and bitter to light and sweet. *Common varieties include Adnams Broadside; Greene King I.P.A.; Newcastle Brown Ale; Well's Waggle Dance.*

BITTER. This is the generic name given to bitter types of ale. They vary greatly in strength; bitters with the word "best" after their name are medium; "premium," "strong," or "special" are the strongest. *Bitters to try include London Pride and Courage Directors.*

London Pride

LAGER. Often imported, these carbonated, light, pale beers are usually mass produced, and they're extremely popular. Lager is always served chilled. What Americans call beer, the British call lager, including beers from continental Europe.

STOUT. Something of an acquired taste, stouts are dark beers made with roasted barley or malt. A stronger variant, known as porter, was popular in the 18th and 19th centuries, and a handful of bottled kinds are sold in pubs today. *Try Guinness (the Irish favorite) or Fuller's London Porter.*

Fuller's London Porter

WHEAT BEER. These beers brewed from wheat are mostly imported from Europe. They are often white in color and have a malty taste. *Try Hoegaarden or Erdinger.*

MORE CHOICES

CIDER. Made with apples, cider is like its American namesake—but alcoholic. Ciders can be sweet or dry. Try Magners or Strongbow.

LAGER TOPS. A pint of lager with a splash of lemonade on top is a lager top. A 50/50 version of the same thing is called a shandy; this traditional summer afternoon drink is worth a try.

SNAKEBITE. Half lager and half cider, snakebite is usually served with a splash of blackcurrant cordial as a "snakebite and black."

(top) Magners cider, (bottom) Newcastle Brown Ale

EATING AT THE PUB

(left) Traditional ploughman's lunch, (right) Steak and kidney pie

In the 1980s, the best you might hope for in a pub was a sandwich or a plate of cold meats and cheese. The gastropub revolution of the 1990s forced everybody to raise their game. Popular chain pubs, such as Wetherspoons and The Slug and Lettuce, offer decent meals, especially at lunchtime. Don't want a full meal? Most pubs will fix you a bowl of chips (thick-cut French fries) or other hot nibbles. If pubs have specials boards or a menu prominently displayed outside, they're probably worth a shot for a meal. Pub fare includes anything from lasagna to burgers, but look for these traditional favorites:

- Savory pies, such as steak and ale or chicken and bacon. Just make sure they're homemade.
- Bangers and mash (sausage links and mashed potato), especially if the sausages are "butchers" or "local."
- Ploughman's lunch, with cheese, pickles, and crackers.
- Fish and chips may seem like a good pick, but avoid it in city pubs because proper fish and chips shops are usually better. Near the coast, though, pubs that advertise local seafood may be the best place for fish and chips.
- Sunday roasts, another culinary tradition, are hearty feasts—and pubs are usually the best places to sample them. Even pubs not noted for their food can pull out excellent roasts at Sunday lunchtime, and the best places get packed; you may need a reservation. The centerpiece is roast beef, chicken, pork, or lamb, served with roast potatoes and vegetables, covered in thin, rich, dark gravy. Each meat has its traditional accompaniment; Yorkshire pudding (light, fluffy batter, resembling a soufflé) and horseradish sauce with beef; mint jelly with lamb. It's a treat to savor.

PUB QUIZZES AND GAMES

Many pubs hold general knowledge quizzes on a weekday evening, and anybody can enter. It's usually a pound each, which goes into a pot as prize money. Quizzes are a fun and relaxed way to socialize with locals, although it helps to know some British sports and pop culture.

Video gaming machines are a common, if jarringly modern feature, in many pubs. They're the latest additions to a longtime custom, though. Traditional pub games include darts, dominoes, and chess—plus more arcane pastimes now found only rarely in the countryside. These include bar billiards, a miniature version of pool crossed with skittles; and Nine Men's Morris, similar to backgammon.

historic walking tours that run from late April through October. ✉ *48–51 Broad St.* ☎ *01865/792792* 🌐 *bookshop.blackwell.co.uk/stores/oxford-bookshop.*

Fodor's Choice ★ **Covered Market.** This is a fine place for a cheap sandwich and a leisurely browse; the smell of pastries and coffee follows you from cake shop to jeweler to cheesemonger. ✉ *High St.* 🌐 *www.oxford-coveredmarket.co.uk.*

Scriptum. Cards, stationery, handmade paper, and leather-bound journals can be purchased here, as well as quills, sealing wax, and Venetian masks. ✉ *3 Turl St.* ☎ *01865/200042* 🌐 *www.scriptum.co.uk.*

Shepherd & Woodward. This traditional tailor specializes in university gowns, ties, and scarves. ✉ *109–113 High St.* ☎ *01865/249491* 🌐 *www.shepherdandwoodward.co.uk.*

Taylors Deli. If you're planning a picnic, Taylors Deli has everything you need. There are cakes and pastries, as well as first-rate teas and coffees. There's a shop on the High Street as well. ✉ *31 St. Giles* ☎ *01865/558853* 🌐 *www.taylorsoxford.co.uk.*

University of Oxford Shop. Run by the university, the University of Oxford Shop sells authorized clothing, ceramics, and tea towels, all emblazoned with university crests. ✉ *106 High St.* ☎ *01865/247414* 🌐 *www.oushop.com.*

SPORTS AND THE OUTDOORS

BIKING

Bainton Bikes. Bicycles can be rented from Bainton Bikes, a family-owned company that's happy deliver to your hotel. You can also hire a two-wheeler outside the train station in the summer. Prices start at around £10. The shop also provides free support during your hire, including puncture repair. ✉ *78 Walton St.* ☎ *01865/311610* 🌐 *www.baintonbikes.com.*

PUNTING

Fodor's Choice ★ You may choose, like many an Oxford student, to spend a summer afternoon **punting,** while dangling your champagne bottle in the water to keep it cool. Punts—shallow-bottom boats that are poled slowly up the river—can be rented in several places, including at the foot of the Magdalen Bridge.

Cherwell Boathouse. From mid-March through mid-October, Cherwell Boathouse rents boats, and if you call ahead, someone to punt it. Rentals are £15 (£18 on weekends) per hour or £75 (£90 on weekends) per day and should be booked ahead. The facility, a mile north of the heart of Oxford, also includes a stylish restaurant. ✉ *Bardwell Rd.* ☎ *01865/515978* 🌐 *www.cherwellboathouse.co.uk.*

Salter's Steamers. At the St. Aldates Road end of Folly Bridge, Salter's Steamers rents out punts and skiffs (rowboats) for £20 per hour, £60 per half day, and £100 per day. Chauffeured punts are £60 per hour, booked in advance. Day cruises are also run from Christ Church meadows to nearby Abingdon. ✉ *Folly Bridge* ☎ *01865/243421* 🌐 *www.salterssteamers.co.uk.*

SPECTATOR SPORTS

Eights Week. At the end of May, during Oxford's Eights Week, men and women from the university's colleges compete to be "Head of the River." Because the river is too narrow for the eight-member teams to race side by side, the boats set off one behind another. Each boat tries to catch and bump the one in front. ✉ *Oxford.*

OXFORDSHIRE

The River Thames takes on a new graciousness as it flows along the borders of Oxfordshire for 71 miles; with each league it increases in size and importance. Three tributaries swell the river as it passes through the landscape: the Windrush, the Evenlode, and the Cherwell. Tucked among the hills and dales are one of England's impressive stately homes, an Edenic little town, and a former Rothschild estate. Closer to London in Hertfordshire is St. Albans, with its cathedral and Roman remains.

6

WOODSTOCK AND BLENHEIM PALACE

8 miles northwest of Oxford on A44.

Handsome 17th- and 18th-century houses line the trim streets of Woodstock, at the eastern edge of the Cotswolds. It's best known for nearby Blenheim Palace, and in summer tour buses clog the village's ancient streets. On a quiet fall or spring afternoon, however, Woodstock is a sublime experience: a mellowed 18th-century church and town hall mark the central square, and along its backstreets, you can find flower-bedecked houses and quiet lanes right out of a 19th-century etching.

GETTING HERE AND AROUND

The public bus service S3 runs (usually every half hour) between Oxford and Woodstock and costs £3.40 one-way. It can drop you at the gates of Blenheim Palace.

EXPLORING

Fodor's Choice ★ **Blenheim Palace.** This grandiose palace has the distinction of being the only historic house in Britain to be named a World Heritage Site. Designed by Sir John Vanbrugh in the early 1700s in collaboration with Nicholas Hawksmoor, Blenheim was given by Queen Anne and the nation to General John Churchill, first duke of Marlborough, in gratitude for his military victories (including the Battle of Blenheim) against the French in 1704. The exterior is nothing short of sumptuous, with huge columns, enormous pediments, and obelisks, all exemplars of English Baroque. Inside, lavishness continues in extremes: you can join a free guided tour or simply walk through on your own. In most of the opulent rooms family portraits look down at sumptuous furniture, elaborate carpets, fine Chinese porcelain, and immense pieces of silver. Exquisite tapestries in the three state rooms illustrate the first duke's victories. Book a tour of the current duke's private apartments for a more intimate view of ducal life. For some visitors, the most memorable room is the small, low-ceiling chamber where Winston Churchill (his father was the younger brother of the then-duke) was born in 1874; you can also see his paintings, his toy soldier collection, and a room devoted to his private letters (those he sent home from school in Malborough as a young boy are both touching and tragic). He's buried in nearby Bladon.

Sir Winston wrote that the unique beauty of Blenheim lay in its perfect adaptation of English parkland to an Italian palace. Its 2,000 acres of grounds, the work of Capability Brown, 18th-century England's best-known landscape gardener, are arguably the best example of the "cunningly natural" park in the country. Looking across the park to Vanbrugh's semi-submerged Grand Bridge makes for an unforgettable vista. Blenheim's formal gardens include notable water terraces and an Italian garden with a mermaid fountain, all built in the 1920s.

The Pleasure Gardens, reached by a miniature train that stops outside the palace's main entrance, contain some child-pleasers, including a butterfly house, a hedge maze, and giant chess set. The herb-and-lavender garden is also delightful. Blenheim Palace stages a concert of Beethoven's *Battle Symphony* in mid-July, combined with a marvelous fireworks display. There are many other outdoor events throughout the summer, including jousting tournaments. Allow at least three hours for a full visit. ✉ *Off A4095, Woodstock* ☎ *01993/810530, 0800/849–6500 recorded information (24-hr)* 🌐 *www.blenheimpalace.com* 🎫 *Palace, park, and gardens £22.50; park and gardens £13.50* ⏲ *Palace and Pleasure Garden mid-Feb.–Oct., daily 10:30–5:30; Nov.–mid-Dec., Wed.–Sun. 10:30–4:30. Park and Visitor Centre mid-Feb.–mid-Dec., daily 9–6 or dusk; last admission 45 min before closing.*

WHERE TO EAT AND STAY

$ BRITISH Fodor's Choice ★ ✕ **Falkland Arms.** It's worth detouring a bit for this supremely appealing pub on the village green at Great Tew, about 8 miles northwest of Woodstock. The bar stocks fruit wines and snuff as well as local ales, and there's a fine selection of mugs and jugs hanging from the beams. The small restaurant chalks up a traditional but creative menu, which includes dishes like baked salmon with pine nut and watercress crust alongside pub classics such as beer-battered fish-and-chips or a tasty homemade pie of the day. Sandwiches and Ploughman's lunches are available in the afternoon. Book ahead on weekends. If you can't bear to leave, a spiral stone staircase leads to five guest rooms (£100 per night). $ *Average main: £13* ✉ *19–21 The Green, Great Tew* ☎ *01608/683653* 🌐 *www.falklandarms.co.uk* ✍ *Reservations essential.*

$$ HOTEL **The Feathers.** Antiques-bedecked guest rooms fill this stylish inn, which was cobbled together from five 17th-century houses in the heart of town. **Pros:** beautiful modern design; great food; good for gin drinkers. **Cons:** two-night minimum stay on weekends in summer; narrow stairs for top rooms; no hotel parking. $ *Rooms from: £123* ✉ *Market St., Woodstock* ☎ *01993/812291* 🌐 *www.feathers.co.uk* *16 rooms, 5 suites* 🍽 *Breakfast.*

$$$ HOTEL **Macdonald Bear.** Tudoresque wood paneling, beamed ceilings, wattle-and-daub walls, and blazing fireplaces help define this as an archetypal English coaching inn. **Pros:** plenty of character; historic house. **Cons:** creaky old floors; you can knock yourself silly on those old beams;

Fountains and formal Italian gardens set off the monumental baroque pile that is Blenheim Palace.

some rooms are "haunted". $ *Rooms from: £206* ✉ *Park St., Woodstock* ☎ *0811/879 9113 local, 01993/811124 international* 🌐 *www.macdonaldhotels.co.uk/our-hotels/macdonald-bear-hotel* *46 rooms, 8 suites* 🍽 *Breakfast.*

EN ROUTE

After taking in Blenheim Palace, stop by **Bladon**, 2 miles southeast of Woodstock on A4095 and 6 miles northwest of Oxford, to see the small, tree-lined churchyard that's the burial place of Sir Winston Churchill. His grave is all the more impressive for its simplicity.

AYLESBURY

22 miles east of Oxford, 46 miles northwest of London.

Aylesbury makes a good base for exploring the surrounding countryside, including stately homes and gardens. It's a pretty, historic place with a 13th-century church surrounded by small Tudor lanes and cottages. This market town has been associated with the Aylesbury duck since the 18th century, when flocks were walked 40 miles to the London markets. Kids appreciate a visit to the Roald Dahl's Children's Gallery, which is open all year.

GETTING HERE AND AROUND

From London, Chiltern Railways runs frequent trains from Marylebone Station (one hour). The town is easily accessible from Oxford by Arriva Bus 280, which runs every 30 minutes; travel time is 80 minutes. If you're driving from Oxford, take A40 and A418. From London, follow M1 and A41 and allow 90 minutes.

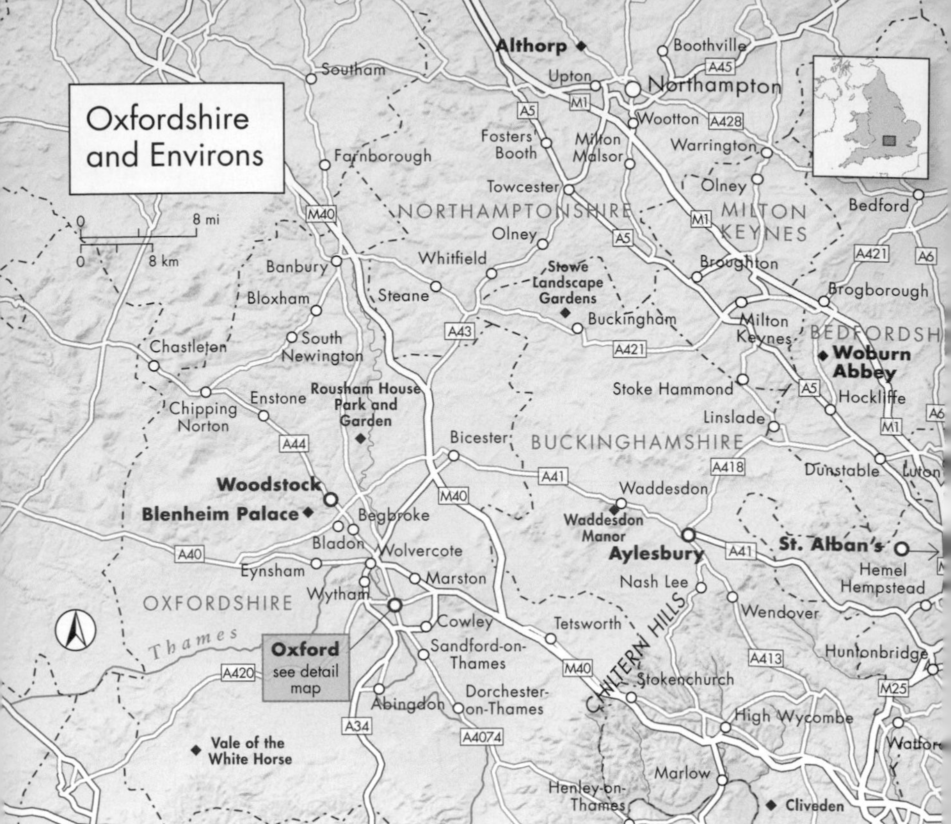

ESSENTIALS

Visitor Information Aylesbury Tourist Information Centre. ✉ *King's Head Passage, off Market Sq.* ☎ *01296/330559* 🌐 *www.visitbuckinghamshire.org.*

EXPLORING

Fodor's Choice ★ **Stowe Landscape Gardens.** This superb example of a Georgian garden was created for the Temple family by the most famous gardeners of the 18th century. Capability Brown, Charles Bridgeman, and William Kent all worked on the land to create 980 acres of pleasing greenery in the valleys and meadows. More than 40 striking monuments, follies, and temples dot the landscape of lakes, rivers, and pleasant vistas; this is a historically important place, but it's not for those who want primarily a flower garden. Allow at least half a day to explore the grounds. Stowe House, at the center, is now a fancy school with some magnificently restored rooms; it's open for tours most afternoons, but the actual schedule is notoriously changeable, so do call ahead or check 🌐 *www.stowe.co.uk* for more information. The gardens are about 3 miles northwest of Buckingham, which is 14 miles northwest of Aylesbury. You enter the gardens through the New Inn visitor center, where there are period parlor rooms to explore. ✉ *New Inn Farm, off A422, Stowe* ☎ *01280/817156, 01280/818166 for information, 01280/818002 for tours* 🌐 *www.nationaltrust.org.uk/stowegardens* 🎟 *£15; house only £6*

THAMES VALLEY HIKING AND BIKING

The Thames Valley is a great area to explore on foot or by bike. It's not too hilly, and pubs and easily accessible lodgings dot the riverside and small towns. The Thames is almost completely free of car traffic along the Thames Path, a 184-mile national trail that traces the river from the London flood barrier to the river's source near Kemble, in the Cotswolds. The path follows towpaths from the outskirts of London, through Windsor, Oxford, and Lechlade.

Good public transportation in the region makes it possible to start and stop easily anywhere along this route. In summer the walking is fine and no special gear is necessary, but in winter the path often floods—check before you head out.

For the best information on the Thames paths, contact the National Trails Office or the Ramblers' Association, both good sources of information, advice, and maps. The Chiltern Conservation Board promotes walking in the Chilterns peaks.

Biking is perhaps the best way to see the Chilterns. Routes include the 99-mile Thames Valley Cycle Route from London to Oxford, and the 87-mile Ridgeway Path from Uffington that follows the Chilterns; the National Trails Office has information. The Thames Path also has plenty of biking opportunities.

CONTACTS AND RESOURCES

Chiltern Conservation Board. ✉ *Aylesbury* ☎ *01844/355500* 🌐 *www.chilternsaonb.org.*

Chiltern Way. ✉ *Aylesbury* ☎ *01494/771250* 🌐 *www.chilternsociety.org.uk.*

National Trails. ✉ *Aylesbury* 🌐 *www.nationaltrail.co.uk.*

Ramblers' Association. ✉ *Aylesbury* ☎ *020/7339–8500* 🌐 *www.ramblers.org.uk.*

⏲ *Gardens daily 10–6; last admission 90 min before closing. House generally 5 or 6 days per week, 11–5; last admission 30 min before closing. Call or check Stowe website for up-to-date schedules.*

Fodor's Choice ★ **Waddesdon Manor.** Many of the regal residences created by the Rothschild family throughout Europe are gone now, but this one is still a vision of the 19th century at its most sumptuous. G.H. Destailleur built the house in the 1880s for Baron Ferdinand de Rothschild in the style of a 16th-century French château, with perfectly balanced turrets and towers and walls of creamy stone. Although intended only for summer weekend house parties, it was lovingly furnished over 35 years with Savonnerie carpets, Sèvres porcelain, furniture made by Riesener for Marie Antoinette, and paintings by Guardi, Gainsborough, and Reynolds. An exquisite 21st-century broken porcelain chandelier by Ingo Maurer in the Blue Dining Room brings the collection up-to-date. The gardens are equally extraordinary, with an aviary, colorful plantings, and winding trails that provide panoramic views. In the restaurant you can dine on English or French fare and order excellent Rothschild wines if your pocketbook can take the hit. To learn more about the house and its wines, there's a 20-minute talk daily at 2 pm in the wine cellar. Admission is by timed ticket; arrive early or book in advance. ✉ *Silk St., Waddesdon* ✣ *On A41 west of Aylesbury* ☎ *01296/653226* 🌐 *www.waddesdon.org.uk* 🎫 *House and gardens £18; gardens only £8* ⏲ *House late Mar.–late Oct., Wed.–Fri. noon–4; last entry 50 min before closing, Sat.–Sun. 11–4; last entry 50 min before closing. Gardens late Mar.–late Oct., Wed.–Sun. 10–5; last entry 1 hr before closing.*

WHERE TO STAY

$ B&B/INN **Five Arrows.** Fancifully patterned brick chimneys and purple gables decorate this elegant building next to the main entrance of Waddesdon Manor. **Pros:** historic building; lovely grounds. **Cons:** some rooms are small; on a busy main road. $ *Rooms from: £90* ✉ *High St., Waddesdon* ☎ *01296/651727* 🌐 *www.thefivearrows.co.uk* *14 rooms, 2 suites* 🍽 *Breakfast.*

$$$$ HOTEL Fodor's Choice ★ **Hartwell House.** Part Jacobean, part Georgian, this magnificent stately home provides formal luxury in an opulent country setting. **Pros:** truly elegant; soothing views of the gardens. **Cons:** may feel too formal; spa is open to the public. $ *Rooms from: £270* ✉ *Oxford Rd.* ☎ *01296/747444* 🌐 *www.hartwell-house.com* *33 rooms, 13 suites* 🍽 *Breakfast.*

ST. ALBANS

25 miles east of Aylesbury, 20 miles northwest of London.

A lively town on the outskirts of London, St. Albans is known for its historic cathedral, and it also holds reminders of a long history. From AD 50 to 440, the town, then known as Verulamium, was one of the largest communities in Roman Britain. You can explore this past in the Verulamium Museum and splendid Roman sites around the area. For activities more focused on the present, every Wednesday and Saturday the Market Place on St. Peter's Street bustles with traders from all over England selling everything from fish and farm produce to clothing and CDs. A 20-minute drive away from St. Albans is Warner Bros. Harry Potter Studio Tour, which has sets and props from the successful films.

GETTING HERE AND AROUND

About 20 miles northwest of London, St. Albans is off the M1 and M25 highways, about an hour's drive from the center of the capital. Thameslink has frequent trains from London's St. Pancras Station, arriving at St. Albans City station in 30 minutes. The main train station is on Victoria Street, in the town center. A second station on the south side of town, St. Albans Abbey Station, serves smaller towns in the surrounding area. Trains on this line are operated by London Midland. Bus service is slow and not direct. Central St. Albans is small and walkable. There's a local bus service, but you're unlikely to need it. Taxis usually line up outside the train stations.

ESSENTIALS

Train Contacts London Midland. ☎ *0121/364–2040* 🌐 *www.londonmidland.com.*

Visitor Information St. Albans Tourist and Information Centre. ✉ *Town Hall, Market Pl.* ☎ *01727/864511* 🌐 *www.enjoystalbans.com.*

EXPLORING

TOP ATTRACTIONS

Fodor's Choice ★ **Hatfield House.** Six miles east of St. Albans, this outstanding brick mansion surrounded by lovely formal gardens stands as a testament to the magnificence of Jacobean architecture. Robert Cecil, earl of Salisbury, built Hatfield in 1611, and his descendants still live here. The interior, with its dark-wood paneling, lush tapestries, and Tudor and Jacobean portraits, reveals much about the era. The King James Drawing Room is an exercise in ostentatious grandeur, with its gilded ceiling and portrait-covered walls. By contrast, the Chinese Bedroom is a rather charming example of the later, 19th-century infatuation with Far Eastern design. The Marble Hall, with its intricate carved wooden panels, is one of the most impressive rooms in the house, although perhaps the building's finest single feature is the ornate Grand Staircase, with carved wooden figures on the banisters. The knot garden, near the Tudor Old Palace, where the first Queen Elizabeth spent much of her youth, is a highlight of the West Garden. Wednesday is the only day on which the East Garden, with topiaries, parterres, and rare plants, is open to the public. The Park has lovely woodland paths and masses of bluebells. There are various markets, theater performances, and shows throughout the season, including open air film screenings, and occasionally, Elizabethan banquets. Check the website for the schedule. ✉ *Great North Rd., Hatfield* ☎ *01707/287010* 🌐 *www.hatfield-house.co.uk* 🎫 *House, West Garden, and Park £16.50; West Garden and Park £10; East Garden £4; park £5* ⏲ *House Easter–Sept., Wed.–Sun. and holiday Mon. 11–4:30. West Garden Tues.–Sun. and holiday Mon. 10–5:30. East Garden Wed. 11–4:30. Park Tues.–Sun. and holiday Mon. 10–5:30 or dusk.*

St. Albans Cathedral. Medieval pilgrims came from far and wide to the hilltop St. Albans Cathedral to honor its patron saint, a Roman soldier turned Christian martyr. His red-canopied shrine beyond the choir has a rare loft from where guards kept watch over gifts that were left. Construction of the mainly Norman cathedral began in the early 11th century, but the nearly 300-foot-long nave dates from 1235; the pillars are decorated with 13th- and 14th-century paintings. The tower is even more historic, and contains bricks from ancient Roman buildings. There is a free tour of highlights at 1:05 daily, and more extensive free tours at 11:30 and 2:30 from Monday to Friday, 11:30 and 2 on Saturday, and 2:30 on Sunday. Tower tours (£8) take place on selected dates, mostly on Saturdays. Call or check the website for schedule. ✉ *Holywell Hill* ☎ *01727/860780* 🌐 *www.stalbanscathedral.org* 🎫 *Free (donations welcome); tower tours £8* ⏲ *Daily 8:30–5:45.*

FAMILY **Verulamium Museum.** With exhibits on everything from food to burial practices, the Verulamium Museum, on the site of the ancient Roman city, explores life 2,000 years ago. The re-created Roman rooms contain colorful mosaics that are some of the finest in Britain. Every second weekend of the month, "Roman soldiers" invade the museum and demonstrate the skills of the Imperial Army. ✉ *St. Michael's St.* ☎ *01727/751810* 🌐 *www.stalbansmuseums.org.uk* 🎫 *£5* ⏲ *Mon.–Sat. 10–5:30, Sun. 2–5:30; last admission 30 min before closing.*

6

FAMILY Fodor's Choice ★ **Warner Bros. Harry Potter Studio Tour.** Muggles, take note: this spectacular attraction just outside Watford gives you a good three hours of the magical world of Harry Potter. From the Great Hall of Hogwarts—faithfully restored—to magical props beautifully displayed in a vast studio space, each section of this attraction showcases the real sets, props, and special effects used in the eight movies. Visitors enter the Great Hall, a fitting stage for costumes from each Hogwarts house. You can admire the intricacies of the huge Hogwarts Castle model, ride a broomstick, try butterbeer, explore Platform 9¾, or just take refuge in the comforting confines of Dumbledore's office. The new Hogwarts Express section—in a faithfully reproduced King's Cross Station—allows you to walk through the actual steam train and see what it's like to ride with Harry and the gang. Tickets, pegged to a 30-minute arrival time slot, must be prebooked online. The studio tour is a 20-minute drive from St. Albans. You can also get here by taking a 20-minute train ride from London's Euston Station to Watford Junction (then a 15-minute shuttle bus ride). Via car from London, use M1 and M25—parking is free. ✉ *Studio Tour Dr., Leavesden* ☎ *0845/084–0900* 🌐 *www.wbstudiotour.co.uk* 🎟 *£35* ⏲ *Daily times vary; generally 10–8 in summer months; last tour slot 2½–3½ hrs before closing. Call or check website to confirm daily times.*

WORTH NOTING

Roman Theater. Your imagination can take you back to AD 130 as you walk around the ruins of this 2,000-seat Roman Theater, one of the few in the country. Next to the theater are the scant ruins of a Roman town house, shops, and a shrine. ✉ *Bluehouse Hill* ☎ *01727/835035* 🎟 *£2.50* ⏲ *Easter–Nov., daily 10–5; Dec.–Easter, daily 10–4.*

Shaw's Corner. From 1906 to his death in 1950, the famed Irish playwright George Bernard Shaw lived in the small village of Ayot St. Lawrence, 9 miles northeast of St. Albans. Today his small Edwardian home, Shaw's Corner, remains much as he left it. The most delightful curiosity is his little writing hut in the garden, which can be turned to face the sun. ✉ *Off Hill Farm La., Ayot St. Lawrence* ☎ *01438/821968* 🌐 *www.nationaltrust.org.uk/shawscorner* 🎟 *£7.50* ⏲ *House mid-Mar.–Oct., Wed.–Sun. 1–5. Gardens mid-Mar.–Oct., Wed.–Sun. noon–5:30; last admission 1 hr before closing.*

FAMILY **Verulamium Park Hypocaust.** Adjacent to the Verulamium Museum, this park contains the usual—playground, wading pool, lake—and the unusual—Roman ruins that include part of the town hall and a hypocaust, or central-heating system. The hypocaust dates to AD 200 and included one of the first heated floors in Britain. Brick columns supported the floor, and hot air from a nearby fire was drawn underneath the floor to keep bathers warm. ✉ *St. Michael's St.* ☎ *01727/751810* 🌐 *www.stalbansmuseums.org.uk* 🎟 *Free* ⏲ *Hypocaust Apr.–Sept., Mon.–Sat. 10–4:30, Sun. 2–4:30; Oct.–Mar., Mon.–Sat. 10–3:45, Sun. 2–3:45; last admission 30 min before closing.*

WHERE TO EAT AND STAY

$ BELGIAN ✕ **Waffle House.** Indoors or out, you can enjoy a great budget meal at the 16th-century Kingsbury Watermill, near the Verulamium Museum. The organic flour for the sweet-and-savory Belgian waffles comes from

Redbournbury Watermill, north of the city. In the main dining room, you can see the wheel churn the water of the River Ver. It's also open for early dinners until 7 pm Thursday through Saturday. *Average main: £8* *Kingsbury Watermill, St. Michael's St.* *01727/853502* *www.wafflehouse.co.uk* *No dinner.*

$ BRITISH **Ye Olde Fighting Cocks.** Some claim this is England's oldest pub, but it should come as no surprise that the title is hotly contested. Still, this octagonal building certainly looks suitably aged. The building was moved to this location in the 16th century, but the foundations date back 800 years before that. The small rooms with low ceilings make a cozy stop for a pint and good home-cooked food. Be prepared for crowds. *Average main: £12* *16 Abbey Mill La.* *01727/869152* *www.yeoldefightingcocks.co.uk* *No dinner Sun.*

$$ HOTEL **St. Michael's Manor.** In the same family for three generations, this luxurious 16th-century manor house close to the center of St. Albans is set in 5 acres of sweeping grounds. **Pros:** spacious rooms; excellent food; beautiful grounds. **Cons:** a little too grand for some. *Rooms from: £150* *Fishpool St.* *01727/864444* *www.stmichaelsmanor.com* *30 rooms, 5 suites* *Breakfast.*

6

WOBURN ABBEY

30 miles west of St. Albans, 10 miles northeast of Aylesbury.

A stunning drive through the deer park at Woburn Abbey leads to a superb art collection within a Georgian mansion and roaming wildlife in a safari park.

GETTING HERE AND AROUND

Woburn Abbey is easily accessible for drivers from M1 at Junction 12 or 13; a car is needed to tour the safari park. The nearest train station, Flitwick, is a 15-minute taxi ride away. Frequent trains connect with St. Albans and London's St. Pancras Station in 30 minutes.

EXPLORING

FAMILY **Woburn Abbey.** Still the ancestral residence of the duke of Bedford, Woburn Abbey houses countless Grand Tour treasures and old master paintings, including 20 stunning Canalettos that practically wallpaper the crimson dining salon, and excellent works by Gainsborough and Reynolds. The Palladian mansion contains a number of etchings by Queen Victoria, who left them behind after she stayed here. Outside, 10 species of deer roam grounds that include an antiques center and small restaurant. The adjacent **Woburn Safari Park** is a popular drive-through wildlife experience, home to big game from around the world. Be prepared for fearless monkeys who like to go for a ride on your car. There are plenty of play areas, a boating lake with swan boats, and walkabouts with small animals such as wallabies. Allow at least half a day for the safari park. If you buy a joint ticket with the house, you can use it on another day. *A4012, off A5, Woburn* *01525/290333 abbey, 01525/290407 safari park* *www.woburn.co.uk* *House, gardens, and deer park £15; gardens and deer park only £7; safari park £23; combination ticket £27* *House late Mar.–Oct., daily 11–5. Safari Park Apr.–late Oct., daily 10–6. Gardens late Mar.–Oct., daily 10–5 or dusk.*

WHERE TO STAY

$$ HOTEL **The Woburn Hotel.** In the center of this small Georgian town, this former coaching inn has uncluttered and comfortable bedrooms. **Pros:** close to Woburn Abbey; light-filled spaces. **Cons:** standard rooms are small; small bathrooms. *Rooms from: £105 George St., Woburn 01525/290441 www.thewoburnhotel.co.uk 48 rooms, 7 suites Breakfast.*

ALTHORP

5 miles west of Northampton, 27 miles northwest of Woburn Abbey.

Althorp, known as the childhood home and burial place of Princess Diana, has fine architecture and paintings, both old masters and new.

GETTING HERE AND AROUND

Signposted at Junction 16 of M1, Althorp is most easily reached by car. However, if you ask the driver, Stagecoach Bus 96 from Northampton's train station will drop you here (Monday through Saturday). Buses run every hour.

ESSENTIALS

Bus Contacts Stagecoach. *0871/200–2233 Traveline www.stagecoachbus.com.*

EXPLORING

Althorp House. Deep in the heart of Northamptonshire sits the ancestral home of the Spencers, also known as the family home of Princess Diana. Here, on a tiny island in a lake known as the Round Oval, is Diana's final resting place and the lakeside temple is dedicated to her memory. Diana and her siblings found the house too melancholy, calling it "Deadlock Hall." The house no longer has any Diana memorabilia or exhibits, but it does have rooms filled with paintings by Van Dyck, Reynolds, and Rubens—all portraits of the Spencers going back 500 years—and an entry hall that architectural historian Nikolaus Pevsner called "the noblest Georgian room in the country." Two paintings by contemporary artist Mitch Griffiths stand out in complete contrast. A literary festival is held here in mid-June. On the west side of the estate park is Great Brington, the neighboring village where the church of St. Mary the Virgin holds the Spencer family crypt; it's best reached by the designated path from Althorp. A major festival takes place here over a week in June. *Rugby Rd., off A428, Northampton 01604/770107 www.spencerofalthorp.com £19 May, June–late July, and Sept., Sun., 1–5; late July and Aug., daily 1–5; also daily during Althorp Literary Festival; last entry 3:45 (house), 4 (grounds).*

BATH AND THE COTSWOLDS

WELCOME TO BATH AND THE COTSWOLDS

TOP REASONS TO GO

★ **Architecture of Bath:** Bath is perhaps the most perfectly preserved and harmonious English city. Close up, the elegance and finesse of the Georgian buildings is a perpetual delight.

★ **Hidcote Manor Gardens:** In a region rich with imaginative garden displays, Hidcote lays good claim to eminence. Exotic shrubs from around the world and the famous "garden rooms" are the highlights of this Arts and Crafts masterpiece.

★ **Perfect villages:** With their stone cottages, Cotswold villages tend to be improbably picturesque; the hamlets of Upper and Lower Slaughter are among the most seductive.

★ **Roman Baths:** Take a break from Bath's Georgian elegance and return to its Roman days on a tour around this ancient bath complex.

1 Bath and Nearby. With the Roman Baths—renovated and embellished in the 18th century—and the late-medieval Bath Abbey at its heart, Bath is one of the country's comeliest towns. You can also soak up its thriving cultural scene and many shops.

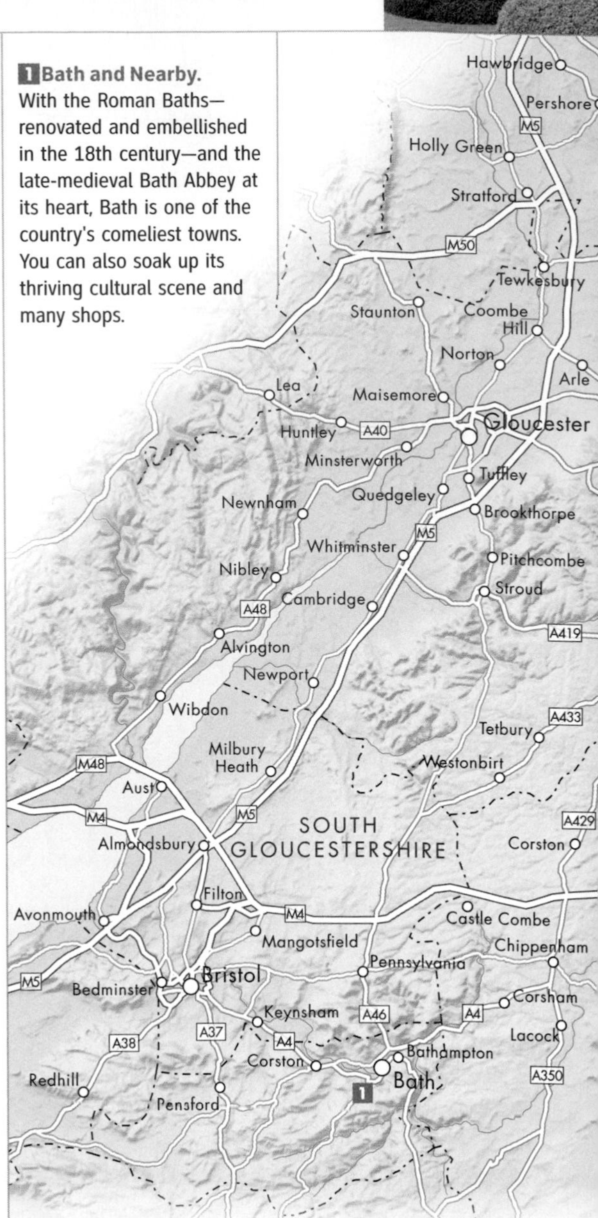

2 The Cotswolds. With a scattering of picture-postcard towns and villages separated by sequestered valleys and woods, the Cotswolds are rural England at its best. Nearby Cheltenham, a larger town, with busy cafés and shops, provides a lively counterpoint.

GETTING ORIENTED

The major points of interest in this part of west-central England—Bath, the Cotswolds, and Cheltenham—are one way to organize your explorations. Bath, in the southwestern corner of this area, is a good place to start; it can also be visited on a day trip out from London. The Cotswolds, about two hours northwest of London by car, cover some of southern England's most beautiful terrain. The area's small roads make for wonderful exploring, but public transportation is limited. To the west of the Cotswolds lies the city of Cheltenham, an elegant former spa town.

GREAT WALKS IN THE COTSWOLDS

The gentle Cotswolds countryside, designated an Area of Outstanding Natural Beauty, is threaded with more than 3,000 miles of pleasant walking routes that enable you to appreciate these upland tracts at their best. It's easy to plan an afternoon walk or a multiday exploration.

(above) The Cotswold Way traverses some of England's loveliest countryside; (right, top) Stone bridge at Lower Slaughter; (right, below) Helpful sign on the Cotswold Way

The Cotswolds are a delight: wherever you turn, green areas are dotted with church steeples and stone roofs, restful on the eye and nourishing for the soul. To enjoy them to the fullest, do as the locals do—hoist on some walking shoes, don a sun (or rain) hat, and set forth on foot. Waymarked routes crisscross the area, and none of them are too challenging. No specialized equipment is required; it's healthy and it's free. Walks come in all lengths, but unless you decide to tackle one of the more ambitious regional trails, it may be easiest to pick a circular route. Just look for the "Public Footpath" and "Public Bridleway" signs, which indicate a right of way even when this passes through private property. Before you know it, you'll be opening gates and crossing stiles on the trails along with everyone else.

BRING WITH YOU

Light walking shoes or boots are essential, as are rain gear (even if it's sunny out), water, and a map. The walks may not be strenuous, but wear pants you won't mind getting dirty as you pass through fields. A fleece will keep the wind at bay, though in cold weather bundle up as needed. Carry a day pack for anything you don't want to hold or wear; you'll need your hands free to open gates along the trails.

CHOOSE YOUR WALKING ROUTE

The most celebrated route traversing the area is the **Cotswold Way** (🌐 *www.nationaltrail.co.uk*), a 102-mile national trail that traces the escarpment marking the western edge of the Cotswolds, stretching north to south between Chipping Campden and Bath, and taking in Broadway, Winchcombe, and Painswick, among many other villages. The trail has incomparable views across the Severn Vale to the Malvern Hills and takes you through varied scenery: limestone grasslands crossed by dry-stone walls, beech woodlands, and stone-built villages with ancient churches. You can select a route rather than walk the entire trail, which might take 7–10 days.

The **Heart of England Way** (🌐 *www.heartofenglandway.org*) runs a linear route from Bourton-on-the-Water north to Lower Slaughter, Bourton-on-the-Hill, and Chipping Campden, and continues north into the West Midlands. It's 104 miles in all, and the Cotswold section takes in hills and deep wooded valleys.

The **Warden's Way** and the **Windrush Way** both run between Winchcombe and Bourton-on-the-Water, 14-mile rambles that link the Cotswold Way (at Winchcombe) with the Oxfordshire Way (at Bourton-on-the-Water). The Warden's Way takes you through Upper and Lower Slaughter; the Windrush Way follows the meandering River Windrush and touches on Sudeley Castle, but without entering any village en route.

Part of the Cotswold Way can be incorporated into an easy circular route between **Chipping Campden and Broadway**, along mostly level ground but including the elevated viewpoints of Dover's Hill and Broadway Tower. The circular route adds up to around 12 miles.

One of the most scenic Cotswolds walks explores the **Coln Valley,** a 6-mile (10-km) circular route beginning and ending at Bibury. The path follows the banks of the lovely River Coln for part of the way, through meadows and woodland.

RESOURCES

Tourist information centers carry local walking maps and publications describing longer trails. The most useful map for walkers in the area is Ordnance Survey Explorer OL45 (1:25,000). The **National Trail** website (🌐 *www.nationaltrail.co.uk*) outlines circular walks of 5–10 miles from the Cotswold Way.

Cotswold Voluntary Wardens conduct free guided walks of 4–10 miles (no booking needed). The free *Cotswold Lion* newspaper at tourist offices lists these. The website of the Cotswolds Area of Outstanding National Beauty (🌐 *www.cotswoldsaonb.org.uk*) is another resource.

Walk the Landscape (🌐 *www.walkthelandscape.co.uk*) organizes guided and self-guided hikes with luggage transfer and accommodation.

Compass Holidays (🌐 *www.compass-holidays.com*) arranges short self-guided walking trips in the Cotswolds, and **Sherpa Van** (🌐 *www.sherpavan.com*) offers a luggage transfer and accommodation booking service.

7

Updated by
Kate Hughes

The rolling uplands of the Cotswolds represent the quintessence of rural England, as immortalized in countless books, paintings, and films. In eloquently named settlements from Bourton-on-the-Water to Stow-on-the-Wold, you can taste the glories of the old English village—its stone slate roofs, low-ceiling rooms, and gardens; the atmosphere is as thick as honey, and equally as sweet. On the edge of the Cotswolds is Bath, among the most alluring small cities in Europe.

The blissfully unspoiled Cotswolds, deservedly popular with visitors and convenient to London, occupy much of the county of Gloucestershire, in west-central England. They also take in slices of neighboring Oxfordshire, Worcestershire, and Somerset. Together these make up a sweep of land stretching from close to Stratford-upon-Avon and Shakespeare Country in the north almost as far as the Bristol Channel in the south. On the edge of the area, two historic towns have absorbed, rather than compromised. Bath, offering up "18th-century England in all its urban glory," to use a phrase by writer Nigel Nicolson, is one. The other is Regency-era Cheltenham, which, like Bath, is a spa town with elegant architecture.

Bath rightly boasts of being the best-planned town in England. Although the Romans founded the city when they discovered here the only true hot springs in England, its popularity during the 17th and 18th centuries luckily coincided with one of Britain's most creative architectural eras. Today people come to walk in the footsteps of Jane Austen, visit Bath Abbey and the excavated Roman baths, shop in an elegant setting, or have a modern spa experience at the stunning Thermae spa.

North of Bath are the Cotswolds—a region that more than one writer has called the very soul of England. This idyllic region, which from medieval times grew prosperous on the wool trade, remains a vision of rural England. Here are time-defying churches, sleepy hamlets, sequestered ancient farmsteads, and such fabled abodes as Sudeley Castle. The

Cotswolds can hardly claim to be undiscovered, but the area's poetic appeal has survived the tour buses and antiques shops.

BATH AND THE COTSWOLDS PLANNER

WHEN TO GO

This area contains some of England's most popular destinations, and it's best to avoid weekends in the busier areas of the Cotswolds. During the week, even in summer, you may hardly see a soul in the more remote spots. Bath is particularly congested in summer, when students flock to its language schools. On the other hand, Cheltenham is a relatively workaday place that can absorb many tour buses comfortably.

Book your room well ahead if you visit during the two weeks in May and June when the Bath International Music Festival hits town, or if you visit Cheltenham during the National Hunt Festival (horse racing) in mid-March. Note that the private properties of Hidcote Manor, Snowshill Manor, and Sudeley Castle close in winter; Hidcote Manor Garden is at its best in spring and fall.

PLANNING YOUR TIME

Bath and Cheltenham are the most compelling larger towns in the region, and the obvious centers for an exploration of the Cotswolds. Cheltenham is closer to the heart of the Cotswolds and is far less touristy, but it has less immediate appeal. Bath is 29 miles from Cirencester in the southern Cotswolds, and 45 miles from Stow-on-the-Wold in the north. It's also worth finding accommodations in the smaller Cotswold settlements, though overnight stops in this well-heeled area can be costly. Good choices include Cirencester, Stow-on-the-Wold, and Broadway.

You can get a taste of Bath and the Cotswolds in three hurried days; a weeklong visit gives you plenty of time for the slow wandering this small region deserves. Near Bath, it's an easy drive to Lacock and Castle Combe, two stately villages on the southern edge of the Cotswolds, and Winchcombe makes a good entry into the area from Cheltenham. At the heart of the Cotswolds, Stow-on-the-Wold, Bourton-on-the-Water, and Broadway should on no account be missed. Within a short distance of these, Chipping Campden and Moreton-in-Marsh are less showy, with a more relaxed feel. Northleach is fairly low-key but boasts a fine example of a Cotswold wool church, while Bibury and Upper and Lower Slaughter are tiny settlements that can easily be appreciated on a brief passage. On the southern fringes of the area, Burford, Tetbury, and Cirencester have antiques and tea shops galore while avoiding the worst of the crowds.

GETTING HERE AND AROUND

AIR TRAVEL

This area is about two hours from London; Bristol and Birmingham have the closest regional airports.

BUS TRAVEL

National Express buses head to the region from London's Victoria Coach Station. Megabus, a budget bus company best booked online, also serves Cheltenham and Bath from London. It takes about three hours to get to both Cheltenham and to Bath. Bus service between some towns can be extremely limited. The First company covers the area around Bath. Stagecoach, Johnson's Coaches, Cotswold Green, Swanbrook, Marchant's, and Pulham's Coaches operate in the Cotswolds region. Traveline has comprehensive information about all public transportation.

Contacts Cotswold Green. ☎ *01453/835153.* **First.** ☎ *0871/200–2233* 🌐 *www.firstgroup.com.* **Johnson's Coaches.** ☎ *01564/797070* 🌐 *www.johnsonscoaches.co.uk.* **Marchant's.** ☎ *01242/257714* 🌐 *www.marchants-coaches.com.* **Megabus.** ☎ *0871/266–3333 for general inquiries, 0900/160–0900 for bookings; calls cost 60p per minute* 🌐 *www.megabus.com.* **National Express.** ☎ *0871/781–8181* 🌐 *www.nationalexpress.com.* **Pulham's Coaches.** ☎ *01451/820369* 🌐 *www.pulhamscoaches.com.* **Stagecoach.** ☎ *0871/200–2233* 🌐 *www.stagecoachbus.com.* **Swanbrook.** ☎ *01452/712386* 🌐 *www.swanbrook.co.uk.* **Traveline.** ☎ *0871/200–2233* 🌐 *www.traveline.info.* **Wessex.** ☎ *0117/986–9953* 🌐 *www.wessexbus.com.*

CAR TRAVEL

A car is the best way to make a thorough tour of the area, given the limitations of public transportation. M4 is the main route west from London to Bath and southern Gloucestershire; expect about a two-hour drive. From Exit 18, take A46 south to Bath. From Exit 20, take M5 north to Cheltenham; from Exit 15, take A419 to A429 north to the Cotswolds. From London you can also take M40 and A40 to the Cotswolds, where a network of minor roads link the villages.

TRAIN TRAVEL

First Great Western trains serve the region from London's Paddington Station; First Great Western and CrossCountry trains connect Cheltenham and Birmingham. Travel time from Paddington to Bath is about 90 minutes. Most trains to Cheltenham (two hours and 20 minutes) involve a change at Swindon or Bristol Parkway. Train service within the Cotswold area is extremely limited, with Kemble (near Cirencester) and Moreton-in-Marsh being the most useful stops, both serviced by regular trains from London Paddington. A three-day or seven-day Heart of England Rover pass is valid for unlimited travel within the region. National Rail Enquiries can help with schedules and other information.

Contacts National Rail Enquiries. ☎ *0845/748–4950* 🌐 *www.nationalrail.co.uk.*

RESTAURANTS

Good restaurants dot the region, thanks to a steady flow of fine chefs seeking to cater to wealthy locals and waves of demanding visitors. The country's food revolution is in full evidence here. Restaurants have never had a problem with a fresh food supply: excellent regional produce, salmon from the rivers Severn and Wye, local lamb and pork, venison from the Forest of Dean, and pheasant, partridge, quail, and grouse in season. Also look for Gloucestershire Old Spot pork, bacon (try a delicious Old Spot bacon sandwich), and sausage on area menus.

HOTELS

The hotels of this region are among Britain's most highly rated—from bed-and-breakfasts in village homes and farmhouses to luxurious country-house hotels. Many hotels present themselves as deeply traditional rural retreats, but some have opted for a sleeker, fresher style, with boldly contemporary or minimalist furnishings. Spas are becoming increasingly popular at these hotels. Book ahead whenever possible and brace yourself for some high prices. B&Bs are a cheaper alternative to the fancier hotels, and most places offer two- and three-day packages. Note that the majority of lodgings in Bath and many in the Cotswolds require a two-night minimum stay on weekends and holidays; rates are often higher on weekends. Accommodation in Cheltenham and the Cotswolds is especially hard to find during the week of Cheltenham's National Hunt Festival in March.

There are numerous possibilities for renting a cottage in and around Bath and the Cotswolds, and accommodations are usually available by the week. Check out Manor Cottages or Jigsaw Holidays for a range of self-catering options. ⇨ *Hotel reviews have been shortened. For full information, visit Fodors.com.*

Contacts Jigsaw Holidays. ☎ *01993/849484* 🌐 *www.jigsawholidays.co.uk.* **Manor Cottages.** ☎ *01993/824252* 🌐 *www.manorcottages.co.uk.*

7

WHAT IT COSTS IN POUNDS

	$	$$	$$$	$$$$
Restaurants	under £15	£15–£19	£20–£25	over £25
Hotels	under £100	£100–£160	£161–£220	over £220

Restaurant prices are the average cost of a main course at dinner or, if dinner is not served, at lunch. Hotels prices are the lowest cost of a standard double room in high season, including 20% V.A.T.

VISITOR INFORMATION

The South West Tourism website has information about the entire region; the Cotswolds site is a government one that has a useful section on tourism. The major towns have Tourist Information Centres that provide advice and help with accommodations.

Contacts The Cotswolds. 🌐 *www.cotswolds.com.* **South West Tourism.** 🌐 *www.visitsouthwest.co.uk.*

BATH AND NEARBY

On the eastern edge of the county of Somerset, the city of Bath has strong links with the Cotswolds stretching north, the source of the wool that for centuries underpinned its economy. The stone mansions and cottages of that region are recalled in Bath's Georgian architecture

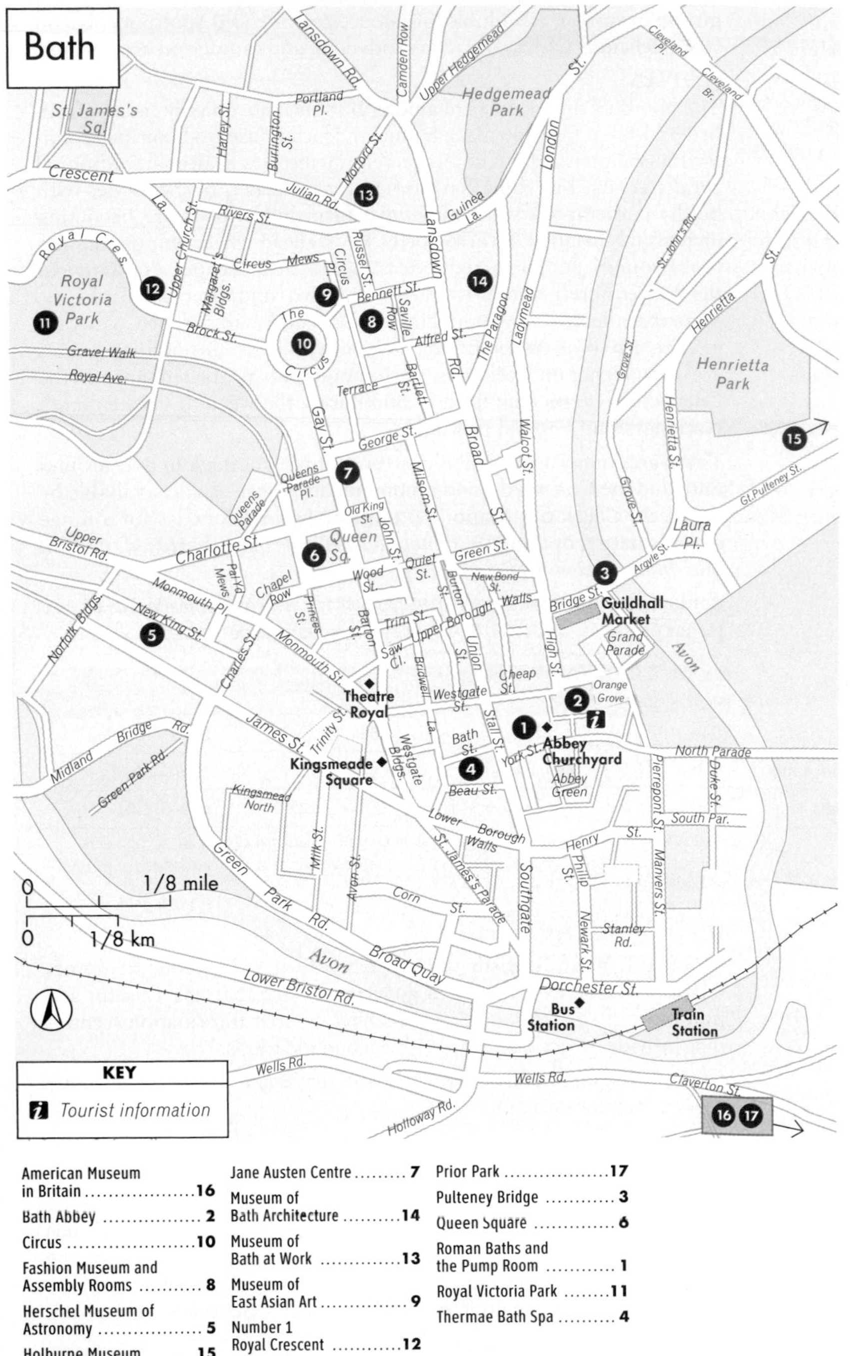

American Museum in Britain ... 16
Bath Abbey ... 2
Circus ... 10
Fashion Museum and Assembly Rooms ... 8
Herschel Museum of Astronomy ... 5
Holburne Museum ... 15
Jane Austen Centre ... 7
Museum of Bath Architecture ... 14
Museum of Bath at Work ... 13
Museum of East Asian Art ... 9
Number 1 Royal Crescent ... 12
Prior Park ... 17
Pulteney Bridge ... 3
Queen Square ... 6
Roman Baths and the Pump Room ... 1
Royal Victoria Park ... 11
Thermae Bath Spa ... 4

and in the mellow stone that it shares with two of the villages across the Wiltshire border, Lacock and Castle Combe.

BATH

13 miles southeast of Bristol, 115 miles west of London.

Fodor's Choice ★

"I really believe I shall always be talking of Bath. Oh! Who can ever be tired of Bath," enthuses Catherine Morland in Jane Austen's *Northanger Abbey,* and today plenty of people agree with these sentiments. In Bath, a UNESCO World Heritage Site, you're surrounded by magnificent 18th-century architecture, a lasting reminder of the vanished world described by Austen. In the 19th century the city lost its fashionable luster and slid into a refined gentility that still remains. Bath is no museum, though: it's lively, with good dining and shopping, excellent art galleries and museums, the remarkable excavated Roman baths, and theater, music, and other performances all year. Many people rush through Bath in a day, but there's enough to do to merit an overnight stay—or more. In summer, the sheer volume of sightseers may hamper your progress.

The Romans put Bath on the map in the 1st century when they built a temple here, in honor of the goddess Minerva, and a sophisticated network of baths to make full use of the mineral springs that gush from the earth at a constant temperature of 116°F (46.5°C). **■TIP→ Don't miss the remains of the baths, one of the city's glories.** Visits by Queen Anne in 1702 and 1703 brought attention to the town, and soon 18th-century "people of quality" took it to heart. Assembly rooms, theaters, and pleasure gardens were built to entertain the rich and titled when they weren't busy attending the parties of Beau Nash (the city's master of ceremonies and chief social organizer, who helped increase Bath's popularity) and having their portraits painted by Gainsborough.

7

GETTING HERE AND AROUND

Frequent trains from Paddington and National Express buses from Victoria connect Bath with London. The bus and train stations are close to each other south of the center. By car from London, take M4 to Exit 18, from which A46 leads 10 miles south to Bath.

Drivers should note that parking is extremely limited within the city, and any car illegally parked will be ticketed. Fees for towed cars can be hundreds of pounds. Public parking lots in the historic area fill up early, but the park-and-ride lots on the outskirts provide inexpensive shuttle service into the center, which is pleasant to stroll around.

TIMING

Schedule a visit to Bath during the week, as weekends see an influx of visitors. The city gets similarly crowded during its various festivals, though the added conviviality and cultural activity during these events are big draws in themselves.

TOURS

City Sightseeing. Fifty-minute guided tours of Bath are run by City Sightseeing on open-top buses year-round, leaving two to four times an hour from High Street, near the abbey. Tickets, valid for 24 hours, give

The remains of the Roman Baths evoke the days when the Romans gathered here to socialize and bathe.

discounts on entry to some of Bath's top attractions. ☎ *01225/444102* 🌐 *www.city-sightseeing.com* 🎫 *From £14.*

Mad Max Tours. During summer, Mad Max Tours runs full-day tours through the Cotswolds on Monday, Wednesday, and Saturday departing at 9 am and stopping at Tetbury, Bampton, Burford, Bibury and Arlington Row, as well as Castle Combe, Lacock, Avebury, and Stonehenge on Tuesday and Friday starting at 8:30 am. The departure point is the Best Western Hotel, North Parade, near Bath Abbey. ☎ *0799/050–5970* 🌐 *www.madmaxtours.co.uk* 🎫 *From £35.*

Mayor of Bath's Honorary Guides. Free two-hour walking tours of Bath are offered year-round by the Mayor of Bath's Honorary Guides. Individuals can just show up outside the main entrance to the Pump Room. Tours are Sunday through Friday at 10:30 and 2, Saturday at 10:30, and there's an additional tour at 7 pm Tuesday and Thursday from May to September. ☎ *01225/477411* 🌐 *www.bathguides.org.uk.*

ESSENTIALS

Visitor Information Bath Tourist Information Centre. ✉ *Abbey Chambers, Abbey Churchyard* ☎ *0844/847–5257, 0906/711–2000 calls cost 50p a minute* 🌐 *www.visitbath.co.uk.*

EXPLORING

TOP ATTRACTIONS

Bath Abbey. Dominating Bath's center, this 15th-century edifice of golden, glowing stone has a splendid west front, with carved figures of angels ascending ladders on either side. Notice, too, the miter, olive tree, and crown motif, a play on the name of the building's founder, Bishop

Oliver King. More than 50 stained-glass windows fill about 80% of the building's wall space, giving the interior an impression of lightness. The abbey was built in the Perpendicular (English late-Gothic) style on the site of a Saxon abbey, and the nave and side aisles contain superb fan-vaulted ceilings. Look for the 21st-century expressively carved angels on the choir screens. There are five services on Sunday, including choral evensong at 3:30. Forty-five-minute **tower tours**, allowing close-up views of the massive bells and panoramic cityscapes from the roof, take place daily except Sundays; the 212 dizzying steps demand a level of fitness. ✉ *Abbey Churchyard* ☎ *01225/422462* 🌐 *www.bathabbey.org* 🎫 *Abbey £2.50 suggested donation, tower tours £6* ⏲ *Abbey Mon. 9:30–5:30, Tues.–Fri. 9–5:30, Sat. 9–6, Sun. 1–2:30 and 4:30–5:30. Tower tours Mon.–Sat., hourly Jan.–Mar., 11–4; Apr.–Aug., 10–5; Sept. and Oct., 10–4; Nov. and Dec., 11–3.*

Circus. John Wood designed the masterful Circus, a circle of curving, perfectly proportioned Georgian houses interrupted just three times for intersecting streets. Wood died shortly after work began; his son, the younger John Wood, completed the project. Notice the carved acorns atop the houses: Wood nurtured the myth that Prince Bladud founded Bath, ostensibly with the help of an errant pig rooting for acorns (this is one of a number of variations of Bladud's story). A garden with large plane trees fills the center of the Circus. The painter Thomas Gainsborough (1727–88) lived at No. 17 from 1760 to 1774. ✉ *Intersection of Bennett, Brock, and Gay Sts.*

7

QUICK BITES

Bea's Vintage Tea Rooms. After surveying the Royal Crescent and the Circus, fast-forward into the 1940s with a visit to these charming tearooms. Breakfasts, light lunches, and afternoon teas are all served on vintage china and hand-embroidered tablecloths. Teapots come with egg timers for the correct length of brew. ✉ ***6–8 Saville Row*** ☎ ***01225/464552*** 🌐 ***www.beasvintagetearooms.com*** ⏲ ***No dinner.***

Fodor's Choice ★

Fashion Museum and Assembly Rooms. In its role as the **Assembly Rooms**, this neoclassical building was one of the leading centers for social life in 18th-century Bath. Jane Austen came here often, and it's in the Ballroom that Catherine Morland has her first, disappointing encounter with Bath's beau monde in *Northanger Abbey*; the Octagon Room is the setting for an important encounter between Anne Elliot and Captain Wentworth in *Persuasion*. Built by John Wood the Younger in 1771, the building was badly damaged by wartime bombing in 1942 but was faithfully restored. Its stunning chandeliers are the 18th-century originals. Throughout the year, classical concerts are given here, just as they were in bygone days. The Assembly Rooms are also known today for the entertaining **Fashion Museum**, displaying apparel from Jacobean times up to the present. You can see examples of what would have been worn in the heydays here, as well as glamorous frocks from the 20th century—a dress of the year is an annual addition. Besides admiring the changing exhibits, you can have fun trying on corsets and crinolines. An audio guide and daily guided tours at noon and 3:30 are included in the admission. ✉ *Bennett St.* ☎ *01225/477789* 🌐 *www.*

fashionmuseum.co.uk 🎫 *£2.50 for Assembly Rooms; £8.25 for Assembly Rooms and Fashion Museum; £18 combined ticket includes Roman Baths* ⏲ *Mar.–Oct., daily 10:30–6; Nov.–Feb., daily 10:30–5; last admission 1 hr before closing.*

JANE AUSTEN IN BATH

Though born and brought up in Hampshire, Jane Austen had close connections with Bath and lived here from 1801 to 1806. She wasn't overly fond of the place, peppering her letters with caustic comments about it (interspersed with gossip and effusions on bonnets and trimmings). Austen wrote her sister, Cassandra, that she left "with what happy feelings of escape." However, she is thought to have fallen in love here, and she received her only known offer of marriage while in Bath. Bath's eight-day Jane Austen Festival celebrates the writer in late September.

Fodor's Choice ★ **Holburne Museum.** One of Bath's gems, this elegant 18th-century building and its modern extension house a superb collection of 17th- and 18th-century decorative arts, ceramics, and silverware. Highlights include paintings by Gainsborough (*The Byam Family,* on indefinite loan) and George Stubbs (*Reverend Carter Thelwall and Family*), and a hilarious collection of caricatures of the Georgian city's fashionable elite. In its original incarnation as the Sydney Hotel, the house was one of the pivots of Bath's high society, which came to perambulate in the pleasure gardens (Sydney Gardens) that still lie behind it. One visitor was Jane Austen, whose main Bath residence was No. 4 Sydney Place, a brief stroll from the museum. There's an excellent café and tea garden on-site. ✉ *Great Pulteney St.* ☎ *01225/388569* 🌐 *www.holburne.org* 🎫 *Free; suggested donation £3* ⏲ *Mon.–Sat. 10–5, Sun. and national holiday Mon. 11–5.*

Jane Austen Centre. The one place in Bath that gives Austen any space provides a briefly diverting exhibition about the influence of Bath on her writings; *Northanger Abbey* and *Persuasion* are both set primarily in the city. The center is brought to life by characters in costume, and displays and a short film give a pictorial overview of life in Bath around 1800. Immerse yourself further by dressing up in costume; assistants are on hand to take your photo. The cozy Georgian house, a few doors up from where the writer lived in 1805 (one of several addresses she had in Bath), also includes the Austen-themed Regency Tea Rooms, open to the public. ✉ *40 Gay St.* ☎ *01225/443000* 🌐 *www.janeausten.co.uk* 🎫 *£9* ⏲ *Late Mar.–June, Sept., and Oct, daily 9:45–5:30; July and Aug., daily 9–6; Nov.–late Mar., Sun.–Fri. 11–4:30, Sat. 9:45–5:30.*

Fodor's Choice ★ **Number 1 Royal Crescent.** The majestic arc of the Royal Crescent, much used as a film location, is the crowning glory of Palladian architecture in Bath. The work of John Wood the Younger, these 30 houses fronted by 114 columns were laid out between 1767 and 1774. The first house to be built, on the corner of Brock Street and the Royal Crescent, was Number 1 Royal Crescent. The museum now crystallizes a view of the English class system in the 18th century—the status, wealth, and elegance of the upstairs in contrast with the extensive servants' quarters and kitchen downstairs. You can witness the predilections of the first resident, Henry Sandford, in the cabinet of curiosities and the electrical machine, as well as a Georgian love of display in the sumptuous dessert table arrangement in the dining room. Several varieties of historic mousetraps make their appearance downstairs. Everything is presented with elegant attention to authenticity and detail. ✉ *Royal Crescent* ☎ *01225/428126* 🌐 *no1royalcrescent.org.uk* 🎟 *£9; joint ticket with Museum of Bath Architecture £11.50* ⏲ *Feb.–mid-Dec., Mon. noon–5:30, Tues.–Sun. 10:30–5:30; last admission 1 hr before closing.*

Pulteney Bridge. Florence's Ponte Vecchio inspired this 18th-century span, one of the most famous landmarks in the city and the only work of Robert Adam in Bath. It's unique in Great Britain because shops line both sides of the bridge. ✉ *Between Bridge St. and Argyle St.*

Queen Square. Palatial houses and the Francis Hotel surround the garden in the center of this square designed by the older John Wood. An obelisk financed by Beau Nash celebrates the 1738 visit of Frederick, prince of Wales. ✉ *South end of Gay St.*

Fodor's Choice ★ **Roman Baths and the Pump Room.** The hot springs have drawn people here since prehistoric times, so it's quite appropriate to begin an exploration of Bath at this excellent museum on the site of the ancient city's primary "watering hole." Roman patricians would gather to immerse themselves, drink the mineral waters, and socialize. With the departure of the Romans, the baths fell into disuse. When bathing again became fashionable at the end of the 18th century, this magnificent Georgian building was erected.

Almost the entire Roman bath complex was excavated in the 19th century, and the museum displays relics that include a memorable mustachioed, Celtic-influenced Gorgon's head, fragments of colorful curses invoked by the Romans against their neighbors, and information about Roman bathing practices. The **Great Bath** is now roofless, and the statuary and pillars belong to the 19th century, but much remains from the original complex (the Roman characters strutting around, however, are 21st-century) and the steaming, somewhat murky waters are undeniably evocative. Free tours take place hourly, and you can visit after 6:30 pm in July and August to experience the baths lighted by torches. Wear sensible shoes as the ancient stones are uneven and can be slippery.

Adjacent to the Roman bath complex is the famed **Pump Room,** built in 1792–96, a rendezvous for members of 18th- and 19th-century Bath society. Here Catherine Morland and Mrs. Allen "paraded up and down for an hour, looking at everybody and speaking to no one," to quote from Jane Austen's *Northanger Abbey.* Today you can take in the elegant space—or you can simply, for a small fee, taste the fairly vile mineral water. Charles Dickens described it as tasting like warm flatirons. The tourist office offers a £66 package that includes a visit to the Roman Baths, a three-course lunch or champagne afternoon tea, and a two-hour Thermae Bath spa session. ✉ *Abbey Churchyard* ☎ *01225/477785* 🌐 *www.romanbaths.co.uk* 🎟 *Roman Baths £14 (£14.50 in July and Aug.); £18 combined ticket includes the Fashion Museum and Assembly Rooms* ⏲ *Mar.–June, Sept., and Oct., daily 9–6; July and Aug., daily 9 am–10 pm; Nov.–Feb., daily 9:30–5:30; last admission 1 hr before closing.*

Thermae Bath Spa. One of the few places in Britain where you can bathe in natural hot-spring water, and in an open-air rooftop location as well, this striking complex designed by Nicholas Grimshaw consists of a Bath-stone building surrounded by a glass curtain wall. The only difficulty is in deciding where to spend more time—in the sleekly luxurious, light-filled Minerva Bath, with its curves and gentle currents, or in the smaller, open-air rooftop pool for the unique sensation of bathing with views of Bath's operatic skyline (twilight is particularly atmospheric here). Two 18th-century thermal baths, the Cross Bath and the Hot Bath, are back in use too (the latter for treatments only). End your session in the crisp third-floor café and restaurant. ■ **TIP→ It's essential to book spa treatments ahead of time.** Towels, robes, and slippers are available for rent. Note that changing rooms are co-ed. Weekdays are the quietest time to visit. You must be 16 to bathe here and 18 to book a spa treatment. A separate, free **Visitor Centre** (April through October, Monday through Saturday 10–5, Sunday 11–4) opposite the entrance gives an overview of the project and provides audio guides (£2) for a brief tour of the exterior. ✉ *Hot Bath St.* ☎ *01225/331234* 🌐 *www.thermaebathspa.com* 🎫 *£32 for 2 hrs (£35 on Sat.) and £10 for each additional hour* ⏲ *Daily 9 am–9:30 pm; last admission at 7.*

WORTH NOTING

American Museum in Britain. A 19th-century Greek Revival mansion in a majestic setting on a hill 2½ miles southeast of the city holds the only museum of American decorative arts outside the United States. Rooms are furnished in historical styles, such as the 17th-century Conkey's Tavern, the beautifully elegant Greek Revival room, and the lavish, richly red New Orleans bedroom from the 1860s. Other galleries explore historical themes (the settlement of the West, the Civil War) or contain a large collecion of quilts, as well as porcelain and Shaker objects; a separate building is devoted to folk art, including a fine collection of decoy wildfowl. The parkland includes a reproduction of George Washington's garden at Mount Vernon. Take a bus headed to the University of Bath and get off at the Avenue where signs point to the museum, half a mile away. The City Sightseeing bus also drops off here. ✉ *Claverton Manor, off A36* ☎ *01225/460503* 🌐 *www.americanmuseum.org* 🎫 *£9* ⏲ *Mar.–July, Sept., and Oct., Tues.–Sun. and holiday Mon. noon–5; Aug., daily noon–5; late Nov.–mid-Dec., Tues.–Sun. noon–4:30; last admission 1 hr before closing.*

Herschel Museum of Astronomy. In the garden of this modest Bath town house, which he shared with his sister Caroline (an astronomer in her own right), William Herschel (1738–1822) identified the planet Uranus. He used a handmade telescope of his own devising and this small museum, devoted to his studies and discoveries, shows his telescopes, the workshop abutting the kitchen, where he cast his speculum metal mirrors, as well as orreries, caricatures, and musical instruments of his time (Herschel was the organist at Bath's Octagon Chapel). ✉ *19 New King St.* ☎ *01225/446865* 🌐 *www.herschelmuseum.org.uk* 🎫 *£6* ⏲ *Weekdays 1–5, weekends and holiday Mon. 11–5; last admission at 4:15.*

Museum of Bath Architecture. This absorbing museum in the Georgian Gothic-style Countess of Huntingdon's Chapel is an essential stop on any exploration of Bath, particularly for fans of Georgian architecture. It illustrates the evolution of the city, with examples of everything from window design and wrought-iron railings to marbling and other interior decoration, while an informative film puts what you see into context. ✉ *The Paragon* ☎ *01225/333895* 🌐 *www.museumofbatharchitecture.org.uk* 🎫 *£5.50; joint ticket with Number 1 Royal Crescent £11.50* 🕒 *Mid-Feb.–Nov., Tues.–Fri. 2–5, weekends 10.30–5; last admission 30 min before closing.*

Museum of Bath at Work. The core of this industrial-history collection, which gives a novel perspective on the city, is an engineering works and fizzy drinks factory. This building once belonged to Bath entrepreneur Jonathan Bowler, who started his many businesses in 1872. The collection includes the original clanking machinery and offers glimpses into Bath's stone industry and cabinetmaking. Look out for the Bath in Particular exhibition, an illuminating collection chosen by locals. ✉ *Julian Rd.* ☎ *01225/318348* 🌐 *www.bath-at-work.org.uk* 🎫 *£5 including audioguide* 🕒 *Apr.–Oct., daily 10:30–5; Nov. and Jan.–Mar., weekends 10:30–5; last admission at 4.*

Museum of East Asian Art. Intimate galleries on three floors display ancient and modern pieces, mostly from China but with other exhibits from Japan, Korea, and Southeast Asia. Highlights are the Chinese jade figures, especially the animals, both mythical and real, Buddhist objects, and Japanese lacquerware and prints. Don't miss the charming *netsuke* (toggles) and *inro* (seal cases) on the staircase to the lower ground floor. ✉ *12 Bennett St.* ☎ *01225/464640* 🌐 *www.meaa.org.uk* 🎫 *£3* 🕒 *Tues.–Sat. 10–5, Sun. noon–5; last admission at 4:30.*

Prior Park. A vision to warm Jane Austen's heart, Bath's grandest house lies a mile or so southeast of the center, with splendid views over the Georgian townscape. Built around 1738 by John Wood the Elder of honey-color limestone, the Palladian mansion was the home of quarry owner and philanthropist Ralph Allen (1693–1764), whose guests included such luminaries as poet Alexander Pope and novelists Henry Fielding and Samuel Richardson. Today it's a school and the interior is not open to the public, but you may wander through the beautiful grounds, designed by Capability Brown and embellished with a Palladian bridge and lake. A leisurely circuit of the park should take around an hour. ■ **TIP→ The parking here is reserved for people with disabilities, so take a taxi or bus from the center. The City Sightseeing bus also calls here.** ✉ *Ralph Allen Dr.* ☎ *01225/833422* 🌐 *www.nationaltrust.org.uk* 🎫 *£6.20* 🕒 *Feb.–Oct., daily 10–5:30; Nov.–Jan., weekends 10–4; last admission 1 hr before closing.*

FAMILY **Royal Victoria Park.** Originally designed as an arboretum, this tidy expanse of lawns and shady walks just west of the Royal Crescent provides the perfect setting for pleasant strolls and leisurely picnics. The park has a pond, a **Botanic Garden,** and an adventure playground with plenty for kids. Hot-air balloon launches and open-air shows at festival time enliven the atmosphere. ✉ *Upper Bristol Rd.* 🎫 *Free* 🕒 *Daily 24 hrs.*

7

CLOSE UP

Bath's Georgian Architecture

Bath wouldn't be Bath without its distinctive 18th-century Georgian architecture, much of which was conceived by John Wood the Elder (1704–54), an antiquarian and architect. Wood saw Bath as a city destined for almost mythic greatness. Arriving in Bath in 1727, he sought a suitable architectural style, and found it in the Palladian style, made popular in Britain by Inigo Jones.

ELEMENTS OF STYLE

Derived from the Italian architect Andrea Palladio (1508–80), who in turn was inspired by ancient Roman architecture, Palladianism accentuated symmetry and proportion. The plain facades of buildings, dignified with columns, pilasters, and pediments over doors and windows, often contrasted with rich interiors. The Building of Bath Collection has more information.

BUILDINGS TO SEE

Wood created a harmonious city, building graceful terraces (row houses), crescents (curving rows of houses), and villas of the same golden local limestone used by the Romans. Influenced by nearby ancient stone circles as well as round Roman temples, Wood broke from convention in his design for Bath's Circus, a circle of houses broken only three times for intersecting streets.

After the death of Wood the Elder, John Wood the Younger (1728–82) carried out his father's plans for the Royal Crescent, a regal crescent of 30 houses. Today you can stop in at Number 1 Royal Crescent for a look at one of these homes—it's like eavesdropping on the 18th century. He also built the Assembly Rooms, which are open to the public.

WHERE TO EAT

$ MODERN BRITISH **Bathwick Boatman.** Set right on the river, a five-minute stroll from the Holburne Museum, this former rowing club house still contains boats—elegant antique skiffs suspended from the ceiling—but also delivers on food. On warm summer nights enjoy sitting on the veranda by candlelight (in winter tucked up with a throw) and enjoy crispy whitebait, goat curry with mango chutney, or beef bourguignonne , topped off with bread-and-butter pudding and brandy ice cream. If you come during the day, you could work up an appetite by taking out a skiff or canoe from the next-door boat station. *Average main: £13* *Forester Rd.* *01225/428844* *www.bathwickboatman.com* *Closed Mon.* *No credit cards.*

$ MODERN BRITISH **Boston Tea Party.** Sit in this bustling café and watch the comings and goings of the Bath square outside and take your pick from the all-day menu. Choose the sourdough eggy bread with smoked bacon and avocado, perhaps, or a croque monsieur (toasted cheese-and-ham sandwich), with a wide range of teas, coffees, and smoothies. Closing time is 7 pm. *Average main: £7* *19 Kingsmead Sq.* *01225/313901* *www.bostonteaparty.co.uk* *No credit cards.*

$$ FRENCH **Casanis.** Dappled sunlight on the stripped wood floor, small tables covered with white linens, and Provençal antiques and bottles of pastis make this place seem like a chic corner of France. Chef Laurent

Couvreur puts his stamp on the beautifully presented and amiably served classic dishes, including blue cheese and leek tart with walnut and Parmesan dressing, quail with a braised lentil ragout, and pear and vanilla crumble with salted caramel ice cream. Round off your meal with a selection of tasty cheeses. The £18 two-course lunch menu is a steal. *Average main: £19* *4 Saville Row* *01225/780055* *www.casanis.co.uk* *No credit cards* *Closed Sun. and Jan.*

$$ MODERN BRITISH **Circus Cafe and Restaurant.** You could linger all day in this sophisticated eatery on the corner of the Circus. There's always a good crowd for morning coffee, elevenses (brunch), afternoon tea, and cocktails, not to mention lunch and dinner, all of which are dispensed with efficient cordiality. If you can take your attention off the crumpets with Marmite, the spinach and nutmeg soup, or the breast of duck served on sweet potatoes with sloe gin sauce, you can discuss the colorful modern art on the walls. Desserts include cardamom rice pudding with honey and cumin-glazed figs. Ingredients are locally sourced and wines come from small growers. *Average main: £18* *34 Brock St.* *01225/466020* *www.thecircuscafeandrestaurant.co.uk* *No credit cards* *Closed Sun.*

$ INDIAN **Eastern Eye.** Delicious Indian dishes are the main draw, but the three magnificent glass domes of the large Georgian interior and the arresting South Asian murals, mean that a meal here becomes an event. Specialties of the house include *mughlai* chicken (flavored with egg, ginger, and garlic and fried in a sauce of yogurt, coconut, and poppy seeds) and salmon *bhaja* (pan-fried with Bengali spices and served with diced potatoes). All the classic dishes are on the capacious menu and are easy on the wallet. *Average main: £13* *8a Quiet St.* *01225/422323* *www.easterneye.com* *No credit cards.*

$ ITALIAN **Jamie's Italian.** Part of a chain owned by celebrity chef Jamie Oliver, this buzzing brasserie is a cheerful counterpoint to Bath's predominantly sedate tone. The dining areas, spread over two floors and including a rooftop terrace, have a contemporary, slightly industrial feel. Expect dishes typical of Oliver's straightforward Italian rustic style, such as bruschetta, crispy polenta chips, or lamb chops grilled under a brick. Desserts include ice creams with a variety of toppings. It can get busy, but you can take advantage of the all-day service by coming during off-peak hours. *Average main: £14* *10 Milsom Pl.* *01225/432340* *www.jamieoliver.com* *No credit cards.*

$ ECLECTIC **Jazz Café.** Squeeze past the gentlemen deep in their papers and trendy mothers to nab a table in this cozy and amiable café. Famous for its all-day breakfasts, the café is also a good spot for a quick lunch, with soups, salads, sandwiches, and fine appetizers. Daily specials might include spicy beef chili, a tart of the day, or lamb pita sandwich. Get here early, as the place closes at 5 pm (4 on Sunday). *Average main: £8* *Kingsmead Sq.* *01225/329002* *www.bathjazzcafe.co.uk* *No credit cards* *No dinner.*

$$$$ MODERN BRITISH **Menu Gordon Jones.** It's worth stepping away from the center of town to sample the ingenious flights of gastronomic fancy that chef Gordon Jones conjures up in his tiny open kitchen. There is no set menu, but each course is carefully explained before it's served; there might be smoked

eel with maple syrup and purple potatoes, a crisp haggis, roasted turbot with giant raisins and caper dressing, and blackberry sorbet with marinated cucumber. You can choose a wine flight to accompany the tasting menus (five-course lunch £40, six-course dinner £50). The location is unprepossessing and the decor plain, enlivened by a few antlers and phials of oil, but the service is friendly and unstuffy; if you want to talk with the chef about your snail caviar, he will willingly do so. Book well in advance; lunch is easier to reserve than dinner. *Average main: £50* *2 Wellsway* *01225/480871* *www.menugordonjones.co.uk* *No credit cards* *Closed Mon.* *Reservations essential.*

$$ MODERN BRITISH **The Pig Near Bath.** The latest outpost of the growing Pig empire is an excellent funky but chic "restaurant with rooms" in a converted country house set in a deer park in the bucolic Mendip Hills. As in the New Forest original, the "25 Mile Menu" is all about the local and seasonal (and the porcine); kale, rocket, and other leaves and veggies are sourced from the Pig's kitchen garden; apples, pears, and apricots come from its orchard; and pork, chicken, quail, and venison are provided by animals raised on the property. Salmon, pancetta, and bacon are smoked on-site. The results are exceptionally fresh and flavorsome dishes like loin of home-reared venison or "Kentucky-fried" wild rabbit. Dining alfresco in summer, when the wood-fired oven gets going, is a delight. The 29 comfortable and reasonably priced rooms (from £149) are decorated with an elegant simplicity and have glorious views. It's located about 8 miles from Bath, off the A368. *Average main: £16* *Hunstrete House, Pensford* *01761/49049* *www.thepighotel.com* *No credit cards.*

$ BRITISH **Pump Room.** The 18th-century Pump Room, with views over the Roman Baths, serves morning coffee, lunches, and afternoon tea, to music by a pianist or string trio who play every day. The stately setting is the selling point rather than the food, but do sample the West Country cheese board and the homemade cakes and pastries. Light or full lunches are on offer, and the place is usually open for dinners in July, August, and December and during the major festivals (reservations are essential). Be prepared to wait in line for a table during the day. *Average main: £14* *Abbey Churchyard* *01225/444477* *www.romanbaths.co.uk* *No credit cards* *No dinner Jan.–June and Sept.–Nov.*

$$ ITALIAN **Rustico.** Favorite places to sit in this traditional and cozy corner of Cotswold Italy are among the scatter of cushions in the window or, on a sunny day, outside on the pavement. The welcoming staff gladly serves you, as the name might imply, with good old-fashioned country fare—homemade pastas like grandma used to make, lashings of seafood casserole, handsome steaks, and pork in sage and white wine sauce, for instance. Leave room for the light and fluffy tiramisu. *Average main: £15* *2 Margaret's Bldgs., Cheltenham* *01225/310064* *www.rusticobistroitaliano.co.uk* *No credit cards* *Closed Mon.*

$ BRITISH **Sally Lunn's.** Small and slightly twee, this tourist magnet near Bath Abbey occupies the oldest house in Bath, dating to 1482. It's famous for the Sally Lunn bun, a semisweet bread served here since 1680. You can choose from more than 30 sweet and savory toppings to accompany your bun, or turn it into a meal with salmon or a steak. There are also economical lunch and early-evening menus. Daytime diners can view the small kitchen museum in the cellar (30p for non-dining visitors). *Average main: £12 4 N. Parade Passage 01225/461634 www.sallylunns.co.uk No credit cards.*

$$ FRENCH **Tilleys Bistro.** This intimate, bow-windowed French eatery presents alluring meat, vegan, and vegetarian dishes offered in small, medium, and large portions. Choices include medallions of pork *à la dijonnaise* (fried tenderloin and mushrooms in a brandy, cream, and mustard sauce), roasted *aubergine à la Tunisienne* (eggplant cooked with chickpeas, dates, and apricots), and a selection of meats from a Bristol charcuterie. Pre-theater meals are available weekdays between 6 and 7 pm. *Average main: £16 3 N. Parade Passage 01225/484200 www.tilleysbistro.co.uk No credit cards No lunch Sun.*

WHERE TO STAY

$ B&B/INN **Albany Guest House.** Homey and friendly, this Edwardian house close to the Royal Crescent has simply furnished rooms decorated with neutral shades of beige and cream. **Pros:** spotless rooms; convenient location; excellent breakfasts. **Cons:** some rooms are very small; limited parking. *Rooms from: £85 24 Crescent Gardens 01225/313339 www.albanybath.co.uk No credit cards 6 rooms Breakfast.*

$$ B&B/INN **Bath Paradise House.** Don't be put off by the 10-minute uphill walk from the center of Bath—you'll be rewarded by a wonderful view of the city from the lovely garden and upper stories of this Georgian guesthouse. **Pros:** great attention to detail; spectacular views from some rooms. **Cons:** uphill walk; books up far in advance. *Rooms from: £130 88 Holloway 01225/317723 www.paradise-house.co.uk No credit cards 12 rooms Breakfast.*

$ B&B/INN **Cranleigh.** On a quiet hilltop above the city center, this Victorian guesthouse has wonderful views of the Avon Valley. **Pros:** quiet rooms; period furnishings; many choices at breakfast; free parking. **Cons:** far from center; along a busy road; steps to climb. *Rooms from: £80 159 Newbridge Hill 01225/310197 cranleighbath.com No credit cards 9 rooms Breakfast.*

$$ HOTEL **Dukes Hotel.** True Georgian grandeur is evident in the refurbished rooms of this Palladian-style mansion–turned–elegant small hotel, which comes with one of the best addresses in Bath. **Pros:** excellent central location; free parking; friendly and helpful service. **Cons:** some rooms are small; steps to climb. *Rooms from: £120 53–54 Great Pulteney St., entrance on Edward St. 01225/787960 www.dukesbath.co.uk No credit cards 11 rooms, 6 suites Breakfast.*

$$ HOTEL **Halcyon Apartments.** For those who like more privacy and to fend for themselves, these spacious and chic, contemporary apartments fit the bill; breakfast is included in the rate. **Pros:** central location; good for those who are independent; parking. **Cons:** not for those who like to be waited on; advance notice of check-in needed; plenty of stairs. *Rooms from: £138 15a George St. 01225/585100 www.thehalcyon.com 7 apartments Breakfast No credit cards.*

$$ HOTEL **Harington's Hotel.** It's rare to find a compact hotel in the cobblestone heart of Bath, and this informal three-story lodging converted

7

from a group of Georgian town houses fits the bill nicely. **Pros:** good breakfasts; helpful staff. **Cons:** occasional street noise from revelers; steps to climb; many small rooms. *Rooms from: £140* ✉ *Queen St.* ☎ *01225/461728* 🌐 *www.haringtonshotel.co.uk* *No credit cards* *13 rooms* *Breakfast.*

$$ B&B/INN **Marlborough House.** A warm, informal welcome greets all who stay at this Victorian establishment not too far from the Royal Crescent, where each room charms with period furniture, fresh flowers, and antique beds. **Pros:** obliging and helpful hosts; immaculate rooms; parking available. **Cons:** walk to the center is along a busy road; minimum two-night stay at weekends. *Rooms from: £145* ✉ *1 Marlborough La.* ☎ *01225/318175* 🌐 *www.marlborough-house.net* *No credit cards* *6 rooms* *Breakfast.*

$$ HOTEL **Queensberry Hotel.** Intimate and elegant, this boutique hotel in a residential street near the Circus occupies three 1772 town houses built by John Wood the Younger for the marquis of Queensberry; it's a perfect marriage of chic sophistication, homey comforts, and attentive service. **Pros:** efficient service; tranquil ambience; valet parking. **Cons:** occasional street noise; no tea/coffee-making facilities in rooms. *Rooms from: £160* ✉ *7 Russel St.* ☎ *01225/447928* 🌐 *www.thequeensberry.co.uk* *No credit cards* *26 rooms, 3 suites* *Breakfast.*

$$$$ HOTEL **The Royal Cescent.** You can't get a more prestigious address in Bath than the Royal Crescent, and this hotel, discreetly plumb center, overlooks parkland and the town. **Pros:** historic building; total comfort; great location. **Cons:** most bedrooms are very modern in feel; some rooms have no views. *Rooms from: £300* ✉ *16 Royal Crescent* ☎ *01225/823333* 🌐 *www.royalcrescent.co.uk* *No credit cards* *27 rooms, 18 suites* *Breakfast.*

$$ B&B/INN **Three Abbey Green.** Just steps from Bath Abbey, a gorgeous square dominated by a majestic plane tree is home to this welcoming B&B. **Pros:** superb location; airy rooms. **Cons:** some noise from pub-goers; only two suites have bathtubs; no parking. *Rooms from: £120* ✉ *3 Abbey Green* ☎ *01225/428558* 🌐 *www.threeabbeygreen.com* *No credit cards* *8 rooms, 2 suites* *Breakfast.*

NIGHTLIFE AND PERFORMING ARTS

FESTIVALS

Bath Comedy Festival. Running for 10 days, April's Bath Comedy Festival features comedy events at venues throughout the city. ✉ *Bath Box Office, Abbey Chambers, Abbey Courtyard* ☎ *01225/463362* 🌐 *www.bathcomedy.com.*

Fodor's Choice ★ **Bath International Music Festival.** Held over 12 days in May and June, the Bath International Music Festival presents classical, jazz, and world-music concerts, dance performances, and exhibitions in and around Bath, many in the Assembly Rooms and Bath Abbey. ✉ *Bath Box Office, Abbey Chambers, Abbey Churchyard* ☎ *01225/463362* 🌐 *www.bathfestivals.org.uk.*

Bath Literature Festival. The 10-day Bath Literature Festival in early March features readings and talks by writers, mostly in the 18th-century

Guildhall on High Street. ✉ *Bath Box Office, Abbey Chambers, Abbey Churchyard* ☎ *01225/463362* 🌐 *www.bathfestivals.org.uk.*

Jane Austen Festival. Celebrating the great writer with films, plays, walks, and talks over nine days in mid-September, the Jane Austen Festival is a feast for Janeites. ✉ *Bath* ☎ *01225/443000* 🌐 *www.janeaustenfestival bath.co.uk.*

NIGHTLIFE

The Bell. Owned by a co-op, and a favorite among locals, the Bell has live music—jazz, blues, and folk—on Monday, Wednesday, and Sunday, as well as a selection of real ales, good food, computer access, and even self-service laundry. ✉ *103 Walcot St.* ☎ *01225/460426.*

Circo. The buzzing cellar bar whips up a sassy cocktail or glass of champagne in its dark and moody vaults, with music to match. There are quieter spaces, too, and a nice selection of canapés and sharing plates. ✉ *2–3 South Parade* ☎ *01225/444100.*

Raven. Pub aficionados will relish the friendly, unspoiled ambience of the Raven, a great spot for a pie and a pint. There are regular arts, science, and storytelling nights upstairs. ✉ *Queen St.* ☎ *01225/425045* 🌐 *www.theravenofbath.co.uk.*

PERFORMING ARTS

Theatre Royal. A gemlike Regency playhouse from 1805, the Theatre Royal has a year-round program that often includes pre- or post-London tours. You must reserve the best seats well in advance, but you can line up for same-day standby seats or standing room. **■ TIP→ Take care with your seat location—sight lines can be poor.** ✉ *Box Office, Saw Close* ☎ *01225/448844* 🌐 *www.theatreroyal.org.uk.*

SHOPPING

Bartlett Street Antiques Centre. This place has more than 60 showcases and stands selling every kind of antique imaginable, including silver, porcelain, and jewelry. ✉ *Bartlett St.* 🌐 *www.bartlettstreetantiques centre.com.*

Bath Christmas Market. For 18 days in late November and early December, the outdoor Bath Christmas Market sells gift items—from handcrafted toys to candles, cards, and edible delights—in 170 chalet-style stalls concentrated in the area just south of the Abbey. ✉ *York St.* ☎ *0844/847–5257* 🌐 *www.bathchristmasmarket.co.uk.*

Bath Sweet Shop. The city's oldest candy store, Bath Sweet Shop boasts of stocking some 350 different varieties, including traditional licorice torpedoes, pear drops, and aniseed balls. Sugar-free treats are available. ✉ *8 N. Parade Passage* ☎ *01225/428040.*

Beaux Arts Ceramics. This shop, close by the Abbey, carries the work of prominent potters, sculptors, painters, and printmakers. ✉ *12–13 York St.* ☎ *01225/464850* 🌐 *www.beauxartsbath.co.uk.*

Guildhall Market. The covered Guildhall Market, open Monday through Saturday 9–5, is the place for everything from jewelry and gifts to delicatessen food, secondhand books, bags, and batteries. There's a café, too. ✉ *Entrances on High St. and Grand Parade* 🌐 *www.bathguildhall market.co.uk.*

7

The charm of tiny Castle Combe, with its one main street of stone cottages, far exceeds its size.

SPORTS AND THE OUTDOORS

Bath Boating Station. To explore the River Avon by rented skiff, punt, or canoe, head for the Bath Boating Station, behind the Holburne Museum. It's open April to September. ✉ *Forester Rd.* ☎ *01225/312900* 🌐 *www.bathboating.co.uk*.

CASTLE COMBE

12 miles northeast of Bath, 5 miles northwest of Chippenham.

Fodor's Choice ★ This Wiltshire village lived a sleepy existence until 1962, when it was voted the "prettiest village" in England—without any of its inhabitants knowing that it had even been a contender. The village's magic is that it's so toylike, so delightfully all-of-a-piece: you can see almost the whole town at one glance from any one position. Castle Combe consists of little more than a brook, a pack bridge, a street (which is called the Street) of simple stone cottages, a market cross from the 13th century, and the Perpendicular-style church of St. Andrew. The grandest house in the village (on its outskirts) is the Upper Manor House, which was built in the 15th century by Sir John Fastolf and is now the Manor House Hotel. If you're coming by car, use the village car park at the top of the hill and walk down.

GETTING HERE AND AROUND

Regular buses and trains go to Chippenham, where you can pick up a bus for Castle Combe, but it's easier to drive or join a tour.

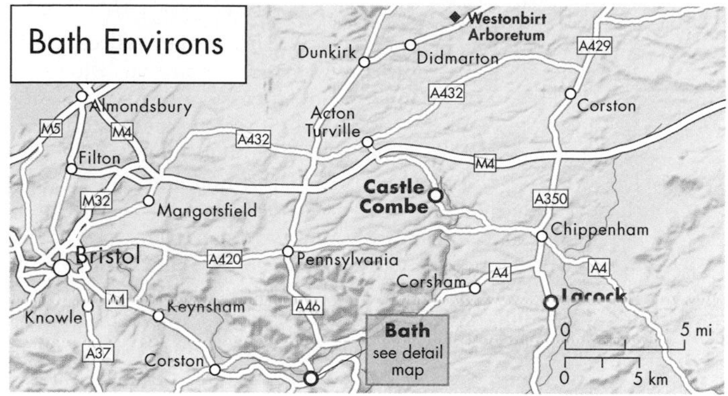

WHERE TO STAY

$$$$ HOTEL **Lucknam Park Hotel & Spa.** As you drive up Lucknam Park's mile-long avenue of lime and beech trees towards the 18th century Palladian mansion, you may feel like you've bagged an invitation to stay with Jane Austen's demanding dragon, Lady Catherine de Burgh. **Pros:** attentive service; country estate setting; well-equipped spa. **Cons:** pricey; some rooms on the small side; a little off the beaten track. *Rooms from: £325 Colerne, Chippenham 01225/742777 www.lucknampark.co.uk No credit cards 31 rooms, 11 suites Breakfast.*

$$$$ HOTEL Fodor's Choice ★ **Manor House Hotel.** Secluded in a 23-acre park on the edge of the village, this partly 14th-century manor house has guest rooms—some in mews cottages—that brim with antique character. **Pros:** romantic getaway; rich historical setting; good golf course. **Cons:** some rooms outside of main house; not for those who dislike sound of constant running water; very manicured flower beds. *Rooms from: £240 Castle Combe 01249/782206 www.manorhouse.co.uk No credit cards 48 rooms Breakfast.*

LACOCK

8 miles southeast of Castle Combe, 12 miles east of Bath.

Fodor's Choice ★ Owned by the National Trust, this lovely Wiltshire village is the victim of its own charm, its unspoiled gabled and stone-tile cottages drawing tour buses aplenty. Off-season, however, Lacock slips back into its profound slumber, the mellow stone and brick buildings little changed in 500 years and well worth a wander. Besides Lacock Abbey, there's the handsome church of St. Cyriac (built with money earned in the wool trade), a 14th-century tithe barn, and, in the village, a few antiques shops and a scattering of pubs that serve bar meals in atmospheric surroundings.

GETTING HERE AND AROUND

All buses from Bath to Lacock involve a change and take 60 to 110 minutes, so it's best to drive or join a tour.

7

EXPLORING

Lacock Abbey. Well-preserved Lacock Abbey reflects the fate of many religious establishments in England—a spiritual center became a home. The abbey, at the town's center, was founded in the 13th century and closed down during the dissolution of the monasteries in 1539, when its new owner, Sir William Sharington, demolished the church and converted the cloisters, sacristy, chapter house, and monastic quarters into a private dwelling. The house passed to the Talbot family, the most notable descendant of whom was William Henry Fox Talbot (1800–77), who developed the world's first photographic negative. You can see the oriel window, the subject of this photograph in the upper rooms of the abbey, along with a rare 16th-century purpose-built strong room in the octagonal tower. Look for the sugar lump on the goat's nose in the Great Hall. The last descendant, Matilda Talbot, donated the property as well as Lacock itself to the National Trust in the 1940s. The abbey's grounds and Victorian woodland are also worth a wander. Harry Potter fans, take note: Lacock Abbey was used for some scenes at Hogwarts School in the film *Harry Potter and the Sorcerer's Stone.*

The **Fox Talbot Museum,** in a 16th-century barn at the gates of Lacock Abbey, commemorates the work of Fox Talbot as well as other pioneers and contemporary artists in this field. ✉ *High St.* ☎ *01249/730459* 🌐 *www.nationaltrust.org.uk* 🎫 *£11.60; excluding Abbey rooms £9.40* 🕒 *Abbey rooms mid-Feb.–Oct., daily 11–5; early Nov.–mid. Dec., weekends noon–4. Cloister, museum, and grounds mid-Feb.–Oct., daily 10:30–5:30; Nov.–mid-Feb., daily 11–4. Last admission 45 min before closing.*

WHERE TO EAT

$$ BRITISH

✕ **Sign of the Angel.** Creak open the heavy door, be greeted by the hearty fire in the huge chimney beast and you could be forgiven thinking that you stepped back a few centuries. Some food, such as roast loin of beef with Yorkshire pudding, roast pork with apple fritters, or the seasonal pie of the day is as traditional as this inn which has been here since the 15th century, but modern touches—orange butter sauce, for instance, adds an extra dimension. It's the perfect spot for a cream tea, and upstairs are five beautifully rustic rooms in which to stay. [$] *Average main: £17* ✉ *6 Church St.* ☎ *01249/730230* 🌐 *www.signoftheangel.co.uk* 🕒 *Closed Mon.*

THE COTSWOLDS

A gently undulating area of limestone uplands, the Cotswolds are among England's best-preserved rural districts, and the quiet but lovely grays and ambers of the stone buildings here are truly unsurpassed. Much has been written about the area's age-mellowed towns, but the architecture of the villages actually differs little from that of villages elsewhere in England. Their distinction lies in their surroundings: the valleys are lush and rolling, and cozy hamlets appear covered in foliage from church tower to garden gate. Beyond the town limits, you can explore, on foot or by car, the "high wild hills and rough uneven ways" that Shakespeare wrote about.

Over the centuries, quarries of honey-color stone have yielded building blocks for many Cotswold houses and churches and have transformed little towns into realms of gold. Make Chipping Campden, Moreton-in-Marsh, or Stow-on-the-Wold your headquarters and wander for a few days. Then ask yourself what the area is all about. Its secret seems shared by two things—sheep and stone. These were once the great sheep-rearing areas of England, and during the peak of prosperity in the Middle Ages, Cotswold wool was in demand the world over. This made the local merchants rich, but many gave back to the Cotswolds by restoring old churches (the famous "wool churches" of the region) or building rows of limestone almshouses now seasoned to a glorious golden-gray. These days the wool merchants have gone but the wealth remains—the region includes some of the most exclusive real estate in the country.

One possible route is to begin with Cheltenham—the largest town in the area and a gateway to the Cotswolds, but slightly outside the boundaries and more of a small city in atmosphere—then move on to the beauty spots in and around Winchcombe. Next are Sudeley Castle, Stanway House, and Snowshill Manor, among the most impressive houses of the region; the oversold village of Broadway; Chipping Campden—the Cotswold cognoscenti's favorite; and Hidcote Manor, one of the most spectacular gardens in England. Then circle back south, down through Moreton-in-Marsh, Stow-on-the-Wold, Upper Slaughter, Lower Slaughter, and Bourton-on-the-Water, and end with Bibury and Tetbury. This is definitely a region where it pays to go off the beaten track to take a look at that village among the trees.

CHELTENHAM

50 miles north of Bath, 13 miles east of Gloucester, 99 miles west of London.

Although Cheltenham has acquired a reputation as snooty—the population (around 110,000) is generally well-heeled and conservative—it's also cosmopolitan. The town has excellent restaurants and bars, fashionable stores, and a thriving cultural life. Its primary claim to renown, however, is its architecture, rivaling Bath's in its Georgian elegance, with wide, tree-lined streets, crescents, and terraces with row houses, balconies, and iron railings.

Like Bath, Cheltenham owes part of its fame to mineral springs. By 1740 the first spa was built, and after a visit from George III and Queen Charlotte in 1788, the town dedicated itself to idleness and enjoyment. "A polka, parson-worshipping place"—in the words of resident Lord Tennyson—Cheltenham gained its reputation for snobbishness when stiff-collared Raj majordomos returned from India to find that the springs—the only purely natural alkaline waters in England—were the most effective cure for their "tropical ailments."

Great Regency architectural set pieces—Lansdown Crescent, Pittville Spa, and the Lower Assembly Rooms, among them—were built solely to adorn the town. The Rotunda building (1826) at the top of Montpellier Walk—now a bank—contains the spa's original "pump room," in which the mineral waters were on tap. More than 30 statues adorn the storefronts of Montpellier Walk. Wander past Imperial Square, with its ironwork balconies, past the ornate Neptune's Fountain, and along the Promenade. In spring and summer lush flower gardens enhance the town's buildings, attracting many visitors.

GETTING HERE AND AROUND

Trains from London Paddington and buses from London Victoria head to Cheltenham. The train station is west of the center, and the bus station is centrally located off Royal Well Road. Drivers should leave their vehicles in one of the numerous parking lots. The town center is easily negotiable on foot. Cheltenham's tourist office arranges walking tours (£5) of the town at 11 on Saturday from April until mid-November.

TOURS

The Wilson Tourist Information Centre. The center arranges walking tours of the town at 11 on Saturday from April through October and on Sundays in July and August. ✉ *Cheltenham Art Gallery and Museum, Clarence St.* ☎ *01242/237431* 🌐 *www.visitcheltenham.com* 🎫 *From £5.*

EXPLORING

Pittville Pump Room. The grandest of the remaining spa buildings, the pump room is set amid parkland, a 20-minute walk from the town center. The classic Regency structure, built in the late 1820s, now serves mainly as a concert hall and a theatrical venue but still offers its musty mineral waters to the strong of stomach. It's wise to check before visiting as there's often a function taking place. ✉ *E. Approach Dr., Pittville* ☎ *0844/576–2210* 🌐 *www.cheltenhamtownhall.org.uk* 🎫 *Free* 🕘 *Daily 10–4.*

Fodor's Choice ★

The Wilson, Cheltenham Art Gallery and Museum. Reenovated in 2013, this museum and art gallery shows off its treasures with aplomb. From the 1880s onward, Cheltenham was at the forefront of the Arts and Crafts movement and this is still demonstrated by the fine displays of William Morris textiles, furniture by Charles Voysey, and wood and metal pieces by Ernest Gimson. Decorative arts, such as Chinese ceramics, are also well represented, and British artists, including Stanley Spencer, Vanessa Bell, and Jake and Dinos Chapman, make their mark. The Summerfield Galleries demonstrate life through the ages in easily digestible chunks. Exhibits on Cheltenham's history complete the picture; one is devoted to Edward Wilson, who traveled with Robert Scott to the Antarctic on Scott's ill-fated 1912 expedition. ✉ *Clarence St.* ☎ *01242/237431* 🌐 *www.thewilson.org.uk* 🎫 *Free* 🕘 *Daily 9:30–5:15.*

OFF THE BEATEN PATH

Fodor's Choice ★

Gloucester Cathedral. In the center of Gloucester, magnificent Gloucester Cathedral, with its soaring, elegant exterior, was originally a Norman abbey church, consecrated in 1100. Reflecting different periods, the cathedral mirrors perfectly the slow growth of ecclesiastical taste and the development of the Perpendicular style. The interior has largely been spared the sterilizing attentions of modern architects and is almost completely Norman, with the massive pillars of the nave left untouched since their completion. The fan-vaulted roof of the 14th-century cloisters is the finest in Europe, and the cloisters enclose a peaceful garden (used in the filming of *Harry Potter and the Sorcerer's Stone*).

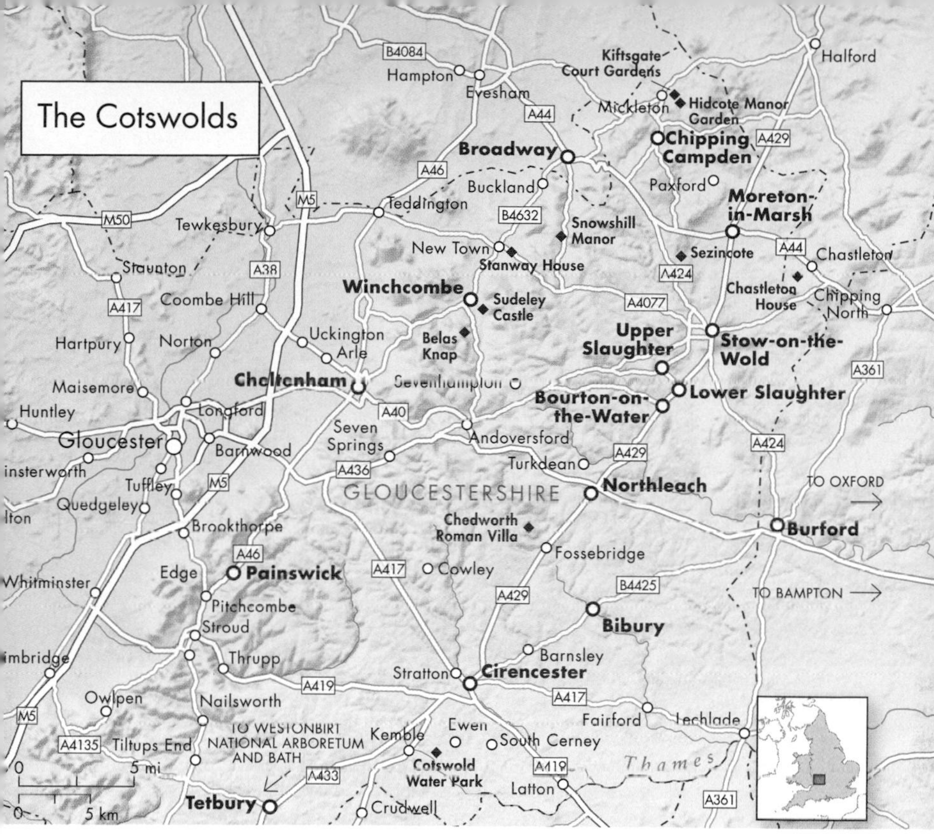

■TIP→ Don't miss the Whispering Gallery, which has a permanent exhibition devoted to the splendid, 14th-century stained glass of the Great East Window. Tours of the tower (269 steps up) are available, as are guided tours. Gloucester is 13 miles southwest of Cheltenham and reachable from there on frequent buses and trains. ✉ *Westgate St.* ☎ *01452/528095* 🌐 *www.gloucestercathedral.org.uk* 🎫 *£5 requested donation, photography permit £3, tower tours £4, Whispering Gallery £2* ⏲ *Daily 7:30–6, except during services. Tower tours Apr.–Oct., Wed.–Fri. 2:30, Sat. 1:30 and 2:30, national holidays 11:30, 1:30, and 2:30; also Mon. and Tues. at 2:30 during school vacations. Whispering Gallery Apr.–Oct., weekdays 10:30–4, Sat. 10:30–3:30.*

WHERE TO EAT

$$ BISTRO ✕ **Bistrot Coco.** Stone steps lead down to this intimate basement bistro where red lamps fringed with tassels, a wood-burning stove, and a little bar with a ceiling papered with French icons like the Eiffel Tower are the backdrop for classic French dishes. The menu changes frequently; there could be fresh asparagus, ham hock terrine, a warm goat's cheese salad, or navarin of lamb, which you can accompany with a glass or two from the carefully selected wine list. There's a sheltered courtyard for warm days and a two-course lunch for £10. 💲 *Average main: £15* ✉ *30 Cambray Pl.* ☎ *01242/534000* ▬ *No credit cards* ⏲ *Closed Sun.*

A tour of Gloucester Cathedral provides a visual lesson in architectural styles from Norman through Perpendicular Gothic.

$$ MODERN BRITISH ✕ **The Daffodil.** This restaurant proves that turning up the wow quotient doesn't always mean a drop in culinary standards. Housed in a former art deco cinema, the place is themed along 1920s lines. It's dimly lit, with sweeping staircases and an open kitchen where the screen once stood; the best view is from the Circle Bar where you can also sip cocktails. The menu features twice-baked Double Gloucester soufflé, calves liver with mustard mash, and curry spiced chicken breast. Afterward, indulge in a popcorn panna cotta, or a platter of cheeses with walnut bread. Tasting dishes for two are also available, and early-evening and lunch menus are a good deal. There's live jazz on Monday evening and during lunchtime on Saturday. *Average main: £17* ✉ *18–20 Suffolk Parade* ☎ *01242/700055* 🌐 *www.thedaffodil.com* ⏲ *Closed Sun.* ✍ *Reservations essential.*

$$ MODERN BRITISH ✕ **Purslane.** Daughters treating their mothers, ladies who shop, and gentlemen cutting a dash all come here, lured by the imaginative and well-presented menu and cool, unfussy surroundings. The freshest of Cornish fish, Salcombe Bay crab, and Forest of Dean ham are accompanied by unusual, but delicious vegetables like borage, wild garlic, and sea cabbage. The accent is on fish, but you will also find hay-baked Cotswold lamb, vegetarian dishes, and plenty of local cheeses. Service is friendly and knowledgeable. *Average main: £16* ✉ *16 Rodney Rd.* ☎ *01242/321639* 🌐 *www.purslane-restaurant.co.uk* ▭ *No credit cards* ⏲ *Closed Sun. and Mon.*

$ CAFÉ ✕ **Well Walk Tea Room.** Squeeze past all the antiques and knickknacks in this pretty bow-fronted shop and tearoom for a soup, pasta, or sandwich lunch, or treat yourself to an afternoon tea with crumpets and cakes. Along with traditional English Breakfast and Earl Grey, you can sample nettle and sweet fennel, jasmine, green, and white tea. In summer ask for a refeshing homemade lemonade. *Average main: £3* *5–6 Well Walk* *01242/574546* *www.wellwalktearoom.co.uk* *No credit cards* *Closed Mon. No dinner.*

WHERE TO STAY

$ B&B/INN **The Bradley.** The thoughtful and hospitable owners take great pride in this town house, near the center, that has been in the same family for more than 100 years. **Pros:** good value; attentive hosts; well-designed rooms. **Cons:** lots of stairs to top rooms; no private parking. *Rooms from: £88* *19 Bayshill Rd.* *01242/519077* *www.thebradleyhotel.co.uk* *No credit cards* *5 rooms, 1 suite* *Breakfast.*

$$$$ HOTEL **Cowley Manor.** Good-bye, floral prints: this Georgian mansion on 55 acres brings country-house style into the 21st century with a mellow atmosphere and modern fabrics and furnishings. **Pros:** beautiful grounds; excellent spa facilities; relaxed vibe. **Cons:** slightly corporate feel; spa is set away from the main house. *Rooms from: £245* *Off A435, Cowley* *01242/870900* *www.cowleymanor.com* *No credit cards* *30 rooms* *Breakfast.*

$$ B&B/INN **Hanover House.** Centrally located, this family-run guesthouse dating from 1848 brims with character, and richly colored cushions, flowers, a decanter of sherry, and myriad books enliven the bright and airy rooms. **Pros:** fun; convenient location; award-winning breakfasts. **Cons:** not for those who wish to remain anonymous; all guests share one large table at breakfast. *Rooms from: £110* *65 St. George's Rd.* *01242/541297* *www.hanoverhouse.org* *No credit cards* *3 rooms* *Breakfast.*

NIGHTLIFE AND PERFORMING ARTS

Cheltenham Jazz Festival. Held over a week in late April and early May, the Cheltenham Jazz Festival presents noted musicians from around the world. *Cheltenham* *0844/880–8094 box office* *www.cheltenhamfestivals.com.*

Everyman Theatre. The late-Victorian Everyman Theatre is an intimate venue for opera, dance, concerts, and plays. **TIP→ You can often catch pre- or post-West End productions here, at a fraction of big-city prices.** *Regent St.* *01242/572573* *www.everymantheatre.org.uk.*

Festivals Box Office. For information on the town's ambitious lineup of festivals, contact the Festivals Box Office. *15 Suffolk Parade* *0844/880–8094 box office* *www.cheltenhamfestivals.com.*

Fodor's Choice ★ **Literature Festival.** The 10-day Literature Festival in October brings together world-renowned authors, actors, and critics for hundreds of readings, lectures, and other events. *Cheltenham* *0844/880–8094 box office* *www.cheltenhamfestivals.com.*

Music Festival. Cheltenham's famous Music Festival, held over 10 days in early July, highlights new compositions, often conducted by the composers themselves, plus a wide variety of choral and instrumental classical pieces. *Cheltenham* *0844/880–8094 box office* *www.cheltenhamfestivals.com.*

Science Festival. For five days in early June, the Science Festival attracts leading scientists and writers. ✉ *Cheltenham* ☎ *0844/880–8094 tickets* 🌐 *www.cheltenhamfestivals.com.*

SHOPPING

This is serious shopping territory. A stroll along Montpellier Walk and then along the flower-bedecked Promenade brings you to high-end specialty stores and boutiques. A bubble-blowing Wishing Fish Clock, designed by Kit Williams, dominates the Regent Arcade, a modern shopping area behind the Promenade. A farmers' market enlivens the Promenade on the second and last Friday of the month.

Cavendish House. The town's oldest department store, now run by House of Fraser, stocks designer fashions. ✉ *32–48 The Promenade* ☎ *01242/521300.*

Feva. Eye-catching women's clothing in bright, splashy colors, as well as accessories like shoes, belts, and handbags, are on display at Feva. More-formal wear is sold on the upper floor. ✉ *20 Regent St.* ☎ *01242/222998.*

Martin. This shop carries a good stock of classic and modern jewelry. ✉ *19 The Promenade* ☎ *01242/522821.*

Q and C Militaria. A treasure trove for military buffs, Q and C Militaria offers badges and medals, breastplates, helmets, coats of arms, and books. It's run by ex-soldiers. ✉ *22 Suffolk Rd.* ☎ *01242/519815.*

SPORTS AND THE OUTDOORS

Cheltenham Racecourse. Important steeplechase races take place at Cheltenham Racecourse, north of the town center. The Gold Cup awards crown the last day of the National Hunt Festival in mid-March. ✉ *Prestbury Park* ☎ *0844/579–3003 ticket line, 01242/513014 tickets and inquiries* 🌐 *cheltenham.thejockeyclub.co.uk.*

WINCHCOMBE

7 miles northeast of Cheltenham.

Fodor's Choice ★ The sleepy, unspoiled village of Winchcombe (population 4,500), once the capital of the Anglo-Saxon kingdom of Mercia, has some attractive half-timber and stone houses, as well as a clutch of appealing old inns serving food. A good place to escape the crowds, it's near Sudeley Castle and is also on several walking routes: the Cotswold Way; the Warden's Way and Windrush Way, both linking Winchcombe with Bourton-on-the-Water; and the Winchcombe Way, a 42-mile figure-eight trail around the northern Cotswolds. A three-day walking festival (🌐 *www.winchcombewelcomeswalkers.com*) takes place here in mid-May.

GETTING HERE AND AROUND

Hourly Marchant's buses take 20 minutes to get to Winchcombe from Cheltenham (no Sunday service). By car, take B4632, leading over the steep and panoramic Cleeve Hill.

ESSENTIALS

Visitor Information Winchcombe Tourist Information Centre. ✉ *Town Hall, High St.* ☎ *01242/602925* 🌐 *www.winchcombe.co.uk.*

EXPLORING

Belas Knap Long Barrow. A bracing 2-mile walk south of Winchcombe on the Cotswold Way, one of Britain's national walking trails, leads to the hilltop site of Belas Knap, a Neolithic long barrow, or submerged burial chamber, above Humblebee Wood. ■ **TIP→ The site isn't much to see, but you hike through one of the most enchanting natural domains in England, with views stretching over to Sudeley Castle.** ✉ *Winchcombe* ☎ *0870/333–1181* 🌐 *www.english-heritage.org.uk/daysout/properties/belas-knap-long-barrow.*

FAMILY **Gloucestershire and Warwickshire Railway.** Less than a mile north of Winchcombe at Greet, this steam-hauled train chugs its way along the foot of the Cotswolds connecting Winchcombe with Toddington and Cheltenham Racecourse. From Cheltenham the round-trip is 25 miles, but you can take a shorter trip from Winchcombe to Toddington. ✉ *Winchcombe Station, Greet Rd., Greet* ☎ *01242/621405* 🌐 *www.gwsr.com* 🎫 *£12 return to Ceheltenham, £10 to Toddington* ⏲ *June–Sept., Tues.–Thurs. and weekends 10–5; Apr., May, and Oct., Tues., Wed., and weekends 10–5; Mar. and Dec., weekends 10–5.*

St. Peter's Church. Almost 40 outlandish gargoyles adorn this mid-15th-century Perpendicular-style building, a typical Cotswold wool church full of light. The interior displays an embroidered altar frontal said to have been worked by Catherine of Aragon, first wife of King Henry VIII. Look for the Winchcombe Imp, an unusual figure for a rood screen, now at the back of the church. ✉ *Gloucester St.* ☎ *01242/602067.*

7

Sudeley Castle. One of the grand showpieces of the Cotswolds, Sudeley Castle was the home and burial place of Catherine Parr (1512–48), Henry VIII's sixth and last wife, who outlived him by one year. Here Catherine undertook, in her later years, the education of the ill-fated Lady Jane Grey and the future queen, Princess Elizabeth. Sudeley, for good reason, has been called a woman's castle. The term "castle" is misleading, though, for it looks more like a Tudor-era palace, with a peaceful air that belies its turbulent history. In the 17th century Charles I took refuge here, causing Oliver Cromwell's army to besiege the castle. It remained in ruins until the Dent-Brocklehurst family stepped in with a 19th-century renovation.

The 14 acres of gardens, which include the roses of the Queen's Garden (best seen in June) and a Tudor knot garden, are the setting for Tudor fun days in summer. Inside the castle, visitors see the West Wing, with the Long Room where exhibitions illustrate the castle's history, and the East Wing which contains the private apartments of Lord and Lady Ashcombe, where you can see paintings by Van Dyck, Rubens, Turner, and Reynolds. Rare and exotically colored birds strut in the pheasantry. The 11 cottages and apartments on the grounds are booked for a minimum of three-night stays. The castle is a mile southeast of Winchcombe. ✉ *Off B4632* ☎ *01242/602308, 01242/609481 cottages* 🌐 *www.sudeleycastle.co.uk* 🎫 *£14* ⏲ *Mid-Mar.–Oct., daily 10–5.*

As enchanting as the house, the gardens at Sudeley Castle provide a perfect spot for summer meanderings.

WHERE TO EAT

$$ MODERN BRITISH

✕ **Wesley House.** Wooden beams and stone walls distinguish this 15th-century half-timber building, where the elegant dining room and sunny conservatory make a fine backdrop for superior Modern British dishes. The seasonal menu might include braised chicory tart as a starter, and roast Cotswold lamb with smoked eggplant compote to follow. Fixed-price lunch and evening menus are a good value. You can eat and drink less formally in the adjoining snug or bar and grill, where sharing platters of cheeses, cured meats, or fish lets you sample a bit of everything. Upstairs, five small guest rooms have twisted beams and sloping ceilings, including the Preacher's Room, where John Wesley used to stay. *Average main: £18 ✉ High St. ☎ 01242/602366 🌐 www.wesleyhouse.co.uk ▭ No credit cards ⏲ No dinner Sun. and Mon.*

BROADWAY

8 miles north of Winchcombe, 17 miles northeast of Cheltenham.

The Cotswold town to end all Cotswold towns, Broadway has become a favorite of day-trippers. William Morris first discovered the delights of this village, and J. M. Barrie, Vaughan Williams, and Edward Elgar soon followed. Today you may want to avoid Broadway in summer, when it's clogged with cars and buses. Named for its handsome, wide main street (well worth a stroll), the village includes numerous antiques shops, tea parlors, and boutiques. Step into Broadway's back-roads and alleys and you can discover any number of honey-color houses and colorful gardens.

GETTING HERE AND AROUND

Broadway can be reached by car via A44; park in one of the parking lots signposted from the main street. Johnson's Coaches connects the town with Stratford-upon-Avon, Chipping Campden, and Moreton-in-Marsh; Marchants connects Broadway with Winchcombe and Cheltenham. No buses run on Sunday. You'll need a car to reach Broadway Tower, Stanway House, and Snowshill Manor.

ESSENTIALS

Visitor Information Broadway Tourist Information Centre. ✉ *Russell Sq.* ☎ *01386/852937* 🌐 *www.beautifulbroadway.com.*

EXPLORING

Broadway Tower Country Park. Among the attractions of this park on the outskirts of town is its crenelated tower, an 18th-century "folly" built by the sixth earl of Coventry and later used by William Morris as a retreat. The panoramic view from the top takes in three counties and looks over peaceful countryside and wandering deer. There are plenty of nature trails and good spots for picnics, as well as a café. Wall panels on the three floors inside describe the tower's connection with the local Arts and Crafts movement and World War II. Note that the spiral staircase is narrow and steep. A nuclear bunker is open on weekends during the summer. ✉ *Off A44* ☎ *01386/852390* 🌐 *www.broadwaytower.co.uk* 🎫 *Park free, tower £4.80, bunker £3.50* ⏲ *Daily 10–5, or dusk in winter.*

7

FAMILY
Fodor's Choice ★

Snowshill Manor. Three miles south of Broadway and 13 miles northeast of Cheltenham, Snowshill is one of the most unspoiled of all Cotswold villages. Snuggled beneath Oat Hill, with little room for expansion, the hamlet is centered on an old burial ground, the 19th-century St. Barnabas Church, and Snowshill Manor, a splendid 17th-century house that brims with the collections of Charles Paget Wade, gathered between 1919 and 1956. Over the door of the house is Wade's family motto, *Nequid pereat* ("Let nothing perish"). The rooms are bursting with Tibetan scrolls, spinners' tools, ship models, Persian lamps, and bric-a-brac; the Green Room displays 26 suits of Japanese samurai armor. Children love the place. Outside, an imaginative terraced garden provides an exquisite frame for the house. ■ **TIP→ Admission is by timed tickets issued on a first-come, first-served basis, so arrive early in peak season.** ✉ *Off A44, Snowshill* ☎ *01386/852410* 🌐 *www.nationaltrust.org.uk* 🎫 *£10.20; garden only £5.50* ⏲ *House Apr.–June, Sept.–Oct., Wed.–Sun. and holiday Mon. noon–5; July and Aug., Wed.–Mon. 11:30–4:30; Nov., weekends 10:30–3:30. Garden Apr.–June and Sept.–Oct., Wed.–Sun. and holiday Mon. 11–5:30; July and Aug., Wed.–Mon. 11–5; Nov., weekends 10:30–3:30. Last admission 1 hr before closing.*

Stanway House. This perfect Cotswold manor of glowing limestone, Stanway House dates from the Jacobean era. Its triple-gabled gatehouse is a Cotswold landmark, and towering windows dominate the house's Great Hall. They illuminate a 22-foot-long shuffleboard table from 1620 and an 18th-century bouncing exercise machine. The other well-worn rooms are adorned with family portraits, tattered tapestries, vintage armchairs, and, at times, Lord or Lady Neidpath themselves, the current owners. The partly restored baroque water garden has a modern fountain that shoots up 300 feet. The tallest in Britain, it shoots at 2:45 and 4. To get to Stanway, about 5 miles south of Broadway, take B4632 south from town, turning left at B4077. ✉ *Off B4077, Stanway* ☎ *01386/584469* 🌐 *www.stanwayfountain.co.uk* *House and fountain £7; fountain only, £4.50* ⏲ *Jun.–Aug., Tues. and Thurs. 2–5.*

WHERE TO EAT

$$$ MODERN BRITISH ✕ **Russell's.** With a courtyard at the back and a patio at the front, this chic "restaurant with rooms" is perfect for a light lunch at midday or a full meal in the evening. The restaurant, in a former furniture factory belonging to local designer George Russell, is modern, airy, and stylish. Menus concentrate on Modern British dishes, with such temptations as pressed pig's head terrine, Bibury trout, and a calorific dessert of Battenburg cake, donut, and profiterole topped with chocolate and cream. The less expensive fixed-price menu is just as tempting, and there's also an attached fish-and-chip shop. Seven boutique-style rooms upstairs are very sleek. $ *Average main: £21* ✉ *20 High St.* ☎ *01386/853555* 🌐 *www.russellsofbroadway.co.uk* ▭ *No credit cards* ⏲ *No dinner Sun.*

$ MODERN BRITISH FAMILY ✕ **The Swan.** In the center of Broadway, this pub-restaurant makes a handy stop for a snack, lunch, drink, or something more substantial. Service may be occasionally slapdash and the place can get congested, but on a weekday it's cozy and convivial, with an open fire in winter and comfortable seating. The imaginative decor blends the traditional and trendy with large mirrors, log-studded walls, and eye-catching knickknacks. Among the hot dishes you're likely to find slow-cooked corned salt-beef hash or sticky crispy duck salad; tapots (small British tapas-style dishes) and tasting platters are a popular alternative. There's a good wine cellar and plenty of cask ales, as well as a childrens' menu. $ *Average main: £13* ✉ *2 The Green* ☎ *01386/852278* 🌐 *www.theswanbroadway.co.uk* ▭ *No credit cards.*

WHERE TO STAY

$$$$ HOTEL **Buckland Manor.** As an alternative to the hustle and bustle of Broadway, you can travel the 2 miles to the idyllic hamlet of Buckland and splurge at this exceptional country house, which has more of a feel of a genteel family home than a hotel. **Pros:** beautiful setting; elegant guest rooms; large bathrooms with high-quality toiletries. **Cons:** some rooms are small; restaurant quite formal; steep prices. $ *Rooms from: £270* ✉ *Off B4632, Buckland* ☎ *01386/852626* 🌐 *www.bucklandmanor.co.uk* ▭ *No credit cards* *15 rooms* 🍽 *Breakfast.*

$$$$ HOTEL **Dormy House Hotel.** Luxury rules at this converted 17th-century farmhouse overlooking the Vale of Evesham from high on the Cotswolds ridge. **Pros:** unstuffy service; good food; great views. **Cons:** steep prices; isolated; can get very busy. $ *Rooms from: £230* ✉ *Willersey Hill* ☎ *01386/852711* 🌐 *www.dormyhouse.co.uk* ▭ *No credit cards* *34 rooms, 6 suites* 🍽 *Breakfast.*

$$$ B&B/INN **Mill Hay House.** If the rose garden, trout-filled pond, and sheep on the hill at this 18th-century Queen Anne house aren't appealing enough, then the stone-flagged floors, leather sofas, and grandfather clocks should satisfy. **Pros:** delightful owners; beautifully landscaped gardens; gourmet breakfasts. **Cons:** books up quickly; no young children admitted.

Rooms from: £185 ✉ *Snowshill Rd.* ☎ *01386/852498* 🌐 *www.millhay.co.uk* ▭ *No credit cards* *2 rooms, 1 suite* *Breakfast.*

$ B&B/INN **Old Station House.** With its acre of lawns and gardens, this former stationmaster's home, now a bed-and-breakfast, makes a peaceful refuge from the tourist traffic of Broadway, a 10-minute walk away. **Pros:** thoughtful and welcoming hosts; peaceful location; Wi-Fi. **Cons:** outside the village; lacks old-world ambience; not good for young families. *Rooms from: £95* ✉ *Station Rd.* ☎ *01386/852659* 🌐 *www.broadwaybedandbreakfast.com* ▭ *No credit cards* *5 rooms* *Breakfast.*

$$ B&B/INN **The Olive Branch.** Right on the main drag, this 16th-century cottage has authentic period charm and is strewn with antique knickknacks: a brass wind-up gramophone has a place of pride. **Pros:** cottage character; central location; hospitable hosts. **Cons:** small bathrooms; narrow stairs; low ceilings. *Rooms from: £105* ✉ *78 High St.* ☎ *01386/853440* 🌐 *www.theolivebranch-broadway.com* ▭ *No credit cards* *8 rooms* *Breakfast.*

CHIPPING CAMPDEN

4 miles east of Broadway, 18 miles northeast of Cheltenham.

Fodor's Choice ★ Undoubtedly one of the most beautiful towns in the area, Chipping Campden, with its population of about 2,500, is the Cotswolds in a microcosm. It has St. James, the region's most impressive church; frozen-in-time streets; a silk mill that was once the center of the Guild of Handicraft; and pleasant, untouristy shops. One of the area's most seductive settings unfolds before you as you travel on B4081 through sublime English countryside and happen upon the town, tucked in a slight valley. North of town is lovely Hidcote Manor Garden. **TIP→ Chipping Campden can easily be reached on foot along a level section of the Cotswold Way from Broadway Tower, outside Broadway; the walk takes about 75 minutes.**

GETTING HERE AND AROUND

By car, Chipping Campden can be reached on minor roads from A44 or A429. There's a small car park in the center and spaces on the outskirts of the village. By bus, take Johnson's Coaches from Stratford-upon-Avon, Broadway, and Moreton-in-Marsh, or Pulham's Coaches from Bourton-on-the-Water and Cheltenham, changing at Moreton-in-Marsh (no Sunday service).

ESSENTIALS

Visitor Information Chipping Campden Tourism Information Centre. ✉ *The Old Police Station, High St.* ☎ *01386/841206* 🌐 *www.chippingcampdenonline.org.*

EXPLORING

TOP ATTRACTIONS

Fodor's Choice ★ **Hidcote Manor Garden.** Laid out around a Cotswold manor house, Hidcote Manor Garden is arguably the most interesting and attractive large garden in Britain. Crowds are large at the height of the season, but it's worthwhile anytime. A horticulturist from the United States,

Continued on page 463

GLORIOUS ENGLISH GARDENS

by Kate Hughes

The English have been masters of the garden for centuries; gardening is in the blood. No one, from the owner of vast acres in the country to a town dweller with a modest window box, is able to resist this pull. Since the 18th century they have also been inveterate garden visitors, with people from around the world following in their wake. Here's how to make the most of your garden visit, from the variety of styles you'll see to the best bets for all tastes around England.

Magnificent vista of the Palladian bridge and lake at Stourhead gardens.

For many people the quintessential English garden conjures up swaths of close-clipped lawns (the landscape garden), beds of roses, or colorful flowers (the herbaceous border) lining a path to a cottage door framed with honeysuckle.

This is not the whole story, however. Cathedrals and colleges yield up their sequestered cloister gardens; grand houses their patterned beds of flowers by the thousand; manor houses their amusing topiary shapes, orchards, and wildflower meadows; sweeping landscaped parks their classical temples and serpentine lakes; a Cornish ravine its jungle tumbling down to the sea. And this is not to mention the magnificent glasshouses and biomes of the botanical gardens housing spectacular plant treasures. Around the country, gardens large and small invite exploration.

GARDEN STYLES THROUGH THE AGES

In the gardens you'll be visiting, one theme remains constant no matter the style: the combination of usefulness and beauty. Gardens were larders as well as ornaments; plants were grown and birds and animals kept both for decoration and for eating. Behind each great garden was wealth, and gardens became as great a status symbol as the houses they surrounded. Growing the best pineapple, building the most elaborate terraces, flooding a valley to make a lake were all signs that you had made it in the world.

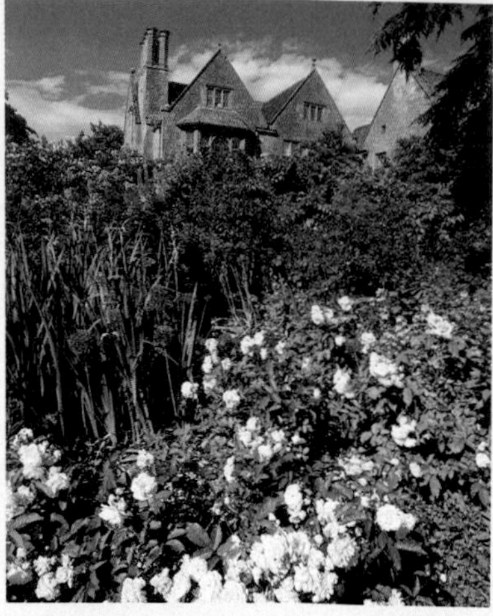

Clockwise from top left: Stowe Landscape Gardens; Chatsworth; Hidcote Manor Garden; Hampton Court Palace (formal Privy Garden)

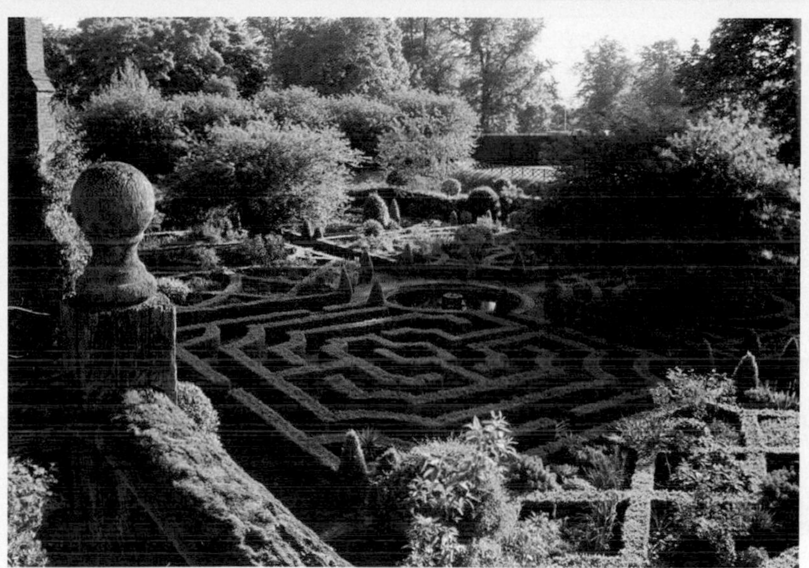

SYMBOLS AND PATTERNS: TUDOR GARDENS

Since Tudor times the rose has been the emblem of England, and it still is the most loved English flower. Musk roses entwine the arbors in the garden created to impress Queen Elizabeth I on her visit to Kenilworth Castle in 1575, now magnificently restored. Here the formal arrangement of trellises, obelisks, fountain, statues, and aviary set in gravel paths and overlooked by a viewing platform exemplify gardens of the time. Also here is the first uniquely English garden feature—the knot garden. Low evergreen hedges, most famously planted with box, were interlaced in geometric patterns, the spaces filled with flowers and herbs. Good examples of knot gardens can be found at Hampton Court Palace and Hatfield House.

WEALTH AND POWER: THE 17TH-CENTURY FORMAL GARDEN

Landed gentry with time on their hands took gardening to their hearts. After the ravages of the Civil War (1642–49) and the Great Fire of London (1666) they felt the lure of the rural idyll, and country houses with small estates proliferated. The garden rectangle in front of the house was divided into smaller rectangles—the forerunner of garden "rooms" as at Sissinghurst and Hidcote Manor—and filled with formal walkways, fishponds, and fountains. Topiary gardens (Levens Hall and Packwood House) became popular, and an increase in foreign travel led to the introduction of a greater variety of bulbs and flowers. In 1621 the first botanic garden was set up in Oxford.

Knot garden at Hatfield House

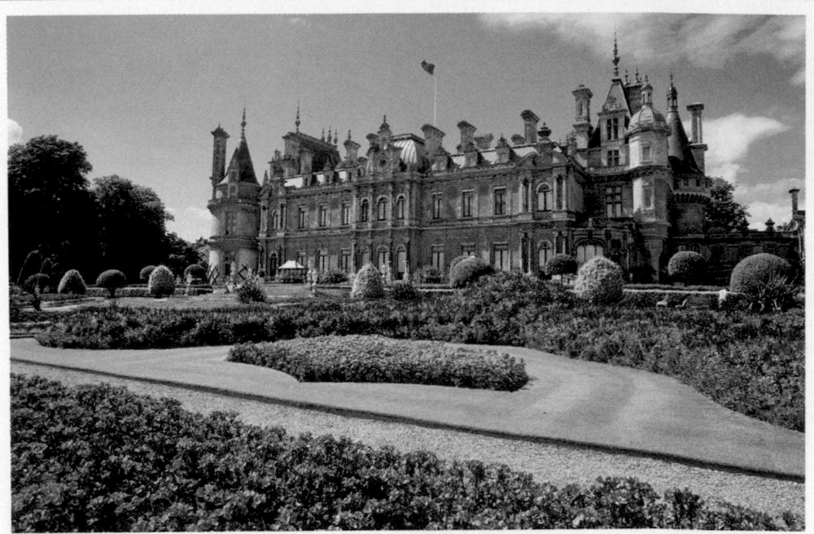

GEOMETRY TO LANDSCAPE: THE 18TH CENTURY

Gradually the formal approach gave way. One product of the fashionable Grand Tour, when aristocratic young bloods were exposed to new landscapes and ideas, was William Kent (1685–1748), the "father of modern gardening." His innovative genius was his English take on the Italian garden, converting the natural landscape into a pleasure ground for the rich, dotting it with statues, obelisks, and classical temples and ornamenting it with trees and serpentine lakes (Rousham and Stowe).

Kent was eclipsed by Lancelot "Capability" Brown (1715–83), who created 100 gardens between 1750 and 1780 (Stowe, Stourhead, Petworth, Kew Gardens). He brought the landscape right to the front door and created lakes and parkland that also provided timber, cover for game, and grazing for sheep and deer.

SHOW AND TECHNOLOGY: THE VICTORIAN PERIOD

This was an age of new technology, variety, and the return of flowers. Wealthy industrialists could afford to move out of town and create rose gardens, ferneries, and rockeries, and display showier flowers such as chrysanthemums, dahlias, and rhododendrons. The invention of the lawn mower in 1830 made the English obsession with close-clipped lawns accessible to all. Bedding schemes and patterns reappeared in the new public parks of the 1830s and 1840s. One spectacular scheme is the parterre (ornamental flower garden with paths) at Waddesdon Manor, planted with lavish displays each spring and summer. Joseph Paxton (1803–1865) head gardener at Chatwsorth, created the first greenhouse, which started a fashion for conservatories and the growing of exotic fruit such as figs and peaches.

The parterre at Waddesdon Manor

ARTS AND CRAFTS: INTO THE 20TH CENTURY

The Arts and Crafts movement drew inspiration from medieval romance and nature and preferred the informal cottage garden look, seen particularly in the Cotswolds (Hidcote Manor, Kiftsgate, Rodmarton Manor). Female gardeners came to the fore. Gertrude Jekyll (pronounced Jee-kill; 1843–1932), often working with the architect Edwin Lutyens (1869–1944), set the fashion for using drifts of single color, and Vita Sackville West (1892–1962) created the enduringly romantic Sissinghurst.

ANYTHING GOES: MODERN TIMES

The reaction to the drab years of the Second World War was to create garden cities and increasingly versatile gardens using all modern materials available. The bold approach and strong colors of Christopher Lloyd (1921–2006) at Great Dixter has remained influential. Environmental awareness has led to more educational gardens, such as the spectacular Eden Project in Cornwall.

Overview of part of Sissinghurst (top); house and garden at Great Dixter (bottom)

BEST IN SHOW AROUND THE COUNTRY

Rousham Park

Practically every house or stately home you visit will be surrounded by a lovingly tended garden, but you will find a profusion of outstanding examples in the Cotswolds (Oxfordshire and Gloucestershire), Kent, and Cornwall. Kent is known as the "Garden of England" for its abundance of orchards and hop gardens; Cornwall's mild climate produces lush gardens, many by the sea; and the mellow honey-colored stone of the Cotswolds makes a perfect backdrop for floral ornament.

FLOWER GARDENS

The first three gardens, created in the 20th century, come top of the garden-visiting league. All show flair for harmonious planting in choice of color, form, and texture within a strong framework. Here flowers hold court.

1 **Hidcote Manor Garden** (Bath and the Cotswolds). The pioneer of "garden rooms" and influential ever since, this garden blends the scent of old roses, long avenues with vistas, and the famous Red Border, especially vibrant from July.

2 **Sissinghurst** (Southeast). Inspired by Hidcote Manor, it's divided into themed spaces: the Purple Border, the Rose Garden, the Cottage Garden, and, most famously, the White Garden.

3 **Great Dixter** (Southeast). Vibrant color combinations surround the delightful 16th-century, half-timbered manor house, also open. The Exotic Garden is at its best in late summer and early autumn.

4 **Rose Garden in the Savill Garden at Windsor** (Thames Valley). The very contemporary Rose Garden has a viewing promontory for the 2,500 headily scented roses in their swaths of pinks, yellows, and reds.

BOTANIC AND TEACHING GARDENS

If you're thinking endless paths of plants and reading labels, think again. These gardens share their expertise through stunning architecture, hands-on activities, and fantastic displays.

5 **Kew Gardens** (London). An 18th-century Chinese Pagoda is the landmark for Kew Gardens and its magnificent 19th-century greenhouses, housing a tropical rain forest and the world's tallest plant. There's also a treetop walkway.

6 **Eden Project** (West Country). Cornwall's "global garden" explores man's relationship with plants with great imagination and a sense of fun. Huge biomes, like see-through golf balls, contain different plants from all climates.

7 **Wisley** (Southeast). Flagship garden for the Royal Horticultural Society, it has a huge modern, elegant glasshouse, full of plants from around the world, plus flower and vegetable gardens and a unique interactive Root Zone.

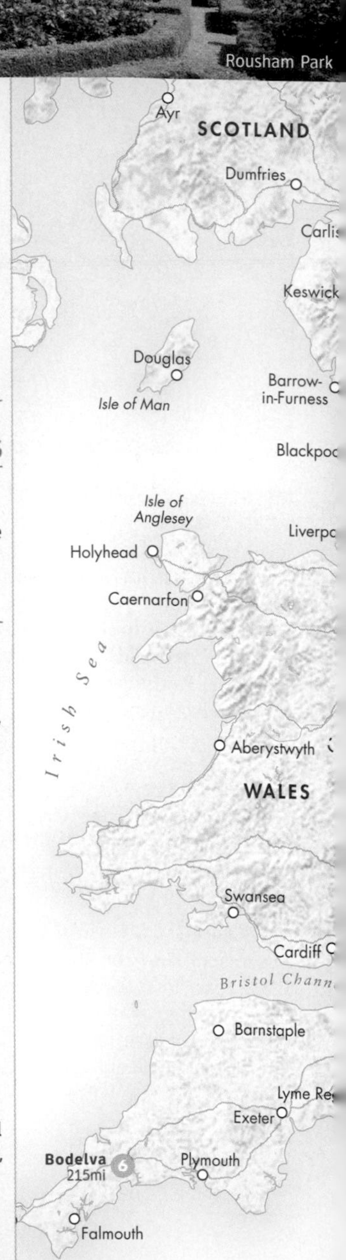

Kew Gardens
Stourhead

LANDSCAPE GARDENS

The 18th-century English landscape garden has much more to offer than sweeping Capability Brown parkland. Adopt an aristocratic air and give yourself time to walk and admire the vistas.

8 Stowe Landscape Gardens (Thames Valley). The grandest stop on the garden visiting circuit for over 200 years, it has no less than 40 temples, enormous grand avenues, a serpentine lake, and even Elysian Fields.

9 Stourhead (South). Quite simply, this masterpiece of a garden set in a valley encompassing a lake is one of the finest landscape gardens in the world. Summer rhododendrons and trees in the fall add to the picture.

10 Rousham Park (Thames Valley). More intimate than Stowe or Stourhead, it makes for an idyllic walk. The walled garden blooms with flowers.

FAMILY FAVORITES

For kids, choose the bigger gardens; they will have special attractions and activities for them. The Eden Project and Kew Gardens are also family friendly.

11 Alnwick Garden (Northeast). This contemporary garden was created with families in mind. Kids will be fascinated by the poison garden, water jets, and Bamboo Maze, and won't forget eating in the wooden Treehouse Café.

12 Chatsworth (Manchester and Liverpool). The grand water Cascade falling the 200-foot length of the steps and the Emperor Fountain shooting 300 feet into the sky provide entertainment, along with the maze, farmyard, and woodland adventure playground.

13 Westonbirt National Arboretum (Bath and the Cotswolds). Play zones are hidden throughout the arboretum. Kids can make dens, balance on logs, build nests, and, of course, climb trees.

* Approximate travel distance from London

MAKING THE MOST OF YOUR GARDEN VISIT

SEASONAL SPLENDOR

The best gardens will have something of interest year-round, though many close in winter. Spring through September yield the most rewards, and each season will have its special offerings: early spring offers snowdrops, followed by daffodils and bluebells. May is the month for azaleas and rhododendrons, roses are in full bloom in June, and by July herbaceous borders of lupins, delphiniums, and foxgloves are showing their true colors. August sees hydrangeas and dahlias coming to the fore, while in September there's a second flowering of roses. The oranges and reds of the fall last through October.

TOURING TIPS

The bigger houses have separate, often less expensive tickets for the gardens and the grounds only, so do ask. Depending on your itinerary, buying an English Heritage (🌐 *www.english-heritage.org.uk*) or National Trust (🌐 *www.nationaltrust.org.uk*) pass or joining the National Trust may save you money on garden admissions.

A car is preferable, as many places are not accessible by train or bus; Web sites often have information on public transportation options if they are available. The most popular gardens, such as Sissinghurst, get very crowded, especially on weekends, so come early or late in the day for a more peaceful visit. Most gardens have a café or restaurant, and nothing is more delightful than a cream tea in an English country garden in June.

Gardens associated with the National Trust are closed in winter, but their grounds remain open.

Eden Project

GOING DEEPER

The indispensable Yellow Book is published annually by the National Gardens Scheme; it is also available in sections by county (free, with donation). The directory lists public and private gardens that are normally closed to the public but have open days for charity throughout the year. Many of them offer teas as well.

FLOWER SHOWS

London claims the two main flower shows, both knockouts that last several days. The Chelsea Flower Show, five days in late May, and, outside the city, Hampton Court Palace Flower Show, six days in early July, represent the cutting edge of design and cover every aspect of gardening.

Major Lawrence Johnston, created the garden in 1907 in the Arts and Crafts style. Johnston was an imaginative gardener and avid traveler who brought back specimens from all over the world. The formal part of the garden is arranged in "rooms" separated by hedges and often with fine topiary work and walls. Besides the variety of plants, what's impressive are the different effects created, from calm open spaces to areas packed with flowers. **■ TIP→ Look for one of Johnston's earliest schemes, the red borders of dahlias, poppies, fuchsias, lobelias, and roses; the tall hornbeam hedges; and the Bathing Pool garden, where the pool is so wide there's scarcely space to walk.** The White Garden was probably the forerunner of the popular white gardens at Sissinghurst and Glyndebourne. If you have time, explore the tiny village of Hidcote Bartrim with its thatched stone houses; it borders the garden and fills a storybook dell. The garden is 4 miles northeast of Chipping Campden. ✉ *Off B4081, Hidcote Bartrim* ☎ *01386/438333* 🌐 *www.nationaltrust.org.uk/hidcote* 🎟 *£10.45* ⏲ *Mid-Feb.–late Feb. and early Nov.–mid-Dec., weekends 11–4; Mar.–Sept., daily 10–6; Oct., daily 10–5; last admission 1 hr before closing.*

St. James. The soaring pinnacled tower of St. James, a prime example of a Cotswold wool church (it was rebuilt in the 15th century with money from wool merchants), announces Chipping Campden from a distance; it's worth stepping inside to see the lofty, light-filled nave. The church recalls the old saying, which became popular because of the vast numbers of houses of worship in the Cotswolds, "As sure as God's in Gloucestershire." ✉ *Church St.* ☎ *01386/841927* 🌐 *www.stjameschurchcampden.co.uk* 🎟 *£3 donation suggested* ⏲ *Mar.–Oct., Mon.–Sat. 10–6, Sun. 2–6; Nov.–Feb., Mon.–Sat. 11–3, Sun. 2–3.*

7

WORTH NOTING

Court Barn Museum. Near the church of St. James, this museum occupies an old agricultural building that has been smartly renovated to showcase the area's prominence in the fields of craft and design. You can admire examples of silverware, ceramics, printing, woodcarving, jewelry, and cutlery, as well as changing exhibitions. Opposite the barn is an important row of almshouses dating from the reign of King James I. ✉ *Church St.* ☎ *01386/841951* 🌐 *www.courtbarn.org.uk* 🎟 *£5* ⏲ *Apr.–Sept., Tues.–Sun. and holiday Mon. 10–5; Oct.–Mar., Tues.–Sun. 10–4.*

Guild of Handicraft. In 1902 the Guild of Handicraft took over this former silk mill. Arts and Crafts evangelist Charles Robert Ashbee (1863–1942) brought 150 acolytes from London, including 50 guildsmen, to revive and practice such skills as cabinetmaking and bookbinding. The operation folded in 1920, but the refurbished building now houses the intriguing and very full workshop of a silversmith and has a café and gallery on the ground floor. ✉ *Sheep St.* ☎ *01386/841100 silversmith, 01386/840345 gallery* 🌐 *www.thegalleryattheguild.co.uk* 🎟 *Free* ⏲ *Workshops weekdays 9–5, Sat. 9–1. Gallery daily 10–5.*

Kiftsgate Court Gardens. While not so spectacular as Hidcote Manor Garden, this intimate, privately owned garden, just a five-minute stroll away, still captivates. It's skipped by the majority of visitors to Hidcote, so you won't be jostled by the crowds. The interconnecting flower beds present harmonious arrays of color, and the contemporary formal water garden adds an elegant contrast. Don't miss the prized Kiftsgate rose, supposed to be the largest in England, flowering gloriously in mid-July. ✉ *Off B4081, Mickleton* ☎ *01386/438777* 🌐 *www.kiftsgate.co.uk* 🎫 *£8* ⏲ *Apr. and Sept., Mon., Wed., and Sun. 2–6; May–July, Sat.–Wed. noon–6; Aug., Sat.–Wed. 2–6.*

Market Hall. The broad High Street, lined with stone houses and shops, follows a captivating curve; in the center, on Market Street, is the Market Hall, a gabled Jacobean structure built by Sir Baptiste Hycks in 1627 "for the sale of local produce." ✉ *Market St.*

WHERE TO EAT

$ BRITISH ✕ **Eight Bells.** Close to St. James Church, this traditional tavern has low beams, a flagstone floor, and a small courtyard. The long menu includes daily specials and such enticing dishes as sun-dried tomato and spinach risotto, gammon steak with parsley sauce, and apple and cinnamon sponge pudding. Ciabatta sandwiches served at lunchtime are easy on the wallet. The service is swift, and the good local ales are worth a taste. There are also six rooms where you can stay. [$] *Average main: £14* ✉ *Church St.* ☎ *01386/840371* 🌐 *www.eightbellsinn.co.uk* 💳 *No credit cards.*

$ CAFÉ ✕ **Huxleys.** At this beamed and buzzing little café, locals drop in to discuss horses and dogs over a glass of wine, families gather around the big round table for lunch, and tired shoppers sink into armchairs for a reviving coffee. Everything is overseen by the Italian manager, Marco Porta, who stocks the menu with light dishes—antipasti, bruschetta, soups, baked potatoes, and salads. He has chosen an English baker for the daily cake specials. There's also a terrace for warm days. It's open until 8 pm–10 pm on weekends. [$] *Average main: £8* ✉ *High St.* ☎ *01386/849077* 🌐 *www.huxleys.org* 💳 *No credit cards* ⏲ *No dinner Sun.–Thurs. in winter.*

WHERE TO STAY

$ B&B/INN **Badgers Hall.** Expect a friendly welcome at this antique B&B above a tearoom just across from the Market Hall, where the spacious, spotless rooms have beamed ceilings and exposed stonework. **Pros:** atmospheric building; attentive hosts; delicious breakfasts. **Cons:** low ceilings; entrance is through tea shop; two-night minimum stay required. [$] *Rooms from: £90* ✉ *High St.* ☎ *01386/840839* 🌐 *www.badgershall.com* 💳 *No credit cards* *3 rooms* *Breakfast* ☞ *No kids under 10.*

$$$ HOTEL **Charingworth Manor.** Views of the countryside are limitless from this 14th-century manor house hotel where mullioned windows and oak beams enhance the sitting room. **Pros:** helpful and friendly staff; great breakfasts; lots of amenities. **Cons:** some low beams in bedrooms; birds leave messages on cars; decor a bit dated. [$] *Rooms from: £180* ✉ *Off B4035, Charingworth* ☎ *01386/593555, 08446/932961* 🌐 *www.classiclodges.co.uk* 💳 *No credit cards* *23 rooms, 3 suites* *Breakfast.*

$$$ HOTEL **Cotswold House Hotel and Spa.** This luxury hotel in the heart of Chipping Campden injects contemporary design into a stately 18th-century manor house, and from the swirling staircase in the entrance to the

CLOSE UP

Arts and Crafts in the Cotswolds

The Arts and Crafts movement flourished throughout Britain in the late-19th and early-20th centuries, but the Cotswolds are most closely associated with it. The godfather of the movement was designer William Morris (1834–96), whose home for the last 25 years of his life, Kelmscott Manor in Gloucestershire, became the headquarters of the school. A lecture by Morris, "The Beauty of Life," delivered in Birmingham in 1880, included the injunction that became the guiding principle of the movement: "Have nothing in your houses which you do not know to be useful or believe to be beautiful."

Driven by the belief that the spirit of medieval arts and crafts was being degraded and destroyed by the mass production and aggressive capitalism of the Victorian era, and aided by a dedicated core of artisans, Morris revolutionized the art of house design and decoration. His work with textiles was particularly influential.

WHERE TO SEE IT

Many of Morris's followers were influenced by the Cotswold countryside, such as the designer and architect Charles Robert Ashbee, who transferred his Guild of Handicraft from London to Chipping Campden in 1902. The village holds the small Court Barn Museum dedicated to local craftwork, including a permanent exhibition of pieces by the original group and those who followed in their wake.

Their work can also be seen at the Wilson, Cheltenham Art Gallery and Museum, and, in its original context, at Rodmarton Manor outside Tetbury—which Ashbee declared the finest application of the movement's ideals. (Farther afield, Blackwell in the Lake District is a notable Arts and Crafts house.)

To see the Arts and Crafts ethic applied to horticulture, visit Hidcote Manor Garden, near Chipping Campden.

7

individually designed guest rooms studded with contemporary art, it's a winning formula. **Pros:** plenty of pampering; pleasant garden. **Cons:** some bathrooms are small. *Rooms from: £185* *The Square* *01386/840330* *www.cotswoldhouse.com* *No credit cards* *20 rooms, 8 suites* *Breakfast.*

$$ HOTEL **Noel Arms Hotel.** Dating to the 14th century, Chipping Campden's oldest inn was built to accommodate foreign wool traders, and even though it's been enlarged, the building retains its exposed beams and stonework. **Pros:** traditional character; friendly staff. **Cons:** rooms can be noisy and overheated; annex overlooks car park. *Rooms from: £120* *High St.* *01386/840317* *www.noelarmshotel.com* *No credit cards* *28 rooms* *Breakfast.*

SHOPPING

Hart. Descendants of an original member of the Guild of Handicraft specialize in fashioning lovely items from silver at this shop. *Guild of Handicraft, Sheep St.* *01386/841100.*

Stuart House Antiques. Three bay windows filled with silverware and copperware, porcelain, Doulton figurines, and Staffordshire figures show you only a fraction of what's available here over two floors overflowing with antiques. ✉ *High St.* ☎ *01386/840995.*

MORETON-IN-MARSH

5 miles south of Chipping Campden, 18 miles northeast of Cheltenham, 5 miles north of Stow-on-the-Wold.

In Moreton-in-Marsh, the houses have been built not around a central square but along a street wide enough to accommodate a market. The village has fine views across the hills. One local landmark, St. David's Church, has a tower of honey-gold ashlar. This town of about 3,500 also possesses one of the last remaining curfew towers, dated 1633; curfew dates to the time of the Norman Conquest, when a bell was rung to "cover-fire" for the night against any invaders.

GETTING HERE AND AROUND

Moreton-in-Marsh is on the A429 north of Cirencester. Park along the main street or in the lot on Station Road. The town has a train station with frequent connections to London Paddington. There are good bus services except on Sundays. Pulham's Coaches connect with Cirencester, Cheltenham Stow-on-the-Wold, and Bourton-on-the-Water; Johnson's Coaches with Stratford-upon-Avon, Chipping Campden, and Broadway. For Sezincote, a car is necessary.

ESSENTIALS

Visitor Information Moreton-in-Marsh Visitor Information Centre. ✉ *Moreton Area Centre, High St.* ☎ *01608/650881* 🌐 *www.cotswolds.com.*

EXPLORING

Sezincote. It comes as somewhat of a surprise to see the blue onion domes and miniature minarets of Sezincote, a mellow stone house and garden tucked into a valley near Moreton-in-Marsh. Created in the early 19th century, Sezincote (pronounced *see*-zinct) was the vision of Sir Charles Cockerell, who made a fortune in the East India Company. He employed his architect brother, Samuel Pepys Cockerell, to "Indianize" the residence with Hindu and Muslim motifs. Note the peacock-tail arches surrounding the windows of the first floor. The exotic garden, Hindu temple folly, and Indian-style bridge were favorites of the future George IV, who was inspired to create that Xanadu of Brighton, the Royal Pavilion. If you come in spring, glorious aconites and snowdrops greet you. Note that children are allowed inside only at the owners' discretion. ✉ *Off A44* ☎ *01386/700444* 🌐 *www.sezincote.co.uk* 🎫 *House and grounds £10; grounds only £5* ⏲ *House May–Sept., Thurs., Fri., and holiday Mon. 2:30–5:30. Grounds Jan.–Nov., Thurs. and Fri. and holiday Mon. 2–6 or dusk.*

Tuesday Market. Supposed to be the largest street market in the Cotswolds, the Tuesday Market takes over the center of the main street between 8 am and 3:30 pm, with a mix of household goods, fruits and vegetables, and some arts-and-crafts and jewelry stalls. It's no newcomer to the market scene either: it was chartered in 1227. ✉ *High St.*

WHERE TO EAT AND STAY

$ MODERN BRITISH **Horse and Groom.** The squash in the car park bears witness to the popularity of this pub, situated between Broadway and Moreton-in-Marsh. Inside there is a scattering of wooden tables and assortment of chairs, open fire, and service with a smile. The chalkboard gives you the dishes of the day, which might be Dexter sirloin steak with watercress, shallot and horseradish butter, or a beetroot-and-thyme risotto. Spiced apple and pear flapjack crumble and steamed ginger pudding are just two of the delicious desserts. There's a pleasant garden for summer days. *Average main: £16 Bourton-on-the-Hill 01386/700413 www.horseandgroom.info No credit cards.*

$$$ HOTEL **Manor House Hotel.** Secret passageways and a priest's hole testify to the age of this 16th-century building, where the mullioned windows, original stonework, and log fires in winter are tastefully balanced by smart, contemporary furnishings in the public areas. **Pros:** accommodating staff; historical ambience; set back from the main road. **Cons:** smallish rooms; lots of stairs, some noise intrusion. *Rooms from: £170 High St. 01608/650501 www.cotswold-inns-hotels.co.uk No credit cards 33 rooms, 2 suites Breakfast.*

STOW-ON-THE-WOLD

5 miles south of Moreton-in-Marsh, 15 miles east of Cheltenham.

At an elevation of 800 feet, Stow is the highest town in the Cotswolds—"Stow-on-the-Wold, where the wind blows cold" is the age-old saying. Built around a wide square, Stow's imposing golden stone houses have been discreetly converted into high-quality antiques stores, shops, and tea parlors. The Square, as it's known, has a fascinating history. In the 18th century Daniel Defoe wrote that more than 20,000 sheep could be sold here on a busy day; such was the press of livestock that sheep runs, known as "tures," were used to control the sheep, and these narrow streets still run off the main square. Today pubs and antiques shops fill the area.

Also here are St. Edward's Church and the Kings Arms Old Posting House, its wide entrance still seeming to wait for the stagecoaches that used to stop here on their way to Cheltenham.

GETTING HERE AND AROUND

Stow-on-the-Wold is well connected by road (A429, A424, and A436) and bus (from Moreton-in-Marsh, Bourton-on-the-Water, Northleach, Cirencester, and Cheltenham). There are car parks off Sheep Street and Fosseway (A429). Chastleton House is reachable only by car.

EXPLORING

Chastleton House. One of the most complete Jacobean properties in Britain opts for a beguilingly lived-in appearance, taking advantage of almost 400 years' worth of furniture and trappings accumulated by many generations of the single family that owned it until 1991. The house was built between 1605 and 1612 for William Jones, a wealthy wool merchant, and has an appealing authenticity: bric-a-brac is strewn around, wood and pewter are unpolished, upholstery is uncleaned. The top floor is a glorious, barrel-vaulted long gallery, and throughout the house you can see exquisite plasterwork, paneling, and tapestries. The gardens include rotund topiaries and the first croquet lawn (the rules of croquet were codified here in 1865). Admission is by timed ticket on a first-come, first-served basis, and there is no advance booking, so it's a good idea to arrive early. Note that there is no tearoom or shop here. Chastleton is 6 miles northeast of Stow, signposted off A436 between Stow and A44. ✉ *Off A436, Moreton-in-Marsh* ☎ *01608/674981, 01494/755560 info line* 🌐 *www.nationaltrust.org.uk* 🎫 *£9.50; garden only £3.50* ⏲ *Mar. and Oct., Wed.–Sun. 1–4; Apr.–Sept., Wed.–Sun. 1–5. Last entry 1 hr before closing.*

WHERE TO EAT AND STAY

$ BRITISH ✕ **Queen's Head.** A convivial stopping-off spot for lunch or dinner, this pub has a courtyard out back that's a quiet retreat on a summer day. Expect to rub shoulders with the locals and their families as well as passing tourists. Besides standard pub grub, including sandwiches, baguettes, and sausage and mash, there are daily specials such as steak-and-kidney pie, suet pudding, and a burger of the week. Opposite on the green are some working stocks that you can try out. $ *Average main: £10* ✉ *The Square* ☎ *01451/830563* ▭ *No credit cards.*

$ B&B/INN 🏨 **Number Nine.** Beyond the traditional Cotswold stone exterior of this former coaching inn—now a bed-and-breakfast—are unfussy, spacious bedrooms done in soothing white and pale colors. **Pros:** helpful and amiable hosts; close to pubs and restaurants. **Cons:** two bathrooms have tubs, not showers; low ceilings; steps to climb. $ *Rooms from: £80* ✉ *9 Park St.* ☎ *01451/870333* 🌐 *www.number-nine.info* ▭ *No credit cards* 🛏 *3 rooms* 🍽 *Breakfast.*

$$ HOTEL 🏨 **Stow Lodge.** A former rectory, this stately, family-run hotel couldn't be better placed, separated from Stow's main square by a tidy garden. **Pros:** central location; hospitable service; good breakfasts. **Cons:** chiming church clock can be disturbing; steep steps to top-floor rooms; no kids under five. $ *Rooms from: £150* ✉ *The Square* ☎ *01451/830485* 🌐 *www.stowlodge.co.uk* ▭ *No credit cards* 🛏 *19 rooms, 1 suite* 🍽 *Breakfast.*

SHOPPING

Stow-on-the-Wold is the leading center for antiques stores in the Cotswolds, with dealers centered on the Square, Sheep Street, and Church Street.

Baggott Church St. Limited. This shop displays fine old furniture, portraits and landscape paintings, silver, and toys, with their price tags tied on with ribbon. ✉ *Church St.* ☎ *01451/830370* 🌐 *www.baggottantiques.com.*

Durham House Antiques. Showcases of jewelry, silver items, and ceramics, along with antiquarian books and period furniture, are on display over two floors. ✉ *48 Sheep St.* ☎ *01451/870404* 🌐 *www.durhamhousegb.com.*

Tudor House. Three floors of showcases contain the finds of 30 antiques dealers presenting anything from tiny mother of pearl pieces and beaded bags to wooden dressers full of plates and jugs. ✉ *40 Sheep St., Stow-on-the-Wold* ☎ *01451/830021* 🌐 *www.tudor-house-antiques.com.*

BOURTON-ON-THE-WATER

4 miles southwest of Stow-on-the-Wold, 12 miles northeast of Cheltenham.

Off A429 on the eastern edge of the Cotswolds, Bourton-on-the-Water is deservedly famous as a classic Cotswold village. Like many others, it became wealthy in the Middle Ages because of wool. The little River Windrush runs through Bourton, crossed by low stone bridges; it's as pretty as it sounds. This village makes a good touring base and has a collection of quirky small museums, but in summer it can be overcrowded. A stroll through Bourton takes you past stone cottages, many converted to small stores and fish-and-chip and tea shops.

GETTING HERE AND AROUND

Bourton-on-the-Water is served by Pulham's Coaches from Stow-on-the-Wold, Moreton-in-Marsh, Cirencester, and Cheltenham. By car, take A40 and A436 from Cheltenham. You may find parking in the center, but if not use the lot outside the village.

ESSENTIALS

Visitor Information Bourton-on-the-Water Visitor Information Centre. ✉ *Victoria St.* ☎ *01451/820211* 🌐 *www.bourtoninfo.com.*

EXPLORING

FAMILY **Cotswold Motoring Museum and Toy Collection.** Housed in an old mill and marked by a topiary vintage Mini car, this museum has seven rooms crammed to the rafters with more than 30 shiny vintage and classic cars, delightful caravans from the 1920s and 1960s, ancient motorbikes and bicyles, road signs from past times, and a shepherd's hut on wheels. If this and the assortment of motoring memorabilia is not enough, there are also children's toys, pedal cars, models, and board games. ✉ *The Old Mill, Sherborne St.* ☎ *01451/821255* 🌐 *www.cotswoldmotoringmuseum.co.uk* 🎫 *£5.25* ⏲ *Mid-Feb.–mid-Dec., daily 10–6.*

FAMILY **Model Village.** Built in 1937, this knee-high model of Bourton-on-the-Water took five years to complete. As you walk down its tiny lanes, you'll see how little has changed over the past decades. The small exhibition at Miniature World shows miniature scenes and rooms; some you can make come to life. ✉ *Old New Inn, High St.* ☎ *01451/820467* 🌐 *www.themodelvillage.com* 🎫 *£3.60; Miniature World £1* ⏲ *Late Mar.–Oct., daily 10–6; Nov.–late Mar., daily 10–4; last admission 15 min before closing.*

WHERE TO EAT AND STAY

$ BRITISH ✕ **Rose Tree.** Plain wooden tables and understated decor are the setting for the wholesome British dishes served in this traditional restaurant beautifully sited on the banks of the Windrush. Try the deep-fried Somerset Brie with cranberry sauce to start, moving on to chicken with spinach, ham and Roquefort cheese or roast cod on a caper mash. Desserts include raspberry pavlova and lemon meringue pie. Sip a cocktail on the riverside terrace while you wait for your order. [$] *Average main: £13* ✉ *Victoria St.* ☎ *01451/820635* 🌐 *www.therosetreerestaurant.co.uk* 💳 *No credit cards.*

CLOSE UP

Antiques and Markets in the Cotswolds

The Cotswolds contain one of the largest concentrations of art and antiques dealers outside London. The famous antiques shops here are, it's sometimes whispered, "temporary storerooms" for the great families of the region, filled with tole-ware, treen, faience firedogs, toby jugs, and silhouettes, plus country furniture, and ravishing 17th- to 19th-century furniture.

The center of antiquing is Stow-on-the-Wold, in terms of volume of dealers. Other towns that have a number of antiques shops are Broadway, Burford, Cirencester, Tetbury, and Moreton-in-Marsh. The Cotswolds have few of those "anything in this tray for £10" shops, however. The **Cotswold Antique Dealers' Association** (07831/850544 🌐 *www.cotswolds-antiques-art.com*) represents 50 or so dealers in the area.

As across England, many towns in the region have market days, when you can purchase local produce (including special treats ranging from Cotswold cheeses to fruit juices), crafts, and items such as clothes, books, and toys. Moreton-in-Marsh has a market on Tuesday, while Cirencester is busy on Monday and Friday. Attending a farmers' market or a general market is a great way to mingle with the locals and perhaps find a special treasure or a tasty treat.

$ HOTEL **Chester House Hotel.** Just steps from the River Windrush, this traditional stone building has been tastefully adapted with contemporary fittings and style. **Pros:** friendly staff; stylish rooms. **Cons:** busy on weekends; coach house rooms overlook car park. *Rooms from: £95* ✉ *Victoria St.* ☎ *01451/820286* 🌐 *www.chesterhousehotel.com* *No credit cards* *22 rooms* *Breakfast.*

SHOPPING

Cotswold Perfumery. This popular shop carries many perfumes that are manufactured on the premises by hand, and also stocks perfume bottles, diffusers, and essential oils, as well as jewelry. ✉ *Victoria St.* ☎ *01451/820698* 🌐 *www.cotswold-perfumery.co.uk* *Factory tour £5* *Mon.–Sat. 9:30–5, Sun. 10:30–5.*

LOWER SLAUGHTER AND UPPER SLAUGHTER

2 miles north of Bourton-on-the-Water, 15 miles east of Cheltenham.

Fodor's Choice ★ To see the quieter, more typical Cotswold villages, seek out the evocatively named Lower Slaughter and Upper Slaughter (the names have nothing to do with mass murder, but come from the Saxon word *sloh,* which means "a marshy place"). Lower Slaughter is one of the "water villages," with Slaughter Brook running down the center road of the town. Little stone footbridges cross the brook, and the town's resident gaggle of geese can often be seen paddling through the sparkling water. Nearby, Lower and Upper Swell are two other quiet towns to explore.

GETTING HERE AND AROUND

The Slaughters are best explored by car.

EXPLORING

Warden's Way. Connecting the two Slaughters is the Warden's Way, a mile-long pathway that begins in Upper Slaughter at the town-center parking lot and passes stone houses, green meadows, ancient trees, and a 19th-century corn mill with a waterwheel and brick chimney. The Warden's Way continues south to Bourton-on-the-Water; the full walk from Winchcombe to Bourton is 14 miles. You can pick up maps from local tourist offices. ✉ *Lower Slaughter.*

WHERE TO STAY

$$$ HOTEL **Lords of the Manor Hotel.** You'll find refinement and a warm welcome in this rambling 17th-century manor house with Victorian additions, tucked away in a quintessential Cotswold village. **Pros:** heavenly setting; understated elegance; outstanding food. **Cons:** some rooms on the small side; limited Wi-Fi; packages book up quickly. *Rooms from: £225* ✉ *Off A429, Upper Slaughter* ☎ *01451/820243* 🌐 *www.lordsofthemanor.com* *No credit cards* *26 rooms* *Breakfast.*

NORTHLEACH

7 miles southwest of Lower and Upper Slaughter, 14 miles southeast of Cheltenham.

Just off the Fosse Way (and bypassed by the busy A40), little Northleach—population around 2,000—has remained one of the least spoiled of Cotswold towns. Trim cottages, many with traditional stone-tile roofs, line the streets that converge on the spacious central square. By the 13th century Northleach had acquired substantial wealth thanks to the wool trade. The wool of the local Cotswold Lion sheep (so called because of their thick, manelike fleece) was praised above all others by weavers in Flanders, to whom it was exported.

GETTING HERE AND AROUND

Pulham's Coaches links Northleach with Bourton-on-the-Water and Cheltenham. It's an out-of-the-way village—signposted from A40 and A429—where you should be able to park near the central square and walk to the sights.

EXPLORING

Mechanical Music Museum. At this shop, the diverting tour lets you hear pianolas, music boxes, and other mechanical instruments from times past. You can even listen to the maestros Grieg, Paderewski, Rachmaninov, and Gershwin on piano rolls. The well-stocked shop stocks antique and modern music boxes, mechanical toys, piano rolls, books, and more. ✉ *The Oak House, High St.* ☎ *01451/860181* 🌐 *www.mechanicalmusic.co.uk* *£8* *Daily 10–5; last tour at 4.*

St. Peter and St. Paul. Besides its soaring pillars and clerestory windows, this 15th-century light-filled church, known as the cathedral of the Cotswolds, contains notable memorial brasses, monuments to the merchants who endowed the church. Each merchant has a wool sack and sheep at his feet. ✉ *Mill End* ☎ *01451/861132* 🌐 *www.northleach.org* *Free* *Daily 10–dusk.*

7

WHERE TO EAT AND STAY

$$ MODERN BRITISH **Wheatsheaf Inn.** This pub, traditional on the outside, comfortably comtemporary and stylish on the inside, offers a snug coffee lounge and adjoining restaurant, which specializes in Modern British fare. On the menu you might see such light dishes as beetroot soup or Jerusalem artichoke risotto, followed by pigeon pie or saffron-baked cod with clams. The courtyard garden makes an ideal spot for an elderfower and mint cocktail and alfresco dining. The inn also offers 13 stylish, uncluttered bedrooms and a spa. *Average main: £19* *West End* *01451/860244* *www.cotswoldswheatsheaf.com* *No credit cards.*

$$ B&B/INN **Yew Tree Cottage.** For a peaceful stay in a traditional Cotswold cottage, you can't beat this guesthouse. **Pros:** full of character; charming hostess. **Cons:** a bit remote; dogs in the house. *Rooms from: £100* *Off A429, Turkdean* *01451/860222* *www.bestcotswold.com* *No credit cards* *2 rooms* *Breakfast.*

BURFORD

9 miles east of Northleach, 18 miles north of Swindon, 18 miles west of Oxford.

Burford's broad main street leads steeply down to a narrow bridge across the River Windrush. The village served as a stagecoach stop for centuries and has many historic inns; it's now a popular stop for tour buses and seekers of antiques.

GETTING HERE AND AROUND

Burford can be easily reached by bus from Oxford and Northleach. Once here, it's easy to stroll around. Drivers should park as soon as possible; there are possibilities on and off High Street.

ESSENTIALS

Visitor Information Burford Visitor Information Centre. *33a High St.* *01993/823558* *www.oxfordshirecotswolds.org.*

EXPLORING

St. John the Baptist. Hidden away at the end of a lane at the bottom of High Street is the splendid parish church of St. John the Baptist, its interior a warren of arches, chapels, and shrines. The church was remodeled in the 15th century from Norman beginnings. Among the monuments is one dedicated to Henry VIII's barber, Edmund Harman, that depicts four Amazonian Indians; it's said to be the first depiction of native people from the Americas in Britain. Also look for the elaborate Tanfield monument and the grave of Christopher Kempster, master mason to Christopher Wren during the rebuilding of St. Paul's Cathedral in London. *Lawrence La.* *01993/823788* *www.burfordchurch.org* *Suggested donation £2* *Mon.–Sat. 9–5, Sun. 9–10 and 1–5.*

WHERE TO EAT AND STAY

$$ MODERN BRITISH **The Angel at Burford.** At this informal eatery in a 16th-century coaching inn, the farmhouse-style tables are filled with traditional dishes like chicken breast with chestnut sauce, or rib-eye steaks with mushrooms and fries. A secluded, sunny garden is a perfect place for a lunchtime baguette or sandwich. There are three individually furnished guest

Blue skies, stone buildings, a peaceful brook: villages such as Upper Slaughter demonstrate the enduring appeal of the Cotswolds.

rooms upstairs. *Average main: £16* *14 Witney St.* *01993/822714* *www.theangelatburford.co.uk* *No credit cards.*

$$$ HOTEL **The Lamb Inn.** Step through the door of this ancient coaching inn and be greeted by huge flagstones, gateleg tables, armchairs, and a roaring fire, then wind your way along the tartan carpet through creaking passages and stairways to the immaculate and cozy bedrooms. **Pros:** idyllic location; attentive service; historical building. **Cons:** some rooms are small; some street parking; very pet-friendly, so not for non-dog lovers. *Rooms from: £165* *Sheep St.* *01993/823155* *www.cotswold-inns-hotels.co.uk* *No credit cards* *17 rooms* *Breakfast.*

EN ROUTE

Fans of the television drama *Downton Abbey* probably already know that the interior shots of the series are filmed at Highclere Castle in southern Winchester (⇨ *see Chapter 4: The South*), but they might be interested to learn that most of the exterior shots are concentrated on the Oxfordshire village of **Bampton**, on the eastern edge of the Cotswolds. Visitors can walk the sleepy streets of mellow stone, see the library in Church View which doubled as the Downton Cottage Hospital, and visit the church of St. Mary, the setting of both Mary and Edith's weddings. Lady Sybil and Branson planned their elopement in the Swan Inn at the nearby village of Swinbook, 2 miles east of Burford.

Bampton is 6 miles southeast of Burford and 18 miles southwest of Oxford, from where there is a regular bus. Drivers should take the road signed Brize Norton off the A40.

BIBURY

10 miles southwest of Burford, 6 miles northeast of Cirencester, 15 miles north of Swindon.

The tiny town of Bibury, with a population of less than 1,000, sits idyllically beside the little River Coln on B4425; it was famed Arts and Crafts designer William Morris's choice for Britain's most beautiful village. Fine old cottages, a river meadow, and the church of St. Mary's are some of the delights here.

GETTING HERE AND AROUND

There are a few buses to Bibury operated on weekdays only by Pulham's Coaches from Cirencester which continue on to Bourton-on-the-Water. You'll need a car to reach Chedworth Roman Villa.

EXPLORING

Arlington Row. The town has a famously pretty and much-photographed group of 17th-century weavers' cottages made of stone. ✉ *Bibury.*

FAMILY **Chedworth Roman Villa.** The remains of a mile of walls are what's left of one of the largest Roman villas in England, beautifully set in a wooded valley on the eastern fringe of the Cotswolds. Thirty-two rooms, including two complete bath suites, have been identified, and covered walkways take you over the colorful mosaics, some of the most complete in England. Audio guides are available, and there's a small museum. Look out for the rare large snails, fattened on milk and herbs during Roman times, in the grounds; they come out on warm, wet days. There's a café here, but it's also an ideal place for a picnic. **■ TIP→ Look carefully for the signs for the villa: from Bibury, go across A429 to Yanworth and Chedworth. The villa is also signposted from A40. Roads are narrow.** The site is 6 miles northwest of Bibury and 10 miles southeast of Cheltenham. ✉ *Off A429, Yanworth* ☎ *01242/890256* 🌐 *www.nationaltrust.org.uk* 🎟 *£9* ⏲ *Mid-Feb.–Mar. and Nov., daily 10–4; Apr.–Oct., daily 10–5.*

WHERE TO STAY

$$$ HOTEL **Swan Hotel.** Few inns can boast of a more idyllic setting than this mid-17th-century coaching inn, originally a row of cottages on the banks of the gently flowing River Coln. **Pros:** idyllic spot; helpful staff. **Cons:** busy with day-trippers, and wedding parties on weekends; most standard rooms lack views. $ *Rooms from: £170* ✉ *B4425* ☎ *01285/740695* 🌐 *www.cotswold-inns-hotels.co.uk* ▭ *No credit cards* 🛏 *18 rooms, 4 suites* 🍽 *Breakfast.*

CIRENCESTER

6 miles southwest of Bibury, 9 miles south of Chedworth, 14 miles southeast of Cheltenham.

A hub of the Cotswolds since Roman times, when it was called Corinium, Cirencester (pronounced *siren*-sester) was second only to London in importance. Today this old market town is the area's largest, with a population of 19,000. It sits at the intersection of two major Roman roads, the Fosse Way and Ermin Street (now A429 and A417). In the

Middle Ages Cirencester grew rich on wool, which funded its 15th-century parish church. It preserves many mellow stone buildings dating mainly from the 17th and 18th centuries and bow-fronted shops that still have one foot in the past.

GETTING HERE AND AROUND

Cirencester has hourly bus service from Cheltenham and less frequent service from Moreton-in-Marsh, Tetbury, and Kemble (for rail links). By road, the town can be accessed on A417, A419, and A429. Its compact center is easily walkable.

ESSENTIALS

Visitor Information Cirencester Visitor Information Centre. ✉ *Corinium Museum, Park St.* ☎ *01285/654180* 🌐 *www.cirencester.gov.uk.*

EXPLORING

FAMILY Fodor's Choice ★ **Corinium Museum.** Not much of the Roman town remains visible, but the museum displays an outstanding collection of Roman artifacts, including jewelry and coins, as well as mosaic pavements and full-scale reconstructions of local Roman interiors. Spacious and light-filled galleries that explore the town's history in Roman and Anglo-Saxon times and in the 18th century include plenty of hands-on exhibits for kids. ✉ *Park St.* ☎ *01285/655611* 🌐 *www.coriniummuseum.org* 🎟 *£4.95* ⏲ *Apr.–Oct., Mon.–Sat. 10–5, Sun. 2–5; Nov.–Mar., Mon.–Sat. 10–4, Sun. 2–4.*

St. John the Baptist. At the top of Market Place is this magnificent Gothic parish church, known as the cathedral of the "woolgothic" style. Its gleaming, elaborate three-tier, three-bay south porch is the largest in England and once served as the town hall. The chantry chapels and many coats of arms bear witness to the importance of the wool merchants as benefactors of the church. A rare example of a delicate 15th-century wineglass pulpit sits in the nave. ✉ *Market Pl.* ☎ *01285/659317* 🌐 *www.cirenparish.co.uk* 🎟 *£3 donation suggested* ⏲ *Daily 10–5 (10–4 in winter).*

QUICK BITES

Made by Bob. The energy and buzz of this plate-glass and chrome eatery, situated right by the Cornhall in the center of town, will set you up as much as the coffee and pastry, afternoon tea and a bun, or soup and focaccia lunches. You can always pick something up from the delicatessen for a picnic if you prefer. ✉ ***Unit 6 The Cornhall, 26 Market Pl.*** ☎ ***01285/641818*** 🌐 ***www.foodmadebybob.com*** ⏲ ***Closed Sun.***

WHERE TO EAT AND STAY

$$ MODERN BRITISH ✕ **Jesse's.** The fish is chilling on the counter and the charcoal is glowing in the oven as you sit at your mosaic-topped table and watch the chefs at work. Tucked away in a little courtyard, the bistro is intimate yet roomy, bustling yet snug. Treat yourself to a chilled sherry, then be tempted by game terrine with toasted chocolate and beetroot bread, local Gatcombe lamb, or fish straight up from Cornwall. You'll be spoiled for choice by the excellent choices on the British cheese board. It's advisable to book a table in advance. 💲 *Average main: £17* ✉ *The Stableyard, Black Jack St.* ☎ *01285/641497* 🌐 *www.jessesbistro.co.uk* 💳 *No credit cards* ⏲ *Closed Sun. No dinner Mon.*

7

$$$$ HOTEL **Barnsley House.** A honey-and-cream Georgian mansion, the former home of garden designer Rosemary Verey has been discreetly modernized and converted into a luxurious retreat without sacrificing its essential charm. **Pros:** romantic setting; great attention to detail. **Cons:** some rooms at the top of three flights of stairs; no kids under 14. *Rooms from: £300* ✉ *B4425, Barnsley* ☎ *01285/740000* 🌐 *www.barnsleyhouse.com* ▭ *No credit cards* *9 rooms, 9 suites* *Breakfast.*

$ B&B/INN **Ivy House.** Delicious breakfasts, hospitable owners, and reasonable rates enhance a stay at this stone Victorian house, close to the center of town. **Pros:** homemade granola at breakfast; child-friendly atmosphere. **Cons:** on a main road; some rooms on the small side. *Rooms from: £87* ✉ *2 Victoria Rd.* ☎ *01285/656626* 🌐 *www.ivyhousecotswolds.com* ▭ *No credit cards* *4 rooms* *Breakfast.*

SHOPPING

Corn Hall. This is the venue for a home, garden, and fashion market Monday through Thursday, an antiques market on Friday, and a crafts market on Saturday. ✉ *Market Pl.* 🌐 *www.cornhallcirencester.com.*

Makers and Designers Emporium. Better known as MADE, this shop is a cornucopia of unusual designer items, including stationery, textiles, housewares, toys, and jewelry. ✉ *9 Silver St.* ☎ *01285/658225* 🌐 *www.made-gallery.com.*

Market Place. Every Monday and Friday, Cirencester's central Market Place is packed with stalls selling a motley assortment of goods, mainly household items but some local produce and crafts, too. A farmers' market takes place here every second and fourth Saturday of the month. ✉ *Cirencester.*

SPORTS AND THE OUTDOORS

FAMILY **Cotswold Water Park.** You can indulge in water sports such as waterskiing and windsurfing at the Cotswold Water Park, 4 miles south of Cirencester. This group of 150 lakes covers 40 square miles and has multiple entrances. There's swimming March through October, and plenty to do for walkers, cyclists, and kayakers as well. You pay individual charges for the activities, and you can rent equipment on-site. ✉ *B4696, South Cerney* ☎ *01793/752413* 🌐 *www.waterpark.org* *Free* *Individual operators have varying opening hrs.*

PAINSWICK

16 miles northwest of Cirencester, 8 miles southwest of Cheltenham, 5 miles south of Gloucester.

Fodor's Choice ★ An old Cotswold wool town of around 2,000 inhabitants, Painswick has become a chocolate-box picture of quaintness, attracting day-trippers and tour buses. But come during the week and you can discover the place in relative tranquillity. The huddled gray-stone houses and inns date from as early as the 14th century and include a notable group from the Georgian era. It's worth a stroll through the churchyard of St. Mary's, renowned for its table tombs and monuments and its 100 yew trees planted in 1792. The Cotswold Way passes near the center of the village, making it easy to take a pleasant walk in the countryside.

GETTING HERE AND AROUND
Painswick is on A46 between Stroud and Cheltenham. Stagecoach runs hourly bus connections with Stroud (15 minutes) and Cheltenham (35 minutes), with reduced service on Sunday.

ESSENTIALS
Visitor Information Painswick Visitor Information Centre. ✉ *Grave Diggers Hut, St Mary's Church* ☎ *0750/3516924* 🌐 *www.painswicktouristinfo.co.uk.*

SPECIAL DAYS

Painswick's annual Clypping Ceremony, on the first Sunday after September 19, has nothing to do with topiaries—the name derives from the Anglo-Saxon word "clyppan," meaning "encircle." Children with garlands make a ring around the parish church as traditional hymns are sung. The idea is to affirm the church and the faith it stands for. Another good time to visit is the town's Victorian Market Day in early July.

EXPLORING

Painswick Rococo Garden. Half a mile north of town, this delightful garden is a rare survivor from the exuberant rococo period of English garden design (1720–60). After 50 years in its original form, the 6-acre garden became overgrown. Fortunately the rediscovery of the 1748 painting of the garden by Thomas sparked, in the 1980s, a full-scale restoration. Now you can view the original structures—such as the pretty Gothic Eagle House and curved Exedra—take in the asymmetrical vistas, and try the modern maze, which, unusually, has three jails you can discover. It's also famous for its snowdrops which bloom in January and February. There's a restaurant and a shop as well. ✉ *B4073* ☎ *01452/813204* 🌐 *www.rococogarden.org.uk* 🎫 *£7* 🕐 *Mid-Jan.–Oct., daily 11–6; last admission at 5.*

WHERE TO EAT AND STAY

$$ BRITISH ✕ **Falcon Inn.** With views of the church of St. Mary's, this pub dating from 1554 offers a reassuringly traditional and charming milieu for food and refreshment. Light meals are available at lunchtime, teas in the afternoon, and for the evening meal you might start with deep-fried calamari and whitebait with caper sauce, then try the rump of lamb with minted mashed potato for your main course. The spotted Dick (sponge with dried fruits) and custard makes a classic old-school end to the meal. The inn's grounds hold what is claimed to be the world's oldest bowling green. There are 11 well-furnished bedrooms upstairs. $ *Average main: £15* ✉ *New St.* ☎ *01452/814222* 🌐 *www.falconinn-cotswolds.co.uk* 💳 *No credit cards.*

$ HOTEL **Cardynham House.** In the heart of the village, this 15th- to 16th-century former wool merchant's house, which retains its beamed ceilings, Jacobean staircase, and Elizabethan fireplace, has four-poster beds in almost all of its rooms. **Pros:** romantic and quirky; great food in restaurant. **Cons:** some low ceilings; mainly small bathrooms. $ *Rooms from: £90* ✉ *The Cross, Tibbiwell St.* ☎ *01452/814006, 01452/810030 restaurant* 🌐 *www.cardynham.co.uk* 💳 *No credit cards* 🛏 *9 rooms* 🍽 *Breakfast.*

With its majestic trees, Westonbirt National Arboretum is the perfect place to take in fall's splendor.

TETBURY

12 miles south of Painswick, 8 miles southwest of Cirencester.

With about 5,300 inhabitants, Tetbury claims royal connections. Indeed, the soaring spire of the church that presides over this Elizabethan market town is within sight of Highgrove House, the Prince of Wales's abode. The house isn't open to the public, but you can book well in advance for a tour of the gardens. Tetbury is known as one of the area's antiques centers.

GETTING HERE AND AROUND

Tetbury is connected to Cirencester by buses operated by Cotswold Green. There are no Sunday services. It's easy to stroll around the compact town.

ESSENTIALS

Visitor Information Tetbury Tourist Information Centre. ✉ *33 Church St.* ☎ *01666/503552* 🌐 *www.visittetbury.co.uk.*

EXPLORING

Fodor's Choice ★ **Highgrove House.** Highgrove House is the much loved country home of Prince Charles and Camilla, Duchess of Cornwall. Here the prince has been making the 37-acre estate his personal showcase for traditional and organic growing methods and conservation of native plants and animals since 1980. Joining a tour of 26 people, you can appreciate the amazing industry on the part of the royal gardeners who have created the orchards, kitchen garden, and woodland garden almost from nothing. Look for the stumpery, the immaculate and quirky topiaries, and the national collection of hostas. You can sample the estate's produce in the restaurant and shop, or from its retail outlet in Tetbury. Tickets go on sale in February and sell out quickly, though extra dates are released through the year via a mailing list. Be sure to book well ahead. Allow three to four hours for a visit to the garden, which is 1½ miles southwest of Tetbury. Those under 12 aren't permitted. ✉ *Off A433, Doughton* ☎ *020/7766–7310 book tours* 🌐 *www.highgrovegardens.com* 🎫 *£24.50, prebooked only* 🕒 *Early Apr.–late Oct., weekdays plus occasional weekends.*

Market House. In the center of Tetbury, look for the eye-catching Market House, dating from 1655. Constructed of white-painted stone, it's built up on rows of Tuscan pillars. Various markets are held here during the week. ✉ *Market Sq.*

Rodmarton Manor. One of the last English country houses constructed using traditional methods and materials, Rodmarton Manor (built 1909–29) is furnished with specially commissioned pieces in the Arts and Crafts style. Ernest Barnsley, a follower of William Morris, worked on the house and gardens. The notable gardens—wild, winter, sunken, and white—are divided into "rooms" bounded by hedges of holly, beech, and yew. The manor is 5 miles northeast of Tetbury. ✉ *Off A433, Rodmarton* ☎ *01285/841442* 🌐 *www.rodmarton-manor.co.uk* 🎫 *£8; garden only £5* 🕒 *Apr.–Sept., Wed., Sat., and holiday Mon. 2–5.*

St. Mary the Virgin. This church, a fine example of 18th-century neo-Gothic style, has a galleried interior with pews and fine slender pillars. The entrance porch has a striking contemporary mural of the Annuciation. Donations are welcome. ✉ *Church St.* ☎ *01666/500088* 🌐 *www.tetburychurch.co.uk* 🎫 *Free* 🕒 *Daily 9–5.*

7

QUICK BITES

Snooty Fox. Just steps from Market House and at the heart of village life, the Snooty Fox is a bustling inn and restaurant with leather armchairs and an open fire in winter and a patio to use in summer. Real ales and local ciders are served at the bar, and teas, coffees, and hot and cold meals are available all day. ✉ *Market Pl.* ☎ *01666/502436* 🌐 www.snooty-fox.co.uk.

FAMILY **Westonbirt National Arboretum.** Spread over 600 acres and with 17 miles of paths, this arboretum contains one of the most extensive collections of trees and shrubs in Europe. A lovely place to spend an hour or two, it's 3 miles southwest of Tetbury and 10 miles north of Bath. The best times to come for color are in late spring, when the rhododendrons, azaleas, and magnolias are blooming, and in fall, when the maples come into their own. Open-air concerts take place in summer, and there are exhibitions throughout the year. A gift shop, café, and restaurant are on the grounds. ✉ *Off A433* ☎ *01666/880220* 🌐 *www.forestry.gov.uk/westonbirt* 🎫 *£8 Mar.–Sept.; £9 Oct. and Nov.; £6 Dec.–Feb.* 🕒 *Apr.–Aug., daily 9–8; Sept.–Mar., daily 9–5.*

WHERE TO EAT AND STAY

$ MODERN BRITISH ✕ **The Royal Oak.** This mellow-stone gabled pub, located in the snug village of Leighterton just 5 miles west of Tetbury, likes to satisfy the good crowd that assembles here with the best local fare in the area. Draw up a stool at the bar or take a kitchen chair at one of the many wooden tables to try the squid, chorizo, and tomato stew, or cauliflower, squash, and chickpea tagine. Finish with an adventurous quince-and-hazelnut crumble. There's also a sheltered walled garden for summer dining. *Average main: £14 1 The Street, Leighterton 0166/890250 www.royaloakleighterton.co.uk No credit cards No dinner Sun.*

$$$$ HOTEL FAMILY Fodor's Choice ★

Calcot Manor. In an ideal world everyone would sojourn in this oasis of opulence at least once; however, the luxury never gets in the way of the overall air of relaxation, a tribute to the warmth and efficiency of the staff. **Pros:** delightful rural setting; excellent spa facilities; children love it. **Cons:** all but 12 rooms are separate from main building; some traffic noise; steep prices. *Rooms from: £250 A4135 01666/890391 www.calcotmanor.co.uk No credit cards 26 rooms, 9 suites Breakfast.*

SHOPPING

Tetbury is well-known for its antiques shops, some of which are incorporated into small malls.

Highgrove Shop. This pleasant, though pricey, shop sells organic products and gifts inspired by Prince Charles's gardens. *10 Long St. 0845/521–4342 www.highgroveshop.com.*

House of Cheese. Farm-produced cheeses, all wonderfully fresh and flavorsome, are on offer at the House of Cheese. Pâtés, preserves, and olivewood cheeseboards are other goodies at this tiny shop. *13 Church St. 01666/502865 www.houseofcheese.co.uk Closed Mon.*

Long Street Antiques. This spacious and elegant shop offers everything from jewelry and kitchenalia to oak and mahogany furniture. *14 Long St. 01666/500850 www.longstreetantiques.com.*

8

STRATFORD-UPON-AVON AND THE HEART OF ENGLAND

WELCOME TO STRATFORD-UPON-AVON AND THE HEART OF ENGLAND

TOP REASONS TO GO

★ **Shakespeare in Stratford:** To see a play by Shakespeare in the town where he was born—and perhaps after you've visited his birthplace or other sites—is a magical experience.

★ **The city of Birmingham:** The revamped city center shows off its superb art collections and cultural facilities, international cuisine, and renowned Jewellery Quarter.

★ **Half-timber architecture:** Black-and-white half-timber houses are a mark of pride throughout the region; there are concentrations of buildings from medieval times to the Jacobean era in Chester, Shrewsbury, and Ludlow.

★ **Ironbridge Gorge:** Recall the beginnings of England's Industrial Revolution at this fine complex of industrial-heritage museums.

★ **Warwick Castle:** Taking in the history—and some modern kitsch—at this sprawling medieval castle is a fun day out and great for the whole family.

GETTING ORIENTED

1 Stratford-upon-Avon. The birthplace of Shakespeare, the bustling historic town of Stratford-upon-Avon is liberally dotted with 16th-century buildings the playwright would recognize.

2 Around Shakespeare Country. Warwickshire—the county of which Stratford is the southern nexus—has sleepy villages and thatch-roof cottages, as well as stately homes and sprawling Warwick Castle.

3 Birmingham. Britain's second-largest city, once known as "the city of 1,001 trades," now makes the most of its industrial past through some outstanding museums and the biggest canal network outside Venice. There's also buzzing nightlife and an excellent restaurant scene.

4 Great Malvern and Hereford. This region includes the cathedral town of Hereford and bucolic villages set amid lush orchards. Providing a backdrop to it all are the volcanic ridges of the Malvern Hills, where you'll find genteel Great Malvern and Ledbury.

5 Shrewsbury and Chester. The northern, most varied part of the region, studded with its characteristic half-timber buildings, embraces the World Heritage Site of Ironbridge Gorge, the Shropshire hills, and ancient Shrewsbury and Chester, as well as Ludlow with its gastronomic delights.

Stratford-upon-Avon is northwest of London in the midland county of Warwickshire, known as Shakespeare Country. Tiny villages surround it; to the north are two magnificent castles, Warwick and Kenilworth. A little farther northwest is the region's main city, Birmingham. To the southwest, along the Malvern Hills, lie the peaceful spa town of Great Malvern and the prosperous agricultural city of Hereford. The western part of the region, bordering Wales, is hugged by the River Severn. The small city of Shrewsbury is here, close to Ironbridge with its industrial-heritage museums. To its south lies Ludlow, an architectural and culinary hot spot; at the northwestern edge of the region is the ancient city of Chester.

GREAT INDIAN FOOD IN ENGLAND

(above) Chilis add heat to Indian food; you can cool things down with some bread; (right, top) Rogan josh, a spicy choice; (right, below) Chicken tikka masala, a favorite

"Going for an Indian" or "going for a curry"—the two are synonymous—is part of English life. On even the smallest town's main street you'll usually find an Indian restaurant or take-out place, from inexpensive to high-end.

British trade with, and subsequent rule over, India for the two centuries before 1947 has ensured an enduring national appetite for spices. The town of Cheltenham used to be known as an Anglo-Indian paradise because so many "curry-eating colonels" used to retire there. Immigration from Pakistan and Bangladesh in the mid-20th century led to a concentration of restaurants in Birmingham, Manchester, and London. Today you can also find South Indian, Nepalese, and Sri Lankan establishments. The exotic mix of herbs and spices gives Indian food its distinctive appeal. Typically, ginger, garlic, cilantro, cumin, cardamom, fenugreek, and cayenne enhance fresh vegetables and meat (chicken or lamb), fish, or cheese (paneer). Fresh cilantro is a common garnish. But it's the addition of chili that makes things hot: feel free to ask advice when ordering.

ACCOMPANIMENTS

Starters include lime pickle, mango chutney, and *raita* (diced cucumber in mint yogurt), all scooped up with *pappadams* (crispy, fried tortillalike disks made from chickpeas). For the main course, there's plain or pilau Basmati rice, naan bread from the tandoor (barrel-shape clay oven), or chapatis (flat bread). Side dishes include onion or eggplant *bhajis* (spiced fritters) and *sag aloo* (potato with spinach).

Curry is a general term for dishes with a hot, spicy sauce. The strength of each dish is given in italics after the description.

BALTI

Literally meaning "bucket," a *balti* dish is a popular Birmingham invention dating to the 1970s. Different combinations of meat, spices, and vegetables are stir-fried and served at the table in a small wok with handles. Naan or chapatis are accompaniments. *Mild to Medium.*

BIRYANI

Made with stir-fried chicken or lamb, almonds, and golden raisins, this rice-based dish has a dry texture. It can be served with a vegetable curry. *Medium.*

CHICKEN TIKKA MASALA

A British-Bangladeshi invention, this is reputedly the nation's favorite dish. Boneless chunks of chicken breast are marinated in yogurt and garam masala (dry-roasted spices), threaded on a skewer, and cooked in a tandoor. The accompanying creamy, tomato-based sauce is either orange-red from turmeric and paprika or deep red from food coloring. *Mild.*

DHANSAK

Meat or prawns are combined with a thick sweet-and-sour sauce and a red or yellow dal (lentil stew) in a dish that originated in Persia. *Medium to hot.*

DOPIAZA

The name means two or double onions, so expect lots of onions, mixed with green bell peppers. The sauce is reduced, producing concentrated flavors. *Medium hot.*

JALFREZI

This dish derived from British rule in India, when the Indian cook would heat up leftover cold roast meat and potatoes. Fresh meat is cooked with green bell peppers, onions, and plenty of green chilis in a little sauce. *Hot.*

KORMA

Mild and sweet, this curry is very popular. Chicken or lamb is braised in a creamy or yogurt-based sauce to which almonds and coconut are added. *Mild.*

ROGAN JOSH

A staple dish, rogan josh is quite highly spiced. Its deep red color originally came from dried red Kashmiri chilis, but now red bell peppers and tomatoes are used. *Medium hot.*

TANDOORI CHICKEN

Chicken pieces are marinated in a yogurt and spice paste, and then cooked in a tandoor. The red color comes from cayenne pepper, chili powder, or food coloring. It's served dry with slices of lemon or lime, naan, and salad. *Mild.*

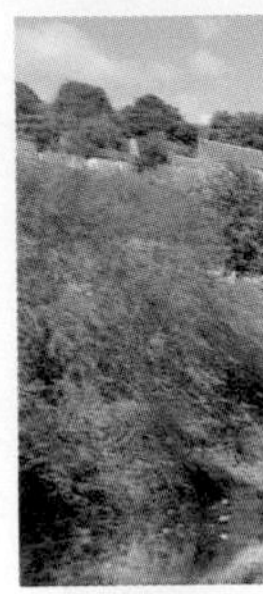

Updated by Kate Hughes And Jack Jewers

The lyricism of England's geographical heartland is found in the remote, half-timber market towns of Herefordshire, Worcestershire, and Shropshire, and in the bucolic villages of Warwickshire. It melts away around the edges of Birmingham—England's second largest city, often maligned by Brits as a grubby postindustrial metropolis, but forging a new identity for itself as a cultural hub.

However, it's the countryside around here that most invokes the England of our imaginations—nowhere more so than Stratford-upon-Avon, birthplace of perhaps the nation's most famous son, William Shakespeare. You get new insight into the great playwright when you visit the stretch of country where he was born and raised. The sculpted, rolling farmland of Warwickshire may look nothing like the forested countryside of the 16th century, but plenty of sturdy Tudor buildings that Shakespeare knew survive to this day (including his birthplace). There's beauty in this—but also the possibility of tourist overkill. Stratford itself, with its Shakespeare sites and the theaters of the Royal Shakespeare Company, sometimes can get to feel like "Shakespeare World." And while Shakespeare himself would recognize plenty of the ancient, timber-framed buildings that line the main shopping streets, the same cannot be said of the bland, cookie-cutter chain stores that occupy most of these buildings today.

Still, there's much more to see—magnificent castles, bucolic churches, and gentle countryside—in this famously lovely part of England. Stop in at Charlecote, a grand Elizabethan manor house, and Baddesley Clinton, a superb example of late-medieval domestic architecture. The huge fortresses of Warwick Castle and Kenilworth Castle provide glimpses into the past.

To the west, some of England's prettiest countryside lies along the 108-mile border with Wales in the counties of Herefordshire, Worcestershire, and Shropshire. The Welsh borders are remote and tranquil, dotted with small villages and market towns full of 13th- and 14th-century black-and-white half-timber buildings, the legacy of a forested countryside. The Victorians were responsible for the more recent fashion of painting these structures black and white. The more elaborately decorated half-timber buildings in market towns such as Shrewsbury and Chester are monuments to wealth, dating mostly from the early 17th century. More half-timbered structures are found in Ludlow, now a culinary center nestled in the lee of its majestic ruined castle.

In the 18th century, in a wooded stretch of the Severn Gorge in Shropshire, the coke blast furnace was invented and the first iron bridge was erected (1779), heralding the birth of the Industrial Revolution. You can get a sense of this history at the museums at Ironbridge Gorge.

The ramifications of that technological leap are what led to the rapid growth of Birmingham, the capital of the Midlands. Its industrial center, which suffered decades of decline in the 20th century, inspired culture as diverse as the heavy metal sound of Black Sabbath and the dark realm of Mordor in J.R.R. Tolkien's *The Lord of the Rings*. Today an imaginative makeover and active, varied cultural life are draws for anyone interested in the rebirth of modern urban Britain.

STRATFORD-UPON-AVON AND THE HEART OF ENGLAND PLANNER

WHEN TO GO

The Shakespeare sights get very crowded on weekends and school vacations; Warwick Castle usually brims with visitors, so arrive early in the day. Throughout the region, some country properties fill up quickly on weekends. Most rural sights have limited opening hours in winter and some stately homes have limited hours even in summer, which is when the countryside is at its most appealing. The open-air performances at Ludlow Castle take place at the end of June; the Autumn in Malvern Festival happens on weekends in October.

8

PLANNING YOUR TIME

Stratford-upon-Avon is ideal for day visits from London or as a base for exploring nearby, but even ardent Shakespeare lovers probably won't need more than a day or two here. Warwick can be explored in an hour or two, but allow half a day to tackle the many lines at busy Warwick Castle. A drive through the area's country lanes is a pleasant way to spend a day; a stop at any stately home will take a few hours. You're also near the northern Cotswolds if you want to explore the countryside further.

The museums and major sights of Birmingham can be covered in a day, and it's a good city for modern, budget hotels. However, the smaller cities of Hereford, Shrewsbury, and Chester have more obvious charms. If you want to walk the hills, Great Malvern or Ledbury are good gateways for the Malvern Hills. In the north of the region, Ironbridge Gorge and Chester demand a full day each. Ludlow and Shrewsbury take less time. Once you've gone as far north as this, you could consider going on to Liverpool, or hopping across the border into North Wales.

GETTING HERE AND AROUND

AIR TRAVEL

The region is served by Birmingham International Airport, 6 miles east of the city center. It has connections to all of Britain's major cities and limited service to the United States.

Contacts Birmingham International Airport. ✉ *A45, off M42, Birmingham* ☎ *0870/222–0072* 🌐 *www.birminghamairport.co.uk.*

BUS TRAVEL

The cheapest way to travel is by bus, and National Express serves the region from London's Victoria Coach Station. You can reach Birmingham in less than three hours; Hereford and Shrewsbury take between four and five hours. It also operates services from London's Heathrow (2¾ hours) and Gatwick (4 hours) airports to Birmingham.

Stagecoach serves local routes throughout the Stratford and Birmingham areas. Megabus, a budget service booked online, runs double-decker buses from Victoria Station in London to Birmingham. The First bus company has service between Birmingham, Hereford, and Ludlow.

Contacts First. ☎ *0871/200–2233* 🌐 *www.firstgroup.com.* **Megabus.** ☎ *0141/352–4444 for inquiries, 0900/160–0900 booking line; calls cost 61p per minute (mobiles more)* 🌐 *www.megabus.com.* **National Express.** ☎ *0871/781–8178* 🌐 *www.nationalexpress.com.* **Stagecoach.** ☎ *0845/600–1314* 🌐 *www.stagecoachbus.com.*

CAR TRAVEL

To reach Stratford (100 miles), Birmingham (120 miles), Shrewsbury (150 miles), Ludlow (140 miles), and Chester (180 miles) from London, take M40. For the farther areas, keep on it until it becomes M42, or take M1/M6. M4 and then M5 from London take you to Hereford in just under three hours. Driving can be difficult in the region's western reaches—especially in the hills and valleys west of Hereford, where steep, twisting roads often narrow down into mere trackways.

Around Stratford, one pleasure of this rural area is driving the smaller "B" roads, which lead deep into the countryside. Local public bus service isn't sufficient for most sightseeing journeys around Warwickshire. Renting a car or taking a tour bus are the two best options, although trains serve the major towns.

TRAIN TRAVEL

Stratford has good train service and can be seen as a day trip from London if your time is limited (a matinee is your best bet if you want to squeeze in a play). Chiltern Railways trains leave from London Marylebone Station and take 2 hours direct, or 2½ hours with transfers. They also go to Warwick. A one-day (£35) or four-day (£50) Shakespeare Explorer ticket can offer big savings if you're going to stay in the region. London Midland serves the area from Birmingham (about 40 miles from Stratford). From London, Virgin and London Midland trains leave from Euston while Chiltern Railways trains leave from Marylebone. Trains from Euston tend to be quicker (around 1½ hours). Travel times from Paddington to Hereford and Ludlow are about 3 hours (most change at Newport); Euston to Shrewsbury, with a change at Crewe or Birmingham, is 2½ hours; and to Chester, direct or with a change at Crewe, takes 2 hours. West Midlands Day Ranger tickets (£22.50) and Heart of England Rover tickets, which can be used for three non-consecutive days over a week (£74), allow unlimited travel on trains throughout the region.

Contacts Chiltern Railways. ☎ *0845/600–5165* 🌐 *www.chilternrailways.co.uk.* **London Midland.** ☎ *0344/811–0133* 🌐 *www.londonmidland.com.* **National Rail Enquiries.** ☎ *0845/748–4950* 🌐 *www.nationalrail.co.uk.*

RESTAURANTS

Stratford has many reasonably priced bistros and unpretentious eateries offering a broad choice of international fare; Warwick and Kenilworth both have good restaurant options. Birmingham has good international restaurants but is probably most famous for its Indian and Pakistani "curry houses"; you'll find good choices both in the city center and out of town. The city hosts the annual Taste of Birmingham Festival in July. In the rest of the Midlands, casual spots dominate, although Ludlow has some exceptionally good restaurants.

HOTELS

Stratford and Warwick have accommodations to fit every wallet. Because Stratford is so popular with theatergoers, book well ahead. Most hotels offer discounted two- and three-day packages. Near Stratford, a number of top-notch country hotels guarantee discreet but attentive service—at fancy prices. Birmingham's hotels, geared to the convention crowd and often booked well in advance, are mostly bland and impersonal, but a few are sophisticated; look for weekend discounts. In the country-side, many ancient inns and venerable Regency style houses have been converted into hotels. ⇨ *Hotel reviews have been shortened. For full information, visit Fodors.com.*

WHAT IT COSTS IN POUNDS

	$	$$	$$$	$$$$
Restaurants	under £15	£15–£19	£20–£25	over £25
Hotels	under £100	£100–£160	£161–£220	over £220

Restaurant prices are the average cost of a main course at dinner, or if dinner is not served, at lunch. Hotels prices are the lowest cost of a standard double room in high season, including 20% V.A.T.

VISITOR INFORMATION

Traveline can field all general transportation inquiries. Local tourist offices can recommend day or half-day tours of the region and will have the names of registered Blue Badge guides.

Contacts Heart of England Tourist Board. ☎ *01905/887690* 🌐 *www.visitheartofengland.com.* **Shakespeare Country.** ☎ *0871/978–0800* 🌐 *www.shakespeare-country.co.uk.* **Traveline.** ☎ *0871/200–2233* 🌐 *www.traveline.info.*

8

With its thatch roof, half-timbering, and countryside setting, Anne Hathaway's Cottage is a vision from the past.

STRATFORD-UPON-AVON

Even under the weight of busloads of visitors, Stratford, on the banks of the slow-flowing River Avon, has somehow hung on to much of its ancient character and on a good day, can still feel like an English market town. It doesn't take long to figure out who's the center of attention here. Born in a half-timber, early-16th-century building in the center of Stratford on April 23, 1564, William Shakespeare died on April 23, 1616, his 52nd birthday, in a more imposing house at New Place. Although he spent much of his life in London, the world still associates him with "Shakespeare's Avon."

Here, in the years between his birth and 1587, he played as a young lad, attended grammar school, and married Anne Hathaway; and here he returned as a prosperous man. You can see Shakespeare's whole life here: his birthplace on Henley Street; his burial place in Holy Trinity Church; Anne Hathaway's Cottage; the home of his mother, Mary Arden, at Wilmcote; New Place; and the neighboring Nash's House, home of Shakespeare's granddaughter.

By the 16th century, Stratford was a prosperous market town with thriving guilds and industries. Half-timber houses from this era have been preserved, and they're set off by later architecture, such as the elegant Georgian storefronts on Bridge Street, with their 18th-century porticoes and arched doorways.

Most sights cluster around Henley Street (off the roundabout as you come in on the A3400 Birmingham road), High Street, and Waterside, which skirts the public gardens through which the River Avon flows.

Bridge and Sheep streets (parallel to Bridge) are Stratford's main thoroughfares and the site of most banks, shops, and eateries. Bridgefoot, between the canal and the river, is next to Clopton Bridge—"a sumptuous new bridge and large of stone"—built in the 15th century by Sir Hugh Clopton, once lord mayor of London and one of Stratford's richest and most philanthropic residents.

GETTING HERE AND AROUND

Stratford lies about 100 miles northwest of London; take M40 to Junction 15. The town is 37 miles southeast of Birmingham by A435 and A46 or by M40 to Junction 15.

Chiltern Railways serves the area from London's Marylebone Station. Six direct trains a day take just over two hours to reach Stratford; other trains require changing at Birmingham. London Midland operates direct routes from Birmingham's Snow Hill Station (journey time under an hour). Stratford has two stations, Stratford Parkway, northwest of the center at Bishopston, and Stratford at the edge of the town center on Alcester Road, from which you can take a taxi or walk the short distance into town.

Stratford's center is small and easily walkable—it's unlikely you'd need to use the local bus service.

PLANNING YOUR TIME

If you have only a day here, arrive early and confine your visit to two or three Shakespeare Birthplace Trust properties, a few other town sights, a pub lunch, and a walk along the river, capped off by a stroll to the cottage of Anne Hathaway. If you don't like crowds, avoid visiting on weekends and school vacations, and take in the main Shakespeare shrines in the early morning to see them at their least frenetic. One high point of Stratford's calendar is the Shakespeare Birthday Celebrations, usually on the weekend nearest to April 23.

TOURS

City Sightseeing. Hop-on, hop-off guided tours of Stratford are run by City Sightseeing, and you can combine the tour (about an hour with no stops) with entry to either three or five Shakespeare houses. *01789/412680 www.city-sightseeing.com From £12.50.*

Shakespeare Birthplace Trust. The main places of Shakespearean interest (Anne Hathaway's Cottage, Hall's Croft, Mary Arden's House, New Place and Nash's House, Shakespeare's Birthplace, and Shakespeare's Grave) are run by the Shakespeare Birthplace Trust. Buy a money-saving combination ticket to five properties for £23.90, or pay separate entry fees if you're visiting only one or two. Family tickets are an option, too. Advance booking online gives you a 10% discount and tickets are valid for a year. Tickets for Hall's Croft, New Place, and Nash's House are available only as a rather pricey (£15.90) joint ticket, which includes the birthplace and grave. *01789/204016 www.shakespeare.org.uk.*

Stratford Town Walk. This walking tour runs year-round and also offers ghost-themed walks and cruises. *07855/576–0377, 01789/292478 www.stratfordtownwalk.co.uk From £5 Weekdays at 11, weekends at 11 and 2.*

8

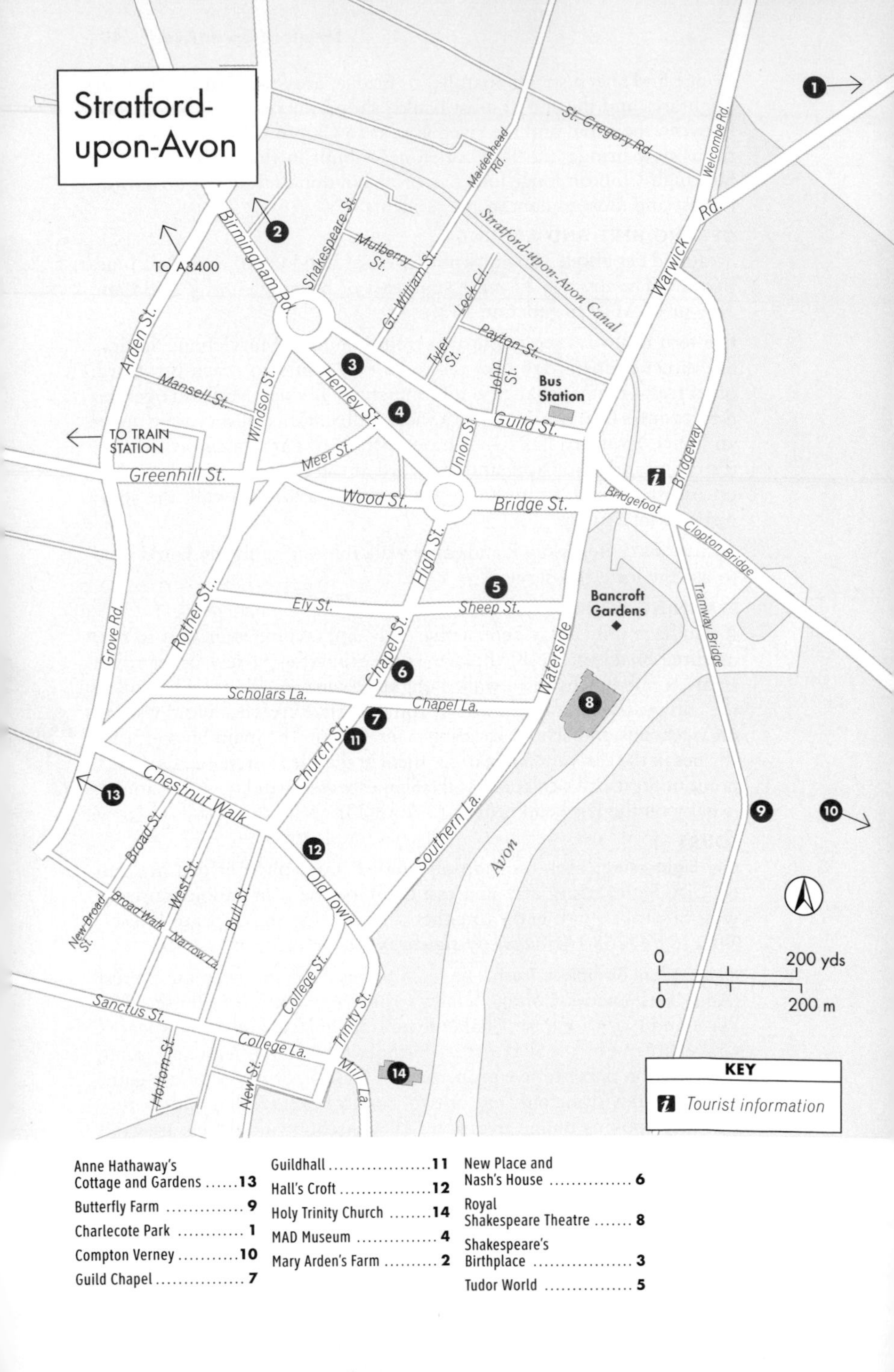

Anne Hathaway's Cottage and Gardens 13
Butterfly Farm 9
Charlecote Park 1
Compton Verney 10
Guild Chapel 7
Guildhall 11
Hall's Croft 12
Holy Trinity Church 14
MAD Museum 4
Mary Arden's Farm 2
New Place and Nash's House 6
Royal Shakespeare Theatre 8
Shakespeare's Birthplace 3
Tudor World 5

ESSENTIALS

Visitor Information Stratford-upon-Avon Tourist Information Centre. ✉ *Bridgefoot* ☎ *01789/264293* 🌐 *www.discover-stratford.com.*

EXPLORING

TOP ATTRACTIONS

Fodor's Choice ★ **Anne Hathaway's Cottage and Gardens.** The most picturesque of the Shakespeare Trust properties, on the western outskirts of Stratford, was the family home of the woman Shakespeare married in 1582. The "cottage," actually a substantial Tudor farmhouse, has latticed windows and a grand thatch roof. Inside is period furniture, including the settle where Shakespeare reputedly conducted his courtship, and a rare carved Elizabethan bed; outside is a garden planted in lush Edwardian style with herbs and flowers. A stroll through the adjacent orchard takes you to willow cabins where you can listen to sonnets and view sculptures with Shakespearean themes, while the nearby arboretum has trees, shrubs, and roses mentioned in Shakespeare's works. **■ TIP→ The best way to get here is on foot, especially in late spring when the apple trees are in blossom.** The signed path runs from Evesham Place (an extension of Grove Road) opposite Chestnut Walk. Pick up a leaflet with a map from the tourist office; the walk takes a good half hour. ✉ *Cottage La., Shottery* ☎ *01789/295517* 🌐 *www.shakespeare.org.uk* 🎟 *£9.50; £23.90 with the Five House Pass which includes Hall's Croft, Mary Arden's Farm, New Place and Nash's House, Shakespeare's Birthplace, and Shakespeare's Grave* ⏲ *Mid-Mar.–Oct., daily 9–5; Nov.–mid-Mar., daily 10–4.*

Charlecote Park. A celebrated house in the village of Hampton Lucy, Charlecote Park was built in 1572 by Sir Thomas Lucy to entertain Queen Elizabeth I (in her honor, the house is shaped like the letter "E"). Shakespeare knew the house and may even have poached deer here. Overlooking the River Avon, the redbrick manor is striking and sprawling. It was renovated in neo-Elizabethan style by the Lucy family, represented here by numerous portraits, during the mid-19th century; a carved ebony bed is one of many spectacular pieces of furniture. The Tudor gatehouse is unchanged since Shakespeare's day, and a collection of carriages, a Victorian kitchen, and a small brewery occupy the outbuildings. Indulge in a game of croquet near the quirky, thatched, Victorian-era summer hut, or explore the deer park landscaped by Capability Brown. Interesting themed tours and walks take place in summer—call in advance to find out what's on offer. The house is 6 miles northeast of Stratford; by car take the B4086. ✉ *B4086, off A429, Hampton Lucy* ☎ *01789/470277* 🌐 *www.nationaltrust.org.uk* 🎟 *£10.05, £6.80 in winter; grounds only £6.80* ⏲ *House mid-Feb.–Mar., Thurs.–Tues. noon–3:30; Apr.–Oct., Thurs.–Tues. 11–4:30; Nov.–Dec., weekends noon–3:30. Park and gardens daily 10:30–5:30 or dusk. Last entry 30 min before closing.*

Holy Trinity Church. The burial place of William Shakespeare, this 13th-century church sits on the banks of the Avon with a graceful avenue of lime trees framing its entrance. Shakespeare's final resting place is in

8

the chancel, rebuilt in 1465–91 in the late Perpendicular style. He was buried here not because he was a famed poet but because he was a lay rector of Stratford, owning a portion of the township tithes. On the north wall of the sanctuary, over the altar steps, is the famous marble bust created by Gerard Jansen in 1623 and thought to be a true likeness of Shakespeare. The bust offers a more human, even humorous, perspective when viewed from the side. Also in the chancel are the graves of Shakespeare's wife, Anne; his daughter Susanna; his son-in-law John Hall; and his granddaughter's husband, Thomas Nash. Nearby, the Parish Register is displayed, containing Shakespeare's baptismal entry (1564) and his burial notice (1616). ✉ *Trinity St.* ☎ *01789/266316* 🌐 *www.stratford-upon-avon.org* 🎫 *£2 for chancel* ⏲ *Mar. and Oct., Mon.–Sat. 9–5, Sun. 12:30–5; Apr.–Sept., Mon.–Sat. 8:30–6, Sun. 12:30–5; Nov.–Feb., Mon.–Sat. 9–4, Sun. 12:30–5; last admission 20 min before closing.*

FAMILY **MAD Museum.** Push buttons and pedals to your heart's content to make the exhibits in the Museum of Mechanical Art and Design come alive. Witty, beautiful, and intricate automata and examples of kinetic art will clank, whirr, and rattle away. Marbles and Ping-Pong balls thread and bounce through looping runs, a typewriter play tunes on glasses and bottles, and two trains chuff around high up on the walls. Kids will love constructing their own marble run and grown-ups will marvel at the Kitchenator display. There's also a shop full of weird and wonderful things to buy. ✉ *4–5 Henley St.* ☎ *01789/269356* 🌐 *themadmuseum.co.uk* 🎫 *£6.80* ⏲ *Apr.–Sept., weekdays 10–5, weekends 10–5:30; Oct.–Mar., weekdays 10:30–4:30, weekends 10–5:30.*

FAMILY **Mary Arden's Farm.** A working farm, where food is grown using methods common in the 16th century, is the main attraction at Mary Arden's House (the childhood home of Shakespeare's mother) and Palmer's Farm. This bucolic stop is great for kids, who can try their hand at basket weaving and gardening, listen as the farmers explain their work in the fields, and watch the cooks prepare food in the Tudor farmhouse kitchen. It all brings the past to life. There are crafts exhibits, a café, and a garden. The site is 3 miles northwest of Stratford; you need to walk or drive here, or else go with a tour. ✉ *Off A3400, Wilmcote* ☎ *01789/293455* 🌐 *www.shakespeare.org.uk* 🎫 *£12.50; £23.90 with the Five House Pass which includes Anne Hathaway's Cottage and Gardens, Hall's Croft, Mary Arden's Farm, Nash's House and New Place, Shakespeare's Birthplace, and Shakespeare's Grave* ⏲ *Mid-Mar.–Oct., daily 10–5.*

Fodor's Choice ★ **Royal Shakespeare Theatre.** Set amid gardens along the River Avon, the Stratford home of the world-renowned Royal Shakespeare Company has a viewing tower and well-regarded rooftop restaurant among its amenities. The company, which presents some of the world's finest productions of Shakespeare's plays, has existed since 1879. Shows are also staged in the Swan. ■ **TIP→ Book ahead for the popular backstage tour.** ✉ *Waterside* ☎ *0844/800–1110 ticket hotline* 🌐 *www.rsc.org.uk* 🎫 *Backstage tour £7.50, front of house tour £5.50, open-air tour £6.50, tower visit £2.50.*

Fodor's Choice ★ **Shakespeare's Birthplace.** A half-timber house typical of its time, the playwright's birthplace is a much-visited shrine that has been altered and restored since he lived here. Passing through the modern visitor center, you are immersed in the world of Shakespeare through an exhibition that displays the First Folio, deeds to his properties, what is thought to be his signet ring, busts, and other memorabilia. The house itself is across the garden from the visitor center. Colorful wall decorations and the furnishings reflect comfortable, middle-class Elizabethan domestic life. Shakespeare's father, John, a glove maker and wool dealer, purchased the house; a reconstructed workshop shows the tools of the glover's trade. Mark Twain and Charles Dickens were both pilgrims here, and you can see the signatures of Thomas Carlyle and Walter Scott scratched into Shakespeare's windowpanes. In the garden, actors present excerpts from the plays. There's also a café and bookshop on the grounds. ✉ *Henley St.* ☎ *01789/201822* 🌐 *www.shakespeare.org.uk* 🎟 *£15.90, includes entry to Hall's Croft, Nash's House and New Place, and Shakespeare's Grave* ⏲ *Mid-Mar.–June, Sept., and Oct., daily 9–5; July and Aug., daily 9–6; Nov.–mid-Mar., daily 10–4.*

QUICK BITES

Hobsons Patisseries. Visitors and locals alike head for the half-timber Hobsons Patisserie to indulge in the famous savory pies or scrumptious afternoon teas. ✉ *1 Henley St.* ☎ *01789/293330.*

WORTH NOTING

FAMILY **Butterfly Farm.** Europe's largest displays of exotic butterflies, spiders, caterpillars, and insects from all over the world are housed in a tropical greenhouse, a two-minute walk past the Bridgefoot footbridge. Kids can watch as butterflies emerge from pupae or take a look at a toxic black widow spider. ✉ *Swan's Nest La.* ☎ *01789/299288* 🌐 *www.butterflyfarm.co.uk* 🎟 *£6.25* ⏲ *Apr.–Sept., daily 10–6; Oct.–Mar., daily 10–5.*

Compton Verney. A neoclassical country mansion remodeled in the 1760s by Robert Adam has been repurposed by the Peter Moores Foundation as an art museum with more than 800 works. The house is set in 120 acres of rolling parkland and lake landscaped by Capability Brown. The works of art are intriguingly varied and beautifully displayed in restored rooms: British folk art and portraits, textiles, Chinese pottery and bronzes, southern Italian art from 1600 to 1800, and German art from 1450 to 1600 are the main focus. Daily tours take place at noon and 2:30. It's 9 miles east of Stratford; by car, take the B4086. ✉ *Off B4086, near Kineton* ☎ *01926/645500* 🌐 *www.comptonverney.org.uk* 🎟 *£7.25; extra charge for exhibitions* ⏲ *Mar.–mid-Dec., Tues.–Sun. and holiday Mon. 11–5; last entry 30 min before closing.*

Guild Chapel. This chapel is the noble centerpiece of Stratford's Guild buildings, including the Guildhall, the Grammar School, and the almshouses—all well known to Shakespeare. The ancient structure was rebuilt in the late Perpendicular style in the first half of the 15th century, thanks to the largesse of Stratford resident Hugh Clopton. Its otherwise plain interior includes fragments of a remarkable medieval fresco of the Last Judgment painted over in the 16th century and uncovered in a 20th-century reconstruction. The curfew bell still rings at 7 o'clock every evening. ✉ *Chapel La. , at Church St.* ☎ *01789/207111* 🎟 *Free, donations welcome* ⏲ *Daily 10–4.*

Guildhall. Dating back to 1416, the Guildhall is occupied by King Edward's Grammar School, which Shakespeare probably attended as a boy; it's still used as a school. On the first floor is the Guildhall proper, where traveling acting companies performed. Many historians believe that it was after seeing the troupe known as the Earl of Leicester's Men in 1587 that Shakespeare got the acting bug and set off for London. The Guildhall is only open a few days a year, sometimes during school vacations. Some investigating is usually required to find out what days these are. Immediately beyond the Guildhall on Church Street is a row of 15th-century timber-and-daub almshouses, built for the poor and now serving as housing for pensioners. ✉ *Church St.*

Hall's Croft. One of the finest surviving Jacobean (early 17th-century) town houses, this impressive residence has a delightful walled garden. Hall's Croft was the home of Shakespeare's elder daughter, Susanna, and her husband, Dr. John Hall, a wealthy physician who, by prescribing an herbal cure for scurvy, was well ahead of his time. One room is furnished as a medical dispensary of the period, and throughout the building are fine examples of heavy oak Jacobean furniture, including a child's high chair and some 17th-century portraits. The café serves light lunches and afternoon teas. ✉ *Old Town* ☎ *01789/292107* 🌐 *www.shakespeare.org.uk* 🎟 *£15.90, includes admission to Shakespeare's Birthplace, New Place and Nash's House, and Shakespeare's Grave* ⏲ *Mid-Mar.–Oct., daily 10–5; Nov.–mid-Mar., daily 11–4.*

New Place and Nash's House. Originally built in 1483 "of brike and tymber" for a lord mayor of London, **New Place** was Stratford's grandest piece of real estate when Shakespeare bought it in 1597 for £60. Along with a celebrated mulberry tree, revered for being planted by Shakespeare himself, the house was torn down in 1759 by the Reverend Francis Gastrell, who was angry at the hordes of Shakespeare-related sightseers. This in turn provoked the wrath of the local inhabitants, who drove him out of town. Now imaginatively reinterpreted to mark the 400th anniversary of Shakespeare's death in 1616, it shows the footprint of the original house and focuses on a deep, illuminated pool. Next door is **Nash's House,** the residence of Thomas Nash, who married Shakespeare's last direct descendant, his granddaughter Elizabeth Hall; it holds finds from recent excavations of the area. The gardens contain a restored Elizabethan knot garden and a fine display of cloud topiary. Currently closed for renovations, the site reopens in April 2016. ✉ *Chapel St.* ☎ *01789/292325* 🌐 *www.shakespeare.org.uk* 🎟 *£15.90, includes admission to Shakespeare's Birthplace, Hall's Croft, and Shakespeare's Grave* ⏲ *Mid-Mar.–Oct., daily 10–5; Nov.–mid-Mar., daily 11–4.*

FAMILY **Tudor World.** Tread carefully over the cobbles and enter Tudor World to find a dimly lighted and quirky maze of displays that explore, with the help of Tudor mannequins, aspects of the 16th century—the plague years, early medicine, bearbaiting, punishment, and alleged ghosts. Kids

Stratford-upon-Avon has plenty of pubs and restaurants when you need a break from the Shakespeare trail.

will enjoy peering round the curtains and opening the boxes of smells. At night, adults-only "ghost tours" (£7.50; nightly at 6) explore the house's paranormal history in spooky detail. ✉ *The Shrieves House Barn, 40 Sheep St.* ☎ *01789/298070* 🌐 *www.falstaffexperience.co.uk* 🎫 *£5.50* ⏲ *Daily 10:30–5:30.*

WHERE TO EAT

$ BRITISH Fodor's Choice ★ ✕ **The Black Swan/The Dirty Duck.** The only pub in Britain to be licensed under two names (the more informal one came courtesy of American GIs who were stationed here during World War II), this is one of Stratford's most celebrated pubs—it's attracted actors since the 18th-century thespian David Garrick's days. A little veranda overlooks the theaters and the river here. Along with your pint of bitter, you can choose from the extensive menu of baked potatoes, steaks, burgers, and grills; there are also good-value set menus. Few people come here for the food, though you will need to book ahead for dinner: the real attraction is the ambience and your fellow customers. [$] *Average main: £8* ✉ *Waterside* ☎ *01789/297312* 🌐 *www.oldenglishinns.co.uk.*

$$ MODERN BRITISH ✕ **Church Street Town House.** Theatergoers tucking into an early supper to the strains of the grand piano in the Blue Bar, grandmothers enjoying afternoon tea in the Library, and couples lingering over their candlelit suppers can all happily be found here. Plush armchairs, red drapes, and oil paintings add to the intimacy and refinement of this 18th-century town house. The chef aims to keep flavors to the fore and uses local produce in such dishes as oat-crusted calves' liver with smoked garlic mash and spinach or grilled haddock with parsley and Parmesan crumb.

There's an excellent choice of cheeses. You could finish with a glass of port in one of the dozen bedrooms, should you wish to linger. *Average main: £16* ✉ *16 Church St.* ☎ *01789/262222* 🌐 *www.churchstreettownhouse.com.*

$ INDIAN ✕ **Hussain's.** The luxuriant marigolds in the window might draw you in, but locals will tell you that the Indian dishes are excellent here. The extensive menu lists plenty of balti and rogan josh dishes: for something mild, try the tandoori chicken with mild spices, cream, ground almonds, and mixed fruits, or increase the heat a bit with *jhinga bhuna* (king-size prawns in a spicy tomato sauce with onions, green peppers, and coriander). Wash it all down with Cobra draft beer. *Average main: £9* ✉ *6A Chapel St.* ☎ *01789/267506* 🌐 *www.hussains-restaurant.com* ⏲ *No lunch Mon.–Wed.*

$ SOUTHERN ITALIAN ✕ **Il Moro.** Chef Massimilliano Melis takes pride in serving up Italian dishes with a Sardinian emphasis in this slick, family-run restaurant. You could start with an aperitivo on the roof terrace, followed by fresh pea and *fregola* (pasta made with semolina) soup, and then move on to pork with Pecorino cheese, pancetta, and rocket salad. Try a Sardinian dessert wine or homemade truffles to round off the meal. *Average main: £14* ✉ *27 Henley St., at Windsor St.* ☎ *01789/415770* 🌐 *www.ilmoro.co.uk* ⏲ *Closed Sun.*

$ BRITISH ✕ **Lambs of Sheep Street.** Sit downstairs to appreciate the hardwood floors and oak beams of this local epicurean favorite; upstairs, the look is a bit more contemporary. The updates of tried-and-true dishes include salmon cakes with sorrel sauce, and slow-roasted Cotswold lamb shank with creamed potatoes. Desserts are fantastic here, and daily specials keep the menu seasonal. The two- and three-course fixed-price menus (£14 and £18) for lunch or pretheater dining on weekdays are good deals. *Average main: £14* ✉ *12 Sheep St.* ☎ *01789/292554* 🌐 *www.lambsrestaurant.co.uk* ⏲ *No lunch Mon.* *Reservations essential.*

$ FRENCH ✕ **Le Bistrot Pierre.** There's always a satisfied hum in the air at this large, modern, and bustling bistro, part of a small chain, that's close to the river. It's French and make no mistake about it: olives from Provence, sausage from the Beaujolais region, pâtés, mussels in a Roquefort sauce, beef bourguignonne , and rustic French cheeses all appear on the menu. Croque monsieur (toasted ham and cheese sandwich) is a popular lunchtime dish. Vegetarians are well catered to, and the service is amicable and attentive. *Average main: £14* ✉ *Swan's Nest La.* ☎ *01789/264804* 🌐 *www.lebistrotpierre.co.uk.*

$ MODERN BRITISH ✕ **Opposition.** Hearty, warming meals are offered at this informal, family-style restaurant in a 16th-century building on the main dining street near the theaters. The English and international dishes—chicken roasted with banana and served with curry sauce and basmati rice, for instance—win praise from the locals. There's a good range of lighter and vegetarian options and fixed-price menus as well. Make reservations a month ahead in summer. *Average main: £14* ✉ *13 Sheep St.* ☎ *01789/269980* 🌐 *www.theoppo.co.uk* ⏲ *Closed Sun.*

$$ ITALIAN ✕ **Sorrento.** Family-run, this Italian restaurant takes a respectable, old-fashioned approach to service. Upon arrival, sip an aperitif in the lounge before you're escorted to your table for a silver-service, white-tablecloth

meal. The menu of traditional favorites is cooked from family recipes and includes a starter of goat cheese with roast peppers and beetroot salad, and main dishes of deep-fried calamari or linguini lobster with cockles and mussels in a garlic-and-chili sauce. There's also a hearty risotto of the day. Pretheater dinners are a good value. *Average main: £16 8 Ely St. 01789/297999 www.sorrentorestaurant.co.uk Closed Sun. and Mon.*

$ BISTRO **The Vintner.** The imaginative, bistro-inspired menu varies each day at this café and wine bar. Pork fillet with caper butter is a popular main course, as are the steak and the selection of tapas; a children's menu is also available. To dine before curtain time, arrive early or make a reservation. The building, largely unaltered since the late 1400s, has lovely flagstone floors and oak beams. *Average main: £14 5 Sheep St. 01789/297259 www.the-vintner.co.uk.*

WHERE TO STAY

$$$ HOTEL **Arden Hotel.** Bedrooms are spacious and discreet with splashes of green, violet, and dark crimson in this redbrick boutique hotel across the road from the Royal Shakespeare Theatre. **Pros:** convenient to the Shakespeare theater; crisp and modern style; large bathrooms. **Cons:** gets booked up quickly; plastic, not real, orchids. *Rooms from: £180 Waterside 01789/298682 www.theardenhotelstratford.com 45 rooms Breakfast.*

$$ B&B/INN **The Bell.** Just a few miles south of Stratford, this "pub with rooms" oozes imagination and individuality, with sophisticated and funky guest rooms that have beautiful bathrooms and mix antiques with brightly colored ornaments and cushions, crystal chandeliers, even a large golden coronet. **Pros:** rural setting; excellent food; friendly service. **Cons:** on a main road. *Rooms from: £110 Shipston Rd., Alderminster 01789/450414 www.thebellald.co.uk 8 rooms, 1 suite Breakfast.*

$$ B&B/INN **Cherry Trees.** Although it's nothing fancy from the outside, this modern house near the river offers three beautifully and individually furnished suites in a tranquil location with a chic rear garden. **Pros:** welcoming hosts; great breakfasts; convenient to in-town sights. **Cons:** too small for some. *Rooms from: £110 Swan's Nest La. 01789/292989 www.cherrytrees-stratford.co.uk 3 suites Breakfast.*

$$ HOTEL **Ettington Park Hotel.** Built on land owned by the Shirley family since the 12th century, this Victorian Gothic mansion is a soothing retreat for theatergoers who don't want to cope with Stratford's crowds. **Pros:** gorgeous building; spacious rooms; relaxing lounge. **Cons:** a bit too formal for some; well outside Stratford; many wedding guests on weekends. *Rooms from: £140 Off A3400, Alderminster 0845/072–7454 www.handpickedhotels.co.uk 42 rooms, 6 suites Breakfast.*

$$ HOTEL **Falcon Hotel.** Licensed as an alehouse since 1640, this black-and-white timber-frame hotel in the center of town has an excellent location as well as a light, airy interior that looks out to a pleasant garden. **Pros:** great location; old portion of the building is charming; friendly staff. **Cons:** piped music can be intrusive; rooms can be hot; £5 parking

8

charge. *Rooms from: £115* *Chapel St.* *01789/279953* *www.sjhotels.co.uk* *83 rooms* *Breakfast.*

$$ HOTEL FAMILY **Holiday Inn Stratford-upon-Avon.** This spick-and-span, good-value hotel's selling points are an excellent location near the center of the historic district and views across the river. **Pros:** good location; handy for families; free accommodation and dinners for kids under 13. **Cons:** modern and featureless; big and impersonal. *Rooms from: £125* *Bridgefoot* *0871/942–9270 for reservations, 01789/279988 for inquiries* *www.holidayinn.com* *259 rooms, 2 suites* *Breakfast.*

$$ HOTEL **Macdonald Alveston Manor.** This redbrick Elizabethan manor house across the River Avon has plenty of historic details, as well as a modern spa with a long list of treatments. **Pros:** nice mix of historic and modern; you can warm yourself by a fire in winter. **Cons:** modern rooms are less interesting; there's no elevator and lots of stairs; parking fee. *Rooms from: £150* *Clopton Bridge* *0844/879–9138* *www.macdonald-hotels.co.uk* *110 rooms, 3 suites* *Breakfast.*

$$$ HOTEL **Menzies Welcombe Hotel Spa & Golf Club.** With its mullioned bay windows, gables, and tall chimneys, this hotel in an 1886 neo-Jacobean-style building evokes the luxury of bygone days. **Pros:** great for golfers; good spa facilities; gorgeous grounds and gardens. **Cons:** dining too formal for some; need a car to get here. *Rooms from: £165* *Warwick Rd.* *01789/295252* *www.menzies-hotels.co.uk* *78 rooms* *Breakfast.*

$$ HOTEL **Mercure Stratford-Upon-Avon Shakespeare Hotel.** Built in the 1400s, this Elizabethan town house in the heart of town is a vision right out of *The Merry Wives of Windsor*, with its nine gables and long, stunning, black-and-white half-timber facade. **Pros:** historic building; relaxing lounge. **Cons:** some very small bedrooms; charge for parking. *Rooms from: £140* *Chapel St.* *01789/294997* *www.mercure.com* *63 rooms, 10 suites* *Breakfast.*

$$ HOTEL **The Stratford.** Although this modern hotel may lack the period charm of older hotels, its up-to-date facilities, spacious rooms, and ample grounds make it a good option if Tudor beamed ceilings aren't a must. **Pros:** friendly; handy location near train station; lots of modern conveniences. **Cons:** largely used as a conference hotel; rooms lack personality; parking charge. *Rooms from: £120* *Arden St.* *01789/271000* *www.qhotels.co.uk* *102 rooms* *Breakfast.*

$ B&B/INN **Victoria Spa Lodge.** This good-value B&B, run by the same family for 30 years, lies 1½ miles outside town, within view of the Stratford Canal; the grand, clematis-draped building dates from 1837. **Pros:** beautiful building; full of character; family-friendly. **Cons:** away from the town center; too old-fashioned for some. *Rooms from: £70* *Bishopton La., Bishopton* *01789/267985* *www.victoriaspa.co.uk* *7 rooms* *Breakfast.*

$$ HOTEL Fodor's Choice ★ **White Swan.** None of the character of this black-and-white timbered hotel, which claims to be the oldest building in Stratford, has been lost in its swanky but sympathetic update. **Pros:** antiquity; generous bathrooms; friendly service. **Cons:** charge for parking, which is not on-site; stripey carpet may cause dizziness. *Rooms from: £145* *Rother St.*

☎ *01789/297022* 🌐 *www.white-swan-stratford.co.uk* *37 rooms, 4 suites* *Breakfast.*

NIGHTLIFE AND PERFORMING ARTS

FESTIVALS

Shakespeare Birthday Celebrations. These festivities take place on and around the weekend closest to April 23. The events, spread over several days, include lectures, free concerts, processions, and impromptu performances. ✉ *Stratford-upon-Avon* ☎ *01789/264293* 🌐 *www.shakespearesbirthday.org.uk.*

THEATER

Fodor's Choice ★ **Royal Shakespeare Company.** One of the finest repertory troupes in the world and long the backbone of the country's theatrical life, the company performs plays year-round in Stratford and at venues around Britain. The stunning Royal Shakespeare Theatre, home of the RSC, has a thrust stage based on the original Globe Theater in London. The Swan Theatre, part of the theater complex and also built in the style of Shakespeare's Globe, stages plays by Shakespeare and contemporaries such as Christopher Marlowe and Ben Jonson, as well as works by contemporary playwrights. Prices range from £5 to £50. **■ TIP→ Seats book up fast, but day-of-performance and returned tickets are sometimes available.** ✉ *Waterside* ☎ *0844/800–1110 ticket hotline* 🌐 *www.rsc.org.uk.*

SHOPPING

Chain stores and shops sell tourist junk, but this is also a good place to shop for high-quality (and high-price) silver, jewelry, and china. There's an open **market** (great for bargains) every Friday in the Market Place at Greenhill and Meer streets.

Antiques Centre. This building contains around 50 stalls displaying jewelry, silver, linens, porcelain, and memorabilia. ✉ *60 Ely St.* *Open daily.*

B&W Thornton. Above Shakespeare's Birthplace, B&W Thornton stocks Moorcroft pottery and glass. ✉ *23 Henley St.* ☎ *01789/269405* 🌐 *www.bwthornton.co.uk* *Open daily.*

Chaucer Head Bookshop. This is the best of Stratford's many secondhand bookshops. ✉ *21 Chapel St.* ☎ *01789/415691* 🌐 *www.chaucerhead.com* *Closed Sun.*

Lakeland. A great range of kitchen and housewares are available at Lakeland. ✉ *1/5 Henley St.* ☎ *01789/262100* 🌐 *www.lakeland.co.uk* *Open daily.*

Shakespeare Bookshop. Run by the Shakespeare Birthplace, the Shakespeare Bookshop carries Elizabethan plays, Shakespeare studies, children's books, and general paraphernalia. ✉ *Shakespeare's Birthplace, Henley St.* ☎ *01789/292176* 🌐 *www.shakespeare.org.uk.*

8

SPORTS AND THE OUTDOORS

Avon Boating. From Easter to October, Avon Boating rents boats and punts by the hour and runs half-hour river excursions (£5.50). A Venetian gondola can be rented for £100 for 40 minutes. ✉ *The Boatyard, Swan's Nest La.* ☎ *01789/267073* 🌐 *www.avon-boating.co.uk.*

Bancroft Cruisers. A family-run business, Bancroft Cruises runs regular 45-minute guided excursions along the Avon (£5.50). ✉ *Moathouse, Bridgefoot* ☎ *01789/269669* 🌐 *www.bancroftcruisers.co.uk.*

AROUND SHAKESPEARE COUNTRY

This section of Warwickshire is marked by gentle hills, green fields, slow-moving rivers, quiet villages, and time-burnished halls, churches, and castles (Warwick and Kenilworth are the best examples and well worth visiting). Historic houses such as Baddesley Clinton and Packwood House Court are another reason to explore. All the sights are close enough to Stratford-upon-Avon that you can easily use the town as a base if you wish.

HENLEY-IN-ARDEN

8 miles northwest of Stratford.

A brief drive out of Stratford will take you under the Stratford-upon-Avon Canal aqueduct to pretty Henley-in-Arden, whose wide main street is an architectural pageant of many periods. This area was once the Forest of Arden, where Shakespeare set one of his greatest comedies, *As You Like It.* Among the buildings to look for are the former Guildhall, dating from the 15th century, and the White Swan pub, built in the early 1600s. Near Henley-in-Arden are two stately homes worth a stop, Packwood House and Baddesley Clinton.

GETTING HERE AND AROUND

The town is on the A3400. London Midland trains for Henley-in-Arden depart every hour from Stratford; the journey takes about 15 minutes. Train service from Birmingham New Street takes about 45 minutes, and trains leave every hour. The town heritage center is open Easter through October.

ESSENTIALS

Visitor Information Henley-in-Arden Heritage Center. ✉ *Joseph Hardy House, 150 High St.* ☎ *01564/795919* 🌐 *www.heritagehenley.org.uk.*

EXPLORING

Fodor's Choice ★ **Baddesley Clinton.** The eminent architectural historian Sir Nikolaus Pevsner described this as "the perfect late medieval manor house. The entrance side of grey stone, the small, creeper-clad Queen Anne brick bridge across the moat, the gateway with a porch higher than the roof and embattled—it could not be better." Set off a winding backroad, this grand manor dating from the 15th century retains its great fireplaces, 17th-century paneling, and three priest holes (secret chambers for Roman Catholic priests, who were hidden by sympathizers when

Catholicism was banned in the 16th and 17th centuries). The café is an idyllic spot. Admission to the house is by timed ticket; Baddesley Clinton is 2 miles east of Packwood House and 15 miles north of Stratford-upon-Avon. ✉ *Rising La., off A4141 near Chadwick End* ☎ *01564/783294* 🌐 *www.nationaltrust.org.uk* 🎫 *£10.05; garden only £6.80* ⏲ *House mid-Feb.–Oct., daily 11–5; Nov.–mid-Feb., daily 11–4. Grounds mid-Feb.–Oct., daily 9–4; Nov.–mid-Feb., daily 9–5; last admission 30 min before closing.*

Packwood House. Garden enthusiasts are drawn to Packwood's re-created 17th-century gardens, highlighted by an ambitious topiary Tudor garden in which yew trees represent Jesus's Sermon on the Mount. With tall chimneys, the house combines redbrick and half-timbering. Exquisite collections of 16th-century furniture and tapestries in the interior's 20th-century version of Tudor architecture make this one of the area's finest historic houses open to the public. It's 5 miles north of Henley-in-Arden and 12 miles north of Stratford-upon-Avon. ✉ *Off B4439, 2 miles east of Hockley Heath* ☎ *01564/782024* 🌐 *www.nationaltrust.org.uk* 🎫 *Mid-Feb.–Oct., house £10.05, garden only £6.80; Nov.–mid-Feb., house £6.80, garden only £4.70* ⏲ *House and garden mid-Feb.–mid-July, Sept., and Oct., Tues.–Sun. 11–5; mid-July–Aug., daily 11–5; Nov.–mid-Feb., Tues.–Sun. 11–3; last admission 30 min before closing.*

WARWICK

8 miles east of Henley-in-Arden, 4 miles south of Kenilworth, 9 miles northeast of Stratford-upon-Avon.

Most famous for Warwick Castle—that vision out of the feudal ages—the town of Warwick (pronounced *war*-ick) is an interesting architectural mix of Georgian redbrick and Elizabethan half-timbering.

8

GETTING HERE AND AROUND

Frequent trains to Warwick leave London's Marylebone Station; travel time is about 90 minutes. The journey between Stratford-upon-Avon and Warwick takes around 30 minutes by train or bus. Stagecoach bus 16 is more frequent, running every hour.

ESSENTIALS

Visitor Information Warwick Tourist Information Centre. ✉ *Court House, Jury St.* ☎ *01926/492212* 🌐 *www.visitwarwick.co.uk.*

EXPLORING

Collegiate Church of St. Mary. Crowded with gilded, carved, and painted tombs, the **Beauchamp Chapel** of this church is the essence of late-medieval and Tudor chivalry—although it was built (1443–64) to honor the somewhat-less-than-chivalrous Richard Beauchamp, who consigned Joan of Arc to the flames. Alongside his impressive effigy in gilded bronze lie the fine tombs of Robert Dudley, earl of Leicester, adviser and favorite of Elizabeth I, and Dudley's brother Ambrose. The church's chancel, distinguished by its flying ribs, a feature unique to a parish church, houses the alabaster table tomb of Thomas Beauchamp and his wife; the adjacent tiny Dean's chapel has exquisite miniature fan vaulting. In the Norman crypt, look for the rare ducking stool (a chair

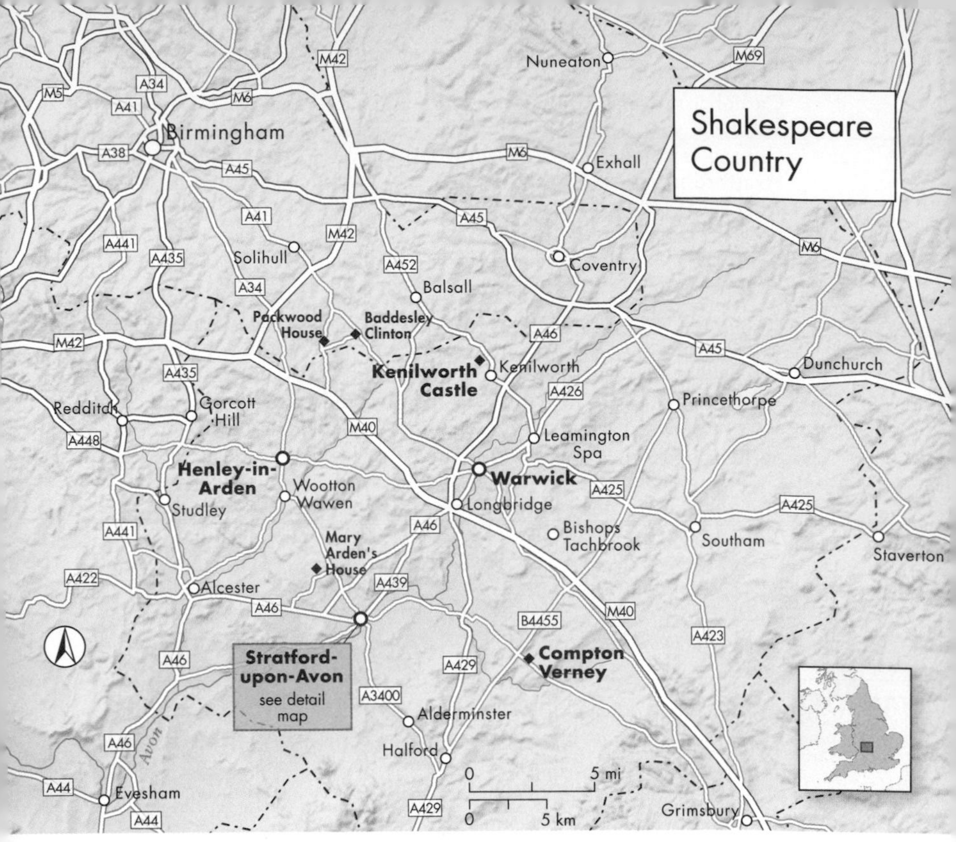

in which people were tied for public punishment). There's a brass-rubbing center, and you can climb the tower in summer. It's a five-minute walk from Warwick Castle. ✉ *Old Sq., Church St.* ☎ *01926/403940* 🌐 *www.stmaryswarwick.org.uk* 🎟 *£2 donation suggested; tower £2.50* 🕓 *Apr.–Sept., daily 10–6 (last entry 5:15); Oct.–Mar., daily 10–4:30.*

Lord Leycester Hospital. Unattractive postwar development has spoiled much of Warwick's town center, but look for the 15th-century half-timber Lord Leycester Hospital, a home for old soldiers since the earl of Leicester dedicated it to that purpose in 1571. Within the complex are a chapel, an impressive beamed hall containing a small museum, and a fine courtyard with a wattle-and-daub balcony and 500-year-old gardens with a pineapple pit. Try a cream tea in the Brethren's Kitchen. ✉ *High St.* ☎ *01926/491422* 🌐 *www.lordleycester.com* 🎟 *£5.90* 🕓 *Apr.–Sept., Tues.–Sun. 10–5; Oct.–Mar., Tues.–Sun. 10–4.*

FAMILY **St. John's House Museum.** Kids as well as adults appreciate the well-thought-out St. John's House Museum, with its period costumes and scenes of domestic life, as well as a Victorian schoolroom and kitchen. Beautiful gardens surround the Jacobean building near the castle. ✉ *Smith St.* ☎ *01926/412132* 🌐 *heritage.warwickshire.gov.uk* 🎟 *Free* 🕓 *Apr.–Sept., Tues.–Sat. 10–5; Oct.–Mar., Tues.–Sat. 10–4.*

FAMILY
Fodor's Choice ★
Warwick Castle. The vast bulk of this medieval castle rests on a cliff overlooking the Avon—"the fairest monument of ancient and chivalrous splendor which yet remains uninjured by time," to use the words of Sir Walter Scott. Today the company that runs the Madame Tussauds wax museums owns the castle, and the exhibits and diversions can occupy a full day. Warwick is a great castle experience for kids, though it's pricey (there are family rates). Warwick's two soaring towers, bristling with battlements, can be seen for miles: the 147-foot-high Caesar's Tower, built in 1356, and the 128-foot-high Guy's Tower, built in 1380. The castle's most powerful commander was Richard Neville, earl of Warwick, known during the 15th-century Wars of the Roses as the Kingmaker. Warwick Castle's monumental walls enclose an impressive armory of medieval weapons, as well as state rooms with historic furnishings and paintings by Peter Paul Rubens, Anthony Van Dyck, and other old masters. Twelve rooms are devoted to an imaginative wax exhibition, "A Royal Weekend Party—1898." Other exhibits display the sights and sounds of a great medieval household as it prepares for an important battle and of a princess's fairy-tale wedding. At the Mill and Engine House, you can see the turning water mill and the engines used to generate electricity early in the 20th century. In the spooky dungeon exhibit, you can wander by wax re-creations of decaying bodies, chanting monks, witches, executions, and "the labyrinth of lost souls"—a modern mirror maze. Elsewhere, a working trebuchet (a kind of catapult), falconry displays, and rat-throwing (stuffed, not live) games add to the atmosphere. Below the castle strutting peacocks patrol the 60 acres of grounds elegantly landscaped by Capability Brown in the 18th century. **■ TIP→ Arrive early to beat the crowds. If you book online, you save 20% on ticket prices.** Lavish medieval banquets (extra charge) and special events, including festivals, jousting tournaments, and a Christmas market, take place throughout the year, and plenty of food stalls serve lunches. For the ultimate castle experience, you can glamp (glamorously camp) in a medieval tent or stay in your own luxury suite in Ceasar's Tower, ✉ *Castle La., off Mill St.* ☎ *01926/495421, 0871/265–2000 24-hr information line, 01926/406–660 for accommodations* 🌐 *www.warwick-castle.com* 🎫 *castle, Dragon Tower, and dungeon £30.60; castle and dungeon £28.20; castle £22.80; parking £6* 🕒 *Late July and Aug., daily 10–6; mid-Sept.–mid-July, daily 10–5; last admission 30 min before closing.*

QUICK BITES

Undercroft. After a vigorous walk around the ramparts at Warwick Castle, you can drop by the cream-, crimson-, and gold-vaulted 14th-century Undercroft for a spot of tea or a hot meal from the cafeteria. ✉ ***Warwick*** ☎ ***01926/495421.***

WHERE TO EAT AND STAY

$$
THAI
✗ **The Art Kitchen.** Thai chefs enjoy fine-tuning the recipes at this chic and contemporary restaurant. The green and red curries are favorites, especially the chicken or lamb Masaman curry. Also consider the sea bass with garlic and pepper sauce. If you're not big on making decisions, you could always opt for the "salt, hot, sour, and sweet" menu, which includes a delicious coconut pancake. The service is always courteous,

8

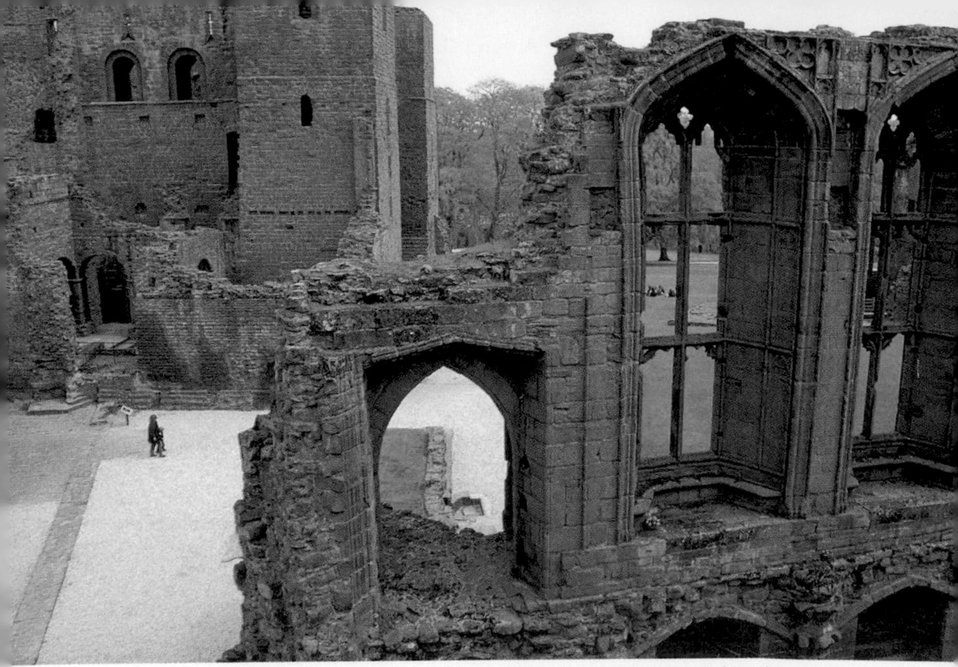

Now in impressive ruins, mighty Kenilworth Castle once hosted Queen Elizabeth I. Today it has gardens, exhibitions, and a great setting.

and the art that peppers the walls is for sale. *Average main: £16* ✉ *7 Swan St.* ☎ *01926/494303* 🌐 *www.theartkitchen.com.*

$ MODERN BRITISH ✕ **Rose & Crown.** Plain wood floorboards, comfy sofas, sturdy wooden tables, and solidly good food and drink set the tone at this contemporary gastro-pub with rooms on the town's main square. It's popular with locals, and the owners take pride in offering seasonal food that mixes British and international influences. There are five different sharing boards—cheese, fish, cold cuts, veggie, and favorites—and a wide range of food is served all day. Thirteen moderately priced bedrooms provide stylish lodging in the pub and across the lane. *Average main: £13* ✉ *30 Market Pl.* ☎ *01926/411117* 🌐 *www.roseandcrownwarwick.co.uk.*

$$$ HOTEL **Mallory Court Hotel.** This elegant country-house hotel 6 miles southeast of Warwick makes a quiet, luxurious getaway; it has 30 rooms but still manages to feel as if you're just visiting wealthy friends. **Pros:** good for pampering; excellent restaurant. **Cons:** outside town; lots of weekend weddings; some traffic noise. *Rooms from: £165* ✉ *Harbury La., Bishops Tachbrook* ☎ *01926/330214* 🌐 *www.mallory.co.uk* *31 rooms* *Breakfast.*

KENILWORTH CASTLE

5 miles north of Warwick.

The sprawling, graceful red ruins of Kenilworth Castle loom over the green fields of Warwickshire, surrounded by the low grassy impression of what was once a lake.

GETTING HERE AND AROUND

The local Stagecoach company offers bus services to and from Stratford and Warwick on the 16 and X17 route. The castle is 1½ miles from the town center.

ESSENTIALS

Visitor Information Kenilworth Library and Information Centre. ✉ *Kenilworth Library, 11 Smalley Pl., Kenilworth* ☎ *0300/555–8171* 🌐 *www.warwickshire.gov.uk/kenilworthlibrary.*

EXPLORING

Fodor's Choice ★ **Kenilworth Castle.** The ruins of the castle and its surrounding grounds reflect several highlights of English history. In 1326 King Edward II was imprisoned here and forced to renounce the throne before he was transferred to Berkeley Castle and allegedly murdered with a red-hot poker. Here the ambitious Robert Dudley, earl of Leicester, one of Elizabeth I's favorites, entertained her four times, most notably in 1575 with 19 days of revelry. The top of the keep (central tower) has commanding views of the countryside, one good indication of why this was such a formidable fortress from 1120 until it was dismantled by Oliver Cromwell after the civil war in the mid-17th century. Still intact are its keep, with 20-foot-thick walls; its great hall built by John of Gaunt in the 14th century; and its curtain walls, the low outer walls forming the castle's first line of defense. You can climb the stairs to the viewing platforms for the view that Elizabeth would have had when she stayed and visit the restored gatehouse where an excellent exhibition explores her relationship with Leicester. A stunning re-created Elizabethan garden with arbors, aviary, and an 18-foot high Carrara marble fountain provides further interest for an hour or two. This is a good place for a picnic and contemplation of the passage of time. The fine gift shop sells excellent replicas of tapestries and swords. ✉ *Off A452, Kenilworth* ☎ *01926/852078* 🌐 *www.english-heritage.org.uk* 🎟 *£9.60* ⏲ *Apr.–Sept., daily 10–6; Oct., daily 10–5; Nov.–Mar., weekends 10–4; last admission 30 min before closing.*

WHERE TO EAT

$ BRITISH ✕ **Clarendon Arms.** A location close to Kenilworth Castle helps make this pub a good spot for lunch and some good hand-pulled ales. You can order fine home-cooked food, including steaks and grills from the bar. Another option is to sample more upmarket fare with an international slant at the next-door Harrington's restaurant, under the same management. [$] *Average main: £10* ✉ *44 Castle Hill, Kenilworth* ☎ *01926/852017* 🌐 *www.clarendonarmspub.co.uk.*

BIRMINGHAM

25 miles north of Stratford-upon-Avon and 120 miles northwest of London.

Though not the U.K.'s most visually appealing city—thanks to the decline of heavy industry, bombing during World War II, and some drab civic architecture in the decades afterwards—21st-century Birmingham is a vibrant and diverse metropolis, in the midst of a major cultural rebirth.

8

The city first flourished in the boom years of the 19th-century's Industrial Revolution, allowing its inventive citizens to accumulate enormous wealth that was evident in the city streets; at one time the city had some of the finest Victorian buildings in the country. It still has some of the most ravishingly beautiful Pre-Raphaelite paintings, on view in the Birmingham Museum and Art Gallery.

Today art galleries, theater, museums, ballet, and a symphony orchestra all thrive here. Creative redevelopment and public art are also making areas more attractive for the city's 2.6 million residents. The redeveloped Bullring shopping center, part of which has a striking, curving facade of 15,000 aluminum disks, has won widespread critical acclaim.

The city has a distinctive, almost singsong local accent—known as "Brummie"—that's often the butt of unfair jokes in the U.K. In 2008 the London *Times* reported a survey finding it to be the accent Brits most associated with stupidity, even more so than being unable to speak at all. A favorite local rebuttal is to point out that Shakespeare, born and raised just 25 miles away, would have had a Brummie accent.

GETTING HERE AND AROUND

Bus 900 runs from the airport to the city center every 20 minutes; a taxi will cost you around £25. Try to avoid the city's convoluted road network. Drivers are often surprised that Birmingham's inner ring road twists through the city center. Parking in the center is free from 6 pm to 8 am.

New Street train station is right in the center of the city, close to the Bullring shopping center. The bus station is at Oxford Street, a few minutes' walk from the Bullring.

Most of the central sights, which are well signposted, form a tight-knit group. The easiest way to get around the city is on foot, though you'll need a bus for the Barber Institute and Cadbury World, and a short Metro (tram) trip for the Jewellery Quarter. A Daytripper ticket covering bus, train, and Metro travel costs £6.20. The tourist information center, the best place to pick up a map, is close to the public bus and rail stations. It has details for heritage walks.

PLANNING YOUR TIME

A full day gives you time to linger in the Jewellery Quarter and browse the art museums. Much of Birmingham is now pedestrian-friendly, the downtown shopping area transformed into arcades and buses-only streets. You can also explore restored canals and canal towpaths.

ESSENTIALS

Visitor Information Visit Birmingham. ✉ *New St. and Corporation St.* ☎ *0844/888–3883* 🌐 *www.visitbirmingham.com.*

EXPLORING

TOP ATTRACTIONS

Fodor's Choice ★ **Barber Institute of Fine Art.** Part of the University of Birmingham, the museum has a small but astounding collection of European paintings, prints, drawings, and sculpture, including works by Botticelli, Van Dyck, Gainsborough, Turner, Manet, Monet, Degas, Van Gogh, and Magritte.

They also have a lively program of temporary exhibitions; recent highlights have included "degenerate art" banned by the Nazis in the 1930s and the aesthetic heritage of the Roman Empire in Britain. The museum is 3 miles from the city center; to get here, take a train from New Street Station south to University Station or Bus 61, 63, or 98 from the city center. ✉ *Off Edgbaston Park Rd., near East Gate, Edgbaston* ☎ *0121/414–7333* 🌐 *www.barber.org.uk* 🎟 *Free* 🕑 *Weekdays 10–5, weekends 11–5.*

Birmingham Back to Backs. Of the 20,000 courts of back-to-back houses (constructed around a courtyard and thus backing onto each other) built in the 19th century for the city's expanding working-class population, this is the only survivor. Three houses tell the stories of families, headed by a watchmaker, a locksmith, and a glassworker, who lived here between the 1840s and the 1930s. A few houses are available for overnight stays. Admission is by timed ticket, booked in advance; allow one hour for the tour and be prepared for steep stairs. ✉ *55–63 Hurst St., City Centre* ☎ *0121/666–7671* 🌐 *www.nationaltrust.co.uk* 🎟 *£8 (booking essential)* 🕑 *Feb.–mid-July and Sept.–mid Dec., Tues.–Thurs. 1–5, Fri.–Sun. 10–5; mid. July–Aug., Tues.–Sun. 10–5. Also public holidays 10–5 (but closed next day).*

Fodor's Choice ★ **Birmingham Museum and Art Gallery.** Vast and impressive, this museum holds a magnificent collection of Victorian art and is known internationally for its works by the Pre-Raphaelites. All the big names are here—among them Rubens, Renoir, Constable, and Francis Bacon—reflecting the enormous wealth of 19th-century Birmingham and the aesthetic taste of its industrialists. Galleries of metalwork, silver, and ceramics reveal some of the city's history, and works from the Renaissance, the Arts and Crafts movement, and the present day are also well represented. A new gallery displays part of the incredible **Staffordshire Hoard,** the greatest collection of Anglo-Saxon treasure ever discovered. The 3,500-strong haul was unearthed in a field 16 miles north of Birmingham in 2009; among the hundreds of items on permanent display here include helmets, gold, jewelry, and metalwork. ✉ *Chamberlain Sq., City Centre* ☎ *0121/348–8007* 🌐 *www.birminghammuseums.org.uk/bmag* 🎟 *Free* 🕑 *Sat.–Thurs. 10–5, Fri. 10:30–5.*

FAMILY Fodor's Choice ★ **Black Country Living Museum.** It was in the town of Dudley, in the 17th century, that coal was first used for smelting iron. The town became known as the capital of the region still known as the Black Country—a term that arose from the resulting air pollution. This 26-acre museum consists of an entire village made up of buildings from around the region, including a chain maker's workshop; a trap-works where animal snares were fashioned; his-and-hers hardware stores (pots and pans for women, tools and sacks for men); a druggist; and a general store where costumed women describe life in a poor industrial community in the 19th century. You can also sit on a hard bench and watch Charlie Chaplin in the 1920s cinema peer into the depths of a mine or ride on a barge through a tunnel to experience canal travel of yesteryear. For sustenance there are two cafés: the 1930s-era Fried Fish Shop that serves fish-and-chips cooked in beef drippings, and the Bottle & Glass pub for ales and drinks. ■ **TIP→ To avoid the numerous school parties, visit on the weekend or during school vacations.** The museum, 3

8

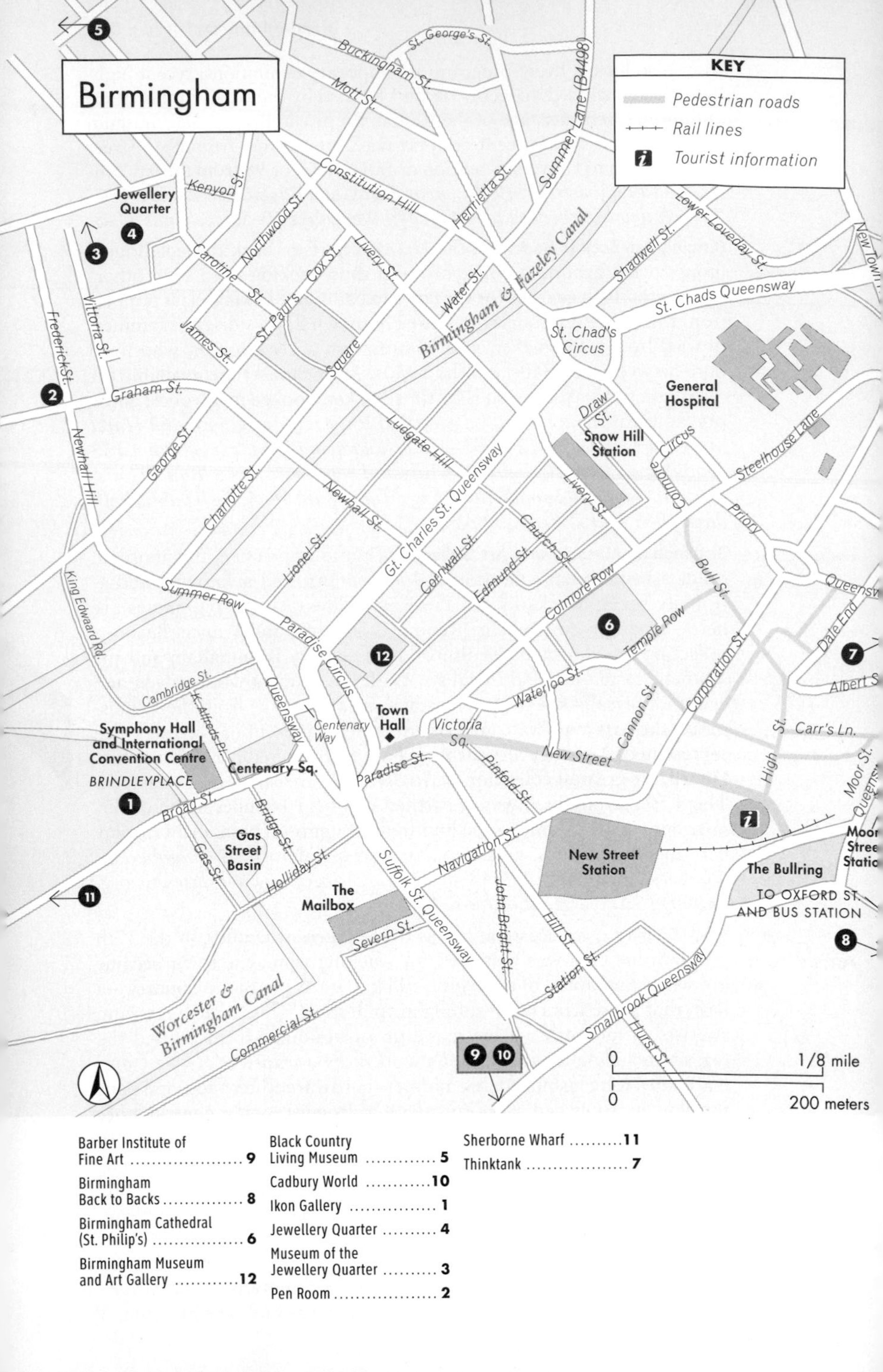

Barber Institute of Fine Art **9**
Birmingham Back to Backs **8**
Birmingham Cathedral (St. Philip's) **6**
Birmingham Museum and Art Gallery **12**
Black Country Living Museum **5**
Cadbury World **10**
Ikon Gallery **1**
Jewellery Quarter **4**
Museum of the Jewellery Quarter **3**
Pen Room **2**
Sherborne Wharf **11**
Thinktank **7**

CLOSE UP

Cruising Birmingham's Canals

With eight canals and 34 miles of waterways, Birmingham has more canals in its center than Venice. The city is at the heart of a system of waterways built during the Industrial Revolution to connect inland factories to rivers and seaports—by 1840 the canals extended more than 4,000 miles throughout the British Isles. These canals, which carried 9 million tons of cargo a year in the late 19th century and helped make the city an industrial powerhouse, have undergone extensive cleanup and renovation, and are now a tourist attraction.

A walk along the Birmingham Canal Main Line near the Gas Street Basin will bring you to modern shops, restaurants, and more developments such as Brindleyplace in one direction and the Mailbox in the other, and you can see the city from an attractive new perspective. Contact the city tourist offices for maps of pleasant walks along the towpaths and canal cruises on colorfully painted barges.

miles from the M5, is best reached by car. Leave M5 at Junction 2 by A4123, and then take A4037 at Tipton. Trains from Birmingham New Street to Tipton Station take 16 minutes; buses from the train station run past the museum, which is 1 mile away. ✉ *Tipton Rd., Dudley* ☎ *0121/557–9643* 🌐 *www.bclm.co.uk* 🎟 *£16.50; parking £3* 🕒 *Late Mar.–Oct., daily 10–5; Nov.–late Mar., Wed.–Sun. 10–4.*

Jewellery Quarter. For more than two centuries, jewelers have worked in the district of Hockley, northwest of the city center; today around 200 manufacturing jewelers continue the tradition in the Jewellery Quarter, producing more than a third of the jewelry made in Britain. **■TIP→ A free booklet from the tourist office gives you the lowdown on shopping in the area.** The city's Assay Office hallmarks 12 million items each year with the anchor symbol denoting Birmingham origin. The ornate green and gilded Chamberlain Clock, at the intersection of Vyse Street, Warstone Lane, and Frederick Street, marks the center of the district. Shops are closed Sunday. The quarter is two stops along Metro Line 1 from Snow Hill Station. ✉ *Hockley* 🌐 *www.jewelleryquarter.net.*

Museum of the Jewellery Quarter. The museum is built around the workshops of Smith & Pepper, a firm that operated here for more than 80 years. Little changed here from when the firm was founded in 1899 to when it finally closed its doors in 1981. A factory tour (about an hour) and exhibits explain the history of the neighborhood and the jeweler's craft, and you can watch demonstrations of jewelry being made in the traditional way. The Earth's Riches gallery displays intriguing jewelry made from an assortment of natural materials, and the shop sells pieces by local artists. ✉ *75–79 Vyse St., Jewellery Quarter* ☎ *0121/554–3598* 🌐 *www.jewelleryquarter.net* 🎟 *£5* 🕒 *Tues.–Sat. and holiday Mon. 10:30–4. Closed Sun. and Mon.*

Sherborne Wharf. Birmingham has around 100 miles of navigable canals, and you can take a ride on a barge from Sherborne Wharf. Trips leave daily Easter through October at 11:30, 1, 2:30, and 4, and on weekends the rest of the year, departing from the International Convention Centre Quayside. An hour-long trip costs £8. ✉ *Sherborne St., City Centre* ☎ *0121/455–6163* 🌐 *www.sherbornewharf.co.uk.*

FAMILY **Thinktank.** This interactive museum in the state-of-the-art Millennium Point center allows kids to explore science and the history of Birmingham over four floors of galleries. They can watch giant steam engines at work, explore deep space, program a robot to play the drums, and help perform a hip operation; it's a great rainy day activity for families. The planetarium has shows throughout the day (included in the ticket price). The museum is a 10-minute walk from Moor Street railway station. ✉ *Millennium Point, Curzon St., Digbeth* ☎ *0121/202–2222* 🌐 *www.birminghammuseums.org.uk/thinktank* 🎫 *£12.50* 🕓 *Daily 10–5; last admission 1 hr before closing.*

WORTH NOTING

Birmingham Cathedral. The early-18th-century Cathedral of St. Philip, a few blocks from Victoria Square, contains some lovely plasterwork in its elegant, gilded Georgian interior. The stained-glass windows behind the altar, designed by the Pre-Raphaelite Edward Burne-Jones (1833–98) and executed by William Morris (1834–96), glow with sensuous hues. ✉ *Colmore Row, City Centre* ☎ *0121/262–1840* 🌐 *www.birminghamcathedral.com* 🎫 *Free; suggested donation £2* 🕓 *Weekdays 8–6:30, weekends 9–5.*

FAMILY **Cadbury World.** The village of Bournville (4 miles south of the city center) contains this museum devoted to—what else?—chocolate. In 1879 the Quaker Cadbury brothers moved the family business from the city to this "factory in a garden." The museum traces the history of the cocoa bean and the Cadbury dynasty. The rain-forest walk, Cadabra ride, and exhibits may seem kitschy, but Cadbury World is extremely popular. You can watch (and smell) chocolates being made by hand, enjoy free samples, and then stock up from the cut-price shop. The restaurant has specialty chocolate cakes as well as lunches. Opening times change almost daily, and reservations are essential; call or go online to check times and book tickets. ✉ *Off A38, Bournville* ☎ *0844/880–7667* 🌐 *www.cadburyworld.co.uk* 🎫 *£16.50* 🕓 *Mid–late Jan., Wed., Thurs., and weekends; Feb.–Nov., daily; Dec., Tues.–Thurs. and weekends; times vary by wk but generally 10–3 weekdays, 9:30–4 weekends (call to check); reservations essential.*

Ikon Gallery. Converted from a Victorian Gothic–style school, this gallery is among the city's top venues for contemporary art from Britain and abroad. The bright, white interior is divided into comparatively small display areas, making the shows easily digestible. Exhibitions change every few months, with several running continuously. ✉ *Brindleyplace, 1 Oozells Sq., City Centre* ☎ *0121/248–0708* 🌐 *www.ikon-gallery.co.uk* 🎫 *Free* 🕓 *Tues.–Sun. and holiday Mon. 11–6.*

QUICK BITES

Malt House. The balcony of the redbrick Malt House is just the place to linger over a drink or eat lunch as you watch canal life go by. ✉ ***75 King Edward's Rd.*** ☎ ***0121/633–4171*** 🌐 ***www.taylor-walker.co.uk/pub/malt-house-birmingham/p0937.***

Pen Room. During the 19th century, Birmingham was the hub of the world pen trade. This compact museum in a former factory illustrates that heyday through an overwhelming and decorative array of nibs, quills, fountain pens, inks, and all the paraphernalia of the pre-ballpoint era. You can try your hand at calligraphy and make your own nib. ✉ *Unit 3, the Argent Centre, 60 Frederick St., Jewellery Quarter* ☎ *0121/236–9834* 🌐 *www.penroom.co.uk* 🎫 *Free; suggested donation £2* ⏲ *Mon.–Sat. 11–4, Sun. 1–4.*

EAT BALTI IN BRUM

Birmingham is home to the *balti,* a popular cuisine created in the mid-1970s by the Pakistani community. The food is cooked and brought to the table in a wok-like dish and eaten with naan, not rice. Curry and other spices season the meat and vegetables. There are more than 30 restaurants in the "Balti Triangle" of the Moseley and Sparkbrook districts.

WHERE TO EAT

$$ MODERN FRENCH ✕ **Annexe.** There's something very jazz age about the ambience at this playful yet sophisticated French restaurant. An occasional but imaginative program of live entertainment means that your dinner could be accompanied by anything from a 1930s-style gypsy band to a silent film screening. The classic-with-a-twist ethos carries through to the menu; try the lemon- and thyme-scented swordfish, or the twice-baked blue cheese soufflé. The two-course lunch menu is an excellent value at just £12.50. 💲 *Average main: £18* ✉ *220 Corporation St., City Centre* ☎ *0121/236–1171* 🌐 *www.annexe.co.*

$ INDIAN ✕ **Itihaas.** Birmingham has some of the country's finest Indian restaurants, and this is one of the best in the city. The style is traditional and colonial; potted palms and portraits rub shoulders with Raj-style antiques. The cooking concentrates on north Indian dishes like *koila murgh* (chicken marinated in yogurt and seared over charcoal) and *hara bara gosth* (a casserole of lamb cooked with garlic, chili, and spinach). The weekday lunchtime menu, served tapas-style, is a deal at £8.95. They also have a second outlet in the food court at Selfridge's. 💲 *Average main: £12* ✉ *18 Fleet St., City Centre* ☎ *0121/212–3383* 🌐 *www.itihaas.co.uk* ⏲ *No lunch weekends.*

$$$$ MODERN BRITISH ✕ **Love's.** Overlooking a spruced-up stretch of canal bobbing with barges, this contemporary eatery takes you on an imaginative journey through the British culinary landscape. Chef Steve Love accompanies his Herefordshire rib eye with slow-cooked ox cheek and pickled carrots, while his fillet of coley comes with celery porridge. The excellent wine list has been nominated for national awards. All menus are fixed-price; the tasting menu is £75. Reservations are recommended. 💲 *Average main: £75* ✉ *3 Canal Sq., City Centre* ☎ *0121/454–5151* 🌐 *www.loves-restaurant.co.uk* ⏲ *Closed Mon., Tues., and Sun. (except lunch, last Sun. of every month).*

$$$ MODERN BRITISH ✕ **Opus.** This stylish, modern restaurant specializes in local, seasonal British flavors. Expect Aberdeen beef with duck fat chips, or perhaps some grilled sole with rich brown shrimp butter. Meat is free range

and fish is freshly caught. Adventurous diners may want a seat at the chef's table, right in the heart of the kitchen. After establishing how much interaction you're comfortable with, the kitchen staff will either chat to you as they prepare the food, or just leave you to enjoy the special five-course meal (£75) while you observe the action. *Average main: £22 54 Cornwall St., City Centre 0121/200–2323 www.opusrestaurant.co.uk Closed Sun.*

$$$$ MODERN BRITISH **Purnell's.** Business moguls and sophisticated foodies can be found sampling an aperitif in a comfy armchair before moving to the sleek, slate-floor dining room at Purnell's. This high spot in the business district, in a Victorian terra-cotta and redbrick building, is where chef Glyn Purnell creates his adventurous Modern British fare. In addition to a few à la carte options, you can choose from a couple of different, whole-table tasting menus—depending on how adventurous you're feeling. The "Now" menu doesn't stray far from traditional British tastes—roast brill, Herefordshire beef with black truffle, followed by comfort food desserts. "Reminisce" is much more playful; you could be presented with haddock and eggs served with cornflakes to start, followed by beef carpaccio with octopus in red wine. **TIP→ Prices at lunchtime are half what they are in the evening.** *Average main: £55 55 Cornwall St., City Centre 0121/212–9799 www.purnellsrestaurant.com Closed Sun. and Mon. No lunch Sat.*

$ INDIAN Fodor's Choice ★ **Pushkar.** A vogueish dining room is the perfect setting for the inventive Punjabi cuisine at this popular curry palace and cocktail bar on bustling Broad Street. Try seared fillet of sea bass on a bed of spiced mash with mango, ginger, and coconut, or the slow-braised lamb with spinach, garlic, and cumin, and you'll find out why Pushkar is a rich part of the superb Birmingham curry scene. *Average main: £13 245 Broad St., City Centre 0121/643–7978 www.pushkardining.com.*

$$$$ FRENCH Fodor's Choice ★ **Simpsons.** Choose between the conservatory with garden views or the inner dining space of this elegant and gleaming Georgian villa known for French-influenced cuisine. Either way, the light and immaculate surroundings and assured and welcoming service make it easy to savor specialties such as Cornish lamb with pomegranate and eggplant, and scallops served with creamed parsley. There are four luxurious themed guest rooms for those who wish to stray no farther (Tuesdays to Saturdays only; £160–225) and a cooking school. It's a mile south of the city center. *Average main: £28 20 Highfield Rd., Edgbaston 0121/454–3434 www.simpsonsrestaurant.co.uk No dinner Sun.*

WHERE TO STAY

$ HOTEL **The Bloc Hotel.** There are few frills—and even less space—at this budget hotel in the Jewellery Quarter, with its "pod"-style bedrooms, but the beds are comfortable, the bathrooms decent, guest rooms have wall-mounted flat screen TVs, and there's no shortage of designer touches. **Pros:** comfortable rooms; unbeatable price; well designed. **Cons:** absolutely no storage space aside from a couple of hooks and a space under the bed; breakfast costs extra and is not available on weekends. *Rooms from: £46 Caroline St., City Centre 0121/212–1223 www.blochotels.com 73 rooms No meals.*

$ HOTEL **Eaton Hotel.** Fronted by an elegant, gleaming white facade, this mansion in leafy Edgbaston provides a peaceful, cozy stay two miles from the bustle of Birmingham's center. **Pros:** complimentary parking; good breakfasts; frequent buses to center. **Cons:** not in center. *Rooms from: £87 ✉ 279 Hagley Rd., Edgbaston ☎ 0121/454–3311 🌐 www.eatonhotel.co.uk 54 rooms Breakfast.*

$ HOTEL **Hilton Garden Inn.** An excellent central location near the waterside nightlife scene is just one perk to staying at this smoothly run hotel. **Pros:** good location; free Wi-Fi; frequent special offers. **Cons:** mostly for business travelers. *Rooms from: £60 ✉ 1 Brunswick Sq., Brindleyplace, City Centre ☎ 0121/643–1003 🌐 www.placeshilton.com/brindleyplace 238 rooms No meals.*

$$ HOTEL **Hotel du Vin & Bistro.** A Victorian hospital in the city center got a makeover from this super-hip chain, but retains such original details as the ironwork double stairway and marble columns. **Pros:** chic and comfortable; central location. **Cons:** expensive valet parking. *Rooms from: £119 ✉ 25 Church St., City Centre ☎ 0121/200–0600 🌐 www.hotelduvin.com/locations/birmingham 56 rooms, 10 suites No meals.*

$ HOTEL **Macdonald Burlington Hotel.** Housed in one of the city's grand Victorian buildings, this traditional hotel is a surprisingly good value option in the center of Birmingham. **Pros:** close to New Street Station and shops; very good weekend rates. **Cons:** attracts a mainly business clientele. *Rooms from: £76 ✉ Burlington Arcade, 126 New St., City Centre ☎ 0844/879–9019 🌐 www.macdonaldhotels.co.uk/our-hotels/macdonald-burlington-hotel/ 112 rooms Breakfast.*

$ HOTEL **Malmaison.** Retail therapy is on your doorstep at this chic hotel in the Mailbox shopping center, where large windows make the guest rooms light and airy by day, and there's subtle lighting by night. **Pros:** handy for shopping and dining; near canal-side attractions; in-hotel spa. **Cons:** drab views; expensive parking (cheaper alternatives are close by); breakfast not included; a bit scruffy in places. *Rooms from: £65 ✉ 1 Wharfside St., City Centre ☎ 0121/246–5000 🌐 www.malmaison.com/locations/birmingham 189 rooms, 10 suites No meals.*

$$ RENTAL Fodor's Choice ★ **Staying Cool at the Rotunda.** The 19th and 20th floors of the Rotunda, an iconic, cylindrical office building from 1965, now contain spacious one- and two bedroom apartments, designed to the hilt in sleek mid-century style. **Pros:** well-stocked kitchens; dreamy beds; Mac entertainment systems with free Wi-Fi. **Cons:** no designated parking. *Rooms from: £123 ✉ 150 New St., City Centre ☎ 0121/285–1250 🌐 www.stayingcool.com 15 apartments No meals.*

NIGHTLIFE AND PERFORMING ARTS

NIGHTLIFE

The city's thriving nightlife scene is concentrated around Broad Street and Hurst Street, as well as the Brindleyplace and Mailbox areas.

Bar Epernay. This champagne bar and brasserie has a revolving piano and a warming brazier, making it perfect for relaxing after a day's sightseeing. *✉ 171 Wharfside St., City Centre ☎ 0121/632–1430 🌐 www.bar-epernay.co.uk.*

8

The Fighting Cocks. This handsome, trendy pub is full of polished wood tables, colorful cushions, and stained-glass windows. The beer selection is huge and the high-class pub food is delicious. This place gets rammed to the rafters for the traditional "roasts"—beef, pork, lamb, chicken, or nut—on Sunday at lunchtime. ✉ *1 St. Mary's Row, Moseley* ☎ *0121/449–0811* 🌐 *www.thefightingcocksmoseley.co.uk.*

Jam House. This excellent drinking, dining, and dancing venue has live jazz, soul, or funk nightly. ✉ *3–5 St. Paul's Sq., Jewellery Quarter* ☎ *0121/200–3030* 🌐 *www.thejamhouse.com/birmingham.*

Old Joint Stock. The spacious and high-domed Old Joint Stock serves good ales and pies, and there's a theater attached. ✉ *4 Temple Row W, off Colmore Row, City Centre* ☎ *0121/200–1892 for pub, 0121/200–0946 for theater bookings* 🌐 *www.oldjointstocktheatre.co.uk.*

Vaults. The bar at the Vaults is perfect for an intimate drink. Another option is to reserve your own private brick-vaulted booth, draw the curtain, adjust the music, and relax. ✉ *Newhall Pl., Jewellery Quarter* ☎ *0121/212–9837* 🌐 *www.vaultsbirmingham.com.*

PERFORMING ARTS

Birmingham's performing arts companies are well regarded throughout the country. Catch a performance if you can.

BALLET

Fodor's Choice ★ **Birmingham Royal Ballet.** The second company of the Royal Ballet, the touring Birmingham Royal Ballet is based at the Hippodrome Theatre, which also plays host to visiting companies such as the Welsh National Opera. ✉ *Thorp St., City Centre* ☎ *0844/338–5000 Birmingham Hippodrome* 🌐 *www.brb.org.uk.*

CONCERTS

The L.G. Arena. The top names in rock and pop play at the L.G. Arena, part of the massive National Exhibition Centre (universally known as "the N.E.C."). The venue is close to the airport. ✉ *Off M42* ☎ *0844/338–8000 for box office* 🌐 *www.lgarena.co.uk.*

Symphony Hall. This is the home of the distinguished City of Birmingham Symphony Orchestra and a venue for jazz, pop, and classical concerts. ✉ *International Convention Centre, Broad St., City Centre* ☎ *0121/345–0600* 🌐 *www.thsh.co.uk.*

Town Hall Birmingham. The splendidly refurbished neoclassical Town Hall Birmingham holds a wide range of events, including organ recitals, opera, and folk concerts. ✉ *Paradise St., City Centre* ☎ *0121/345–0600* 🌐 *www.thsh.co.uk.*

THEATER

Birmingham Repertory Theatre. Founded in 1913, the newly refurbished Birmingham Repertory Theatre is equally at home with modern or classical works. It's one of England's oldest and most esteemed theater companies. ✉ *Centenary Sq., Broad St., City Centre* ☎ *0121/236–4455* 🌐 *www.birmingham-rep.co.uk.*

New Alexandra Theatre. The New Alexandra Theatre welcomes touring companies on their way to or from London's West End. ✉ *Station*

St., City Centre ☎ *0844/871–3011* 🌐 *www.atgtickets.com/venues/new-alexandra-theatre-birmingham.*

FILM

Electric Cinema. This movie theater is a genuine survivor from the art deco age, and a class act to boot. Sofas and waiter service enhance the decadent viewing experience. ✉ *47–49 Station St., City Centre* ☎ *0121/643–7879* 🌐 *www.theelectric.co.uk.*

SHOPPING

SHOPPING CENTERS

Fodor's Choice ★ **Bullring.** The glass-roof Bullring has three floors of shiny retail delight, including two department stores, Debenhams and the stunningly curved Selfridges, covered with aluminum disks. Don't miss Selfridges's awesome Food Hall. ✉ *Between New St. and High St., City Centre* ☎ *0121/632–1526* 🌐 *www.bullring.co.uk.*

The Mailbox. Once a Royal Mail sorting office, the Mailbox is now filled with trendy shops and designer outlets such as Harvey Nichols and Armani, as well as some fine restaurants. ✉ *150 Wharfside St., City Centre* ☎ *0121/632–1000* 🌐 *www.mailboxlife.com.*

JEWELLERY QUARTER

Crescent Silver. This shop sells a range of interesting silver jewelry and gifts. ✉ *83–85 Spencer St., Jewellery Quarter* ☎ *0121/236–9006* 🌐 *www.jewelleryquarter.net.*

St. Paul's Gallery. An entertaining and quirky treasure trove, St. Paul's Gallery specializes in hand-signed fine-art prints of album covers, past and present. ✉ *94–108 Norwood St., Jewellery Quarter* ☎ *0121/236–5800* 🌐 *www.stpaulsgallery.com.*

GREAT MALVERN AND HEREFORD

In the arc of towns to the west of Birmingham and around the banks of the River Wye to the south, history and tradition rub up against deepest rural England. Great Malvern and the cathedral town of Hereford are great bases from which to soak up the bucolic flavor of the Malvern Hills and Elgar country, or to view the spectacular swing of the Wye at the wonderfully named Symonds Yat.

GREAT MALVERN

47 miles southwest of Birmingham, 18 miles northeast of Hereford.

Great Malvern feels a bit like a seaside resort, though instead of the ocean your eyes plunge into an expanse of green meadows rolling away into the Vale of Evesham. This attractive Victorian spa town's architecture has changed little since the mid-1800s. Its Winter Gardens complex with a theater, cinema, and gardens makes the town a good base for walks in the surrounding Malvern Hills. These hills, with their long, low, purple profiles rising from the surrounding plain, inspired much of the music of Sir Edward Elgar (1857–1934), who composed "Pomp

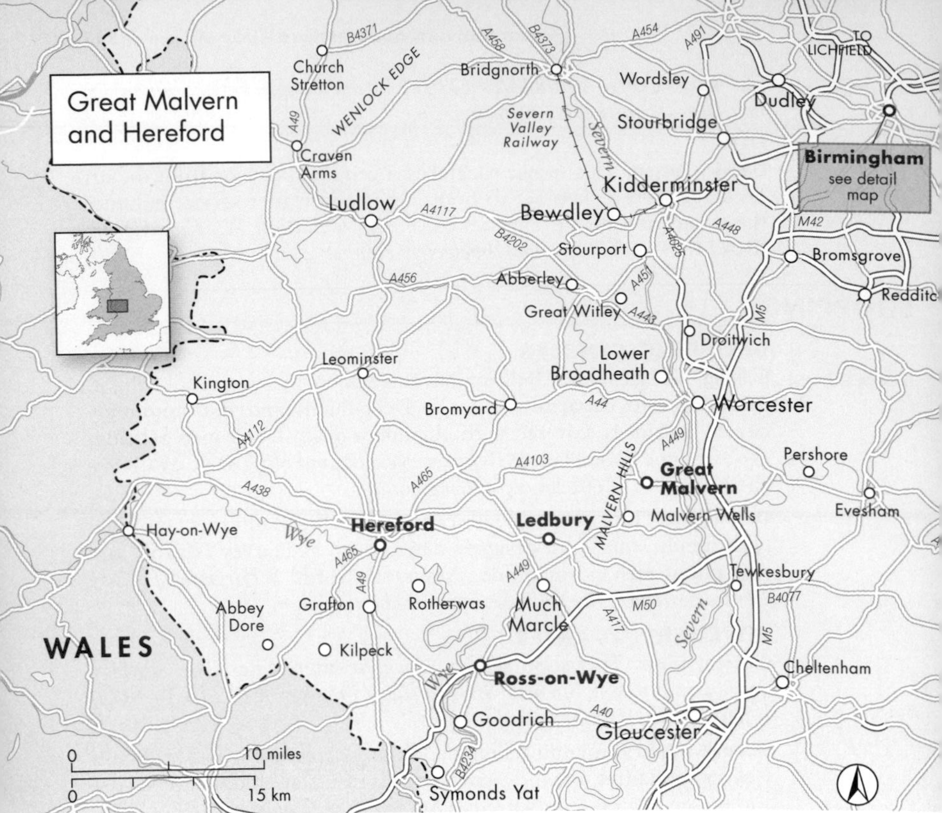

and Circumstance." They also inspired his remark that "there is music in the air, music all around us."

GETTING HERE AND AROUND

Great Malvern is off the A449 road; getting here from Hereford will take 30 minutes or so by car. There are also frequent trains and buses run by First (30 minutes by train, one hour by bus). Birmingham is an hour away by car and rail.

ESSENTIALS

Visitor Information Malvern Tourist Information Centre. ✉ *21 Church St.* ☎ *01684/892289* 🌐 *www.visitthemalverns.org.*

EXPLORING

Great Malvern Priory. A solidly built early-Norman Benedictine abbey restored in the mid-19th century, the priory dominates the steep streets downtown. The fine glass spans from the 15th century—including a magnificent east window and the vibrantly blue Magnificat window in the north transept—to the beautifully evocative Millennium Windows, installed in 1999. There's also a splendid set of misericords (the elaborately carved undersides of choir seats). ✉ *Church St.* ☎ *01684/561020* 🌐 *www.greatmalvernpriory.org.uk* 🎫 *Free* 🕘 *Mon.–Sat. 9–5.*

OFF THE BEATEN PATH

Worcester Cathedral. There are few more quintessentially English sights than that of Worcester Cathedral, its towers overlooking the green expanse of the county cricket ground, and its majestic image reflected in the swift-flowing waters of the River Severn. A cathedral has stood on this site since 680, and much of what remains dates from the 13th and 14th centuries. Notable exceptions are the Norman crypt (built in the 1080s), the largest in England, and the ambulatory, a cloister built around the east end. The most important tomb in the cathedral is that of King John (1167–1216), one of the country's least-admired monarchs, who alienated his barons and subjects through bad administration and heavy taxation and in 1215 was forced to sign that great charter of liberty, the Magna Carta. ■**TIP→ Don't miss the beautiful decoration in the vaulted chantry chapel of Prince Arthur, Henry VII's elder son, whose body was brought to Worcester after his death at Ludlow in 1502.** The medieval library (accessible by prebooked tour only) holds around 300 medieval manuscripts, dating from the 10th century onwards. Worcester is 7 miles north of Great Malvern. ✉ *College Yard, at High St., Worcester* ☎ *01905/732900, 01905/732922 for library tour bookings* 🌐 *www.worcestercathedral.co.uk* *Free; cathedral tours £4; library tours £5* ⏲ *Daily 7:30–6. Tours Mar.–Nov., Mon.–Sat. 11 and 2:30; Dec.–Feb., Sat. 11 and 2:30.*

WHERE TO EAT AND STAY

$$ MODERN FRENCH Fodor's Choice ★

✕ **L'amuse Bouche.** One of Malvern's best restaurants L'amuse Bouche specializes in French cuisine with a contemporary edge. Start with some scallops with fresh tarragon before sampling some cod fish cakes with chili and cilantro, or maybe some simple pork belly served with English apples. The restaurant is part of the Cotford Hotel; if you feel like making a night of it, the pleasantly traditional rooms start at around £130. $ *Average main: £18* ✉ *Cotford Hotel, 51 Graham Rd.* ☎ *01684/572427* 🌐 *www.cotfordhotel.co.uk/lamuse-bouche-restaurant* ⏲ *No lunch Mon.–Sat.* *Reservations essential.*

$ HOTEL Fodor's Choice ★

Cottage in the Wood. On shady grounds, this family-run hotel sits high up the side of the Malvern Hills, with splendid views of the landscape. **Pros:** tremendous views; good food; free Wi-Fi. **Cons:** three separate buildings; steep and narrow approach; cheaper rooms don't have the best views. $ *Rooms from: £84* ✉ *Holywell Rd.* ☎ *01684/588860* 🌐 *www.cottageinthewood.co.uk* *30 rooms* *Breakfast; Some meals.*

NIGHTLIFE AND PERFORMING ARTS

Malvern has links with Sir Edward Elgar as well as with George Bernard Shaw, who premiered many of his plays here.

Autumn in Malvern Festival. The Autumn in Malvern Festival takes place on weekends throughout late September and October. Classical music is the mainstay of the festival (local hero Elgar is featured heavily) with plenty of literary events as well. ✉ *Great Malvern* ☎ *01684/892277 for tickets* 🌐 *www.malvernfestival.co.uk.*

8

Worcester Cathedral has a blissfully English setting near the River Severn.

LEDBURY

10 miles southwest of Great Malvern on A449.

Among the 16th-century black-and-white half-timber buildings in the center of Ledbury, take special note of the Feathers Hotel and the Talbot Inn. They're considered to be among the finest timber-framed buildings of their age left in England. The cobbled Church Lane, almost hidden behind the 17th-century market house, is crowded with other medieval half-timber buildings and leads to St. Michael's Church.

GETTING HERE AND AROUND

If you're driving, Ledbury is 25 minutes from Hereford via A438 and 15 minutes from Great Malvern via A449. There are local buses from both Hereford and Great Malvern, which have rail links with the rest of the country.

ESSENTIALS

Visitor Information Ledbury Tourist Information Centre. ✉ *Ice Bytes Café, 38 The Homend* ☎ *0844/567–8650* 🌐 *www.visitledbury.co.uk.*

EXPLORING

FAMILY **Eastnor Castle.** Completed in 1820, Eastnor Castle, a turreted Norman Revival extravaganza on the eastern outskirts of Ledbury, includes some magnificent neo-Gothic salons designed by 19th-century architect Augustus Pugin. The Hervey-Bathurst family has restored other grand rooms, full of tapestries, gilt-framed paintings, Regency chandeliers, old armchairs, and enormous sofas, making Eastnor a must-see for lovers of English interior decoration. In the Little Library, look out for the rare game of Life Pool, originally played on the billiards table.

EATING WELL IN THE HEART OF ENGLAND

"The Malvern water," said John Wall in 1756, "is famous for containing nothing at all." The famously pure water is still bottled in the town and exported worldwide; it's said that the Queen never travels without it.

Outside Birmingham, this area is rich farming country where the orchards produce succulent fruit, especially apples and plums. Hereford cider is popular because it tastes much sweeter than the cider brewed farther south in Devon.

The meat and milk products, which come from the local red-and-white Hereford breed of cattle, are second to none. Cheshire cheese, one of the country's oldest cheeses, is noted for its rich, crumbly texture; blue-veined Shropshire cheese is more unusual and worth trying. Ludlow produces a formidable assortment of local meat products and is noted for its sausages.

In the grounds there's a knight's maze and adventure playground to keep kids amused. ✉ *A438* ☎ *01531/633160* 🌐 *www.eastnorcastle.com* 🎫 *House and grounds £10.50; grounds only, £7* 🕑 *Easter–last Sun. in Sept., grounds daily 11–5:30, castle daily 11:30–4:30 (last admission 4).*

Fodor's Choice ★ **Hellens Manor.** Just outside the village of Much Marcle, 4 miles southwest of Ledbury, lies the beautiful 17th-century manor of Hellens, kept like a time capsule in virtually unspoiled condition. The gloom and dust are part of the experience of visiting; candles illuminate the interior and there's no central heating. Part of the house dates from the 13th century and contains fine old-master paintings. Take a walk in the gardens and, if you have time, also check out the 13th-century village church. The house is ½ mile east of A449. ✉ *Off B4024 and Monks Walk, Much Marcle* ☎ *01531/660504* 🌐 *www.hellensmanor.com* 🎫 *£7* 🕑 *Apr.–Sept., Wed., Thurs., Sun., and holiday Mon., guided tours at 2, 3, and 4.*

Ledbury Heritage Centre. In the old grammar school, this museum traces the history of the building, town, railroad, and canal, mostly through local postcards. It also has displays on two literary celebrities linked to the area, John Masefield and Elizabeth Barrett Browning. ✉ *Church La.* ☎ *01432/260692* 🎫 *Free* 🕑 *Easter–Oct., daily 10:30–4:30.*

WHERE TO STAY

$$ HOTEL **Feathers Hotel.** You can't miss the striking black-and-white facade of this centrally located hotel, which dates from the 16th century; its interior has a satisfyingly antique flavor, with wooden beams, creaking staircases, and ancient floorboards, and some rooms have four-posters. **Pros:** guest rooms retain period feel; indoor heated pool; discounts for booking online. **Cons:** some guest rooms on the small side; some steps to climb. 💲 *Rooms from: £145* ✉ *High St.* ☎ *01531/635266* 🌐 *www.feathers-ledbury.co.uk* *22 rooms* 🍽 *Breakfast.*

8

ROSS-ON-WYE

10 miles southwest of Ledbury.

Perched high above the River Wye in the Malvern Hills, Ross-on-Wye seems oblivious to modern-day intrusions and remains at heart a small market town. Its steep streets come alive on Thursday and Saturday—market days—but they're always a happy hunting ground for antiques. Nearby towns have sights from a castle to a scenic overlook on the river.

GETTING HERE AND AROUND

A449 connects Ross-on-Wye with Great Malvern and Ledbury, and M50 leads directly to Ross from Junction 8 of M5. Stagecoach buses run from Ledbury (30 minutes) and have frequent connections with Hereford (50 minutes) and Gloucester (45 minutes).

ESSENTIALS

Visitor Information Ross-on-Wye Tourist Information Centre. ✉ *Market House, Market Pl.* ☎ *01989/562768* 🌐 *www.visitherefordshire.co.uk.*

EXPLORING

Goodrich Castle. Looming dramatically over the River Wye at Kerne Bridge, from the south the castle looks like a fortress from the Rhineland amid the green fields; you quickly see its grimmer face from the battlements on its north side. Dating from the late 12th century, the red sandstone castle is surrounded by a deep moat carved out of solid rock, from which its walls appear to soar upward. Built to repel Welsh raiders, it was destroyed in the 17th century during the Civil War. The town of Goodrich is 3 miles south of Ross-on-Wye on B4234. ✉ *Castle La., Goodrich* ☎ *01600/890538* 🌐 *www.english-heritage.org.uk* 🎫 *£6.70* ⏲ *Late Feb.–Mar., weekends 10–4; Apr.–Sept., daily 10–6; Oct., daily 10–5.*

Symonds Yat and King Arthur's Cave. Six miles south of Ross-on-Wye, outside the village of Symonds Yat (a local dialect word for "gate"), the 473-foot-high Yat Rock commands superb views of the River Wye as it winds through a narrow gorge in a great 5-mile loop. It's best approached from the south on B4432, from which it's a short walk. A small ferry takes passengers across the river (£1). About a mile northeast of Symonds Yat is **King Arthur's Cave**; although any link to the legendary monarch is, well, just a legend, several important Paleolithic finds have been made in the cave, including flint tools and the bones of a woolly mammoth and a sabre-tooth cat. Today it is home to a colony of bats. To find the cave, take the exit marked Symonds Yat West from A40. Park at the rest area just before Downard Park camp site and follow the track a short way into the woods. ✉ *Symonds Yat.*

WHERE TO STAY

$$ HOTEL **Chase Hotel.** The public areas in this nicely renovated Georgian-style country house retain some original elements of the building's history. **Pros:** 11 acres of peaceful grounds; country-house appeal. **Cons:** popular with wedding parties; strict rules against bringing in food. [$] *Rooms from: £140* ✉ *Gloucester Rd.* ☎ *01989/763161* 🌐 *www.chasehotel.co.uk* 🛏 *36 rooms* 🍽 *Breakfast.*

SPORTS AND THE OUTDOORS

Symonds Yat Canoe Hire. This well-regarded company rents canoes and kayaks by the day or half day. It's a popular way to experience the River Wye. Prices start at £23 for a two-person canoe, and it's cash only. ✉ *Leisure Park, off A40, Symonds Yat West* ☎ *01600/891069, 07860/848136* 🌐 *www.canoehire.com.*

HEREFORD

9 miles northwest of Ross-on-Wye, 56 miles southwest of Birmingham, 54 miles northeast of Cardiff.

Before 1066 Hereford was the capital of the Anglo-Saxon kingdom of Mercia and, earlier still, the site of Roman, Celtic, and Iron Age settlements. Today people come primarily to see the massive Norman cathedral, but quickly discover the charms of this busy country town. Hereford is the center of a wealthy agricultural area known for its cider, fruit, and cattle—the white-faced Hereford breed has spread across the world.

GETTING HERE AND AROUND

The bus and train stations are about half a mile northeast of the center. A train from Birmingham will take around 1½ hours. Traveling by car, take M50 off Junction 8 of the M5, then A417 and A438 to Hereford. First buses cover the local area, and the city is compact enough to cover on foot.

ESSENTIALS

Visitor Information Hereford Tourist Information Centre. ✉ *1 King St.* ☎ *01432/268430* 🌐 *www.visitherefordshire.co.uk.*

8

EXPLORING

Cider Museum. A farm's cider house (the alcoholic, European kind) and a cooper's workshop have been re-created at the Cider Museum, where you can tour ancient cellars with huge oak vats. Cider brandy is made here, and the museum sells its own brand, along with other cider items. ✉ *Pomona Pl., at Whitecross Rd.* ☎ *01432/354207* 🌐 *www.cidermuseum.co.uk* 🎫 *£5.50* ⏲ *Apr.–Oct., Mon.–Sat. 10–5, Sun. on holiday weekends 11–3; Nov.–Mar., Mon.–Sat. and Sun. on holiday weekends, 11–3; last admission 45 min before closing.*

Fodor'sChoice ★ **Hereford Cathedral and Mappa Mundi.** Built of local red sandstone, Hereford Cathedral retains a large central tower and some fine 11th-century Norman carvings, although most of the interior is 19th century. There are also some exquisite contemporary stained-glass windows in the Audley Chapel. However, its main attractions are two great treasures: a 12th-century chair, to the left of the high altar, one of the oldest pieces of furniture in the country and reputedly used by King Stephen (1092–1154); and the **Mappa Mundi,** the largest medieval map of the world still in existence. Drawn in about 1300, it's a fascinating glimpse of how the medieval mind viewed the world: Jerusalem is shown dead center, the Garden of Eden at the edge, Europe and Africa are the wrong way round—and, of course, there are no Americas. In addition to land masses, the map details 500 individual drawings, including cities, Biblical stories, mythical creatures, and images of how people in different corners of the globe were thought to look—the last two frequently overlapping in wildly imaginative fashion. The map is held inside a chained library, containing some 1,500 books, among them an 8th-century copy of the Four Gospels. Chained libraries, in which books were attached to cupboards to discourage theft, are extremely rare: they date from medieval times, when books were as precious as gold. The Cathedral also holds a copy of the 1217 version of the Magna Carta—it's not on permanent display, but is sometimes brought out for temporary exhibits. Tours of the cathedral (without the library), tower, and garden run through summer; however, some are dependent on weather and are liable to change, so calling to confirm times is strongly recommended. ✉ *Cathedral Close* ☎ *01432/374200* 🌐 *www.herefordcathedral.org* 🎫 *Cathedral free (suggested dontation £5); Mappa Mundi and chained library exhibition £6; cathedral tours £4; tower tours £4; garden tours £5* ⏲ *Cathedral Mon.–Sat. 9:15–5:30, Sun. 9:15–3:30; Mappa Mundi and chained library exhibition Apr.–Oct., Mon.–Sat. 10–5, Nov.–Mar., Mon.–Sat. 10–4; Cathedral tours Mon.–Sat. 11; Tower tours Apr.–Oct., Wed. and Thurs. 11:30–2:30; Garden tours June–Sept., Wed. and Sat. 2:30.*

Old House. The half-timber Old House, crisscrossed with black beams and whitewashed walls, is a fine example of domestic Jacobean architecture. Built in 1601, the house started out as a private home, before spending years as a butcher's shop and then a bank, but has been preserved as a museum since the 1930s. It's kept in the style it would have been in the early 17th century; across the three floors you can explore a kitchen, dining hall, parlor, and bedrooms complete with four-poster beds. Look for the rare wall paintings and the unusual dog's door between the nursery and master bedroom. ✉ *High Town* ☎ *01432/260694* 🌐 *www.herefordshire.gov.uk* 🎫 *Free* ⏲ *Tues.–Thurs. and Sat. 10–4.*

WHERE TO EAT AND STAY

$ BRITISH ✕ **Café @ All Saints.** A good spot for lunch, this coffee bar and restaurant occupies the western end and gallery of this community-minded church, granting a rare opportunity to indulge body and spirit at one sitting. The imaginative menu is worth every penny, and the shepherd's pie is a winner. For something lighter, try the tasty sandwiches (roast mushroom and tofu, for example), salads, cakes, and local ice creams. Breakfasts are good here, too. 💲 *Average main: £7* ✉ *High St.* ☎ *01432/370415* 🌐 *www.cafeatallsaints.co.uk* ⏲ *Closed Sun. No dinner.*

$$ HOTEL 🏨 **Castle House.** These conjoined Georgian villas next to the moat (all that remains of Hereford Castle) offer luxurious lodgings, a warm welcome, and good food. **Pros:** close to cathedral; quiet setting; lovely garden. **Cons:** cost a little high for what you get. 💲 *Rooms from: £150* ✉ *Castle St.* ☎ *01432/356321* 🌐 *www.castlehse.co.uk* 🛏 *15 rooms, 9 suites* 🍽 *Breakfast.*

$ HOTEL 🏨 **Sink Green Farm.** Peace and seclusion await 3 miles southeast of Hereford at this informal working farm, which dates back to the 16th century, as do magnificent views of the Wye Valley—and a hot tub from which to enjoy them. **Pros:** friendly and casual; lovely garden; river walks; free Wi-Fi. **Cons:** car needed to get around. *Rooms from: £80 The Straight Mile, B4399, Rotherwas 01432/870223 www.sinkgreenfarm.co.uk No credit cards 4 rooms Breakfast.*

SHOPPING

Hereford has a market in the city center on Wednesday and Saturday where you can browse food, crafts, and general bric-a-brac.

Capuchin Yard. The stores in Capuchin Yard display handmade items ranging from shoes to hats to knitwear. Other outlets feature fine ceramics. *29 Church St.*

SHREWSBURY AND CHESTER

Rural Shropshire, one of the least populated English counties, is far removed from most people's preconceptions of the industrial Midlands. Within its spread are towns long famed for their beauty, such as Ludlow. Two important cities of the region, Shrewsbury and Chester, are both renowned for their medieval heritage and their wealth of half-timber buildings. The 6-mile stretch of the Ironbridge Gorge, however, gives you the chance to experience the cradle of the Industrial Revolution with none of the reeking smoke that gave this region west of Birmingham its name—the Black Country—during the mid-19th century. Now taken over by the Ironbridge Gorge Museum Trust, the bridge, the first in the world to be built of iron and opened in 1781, is the centerpiece of this vast museum complex.

SHREWSBURY

55 miles north of Hereford, 46 miles south of Chester, 48 miles northwest of Birmingham.

One of England's most important medieval towns, Shrewsbury (pronounced *shrose*-bury), the county seat of Shropshire, lies within a great horseshoe loop of the Severn. It has numerous 16th-century half-timber buildings—many built by well-to-do wool merchants—plus elegant ones from later periods. Today the town retains a romantic air—there are many bridal shops along with churches—and it can be a lovely experience to stroll the Shrewsbury "shuts." These narrow alleys overhung with timbered gables lead off the central market square, which was designed to be closed off at night to protect local residents. You can also relax in Quarry Park on the river.

A good starting point for exploring the city is the small square between Fish Street and Butcher Row. These streets are little changed since medieval times, when some of them took their names from the principal trades carried on there, but Peacock Alley, Gullet Passage, and Grope Lane clearly got their names from somewhere else.

GETTING HERE AND AROUND

The train station is at the neck of the river that loops the center, a little farther out than the bus station on Raven Meadows. A direct train service runs here from Hereford (50 minutes) and Birmingham (one hour). If you're coming from London by car, take M40 and M42 north, then M6 and M54, which becomes A5 to Shrewsbury; the trip is 150 miles. The streets are full of twists, but the town is small enough not to get lost. Walking tours of Shrewsbury depart from the tourist office at 2:30 Monday to Saturday, May through October (also at 11 on Sundays until the end of September) and Saturdays only from November to March (£4.50).

ESSENTIALS

Visitor Information **Shrewsbury Visitor Information Centre.** ✉ *Shrewsbury Museum and Art Gallery, The Square* ☎ *01743/258888* 🌐 *www.visitshrewsbury.com.*

EXPLORING

Attingham Park. Built in 1785 by George Steuart (architect of the church of St. Chad in Shrewsbury) for the first Lord Berwick, this elegant stone mansion has a three-story portico, with a pediment carried on four tall columns. The building overlooks a sweep of parkland, part of which is home to around 300 deer. Inside the house are painted ceilings and delicate plasterwork, a fine picture gallery designed by John Nash (1752–1835), and 19th-century Neapolitan furniture. Attingham Park is 4 miles southeast of Shrewsbury. ✉ *B4380, off A5* ☎ *01743/708123* 🌐 *www.nationaltrust.org.uk/attingham-park* 🎫 *£11.50; park and grounds only £7* 🕒 *House Jan.–Feb. (tours only), Fri.–Sun. 11–3; Mar.–Oct., daily 10:30–5:30; last admission 1 hr before closing. Park and grounds Mar.–Oct., daily 9–6; Nov.–Feb., daily 9–5.*

Shrewsbury Abbey. Now unbecomingly surrounded by busy roads, the abbey was founded in 1083 and later became a powerful Benedictine monastery. The abbey church has survived many ups and downs, and retains a 14th-century west window above a Norman doorway. A more recent addition is a memorial to World War I poet Wilfred Owen. To reach the abbey from the center, cross the river by the English Bridge. ✉ *Abbey Foregate* ☎ *01743/232723* 🌐 *www.shrewsburyabbey.com* 🎫 *Free* 🕒 *Apr.–Oct., daily 10–4; Nov.–Mar., daily 10:30–3; last entry 15 min before closing.*

Shrewsbury Castle. Guarding the northern approaches to the town, the sandstone castle rises over the River Severn at the bottom of Pride Hill. Originally Norman, it was dismantled during the civil war and later rebuilt by Thomas Telford, the Scottish engineer who designed many notable buildings and bridges in the early 19th century. Military history buffs will enjoy the **Shropshire Regimental Museum** based in the castle, although there's enough history about the area and its people thrown in to satisfy even the casually interested. **■ TIP→ The numerous benches in the gardens are good for a quiet sit-down.** ✉ *Castle Gates* ☎ *01743/358516* 🌐 *www.shrewsburymuseums.com* 🎫 *£3; grounds free* 🕒 *Late May–mid-Sept., Mon.–Wed., Fri., and Sat. 10:30–5, Sun. 10:30–4; mid-Sept.–mid-Dec., Mon.–Wed., Fri., and Sat. 10:30–4; mid-Dec.–mid-Feb., grounds only daily 9–5; mid-Feb.–late May, Mon.–Wed., Fri., and Sat., and Easter Sun. 10:30–4.*

Shrewsbury Museum and Art Gallery. Recently expanded and moved to a new site in the town's former Music Hall, this museum chronicles the history of the area, from prehistoric times to the present day. One

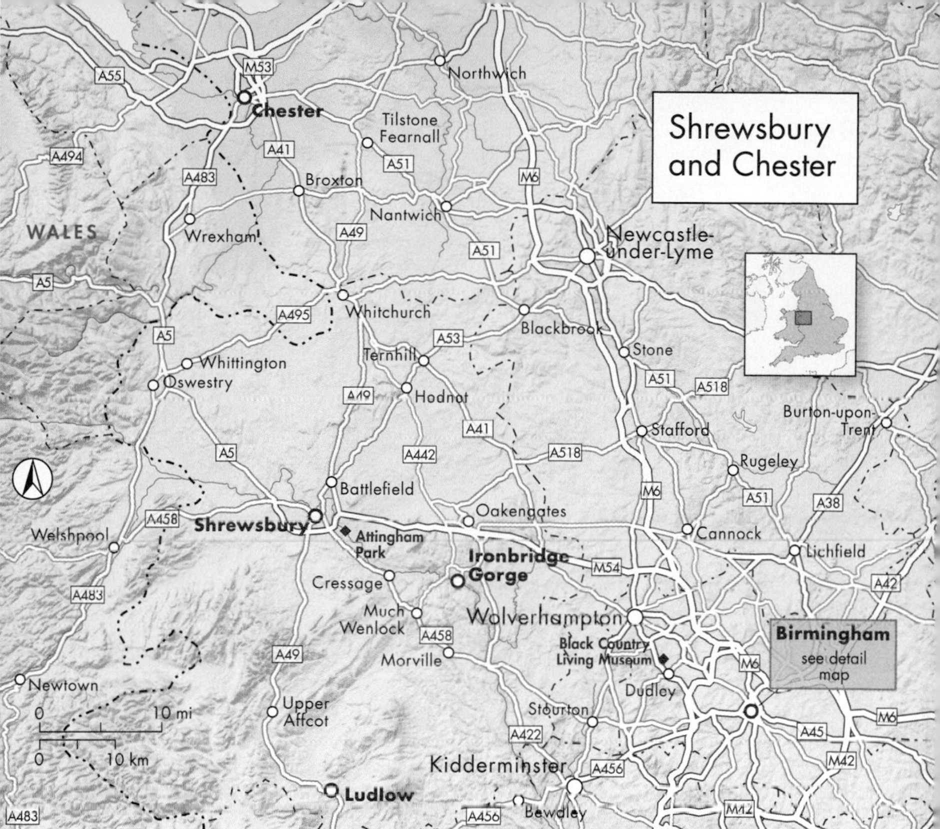

gallery tells the story of Roman occupation; some genuine finds include a unique silver mirror from nearby Wroxeter. Another gallery focuses on the boom years of the 19th century, including a display on the life of Shrewsbury's most famous son, Charles Darwin. Special exhibitions change regularly; recent headliners have included a fascinating collection of Egyptian mortuary relics. ✉ *The Square* ☎ *01743/258885* 🌐 *www.shrewsburymuseum.org.uk* 🎫 *£4* 🕒 *Daily 10:30–4:30.*

St. Chad. On a hilltop west of the town center, this church designed by George Steuart, the architect of Attingham Park, is one of England's most distinctive ecclesiastical buildings. Completed in 1792, the round Georgian church is surmounted by a tower that is in turn square, octagonal, and circular—and finally topped by a dome. When being built, it provoked riots among townsfolk averse to its radical style. The interior has a fine Venetian east window and a brass Arts and Crafts pulpit. ✉ *St. Chad's Terr.* ☎ *01743/365478* 🌐 *www.stchadschurchshrewsbury.com* 🎫 *Free* 🕒 *Mon.–Sat. 8–5:30, Sun. 9–6, public holidays 11–5:30.*

WHERE TO EAT

$$
MODERN BRITISH

✕ **Draper's Hall.** The dark-wood paneling, antique furniture, and intimate lighting of this 16th-century hall make this a distinctive dining spot for up-to-date Modern British cuisine. You might try the Welsh lamb with mint and red currant, or wild sea trout served with saffron rouille.

The sprawling Ironbridge Gorge Museum interprets the country's industrial history and includes a re-created Victorian town.

For dessert you could sample the baked chocolate fondant or a seleciton of local cheeses. The restaurant also has rooms available for £110 per night. *Average main: £18* *10 St. Mary's Pl.* *01743/344679* *www.drapershallrestaurant.co.uk* *No dinner Sun.*

$$ BRITISH **Porterhouse SY1.** Whether you eat in the sleek, dark-wood restaurant or the foliage-filled courtyard, you'll be tucking into good local and seasonal produce here. You can try the tender rib-eye steak, some well-prepared Shropshire lamb, or perhaps a local catch of the day, although locals swear by the pulled pork burger. Desserts, like the baked banoffee (a combination of banana and toffee) cheesecake, are unapologetically indulgent. A few bedrooms are available should you wish to linger longer. *Average main: £15* *15 St. Mary's St.* *01743/358870* *www.porterhousesy1.co.uk* *No dinner Sun.*

WHERE TO STAY

$$ HOTEL **Albright Hussey Manor.** Lovely gardens surround this Tudor manor house, originally the home of the Hussey family, which dates back to 1524; black-and-white half-timbering combines with a later red-brick-and-stone extension. **Pros:** friendly service; fine food; beautiful grounds. **Cons:** popular venue for weddings; could do with a face-lift; newer rooms less attractive. *Rooms from: £120* *Ellesmere Rd.* *01939/290523* *www.albrighthussey.co.uk* *22 rooms, 4 suites* *Breakfast; Some meals.*

$$ HOTEL **The Lion Hotel.** The myriad corridors of this famous coaching inn in the heart of town creak with more than 600 years of history; rooms are small and traditionally furnished, but the glorious lounge, with its high ceiling, oil paintings, and carved-stone fireplace, sets the Lion

apart. **Pros:** historic appeal; good breakfasts. **Cons:** prone to wedding parties on weekends; unlike the public rooms, many guest rooms have tired decor in need of an upgrade. *Rooms from: £108* ✉ *Wyle Cop* ☎ *01743/353107* 🌐 *www.thelionhotelshrewsbury.co.uk* *59 rooms* *Breakfast.*

NIGHTLIFE AND PERFORMING ARTS

Theatre Severn. This theater covers all the lively arts: classical and popular music, dance, and drama. ✉ *Frankwell Quay* ☎ *01743/281281* 🌐 *www.theatresevern.co.uk.*

SHOPPING

Parade. Behind St. Mary's church, this shopping center is in a neoclassical building from 1830 that once held the Royal Infirmary. One of the most appealing malls in England, it has 30 attractive boutiques, a coffee shop, and a river terrace. ✉ *St. Mary's Pl.* ☎ *01743/343178* 🌐 *www.paradeshops.co.uk.*

IRONBRIDGE GORGE

4 miles east of Much Wenlock, 15 miles east of Shrewsbury, 28 miles northwest of Birmingham.

Fodor's Choice ★ The River Severn and its tree-cloaked banks make an attractive backdrop to this cluster of villages; within a mile of the graceful span of the world's first iron bridge are fascinating museums exploring the area's industrial past and the reasons why it's been described as the "cradle of the Industrial Revolution."

GETTING HERE AND AROUND

To drive here from Shrewsbury, take A5 east, A442 south, and then A4169 west before following the brown signs for Ironbridge. On weekends and bank holidays from Easter to late October, the Gorge Connect Bus shuttles passengers between Ironbridge's museums every 30 minutes; it's free of charge to museum passport holders.

ESSENTIALS

Visitor Information Ironbridge Visitor Information Centre. ✉ *The Museum of the Gorge, The Wharfage, Telford* ☎ *01952/433424* 🌐 *www.ironbridge.org.uk.*

EXPLORING

FAMILY Fodor's Choice ★ **Ironbridge Gorge Museum.** The 10 sites that make up the Ironbridge Gorge Museum—a World Heritage Site spread over 6 square miles—preserve the area's fascinating industrial history in spectacular fashion. The best starting point is the **Museum of the Gorge**, which has a good selection of literature and an audiovisual show on the gorge's history. In nearby Coalbrookdale, the **Museum of Iron** explains the production of iron and steel. You can see the blast furnace built by Abraham Darby, who developed the original coke process in 1709. The adjacent **Enginuity** exhibition is a hands-on, feet-on interactive exploration of engineering that's good for kids. From here, drive the few miles along the river until the arches of the **Iron Bridge** come into view. Designed by T.F. Pritchard, smelted by Darby, and erected between 1777 and 1779, this graceful arch spanning the River Severn can best be seen—and photographed—from the towpath, a riverside walk edged with wildflowers and shrubs. The tollhouse on the far side houses an exhibition on the bridge's history and restoration.

A mile farther along the river is the **Jackfield Tile Museum,** a repository of decorative tiles from the 19th and 20th centuries. Another half mile brings you to the **Coalport China Museum.** Exhibits show some of the factory's most beautiful wares, and craftspeople give demonstrations; visit the restrooms for the unique communal washbasins. A short walk from Coalport is the **Tar Tunnel**, part of a 1787 tar mine; note the black bitumen still seeping through the walls. Nearby is Ironbridge's star attraction: **Blists Hill Victorian Town,** where you can see old mines, furnaces, and a wrought-iron works. The main draw is the re-creation of the "town" itself, with its doctor's office, bakery, grocer's, candle maker's, sawmill, printing shop, and candy store. At the entrance you can change some money for specially minted pennies and make purchases from the shops. Shopkeepers, the bank manager, and the doctor's wife are on hand to give you advice. If you don't fancy the refreshments at the Fried Fish shop, you could drop into the **New Inn** pub (in Blists Hill) for a traditional ale or ginger beer, and join one of the sing-alongs around the piano that take place a couple of times every afternoon; or, for something more formal, try the **Club Room** restaurant next door. Allow at least a full day to appreciate all the major sights, and perhaps to take a stroll around the famous iron bridge or hunt for Coalport china in the stores clustered near it. On weekends and national holidays from April through October, a shuttle bus takes you between sites. Family tickets are great value at £50 to £68—and they're good for a year. ✉ *B4380, Telford* ☎ *01952/433424* 🌐 *www.ironbridge.org.uk* 🎫 *Passport ticket (all attractions, valid 1 year) £28. Individual sites: Blists Hill £16.50; Enginuity £9; Coalport China Museum £9; Jackfield Tile Museum £9; Museum of Iron £9; Darby Houses £5.50; Museum of Iron and Darby Houses £9.50; Broseley Pipeworks £5.50; Museum of the Gorge £4.50; Tar Tunnel £3.50* ⏲ *Site and Museums: Apr.–Oct., daily 10–5; Nov.–Mar., daily 10–4. Tar Tunnel: Apr.–Oct., daily 10:30–4; closed Nov.–Mar. Last admission 1 hr before closing.*

WHERE TO EAT AND STAY

$$$$ MODERN BRITISH ✕ **Restaurant Severn.** This discreet restaurant, set back from the main road in the center of Ironbridge, delivers fine-quality food prepared with care and attention. Chefs Beb and Eric Bruce prepare delicious fixed-price dinner menus of classic English fare with ingredients from their own smallholding; options include duo of duckling with orange and honey sauce, and a classic beef Wellington. You can round off the meal with a slice of apple Charlotte (a traditional English dessert, like apple pie but with a crust made of sweetened toast) or glazed lemon tart with passion fruit sorbet. Prices go up by a few pounds on weekends. $ *Average main: £28* ✉ *33 High St., Ironbridge* ☎ *01952/432233* 🌐 *www.restaurantseven.co.uk* ⏲ *Closed Mon., Tues., and Sun. No lunch (except one Sun. a month).*

$$ HOTEL 🏨 **Hundred House Hotel.** The low beams, stained glass, wood paneling, and patchwork cushions that greet you as you enter this Georgian inn set the tone for the whimsical guest rooms, fancifully named

after herbs and flowers (the latter, of course, being the most colorful). **Pros:** full of fanciful touches and quirky nooks and corners; good food. **Cons:** not for those who favor the plain and simple. $ *Rooms from: £120 ✉ Bidgnorth Rd. (A442), Norton ☎ 01952/580240 🌐 www.hundredhouse.co.uk 10 rooms Breakfast.*

$ B&B/INN Fodor's Choice ★ **Library House.** Built in 1740 and at one time the village's library, this small guesthouse sits on the hillside near the Ironbridge museums and just a few steps from the bridge. **Pros:** welcoming hosts; good location; free parking passes for the town. **Cons:** not for families with young children; no restaurant. $ *Rooms from: £95 ✉ 11 Severn Bank, Telford ☎ 01952/432299 🌐 www.libraryhouse.com 4 rooms Breakfast.*

LUDLOW

22 miles south of Ironbridge Gorge, 29 miles south of Shrewsbury, 24 miles north of Hereford.

Fodor's Choice ★ Medieval, Georgian, and Victorian buildings jostle for attention in pretty Ludlow, which has a finer display of black-and-white half-timber buildings than even Shrewsbury. Dominating the center is the Church of St. Lawrence, its extravagant size a testimony to the town's prosperous wool trade. Cross the River Teme and climb Whitcliffe for a spectacular view of the church and the Norman castle.

Several outstanding restaurants have given the town of just 10,000 a reputation as a culinary hot spot. Ludlow is now the national headquarters of the Slow Food movement, which focuses on food traditions and responsible production.

GETTING HERE AND AROUND

From London Paddington, the journey time via train is 3 hours (changing at Newport), from Shrewsbury 30 minutes, and from Birmingham 2 hours with a change in Hereford. The train station is a 15-minute walk southwest to the center. Driving from London, take M40, M42, and A448 to Kidderminster, then A456 and A4117 to Ludlow. The town has good parking and is easily walkable.

ESSENTIALS

Visitor Information Ludlow Visitor Information Centre. ✉ *Ludlow Assembly Rooms, 1 Mill St.* ☎ *01584/875053* 🌐 *www.ludlow.org.uk.*

EXPLORING

Ludlow and the Marches Food Festival. The festival takes place over a weekend in mid-September and has demonstrations and tastings of local sausages, ale, and cider. ✉ *Ludlow* ☎ *01584/873957* 🌐 *www.foodfestival.co.uk.*

Ludlow Castle. The "very perfection of decay," according to author Daniel Defoe, the ruins of this red sandstone castle date from 1085. No wonder the massive structure dwarfs the town: it served as a vital stronghold for centuries and was the seat of the Marcher Lords who ruled "the Marches," the local name for the border region. The two sons of Edward IV—the little princes of the Tower of London—spent time here before being dispatched to London and before their death in 1483. Follow the terraced walk around the castle for a lovely view of

8

the countryside. ✉ *Castle Sq.* ☎ *01584/873355* 🌐 *www.ludlowcastle.com* 🎟 *£5.50* ⏲ *Jan.–mid-Feb., weekends 10–4; mid-Feb.–mid-Mar. and Oct.–Dec., daily 10–4; Apr.–Sept. daily 10–5; last admission 30 min before closing.*

OFF THE BEATEN PATH

Stokesay Castle. This 13th-century fortified manor house built by a wealthy merchant is among the finest of its kind in England. Inside the main hall, the wooden cruck roof and timber staircase (a rare survival) demonstrate state-of-the-art building methods of the day. Outside, the cottage-style garden creates a bewitching backdrop for the magnificent Jacobean timber-frame gatehouse. The castle is 7 miles northwest of Ludlow. ✉ *Off A49, Craven Arms* ☎ *01588/672544* 🌐 *www.english-heritage.org.uk/stokesay-castle* 🎟 *£6.70* ⏲ *Apr.–Oct., daily 10–5; Nov.–Mar., weekends 10–4.*

WHERE TO EAT

$$$$ MODERN BRITISH

✕ **Mr. Underhill's.** Occupying a converted mill building beneath the castle, this Michelin-starred restaurant looks onto the wooded River Teme and is stylish, light, and informal. The superb Modern British cuisine makes inventive use of fresh, seasonal ingredients. The fixed-price menus, which change daily, could include thick white fish soup served with marmalade ice cream, or a slow roasted side of local Marches beef with parsnip and spinach puree. Book well ahead, especially on weekends. Rooms and suites are available should you want to make a night of it; prices start at about £220. 💲 *Average main: £68* ✉ *Dinham Weir* ☎ *01584/874431* 🌐 *www.mr-underhills.co.uk* ⏲ *Closed Mon. and Tues. No lunch* ✍ *Reservations essential.*

WHERE TO STAY

$ HOTEL

🏨 **The Cliffe at Dinham.** Built in the 1850s, this friendly, redbrick inn near Ludlow Castle has comfortable bedrooms with plenty of natural light, which are simply decorated with heavy pine furniture. **Pros:** lovely staff; great view of the castle; free Wi-Fi. **Cons:** not all rooms have good views; bar area a little bland. 💲 *Rooms from: £75* ✉ *Dinham* ☎ *01584/872063* 🌐 *www.thecliffehotel.co.uk* 🛏 *17 rooms* 🍽 *Breakfast.*

$$ HOTEL

🏨 **The Feathers.** Even if you're not staying here, take time to admire the extravagant half-timber facade of this hotel, built in the early 17th century and described by the historian Jan Morris in the *New York Times* as "the most handsome inn in the world." The interior is equally impressive—dripping with ornate plaster ceilings, carved oak, paneling, beams, and creaking floors. **Pros:** ornate plasterwork; unpretentious feel. **Cons:** most guest rooms lack the old-fashioned feel. 💲 *Rooms from: £135* ✉ *21 Bullring* ☎ *01584/875261* 🌐 *www.feathersatludlow.co.uk* 🛏 *40 rooms* 🍽 *Breakfast; Some meals.*

$ B&B/INN Fodor's Choice ★

🏨 **Fishmore Hall.** Saved from dereliction in the late 2000s, Fishmore Hall has been beautifully converted from a crumbling old mansion into a relaxing, contemporary lodge with good-size guest rooms decorated in soothing color schemes, with heavy wood furniture and silk drapes. **Pros:** lovely location; well-designed rooms; beautiful views. **Cons:** restaurant is pricey; a little out of town. 💲 *Rooms from: £99* ✉ *Fishmore Rd.* ☎ *01584/875148* 🌐 *www.fishmorehall.co.uk* 🛏 *15 rooms* 🍽 *Breakfast.*

$ B&B/INN FAMILY **Timberstone.** The Read family has turned a rambling stone cottage in the Clee Hills into a welcoming haven with rooms furnished in neutral tones in a soothing, contemporary style. **Pros:** relaxing and hospitable; geared to families; great food. **Cons:** far from the center of Ludlow. *Rooms from: £95 B4363, Clee Stanton 01584/823519 www.timberstoneludlow.co.uk 4 rooms Breakfast; Some meals.*

CHESTER

75 miles north of Ludlow, 46 miles north of Shrewsbury.

Cheshire's thriving center is Chester, a city similar in some ways to Shrewsbury, though it has many more black-and-white half-timber buildings (some built in Georgian and Victorian times), and its medieval walls still stand. History seems more tangible in Chester than in many other ancient cities, as modern buildings haven't been allowed to intrude on the center. A negative result of this perfection is that Chester has become a favorite tour bus destination, with gift shops, noise, and crowds aplenty.

Chester has been a prominent city since the late 1st century, when the Roman Empire expanded north to the banks of the River Dee. The original Roman town plan is still evident: the principal streets, Eastgate, Northgate, Watergate, and Bridge Street, lead out from the Cross—the site of the central area of the Roman fortress—to the four city gates. The partly excavated remains of what is thought to have been the country's largest Roman amphitheater lie to the south of Chester's medieval castle.

8

GETTING HERE AND AROUND

There's a free shuttle bus to the center if you arrive by train, and buses pull up at Vicar's Lane in the center (Monday to Saturday). Chester is 180 miles from London and about 2 hours by train; some trains change at Crewe. If you're driving and here for a day only, use the city's Park and Ride lots, as central parking lots fill quickly, especially in summer.

Guided walks leave the town hall daily at 10:30 with an additional tour at 11:30 from May to October (£6). In summer the 10:30 tour ends with a proclamation from the Town Crier, who is dressed in traditional attire.

ESSENTIALS

Visitor and Tour Information Chester Tourist Information Centre. *Town Hall, Northgate St. 0845/647–7868 www.visitchester.com.* **City Sightseeing.** *0845/647–7868, 01244/381461 weekdays only www.city-sightseeing.com.*

EXPLORING

TOP ATTRACTIONS

Chester Cathedral. Tradition has it that in Roman times a church of some sort stood on the site of what is now Chester Cathedral, but records indicate construction around AD 900. The earliest work traceable today, mainly in the north transept, is that of the 11th-century Benedictine abbey. After Henry VIII dissolved the monasteries in the 16th century, the abbey church became the cathedral church of the new diocese of Chester. The misericords in the choir stalls reveal carved

Lined with handsome brick, stone, and half-timber buildings, Chester's compact center is perfect for shopping and strolling.

figures of people and animals, both real and mythical, and above is a gilded and colorful vaulted ceiling. Cathedral at Height tours (£8) take you to parts of the building usually off-limits to visitors, including the roof—from which you can see two countries (England and Wales) and five separate counties. Reservations are essential. ✉ *St. Werburgh St., off Market Sq.* ☎ *01244/500959* 🌐 *www.chestercathedral.com* 🎫 *Free; suggested donation £3; audio guides £1* ⏲ *Mon.–Sat. 9–5, Sun. 11–4.*

City walls. Accessible from several points, the city walls provide splendid views of Chester and its surroundings. The whole circuit is 2 miles, but if your time is short, climb the steps at Newgate and walk along toward Eastgate to see the great ornamental **Eastgate Clock,** erected to commemorate Queen Victoria's Diamond Jubilee in 1897. Lots of small shops near this part of the walls sell old books, old postcards, antiques, and jewelry. Where the **Bridge of Sighs** (named after the enclosed bridge in Venice that it closely resembles) crosses the canal, descend to street level and walk up Northgate Street into Market Square. ✉ *Chester.*

Rows. Chester's unique Rows, which originated in the 12th and 13th centuries, are essentially double rows of stores, one at street level and the other on the second floor with galleries overlooking the street. The Rows line the junction of the four streets in the old town. They have medieval crypts below them, and some reveal Roman foundations. **■ TIP→ You can view some of these Roman foundations in the basement of fast food restaurant Spudulike at 39 Bridge Street.** ✉ *Chester.*

WORTH NOTING

ChesterBoat. This company runs excursions on the River Dee every 30 minutes daily from 11–5 (late March through October) and hourly from 11–4 on weekends (November through March). Special themed cruises include retro disco nights; see the website for listings. ✉ *Boating Station, Souters La.* ☎ *01244/325394* 🌐 *www.chesterboat.co.uk* 🎫 *£6.50.*

FAMILY **Chester Zoo.** Well-landscaped grounds and natural enclosures make the 80-acre zoo one of Britain's most popular and also one of the largest. Highlights include Chimpanzee Island, the jaguar enclosure, and the Islands in Danger tropical habitat. Baby animals are often on display. Eleven miles of paths wind through the zoo, and you can use the waterbus boats or the overhead train to tour the grounds. Fun 10-minute animal talks, aimed at kids, take place at various locations around the zoo throughout the day. The zoo is 2 miles north of Chester. ✉ *A41* ☎ *01244/380280* 🌐 *www.chesterzoo.org* 🎫 *Apr.–Oct. £22.50; Nov.–Mar. £16.50; waterbus £2; monorail £2* ⏲ *Late Apr.–late May, Sept., and Nov.–mid-Feb., daily 10–5; late May–Aug. and holiday weekends, daily 10–6; Oct., daily 10–4:30; last admission 30 min before closing.*

Grosvenor Museum. Start a visit to this museum with a look at the Roman Stones Gallery, which displays Roman-era tombstones previously used to repair city walls. (Keep an eye out for the wounded barbarian.) Afterward you can skip a few centuries to explore the period house for a tour from 1680 to the 1920s. ✉ *27 Grosvenor St.* ☎ *01244/972197* 🌐 *grosvenormuseum.westcheshiremuseums.co.uk* 🎫 *Free* ⏲ *Mon.–Sat. 10:30–5, Sun. 1–4.*

WHERE TO EAT

$ BRITISH ✕ **Albion.** You feel as if you're stepping back in time at this Victorian pub; the posters, advertisements, flags, and curios tell you the idiosyncratic landlord keeps it as it would have been during World War I. The candlelit restaurant forms one of the three snug rooms and, unsurprisingly, serves up traditional fare such as corned beef hash, Staffordshire oatcakes, and gammon (thick-sliced ham) with pease pudding. You can stay overnight here as well. 💲 *Average main: £10* ✉ *Park St.* ☎ *01244/340345* 🌐 *www.albioninnchester.co.uk* ⏲ *No dinner Sun.*

$ BISTRO ✕ **Chez Jules.** Once a fire station, this bustling bistro is now unashamedly French and rustic, with red-and-white-check tablecloths and a menu chalked up on the blackboard. Start perhaps with some *moules marinières* (mussels cooked in a white wine and onion sauce) or French onion soup, followed by grilled sea bass or a classic rib-eye steak with Café du Paris butter. The two-course early-bird menu is a great value at £12 (available until 6 pm). 💲 *Average main: £8.50* ✉ *71 Northgate St.* ☎ *01244/400014* 🌐 *www.chezjules.com.*

$$$$ FRENCH ✕ **Simon Radley at the Chester Grosvenor.** Named for its noted chef, this Michelin-starred restaurant has a sophisticated panache and prices to match. Expect the seasonal but not the usual, including named dishes: Herdwick is spring lamb with asparagus and spearmint peas, while Caramélia is a dessert of chocolate caramel, torched banana, and spiced rum. There's a fixed-price dinner (£75) as well as a daily tasting menu (£99). The huge wine cellar has more than a thousand bins. Reservations are essential on weekends, and children must be at least 12. 💲 *Average*

main: £75 ✉ *Chester Grosvenor Hotel, Eastgate St.* ☎ *01244/324024* 🌐 *www.chestergrosvenor.com/simon-radley-restaurant* ⊙ *No dinner Mon. and Sun. Closed 1st 3 wks in Jan.* *Reservations essential* *Jacket required.*

WHERE TO STAY

$ HOTEL **Abode Chester.** Perched at a busy traffic intersection on the edge of Chester's old town, this gleaming, modern hotel from the trendy Abode chain may not occupy the city's most romantic spot, but it's well run and comfortable. **Pros:** spacious guest rooms; good food; great bar. **Cons:** lacks historic charm of older hotels; parking lot is hard to find (take the almost-hidden exit from the roundabout that looks like it's just for deliveries). $ *Rooms from: £94* ✉ *Grosvenor Rd.* ☎ *01244/347000* 🌐 *www.abodehotels.co.uk/chester* *85 rooms* *Breakfast; Some meals.*

$$$ HOTEL Fodor's Choice ★ **Chester Grosvenor Hotel.** Handmade Italian furniture and swaths of French silk fill this deluxe downtown hotel in a Tudor-style building. **Pros:** pampering luxury; superb food; excellent service and facilities. **Cons:** no private parking. $ *Rooms from: £175* ✉ *Eastgate St.* ☎ *01244/324024* 🌐 *www.chestergrosvenor.com* *66 rooms, 14 suites* *No meals; Breakfast.*

$ B&B/INN **Chester Recorder House.** This Georgian redbrick house has the perfect location right on the city wall and overlooking the River Dee. Meander through the picture-filled passages to find the rooms, the best of which have four-poster beds. **Pros:** within easy reach of the center; excellent breakfasts. **Cons:** no elevator. $ *Rooms from: £85* ✉ *19 City Walls* ☎ *01244/326580* 🌐 *www.recorderhotel.co.uk* *11 rooms* *Breakfast.*

$ B&B/INN **Grove Villa.** This family-run B&B in an early-19th-century house has an appealing location on the banks of the River Dee and guest rooms with four-poster or half-tester beds; two rooms overlook the river. **Pros:** beautiful river location; breakfast around a communal table. **Cons:** no credit cards; no Internet connection. $ *Rooms from: £73* ✉ *18 The Groves* ☎ *01244/349713* 🌐 *www.grovevillachester.com* *No credit cards* *3 rooms* *Breakfast.*

SHOPPING

Chester Market. This indoor market, near the Town Hall, has more than 50 stalls. It's open Monday to Saturday until 5 pm. ✉ *6 Princess St.* 🌐 *www.chestermarket.com.*

9

MANCHESTER, LIVERPOOL, AND THE PEAK DISTRICT

WELCOME TO MANCHESTER, LIVERPOOL, AND THE PEAK DISTRICT

TOP REASONS TO GO

★ **Manchester theater and nightlife:** The city's theater scene keeps getting more exciting, while bustling café-bars and pubs, together with ornate Victorian-era beer houses, mean there's plenty of ways to continue your night out in style.

★ **Liverpool culture, old and new:** This once-run-down merchant city, already a must-see for fans of the Fab Four, has reinvented itself as a cultural hub with plenty of dining, lodging, and nightlife hot spots.

★ **Outdoor activities in the Peak District:** Even a short hike in Edale or High Peak reveals the craggy, austere beauty for which the area is famous, but cycling, caving, and other sports make the Peaks a veritable natural playground.

★ **Grand country houses:** The stately Chatsworth House and the Tudor manor Haddon Hall will enchant fans of both *Downton Abbey* and quintessentially English architecture alike.

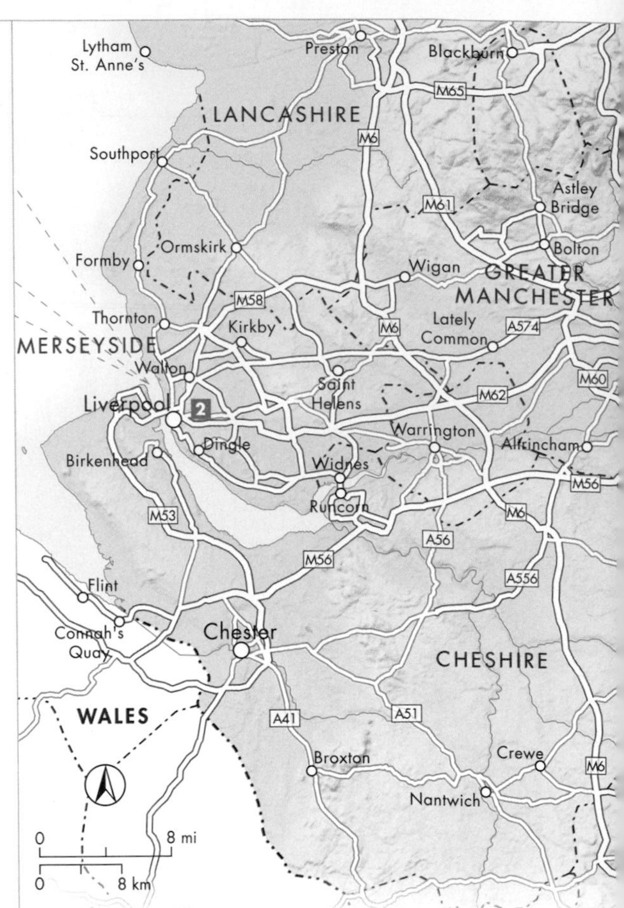

1 Manchester. This vibrant city mixes a compelling industrial heritage with cutting-edge urban design and thriving music and club scenes. Great museums and art galleries justify its blossoming status as the U.K.'s second city of culture.

2 Liverpool. The imposing waterfront, the pair of cathedrals, and the grand architecture make it clear that this city—now undergoing a postindustrial rebirth—is more than just the Beatles. Even so, the many museums don't leave out the city's place in rock-and-roll history.

GETTING ORIENTED

Manchester lies at the heart of a tangle of motorways in the northwest of England, about a half hour across the Pennines from Yorkshire. It's 70 miles from the southern edge of the Lake District. The city spreads west toward the coast and the mouth of the River Mersey and Liverpool. To see any great natural beauty, you must head east to the Peak District, a national park less than an hour's drive southeast of Manchester. It's also where you'll find two of the grandest and best-preserved historic homes in all of Britain: Chatsworth and Haddon Hall.

9

3 The Peak District. Britain's first national park is studded with an array of stately homes, but the real stars of the show are its dramatic moors, sylvan dales, atmospheric limestone caverns, and superb walking trails.

THE BEATLES IN LIVERPOOL

(above) The Beatles' music and style—and their haircuts—rocked the 1960s; (right, top) Mendips, John's childhood home and now a National Trust site; (right, bottom) The rebuilt Cavern

This distinctive northern English city was the birthplace of the Beatles, who changed rock music forever using recording techniques unheard of at the time. The Fab Four became counterculture icons who defined the look and sound of the 1960s, but despite their international success, they remained true sons of Liverpool.

Reinvigorated over the past decade and a half, this city remains a site of pilgrimage for fans more than half a century after the Beatles' early gigs here. Liverpool may no longer be the rough, postwar city the Beatles grew up in, but it makes the most of its connections to Paul McCartney, John Lennon, George Harrison, and Ringo Starr. John's and Paul's childhood homes, Mendips and 20 Forthlin Road, are in south Liverpool; both are National Trust sites. You can take in a show at Mathew Street's (re-created) Cavern Club, where the band played in its early days, or tour Penny Lane, Strawberry Fields, and other mop-top nostalgia spots. Located on two sites at Albert Dock and Pier Head, the Beatles Story museum provides a state-of-the-art overview of the group's career.

THEIR WORDS

"I knew the words to 25 rock songs, so I got in the group. 'Long Tall Sally' and 'Tutti Frutti,' that got me in. That was my audition."
—Paul McCartney

"Paul wasn't quite strong enough, I didn't have enough girl appeal, George was too quiet, and Ringo was the drummer. But we thought that everyone would be able to dig at least one of us, and that's how it turned out."
—John Lennon

FOLLOW IN THE FOOTSTEPS

SEE THE MAIN SIGHTS

The three key shrines of Beatle-dom in Liverpool are John's and Paul's childhood homes in south Liverpool, and the legendary Cavern Club on Mathew Street downtown, where the Beatles were discovered by their future manager Brian Epstein in 1961. A combined ticket for both Beatle homes includes a bus between the city center and the two sites.

CHECK OUT THE BEATLES STORY

At two venues at the Albert Dock and Pier Head, entertaining scenes re-create stages in the Fab Four's lives, from early gigs in Germany and the Cavern Club to each member's solo career, with 3-D computer animations, band artifacts, and more.

CHOOSE THE RIGHT TOUR

The two-hour Magical Mystery Tour (🌐 *www.cavernclub.org*) departing from the Albert Dock Visitor Centre is a great way to zoom around Penny Lane, Strawberry Field, and other landmarks it would otherwise be difficult to find. Liverpool Beatles Tours (🌐 *www.beatlestours.co.uk*) can cram in every Beatles haunt on four-hour or full-day tours. Other options are private guides or personalized tours.

SLEEP WITH THE BEATLES . . . AND SHOP, TOO

Within earshot of the Cavern on the corner of Mathew Street is the Hard Day's Night Hotel, with Lennon- and McCartney-themed suites, Yellow Submarine jukeboxes, and an inviting bar. At 31 Mathew Street the Beatles Shop packs in memorabilia and souvenirs from vintage posters and vinyls to mugs.

GO TO BEATLEWEEK

The annual **International Beatleweek** (🌐 *www.cavernclub.org*) is usually held the last week in August. Attend John and Yoko fancy-dress parties, listen to Beatles tribute bands, and attend record fairs, exhibitions, and conventions.

TAKING STOCK

When these four local rapscallions appeared on the Liverpool pop circuit in the early 1960s, they were just another group of lads struggling to get gigs on the city's "Merseybeat" scene. What followed was extraordinary: Beatlemania swept over fans around the world, including the United States, which the group first visited in 1964. Before their 1969 breakup, the Beatles achieved phenomenal commercial and creative success, bringing bohemianism to the masses and embodying a generation's ideals of social liberation and peace. They reinvented pop music, bridging styles and genres as diverse as Celtic folk, psychedelia, and Indian raga, starring in epoch-making movies such as *A Hard Day's Night* and *Help!*, and causing such hysteria they couldn't even hear their own guitars on stage. Though adulation followed them everywhere, the Beatles remained obstinate "Scousers," showing a grounded charm and irreverent humor characteristic of their native city.

Updated by Rhonda Carrier

For those looking for picture-postcard England, the northwest region of the country might not appear at the top of many sightseeing lists, but it has plenty more to offer. Manchester, Britain's third-largest city by size and second by cultural significance, bustles with redevelopment, and Liverpool is undergoing similar revitalization. Yes, the 200 years of smokestack industry that abated only in the 1980s have taken a toll on the landscape, yet the region does have some lovely scenery inland, in Derbyshire (pronounced *Dar-be-sha*)—notably the spectacular Peak District, a national park at the southern end of the Pennine range.

Manchester and Liverpool, the economic engines that propelled Britain in the 18th and 19th centuries, are sloughing off their mid-20th-century decline and celebrating their rich industrial and maritime heritage through some excellent museums—either in converted Victorian edifices, strikingly modern buildings, or, in the case of the Manchester Art Gallery and Whitworth Art Gallery, a stunning combination of the two.

The cities, each with a population of about 500,000, have reestablished themselves as centers of sporting and musical excellence, as well as hot spots for culture and nightlife. Since 1962 the Manchester United, Everton, and Liverpool football (soccer in the United States) clubs have between them won everything worth winning in Britain and Europe. The Beatles launched the Mersey sound of the '60s; contemporary Manchester groups still punch above their weight on both sides of the Atlantic. On the classical side of music, Manchester is also the home of Britain's oldest leading orchestra, the Hallé (founded in 1857)—just one legacy of 19th-century industrialists' investments in culture.

As you head inland to the Peak District, nature comes to the forefront in the form of crags that rear violently out of the plains. The Pennines, a line of hills that begins in the Peak District and runs as far north as Scotland, are sometimes called the "backbone of England." In this landscape of rocky outcrops and undulating meadowland you'll see nothing for miles but sheep, dry-stone walls (built without mortar), and farms, interrupted—spectacularly—by 19th-century villages and stately homes. In and around this area are Victorian-era spas such as Buxton, pretty towns such as Bakewell, and magnificent houses such as Chatsworth and Haddon Hall. The delight of the Peak District is being able to ramble for days in rugged countryside but still enjoy the pleasures of civilization.

MANCHESTER, LIVERPOOL, AND THE PEAK DISTRICT PLANNER

WHEN TO GO

Manchester has a reputation as one of the wettest cities in Britain, and visiting in summer won't guarantee dry weather. Nevertheless, the damp and/or cold shouldn't spoil a visit because of the many indoor sights and cultural activities here and in Liverpool. Summer is the optimum time to see the Peak District, especially because traditional festivities take place in many villages. The only time to see the great houses of Derbyshire's Wye Valley is from spring through fall.

PLANNING YOUR TIME

It's possible to see the main sights of Manchester or Liverpool in two days, but you'd have to take the museums at a real gallop. In Manchester, the Museum of Science and Industry and the Imperial War Museum North could easily absorb a day by themselves, as could the Albert Dock and waterfront area of Liverpool, where the Beatles Story's main venue, the Tate Liverpool, and the Merseyside Maritime and International Slavery museums, as well as the neighboring Museum of Liverpool, all vie for your attention. In Liverpool, an additional half day is needed to see the homes of John Lennon and Paul McCartney. The excellent nightlife of each city demands at least an overnight stay at each. You can explore the Peak District on a day trip from Manchester in a pinch, but allow longer to visit the stately homes or to hike.

GETTING HERE AND AROUND

AIR TRAVEL

Both Manchester and Liverpool are well served by their international airports. Manchester, the third-largest airport in the country (and the busiest outside London), has the greater number of flights, including some from the United States. East Midlands Airport southwest of Derby also provides an alternative international air route into the region.

Airports East Midlands Airport. ✉ *Castle Donington* ☎ *0871/919–9000* 🌐 *www.eastmidlandsairport.com.* **Liverpool John Lennon Airport.** ✉ *Hale Rd., Liverpool* ☎ *0871/521–8484* 🌐 *www.liverpoolairport.com.* **Manchester Airport.** ✉ *Manchester* ☎ *0871/271–0711* 🌐 *www.manchesterairport.co.uk.*

BUS TRAVEL

National Express buses serve the region from London's Victoria Coach Station. Average travel time to Manchester or Liverpool is five hours. To reach Matlock, Bakewell, and Buxton you can take a bus from London to Derby and change to the TransPeak bus service, though you might find it more convenient to travel first to Manchester.

Bus Contacts National Express. ☎ *0871/781–8178* 🌐 *www.nationalexpress.com.* **TransPeak.** ☎ *0843/523–6036* 🌐 *www.highpeakbuses.com.*

CAR TRAVEL

If you're traveling by road, expect heavy traffic out of London on weekends. Travel time to Manchester or Liverpool from London via the M6 is 3 to 3½ hours. Although a car may not be an asset in touring the centers of Manchester and Liverpool, it's helpful in getting around the Peak District. The bus service there is quite good, but a car allows the most flexibility.

Roads within the region are generally very good, but the deeper you get into the countryside, the more likely you are to encounter narrow, one-lane farm roads once you turn off the main routes. In summer, Peak District traffic is very heavy; watch out for speeding motorbikes, especially on the A6. In winter, know the weather forecast, as moorland roads can quickly become impassable.

In Manchester and Liverpool, try to sightsee on foot to avoid parking issues. In the Peak District, park in signposted parking lots whenever possible.

TRAIN TRAVEL

Virgin Trains serves the region from London's Euston Station. Direct services to Manchester and Liverpool take between 2 and 2½ hours. There are trains between Manchester's Piccadilly Station and Liverpool's Lime Street roughly three times an hour during the day; the trip takes 50 minutes. (Trains also go less frequently from Manchester's Victoria and Oxford Road stations.) Get schedules and other information through National Rail Enquiries.

To reach Buxton in the Peak District from London, take the train to Manchester that stops at Stockport and change there; to Buxton it's another 45-minute ride. The local service—one train an hour—from Manchester Piccadilly to Buxton takes one hour.

Train Contacts National Rail Enquiries. ☎ *08457/484950* 🌐 *www.nationalrail.co.uk.*

TRANSPORTATION DISCOUNTS AND DEALS

A Wayfarer ticket (£12; £23 for groups of up to 2 adults and 2 children) covers a day's travel on all forms of transport in Manchester, Lancashire, Cheshire, Staffordshire, Derbyshire, and the Peak District. See 🌐 *www.tfgm.com* or call ☎ *0871/200–2233* for information.

RESTAURANTS

Dining options in Manchester and Liverpool vary from smart cafés offering Modern British, Continental, or global fare to world-class international restaurants for all budgets. Manchester has one of Britain's biggest Chinatowns, and locals also favor the 40-odd Bangladeshi,

Pakistani, and Indian restaurants along Wilmslow Road in Rusholme, a mile south of the city center, known as Curry Mile.

One local dish that has survived is Bakewell pudding (*never* called "tart" in these areas, as its imitations are elsewhere in England). Served with custard or cream, the pudding—a pastry covered with jam and a thin layer of almond-flavor filling—is a real joy of visiting Bakewell.

HOTELS

Because the larger city-center hotels in Manchester and Liverpool rely on business travelers during the week, they may markedly reduce their rates on weekends. Smaller hotels and guesthouses abound, often in nearby suburbs, many just a short bus ride from downtown. The Manchester and Liverpool visitor centers operate room-booking services. Also worth investigating are serviced apartments, which are becoming more popular in the cities. The Peak District has inns, bed-and-breakfasts, and hotels, as well as a network of youth hostels and campsites. Local tourist offices have details; reserve well in advance for Easter and summer. ⇨ *Hotel reviews have been shortened. For full information, visit Fodors.com.*

WHAT IT COSTS IN POUNDS				
	$	$$	$$$	$$$$
Restaurants	under £15	£15–£19	£20–£25	over £25
Hotels	under £100	£100–£160	£161–£220	over £220

Restaurant prices are the average cost of a main course at dinner, or if dinner is not served, at lunch. Hotels prices are the lowest cost of a standard double room in high season, including 20% V.A.T.

MANCHESTER

Central Manchester is alive with the vibe of cutting-edge popular music and a swank, often fancy café, cocktail bar, and restaurant culture. The city's once-grim industrial landscape, redeveloped since the late 1980s, includes tidied-up canals, cotton mills transformed into loft apartments, and stylish contemporary architecture that has pushed the skyline ever higher. Beetham Tower, the 11th-tallest building in Britain (the tallest outside London), stands proud and prominent above it all. Bridgewater Hall and the Lowry, as well as the Imperial War Museum North, are among the outstanding cultural facilities. It still rains a lot here, but even the rain-soaked streets can be part of the city's charm, in a bleak, northern kind of way.

The now-defunct Haçienda Club marketed the 1980s rock band New Order to the world, and Manchester became the clubbing capital of England. Other Manchester-based bands like Joy Division, the Smiths, Stone Roses, Happy Mondays, and Oasis also rose to the top of the charts throughout the '70s, '80s, and '90s. The extraordinary success of the Manchester United football club (which now faces a stiff challenge from its newly rich neighbor, Manchester City, owing to a stupendous injection of cash from its oil-rich Middle Eastern owner) has kept the eyes of sports fans around the world fixed firmly on Manchester.

GETTING HERE AND AROUND

Manchester Airport has many international flights, so you might not even have to travel through London. There are frequent trains from the airport to Piccadilly Railway Station (15–20 minutes), new Metrolink trams to the city center (50 minutes), and buses to Piccadilly Gardens Bus Station (one hour). A taxi from the airport to Manchester city center costs around £25. For details about public transportation in Manchester, see *www.tfgm.co* or call *0871/200–2233*.

Driving to Manchester from London (3 to 3½ hours), take the M1 north to the M6, then the M62 east, which becomes the M602 as it enters Greater Manchester.

Trains from London's Euston Station drop passengers at the centrally located Piccadilly railway station. The journey takes just over two hours. Manchester Central Coach Station, a few hundred yards west of Piccadilly railway station, is the main bus station for regional and long-distance buses.

Most local buses leave from Piccadilly Gardens bus station, the hub of the urban bus network. Metroshuttle operates three free circular routes around the city center; service runs every five to 10 minutes Monday to Saturday from 7 to 7 and Sunday and public holidays from 10 to 6.

The ever-expanding Metrolink electric tram service runs through the city center and out to the suburbs and the airport. The Eccles extension has a stop for the Lowry (Harbour City) and the Altrincham line a stop for Manchester United Stadium (Old Trafford). Buy a ticket from the platform machine before you board.

SystemOne Travelcards allowing unlimited travel cost between £5.20 and £8.60, depending on the times of day, number of days, and modes of transport you want to include (for example, unlimited buses and trams after 9:30 am cost £5.70 with a Daysaver); buy from the driver (buses only) or a ticket machine.

TOURS

Manchester Guided Tours. Group tours run by this tourism board-recommended firm include Chinatown and the Town Hall. *07505/685942* *www.manchesterguidedtours.com* *From £6.*

City Centre Cruises. Take a three-hour round-trip cruise on a barge to the Manchester Ship Canal; some include a traditional Sunday lunch. Another of their full-day river tours includes entry to the Manchester United football stadium tour and museum. Times vary; call or go online for departure schedule. *0161/902–0222* *www.citycentrecruises.co.uk* *From £25.*

ORIENTATION

Manchester is compact enough that you can easily walk across the city center in 40 minutes. Deansgate and Princess Street, the main thoroughfares, run roughly north–south and west–east; the lofty terra-cotta Victorian **Town Hall** sits in the middle, close to the fine **Manchester Art Gallery.** Dominating the skyline at the southern end of Deansgate

Manchester was an industrial powerhouse; learn all about this history at the engaging Museum of Science and Industry.

is Manchester's highest building, Beetham Tower, which houses a Hilton Hotel and marks the beginning of the **Castlefield Urban Heritage Park,** with the Museum of Science and Industry and the canal system. The **Whitworth Art Gallery** is a bus ride from downtown; otherwise, all other central sights are within easy walking distance of the Town Hall. Take a Metrolink tram 2 miles south for the Salford Quays dockland area, with the **Lowry** and the **Imperial War Museum North**; you can spend half a day or more in this area. ■**TIP→ Keep in mind that the museums mentioned above are both excellent and free.**

9

FESTIVALS

Fodor's Choice ★ **Manchester International Festival.** This biennial multi-arts festival has played a major role in Manchester's cultural development since it launch in 2007. With international artists like Björk and Marina Abramović making appearances, it often premiers events that go on to tour nationally or globally. Events take place in some of the city's most popular performing arts spaces, as well as obscure locations such as disused buildings. ✉ *Manchester* 🌐 *www.mif.co.uk.*

ESSENTIALS

Transportation Contacts Metrolink. ☎ *0161/205–2000* 🌐 *www.metrolink.co.uk.* **Transport for Greater Manchester.** ☎ *0871/200–2233* 🌐 *www.tfgm.com.*

Visitor Information Manchester Visitor Information Centre. ✉ *40–50 Piccadilly Plaza, Portland St., City Centre* ☎ *0871/222–8223* 🌐 *www.visitmanchester.com.*

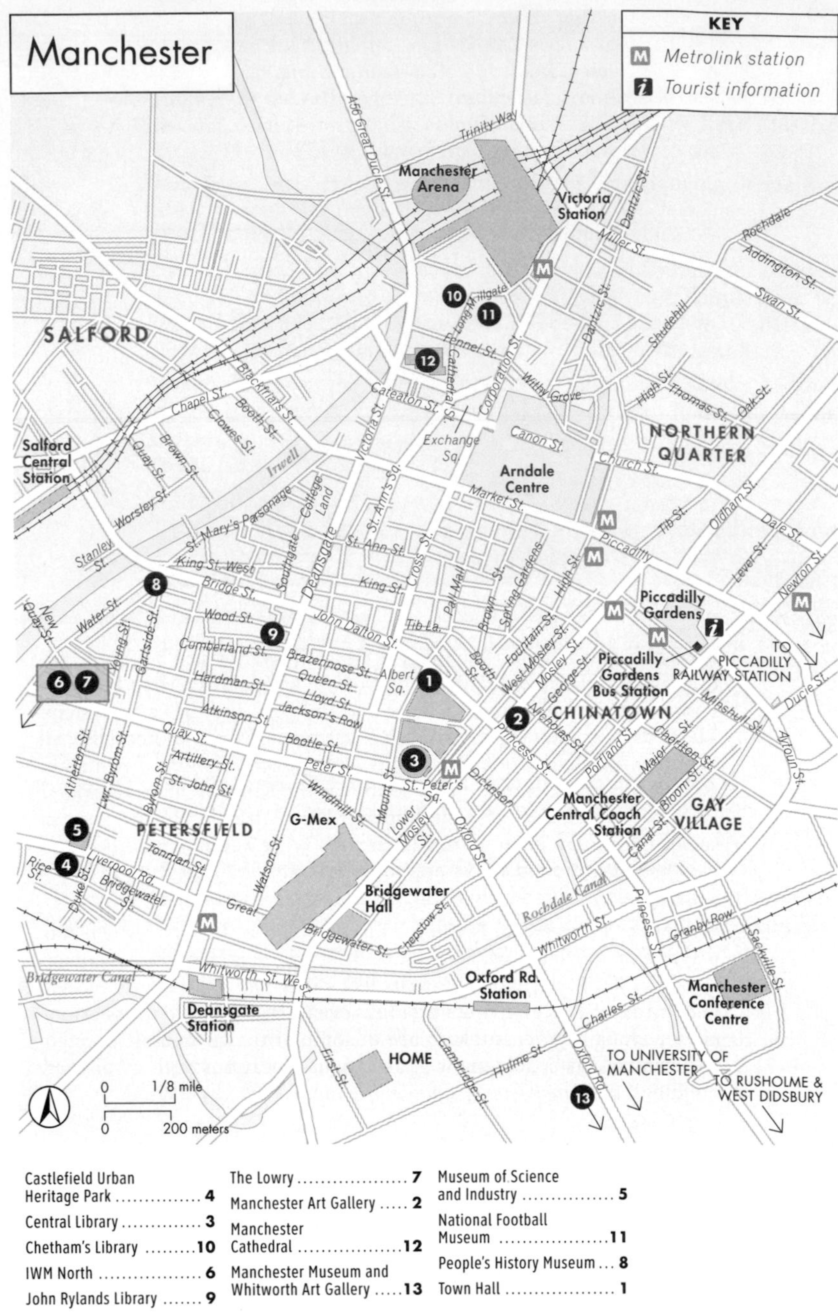

Castlefield Urban Heritage Park 4
Central Library 3
Chetham's Library 10
IWM North 6
John Rylands Library 9
The Lowry 7
Manchester Art Gallery 2
Manchester Cathedral 12
Manchester Museum and Whitworth Art Gallery 13
Museum of Science and Industry 5
National Football Museum 11
People's History Museum ... 8
Town Hall 1

EXPLORING

TOP ATTRACTIONS

FAMILY **Castlefield Urban Heritage Park.** Site of an early Roman fort, the district of Castlefield was later the center of the city's industrial boom, which resulted in the building of Britain's first modern canal in 1764 and the world's first railway station in 1830. It has been beautifully restored into an urban park with canal-side walks, landscaped open spaces, and refurbished warehouses. The 7-acre site contains the reconstructed gate to the Roman fort of Mamucium, the buildings of the **Museum of Science and Industry,** and several bars and restaurants, many with outdoor terraces. You can easily spend a day here. ✉ *Liverpool Rd., Castlefield.*

Fodor's Choice ★ **Central Library.** This 1930s structure was once the biggest municipal library in the world, and today its circular exterior, topped by a line of Doric columns and a massive Corinthian portico facing St. Peter's Square, is a major focus for Manchester's most prestigious civic quarter. Notable sights within the library are the **British Film Institute Mediatheque,** a free-to-view collection of 2,000 films and TV programs relating to the UK and its people; the Media Lounge with creative software and gaming stations; the Music Library with a DJ-mixing desk and instrument collection that is free to use; and the Children's Library, as well as free Wi-Fi, displays on local history, and a convenient café. ✉ *St. Peter's Sq., City Centre* ☎ *0161/234–1983* 🌐 *www.manchester.gov.uk/centrallibrary* ⏲ *Mon.–Thurs. 9–8, Fri.–Sat. 9–5.*

FAMILY Fodor's Choice ★ **IWM North.** The thought-provoking exhibits in this striking, aluminum-clad building, which architect Daniel Libeskind described as representing three shards of an exploded globe, present the reasons for war and show its effects on society. Hourly Big Picture audiovisual shows envelop you in the sights and sounds of conflicts while a timeline from 1914 to the present-day examines objects and personal stories from veterans showing how war changes lives. The Air Shard, a 100-foot viewing platform, gives a bird's-eye view of the city. Excellent special exhibitions cover everything from life in Britain during the Blitz to artistic responses to conflict. The museum is on the banks of the Manchester Ship Canal in The Quays,across the footbridge from the Lowry. It's a five-minute walk from the MediaCityUK stop of the Metrolink tram. ✉ *Trafford Wharf Rd., Trafford Wharf* ☎ *0161/836–4000* 🌐 *www.iwm.org.uk/visits/iwm-north* ⏲ *Daily 10–5; last admission 30 min before closing.*

Fodor's Choice ★ **John Rylands Library.** Owned by the University of Manchester, this Gothic Revival masterpiece designed by Alfred Waterhouse was built by Enriqueta Augustina Rylands as a memorial to her husband, a cotton magnate. Constructed of red sandstone in the 1890s, the library resembles a cathedral and contains some outstanding collections of illuminated manuscripts and beautifully illustrated books. Among the many highlights are the oldest known fragment of the New Testament in existence, dating from around AD 100; an original Gutenberg Bible; and several works by William Caxton (c.1417–92), who introduced the printing press to the English-speaking world. A lively temporary exhibition and events program includes printing press demonstrations,

9

photography tours, and children's storytelling sessions based on elements of the building's decor. The café hosts regular tasting events involving recipes gleaned from historic cooking books in the library's collections. ✉ *150 Deansgate, Millennium Quarter* ☎ *0161/306–0555* 🌐 *www.library.manchester.ac.uk* 🎟 *Free* ⏲ *Tues.–Sat. 10–5, Sun. and Mon. noon–5; last entry 30 min before closing.*

FAMILY **The Lowry.** Clad in perforated steel and glass, this arts center is one of the highlights of the Salford Quays waterways. L. S. Lowry (1887–1976) was a local artist, and one of the few who painted the industrial landscape; galleries here showcase his work alongside that of contemporary artists. The theater, Britain's largest outside London, has three spaces showcasing everything from West End musicals and new works by up-and-coming theater companies to some of the U.K.'s most popular stand-up comedians. The nearest Metrolink tram stop is Harbour City, a 10-minute walk away. ✉ *Pier 8, Salford Quays* ☎ *0843/208–6000* 🌐 *www.thelowry.com* 🎟 *Free, tours £5* ⏲ *Mon.–Sat. 10–8 (later on nights when performances are happening), Sun. and holiday Mon. 10–6. Galleries Sat. 10–5, Sun.–Fri. 11–5.*

FAMILY **Manchester Art Gallery.** Behind an impressive classical portico, this splendid museum and its sparkling modern atrium houses an outstanding collection of paintings by the Pre-Raphaelites and their circle, notably Ford Madox Brown's masterpiece *Work*, Holman Hunt's *The Hireling Shepherd,* and Dante Gabriel Rossetti's *Astarte Syriaca*. British artworks from the 18th and the 20th centuries are also well represented. The second-floor Craft and Design Gallery shows off the best of the decorative arts in ceramics, glass, metalwork, and furniture. The Clore Art Studio is a creative space for families. ✉ *Mosley St., City Centre* ☎ *0161/235–8888* 🌐 *www.manchestergalleries.org.uk* 🎟 *Free* ⏲ *Fri.–Wed. 10–5; Thurs. 10–9; last admission 30 min before closing.*

FAMILY Fodor's Choice ★ **Manchester Museum.** Run by the University of Manchester, this museum and its superb Gothic Revival building embraces anthropology, natural history, and archaeology. It features one of the U.K's largest ancient Egyptian collections as part of its extensive Ancient Worlds galleries; there's also a beautiful Living Worlds gallery designed to raise questions about our attitude towards nature; a vivarium complete with live frogs and other amphibians and reptiles; and a Nature Discovery gallery for children under five. A lively events program for all ages helps lure in repeat visitors. ✉ *Oxford Rd., University Quarter* ☎ *0161/275–2648* 🌐 *www.museum.manchester.ac.uk* ⏲ *Daily 10–5.*

FAMILY Fodor's Choice ★ **Museum of Science and Industry.** The museum's five buildings, one of which is the world's oldest passenger rail station (1830), hold marvelous collections relating to the city's industrial past and present; the next few years promise further expansion into the buildings' vaulted basement spaces. You can walk through a reconstructed Victorian sewer, be blasted by the heat and noise of working steam engines, see cotton looms whirring in action, and watch a planetarium show. The Air and Space Gallery fills a graceful cast-iron-and-glass building, constructed as a market hall in 1877. ■ **TIP→ Allow at least half a day to get the most out of all the sites, temporary exhibitions, talks, and events.**

Castlefield Urban Heritage Park, Liverpool Rd., main entrance on Lower Byrom St., Castlefield 0161/832–2244 www.mosi.org.uk Free, charges vary for special exhibits Daily 10–5.

People's History Museum. Not everyone in 19th-century Manchester owned a cotton mill or made a fortune on the trading floor. This museum recounts powerfully the struggles of working people in the city and in the U.K. as a whole since the Industrial Revolution. Displays include the story of the 1819 Peterloo Massacre—when the army attacked a crowd of civil rights protesters in Manchester's St. Peter's Square, killing 15 and almost sparking revolution—together with an unrivaled collection of trade union banners, tools, toys, utensils, and photographs, all illustrating the working lives and pastimes of the city's people. *Left Bank, City Centre 0161/838–9190 www.phm.org.uk Free Daily 10–5.*

NEED A BREAK?

Central Library Café. The ground-floor café of this glorious domed neoclassical rotunda is a fine spot to catch a quick bite to eat at any time of the day, plus a place to take advantage of the free Wi-Fi. Surrounded by displays on the city's history, feast on porridge with regional honey or barms (bread rolls) with Lancashire bacon, sausage, or field mushrooms. ***St Peter's Sq., City Centre 0161/234–1979 www.manchester.gov.uk/centrallibrary.***

Town Hall. Manchester's imposing Town Hall, with its 280-foot-tall clock tower, speaks volumes about the city's 19th-century sense of self-importance. Alfred Waterhouse designed the Victorian Gothic building (1867–76); extensions were added just before World War II. Over the main entrance is a statue of Roman general Agricola, who founded Mamucium in AD 79. Just inside the entrance, the Sculpture Hall has a magnificent low vaulted ceiling; now used as an atmospheric café, its walls are lined with Gothic-style alcoves and statues of famous Mancunians. The Great Hall is decorated with murals of the city's history, painted between 1852 and 1865 by the Pre-Raphaelite Ford Madox Brown, which the public can view for free so long as the room isn't being used by officials. Clock tower tours are available from companies like Manchester Guided Tours and New Manchester Walks. *Albert Sq., public entrance on Lloyd St., City Centre 0161/234–4433 www.manchester.gov.uk/townhall Free Weekdays 9–4, Sat. 11–4.*

FAMILY
Fodor's Choice ★

Whitworth Art Gallery. After a vast redevelopment project doubling its overall size, this University of Manchester–owned art museum reopened in early 2015 to reveal its integration into the surrounding parkland through the creation of an art garden, a sculpture terrace, an orchard garden, and a landscape gallery. Some of the free events and activities take you out into the park itself, in the form of messy play for kids, walks, and self-guided trails. The renowned collections inside the gallery embrace British watercolors, old-master drawings, postimpressionist works, wallpapers, and an outstanding textile gallery befitting a city built on textile manufacturing. There's also a new learning studio for families and a "café in the trees" with floor-to-ceiling windows and a seasonal British menu. *University of Manchester, Oxford Rd.,*

CLOSE UP

Manchester's History: Cottonopolis

Manchester's spectacular rise from a small town to the world's cotton capital—with the nickname Cottonopolis—in only 100 years began with the first steam-powered cotton mill, built in 1783. Dredging made the rivers Irwell and Mersey navigable to ship coal to the factories. The world's first passenger railway opened in 1830, and construction of the Manchester Ship Canal in 1894 provided the infrastructure for Manchester to dominate the industrial world.

A few people acquired great wealth, but factory hands worked under appalling conditions. Working-class discontent came to a head in 1819 in the Peterloo Massacre, when soldiers killed 15 workers at a protest meeting. The conditions under which factory hands worked were later recorded by Friedrich Engels (co-author with Karl Marx of the *Communist Manifesto*), who managed a cotton mill in the city. More formal political opposition to the government emerged in the shape of the Chartist movement (which campaigned for universal suffrage) and the Anti–Corn Law League (which opposed trade tariffs), forerunners of the British trade unions. From Victorian times until the 1960s, daily life for the average Mancunian was so oppressive that it bred the desire to escape, although most stayed put and endured the harsh conditions.

University Quarter ☎ *0161/275–7450* 🌐 *www.whitworth.manchester.ac.uk* 🎟 *Free* 🕒 *Fri.–Wed. 10–5, Thurs. 10–9.*

WORTH NOTING

Chetham's Library. The oldest public library in the English-speaking world (founded in 1653), as well as the meeting place of Marx and Engels when the former visited Manchester, is now an accredited museum. Among its collection of over 100,000 printed works—including some 16th- and 17th-century books and journals—is the economics book that Marx read here. ✉ *Long Millgate* ☎ *0161/834–7961* 🌐 *www.chethams.org.uk* 🕒 *Mon.–Fri. 9–12:30 and 1:30–4:30.*

Manchester Cathedral. The city's sandstone cathedral, set beside the River Irwell and originally a medieval parish church dating in part from the 15th century, is unusually broad for its length and has the widest medieval nave in Britain. Inside, angels with gilded instruments look down from the roof of the nave, and misericords (the undersides of choristers' seats) in the early 16th-century choir stalls reveal intriguing carvings. The octagonal chapter house dates from 1485. There are free daily guided tours year-round, and on weekends and school holidays kids get free Explorer Trails (interactive tours meant to engage kids with different parts of the cathedral). ✉ *Victoria St., City Centre* ☎ *0161/833–2220* 🌐 *www.manchestercathedral.org* 🎟 *Free* 🕒 *Daily 8:30–6:30; tours weekdays 11 and 2, Sat. 1, Sun. 2.*

FAMILY **National Football Museum.** This striking, glass-skinned triangle of a building includes a galaxy of footballing (soccer) memorabilia, from historic trophies, souvenirs, and shirts (many of them match-worn and signed by legends of the sport) to such near-sacred items as the ball from the

1966 World Cup—the last time England won the sport's ultimate prize. Other exhibits explore football's role in English popular culture. In the interactive Football Plus+ zone you can pick up a microphone and develop your commentary style or test your ball skills in a range of activities, including a tense penalty shoot-out; these require paid tickets. ✉ *Urbis Bldg., Cathedral Gardens, City Centre* ☎ *0161/605–8200* 🌐 *www.nationalfootballmuseum.com* 🎟 *Free; charge for activities.* 🕒 *Mon.–Sat. 10–5, Sun. 11–5.*

WHERE TO EAT

$$$$ MODERN EUROPEAN ✕ **Manchester House.** Bursting onto the Manchester dining scene in 2013 courtesy of chef-prodigy Aiden Byrne, formerly of the Dorchester Hotel in London, this fine-dining restaurant is a glitzy spot in a somewhat incongruous 1960s tower block. Though it's the kind of place where many of the staff look like models, the food itself warrants serious attention: you'll find dishes such as the starter of squab pigeon with cherries, pistachios, and violet mustard, mains including John Dory poached in carrot butter, dried oranges, and bouillabaisse and a dessert of Lapsang souchong panna cotta with white miso and plums four ways. Don't miss the 12th-floor lounge-bar; it's the perfect place for an aperitif, nightcap, or afternoon tea with a view. Note that on Saturdays you're restricted to the 12-course tasting menu (£95). For a splurge with friends, book the Chef's Table experience with a front-row view of the bustling kitchen. $ *Average main: £35* ✉ *Tower 12, 18–22 Bridge St., Spinningfields* ☎ *0161/835–2557* 🌐 *www.manchesterhouse.uk.com* 🕒 *Closed Sun. and Mon.*

$$ BRITISH ✕ **Mr. Thomas's Chophouse.** The city's oldest restaurant, dating from 1872, dishes out good old British favorites such as crispy corned beef hash with poached eggs and HP brown sauce and steak and kidney pudding to diners in a Victorian-styled room with original tiling. Desserts are a bit more modern: try the bread and butter pudding layered with peanut butter and topped with white chocolate ice cream. Mr. Sam's Chophouse in Chapel Walks and the newer Albert Square Chophouse serves similar fare. $ *Average main: £16* ✉ *52 Cross St., City Centre* ☎ *0161/832–2245* 🌐 *www.tomschophouse.com* 💳 *No credit cards.*

$ INDIAN ✕ **Mughli Restaurant and Charcoal Pit.** At this long-standing north Indian and Pakistani restaurant, meals start with enticing shared dishes from a street food–based appetizers menu before proceeding to main courses both classic and contemporary; all are served around an open charcoal pit. Modern decor, Bollywood posters, and a serious cocktail menu have made this one of the more stylish options on Rusholme's "Curry Mile." $ *Average main: £9* ✉ *28–32 Wilmslow Rd., Rusholme* ☎ *0161/248–0900* 🌐 *www.mughli.com* 💳 *No credit cards.*

$$ MODERN AMERICAN ✕ **Neighbourhood.** Industrial chic decor and a decidedly gritty location amidst the tower blocks of Spinningfields can make the cozy name of this restaurant/bar seem ironic. But luckily this place is as fun as any Manhattan neighorhood it claims to be inspired by, with over-the-top cocktails like the Oppulentini (a martini with a crab oyster garnish) and quirky modern American dishes like the "shrimp, crackle, and pop" (shrimp in shellfish bisque, with an explosive Rice Krispie topping) and

9

buttermilk-marinated chicken "lollipops" (skewers). The menu also features burgers, steaks, and a raw bar with oysters, ceviche, and tartares. *Average main: £19 The Avenue North, Spinningfields 0161/832–6334 www.neighbourhoodrestaurant.co.uk No credit cards.*

$$ MODERN BRITISH Fodor's Choice ★ **The Rose Garden.** An intimate spot with fresh modern interiors, the Rose Garden is a standout option on a hip suburban street known for its lively dining scene. The menu changes seasonally but always features surprising and engaging dishes; you could choose from a starter of wild boar rillettes with crackling, apple, and radish salad, or a main of duck breast and rhubarb with wilted greens and polenta chips. Save room for the equally intriguing desserts. *Average main: £16 218 Burton Rd., West Didsbury 0161/478–0747 www.therosegardendidsbury.com No lunch Mon.–Sat. No credit cards.*

$$$$ MODERN BRITISH **Season's Eatings at Trove.** This monthly supper club is the brainchild of two female chefs intent on showcasing seasonal local produce prepared in inventive ways. A short train or bus ride from city center, Trove is a funky neighborhood café and bakery that creates a convivial buzz every first Thursday of the month with a four-course tasting menu that can include celeriac with cured egg yolk and chestnuts, and Jerusalem artichoke with passion fruit and hazelnut. The price includes a welcome cocktail, water, and artisan bread; you can bring your own alcohol. The chefs also have a seasonal club at the Fig and Sparrow in the Northern Quarter, and occasional pop-ups elsewhere in the city. *Average main: £33.50 1032 Stockport Rd. No phone www.trovefoods.co.uk Only open 1st Thurs. of every month Reservations essential No credit cards.*

$ THAI **Siam Smiles.** Quite possibly the most unassuming restaurant in all Manchester, this no-frills basement joint in a Chinatown supermarket serves authentic Thai food to a largely non-Western crowd from a small, noodle-centric menu. Standouts include Som Tam salad with papaya, cabbage, carrots, red chilli, peanuts, and dried shrimp, and Grill E-san fermented sausages with raw Chinese leaves, ginger, and red chili. You can bring in your own alcohol or grab soft drinks from nearby supermarket shelves. *Average main: £6 48a George St., Chinatown 0161/237–1555 Reservations not accepted.*

WHERE TO STAY

$ HOTEL **Abel Heywood.** In a city with so many chain hotels, the arrival of this well-priced boutique hotel and bar in the funky Northern Quarter came as a relief. **Pros:** in-room visitor guide to the Northern Quarter and Manchester; free Wi-Fi. **Cons:** rooms are small; some rooms have noise from the kitchen. *Rooms from: £70 38 Turner St., Northern Quarter 0161/819–1441 www.abelheywood.co.uk 15 rooms No meals.*

$$ HOTEL Fodor's Choice ★ **Hotel Gotham.** Located in an iconic art deco building, the offbeat Hotel Gotham reinvigorated the Manchester hotel scene with its 1930s New York theme; it also takes design cues from the building's former incarnation as a bank. **Pros:** guests get access to Brass, the private member's bar with a rooftop terrace; free mini-cocktails on check-in; gorgeous, unique decor; fantastic and fun restaurant. **Cons:** no bathtubs

except in certain suites; some rooms have small windows. *$ Rooms from: £150 ✉ 100 King St., City Centre ☎ 0844/815–9833 ⊕ www.hotelgotham.co.uk ⇌ 67 rooms ¶ No meals.*

$$ HOTEL FAMILY Fodor'sChoice ★ **The Lowry Hotel.** Luxurious and inviting, this elegant property occupies a striking curved glass building overlooking the River Irwell and Santiago Calatrava's Trinity Bridge and is a magnet for celebrity visitors to the city. **Pros:** a quiet location within an easy stroll of the center; spacious rooms. **Cons:** rooms facing Chapel Street are rather bleak; cheapest rates don't include breakfast. *$ Rooms from: £129 ✉ 50 Dearman's Pl., City Centre ☎ 0161/827–4000 ⊕ www.thelowryhotel.com ⇌ 157 rooms, 7 suites ¶ No meals.*

$ HOTEL **The Oxnoble at Potato Wharf.** Opposite the Museum of Science and Industry, this friendly and relaxed gastro-pub and hotel has simple, modern rooms with free Wi-Fi. **Pros:** friendly staff; bargain prices. **Cons:** no-frills decor; noise from the bar reaches some of the rooms. *$ Rooms from: £50 ✉ 71 Liverpool Rd., Castlefield ☎ 0161/839–7760 ⊕ www.theox.co.uk ▭ No credit cards ⇌ 10 rooms ¶ No meals.*

$ RENTAL Fodor'sChoice ★ **RoomZZZ.** The stylishly modern serviced apartments in this old cotton warehouse are all about self-contained autonomy, but the lobby and corridors have the feel of a boutique hotel. **Pros:** central location on Chinatown's doorstep; rooms have shutters and black-out blinds; free Wi-Fi. **Cons:** tends to attract party groups; some rooms are in the basement. *$ Rooms from: £99 ✉ 36 Princess St., Chinatown ☎ 0161/236–2121 ⊕ www.roomzzz.co.uk ▭ No credit cards ⇌ 59 apartments ¶ No meals.*

NIGHTLIFE AND PERFORMING ARTS

Manchester vies with London as Britain's capital of youth culture, but has vibrant nightlife and entertainment options for all ages. Spending time at a bar, pub, or club is definitely an essential part of any trip. For event listings, check out the free *Manchester Evening News*, widely available throughout the city, or websites like ⊕ *www.manchesterconfidential.co.uk* or ⊕ *www.manchesterwire.co.uk*.

9

NIGHTLIFE

BARS

Cloud 23. This dressy champagne and cocktail bar in the city's tallest building has stunning 360-degree views. Some of its inventive concoctions are named after key figures in Manchester's history, from Roman emperors to industrialists: Mr. Mercer's Cotton Peculiar (rum, spiced syrup, passion fruit, ice cream, and ginger beer) recalls a Lancashire chemist. *✉ Hilton Manchester Deansgate, Beetham Tower, 303 Deansgate, City Centre ☎ 0161/870–1670, ⊕ www.cloud23bar.com.*

Dry Bar. The Northern Quarter's original café-bar, opened by Tony Wilson Factory Records, gets packed with young people dancing and (despite the name) drinking. There's also a basement club and live music space. *✉ 28–30 Oldham St., Northern Quarter ☎ 0161/236–9840 ⊕ www.drybar.co.uk.*

Folk. Bars and restaurants come and go on trendy, ever-evolving Burton Road, but this bar that also doubles as a café and deli has stood the test

Manchester's pubs and café-bars, whether Victorian or modern, are well worth a stop.

of time thanks to its heated terrace (complete with palm trees), eclectic tunes by live DJs, chic interiors, and good food. ✉ *169 Burton Rd., West Didsbury* ☎ *0161/445–2912* 🌐 *www.folkcafebar.co.uk.*

Kosmonaut. With stripped-down decor, exposed brick walls, old tiles, and leather benches, this bar exudes a hipster vibe thanks to the Ping-Pong table and changing art exhibitions. The wine list and beer selection are great, although it's the cocktail menu that draws the biggest crowds. ✉ *10 Tariff St., Northern Quarter* ☎ *0161/236–7171* 🌐 *www.kosmonaut.co.*

The Liars Club. This self-described "tiki dive bar" serves up generously sized cocktails in its kitschy Caribbean beach–style bar. Order a zombie if you like your drinks set on fire. They also serve a hundred types of rum. ✉ *19A Back Bridge St., City Centre* ☎ *0161/834–5111* 🌐 *www.theliarsclub.co.uk.*

The Molly House. This lively Gay Village bar has an outstanding selection of beers from around the world, in addition to good wine and cocktail lists. The tapas nibbles are delicious and surprisingly inexpensive. ✉ *26 Richmond St., City Centre* ☎ *0161/237–9329* 🌐 *www.themollyhouse.com.*

Wood Wine and Deli. This wine bar and café charms with its quirky, rough-and-ready wooden bar counter built by a local artist; expanding on the theme, wooden boards are used for the meat and cheese sharing platters. There's beer and spirits in addition to a long wine list. ✉ *Smithfield Buildings, 44 Tib St., Northern Quarter* ☎ *0161/478–7100.*

PUBS

The Angel. You won't find any televisions in this atmospheric real ale pub serves that beers from small independent breweries. British comfort food is also offered in both the bar and its cozy restaurant that comes with a log fire and local art. ✉ *6 Angel St., Northern Quarter* ☎ *0161/833–4786* 🌐 *www.theangelmanchester.com.*

The Briton's Protection. You can sample more than 230 whiskies and bourbons at this gorgeous pub with stained-glass windows, cozy back rooms, a spacious beer garden, and a mural of the Peterloo Massacre. ✉ *50 Great Bridgewater St., Peter's Fields* ☎ *0161/236–5895* 🌐 *www.britons-protection.com.*

Dukes 92. Once a stable block for horses working the canals, it's now a great spot for a pub lunch or drink, especially in the summer thanks to its waterside terrace and balcony. ✉ *18 Castle St., Castlefield* ☎ *0161/839–3522* 🌐 *www.dukes92.com.*

Marble Arch. This handsome, unspoiled Victorian pub specializes in craft beers brewed by local firm Manchester Marble and offers a dedicated cheese menu. ✉ *73 Rochdale Rd., Northern Quarter* ☎ *0161/832–5914* 🌐 *www.marblebeers.com/marble-arch.*

The Oast House. This unique pub occupies a 16th-century oasthouse (where brewers roasted hops) that was brought, brick by brick, to Manchester from Kent. The emphasis is on craft beers and ales, accompanied by deli and rotisserie-style meats. The large terrace also offers some barbeque options. ✉ *The Avenue Courtyard, Crown Sq.* ☎ *0161/829–3830* 🌐 *www.theoasthouse.uk.com.*

Peveril of the Peak. An iconic throwback Victorian pub with a green-tile exterior, Peveril of the Peak draws a crush of locals to its tiny rooms. ✉ *127 Great Bridgewater St., Peter's Fields* ☎ *0161/236–6364.*

DANCE CLUBS

42nd Street. Off Deansgate, 42nd Street plays retro, indie, singalong anthems, and classic rock, with Manchester's proud musical heritage at the fore. ✉ *2 Bootle St., City Centre* ☎ *0161/831–7108* 🌐 *www.42ndstreetnightclub.co.uk.*

Fodor's Choice ★ **Factory 251.** This club and occasional live music venue brings the old offices of the legendary Factory Records to life with sounds ranging from drum 'n' bass to indie. ✉ *118 Princess St., City Centre* ☎ *0161/272–7251* 🌐 *www.factorymanchester.com.*

Gorilla. Nestled under old railway arches, Gorilla is a live music venue and gin parlour with an intimate vibe. ✉ *54-58 Whitworth St., University Quarter* ☎ *0161/407–0301* 🌐 *www.thisisgorilla.com.*

Sakura. Asian-inspired and futuristic decor meet in this glam club and bar offering an eclectic soundtrack for those ready to dance. ✉ *Arch 2, Deansgate Locks, Whitworth St., Peter's Fields* ☎ *0161/832–0234* 🌐 *www.sakuramanchester.com.*

Sankey's. Electro, techno, and hardcore music draw crowds of young people to this long-standing venue that sometimes draws comparisons to Ibiza in summer. ✉ *Radium St., Northern Quarter* ☎ *0161/661–9668* 🌐 *www.sankeys.info.*

GAY CLUBS

Gay Village. This neighborhood lines up stylish bars and cafés along the Rochdale Canal; Canal Street is its heart. There are certainly several gay bars, but most attract a mixed crowd. ✉ *Canal St.*

LIVE MUSIC

Fodor's Choice ★ **Albert Hall.** One of the city's most exciting venues, this former Wesleyan chapel was abandoned and forgotten about for over four decades; it's now a superb indie music hall retaining many of the site's original features, including an organ and stained-glass windows. ✉ *27 Peter St., City Centre* ☎ *0844/858–8521* 🌐 *www.alberthallmanchester.com.*

Band on the Wall. This famous venue has a reputation for hosting both established and pioneering acts. ✉ *25 Swan St., Northern Quarter* ☎ *0161/834–1786* 🌐 *www.bandonthewall.org.*

Fodor's Choice ★ **The Deaf Institute.** Good acoustics characterize the intimate domed music hall of this landmark building (a one-time institute for deaf and mute people) that regularly hosts cutting-edge indie acts. There are also club nights, open mics, and quiz nights. ✉ *135 Grosvenor St., University Quarter* ☎ *0161/276–9350* 🌐 *www.thedeafinstitute.co.uk.*

Manchester Arena. Europe's largest indoor arena hosts shows by major rock and pop stars, as well as large-scale sporting events. ✉ *21 Hunts Bank, Hunt's Bank* ☎ *0844/847–8000 box office,* 🌐 *www.manchester-arena.com.*

Night & Day Café. A major player in Manchester's musical history, many bands who played here eventually went on to huge success, including Elbow. Now this venue and café-bar covers all genres, from indie and folk to jazz and electronica. ✉ *26 Oldham St., Northern Quarter* ☎ *0161/236–1822* 🌐 *www.nightnday.org.*

O2 Apollo Manchester. Housed in an art-deco venue, the 3,500-seat venue (known by locals as just "the Apollo") showcases live rock and comedy acts before a mixed-age crowd. ✉ *Stockport Rd., Ardwick Green* ☎ *08444/777677* 🌐 *www.o2apollomanchester.co.uk.*

The Roadhouse. This intimate venue hosts rock, pop, funk, and indie bands, plus club nights. ✉ *8 Newton St., City Centre* ☎ *0161/237–9789* 🌐 *www.theroadhouselive.co.uk.*

Sound Control. Formerly a cult music shop frequented by the likes of local legends Johnny Marr and Noel Gallagher, this three-story venue has two live music spaces and a basement club. ✉ *1 New Wakefield St., University Quarter* ☎ *0161/236–0340* 🌐 *www.soundcontrolmanchester.co.uk.*

PERFORMING ARTS

Bridgewater Hall. Dramatically modern Bridgewater Hall is home to Manchester's renowned Hallé Orchestra and the BBC Symphony Orchestra, but also hosts a varied light-entertainment program. The venue sits on 280 springs to reduce external noise. ✉ *Lower Mosley St., Peter's Fields* ☎ *0161/907–9000* 🌐 *www.bridgewater-hall.co.uk.*

Fodor's Choice ★ **HOME.** This 2015 venue takes off where the Cornerhouse left off and also provides a new home for the Library Theatre Company. Within it you'll find a main 450-seat theater, a studio theater space, a gallery, five cinema screens, and digital production and broadcast facilities, as well a bar, a café, and a bookshop. ✉ *2 Tony Wilson Pl. at First St., University Quarter* ☎ *0161/228–7621* 🌐 *www.homemcr.org.*

The Kings Arms. Live music, plays, and comedy feature on the bill of this intimate space located above a traditional pub. ✉ *11 Bloom St., Salford Quays* ☎ *0161/832–3605.*

Palace Theatre. One of the city's largest houses, the Palace Theatre presents mainly touring musicals and tribute acts. ✉ *97 Oxford St., City Centre* ☎ *0844/871–3019* 🌐 *www.atgtickets.com/venues/manchester.*

Fodor's Choice ★ **Royal Exchange Theatre.** Housed in the city's one-time cotton exchange, this innovative venue for classic and contemporary works includes a glass-and-metal structure cradling a theater-in-the-round, plus a studio space. ✉ *St. Ann's Sq., City Centre* ☎ *0161/833–9833* 🌐 *www.royalexchange.co.uk.*

Three Minute Theatre. Also known as the 3MT Venue, the self-described "vintage recycled boutique theater" hosts innovative plays, music, comedy, poetry, and film in an intimate, bohemian setting. ✉ *Afflecks Arcade, 35–39 Oldham St., Northern Quarter* ☎ *0161/834–4517* 🌐 *www.threeminutetheatre.co.uk.*

SHOPPING

The city is nothing if not fashion conscious; take your pick from glitzy department stores, huge retail outlets, designer shops, and idiosyncratic boutiques. Famous names are centered on Exchange Square (including branches of big name department stores Harvey Nichols and Selfridges), Deansgate, and King Street, and designer boutiques are colonizing nearby Spinningfields; the Northern Quarter provides edgier style for young trendsetters as well as a wide variety of vinyl record and music shops. Outside the city, the vast Trafford Centre mall houses a multitude of store, entertainment options, and eateries under one roof.

Afflecks. With a collection that ranges from top hats to punk skinny jeans and skatewear, this emporium has been purveying indie fashion and lifestyle paraphernalia to its many fans for decades. ✉ *52 Church St., Northern Quarter* ☎ *0161/839–0718* 🌐 *www.afflecks.com.*

Barton Arcade. This charming Victorian arcade houses various specialty stores including women's fashion, bridalwear, and jewelry. ✉ *51–63 Deansgate, City Centre* 🌐 *www.bartonarcade.com.*

Fodor's Choice ★ **Manchester Craft and Design Centre.** A Victorian market building has been tranformed into this vibrant, airy space that houses 30 resident artists and craftmakers with workshop-cum-retail outlets. There's also a wonderful café. ✉ *17 Oak St., Northern Quarter* ☎ *0161/832–4274* 🌐 *www.craftanddesign.com.*

SPORTS AND THE OUTDOORS

FOOTBALL

Football (soccer in the United States) is *the* reigning passion in Manchester. Locals tend to be torn between Manchester City and Manchester United, the two local clubs based in neighboring Trafford. Matches for both clubs are usually sold out months in advance, though you have more of a chance with Manchester City; stadium tours can be a good alternative if you can't snag match tickets.

Manchester City. This football club, a favorite with locals, plays at the Etihad (City of Manchester) Stadium. ✉ *Rowsley St., SportCity* ☎ *0161/444–1894* 🌐 *www.mcfc.co.uk.*

Manchester City Etihad Stadium. This is the place to see Man City in action and also to inspect club memorabilia, visit the changing rooms, and explore the pitch. There are also daily tours, including on match days. ✉ *Etihad Campus, Rowsley St., SportCity* ☎ *0161/444–1894* 🌐 *www.mcfc.co.uk* 🎫 *£15.*

Manchester United. One of the biggest clubs in soccer (and the world's second-richest sports team, after Spanish club Real Madrid), Manchester United has home matches at Old Trafford. ✉ *Sir Matt Busby Way, Trafford Wharf* ☎ *0161/868–8000* 🌐 *www.manutd.com.*

Old Trafford. Manchester United's home stadium attracts fans from near and far for matches as well as the museum and tour, which takes you behind the scenes into the changing rooms and players' lounge, and down the tunnel. ✉ *Sir Matt Busby Way, Trafford Wharf* ☎ *0161/868–8000* 🌐 *www.manutd.com* 🎫 *£18.*

LIVERPOOL

A city lined with one of the most famous waterfronts in England, celebrated around the world as the birthplace of the Beatles, and still the place to catch that "Ferry 'Cross the Mersey," Liverpool reversed a downturn in its fortunes with developments in the late 1980s, such as the impressively refurbished Albert Dock area. In 2004, UNESCO named six historic areas in the city center together as one World Heritage Site, in recognition of the city's maritime and mercantile achievements during the height of Britain's global influence. The city's heritage, together with famous attractions and a legacy of cultural vibrancy that includes an ever-growing events program, draws in an increasing number of visitors each year—in turn impacting its growing hotel and dining scenes.

The 1960s produced Liverpool's most famous export: the Beatles. The group was one of hundreds influenced by the rock and roll they heard from visiting American GIs and merchant seamen in the late 1950s, and one of many that played local venues such as the Cavern (demolished but rebuilt nearby). All four Beatles were born in Liverpool, but the group's success dates from the time they left for London. Nevertheless, the city has milked the group's Liverpool connections for all they're worth, with a multitude of local attractions such as Paul McCartney's and John Lennon's childhood homes.

GETTING HERE AND AROUND

Liverpool John Lennon Airport, about 5 miles southeast of the city, receives mostly domestic and European flights. The Arriva 500 bus service runs to the city center up to every 30 minutes; other buses to the center are the 80A, 82A, and 86A. A taxi to the center of Liverpool costs around £20.

Long-distance National Express buses, including a service from London, use the Norton Street Coach Station, while local buses depart from Sir Thomas Street, Queen Square, and the Liverpool One Bus Station. Train service on Virgin Trains from London's Euston Station takes 2½ hours.

If you're walking (easier than driving), you'll find the downtown sights well signposted. Take care when crossing the busy inner ring road separating the Albert Dock from the rest of the city. The circular Citylink buses ("Cumfybus") link Queen Square bus station with the Albert Dock (Gower Street stop).

TOURS

Magical Mystery Tours. This ever-popular tour departs daily from the Albert Dock visitor center. The bus—decked out in full psychedelic colors—takes you around all the Beatles-related high points, including Penny Lane and Strawberry Fields, in two hours. The ticket price includes entry to the Cavern Club on the evening of your tour day. The firm also offers private tours. ✉ *City Centre* ☎ *0151/703–9100* 🌐 *www.cavernclub.org/cavern-citytours* 🎫 *£17.*

Mersey Guides. This is your point of contact for dozens of different tours of the city, bringing together professional local guides with in-depth knowledge on topics as diverse as Manchester's medical history and its spies. ☎ *07940/933073* 🌐 *www.showmeliverpool.com.*

ORIENTATION

Liverpool has a fairly compact center, and you can see most of the city highlights on foot. The skyline helps with orientation: the Radio City tower on **Queen Square** marks the center of the city. The Liver Birds, on top of the **Royal Liver Building,** signal the waterfront and River Mersey. North of the Radio City tower lie Lime Street Station and William Brown Street, a showcase boulevard of municipal buildings, including the outstanding **Walker Art Gallery** and **World Museum Liverpool.** The city's other museums, including the dazzling Museum of Liverpool and the two-venue **Beatles Story,** are concentrated westward on the waterfront in the **Albert Dock** and **Pier Head** area, a 20-minute walk or five-minute bus ride away. **Hope Street,** to the east of the center, connects the city's two cathedrals, both easily recognizable on the skyline. On nearby Berry Street the red, green, and gold **Chinese Arch,** the largest multiple-span arch outside China, marks the small Chinatown area. ■**TIP→ Allow extra time to tour the childhood homes of Paul McCartney and John Lennon, as they lie outside the city center.**

ESSENTIALS

Bus Contacts Cumfybus. ☎ *01704/227321* 🌐 *www.cumfybus.co.uk.* **Merseytravel.** ☎ *0151/227–5181* 🌐 *www.merseytravel.gov.uk.*

Visitor Information Visit Liverpool. ✉ *Liverpool John Lennon Airport* ☎ *0151/223–2008* 🌐 *www.visitliverpool.com.* **Visit Liverpool.** ✉ *Anchor Courtyard, Albert Dock, Waterfront.* **Visit Liverpool.** ✉ *Lime Street Station, Lime St., Platform 7, City Centre.*

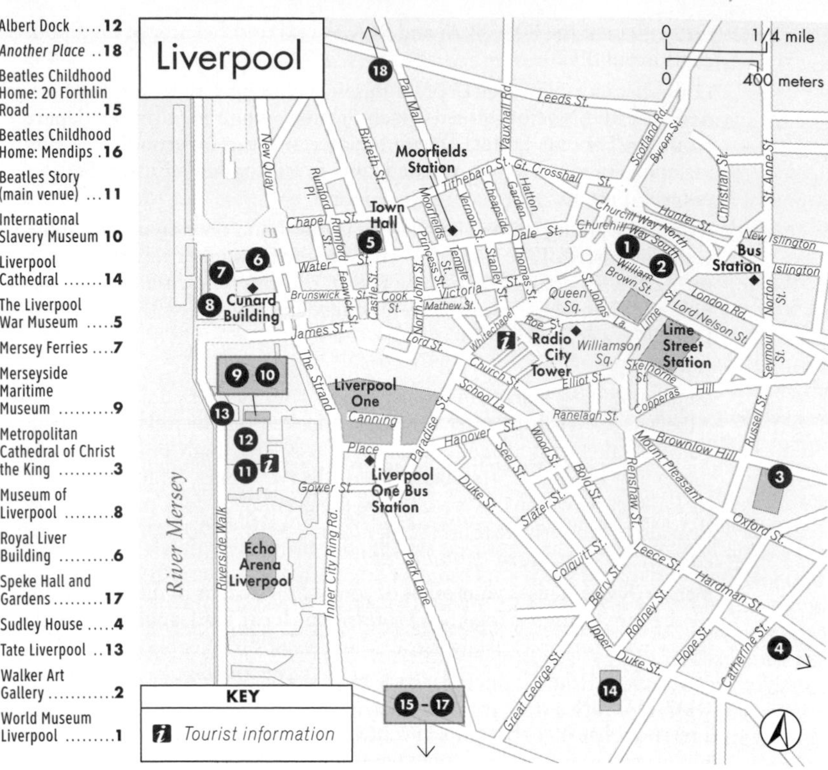

EXPLORING

TOP ATTRACTIONS

Albert Dock. To understand the city's prosperous maritime past, head for these 7 acres of restored waterfront warehouses built in 1846. Named after Queen Victoria's consort, Prince Albert, the dock provided storage for silk, tea, and tobacco from the Far East until it was closed in 1972. Today the fine colonnaded brick buildings contain the **Merseyside Maritime Museum,** the **International Slavery Museum, Tate Liverpool,** and the main venue of the **Beatles Story.** When weather allows, you can sit at an outdoor café overlooking the dock; there are also bars, restaurants, and even hotels on the site. For a bird's-eye view of the Albert Dock area, take the rotating Echo Wheel—Liverpool's 60-meter-tall version of the London Eye. ■ **TIP→ Much of the pedestrian area of the Albert Dock and waterfront area is cobblestone, so wear comfortable shoes.** ✉ *Off Strand St. (A5036), Waterfront* ☎ *0151/223–2008 visitor center* 🌐 *www.albertdock.com.*

Fodor's Choice ★ ***Another Place.*** A hundred naked, life-size, cast-iron figures by sculptor Antony Gormley stand proudly on the 2 miles of foreshore at Crosby Beach, weathered by sand and sea. Unlike most other statues, you are permitted to interact with these and even clothe them if you wish. Check tide times before you go and be aware that it's not safe to walk out to the farthest figures. The site is 6 miles north of downtown Liverpool; to get here, take the Merseyrail Northern Line train to Waterloo, Hall Rd., Blundellsands, or Crosby from Moorfields Station. A taxi will cost around £25. ✉ *Mariners Rd., Crosby Beach* ☎ *01704/533333 for tide times* 🌐 *www.visitliverpool.com* 🎫 *Free.*

Fodor's Choice ★ **The Beatles' Childhood Homes.** A must-see for Beatles pilgrims, this tour takes you to Mendips, the 1930s middle-class, semidetached house that was the home of John Lennon from 1946 to 1963, and 20 Forthlin Road, Paul McCartney's childhood home. After his parents separated, John joined his aunt Mimi at Mendips; she gave him his first guitar but banished him to the porch, saying, "The guitar's all very well, John, but you'll never make a living out of it." Meanwhile, Forthlin Road is a modest 1950s council house where a number of the Beatles' songs were written. The tour leaves from the Jury's Inn next to Albert Dock (mornings) or Speke Hall (afternoons). **■ TIP→ Advanced bookings are essential—places are strictly limited to 15.** ✉ *City Centre* ☎ *0844/800–4791* 🌐 *www.nationaltrust.org.uk/beatles-childhood-homes* 🎫 *£20, includes Speke Hall gardens* ⏲ *Mid-Mar.–Oct., Wed.–Sun. and holiday Mon., Jury's Inn departure 10, 11, 2:15, Speke Hall departure 3:15; early Mar. and Nov., Wed.–Sun., Jury's Inn departure, 10, 11, and 2:15.*

Fodor's Choice ★ **Beatles Story.** Entertaining scenes at this popular attraction in the Albert Dock complex re-create stages in the Beatles' story (and their later careers as solo artists). You'll find everything from the enthusiastic early days in Germany and the Cavern Club to the White Room, where "Imagine" seems to emanate from softly billowing curtains. A second location at the Mersey Ferries Terminal at Pier Head is included in the admission price; here you can see *Fab4D*, a 3-D show with computer animation. On-site shops sell every conceivable kind of souvenir a Fab Four fan could wish for. ✉ *Britannia Vaults, Albert Dock, Waterfront* ☎ *0151/709–1963* 🌐 *www.beatlesstory.com* 🎫 *£15* ⏲ *Apr.–Oct., daily 9–7:30; Nov.–Mar., daily 10–6; last admission 1 hr before closing.*

9

International Slavery Museum. In the same building as the Merseyside Maritime Museum, this museum's four dynamic galleries recount the history of transatlantic slavery and trace its significance in contemporary society. "Life in West Africa" reproduces a Nigerian Igbo compound; life aboard slave ships bound for the Americas is revealed in the "Enslavement and the Middle Passage" section; and "Legacies of Slavery" examines the effect of the African diaspora on contemporary society. The Campaign Zone hosts temporary exhibitions focusing on contemporary slavery issues such as human trafficking and child labor; visitors are encouraged to lobby politicians about these injustices. ✉ *Albert Dock, Hartley Quay, off A5036, Waterfront* ☎ *0151/478–4499* 🌐 *www.liverpoolmuseums.org.uk* 🎫 *Free* ⏲ *Daily 10–5.*

Liverpool Cathedral. The world's fifth largest Anglican cathedral, this Gothic-style edifice was begun in 1903 by architect Giles Gilbert Scott and finally finished in 1978. A custom-built theater shows "the Great Space," a 10-minute panoramic film on the history of the cathedral. The tower is a popular climb; two elevators and 108 steps take you to breathtaking views. From March to October, "Twilight Tower" tickets

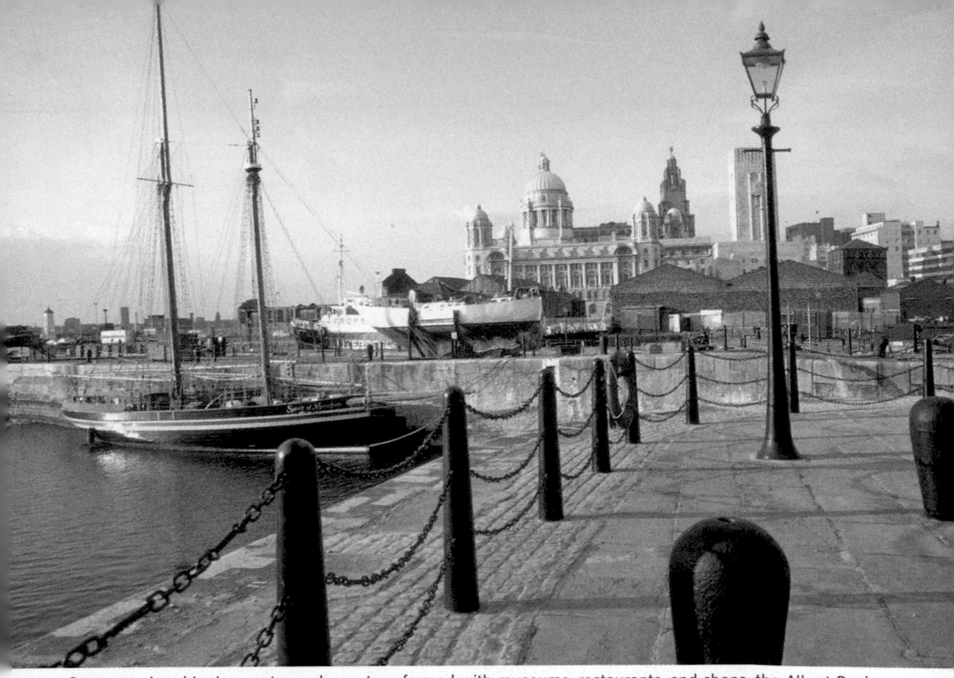

Once a major shipping center and now transformed with museums, restaurants, and shops, the Albert Dock has views of the green dome of the Royal Liver Building.

give you a spectacular view of sunset over the city from the top of the tower. Guided tours of the cathedral take place at 10 am, Monday to Saturday, and at noon on Sunday. ✉ *St. James Mount, City Centre* ☎ *0151/709–6271* 🌐 *www.liverpoolcathedral.org.uk* 🎫 *Free; £3 suggested donation; £5 combined ticket for film, tower, and audio tour; Twilight Tower £5 (booking essential)* 🕓 *Daily 8–6. Tower weekdays 10–4:30, Sat. 9–4:30, Sun. around 11:45–3:30. Twilight Tower times according to sunset.*

FAMILY Fodor's Choice ★

Merseyside Maritime Museum. This wonderful museum captures the triumphs and tragedies of Liverpool's seafaring history over five floors. Besides exhibits of maritime paintings, models, ceramics, and ships in bottles, it brings to life the ill-fated stories of the *Titanic* and *Lusitania;* the Battle of the Atlantic; and the city's role during World War II. The basement is home to Seized, the gallery for the Border Force National Museum, which explores the heroes and villains of the world of smuggling, together with the story of mass emigration from the port in the 19th century. ✉ *Albert Dock, Hartley Quay, off A5036, Waterfront* ☎ *0151/478–4499* 🌐 *www.liverpoolmuseums.org.uk* 🎫 *Free* 🕓 *Daily 10–5.*

Royal Liver Building. Best seen from the ferry, the 322-foot-tall Royal Liver (pronounced *lie-ver*) Building with its twin towers is topped by two 18-foot-high copper birds representing the mythical Liver Birds, the town symbol; local legend has it that if they fly away, Liverpool will cease to exist. For decades Liverpudlians looked to the Royal Liver Society for assistance—it was originally a burial club to which families

CLOSE UP

Liverpool's History: Shipping Center

Liverpool, on the east bank of the Mersey River estuary, at the point where it merges with the Irish Sea, developed from the 17th century through the slave trade. It became Britain's leading port for ferrying Africans to North America and for handling sugar, tobacco, rum, and cotton, which began to dominate the local economy after the abolition of the slave trade in 1807.

Because of its proximity to Ireland, the city was also the first port of call for those fleeing famine, poverty, and persecution in that country. Similarly, Liverpool was often the last British port of call for thousands of mostly Jewish refugees fleeing Eastern Europe.

Many of the best-known liner companies were based in Liverpool, including Cunard and White Star, whose most famous vessel, the *Titanic*, was registered in Liverpool. The city was dealt an economic blow in 1894 with the opening of the Manchester Ship Canal, which allowed traders to bypass Liverpool and head to Manchester, 35 miles east. Britain's entry into the European Common Market saw more trade move from the west coast to the east, and the postwar growth of air travel diverted passengers from the sea. But as a sign of the city's revival, oceangoing liners returned to the city in 2008 after the building of a new cruise liner terminal at the Pier Head.

paid contributions to ensure a decent send-off. ✉ *Water St., off A5036, Waterfront.*

Speke Hall and Gardens. This black-and-white mansion 6 miles from downtown Liverpool is one of the best examples of half-timbering in Britain. Built around a cobbled courtyard, the great hall dates to 1490; an elaborate western bay with a vast chimneypiece was added in 1560. The house, owned by the National Trust, was heavily restored in the 19th century, though a Tudor priest hole and Jacobean plasterwork remain intact. The Victorian landscaped gardens enjoy views over the Mersey toward North Wales. Speke Hall is on the east side of the airport. The Arriva 500 bus drops you a pleasant 10-minute walk away; ask the driver to let you off at the nearest stop. ✉ *The Walk, Speke* ☎ *0151/427–7231* 🌐 *www.nationaltrust.org.uk/speke-hall* 🎫 *£9.20; gardens only £5.70* ⏲ *Mid-Mar.–Oct., Wed.–Sun. and holiday Mon. 11–5; Nov.–early Dec. and early Mar., weekends 11–4; entry to house by guided tour only until 12:30; last admission 30 min before closing.*

FAMILY Fodor's Choice ★ **Tate Liverpool.** An offshoot of the London-based art galleries of the same name, Tate Liverpool is located in a handsome conversion of Albert Dock warehouses by the late James Stirling, one of Britain's leading 20th-century architects. There is no permanent collection; challenging exhibitions of modern and contemporary art change every couple of months. A free introductory tour begins daily at 2:40 and there are free daily talks, too, as well as children's activities, an excellent gift shop, and a dockside café-restaurant. ✉ *Albert Dock, The Colonnades, Waterfront* ☎ *0151/702–7400* 🌐 *www.tate.org.uk* 🎫 *Free; charges for*

9

certain special exhibitions vary ⏲ *Early Apr.–early Oct., daily 10–5:50 (last admission 5); early Oct.–early Apr., daily 10–5 (last admission 4).*

FAMILY Fodor's Choice ★ **Walker Art Gallery.** With a superb display of British art and some outstanding Italian and Flemish works, this is one of the best British art collections outside London. Don't miss the unrivaled collection of paintings by 18th-century Liverpudlian equestrian artist George Stubbs, or works by J.M.W. Turner, Claude Monet, Frederic Lord Leighton, and the Pre-Raphaelites. Modern artists are included, too; on display is one of David Hockney's typically Californian pool scenes. Other excellent exhibits showcase classical Greek and Roman sculptures as well as china, silver, and furniture that once adorned the mansions of Liverpool's industrial barons. There are temporary exhibitions and a dedicated children's art space and gallery trail. The café holds center stage in the airy museum lobby. ✉ *William Brown St., City Centre* ☎ *0151/478–4199* 🌐 *www.liverpoolmuseums.org.uk* 🎫 *Free* ⏲ *Daily 10–5.*

FAMILY **World Museum Liverpool.** You can travel from the prehistoric to the space age through the stunning displays in these state-of-the-art galleries. Ethnology, the natural and physical sciences, and archaeology all get their due over five floors; highlights include a collection of Egyptian mummies in the Ancient World Gallery, and a beautiful assemblage of Javanese shadow puppets in the World Cultures Gallery. There's plenty to keep kids amused, from fish and other sea creatures in the Aquarium and monster bugs in the Bug House to life-size casts of prehistoric monsters in the Dinosaurs Gallery, plus a busy program of events and activities. ✉ *William Brown St., City Centre* ☎ *0151/478–4393* 🌐 *www.liverpoolmuseums.org.uk* 🎫 *Free* ⏲ *Daily 10–5.*

WORTH NOTING

The Liverpool War Museum. Winston Churchill said that the threat of a U-Boat attack from the Atlantic was his greatest fear during World War II. At this evocative war museum you can explore the warren of rooms under the city streets that served the top-secret "Western Approaches Command HQ" from 1941 to 1945. The lofty Operations Room, full of the state-of-the-art technology of the time, is especially interesting. ✉ *1–3 Rumford St., off Chapel St., City Centre* ☎ *0151/227–2008* 🌐 *www.liverpoolwarmuseum.co.uk* 🎫 *£6* ⏲ *Mar.–Oct., Mon.–Thurs. and Sat. 10:30–4:30; last admission 1 hr before closing.*

Mersey Ferries. Hop on a ferry across the River Mersey to Birkenhead and Seacombe, where you'll see fine views of the city—a journey celebrated in "Ferry 'Cross the Mersey," Gerry and the Pacemakers' 1964 hit song. With these 50-minute cruises, you can get combined tickets with Spaceport (a space-travel themed museum and planetarium) and/or with U-Boat Story (a docked German World War II museum with interactive displays), both on the other side of the water. It was from Pier Head that 9 million British, Irish, and other European emigrants set sail between 1830 and 1930 for new lives in North America, Australia, and Africa. ✉ *Pier Head Ferry Terminal, off A5036, Waterfront* ☎ *0151/330–1444* 🌐 *www.merseyferries.co.uk* 🎫 *£8.50 round-trip; with Spaceport or U-Boat Story £13, with both £16* ⏲ *Ferries every 20 min weekdays 7:20–9:40 and 4:10–6:45 (Apr.–Oct. 5–6:40); cruises*

Apr.–Oct., hourly weekdays 10–4, weekends 10–6; Nov.–Mar., hourly weekdays 10–3, weekends 10–4.

Metropolitan Cathedral of Christ the King. Consecrated in 1967, this Roman Catholic cathedral is a modernistic, funnel-like structure of concrete, stone, and mosaic, topped with a glass lantern. Long, narrow, blue-glass windows separate chapels, each with modern works of art. An earlier design by classically inspired architect Edwin Lutyens was abandoned when World War II began (the current design is by Frederick Gibberd), but you can still take a look at Lutyen's vast brick-and-granite crypt and barrel-vaulted ceilings. ✉ *Mount Pleasant, City Centre* ☎ *0151/709–9222* 🌐 *www.liverpoolmetrocathedral.org.uk* 🎟 *Free; suggested donation £2.50; crypt and treasury £3* ⏲ *Daily 7:30–6.*

FAMILY **Museum of Liverpool.** Clad in Jura stone and shaped like a ship, with a spectacular spiral staircase running from the atrium to each floor, this ambitious museum tells the story of the city from its earliest settlement in the Neolithic Age. Highlights include an extraordinary 3-D map with different perspectives of the city as you move around it, an engrossing film about soccer culture, and an interactive timeline peeling away layers of Liverpool's history. ✉ *Pier Head, Waterfront* ☎ *0151/478–4545* 🌐 *www.liverpoolmuseums.org.uk* 🎟 *Free* ⏲ *Daily 10–5.*

Sudley House. This handsome 19th-century mansion next to Liverpool John Moore's University contains the extraordinary art collection amassed by shipping magnate George Holt (1825–96). Paintings on display include works by J.M.W. Turner, Thomas Gainsborough, Dante Gabriel Rossetti, and Joshua Reynolds. The interior of the building itself is an immaculately maintained example of high Victorian domestic style. Permanent displays include a collection of historic children's toys and women's fashion from the 18th century to the present day. Sudley House is about 5 miles southeast of the city center. To drive, take the A5036 along the river heading south; alternatively, Bus No. 61 to Elmswood Road, 80 or 80A to Rose Lane, or 82 to Aigburth Road. ✉ *Mossley Hill Rd., Aigburth* ☎ *0151/478–4016* 🌐 *www.liverpoolmuseums.org.uk* 🎟 *Free* ⏲ *Daily 10–5.*

9

WHERE TO EAT

$$$ MODERN BRITISH Fodor's Choice ★ ✕ **The Art School.** A 2014 arrival on the Liverpool fine-dining scene, the Art School is a chic modern space with a glass window that lets you look into the kitchen and watch the chefs at work. In a former life, this was the lantern room of the Victorian-era Home for Destitute Children. Chef Paul Askew is a champion of local produce, which features heavily in the ambitious but well-executed dishes like the Menai mackerel with blood orange dressing, ricotta, spinach dumpling, and golden beets, or Highland venison carpaccio with horseradish snow, Parmesan shavings, Lilliput capers, and winter leaves. You can choose from five menus, including the excellent value prix-fixe option. $ *Average main: £22.50* ✉ *1 Sugnall St., City Centre* ☎ *0151/230–8600* 🌐 *www.theartschoolrestaurant.co.uk* ⏲ *Closed Sun. and Mon.* 💳 *No credit cards.*

$$ ITALIAN **Bacaro.** This stylish place is a lively take on the working men's canteens of backstreet Venice, known as *baracos*. It also describes itself as a Campari bar offering small plates and charcuterie, so order a few *cichetti* (sharing plates) and enjoy; options include cured meats, fried mixed fish, meatballs, and *pizzette* (mini-pizzas). Don't miss the Venetian slow-cooked duck ragout tagliatelle with garlic crumb, or a slice of chocolate pudding for dessert. Eating at the bar makes for a particularly sociable experience. *Average main: £15 ✉ 47 Castle St. ☎ 0151/665–0047 ⊕ www.salthousebacaro.com.*

$ LEBANESE FAMILY Fodor's Choice ★ **Bakchich.** Those who like good food at great prices head to Bakchich, a Lebanese street food joint featuring a large communal table with smaller tables dotted around it. On offer are delicious hot and cold mezze, wraps, and salads; don't miss the *jawaneh machwi* (charcoal-grilled chicken wings with garlic and harissa sauce). The nonalcoholic drink list includes fresh lemonade and smoothies—try the pomegranate with orange blossom. Take note that portions are huge. There's also a small but tasty kids' menu. *Average main: £7 ✉ 54 Bold St., Crosby Beach ☎ 0151/707–1255 ⊕ www.bakchich.co.uk.*

$ JAPANESE **Etsu.** Minimalist decor, a friendly staff, and a polished Japanese menu greet you at this inconspicuous street-corner locale just off the Strand. The traditional sushi, noodle soups, and tempuras are all made with the freshest ingredients and the bento boxes are a great deal at lunchtime. *Average main: £14 ✉ 25 The Strand, entrance on Brunswick St., City Centre ☎ 0151/236–7530 ⊕ www.etsu-restaurant.co.uk ▭ No credit cards ⊙ Closed Mon. No lunch Wed. and weekends.*

$ CATALAN FAMILY Fodor's Choice ★ **Lunya.** An 18th-century warehouse on the edge of the Liverpool One shopping district houses Lunya, an impressive Catalan fusion restaurant and deli. Feast on classic and creative tapas dishes such as pan-fried cod with wilted spinach, langoustine, and lobster bisque, or acorn-fed pork, cooked rare, with shallot purée and caramelized red onions. An extensive breakfast menu makes this a great place to start your day, while the children's menu tempts those with junior foodies. *Average main: £9 ✉ 18–20 College La., City Centre ☎ 0151/706–9770 ⊕ www.lunya.co.uk.*

$ MODERN EUROPEAN Fodor's Choice ★ **Oh Me Oh My.** Billing itself as a secret space for in-the-know Liverpool residents, this hidden-away tea room and restaurant takes on an old-school grandeur from its location in the former Bank of West Africa building. Music ups the nostalgic theme—think everything from 1950s movie soundtracks to soul—while the menu embraces European classics and more modern inventions, from French onion soup to sage and lemon chicken with saffron rice and red pepper coulis. It's also a great spot for breakfast and afternoon tea. *Average main: £6 ✉ West Africa House, 25 Water St., City Centre ☎ 0151/227–4810 ⊕ www.ohmeohmyliverpool.co.uk ⊙ Closed Sat. and Sun. No dinner.*

$$$ MODERN EUROPEAN **Panoramic 34.** For some, the waterfront and city views through the floor-to-ceiling windows of this 34th-floor restaurant might outdo the food. But there's no denying the ambitiousness and wonderful sense of playfulness behind the modern European menu; think smoked eel beignet with Yorkshire rhubarb and pickled pear salad as a starter, and sea-salted popcorn with cornflake ice cream for dessert. You can also

just come here to soak up the views over afternoon tea or a cocktail. *$ Average main: £20 ✉ West Tower, Brook St., 34th fl., Waterfront ☎ 0151/236–5534 🌐 www.panoramic34.com ⊗ Closed Mon.*

$ ECLECTIC **The Pen Factory.** An all-day café and restaurant, the Pen Factory focuses on seasonal tapas-style small plates in the evening, but by day serves breakfast pastries, soups, salads, and sandwiches. There are also daily specials such as Provençal beef with roasted garlic mash as well as craft beer, wine, and cocktails. As befits its location in the basement of the old theater annex, the vibe is rough-hewn industrial chic. *$ Average main: £7 ✉ 13 Hope St., City Centre ☎ 0151/709–7887 🌐 www.pen-factory.co.uk ⊗ Closed Sun. and Mon.*

WHERE TO STAY

$ HOTEL FAMILY **Crowne Plaza Liverpool City Centre.** This chain hotel stands out from the crowd with its waterfront location, where the city's main sights are all virtually on its doorstep, including the iconic Royal Liver Building. **Pros:** great views and central location; excellent gym and fitness facilities. **Cons:** bland furnishings. *$ Rooms from: £80 ✉ St. Nicholas Pl., off A5036, Waterfront ☎ 0151/243–8000 🌐 www.cpliverpool.com ▭ No credit cards ⇆ 159 rooms ¶◎¶ No meals.*

$ HOTEL **Hope Street Hotel.** Liverpool's first boutique hotel occupies a converted carriage warehouse built in the style of a Venetian palazzo. **Pros:** beautiful design; frequent upgrades; can find good deals in the off-season. **Cons:** staff can seem distracted. *$ Rooms from: £80 ✉ 40 Hope St., City Centre ☎ 0151/709–3000 🌐 www.hopestreethotel.co.uk ⇆ 85 rooms, 4 suites ¶◎¶ No meals.*

$ HOTEL FAMILY Fodor's Choice ★ **The Nadler Liverpool.** Formerly known as Base2stay, the Nadler succeeds in its aim to bring affordable luxury to central Liverpool with its stylish rooms with mini-kitchens and free Wi-Fi, located in an impressive 1850s industrial building. **Pros:** every room has a HDTV with free music, games, and an interactive directory; great value; interesting building. **Cons:** some doubles have zipped twin beds; no dining on-site. *$ Rooms from: £59 ✉ 29 Seel St., City Centre ☎ 0151/705–2626 🌐 www.thenadler.com/liverpool.shtml ⇆ 106 rooms ¶◎¶ No meals ▭ No credit cards.*

$ RENTAL FAMILY **Premier Apartments.** These spacious and airy apartments in the heart of downtown have everything you need for an independent stay—including the option of grocery delivery to your door, and children's amenities. **Pros:** a five-minute walk from Lime Street Station; roomier than a hotel. **Cons:** the optional breakfast boxes are pricey at £10; Wi-Fi costs extra. *$ Rooms from: £60 ✉ 7 Hatton Garden, City Centre ☎ 0151/227–9467 🌐 www.premierapartmentsliverpool.com ⇆ 62 apartments ¶◎¶ No meals.*

$$ HOTEL **The Raquet Club.** Occupying a former private gentleman's club, this family-run hotel continues to exude a clubby feel with its soft leather sofas and antiques. **Pros:** very attentive and welcoming staff; intimate alternative to Liverpool's chain hotels. **Cons:** often hosts weddings; can get booked up well in advance. *$ Rooms from: £100 ✉ The Hargreaves Bldg., 5 Chapel St., City Centre ☎ 0151/236–6676 🌐 www.racquetclub.org.uk ⇆ 8 rooms ¶◎¶ No meals.*

9

$ HOTEL Fodor's Choice ★ **Z Liverpool.** Modern urban style on a budget and a super-central location make the Z a superb addition to the Liverpool hotel scene. **Pros:** thoughtful design features; free wine and cheese in the evening. **Cons:** street noise from some rooms; not all rooms have windows. *Rooms from: £39* ✉ *2 North John St., City Centre* ☎ *0151/ 556–1770* 🌐 *www.thezhotels.com* *92 rooms* *No meals; Breakfast.*

NIGHTLIFE AND PERFORMING ARTS

NIGHTLIFE

Alma de Cuba. A church transformed into a luxurious bar, Alma de Cuba has a huge mirrored altar and hundreds of dripping candles. They also serve a popular Sunday brunch with a live gospel choir. ✉ *St. Peter's Church, Seel St., City Centre* ☎ *0834/504–6494* 🌐 *www.alma-de-cuba.com.*

Arts Club. Music, art, science events, and casual dining are all in the mix at this long-standing venue reinvented as a creative space and bar. ✉ *90 Seel St., City Centre* ☎ *0151/559–3773* 🌐 *www.artsclubliverpool.com.*

Berry and Rye. Hidden away behind an unassuming and umarked facade, Berry and Rye is a Prohibition-era speakeasy that brings together expertly mixed cocktails and cakes in a stylish candlelit space. ✉ *48 Berry St, City Centre* ☎ *0151 /345–7271* 🌐 *No website.*

Camp and Furnace. This huge bar, live music venue, and restaurant complex occupies a former Edwardian foundry and blade-making factory, retaining the suitably industrial vibe. Three rooms host live musical performances throughout the week while regular Friday events bring together dance music, cocktails, and food, some of it grilled on a giant barbeque. ✉ *67 Greenland St., City Centre* ☎ *0151/708–2890* 🌐 *www.campandfurnace.com.*

Fodor's Choice ★ **Cavern Club.** While not the original venue—that was demolished years ago—the Cavern Club is still a top music spot, drawing in rock-and-roll fans with its live acts including Beatles tribute bands. ✉ *10 Mathew St., City Centre* ☎ *0151/236–9091* 🌐 *www.cavernclub.org.*

Heebie Jeebies. A roster of local indie bands and talented DJs makes this two-story club with a courtyard a top option for the young alternative crowd. ✉ *80–82 Seel St., City Centre* ☎ *0151/709–3678.*

Leaf on Bold Street. Teashop meets bar and live music venue at Leaf on Bold Street, a bohemian spot in a former art-deco cinema. Inside you'll also find a café, an art gallery, club nights, and vintage clothes markets. ✉ *65–67 Bold St.* ☎ *0151/707–7747* 🌐 *www.thisisleaf.co.uk.*

The Kazimier. This mid-sized, split-level venue hosts live music, avant-guard club nights, and theater and film events. It also has a year-round garden with an open kitchen and charcoal grill. ✉ *4–5 Wolstenholme Sq.* ☎ *0151/324–1723* 🌐 *www.thekazimier.co.uk.*

The Shipping Forecast. Big-name acts mean this intimate basement venue often gets packed to the rafters, but that only adds to the clubby vibe. There are also club nights that range from hip-hop to indie, plus a menu of well-executed American comfort food classics. ✉ *15 Slater St., City Centre* ☎ *0151/709–6901* 🌐 *www.theshippingforecastliverpool.com.*

PERFORMING ARTS

FILM

FACT Centre. The Foundation for Art and Creative Technology offers up a unique mix of exhibitions, films, and participant-led art projects, plus a café. ✉ *88 Wood St., City Centre* ☎ *0151/707–4444* 🌐 *www.fact.co.uk.*

PERFORMING ARTS VENUES

Fodor's Choice ★ **Bluecoat.** The city center's oldest building is now a creative hub encompassing visual arts, live art, literarture, music, and dance, along with a café and bistro. ✉ *School La., City Centre* ☎ *0151/702–5324* 🌐 *www.thebluecoat.org.uk.*

Liverpool Empire. This theater presents musicals, live music acts, and occasionally dance and opera. ✉ *Lime St., City Centre* ☎ *0844/847–7615* 🌐 *www.atgtickets.com/venues/liverpool-empire.*

Philharmonic Hall. This large art-deco concert hall and sometime cinema plays host to concerts by the resident Royal Liverpool Philharmonic Orchestra, as well as contemporary rock, pop, folk, roots, jazz, and blues performances. ✉ *Hope St., City Centre* ☎ *0151/709–3789* 🌐 *www.liverpoolphil.com.*

THEATER

Everyman Theatre. After a radical 2014 rebuild, this vibrant theater focuses on British playwrights and experimental productions from around the world, as well as hosting a writers' workspace. There's also a sidewalk café and a basement bistro. A sister theater, the Everyman Playhouse in Williamson Square, stages slightly more mainstream productions. ✉ *5–11 Hope St., City Centre* ☎ *0151/709–4776 box office (both theaters)* 🌐 *www.everymanplayhouse.com.*

Royal Court Theatre. Undergoing refurbishment and expansion at the time of this writing, the art-deco Royal Court Theatre is one of the city's most appealing sites for stand-up comedy, theater, and more. Visitors can also take a heritage tour of the building. ✉ *1 Roe St., City Centre* ☎ *0151/709–4321* 🌐 *www.royalcourtliverpool.co.uk.*

SHOPPING

The Beatles Shop. All the mop-top knickknacks of your dreams are available at this hugely popular, official Beatles souvenir shop. ✉ *31 Mathew St., City Centre* ☎ *0151/236–8066* 🌐 *www.thebeatleshop.co.uk.*

Holts Arcade. Here at the Holts Arcade, the history behind the historic shopping center is almost as interesting as what you can buy. Once part of a shipping office building, it now houses stores selling antiques, bespoke menswear, and more. ✉ *India Buildings, Water St., City Centre.*

Fodor's Choice ★ **Liverpool One.** The city's largest shopping complex comprises four districts (Peter's Lane, South John Street, Paradise Street, and Hanover Street) totaling more than 160 stores, from small independent shops to

9

international chains, plus restaurants and leisure amenities. ✉ *Paradise St., City Centre* ☎ *0151/232–3100* 🌐 *www.liverpool-one.com.*

Metquarter. This luxury shopping district is the place for upmarket boutiques, designer names, and cutting-edge fashions. ✉ *35 Whitechapel, City Centre* ☎ *0151/224–2390* 🌐 *www.metquarter.com.*

SPORTS AND THE OUTDOORS

FOOTBALL

Football matches are played on weekends and, increasingly, some weekdays. Tickets for Liverpool sell out months in advance; you should have more luck with Everton.

Anfield Stadium. If you can't get tickets to a match at this stadium, you can take a trip into the dressing rooms and down the tunnel of Anfield Football Stadium as part of a tour and/or visit the interactive museum. As of this writing, the stadium was undergoing expansion from 45,000 to 59,000 capacity in time for the 2016/17 season. ✉ *Anfield Rd., Anfield* ☎ *0151/260–6677* 🌐 *www.liverpoolfc.com* 🎫 *£17.*

Everton Football Club. One of Liverpool's two great football teams, Everton plays at the 40,000-capacity Goodison Park. ✉ *Goodison Rd.* ☎ *0871/663–1878* 🌐 *www.evertonfc.com.*

Liverpool Football Club. One of England's top teams, Liverpool plays at Anfield, 2 miles north of the city center. ✉ *Anfield Rd., Anfield* ☎ *0843/170–5000* 🌐 *www.liverpoolfc.tv.*

HORSE RACING

Aintree Racecourse. Britain's most famous horse race, the Grand National Steeplechase, has been run here almost every year since 1839. The race is held in March or April; book well ahead to attend (the event is also televised). Admission starts at around £20, depending on the race day and your level of access. ✉ *Ormskirk Rd., Aintree* ☎ *0844/579–3001* 🌐 *aintree.thejockeyclub.co.uk.*

THE PEAK DISTRICT

Heading southeast, away from the urban congestion of Manchester and Liverpool, it's not far to the southernmost contortions of the Pennine Hills. Here, about an hour southeast of Manchester, sheltered in a great natural bowl, is the spa town of Buxton: at an elevation of more than 1,000 feet, it's the second-highest town in England. Buxton makes a convenient base for exploring the 540 square miles of the Peak District, Britain's oldest—and, its fans say, most beautiful—national park. About 38,000 people live in the towns throughout the park.

"Peak" is perhaps misleading; despite being a hilly area, it contains only gentle rises that don't reach much higher than 2,000 feet. Yet a trip around destinations such as Bakewell, Matlock, Castleton, and Edale, as well as around the grand estates of Chatsworth House and Haddon Hall involves negotiating fairly perilous country roads, each of which repays the effort with enchanting views.

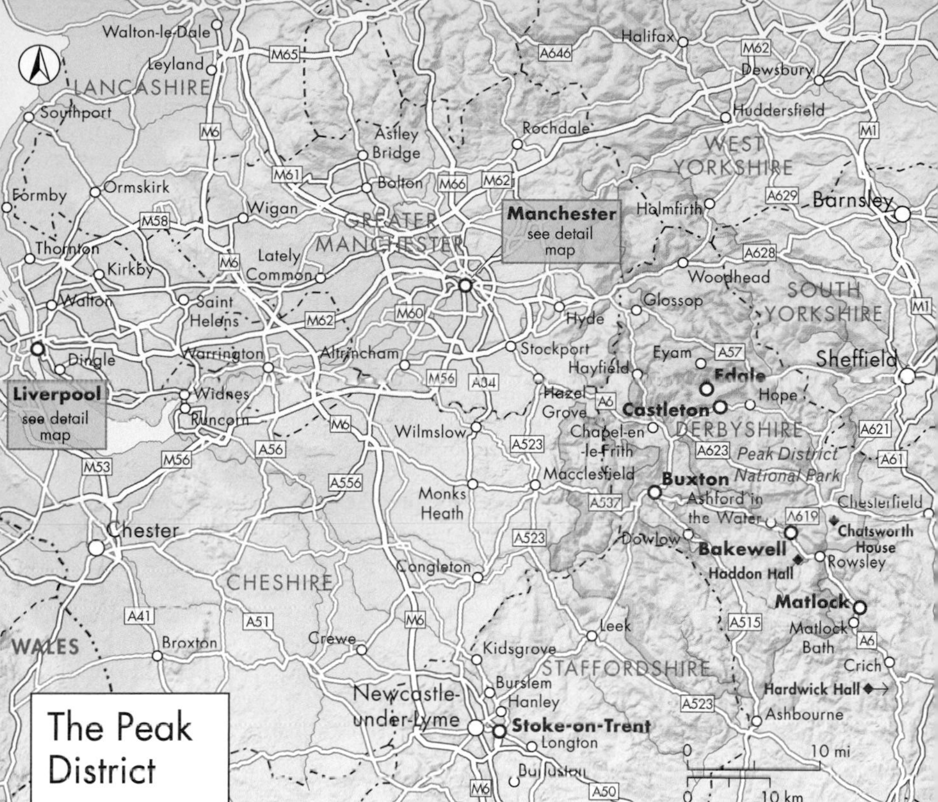

Outdoor activities are popular in the Peaks, particularly caving (or "potholing"), walking, and hiking. Bring all-weather clothing and waterproof shoes.

BUXTON

25 miles southeast of Manchester.

Just outside the national park yet almost entirely surrounded by it, Buxton makes a good base for Peak District excursions but it has its own attractions as well. The town's spa days left a notable legacy of 18th- and 19th-century buildings, parks, and open spaces that give the town an air of faded grandeur. The Romans arrived in AD 79 and named Buxton Aquae Arnemetiae, loosely translated as "Waters of the Goddess of the Grove." The mineral springs, which emerge from 3,500 to 5,000 feet below ground at a constant 82°F, were believed to cure assorted ailments; in the 18th century the town became established as a popular spa, a minor rival to Bath. You can still drink water from the ancient St. Ann's Well, and it's also sold throughout Britain.

GETTING HERE AND AROUND

Some National Express bus services to London and all TransPeak bus services to Derby from Manchester stop at Buxton, departing from Manchester's Central Coach Station. If you're driving from Manchester, take A6 southeast to Buxton. The journey takes one hour. The hourly train from Manchester to Buxton also takes an hour.

ESSENTIALS

Visitor Information Buxton Tourist Information Centre. ✉ *Pavilion Gardens, Water St.* ☎ *01298/25106* 🌐 *www.visitpeakdistrict.com.*

EXPLORING

Buxton Museum and Art Gallery. This is a good place to see Blue John, a colorful, semiprecious mineral found only in the Peak District (the name comes from *bleu jaune*—literally "blue yellow"—a term supposedly coined by visiting French mineworkers). There are also displays of local archaeological finds and pieces made from Derbyshire black marble, and a small art gallery. ✉ *Terrace Rd.* ☎ *01629/533540* 🌐 *www.derbyshire.gov.uk/leisure/buxton_museum* 🎫 *Free* ⏲ *Tues.–Fri. 9:30–5:30, Sat. 9:30–5, Sun. 10:30–5.*

Buxton Opera House. Built in 1903, this lovely Edwardian edifice is one of England's best examples of Frank Matcham theater design, with its marble columns, carved cherubs, and golden leaf. A varied performance program includes classical music, opera, dance, drama, and comedy. ✉ *Water St.* ☎ *0845/127–2190* 🌐 *www.buxtonoperahouse.org.uk.*

Pavilion Gardens. Surrounded by 25 acres of pretty gardens, the 1870s Pavilion and its ornate iron-and-glass roof was originally a concert hall and ballroom. It remains a lively place with an arts center, three cafés, and a gift boutique, as well as a miniature train and play areas. ✉ *St. John's Rd.* ☎ *01298/23114* 🌐 *www.paviliongardens.co.uk.*

FAMILY
Fodor's Choice ★

Poole's Cavern and Buxton Country Park. The Peak District's extraordinary geology can be seen up close in this large limestone cave far beneath the 100 acres of Buxton Country Park. Inhabited in prehistoric times, the cave contains, in addition to the standard stalactites and stalagmites, the source of the River Wye, which flows through Buxton. The Country Park paths take you up to Grin Low, home to the Victorian fortified hill marker Solomon's Tower, the remains of several Bronze Age burial chambers, and views of Mam Tor and Kinder Scout; there's also a fun Go Ape! treetop adventure course on site. Admission to the cave includes a guided tour lasting nearly an hour. ✉ *Green La.* ☎ *01298/26978* 🌐 *www.poolescavern.co.uk* 🎫 *£9* ⏲ *Mar.–Oct., daily 9:30–5 (tours every 20 min, last tour 4:30); Nov.–Feb., weekday tours at 10:30, 12:30, and 2:30, weekends every 20 min 9:30–4.*

WHERE TO EAT AND STAY

$$
MODERN BRITISH
Fodor's Choice ★

✕ **Columbine.** The husband-and-wife team behind Columbine are known for their fine use of local ingredients and flavors, from sautéed sea bass in a sauce of lemon, ginger, and spring onion to beef medallions with blue Stilton sauce and garlic mushrooms. The cozy venue, with upstairs and downstairs cellar seating, is an excellent spot for pre- and post-theater meals. 💲 *Average main: £16* ✉ *7 Hall Bank* ☎ *01298/78752* www.columbinerestaurant.co.uk No credit cards Closed Sun. year-round and Tues. Nov–Apr. No lunch.

$ B&B/INN **Buxton Victorian Guesthouse.** One of a group of row houses built by the duke of Devonshire in 1860, this handsomely decorated property stands in the center of Buxton. **Pros:** peaceful location on Pavilion Gardens; delightful hosts. **Cons:** often booked up well in advance. *Rooms from: £88 3A Broad Walk 01298/78759 www.buxtonvictorian.co.uk No credit cards 4 rooms, 1 apartment Breakfast.*

$ B&B/INN FAMILY **Old Hall.** In a refurbished 16th-century building claiming to be England's oldest hotel and rumoured to have once accommodated Mary Queen of Scots, this hotel overlooks the ornate Buxton Opera House and often offers guest the option of prime tickets for big shows there. **Pros:** family-friendly, with toys for kids; good dining options; cool historic building. **Cons:** no private parking; decor is a little boring. *Rooms from: £79 The Square 01298/22841 www.oldhallhotelbuxton.co.uk No credit cards 38 rooms Breakfast.*

$ B&B/INN FAMILY **Stoneridge.** This handsome Edwardian B&B has been richly restored, with bedrooms in brown and cream and furnished with modern pieces. **Pros:** family-friendly; secluded and tranquil garden. **Cons:** no tubs in bathrooms. *Rooms from: £80 9 Park Rd. 01298/26120 www.stoneridge.co.uk 4 rooms Breakfast.*

NIGHTLIFE AND PERFORMING ARTS

Buxton Festival. The renowned Buxton Festival, held for two weeks during mid-July each year, includes opera, drama, and concerts. *The Square 0845/127–2190 box office www.buxtonfestival.co.uk.*

SHOPPING

Buxton has a wide varierty of stores, especially around Spring Gardens, the main shopping street.

Cavendish Arcade. Stores in the beautifully tiled Cavendish Arcade, on the site of the old thermal baths, sell chocolates, fashion, homewares, gifts, and natural handmade products. *The Crescent www.cavendisharcade.co.uk.*

9

BAKEWELL

12 miles southeast of Buxton.

In Bakewell, a medieval bridge crosses the winding River Wye in five graceful arches while a 9th-century Saxon cross that stands outside the parish church reveals the town's great age. Narrow streets and houses built out of the local gray-brown stone also make the town extremely appealing. Ceaseless traffic through the streets can take the shine off—though there's respite down on the quiet riverside paths.

This market town is the commercial hub of the Peak District, for locals and visitors. The crowds are really substantial on market day (Monday), attended by area farmers. For a self-guided hour-long stroll, pick up a map at the tourist office, where the town trail begins. A small photography exhibition upstairs explores the landscape of the Peak District.

GETTING HERE AND AROUND
TransPeak buses to Derby from Manchester's Central Coach Station stop at Bakewell, as do some National Express buses to London. By car, Bakewell is a 1½-hour drive southeast on the A6 from Manchester.

ESSENTIALS
Visitor Information Bakewell Visitor Centre. ✉ *Old Market Hall, Bridge St.* ☎ *01629/816558* 🌐 *www.visitpeakdistrict.com.*

BAKEWELL PUDDING

Bakewell is the source of Bakewell pudding, said to have been created inadvertently, when, sometime in the 19th century, a cook at the town's Rutland Arms Hotel (which is still in business) dropped some rich cake mixture over jam tarts and baked it. Every local bakery and tearoom claims an original recipe, so it's easy to spend a gustatory afternoon tasting rival puddings.

EXPLORING

Caudwell's Mill. This unique roller flour mill still runs most days, and visitors can experience the result in the on-site shop in the form of cookies, flours, and yeast. Among the displays are hands-on models and mechanical features. ✉ *Rowsley* ☎ *01629/734374* 🌐 *www.caudwellsmill.co.uk* 🎟 *£4.50* ⏲ *Daily 10–5; last admission at 4:15.*

FAMILY
Fodor's Choice ★

Chatsworth House. One of England's greatest country houses, Chatsworth House, known as the Palace of the Peak, is the ancestral home of the dukes of Devonshire and stands in vast parkland grazed by deer and sheep. Originally an Elizabethan house, it was altered over several generations starting in 1686, and the architecture now has a hodgepodge look, though the Palladian facade remains untouched. The house is surrounded by woods, elaborate gardens, greenhouses, rock gardens, and a beautiful water cascade —all designed by Capability Brown in the 18th century and, in the 19th, Joseph Paxton, an engineer as well as a brilliant gardener. ■ **TIP→ Plan on at least a half day to explore the grounds; avoid Sunday if you can as it gets very crowded.** Inside are intricate carvings, superb furniture, Van Dyck portraits, Sir Joshua Reynolds's *Georgiana, Duchess of Devonshire and Her Baby,* John Singer Sargent's enormous *Acheson Sisters*, and a few fabulous rooms, including the Sculpture Gallery, the library, and the Painted Hall. Chatsworth is 4 miles northeast of Bakewell. On the estate there is also a working farm with milking demonstrations, as well as an adventure playground. There are also cafés, restaurants, a tea shop, and a farm shop; you can stay on the estate in several cottages scattered throughout the grounds. ✉ *Off B6012* ☎ *01246/565300* 🌐 *www.chatsworth.org* 🎟 *House, gardens, farm, and adventure playground £22; house and gardens £20; gardens only £12; farmyard and adventure playground £6; parking £3 (free with online tickets)* ⏲ *Late-Mar.–late Dec., house daily 11–5:30; gardens daily 11–6, farmyard and adventure playground daily including Feb. school holidays 10:30–5:30; last admission 1 hr before closing.*

Eyam Plague Village. After a local tailor died of the plague in this tiny, idyllic, gray-stone village in 1665, locals isolated themselves from the outside world rather than risk the spread of Black Death (the area had hitherto been spared). They succeeded in containing the disease, but at huge cost; by the time it had run its course, most of the residents were dead. Their heroism is commemorated in florid memorials in the village churchyard. The small **Eyam Museum** puts everything into context (open late March to October, Tuesday to Sunday and holiday Mondays, 10 to 4:30; admission £2.50), while **Eyam Hall and Craft Centre**, run by the National Trust, hosts history walks on the topic. Eyam is 6 miles north of Bakewell off A623. ✉ *Hawkwill Rd., Eyam* ☎ *01433/631371 museum* 🌐 *www.eyamplaguevillage.co.uk*.

QUICK BITES

Eyam Tea Rooms & Bistro. Surrounded by blooming potted plants in summer, this sweet little tea room, a stone's throw from the village church, serves afternoon tea and traditional lunches along with a bistro evening once a month. ✉ ***The Square, Eyam*** ☎ ***01433/631274*** 🌐 ***www.uk-eshop.co.uk/browns.***

Fodor's Choice ★

Haddon Hall. One of England's finest stately homes, and perhaps the most authentically Tudor of all the great houses, Haddon Hall bristles with intricate period detail. Built between 1180 and 1565, the house passed into the ownership of the dukes of Rutland and remained largely untouched until the early 20th century, when the ninth duke undertook a superlative restoration that revealed a series of early decorative 15th-century frescoes in the chapel. The finest of the intricate plasterwork and wooden paneling is best seen in the superb Long Gallery on the first floor. Baking is still done in the bread ovens in the well-preserved Tudor kitchen, using authentic Tudor methods. Here, too, is the unique collection of Gothic dole cupboards, some original to the house, which would have been filled with food and placed outside for those in need. A popular filming location, Haddon's starring roles include *The Princess Bride* (1985), *Pride and Prejudice* (2005), and *The Other Boleyn Girl* (2008). ✉ *A6* ☎ *01629/812855* 🌐 *www.haddonhall.co.uk* 🎫 *£12, parking £2* ⏲ *Apr. and Oct. (and Easter week), Sat.–Mon. noon–5; May–Sept., daily noon–5; 10 days in December 10:30–4; last admission 1 hr before closing.*

9

WHERE TO EAT AND STAY

$$ INTERNATIONAL

✕ **Devonshire Arms.** Part of the Chatsworth Estate (2 miles from the house itself), this stone 18th-century coaching inn has a cozy bar and a modern brasserie, both serving impressive global dining using local ingredients when possible, many of them from Chatsworth farms. Think everything from estate pheasant with mashed potatoes and sweet red cabbage soaked in raisin sauce, to a tikka masala curry of slow-cooked estate venison with pilau rice and spicy pickles. There are also 14 rooms decorated by the Duchess of Devonshire herself (from around £100 per night). 💲 *Average main: £16* ✉ *B6012, Beeley* ☎ *01629/733259* 🌐 *www.devonshirebeeley.co.uk* 💳 *No credit cards.*

$$$$ MODERN BRITISH Fodor's Choice ★

✕ **Fischer's.** A stately Edwardian manor on the edge of the Chatsworth estate, 4 miles north of Bakewell, Fischer's houses an intimate and fairly formal restaurant. All evening meals and most lunches are fixed-price; dishes rely heavily on high-quality local ingredients including wild venison, John Dory and Cornish dover sole, Derbyshire pork and

The Emperor Fountain enhances the bucolic landscape at Chatsworth, one of England's most magnificent stately homes.

lamb, and Yorkshire rhubarb, all used with imagination and aplomb. If you can't decide, there's a 10-course tasting menu of specialty dishes (£80, or £128 with wines). With 11 elegant bedrooms (from £150), you might consider staying the night; there's also a cottage that sleeps two a five-minute walk away. *Average main: £55 Baslow Hall, Calver Rd., Baslow 01246/583259 www.fischers-baslowhall.co.uk No credit cards.*

$ BRITISH **The Old Original Bakewell Pudding Shop.** Given the plethora of local rivals, it takes a bold establishment to claim its Bakewell puddings as "original," but those served here are among the best you'll find. A British favorite, the "pudding" in question is actually a dense, sugary pie with a jam and almond filling and a puff pastry crust, eaten cold or hot with custard or cream. A more common varient, the Bakewell tart, is made with shortcrust pastry, but aficionados consider the pudding to be more authentic. The oak-beam dining room also turns out commendable main courses including steak-and-ale pie. *Average main: £8 The Square 01629/812193 www.bakewellpuddingshop.co.uk No credit cards No dinner.*

$$ B&B/INN **River Cottage.** This charming riverside B&B occupies an 18th-century house and mixes modern conveniences such as flat-screen TVs with antique French beds in most rooms. **Pros:** close to fun village pubs; beautiful garden. **Cons:** not all bathrooms are ensuite. *Rooms from: £115 Buxton Rd., Ashford-in-the-Water 01629/813327 www.rivercottageashford.co.uk 4 rooms Breakfast.*

MATLOCK

8 miles southeast of Bakewell, 5 miles south of Haddon Hall.

In the heart of the Derbyshire Dales just outside Peak District National Park, Matlock and its near neighbor Matlock Bath are former spa towns compressed into a narrow gorge on the River Derwent. The area's beautiful scenery led Daniel Defoe to nickname this area "Little Switzerland." Some surviving Regency buildings in Matlock testify to its former importance, although it's less impressive an ensemble than that presented by Buxton.

Matlock Bath Illuminations, a flotilla of lighted and decorated boats, shimmers after dark on weekends in September and October, along the still waters of the Derwent; on Saturdays there are also firework displays.

GETTING HERE AND AROUND

One National Express bus a day from Manchester's Central Coach Station to London stops at Matlock, leaving Manchester at 6:30 am. On weekends, one TransPeak bus from Manchester to Derby (leaving at 9:15 am) calls at Matlock. The town is about a 1-hour, 40-minute drive southeast on the A6 from Manchester.

ESSENTIALS

Visitor Information Matlock Visitor Information Point. ✉ *Matlock Station, off A6* ☎ *01629/761103* 🌐 *www.visitpeakdistrict.com.*

EXPLORING

FAMILY
Fodor's Choice ★

Crich Tramway Village. A 15 minute drive outside Matlock, this period village includes the **National Tramway Museum of Antique Vehicles** and a tram restoration workshop with a public viewing gallery. On the vintage streets, you can board old trams that take you to the surrounding countryside and back. Spend your pennies in the old-fashioned sweets shop or ice cream parlor before exploring the woodland walk and play areas. ✉ *Crich Village* ☎ *01773/854321* 🎟 *£14* ⏲ *Late Mar.–early Nov. daily 10–5:30.*

Hardwick Hall. Few houses in England evoke the late Elizabethan era as vividly as Hardwick Hall, a beautiful stone mansion and walled gardens 10 miles east of Matlock. The vast state apartments well befit their original chatelaine, Bess of Hardwick, who, by marrying a succession of four rich husbands, was second only to Queen Elizabeth in her wealth when work on this house began. She took possession in 1597, and four years later made an inventory of the important rooms and their contents—furniture, tapestries, and embroideries. Unique patchwork hangings, probably made from clerical copes and altar frontals taken from monasteries and abbeys, grace the entrance hall, and superb 16th- and 17th-century tapestries cover the walls of the main staircase and first-floor High Great Chamber. Access is signposted from Junction 29 of the M1 motorway. ✉ *Doe Lea, Chesterfield* ☎ *01246/850430* 🌐 *www.nationaltrust.org.uk/hardwick* 🎟 *£15; gardens only £7.30; parking £3* ⏲ *Mar.–Oct., Wed.–Sun. noon–4:30. Gardens daily 9–6; last admission 30 min before closing. Grounds daily 8–dusk.*

FAMILY **Heights of Abraham.** A cable-car ride across the River Derwent takes you to this country park on the crags above the small village of Matlock Bath. The ticket includes access to the woodland walks and nature trails of the 60-acre park, guided tours of a cavern and a former lead mine where workers toiled by candlelight, and entry to a local fossils exhibition. There are also two adventure playgrounds and a restaurant. ✉ *A6, Matlock Bath* ☎ *01629/582365* 🌐 *www.heightsofabraham.com* 🎟 *£14.50 cable car, park, exhibition, and caverns* ⏲ *Mid-Feb.–late Feb. and late-Mar.–Oct., daily 10–4:30; early to mid-Mar., weekends 10–4:30.*

FAMILY **Red House Stables and Carriage Museum.** This quaint museum contains a collection of historic carriages, including the last remaining London to Holyhead Royal Mail coach in Britain, dating from around 1826. Trips through the local countryside on some of the carriages are available for around £30 per person an hour (booking ahead is advisable). ✉ *Old Rd.* ☎ *01629/733583* 🌐 *www.redhousestables.co.uk* 🎟 *£5* ⏲ *Apr.–Oct., Mon.–Sat. 10–5, Sun. 10–3; Nov.–Mar., Mon.–Sat. 10–4, Sun. 10–2.*

WHERE TO EAT AND STAY

$$$$ MODERN BRITISH Fodor's Choice ★ ✕ **Stones.** This charming restaurant with a river terrace serves top-notch Modern British food as well as a monthly traditional Sunday lunch. The set menus take regional flavors and infuse them with contemporary flair; an inventive tasting menu is offered at £48.50 per person. You might start with seared scallops with apple and horseradish before sampling the lamb with fennel puree and potato rosti, or maybe the catch of the day, served with parsley and caper velouté. Imaginatively presented desserts might include passion fruit panna cotta served with a sorbet of mango and lime. ■ **TIP→ Prices drop considerably at lunch to just £18 for two courses.** $ *Average main: £27* ✉ *1C Dale Rd.* ☎ *01629/56061* 🌐 *www.stones-restaurant.co.uk* 💳 *No credit cards* ⏲ *No lunch Tues. Closed Sun. and Mon.*

$ B&B/INN **Sheriff Lodge.** Huge beds and luxury bedding demonstrate the hosts' commitment to guest comfort at this intimate B&B in a lovely garden with views across the valley towards Riber Castle. **Pros:** hearty breakfasts with homemade breads; a genuinely warm welcome from hosts. **Cons:** elements of room decor might not be to everyone's taste. $ *Rooms from: £84* ✉ *The Dimple, Dimple Rd.* ☎ *01629/760760* 🌐 *www.sherifflodge.co.uk* *5 rooms* 🍽 *Breakfast.*

SPORTS AND THE OUTDOORS

High Peak Trail. One of the major trails in the Peak District, High Peak Trail runs for 17 miles from Cromford (just south of Matlock Bath) to Dowlow, following the route of an old railroad. ✉ *Matlock* 🌐 *www.peakdistrict.gov.uk.*

CASTLETON

24 miles northwest of Matlock, 10 miles northwest of Chatsworth, 9 miles northeast of Buxton.

The area around Castleton, in the Hope Valley, contains the most famous manifestations of the geology of the Peak District. A number of caves and mines are open to the public, including some former lead mines and Blue John mines (amethystine spar; the unusual name is a corruption of the French *bleu-jaune*, meaning "blue yellow"). The limestone caverns attract many people, which means that pretty Castleton is marred by a certain commercialization. Summer brings the crowds, many of which poke around in the numerous shops displaying Blue John jewelry and wares.

GETTING HERE AND AROUND

Hope Rail Station, 1½ miles from the center of Castleton, is served by rail on the Manchester Piccadilly–Sheffield line every one to two hours. The journey takes 50 minutes. By car, Castleton is a one-hour drive southeast on the A6 from Manchester.

ESSENTIALS

Visitor Information Castleton Visitor Centre. ✉ *Buxton Rd.* ☎ *01629/816572* 🌐 *www.visitpeakdistrict.com.*

EXPLORING

FAMILY **Peak Cavern.** Caves riddle the entire town and the surrounding area, and in the massive Peak Caverns, rope making has been done on a great ropewalk for more than 400 years. You can still see the remains of the 17th-century rope makers' village. Some trivia to keep kids amused: the Peak Caverns were traditionally called the "Devil's Arse," due to the flatulent noise that water makes when draining out of the caves. ✉ *Off Goosehill* ☎ *01433/620285* 🌐 *www.peakcavern.co.uk* 🎫 *£9.75 Peak Cavern; £16 joint ticket with Speedwell Caverns* ⏲ *Apr.–Oct., daily 10–5, tours hourly; Nov.–Mar., weekday tours 11 and 2, weekend and holiday tours hourly 10–5.*

Peveril Castle. In 1176 Henry II added the square tower to this Norman castle, whose ruins occupy a dramatic crag above the town. The castle has superb views—from here you can still clearly see a curving section of the medieval defensive earthworks in the town center below. Peveril Castle is protected on its west side by a 230 foot-deep gorge formed by a collapsed cave; unsurprisingly, it was considered to be the best-defended castle in England in its day, and was never captured or besieged. However, its relative lack of strategic importance meant that the castle wasn't well maintained, and in 1609 it was finally abandoned altogether. Park in the town center, from which it's a steep climb up. ✉ *Market Pl.* ☎ *01433/620613* 🌐 *www.english-heritage.org.uk* 🎫 *£4.80* ⏲ *Apr.–Oct., daily 10–5; Nov.–Mar., weekends 10–4.*

FAMILY Fodor's Choice ★ **Speedwell Cavern.** The area's most exciting cavern by far is Speedwell Cavern, with 105 slippery steps leading down to old lead-mine tunnels blasted out by 19th-century miners. Here you transfer to a small boat for the claustrophobic ¼-mile trip through an illuminated access tunnel to the cavern itself. At this point you're 600 feet underground, with views farther down to the so-called Bottomless Pit, a cavern entirely filled with water. An on-site shop sells items made of Blue John, a mineral found nowhere else in the world. Speedwell Cavern is at the bottom of Winnats Pass, 1 mile west of Castleton. ✉ *Winnats Pass* ☎ *01433/623018* 🌐 *www.speedwellcavern.co.uk* 🎫 *£10.50; £16* *combination ticket with Peak Cavern ⊙ Apr.–Oct., daily 10–5; Nov.–Mar., daily 10–4; last tour 1 hr before closing.*

WHERE TO EAT AND STAY

$ BRITISH **The Bull's Head.** This handsome brick inn is a cozy spot for traditional and modern British food, served in front of roaring log fires in winter and a courtyard garden in summer. You can share a mixed seafood board, or sample the eight-hour slow-roasted belly pork on black pudding mash with apple and cider gravy. Five snug B&B rooms take in views of Peveril Castle and Mam Tor (from £70 per night); there are also two cottages nearby available for guests. *Average main: £12 ✉ Cross St., Casteton ☎ 01433/620256 🌐 www.bullsheadcastleton.co.uk.*

$ B&B/INN **Underleigh House.** Peaceful is the word for the location of this creeper-clad cottage and barn at the end of a lane in beautiful hiking country. **Pros:** superb views; free Wi-Fi; ample breakfasts. **Cons:** minimum stays on weekends. *Rooms from: £100 ✉ Off Edale Rd., Hope ☎ 01433/621372 🌐 www.underleighhouse.co.uk 3 rooms, 2 suites Breakfast.*

EN ROUTE **Winnats Pass.** Heading northwest to Edale, the most spectacular driving route is over Winnats Pass, through a narrow, boulder-strewn valley. The name means "wind gate," due to the wind tunnel effect of the peaks on each side. Beyond are the tops of Mam Tor (where there's a lookout point) and the hamlet of Barber Booth, after which you run into Edale. *✉ Castleton.*

EDALE

5 miles northwest of Castleton.

At Edale, an extremely popular hiking center, you're truly in the Peak District wilds. This sleepy, straggling village, in the shadow of Mam Tor and Lose Hill and the moorlands of the high plateau known as Kinder Scout (2,088 feet), lies among some of the most breathtaking scenery in Derbyshire. England has little wilder scenery than Kinder Scout, with its ragged edges of grit stone and its interminable leagues of heather and peat.

GETTING HERE AND AROUND

Edale Rail Station has hourly services from Manchester (40 minutes) and Sheffield (30 minutes). By car, Edale is a one-hour drive southeast on the A6 from Manchester.

ESSENTIALS

Visitor Information The Moorland Centre. *✉ Fieldhead ☎ 01433/670207 🌐 www.visitpeakdistrict.com.*

EXPLORING

FAMILY **Chestnut Centre: Otter, Owl, and Wildlife Park.** This family-run conservation park counts South American giant otters, Scottish wildcats, and 17 species of owls among its inhabitants. During school breaks, there are nature quiz trails and informational staff talks. *✉ Castleton Rd., Chapel-en-le-Frith ☎ 01298/814099 🌐 www.chestnutcentre.co.uk £7.75 ⊙ Spring/summer daily 10:30–5:30, fall/winter daily 10:30–4:30 or dusk (weekends only in Jan.); last admission 90 min before closing.*

Pennine Way. The 250-mile-long Pennine Way starts in the village of Edale, 4 miles northeast of Castleton, and crosses Kinder Scout, a moorland plateau and nature reserve. If you plan to attempt this, seek local advice first, because bad weather can make the walk treacherous. However, several much shorter routes into the Edale Valley, such as the 8-mile route west to Hayfield, give you a taste. ✉ *Edale* 🌐 *www.nationaltrail.co.uk.*

WHERE TO EAT

$ BRITISH

✕ **Old Nag's Head.** This pub at the top of the village has marked the official start of the Pennine Way since 1965. Call in at the Hiker's Bar, sit by the fire, and tuck into hearty meals such as winter steak and game pie, or the hiker's special of pasties and chips. Be sure to order a hot toddy, too. There are also two cottages for rent on the premises. [$] *Average main:* ✉ *Grinsbrook Booth* ☎ *01433/670291* 🌐 *www.the-old-nags-head.co.uk.*

STOKE-ON-TRENT

55 miles southeast of Liverpool.

Just west of the Peak District, the area known as the Potteries is still the center of Britain's ceramics industry, though production is increasingly being transferred overseas. There are, in fact, six towns, now administered as "the city of Stoke-on-Trent." Famous names such as Wedgwood, Royal Doulton, Spode, and Coalport carry on, though they've been taken over by other companies.

The most famous manufacturer, Josiah Wedgwood, established his pottery works at Etruria, near Burslem, in 1759. More recent innovators include the very collectible Clarice Cliff, who strove to brighten plain whiteware in the 1920s with her colorful geometric and floral designs. Also bold and colorful were the classic art deco pieces of Susie Cooper. Museums portray the history of this area, and there's still plenty of shopping, with good prices for seconds.

GETTING HERE AND AROUND

Stoke-on-Trent is on the main rail route between London (90 minutes) and Manchester (an hour). If you're driving, it's just off junctions 15 and 16 on the M6 motorway. National Express coaches between Manchester and Birmingham, and between London and Colne or Southport, call here. Traveline West Midlands (🌐 *www.travelinemidlands.co.uk*) has information on local bus services.

ESSENTIALS

Visitor Information Tourist Information Centre. ✉ *The Potteries Museum & Art Gallery, Bethsheba St.* ☎ *01782/236000* 🌐 *www.visitstoke.co.uk.*

EXPLORING

Emma Bridgewater. This highly successful local firm is known across Britain for its whimsical pottery designs. The 45-minute factory tour shows how Emma Bridgewater herself adapted 200-year-old techniques, and you can book a session in the decorating studio to try your hand at designs of your own. There's also a gift shop, a cute café, and a walled country-style garden in the summer. ✉ *Lichfield St., Hanley*

01782/201328 www.emmabridgewaterfactory.co.uk Tour: £2.50; refunded when you spend £13 in gift shop Mon.–Sat. 9:30–5:30, Sun. 10–4.

Gladstone Pottery Museum. The country's only remaining old-style Victorian pottery factory, the Gladstone Pottery Museum's traditional bottle kilns are surrounded by original workshops where you can watch demonstrations of the old skills of throwing, casting, and decorating. *Uttoxeter Rd., Longton 01782/237777 www.stokemuseums.org.uk £7.50 Apr.–Sept., Tues.–Sat. and holiday Mon. 10–5; Oct.–Mar., Tue.–Sat. and holiday Mon. 10–4; last admission 1 hr before closing.*

The Potteries Museum & Art Gallery. This modern museum and gallery displays a 5,000-piece ceramic collection of international repute and is recognized worldwide for its unique Staffordshire pottery, as well as for a number of items from the Staffordshire Hoard, the largest collection of Anglo-Saxon gold and metalworks ever found. Other highlights are an original World War II Spitfire plane and works by Picasso, Degas, and Dürer. You'll also find the area's tourism information headquarters here. *Bethesda St., Hanley 01782/232323 www.stokemuseums.org.uk Free Mon.–Sat. 10–5, Sun. 2–5.*

FAMILY **World of Wedgwood.** Opened in 2015 to replace the former museum and visitor center, this attraction on the Wedgewood Estate's 240-acre garden factory site offers a new and improved factory tour, a museum, creative studios hosting activities and events, woodland walks, and a children's play area. There's also a restaurant, a café, and the obligatory pottery and gift store. *Wedgewood Dr., Off A5035, Barlaston 01782/204141 www.wedgwoodvisitorcentre.com Factory tour and museum £15 (separate tickets available) Weekdays 10–5, weekends 10–4.*

WHERE TO STAY

$$ HOTEL **Upper House Hotel.** A handsome mansion located among gardens and woodlands, the Upper House Hotel was built in 1845 for Francis Wedgwood, heir to the family property firm. **Pros:** good food on-site; lovely views. **Cons:** popular with weddings; the quality of service can vary. *Rooms from: £105 The Green, Barlaston 01782/373790 www.theupperhouse.com 24 rooms No meals.*

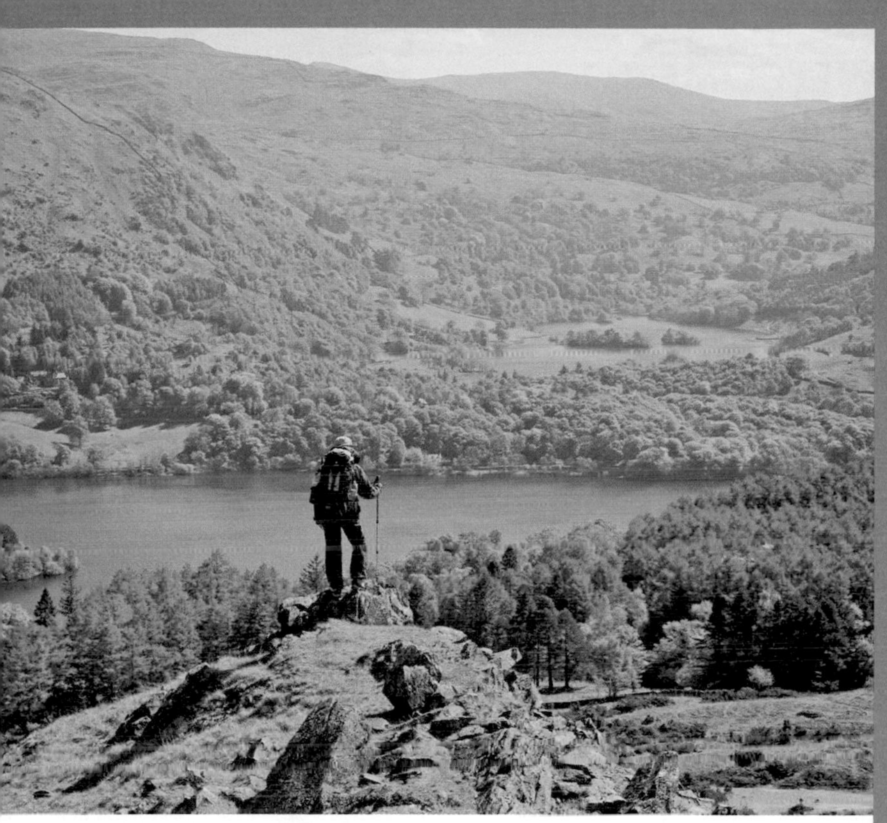

THE LAKE DISTRICT

10

WELCOME TO THE LAKE DISTRICT

TOP REASONS TO GO

★ **Hiking the trails:** Whether it's a demanding trek or a gentle stroll, walking is the way to see the Lake District at its best.

★ **Messing about in boats:** There's nowhere better for renting a small boat or taking a cruise. The Coniston Boating Centre and Derwent Water Marina near Keswick are possible places to start.

★ **Literary landscapes:** The Lake District has a rich literary history, in the children's books of Beatrix Potter, in the writings of John Ruskin, and in the poems of Wordsworth. Stop at any of the writers' homes to enrich your experience.

★ **Pints and pubs:** A pint of real ale in one of the region's inns, such as the Drunken Duck near Hawkshead, may never taste as good as after a day of walking.

★ **Sunrise at Castlerigg:** The stone circle at Castlerigg, in a hollow ringed by peaks, is a reminder of the region's ancient history.

GETTING ORIENTED

The Lake District is in northwest England, some 70 miles north of the industrial belt that stretches from Liverpool to Manchester, and south of Scotland. The major gateway from the south is Kendal, and from the north, Penrith. Both are on the M6 motorway. Main-line trains stop at Oxenholme, near Kendal, with a branch linking Oxenholme to Kendal and Windermere. Windermere, in the south, is the most obvious starting point and has museums, cafés, and gift shops. But the farther (and higher) you can get from the southern towns, the more you'll appreciate the area's spectacular landscapes. Lake District National Park breaks into two reasonably distinct sections: the gentler, rolling south and the craggier, wilder north.

1 The Southern Lakes. The southern lakes and valleys contain the park's most popular destinations, and thus those most overcrowded in summer. The region incorporates the largest body of water, Windermere, as well as most of the quintessential Lakeland towns and villages: Bowness, Ambleside, Grasmere, Elterwater, Coniston, and Hawkshead. To the east and west of this cluster of habitation, the valleys and fells climb to some beautiful upland country.

2 Penrith and the Northern Lakes. In the north, the landscape opens out across the bleaker fells to reveal challenging, spectacular walking country. Here, in the northern lakes, south of Keswick and Cockermouth, you have the best chance to get away from the crowds. This region's northwestern reaches are largely unexplored, while the northeast is home to Penrith, a bustling market town.

10

CLASSIC ENGLISH DESSERTS

The English love to round off lunch or dinner with something sweet. British food is experiencing an ongoing revival that has cooks bringing back favorites such as fool, trifle, spotted dick, and sticky toffee pudding, and making the most of seasonal fruits and traditional spices.

(above) A dense texture and toffee sauce make sticky toffee pudding perfect for winter; (right, top) Trifle variation with strawberries and mascarpone; (right, bottom) Eton mess can use mixed berries.

"Sweet," "afters," and "pudding" all refer informally to dessert; "sweets" are simply candies, though. In England dessert is as likely to be a delicate creamy confection as a warming fruit pie or a rich, hearty pudding. Winter is the perfect time for steamed puddings, made with currants, dried fruits, and spices such as cinnamon, nutmeg, cloves, and ginger, or for hot fruit crumbles with custard. The warmer months bring an avalanche of fresh berries, and with them light, creamy desserts such as syllabub and fool come into their own. For many, the classic desserts such as sticky toffee pudding and spotted dick capture memories of growing up in the 20th century. Today dessert bars are becoming a trend in cities including London.

SPECIAL INGREDIENTS

Desserts may use wine and brandy, and other special items. These include **currants**—dried small black grapes—as well as dried fruits, candied fruit peel, and spices. **Quinces,** hard, applelike fruits, can be combined with apples in a crumble or turned into a paste to accompany cheese. **Damsons** are acidic plums, made into jams, jellies, or wine.

HOT STEAMED PUDDINGS

These puddings are cooked slowly over boiling water. Sticky toffee pudding is a dark sponge cake, made with finely chopped dates or prunes, and covered in a thick toffee sauce. The oddly named spotted dick is traditionally made with suet and steamed in a hot cloth, "spotted" with currants and other dried fruits, and served with custard. Another classic, Christmas pudding, dates from medieval times. Also known as plum pudding, it contains brandy, currants, and dried fruit, and is strong-flavored. Before the pudding steams for many hours, each family member stirs the mixture and makes a wish.

FRUIT CRUMBLES

Crumbles, similar to American crisps, were invented during wartime rationing when butter, flour, and sugar were too scarce to make pastry for pie. Tart Bramley apples native to England work well with cinnamon and cloves. Don't pass up rhubarb crumble, especially around February when the delicate bright pink variety of rhubarb from Yorkshire makes its brief appearance.

TRIFLE, FOOL, AND SYLLABUB

Dating from Tudor times, fool is simply a sharp fruit, usually gooseberry, swirled with whipped cream and a little sugar. Trifle evolved from fool, and begins with a layer of sponge cake (soaked in port, sherry, or Madeira wine) and

Jell-O or jam, topped with custard and whipped cream. Light but flavorful, syllabub is made from wine or brandy infused overnight with lemon and sugar, and whipped with cream.

ETON MESS

Invented at the famous Eton College, after, it's said, a Labrador dog accidentally sat on a picnic basket, Eton Mess is still served at the annual prize-giving ceremony. This unfussy summer dessert consists of strawberries mixed with whipped cream and crushed meringue.

SUMMER PUDDING

Fresh summer berries, bread, and a little sugar are all that should go into a summer pudding. Left for several hours so that the sweet and sharp flavors develop, the pudding turns out a deep red color and is often served with a touch of cream.

MORE FAVORITES

Grasmere gingerbread from the Lake District is a dense spicy cake flavored with ginger and golden syrup. Eccles cakes, from Eccles in Lancashire, are round pastry cases, slashed three times for the Holy Trinity and filled with syrupy currants. Bakewell pudding or tart has a layer of jam and almond sponge, topped with flaked almonds or white icing.

Updated by Julius Honnor

"Let nature be your teacher." Wordsworth's ideal comes true in this popular national park of jagged mountains, waterfalls, wooded valleys, and stone-built villages. No mountains in Britain give a greater impression of majesty; deeper and bluer lakes can be found, but none that fit so readily into the surrounding scene. Outdoors enthusiasts flock to this region for boating or hiking, while literary types visit the homes of Beatrix Potter, William Wordsworth, and other favorite writers.

In 1951 the Lake District National Park was created here from parts of the old counties of Cumberland, Westmorland, and Lancashire. The Lake District is a contour map come to life, covering an area of approximately 885 square miles and holding 16 major lakes and countless smaller stretches of water. The scenery is key to all the park's best activities: you can cross it by car in about an hour, but this is an area meant to be walked or boated or climbed. The mountains aren't high by international standards—Scafell Pike, England's highest peak, is only 3,210 feet above sea level—but they can be tricky to climb. In spring, many summits remain snowcapped long after the weather below has turned mild.

The poets Wordsworth and Coleridge, and other English writers, found the Lake District an inspiring setting for their work, and visitors have followed ever since, to walk, go boating, or just relax and take in the views. Seeing the homes and other sights associated with these writers can occupy part of a trip.

This area can be one of Britain's most appealing reservoirs of calm, though in summer the lakeside towns can lose their charm when cars and tour buses clog the narrow streets. Similarly, the walks and hiking trails that crisscross the region seem less inviting when you share them with a crowd. Despite the challenges of popularity, the Lake District has managed tourism and the landscape in a manner that retains the character of the villages and the natural environment. Explore beyond Windermere and Keswick to discover little farming communities eking out a living despite the occasionally harsh conditions.

Today, too, a new generation of hotel and restaurant owners is making more creative use of the local foods and other assets of the Lakeland fells, and chic modern or foodie-oriented establishments are springing up next to traditional tearooms and chintz-filled inns.

Off-season visits can be a real treat. All those inns and bed-and-breakfasts that turn away crowds in summer are eager for business the rest of the year (and their rates drop accordingly). It's not an easy task to find a succession of sunny days in the Lake District—some malicious statisticians allot to it about 250 rainy days a year—but when the sun breaks through and brightens the surfaces of the lakes, it's an away-from-it-all place to remember.

LAKE DISTRICT PLANNER

WHEN TO GO

The Lake District is one of the rainiest areas in Britain, but June, July, and August hold the best hope of fine weather, and summer is the time for all the major festivals. You will, however, be sharing the lakes with thousands of other people. If you travel at this time, turn up early at popular museums and attractions and expect to work to find parking. April and May, as well as September and October, are good alternatives. Later and earlier in the year there'll be even more space and freedom, but many attractions close, and from December to March, snow and ice can sometimes block high passes and may preclude serious hill walking without heavy-duty equipment.

PLANNING YOUR TIME

You could spend months tramping the hills, valleys, and fells of the Lake District, or, in three days you could drive through the major towns and villages. The key is not to do too much in too short a time. If you're traveling by public transportation, many places will be off-limits. As a base, Windermere has the best transport links, but it can be crowded and it has less character than some of the smaller towns like Ambleside and Keswick, which also have plenty of sleeping and eating options. For a more intimate version of village life, try Coniston, Hawkshead, or Grasmere. Keep in mind that the northern and western lakes have the most dramatic scenery and offer the best opportunity to escape the summertime hordes.

The Lake District may be compact, but it's not a place to hurry. Allow plenty of time for walking: paths can be steep and rocky, and in any case you'll want to stop frequently to look at the great views. A good day's walking with a picnic can be done from nearly anywhere. Driving brings its own speed inhibitors, from sheep on the roads to slow tractors.

You're likely to be based down near lake level, but try to experience the hills, too. If you're short of time, a drive over one of the high passes such as Honister will give you a glimpse of the enormity of the landscape.

GETTING HERE AND AROUND

AIR TRAVEL

Manchester Airport has its own rail station with direct service to Carlisle, Windermere, and Barrow-in-Furness. Manchester is 70 miles from the southern part of the Lake District.

Contact Manchester Airport. ✉ *M56, Near Junctions 5 and 6* ☎ *08712/710711* 🌐 *www.manchesterairport.co.uk.*

BOAT TRAVEL

Whether you rent a boat or take a ride on a modern launch or vintage vessel, getting out on the water is a fun (and often useful) way to see the Lake District. Windermere, Coniston Water, and Derwentwater all have boat rental facilities.

BUS TRAVEL

National Express serves the region from London's Victoria Coach Station and from Manchester's Chorlton Street Station. Average travel time to Kendal is just over 7 hours from London; to Windermere, 7½ hours; and to Keswick, 8¼ hours. From Manchester there's one bus a day to Windermere via Ambleside, Grasmere, and Keswick. There's direct bus service to the Lake District from Carlisle, Lancaster, and York.

Stagecoach in Cumbria provides local service between Lakeland towns and through the valleys and high passes. Bus service between main tourist centers is fairly frequent on weekdays, but much reduced on weekends and bank holidays. Don't count on reaching the more remote parts of the area by bus. Off-the-beaten-track touring requires a car or strong legs. A one-week Cumbria Goldrider ticket (£26), available on the bus, is valid on all routes. Explorer tickets (£10.30) are valid for a day on all routes. Contact Traveline for up-to-date timetables.

Contacts National Express. ☎ *08717/818178* 🌐 *www.nationalexpress.com.* **Stagecoach.** ☎ *0871/200–2233* 🌐 *www.stagecoachbus.com.* **Traveline.** ☎ *0871/200–2233* 🌐 *www.traveline.info.*

CAR TRAVEL

A car is almost essential in the Lake District; bus service is limited and trains can get you to the edge of the national park but no farther. You can rent cars in Penrith and Kendal. Roads within the region are generally good, although minor routes and mountain passes can be steep and narrow. Warning signs are often posted if snow or ice has made a road impassable; check local weather forecasts in winter before heading out. In July and August and during the long public holiday weekends, expect heavy traffic. The Lake District has plenty of parking lots; use them to avoid blocking narrow lanes.

To reach the Lake District by car from London, take M1 north to M6, getting off either at Junction 36 and joining A590/A591 west (around the Kendal bypass to Windermere) or at Junction 40, joining A66 direct to Keswick and the northern lakes region. Travel time to Kendal is about four to five hours, to Keswick five to six hours. Expect heavy traffic out of London on weekends.

TRAIN TRAVEL

There are direct trains from Manchester and Manchester airport to Windermere. For schedule information, call National Rail Enquiries. Two train companies serve the region from London's Euston Station: take a Virgin or Northern Rail train bound for Carlisle, Edinburgh, or Glasgow and change at Oxenholme for the branch line service to Kendal and Windermere. Average travel time from London to Windermere (including the change) is 3¼ hours. If you're heading for Keswick, you can either take the train to Windermere and continue from there by Stagecoach bus (Bus 554/555/556; 70 minutes) or stay on the main London–Carlisle train to Penrith Station (4 hours), from which Stagecoach buses (Bus X5) also run to Keswick (45 minutes). Direct trains from Manchester depart for Windermere five times daily (travel time 2 hours). First North Western runs a local service from Windermere and Barrow-in-Furness to Manchester Airport. National Rail can handle all questions about trains.

Train connections are good around the edges of the Lake District, but you must take the bus or drive to reach the central Lakeland region. Trains are sometimes reduced, or nonexistent, on Sunday.

Contacts National Rail Enquiries. ☎ *08457/484950* 🌐 *www.nationalrail.co.uk.* **Northern Rail.** ☎ *0844/241–3454* 🌐 *www.northernrail.org.* **Virgin Trains.** ☎ *08719/774222* 🌐 *www.virgintrains.co.uk.*

NATIONAL PARK

The Lake District National Park head office (and main visitor center) is at Brockhole, north of Windermere. Helpful regional national-park information centers sell books and maps, book accommodations, and provide walking advice.

Contacts Bowness Bay Information Centre. ✉ *Glebe Rd., Bowness-on-Windermere* ☎ *015394/42895* 🌐 *www.lakedistrict.gov.uk.* **Keswick Information Centre.** ✉ *Moot Hall, Main St., Keswick* ☎ *017687/72645* 🌐 *www.keswick.org.* **Lake District Visitor Centre.** ✉ *Brockhole, Ambleside Rd., Windermere* ☎ *015394/46601* 🌐 *www.brockhole.co.uk.* **Ullswater Information Centre.** ✉ *Beckside Car Park, off Greenside Rd., Glenridding* ☎ *017684/82414* 🌐 *www.lakedistrict.gov.uk.*

10

TOURS

Cumbria Tourist Guides. This organization of Blue Badge–accredited guides, who are all experts on the area, offers a large range of customized tours, from low-impact country ambles to brewery crawls. ☎ *01228/562096* 🌐 *cumbriatouristguides.co.uk* 🎫 *From £25.*

English Lakeland Ramblers. Arrange single base and inn-to-inn guided tours of the Lake District from the U.S. through this organization. ☎ *703/680–4276, 800/724–8801* 🌐 *www.ramblers.com* 🎫 *From $2,850.*

Fodor's Choice ★ **Head to the Hills.** With more than 80 lakes, meres, and tarns, Cumbria is a great place for open-water swimming. Head to the Hills have specialized swimming wet suits and a wealth of knowledge and enthusiasm about the best places to swim. Guided trips range from a couple of hours to weekends with accommodation and food included. As a way to see the lakes, the view and the experience from the water is hard to beat. ✉ *2 Compston Rd., Ambleside* ☎ *015394/33826* 🌐 *www.headtothehills.co.uk*.

Lake District Walker. This outfitter offers guided day hikes for different abilities. ☎ *0844/693–3389* 🌐 *www.thelakedistrictwalker.co.uk* 🎫 *From £16*.

Lakes Supertours. This company offers minibus sightseeing tours with skilled local guides. ✉ *1 High St., Windermere* ☎ *015394/42751* 🌐 *www.lakes-supertours.com* 🎫 *From £35*.

Mountain Goat. Half- and full-day tours, some of which really get off the beaten track, depart from Bowness, Windermere, Ambleside, and Grasmere. ✉ *Victoria St., Windermere* ☎ *015394/45161* 🌐 *www.mountain-goat.co.uk* 🎫 *From £29*.

RESTAURANTS

Lakeland restaurants increasingly reflect a growing British awareness of good food. Local sourcing and international influences are common, and even old Cumberland favorites are being creatively reinvented. Pub dining in the Lake District can be excellent—the hearty fare often makes use of local ingredients such as Herdwick lamb, and real ales are a good accompaniment. If you're going walking, ask your hotel or B&B about making you a packed lunch. Some local delicatessens also offer this service.

HOTELS

Your choices include everything from small country inns to grand lakeside hotels; many hotels offer the option of paying a higher price that includes dinner as well as breakfast. The regional mainstay is the bed-and-breakfast, from the house on Main Street to an isolated farmhouse. Most country hotels and B&Bs gladly cater to hikers and can provide on-the-spot information. Wherever you stay, book well in advance for summer visits, especially those in late July and August. In winter many accommodations close for a month or two. On weekends and in summer it may be hard to get a reservation for a single night. Internet access is improving, and an increasing number of hotels and cafés offer Wi-Fi access. ⇨ *Hotel reviews have been shortened. For full information, visit Fodors.com.*

WHAT IT COSTS IN POUNDS

	$	$$	$$$	$$$$
Restaurants	under £15	£15–£19	£20–£25	over £25
Hotels	under £100	£100–£160	£161–£220	over £220

Restaurant prices are the average cost of a main course at dinner, or if dinner is not served, at lunch. Hotels prices are the lowest cost of a standard double room in high season, including 20% V.A.T.

VISITOR INFORMATION

Contacts Cumbria Tourism. ✉ *Windermere Rd., Staveley* ☎ *01539/822222* 🌐 *www.golakes.co.uk.*

The design of the famous, fanciful topiary garden at Levens Hall dates back to the 17th century.

THE SOUTHERN LAKES

Among the many attractions here are the small resort towns clustered around Windermere, England's largest lake, and the area's hideaway valleys, rugged walking centers, and monuments rich in literary associations. This is the easiest part of the Lake District to reach, with Kendal, the largest town, just a short distance from the M6 motorway. An obvious route from Kendal takes in Windermere, the area's natural touring center, before moving north through Ambleside and Rydal Water to Grasmere. Some of the loveliest Lakeland scenery is to be found by then turning south, through Elterwater, Hawkshead, and Coniston.

KENDAL

70 miles north of Manchester.

The southern gateway to the Lake District is the "Auld Gray Town" of Kendal, outside the national park and less touristy than the towns to the northwest. You may want to stay closer to the action, but the town has some worthwhile sights. Nearby hills frame Kendal's gray stone houses and provide some delightful walks; you can also explore the ruins of Kendal Castle. **■TIP→ Pack a slab of Kendal mint cake, the local peppermint candy that British walkers and climbers swear by. It's for sale around the region.**

The town's motto, "Wool Is My Bread," refers to its importance as a textile center in northern England before the Industrial Revolution. It was known for manufacturing woolen cloth, especially Kendal Green, which archers favored. Away from the main road are quiet courtyards

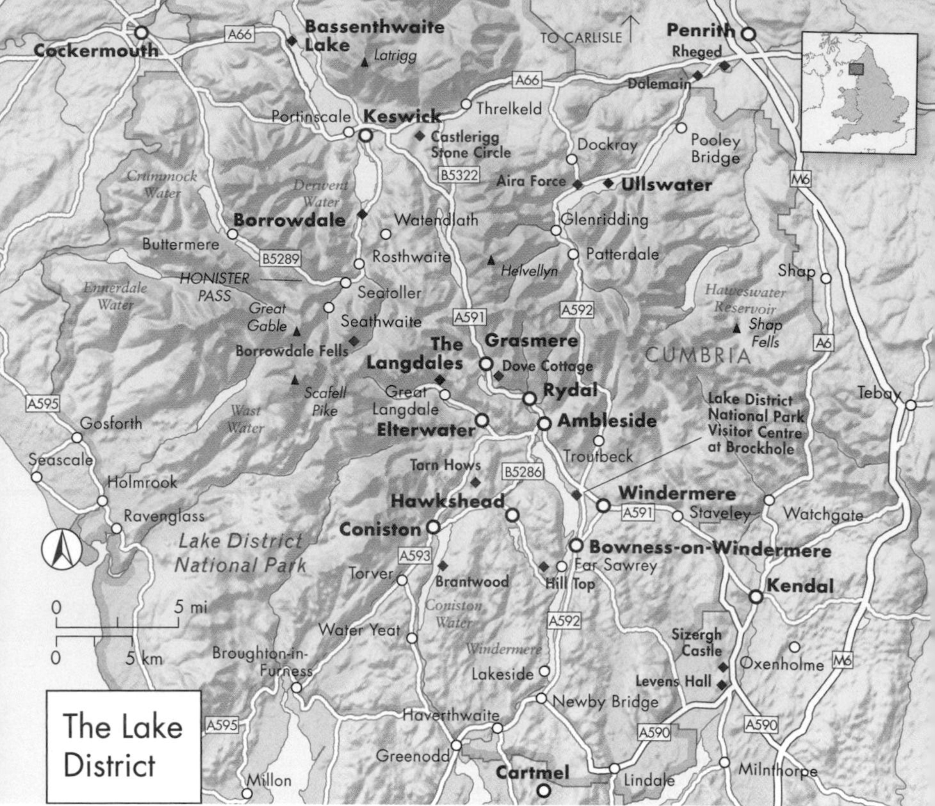

and winding medieval streets known as "ginnels." Wool merchants used these for easy access to the River Kent.

GETTING HERE AND AROUND

Kendal is just off the M6, about 70 miles north of Manchester. It has train service via a branch line from Oxenholme, and National Express bus service from London as well. It's the largest town in the area but is still plenty small enough to walk around.

ESSENTIALS

Visitor Information Kendal Tourist Information Centre. ✉ *Made in Cumbria, 25 Stramongate* ☏ *01539/735891* 🌐 *www.exploresouthlakeland.co.uk.*

EXPLORING

Fodor's Choice ★ **Abbot Hall.** The region's finest art gallery, Abbot Hall occupies a Palladian-style Georgian mansion built in 1759. In the permanent collection are works by Victorian artist and critic John Ruskin, who lived near Coniston, and by 18th-century portrait painter George Romney, who worked in Kendal. *The Great Picture*, a grand 17th-century triptych of the life of Lady Ann Clifford, is attributed to Flemish painter Jan Van Belcamp. The gallery also owns some excellent contemporary art, including work by Barbara Hepworth, Ben Nicholson, Winifred Nicholson, and L.S. Lowry, and the always interesting temporary exhibitions showcase the best of British art. There's also an excellent café. Abbot

Hall is on the River Kent, next to the parish church. The **Museum of Lakeland Life** (*www.lakelandmuseum.org.uk*), with exhibits on blacksmithing and wheelwrighting and a wonderful re-creation of a period pharmacy, is in the former stable block of the hall, on the same site. *Off Highgate 01539/722464 www.abbothall.org.uk Abbot Hall £6.35; Museum of Lakeland Life £5; combined ticket £8.60 Mar.–Oct., Mon.–Sat. 10:30–5; Nov.–mid-Dec. and mid-Jan.–Feb., Mon.–Sat. 10:30–4.*

FAMILY **Levens Hall.** An Elizabethan house and the home of the Bagot family since 1590, Levens Hall is famous for its topiary garden, probably the most distinctive in the world. Laid out in 1694, the garden retains its original design, and the yew and beech hedges, cut into complex shapes that resemble enormous chess pieces, rise among a profusion of flowers. The house contains a stunning medieval hall with oak paneling, ornate plasterwork, Jacobean furniture, and Cordova goat-leather wallpaper. You can easily spend a couple of hours here admiring the place or getting lost in the living willow labyrinth. There's a play area for children. Levens Hall is 4 miles south of Kendal. *Off A590, Levens 015395/60321 www.levenshall.co.uk £12.50; gardens only £9 Early Apr.–early Oct., Sun.–Thurs. house noon–4:30, gardens 10–5; last admission to house at 4.*

Sizergh Castle. One of the Lake District's finest fortified houses, Sizergh Castle has a 58-foot-tall tower that dates from 1340, more than 1,600 acres of grounds, and the national fern collection. Expanded in Elizabethan times, the castle includes outstanding oak-paneled interiors with intricately carved chimneypieces and oak furniture. The estate has ancient woodland, and there are good walks here. Sizergh is 3½ miles south of Kendal. *Off A591, Sizergh 015395/60951 www.nationaltrust.org.uk/sizergh £9.90; gardens only £6.10 Castle mid-Mar.–Oct., Sun.–Thurs. noon–4 (also 11–noon and 4–5 by guided tour). Gardens mid-Mar.–Oct., Mon.–Sun. 10–5.*

WHERE TO EAT AND STAY

The Brewery Arts Centre has other good dining options in Kendal, including the Grain Store restaurant and the theatrical Warehouse Café.

10

$$ MODERN BRITISH **The New Moon.** Small but sleek, this restaurant with an open fire and artfully battered floorboards has won a good local reputation for high-quality dishes. The vegetarian selections are always worthwhile, and the sometimes-adventurous Modern British cooking shows Mediterranean flourishes. Damson plum-and-pork sausages come with mashed potatoes and a red wine jus, and the fresh mussels are cooked in a curry sauce. Excellent lunches and the fixed-price early dinners (5:30–7 weekdays) are especially good values. *Average main: £15 129 Highgate 01539/729254 www.newmoonrestaurant.co.uk Closed Sun. and Mon.*

$ B&B/INN **Beech House.** Old-fashioned charm combines with modern luxuries like heated bathroom floors in this comfortable, ivy-clad town house a five-minute walk up the hill from the center of town in a conservation area. **Pros:** homey rooms; locally made toiletries; private parking. **Cons:** steep walk up the hill to get here; two-night minimum on weekends. $ *Rooms from: £80* ✉ *40 Greenside* ☎ *01539/720385* 🌐 *www.beechhouse-kendal.co.uk* 🛏 *6 rooms* 🍽 *Breakfast.*

NIGHTLIFE AND PERFORMING ARTS

Brewery Arts Centre. A contemporary complex in a converted brewery, the Brewery Arts Centre includes a gallery, theater, cinemas, and workshop spaces. The Grain Store, overlooking lovely gardens, serves lunch and dinner; the Warehouse Café offers tasty toasted sandwiches and occasional live performances; and Vats Bar has good beer and wine. In November the Mountain Film Festival presents productions aimed at climbers and walkers. ✉ *Highgate* ☎ *01539/725133* 🌐 *www.breweryarts.co.uk* 🎟 *Free* 🕓 *Mon.–Sat. 9 am–11 pm.*

SHOPPING

Kendal has a pleasant mix of chains, factory outlet stores, specialty shops, and traditional markets. The most interesting stores are tucked away in the quiet lanes and courtyards around Market Place, Finkle Street, and Stramongate. There's been a **market** in Kendal since 1189, and outdoor market stalls still line the center of town along Stramongate and Market Place every Wednesday and Saturday.

WINDERMERE AND BOWNESS-ON-WINDERMERE

10 miles northwest of Kendal.

For a natural touring base for the southern half of the Lake District, you don't need to look much farther than Windermere, though it does get crowded in summer. The resort became popular in the Victorian era when the arrival of the railway made the remote and rugged area accessible. Wordsworth and Ruskin opposed the railway, fearing an influx of tourists would ruin the tranquil place. Sure enough, the railway terminus in 1847 brought with it Victorian day-trippers, and the original hamlet of Birthwaite was subsumed by the new town of Windermere, named after the lake.

Windermere has continued to flourish, despite being a mile or so from the water; the development now spreads to envelop the slate-gray lakeside village of Bowness-on-Windermere. Bowness is the more attractive of the two, but they're so close it doesn't matter where you stay.

GETTING HERE AND AROUND

Windermere is easily reached by car, less than a half hour off the M6. There's also a train station at the eastern edge of town; change at Oxenholme for the branch line to Kendal and Windermere.

Bus 599, leaving every 20 minutes in summer (hourly the rest of the year) from outside the Windermere train station, links the town with Bowness.

The Windermere Ferry, which carries cars and pedestrians, crosses from Ferry Nab on the Bowness side of the lake to reach Far Sawrey and the road to Hawkshead. With year-round ferry service between Ambleside, Bowness, Brockhole, and Lakeside, Windermere Lake Cruises is a pleasant way to experience the lake.

Walk through an underwater tunnel and learn about the Lake District's fish, frogs, and otters at the Lakes Aquarium near Windermere.

ESSENTIALS

Contacts Windermere Ferry. ✉ *Windermere* ☎ *01228/227653* 🌐 *www.cumbria.gov.uk.* **Windermere Lake Cruises.** ✉ *Windermere* ☎ *015394/43360* 🌐 *www.windermere-lakecruises.co.uk.*

EXPLORING

TOP ATTRACTIONS

Fodor'sChoice ★ **Blackwell.** From 1898 to 1900, architect Mackay Hugh Baillie Scott (1865–1945) designed Blackwell, a quintessential Arts and Crafts house with carved paneling, delicate plasterwork, and a startling sense of light and space. Originally a retreat for a Manchester brewery owner, the house is a refined mix of modern style and the local vernacular. Lime-washed walls and sloping slate roofs make it fit elegantly into the landscape above Windermere, and the artful integration of decorative features into stained glass, stonework, friezes, and wrought iron gives the house a sleekly contemporary feel. Accessibility is wonderful here: nothing is roped off and you can even play the piano. There's some Bailie Scott furniture too, and an exhibition space upstairs. Peruse the shop and try the honey-roast ham in the excellent tearoom. The grounds are also worth a visit: they often host contemporary sculpture installations. ✉ *B5360, Windermere* ☎ *015394/46139* 🌐 *www.blackwell.org.uk* 🎫 *£7.70* ⏲ *Apr.–Oct., daily 10:30–5; Nov., Dec., and Jan.–Mar., daily 10:30–4.*

FAMILY Fodor'sChoice ★ **Lakes Aquarium.** On the quayside at the southern end of Windermere, this excellent aquarium has wildlife and waterside exhibits. One highlight is an underwater tunnel walk along a re-created lake bed, complete with diving ducks and Asian short-clawed otters. Piranhas, rays, and tropical frogs also have their fans, and there are some unexpected treats such as marmosets. A friendly, knowledgeable staff is eager to talk about the animals. **■TIP→ Animal handling takes place daily at 12:45 in the rain-forest areas.** Tickets are cheaper if booked in advance online. ✉ *C5062, Lakeside* ☎ *015394/30153* 🌐 *www.lakesaquarium.co.uk* 🎫 *£5.95; £11.85 combined ticket with Lakeside & Haverthwaite Railway Company* ⏲ *Daily 9–6; last admission 1 hr before closing.*

OFF THE BEATEN PATH

Orrest Head. To escape the traffic and have a view of Windermere, set out on foot and follow the signs to the left of the Windermere Hotel to Orrest Head. The shady, uphill path winds through Elleray Wood, and after a 20-minute hike you arrive at a rocky little summit (784 feet) with a panoramic view that encompasses the Yorkshire fells, Morecambe Bay, and the beautiful Troutbeck Valley. ✉ *Windermere.*

Windermere. No sights in Windermere or Bowness compete with that of Windermere itself. At 11 miles long, 1½ miles wide, and 220 feet deep, the lake is England's largest and stretches from Newby Bridge almost to Ambleside, filling a rocky gorge between thickly wooded hills. The cold waters are superb for fishing, especially for Windermere char, a rare lake trout. In summer, steamers and pleasure craft travel the lake, and a trip across the island-studded waters, particularly the round-trip from Bowness to Ambleside or down to Lakeside, is wonderful. Although the lake's marinas and piers have some charm, you can bypass the busier stretches of shoreline (in summer they can be packed solid) by walking beyond the boathouses. Here, from among the pine trees, are fine views across the lake. Windermere Lake Cruises offers a variety of excursions. ✉ *Windermere* 🌐 *www.windermere-lakecruises.co.uk.*

WORTH NOTING

FAMILY **Brockhole.** A lakeside 19th-century mansion with 30 acres of terraced gardens sloping down to the water, Brockhole serves as the park's official visitor center and has some exhilarating activities: "treetop trek"—a rope bridge and zip-line route high up through oak trees—and the U.K.'s only "treetop nets," allowing everyone over the age of three to climb and bounce around safely among the twigs and leaves more than 25 feet up, supported by elastic ropes. There's also a 30-foot climbing wall. The gardens, designed in the Arts and Crafts style by Thomas Mawson, are at their best in spring, when daffodils punctuate the lawns and azaleas burst into bloom. There's an adventure playground, pony rides, mini golf, and rowboats for rent. The bookstore carries hiking guides and maps, and you can picnic here or eat at the café-restaurant. Bus 555/559 goes to the visitor center from Windermere, and boats from Waterhead stop at a pier. Windermere Lake Cruises has seasonal ferry service to Brockhole from Waterhead in Ambleside. ✉ *Ambleside Rd., Windermere* ☎ *015394/46601* 🌐 *www.brockhole.co.uk* 🎫 *Free; treetop trek from £20; treetop nets £16* ⏲ *Mid-Feb.–Oct., daily 10–5, gardens daily 10–dusk; Nov.–mid-Feb., daily 10–4, gardens daily 8:30–7. Treetop activities weekends, holidays, and all summer.*

Hawkshead Brewery. It may not have the Lake District's most picturesque setting—in Staveley, between Windermere and Kendal—but for beer lovers, there are few better places than this brewery, which brews and serves 14 beers, including some champion pints. Sample the wares and "beer tapas" (sweetcorn and coriander fritters, breaded whitebait) at the large bar, or have something more substantial upstairs, with views of the vats. Brewery tours happen Wednesday, Friday, Saturday, and Sunday at 2 pm. Keep an eye on the website for details of live music and beer festivals. ✉ *Mill Yard, Staveley* ☎ *01539/822644* 🌐 *hawksheadbrewery.co.uk* 🎫 *Free; tours £8.*

FAMILY **Lakeside & Haverthwaite Railway Company.** Vintage steam trains chug along on the 18-minute, 4-mile branch line between Lakeside and Haverthwaite, giving you a great view of the lake's southern tip. You can add on a lake cruise for another perspective on the region's natural beauty. Departures from Lakeside coincide with ferry arrivals from Bowness and Ambleside. ✉ *A590, Haverthwaite* ☎ *015395/31594* 🌐 *www.lakesiderailway.co.uk* 🎫 *£6.60 round-trip; £11.85 combined ticket with Lakeside Aquarium* ⏲ *Apr.–Oct., daily 10:30–6.*

FAMILY **World of Beatrix Potter.** A touristy attraction aimed at kids interprets the author's 23 tales with three-dimensional scenes of Peter Rabbit and more. Skip it if you can and visit Potter's former home at Hill Top and the Beatrix Potter Gallery in Hawkshead. ✉ *The Old Laundry, Crag Brow, Bowness-on-Windermere* ☎ *0844/504–1233* 🌐 *www.hop-skip-jump.com* 🎫 *£6.95* ⏲ *Apr.–Sept., daily 10–5:30; Oct.–Mar., daily 10–4:30; closed 1 wk end of Jan.*

WHERE TO EAT

$ BRITISH ✕ **Angel Inn.** Up the steep slope from the water's edge in Bowness, this spacious, stylish pub serves good home-cooked fare as well as a fine collection of beers that includes its own Hawkshead brew. Specials, chalked on a board, may include dishes such as roasted cod with pak choi or goat cheese and fig tart. Leather sofas and open fires make the Angel a cozy place; service is low-key and friendly, with crayons for kids and games to play. The decoration is bright, minimal, and contemporary, with wooden floors and off-white walls. Thirteen comfortable, good-value bedrooms complete the picture. $ *Average main: £14* ✉ *Helm Rd., Bowness-on-Windermere* ☎ *015394/44080* 🌐 *www.theangelinnbowness.com.*

$ BRITISH FAMILY ✕ **Masons Arms.** With fabulous views over the rolling countryside of the Winster Valley to the east of Windermere, the Masons Arms is a slate-floored traditional old inn serving local ales and good pub food. In winter there's an open log fire; in summer outdoor seating beckons. Dark wooden beams hold up low ceilings. It's more formal than some of its Lake District counterparts—staff wear ties—but service is friendly. Old mirrors and tankards decorate the walls, and there's a speciality gin list as well as stews and pheasant sausages. Five suites and two cottages provide stylish places to sleep, should you wish to stay. $ *Average main: £12* ✉ *Strawberry Bank, Windermere* ☎ *015395/ 68486* 🌐 *www.masonsarmsstrawberrybank.co.uk.*

$ BRITISH FAMILY ✕ **Wild & Co.** Opened in 2014 by an English-Italian couple, Wild & Co is an excellent café by day and a fashionable bar-restaurant by night. Local linocuts line the walls and fresh flowers decorate the wooden tables. Locally sourced and homegrown ingredients are expertly turned into dishes such as slow-cooked ragu of Lakeland venison with pappardelle, and confit of Goosnargh duck with black pudding cassoulet and savory granola; a thoughtful children's menu is available, too. Delicious homemade cakes make a good accompaniment to the excellent coffee or tea. *Average main: £14 31–33 Crescent Rd., Windermere 015394/43877 www.wildandco.co.uk Closed Tues.*

WHERE TO STAY

$ B&B/INN Fodor's Choice ★ **1 Park Road.** On a quiet corner, this upmarket boutique B&B has spacious guest rooms with carefully chosen fabrics, feature wallpaper, comfortable mattresses, and contemporary touches such as music-player docking stations. **Pros:** welcoming and stylish; picks guests up from the station; good food, wine, and beer. **Cons:** a 15-minute walk to the lake. *Rooms from: £84 1 Park Rd., Windermere 015394/42107 www.1parkroad.com 6 rooms Breakfast.*

$$$$ HOTEL Fodor's Choice ★ **Gilpin Hotel.** Hidden among 22 acres of grounds with meandering paths leading to sleek, spacious lodges, this rambling country-house hotel pampers you in a low-key way. **Pros:** plenty of pampering; notable food; a policy of no weddings or conferences. **Cons:** a little out of the way; expensive rates; no children under seven. *Rooms from: £335 Crook Rd., Bowness-on-Windermere 2 miles east of Windermere 015394/88818 thegilpin.co.uk 15 rooms, 12 suites Some meals.*

$ B&B/INN **Ivy Bank.** One of Windermere's smartest bed-and-breakfasts, spotless Ivy Bank is in a quiet, leafy part of town. **Pros:** bike storage; good walks nearby; family room. **Cons:** most rooms have showers, but no tubs. *Rooms from: £80 Holly Rd., Windermere 015394/42601 www.ivy-bank.co.uk 5 rooms Breakfast.*

$$$ HOTEL Fodor's Choice ★ **Miller Howe.** A lovely location, lake views, and superb service help set this luxurious Edwardian country-house hotel apart. **Pros:** more than 5 acres of grounds; great lake views; staff that take care of the little extras. **Cons:** sometimes closes for a couple of weeks in winter. *Rooms from: £210 Rayrigg Rd., Bowness-on-Windermere 015394/42536 www.millerhowe.com 15 rooms Some meals.*

$$$ HOTEL Fodor's Choice ★ **Punch Bowl Inn.** An outstanding inn and restaurant, the Punch Bowl is a stylish but down-to-earth retreat in the peaceful Lyth Valley, between Windermere and Kendal. **Pros:** contemporary design; relaxed atmosphere; excellent food. **Cons:** a little way from the area's main sights. *Rooms from: £165 Off A5074, Crosthwaite 015395/68237 www.the-punchbowl.co.uk 9 rooms Breakfast.*

$ B&B/INN **Rum Doodle.** Named after a classic climbing novel, Rum Doodle is an immaculately and imaginatively designed B&B. **Pros:** wonderfully stylish with lots of fun quirks; friendly welcome. **Cons:** some distance from both Bowness and Windermere centers. *Rooms from: £99 Sunny Bank Rd., Windermere 015394/45967 www.rumdoodlewindermere.com . 9 rooms Breakfast.*

$$$ HOTEL **The Samling.** On its own sculpture-dotted 67 acres above Windermere, this place oozes exclusivity from every carefully fashioned corner. **Pros:** you'll feel like a star, and may sit next to one at breakfast, too. **Cons:** exclusivity doesn't come cheap. *Rooms from: £220 Ambleside Rd., Windermere 01539/431922 www.thesamlinghotel.co.uk 5 rooms, 6 suites Breakfast.*

SHOPPING

The best selection of shops is at the Bowness end of Windermere, on Lake Road and around Queen's Square: clothing stores, crafts shops, and souvenir stores of all kinds.

Fodor's Choice ★ **More? The Artisan Bakery** Between Kendal and Windermere, this bakery is the place to stop for mouthwatering, award-winning bread, cakes, and sandwiches. It also brews fine coffee. ✉ *Mill Yard, Staveley* ☎ *015398/22297* 🌐 *www.moreartisan.co.uk.*

Peter Hall & Son. This woodcraft workshop, between Kendal and Windermere, sells finely honed furnishings, boxes, and bowls, among other items. ✉ *Danes Rd., Staveley* ☎ *01539/821633* 🌐 *www.peter-hall.co.uk* ⏲ *Closed Sun.*

SPORTS AND THE OUTDOORS

BIKING

Country Lanes Cycle Hire. This shop rents a variety of bikes from £20 per day. ✉ *Windermere Railway Station, off A591, Windermere* ☎ *015394/44544* 🌐 *www.countrylaneslakedistrict.co.uk.*

BOATING

Windermere Lake Holidays. This company rents a wide range of vessels, from small sailboats to houseboats. ✉ *Mereside, Ferry Nab, Bowness-on-Windermere* ☎ *015394/43415* 🌐 *www.lakewindermere.net.*

AMBLESIDE

7 miles northwest of Windermere.

Unlike Kendal and Windermere, Ambleside seems almost part of the hills and fells. Its buildings, mainly of local stone and many built in the traditional style that forgoes the use of mortar in the outer walls, blend perfectly into their setting. The small town sits at the northern end of Windermere along A591, making it a popular center for Lake District excursions. It has recently seen a sharp rise in great-quality restaurants, and the numerous outdoor shops are handy for walkers. Ambleside does, however, suffer from overcrowding in high season. Wednesday, when the local market takes place, is particularly busy.

GETTING HERE AND AROUND

An easy drive along A591 from Windermere, Ambleside can also be reached by ferry.

ESSENTIALS

Visitor Information Ambleside Tourist Information Centre. ✉ *The Hub, Central Bldgs., Market Cross, Rydal Rd* ☎ *0844/225–0544.*

EXPLORING

Armitt Museum. Ambleside's fine local museum is a scholarly place, focusing on influential German artist Kurt Schwitters and Beatrix Potter. Schwitters lived out his final years in Ambleside, and the museum now has a room filled with his art. The museum also shows the less well-known aspects of Beatrix Potter, revealing her work as an important scientific and intellectual figure. Exhibits shed light on her as a naturalist, mycologist, sheep breeder, and conservationist. A large collection of her natural-history watercolors and a huge number of photographic portraits can be viewed by appointment in the excellent library upstairs. ✉ *Rydal Rd.* ☎ *015394/31212* 🌐 *www.armitt.com* 🎫 *£3.50* ⏲ *Mon.–Sat. 10–5; last admission at 4:30.*

Bridge House. This tiny 17th-century stone building, once an apple store, perches on an arched stone bridge spanning Stone Beck. It may have been built here to avoid land tax. This much-photographed building holds a shop and an information center. ✉ *Rydal Rd.* ☎ *015394/35599* 🎫 *Free* ⏲ *Easter–Oct., daily 10–5.*

WHERE TO EAT

$ VEGETARIAN Fodor's Choice ★ **✕ Fellinis.** Billing itself as "Vegeterranean" to reflect its Mediterranean culinary influences, Fellinis is one of Cumbria's finest foodie destinations. Upstairs is a plush studio cinema screening art-house releases, while downstairs the restaurant rustles up sumptuous concoctions for a sophisticated crowd. The menu's imaginative dishes might start with blue cheese mousse, then continue with baby spinach crêpes filled with wild mushrooms, tarragon, and Brie. The large, open dining room has soft seating, bold patterns, oversize lamp shades, and a chill, jazzy soundtrack. White tablecloths, contemporary art, and fresh flowers enhance the modern sensibility. [$] *Average main: £12* ✉ *Church St.* ☎ *01539/433845* 🌐 *www.fellinisambleside.com* ⏲ *No lunch.*

$$$ MODERN BRITISH **✕ Lake Road Kitchen.** Cuttlefish shells piled in the window and a Nordic-style wood-paneled interior give a clue as to the culinary style of Lake Road Kitchen, one of the brace of new Ambleside restaurants creating a buzz all over the region. Eighty percent of everything green on the menu is foraged; the remainder comes from the highest-quality, mainly local suppliers. Dishes may include grilled octopus with fermented wild garlic puree and wild herbs, or guinea hen with seaweed and wild primrose pie. Every dish is creatively conceived and expertly put together, creating food of the highest order. The arrival of chef James Cross, from Per Se in New York and Noma in Copenhagen, is a huge coup for Ambleside, and the talk of the town. [$] *Average main: £25* ✉ *Lake Rd.* ☎ *015394/22012* 🌐 *www.lakeroadkitchen.co.uk* ⏲ *No lunch. Closed Mon. and Tues.* ✍ *Reservations essential.*

$$$ BRITISH Fodor's Choice ★ **✕ Old Stamp House.** The quality of locally sourced and foraged food has been raised to a new level by this startlingly good restaurant, which together with the Lake Road Kitchen has given Ambleside unexpected status on the British gastro map. Chef Ryan Blackburn's menu is anchored to Cumbrian traditions but at the same time mouthwateringly creative and contemporary. Look for beetroot meringues with horseradish as an amuse-bouche and black pudding balls with fruit sauce between courses. Main dishes may pair Lakeland lamb with goat cheese gnocchi or Whitehaven turbot with spiced mead. The restaurant has an unprepossessing setting, down steps in a dim room, but there's history in the whitewashed, rough-hewn walls: Wordsworth once worked here as "Distributer of Stamps." [$] *Average main: £22* ✉ *Church St.* ☎ *015394/32775* 🌐 *www.oldstamphouse.com* ⏲ *No lunch Tues. Closed Sun.–Mon.* ✍ *Reservations essential.*

$ VEGETARIAN **✕ Rattle Gill.** Hidden away up a winding lane past the old mill waterwheel, homey Rattle Gill is a deservedly popular little café serving great homemade cakes, soups, sandwiches, and salads. The tasting plate of cakes is an especially good option. Local art hangs on the berry-red walls, and old exposed beams give the place extra atmosphere. It's child-friendly, with books to read, and there are seats outside above the stream for good weather. *Average main: £7 2 Bridge St. 7975/912990 www.rattlegill.com No dinner. Closed Mon.–Tues.*

WHERE TO STAY

$ B&B/INN **3 Cambridge Villas.** It's hard to find a more welcoming spot than this lofty Victorian house right in the center of town, thanks to hosts who know a thing or two about local walks. **Pros:** especially good value for single travelers; warm family welcome; central location. **Cons:** some rooms are a little cramped; can occasionally be noisy. *Rooms from: £80 3 Church St. 015394/32307 www.3cambridgevillas.co.uk 7 rooms, 5 with bath Breakfast.*

$$ B&B/INN **Nanny Brow.** Outside Ambleside toward the Langdales, this smart guesthouse feels more like a hotel, with a huge lounge, named rooms, antique furniture, and award-winning breakfasts. **Pros:** great setting and views; easy access to the Fells. **Cons:** no evening meals; a bit out of the way, especially without a car. *Rooms from: £150 Clappersgate Off the A593 between Clappersgate and Skelwith Bridge 015394/33232 www.nannybrow.co.uk 13 rooms Breakfast.*

$ B&B/INN **Rooms at the Apple Pie.** Converted from what were once the offices of Beatrix Potter's solicitor husband, this Ambleside café has branched out into accommodations, with eight simple but stylishly furnished rooms decorated with photos of delights from the café next door. **Pros:** scrumptious breakfasts; central location; five parking spaces. **Cons:** not staffed 24 hours a day; breakfast is extra. *Rooms from: £75 Rydal Rd., Keswick 015394/33679 www.roomsattheapplepie.co.uk 8 rooms No meals.*

$$ HOTEL **Waterhead.** If you want hotel benefits, Waterhead is a good bet: near the water's edge, with good views, it's comfortable and spotless, with excellent service and amenities that include music docks, underfloor heating, espresso machines, and even the occasional trouser press. **Pros:** welcoming and professional; a stone's throw from Lake Windermere. **Cons:** style is a little dated; a walk from Ambleside's best pubs and restaurants. *Rooms from: £139 Lake Rd. 015394/32566 www.waterhead-hotel.co.uk 41 rooms Breakfast.*

SPORTS AND THE OUTDOORS

The fine walks in the vicinity include routes north to Rydal Mount or southeast over Wansfell to Troutbeck. Each walk will take up to a half day, there and back. Ferries from Bowness-on-Windermere dock at Ambleside's harbor, called Waterhead. **TIP→ To escape the crowds, rent a rowboat at the harbor for an hour or two.**

RYDAL

1 mile northwest of Ambleside.

The village of Rydal, on the small glacial lake called Rydal Water, is rich with Wordsworthian associations.

10

One of the Lake District's literary landmarks, Dove Cottage near Grasmere was where poet William Wordsworth wrote many famous works.

EXPLORING

Dora's Field. One famous beauty spot linked with Wordsworth is Dora's Field, below Rydal Mount next to the church of **St. Mary's** (where you can still see the poet's pew). In spring the field is awash in yellow daffodils, planted by William Wordsworth and his wife in memory of their beloved daughter Dora, who died in 1847. ✉ *A591.*

Rydal Mount. If there's one poet associated with the Lake District, it is Wordsworth, who made his home at Rydal Mount from 1813 until his death. Wordsworth and his family moved to these grand surroundings when he was nearing the height of his career, and his descendants still live here, surrounded by his furniture, his books, his barometer, and portraits. You can see the study in which he worked, Dorothy's bedroom, and the 4½-acre garden, laid out by the poet himself, that gave him so much pleasure. ■ **TIP→ Wordsworth's favorite footpath can be found on the hill past White Moss Common and the River Rothay.** Spend an hour or two walking the paths and you may understand why the great poet composed most of his verse in the open air. A tearoom in the former saddlery provides cakes and drinks; in winter it moves into the dining room. ✉ *Off A591* ☎ *015394/33002* 🌐 *www.rydalmount.co.uk* 🎟 *£7.25; garden only £4.50* ⏲ *Mar.–Oct., daily 9:30–5; Nov., Dec., and Feb., Wed.–Sun. 11–4.*

GRASMERE

3 miles north of Rydal, 4 miles northwest of Ambleside.

Fodor's Choice ★ Lovely Grasmere, on a tiny, wood-fringed lake, is made up of crooked lanes in which Westmorland slate–built cottages hold shops and galleries. The village is a focal point for literary and landscape associations because this area was the adopted heartland of the Romantic poets, notably Wordsworth and Coleridge. The Vale of Grasmere has changed over the years, but many features Wordsworth wrote about are still visible. Wordsworth lived on the town's outskirts for almost 50 years and described the area as "the loveliest spot that man hath ever known."

GETTING HERE AND AROUND

On the main A591 between Ambleside and Keswick, Grasmere is easily reached by car.

ESSENTIALS

Visitor Information Grasmere Tourist Information Centre. ✉ *Church Stile* ☎ *015394/35665* 🌐 *www.nationaltrust.org.uk/allan-bank-and-grasmere.*

EXPLORING

FAMILY Fodor's Choice ★ **Allan Bank.** Rope swings on the grounds, picnics in atmospheric old rooms, free tea and coffee, and huge blackboards you can write on: Allan Bank is unlike most other historic houses cared for by the National Trust. On a hill above the lake near Grasmere village, this grand house was once home to poet William Wordsworth as well as to Canon Rawnsley, the founder of the National Trust. Seriously damaged by fire in 2011, it has been partially restored but also left deliberately undecorated. It offers a much less formal experience than other stops on the Wordsworth trail. There are frequent activities for both children and adults: arts and crafts but also music and astronomy. Red squirrels can be seen on the 30-minute woodland walk through the beautiful grounds. ✉ *Off A591* ☎ *015394/35143* 🌐 *www.nationaltrust.org.uk/allan-bank-and-grasmere* 🎫 *£5.70* ⏲ *Mid-Mar.–Dec., daily 10–5.*

Dove Cottage and Wordsworth Museum. William Wordsworth lived in Dove Cottage from 1799 to 1808, a prolific and happy time for the poet. During this time he wrote some of his most famous works, including "Ode: Intimations of Immortality" and *The Prelude*. Built in the early 17th century as an inn, this tiny, dim, and, in some places, dank, house is beautifully preserved, with an oak-paneled hall and floors of Westmorland slate. It first opened to the public in 1891 and remains as it was when Wordsworth lived here with his sister, Dorothy, and wife, Mary. Bedrooms and living areas contain much of Wordsworth's furniture and many personal belongings. Coleridge was a frequent visitor, as was Thomas De Quincey, best known for his 1822 autobiographical masterpiece *Confessions of an English Opium-Eater*. De Quincey moved in after the Wordsworths left. You visit the house on a timed guided tour, and the ticket includes admission to the spacious, modern Wordsworth Museum, which documents the poet's life and the literary contributions of Wordsworth and the Lake Poets. The museum includes space for major art exhibitions. The **Jerwood Centre,** open to researchers by appointment, houses 50,000 letters, first editions, and

10

CLOSE UP

Poetry, Prose, and the Lakes

The Lake District's beauty has whetted the creativity of many a famous poet and artist over the centuries. Here's a quick rundown of some of the writers inspired by the area's vistas.

William Wordsworth (1770–1850), one of the first English Romantics, redefined poetry by replacing the mannered style of his predecessors with a more conversational style. Many of his greatest works, such as *The Prelude,* draw directly from his experiences in the Lake District, where he spent the first 20 and last 50 years of his life. Wordsworth and his work had an enormous effect on Coleridge, Keats, Shelley, Byron, and countless other writers. Explore his homes in Cockermouth, Rydal, and Grasmere, among other sites.

John Ruskin (1819–1900), writer, art critic, and early conservationist, was an impassioned champion of new ways of seeing. He defended contemporary artists such as William Turner and the Pre-Raphaelites. His five-volume masterwork, *Modern Painters,* changed the role of the art critic from that of approver or naysayer to that of interpreter. Stop by Coniston to see his home and the Ruskin Museum.

Thomas De Quincey (1785–1859) wrote essays whose impressionistic style influenced many 19th-century writers, including Poe and Baudelaire. His most famous work, *Confessions of an English Opium-Eater* (1822), is an imaginative memoir of his young life, which indeed included opium addiction. He settled in Grasmere in 1809.

Beatrix Potter (1866–1943) never had a formal education; instead, she spent her childhood studying nature. Her love of the outdoors, and Lakeland scenery in particular, influenced her delightfully illustrated children's books, including *The Tale of Peter Rabbit* and *The Tale of Jemima Puddle-Duck.* Potter also became a noted conservationist who donated land to the National Trust. The story of her life was made into the 2006 film *Miss Potter,* starring Renée Zellweger and Ewan McGregor. Today you can visit Hill Top, the writer-artist's home in Hawkshead.

manuscripts. Afternoon tea is served at a café next to the car park. ✉ *A591, south of Grasmere* ☎ *015394/35544* 🌐 *www.wordsworth.org.uk* 🎫 *£7.50* ⏲ *Mar.–Oct., daily 9:30–5; Nov.–Feb., daily 9:30–4:30.*

QUICK BITES

Heidi's. This bustling, cozy little café and deli is lined with jars of locally made jams and chutneys. Bang in the center of Grasmere, it's great for coffee and a homemade pastry or flapjack (bars made with syrup, butter, and oats). ✉ ***Red Lion Sq.*** ☎ ***015394/35248*** 🌐 ***www.heidisgrasmerelodge.co.uk.***

St. Oswald's. William Wordsworth, his wife Mary, his sister Dorothy, and four of his children are buried in the churchyard of this church on the River Rothay. The poet planted eight of the yew trees here. As you leave the churchyard, stop at the Gingerbread Shop, in a tiny cottage, for a special local treat. ✉ *Stock La.* 🌐 *www.grasmereandrydal.org.uk.*

WHERE TO EAT

$$ BRITISH Fodor's Choice ★ **The Jumble Room.** A small stone building dating to the 18th century, Grasmere's first shop is now a friendly, fashionable, and colorful restaurant, with children's books, bold animal paintings, and hanging lamps. A dedicated local fan base means the place always buzzes, and the owners' enthusiasm is contagious. The food is an eclectic mix of international and traditional British: excellent fish-and-chips and beefsteak appear on the menu with polenta gnocchi with beetroot, pesto, and thyme-roasted pumpkin. Lunches are lighter and cheaper, with good soups and homemade puddings; bread is baked fresh every day. Note: hours change frequently, so call ahead. *Average main: £17 Langdale Rd. 015394/35188 www.thejumbleroom.co.uk Closed Mon. and Tues. No lunch in winter.*

$$ MODERN BRITISH Fodor's Choice ★ **Tweedies Bar.** One of the region's best gastro-pubs, Tweedies attracts many locals as well as visitors. Delicious updated British classics include pork belly with sage mash, black pudding, fennel, apple, and radish salad. Everything is served in a smart, cozy, wood-filled contemporary pub with mellow music, flickering candles, a slate floor, and a fireplace. The Lodge Restaurant in the Dale Lodge Hotel next door serves the same menu in a more formal setting. Several of Cumbria's best beers are on tap alongside a good selection of world beers. *Average main: £16 Langdale Rd. 015394/35300 www.tweediesbargrasmere.co.uk.*

WHERE TO STAY

$ B&B/INN **Banerigg House.** A cozy family home less than a mile south of the village, Banerigg House has unfussy, well-appointed rooms, most with lake views. **Pros:** very welcoming hosts; good value for single rooms; canoes available. **Cons:** a little out of town; the house has an awkward turn onto the busy road. *Rooms from: £82 Lake Rd. 015394/35204 www.guesthouse-cumbria.co.uk 6 rooms, 5 with bath Breakfast.*

$ B&B/INN Fodor's Choice ★ **Heidi's Grasmere Lodge.** Small but sumptuous, this lodging has a distinctly feminine sensibility, with floral wallpaper, curly steel lamps, and painted woodwork. **Pros:** chic bathrooms with whirlpool tubs; warm welcome. **Cons:** no children allowed; so pristine you may worry about your muddy boots. *Rooms from: £89 Red Lion Sq. 015394/35248 www.heidisgrasmerelodge.co.uk 6 rooms Breakfast.*

$$$ B&B/INN **Moss Grove Organic.** A Victorian building in the heart of Grasmere, the chic and spacious Moss Grove Organic puts an emphasis on its environmental credentials. **Pros:** plenty of room; huge chunky furniture; modern design with a conscience. **Cons:** tight parking; not the place for a big fry-up breakfast. *Rooms from: £179 Red Lion Sq. 015394/35251 www.mossgrove.com 11 rooms Breakfast.*

$$ B&B/INN **Raise View.** Out of the center of Grasmere toward Dunmail Raise (hence the name), Raise View has some of Grasmere's more stylish rooms and a reputation for hospitality. **Pros:** high quality, homey accommodation; gorgeous views; generous breakfast. **Cons:** on the edge of town; usually need to book well in advance. *Rooms from: £116 White Bridge 015394/35215 www.raiseviewhouse.co.uk 7 rooms Breakfast.*

SHOPPING

Fodor's Choice ★ **Grasmere Gingerbread Shop.** The smells wafting across the churchyard draw many people to the Grasmere Gingerbread Shop. Since 1854 Sarah Nelson's gingerbread has been sold from this cramped 17th-century cottage, which was once the village school. The delicious treats, still made from a secret recipe, are sold by costumed ladies and packed into attractive tins for the journey home or to eat right away. ✉ *Church Cottage* ☎ *015394/35428* 🌐 *www.grasmeregingerbread.co.uk.*

SPORTS AND THE OUTDOORS

Loughrigg Terrace. The most panoramic views of lake and village are from the south of Grasmere, from the bare slopes of Loughrigg Terrace, reached along a well-signposted track on the western side of the lake or through the woods from parking lots on the A591 between Grasmere and Rydal Water. It's less than an hour's walk from the village, though your stroll can be extended by continuing around Rydal Water, passing Rydal Mount, detouring onto White Moss Common before returning to Dove Cottage and Grasmere, a 4-mile (three-hour) walk in total. ✉ *Grasmere.*

ELTERWATER AND THE LANGDALES

2½ miles south of Grasmere, 4 miles west of Ambleside.

The delightful village of Elterwater, at the eastern end of the Great Langdale Valley on B5343, is a good stop for hikers. It's barely more than a cluster of houses around a village green, but from here you can choose from a selection of excellent circular walks. Great Langdale winds up past hills known as the Langdale Pikes towards Great End and England's highest hill, Scafell Pike. To the south, Little Langdale is another of Cumbria's most beautiful valleys with walks aplenty. At its head, the high passes of Wrynose and Hardknott lead west across wild fells to Eskdale and one of the most beautiful and remote lakes, Wast Water. Beyond that, at Ravenglass, the national park reaches all the way to the Cumbrian coast. Between the two Langdales are plenty more great walking opportunities over fells and past far-flung beauty spots such as Blea Tarn.

WHERE TO EAT AND STAY

$ BRITISH ✕ **Britannia Inn.** At this 500-year-old pub, restaurant, and inn in the heart of superb walking country, antiques, comfortable chairs, and prints and oil paintings furnish the cozy, beamed public rooms. The whole family can relax with a bar meal and Cumbrian ale on the terrace while taking in the village green and the rolling scenery beyond. The hearty traditional British food—from grilled sea bass fillet to thyme-breaded Brie—is popular with locals, as are the many whiskies and ales, including a specially brewed Britannia Gold beer. The nine simple guest rooms (eight of which are en suite) are more modern in style, with large, comfy beds. Accommodation includes use of the nearby Langdale Spa's pool, sauna, and fitness room. [$] *Average main: £13* ✉ *B5343* ☎ *015394/37210* 🌐 *thebritanniainn.com.*

$ BRITISH ✕ **Sticklebarn.** The National Trust owns other pubs, but Sticklebarn is the first one it has run. With its own water supply and hydroelectric power, the pub's aim is sustainability. The kitchen uses as much produce as possible from the immediate area, and makes its own gin and vodka. Most of the menu is traditional pub fare—burgers, macaroni and cheese, and lamb stew, for example—aimed at the Langdale walkers that fill the rustic, wood-beamed dining room. Tables spill out onto the terrace in sunny weather. There's also a wood-fired pizza oven. *Average main: £12 Great Langdale 01539/437356 www.nationaltrust.org.uk/sticklebarn-and-great-langdale.*

$$ HOTEL **Old Dungeon Ghyll Hotel.** There's no more comforting stop after a day outdoors than the Hiker's Bar of this 300-year-old hotel at the head of the Great Langdale Valley. **Pros:** ideally situated for walking; wonderfully isolated; spectacular views all around. **Cons:** no-nonsense approach not to everyone's taste. *Rooms from: £116 Off B5343, Great Langdale 015394/37272 www.odg.co.uk 12 rooms Some meals.*

SPORTS AND THE OUTDOORS

There are access points to Langdale Fell from several spots along B5343, the main road; look for information boards at local parking places. You can also stroll up the river valley or embark on more energetic hikes to Stickle Tarn or to one of the summits of the Langdale Pikes. Beyond the Old Dungeon Ghyll Hotel, the Great Langdale Valley splits in two around a hill known as the Band—a path up its spine has particularly good views back down over the valley and can be continued to the summit of Scafell Pike.

CONISTON

5 miles south of Elterwater.

This small lake resort and boating center attracts climbers to the steep peak of the **Old Man of Coniston** (2,635 feet), which towers above the slate-roof houses. It also has sites related to John Ruskin. Quieter than Windermere, Coniston is a good introduction to the pastoral and watery charms of the area, though the small town itself can get crowded in summer.

GETTING HERE AND AROUND

The Coniston Launch connects Coniston Pier with Ruskin's home at Brantwood and some other stops around the lake, offering hourly service (£10.50 for a day-long, "hop-on, hop-off" ticket; £17.15 including entry to Brantwood) on its wooden Ruskin and Ransome launches.

ESSENTIALS

Visitor Information Coniston Launch. *Coniston 017687/75753 www.conistonlaunch.co.uk.* **Coniston Tourist Information Centre.** *Ruskin Ave. 015394/41533 www.conistontic.org.*

EXPLORING

Fodor's Choice ★ **Brantwood.** On the eastern shore of Coniston Water, Brantwood was the cherished home of John Ruskin (1819–1900), the noted Victorian artist, writer, critic, and social reformer, after 1872. The rambling 18th-century house (with Victorian alterations) is on a 250-acre estate that stretches high above the lake. Here, alongside mementos such as his

Continued on page 618

DID YOU KNOW?
The rewards of a hike to Catbells include panoramic views that are beautiful at any time of year. Derwentwater stretches before you, and to the north are the town of Keswick and the mountains of Skiddaw and Blencathra.

HIKING IN THE LAKE DISTRICT

by Julius Honnor

From easy strolls around lakes to mountain climbs, the Lake District has some of England's best hiking. The landscape is generally accessible but also spectacular, with crashing streams cascading from towering mountains into the rivers and lakes that define the region. The scenery that inspired Wordsworth and Ruskin, among many others, is best experienced on an exhilarating walk.

With its highest mountain topping out at just 3,209 feet, the Lake District has peaks that are sometimes sniffed at by hardcore hikers, but they provide a stunning and not always benevolent setting. In winter the peaks are often ice- and snow-bound, and even routes at lower levels can occasionally be impassable.

There is plenty of variety to suit all abilities and enthusiasms, and almost everywhere you go in the national park you'll come across wooden footpath signs pointing the way over stiles and across fields. Paths are usually well maintained and, especially in summer, the most popular trails can be busy with booted walking hordes. Many people don't venture far from their cars, however, and peace and solitude are usually only a hillside or two away.

Many lakes and tarns (small mountain lakes) have paths that skirt their edges, though to see the best of the region you should head upward into the fells (mountains) and valleys, where the landscape becomes increasingly grand. Some of the best routes combine a boat ride with a walk up a fellside. When your walk is over, be sure to reward yourself with a pint at the pub.

Above: View of Troutbeck Park, a farm near Troutbeck that writer Beatrix Potter left to the National Trust

CHOOSE YOUR BEST DAY HIKE

Trails are abundant in the Lake District: you can walk just about anywhere, but a little planning will be rewarded. It's worthwhile to buy a good Ordnance Survey map, too. The routes included here, from 90 minutes to 5 hours, all show the national park at its best, from the southern lakes to the wilder, bleaker northern lakes. A couple of the trails are fairly popular, well-trodden routes; others take you off the most beaten paths. Several include a boat trip for extra enjoyment—just don't miss the last boat home.

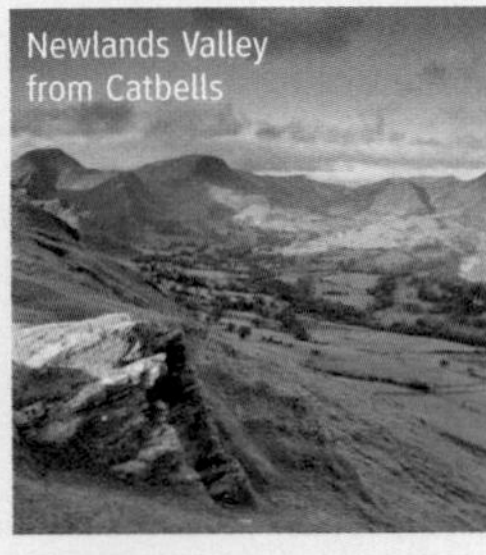
Newlands Valley from Catbells

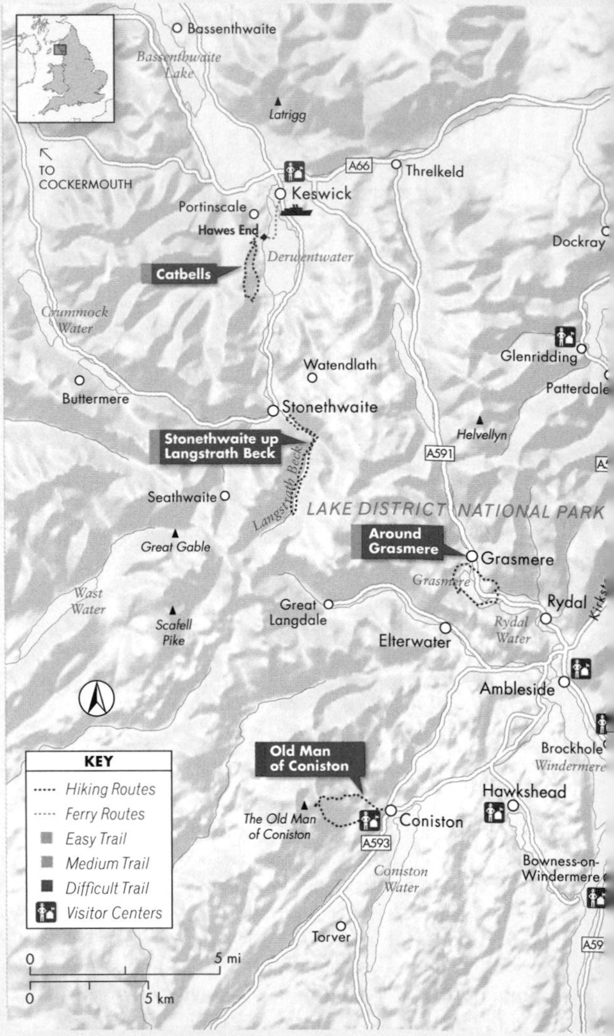

CATBELLS

Medium; 3.6 miles walking, plus boat ride to and from Keswick; 1 hour, 30 minutes walking
Starting point: Hawes End

This classic, popular Lakes route climbs the long, fairly gently sloping hill of Catbells, above Derwentwater. You'll need to catch the ferry from Keswick to the beginning of the route at Hawes End.

From the ferry landing stage, climb straight uphill before heading right (south) along the spine of the hill to the summit. From Catbells, the views over Derwenwater and beyond to the high fells of Skiddaw and Blencathra are breathtaking. Take the lower path, nearer the lake, on the return in order to make this a circular route. The route can be

Borrowdale

On Pillar mountain, western Lake District

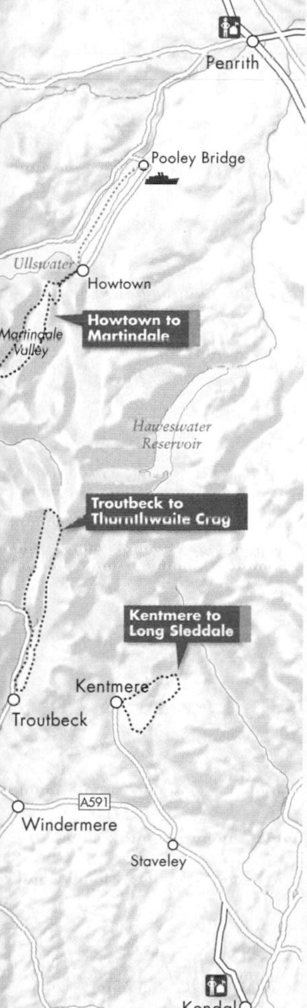

shortened by catching a boat back from High Brandelhow or Low Brandelhow (other landing stages) instead of Hawes End.

STONETHWAITE UP LANGSTRATH BECK

Easy; 6 miles; 2 hours, 30 minutes
Starting point: Stonethwaite

In the high valleys in the middle of the Lake District, rivers become streams and wind through a wonderfully wild, largely treeless landscape away from the lakes themselves. Running south from Derwentwater, Borrowdale is one of the most beautiful valleys around, but for even more spectacular walking country continue to the hamlet of Stonethwaite, from where the road becomes a track and then a path as it leads up beside the beck, the valley opening out into moorland. At the bottom of the valley, the climb is a fairly gentle one.

Red deer

About 3 miles upstream, cross a bridge and return on the other side of the stream. The Langstrath Inn makes a good food and drink spot at the end of the walk.

TROUTBECK TO THORNTHWAITE CRAG

Difficult; 9.8 miles; 4–5 hours
Starting point: Troutbeck

Windermere is more known for its boating, but you can find great mountain routes. Starting in the village of Troutbeck, 3 miles north of Windermere, this walk drops down into the valley, following the stream of Hagg Gill and climbing around a hill known as the Troutbeck Tongue. The trail then rises onto the ridge of Thornthwaite Crag, from where there are vertiginous views. Parts of this upper section are steep. For the return to Troutbeck, head west into the valley of the Trout Beck (stream) itself. Back in the village of Troutbeck, the Queen's Head Hotel is a great pub for food and drink.

KENTMERE TO LONG SLEDDALE

Medium; 4.5 miles; 2 hours, 30 minutes
Starting point: Kentmere

Looking away from Martindale, toward Ullswater.

Easily accessible from popular centers in the south of the region such as Windermere or Kendal, Kentmere and Long Sleddale are nevertheless in a part of the national park that many visitors bypass in their haste to get to the lakes—and that's a shame. These two valleys are beautiful examples of rural Cumbria, and the easy climb from one to another has some great views.

For a circular route, head south along the road from the village of Kentmere before heading left up the hill and across high moorland and down into the grand valley of Long Sleddale. The trail is a pleasant loop.

HOWTOWN TO MARTINDALE
Medium; 7.6 miles plus optional boat ride from Pooley Bridge; 3 hours, 30 minutes plus 25-minute boat ride
Starting point: Howtown

To get to Howtown, you can drive the long, narrow road down the eastern side of Ullswater; but to arrive at this spot in style, catch an antique Ullswater Steamer from Pooley Bridge at the lake's northern end.

Martindale is a magically hidden valley, enclosed on all sides by large fells. Climbing the steep switchback road up the bare hillside of Hallin Fell to the pass from the hamlet of Howtown, there is nothing to suggest the beautifully pastoral landscape beyond. Sheep graze at lower levels; higher up the steep sides of the valley are wild and rocky.

To turn this into a circular route, turn left at the top of the valley and return along the ridge of Beda Fell. In Howtown, the eponymous hotel serves food and drink and will make you a take-out lunch.

AROUND GRASMERE
Easy; 3.4 miles (can easily be extended to go around Rydal Water); 1 hour, 30 minutes
Starting point: Grasmere village

Rich with literary and artistic traditions, Grasmere is a bijou little lake easily walked around in an afternoon.

Starting in the village, where there is parking, head counter-clockwise around the lake, skirting the lower edge of Loughrigg Terrace. At the southeastern end of the lake, follow the stream through woods that link Grasmere to Rydal Water. If you want something a little longer, the walk can be extended around Rydal before you cross the A591 and return to Grasmere across White Moss Common.

In Grasmere, Tweedies Bar is a good place for a post-stroll pint.

OLD MAN OF CONISTON
Difficult; 4.6 miles; 2 hours, 30 minutes to 3 hours
Starting point: Coniston village

Of all the area's classic peaks, the Old Man of Coniston is one of the most accessible. Though it's a

LAKELAND LINGO

If someone tells you to walk along the "beck" to the "force" and then climb the "fell" to the "tarn," you've just been told to hike along the stream or river (beck) to the waterfall (force) before climbing the hill or mountain (fell) to reach a small mountain lake (tarn).

You should also keep in mind that town or place names in the Lake District can be the same as the name of the lake on which the town stands. For example, Windermere is both the town and the lake itself—a "mere" is a lake in Old English.

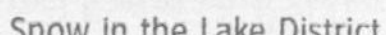
Snow in the Lake District

View of the Langdale Fells

fairly steep route that can be difficult in winter, the paths are well-trodden and well-maintained and it doesn't require any climbing to reach the summit, 2,634 feet up. From the top on a clear day, there are extraordinary views down to Coniston Water and around and beyond the Furness Fells. Set off from the center of the village of Coniston, where the Black Bull Inn offers good hearty food and some excellent ales. Multiple paths to the summit make it easy to turn the walk into a circular route.

PREPARING FOR YOUR HIKE

CHOOSING A HIKE

A glance at a map of the Lake District National Park reveals a lacework mesh of footpaths; stop your car at random on a country road and there will probably be a path somewhere nearby. In the Lake District meticulous planning is not necessarily required in order to go for a walk: possibilities for short strolls abound.

The walks suggested offer good options; for other choices and for maps, stop in any town visitor information office or at the Lake District National Park Visitor Centre at Brockhole. There are trails from this visitor center. You can also join a guided hike. *(For more information on these offices, see the towns in this chapter and the Lake District Planner.)*

WHAT TO WEAR

Check the weather, but expect the unexpected. Good clothing, and clothing for rain, is essential: even at the height of summer, wet weather can roll in from the west and spoil a sunny day. Higher up, too, temperatures are noticeably colder than at lake level, and it's usually much breezier. Generally a good pair of walking boots will suffice, and for lakeside walks you'd probably get by with flat-soled shoes. For the highest routes, snow and ice in winter can linger until spring and a set of slip-on spikes can be useful. The national park is overflowing with shops selling walking clothes, maps, and equipment.

WHAT TO BRING

Carry plenty of water and lightweight, high-energy food—or whatever you want for a picnic. Kendal mint cake is a favorite snack. Don't forget sunscreen and insect repellent. Bring a map: Ordnance Survey maps, available in area bookstores and visitor centers, are the best.

mahogany desk, are Ruskin's own paintings, drawings, and books. On display is art that this great connoisseur collected, and in cerebral corners such as the Ideas Room visitors are encouraged to think about meaning and change. Ruskin's Rocks explores his fascinations with stones and music with a brilliant bit of modern technology. A video on Ruskin's life shows the lasting influence of his thoughts, and the Severn Studio has rotating art exhibitions. Ruskin himself laid out the extensive grounds; take time to explore the gardens and woodland walks, which include some multi-layered significance: Ziggy Zaggy, for example, originally a garden built by Ruskin to reflect Dante's Purgatorial Mount, is now an allegory of the seven deadly sins. Brantwood hosts a series of classical concerts on some Saturdays as well as talks, guided walks, and study days. ✉ *Off B5285* ☎ *015394/41396* 🌐 *www.brantwood.org.uk* 🎫 *£7.50; gardens only £5.20* ⏲ *Mid-Mar.–Nov., daily 10:30–5; Dec.–mid-Mar., Wed.–Sun. 10:30–4.*

Coniston Boating Centre. The National Trust's restored Victorian steam yacht and the slightly more utilitarian Coniston Launch both leave from the town's spruced up waterside satellite, a 15-minute stroll from the center. There's a parking lot, a smart café, and various boat and bike hire options, too. Originally launched in 1859 and restored in the 1970s, the Steam Yacht (🌐 *www.nationaltrust.org.uk/gondola*) runs between Coniston Pier, Brantwood, and Park-a-Moor at the south end of Coniston Water daily from April through October (half-lake cruise £11). The Coniston Launch (🌐 *www.conistonlaunch.co.uk*) runs similar routes and is marginally cheaper, though also a little less romantic. Both will get you across the lake to Brantwood, and a stop at Monk Coniston jetty, at the lake's northern tip, connects to the footpaths through the Monk Coniston Estate and the beauty spot of Tarn Hows. ✉ *Coniston Pier* ☎ *015394/41366* 🌐 *www.conistonboatingcentre.co.uk.*

Coniston Water. The lake came to prominence in the 1930s when Arthur Ransome made it the setting for *Swallows and Amazons,* one of a series of novels about a group of children and their adventures. The lake is about 5 miles long, a tempting stretch that drew Donald Campbell here in 1959 to set a water-speed record of 260 mph. He was killed when trying to beat it in 1967. His body and the wreckage of *Bluebird K7* were retrieved from the lake in 2001. Campbell is buried in St. Andrew's church in Coniston, and a stone memorial on the village green commemorates him. ✉ *Coniston.*

Monk Coniston Estate. Two miles north of Coniston on the A593, just past Beatrix Potter's beautifully situated Yew Tree Farm, is a small National Trust car park from where paths lead up through oak woods beside the tumbling stream of Tom Gill to Tarn Hows, a celebrated Lake District beauty spot, albeit a man-made one, created when the gill was dammed in the mid-19th century. The paths are steep in places but two waterfalls make it well worth the effort. ✉ *Coniston.*

Ruskin Museum. This repository of fascinating and thought-provoking manuscripts, personal items, and watercolors by John Ruskin illuminates his thinking and influence. There is also a focus on speedboat racer Donald Campbell; his *Bluebird K7,* dragged up from Coniston

Water, will eventually rest here once it has been painstakingly put back together. Good local-interest exhibits include copper mining, geology, lace, and more. Upstairs, the Dawson Gallery occasionally hosts high-profile artists. ✉ *Yewdale Rd.* ☎ *015394/41164* 🌐 *www.ruskinmuseum.com* 🎫 *£6* 🕑 *Mid-Mar.–mid-Nov., daily 10–5:30; mid-Nov.–mid-Mar., Wed.–Sun. 10:30–3:30.*

WHERE TO EAT AND STAY

$ BRITISH ✕ **Black Bull Inn.** Attached to the Coniston Brewing Company, whose ales are on tap here, the Black Bull is an old-fashioned pub in the heart of the village. It can feel a little dated but it's a good pick for simple, hearty food and exemplary beer. Old photos of Donald Campbell's boat *Bluebird* decorate the walls, and there are wooden beams and benches. The menu lists daily specials as well as sandwiches for lunch or shrimp from Morecambe Bay. $ *Average main: £10* ✉ *Coppermines Rd.* ☎ *015394/41335* 🌐 *www.conistonbrewery.com.*

$ BRITISH Fodor's Choice ★ ✕ **Jumping Jenny.** Named after Ruskin's beloved boat, the wood-beamed tearoom at Brantwood offers an elevated mix of classical music and delicious homemade cakes. It occupies the converted coach house and has a log fire and lake views. Pop in for morning coffee, lunch (sophisticated soups such as carrot and celeriac, pastas, sandwiches, and salads), or afternoon tea with several varieties of flapjack. You can sit on the terrace in season for a great view across Coniston Water. $ *Average main: £10* ✉ *Off B5285* ☎ *015394/41715* 🌐 *www.jumpingjenny.net* 🕑 *No dinner. Closed Mon. and Tues. in winter.*

$$ HOTEL Fodor's Choice ★ 🏨 **Bank Ground Farm.** Used by Arthur Ransome as the setting for *Swallows and Amazons*, 15th-century Bank Ground is beautifully situated on the eastern shore of Coniston Water, opposite the village of Coniston on the western shore. **Pros:** stunning lake views; homey atmosphere; traditional welcome. **Cons:** a fair walk from the village. $ *Rooms from: £100* ✉ *Off B5285* ☎ *015394/41264* 🌐 *www.bankground.com* 🕑 *Guesthouse closed Nov.–Easter* 🛏 *7 rooms, 4 cottages* 🍽 *Breakfast.*

$ B&B/INN 🏨 **Lakeland House.** In the middle of Coniston, Lakeland House has smart, modern rooms with bold wallpaper, beamed ceilings, and slate-floored bathrooms. **Pros:** café downstairs means drinks and snacks are never far away; good value. **Cons:** not as homey as a traditional B&B. $ *Rooms from: £85* ✉ *Tilberthwaite Ave., Keswick* ☎ *015394/41303* 🌐 *www.lakelandhouse.co.uk* 🛏 *12 rooms* 🍽 *Breakfast.*

10

SHOPPING

Heritage Meats. Once owned by Beatrix Potter, Yew Tree Farm is nestled in some especially attractive hills. The owners have a conservation-based approach to farming and sell great free-range meat. If you're staying nearby in a self-catering cottage, ring ahead to arrange to pick up some Herdwick chops or wild Lakeland game. ✉ *A593* ☎ *015394/41433* 🌐 *www.heritagemeats.co.uk.*

SPORTS AND THE OUTDOORS

HIKING

Steep tracks lead up from the village to the **Old Man of Coniston.** The trail starts near the Sun Hotel on Brow Hill and goes past an old copper mine to the peak, which you can reach in about two hours. It's one of the

Lake District's most satisfying hikes—not too arduous but high enough to feel a sense of accomplishment and get fantastic views (west to the sea, south to Morecambe Bay, and east to Windermere). Experienced hikers include the peak in a seven-hour circular walk from the village, also taking in the heights and ridges of Swirl How and Wetherlam.

HAWKSHEAD

3 miles east of Coniston.

In the Vale of Esthwaite, this small market town is a pleasing hodgepodge of tiny squares, cobbled lanes, and whitewashed houses. There's a good deal more history here than in most local villages, however. The Hawkshead Courthouse, just outside town, was built by the monks of Furness Abbey in the 15th century. Hawkshead later derived much wealth from the wool trade, which flourished here in the 17th and 18th centuries.

As a thriving market center, Hawkshead could afford to maintain the **Hawkshead Grammar School,** at which William Wordsworth was a pupil from 1779 to 1787; he carved his name on a desk inside, now on display. In the village, Ann Tyson's House claims the honor of having provided the young William with lodgings. The twin draws of Wordsworth and Beatrix Potter—apart from her home, Hill Top, there's a Potter gallery—conspire to make Hawkshead crowded year-round.

GETTING HERE AND AROUND

Hawkshead is east of Coniston on B5285 and south of Ambleside via B5286. An alternative route is to cross Windermere via the car ferry from Ferry Nab, south of Bowness. Local buses link the village to others nearby.

ESSENTIALS

Visitor Information Hawkshead Tourist Information Centre. ✉ *Main St.* ☎ *015394/36946* 🌐 *www.hawksheadtouristinfo.org.uk.*

EXPLORING

FAMILY Fodor's Choice ★ **Beatrix Potter Gallery.** In the 17th-century solicitor's offices formerly used by Potter's husband, the Beatrix Potter Gallery displays a selection of the artist-writer's original illustrations, watercolors, and drawings. There's also information about her interest in conservation and her early support of the National Trust. The house looks almost as it would have in her day, though with touch screens in wooden frames and a children's play area upstairs. Admission is by timed ticket when the place gets busy. ✉ *Main St.* ☎ *015394/36355* 🌐 *www.nationaltrust.org.uk/beatrix-potter-gallery* 🎫 *£5.40* ⏲ *Mid-Feb.–mid-Mar., Sat.–Thurs. 10:30–3:30; mid-Mar.–Oct., Sat.–Thurs. 10:30–5.*

Fodor's Choice ★ **Hill Top.** Children's author and illustrator Beatrix Potter (1866–1943), most famous for her *Peter Rabbit* stories, called this place home. The house looks much the same as when Potter bequeathed it to the National Trust, and fans will recognize details such as the porch and garden gate, old kitchen range, Victorian dollhouse, and four-poster bed, which were depicted in the book illustrations. **■ TIP→ Admission to this often-crowded spot is by timed ticket; book in advance and**

Children's writer Beatrix Potter used details from her house at Hill Top, near Hawkshead, in the illustrations for her stories.

avoid summer weekends and school vacations. Hill Top lies 2 miles south of Hawkshead by car or foot, though you can also approach via the car ferry from Bowness-on-Windermere. ✉ *Off B5285, Near Sawrey* ☎ *015394/36269* 🌐 *www.nationaltrust.org.uk/hill-top* 🎟 *£9.50* ⏲ *House mid-Feb.–Mar., Sat.–Thurs. 10:30–3:30; Apr., May, Sept., and Oct., Sat.–Thurs. 10:30–4:30; June–Aug., Sat.–Thurs. 10–5:30. Gardens mid-Feb.–Mar., daily 10:15–4; Apr., May, Sept., and Oct., daily 10–5; June–Aug., daily 9:45–5:45; Nov. and Dec., daily 10–4.*

WHERE TO EAT

$ BRITISH Fodor's Choice ★ ✕ **Tower Bank Arms.** With a porch that appears in a Beatrix Potter story and a location just a rabbit's hop from the author's home, you might expect this pub to be something of a tourist trap. It's anything but. There's a slate floor, a crackling open fire, and a bar that stocks some of the best beers around, usually including some of the great ales from the nearby Barngates Brewery. There's a friendly welcome and the meals are tasty and copious, making use of local ingredients; the beef-and-ale stew is especially good. Four bedrooms upstairs (starting at £95) offer a good-value alternative to pricier lodgings. 💲 *Average main: £12* ✉ *Off B5285, Near Sawrey* ☎ *015394/36334* 🌐 *www.towerbankarms.co.uk.*

WHERE TO STAY

$$ HOTEL Fodor's Choice ★ 🏨 **Drunken Duck Inn.** After four centuries, this friendly old coaching inn remains an outstanding place for both food and lodging. **Pros:** superchic rural style; excellent dining and drinking. **Cons:** hunting paraphernalia may put you off your beer; can feel isolated. 💲 *Rooms from: £140* ✉ *Off B5286, Barngates* ☎ *015394/36347* 🌐 *www.drunkenduckinn.co.uk* 🛏 *16 rooms* 🍽 *Some meals.*

CLOSE UP

What's Real About Real Ale?

The English can be passionate about their drink, as the growing interest in real ale shows. It differs from other beers by the use of natural ingredients and the fact that it's matured by fermentation in the barrel from which the ale is served. The process doesn't use carbon dioxide, so pure taste wins out over fizz.

The **Directory of U.K. Real Ale Breweries** (*www.quaffale.org.uk*) lists 35 operating real-ale breweries in Cumbria, of which the Coniston Brewing Company, Barngates Brewery (at the Drunken Duck Inn), and Hawkshead (in Staveley, between Kendal and Windermere) are three of the best. Most real ales are caramel in color and hoppy, malty, and slightly bitter to taste. A pint of ale is the usual quantity to be consumed, though a half is acceptable; you can also find it in bottles.

Most pubs in the Lake District offer some sort of local brew—the better ones take enormous pride in their careful tending of the beer, from barrel to glass. Interested in the subject, or just in the taste? Check out the website of the **Campaign for Real Ale** (*www.camra.org.uk*).

$$$$ B&B/INN **Randy Pike.** Built in the 19th century as the shooting lodge for Wray Castle, Randy Pike is filled with stylish, imaginative, and playful touches. **Pros:** plenty of space; good food; big garden. **Cons:** a little out of the way; pricey rates. *Rooms from: £225* *Off B5286, between Outgate and Clappersgate* *015394/36088* *www.randypike.co.uk* *3 rooms* *Breakfast.*

$ B&B/INN Fodor's Choice ★ **Yewfield.** With the laid-back friendliness of a B&B and the sophisticated style of a country house, Yewfield is a very good value—especially if you can score one of the rooms at the front of the house with a great view across the valley. **Pros:** out-of-the-way location; pretty garden; apartments are great for weeklong stays. **Cons:** not good for families with young kids. *Rooms from: £98* *Hawkshead Hill* *015394/36765* *www.yewfield.co.uk* *Closed Dec. and Jan.* *19 rooms, 2 apartments* *Breakfast.*

SPORTS AND THE OUTDOORS

Grizedale Forest Park. Stretching southwest from Hawkshead and blanketing the hills between Coniston and Windermere, Grizedale Forest Park has a thick mix of oak, pine, and larch woods crisscrossed with biking and walking paths. Forty permanent outdoor sculptures are scattered beside the trails and more are planned. The **visitor center** has information, maps, a café, and an adventure playground. *Off B5286* *01229/860010* *www.forestry.gov.uk/grizedaleforestpark.*

Grizedale Mountain Bikes. If you have the urge to explore the trails of the national park, Grizedale Mountain Bikes rents all the right equipment from £25 per day. *Grizedale Forest Park Visitor Centre, off B5286* *01229/860369* *www.grizedalemountainbikes.co.uk.*

CARTMEL

17 miles south of Hawkshead.

The village of Cartmel is the southern Lakeland area's most attractive, set in a gentler Cumbrian landscape of hills and fields beyond the trees of Grizedale and the southern tip of Windermere. It comes alive when more than 20,000 people descend on Cartmel Racecourse for steeplechasing on holiday weekends in May and August. Dominating the town is the ancient priory, now the village church. **Market Square** has pubs, bookshops, and the village shop, rightly famed for its delicious sticky toffee pudding. Helped by the L'Enclume restaurant, the town has a large and growing foodie reputation and some excellent gourmet shops, including a great cheese shop.

EXPLORING

Cartmel Priory. Founded in 1190, the huge Cartmel Priory survived the dissolution of the monasteries in the 16th century because it was also the village church. Four monks and 10 villagers were hanged, however. The 25 wooden misericords are from 1440 and include a carved depiction of the Green Man, with a face made of leaves. ✉ *Priest La.* ☎ *015395/36261* 🌐 *www.cartmelpriory.org.uk* 🎫 *Free; tours £3* ⏲ *Daily 10–5:30. Tours Apr.–Oct., Wed. 11 and 2.*

Holker Hall. The red sandstone towers of Holker Hall rise above elegant English gardens. The Cavendish family still lives in the house, which has a fine cantilevered staircase and a library with more than 3,000 books; much of the house was rebuilt in Elizabethan style after an 1871 fire. Topiaries, a labyrinth, and an enormous lime tree are the highlights of the 25 acres of gardens. The three-day Holker Festival in early June celebrates the gardens and local culture and food. ✉ *Off A5278, Cark-in-Cartmel* ✢ *2 miles west of Cartmel* ☎ *015395/58328* 🌐 *www.holker.co.uk* 🎫 *House and gardens £12; gardens only £8* ⏲ *House Apr.–Oct., Sun.–Fri. 11–4. Gardens Mar.–Oct., Sun.–Fri. 10:30–4:30 (5:30 in July and Aug.).*

WHERE TO EAT

$$$$
MODERN BRITISH
Fodor's Choice ★

✕ **L'Enclume.** The village of Cartmel has earned a place on England's culinary map with this ambitious restaurant with rooms. The restaurant is in what was once a forge, now converted to a bright, contemporary, and airy space with dark wooden beams, stark white walls, and splashes of color. Chef Simon Rogan's innovative food incorporates long-forgotten herbs and cutting-edge techinques. The set menu (£120) comes with up to 12 courses; if that sounds like a bit much, go for the simpler lunch menu (£45). Dishes might include potatoes in onion ashes and lovage, or roast cauliflower with young squid and elderberry vinegar. Some things work better than others at this outpost of molecular gastronomy, but boredom is never a risk. Nearby Rogan and Company (🌐 *simonrogan.co.uk*), run by the same team, has a slightly less elevated menu. L'Enclume's 17 elegant rooms (from £99) are in three different buildings around the village. $ *Average main: £120* ✉ *Cavendish St.* ☎ *015395/36362* 🌐 *www.lenclume.co.uk/sr* ⏲ *No lunch Mon.* ✍ *Reservations essential.*

10

SHOPPING

Cartmel Cheeses. A huge range of delicious cheeses, mostly British, can be purchased in this welcoming, pungent little shop. Free tastings are often available. ✉ *1 Unsworth Yard* ☎ *015395/58623* 🌐 *www.cartmelcheeses.co.uk* ⏲ *Closed Mon. Oct.–Apr.*

Cartmel Village Shop. This fabulous delicatessen, famous for its deliciously rich sticky toffee pudding, is also a great place to purchase picnic provisions. ✉ *The Square* ☎ *015395/36280* 🌐 *www.cartmelvillageshop.co.uk.*

PENRITH AND THE NORTHERN LAKES

The scenery of the northern lakes is considerably more dramatic—some would say bleaker—than much of the landscape to the south, a change that becomes apparent on your way north from Kendal to Penrith. A 30-mile drive on the A6 takes you through the wild and desolate Shap Fells, which rise to a height of 1,304 feet. This is one of the most notorious moorland crossings in the country: even in summer it's a lonely place to be, and in winter, snow on the road can be dangerous. From Penrith the road leads to Ullswater, possibly the grandest of all the lakes; then there's a winding route west past Keswick, south through the marvelous Borrowdale Valley, and on to Cockermouth. Outside the main towns such as Keswick it can be easier to escape the summer crowds in the northern lakes.

PENRITH

30 miles north of Kendal.

The red-sandstone town of Penrith was the capital of old Cumbria, part of the Scottish kingdom of Strathclyde in the 9th and 10th centuries. It was rather neglected after the Normans arrived, and the Scots sacked it on several occasions. Penrith has been a thriving market town for centuries; the market still takes place on Tuesday, and it continues to be known for good shopping.

The tourist information center, in the Penrith Museum, has information about the historic town trail, which takes you through narrow byways to the plague stone on King Street, where food was left for the stricken, to St. Andrew's churchyard and its 1,000-year-old "hog back" tombstones (stones carved as stylized "houses of the dead"), and finally to the ruins of Penrith Castle.

GETTING HERE AND AROUND

Penrith is just off the M6, 30 miles north of Kendal and 100 miles north of Manchester. Both the M6 and the alternative A6 cross the Pennines spectacularly at Shap Fells. From Windermere you can reach Penrith by going over the Kirkstone Pass to Ullswater. There are some direct trains from Euston Station in London to Penrith; sometimes it's necessary to change.

ESSENTIALS

Visitor Information Penrith Tourist Information Centre. ✉ *Penrith Museum, Middlegate* ☎ *01768/867466* 🌐 *www.visiteden.co.uk.*

EXPLORING

TOP ATTRACTIONS

FAMILY **Lowther Castle.** On 130 acres of parkland and gardens, the 1806 Lowther Castle fell into disrepair during the second half of the 20th century. Once used as a chicken farm, this fairy-tale structure is currently being carefully restored. Its turrets can be seen from all over the grounds, which are carpeted with wildflowers, dotted with living willow sculptures, and filled with tree swings and other play areas for the kids. The gallery has ornate Italian plaster decoration, and the café is a fine spot for afternoon tea and cake. ✉ *Off A6, Lowther* ☎ *01931/712192* 🌐 *www.lowthercastle.org* 🎫 *£8* ⏲ *Daily 10–5.*

Fodor'sChoice ★ **The Watermill.** This fully functioning stone-ground flour mill is well worth a visit for its delicious baked goods and for a tour of the fascinating workings of the mill itself. There's been a mill here since the 13th century, and the current structure was built in 1760. Tours are officially self-guided (take an information sheet), but the miller will probably take a break to show you around. Just up the road is the Bronze Age stone circle of Long Meg and her Daughters. According to folklore, the 51 stones (27 of which are still upright) were a coven of witches turned to stone by a Scottish wizard. ✉ *Off A66, 6 miles northeast of Penrith, Little Salkeld* ☎ *01768/881523* 🌐 *www.organicmill.co.uk* ⏲ *Mid Jan.–Christmas, daily 10:30–5* ⏲ *£2.*

WORTH NOTING

Dalemain. Home of the Hasell family since 1679, Dalemain began with a 12th-century peel tower built to protect the occupants from raiding Scots, and is now a delightful hodgepodge of architectural styles. An imposing Georgian facade of local pink sandstone encompasses a medieval hall and extensions from the 16th through the 18th century. Inside are a magnificent oak staircase, furniture dating from the mid-17th century, a Chinese drawing room, a 16th-century room with intricate plasterwork, and many fine paintings, including masterpieces by Van Dyck. The gardens are worth a look, too, and deer roam the estate. At the end of winter, the house hosts the World Marmalade Awards and Festival. Dalemain is 3 miles southwest of Penrith. ✉ *A592* ☎ *017684/86450* 🌐 *www.dalemain.com* 🎫 *£11; gardens only £8* ⏲ *House Apr.–Sept., Sun.–Thurs. 11:15–4; Oct., Sun.–Thurs. 11:15–3. Gardens Apr.–Oct., Sun.–Thurs. 10:30–5; Nov.–mid-Dec., Sun.–Thurs. 11–3.*

Penrith Castle. The evocative remains of this 15th-century redbrick castle stand high above a steep, now-dry moat. Home of the maligned Richard, duke of Gloucester (later Richard III), who was responsible for keeping peace along the border, it was one of England's first lines of defense against the Scots. By the Civil War the castle was in ruins, and the townsfolk used some of the fallen stones to build their houses. The ruins stand in a park, across from the town's train station. ✉ *Off Castlegate* ☎ *0870/333–1181* 🌐 *www.english-heritage.org.uk* 🎫 *Free* ⏲ *June–Sept., daily 7:30 am–9 pm; Oct.–May, daily 7:30–4:30.*

Penrith Museum. In a 16th-century building that served as a school from 1670 to the 1970s, this museum contains neolithic axe heads, interesting fossils, and an informative film about the Cumbrian fells and fell walking. The Penrith Tourist Information Centre is here. ✉ *Middlegate* ☎ *01768/865105* 🌐 *www.eden.gov.uk/museum* 🎫 *Free* 🕙 *Apr.–Oct., Mon.–Sat. 10–5, Sun. 11–4; Nov.–Mar., Mon.–Sat. 10–5.*

FAMILY **Rheged.** Named for the Celtic kingdom of Cumbria, Rheged is a modern, grass-covered visitor center with activities for kids and some interesting free exhibits about the history, culture, and other aspects of the Lake District. A gallery hosts rotating art and photography exhibits, and a massive theater shows 3-D and large-format movies. Shops showcase Cumbrian food and drink and crafts, and three different cafés offer drinks and light meals. Rheged is 2 miles southwest of Penrith and 1 mile west of Junction 40 on the M6. ✉ *A66* ☎ *01768/868000* 🌐 *www.rheged.com* 🎫 *Free; movie £6.50* 🕙 *Daily 10–5:30.*

WHERE TO EAT AND STAY

$$ MODERN BRITISH ✕ **Four and Twenty.** High ceilings, shabby chic chairs, and old-fashioned filament bulbs in jars set the scene for this handsome conversion of what was once a bank: the restaurant's name references the financially themed nursery rhyme. Blue cheese soufflé, tenderloin of pork wrapped in pancetta, and passion-fruit cheesecake with dark chocolate sorbet are among the dishes rustled up in the open kitchen; the small bar has Estrella beer on tap. Book ahead, especially for weekend evenings. 💲 *Average main: £16* ✉ *42 King St.* ☎ *01768/210231* 🌐 *www.fourandtwentypenrith.co.uk* 🕙 *Closed Sun. and Mon.*

$$ BRITISH Fodor's Choice ★ ✕ **George and Dragon.** This pub and restaurant makes good use of local produce for tasty traditional dishes, including wild-mushroom and black-pudding fricassee. Sausages come from the Eden Valley, brown trout from the River Lowther, and many of the greens are grown in the gardens at Askham Hall. The inn is also a well-tended spot for a pint of local beer, with handsome slate floors, roaring wood fires, and hanging hops. Bonnie Prince Charlie was once involved in a battle here, and the remains of 12 Scottish rebels were discovered in the pub's back garden. For an overnight stay, choose from 12 smart, individually designed guest rooms with furnishings from the Lowther family's collection. 💲 *Average main: £15* ✉ *A6, south of Penrith, Clifton* ☎ *01768/865381* 🌐 *www.georgeanddragonclifton.co.uk* 🕙 *No lunch Mon.*

$$$ B&B/INN Fodor's Choice ★ 🏨 **Askham Hall.** Ancient hub of the Lowther Estate, beautiful Askham Hall's spectacular gardens and fairy-tale rooms are now open to guests. **Pros:** royally stylish; beautiful gardens and surrounding countryside. **Cons:** not in the heart of the Lake District. 💲 *Rooms from: £170* ✉ *Off A6, Askham* ☎ *01931/712348* 🌐 *www.askhamhall.co.uk* 🛏 *12 rooms* 🍽 *Breakfast.*

$ B&B/INN 🏨 **Brooklands.** The welcome is friendly, the breakfast is hearty (salmon cakes and omelets are among the options), and the rooms have patterned wallpaper and heavy, luxurious fabrics at this Victorian terraced house. **Pros:** well-looked-after B&B; bathrobes in room; fancy toiletries. **Cons:** a drive from the spectacular Lakeland scenery. 💲 *Rooms from: £80* ✉ *2 Portland Pl.* ☎ *01768/863395* 🌐 *www.brooklandsguesthouse.com* 🛏 *8 rooms* 🍽 *Breakfast.*

SHOPPING

Penrith is a diverting place to shop, with its narrow streets and arcades chockablock with family-run specialty shops. Major shopping areas include Devonshire Arcade, with its brand-name stores; the pedestrian-only Angel Lane and Little Dockray; and Angel Square.

Brunswick Yard. Clocks, hip flasks, doors, tools, kettles, toys, furniture, and all sorts of old treasure can be found in this wonderful antiques shop and salvage yard just up the hill from the town center. ✉ *Brunswick Rd.* ☎ *07887/867741* 🌐 *www.brunswick-yard.co.uk.*

Fodor's Choice ★ **James & John Graham of Penrith Ltd.** Artisanal cheese and the best of Cumbria's local produce, including the town's famously good toffee, are available at this mouthwateringly good bakery and deli. ✉ *Market Sq.* ☎ *01768/862281* 🌐 *www.jjgraham.co.uk.*

New Hedgehog Bookshop. This welcoming little bookshop has a well-chosen selection of children's books on the ground floor and adult books upstairs. Look for occasional promotions such as free rhubarb with every book. ✉ *19 Little Dockray* ☎ *01768/863003.*

ULLSWATER

6 miles southwest of Penrith.

Hemmed in by towering hills, Ullswater, the region's second-largest lake, is one of the least developed, drawing people for its calm waters and good access to the mountain slopes of Helvellyn. The A592 winds along the lake's pastoral western shore, through the adjacent hamlets of **Glenridding** and **Patterdale** at the southern end. Lakeside strolls, great views, tea shops, and rowboat rentals provide the full Lakeland experience.

ESSENTIALS

Visitor Information Ullswater Tourist Information Centre. ✉ *Beckside Car Park, off A592, Glenridding* ☎ *017684/82414* 🌐 *www.lakedistrict.gov.uk.*

EXPLORING

Aira Force. A spectacular 65-foot waterfall pounds under a stone bridge and through a wooded ravine to feed into Ullswater. From the parking lot it's a 10-minute walk to the falls, with more-serious walks on Gowbarrow Fell and to the village of Dockray beyond. A new 1¼-mile footpath allows visitors to leave their cars at Glencoyne Bay, to the south, and walk through a deer park. ■ **TIP→ Bring sturdy shoes, especially in wet or icy weather, when the paths can be treacherous.** Just above Aira Force in the woods of Gowbarrow Park is the spot where, in 1802, William Wordsworth's sister Dorothy observed daffodils that, as she wrote, "tossed and reeled and danced and seemed as if they verily laughed with the wind that blew upon them." Two years later Wordsworth transformed his sister's words into the famous poem "I Wandered Lonely as a Cloud." Two centuries later, national park wardens patrol Gowbarrow Park in season to prevent tourists from picking the few remaining daffodils. ✉ *A592, near A5091* 🌐 *www.nationaltrust.org.uk/aira-force-and-ullswater* 🎫 *Parking £3.50–£5.50.*

10

Helvellyn. West of Ullswater's southern end, the brooding presence of Helvellyn (3,118 feet), one of the Lake District's most formidable mountains and England's third highest, recalls the region's fundamental character. It's an arduous climb to the top, especially via the challenging ridge known as Striding Edge, and the ascent shouldn't be attempted in poor weather or by inexperienced hikers. Signposted paths to the peak run from the road between Glenridding and Patterdale and pass by **Red Tarn,** which is the highest small mountain lake in the region at 2,356 feet. ✉ *Glenridding.*

Fodor's Choice ★ **Ullswater Steamers.** These antique vessels, including a 19th-century steamer that is said to be the oldest working passenger ship in the world, run the length of Ullswater between Glenridding in the south and Pooley Bridge in the north, via Howtown on the eastern shore. It's a pleasant tour, especially if you combine it with a lakeside walk. One-way trips start at £6.40, or you can sail the entire day for £13.60. ✉ *Pier House, off A592, Glenridding* ☎ *017684/82229* 🌐 *www.ullswater-steamers.co.uk.*

WHERE TO STAY

$$$ HOTEL **Howtown Hotel.** Near the end of the road on the isolated eastern side of Ullswater, this gloriously quiet family-run hotel is low-key and low-tech. **Pros:** exceptionally quiet; spectacular location; dinner included in price. **Cons:** not for those who must be plugged in; a bit remote; books up fast. $ *Rooms from: £178* ✉ *Howtown Rd., Howtown* ☎ *017684/86514* 🌐 *www.howtown-hotel.co.uk* ▭ *No credit cards* ⏲ *Closed Nov.–Mar.* *12 rooms, 4 cottages* 🍴 *Some meals.*

$$$ B&B/INN **Rampsbeck.** Dark carved wood, antique tiles, and a stunning location overlooking Ullswater give the Rampsbeck plenty of country-house style, and the hotel also manages to be more relaxed than some of its competition. **Pros:** great lake position; quiet. **Cons:** isolated from other amenities. $ *Rooms from: £170* ✉ *Watermillock* ☎ *017684/86442* 🌐 *www.rampsbeck.co.uk* *19 rooms* 🍴 *Breakfast.*

KESWICK

14 miles west of Ullswater.

Fodor's Choice ★ The great mountains of Skiddaw and Blencathra brood over the gray slate houses of Keswick (pronounced *kezz*-ick), on the scenic shores of Derwentwater. The town is a natural base for exploring the rounded, heather-clad Skiddaw range to the north, while the hidden valleys of Borrowdale and Buttermere (the latter reached by stunning Honister Pass) take you into the rugged heart of the Lake District. Nearby, five beautiful lakes are set among the three highest mountain ranges in England. The tourist information center here has regional information and is the place to get fishing permits for Derwentwater.

Keswick's narrow, cobbled streets have a grittier charm compared to the refined Victorian elegance of Grasmere or Ambleside. However, it's the best spot in the Lake District to purchase mountaineering gear and outdoor clothing. There are also many hotels, guesthouses, restaurants, and pubs.

The most expert climbers will attempt an ascent of Helvellyn along the perilously narrow Striding Edge even in winter.

GETTING HERE AND AROUND

Keswick is easily reached along A66 from Penrith, though you can get there more scenically via Grasmere in the south. Buses run from the train station in Penrith to Keswick. The town center is pedestrianized.

■ **TIP→ Traffic can be horrendous in summer, so consider leaving your car in Keswick.** The open-top Borrowdale bus service between Keswick and Seatoller (to the south) runs frequently, and the Honister Rambler minibus is perfect for walkers aiming for the high fells of the central lakes; it makes stops from Keswick to Buttermere. The Keswick Launch service on Derwentwater links to many walks as well as the Borrowdale bus service.

ESSENTIALS

Visitor Information Keswick Information Centre. ✉ *Moot Hall, Market Sq.* ☎ *017687/72645* 🌐 *www.keswick.org.*

EXPLORING

Fodor's Choice ★ **Castlerigg Stone Circle.** A Neolithic monument about 100 feet in diameter, this stone circle was built around 3,000 years ago on a hill overlooking St. John's Vale. The brooding northern peaks of Skiddaw and Blencathra loom to the north, and there are views of Helvellyn to the south. The 38 stones aren't large, but the site makes them particularly impressive. Wordsworth described them as "a dismal cirque of Druid stones upon a forlorn moor." The site, always open to visitors, is 4 miles east of Keswick. There's usually space for cars to park beside the road that leads along the northern edge of the site: head up Eleventrees off Penrith Road at the eastern edge of Keswick. ✉ *Off A66* 🌐 *www.english-heritage.org.uk* 🎫 *Free.*

CLOSE UP

Festivals and Folk Sports

With everything from rushbearing to Westmorland wrestling to traditional music, the Lake District hosts some of Britain's most unusual country festivals as well as some excellent but more typical ones.

MAJOR EVENTS

Major festivals include the Keswick Film Festival (February), Words by the Water (a literary festival in Keswick, March), Keswick Jazz Festival (May), Cockermouth and Keswick carnivals (June), Ambleside and Grasmere rushbearing (August), and the Lake District Summer Music (regionwide, in August)—but there are many others. Horse racing comes to Cartmel over May and August holiday weekends.

SPECIAL ACTIVITIES

Rushbearing dates back to medieval times, when rushes covered church floors; today processions of flower-bedecked children and adults bring rushes to churches in a number of villages. Folk sports, often the highlights at local festivals, include Cumberland and Westmorland wrestling, in which the opponents must maintain a grip around each other's body. Fell running, a sort of cross-country run where the route goes roughly straight up and down a mountain, is also popular.

A calendar of events is available at tourist information centers or on the Cumbria Tourism website, 🌐 *www.golakes.co.uk*.

FAMILY **Cumberland Pencil Museum.** Legend has it that shepherds found graphite on Seathwaite Fell after a storm uprooted trees in the 16th century. The Derwent company still makes pencils here, and the museum contains the world's longest colored pencil (it takes 28 men to lift it), a pencil produced for World War II spies that contains a rolled-up map, and displays about graphite mining. There's a café and plenty of opportunities for kids to draw. ✉ *Southey Works, Carding Mill La.* ☎ *017687/73626* 🌐 *www.pencilmuseum.co.uk* 🎫 *£4.50* ⏲ *Daily 9:30–5; last admission at 4.*

QUICK BITES

Java and Chocolate. With seats out on the main square, Java is a great spot for people-watching, or just for consuming excellent tea, coffee, flapjacks, and caramel slices. ✉ ***23 Main St.*** ☎ ***017687/72568.***

Derwentwater. To understand why Derwentwater is considered one of England's finest lakes, take a short walk from Keswick's town center to the lakeshore and past the jetty, and follow the **Friar's Crag** path, about a 15-minute level walk from the center. This pine-tree-fringed peninsula is a favorite vantage point, with its view of the lake, the ring of mountains, and many tiny islands. Ahead, crags line the **Jaws of Borrowdale** and overhang a mountain ravine—a scene that looks as if it emerged from a Romantic painting. ✉ *Keswick.*

Keswick Launch Company. For the best lake views, take a wooden-launch cruise around Derwentwater. Between late March and November, circular cruises set off every half hour in alternate directions from a dock; there's a more limited (roughly hourly) winter timetable. You can also rent a rowboat here in summer. Buy a hop-on, hop-off Around the Lake ticket (£9.95) and take advantage of the seven landing stages around the lake that provide access to hiking trails, such as the two-hour climb up and down Cat Bells, a celebrated lookout point on the western shore of Derwentwater. ■ **TIP→ Buy slightly discounted tickets at the Moot Hall information office in the center of town.** ✉ *Lake Rd.* ☎ *017687/72263* 🌐 *www.keswick-launch.co.uk*.

WHERE TO EAT

$ BRITISH Fodor's Choice ★ ✕ **Café Bar 26.** A metropolitan bar in a town where cozy tearooms are more the norm, Café Bar 26 has wooden beams, mellow brick-color walls, flickering candlelight, excellent coffee, Wi-Fi, and live music every Saturday. There's a short wine list, tasty homemade pizzas, and tapas. In the middle of the day, lunch options include potted shrimp, burgers, and fish cakes. The four spacious bedrooms upstairs are an excellent value for an overnight stop. 💲 *Average main: £7* ✉ *26 Lake Rd.* ☎ *017687/80863* 🌐 *www.cafebar26.co.uk*.

$$ MODERN BRITISH ✕ **Morrels.** One of the town's better eateries, Morrels has local art and wooden floors that give a sophisticated edge to the bar and dining area. Modern British fare is the specialty at this mellow place: a tomato, olive, and pine-nut compote complements the mackerel fillet, and the fish cakes come spiced with a bean-and-corn salsa. The restaurant opens afternoons at 5:30 for anyone going to the town's theater. A couple of equally stylish apartments upstairs are available for short-term rentals. 💲 *Average main: £15* ✉ *34 Lake Rd.* ☎ *017687/72666* 🌐 *www.morrels.co.uk* ⏲ *Closed Mon. No lunch.*

$ CAFÉ ✕ **Square Orange Café Bar.** Young locals and windblown walkers gather here for excellent coffee or tea, fruit-flavored cordials, and some serious hot chocolate. The music is laid-back, the walls are hung with paintings and photos, and there are homemade pizzas, tapas, and pints of local beer for long rainy days or cold winter nights. Wednesday nights mean live acoustic music. 💲 *Average main: £8* ✉ *20 St. John's St.* ☎ *017687/73888* 🌐 *www.thesquareorange.co.uk*.

WHERE TO STAY

$ B&B/INN FAMILY 🏨 **Ferndene.** Exceptionally friendly, this spotless B&B a 10-minute walk from the lake is carefully tended by its kindly owners, who offer plenty of advice on walking and local sights when you want it. **Pros:** family-focused; good value; bicycle storage. **Cons:** lacks style of more expensive lodgings. 💲 *Rooms from: £80* ✉ *6 St. John's Terr.* ☎ *017687/74612* 🌐 *www.ferndene-keswick.co.uk* 🛏 *6 rooms* 🍽 *Breakfast.*

$$ HOTEL 🏨 **Highfield Hotel.** Slightly austere on the outside but charming within, this Victorian hotel overlooks the lawns of Hope Park and has accommodations with great character, including rooms in the turret and the former chapel. **Pros:** good service; tasty food; great views. **Cons:** some small downstairs bedrooms. 💲 *Rooms from: £100* ✉ *The Heads* ☎ *017687/72508* 🌐 *www.highfieldkeswick.co.uk* ⏲ *Closed Jan.* 🛏 *18 rooms* 🍽 *Some meals.*

$$ B&B/INN Fodor's Choice ★ 🏨 **Howe Keld.** In a town that overflows with B&Bs, this comfortable town house stands out because of its contemporary flair and pampering touches. **Pros:** famously filling breakfasts; good ecological practices; one room accessible for people with disabilities. **Cons:** a short distance

The setting of the Castlerigg Stone Circle, ringed by stunning mountains, makes this Neolithic monument deeply memorable.

from the heart of town; backs onto a busy road. *Rooms from: £116* *5–7 The Heads* *017687/72417* *www.howekeld.co.uk* *Closed Jan.* *14 rooms* *Breakfast.*

$ B&B/INN **The Lookout.** Up the hill from the town center, this friendly and economical B&B lives up to its name, with balconies gazing out onto the high fells. **Pros:** welcoming hosts; stylish rooms; great views. **Cons:** some distance from Keswick's amenities. *Rooms from: £95* *Chestnut Hill* *017687/80407* *www.thelookoutkeswick.co.uk* *3 rooms* *Breakfast.*

NIGHTLIFE AND PERFORMING ARTS

Keswick Film Club. With an excellent festival in February and a program of international and classic films, the Keswick Film Club lights up the beautiful 100-year-old redbrick Alhambra Cinema on St. John's Street and the Theatre by the Lake. *Keswick* *017687/72195* *www.keswickfilmclub.org.*

Keswick Jazz Festival. Held each May, the popular Keswick Jazz Festival consists of four days of music. Reservations are accepted from November. *Keswick* *017687/74411* *www.keswickjazzfestival.com.*

Theatre by the Lake. In one of Cumbria's most vibrant cultural settings, the company at the Theatre by the Lake presents classic and contemporary productions year-round. The Keswick Music Society season runs from September through January, and the Words by the Water literary festival takes place here in March. *Lake Rd.* *017687/74411* *www.theatrebythelake.com.*

SHOPPING

Keswick has a good choice of bookstores, crafts shops, and wool-clothing stores tucked away in its cobbled streets, as well as excellent outdoor shops. Keswick's market is held Saturday.

George Fisher. The area's largest and best outdoor equipment store, George Fisher sells sportswear, travel books, and maps; staff are faultlessly friendly, helpful, and well informed. Daily weather information is posted in the window, and there's a children's play den. ✉ *2 Borrowdale Rd.* ☎ *017687/72178* 🌐 *www.georgefisher.co.uk.*

Needle Sports. This company stocks all the best equipment for mountaineering and for rock and ice climbing. ✉ *56 Main St.* ☎ *017687/72227* 🌐 *www.needlesports.com.*

Thomasons. A butcher and delicatessen, Thomasons sells some very good meat pies—just the thing for putting in your pocket before you climb a Lakeland fell. ✉ *8–10 Station St.* ☎ *017687/80169.*

SPORTS AND THE OUTDOORS

BIKING

Keswick Bikes. This company rents bikes (from £25 per day) and provides information on all the nearby trails. Guided tours can be arranged with advance notice. ✉ *133 Main St.* ☎ *017687/73355* 🌐 *www.keswickbikes.co.uk.*

WATER SPORTS

Derwent Water Marina. Rental boats in all shapes and sizes and instruction in canoeing, sailing, and windsurfing can be had at Derwent Water Marina. Other water-related activities include ghyll scrambling—the fine art of walking up or down a steep Lakeland stream. A two-day sailing or windsurfing course costs £198. ✉ *Portinscale* ☎ *017687/72912* 🌐 *www.derwentwatermarina.co.uk.*

EN ROUTE

The most scenic route from Keswick, B5289 south, runs along the eastern edge of Derwentwater, past turnoffs to natural attractions such as Ashness Bridge, the idyllic tarn of Watendlath, the Lodore Falls (best after a good rain), and the precariously balanced Bowder Stone. Farther south is the tiny village of **Grange,** a walking center at the head of Borrowdale, where there's a riverside café.

10

BORROWDALE

7 miles south of Keswick.

Fodor's Choice ★

South of Keswick and its lake lies the valley of Borrowdale, whose varied landscape of green valley floor and surrounding crags has long been considered one of the region's most magnificent treasures. **Rosthwaite,** a tranquil farming village, and **Seatoller,** the southernmost settlement, are the two main centers (both are accessible by bus from Keswick), though they're little more than clusters of aged buildings surrounded by glorious countryside.

GETTING HERE AND AROUND

The valley is south of Keswick on B5289. The Borrowdale bus service between Keswick and Seatoller runs frequently.

EXPLORING

Fodor's Choice ★ **Borrowdale Fells.** These steep fells rise up dramatically behind Seatoller. Get out and walk whenever inspiration strikes. Trails are well signposted, or you can pick up maps and any gear in Keswick. ✉ *Seatoller.*

Scafell Pike. England's highest mountain at 3,210 feet, Scafell (pronounced *scar*-fell) Pike is visible from Seatoller. One route up the mountain, for experienced walkers, is from the hamlet of Seathwaite, a mile south of Seatoller. ✉ *Seatoller.*

WHERE TO STAY

$$ B&B/INN **Hazel Bank Country House.** Though this stately, carefully restored home retains original elements from its days as a grand Victorian country pile, its welcoming owners have invested in handsome local furniture and stripped away some of the chintz, opening up inspiring views across the pristine lawns to the valley and the central Lakeland peaks beyond. **Pros:** serene location; immaculate gardens. **Cons:** not near many amenities. $ *Rooms from: £156* ✉ *Off B5289, Rosthwaite* ☎ *017687/77248* 🌐 *www.hazelbankhotel.co.uk* *8 rooms, 1 cottage* 🍽 *Breakfast.*

$$ HOTEL FAMILY **Langstrath Country Inn.** In the tranquil hamlet of Stonethwaite, the welcoming Langstrath was originally built as a miner's cottage in the 16th century but has expanded into a spacious inn with chunky wooden tables and logs burning on a slate open fire. **Pros:** great walks right out the door; children welcomed and looked after; wonderfully peaceful. **Cons:** few other places to eat or shop nearby. $ *Rooms from: £106* ✉ *Off B5289, Stonethwaite* ☎ *017687/77239* 🌐 *www.thelangstrath.com* ⏲ *Closed Dec. and Jan.* *8 rooms* 🍽 *Breakfast.*

COCKERMOUTH

15 miles northwest of Borrowdale, 14 miles northwest of Seatoller.

This small but bustling town, at the confluence of the rivers Derwent and Cocker, has colorful buildings, history, and narrow streets that are a delight to wander. The ruined 13th-century castle is open only on special occasions. Over a weekend in September the town holds the Taste Cumbria Food Festival.

GETTING HERE AND AROUND

The most straightforward access to the town is along the busy A66 from Penrith. For a more scenic, roundabout route, head over the Whinlatter or Honister passes from Keswick.

ESSENTIALS

Visitor Information Cockermouth Tourist Information Centre. ✉ *4 Kings Arms La.* ☎ *01900/822634* 🌐 *www.cockermouth.org.uk.*

EXPLORING

Fodor's Choice ★ **Castlegate House Gallery.** One of the region's best galleries, Castlegate displays and sells outstanding contemporary work, many by Cumbrian artists. There's a wonderful permanent collection, and changing exhibitions focus on paintings, sculpture, glass, ceramics, and jewelry. ✉ *Castlegate* ☎ *01900/822149* 🌐 *www.castlegatehouse.co.uk* ⏲ *Mon. and Wed.–Sat. 10–5.*

Fodor'sChoice ★ **Wordsworth House.** Cockermouth was the birthplace of William Wordsworth and his sister Dorothy, whose childhood home was this 18th-century town house, carefully kept as it would have been in their day. There is no sense of dusty preservation here, though, and nothing is roped off; the house achieves a rare sense of natural authenticity, with clutter and period cooking in the kitchen and herbs and vegetables growing outside in the beautiful traditional Georgian garden. A café makes good use of the homegrown produce. Enthusiastic staff are both knowledgable and approachable, and the busy calendar of activities adds to the sense of a house still very much alive. ✉ *Main St.* ☎ *01900/824805* 🌐 *www.nationaltrust.org.uk/wordsworth-house* 🎫 *£7.09* 🕑 *Mid-Mar.–Oct., Sat.–Thurs. 11–5; last admission at 4.*

WHERE TO EAT AND STAY

$ BRITISH ✕ **Bitter End.** Flocked floral wallpaper, old lamps, an open fire, and a handsome wooden floor set the tone at this appealing pub. Homey and intimate, the pub serves big, tasty portions of traditional British food such as lamb cobbler and fish-and-chips and well-kept, locally brewed beer. Excellent Sunday lunches are popular with locals. [$] *Average main: £11* ✉ *15 Kirkgate* ☎ *01900/828993* 🌐 *www.bitterend.co.uk.*

$$ VEGETARIAN ✕ **Quince & Medlar.** Sophisticated and imaginative vegetarian cuisine, served by candlelight, is the specialty at this refined, wood-paneled Georgian town house. You'll probably be offered a drink in the sitting room before being called to your table; you choose from at least six main courses, such as wild mushroom filo cup with baked cheese soufflé, paprika-roasted pine nuts, sweet potato, and a watercress sauce. Delicious desserts may include almond, apricot, and amaretto ice cream. [$] *Average main: £15* ✉ *13 Castlegate* ☎ *01900/823579* 🌐 *www.quinceandmedlar.co.uk* 🕑 *Closed Sun. and Mon. No lunch* ✍ *Reservations essential.*

$ B&B/INN Fodor'sChoice ★ 🏨 **Six Castlegate.** After a day of exploring, relax in style at this elegant B&B in a Georgian town house with spacious rooms immaculately decorated in pale, natural tones; all have good views, generous showers, and comfortable beds. **Pros:** modern facilities and antique style blend nicely; near galleries and attractions; exceptional value. **Cons:** road noise in some rooms. [$] *Rooms from: £70* ✉ *6 Castlegate* ☎ *01900/826786* 🌐 *www.sixcastlegate.co.uk* 🛏 *6 rooms* 🍽 *Breakfast.*

10

BASSENTHWAITE LAKE

5 miles east of Cockermouth, 3 miles north of Keswick.

Bassenthwaite is the only body of water officially called a lake in the Lake District; the others are known as "meres" or "waters." Bird-watchers know this less-frequented lake well because of the many species of migratory birds found here, including ospreys (check out 🌐 *www.ospreywatch.co.uk*). The shoreline habitat is the best preserved in the national park—in part because most of it is privately owned, and also because motorboats are not allowed. Posh accommodations and good restaurants dot the area, and popular walks include the climb up Skiddaw (3,054 feet), which, on a clear day, has panoramic views of the Lake District, the Pennines, Scotland, and the Isle of Man from its summit.

EXPLORING

Lakes Distillery. England's largest whisky distillery, converted from a Victorian model farm, is a huge new venture and a great visitor attraction. Hour-long tours get you up close to the process and include a history of illicit distilling in the area and a thrilling aerial film that follows the River Derwent from source to sea. Visits include a tasting of either gin or whisky; the home-produced whisky will be ready in 2017, and the distillery's own gin will use Lake District juniper berries. The already popular bistro, in the old milking parlor, offers high-quality dishes such as a distiller's lunch—a take on the traditional ploughman's—and wood pigeon breast with crème fraîche and beetroot salad. Desserts are especially good, and seating spills out into the courtyard in good weather. ✉ *Setmurthy, Nr Bassenthwaite Lake* ☎ *017687/88857* 🌐 *www.lakesdistillery.com* 🎫 *£12.50* ⏲ *Tours daily 11–5.*

WHERE TO STAY

$$ B&B/INN Fodor's Choice ★ **The Pheasant.** Halfway between Cockermouth and Keswick at the northern end of Bassenthwaite Lake, this traditional 18th-century coaching inn exudes English coziness without the usual Lakeland fussiness. **Pros:** atmosphere of a well-loved local inn; fantastic bar; great food. **Cons:** a little out of the way. $ *Rooms from: £150* ✉ *Off A66* ☎ *017687/76234* 🌐 *www.the-pheasant.co.uk* 🛏 *15 rooms, 3 suites* 🍽 *Some meals.*

EAST ANGLIA

WELCOME TO EAST ANGLIA

TOP REASONS TO GO

★ **Cambridge:** A walk through the colleges is grand, but the best views of the university's buildings and immaculate lawns (and some famous bridges) are from a punt on the river.

★ **Constable country:** In the area where Constable grew up, you can walk or row downstream from Dedham straight into the setting of one of the English landscape painter's masterpieces at Flatford Mill.

★ **Lincoln's old center:** The ancient center of the city has a vast, soaring cathedral, a proper rampart-ringed castle, and winding medieval streets.

★ **Wild North Sea coast:** North Norfolk has enormous sandy beaches (great for walking) and opportunities to see seals and birds, especially on the salt marshes around Blakeney.

★ **Lavenham:** This old town is the most comely of the tight-knit cluster of places that prospered from the medieval wool trade, with architecture including timber-frame houses gnarled into crookedness by age.

1 Cambridge. The home of the ancient university is East Anglia's liveliest town. The city center is perfect for ambling around the colleges, museums, and King's College Chapel, one of England's greatest monuments.

2 Ely and Central Suffolk. The villages within a short drive of Cambridge remain largely unspoiled. Ely's lofty cathedral dominates the surrounding flatlands, and Sudbury, Long Melford, Lavenham, and Bury St. Edmunds preserve their rich historical flavor.

3 The Suffolk Coast. Idyllic villages such as Dedham and Flatford form the center of what's been dubbed "Constable Country," while the nearby Suffolk Coast includes such atmospheric seaside towns as Woodbridge and Aldeburgh.

Blakeney
A149
Holkham Hall
Wells-next-the-Sea
A148
Fakenham
A148
Blickling Hall
A140
4
A149
NORFOLK
A47
Swaffham
Norwich
A47
Great Yarmouth
A146
Mundford
A11
A140
Lowestoft
Thetford
A143
A12
Scole
A143
North Sea
SUFFOLK
Bury St. Edmunds
3
2
Stowmarket
Aldeburgh
A134
Lavenham
A14
A12
Woodbridge
Ipswich
Orford
Long Melford
Sudbury
Flatford
Felixstowe
Halstead
Dedham
Harwich
Harwich Harbour
Colchester
A12
Kelvedon
Clacton on Sea
0 10 mi
0 10 km

GETTING ORIENTED

East Anglia, in southeastern England, can be divided into distinct areas for sightseeing. The central area surrounds the ancient university city of Cambridge and includes Ely, with its magnificent cathedral rising out of the flatlands, and the towns of inland Suffolk. The Suffolk Heritage Coast is home to historic small towns and villages; while the northeast, with the region's capital, Norwich, encompasses the waterways of the Broads and the beaches and salt marshes of the North Norfolk coast. Farther north, in Lincolnshire, the historic town of Stamford sits just south of the city of Lincoln, famous for its tall, fluted cathedral towers.

4 Norwich and North Norfolk. Sights in Norwich include its cathedral and castle. To the north and west you'll find the stately homes of Blickling Hall, Houghton Hall, and Sandringham, plus quiet coastal resorts such as Blakeney and Wells-next-the-Sea.

5 Stamford and Lincoln. On the western fringes of East Anglia, Lincoln is worth visiting for its Norman cathedral, whereas Stamford is best known for Burghley House, an impressive Elizabethan mansion.

EAST ANGLIA'S SEAFOOD BOUNTY

Perhaps unsurprisingly in an island nation, the harvest of the rivers and the sea forms an essential part of the British culinary tradition. Few regions are so closely associated with a love of good seafood as East Anglia.

(above) Fish-and-chips taste perfect during a day by the sea in East Anglia; (right, top) Cromer crab dressed with lemon mayonnaise; (right, bottom) Potted shrimp, a tasty appetizer

The coastlines of Essex, Suffolk, and Norfolk overflow with towns that specialize in one type of seaborne bounty or another. Shrimp, crab, and oysters are still caught using centuries-old methods; and lobsters, crabs, and mussels from Norfolk are sent to the top restaurants in London. Changing tastes tell a kind of social history of their own: oysters, now an expensive luxury, were once considered peasant food; and a new generation of chefs, eager to reconnect with forgotten ingredients and methods, is rediscovering old-fashioned flavors such as eel and samphire. Then there's that most famous of British seafood dishes—humble fish-and-chips. Some of the best in the country can be found in Suffolk towns such as Aldeburgh, where savvy fish-and-chip shop owners have installed webcams so customers can check how far the line stretches down the street.

SEA SALT

Evidence suggests that sea salt has been harvested in East Anglia for 2,000 years. It's popular today—but only one regional company still produces sea salt in the local style. Based in and named after the harbor town of Maldon in Essex, Maldon Crystal Salt Company uses a distinctive method that yields thin, flaky crystals with a delicate piquancy. Praised by chefs, Maldon salt is widely available at English supermarkets.

CHOOSING YOUR FISH-AND-CHIPS
The key word is simplicity: very fresh fish, deep-fried in batter, served immediately. Chips (slices of fried potato) must be thick cut and slightly soft, not crisp like fries, and sprinkled with salt and vinegar. The kind you get in fish-and-chips shops is almost always better than pub offerings. Cod, plaice, and haddock are the most popular choices, but the concern about cod overfishing means that you may see pollock, coley, or skate as alternatives.

CROMER CRAB
Known for their juicy flesh and higher-than-average white meat content, the best East Anglian crab comes from the area around Cromer in Norfolk. It's often served in salads, pasta dishes, and savory crab cakes.

EEL
A staple of the East Anglian diet for centuries but long out of favor, the humble eel is making a comeback at fashionable restaurants. Eels are usually served smoked (on their own, or in soups or salads) or jellied in a flavored stock with the consistency of aspic.

MUSSELS
This type of small clam is particularly associated with the towns of Brancaster and Stiffkey. Cheap and versatile, mussels can be served on their own; with other seafood; or in soups and stews.

OYSTERS
The Essex coast has been producing oysters since Roman times. A luxury item, oysters are usually served raw with few accompaniments, as a main course by the dozen, or as a starter by the half dozen.

SAMPHIRE
A green sea vegetable that grows wild on shores and marshland, samphire is abundant in East Anglia, where it's an accompaniment to local seafood. Crisp and slightly salty, it's often described as "tasting like the sea."

SHERINGHAM LOBSTER
This well-regarded lobster is usually served with melted butter, or with fries as a kind of upper-class cousin of fish-and-chips. Lobster bisque—a rich, creamy soup—is also popular.

SHRIMP
Caught primarily off the coasts of Lancashire and East Anglia, the British shrimp is a type of shellfish similar to, but much smaller than, prawns. Potted shrimp is a traditional starter, made with butter, mace, and nutmeg.

YARMOUTH BLOATERS
A form of cured herring produced in Great Yarmouth, near Norwich, these fat, slightly salted fish aren't gutted before being smoked. This gives them a particularly strong, almost gamey flavor.

Updated by Jack Jewers

One of those beautiful English inconsistencies, East Anglia has no spectacular mountains or rivers to disturb the quiet, storied land of rural delights. Occupying an area of southeastern England that pushes out into the North Sea, its counties of Essex, Norfolk, Suffolk, Lincolnshire, and Cambridgeshire feel cut off from the pulse of the country. Among its highlights is Cambridge, a lovely and ancient university city. East Anglia also has four of the country's greatest stately homes: Holkham Hall, Blickling Hall, Houghton Hall, and Sandringham—where the Queen spends Christmas.

In times past East Anglia was one of the most important centers of power in northern Europe. Towns like Lincoln were major Roman settlements, and the medieval wool trade brought huge prosperity to the higgledy-piggledy streets of tiny Lavenham. Thanks to its relative lack of thoroughfares and canals, however, East Anglia was mercifully untouched by the Industrial Revolution. The area is rich in idyllic, quintessentially English villages: sleepy, sylvan settlements in the midst of otherwise deserted lowlands. Even the towns feel small and manageable; the biggest city, Norwich, has a population of just 130,000. Cambridge, with its ancient university, is the area's most famous draw, along with incomparable cathedrals, at Ely and Lincoln particularly, and one of the finest Gothic buildings in Europe, King's College Chapel.

And yet, despite all of these treasures, the real joy of exploring East Anglia is making your own discoveries. Spend a couple of days exploring the hidden byways of the fens, or just taking in the subtle beauties of the many England-like-it-looks-in-the-movies villages. If you find yourself driving down a small country lane and an old church or mysterious, ivy-covered ruin peeks out from behind the trees, give in to your curiosity and look inside. Such hidden places are East Anglia's best-kept secrets.

EAST ANGLIA PLANNER

WHEN TO GO

Summer and late spring are the best times to visit East Anglia. Late fall and winter can be cold, windy, and rainy, though this is England's driest region and crisp, frosty days here are beautiful. To escape crowds, avoid the popular Norfolk Broads in late July and August. You can't visit most of the Cambridge colleges during exam period (late May to mid-June), and the competition for hotel rooms heats up during graduation week (late June). The Aldeburgh Festival of Music and the Arts, one of the biggest events on the British classical music calendar, takes place in June.

PLANNING YOUR TIME

Cambridge is the region's most interesting city, and ideally you should allow two days to absorb its various sights. (In a pinch you could do it as a day trip from London, but only with an early start and a good pair of walking shoes.) You could easily use the city as a base for exploring Ely, Bury St. Edmunds, Lavenham, Long Melford, and Sudbury, although accommodations are available in these towns as well. The Suffolk Coast has enticing overnight stops in such small towns as Dedham and Aldeburgh. In the northern part of the region, Norwich makes a good place to stop for the night, and has enough sights to keep you interested for a day. If here to see the coast, you'll do better staying in villages such as Blakeney or Wells. Allow several hours to see the large Blickling Hall, near Norwich, and Burghley House, outside Stamford. Lincoln, notable for its cathedral, and Stamford are west and north of Norfolk if you want to work them into an itinerary.

GETTING HERE AND AROUND

AIR TRAVEL

Norwich International Airport serves a limited number of domestic and international destinations, though not the United States. London Stansted Airport, 30 miles south of Cambridge, is used mainly for European flights. The vast majority of travelers to the region arrive by train, car, or bus.

Airports London Stansted Airport. ✉ *Bassingbourn Rd., Bishop's Stortford* ☎ *0844/335–1803* 🌐 *www.stanstedairport.com.* **Norwich International Airport.** ✉ *Amsterdam Way, off A140, Norwich* ☎ *01603/411923* 🌐 *www.norwichairport.co.uk.*

BUS TRAVEL

National Express buses serve the region from London's Victoria Coach Station. Average travel times are 3 hours to Cambridge and Norwich, 2½ hours to Bury St. Edmunds, and 4½ hours to Lincoln.

Long-distance buses are useful for reaching the region and traveling between its major centers, but for smaller hops, local buses are best. First and Stagecoach buses cover the Cambridge, Lincolnshire, and Norwich areas. Information about local Norfolk service and county service is available from the Norfolk Bus Information Centre. Traveline can answer public transportation questions.

A FirstDay ticket, which covers a day of unlimited bus travel around Norwich and the Norfolk coast, costs £14, while a FirstWeek pass, good for seven days, costs £26. These tickets cover all buses except the Park and Ride shuttles that link parking lots with the town center. There are also various local passes that cost from around £4 to £10 daily, £10 to £21 weekly. You can buy any of these tickets from the driver.

Bus Contacts Norfolk Bus Information Centre. ☎ *0845/300–6116.* **Stagecoach.** ☎ *0871/834–0010* 🌐 *www.stagecoachbus.com/cambridge.* **Traveline.** ☎ *0871/200–2233, 84268 text "Traveline" from mobile phone for link to bus finder* 🌐 *www.traveline.org.uk.*

CAR TRAVEL

If you're driving from London, Cambridge (54 miles) is off M11. At Exit 9, M11 connects with A11 to Norwich (114 miles); A14 off A11 goes to Bury St. Edmunds. A12 from London goes through east Suffolk via Ipswich. For Lincoln (131 miles), take A1 via Huntingdon, Peterborough, and Grantham to A46 at Newark-on-Trent. A more scenic alternative is to leave A1 at Grantham and take A607 to Lincoln.

East Anglia has few fast main roads besides those mentioned here. Once off the A roads, traveling within the region often means taking country lanes that have many twists and turns. Going even just a few miles can take much longer than you think.

TRAIN TRAVEL

The entire region is well served by trains from London's Liverpool Street and King's Cross stations. The quality and convenience of these services varies enormously, however. Cambridge trains leave from King's Cross and Liverpool Street, take about 45 minutes to an hour, and cost about £23. On the other hand, getting to Lincoln from King's Cross entails at least one transfer, takes two to three hours, and costs between £30 and £90, depending on when you travel. **■ TIP→ Tickets for trains between London and Lincoln can be a fraction of the price if you buy online in advance.** A good way to save money on local trains in East Anglia is to buy an Anglia Plus Ranger Pass. It costs £17 for one day or £34 for three days, and allows unlimited rail travel in Norfolk, Suffolk, and part of Cambridgeshire. You can add up to four kids for an extra £2 each.

Train Contacts Abellio Greater Anglia. ☎ *0345/600–7245* 🌐 *www.abelliogreateranglia.co.uk.* **East Midlands Trains.** ☎ *0845/712–5678* 🌐 *www.eastmidlandstrains.co.uk.* **First Capital Connect.** ☎ *0845/026–4700* 🌐 *www.firstcapitalconnect.co.uk.* **National Rail Enquiries.** ☎ *0845/748–4950* 🌐 *www.nationalrail.co.uk.*

RESTAURANTS

In summer the coast gets so packed with people that reservations are essential at restaurants. Getting something to eat at other than regular mealtime hours isn't always possible in small towns; head to cafés if you want a midmorning or after-lunch snack. Look for area specialties, such as crab, lobster, duckling, Norfolk black turkey, hare, and partridge, on menus around the region. In Norwich there's no escaping the hot, bright-yellow Colman's mustard, which is perfect smeared gingerly on some sausage and mash.

HOTELS

The region is full of centuries-old, half-timber inns with rooms full of roaring fires and cozy bars. Bed-and-breakfasts are a good option in pricey Cambridge. It's always busy in Cambridge and along the coast in summer, so reserve well in advance. ⇨ *Hotel reviews have been shortened. For full information, visit Fodors.com.*

WHAT IT COSTS IN POUNDS				
	$	$$	$$$	$$$$
Restaurants	under £15	£15–£19	£20–£25	over £25
Hotels	under £100	£100–£160	£161–£220	over £220

Restaurant prices are the average cost of a main course at dinner, or if dinner is not served, at lunch. Hotels prices are the lowest cost of a standard double room in high season, including 20% V.A.T.

VISITOR INFORMATION

Broads Authority. ✉ *Yare House, 62 Thorpe Rd., Norwich* ☎ *01603/610734* 🌐 *www.broads-authority.gov.uk.* **East of England Tourism.** ✉ *Dettingen House, Dettingen Way, Bury St. Edmunds* ☎ *0333/3204202* 🌐 *www.visiteastofengland.com.*

CAMBRIDGE

Fodor's Choice ★ With the spires of its university buildings framed by towering trees and expansive meadows, and its medieval streets and passages enhanced by gardens and riverbanks, the city of Cambridge is among the loveliest in England. The city predates the Roman occupation of Britain, but there's confusion over exactly how and when the university was founded. The most widely accepted story is that it was established in 1209 by a pair of scholars from Oxford, who left their university in protest over the wrongful execution of a colleague for murder.

Keep in mind there's no recognizable campus: the scattered colleges *are* the university. The town reveals itself only slowly, filled with tiny gardens, ancient courtyards, imposing classic buildings, alleyways that lead past medieval churches, and wisteria-hung facades. Perhaps the best views are from the Backs, the green parkland that extends along the River Cam behind several colleges. This sweeping openness, a result of the larger size of the colleges and lack of industrialization in the city center, is what distinguishes Cambridge from Oxford.

This university town may be beautiful, but it's no museum. Well-preserved medieval buildings sit cheek-by-jowl next to the latest in modern architecture (for example, the William Gates Building, which houses Cambridge University's computer laboratory) in this growing city dominated culturally and architecturally by its famous university (students make up around one-fifth of the city's 109,000 inhabitants), and beautified by parks, gardens, and the quietly flowing River Cam.

GETTING HERE AND AROUND

Good bus (three hours) and train (one hour) services connect London and Cambridge. The long-distance bus terminal is on Drummer Street, very close to Emmanuel and Christ's colleges. Several local buses connect the station with central Cambridge, including the frequent Citi 7 and 8 services, although any bus listing City Centre or Emmanuel Street among its stops will do. The journey takes just under 10 minutes. If you're driving, don't attempt to venture very far into the center—parking is scarce and pricey. The center is amenable to explorations on foot, or you could join the throng by renting a bicycle.

Stagecoach sells Dayrider (£3.90) tickets for all-day bus travel within Cambridge, and Megarider tickets (£13) for seven days of travel within the city. You can extend these to cover the whole county of Cambridgeshire (£6 and £23.50, respectively). Buy any of them from the driver.

TIMING

In summer and over the Easter and Christmas holidays Cambridge is devoid of students, its heart and soul. To see the city in full swing, visit from October through June. In summer there are arts and music festivals, notably the Strawberry Fair and the Arts Festival (both June) and the Folk Festival (late July to early August). The May Bumps, intercollegiate boat races, are, confusingly, held the first week of June. This is also the month when students celebrate the end of exam season, so expect to encounter some boisterous nightlife.

TOURS

City Sightseeing. This company operates open-top bus tours of Cambridge, including the Backs, colleges, and Botanic Gardens. Tours can be joined at marked bus stops in the city. Ask the tourist office about additional tours. ✉ *Cambridge Train Station, Station Rd.* ☎ *01223/433250* 🌐 *www.city-sightseeing.com* 🎫 *From £14.*

Visit Cambridge. Walking tours, as well as other tours, are led by an official Blue Badge guide. The two-hour tours leave from the tourist information center at Peas Hill. Hours vary according to the tour, with the earliest leaving at 11 am and the latest at 1 or 2 pm. ✉ *Peas Hill* ☎ *0871/226–8006* 🌐 *www.visitcambridge.org/official-tours* 🎫 *From £18.50.*

ESSENTIALS

Visitor Information Cambridge University. ☎ *01223/337733* 🌐 *www.cam.ac.uk.*

EXPLORING

Exploring the city means, in large part, exploring the university. Each of the 25 oldest colleges is built around a series of courts, or quadrangles, framing manicured, velvety lawns. Because students and fellows (faculty) live and work in these courts, access is sometimes restricted, and you're asked not to picnic in the quadrangles at any time.

Visitors aren't normally allowed into college buildings other than chapels, dining halls, and some libraries; some colleges charge admission

Cricket, anyone? Audley End, a 17th-century house, serves as an idyllic backdrop for a cricket match.

for certain buildings. Public visiting hours vary from college to college, depending on the time of year, and it's best to call or to check with the city tourist office. Colleges close to visitors during the main exam time, late May to mid-June. Term time (when classes are in session) means roughly October to December, January to March, and April to June; summer term, or vacation, runs from July to September. **■ TIP→ Bring a pair of binoculars, as some college buildings have highly intricate details, such as the spectacular ceiling at King's College Chapel.** When the colleges are open, the best way to gain access is to join a walking tour led by an official Blue Badge guide—many areas are off-limits unless you do. The 90-minute and two-hour tours (£10 to £17.50) leave up to four times daily from the city tourist office. The other traditional view of the colleges is gained from a punt—the boats propelled by pole on the River Cam.

TOP ATTRACTIONS

OFF THE BEATEN PATH

Audley End House and Gardens. A famous example of early-17th-century architecture, Audley End was once owned by Charles II, who bought it as a convenient place to break his journey on the way to the Newmarket races. Although the palatial building was remodeled in the 18th and 19th centuries, the Jacobean style is still on display in the magnificent Great Hall. You can walk in the park, landscaped by Capability Brown in the 18th century, and the fine Victorian gardens. Two exhibits focus on the lives of domestic servants in the late 19th century. A 2014 renovation opened up the Nursery Suite, bedecked in 1830s style, and the Coal Gallery, which once provided hot water for the family upstairs (though not the servants). The Service Wing lets you

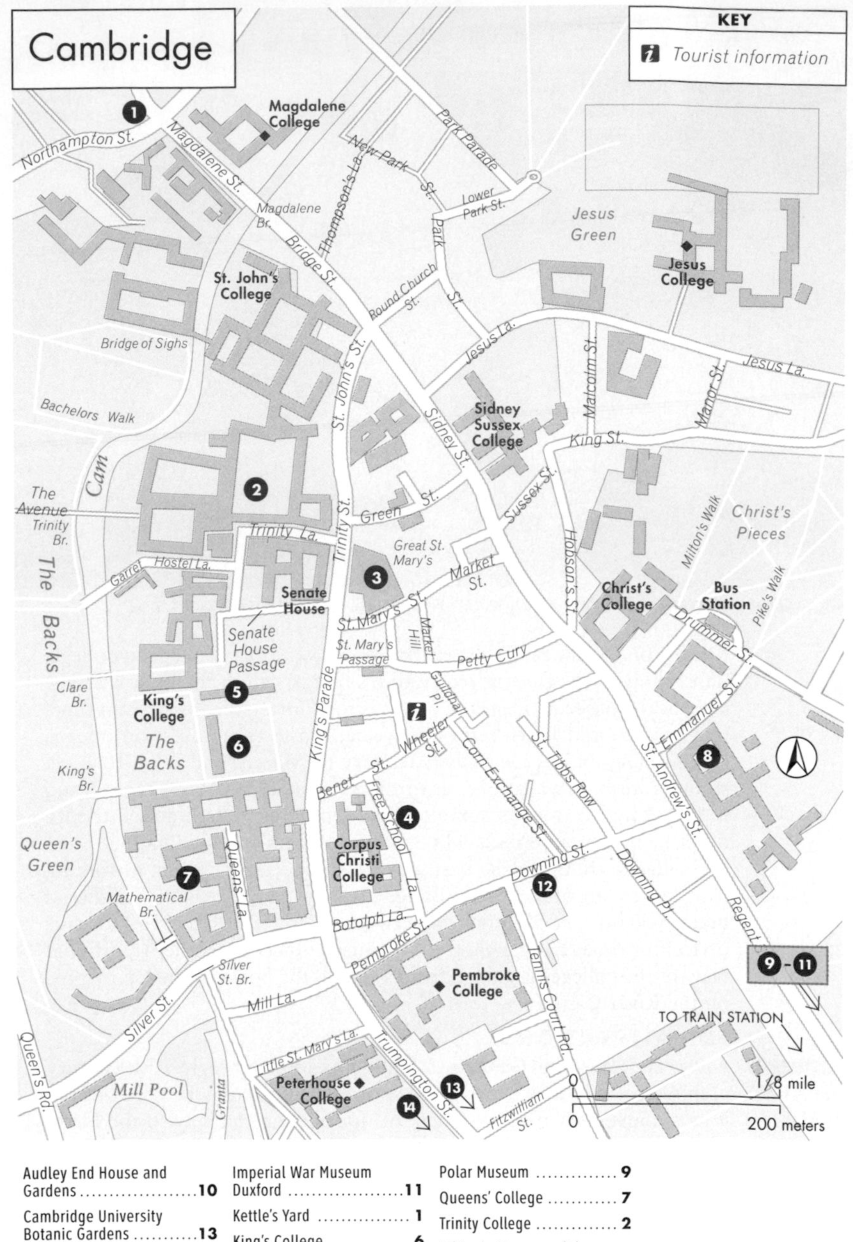

Audley End House and Gardens 10

Cambridge University Botanic Gardens 13

Emmanuel College 8

Fitzwilliam Museum 14

Great St. Mary's 3

Imperial War Museum Duxford 11

Kettle's Yard 1

King's College 6

King's College Chapel 5

Museum of Archaeology and Anthropology 12

Polar Museum 9

Queens' College 7

Trinity College 2

Whipple Museum of the History of Science 4

look "below stairs" at the kitchen, scullery (where fish were descaled and chickens plucked), and game larder (where pheasants, partridges, and rabbits were hung), while the Stable Yard give kids the chance to see old saddles and tack and don Victorian riding costumes. The house is in Saffron Waldon, 14 miles south of Cambridge. ✉ *Off London Rd., Saffron Waldon* ☎ *01799/522842* 🌐 *www.english-heritage.org.uk* 🎫 *£16.50 Apr.–Oct., £10 Nov.–Mar. (stables, service wing, and gardens only)* 🕒 *Apr.–Sept., daily noon–5 (stables, service wing, and gardens 10–6); Oct., daily noon–4 (stables, service wing, and gardens 10–5); Nov.–Mar., weekends 10–4.*

Emmanuel College. The master hand of architect Christopher Wren (1632–1723) is evident throughout much of Cambridge, particularly at Emmanuel, built on the site of a Dominican friary, where he designed the chapel and colonnade. A stained-glass window in the chapel has a likeness of John Harvard, founder of Harvard University, who studied here. The college, founded in 1584, was an early center of Puritan learning; a number of the Pilgrims were Emmanuel alumni, and they remembered their alma mater in naming Cambridge, Massachusetts. ✉ *St. Andrew's St.* ☎ *01223/334200* 🌐 *www.emma.cam.ac.uk* 🎫 *Free* 🕒 *Daily 9–6, except exam period.*

Fodor's Choice ★

Fitzwilliam Museum. In a Classical Revival building renowned for its grand Corinthian portico, this museum, founded by the seventh viscount Fitzwilliam of Merrion in 1816, has one of Britain's most outstanding collections of art and antiquities. Highlights include two large Titians, an extensive collection of French Impressionist paintings, and many works by Matisse and Picasso. The opulent interior displays its treasures to marvelous effect, from Egyptian pieces such as inch-high figurines and painted coffins, to sculptures from the Chinese Han dynasty of the 3rd century BC. Other collections of note here are a fine assortment of medieval illuminated manuscripts and a fascinating room full of armor and muskets. ✉ *Trumpington St.* ☎ *01223/332900* 🌐 *www.fitzmuseum.cam.ac.uk* 🎫 *Free* 🕒 *Tues.–Sat. 10–5, Sun. noon–5.*

Great St. Mary's. Known as the "university church," Great St. Mary's has its origins in the 11th century, although the current building dates from 1478. The main reason to visit is to climb the 113-foot tower, which has a superb view over the colleges and marketplace (though it may be closed in bad weather). Also here is the Michaelhouse Centre, a small café, gallery, and performing arts venue with frequent free lunchtime concerts. Tours must be booked in advance; contact Helen Long at *01223/462914.* ✉ *Market Hill, King's Parade* ☎ *01223/741720* 🌐 *www.gsm.cam.ac.uk* 🎫 *Free; tower £3.80; guided tours £10* 🕒 *Church Mon.–Sat., 10–5, Sun. 12:30–5. Tower May–Aug., Mon.–Sat. 10–4:30, Sun. 12:45–4:30; Sept.–Apr., Mon.–Sat. 10–4, Sun. 12:45–4.*

OFF THE BEATEN PATH

Imperial War Museum Duxford. Europe's leading aviation museum houses a remarkable collection of 180 aircrafts from Europe and the United States. The former airfield is effectively a complex of several museums under one banner. The **Land Warfare Hall** features tanks and other military vehicles. The striking **American Air Museum**, which has just undergone a year-long renovation, honors the 30,000 Americans killed

A must-see at Cambridge is King's College Chapel, a masterpiece of Perpendicular Gothic style.

in action flying from Britain during World War II. It contains the largest display of American fighter planes outside the United States. **AirSpace** holds a vast array of military and civil aircraft in a 3-acre hangar. Directly underneath is the **Airborne Assault Museum,** which chronicles the history of airborne forces, such as the British Parachute Regiment, which played a pivotal role in the Normandy Landings. There are also hangars where you can see restoration work on World War II planes and exhibitions on maritime warfare and the Battle of Britain. See the planes in action with the historic air shows that are held on a handful of dates every summer; check the website for details. ✉ *A505, Duxford* ☎ *01223/835000* 🌐 *duxford.iwm.org.uk* 🎫 *£18* 🕒 *Mid-Mar.–late Oct., daily 10–6; late Oct.–mid-Mar., daily 10–4 (Land Warfare Hall noon–4); last admission 1 hr before closing.*

King's College. Founded in 1441 by Henry VI, King's College has a magnificent late-15th-century chapel that is its most famous landmark. Other notable architecture is the neo-Gothic Porters' Lodge, facing King's Parade, which was a comparatively recent addition in the 1830s, and the classical Gibbs building. ■ **TIP→ Head down to the river, from where the panorama of college and chapel is one of the university's most photographed views.** Past students of King's College include the novelist E.M. Forster, the economist John Maynard Keynes, and the World War I poet Rupert Brooke. ✉ *King's Parade* ☎ *01223/331212* 🌐 *www.kings.cam.ac.uk* 🎫 *£8, includes chapel* 🕒 *Term time: Mon. 9:45–3:30, Tues.–Fri. 9:30–3:30, Sat. 9:30–3:15, Sun. 1:15–2:30. Out of term: Mon. 9:45–4:30, Tues.–Sun. 9:30–4:30.*

Fodor's Choice ★ **King's College Chapel.** Based on Sainte-Chapelle, the 13th-century royal chapel in Paris, this house of worship is perhaps the most glorious flowering of Perpendicular Gothic in Britain. Henry VI, the king after whom the college is named, oversaw the work. From the outside, the most prominent features are the massive flying buttresses and the fingerlike spires that line the length of the building. Inside, the most obvious impression is of great space—the chapel was once described as "the noblest barn in Europe"—and of light flooding in from its huge windows. The brilliantly colored bosses (carved panels at the intersections of the roof ribs) are particularly intense, although hard to see without binoculars. An exhibition in the chantries, or side chapels, explains more about the chapel's construction. Behind the altar is *The Adoration of the Magi*, an enormous painting by Peter Paul Rubens. ■ **TIP→ The chapel, unlike the rest of King's College, stays open during exam periods.** Every Christmas Eve, a festival of carols is sung by the chapel's famous choir. It's broadcast on national television and considered a quintessential part of the traditional English Christmas. To compete for the small number of tickets available, join the line at the college's main entrance early—doors open at 7 am. ✉ *King's Parade* ☎ *01223/331212* 🌐 *www.kings.cam.ac.uk* 🎟 *£8, includes college and grounds* ⏲ *Term time: Mon. 9:45–3:30, Tues.–Fri. 9:30–3:30, Sat. 9:30–3:15, Sun. 9:45–4:30. Out of term: Mon. 9:45–5:30, Tues.–Sun. 9:30–4:30. Sometimes closed for events; call ahead to confirm.*

A GIFT FOR SCIENCE

For centuries Cambridge has been among the country's greatest universities, rivaled only by Oxford. Since the time of one of its most famous alumni, Sir Isaac Newton, it's outshone Oxford in the natural sciences. The university has taken advantage of this prestige, sharing its research facilities with high-tech industries. Surrounded by technology companies, Cambridge has been dubbed "Silicon Fen," a comparison to California's Silicon Valley.

QUICK BITES

Pickerel Inn. This 600-year-old inn is home to one of the city's oldest pubs, making it a good stop for an afternoon pint of real ale and bowl of doorstop-sized potato wedges. Watch for the low beams. ✉ ***30 Magdalene St.*** ☎ ***01223/355068*** 🌐 ***www.taylor-walker.co.uk.***

Fodor's Choice ★ **Museum of Archaeology and Anthropology.** Cambridge University maintains some fine museums in its research halls on Downing Street—the wonder is that they're not better known to visitors. At the recently renovated Museum of Archaeology and Anthropology, highlights include an array of objects brought back from Captain Cook's pioneering voyages to the Pacific; Roman and medieval-era British artifacts; and the oldest human-made tools ever discovered, from the African expeditions of British archaeologist Louis Leakey (1903–1972). ✉ *Downing St.* ☎ *01223/333516* 🌐 *maa.cam.ac.uk* 🎟 *Free* ⏲ *Tues.–Sat. 10:30–4:30, Sun. noon–4:30.*

Fodor's Choice ★ **Polar Museum.** Beautifully designed, this museum at Cambridge University's Scott Polar Research Institute chronicles the history of polar exploration. There's a particular emphasis on the British expeditions of the 20th century, including the ill-fated attempt by Robert Falcon Scott to be the first to reach the South Pole in 1912. Norwegian explorer Roald Amundsen reached the pole first; Scott and his men perished on the return journey, but their story became legendary. There are also collections devoted to the science of modern polar exploration; the indigenous people of northern Canada, Greenland, and Alaska; and frequently changing art installations. ✉ *Scott Polar Research Institute, Lensfield Rd.* ☎ *01223/336540* 🌐 *www.spri.cam.ac.uk/museum* 🎫 *Free* ⏲ *Tues.–Sat. 10–4. Closed Sat. of holiday weekends.*

Queens' College. One of the most eye-catching colleges, Queens' is named after Margaret, wife of Henry VI, and Elizabeth, wife of Edward IV. Founded in 1448, the college is tucked away on Queens' Lane, next to the wide lawns that lead down from King's College to the Backs. The secluded "cloister court" looks untouched since its completion in the 1540s. Queens' masterpiece is the **Mathematical Bridge,** the original version of which is said to have been built without any fastenings. The current bridge (1902) is securely bolted. The college is closed to visitors late May to late June. ✉ *Queens' La.* ☎ *01223/335511* 🌐 *www.quns.cam.ac.uk* 🎫 *£3* ⏲ *Daily 10–4:30; closed during exam study periods certain wks Apr.–July. Call to confirm.*

WORTH NOTING

Cambridge University Botanic Gardens. Opened in 1846, these 40 acres contain rare specimens like the jade vine, greenhouses filled with orchids and other tropical beauties, and a rock garden with delicate plants from all over the world. The gardens are a five-minute walk from the Fitzwilliam Museum. ✉ *Cory Lodge, Bateman St.* ☎ *01223/336265* 🌐 *www.botanic.cam.ac.uk* 🎫 *£5* ⏲ *Feb.–Mar. and Oct., daily 10–5; Apr.–Sept., daily 10–6; Nov.–Jan., daily 10–4; conservatories close 30 min before gardens.*

Kettle's Yard. Originally a private house owned by a former curator of London's Tate galleries, Kettle's Yard contains a fine collection of 20th-century art, sculpture, furniture, and decorative arts, including works by Henry Moore, Barbara Hepworth, and Alfred Wallis. A separate gallery shows changing exhibitions of modern art and crafts, and weekly concerts and lectures attract an eclectic mix of enthusiasts. Ring the bell for admission. ✉ *Castle St.* ☎ *01223/748100* 🌐 *www.kettlesyard.co.uk* 🎫 *Free* ⏲ *Tues.–Sun. and holiday Mon. noon–5 (house), 11:30–5 (gallery).*

Trinity College. Founded in 1546 by Henry VIII, Trinity replaced a 14th-century educational foundation and is the largest college in either Cambridge or Oxford, with nearly 700 undergraduates. In the 17th-century great court, with its massive gatehouse, is **Great Tom,** a giant clock that strikes each hour with high and low notes. The college's greatest masterpiece is Christopher Wren's **library,** colonnaded and seemingly constructed with as much light as stone. Among the things you can see here is A. A. Milne's handwritten manuscript of *The House at Pooh Corner.* Trinity alumni include Isaac Newton, William Thackeray, Lord Byron, Alfred Tennyson, and 31 Nobel Prize winners. ✉ *St. John's St.* ☎ *01223/338400* 🌐 *www.trin.cam.ac.uk* 🎫 *£2* ⏲ *College and chapel* *daily 10–4, except exam period and event days. Wren Library weekdays noon–2, Sat. in term time 10:30–12:30. Great Court daily 10–4:30.*

Whipple Museum of the History of Science. This rather delightful, dusty old cupboard of a museum contains all manner of scientific artifacts, instruments, and doodads from the medieval period to the early 20th century. Most fun is the section on astronomy, including a beautiful 18th-century grand orrery—an elaborate three-dimensional model of the solar system, minus the planets that had yet to be discovered at the time. ✉ *Free School La.* ☎ *01223/330906* 🌐 *www.hps.cam.ac.uk/whipple* 🎫 *Free* ⏲ *Weekdays 12:30–4:30. Closed public holidays.*

WHERE TO EAT

$ ITALIAN ✕ **Jamie's Italian.** Run by celebrity chef Jamie Oliver, this is one of the busiest restaurants in Cambridge. In truth, the long queues on weekend nights have more to do with his star power and the no-reservations policy, but the food deserves some praise. The menu is a combination of authentic Italian flavors and modern variations on the classics; you could opt for the pasta *arrabiata,* made with bread crumbs and fiery peppers, or the fillet of sea bream with garlic, wine, capers, and plum tomatoes. The gorgeous building, a former library, is an attraction in itself. The atmosphere is relaxed and casual, and the prices are lower than you'd expect. 💲 *Average main: £14* ✉ *Old Library, Wheeler St.* ☎ *01223/654094* 🌐 *www.jamieoliver.com/italian.*

$$ SEAFOOD ✕ **Loch Fyne.** Part of a Scottish chain that harvests its own oysters, this airy, casual place across from the Fitzwilliam Museum is deservedly popular. The seafood is fresh and well prepared, served in a traditional setting with a modern ambience. Try the Bradan Rost smoked salmon if it's on the menu; it's flavored with Scotch whisky. The restaurant is also open for breakfast. 💲 *Average main: £17* ✉ *37 Trumpington St.* ☎ *01223/362433* 🌐 *www.lochfyne-restaurants.com.*

$$$$ FRENCH Fodor's Choice ★ ✕ **Midsummer House.** Beside the River Cam on the edge of Midsummer Common, this gray-brick building holds a two-Michelin-starred restaurant with a comfortable conservatory and a handful of tables under fruit trees in a lush, secluded garden. Fixed-price menus for lunch and dinner (three to five courses) present innovative French and Mediterranean-influenced dishes. Choices might include roasted sea bass or venison with blue cheese and sloe berries. 💲 *Average main: £48* ✉ *Midsummer Common* ☎ *01223/369299* 🌐 *www.midsummerhouse.co.uk* ⏲ *Closed Sun. and Mon. No lunch Tues.*

$$ BRITISH ✕ **The Oak.** This charming, intimate restaurant is a local favorite. It's near an uncompromisingly busy intersection, but the friendliness of the staff and classic bistro food more than make up for it. Typical mains include Cajun swordfish with green bean salad, or rib-eye steak with truffle butter and fries. Ask to be seated in the lovely walled garden if the weather's fine. 💲 *Average main: £15* ✉ *6 Lensfield Rd.* ☎ *01223/323361* 🌐 *www.theoakbistro.co.uk.*

$$$$ BRITISH ✕ **Restaurant 22.** Pretty stained-glass windows separate this sophisticated little restaurant from bustling Chesterton Road. The setting, in a terrace of houses, is low-key, but the food is creative and eye-catching.

The fixed-price menu changes monthly and includes dishes like Guinea fowl with madeira sauce and pollock with tarragon cream. For dessert, try the coconut parfait with chili sauce if it's available. *Average main: £37* *22 Chesterton Rd.* *01223/351880* *www.restaurant22.co.uk* *Closed Sun. and Mon. No lunch.*

$$$ MODERN BRITISH **River Bar Steakhouse & Grill.** Across the river from Magdalene College, this popular waterfront bar and grill serves delicious steak and burgers, plus specialties such as lobster mac and cheese, and roast chicken with a bourbon barbecue glaze. Light lunches are served in the afternoon, and the evening cocktail list is small but elegant. Try the French 75, which is gin with lemon juice, sugar, and sparkling wine. *Average main: £20* *Quayside, Thompsons La., off Bridge St.* *01223/307030* *www.riverbarsteakhouse.com* *Reservations essential.*

$$$ MEDITERRANEAN **Three Horseshoes.** This early-19th-century pub and restaurant in a thatched cottage has an elegant dining space in the conservatory and more casual tables in the airy bar. Sourcing of ingredients is taken seriously here—the menu lists not only the suppliers, but specific reasons for choosing them—and this is all put to good use in Modern British dishes with hints of the Mediterranean. Start with sugar-cured sea trout with smoked yogurt, then move on to duck breast with pumpkin seeds, or salmon fillet with pancetta and brown shrimp. The long wine list is predominantly Italian, but there are also some good New World choices. Madingley is 5 miles west of Cambridge, about a 10-minute taxi ride. *Average main: £19* *High St., Madingley* *01954/210221* *www.threehorseshoesmadingley.co.uk.*

$$ MODERN BRITISH **The Willow Tree.** Plenty of Cambridge residents are happy to drive 20 minutes out of the city to this stylish little pub in the sleepy village of Bourn. The seasonal menu serves classic British and European dishes with a creative flourish. Typical mains include sea bass and squid stew with skin crisps, and venison haunch with a walnut crust. Or, if you're in the mood for something simpler, steaks, burgers, and pizzas are also available. For dessert try the chocolate torte with affogato sauce, or the cheesecake made with Bailey's Irish Cream liqueur and Maltesers (a British candy made from malted honeycombs and coated in chocolate). Bourn is 10 miles east of Cambridge; take the B1046 for the prettiest drive. *Average main: £15* *29 High St., Bourn* *01954/719775* *www.thewillowtreebourn.com.*

WHERE TO STAY

There aren't many hotels downtown. For more (and cheaper) options, consider one of the numerous guesthouses on the arterial roads and in the suburbs. These average around £40 to £90 per person per night and can be booked through the tourist information center.

$$ B&B/INN **5 Chapel Street.** This sweet Georgian town house and B&B in the northeastern corner of the city is a beautiful 20-minute walk along the river from central Cambridge. **Pros:** quiet location; wonderful host; excellent breakfast. **Cons:** 20-minute walk to the center; some rooms are small. *Rooms from: £100* *5 Chapel St., Chesterton* *01223/514856* *www.5chapelstreet.com* *3 rooms* *Breakfast.*

$$$ HOTEL **DoubleTree by Hilton Cambridge.** This modern establishment makes the most of its peaceful riverside location, and many rooms have sweeping views of the surrounding area. **Pros:** central position; good facilities and service; spacious rooms. **Cons:** price fluctuates wildly over summer season. *Rooms from: £189* *Granta Pl. and Mill La.* *01223/259988* *www.doubletreecambridge.com* *118 rooms, 4 suites* *Breakfast; Some meals.*

$$ B&B/INN Fodor's Choice ★ **Duke House.** This beautifully converted town house (home of the duke of Gloucester when he was a student) is forever cropping up in British newspaper articles about the best B&Bs in the country. **Pros:** beautiful house; great location; suites are quite spacious. **Cons:** books up fast; two-night minimum on weekends; cheaper rooms are small. *Rooms from: £140* *1 Victoria St.* *01223/314773* *www.dukehousecambridge.co.uk* *4 rooms* *Breakfast.*

$ B&B/INN **Finches Bed and Breakfast.** Although it's in a rather inauspicious building, the diminutive Finches is a well-run B&B with prices that make it an excellent value. **Pros:** cheerful staff; quiet location; good level of service. **Cons:** away from the action; no tubs in bathrooms; no credit cards. *Rooms from: £75* *144 Thornton Rd.* *01223/276653* *www.finches-bnb.com* *No credit cards* *3 rooms* *Breakfast.*

$$ HOTEL **Regent Hotel.** A rare small hotel in central Cambridge, this handsome Georgian town house has wooden sash windows that look out over a tree-lined park called Parker's Piece. **Pros:** good view from top rooms; close to bars and restaurants. **Cons:** no parking; a tad scruffy; disappointing breakfasts. *Rooms from: £119* *41 Regent St.* *01223/351470* *www.regenthotel.co.uk* *22 rooms* *Breakfast.*

$$ HOTEL Fodor's Choice ★ **The Varsity.** This stylish boutique hotel with an adjoining spa has wide windows that flood the place with light. **Pros:** beautiful location; gorgeous views; stylish design. **Cons:** not such great views in the cheap rooms; prices rise sharply on weekdays. *Rooms from: £149* *Thompson's La., off Bridge St.* *01223/306030* *www.thevarsityhotel.co.uk* *48 rooms* *Breakfast; No meals.*

$ B&B/INN **Warkworth House.** The location of this B&B could hardly be better, as the Fitzwilliam Museum and several of Cambridge's colleges are within a 15-minute walk. **Pros:** excellent location; lovely hosts; family rooms are great value; some free parking. **Cons:** few frills; no restaurant onsite. *Rooms from: £90* *Warkworth Terr.* *01223/363682* *www.warkworthhouse.co.uk* *5 rooms* *Breakfast.*

NIGHTLIFE AND PERFORMING ARTS

NIGHTLIFE

The city's pubs provide the mainstay of Cambridge's nightlife and shouldn't be missed.

Eagle. This 16th-century coaching inn with a cobbled courtyard has lost none of its old-time character. It also played a minor role in scientific history when on February 28, 1953, a pair of excited Cambridge scientists announced to a roomful of rather surprised lunchtime patrons that they'd just discovered the secret of life: DNA. A plaque outside commemorates the event. ✉ *8 Benet St.* ☎ *01223/505020* 🌐 *www.gkpubs.co.uk/pubs-in-cambridge/eagle-pub.*

Fort St. George. Overlooking the university boathouses, this lovely old pub gets honors for its riverside views. ✉ *Midsummer Common* ☎ *01223/354327* 🌐 *www.gkpubs.co.uk/pubs-in-cambridge/fort-st-george-pub.*

Free Press. A favorite of student rowers, this small pub has an excellent selection of traditional ales. ✉ *7 Prospect Row* ☎ *01223/368337* 🌐 *www.freepresspub.com.*

PERFORMING ARTS

CONCERTS

Cambridge supports its own symphony orchestra, and regular musical events are held in many colleges, especially those with large chapels.

Cambridge Folk Festival. Spread over four days in late July or early August at Cherry Hinton Hall, the Cambridge Folk Festival attracts major international folk singers and groups. ✉ *Cambridge* ☎ *01223/357851* 🌐 *www.cambridgefolkfestival.co.uk.*

Corn Exchange. The beautifully restored Corn Exchange presents classical and rock concerts, stand-up comedy, musicals, opera, and ballet. ✉ *Wheeler St.* ☎ *01223/357851* 🌐 *www.cornex.co.uk.*

King's College Chapel. During regular terms, King's College Chapel has evensong services Monday through Saturday at 5:30, Sunday at 3:30. ■ **TIP→ Your best chance of seeing the full choir is Thursday to Sunday.** ✉ *King's Parade* ☎ *01223/769340* 🌐 *www.kings.cam.ac.uk.*

THEATER

ADC Theatre. Home of the famous *Cambridge Footlights Revue*, the ADC Theatre hosts mainly student and fringe theater productions. ✉ *Park St.* ☎ *01223/300085* 🌐 *www.adctheatre.com.*

Arts Theatre. The city's main repertory theater, built in 1936 by John Maynard Keynes (one of the most influential economists of the 20th century and a Cambridge University alumnus), still supports a full program of plays and concerts and has a good ground-floor bar and two restaurants. ✉ *6 St. Edward's Passage* ☎ *01223/503333* 🌐 *www.cambridgeartstheatre.com.*

SHOPPING

Head to the specialty shops in the center of town, especially in and around Rose Crescent and King's Parade. Bookshops, including antiquarian stores, are Cambridge's pride and joy.

BOOKS

Cambridge University Press Bookshop. In business since at least 1581, the Cambridge University Press runs this store on Trinity Street. ✉ *1 Trinity St.* ☎ *01223/333333* 🌐 *www.cambridge.org/uk/bookshop.*

David's. Near the Arts Theatre, G. David (known locally as just David's) sells antiquarian books. ✉ *16 St. Edward's Passage* ☎ *01223/354619* 🌐 *www.davidsbookshop.co.uk.*

CLOSE UP

Punting on the Cam

To punt is to maneuver a flat-bottom, wooden, gondolalike boat—in this case, through the shallow River Cam along the verdant Backs behind the colleges of Cambridge. One benefit of this popular activity is that you get a better view of the ivy-covered walls from the water. Mastery of the sport lies in your ability to control a 15-foot pole, used to propel the punt. With a bottle of wine, some food, and a few friends, you may find yourself saying things such as, "It doesn't get any better than this." One piece of advice: if your pole gets stuck, let go. You can use the smaller paddle to go back and retrieve it. Hang on to a stuck punt for too long and you'll probably fall in with it.

The lazier-at-heart may prefer chauffeured punting, with food supplied. Students from Cambridge often do the work, and you get a fairly informative spiel on the colleges. For a romantic evening trip, there are illuminated punts.

One university punting society once published a useful "Bluffer's Guide to Punting" featuring detailed instructions and tips on how to master the art. It has been archived online at 🌐 *www.duramecho.com/misc/howtopunt.html.*

Haunted Bookshop. This shop carries a great selection of old, illustrated books and British classics. And (the clue's in the name) apparently it has a ghost, too. ✉ *9 St. Edward's Passage* ☎ *01223/312913* 🌐 *www.sarahkeybooks.co.uk.*

Heffer's. With many rare and imported books, Heffer's boasts a particularly extensive arts section. ✉ *20 Trinity St.* ☎ *01223/463200* 🌐 *www.heffers.co.uk.*

CLOTHING

Ryder & Amies. Need a straw boater? This shop is the official outlet for Cambridge University products, from hoodies to ties to cufflinks. ✉ *22 King's Parade* ☎ *01223/350371* 🌐 *www.ryderamies.co.uk.*

MARKETS

All Saints Garden Art & Craft Market. This market displays the wares of local artists outdoors on Saturday. It's also open Fridays in July and August and some weekends in December (weather permitting). ✉ *Trinity St.* 🌐 *www.cambridge-art-craft.co.uk.*

SPORTS AND THE OUTDOORS

BIKING

City Cycle Hire. This shop charges super cheap rates of £7 per half day, £10 per day, and £20 for a week. All bikes are mountain or hybrid bikes. Advance reservations are essential in July and August. ✉ *61 Newnham Rd.* ☎ *01223/365629* 🌐 *www.citycyclehire.com.*

PUNTING

You can rent punts at several places, notably at Silver Street Bridge–Mill Lane, at Magdalene Bridge, and from outside the Rat and Parrot pub on Thompson's Lane on Jesus Green. Hourly rental costs around £15 to £25. Chauffeured punting, usually by a Cambridge student, is also popular. It costs upwards of £15 per person.

Scudamore's Punting Co. This company rents chauffeured and self-drive punts. Daily, 45-minute tours start at around £18 per person (£13 if booked online). Scudamore's also runs various special tours—for afternoon tea or Halloween, for example. Private tours and punting lessons are also available. High-stakes romantics can even arrange a "Proposal Tour," which includes champagne and roses if your beloved says yes. ✉ *Granta Place, Mill La.* ☎ *01223/359750* 🌐 *www.scudamores.com.*

ELY AND CENTRAL SUFFOLK

This central area of towns and villages within easy reach of Cambridge is testament to the amazing changeability of the English landscape. The town of Ely is set in an eerie, flat, and apparently endless marsh, or fenland. (A medieval term, "the fens," is still used informally to describe the surrounding region.) Only a few miles south and east into Suffolk, however, all this changes to pastoral landscapes of gently undulating hills and clusters of villages including pretty Sudbury and Lavenham.

ELY

16 miles north of Cambridge.

Known for its magnificent cathedral, Ely is the "capital" of the fens, the center of what used to be a separate county called the Isle of Ely (literally "island of eels"). Until the land was drained in the 17th century, Ely was surrounded by treacherous marshland, which inhabitants crossed wearing stilts. Today Wicken Fen, a nature reserve 9 miles southeast of town (off A1123), preserves the sole remaining example of fenland in an undrained state.

Enveloped by fields of wheat, sugar beets, and carrots, Ely is a small, dense town that somewhat fails to live up to the high expectations created by its big attraction, its magnificent cathedral. The shopping area and market square lie to the north and lead down to the riverside, and the medieval buildings of the cathedral grounds and the King's School (which trains cathedral choristers) spread out to the south and west. Ely's most famous resident was Oliver Cromwell, whose house is now a museum.

GETTING HERE AND AROUND

The 9 and 12 buses leave twice an hour from the Drummer Street bus station in Cambridge. The journey to Ely takes around an hour. To drive there from Cambridge, simply take the A10 road going north out of the city. Ely is quite small, so find somewhere to park and walk to the center. Trains from Cambridge to Ely leave three times an hour and take 15 minutes.

ESSENTIALS

Visitor Information Visit Ely. ✉ *Oliver Cromwell's House, 29 St. Mary's St.* ☎ *01353/662062* 🌐 *www.visitely.org.uk.*

EXPLORING

Fodor's Choice ★ **Ely Cathedral.** Known affectionately as the Ship of the Fens, Ely Cathedral can be seen for miles, towering above the flat landscape on one of the few ridges in the fens. In 1083 the Normans began work on the cathedral, which stands on the site of a Benedictine monastery founded by the Anglo-Saxon princess Etheldreda in 673. In the center of the cathedral you see a marvel of medieval construction—the unique octagonal **Lantern Tower,** a sort of stained-glass skylight of colossal proportions, built to replace the central tower that collapsed in 1322. The cathedral's **West Tower** is even taller; the view from the top (if you can manage the 288 steps) is spectacular. Tours of both towers are run daily. The cathedral is also notable for its 248-foot-long **nave,** with its simple Norman arches and Victorian painted ceiling. Much of the decorative carving of the 14th-century **Lady Chapel** was defaced during the Reformation (mostly by knocking off the heads of the statuary), but enough traces remain to show its original beauty.

The cathedral houses a superior **Stained Glass Museum** (🌐 *www.stainedglassmuseum.com*) up a flight of 42 steps. Exhibits trace the history of stained glass from medieval to modern times. Ely Cathedral is a popular location for films; it doubled for Westminster Abbey in *The King's Speech* (2010).

■ **TIP→ There are guided tours of the Cathedral from Monday to Saturday (and Sundays in summer); generally they start at 10:45, noon, and 2, with extra tours in the summer, but times vary so it's a good idea to call ahead.** ✉ *The Gallery* ☎ *01353/667735* 🌐 *www.elycathedral.org* 🎫 *£8 including tour; £14.50 with Octagon Tower or West Tower; £12 with Stained Glass Museum; £18 combined ticket for all sights* ⏲ *Cathedral May–Sept., daily 7–6:30; Oct.–Apr., Mon.–Sat. 7–6:30, Sun. 7–5:30. Stained Glass Museum Mon.–Sat. 10:30–5, Sun. noon–4:30.*

Oliver Cromwell's House. This half-timber medieval building stands in the shadows of Ely Cathedral. During the 10 years he lived here, Cromwell (1599–1658) was leading the rebellious Roundheads in their eventually victorious struggle against King Charles I in the English Civil War. The house contains an exhibition about its controversial former occupant, who was Britain's Lord Protector from 1653 to 1658. It's also the site of Ely's tourist information center. ✉ *29 St. Mary's St.* ☎ *01353/662062* 🌐 *www.visitely.org.uk/cromwell/oliver-cromwells-house* 🎫 *£4.90* ⏲ *Apr.–Oct., daily 10–5; Nov.–Mar., daily 11–4. Last admission 1 hr before closing.*

WHERE TO EAT AND STAY

$$ BRITISH Fodor's Choice ★ ✕ **Old Fire Engine House.** Scrubbed pine tables fill the main dining room of this converted fire station near Ely Cathedral; another room, used when there's a crowd, has an open fireplace and a polished wood floor, and also serves as an art gallery. The menu could include traditional fenland recipes like sea bream with prawn and watercress sauce, as well as more familiar English fare, such as roast leg of lamb with fresh herb stuffing.

Desserts might include treacle pudding (a sticky, steamed cake) or homemade ice cream. Reserve ahead for afternoon tea (£19). *$ Average main: £16.50 ✉ 25 St. Mary's St. ☎ 01353/662582 🌐 www.theoldfireenginehouse.co.uk ⏱ No dinner Sun.*

$ HOTEL **Cathedral House.** This Georgian house, full of interesting period details such as an oriel window and a handsome staircase, makes a pleasant overnight stop in Ely. The bedrooms are small but cozy, with antique furniture. **Pros:** heaps of character; steps from the cathedral; free Wi-Fi; handy parking. **Cons:** small bathrooms; on a busy road; two-night minimum on weekends; late check-in and early check-out times. *$ Rooms from: £90 ✉ 17 St. Mary's St. ☎ 01353/662124 🌐 www.cathedralhouse.co.uk 3 rooms, 1 cottage 🍽 Breakfast.*

DRAINING EAST ANGLIA

Large areas of East Anglia were originally barely inhabited, swampy marshes. Drainage of the wetlands by the creation of waterways was carried out most energetically in the 17th and 18th centuries. The process was far from smooth. Locals, whose fishing rights were threatened, sometimes destroyed the work. Also, as the marshland dried out, it shrank and sank, requiring pumps to stop renewed flooding. Hundreds of windmills were used to pump water away; some of them can still be seen today.

SUDBURY

32 miles southeast of Ely, 16 miles south of Bury St. Edmunds.

An early silk-weaving industry (still in existence, on a smaller scale) as well as the wool trade brought prosperity to Sudbury, which has three fine Perpendicular Gothic churches and some half-timber houses.

Thomas Gainsborough, one of the greatest English portrait and landscape painters, was born here in 1727; a statue of him holding his palette stands on Market Hill. In Charles Dickens's first novel, *The Pickwick Papers,* Sudbury was the model for the fictional Eatanswill, where Mr. Pickwick stands for Parliament.

GETTING HERE AND AROUND

From Cambridge, driving to Sudbury requires a circuitous route that takes about an hour. The A14 is slightly quicker, but the A3107 is more picturesque. There are no easy bus or train connections from Cambridge or Ely.

ESSENTIALS

Visitor Information Sudbury Tourist Information Centre. *✉ The Library, Market Hill ☎ 01787/881320 🌐 www.sudbury.org.uk.*

EXPLORING

Gainsborough's House. The birthplace and family home of Thomas Gainsborough (1727–88) contains many paintings and drawings by the artist and his contemporaries. Although it presents a Georgian facade, with touches of the 18th-century neo-Gothic style, the building is essentially Tudor. The walled garden has a mulberry tree planted in 1620 and a printmaking workshop. The entrance is through the café and shop

on Weavers Lane. ✉ *46 Gainsborough St.* ☎ *01787/372958* 🌐 *www.gainsborough.org* 🎫 *£6.50; £7.50 with 15-min introductory talk; £90 with 1-hr guided tour* ⏲ *Mon.–Sat. 10–5, Sun. 11–5.*

LONG MELFORD

2 miles north of Sudbury, 14 miles south of Bury St. Edmunds.

It's easy to see how this village got its name, especially if you walk the full length of its 2-mile-long main street, which gradually broadens to include green squares and trees, and finally opens into a large triangular green on the hill. Long Melford grew rich on its wool trade in the 15th century, and the town's buildings are an appealing mix, mostly Tudor half-timber or Georgian. Many house antiques shops. Away from the main road, Long Melford returns to its resolutely late-medieval roots.

GETTING HERE AND AROUND

Long Melford is just off the main A134. If you're driving from Sudbury, take the smaller B1064; it's much quicker than it looks on the map. There are several bus connections with Sudbury, Bury St. Edmunds, and Ipswich.

EXPLORING

Holy Trinity Church. This largely 15th-century church, founded by the rich clothiers of Long Melford, stands on a hill at the north end of the village. Close up, the delicate flint flush-work (shaped flints set into a pattern) and huge Perpendicular Gothic windows that take up most of the church's walls have great impact, especially because the nave is 150 feet long. The Clopton Chapel, with an ornate (and incredibly rare) painted medieval ceiling, predates the rest of the church by 150 years. The beautiful Lady Chapel has an unusual cloister; the stone on the wall in the corner is an ancient multiplication table, used when the chapel served as a school in the 17th and 18th centuries. **■TIP→ Tours can be arranged in advance; contact Ann Share at 01787/310498.** ✉ *Main St.* ☎ *01787/310845* 🌐 *www.longmelfordchurch.com* 🎟 *Free* ⏲ *Apr.–Oct., daily 10–6; Nov.–Mar., daily 10–4.*

Melford Hall. Distinguished from the outside by its turrets and topiaries, Melford Hall is an Elizabethan house with its original banqueting room, a fair number of 18th-century additions, and pleasant gardens. Much of the porcelain and other fine pieces here come from the *Santisima Trinidad*, a ship loaded with gifts from the emperor of China and bound for Spain that was captured in the 18th century. Children's writer Beatrix Potter, related to the owners, visited often; there's a small collection of Potter memorabilia. ✉ *Off A134* ☎ *01787/379228* 🌐 *www.nationaltrust.org.uk/melfordhall* 🎟 *£7.50* ⏲ *Apr.–Oct., Wed.–Sun. 1–5; Nov.–Mar., weekends noon–5 (guided tours only).*

WHERE TO STAY

$$ HOTEL **The Bull.** This half-timber Elizabethan building reveals its long history with stone-flagged floors, bowed and twisted oak beams, and heavy antique furniture. **Pros:** historic atmosphere; comfortable bedrooms; friendly staff. **Cons:** minimum stay on summer weekends; popular with wedding parties. $ *Rooms from: £110* ✉ *Hall St.* ☎ *01787/378494* 🌐 *www.oldenglishinns.co.uk/our-locations/the-bull-hotel-long-melford* *25 rooms* 🍽 *Some meals.*

LAVENHAM

4 miles northeast of Long Melford, 10 miles southeast of Bury St. Edmunds.

Fodor's Choice ★ Virtually unchanged since the height of its wealth in the 15th and 16th centuries, Lavenham is one of the most perfectly preserved examples of a Tudor village in England. The weavers' and wool merchants' houses occupy not just one show street but most of the town. The houses are timber-frame in black oak, the main posts looking as if they could last another 400 years, although their walls are often no longer entirely perpendicular to the ground. The town has many examples of so-called "Suffolk pink" buildings—actually a catch-all term for brightly painted colors, including rose, yellow, and apricot; many of these house small galleries selling paintings and crafts.

GETTING HERE AND AROUND

Lavenham is on the A1141 and B1071. Take the latter if possible, as it's a prettier drive. There are hourly buses from Sudbury and Bury St. Edmunds and slightly less frequent buses from Ipswich.

ESSENTIALS

Visitor Information Lavenham Tourist Information Centre. ✉ *Lady St.* ☎ *01787/248207* 🌐 *www.heartofsuffolk.co.uk.*

EXPLORING

Church of St. Peter and St. Paul. Set apart from the village on a hill, this grand 15th-century church was built between 1480 and 1520 by cloth merchant Thomas Spring. The height of its tower (141 feet) was meant to surpass those of the neighboring churches—and perhaps to impress rival towns. The rest of the church is perfectly proportioned, with intricately carved wood. ✉ *Church St.* ☎ *01787/247244* 🎫 *Free* ⏲ *Daily; hrs vary but usually 10–5.*

Lavenham Guildhall. Also known as the Guildhall of Corpus Christi, this higgledy-piggledy timber-framed building dating from 1529 dominates Market Place, an almost flawlessly preserved medieval square. Upstairs is a rather dull exhibition on local agriculture and the wool trade, although looking around the building itself is worth the admission charge. ✉ *Market Pl.* ☎ *01787/247646* 🌐 *www.nationaltrust.org.uk/lavenham-guildhall* 🎫 *£6* ⏲ *Jan.–Feb., weekends 11–4; Mar.–Oct., daily 11–5; Nov.–late Dec., Thurs.–Sun. 11–4.*

Little Hall. This timber-frame wool merchant's house (brightly painted on the outside, in the local custom) contains a display showing the building's progress from its creation in the 14th century to its subsequent "modernization" in the 17th century. It also has a beautiful garden at the back. ✉ *Market Pl.* ☎ *01787/247019* 🌐 *www.littlehall.org.uk* 🎫 *£3.50* ⏲ *Apr.–Oct., Tues.–Thurs., Sat., and Sun. 1–5, holiday Mon. 10–1; last admission 1 hr before closing.*

QUICK BITE

✕ Munnings Tea Room. Probably one of the most photographed buildings in Lavenham, the wonderfully jumbled exterior of this adorable tearoom draws you in as surely as the promise of a delicious scone or slice of cake. Delightfully old fashioned and quirky, this is what the British call a "proper tearoom," where tea is served in real china and diet-busting treats keep you going until dinner. ✉ ***The Crooked House, 7 High St.*** ☎ ***0782/482-5623*** 🌐 ***www.munningstearoom.co.uk.***

WHERE TO EAT

$$$$ | FRENCH | Fodor's Choice ★

✕ Great House. This excellent "restaurant-with-rooms" on the medieval Market Square takes deeply traditional flavors of the British countryside and updates them with a slight French twist in dishes like grilled salmon with spinach fondue, or lamb with onion and thyme pie. The three-course, fixed-price menus use plenty of local ingredients. The lamb, for example, is reared by a local farmer. The five spacious guest rooms have sloping floors, beamed ceilings, well-appointed bathrooms, and antique furnishings. $ *Average main: £35* ✉ *Market Pl.* ☎ *01787/247431*

Colorful and ancient, the timbered houses in pretty towns such as Lavenham recall the days when these buildings housed weavers and wool merchants.

www.greathouse.co.uk *Closed Mon. and Jan. No dinner Sun. No lunch Mon. and Tues.* *Reservations essential.*

$ INDIAN Fodor's Choice ★ **Memsaab.** In a town ready to burst with cream teas, it's a bit of a surprise to find an Indian restaurant, let alone such an exceptional one. Among the classics one would expect from a curry house—from mild kormas to spicy *madrases* and *jalfrezies* (traditional curries made with chili and tomato)—are some finely executed specialties, including Nizami chicken (a fiery dish prepared with yogurt and fresh ginger) and king prawn *bhuna* (with ginger, garlic, and spring onion). The menu also contains regional specialties from Goa and Hyderabad. *Average main: £11* *2 Church St.* *01787/249431* *www.memsaab oflavenham.co.uk.*

WHERE TO STAY

$ B&B/INN **Guinea House.** Still a private home after 600 years, Guinea House attracts travelers seeking more authenticity than your average B&B. **Pros:** quiet central location; intimate feel; one-of-a-kind atmosphere. **Cons:** low ceilings and hobbit-size doorways; no common areas. *Rooms from: £75* *16 Bolton St.* *01787/249046* *www.guineahouse.co.uk* *No credit cards* *2 rooms* *Breakfast.*

$$ B&B/INN Fodor's Choice ★ **Shilling Grange.** This timber-framed house, built in 1425, has been beautifully converted into a chic and comfortable B&B. **Pros:** beautiful and historic house; good balance of history and modern comfort; charming hosts; quiet street. **Cons:** uneven floors and low ceilings; bedroom above lounge can get noise from below; no dinner; 35% booking deposit is nonrefundable. *Rooms from: £130* *Shilling St.* *01787/249423* *www.shillinggrange.com* *3 rooms* *Breakfast.*

$$ HOTEL **Swan Hotel.** This half-timber 14th-century lodging has rambling public rooms, roaring fireplaces, and corridors so low that cushions are strategically placed on beams. **Pros:** lovely old building; atmospheric rooms; new spa. **Cons:** creaky floors; lots of steps to climb; popular wedding venue. *Rooms from: £130* *High St.* *01787/247477* *www.theswanatlavenham.co.uk* *47 rooms, 2 suites* *Some meals.*

BURY ST. EDMUNDS

10 miles north of Lavenham, 28 miles east of Cambridge.

The Georgian streetscape helps make the town one of the area's prettiest, and the nearby Greene King Westgate Brewery adds the smell of sweet hops to the air. The town hall dates from 1774.

Bury St. Edmunds owes its name, and indeed its existence, to Edmund, the last king of East Anglia and medieval patron saint of England, who was hacked to death by marauding Danes in 869. He was subsequently canonized, and his shrine attracted pilgrims, settlement, and commerce. In the 11th century the erection of a great Norman abbey (now only ruins) confirmed the town's importance as a religious center. The tourist office has a leaflet about the ruins and can arrange a guided tour.

GETTING HERE AND AROUND

The 11 bus from Cambridge's Drummer Street bus station takes about an hour to reach Bury St. Edmunds. By car, the town is a short drive from either Lavenham or Cambridge. Trains from Cambridge to Bury St. Edmunds leave once or twice an hour and take about 40 minutes.

ESSENTIALS

Visitor Information Visit Bury St. Edmunds. *Charter Sq.* *01284/764667* *www.visit-burystedmunds.co.uk.*

EXPLORING

TOP ATTRACTIONS

Abbey Ruins and Botanical Gardens. This is all that remains of the Abbey of Bury St. Edmunds, which fell during Henry VIII's dissolution of the monasteries. The Benedictine abbey's enormous scale is evident in the surviving Norman Gate Tower on Angel Hill, (incongruously, but quite appealingly, overlooked by a row of Georgian houses). Besides this, only the fortified Abbot's Bridge over the River Lark and a few ruins are left standing. There are explanatory plaques amid the ruins, which are now the site of the Abbey Botanical Gardens, with roses, elegant hedges, and rare trees, including a Chinese tree of heaven planted in the 1830s. There's also an aviary, a putting green, and a children's play area. *Angel Hill* *01284/764667* *www.english-heritage.org.uk* *Free* *Daily dawn–dusk.*

St. Edmundsbury Cathedral. Although the cathedral dates from the 15th century, its brilliant ceiling and gleaming stained-glass windows are the result of 19th-century restoration by architect Sir Gilbert Scott. Don't miss the memorial near the altar to an event in 1214, when the barons of England took an oath here to force King John to grant the Magna Carta. The cathedral's original Abbey Gate was destroyed in a riot, and it was rebuilt in the 14th century with defense in mind—you can see the arrow slits. From Easter to September, guided tours are available Monday to Saturday at 11:30. There's also a small but popular café. ✉ *Angel Hill* ☎ *01284/748720* 🌐 *www.stedscathedral.co.uk* 🎫 *Free, suggested donation £3* ⏲ *Daily 8:30–6.*

WORTH NOTING

Angel Hill. A walk here is a journey through the history of Bury St. Edmunds. Along one side, the Abbey Gate, Norman Gate Tower, and St. Mary's Church make up a continuous display of medieval architecture. Elegant Georgian houses line Angel Hill on the side opposite St. Mary's Church; these include the Athenaeum, an 18th-century social and cultural meeting place that has a fine Adam-style ballroom. ✉ *Angel Hill.*

Angel Hotel. This splendid, ivy-clad hotel was the location for Sam Weller's meeting with Job Trotter in Dickens's *The Pickwick Papers*. Dickens himself stayed here while he was giving readings at the nearby Athenaeum Hall. Now it's a great place to stop for lunch or afternoon tea. ✉ *3 Angel Hill* ☎ *01284/714000* 🌐 *www.theangel.co.uk.*

OFF THE BEATEN PATH

Ickworth House. The creation of the eccentric Frederick Hervey, fourth earl of Bristol and bishop of Derry, this unusual 18th-century home was owned by the Hervey family until the 1960s. Inspired by his travels, Hervey wanted an Italianate palace and gardens. Today the two wings around a striking central rotunda contain a hotel (east wing) and paintings by William Hogarth, Titian, and Gainsborough (west wing). Behind the house, the rose gardens and vineyards spread out to reach 1,800 acres of woods. A stroll over the hills gives the best vistas of the house, which is 7 miles southwest of Bury St. Edmunds. ✉ *Off A143, Horringer* ☎ *01284/735270* 🌐 *www.nationaltrust.org.uk/ickworth* 🎫 *£13; gardens and park only £6.50* ⏲ *House mid-Mar.–Oct., Thurs.–Tues. noon–4. West Wing Mar.–Oct. daily 10:30–5, Nov.–Feb. daily 10:30–4. Gardens Mar.–Oct. daily 9–5:30, Nov.–Feb. daily 9–5. Park daily 8–8.*

Moyse's Hall Museum. This 12th-century building, probably the oldest extant building in East Anglia, is a rare surviving example of a Norman house. The rooms hold exhibitions on Suffolk throughout the ages. One macabre display relates to the Red Barn Murder, a grisly local case that gained notoriety in a 19th-century play. ✉ *Cornhill* ☎ *01284/706183* 🌐 *www.moyseshall.org* 🎫 *£4; £9 combined ticket with West Stow Anglo Saxon Village* ⏲ *Mon.–Sat. 10–5; Sun. noon–4; last admission 1 hr before closing.*

St. Mary's Church. Built in the 15th century, St. Mary's has a blue-and-gold embossed "wagon" (barrel-shape) roof over the choir. Mary Tudor, Henry VIII's sister and queen of France, is buried here. ✉ *Angel Hill, at Honey Hill* ☎ *01284/754680* 🌐 *www.wearechurch.net* 🎫 *Free* ⏲ *Apr.–Oct., daily 10–4; Nov.–Mar., daily 10–3.*

Theatre Royal. Built in 1819, the Theatre Royal is an outstanding example of Regency design. Guided tours can be booked at the box office. ✉ *6 Westgate St.* ☎ *01284/769505* 🌐 *www.theatreroyal.org* 🎫 *Free; tours £6.50* ⏲ *Tours Feb.–July, Wed., Thurs., and Sat. 11.*

FAMILY **West Stow Anglo Saxon Village.** This family-friendly museum past the outskirts of Bury St. Edmunds has indoor galleries displaying items from the Anglo-Saxon period (410–1066) as well as a reconstruction of a village from that period with thatched-roof houses. Costumed performers give demonstrations of traditional crafts, and there's also a small farm with rare breeds of pigs and chickens. Call ahead in winter as the hours vary. ✉ *Icklingham Rd., West Stow* ☎ *01284/728718* 🌐 *www.weststow.org* 🎫 *£5; £9 combined ticket with Moyse's Hall* ⏲ *Daily 10–5; last admission 1 hr before closing (90 min in winter).*

WHERE TO EAT

$ CAFÉ ✕ **Harriet's Café Tearooms.** In an elegant dining room, Harriet's brings back the tearooms of yesteryear. The staff, dressed in old-style uniforms, serve snacks, sandwiches, or full afternoon teas (£15–£17) while hits from the 1940s play in the background. The café also serves snacks and light lunches on a similarly traditional theme, including jacket potatoes, cottage pie, and fish-and-chips. $ *Average main: £7* ✉ *57 Cornhill Bldgs.* ☎ *01284/756256* 🌐 *www.harrietscafetearooms.co.uk* ⏲ *No dinner.*

$$$ FRENCH Fodor's Choice ★ ✕ **Maison Bleue.** This stylish French restaurant, with the same owners as the Great House in nearby Lavenham, specializes in locally caught seafood. Typical choices include wild halibut with English wild boar chorizo or lobster tail with seaweed tagliatelle, in addition to meatier options like Suffolk lamb. The two-course lunches for under £20 are good value. $ *Average main: £22* ✉ *31 Churchgate St.* ☎ *01284/760623* 🌐 *www.maisonbleue.co.uk* ⏲ *Closed Sun. and Mon.* ✍ *Reservations essential.*

WHERE TO STAY

$ HOTEL FAMILY 🏨 **Ickworth Hotel.** You can live like nobility in the east wing of the Italianate Ickworth House, set on 1,800 acres of grounds. **Pros:** gorgeous grounds; relaxed atmosphere; family-friendly vibe. **Cons:** price is a little steep for what you get; two-night minimum on weekends; "family friendly" can feel more like "overrun with kids". $ *Rooms from: £95* ✉ *Off A143, 5 miles southwest of Bury St. Edmunds, Horringer* ☎ *01284/735350* 🌐 *www.ickworthhotel.co.uk* *24 rooms, 11 apartments, 8 suites* 🍽 *Breakfast.*

$$ B&B/INN 🏨 **The Old Cannon Brewery.** This delightful old inn near the Bury St. Edmunds train station has a handful of bedrooms in its converted Victorian brewhouse. **Pros:** full of character; good food and beer; friendly hosts. **Cons:** pub is noisy until closing time. $ *Rooms from: £120* ✉ *86 Cannon St.* ☎ *01284/768769* 🌐 *www.oldcannonbrewery.co.uk* *5 rooms* 🍽 *Breakfast; Some meals.*

NIGHTLIFE AND PERFORMING ARTS

Nutshell. While you're in Bury St. Edmunds, pop in for a pint of the local Greene King ale at the Nutshell, which claims to be Britain's smallest pub—measuring just 16 feet by 7½ feet. ✉ *17 The Traverse* ☎ *01284/764867* 🌐 *www.thenutshellpub.co.uk.*

THE SUFFOLK COAST

The 40-mile Suffolk Heritage Coast, which wanders northward from Felixstowe up to Kessingland, is one of the most unspoiled shorelines in the country. The lower part of the coast is the most impressive; however, some of the loveliest towns and villages, such as Dedham and the older part of Flatford, are inland. The best way to experience the countryside around here is to be willing to get lost along its tiny, ancient back roads. Try to avoid the coastal area between Lowestoft and Great Yarmouth; it has little to offer but run-down beach resorts.

DEDHAM

62 miles southeast of Cambridge, 15 miles southeast of Bury St. Edmunds.

Fodor's Choice ★ Dedham is the heart of Constable country. Here gentle hills and the cornfields of Dedham Vale, set under the district's delicate, pale skies, inspired John Constable (1776–1837) to paint some of his most celebrated canvases. He went to school in Dedham, a picture-book village that did well from the wool trade in the 15th and 16th centuries and has retained a prosperous air ever since. The 15th-century church looms large over handsomely sturdy, pastel-color houses.

Nearby towns have several other sites of interest to Constable fans. About 2 miles from Dedham is Flatford, where you can see Flatford Mill, one of the two water mills owned by Constable's father. Northeast of Dedham, off A12, the Constable trail continues in East Bergholt, where Constable was born in 1776. Although the town is mostly modern, the older part has some atmospheric buildings like the church of St. Mary-the-Virgin.

GETTING HERE AND AROUND

From the main A12 road, Dedham is easily reached by car via B1029. Public transportation is extremely limited; there's no nearby train station.

EXPLORING

Bridge Cottage. On the north bank of the Stour, this 16th-century home in East Bergholt has a shop, an exhibition about Constable's life, and a pleasant tearoom overlooking the river. You can also rent rowboats here. ✉ *Off B1070, East Bergholt* ☎ *01206/298260* 🌐 *www.nationaltrust.org.uk/flatford* 🎫 *Free* 🕒 *Jan. and Feb. and Nov.–mid-Dec., weekends 10:30–3:30; Mar., Wed.–Sun. 10:30–5; Apr. and Oct., daily 10:30–5; May–Sept., daily 10:30–5:30.*

OFF THE BEATEN PATH

Colchester. Nobody knows for sure whether Colchester is, as it claims, the oldest town in Britain. What's certain, however, is that it was a major stronghold during the Roman occupation. History buffs enjoy the impressive Roman amphitheater, where parts of the walls and floor are visible. Sections of the original Roman walls are also still standing. Colchester Castle was built on the foundations of the huge Roman Temple of Claudius. Colchester is off the A12, 9 miles southwest of Dedham.

Fodor's Choice ★ **St. Mary-the-Virgin.** One of the most remarkable churches in the region, St. Mary-the-Virgin was started just before the Reformation. The doors underneath the ruined archways outside (remnants of a much older church) contain a series of mysterious symbols—actually a coded message left by Catholic sympathizers of the time. The striking interior contains a mini-museum of treasures, including an ancient wall painting of the Virgin Mary in one of the rear chapels, a 14th-century chest, and an extraordinary series of florid memorial stones on the nave wall opposite the main entrance. A unique feature of the church is that its bells are rung from a cage in the graveyard; this was erected as a temporary measure, pending the construction of a tower in 1531 that was never completed. ✉ *Flatford Rd., East Bergholt* ☎ *01206/392646* 🎟 *Free* ⏲ *Daily; hrs vary but usually 10–5.*

Willy Lott's House. A five-minute stroll down the path from Bridge Cottage brings you to this 16th-century structure that is instantly recognizable from Constable's painting *The Hay Wain* (1821). Although the house itself is not open to the public, the road is a public thoroughfare, so you don't have to buy a ticket to see the famous—and completely unchanged—view for yourself. Just stand across from the two trees on the far bank, with the mill on your right, and look upstream. On the outside wall of the mill is a handy reproduction of the painting to help you compose your own photo. ✉ *Flatford Rd., off B1070, East Bergholt.*

WHERE TO EAT AND STAY

$$$$ BRITISH Fodor's Choice ★ ✕ **Le Talbooth.** This sophisticated restaurant is set in a Tudor house beside the idyllic River Stour. There are lighted terraces where food and drinks are served on warm evenings and jazz and steel bands play on Sunday evenings in summer. Inside, original beams, leaded-glass windows, and a brick fireplace add to the sense of history. The superb British fare at lunch and dinner may include Suffolk lamb with pine nuts and raisins, or monkfish served with seaweed and saffron potatoes. For dessert try the white chocolate and peanut parfait, which comes with spiced rum jelly. In summer, evening barbecues are sometimes held on the terrace on Sundays. $ *Average main: £28* ✉ *Gun Hill* ☎ *01206/323150* 🌐 *www.milsomhotels.com/letalbooth* ⏲ *No dinner Sun. mid-Sept.–early June* ✍ *Reservations essential.*

$ BRITISH ✕ **Marlborough Head.** This friendly, 300-year-old pub across from Constable's school in Dedham serves traditional English pub food. Dishes such as bangers and mash (sausages and mashed potato) and roast chicken share the menu with fish-and-chips and burgers. There are also rooms available, one with a four poster bed. $ *Average main: £11* ✉ *Mill La.* ☎ *01206/323250* 🌐 *www.marlborough-head.co.uk* ⏲ *No dinner Sun.*

$$$ HOTEL Fodor's Choice ★ **Maison Talbooth.** Constable painted the rich meadowlands in which this luxurious Victorian country-house hotel is set. **Pros:** good food; lovely views over Dedham Vale; some private hot tubs. **Cons:** restaurant books up fast; prices are high. $ *Rooms from: £215* ✉ *Stratford Rd.* ☎ *01206/322367* 🌐 *www.milsomhotels.com* *10 rooms* *Breakfast.*

SPORTS AND THE OUTDOORS

Boathouse Restaurant. From Dedham, on the banks of the River Stour, you can rent a rowboat from the Boathouse Restaurant. They're available daily during July and August, and on weekends from April to June and September to October (plus occasional weekdays during local school holiday periods). The cost is £14 per hour. ✉ *Mill La.* ☎ *01206/323153* 🌐 *www.dedhamboathouse.co.uk* ⏲ *Apr.–Oct., daily 10–5.*

WOODBRIDGE

18 miles northeast of Dedham.

One of the first good ports of call on the Suffolk Heritage Coast, Woodbridge is a town whose upper reaches center on a fine old market square, site of the 16th-century Shire Hall. Woodbridge is at its best around its old quayside, where boatbuilding has been carried out since the 16th century. The most prominent building is a white-clapboard mill, which dates from the 18th century and is powered by the tides.

GETTING HERE AND AROUND

Woodbridge is on A12. There are a few local buses, but they mostly serve commuters. By train, Woodbridge is 1½ hours from London and just under 2 hours from Cambridge (with connections).

ESSENTIALS

Visitor Information Woodbridge Tourist Information Centre. ✉ *Station Building, Station Rd.* ☎ *01394/382240* 🌐 *www.suffolkcoastal.gov.uk/tourism.*

EXPLORING

Fodor's Choice ★ **Sutton Hoo.** The visitor center at Sutton Hoo tells the story of one of Britain's most significant Anglo-Saxon archaeological sites. In 1938 a local archaeologist excavated a series of earth mounds and discovered a 7th-century burial ship, probably that of King Raedwald of East Anglia. A replica of the 90-foot-long ship stands in the visitor center, which has artifacts and displays about Anglo-Saxon society. Fascinating as it is, nothing can quite make up for the fact that the best finds have been moved to the British Museum in London. Trails around the 245-acre site explore the area along the River Deben. ✉ *Off B1083* ☎ *01394/389700* 🌐 *www.nationaltrust.org.uk/suttonhoo* 🎫 *£8.20* ⏲ *Exhibition mid-Mar.–Nov., daily 10:30–5; Nov.–mid-Mar., weekends 11–4; Estate daily 9–6.*

WHERE TO EAT AND STAY

$ SEAFOOD Fodor's Choice ★ ✕ **Butley Orford Oysterage.** What started as a little café that sold oysters and cups of tea is now a bustling restaurant, with a nationwide reputation. It has no pretenses to grandeur but serves some of the best smoked fish you're likely to taste anywhere. The fish pie is legendary in these parts, and the traditional English desserts are exceptional. The actual smoking (of fish, cheese, and much else) takes place in the adjacent smokehouse, and products are for sale in a shop around the corner. It's open for lunch daily, year-round, but dinner is seasonal; see below for the full list. $ *Average main: £13* ✉ *Market Hill, Orford* ☎ *01394/450277* 🌐 *www.pinneysoforford.co.uk* ⏲ *No dinner Sun.–Tues. Apr.–July and Sept.–Oct., and Sun.–Thurs. Nov.–Mar.*

Continued on page 678

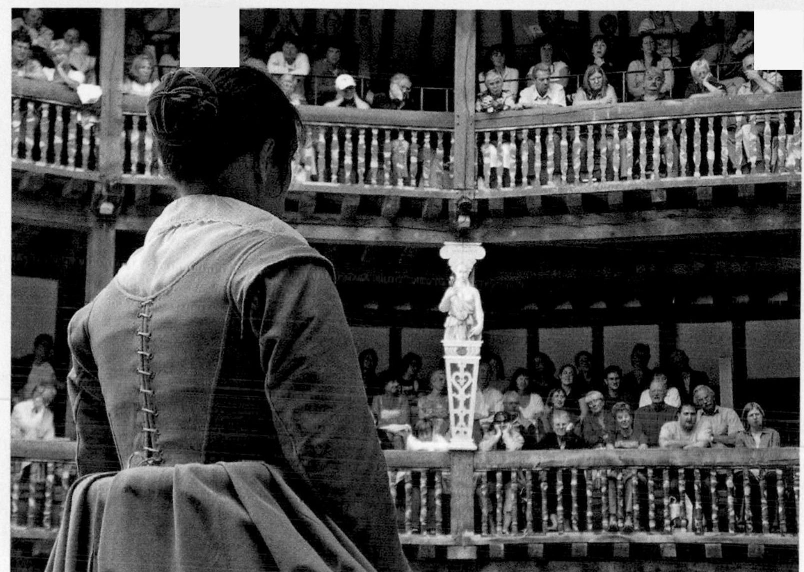

ENGLAND THROUGH THE AGES

English unflappability can cover up a multitude of dark deeds. A landscape, village scene, or ruined castle may present itself as a serene, untroubled canvas, but this is mere show. Trauma and passion are the underlying reality of history; dynastic ambitions, religious strife, and sedition are the subtext. Dig deeper, and what might appear to be a vast, nation-wide museum turns out to be a complex tapestry of narratives and personalities.

On a far-flung corner of Europe, England's geographical position can account for many things: its slowness in absorbing technological and cultural influences from the great Mediterranean civilizations, its speedy adaptation to the global explosion of trade in the early modern era, and its separate, rather aloof identity. But other factors have molded English history too, not least the waves of immigration, settlement and conquest, by Celts, Romans, Danes, and Normans among numerous others. Perhaps the greatest factor of all has been the unforeseen events, accidental meetings, and random coincidences that history delights in throwing up. The careful—sometimes over-zealous—custodianship of England's heritage may pretend otherwise, but behind every object and beneath every ruin lies a tangle of interconnected events. With some context, history is lifted out of the realm of show and into biting reality.

—by Robert Andrews

On stage at Shakespeare's Globe Theatre, London

TIMELINE

3000 BC First building of Stonehenge (later building 2400–1600 BC)

55–54 BC Julius Caesar's exploratory expeditions to England

AD 410 Roman rule of Britain ends

3000 BC · 1000 BC · 0 · AD 900

(clockwise from top left) Avebury Stone Circles in Wiltshire; Roman Baths, Bath; Illuminated manuscript, *Liber Vitae*, 1031; Iron Age coins from Yorkshire

5000 BC–55 BC Early Arrivals

The British Isles had already assumed their current shape by 5000 BC, after the final thawing of the last ice age had resulted in a substantial northwestern promontory being detached from the rest of mainland Europe. However, the influx of different peoples and cultures from the east continued as before. It may have been one of these waves of immigrants that brought agriculture to the islands. Numerous burial sites, hill forts, and stone circles have survived from these early societies, notably in the soft chalk downs of southern England.

55 BC–AD 450 Roman Britain

The emperor Claudius declared Colchester Rome's first British colony soon after the invasion of AD 43, and legionary fortresses in the north were established by AD 75. Resistance included Queen Boudicca's uprising, during which Londinium (London) was razed. However, a Romano-British culture was forged with its northern limit at Hadrian's Wall, built in AD 128. To the south, Celtic Britain became integrated into the Roman Empire with the construction of villas, baths, fortifications, and roads.

450–1066 Anglo-Saxons

Following the withdrawal of the Roman legions, Britain fell prey to invasions by Jutes, Angles, and Saxons from the mainland. The native Celts were pushed back to the fringes of Britain: Cornwall, Wales, northern England, and Scotland. Eventually seven Anglo-Saxon kingdoms emerged, all of which had adopted Christianity by 650. In the 8th century, the Anglo-Saxon kingdoms faced aggressive incomers from Scandinavia, halted only when Alfred the Great, king of Wessex, unified the English against the Viking invaders.

(clockwise from top left) Tower of London; Bayeux Tapestry, scene where the English flee from Normans; Sculpture of King William I on the exterior of Lichfield Cathedral; Reliquary of St. Thomas à Becket, 12th century

1066–1381 Middle Ages: Normans and Plantagenets

The course of England's history altered radically when William, duke of Normandy, invaded and became king of England in 1066. A Norman military and feudal hierarchy was established, French became the language of government, and the country became more centralized. Trading and dynastic links with Europe meant that military campaigns abroad consumed resources, while artistic innovations were more easily absorbed at home—for example, the introduction of Gothic architecture in England's churches and cathedrals. The Plantagenet dynasty came to power in 1154 with the accession of Henry II. A power struggle with the church led to the murder of Henry's archbishop Thomas à Becket in Canterbury Cathedral, which became a center for pilgrimage. The autocratic ambitions of Henry's son John were similarly stymied when he was forced to sign the Magna Carta, promulgating basic principles of English law: no taxation except through Parliament, trial by jury, and property guarantees. In 1348–49, the Black Death (bubonic plague) reduced Britain's population from 4.25 million to 2.5 million.

1381–1485 Twilight of the Middle Ages

English kings invested resources in the Hundred Years War, a struggle to increase their territories in France, but Henry V's gains at Agincourt in 1415 were reversed following the succession of the infant Henry VI. In the domestic Wars of the Roses, the House of York, with a white rose as emblem, triumphed over the House of Lancaster (red rose as emblem), when Edward IV seized the crown. But Edward's brother Richard III was defeated by Henry Tudor, who became Henry VII.

(clockwise from top left) Hampton Court Palace; Elizabeth I; English ships and the Spanish Armada; Queen Mary I; Henry VIII

1485–1603 Tudor Renaissance

The Tudor era saw the political consolidation of the kingdom but a deep religious divide. Henry VIII's break with Rome in order to obtain a divorce from Catherine of Aragon coincided with the Reformation, and he pursued his attack on the church with the dissolution of the monasteries. Protestantism became further entrenched under the short reign of Henry's son, Edward VI, but Catholicism was again in the ascendant under Mary. Elizabeth I strove to heal the sectarian divisions while upholding the supremacy of a Protestant Church of England. Her position was further imperiled by the threat of invasion by Spain, which abated with the defeat of the Spanish Armada in 1588. Elizabeth encouraged piratical attacks on the Spaniards throughout the Atlantic, as well as voyages to the New World, with Walter Raleigh leading expeditions to Virginia in the 1580s. A major flourishing of arts and letters took place during the reign of Good Queen Bess, with such figures as Edmund Spenser and William Shakespeare. When Elizabeth died without an heir, her chief minister, Robert Cecil, invited the Stuart James VI of Scotland to occupy the throne as James I of England.

1603–1660 Stuart England

The Stuarts' attempts to rule independently of Parliament led to disaster. Religious tensions persisted, and Puritans and other dissenters began to seek refuge in the New World. Those who stayed were persecuted under James's son Charles I, who alienated the gentry and merchant classes until war was declared between king and Parliament. The Civil War ended with Charles's trial and execution in 1649 and an interregnum in which Oliver Cromwell, the general who became Parliamentarian leader, was declared Lord Protector.

1620 Pilgrims sail from Plymouth on the *Mayflower*

1660 The Restoration: Charles II restored to the throne

1689 Bill of Rights: Parliament established as England's primary governing body

1795–1815 Napoleonic Wars: Britain and its allies defeat France

1650 | 1700 | 1750 | 1800

(clockwise from top left) *The Great Fire of London* by Turner; George III; West front entrance of St. Paul's Cathedral; Charles II; Chippendale mahogany bonnet-top highboy, 1770s

1660–1714 Restoration

In an uneasy pact with Parliament, Charles I's son was invited back from exile to reign as Charles II. The Restoration led to a revival of the arts, especially in the fields of theater and literature, and a wave of church building. Old divisions resurfaced when Charles was succeeded by James II, whose conversion to Catholicism led to the Glorious Revolution (1688), when Parliament offered the English crown to William of Orange and Mary Stuart, James II's daughter. The thrones of England and Scotland were united in the Act of Union (1707).

1714–1837 Georgian England

With the death of Queen Anne, the Stuart monarchy came to an end and the succession of the new kingdom of Great Britain passed to the Protestant German House of Hanover. But real power now lay with Parliament. George I spent most of his reign in Germany; George II leaned heavily on Robert Walpole (the first "prime minister"); George III was intermittently mad; and George IV's life was marked by dissipation. However, despite losing the Thirteen Colonies in the American Revolution, Britain had by now become the leading European power in the Indian subcontinent. It demonstrated martial supremacy over France in the wars that simmered throughout this period, finally ending in Britain's two victories against Napoleon at Trafalgar and Waterloo. The growing empire, combined with engineering and technical advances at home, helped bring about an early Industrial Revolution in Britain. The process accelerated urbanization, especially in the Midlands and north, and created an urban working class. Partly in response, a new sentimental view of rural England emerged, reflected in the building of stately homes with landscaped estates.

TIMELINE

1832 and 1867 Reform Acts extend the franchise

1887 Victoria celebrates her Golden Jubilee at the height of the British Empire

1914–18 World War I

1840 1865 1880 1915

(clockwise from top left) Queen Victoria in characteristic mourning clothes; Edward VII in coronation robes; Trellis wallpaper Arts and Crafts design by William Morris, 1862; British troops in France, World War I

1837–1901 Victorian Age of Empire

Victoria's reign coincided with the high-water mark of the British Empire, expanding into Africa and consolidating in India. Two parties dominated politics: the Liberals and the Conservatives. These parties supplied such prime ministers as Benjamin Disraeli (Conservative) and William Gladstone (Liberal), who left their mark in reformist measures relating to working conditions, policing, education, health, welfare provision, and the extension of suffrage—all areas highlighted in the literature of the time, notably in the works of Charles Dickens. A network of railways and a nationwide postal service enhanced infrastructure and the growth of industry. In other spheres, the Victorian age harked back to the past, whether in art, as in the Arts and Crafts and Pre-Raphaelite movements, or in architecture, which revived old forms of building from classical to Gothic and Tudor. After Prince Albert's death in 1861, Victoria became a recluse in her Isle of Wight palace, Osborne House, though her golden and diamond jubilees restored her popularity while glorifying the achievements of her long reign.

1901–1918 Edwardian England and World War I

Edward VII, Victoria's son, was a keen sportsman, gambler, and society figure who embodied the blinkered spirit of the country in the aftermath of the Victorian age. The election to Parliament of 29 members of the newly formed Labour Party in 1906 signaled a realignment of politics, though the eruption of World War I sidetracked domestic concerns. The intense fighting across Europe brought about huge loss of life and economic meltdown.

(clockwise from bottom left) Winston Churchill; London Aquatics Centre for the 2012 Olympics; The Beatles; The wedding of Prince William and Catherine Middleton, April 2011 (their son, Prince George, was born in 2013)

1918–1945

Depression and World War II

The interwar period was one of social upheaval, and the unemployment caused by the Great Depression rose to 70% in some areas. At the start of World War II, Hitler's forces pushed the British army into the sea at Dunkirk. The aerial Blitz that followed devastated cities. Winston Churchill's rousing leadership and the support of United States and Commonwealth forces helped turn the tide, with Britain emerging triumphant—but bankrupt.

1945–PRESENT

To Present Day

Elected in 1945, the new Labour government introduced important reforms in welfare and healthcare and initiated the dismantling of the British empire, starting with independence for India and Pakistan in 1947. The years of austerity lasted until the late 1950s, but the following decade saw a cultural explosion that covered every field, from art to music to fashion. British industry had never recovered its former, pre-war strength, however, and inflation and industrial strife marked the 1970s. Britain's entry into the European Economic Community (later to become the European Union) in 1973 did not immediately slow the economic decline. Manufacturing was largely forsaken by Margaret Thatcher (Conservative) and Tony Blair (Labour) in favor of service industries, but Britain's heavy reliance on finance meant that the economy was hit hard by the crash of 2009. The gradual economic recovery that occurred under the Conservative/Liberal Democrat coalition of 2010–2015 helped the Conservatives gain an overall majority in the 2015 elections. This new era of modest hope seemed to effect even the Royal Family; the Duke and Duchess of Cambridge welcomed a new baby, Prince George, in 2013, followed by Pincess Charlotte in 2015.

$$$ B&B/INN Fodor's Choice ★ **Crown and Castle.** Artsy, laid-back, and genuinely friendly, this little gem occupies an 18th-century building in the village of Orford, 10 miles east of Woodbridge. **Pros:** warm service; relaxed atmosphere; good restaurant. **Cons:** need a car to get around; not great for families. *Rooms from: £205 Market Hill, Orford 01394/450205 www.crownandcastle.co.uk 19 rooms Breakfast; Some meals.*

$$ HOTEL Fodor's Choice ★ **Seckford Hall.** The sense of history at this delightfully old-school hotel comes from more than just the magnificent Tudor architecture; several pieces of furniture are castoffs from Buckingham Palace, and one of the beds was supposedly slept in by Elizabeth I. Rooms are large and comfortable, with modern bathrooms (some have whirlpool tubs). **Pros:** antique charm; lovely setting; great atmosphere. **Cons:** no elevator; antique beds are creaky; minimum stay on weekends. *Rooms from: £160 Off A12 01394/385678 www.seckford.co.uk 32 rooms Breakfast; Some meals.*

ALDEBURGH

15 miles northeast of Woodbridge.

Aldeburgh (pronounced *orl*-bruh) is a quiet seaside resort, except in June, when the town fills with people attending the noted Aldeburgh Festival. Its beach is backed by a promenade lined with candy-color dwellings. The 20th-century composer Benjamin Britten lived here for some time. He was interested in the story of Aldeburgh's native son, poet George Crabbe (1754–1832), and turned his life story into *Peter Grimes,* a celebrated opera that perfectly captures the atmosphere of the Suffolk Coast.

GETTING HERE AND AROUND

You have little choice but to drive to Aldeburgh; turn off A12 near Farnham and follow signs. There's no train station and no bus service.

ESSENTIALS

Visitor Information Aldeburgh Tourist Information Centre. *48 High St. 01728/453637 www.visit-suffolkcoast.co.uk.*

EXPLORING

Aldeburgh Beach Lookout. This tiny, disused lookout tower is in the middle of the main beachfront in Aldeburgh and has been converted into a bijou space for contemporary art and performances. Artists take up weekly residences here, welcoming the public on Saturdays to observe what they've created during the week. This isn't just a space for local talent; some big names in the British arts world have taken part in recent years, including the poet Michael Horovitz and painter Eileen Cooper, the first female head of the Royal Academy. *31 Crag Path 01728/452754 www.aldeburghbeachlookout.com Free Sat. 11–4, but hrs vary; check website. Sometimes closed in winter.*

Moot Hall and Aldeburgh Museum. Moot Hall was the place where local elders met to debate and make decisions about the locality. Built of flint and timber, the 16th-century building once stood in the center of a thriving town; the fact that it's now just a few steps from the beach is testament to the erosive powers of the North Sea. Today it contains the Aldeburgh

Museum, a low-key collection that includes finds from an Anglo-Saxon ship burial. ✉ *Market Cross Pl.* ☎ *01728/454666* 🌐 *www.aldeburghmuseumonline.co.uk* 🎫 *£2* ⏲ *Apr., May, Sept., and Oct., daily 2:30–5; June–Aug., daily noon–5. Closed Nov.–Mar.*

WITCHES IN EAST ANGLIA

Aldeburgh wasn't always the peaceful village it is today. In 1646, seven suspected witches were arrested and imprisoned at Moot Hall. They confessed after being tortured, and their public hanging in the town square was overseen by Matthew Hopkins, England's feared "Witchfinder General." From 1645 to 1647, he and his cronies killed around 300 women and children by torture, hanging, or burning. His methods were widely imitated, particularly during the 1692 witch trials in Salem, Massachusetts.

Leiston Abbey & Beach. This Augustinian abbey, founded in 1186, was one of the most important religious orders in the area until it fell victim to Henry VIII's troops during the dissolution of the monasteries. It has a highly unusual feature—a 17th-century church built *inside* (and partially out of) the abbey ruins, effectively making it a church-within-a-church. Just opposite the row of little cottages leading up to the abbey, you'll see a small sign for a walking path to **Leiston Beach.** The track starts rather unpromisingly by crossing a pig farm, but persevere, because the ¼-mile trail across fields, woods, and cliffs is the only way to access this beautiful sandy beach, one of the area's best-kept secrets. The water here is good for swimming, and the seclusion can be heavenly. There are no facilities whatsoever, but plenty of locals make the trek on a sunny day. Look out for the scattered remains of a few brick houses on your way down. These are all that's left of a village that was completely destroyed by coastal erosion in the 1960s. Leiston Abbey is 5½ miles north of Aldeburgh. ✉ *B1122, Theberton* 🌐 *www.english-heritage.org.uk* 🎫 *Free* ⏲ *Daily dawn–dusk.*

WHERE TO EAT AND STAY

$ BRITISH Fodor's Choice ★ ✕ **Aldeburgh Fish and Chip Shop.** A frequent (and deserving) entry on "best fish-n-chips in Britain" lists, Aldeburgh's most celebrated eatery always has a long line of eager customers come frying time. The fish is fresh and local, the batter melts in your mouth, and the chips (from locally grown potatoes) are satisfyingly chunky. Upstairs you can bring your own wine or beer and sit at tables, but for the full experience, join the line and take out the paper-wrapped version. The nearby Golden Galleon, run by the same people, is a good alternative if this place is too crowded. 💲 *Average main: £5.50* ✉ *226 High St.* ☎ *01728/452250* 🌐 *www.aldeburghfishandchips.co.uk* ⏲ *No dinner Sun.–Wed. Closed Mon.*

$ MODERN BRITISH ✕ **The Lighthouse.** An excellent value, this low-key brasserie with tightly packed wooden tables relies exclusively on local produce. The menu focuses on seafood, including oysters and Cromer crabs. All the Modern British dishes are imaginatively prepared. Desserts, such as the Grand Marnier fudge cake, are particularly good. 💲 *Average main: £13* ✉ *77 High St.* ☎ *01728/453377* 🌐 *www.lighthouserestaurant.co.uk.*

$$ HOTEL **Brudenell.** This is the very definition of an English seaside hotel: good food, modest but comfortable rooms, and sweeping views of the sea. **Pros:** laid-back atmosphere; the beach is literally a stone's throw away. **Cons:** rooms are small for the price; car park is tiny. *Rooms from: £140* *The Parade* *01728/452071* *www.brudenellhotel.co.uk* *42 rooms* *Breakfast.*

$ B&B/INN **Dunan House.** A creative, friendly atmosphere pervades this pretty B&B, home to artists Ann Lee and Simon Farr, their cats, and their friendly dog. **Pros:** spacious rooms; delightful hosts; location near the beach. **Cons:** two-night minimum. *Rooms from: £80* *41 Park Rd.* *01728/452486* *www.dunanhouse.co.uk* *3 rooms* *Breakfast.*

NIGHTLIFE AND PERFORMING ARTS

Fodor's Choice ★ **Aldeburgh Festival.** East Anglia's most important arts festival, and one of the best known in Britain, is the Aldeburgh Festival. It's held for two weeks in June in the small village of Snape, 5 miles west of Aldeburgh. Founded by Benjamin Britten, the festival concentrates on music but includes exhibitions, poetry readings, and lectures. A handful of events are aimed specifically at children. *Snape* *01728/687100 for enquiries, 01728/687110 for box office* *www.aldeburgh.co.uk.*

Fodor's Choice ★ **Snape Maltings.** It's worth a stop to take in the peaceful River Alde location of this cultural center. It includes nine art galleries and crafts shops in distinctive large brick buildings once used to malt barley, plus a café and tearoom. There's a farmers' market on the first Saturday of the month, a major food festival in September, and a Benjamin Britten festival in October. Leisurely 45-minute river cruises (£7.50) leave from the quayside in spring and summer. From the Maltings you can stroll out along an elevated trail through some reed marshes for beautiful views—just watch for uneven ground! *Off B1069, Snape* *01728/688303* *www.snapemaltings.co.uk* *Daily 10–5 (some shops, galleries, and restaurants 10–6 in summer).*

NORWICH AND NORTH NORFOLK

Norwich, unofficial capital of East Anglia, is dominated by the 15th-century spire of its impressive cathedral. Norfolk's continuing isolation from the rest of the country, and its unspoiled landscape and architecture—largely bypassed by the Industrial Revolution—have proved to be a draw. Many of the flint-knapped (decorated with broken flint) houses in North Norfolk's newly trendy villages are now weekend or holiday homes. Windmills, churches, and waterways are the area's chief defining characteristics. A few miles inland from the Norfolk coast you reach the Broads, a national park made up of a network of shallow, reed-bordered lakes, many linked by wide rivers. Boating and fishing are great lures; rent a boat for a day or a week and the waterside pubs, churches, villages, and nature reserves are all within easy reach.

NORWICH

63 miles northeast of Cambridge.

It used to be said that Norwich had a pub for each day of the year and a church in which to repent every Sunday. Although this is no longer true, real ales and steeples (including that of its grand cathedral) are still much in evidence in this pleasant city of 130,000. The University of East Anglia brings a cosmopolitan touch, including a lively arts scene and a love of literature evident by the city's many independent bookstores. It's a good base from which to explore the Norfolk Broads and the coast.

Established by the Saxons because of its prime trading position on the rivers Yare and Wensum, the town sits in the triangle between the two waterways. The inner beltway follows the line of the old city wall, much of which is still visible. It's worth walking or driving around after dark to see the floodlit buildings. By the time of the Norman Conquest, Norwich was one of the largest settlements in England, although much was destroyed by the Normans to create a new town. You can see the old flint buildings as you walk down the medieval streets and alleyways. Despite some industrial sites and many modern shopping centers, the town remains engaging.

GETTING HERE AND AROUND

Two Norwich-bound trains per hour leave from London's Liverpool Street station; the journey takes two hours. Buses to Norwich leave London's Victoria Coach Station every couple of hours; the trip takes three hours. The bus and train stations are a 10- to 15-minute walk from the city center. If you're driving, leave your car in any of the numerous lots scattered around the center.

TOURS

Broads Tours. Based in Wroxham, 7 miles northeast of Norwich, Broads Tours has day cruises around the Broads rivers and canals, as well as cruiser boat rentals for a few days or a few weeks. ✉ *Norfolk Broads Direct, The Bridge, Wroxham* ☎ *01603/782207* 🌐 *www.broads.co.uk.*

City Sightseeing. Forty-five-minute open-top bus tours of Norwich leave hourly (starting at 10) from Theatre Street. Prices start at £10. ✉ *Theatre St., across from Theatre Royal* ☎ *01263/587005* 🌐 *www.city-sightseeing.com* 🎫 *From £9.*

ESSENTIALS

Visitor Information Visit Norwich. ✉ *The Forum, Millennium Plain* ☎ *01603/213999* 🌐 *www.visitnorwich.co.uk.*

EXPLORING

Fodor's Choice ★ **Blickling Estate.** Behind the wrought-iron entrance gate to Blickling Estate, two mighty yew hedges form a magnificent frame for this perfectly symmetrical Jacobean masterpiece. The redbrick mansion, 15 miles north of Norwich, has towers and chimneys, Baroque Dutch gables, and, in the center, a three-story timber clock tower. The grounds include a formal flower garden and parkland with woods that conceal a temple, an orangery, and a pyramid. Blickling belonged to a succession of historic figures, including Sir John Fastolf, the model for Shakespeare's Falstaff; Anne Boleyn's family; and finally, Lord Lothian, ambassador

Blickling Estate ...2
Norwich Castle 3
Norwich Cathedral 1
Plantation Garden 5
Sainsbury Centre for the Visual Arts 4

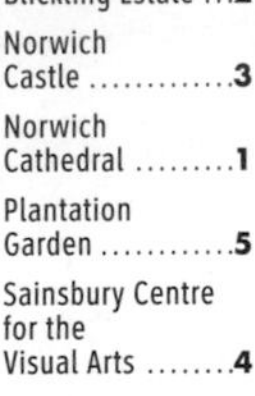

to United States at the outbreak of the World War II. The Long Gallery (127 feet) has an intricate plasterwork ceiling with Jacobean emblems. ✉ *B1354, Blickling* ☎ *01263/738030* 🌐 *www.nationaltrust.org.uk/blickling-estate* 🎫 *£12.70; gardens only £8.30* ⏲ *House Apr.–mid-July and mid-Sept.–early Oct., Wed.–Mon. noon–5; mid-July–early Sept., daily noon–5; mid-Feb.–mid-Mar., Nov., and Dec., weekends 11–3. Gardens mid-Feb.–Oct. daily 10:15–5:30; mid-Nov.–mid-Dec., Thurs.–Sun., 10:15–4; Jan.–mid-Feb., Thurs.–Sun. 10:15–3.*

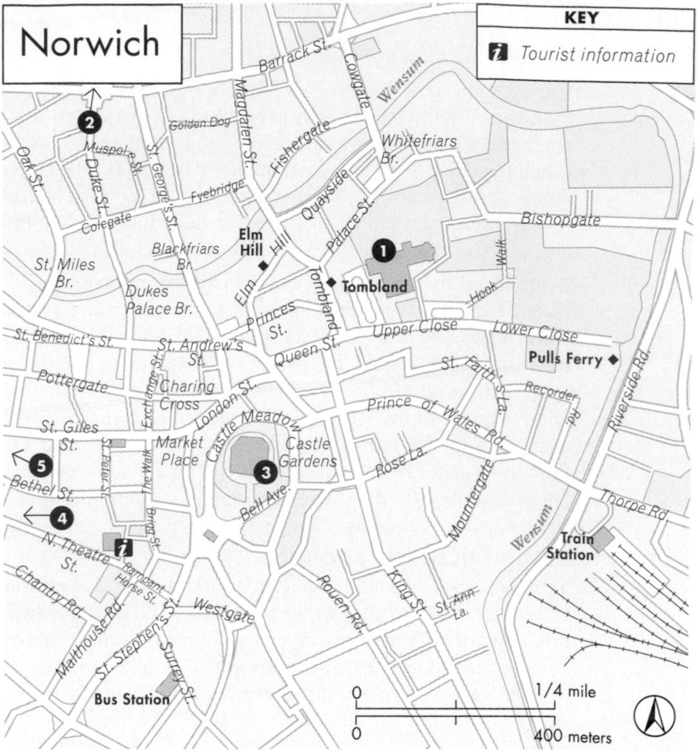

FAMILY **Norwich Castle.** The decorated stone facade of this castle, now a museum on the hill in the center of the city, makes it look like a children's-book illustration. Dating from 1130, the castle is Norman, but a stone keep replaced the original wooden bailey (wall). The thick walls and other defenses attest to its military function. Galleries contain a somewhat eclectic mix of artifacts and interactive displays, covering everything from ancient Egypt to Norman Norfolk and even the history of teapots. One gallery is devoted to the Norwich School of painters who, like John Constable, focused on the everyday landscape and seascape. ■ **TIP→ Admission is £2 the last hour before closing and between noon and 1 on weekdays during school terms.** ✉ *Castle Meadow* ☎ *01603/493625* 🌐 *www.museums.norfolk.gov.uk* 🎫 *£8; special exhibitions around*

£5 ⏲ July–Sept., Mon.–Sat. 10–5, Sun. 1–5; Oct.–June, Mon.–Sat. 10–4:30, Sun. 1–4:30.

Fodor's Choice ★ **Norwich Cathedral.** The grandest example of Norman architecture in Norwich has a towering 315-foot spire and the second-largest monastic cloisters in Britain (only Salisbury's are bigger). The cathedral was begun in 1096 by Herbert de Losinga, who had come from Normandy in 1091 to be its first bishop; his splendid tomb is by the high altar. The remarkable length of the nave is immediately impressive; the similarly striking height of the vaulted ceiling makes it a strain to study the delightful colored bosses, which illustrate Bible stories with great vigor and detail (binoculars are handy). The grave of Norfolk-born nurse Edith Cavell, a British World War I heroine shot by the Germans in 1915, is at the eastern end. There's also a medieval-style herb garden, a Japanese garden, a restaurant, and a coffee shop. Guided tours are run Monday to Saturday at 11, noon, 1, 2, and 3. The Cathedral Close is one of the most idyllic places in Norwich. Keep an eye out for peregrine falcons; they nest in the spire. Past the mixture of medieval and Georgian houses, a path leads down to the ancient water gate, Pulls Ferry. ✉ *62 The Close* ☎ *01603/218300* 🌐 *www.cathedral.org.uk* 🎟 *Free* ⏲ *Cathedral daily 7:30–6:30; herb garden daily 9–5.*

EXPERIENCING NORFOLK'S BROADS

Breathtakingly lovely, the Broads are a network of rivers and canals that stretch for about 150 miles across East Anglia, mostly in North Norfolk. It's a unique landscape of glassy waters, reed-covered marshlands, and impossibly photogenic windmills. At sunset, the whole area turns the color of honey.

The Broads can be seen fleetingly from your car window, but it's nothing compared to floating through them on a boat. You can also see much of the Broads by bike.

For more information visit 🌐 *www.enjoythebroads.com.*

Plantation Garden. Abandoned and overgrown for more than 40 years after World War II, these beautiful Victorian gardens have been painstakingly returned to their former glory by a team of volunteers. Originally planted in 1856, the 2-acre site, dotted with fanciful Gothic follies, includes original features like an Italianate terrace and a huge rockery. It's a particularly tranquil spot when the spring and summer flowers are in full bloom—bring a picnic if the weather's good, or have a bite in the café. The entrance is difficult to find; look for the little gate next to the Beeches Hotel. There's no car park, but you can use the lot at the nearby Black Horse Pub. ✉ *4 Earlham Rd.* ☎ *07504/545810* 🌐 *www.plantationgarden.co.uk* 🎟 *£2* ⏲ *Daily 9–6.*

Sainsbury Centre for the Visual Arts. Designed by Norman Foster, this hangarlike building on the campus of the University of East Anglia holds the collection of the Sainsbury family. It includes a remarkable quantity of 20th-century works, including pieces by Pablo Picasso and Alberto Giacometti. Rotating exhibitions include big-name photography and art shows. Buses 22, 25A, and X25 run from downtown Norwich. ✉ *University of East Anglia, Earlham Rd.* ☎ *01603/593199* *www.scva.org.uk* *Free; special exhibitions £8–12* *Tues.–Fri. 10–6, weekends 10–5.*

WHERE TO EAT AND STAY

$ BRITISH **Adam and Eve.** Said to be Norwich's oldest pub, this place dates back to at least 1249. From noon until 7, the kitchen serves such hearty pub staples as chicken-and-ham pie or cheese-and-ale soup from the short but solid bar menu. Theakston's and Adnams beer are available on tap, as is Aspall's cider. *Average main: £7* *17 Bishopsgate* *01603/667423.*

$ BRITISH **Britons Arms.** A converted pub, this cozy, thatched café and restaurant has famously good homemade cakes as well as pies and tarts. The building, which dates from 1347, has low ceilings, a garden that's open in summer, and a crackling fire in winter. *Average main: £8* *9 Elm Hill* *01603/623367* *www.britonsarms.co.uk* *No credit cards* *Closed Sun. No dinner.*

$ BELGIAN FAMILY **Waffle House.** This is the perfect antidote to all those meat-heavy English breakfasts—waffles, waffles, and more waffles on an imaginative menu. Breakfast choices include toppings like bacon and bananas, while later in the day you can order them with anything from stir-fried vegetables or hummus and avocado to warm chicken and Gouda. Or, skip to dessert and order yours topped with pecans and butterscotch or *banoffee* sauce (a heavenly mix of banana and toffee). *Average main: £8* *39 St. Giles St.* *01603/612790* *www.wafflehousenorwich.co.uk* *Reservations not accepted.*

$ HOTEL **The Maid's Head Hotel.** A charming and eccentric lodging in the middle of Norwich, the Maid's Head claims to be the oldest hotel in England. **Pros:** historic and full of character; modern comforts where they count; good restaurant. **Cons:** low ceilings; restaurant is pricey; breakfast not included in lower rates. *Rooms from: £92* *20 Tombland* *01603/209955* *www.maidsheadhotel.co.uk* *84 rooms, 2 suites* *Breakfast.*

$$ HOTEL Fodor's Choice ★ **The Old Rectory.** This gorgeous, ivy-covered Georgian manor house overlooking manicured lawns and rolling hills is a real find. **Pros:** lovely old building; peaceful setting; friendly staff. **Cons:** away from the center of town; minimum stay some weekends. *Rooms from: £130* *103 Yarmouth Rd., Thorpe St. Andrew* *01603/700772* *www.oldrectorynorwich.com* *7 rooms* *Breakfast.*

NIGHTLIFE AND PERFORMING ARTS

Maddermarket Theatre. Patterned on the layout of Elizabethan theaters, the Maddermarket has been the base of amateur and community theater in Norwich since 1911. *St. John's Alley* *01603/620917* *www.maddermarket.co.uk.*

Norwich Arts Centre. This eclectic venue hosts a busy program of live music, dance, and comedy. *St. Benedict's St.* *01603/660352* *www.norwichartscentre.co.uk.*

Norwich Playhouse. This professional repertory group performs everything from Shakespeare to world premieres of new plays. *42–58 St. George's St.* *01603/598598* *www.norwichplayhouse.org.uk.*

Theatre Royal. Norwich's biggest and best-known theater, the Theatre Royal hosts touring companies staging musicals, ballet, opera, and plays. ✉ *Theatre St.* ☎ *01603/630000* 🌐 *www.theatreroyalnorwich.co.uk.*

SHOPPING

The medieval lanes of Norwich, around Elm Hill and Tombland, contain the best antiques, book, and crafts stores.

Book Hive. Considered by many to be among the best bookstores in England, the Book Hive has a rounded glass facade that gives you a hint of the treasures within. The three-story independent shop specializes in fiction, poetry, art and design, cookery, and children's books. Drop by and you might stumble onto a book reading, cooking class, or other event. ✉ *53 London St.* ☎ *01603/219268* 🌐 *www.thebookhive.co.uk.*

Colman's Mustard Shop. English mustard has a powerful kick—more like Japanese wasabi than its American or French counterparts. This quirky store pays homage to the iconic local brand, Colmans. Founded in the early 19th century, it's now famous in all Britain for its bright yellow packaging. Here you can buy collectibles in addition to 15 varieties of mustard. There's also a quirky little museum devoted to the history of the brand. ✉ *15 Royal Arcade* ☎ *01603/627889* 🌐 *www.mustardshopnorwich.co.uk.*

Norwich Market. Open Monday to Saturday, the city's main outdoor market has been the heart of the city's commerce for 900 years. Two hundred vendors sell everything from jewelry to clothing and food. ✉ *Market Pl.* ☎ *01603/213537* 🌐 *www.norwich.gov.uk* ⏲ *Mon.–Sat. 8:30–5.*

SPORTS AND THE OUTDOORS

Broadland Cycle Hire. Located 8 miles northeast of Norwich, Broadland Cycle Hire charges £16 per day for rental (with discounts for couples and families). The company can recommend several good bike routes around the Broads rivers and canals. ✉ *Horning Rd., Hoveton* ☎ *07887/480331* 🌐 *www.norfolkbroadscycling.co.uk.*

City Boats. A summer trip down the River Yare gives a fresh perspective on Norwich. Longer trips are available down the rivers Wensum and Yare to the nearer parts of the Norfolk Broads. ✉ *Highcraft Marina, Griffin La.* ☎ *01603/701701* 🌐 *www.cityboats.co.uk* ⏲ *Closed Oct.–Mar.*

BLAKENEY

28 miles northwest of Norwich.

The Norfolk coast begins to feel wild and remote near Blakeney, 14 miles west of Cromer. Driving the coast road from Cromer, you pass marshes, sandbanks, and coves, as well as villages. Blakeney is one of the most appealing, with harbors for small fishing boats and yachts. Once a bustling port town exporting corn and salt, it enjoys a quiet existence today, and a reputation for wildlife viewing at Blakeney Point.

CLOSE UP

Walking Paths in East Anglia

East Anglia is a walker's dream, especially if a relatively flat trail appeals to you. The regional website 🌐 *www.visiteastofengland.com* has further details about these paths.

The long-distance footpath known as the **Peddars Way** follows the line of a pre-Roman road, running from near Thetford through heathland, pine forests, and arable fields, and on through rolling chalk lands to the Norfolk coast near Hunstanton.

The **Norfolk Coastal Path** then continues eastward along the coast, joining at Cromer with the delightfully varied **Weaver's Way,** which passes through medieval weaving villages and deeply rural parts of the Norfolk Broads on its 56-mile route from Cromer to Great Yarmouth. Anyone interested in birds should carry binoculars and a field guide, as both of these routes have abundant avian life—both local and migratory.

GETTING HERE AND AROUND

A48 passes through the center of Blakeney. There are few bus connections, though the 46 and CH3 Coasthopper connect the town with Wells-next-the-Sea.

EXPLORING

Blakeney National Nature Reserve. The 1,000 acres of grassy dunes at Blakeney Point are home to nesting terns and about 500 common and gray seals. The 3½-mile walk here from Cley Beach is beautiful, but a boat trip from Blakeney or Morston Quay is fun and educational. An information center and a tearoom at Morston Quay are open according to tides and weather. ✉ *Morston Quay, Quay Rd., Morston* ☎ *01263/740241* 🌐 *www.nationaltrust.org.uk/blakeney* 🎟 *Free* 🕐 *Daily dawn–dusk.*

WHERE TO EAT AND STAY

$ SEAFOOD

✕ **Anchor Inn.** This delightful little gastro-pub in Morston, 1½ miles west of Blakeney, has a cozy, coastal atmosphere. Crab burgers are popular, as are the outstanding servings of fish-and-chips. Less fishy options include homemade meatballs and tagliatelle, and roast Norfolk chicken with buttered kale, potatoes, and parsnips. 💲 *Average main: £14* ✉ *22 The Street, Morston* ☎ *01263/741392* 🌐 *www.morstonanchor.co.uk.*

$$ MODERN BRITISH

✕ **White Horse at Blakeney.** Traditional British food with an imaginative twist is the draw at this former coaching inn. You may find beef brisket with horseradish mash, wilted spinach, and sautéed garlic, or cod fillet with dauphinoise potatoes. You can dine in the bar, the airy conservatory, or the more intimate Long Room. There are also recently refurbished guest rooms with sea views starting at around £80. 💲 *Average main: £17* ✉ *4 High St.* ☎ *01263/740574* 🌐 *www.adnams.co.uk/hotels/the-white-horse.*

$$ HOTEL Fodor's Choice ★

🏨 **Byfords.** In a market town 5 miles southeast of Blakeney, Byfords epitomizes the increasing trendiness of North Norfolk. **Pros:** plush rooms; amiable staff; relaxed atmosphere. **Cons:** minimum stay on weekends. 💲 *Rooms from: £155* ✉ *1–3 Shirehall Plain, Holt* ☎ *01263/711400* 🌐 *www.byfords.org.uk* 🛏 *16 rooms* 🍽 *Breakfast; Some meals.*

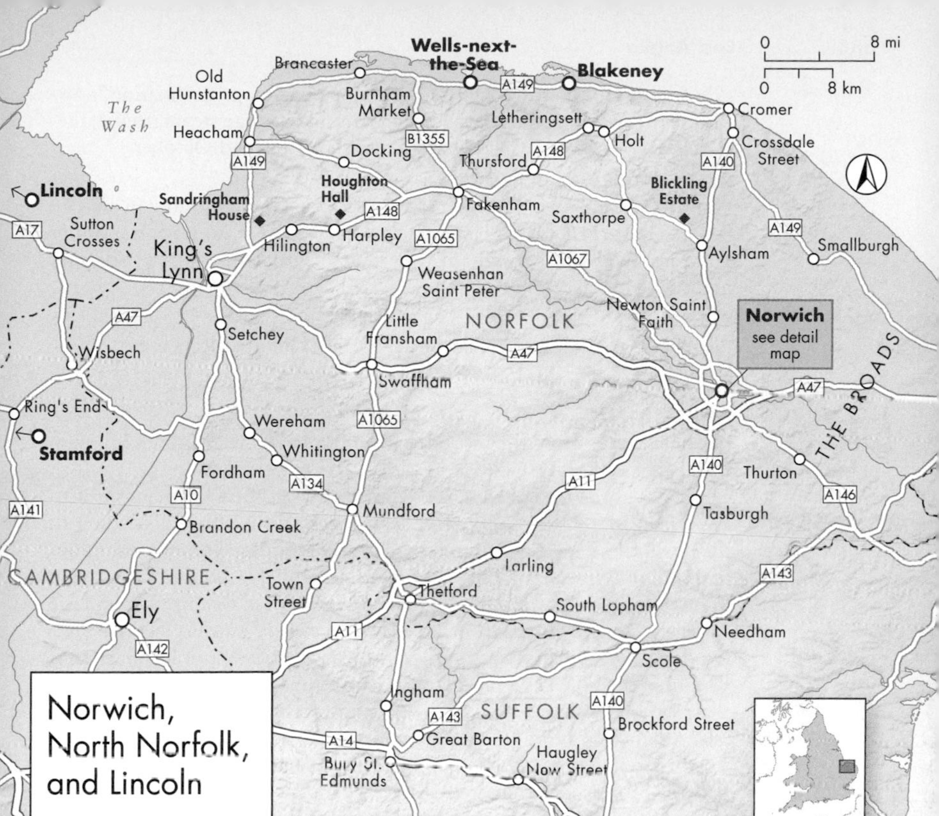

SPORTS AND THE OUTDOORS

Bishop's Boats. This company runs one- or two-hour seal-watching trips daily between March and early November for £10 per person. ✉ *The Quay, at the end of High St.* ☎ *0800/074–0753 toll-free, 01263/740753* 🌐 *www.norfolksealtrips.co.uk.*

Temples Seal Watching Trips. Temples Seal Watching Trips organizes two-hour boat trips out to Blakeney Point, where you can watch seals in their natural environment. Certain sailings drop you off at the Point for an hour before taking you back. Tours cost £10; there are usually two or three daily departures in high season. The ticket office is in Morston, 1½ miles west of Blakeney. ✉ *Anchor Inn, 22 The Street, Morston* ☎ *01263/740791* 🌐 *www.sealtrips.co.uk.*

WELLS-NEXT-THE-SEA

10 miles west of Blakeney, 34 miles northwest of Norwich.

A quiet base from which to explore other nearby towns, the harbor town of Wells-next-the-Sea and the nearby coastline remain untouched, with many excellent places for bird-watching and walking on the sandy beaches of Holkham Bay, near Holkham Hall. Today the town is a mile from the sea, but in Tudor times, when it was closer to the ocean, it served as one of the main ports of East Anglia. The remains of a medieval priory point to the town's past as a major pilgrimage destination in the Middle Ages. Along the nearby beach a narrow-gauge steam train makes the short journey to Walsingham between Easter and October.

GETTING HERE AND AROUND

Wells-next-the-Sea is on the main A149 coastal road, but can also be reached via B1105 from Fakenham. The nearest train station is about 16 miles away in Sheringham. There are regular buses from Sheringham, Fakenham, and Norwich.

ESSENTIALS

Visitor Information Wells-next-the-Sea Tourist Information Centre. ✉ *Staithe St.* ☎ *01328/710885* 🌐 *www.wells-guide.co.uk.*

EXPLORING

Fodor's Choice ★ **Holkham Hall.** One of the most splendid mansions in Britain, Holkham Hall is the seat of the Coke family, the earls of Leicester. In the late 18th century, Thomas Coke went on a grand tour of the Continent, returning with art treasures and determined to build a house according to the new Italian ideas. Centered by a grand staircase and modeled after the Baths of Diocletian, the 60-foot-tall Marble Hall (mostly alabaster, in fact), may well be the most spectacular room in Britain. Beyond are salons filled with works from Coke's collection of masterpieces, including paintings by Gainsborough, Van Dyck, Rubens, and Raphael. Surrounding the house is a park landscaped by Capability Brown in 1762. You'd be hard-pressed to walk through it without spotting several deer. A good way to see the grounds is a half-hour-long lake cruise. The original walled kitchen gardens have been restored and once again provide produce for the estate. The gardens include an adventure playground for children. A major improvement of the visitor facilities is scheduled for completion in 2016; the ambitious plans include a new museum and a large coffee shop and restaurant in what used to be the stable blocks. ✉ *Off A149* ☎ *01328/713111 for tickets, 01328/710227 for estate office* 🌐 *www.holkham.co.uk* 🎫 *Hall, museum, and gardens £13; gardens only £3; park free; parking £2.50* ⏲ *Hall Apr.–Oct., Sun., Mon., and Thurs. noon–4. Gardens and Adventure Play Area Apr.–Oct., daily 10–5. Park Apr.–Oct., daily 9–5, Nov.–Mar., Mon., Wed., and Fri.–Sun. 9–5; Tues. and Thurs. 9:30–5. No vehicle access to park Nov.–Mar.*

Fodor's Choice ★ **Houghton Hall.** Built in the 1720s by the first British prime minister, Sir Robert Walpole, this extraordinary Palladian pile has been carefully restored by its current owner, the seventh marquess of Cholmondeley (pronounced "Chumley"). The double-height Stone Hall and the sumptuous private quarters reveal designer William Kent's preference for gilt, stucco, plush fabrics, and elaborate carvings. Don't leave the grounds without viewing the beautiful medieval simplicity of St. Martin's Church. Candlelight tours, light shows, and other special events are sometimes held on weekends; check the website for the schedule. Houghton Hall is 14 miles southwest of Wells-next-the-Sea. ✉ *Off A148, King's Lynn* ☎ *01485/528569* 🌐 *www.houghtonhall.com* 🎫 *£14; park and grounds only £10* ⏲ *Early June–late Oct., Wed., Thurs.–Sun., and holiday Mon. 11:30–5:30 (house 12:30–5:30); last admission 1 hr before closing.*

Fodor's Choice ★ **Sandringham House.** Not far from the old-fashioned seaside resort of Hunstanton, Sandringham House is where the Royal Family traditionally spends Christmas. The redbrick Victorian mansion was clearly designed for enormous country-house parties, with a ballroom, billiard room, and bowling alley, as well as a shooting lodge on the grounds. The house and gardens close when the Queen is in residence (for about a week in late July), but the woodlands, nature trails, and museum of royal memorabilia in the old stables remain open, as does the church, which is medieval but in heavy Victorian disguise. Tours access most rooms but steer clear of those occupied by current royals. The house is 20 miles southwest of Wells-next-the-Sea. ✉ *Off B1440, Sandringham* ☎ *01485/545400* 🌐 *www.sandringhamestate.co.uk* 🎫 *House, gardens, and museum £13.50; gardens and museum only £9* ⏲ *1st weekend in Apr.–Sept., daily 11–4:30; early–mid-Oct., daily 11–3:30. Gardens 1st weekend in Apr.–Sept., daily 10–6; early–mid-Oct., daily 10–5; last tickets sold 1 hr before closing.*

WHERE TO EAT AND STAY

$$$ MODERN BRITISH ✕ **Hoste Arms.** This renowned gastro-pub is in the village of Burnham Market, 6 miles west of Wells-next-the-Sea. The 17th-century former coaching inn serves such delights as duck breast with rosti potato and parsnip puree, or grilled turbot with Jerusalem artichoke risotto. Accompanying the meals is a good range of fine wines. The bar has an open fire, and there's a conservatory and a large terrace for alfresco lunches. Modern or traditional guest rooms are available from around £130. $ *Average main: £21* ✉ *The Green, Burnham Market* ☎ *01328/738777* 🌐 *www.hostearms.co.uk.*

$$ HOTEL FAMILY **Victoria at Holkham.** A colorful, whimsical hideaway, this hotel on the Holkham Hall estate is more laid-back and family-friendly than the austere Victorian exterior suggests. **Pros:** original character; excellent location; outstanding food. **Cons:** minimum stay on weekends; extremely busy in summer; no elevator. $ *Rooms from: £120* ✉ *Park Rd., Holkham* ☎ *01328/711008* 🌐 *www.holkham.co.uk/victoria* *9 rooms, 1 suite, 4 self-contained lodges* 🍽 *Breakfast.*

SPORTS AND THE OUTDOORS

On Yer Bike Cycle Hire. For upwards of £10 per day (plus a small delivery charge), On Yer Bike Cycle Hire will deliver bikes to your local lodging—and collect them, too. Reservations are required (but no credit cards accepted). ✉ *Nutwood Farm, The Laurels, Wighton* ☎ *01328/820719, 07584/308120 cell phone* 🌐 *www.norfolkcyclehire.co.uk.*

STAMFORD AND LINCOLN

The fens of northern Cambridgeshire pass imperceptibly into the three divisions of Lincolnshire: Holland, Kesteven, and Lindsey. Holland borders the Isle of Ely and the Soke of Peterborough. This marshland spreads far and wide south of the Wash. The chief attractions are two towns: Stamford, to the southwest, and Lincoln, with its magnificent cathedral.

STAMFORD

48 miles northwest of Cambridge.

Serene, honey-hued Stamford, on a hillside overlooking the River Welland, has a well-preserved center, in part because in 1967 it was designated England's first conservation area. This unspoiled town, which grew rich from the medieval wool and cloth trades, has a delightful, harmonious mixture of Georgian and medieval architecture.

GETTING HERE AND AROUND

Stamford is on the A43 and A1. Trains from London (King's Cross and St. Pancras stations) depart about every 30 minutes, and about every hour from Lincoln (all with connections). The journey from London takes between one and two hours, or between two and three from Lincoln due to connections.

ESSENTIALS

Visitor Information Stamford Tourist Information Centre. ✉ *Stamford Arts Centre, 27 St. Mary's St.* ☎ *01780/755611* 🌐 *www.southwestlincs.com.*

EXPLORING

FAMILY
Fodor's Choice ★
Burghley House. Considered one of the grandest houses of the Elizabethan age, this architectural masterpiece is celebrated for its rooftops bristling with pepper-pot chimneys and slate-roof towers. It was built between 1565 and 1587 to the design of William Cecil, when he was Elizabeth I's high treasurer, and his descendants still occupy the house. The interior was remodeled in the late 17th century with treasures from Europe. On view are 18 sumptuous rooms, with carvings by Grinling Gibbons and ceiling paintings by Antonio Verrio (including the Heaven Room and the Hell Staircase—just as dramatic as they sound), as well as innumerable paintings and priceless porcelain. You can tour on your own or join a free 80-minute guided tour beginning daily at 3:30. Capability Brown landscaped the grounds in the 18th century; herds of deer roam free, and open-air concerts are staged in summer. Brown also added the Gothic Revival orangery, where today you can take tea or lunch. More contemporary additions come in the form of the aptly named Garden of Surprise and the adjacent Sculpture Garden, filled with imaginative creations, water jets, and a mirrored maze. The house is closed for a week in late August or early September, when it hosts the international Burghley Horse Trials. Burghley is a mile southeast of Stamford. ✉ *Off A1* ☎ *01780/752451* 🌐 *www.burghley.co.uk* 🎫 *House and gardens £13.50; gardens only £8* 🕒 *House and Gardens mid-Mar.–Oct., Sat.–Thurs. 11–5. Park daily 8–6; last admission 1 hr before closing.*

LINCOLN

53 miles north of Stamford, 93 miles northwest of Cambridge, 97 miles northwest of Norwich.

Fodor's Choice ★
Celts, Romans, and Danes all had important settlements here, but it was the Normans who gave Lincoln its medieval stature after William the Conqueror founded Lincoln Castle as a stronghold in 1068. Four years later William appointed Bishop Remigius to run the huge diocese

stretching from the Humber to the Thames, resulting in the construction of Lincoln Cathedral, the third-largest in England after York Minster and St. Paul's. Since medieval times Lincoln's status has declined. However, its somewhat remote location (there are no major motorways or railways nearby) has helped preserve its traditional character.

The cathedral is on the aptly named Steep Hill; to its south, narrow medieval streets cling to the hillside. Jew's House, on the Strait, dating from the early 12th century, is one of several well-preserved domestic buildings in this area. The name is almost as old as the house itself—it refers to a former resident, Belaset of Wallingford, a Jewish woman who was murdered by a mob in 1290, the same year the Jews were expelled from England (they remained in exile for nearly 400 years). The River Witham flows unobtrusively under the incongruously named High Bridge, a low, vaulted Norman bridge topped by timber-frame houses from the 16th century. West from here you can rent boats, or, in summer, go on a river cruise.

GETTING HERE AND AROUND

There are direct buses (four to five hours) from London, but most rail journeys (two to three hours) involve changing trains. The bus and train stations are south of the center, and it's a steep walk uphill to the cathedral and castle. Drivers will find parking lots around the bus and train stations and in the center at the Lawn and Westgate.

ESSENTIALS

Visitor Information Lincoln Tourist Information Centre. ✉ *9 Castle Hill* ☎ *01522/545458* 🌐 *www.visitlincolnshire.com.*

EXPLORING

FAMILY Fodor's Choice ★ **Lincoln Castle.** Facing the cathedral across Exchequer Gate, this castle was built by William the Conqueror in 1068, incorporating the remains of Roman walls. The castle was used as a debtor's prison from 1787 to 1878. In the chapel you can see cagelike stalls where convicts heard sermons; they were designed this way so inmates couldn't tell who their fellow prisoners were, thus supposedly preserving a modicum of dignity. The castle's star exhibit is an original copy of **Magna Carta**, signed by King John in 1215. This is one of only four surviving copies of the original document, and one of few ever to have left the country—it was secretly moved to Fort Knox for safekeeping during World War II. A major renovation in 2015 opened up the wall walk for the first time, allowing visitors to make a complete circuit of the battlements (totaling more than ¼ of a mile). In addition, a 3D cinema shows a high-tech film about the history of Magna Carta. ✉ *Castle Hill* ☎ *01522/541173* 🌐 *www.lincolncastle.com* 🎫 *All attractions £12; Prison and Magna Carta only £10; Medieval Wall Walk £5; joint ticket with Lincoln Cathedral £16* 🕐 *Apr. and Sept., daily 10–5; May–Aug., daily 10–6; Oct.–Mar., daily 10–4; last entry 45 min before closing.*

Fodor's Choice ★ **Lincoln Cathedral.** Lincoln's crowning glory (properly known as the Cathedral of St. Mary, although nobody calls it that), this was for centuries the tallest building in Europe. The Norman bishop Remigius began work in 1072. The Romanesque church he built was irremediably damaged, first by fire, then by earthquake. Today its most striking

DID YOU KNOW?

In the Heaven Room at Burghley House, 17th-century painter Antonio Verrio shows the classical gods and goddesses of Mount Olympus hard at play. Their frolicking looks almost three-dimensional. In the center of this opulence is a massive 18th-century silver wine cooler, an item the gods (and more earthly lords) might have found useful.

feature is the west front's strikingly tall towers, best viewed from the 14th-century Exchequer Gate in front of the cathedral or from the castle battlements beyond. Inside, a breathtaking impression of space and unity belies the many centuries of building and rebuilding. The stained-glass window at the north end of the transept (known as the Dean's Eye) dates from the 13th century. **■TIP→ Look for the Lincoln Imp on the pillar nearest St. Hugh's shrine; according to legend, an angel turned this creature to stone.**

Through a door on the north side is the chapterhouse, a 10-sided building with one of the oldest vaulted ceilings in the world. It sometimes housed the medieval Parliament of England during the reigns of Edward I and Edward II. The cathedral library, designed by Christopher Wren (1632–1723), was built onto the north side of the cloisters after the original library collapsed. Guided tours of the ground floor are included in the price. You can also book tours of the roof and tower (both £4), but these are popular, so make reservations. For safety reasons, children under 14 are not allowed on those tours. ✉ *Minster Yard* ☎ *01522/561600* 🌐 *www.lincolncathedral.com* 🎫 *Nave free; rest of Cathedral £6; roof and tower tours £4* ⏲ *July and Aug., weekdays 7:15 am–8 pm, weekends 7:15–6; Sept.–June, weekdays 7:15–6, weekends 7:15–5.*

QUICK BITES

Pimento Tearooms. After climbing the aptly named Steep Hill, revive yourself with one of the 23 different teas or 15 coffees available here. Choose a cake or snack to go along with your pick-me-up. ✉ ***26 Steep Hill*** ☎ ***01522/544880.***

Medieval Bishop's Palace. On the south side of Minster Yard, this building has exhibits about the former administrative center of the diocese, plus a garden and working vineyard. ✉ *Minster Yard* ☎ *01522/527468* 🌐 *www.english-heritage.org.uk* 🎫 *£4.90* ⏲ *Mar.–Sept., Wed.–Sun. 10–6; Oct., Wed.–Sun. 10–5; Nov.–Mar., weekends 10–4; last admission 30 min before closing.*

Minster Yard. Surrounding the cathedral on three sides, Minster Yard contains buildings of different periods, including graceful Georgian architecture. A statue of Alfred, Lord Tennyson, who was born in Lincolnshire, stands on the green near the chapter house. ✉ *Minster Yard.*

WHERE TO EAT AND STAY

$
BRITISH

✕ **Brown's Pie Shop.** More than you might imagine from the modest name, Brown's Pie Shop serves the best of old-school British food: succulent beef, great desserts, and some very good, freshly made savory pies. There are also fish specials, steaks, and a small selection of vegetarian dishes. This restaurant, close to the cathedral, serves an inexpensive early-evening menu. 💲 *Average main: £13* ✉ *33 Steep Hill* ☎ *01522/527330* 🌐 *www.brownspieshop.co.uk.*

$$$
MODERN BRITISH
Fodor's Choice ★

✕ **Jew's House.** This intimate restaurant is a much more sedate place than its colorful and sometimes dark history suggests (the name is medieval—check out the story while you're here). It's one of Lincoln's oldest buildings, a rare survivor of 12th-century Norman domestic architecture and worth a visit even if the cosmopolitan menu weren't so outstanding.

Typical main dishes include Lincolnshire lamb with chorizo and beetroot relish, and roast turbot in grapefruit sauce. *Average main: £20* *15 The Strait* *01522/524851* *www.jewshouserestaurant.co.uk* *Closed Sun. and Mon.*

$$ BRITISH **Wig and Mitre.** This pub-café-restaurant serves everything from breakfast to full evening meals in its old-fashioned dining room. The produce comes from the local markets; expect treats like rib-eye with triple-cooked chips (thick-cut fries), or sea bass and crab risotto. *Average main: £15* *30–32 Steep Hill* *01522/535190* *www.wigandmitre.com.*

$ B&B/INN Fodor's Choice ★ **Cathedral View Guest House.** This B&B in the medieval quarter is just a three-minute walk from Lincoln Cathedral and almost as old; those exposed beam roofs you're sleeping under date from the 12th century. **Pros:** historic building in a great location; lovely hosts; good breakfast; private parking lot. **Cons:** some rooms are tiny; some street noise; early checkout. *Rooms from: £80* *6 Eastgate* *01522/537469* *www.cathedralviewlincoln.co.uk* *7 rooms* *Breakfast.*

NIGHTLIFE AND PERFORMING ARTS

Theatre Royal. A fine Victorian auditorium, the Theatre Royal previews plays and musicals before their London runs and also hosts touring productions and comedy. *Clasketgate* *01522/519999* *www.lincolntheatreroyal.com.*

SHOPPING

The best stores are on Bailgate, Steep Hill, and the medieval streets leading directly down from the cathedral and castle.

Cheese Society. Just off Steep Hill, this shop has a great selection of English and French cheeses, including the delicious local Lincoln Blue. There's also an adjacent café. *1 St. Martin's La.* *01522/511003* *www.thecheesesociety.co.uk.*

Harding House Gallery. Steep Hill has good bookstores, antiques shops, and art galleries, including the delightful Harding House Gallery, a cooperative of contemporary visual artists. *Steep Hill* *01522/523537* *www.hardinghousegallery.co.uk.*

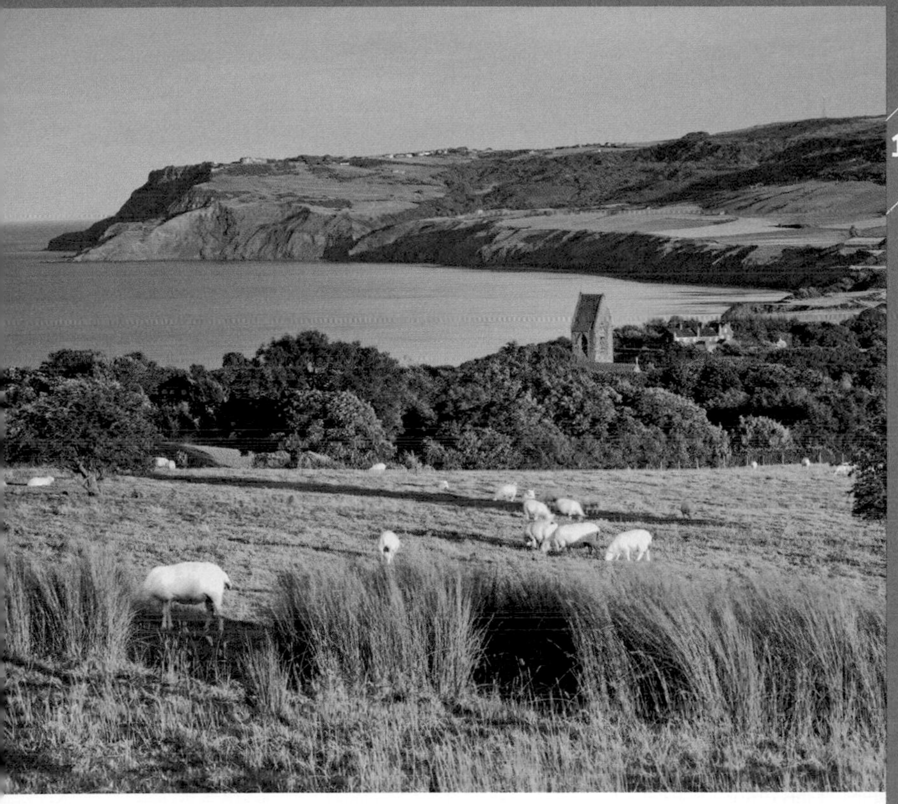

12

YORKSHIRE

WELCOME TO YORKSHIRE

TOP REASONS TO GO

★ **York Minster:** The largest Gothic cathedral in Northern Europe helps make York one of the country's most visited cities. A new interactive exhibit in the undercroft explores the site's history from Roman times onward.

★ **North York Moors:** The wide-open spaces of this national park let walkers find glorious solitude amid the heather-covered hills that glow crimson and purple in late summer and early fall.

★ **Rievaulx Abbey:** The ruins of this great Cistercian abbey can be approached by a tiny lane that provides a view of its soaring arches dramatically appearing out of the trees.

★ **Coastal towns:** Seafront Whitby inspired Bram Stoker to set some of *Dracula* there. Robin Hood's Bay, a village set in a ravine, has an outstanding beach.

★ **Haworth:** Looking as if it were carved from stone, this picture-perfect hillside town in the dales is a lovely place to learn about the Brontë sisters.

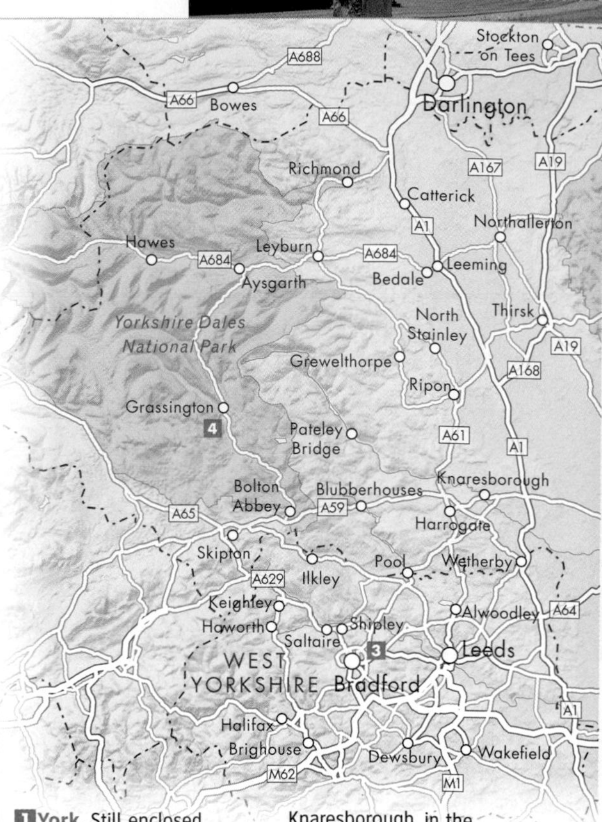

1 York. Still enclosed within its medieval city walls, this beautifully preserved city makes the perfect introduction to Yorkshire. Its towering Minster and narrow streets are alive with history.

2 Around York. Heading away from the city, you'll find the elegant Georgian and Victorian spa town of Harrogate, as well as the historic market town Knaresborough, in the beautiful Nidd Gorge. The Baroque masterpiece, Castle Howard, is also near York.

3 Leeds and Brontë Country. Rocky and bleak, this windswept stretch of country provides an appropriate setting for the dark, dramatic narratives penned by the Brontë sisters in Haworth. Former industrial powerhouse Leeds is being reinvented as a shopping and entertainment hub.

GETTING ORIENTED

Yorkshire is the largest of England's historic counties (and, its proud inhabitants would say, the only one worth visiting). At its heart is the ancient city of York, with its Gothic cathedral and medieval city walls. To the west is the bustling city of Leeds, while a few miles away are the unspoiled hills that form what the tourist office calls Brontë Country—Haworth, where the Brontë family lived, and the valleys and villages of the Yorkshire Dales. North of York is North York Moors National Park. Isolated stone villages, moorland walks, and Rievaulx Abbey are within easy reach. Along the east coast of Yorkshire, beaches and a fascinating history await you in the resort town of Scarborough, the former whaling port of Whitby, and Robin Hood's Bay.

4 The Yorkshire Dales. Waterfalls, ancient woodlands, rugged uplands, and exceptionally scenic valleys make for splendid views. Charming market towns like Richmond and Grassington are well worth exploring.

5 The North York Moors. A short drive north from York, this national park, mostly hilly moorland covered in purple heather, is the perfect place to hike. You'll also find picturesque villages like Hutton-le-Hole, Goathland, and the atmospheric ruins of Rievaulx Abbey.

6 The North Yorkshire Coast. The uniquely steep Robin Hood's Bay, a tiny fishing village, clings to rugged cliffs pounded by the cold North Sea. For a more traditional seaside getaway, head for Scarborough.

GREAT ENGLISH CHEESES

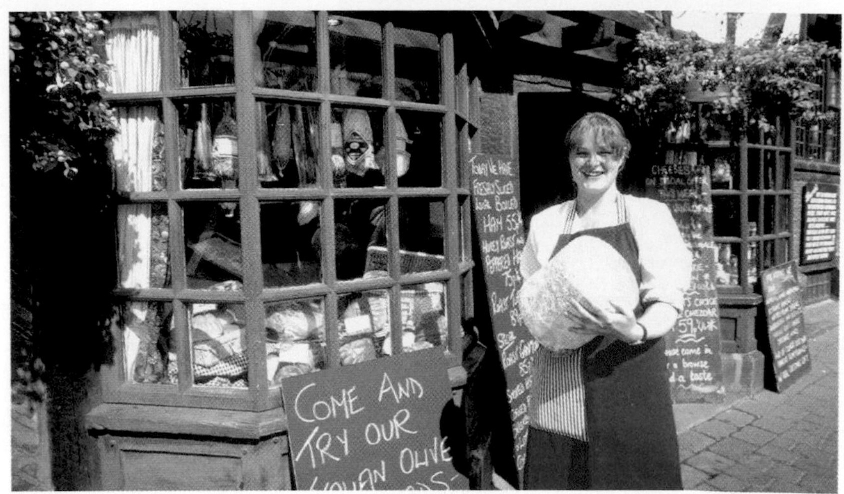

England's lush pastures yield more than 700 types of cheese, which the English eat at any time except breakfast. Smooth and creamy, nutty and tasty, or blue and smelly, cheese turns up in sandwiches and soups, on toast, as a topping, and on cheese boards at the end of a meal. Ask for advice before you choose.

(above) You can buy pieces of cheese both small and large around England; (right, top) Wensleydale cheese; (right, bottom) Strong-flavored Blue Stilton is a classic.

Cheeses come in three strengths: mild, medium, and mature. Young cheese is mild and crumbly; as it ages, the flavor gets sharper and the texture firmer. Protected Designation of Origin (PDO) applies to 14 cheeses that are produced in a designated area. An increasing number of small artisan makers produce distinctive and organic cheeses as well as those made from the milk of goats (Quickes) or sheep (Blacksticks); they aren't afraid to experiment. Cornish Yarg is covered with nettles, Stinking Bishop is washed in perry (an alcoholic drink made from pears), and White Stilton is often stuffed with fruit. Many pubs still serve local cheese as part of a "ploughman's lunch," served with crusty bread, relish, and pickled onion.

ACCOMPANIMENTS

For **ploughman's lunches,** look for fruit chutneys made from raisins, apples, onions, vinegar, and sugar. Branston pickle is a crunchy, spicy-sweet mix of chopped vegetables. Small pickled onions and gherkins are common; piccalilli consists of cauliflower florets pickled in a thick yellow spicy sauce. **Cheese boards** have three or four cheeses, grapes, apples, pears, biscuits, and crackers.

These cheeses are made from cows' milk.

BLUE STILTON

This has been the king of English cheeses since the 18th century. With a strong taste and scent, it's now the cheese traditionally served at Christmas, often with port. Distinguished by blue veins and a crusty exterior, the whole cheeses are wheel-shape and become softer and creamier as they age. As a condition of its PDO status, it must be made in Nottinghamshire, Derbyshire, or Leicestershire. White Stilton is milder, younger, crumbly, and creamy; it's a good dessert cheese often combined with dried fruit.

CHEDDAR

Originally matured only in caves at Cheddar in Somerset, this is the best known of all English cheeses. Ranging from mild to extra-mature (nuttier), it's firm in texture. If you're looking for the best, aim for West Country Farmhouse Cheddar, which has PDO status when it's made traditionally in Devon, Cornwall, Somerset, and Dorset.

CHESHIRE

The oldest named English cheese has appeared on the menu since Roman times. Usually white in color, it has a crumbly texture and salty tang, and is sometimes colored with annatto, a derivative of the achiote tree that gives a yellow hue to orange color.

DOUBLE AND SINGLE GLOUCESTER

Both varieties have a smooth, dense texture and creamy flavor. Double is more common, and its buttery color is due to annatto. Single Gloucester has PDO status; this requires the cheese to be made in Gloucestershire, to be wheel-shaped, and to be natural in color.

LANCASHIRE

This cheese comes in three strengths according to age: creamy, crumbly, and tasty. The creamy, young cheese is ideal for cheese on toast (Welsh rarebit); the crumbly goes well with fruitcake or an apple, or is good in a salad. The rich, nutty tasty variety (matured longer) often turns up in a ploughman's lunch.

SHROPSHIRE BLUE

Contrary to expectation, this cheese has never been made in Shropshire. Now produced exclusively in the East Midlands, it's a soft, mellow, orange-color cheese with blue veins, created by injecting the *penicillium* mold.

WENSLEYDALE

Made all over the country, the cheese is traditionally made at Hawes in Wensleydale in Yorkshire. It has a white, crumbly texture and a salty taste; it's best eaten when young and fresh. Wensleydale is often served with fruitcake, fresh apples, or hot apple dishes.

Updated by Ellin Stein

A hauntingly beautiful region, Yorkshire is known for its wide-open spaces and dramatic landscapes. The hills of the North York Moors and the Yorkshire Dales glow pink and purple with heather in summer, turning to black in winter. Rugged fishing villages like Robin Hood's Bay cling to the edges of cliffs in one of England's most unspoiled areas. Period architecture abounds in York, with its narrow medieval streets, or historic spa towns like Harrogate, while ancient cathedrals, abbeys, and castles provide majestic backdrops to day-to-day life in the area.

Some of the region's biggest attractions are the result of human endeavor: York's towering Gothic cathedral, created by unknown master craftsmen; Castle Howard, Vanbrugh and Hawksmoor's Baroque masterpiece near York; and the Georgian parsonage (now a museum), in the small hilltop village of Haworth, where the Brontë sisters changed literature.

The Yorkshire landscape, however, is just as compelling. The most rugged terrain is the North York Moors, a large windswept moorland (crossed by cultivated valleys), where flocks of Scottish Blackface or Swaledale sheep graze freely. The landscape that inspired the Brontë sisters is found in the West Yorkshire Pennines, with their moors and rocky crags punctuated by gray stone villages. Farther to the north are the lush, green uplands and valleys known as the Yorkshire Dales, where the high rainfall produces swift rivers and sparkling streams. These are wonderfully peaceful places, except in summer, when hundreds of hikers (or "ramblers," as they're known in England) appear over the hills, injecting life into the local economy.

The area isn't all green fields and perfect villages—there's also a gritty, urban aspect to the region. In West Yorkshire, once down-at-heels Leeds has remade itself with trendy restaurants and cafés, along with a buzzing music industry and nightlife scene.

YORKSHIRE PLANNER

WHEN TO GO

To see the heather at its most vibrant, visit in summer (but despite the season, be prepared for some chilly days). It's also the best time to see the coast, as colorful regattas and arts festivals are underway. York Minster makes a splendidly atmospheric focal point for the prestigious York Early Music Festival in early July. Spring and fall bring their own rewards: far fewer crowds and crisp, clear days, although there's an increased risk of rain and fog. The harsh winter is tricky: while the moors and dales are beautiful covered in snow and the coast sparkles on a clear, bright day, storms and blizzards can set in quickly, making the moorland roads impassable and villages at risk of being cut off entirely. In winter, stick to York and the main towns.

PLANNING YOUR TIME

Yorkshire is a vast region and difficult to explore in a short amount of time. If you're in a hurry, you could see the highlights of York or Leeds as a day trip from London; the fastest trains take just two hours. But it's an awful lot to pack into one day, and you're bound to leave out places you'll probably regret missing. Proper exploration—especially of the countryside—requires time and effort. In a few days you could explore York and some highlights such as Castle Howard and Studley Royal Park. You need the better part of a week to take in the small towns, abandoned abbeys, and inspiring moors and coast. It's well worth it: this is the path less traveled. The York Pass (🌐 *www.yorkpass.com*), good for one, two, or three days, can save you money on more than 30 attractions, but check it against your itinerary.

GETTING HERE AND AROUND

AIR TRAVEL

Leeds Bradford Airport, 11 miles northwest of Leeds, has frequent flights from other cities in England and Europe. Look for cheap fares on British Airways, flybe, Jet2, or Ryanair. Another good choice for this region is Manchester Airport, about 40 miles southwest of Leeds. This larger airport is well served by domestic and international carriers.

Airports Leeds Bradford International Airport. ✉ *Leeds* ✈ *Off A658* ☎ *0871/288–2288* 🌐 *www.leedsbradfordairport.co.uk.* **Manchester Airport.** ✉ *M56, near Junctions 5 and 6, Manchester* ☎ *0871/271–0711* 🌐 *www.manchesterairport.co.uk.*

BUS TRAVEL

National Express and Megabus have numerous daily departures from London's Victoria Coach Station to major cities in Yorkshire. Average travel times are 4¼ hours to Leeds, 6 hours to York, and 8 hours to Scarborough. Once you're in the region, local bus companies take over the routes. There are Metro buses from Leeds and Bradford into the more remote parts of the Yorkshire Dales. Other companies are Transdev, and Harrogate & District for services to Ripon, Harrogate, and Leeds; Keighley & District to Haworth; Yorkshire Coastliner for Castle

Howard, Scarborough, Whitby, Malton, and Leeds; Arriva for Whitby, Scarborough, and Middlesbrough; and the volunteer-run DalesBus for Hawes and other destinations, with additional routes on Sundays and holiday Mondays May–September. In York the main local bus operator is Transdev. Traveline has route information.

Bus Contacts **Arriva.** ☎ *0344/800–4411 Customer Service* 🌐 *www.arrivabus.co.uk.* **DalesBus.** ☎ *01756/749400* 🌐 *www.dalesbus.org.* **Harrogate & District.** ☎ *01423/566061* 🌐 *www.harrogatebus.co.uk.* **Keighley & District.** ☎ *01535/603284* 🌐 *www.keighleybus.co.uk.* **Megabus.** ☎ *0141/352–4444* 🌐 *uk.megabus.com.* **MetroLine.** ☎ *0113/245–7676* 🌐 *www.wymetro.com.* **National Express.** ☎ *0871/781–8178* 🌐 *www.nationalexpress.com.* **Transdev York.** ☎ *01904/633990* 🌐 *www.yorkbus.co.uk.* **Traveline.** ☎ *0871/200–2233* 🌐 *www.traveline.info.* **Coastliner.** ☎ *01653/692556* 🌐 *www.yorkbus.co.uk.*

CAR TRAVEL

If you're driving, the M1 is the principal route north from London. This major thoroughfare gets you to Leeds in about three hours. For York (204 miles) and the Scarborough areas, stay on M1 to Leeds (197 miles), and then take A64. For the Yorkshire Dales, take M1 to Leeds, then A65 north and west to Skipton. For the North York Moors, take the A64 and then the A169 north from York to Pickering, then continue north on the A169 to Whitby or west on the A170 to Helmsley. The trans-Pennine motorway, the M62 between Liverpool and Hull, crosses the bottom of this region. North of Leeds, the A1 is the major north–south road, although narrow stretches, roadworks, and heavy traffic make this route slow going at times.

Some of the steep, narrow roads in the countryside off the main routes are difficult drives and can be perilous (or closed altogether) in winter. Main roads often closed by snowdrifts are the moorland A169 and the coast-and-moor A171. If you plan to drive in the dales or moors in winter, check the weather forecast in advance.

TRAIN TRAVEL

Virgin Trains East Coast travel to York and Leeds from London's King's Cross Station. Grand Central trains head to York, Bradford, and Thirsk. Average travel times from King's Cross are 2 hours to York and 2¼ hours to Leeds. Northern Rail trains operate throughout the region. Contact National Rail for train times, and to find out if any discounted Rover tickets are available for your journey.

Train Contacts **Grand Central.** ☎ *0845/603–4852* 🌐 *www.grandcentralrail.com.* **National Rail Enquiries.** ☎ *0845/748–4950* 🌐 *www.nationalrail.co.uk.* **Northern Rail.** ☎ *0845/000–0125* 🌐 *www.northernrail.org.* **Virgin Trains East Coast.** ☎ *0345/722–5333* 🌐 *www.virgintrainseastcoast.com.*

RESTAURANTS

Yorkshire is known for hearty food, though bacon-based breakfasts and lunches of pork pies do tend to pale fairly quickly. Increasingly, the larger towns and cities, particularly Leeds, have developed a foodie scene of sorts. Indian restaurants (often called curry houses) can be very good in northern cities. Out in the countryside, pubs are your best bet for dining. Many serve excellent home-cooked food and locally reared meat (especially lamb) and vegetables. Roast beef dinners generally come with Yorkshire pudding, the tasty, puffy, oven-baked dish made from egg batter known as a popover in the United States. It's generally served with lots of gravy. Be sure to sample local cheeses, especially Wensleydale, which has a delicate flavor and honey aftertaste.

HOTELS

Traditional hotels are limited primarily to major towns and cities; those in the country tend to be guesthouses, inns, bed-and-breakfasts, or pubs with rooms. Many of the better guesthouses are at the edge of town, but some proprietors will pick you up at the main station if you're relying on public transportation—verify before booking. Rooms fill quickly at seaside resorts in July and August, and some places in the moors and dales close in winter. Always call ahead to make sure a hotel is open and has space available. ⇨ *Hotel reviews have been shortened. For full information, visit Fodors.com.*

WHAT IT COSTS IN POUNDS				
	$	$$	$$$	$$$$
Restaurants	under £15	£15–£19	£20–£25	over £25
Hotels	under £100	£100–£160	£161–£220	over £220

Restaurant prices are the average cost of a main course at dinner or, if dinner is not served, at lunch. Hotel prices are the lowest cost of a standard double room in high season, including 20% V.A.T.

VISITOR INFORMATION

Contact Welcome to Yorkshire. ☎ *0113/322–3500* 🌐 *www.yorkshire.com.*

YORK

Fodor's Choice ★

For many people, the first stop in Yorkshire is the historic cathedral city of York. Much of the city's medieval and 18th-century architecture has survived, making it a delight to explore. It's one of the most popular short-stay destinations in Britain and only two hours by train from London's King's Cross Station.

Named "Eboracum" by the Romans, York was the military capital of Roman Britain, and traces of garrison buildings survive throughout the city. After the Roman Empire collapsed in the 5th century, the Saxons built "Eoforwic" on the ruins of a fort, but were soon defeated by Vikings, who called the town "Jorvik" and used it as a base from which to subjugate the countryside. The Normans came in the 11th century and emulated the Vikings by using the town as a military base. They also established the foundations of York Minster, the largest Gothic cathedral in Northern Europe. The 19th century saw large houses built on the outskirts of the city center.

GETTING HERE AND AROUND

If you're driving, take the M1 north from London. Stay on it to Leeds, and then take the A64 northeast for 25 miles to York. The journey should take around 3½ hours. Megabus coaches leave from St. Pancras International station twice a day (4½ hours), and National Express buses depart from London's Victoria Coach Station three times a day (5½ hours). Grand Central and Virgin Trains East Coast run from London's King's Cross Station every 10–30 minutes during the week (2 hours). York Station, just outside the city walls, has a line of taxis out front to take you to your hotel. If you don't have bags, the walk to town takes eight minutes.

York's city center is mostly closed to traffic and very walkable. The old center is a compact, dense web of narrow streets and tiny medieval alleys called "snickelways." These provide shortcuts across the city center, but they're not on maps, so you never quite know where you'll end up, which in York is often a pleasant surprise.

TOURS

City Sightseeing. This tour company runs frequent hop-on, hop-off bus tours of York that stop at the Castle Museum, the Minster, the National Railway Museum, Clifford's Tower, and Jorvik Viking Centre, among other attractions. Tickets are valid for 24 hours. ☎ *01904/634296* 🌐 *www.city-sightseeing.com* 🎫 *From £12.*

Ghost Creeper. Take a "bloodcurdling" tour down narrow passageways and dark streets on weekend nights from November to June, and nightly from July through Halloween. Tours start at 7:30 pm from St. Mary's Graveyard, next to the Jorvik Viking Centre. ✉ *York* ✣ *St. Mary's Churchyard, near Jorvik Viking Centre* ☎ *07947/325239* 🌐 *www.ghostdetective.com* 🎫 *£5.*

FAMILY **Ghost Hunt of York.** This tour for "boils and ghouls" takes a slightly tongue-in-cheek approach to the haunted locations, employing props, illusion, jokes, and audience participation. The tours start at 7:30 pm nightly in the Shambles. ✉ *York* ✣ *Bottom of The Shambles, opposite The Golden Fleece* ☎ *01904/608700* 🌐 *www.ghosthunt.co.uk* 🎫 *£5.*

FAMILY **Ghost Trail of York.** Still going strong after 21 years, the Ghost Trail of York has guides well-versed in local lore, combining traditional spooky tales, Victorian tragedies, and more recent reports of modern ghostly phenomena. The 70-minute tours start at 7:30 pm at the west doors of the Minster. ✉ *York* ✣ *By west doors of The Minster* ☎ *01904/633276* 🌐 *www.ghosttrail.co.uk* 🎫 *£4.*

FAMILY **Original Ghost Walk of York.** Claiming to be the world's first Ghost Walk, the Original Ghost Walk of York presents the city's ghost tales as a combination of "history and mystery," with an emphasis on accuracy and authenticity. The tours depart at 8 pm from in front of the King's Arms Pub near Ouse Bridge. ✉ *Kings Street* ✣ *In front of King's Arms Pub* ☎ *01759/373090* 🌐 *www.theoriginalghostwalkofyork.co.uk* 🎫 *£5.*

York Association of Voluntary Guides. Established more than 60 years ago, this organization arranges short walking tours around the city at least once a day, taking in two medieval gateways, a walk along the ancient walls, and a visit to a medieval church, in addition to well-known sights. The tours are free, but tips are appreciated. ✉ *1 Museum St.* ☎ *01904/550098* 🌐 *www.visityork.org* 🎫 *Free.*

TIMING

In July and August tourists choke the narrow streets and form long lines at the Minster. April, May, June, and September are less crowded, but the weather can be unpredictable. April is also the time to see the embankments beneath the city walls rippling with pale gold daffodils.

ESSENTIALS

Visitor Information Visit York. ✉ *1 Museum St.* ☎ *01904/550099* 🌐 *www.visityork.org.*

EXPLORING

TOP ATTRACTIONS

City of York Walls. Almost 3 miles of original medieval town walls remain around York, more than any other city in England. In the 9th century, invading Vikings buried the original Roman defensive walls, built some 1900 years ago, under earthen ramparts topped with wooden stakes. These in turn were replaced by the current stone walls in the 13th and 14th centuries. In the mid-19th century the walls, which had fallen into disrepair, were restored and maintained for public access, and you can now walk along a narrow paved path at the top and enjoy outstanding views (the whole circuit takes about two hours). In spring, the remains of the Viking embankment at the base are alive with daffodils. The walls are crossed periodically by York's distinctive "bars," or fortified gates: the portcullis on Monk's Bar on Goodramgate is still in working order, and Walmgate Bar in the east is the only gate in England with an intact barbican, although one scarred by the cannonballs during the Civil War. Bootham Bar in Exhibition Square was the defensive bastion for the north road, and Micklegate Bar, in the city's southwest corner, was traditionally the monarch's entrance. To access the path and lookout towers, find a staircase at one of the many breaks in the walls. ✉ *York* ☎ *01904/552270* 🌐 *www.yorkwalls.org.uk* 🕓 *Daily 8 am–dusk.*

FAMILY **Dig.** This reproduction of an archeological dig in and beneath an old church is a great way to inspire an interest in history and archaeology in young people. A venture by the people behind the Jorvik Viking Centre, Dig is supervised by knowledgeable experts. Kids dig in the dirt to "find" Roman or Viking artifacts, and everyone heads to the lab afterwards to learn what previous archaeological finds discovered on the site have revealed about former inhabitants. ✉ *St. Saviour's Church, St. Saviourgate* ☎ *01904/615505* 🌐 *digyork.com* 🎫 *£6.50; joint admission to Jorvik Viking Centre £14.45* 🕓 *Daily 10–5; last admission at 4.*

FAMILY **Jorvik Viking Centre.** This kid-focused exhibition re-creates a 10th-century Viking village. A mixture of museum and carnival ride, you "travel through time" by climbing into a Disney-esque machine that propels you above straw huts and mannequins in Viking garb. Commentary is provided in six languages. Kids get a lot out of it, but adults are

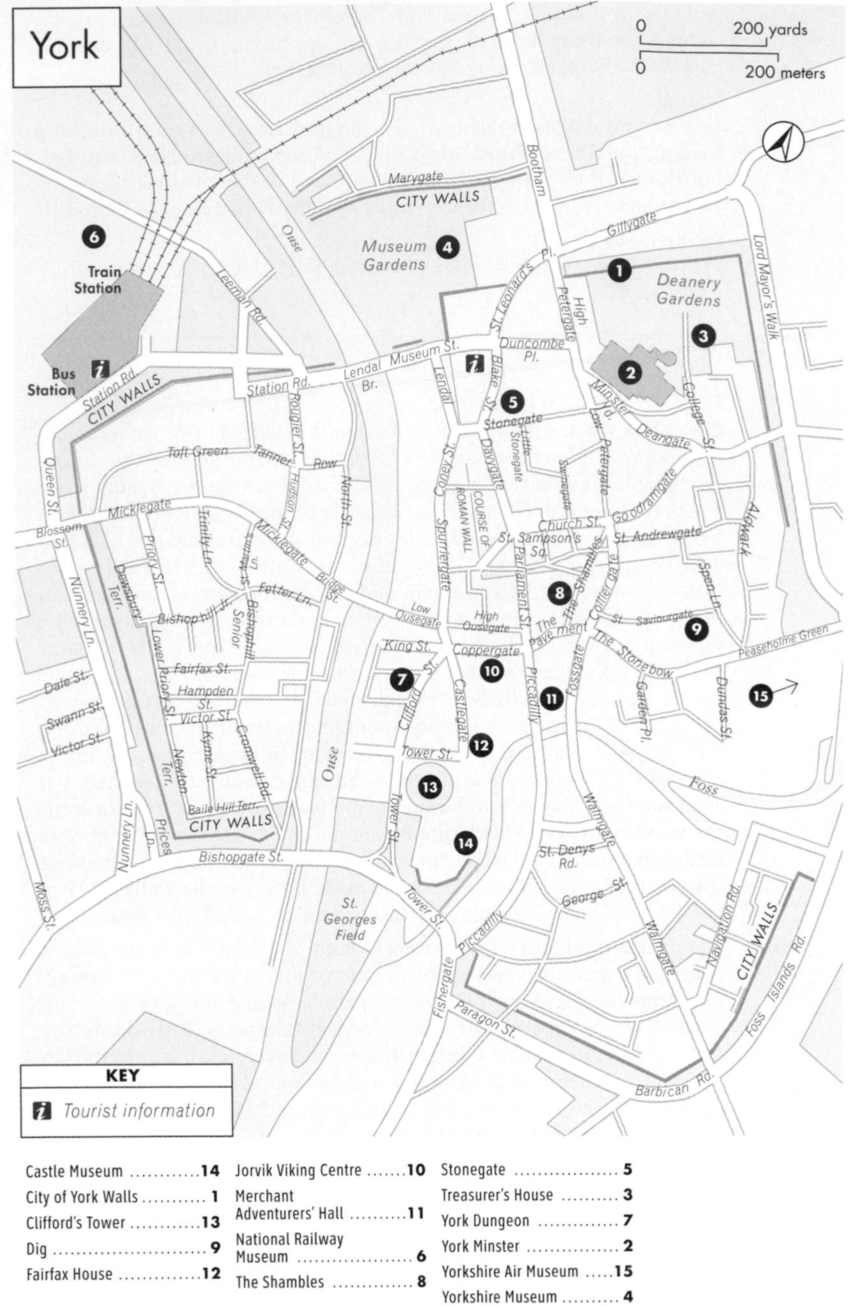
York
0 200 yards
0 200 meters
KEY
Tourist information
Train Station
Bus Station
Museum Gardens
Deanery Gardens
CITY WALLS
Marygate
Bootham
Gillygate
Lord Mayor's Walk
St. Leonard's Pl.
High Petergate
Duncombe Pl.
Museum St.
Lendal Br.
Station Rd.
Leeman Rd.
Ouse
Lendal
Blake St.
Minster Yd.
Stonegate
Little Stonegate
Low Petergate
Deangate
College St.
Toft Green
Tanner Row
Rougier St.
Hudson St.
North St.
Coney St.
Davygate
COURSE OF ROMAN WALL
Swinegate
Goodramgate
Church St.
St. Sampson's Sq.
St. Andrewgate
Aldwark
Queen St.
Micklegate
Blossom St.
Trinity Ln.
Priory St.
St. Martins Ln.
Micklegate Bridge St.
Spurriergate
Parliament St.
The Shambles
Colliergate
Spen Ln.
Nunnery Ln.
Dewsbury Terr.
Fetter Ln.
Bishophill Jr.
Bishophill Senior
Low Ousegate
High Ousegate
The Pavement
St. Saviourgate
Peaseholme Green
King St.
Coppergate
The Stonebow
Lower Priory St.
Fairfax St.
Hampden St.
Victor St.
Clifford St.
Castlegate
Piccadilly
Fossgate
Garden Pl.
Dundas St.
Dale St.
Swann St.
Victor St.
Kyme St.
Cromwell Rd.
Newton Terr.
Tower St.
Foss
Walmgate
Baile Hill Terr.
Nunnery Ln.
Prices Ln.
Bishopgate St.
St. Denys Rd.
Moss St.
St. Georges Field
George St.
Tower St.
Piccadilly
Navigation Rd.
Foss Islands Rd.
Fishergate
Paragon St.
Barbican Rd.
Castle Museum 14
City of York Walls 1
Clifford's Tower 13
Dig 9
Fairfax House 12
Jorvik Viking Centre 10
Merchant Adventurers' Hall 11
National Railway Museum 6
The Shambles 8
Stonegate 5
Treasurer's House 3
York Dungeon 7
York Minster 2
Yorkshire Air Museum 15
Yorkshire Museum 4

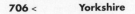

The Shambles, a narrow medieval street in York, once held butchers' shops, but now has stores that serve the city's many shoppers and visitors.

unlikely to learn anything new. A small collection of Viking-era artifacts is on display at the end of the ride. *Coppergate* *01904/615505* *jorvik-viking-centre.co.uk* *£10.25; joint admission to Dig £14.45* *Apr.–Oct., daily 10–6; Nov.–Mar., daily 10–5; last admission 1 hr before closing.*

FAMILY **National Railway Museum.** A must for train-lovers, Britain's biggest railway museum houses part of the national collection of rail vehicles. Don't miss such gleaming giants of the steam era as the *Mallard,* holder of the world speed record for a steam engine (126 mph), and train-buff legend the *Flying Scotsman.* Passenger cars used by Queen Victoria are on display, as is the only Japanese bullet train to be seen outside Japan. You can climb aboard some of the trains and occasionally take a short trip on one. There's also a little tourist train that makes the short journey to York Minster April to November (£2). *Leeman Rd.* *08448/153139* *www.nrm.org.uk* *Daily 10–6.*

The Shambles. York's best-preserved medieval street has shops and residences in half-timbered buildings with overhangs so massive you could almost reach across the narrow gap from one second-floor window to another. Once a hub of butchers (meat hooks are still fastened outside some of the doors), today it's mostly filled with independent shops and remains highly atmospheric. *York* *Off The Stonebow* *www.insideyork.co.uk.*

Stonegate. This narrow, pedestrian-only street lined with Tudor and 18th-century storefronts retains considerable charm. It's been in daily use for almost 2,000 years and was first paved during Roman times.

Today it's a vibrant shopping strip lined with upscale boutiques, jewelers, and quirky one-offs. A passage just off Stonegate, at 52A leads to the remains of a 12th-century Norman stone house attached to a more recent structure. You can still see the old Norman wall and window. ■ **TIP→ Look out for the little red "printer's devil" at No. 33, a medieval symbol of a printer's premises.** At the intersection of Stonegate and High Petergate, Minerva reclines on a stack of books, indicating they were once sold inside. ✉ *Stonegate between Petergate and Davygate.*

WHERE ARE THE GATES?

The Viking conquerors of northern England who held the region for more than a century made York their capital. *Gate* was the Viking word for "street," hence street names such as Goodramgate and Micklegate. Adding to the confusion, the city's entrances, or gates, are called "bars," from an Old English term. As local tour guides like to say, "In York, our streets are called gates, our gates are called bars, and our bars are called pubs."

NEED A BREAK?

Betty's Cafe Tea Rooms. Betty's has been a York institution since 1937. The plate-glass windows with art-nouveau stained glass, the dessert trollies, and solicitous white-aproned staff contribute to an impression of stepping back in time to when afternoon tea was a genteel ritual. The traditional dishes (like pork schnitzel and fried haddock) are so-so, but the tea and cakes are excellent. An in-house store sells a range of specialty coffees and teas, plus pastries and old-fashioned sweets like rose and violet creams. There's a smaller branch at 46 Stonegate. ✉ *6–8 Helen's Sq., off Stonegate* ☎ *01904/659142* 🌐 *www.bettys.co.uk* 🕙 *Closed Sun.*

FAMILY **York Dungeon.** This history-themed attraction takes a tongue-in-cheek approach to exploring the more violent and gory aspects of York's history. Lurid lighting, lots of fake blood, and costumed actors enliven episodes from the careers of infamous residents like highwayman Dick Turpin, revolutionary Guy Fawkes, Viking king Eric Bloodaxe, the Lost Roman Legion Labyrinth, and more, all to a soundtrack of wailing, screaming, and agonized moaning. As you might imagine, it's popular with kids, though not suitable for those under 10. ✉ *12 Clifford St.* ☎ *01904/632599* 🌐 *www.thedungeons.com/york/en* 🎟 *£15.95* 🕙 *Sept.–late Oct., Sun.–Fri. 10:30–4:30, Sat. 10:30–5; Mar. Sun.–Fri. 10:30–4, Sat. 10:30–4:30; Apr.–July, daily from 10 (hrs vary, check website); Nov.–Jan., Sun.–Fri., 10:30–3:30, Sat. 10:30–4:30.*

Fodor's Choice ★ **York Minster.** ⇨ *See highlighted feature in the chapter for more information.* ✉ *Minster Yard* ☎ *01904/557200* 🌐 *www.yorkminster.org* 🎟 *Minster £10, Minster and Tower £15* 🕙 *Minster and Tower Mon.–Sat. 9–6:30 (last admission at 5), Sun. 12:45–5. Undercroft Mon.–Sat. 10–5, Sun. 1–5. Minster Tours Mon.–Sat., hourly 10–3*

FAMILY **Yorkshire Air Museum.** Located on 22 acres of parkland, this is the country's largest World War II airbase that's open to the public. The independent museum showcases more than 60 historic vehicles and aircraft, many of which are still in working condition and are certain to delight aviation enthusiasts. Planes range from early 20th-century biplanes and gliders, such as the Eastchurch Kitten (the only surviving one in the world), to Spitfires, other World War II–era planes, and contemporary fighter jets. There are also exhibits devoted to military vehicles, aircraft weaponry, and Royal Air Force uniforms. The museum is home to a memorial and gardens commemorating British and allied service members who lost their lives in conflict. ✉ *Halifax Way, Elvington* ☎ *01904/608595* 🌐 *www.yorkshireairmuseum.org* 🎫 *£8* ⏲ *Apr.–mid-Nov., daily 10–5; mid-Nov.–Mar., daily 10–4.*

WORTH NOTING

FAMILY **Castle Museum.** In an 18th-century building, whose elegance belies its former role as a debtors' prison, this quirky museum includes a replica York street that recreates the Victorian shopping experience, notable domestic interiors, more than 100 historic patchwork quilts, a toy gallery, and Christmas cards sent during World War I. You can also visit the cell where Dick Turpin, the 18th-century highwayman and folk hero, spent the night before his execution. ✉ *Eye of York* ☎ *01904/687687* 🌐 *www.yorkcastlemuseum.org.uk* 🎫 *£10* ⏲ *Daily 9:30–5.*

Clifford's Tower. This rather battered-looking keep at the top of a steep mound is all that remains of the old York castle. Sitting on a grassy mound, this squat stone tower dates from the early 12th century. The Norman tower that preceded it, built in 1068 by William the Conqueror, was destroyed in 1190 when more than 150 Jews locked themselves inside to protect themselves from a violent mob. Trapped with no food or water, they committed mass suicide by setting their own prison aflame. From the top of the tower you have good views of the city. ✉ *Tower St.* ☎ *01904/646940* 🌐 *www.english-heritage.org.uk* 🎫 *£4.40* ⏲ *Apr.–Sept., daily 10–6; Oct., daily 10–5; Nov.–Mar., daily 10–4; last admission 30 min before closing.*

Fairfax House. This museum of decorative arts, inside an elegant, beautifully decorated Georgian town house, contains crystal chandeliers, silk damask wallpaper, and one of the country's finest collections of 18th-century furniture. Entrance on Monday is restricted to guided tours at 11 and 2. ✉ *Castlegate* ☎ *01904/655543* 🌐 *www.fairfaxhouse.co.uk* 🎫 *£6* ⏲ *Feb.–Dec., Tues.–Sat. 10–5, Sun. 11–4; Mon. by guided tour only; last admission 30 min before closing.*

Merchant Adventurers' Hall. Built between 1357 and 1361 by a wealthy medieval guild, this is the largest half-timbered hall in York. It has fine collections of silver and furniture, along with paintings that provide insight into the history of the Hall and its founders. The building itself is much of the attraction. A riverfront garden lies behind the hall. ✉ *Fossgate* ☎ *01904/654818* 🌐 *www.theyorkcompany.co.uk* 🎫 *£6* ⏲ *Mar.–Oct., Mon.–Thurs. 9–5, Fri. and Sat. 9–3:30, Sun. 11–4; Nov.–mid-Dec., Jan., and Feb., Mon.–Sat. 10–4, Fri. and Sat. 10–3:30; last admission 30 min before closing.*

Treasurer's House. Surprises await inside this large 17th-century town house. With an eye for texture, decoration, and pattern, industrialist

Continued on page 715

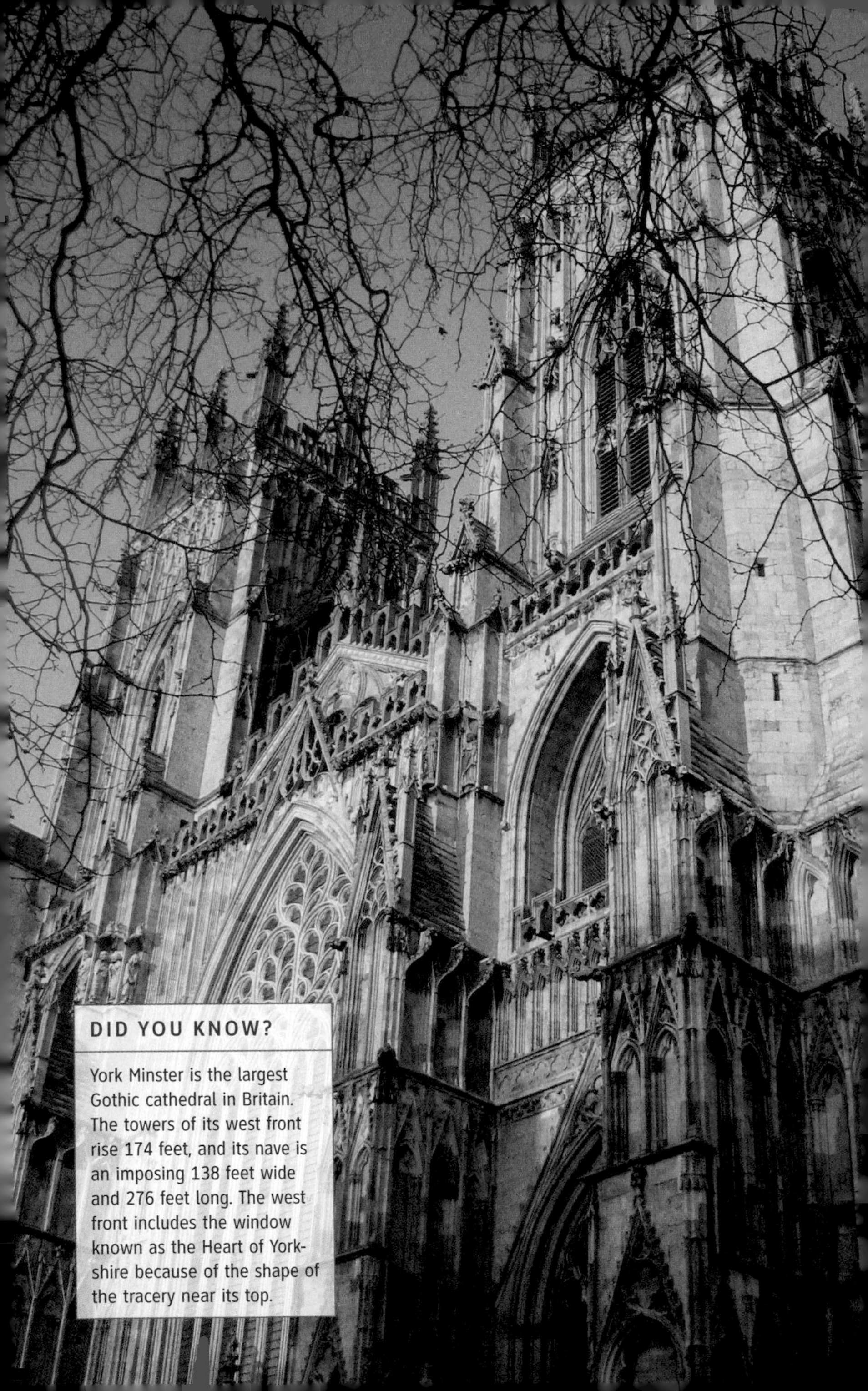

DID YOU KNOW?

York Minster is the largest Gothic cathedral in Britain. The towers of its west front rise 174 feet, and its nave is an imposing 138 feet wide and 276 feet long. The west front includes the window known as the Heart of Yorkshire because of the shape of the tracery near its top.

YORK MINSTER

GOTHIC GRANDEUR

by Christi Daugherty

You can see this vast cathedral from 10 miles away, the tall Gothic towers rising over the flat horizon. The focal point of York, it encompasses centuries of the city's history, and its treasures include 128 dazzling medieval glass windows. The Minster today is a tranquil place, but over the centuries it has survived structural threats and political upheaval.

The present York Minster is the fourth attempt to build a church on this site. The first, a Saxon minster from the 7th century, was built of wood. In the 8th century it was rebuilt in stone. Norman invaders badly damaged the first stone church in 1069 as they conquered the recalcitrant north. They later rebuilt it in their own style, and you can see Norman elements—foundations, masonry, columns—in the undercroft. Marauding Vikings, however, damaged that building. Much of the limestone building you see is the result of the vision of one 13th-century archbishop, Walter de Gray. He wanted to build one of the world's greatest cathedrals, on the scale of Canterbury, with vaulted ceilings soaring hundreds of feet high. York Minster was finally completed in 1472. De Gray stayed with his beloved building beyond the end. He died in 1255, and his effigy lies atop his tomb inside the south transept near the main entrance.

(top left) York Minster interior, (top right) A stone gargoyle, (bottom right) Chapter House ceiling

MINSTER ORIENTATION AND HIGHLIGHTS

The Minster is designed in cruciform, meaning in the shape of a cross. As you walk through the main doors, you're entering the south transept, one of the arms of the cross. These transepts were built in Archbishop de Gray's time in the 13th century. Ahead of you, the grand, soaring, light-filled nave stretches out to your left and right, with massive stained-glass windows at both ends. Across the nave is the northern transept—the other arm of the cross—and off of it a corridor leads to the octagonal Chapter House. The nave's ceiling is supported by flying buttresses on the exterior of the building. In the 13th and 14th centuries, this architectural feature was so experimental that the builders could not be certain the structure would not simply collapse.

Nave

❶ **Nave.** The 14th-century builders of the nave used painted wood for the nave's soaring ceilings out of practicality: they feared stone would be too heavy. A fire in 1840 destroyed the roof, but the vaulting and bosses are exact replicas. Giant stained-glass windows glow from each end: the Heart of Yorkshire to the west, and opposite it the great East Window.

❷ **Great West Window.** The heart-shaped tracery in the window that dominates the west end of the nave dates to 1338, and is remarkable both for its shape and its intricate design.

❸ **Rose Window.** This extraordinary stained-glass window in the south transept has 13th-century stonework, but it has early 16th-century glass in which white and red Tudor roses show the union of the houses of York and Lancaster. It was nearly lost when lightning struck the building in 1984, causing a fire.

❹ **The Five Sisters.** At the end of the north transept, these five tall, blade-shaped windows from around 1260 are rare pieces of medieval glass art made of more than 100,000 pieces of glass. Each blade is more than five feet wide and towers 52 feet high. All were painted on gray-tinged glass using a technique known as grisaille.

The Rose Window

❺ **Chapter House.** With a beautifully painted and gilded ceiling (restored in 1845), the octagonal 13th-century Chapter House is a marvel, lined with exquisite stained glass and decorated with fanciful animals and gargoyles with human faces that could be caricatures of early monks.

❻ **Choir Screen.** Stretching along one section of the nave, an elegantly carved 15th-century stone panel, known as the choir screen, contains almost life-size sculptures of 15 kings of England from William the Conqueror to Henry VI.

Choir Screen

1069 Normans destroy Saxon structure

1220 Walter de Gray begins church

1472 The Minster is consecrated

1829 Arson attack damages choir

1967 Tower is structurally threatened

1200 | 1400 | 1600 | 1800 | 2000

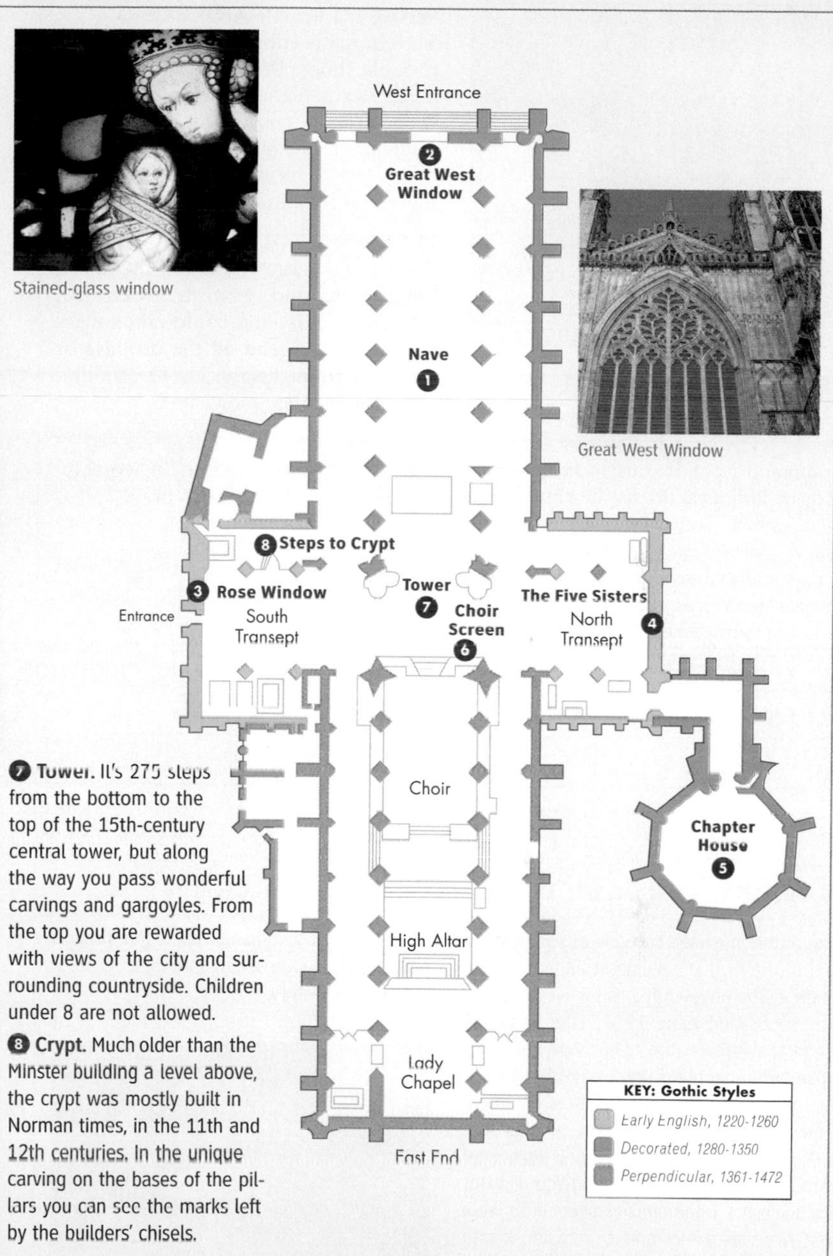

Stained-glass window

Great West Window

7 Tower. It's 275 steps from the bottom to the top of the 15th-century central tower, but along the way you pass wonderful carvings and gargoyles. From the top you are rewarded with views of the city and surrounding countryside. Children under 8 are not allowed.

8 Crypt. Much older than the Minster building a level above, the crypt was mostly built in Norman times, in the 11th and 12th centuries. In the unique carving on the bases of the pillars you can see the marks left by the builders' chisels.

MAKING THE MOST OF YOUR VISIT

Five Sisters

WHEN TO VISIT

The best time to visit is early or late in the day. The church is busiest between 11 am and 2 pm. If you can avoid weekends or holidays, do, as the church can be crowded. You may encounter choir practice in the early evening. Look for occasional evening concerts; attending Evensong service can also be lovely. The building sometimes closes for church events and meetings, and it is closed to visitors (except those attending services) on most major religious holidays.

WHAT TO WEAR AND BRING

The church is enormous, so wear comfortable shoes. Bring binoculars to see the glass and higher carvings. The stone walls keep it cool inside year-round. There are no restrictions on attire. You may want to bring a bottle of water; there's no tea shop.

PLANNING YOUR TIME

A thorough visit, including the crypt, undercroft, and central tower, can take two hours, and could take longer for those who read all the displays or study the stained glass. The Orb exhibit shows some glass at eye level.

FOR FREE

The church is always free for worshippers or those who wish to pray.

TOURS

Free tours may be available without reservations.

WALKING THROUGH HISTORY: THE UNDERCROFT

One of the must-see sections of York Minster isn't in the Gothic building at all, but underneath it. The undercroft was excavated in the late 1960s and early 1970s after a survey found that the central tower was near collapse. While working frantically to shore up the foundations, builders uncovered extensive remains of previous structures on this site. Now the ruins and remnants they uncovered form the basis for the Revealing York Minster exhibit in the Undercroft Museum. You walk past Norman pillars and stonework, Viking gravestones, Saxon carvings and coffins, and the remains of a Roman basilica. The displays put all that you are seeing into the context of the region's history.

York Minster crypt

A WALK IN YORK

York is a fine city for walking, especially along the walls embracing the old center. Start at the Minster and head down Stonegate, a lane dating back to the Middle Ages now lined with shops, which leads directly to Betty's celebrated tearoom. Eventually you'll come to a highly atmospheric shopping street known as the Shambles and farther along, the remains of the old castle.

Make time to stop in at the shops, which are filled with locals as well as tourists; you can find everything from antiques to more contemporary items.

To get a sense of where you are at any point, climb the steps up to the top of the city walls (they are also good for a walk). The River Ouse is bordered in places by walking paths that make for a pleasant stroll.

Frank Green—who lived here from 1897 to 1930—re-created 13 period rooms, including a medieval great hall as a showcase for his collection of antique furniture, ceramics, art, and textiles. Delft tiles decorate the former kitchen (now a shop) and the dining room retains its original 16th-century paneling and 18th-century plasterwork. Stumpwork from the 17th century is the highlight of the textiles in the Tapestry Room. There's an actual Roman road in the cellar, plus a display about Roman York and one resident's account of seeing a ghostly Roman legion in the 1950s. ✉ *Minster Yard* ☎ *01904/624247* 🌐 *www.nationaltrust.org.uk* 🎫 *House and garden £7.20* ⏲ *Mar.–Oct., Sat.–Thurs. 11–5; Feb., Sat.–Thurs. 11–3, by guided tour only; last admission at 4:30.*

Yorkshire Museum. The ecological and archaeological history of the county is the focus of this museum in an early 19th-century Greek Revival–style building with massive Doric columns. Themed galleries focus mostly on Roman, Anglian, Viking, and medieval periods, with nearly 1 million objects, including the 15th-century Middleham Jewel, a pendant gleaming with a large sapphire; a Paleolithic hand axe; and an extremely rare Copperplate Helmet, a 1,200-year-old Viking artifact. ✉ *St. Mary's Lodge, Museum Gardens* ☎ *01904/687687* 🌐 *www.yorkshiremuseum.org.uk* 🎫 *Museum £7.50; gardens and observatory free* ⏲ *Museum daily 10–5. Gardens late Oct.–late Mar., 7:30–6; April–mid-Oct., 7:30–dusk. Observatory Thurs. and Sat., 11:30–2:30.*

WHERE TO EAT

$$ MODERN BRITISH Fodor's Choice ★

✕ **Blue Bicycle.** One of York's best restaurants is in a building that once served as a brothel, a past reflected in its murals featuring undraped women. Downstairs are four intimate walled booths, and at street level is a lively candlelit room. The menu changes with the seasons and concentrates on local seafood. Typical dishes include pan-seared scallops, roast local cod with crayfish tails, and grilled Yorkshire sirloin steak with spring onion mash. The wine list is impressive, and the service can't be friendlier. The restaurant has six self-contained apartments—called the Blue Rooms—in a courtyard to the rear. 💲 *Average main: £19* ✉ *34 Fossgate* ☎ *01904/673990* 🌐 *www.thebluebicycle.com* ✍ *Reservations essential.*

$ **Café Concerto.** Wallpaper made from sheet music reveals the musical theme at this relaxed, intimate bistro in sight of York Minster. The kitchen serves simple rustic classics with an emphasis on local ingredients. Dinner favorites include braised lamb shank with roast potatoes, ground beef cottage pie, and vegetarian moussaka, plus a good selection of desserts. Lunch is mostly soups, salads, and sandwiches, and you can always pop in for tea and carrot or chocolate cake. *Average main: £14 21 High Petergate 01904/610478 www.cafeconcerto.biz.*
BRITISH

$$$ **Le Langhe.** So popular that it has already moved twice to larger premises, this combination café/restaurant/deli specializes in Italian, particularly Piedmontese meats and cheeses. Takeout sandwiches at the deli incorporate a variety of both, as well as artisan olive oils, wines, and other items sourced by the owners. The glass-roofed café serves salads, sandwiches, and house-made pastas such as one with Whitby crab, shallots, and potatoes. All are freshly made with seasonal ingredients. Entreés change daily and might include slow-cooked pork belly, lemon sole, or venison. There's a four-course fixed-price tasting menu for lunch (£24.50) and dinner (£39), served Friday and Saturday in the upstairs restaurant. *Average main: £21 The Old Coach House, Peasholme Green 01904/622584 www.lelanghe.co.uk Reservations essential.*
ITALIAN

$$$ **Melton's.** This former Victorian shop, now restaurant, with an open kitchen beyond a glass door, uses locally sourced Yorkshire produce to create a seasonal, highly imaginative take on Modern British cuisine. Dishes include risotto of spelt, cep mushroom, and lovage; venison with chocolate oil; and rare breed ham hock terrine. Fixed price menus—£23 for two courses, £26 for three—are available at lunch and early dinner. A 10-minute walk from Clifford's Tower, Melton's has an offshoot bar-bistro called Melton's Too on nearby Walmsgate. *Average main: £20 7 Scarcroft Rd. 01904/634341 www.meltonsrestaurant.co.uk Closed Sun. and Mon. and 3 wks at Christmas Reservations essential.*
MODERN BRITISH

$ **Spurriergate Centre.** Churches aren't just for services, as this 15th-century house of worship proves. Resurrected as a cafeteria (there's also a café on the upper floor) using fresh-made local ingredients, St. Michael's is a favorite spot for both tourists and locals to refuel spiritually (you can request use of the prayer room upstairs) as well as physically. You may end up eating beef casserole on the spot where John Wesley prayed in 1768. Don't pass up the cream scones. *Average main: £7 Spurriergate 01904/629393 www.thespurriergatecentre.com No credit cards Closed Sun. No dinner.*
CAFÉ

WHERE TO STAY

$$ **Cedar Court Grand Hotel and Spa.** This handsome, comfortable hotel near the train station—not surprising, considering it was formerly the headquarters of the regional railroad—was built in 1906 and retains many original features, such as solid mahogany doors, beautiful tilework on the stairwells, and art nouveau ironwork. **Pros:** beautiful building; spacious rooms; good location. **Cons:** Continental breakfast only
HOTEL

12

HAUNTED YORK

Given its lengthy history, dark streets, and atmospheric buildings, it's no surprise that York feels as if it could be haunted. Indeed, a body called the Ghost Research Foundation International has determined that, with 500 recorded cases of ghostly encounters, York is the most haunted city in England, and one of the most haunted in the world.

Not everybody believes in earth-bound spirits, but that hasn't stopped the local tourism industry from assuming many do. Should you choose to explore the town's spookier side, try Ghost Creeper, Ghost Hunt, Ghost Trail of York, or the Original Ghost Tour of York.

average; occasional lapses in service. *$ Rooms from: £155 ✉ Station Rise ☎ 01904/380038 🌐 www.cedarcourtgrand.co.uk 107 rooms, 13 suites 🍴 Breakfast.*

$ B&B/INN **Dairy Guest House.** Victorian stained glass, fine woodwork, and intricate plaster cornices are original features of this former dairy near the city walls. **Pros:** nice period details; comfortable rooms. **Cons:** small bathrooms; minimum stay required in summer; few amenities. *$ Rooms from: £70 ✉ 3 Scarcroft Rd. ☎ 01904/639367 🌐 www.dairyguesthouse.co.uk 6 rooms 🍴 Breakfast.*

$$ HOTEL **Grange Hotel.** Built in the early 19th century as the home for two wealthy members of the York clergy, this luxurious boutique hotel decorated with racing memorabilia is reminiscent of a grand country house. **Pros:** spacious rooms; lovely design; good food. **Cons:** can feel a bit fussy; restaurant service uneven. *$ Rooms from: £122 ✉ 1 Clifton ☎ 01904/644744 🌐 www.grangehotel.co.uk 35 rooms, 1 suite 🍴 Breakfast.*

$ B&B/INN **The Hazelwood.** These two tall, elegant Victorian town houses retain many of their original features and stand in a peaceful cul-de-sac; they're away from the hustle and bustle, despite being a short walk from York Minster. **Pros:** good service; lovely building; convenient parking. **Cons:** thin walls; poor water pressure on upper floors. *$ Rooms from: £90 ✉ 24–25 Portland St. ☎ 01904/626548 🌐 www.thehazelwoodyork.com 14 rooms 🍴 Breakfast.*

$$ HOTEL **Hotel du Vin.** A 19th-century orphanage, this historic building has been converted into a swanky hotel that preserves the original exposed brick walls and arched doorways. **Pros:** makes great use of the space; friendly staff; comfortable beds. **Cons:** high parking charges; low bathroom lighting. *$ Rooms from: £129 ✉ 89 The Mount ☎ 0844/748-9268 🌐 www.hotelduvin.com 39 rooms, 5 suites 🍴 Breakfast.*

$$$ HOTEL **Middlethorpe Hall & Spa.** Aimed at those who prize period details like oak-paneled walls, four-poster beds, carved wood bannisters, and window seats, and whose idea of luxury is a bowl of fresh daffodils, this splendidly restored Queen Anne building with mid-18th-century additions feels less like a country-house hotel than an actual country

The Vikings occupied York, and the city recalls this era enthusiastically during the Viking Festival each February.

house. **Pros:** period luxury; gorgeous grounds; attentive staff. **Cons:** poor water pressure; outside city center. *Rooms from: £199* *Bishopthorpe Rd.* *01904/641241* *www.middlethorpe.com* *18 rooms, 11 suites* *Breakfast.*

$$ HOTEL **Mount Royale Hotel.** This hotel has the feel of a relaxing country house despite being close to the city center in an upscale residential neighborhood. **Pros:** large rooms; lovely pool and garden; good service. **Cons:** well outside the town center; some rooms dated. *Rooms from: £130* *117–119 The Mount* *01904/628856* *www.mountroyale.co.uk* *14 rooms, 10 suites* *Breakfast.*

NIGHTLIFE AND PERFORMING ARTS

NIGHTLIFE

Black Swan. In a 15th-century timber-framed building (a pub since the 16th century), complete with flagstone floors and mullioned windows, this pub serves home-cooked bar food and hosts a roster of local folk musicians. *Peasholme Green* *01904/679131* *www.blackswanyork.com.*

Old White Swan. Spreading across five half-timbered, 16th-century buildings on busy Goodramgate, the Old White Swan is known for good its pub lunches and ghosts—it claims to have more than the equally venerable Black Swan. *80 Goodramgate* *01904/540911* *www.nicholsonspubs.co.uk.*

Snickleway Inn. Built in the 15th century, the Snickleway Inn's wood paneling and open brick fireplaces provide a real sense of stepping back in time. ✉ *47 Goodramgate* ☎ *01904/656138* 🌐 *www.thesnicklewayinn.co.uk*.

PERFORMING ARTS

Early Music Festival. Devoted to compositions written before the 18th century, the Early Music Festival is held each July. There's also a Christmas program in early December. ✉ *St. Margaret's Church, Walmgate* ☎ *01904/658338* 🌐 *www.ncem.co.uk*.

FAMILY **Viking Festival.** Held every February, this city-wide Norse-themed festival has more than 60 events, including a long-ship regatta. It ends with the Jorvik Viking combat reenactment, when Norsemen confront their Anglo-Saxon enemies. ✉ *Jorvik Viking Centre, Coppergate* ☎ *01904/615505* 🌐 *jorvik-viking-festival.co.uk*.

York Theatre Royal. In a lovely 18th-century building, the York Theatre Royal hosts theater, dance, music, and comedy performances, as well as readings, lectures, and children's entertainment. ✉ *St. Leonard's Pl.* ☎ *01904/623568* 🌐 *www.yorktheatreroyal.co.uk*.

SHOPPING

Stonegate is the city's main shopping street. Winding down from the Minster toward the river, it's lined with a mix of unique shops and boutiques. Another good shopping street is Petergate, which has mostly chain stores. The Shambles is another prime shopping area, with an eclectic mix of shops geared toward locals and tourists.

Minster Gate Bookshop. This shop in a Georgian town house sells secondhand and antiquarian books, old maps, and prints. ✉ *8 Minster Gate* ☎ *01904/621812* 🌐 *www.minstergatebooks.co.uk*.

Mulberry Hall. This store inside a 1434 timber framed building sells fine bone china from big names like Royal Doulton and Minton, as well as glittering crystal from the likes of Baccarat and Lalique. There are also elegant ornaments, cookware, cutlery, and kitchen essentials. An upstairs traditional tearoom serves light lunches and snacks on Wedgwood china. ✉ *Stonegate* ☎ *01904/620736* 🌐 *www.mulberryhall.co.uk*.

York Antiques Centre. With five showrooms spread over three floors in a Georgian town house, the center sells antiques, collectables, and vintage items—Roman, Georgian, Victorian, Edwardian, and art deco—from more than 100 dealers, who display their wares in "cabinets." ✉ *41 Stonegate* ☎ *01904/635888* 🌐 *www.theantiquescentreyork.co.uk*.

AROUND YORK

West and north of York a number of sights make easy, appealing day trips from the city: the spa town of Harrogate, atmospheric Knaresborough, the ruins of Fountain Abbey, the market town of Ripon, and nearby Newby Hall. If you're heading northwest from York to Harrogate, you might take the less direct B1224 across Marston Moor, where,

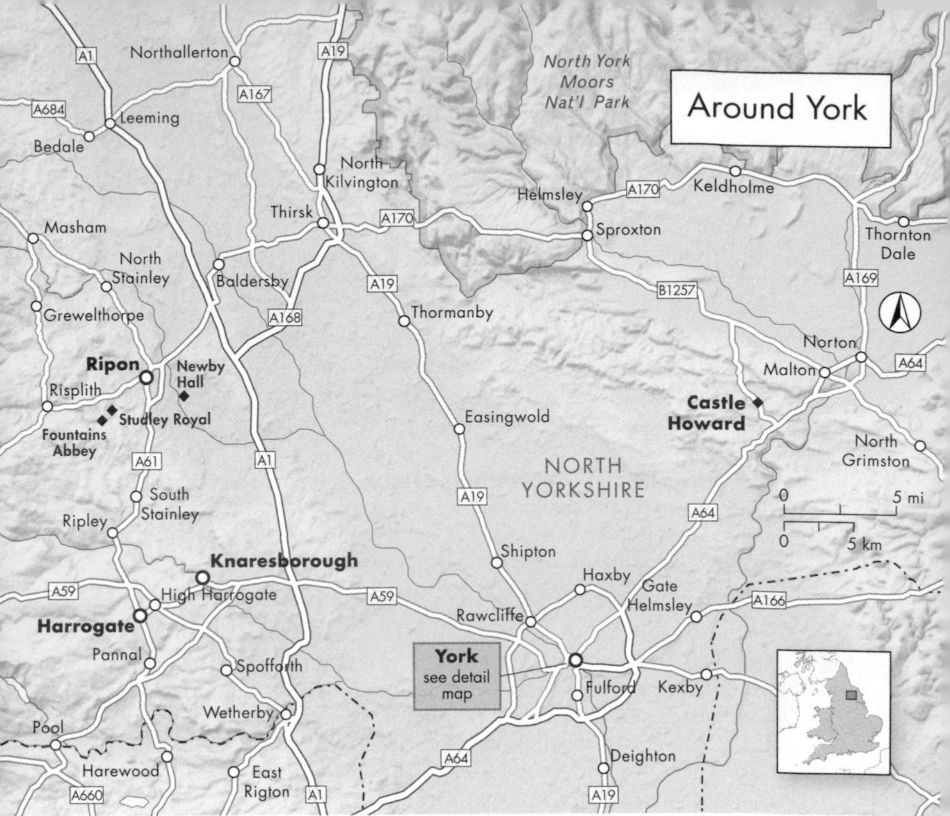

in 1644, Oliver Cromwell won a decisive victory over the Royalists during the English Civil War. A few miles beyond, at Wetherby, you can cut northwest along the A661 to Harrogate. Also nearby toward the northeast is Castle Howard, a magnificent stately home.

HARROGATE

21 miles west of York, 11 miles south of Ripon, 16 miles north of Leeds.

During the Regency and early Victorian periods, it became fashionable for the aristocratic and wealthy to "take the waters" at British spa towns, combining the alleged health benefits with socializing. In Yorkshire the most elegant spa destination was Harrogate, where today its mainly Victorian buildings, parks, and spas still provide a relaxing getaway.

GETTING HERE AND AROUND

Trains from York leave every hour or so, and the journey takes about 30 minutes. There's one direct train daily from London. National Express buses leave from York every hour most days; the journey takes about 40 minutes. By car, Harrogate is off A59 and well marked. It's a walkable town, so you can park in one of its central parking lots and explore on foot.

Within and around Harrogate, the Harrogate & District bus company provides area services, and taxis are plentiful.

ESSENTIALS

Visitor Information Harrogate Tourist Information Centre. ✉ *Royal Baths, Crescent Rd.* ☎ *01423/537300* 🌐 *www.enjoyharrogate.com.*

EXPLORING

Royal Pump Room Museum. This octagonal structure was built in 1842 over the original sulfur well that brought great prosperity to the town. You can still sniff the evil-smelling spa waters here. The museum has displays of bygone spa treatment paraphernalia, alongside a somewhat eccentric collection of fine 19th-century china, clothes, and bicycles. ✉ *Crown Pl.* ☎ *01423/556188* 🌐 *www.harrogate.gov.uk* 🎫 *£4* ⏲ *Apr.–July, Sept.–Oct., Mon.–Sat. 10:30–5, Sun. 2–5; August, Mon.–Sat. 10:30–5, Sun. 12–5; Nov.–Mar., Mon.–Sat. 10:30–4, Sun. 2–4.*

The Stray. Wrapping around the town center, this 200-acre grassy parkland is a riot of color in spring. Many of the mineral springs that first made Harrogate famous bubble below. ✉ *Harrogate* ☎ *01423/841097* 🌐 *www.harrogate.gov.uk.*

Harrogate Turkish Baths and Health Spa. Dating from 1897, these exotic and fully restored Turkish Baths are as enjoyable now as they were for the many Victorians who came to Harrogate. After changing into your bathing suit, relax on luxurious lounge chairs in the stunning mosaic-tile warming room. Move on to increasingly hot sauna rooms, and then soak up eucalyptus mist in the steam room before braving the icy plunge pool. You can also book a massage or facial. Open hours are divided into women-only and mixed sessions, so book in advance. ✉ *Royal Baths, Parliament St.* ☎ *01423/556746* 🌐 *www.turkishbathsharrogate.co.uk* 🎫 *£15.50–£29.50 per session* ⏲ *Daily except holiday Mon.; call for schedule.*

FAMILY **Valley Gardens.** Southwest of the town center, these 17 acres of formal gardens include a children's boating lake, tennis courts, skate park, adventure playground, paddling pool, and little café. ✉ *Valley Dr.* ✣ *Junction with Cornwall Rd. and Royal Parade* ☎ *01423/500600* 🌐 *www.harrogate.gov.uk.*

WHERE TO EAT AND STAY

$ CAFÉ Fodor's Choice ★ ✕ **Betty's Cafe Tea Rooms.** This celebrated Yorkshire tearoom began life in Harrogate in 1919, when a Swiss restaurateur brought his Alpine pastries and chocolates to England. The welcoming interior has changed little since then, and the extensive array of teas not at all. In addition to omelets, quiches, sandwiches, and traditional cakes and pastries, the menu ranges from the Dales (sausages) to the Alps (rösti), and there are now no-gluten options. A pianist plays nightly. Reservations are accepted only for weekend afternoon tea, served in the Imperial Room. 💲 *Average main: £12* ✉ *1 Parliament St.* ☎ *01423/814070* 🌐 *www.bettys.co.uk.*

$$ STEAKHOUSE ✕ **The Moody Cow.** Don't be misled by the uninspiring exterior. This family-friendly Yorkshire take on an American steak house is bright and modern (the conservatory is especially appealing), with an emphasis

on locally sourced food, particularly meat. Specialities include Cajun-spiced breaded chicken marinated in buttermilk (£12.95), baby back barbecue ribs (£14.95 for a full rack), and grilled steak from local herds (sirloin £19.95). For smaller appetites, there are lunchtime "light bites" like a pulled-pork-and-cheddar melt, and fish-eaters are catered to with dishes like pan-fried sea bass and blackened cod. There are even a few vegetarian alternatives plus a salad bar. If you don't feel like hitting the road afterwards, there are 10 modern rooms decorated in chic taupes and browns (from £65). *Average main: £16* *Apperly La., Apperly Bridge* *0113/239–1444* *www.moodycowgrill.co.uk*.

$$$$ INTERNATIONAL Fodor's Choice ★ **The Yorke Arms.** The peaceful rural location of this "restaurant with rooms" in the scenic Nidderdale valley belies the sophistication of its distinctive cooking, which has been consistently rated as one of the top five dining spots not only in Yorkshire, but in the UK. It won its Michelin star with an emphasis on seasonal ingredients, creative combinations of flavors, and elegant presentations, as in appetizers like seared tuna with squid and chorizo, and pheasant with pomegranate and date. Main courses might include a saddle of venison with oxtail in a sloe gin and cherry sauce, or a wild sea bass with tomato, saffron, and shrimp gnocchi. The dessert selection is fabulous, so save room. The dinner menu is pricey, but the set menu at lunch (£40) is a good value. The restaurant is housed in a building that is partially medieval, dating to the 11th century (the monks of nearby Fountains Abbey made cheese in the cellar), and partially an 18th-century coaching inn. The 11 rooms are spacious and charming, four are modern courtyard rooms, and prices start at £172, which includes dinner and breakfast. *Average main: £50* *Ramsgill-in-Nidderdale, Pateley Bridge* *01423/755243* *www.yorke-arms.co.uk* *Closed Sun. and Mon.*

$ HOTEL **Balmoral Hotel.** Contemporary touches mixed with antique pieces, boldly patterned wallpapers, and rich colors characterize these three Victorian houses knocked together to create a boutique hotel. **Pros:** spacious rooms; friendly service. **Cons:** could be cleaner; shabby in places. *Rooms from: £95* *16–18 Franklin Mt.* *01423/508208* *www.balmoralhotel.co.uk* *17 rooms, 3 suites* *Breakfast.*

$$ HOTEL **Hotel du Vin.** This hip hotel sprawls through eight Georgian houses, with stripped-wood floors, clubby leather armchairs, and a purple billiard table setting the tone. **Pros:** tasty food; wonderful wine list; helpful staff; modern vibe. **Cons:** some rooms dark; housekeeping uneven; the bar can take over the lounge. *Rooms from: £115 (room only)* *Prospect Pl.* *01423/856800, 121/616–3613 from U.S.* *www.hotelduvin.com* *40 rooms, 8 suites* *No meals.*

NIGHTLIFE AND PERFORMING ARTS

Harrogate Festival. Throughout July, the town is filled with performances of ballet, contemporary dance, music, comedy, street theater, plus lectures by leading authors and film screenings. *32 Cheltenham Parade* *01423/562303* *www.harrogateinternationalfestivals.com.*

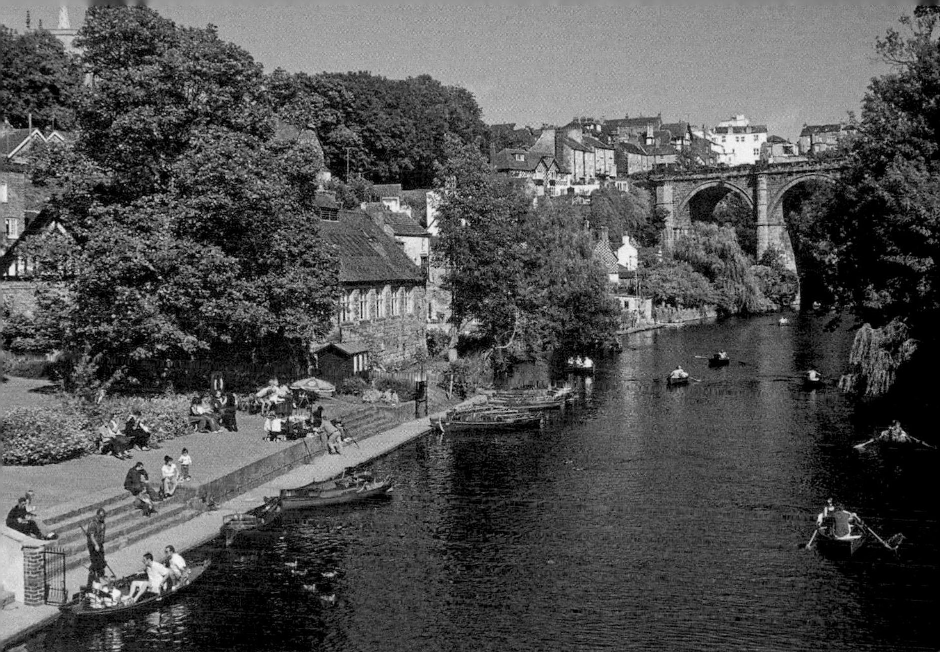

You can paddle on the River Nidd in the pretty town of Knaresborough.

KNARESBOROUGH

3 miles northeast of Harrogate, 17 miles west of York.

At the bottom of a precipitously deep rocky gorge along the River Nidd, the little town of Knaresborough could hardly be more photogenic. It's best seen from a train, crossing the high Victorian viaduct above. In summer you can rent a boat and row down the slow-moving river, or stroll through the town's square, site of a market since the early 14th century. On the top of the hill are the ruins of the castle where Richard II was imprisoned for a night in 1399.

GETTING HERE AND AROUND

Northern Rail trains leave from Leeds every 30 minutes (a 45-minute trip) and from York every hour or so (a 30-minute trip). Local buses travel here from nearby towns, but they're less frequent. By car, the village is on A59 and is well signposted.

The village lies on a precipitous hill. The town is easily walkable, although it helps to be in good shape. There are clearly marked public parking areas.

EXPLORING

Mother Shipton's Cave. Across the river from the center of town and tucked away in a beautiful park is one of England's oldest tourist attractions. According to local lore, the cave is the birthplace of the titular 16th-century prophetess, who supposedly foretold such events as the defeat of the Spanish Armada. The mineral-rich well beside her cave is famously able to petrify soft objects in 3–5 months. Call ahead in winter. ✉ *Prophesy Lodge, High Bridge* ☎ *01423/864600* 🌐 *www.mothershipton.co.uk* 🎟 *£6* ⏲ *Apr.–late Oct., daily 10–5:30; Feb.–Mar., weekends 10–5:30; last admission 30 min before closing.*

RIPON

12 miles north of Knaresborough, 24 miles northwest of York.

Said to be England's second-oldest city and still one of its smallest, Ripon has been the site of a market since the 10th century, and probably before. A basilica was built here in the 7th century, and its chapel remains within the existing building, which is a mostly 12th-century minster. The church was designated a cathedral in the mid-19th century, making Ripon technically a city, despite its population of only about 16,000. Don't miss the Hornblower announcing he's on duty by blowing his horn at 9 pm every evening in the town square, an unbroken tradition that goes back 900 years. Market day, Thursday, is probably the best day to stop by.

GETTING HERE AND AROUND

Ripon is just off A1 via the A61, 12 miles north of Harrogate. There's no train service to Ripon, but local buses run from Harrogate several times a day.

EXPLORING

FAMILY **Newby Hall.** Built under the guidance of Sir Christopher Wren in the 17th century, and given additions and interiors in the 18th century by Robert Adam, this country house is still the home of the original family. Inside is fine decorative art of its period, particularly ornamental plasterwork and Chippendale furniture. Adam's domed Sculpture Hall, devoted to Roman statuary, and Tapestry Hall, boasting priceless Gobelin tapestries, are gorgeous. The 25 acres of gardens are justifiably famous; a double herbaceous border running down to the river separates garden "rooms," each flowering during a different season. A miniature railroad, playground, and pedal boats amuse kids. Entry to the house is restricted to guided tours, run April to September and bookable on the day only ✉ *Skelton-on-Ure* ✥ *Off A1, 6 miles from Ripon exit* ☎ *0845/450–4068* 🌐 *www.newbyhall.com* 🎟 *£14.40; gardens only £10.20* ⏲ *Garden: Apr.–June and Sept., Tues.–Sun. and holiday Mon. 11–5:30; July and Aug., daily 11–5:30; last admission 30 min before closing. House: July and Aug., half-hourly daily 12–3:30; Apr.–Jun. and Sept., weekdays noon and 2 pm.*

Ripon Cathedral. The original 7th-century church here was destroyed by the Vikings, though the Saxon crypt (AD 672) remains. The Romanesque transepts of the current cathedral date from the 12th century, while the west front (circa 1220) is an outstanding example of Early English Gothic. The nave was rebuilt in 1500 in a Perpendicular Gothic style. Note the finely carved choir stalls. ✉ *Liberty Court House, Minster Rd.* ☎ *01765/602072* 🌐 *riponcathedral.info* 🎟 *£5 donation suggested for guided tour* ⏲ *Daily 8:30–6:30.*

Fodor's Choice ★ **Studley Royal Water Garden & Fountains Abbey.** You can easily spend a day at this UNESCO World Heritage Site, an 822-acre complex made up of an 18th-century water garden and deer park, a Jacobean mansion, and, on the banks of the River Skell, Fountains Abbey, the largest monastic ruins in Britain. Here, a neoclassical vision of an ordered universe—with spectacular terraces, classical temples, and a grotto—blends with the majestic Gothic abbey, which was founded in 1132 and completed in the early 1500s. It housed Cistercian monks, called "White Monks" for the color of their robes, who devoted their lives to silence, prayer, and work. Of the surviving buildings, the lay brothers' echoing refectory and dormitory are the most complete. The 12th-century Fountains Mill, perhaps the best preserved in England, displays reconstructed machinery (wool was the abbey's profitable business). The 17th-century Fountains Hall is partially built with stones taken from the abbey. The water garden and Fountains Abbey are 9 miles northwest of Knaresborough, 4 miles southwest of Ripon. ✉ *Ripon* ✣ *Off A1, B6265 exit to Pateley Bridge* ☎ *01765/608888* 🌐 *www.nationaltrust.org.uk/fountainsabbey* 🎟 *£11* ⏲ *Apr.–Oct., daily 10–6; Feb.–Mar., daily 10–5; Nov.–Jan., Sat.–Thurs. 10–4; last admission 1 hr before closing. Deer park dawn–dusk.*

WHERE TO EAT AND STAY

$$ MODERN BRITISH ✕ **Lockwoods.** This family-run eatery with a bistro atmosphere (stripped-brick walls, wood floor, zinc-topped bar) serves breakfast, lunch, and dinner, specializing in simple classics made with seasonal and local ingredients. The lunch menu might have a Vietnamese-style pork belly sandwich or chargrilled chicken Caesar salad, while frequently changing dinner options include braised Gressingham duck leg or 32-day-aged hangar steak with duck fat–fried potatoes. 💲 *Average main: £15* ✉ *83 North St.* ☎ *01765/607555* 🌐 *www.lockwoodsrestaurant.co.uk* ⏲ *Closed Sun. and Mon.*

$$$ HOTEL Fodor's Choice ★ 🏨 **Swinton Park.** If you've ever wanted to experience the *Downton Abbey* lifestyle, head for this luxury hotel situated in a castle complete with battlements, a tower, and a turret. **Pros:** eye-popping castle; gorgeous rooms; beautiful setting. **Cons:** restaurant service patchy; not big on heating. 💲 *Rooms from: £195* ✉ *Swinton Park, Swinton Rd., Masham* ☎ *01765/680900, 1866/810–3039 toll-free from U.S.* 🌐 *www.swintonpark.com* 🛏 *31 rooms, 5 suites* 🍽 *Breakfast.*

CASTLE HOWARD

15 miles northeast of York, 12 miles southeast of Helmsley.

The baroque grandeur of Castle Howard is without equal in northern England. The grounds, enhanced by groves of trees, a twinkling lake, and a perfect lawn, add to the splendor.

GETTING HERE AND AROUND

There's daily scheduled bus service between Malton and Castle Howard, which is well outside any town and several miles off any public road. The nearest train stop is Malton, and you can take a taxi from there. By car, follow signs off A64 from York.

At Castle Howard, a baroque masterpiece, the splendor of the grounds matches the opulence of the sprawling house.

EXPLORING

FAMILY
Fodor's Choice ★

Castle Howard. Standing in the Howardian Hills to the west of Malton, Castle Howard is an outstanding example of English baroque, with a distinctive roofline punctuated by a magnificent central dome. It served as Brideshead, the home of the fictional Flyte family in Evelyn Waugh's tale of aristocratic woe, *Brideshead Revisited,* in both the 1981 TV and 2008 film adaptations. The house was the first commission for playwright-turned-architect Sir John Vanbrugh, who, assisted by Nicholas Hawksmoor, designed it for the 3rd earl of Carlisle, a member of the Howard family. Started in 1701, the central portion took 25 years to complete, with a Palladian wing added subsequently, but the end result was a stately home of audacious grandeur.

A spectacular central hallway with soaring columns supports a hand-painted ceiling that dwarfs all visitors, and there's no shortage of splendor elsewhere: vast family portraits, intricate marble fireplaces, immense tapestries, Victorian silver on polished tables, and a great many marble busts. Outside, the neoclassical landscape of carefully arranged woods, lakes, and lawns led 18th-century bon vivant Horace Walpole to comment that a pheasant at Castle Howard lived better than a duke elsewhere. Hidden throughout the 1,000 acres of formal and woodland gardens are temples, statues, fountains, and a grand mausoleum—even a fanciful children's playground. Hourly tours of the grounds, included in the admission price, fill you in on more background and history. ✉ *Castle Howard, Malton* ✥ *A64 past York, then B1257* ☎ *01653/648333* 🌐 *www.castlehoward.co.uk* 🎫 *House late-Mar.–Oct. and mid-Nov.–mid-Dec. £15; gardens only £9.50; early–mid-Nov. and*

Jan and Feb., gardens only £6 ⏲ House late Mar.–Oct. and mid-Nov.–mid-Dec., daily 11–5; last admission at 4. Grounds Mar.–Dec., daily 10–5; Jan–Feb. daily 10–4; last admission at 4:30 ☞ Frequent early closures for weddings. Check website.

LEEDS AND BRONTË COUNTRY

The busy city of Leeds provides an obvious starting point for a tour of West Yorkshire. From here you can strike out for the traditional wool towns, such as Saltaire, a UNESCO-protected gem, and the Magna museum at Rotherham, which draws long lines for its surprisingly interesting exploration of steel production. But the main thrust of many visits to West Yorkshire is to the west of Leeds, where the stark hills north of the Calder Valley and south of the River Aire form the district immortalized in the equally unsparing novels of the Brontë sisters. Haworth, a gray-stone village, might have faded into obscurity were it not for the enduring fame of the literary sisters. Every summer, thousands toil up the steep main street to visit their former home, but to truly appreciate the setting that inspired their books you need to go farther afield to the ruined farm of Top Withens, which in popular mythology, if not in fact, was the model for Wuthering Heights.

LEEDS

25 miles southwest of York, 43 miles northeast of Manchester.

Once an industrial powerhouse, Leeds has reinvented itself as a vibrant dining, drinking, and shopping destination with numerous cafés, whose outdoor tables defy the northern weather, trendy restaurants, and sleek bars. A large student population keeps the town young and hip, supporting the city's good music shops and funky boutiques.

The 20th century was not kind to Leeds: World War II air raids destroyed the city's most distinguished landmarks, and in the 1960s urban planners replaced much of what was left with undistinguished modern buildings and inner-city highways. The city is currently restoring its surviving Victorian buildings and converting riverfront factories and warehouses into pricey loft apartments and offices buildings.

GETTING HERE AND AROUND

Leeds Bradford Airport, 8 miles northwest of the city, is the main gateway to this part of the country. National Express and Megabus have frequent buses here from London's Victoria Coach Station. The journey takes about 4 hours. East Coast trains depart from London's King's Cross Station to Leeds Station about every 30 minutes during the week. The trip takes about 2¼ hours. Leeds Station is in the middle of central Leeds and usually has a line of taxis waiting out front.

A city of nearly 750,000 people, Leeds has an efficient local bus service. Most visitors never use it as most sights are in the easily walkable downtown.

ESSENTIALS

Visitor Information Leeds Visitor Centre. ✉ *The Headrow* ☎ *0113/242–5242* 🌐 *www.visitleeds.co.uk.*

EXPLORING

TOP ATTRACTIONS

The Calls. East of Granary Wharf, the Calls, now the heart of Leed's gay nightlife, has old riverfront warehouses converted into snazzy bars and restaurants that enliven the cobbled streets. The best have pleasant terraces overlooking the river. ✉ *Leeds.*

Harewood House. The home of the earl of Harewood, a cousin of the Queen, Harewood House (pronounced *har*-wood) is a spectacular 1759 neoclassical mansion designed by York architect John Carr and the period's leading interior designer, Robert Adam. Highlights include important paintings by Gainsborough and Reynolds, fine ceramics, and a ravishingly beautiful collection of Chippendale furniture (Chippendale was born in nearby Otley), notably the magnificent State Bed. The Old Kitchen and Below Stairs exhibition illustrates life from the servants' point of view. Capability Brown designed the handsome grounds, and Charles Barry added a lovely Italian garden with fountains in the 1840s. Also here are a bird garden with numerous rare and endangered species and an adventure playground. The house is 7 miles north of Leeds; you can take Harrogate and District Bus 36. ✉ *Harewood* ✣ *Junction of A61 and A659 (on Leeds-Harrogate road)* ☎ *0113/218–1010* 🌐 *www.harewood.org* 🎫 *£14.50* ⏲ *House Apr.–Oct., daily 11–4; last admission 30 min before closing. Gardens Apr.–Oct., daily 10–5:30; last admission 30 min before closing.*

Leeds Art Gallery. Next door to the Victorian Town Hall, Yorkshire's most impressive art museum has a strong core collection of works by Courbet, Sisley, Constable, Crome, and the internationally acclaimed Yorkshire sculptor Henry Moore, who studied at the Leeds School of Art. The graceful statue on the steps outside the gallery is Moore's *Reclining Woman.* More works by Moore are at the adjacent **Henry Moore Institute,** which also has regular exhibitions of modern sculpture. The **Craft Centre and Design Gallery,** also in the museum, exhibits and sells fine contemporary crafts. ✉ *The Headrow* ☎ *0113/247–8256* 🌐 *www.leeds.gov.uk/museumsandgalleries* ⏲ *Tues.–Sun. 10–5.*

QUICK BITES

New Conservatory. Step into to the cozy, book-lined New Conservatory for fresh sandwiches, hot dishes, and cakes. You can also sit and relax with a cup of tea or a glass of wine. ✉ ***The Albions, Albion Pl., off Briggate*** ☎ ***0113/246–1853*** 🌐 ***www.thenewconservatory-cafebar.co.uk.***

Fodor's Choice ★

Temple Newsam. One of Britain's great country houses, this huge Elizabethan and Jacobean building contains impressive collections of furniture, paintings, and ceramics belonging to the city of Leeds. As the birthplace of Lord Darnley (1545–67), the doomed husband of Mary, Queen of Scots, it's rich in historical significance. Surrounding the house are 1,500 acres of parkland, lakes, gardens, miles of woodland walks, and a farm, where kids can enjoy the new petting zoo. The park and gardens were created by noted 18th-century landscape designer Capability

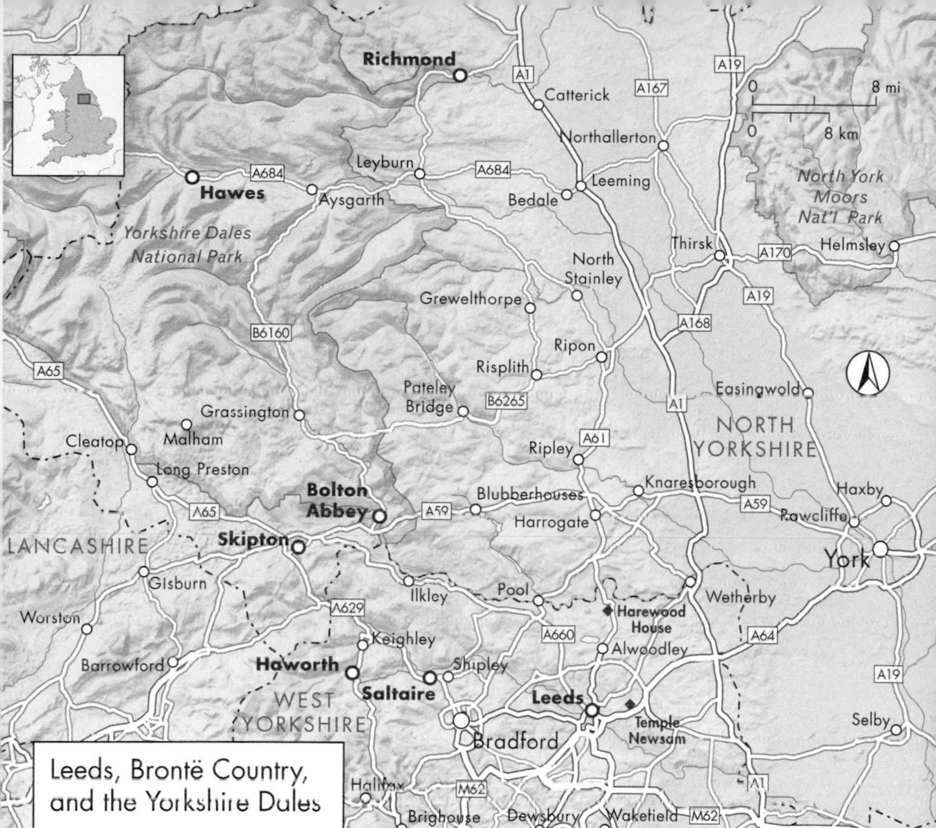

Brown. Temple Newsam is 4 miles east of Leeds on A63; Bus 10 runs directly from Leeds Central Bus station from Easter to mid-September. ✉ *Temple Newsam Rd., off Selby Rd.* ☎ *0113/336–7461* 🌐 *www.leeds.gov.uk/museumsandgalleries* 🎫 *House £4.50, farm £3.60, joint ticket £7.20* 🕒 *House Apr.–May, Tues.–Sun. 10:30–12:30; June–Oct., Tues.–Sun. 10:30–5; Nov.–Mar., Tues.–Sun. 10:30–4. Farm Apr.–Oct., 10–5; Nov.–Mar., 10–4; last admission 45 min before closing.*

Fodor's Choice ★ **Yorkshire Sculpture Park.** This outdoor gallery near Wakefield is in a former 18th-century estate encompassing more than 500 acres of fields, lakes, exotic trees, and rolling hills. The park, garden, and Underground Gallery—three galleries cut into a hillside—are filled with a carefully curated collection that includes works by Henry Moore and Barbara Hepworth, as well as modern sculptors like Antony Gormley, Anthony Caro, and David Nash. You can get here easily from Leeds by train or car. ✉ *West Bretton, Wakefield* ☎ *01924/832631* 🌐 *www.ysp.co.uk* 🎫 *Museum free, parking £2.50 per hr* 🕒 *Galleries Mar.–Oct., daily 10–5. Grounds Mar.–Oct., daily 10–6.*

WORTH NOTING

Granary Wharf. Once at the heart of Leeds's decaying industrial zone, this regenerated development in the Canal Basin along the River Aire is now a trendy hub of chic bars and pleasant cafés. Granary Wharf is reached via the Dark Arches, brick railway tunnels now full of shops, where the River Aire flows under City Station. ✉ *Leeds.*

Hepworth Wakefield. The largest purpose-built British gallery outside of London focuses on 20th-century British art, notably sculptors Henry Moore and Barbara Hepworth, with important works by both. The unique design of slightly skewed concrete building blocks by architect David Chipperfield is combined with the powerful permanent collection and rolling exhibitions devoted to contemporary artists in the Calder gallery. It's in the workaday West Yorkshire town of Wakefield, 12 miles south of Leeds off M1. ✉ *Gallery Walk, Wakefield* ☎ *01924/247360* 🌐 *www.hepworthwakefield.org* 🎫 *Free* ⏲ *Hepworth Tues.–Sun. 10–5 (every 3rd Thurs. 10–9); Calder Tues.–Sun. 10–4.*

OFF THE BEATEN PATH

Magna Science Adventure Centre. A 45-minute drive south from Leeds to Rotherham brings Yorkshire's industrial past squarely into view at Magna, a widely respected science museum housed in a former steelworks. Smoke, flames, and sparking electricity bring one of the original six arc furnaces roaring to life in a sound-and-light show. Four pavilions engagingly illustrate the use of fire, earth, air, and water in the production of steel. ✉ *Sheffield Rd., Templeborough, Rotherham* ✥ *Junction 33 or 35 off M1* ☎ *01709/720002* 🌐 *www.visitmagna.co.uk* 🎫 *£10.95* ⏲ *Daily 10–5.*

FAMILY **Royal Armouries.** Occupying a redeveloped 13-acre dockland site 15 minutes from the city center, this National Museum of Arms and Armour now houses a collection that originally began in the reign of Elizabeth I, when selected objects were displayed at the Tower of London. Five themed galleries—War, Tournament, Self-Defense, Hunting, and Oriental—trace the history of weaponry through some 8,500 objects. The state-of-the-art building is stunningly designed: see a full-size elephant in armor, models of warriors on horseback, and floor-to-ceiling tents, as well as spirited interactive displays and live demonstrations. Shoot a crossbow, direct operations on a battlefield, or, around Easter and the end of August, experience an Elizabethan joust. ✉ *Clarence Dock, Armouries Dr.* ✥ *M621 to Junction 4* ☎ *0113/220–1999* 🌐 *www.royalarmouries.org* ⏲ *Daily 10–5; last admission at 4:30.*

WHERE TO EAT

$$ MODERN BRITISH ✕ **Brasserie Forty 4.** Modern and buzzy, with friendly service and tasty food, this brasserie in a converted grain warehouse has two dining rooms, one with wood tables and terra-cotta walls, the other more formal, with white tablecloths. Both have arched windows overlooking the river, and in summer there's a deck for alfresco dining. The seasonally changing menu usually begins with appetizers like a duck-and-pistachio terrine with orange and honey, or seared king scallops with a crayfish risotto. Elegant main courses include roast chicken breast with wild mushrooms, or venison haunch with spinach and blackberries in a port sauce. From Tuesday to Saturday there's a lunch and early

dinner three-course fixed-price menu for £20. *Average main: £16* *44 The Calls* *0113/234–3232* *www.brasserie44.com* *Closed Sun. and Mon.*

$ BRITISH **The Cross Keys.** A former watering hole for foundry workers, this lovely old inn is now a welcoming restaurant and pub, with exposed brick, wood beams, and open fireplaces. The food is unfussy and reliably good, noted for its use of fresh, local ingredients. The menu, which changes daily, inclines toward old favorites done right, like a salad of grilled sardines, new potatoes, and spring onion, pork-and-apple sausages with mashed potatoes, or beer-battered fish with fries. In summer, you can sit in a sunny courtyard with a glass of wine from the varied wine list or a pint of local ale. Best of all, the prices make it a good value. *Average main: £14* *107 Water La.* *0113/243–3711* *www.the-crosskeys.com.*

$ CAFÉ **Mill Kitchen.** Inside Sunnybank Mills, a converted Victorian textile mill on the outskirts of town that now serves as a live-and-work complex for artists, this café and deli has been winning fans with sandwiches like free-range roast chicken with avocado, salads, tarts, and soups using seasonal, locally sourced produce. Dinner and cocktails are served on Fridays and Saturday nights, when the chefs create a meal from one of their favorite cookbooks. After dining, check out the exhibitions in the complex's 3,500-square-foot art gallery. Buses 16 and 508 take you there from the center. *Average main: £7* *1 The Old Combing, Sunnybank Mills, 83–85 Town St., Farsley* *0113/257–1417* *www.millkitchen.co.uk* *No dinner Sun.–Thurs.*

$ FAST FOOD **Trinity Kitchen.** This shopping center takes five of the best street-food traders and pop-up restaurants from around the country—vans, sheds, carts, or trucks—and installs them on its first floor under the name Trinity Kitchen. Venders change every month, and past lineups have included Smoqued Foods' imaginative tacos (like oak-smoked pork belly and soft shell crab), Meet Frank's gluten-free hot dogs, and Sugar Dumplin's Caribbean BBQ. *Average main: £7* *Trinity Leeds, 27 Albion St.* *0113/394–2415* *www.trinityleeds.com* *No credit cards* *Reservations not accepted.*

$ BRITISH **Whitelocks.** Its full name—Whitelocks First City Luncheon Bar—gives a clue to this small bar's historic antecedents. Claiming to date to 1715, this narrow, atmospheric bar in a quiet alley off bustling Briggate retains 19th- and 20th-century features, like beveled mirrors, copper-topped tables, art-nouveau stained glass, and mosaic tiles. It serves superior pub food with an emphasis on the local and seasonal, like grilled lemon chicken with elderflower salad or homemade beef in ale pie. Beers from local microbreweries are featured, and the prices are friendly. *Average main: £10* *6–8 Turks Head Yard, off Briggate* *0113/245–3950* *www.whitelocksleeds.com.*

WHERE TO STAY

$$ HOTEL **42 The Calls.** This high-tech, high-concept boutique hotel in the fashionable waterfront area makes its home in a converted 18th-century corn mill overlooking the river. **Pros:** riverside location; comfortable rooms; clever use of space. **Cons:** some find it too trendy; street noise

on weekends. Rooms from: £150 42 The Calls 0113/244–0099 www.42thecalls.co.uk 41 rooms Breakfast.

$$ HOTEL **Malmaison.** Once the headquarters of the local tram company, this Edwardian building has been reinvented as a funky hotel. **Pros:** friendly service; tasty food; comfortable beds. **Cons:** some rooms on small side; front rooms may get street noise on weekends; worn public areas. *Rooms from: £115 1 Swinegate 0844/693–0654 www.malmaison.com 99 rooms, 1 suite Breakfast.*

$ HOTEL Fodor's Choice ★ **Quebecs.** This boutique hotel is full of elegant Victorian touches, especially the sweeping oak staircase illuminated by tall stained-glass windows. **Pros:** gorgeous building; stylish rooms; friendly service. **Cons:** limited parking; some rooms have drab outlooks. *Rooms from: £90 9 Quebec St. 0113/244–8989 www.quebecshotel.co.uk 44 rooms, 7 suites Breakfast.*

NIGHTLIFE AND PERFORMING ARTS

NIGHTLIFE

Mojo. This is a real rock-and-roll bar, with the old-school vinyl and look to match. *18 Merrion St. 07815/457814 www.mojobar.co.uk.*

Norman Bar. Distinctive futuristic design, including curved walls, and a vibrant clientele of young professionals are the hallmarks here *36 Call La. 0872/080–8000 www.normanbar.co.uk.*

Roxy Ball Room. This sceney bar in the Trinity Square shopping mall has an extensive menu of craft beers and classic cocktails, but the main attraction is the games: ping-pong, pool, a nine-hole mini-golf course, and even beer pong. Slots can be booked in advance (from £4.50 per half-hour), but a couple of Ping-Pong tables are open for walk-ins. *1st fl., Trinity Sq., Boar La. 0113/322–1781 www.roxyballroom.co.uk.*

The Ship. A tavern for 300 years, this cozy, historic pub has a friendly atmosphere, fine ales, and homemade pub grub. *71A Briggate 0113/246–8031 www.theshipleeds.co.uk.*

PERFORMING ARTS

Leeds Grand Theatre. A leading regional opera company, Opera North, is based at the Leeds Grand Theatre. The lavish Victorian gothic auditorium, opened in 187, hosts touring musicals, ballet, and dramas, in addition to opera. *46 New Briggate 0844/848–2700 www.leedsgrandtheatre.com.*

Leeds International Concert Season. The Victorian Town Hall hosts an international concert season (October through May) that attracts top national and international orchestras. Jazz, world music, rock, and colliery brass bands also play free shows at outdoor bandstands in city parks. *The Headrow 0113/244–3801 www.leedsconcertseason.com.*

West Yorkshire Playhouse. In the heart of Leeds's cultural quarter, this ultramodern theater's adaptable space makes it eminently suitable for staging both new works and classics. *Playhouse Sq., Quarry Hill 0113/213–7700 www.wyp.org.uk.*

SHOPPING

Kirkgate Market. The city has some excellent markets, notably Kirkgate Market, an Edwardian beauty that's one of the largest indoor markets in Europe. ✉ *34 George St.* ☎ *0113/378–1950* 🌐 *www.leedsmarkets.co.uk* ⏲ *Closed Sun.*

Leeds Corn Exchange. Housed in a converted 19th-century mercantile exchange, this glass-roofed shopping mall has independent boutiques, laid-back restaurants, and specialty stores on three levels. ✉ *Call La.* ☎ *0113/234–0363* 🌐 *www.leedscornexchange.co.uk.*

Victoria Quarter. Notable for the soaring glass-covered arches of its beautiful-turn-of-the-century shopping arcades, the spiffy Victoria Quarter combines 19th-century design and 21st-century style. ✉ *4 Cross Arcade* ☎ *0113/245–5333.*

SALTAIRE

12 miles east of Leeds, 8 miles east of Haworth.

GETTING HERE AND AROUND

An old wool-market town, Saltaire has regular bus and train services from the nearby town of Bradford. Drivers should take A650 from Bradford and follow the signs.

ESSENTIALS

Visitor Information Saltaire Visitor Information Centre. ✉ *Salt's Mill, Victoria Rd., Shipley* ☎ *01274/437942* 🌐 *www.saltairevillage.info.*

EXPLORING

Hockney 1853 Gallery. This gallery is devoted to a remarkable exhibition of over 300 works by Bradford-born artist David Hockney. There are two restaurants on-site. ✉ *Salt's Mill, Victoria Rd., Shipley* ☎ *01274/531163* 🌐 *www.saltsmill.org.uk* ⏲ *Weekdays 10–5:30, weekends 10–6.*

Saltaire. A UNESCO World Heritage Site, the former model village of Saltaire was built in the mid-19th century by textile magnate Sir Titus Salt. When he decided to relocate his factories from the dark mills of Bradford to the countryside, he hoped to create an ideal industrial community. The Italianate village is remarkably well preserved, its former mills and houses now turned into shops, restaurants, and galleries. Part of Salt's Mill, the main building, resembles a palazzo. The largest factory in the world when it was built in 1853, it holds an art gallery today, along with crafts and furniture shops. One-hour guided tours (£4.50) of the village depart weekends and some holiday Mondays at 2 pm from the tourist information center. ✉ *Saltaire Rd., Shipley* ☎ *01274/531163* 🌐 *www.saltairevillage.info.*

OFF THE BEATEN PATH

National Media Museum. Bradford, 10 miles west of Leeds, is known for this renowned museum, which traces the history of photographic media. It's a huge and hugely entertaining place, with seven galleries displaying the world's first photographic negative, the latest digital imaging, an IMAX theater, and everything in between. **TIP→ It's popular with children, so come early or late in the day.** ✉ *Little Horton*

The streets and houses of Haworth look much as they did when the Brontë sisters lived and wrote their famous novels in this village near the moors.

Lane, Bradford ☎ *0844/856–3797* 🌐 *www.nationalmediamuseum.org.uk* ⏲ *Daily 10–6.*

HAWORTH: HEART OF BRONTË COUNTRY

8 miles west of Saltaire.

Whatever Haworth might have been in the past, today it's Brontë country. This old stone-built textile village on the edge of the Yorkshire Moors long ago gave up its own personality and allowed itself to be taken over by the literary sisters, their powerful novels, and legions of fans. In 1820, when Anne, Emily, and Charlotte were very young, their father relocated them and their other three siblings away from their old home in Bradford to Haworth. The sisters—Emily (author of *Wuthering Heights,* 1847), Charlotte (*Jane Eyre,* 1847), and Anne (*The Tenant of Wildfell Hall,* 1848) were all affected by the stark, dramatic countryside.

These days, it seems that every building they ever glanced at has been turned into a memorial, shop, or museum. The Haworth Visitor Center has good information about accommodations, maps, books on the Brontës, and inexpensive leaflets to help you find your way to such outlying *Wuthering Heights* sites as Ponden Hall (Thrushcross Grange) and Ponden Kirk (Penistone Crag).

12

GETTING HERE AND AROUND

To reach Haworth by bus or train, buy a Metro Day Rover for bus and rail (£7.90) and take the Metro train from Leeds train station to Keighley and walk to the bus stop, where you change to a Keighley & District bus to Haworth. On weekends and holiday Mondays you can opt to take the Keighley and Worth Valley Railway to continue on to Haworth.

By car, Haworth is an easy 25-mile drive on A629 from Leeds; it's well signposted, and there's plenty of cheap parking in town.

ESSENTIALS

Visitor Information Haworth Visitor Information Centre. ✉ *2–4 West La., Haworth* ☎ *01535/642329* 🌐 *www.visitbradford.com.*

LANDSCAPE AS MUSE

The rugged Yorkshire Moors helped inspire Emily Brontë's 1847 *Wuthering Heights*; if ever a work of fiction grew out of the landscape in which its author lived, it was surely this. "My sister Emily loved the moors," wrote Charlotte. "Flowers brighter than the rose bloomed in the blackest of the heath for her; out of a sullen hollow in a livid hillside her mind could make an Eden. She found in the bleak solitude many and dear delights; and not the least and best loved was liberty."

EXPLORING

Fodor's Choice ★ **Brontë Parsonage Museum.** The best of Haworth's Brontë sights is this somber Georgian (1778) house where the sisters grew up. It displays original furniture (some bought by Charlotte after the success of *Jane Eyre*), portraits, and books. The Brontes moved here when the Reverend Patrick Brontë was appointed to the local church, but tragedy soon struck—his wife, Maria, and their two eldest children died within five years. The museum explores the family's tragic story, bringing it to life with a strong collection of enchanting mementos of the four children. These include tiny books they made when they were still very young; Charlotte's wedding bonnet; and the sisters' spidery, youthful graffiti on the nursery wall. Branwell, the Brontës' only brother, painted several of the portraits on display. ✉ *Church St., Haworth* ☎ *01535/642323* 🌐 *www.bronte.org.uk* 🎫 *£7.50* ⏲ *Apr.–Oct., daily 10–5:30; Nov.–Mar., daily 10–5; last admission 30 min before closing.*

Brontë Waterfall. If you have the time, pack a lunch and walk for 2¾ miles or so from Haworth along a field path, lane, and moorland track to the lovely, isolated waterfall that has, inevitably, been renamed in honor of the sisters. It was one of their favorite haunts, which they wrote about in poems and letters. ✉ *Haworth* ✥ *From Haworth Church on Main St., follow signs* 🌐 *www.haworth-village.org.uk.*

FAMILY **Keighley and Worth Valley Railway.** Haworth is one stop along the route of this scenic 5-mile heritage railway between Keighley and Oxenhope through the picturesque Worth Valley. Many of the trains are pulled by handsome steam engines. Frequent themed special events add to the fun. ✉ *Haworth Station, Station Rd., Haworth* ☎ *01535/647317* 🌐 *www.kwvr.co.uk* 🎫 *£11 round-trip, £16 Day Rover ticket, £35 Family Day Rover ticket* ⏲ *Nov.–Feb., weekends; Mar.–June and Sept.–Oct.,* *weekends and Wed.; June–mid-July, Tues.–Thurs.; Mid-July–Aug., daily ☞ Operates on extra weekdays during school holidays and for special events.*

Main Street. Haworth's steep, cobbled high street has changed little in outward appearance since the early 19th century, but it now acts as a funnel for crowds heading for points of interest: the **Black Bull** pub, where the reprobate Branwell Brontë drank himself into an early grave (his stool is kept in mint condition); the former **post office** (now a bookshop) from which Charlotte, Emily, and Anne sent their manuscripts to their London publishers; and the **church,** with its atmospheric graveyard (Charlotte and Emily are buried in the family vault inside the church; Anne is buried in Scarborough). ✉ *Haworth* 🌐 *www.haworth-village.org.uk/walks.*

Top Withens. A ruined, gloomy mansion on a bleak hilltop farm 3 miles from Haworth, Top Withens is often taken to be the inspiration for the fictional Wuthering Heights. Brontë scholars say it probably isn't; even in its heyday, the house never fit the book's description of Heathcliff's lair. Still, it's an inspirational walk across the moors. There and back from Haworth is a 3½-hour walk along a well-marked footpath that goes past the Brontë waterfall. If you've read *Wuthering Heights,* you don't need to be reminded to wear sturdy shoes and protective clothing. ✉ *Haworth* 🌐 *www.haworth-village.org.uk.*

WHERE TO EAT AND STAY

$ BRITISH ✕ **Haworth Old Hall.** This 16th century building with two magnificent stone fireplaces is now a welcoming pub, and the friendly and efficient service gets high marks. The menu is hearty British food, with mains like pan-fried chicken breast in a brandy, cream, and mushroom sauce; slow-braised lamb shoulder marinated in rosemary and red wine; and a mushroom, lentil, and walnut pot pie. Craft beers (called "real ales" in Britain) are a specialty, and there are two B&B rooms upstairs (£60/night). [$] *Average main: £11* ✉ *Sun St., Haworth* ☎ *01535/642709* 🌐 *www.hawortholdhall.co.uk.*

$$ B&B/INN **The Apothecary Guest House.** Built in 1640, this family-run B&B is located at the top of the cobbled main street, opposite the Brontë church. **Pros:** scenic views; town center location; helpful hosts. **Cons:** rooms at front may have noise from pub; limited breakfast window. [$] *Rooms from: £50* ✉ *86 Main St., Haworth* ☎ *01535/643642* 🌐 *www.theapothecaryguesthouse.co.uk* *7 rooms* 🍽 *Breakfast.*

$ B&B/INN **Ashmount Country House.** A short walk from the Parsonage, this charming stone building was once home to the Brontë sisters' physician, Amos Ingham. **Pros:** lovely period building; ideal location; great views. **Cons:** some bedrooms small; water pressure could be better. [$] *Rooms from: £95* ✉ *Mytholmes La., Haworth* ☎ *01535/645726* 🌐 *www.ashmounthaworth.co.uk* *10 rooms, 2 suites* 🍽 *Breakfast.*

The imposing ruins of Bolton Priory provide a scenic backdrop for a walk along the River Wharfe.

THE YORKSHIRE DALES

To the west of the North York Moors, this landscape has been shaped by limestone: lush green valleys (known as *dales,* the Viking word for valley) lie between white limestone scars (cliffs), while broad uplands are punctuated with dark fells (crags). The limestone cliffs, filled with caves, invite exploration.

As well as dramatic landscapes like the spectacular cliffs and gorges at Malham Cove and Gordale Scar, the area has some breathtaking waterfalls. Ruined priories, narrow roads, drystone walls made without mortar, and babbling rivers make for a quintessentially English landscape, full of paths and trails to explore.

BOLTON ABBEY

12 miles north of Haworth, 24 miles northwest of Leeds.

A leafy, picturesque village amid the rolling hills of the Yorkshire Dales, Bolton Abbey is a famously attractive town with a stone church and an evocative ruined priory. It is on a huge estate owned by the Duke of Devonshire, who still technically owns much of the area—a lingering reminder of the country's feudal past.

GETTING HERE AND AROUND

Bolton Abbey, off the A59 between Skipton and Harrogate, is best reached by car.

EXPLORING

Bolton Abbey. Some of the loveliest Wharfedale scenery comes into view near **Bolton Priory,** the ruins of a 12th-century Augustinian priory that sit on a grassy embankment over a great curve of the River Wharfe. The view inspired J.M.W. Turner to create a number of watercolors of the priory ruins and nearby sites. Close to Bolton Priory and surrounded by romantic woodland scenery, the River Wharfe plunges between a narrow chasm in the rocks (called the Strid) before reaching **Barden Tower,** a ruined medieval hunting lodge that can be visited just as easily as Bolton Priory. Both are part of the 30,000-acre Bolton Abbey estate owned by the dukes of Devonshire. The priory is just a short walk or drive from the village of Bolton Abbey. You can also visit the priory church. Guides are available weekdays from March to October. ✉ *Bolton Abbey, Skipton* ✥ *B6160 off A59* ☎ *01756/718000* 🌐 *www.boltonabbey.com* 🎫 *Parking £8* 🕒 *Late Oct.–mid-Mar., daily 9–6 (last admission 4); mid-Mar.–May and Sept.-late Oct., daily 9–7 (last admission 5:30); May–Aug., daily 9–9 (last admission 6).*

FAMILY **Embsay and Bolton Abbey Steam Railway.** You can take a scenic ride on this preserved heritage railway from the station in Bolton Abbey. Steam trains run every Sunday and daily in summer, but hours vary greatly, so it's best to call ahead. ✉ *Bolton Abbey Station, off A59* ☎ *01756/710614, 01756/795189 recorded timetable* 🌐 *www.embsayboltonabbeyrailway.org.uk* 🎫 *£10 round-trip* 🕒 *Jan.–Mar. and Nov., Sun. only; Apr.–July, Sept., and Oct., Tues. and weekends; Aug., daily; Dec., weekends only.*

WHERE TO STAY

$$$ HOTEL **Devonshire Arms Country House Hotel & Spa.** Originally a 17th-century coaching inn, this luxurious country-house hotel near the River Wharfe is an easy walk from Bolton Abbey. **Pros:** one of the region's best hotels; real country-house atmosphere. **Cons:** you pay for all that charm; some new-wing rooms small. $ *Rooms from: £195* ✉ *Bolton Abbey, Skipton* ✥ *B6160 off A59* ☎ *01756/710441* 🌐 *www.thedevonshirearms.co.uk* 🛏 *37 rooms, 3 suites* 🍽 *Breakfast.*

SKIPTON

6 miles west of Bolton Abbey, 12 miles north of Haworth, 22 miles west of Harrogate.

Skipton in Airedale, capital of the limestone district of Craven, is a country market town with as many farmers as visitors milling in the streets. There are markets Monday, Wednesday, Friday, and Saturday, with a farmers' market on Sunday. Shops selling local produce is the main retail experience.

GETTING HERE AND AROUND

Skipton is off A59 and A65 at the southern edge of the Yorkshire Dales National Park. From Leeds, First Leeds buses run regularly to Skipton. Little Red Bus buses depart once a day on Saturdays from Harrogate. There are regular trains from Leeds; the journey takes about 40 minutes.

ESSENTIALS

Visitor Information **Skipton Tourist Information Centre.** ✉ *Town Hall, High St.* ☎ *01756/792809* 🌐 *www.cravendc.gov.uk.*

EXPLORING

Grassington National Park Centre. This visitor center 10 miles north of Skipton has guidebooks, maps, and bus schedules to help you enjoy a day in Yorkshire Dales National Park. Grassington is deep in the dales on the tiny B6265, also known as the Grassington Road; buses travel here from nearby towns. A small stone village, it makes a good base for exploring Upper Wharfedale. The Dales Way footpath passes through the village, where there are stores, pubs, and cafés. In summer it becomes overwhelmed by day-trippers and hikers, but you can escape them on the many local walks. ✉ *Hebdon Rd., Grassington* ☎ *01756/751690* 🌐 *www.yorkshiredales.org.uk* ⏲ *Apr.–Oct., daily 10–5; Nov.–Dec. and Feb.–Mar., weekends 10–4.*

Skipton Castle. Built by the Normans in 1090, and largely unaltered since the 17th century, Skipton Castle is one of the most complete and best-preserved medieval castles in Britain and still has its original kitchen, great hall, and main bedroom. Following the Battle of Marston Moor during the Civil War, it was the only remaining Royalist stronghold in the north of England, yielding in 1645 only after a three-year siege. So sturdy was the squat little fortification with its rounded battlements (in some places the walls are 12 feet thick) that Oliver Cromwell ordered the removal of the castle roofs. The castle's owner, Lady Anne Clifford, was eventually allowed to replace the roofs thanks to a special Act of Parliament, but only with the stipulation that they not be strong enough to withstand cannon fire. The Act was finally repealed in the 1970s to permit repairs at long last. A yew tree planted in the central Tudor courtyard more than 300 years ago by Lady Anne herself to mark the castle's recovery from its Civil War damage is still flourishing. ✉ *The Bailey* ☎ *01756/792442* 🌐 *www.skiptoncastle.co.uk* 🎫 *£7.30* ⏲ *Mar.–Sept., Mon.–Sat. 10–6, Sun. noon–6; Oct.–Feb., Mon.–Sat. 10–4, Sun. noon–4.*

WHERE TO EAT AND STAY

$$ MODERN BRITISH

✕ **Angel Inn.** The hidden-away hamlet of Hetton is often filled with cars belonging to diners at the Angel Inn, such is the attraction of this highly regarded casual brasserie and more formal restaurant in an early-18th-century building. Both specialize in locally sourced seasonal food, such as beautifully prepared roast lamb, beef, and seafood. Two-course fixed-price menus in the brasserie at lunch and early bird dinner are £14.95 (£18.95 for three courses). In the restaurant, there are three-course fixed-price menus for Saturday dinner (£42) and Sunday lunch (£28). At other times both serve dishes à la carte. The ancient stone barn conversion across the road has five well-equipped guest rooms decorated in an unfussy country style (£150/night), with another four contemporary bedrooms in a more modern building. The elegant country inn is 5 miles north of Skipton. 💲 *Average main: £19* ✉ *Off B6265, Hetton* ☎ *01756/730263* 🌐 *www.angelhetton.co.uk.*

$ BRITISH ✕ **Devonshire Hotel.** With its oak-paneled, candlelit dining room, this traditional inn is an inviting rural dining spot. Old favorites such as shoulder of local lamb and traditional steak-and-ale or fish pies are served with fresh local vegetables. There are also seven comfortable rooms and one suite that have a mix of antiques and modern furniture (£70/night). The inn is 10 miles north of Skipton in the town of Grassington. *Average main: £12 27 Main St., Grassington 01756/752525 www.thedevonshirehotel.co.uk.*

$ B&B/INN **Ashfield House.** Three converted 17th-century stone cottages, once the homes of Grassington lead miners, make up this well-run small hotel off the main street. **Pros:** charming cottages; gorgeous gardens; warm service. **Cons:** design on the fussy side; not a lot of amenities; parking can be tricky. *Rooms from: £50 3 Summers Fold, Grassington 01756/752584 www.ashfieldhouse.co.uk 10 rooms, 2 suites Breakfast.*

$$ B&B/INN **The Devonshire Fell.** This more casual sister property of the Devonshire Arms down the road (guests have access to the larger property's spa and hiking trails) boasts outstanding views over a particularly lovely part of the Yorkshire Dales. **Pros:** lovely views; excellent location; tasty restaurant. **Cons:** skimpy complimentary breakfast; casual service; poor cell phone service. *Rooms from: £109 Burnsall Village, Burnsall Off B3160 01756/729000 www.devonshirefell.co.uk 17 rooms Breakfast.*

SPORTS AND THE OUTDOORS

Avid summer hikers descend in droves on Malham, 12 miles northwest of Skipton, to tour the remarkable limestone formations. Malham Cove, a huge, 260-foot-high natural rock amphitheater, is a mile north of the village and provides the easiest local walk. Taking the 420 steps up to the top is a brutal climb, though you'll be rewarded by magnificent views.

At Gordale Scar, a deep natural chasm between overhanging limestone cliffs, the white waters of a moorland stream plunge 300 feet. It's a mile northeast of Malham by a lovely riverside path.

A walk of more than 3 miles north leads to Malham Tarn, an attractive lake on a slate bed in windswept isolation.

Malham National Park Centre. With informative displays, Malham's National Park Centre gives you some ideas for what to see and do, both in town and in Yorkshire Dales National Park. You can also get a list of bed-and-breakfasts and pub accommodations. *Malham National Park Centre, Chapel Gate, Malham 01729/833200 www.yorkshiredales.org.uk Apr.–Oct., daily 10–5; Nov.–Mar., weekends 10–4.*

HAWES

30 miles north of Skipton.

The best time to visit the so-called cheesiest town in Yorkshire is on Tuesday, when farmers crowd into town for the weekly market. Crumbly, white Wensleydale cheese has been made in the valley for centuries, and it's sold in local stores and at the market. Allow time to explore the cobbled side streets, some of which are filled with antiques shops and tearooms.

GETTING HERE AND AROUND

Hawes is high in the moors on A684. To get here from Grassington, take the B6160 north for 23 miles. There's no train service, but buses travel from Leeds throughout the day on summer weekends.

EXPLORING

Dales Countryside Museum. This museum, in the same former train station as the Hawes National Park Information Centre, traces life in the dales past and present. A traditional rope-making shop opposite also welcomes visitors. ✉ *Station Yard, Burtersett Rd.* ☎ *01969/666210* 🌐 *www.yorkshiredales.org.uk* 🎫 *£4.50* 🕒 *Feb.–Oct., daily 10–5; Nov.–Dec., daily 10–4:30.*

Wensleydale Creamery. Sort of the cheese equivalent of a winery, this museum in a working dairy documents how the famed local cheese—so beloved by the popular animated characters Wallace and Gromit—developed over time. You can watch production (best seen between 10 and 2, but not available every day) from the viewing gallery, and then taste (and buy) the output in the excellent cheese shop. A restaurant serves plenty of samples—try Wensleydale smoked, with ginger, or with apple pie. ✉ *Gayle La.* ☎ *01969/667664* 🌐 *www.wensleydale.co.uk* 🎫 *Tour £2.50* 🕒 *Museum daily 10–4. Shop daily 9–5.*

RICHMOND

24 miles northeast of Hawes.

Tucked into a bend above the foaming River Swale, Richmond has a picturesque network of narrow Georgian streets and terraces opening onto a large cobbled marketplace that dates back to medieval times. The town's history can be traced to the late 11th century, when the Normans swept in, determined to subdue the local population and establish their rule in the north. They built the mighty castle whose massive keep still dominates the skyline.

GETTING HERE AND AROUND

East Coast Trains run regularly from Leeds and from London's King's Cross to the nearest station, Darlington. From here take the No. 27 bus that runs every 30 minutes. The journey from London takes around 2½ hours, from Leeds it takes about 1½ hours. By car, Richmond is on the rural B6274—follow signs off A1.

ESSENTIALS

Visitor Information Richmond Tourist Information Centre. ✉ *2 Queens Rd.* ☎ *01748/050549* 🌐 *richmond.org/tic.*

EXPLORING

Fodor's Choice ★ **Georgian Theatre Royal.** A jewel box built in 1788 and still an active community playhouse, this theater and museum, Britain's most complete Georgian playhouse in its original form, retains original features such as the wooden seating from which patrons watched 18th-century

Shakespearean leading man David Garrick. During the hourly tours from Monday to Saturday between 10 and 4 (mid-February through October), you can see Britain's oldest painted scenery dating back to 1836 and try on theatrical costumes. There's also an extensive theatrical archive that contains scripts, playbills, and images. ✉ *Victoria Rd.* ☎ *01748/823710* 🌐 *www.georgiantheatreroyal.co.uk* 🎟 *£3.50 suggested donation for tours* 🕐 *Tours mid-Feb.–Nov., Mon.–Sat. 10–4:30.*

Richmond Castle. In a commanding position 100 feet over the River Swale is the 12th-century great keep of this castle, one of the three oldest stone-built castles in England and considered to be one of the finest examples of a Norman fortress. If you climb the 130 steps to the top, you are rewarded with sweeping views over the Dales. Originally built around 1071 by the first earl of Richmond to subdue the unruly inhabitants of the North, the castle retains much of its curtain wall and three chapels. There's also an even earlier, two-story structure known as Scolland's Hall, which was built in the 11th century and is believed to be the oldest great hall in England. During World War I, conscientious objectors were imprisoned in the castle, and you can still see their graffiti. A path along the river leads to the ruins of golden-stone Easby Abbey. One historical note: when Henry Tudor (son of the earl of Richmond) became Henry VII in 1485, he began calling his palace in southwest London after the site of his family seat, leading to that part of the city becoming known as Richmond. ✉ *Riverside Rd.* ☎ *01748/822493* 🌐 *www.english-heritage.org.uk* 🎟 *£5* 🕐 *Apr.–Sept., daily 10–6; Oct., daily 10–5; Nov.–Mar., weekends 10–4; last admission 30 min before closing.*

WHERE TO EAT AND STAY

$$ BRITISH

✕ **Black Bull.** New owners mean a new lease of life at this handsome pub with flagstone floors, oak doors, and wood-burning stove. The restaurant in a new contemporary-style glass-and-steel extension specializes in traditional Yorkshire fare, done right. The cooking uses locally sourced ingredients and changes with the seasons, so options might include fresh Lindesfarne oysters (£12.50 for 6), fish pie with Whitby smoked haddock, Scottish salmon, king prawns, and scallops, or charcoal-grilled sirloin steak (£25.95). $ *Average main: £16* ✉ *Back La., Moulton, Moulton* ☎ *01325/377556* 🌐 *www.blackbullmoulton.com.*

$$ BRITISH

✕ **Shoulder of Mutton Inn.** This cozy restaurant in an 18th-century inn on the outskirts of an unspoiled country village is traditional but not fussy, with exposed stone walls, open fireplaces, original oak beams, and windows that look out to panoramic views of the Dales. The same satisfaction is in the food, which incorporates local ingredients whenever possible. Main courses include grilled cod with a crab, lime, and coconut crust and Gressingham duck breast in a Madeira sauce. A bar menu serves traditional pub grub like fish cakes or local sausage with mash. The craft beer selection is outstanding. Dinner is served between 6:30 and 8:45. The inn's six rooms (£70/night) are simple but comfortable. (Just to confuse things, there's a Shoulder of Mutton pub in Middleton Tyas, also outside Richmond, that serves highly regarded pub food.) $ *Average main: £15* ✉ *Kirby Hill* ☎ *01748/822772* 🌐 *www.*

shoulderofmutton.net ⏲ *Restaurant closed Mon. and Tues. No lunch weekdays.*

$$ HOTEL **Frenchgate Hotel and Restaurant.** This three-story Georgian town house on a quiet cobbled street has a bright and welcoming interior and a secluded walled garden for summer days. **Pros:** lovely gardens; good food; luxurious bathrooms. **Cons:** some bedrooms not as nice as others. *Rooms from: £118* ✉ *59–61 Frenchgate* ☎ *01748/822087* 🌐 *www.thefrenchgate.co.uk* *9 rooms* *Breakfast.*

$$ B&B/INN **Millgate House.** This 18th-century house in the center of Richmond has been beautifully restored, with a particularly elegant Regency dining room and sitting room. **Pros:** central location; elegant atmosphere; plenty of privacy. **Cons:** rooms can be a bit chilly. *Rooms from: £110* ✉ *3 Millgate* ☎ *01748/823571* 🌐 *www.millgatehouse.com* *No credit cards* *3 rooms, 2 apartments* *Breakfast.*

THE NORTH YORK MOORS

The North York Moors are a dramatic swath of high moorland starting 25 miles north of the city of York and stretching east to the coast and west to the Cleveland Hills. Only a few pockets remain of the dense forest that once covered the area. The transformation began during the Middle Ages, when the monks of Rievaulx and Whitby abbeys began raising huge flocks of sheep. Over the course of centuries, the sheep have kept the moors deforested, which ensures that the pink heather on which they feed spreads lushly across the hills. A series of isolated, medieval "standing stones" that once served as signposts on the paths between the abbeys are still handy for hikers.

For more than four decades the area has been a national park, ensuring the protection of the bleak moors and grassy valleys that shelter brownstone villages and hamlets. Minor roads and tracks crisscross the hills, but there's no single, obvious route through the region. You can approach from York; another approach is from the coast at Whitby, along the Esk Valley to Danby, which is also accessible on the Esk Valley branch-train line running between Middlesbrough and Whitby. From Danby, minor roads run south over the high moors reaching Hutton-le-Hole, beyond which main roads lead to such interesting market towns as Helmsley, on the moors' edge. Completing the route in this direction leaves you with an easy side trip to Castle Howard before returning to York.

DANBY

49 miles northeast of York, 15 miles west of Whitby.

The old stone village of Danby nestles in the green Esk Valley, a short walk from the summit of the moors. It's been settled since Viking times—Danby means "village where the Danes lived"—and these days it's home to the main information center for Moors National Park. There's also a pub and a cozy bakery with a tearoom. Bring hiking boots and within 10 minutes you can be surrounded by moorland looking down on the village below.

GETTING HERE AND AROUND

From York, take A64 to A169 and then follow the signs across the moor. Northern Rail travels to Danby station throughout the day from nearby towns. To get here from Whitby, take A171 west and turn north for Danby after 12 miles, after which it's a 3-mile drive over Danby Low Moor to the village.

Four Moorsbus routes run over the moors on Sundays and holiday Mondays from March to October: one to Rievaulx Abbey and Hemsley; one to Ryedale; one to the Dalby Forest; and one to the North York Moors National Park and the Cleveland Way trail.

Contacts Moorsbus. ☎ *01482/592929* 🌐 *www.eyms.co.uk.*

EXPLORING

FAMILY **Moors National Park Centre.** On the banks of the River Esk, near Danby, is this flagship visitor center of the North York Moors National Park. There's an exhibition with interactive displays about the park's history, wildlife, and landscape, as well as a gallery with work by local artists and artisans. While parents relax in the tearoom, children can scramble up the kids-only climbing wall or enjoy the beautiful outdoor play area ✉ *Danby Lodge, Lodge La.* ☎ *01439/772737* 🌐 *www.northyorkmoors.org.uk* ⏲ *Jan. and Feb., weekends 10:30–4; mid-Feb.–Mar. and Nov.–Dec., daily 10:30–4; Apr.–July and Sept.–Oct., daily 10–5; Aug., 9:30–5:30.*

EN ROUTE From Danby take the road due west for 2 miles to Castleton, and then turn south over the top of the moors toward Hutton-le-Hole. The narrow road has magnificent views over North York Moors National Park, especially at the old stone **Ralph Cross** (5 miles), which marks the park's highest point. Drive carefully, keeping your eye out for sheep in the road.

HUTTON-LE-HOLE

13 miles south of Danby.

Sleepy Hutton-le-Hole is a charming little place based around a wide village green, with woolly sheep snoozing in the shade of stone cottages. Unfortunately, it can be unbearably crowded in summer. You can always keep driving to either the charming nearby village of Thornton-le-Dale or to the medieval market towns of Helmsley or Pickering.

GETTING HERE AND AROUND

Hutton-le-Hole is on the moors off A170. It has no train station, and is only accessible by bus in summer when the Moors Explorer travels between the small towns in the region.

EXPLORING

FAMILY **Ryedale Folk Museum.** This excellent open-air folk museum explores the rural way of life from the Iron Age to the 1950s through more than 20 historic buildings (some restored, some reconstructed), including a medieval crofter's cottage, a Tudor manor house, a 16th-century glass kiln, a full-scale reconstructed Iron Age dwelling, and the oldest daylight photography studio in the country. There are also demonstrations

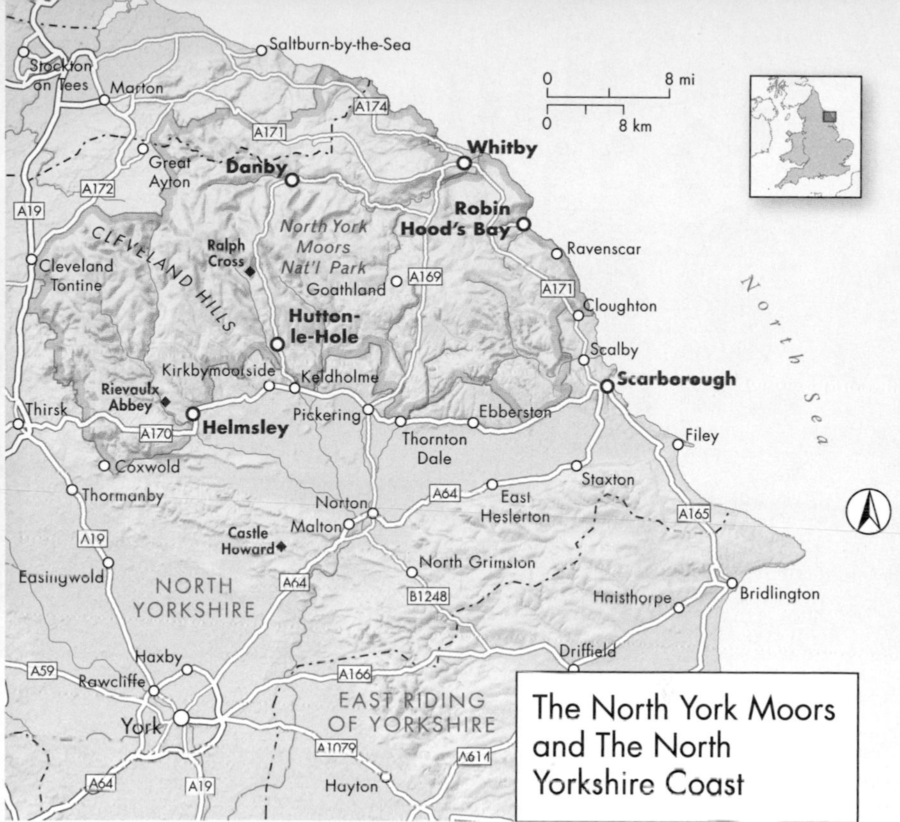

The North York Moors and The North Yorkshire Coast

of bygone traditional craft techniques like wheel hooping, saddlery, and Iron Age wood turning. *Aff A170 01751/417367 www.ryedalefolkmuseum.co.uk £7 Feb. and Mar., Oct. and Nov., 10–4; Apr.–Sept., 10–5:30; last admission 1 hr before closing All entry weather permitting. Call to check.*

HELMSLEY

8 miles southwest of Hutton-le-Hole, 27 miles north of York.

The market town of Helmsley, with its flowering window boxes, stone cottages, churchyard, and arched bridges leading across streams, is the perfect place to spend a relaxing afternoon. You can while away a few hours lingering in its tea shops and tiny boutiques or exploring the craggy remains of its Norman castle. Market day is Friday. Nearby are the impressive ruins of Rievaulx Abbey.

GETTING HERE AND AROUND

There's no train station in Helmsley, but it's served by bus from Scarborough. By car, Helmsley is on A170.

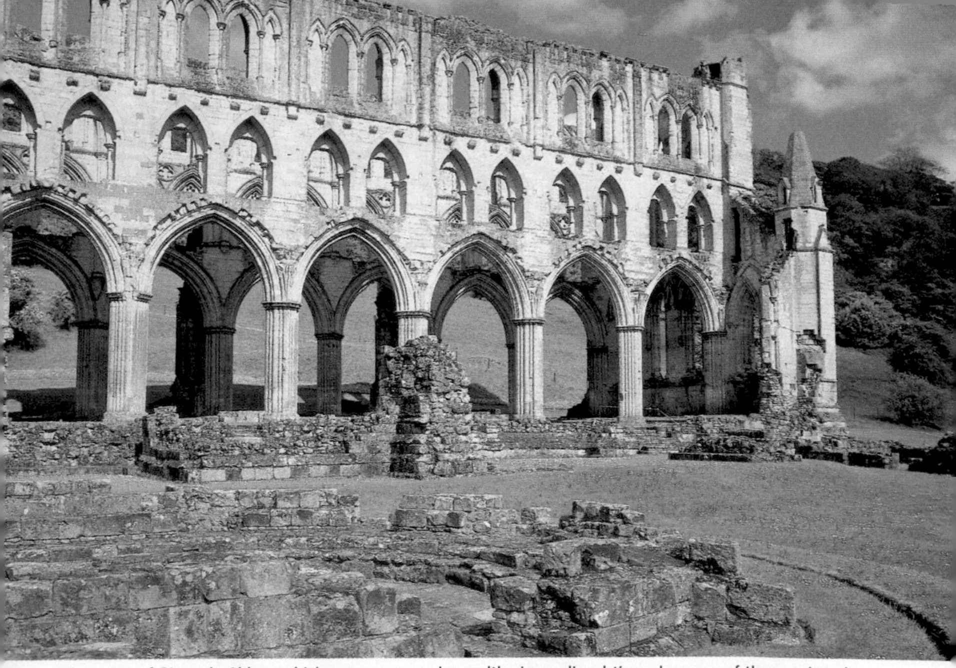

The ruins of Rievaulx Abbey, which was enormously wealthy in medieval times because of the wool trade, show how large the abbey was.

EXPLORING

Fodor's Choice ★ **Rievaulx.** The perfect marriage of architecture and countryside, Rievaulx (pronounced ree- *voh*) Abbey sits in a dramatic setting 2 miles northwest of Helmsley, its soaring arches built to precisely frame a forested hillside rushing down to the River Rye. A French Cistercian sect founded this abbey in 1132, but the monks' life of isolation didn't prevent them from being active in the wool trade. By the end of the 13th century the abbey was massively wealthy and the evocative ruins give a good indication of how vast it once was. Medieval mosaic tiling can still be seen in places, and large parts of the symmetrical cloisters remain. At the entrance to the Chapter House is the original shrine to the first abbot, William.

By the time of Henry VIII, the abbey had shrunk dramatically; only 20 or so monks lived here when the king's soldiers arrived to destroy the building in 1538. After that, the earl of Rutland owned Rievaulx, and he did his best to demolish what was left, with villagers carting away stones from the abbey to build their houses. What remains is a beautiful ghost of the magnificent building that once stood here. From Rievaulx Abbey it's a short climb or drive up the hill to Rievaulx Terrace, an 18th-century escarpment with a magnificent view of the abbey. At either end of the woodland walk are two mid-18th-century follies in the style of small Palladian temples. ✉ *Helmsley* ✣ *Off B1257* ☎ *01439/798228* 🌐 *www.english-heritage.org.uk* 🎟 *£6.20* ⏲ *Apr.–Sept., daily 10–6; Oct., daily 10–5; Nov.–Mar., weekends 10–4.*

Shandy Hall. The Brontës aren't the only literary lions to emerge from this part of Yorkshire. With his eccentric, satirical book *The Life and*

CLOSE UP

Visiting Yorkshire's Monastic Past

Today the ruined abbeys at Fountains, Rievaulx, and Whitby are top attractions where you can learn about the religious life and commercial activities of Yorkshire's great monasteries, and the political machinations that destroyed them. The sites vividly evoke the monks' daily life during the Middle Ages.

THE FALL OF THE MONASTERIES

The sheer number of what were once richly decorated monastic buildings is a testament to the power of medieval Yorkshire's Catholic monastic orders. They became some of the richest in Europe by virtue of the international wool trade conducted from their vast estates with the help of lay workers. The buildings are now mostly romantic ruins, a result of the dissolution of the monasteries during the 16th century following Henry VIII's establishment of the Church of England (with himself as its head) in 1534. This was both a retaliation against the Catholic Church for denying him a divorce (and thus, in his view, a male heir) and a way of appropriating the monasteries' wealth. By 1540 no monasteries remained in England; the king confiscated all their property, redistributed their land, and destroyed or gave away many buildings.

Opinions of Tristram Shandy, Gentleman, Laurence Sterne was experimenting with the post-modern novel even before the traditional form had emerged as a literary genre. Despite the book's often bawdy humor, Sterne was the local parson, living and writing in this charming 15th-century house with 18th-century additions. Restored in the 1990s, it contains the world's largest collection of Sterne's work and memorabilia. There are also 2 acres of grounds, including a walled rose garden. ✉ *Thirsk Bank, Coxwold* ✣ *Off A19* ☎ *01347/868465* 🌐 *www.laurencesternetrust.org.uk* 🎫 *House and garden, £4.50; garden only £2.50* ⏲ *House May–Sept., Wed. and Sun. 2:30–4:30. Gardens May–Sept., Sun.–Fri. 11–4:30.*

WHERE TO STAY

$$ HOTEL **Black Swan Hotel.** A splendid base for exploring the area, this ivy-covered property sits on the edge of Helmsley's market square. **Pros:** historic charm; great location. **Cons:** design is a bit old-fashioned; bathrooms on small side. $ *Rooms from: £129* ✉ *Market Pl.* ☎ *01439/770466* 🌐 *www.blackswan-helmsley.co.uk* *45 rooms, 1 suite* 🍽 *Breakfast.*

$$ B&B/INN **No. 54.** Tea and cakes provide a tasty welcome at this B&B in a stone cottage just off the market square. **Pros:** tasty treats on arrival; comfy beds; pretty courtyard. **Cons:** small rooms; some noise between rooms. $ *Rooms from: £100* ✉ *54 Bondgate* ☎ *01439/771533* 🌐 *www.no54.co.uk* *3 rooms* 🍽 *Breakfast.*

SPORTS AND THE OUTDOORS

Cleveland Way. Helmsley, on the southern edge of the moors, is the starting point of the long-distance moor-and-coastal footpath known as the Cleveland Way. Boots go on at the old cross in the market square, then it's 50 miles or so across the moors to the coast, followed by a

A former smuggling center, the village of Robin's Hood Bay is known for its red-roof cottages as well as its beach.

similar distance south to Filey along the cliffs. The footpath is 110 miles long and takes around nine days start to finish. The trail passes close to Rievaulx Abbey, a few miles outside town. ✉ *Helmsley* 🌐 *www.nationaltrail.co.uk*.

THE NORTH YORKSHIRE COAST

The coastline of the North York Moors paints a dramatic view of spectacular white cliffs covered in pink heather plummeting down to the dark sea hundreds of feet below. The red roofs of Robin Hood's Bay, the sharply curved bay at Whitby, and the gold-and-white buildings of Scarborough capture the imagination at first sight. Most coastal towns still support an active fishing industry, and every harbor offers fishing and leisure trips throughout summer. Beaches at Scarborough and Whitby have patrolled areas: swim between the red-and-yellow flags, and don't swim when a red flag is flying. All the North Sea beaches are ideal for fossil hunting and seashell collecting.

SCARBOROUGH

44 miles northeast of York.

There's no Scarborough Fair, and historians are divided on whether there ever was one, but don't let that stop you from heading to this classic English seaside resort on the North Sea. The liveliest tourist action is on South Bay, a riot of tacky arcades, ice-cream stands, and stores selling "rock" (luridly colored hard candy). Above the former spa are the lemon-hued Victorian and Regency terraces of the genteel South Cliff Promenade, with its views across Cayton Bay and a Victorian funicular linking it to the South Sands below. The South Bay and quieter North Bay are divided by a rocky headland on which sits the ruins of an 11th-century castle. The huddle of streets, alleyways, and red-roof cottages around the harbor gives an idea of what the town was like before it became a resort.

A SPA IS BORN

In 1626, Elizabeth Farrow came upon a stream of acidic water running from a cliff south of Scarborough. This led to the town becoming a hugely popular spa on a par with Harrogate. By the 18th century when icy sea bathing came into vogue, no beaches were busier than Scarborough's. Donkeys and horses drew wheeled cabins called bathing machines into the surf to enable ladies to change into swimming costumes while preserving their modesty. The city's prosperity manifested itself in the handsome Regency and early Victorian residences and hotels you see today.

GETTING HERE AND AROUND

Scarborough is difficult to reach by public transportation. There are no direct trains from London, and a bus from London takes all day. Transpennine Express trains leave from York every hour or so; the journey takes just under an hour. The journey from Leeds by National Express bus takes about three hours. By car, Scarborough is on the coastal A165 road.

ESSENTIALS

Train Information Transpennine Express. ☎ *0845/748–4950* 🌐 *www.tpexpress.co.uk.*

Visitor Information Scarborough Tourist Information Centre. ✉ *Town Hall, St. Nicholas Street* ☎ *01723/383636* 🌐 *www.discoveryorkshirecoast.com.*

EXPLORING

Rotunda Museum. One of the country's first purpose-built museums, this extraordinary cylindrical building was constructed in 1829 to house Jurassic fossils and minerals collected nearby. Designed by William Smith, known as "the father of English geology," it now displays important archaeological finds, evidence of local dinosaurs, and a unique Bronze Age skeleton. Don't miss the frieze illustrating the geology of the nearby coastline. ✉ *Vernon Rd.* ☎ *01723/353665* 🌐 *www.rotundamuseum.org.uk* 🎟 *£4.50* 🕑 *Tues.–Sun. 10–5.*

Scarborough Castle. There have been military structures on this promontory commanding a view of the North and South bays since prehistoric times. Digs have uncovered evidence of fortifications here dating back to 500 BC, and there is still some remaining stonework from a 4th-century Roman signalling station. In 1136, a clifftop stone fortress was built by the earl of Albemarle, and the massive keep that dominates the existing ruins was added by Henry II in 1158, along with the enormous curtain walls that made the castle virtually impregnable. It remained largely unscathed until Cromwell's cannons did their worst during the Civil War. Further demolition came in 1914 when German warships shelled the town, and in 2012 when local vandals significantly damaged the Roman stonework. **■ TIP→ The castle has a spectacular panoramic view of the coast.** ✉ *Castle Rd.* ☎ *01723/372451* 🌐 *www.english-heritage.org.uk* 🎟 *£5.20* ⏲ *Apr.–Sept., daily 10–6; Oct., daily 10–5; Nov.–Mar., weekends 10–4; last admission 30 min before closing.*

FAMILY **Scarborough Sea Life Centre and Marine Sanctuary.** This aquarium and marine sanctuary is a great—if rather expensive—way to entertain the kids for an afternoon. Marine habitats and creatures from around Britain and further afield are represented; otters, penguins, jellyfish, loggerhead turtles, octopuses, and rescued seal pups are particularly popular. ✉ *Scalby Mills, North Bay* ☎ *0871/423–2110* 🌐 *www.visitsealife.com* 🎟 *£16.20* ⏲ *Late Apr.–late July, daily 10–5; late July–early Sept., daily 10–6; early Sept.–late Nov., daliy 10–5; early Nov.–Mar., daily 10–4.*

St. Mary's. Most visitors to this little medieval church near the castle are attracted by the churchyard's most famous occupant: Anne, the youngest Brontë sister. As a governess, Anne accompanied her employers to Scarborough for five summers. Shortly before her death from tuberculosis in 1849, she returned here in the hope the sea air would stimulate a recovery. Her sister Charlotte decided to "lay the flower where it had fallen" and buried Anne above the bay she'd loved. ✉ *Castle Rd.* ☎ *01723/500541* 🌐 *www.scarborough-stmarys.org.uk.*

WHERE TO EAT AND STAY

$ BRITISH ✕ **The Golden Grid.** Everyone has to have fish-and-chips at least once in Scarborough, and this harborfront spot is a classic of its kind. Choose an upstairs window table and tuck into freshly fried, lightly battered cod or haddock. Fresh lobster, oyster, crab, fish pie, plus burgers, sausages, and traditional roast beef with Yorkshire pudding are also available. $ *Average main: £12* ✉ *4 Sandside* ☎ *01723/360922* 🌐 *www.goldengrid.co.uk.*

$$$ ITALIAN Fodor's Choice ★ ✕ **Lanterna.** This unpretentious family-run restaurant prides itself on *not* being trendy but nevertheless is regularly acclaimed as one of the best restaurants in Britain, let alone Yorkshire. It specializes in refined northern Italian dishes such as homemade spaghetti with local velvet crab, as well as seafood specials using catches fresh off the boats in the harbor. Opt for seasonal specials incorporating white truffles or game (October to January) or locally sourced vegetables. With only 30 seats, it books up quickly. $ *Average main: £20* ✉ *33 Queen St.* ☎ *01723/363616* 🌐 *www.lanterna-ristorante.co.uk* ⏲ *Closed Sun. and 2 wks late Oct. No lunch* ✍ *Reservations essential.*

$ HOTEL **Crown Spa Hotel.** The centerpiece of the Regency Esplanade, this grand hotel overlooking the South Bay was originally built to accommodate fashionable 19th-century visitors. **Pros:** Victorian grandeur; modern amenities; free access to health club. **Cons:** inconsistent service. $ *Rooms from: £83* ✉ *7–11 Esplanade, South Cliff* ☎ *01723/357400* 🌐 *www.crownspahotel.com* *115 rooms, 5 suites* 🍽 *Breakfast.*

NIGHTLIFE AND PERFORMING ARTS

Stephen Joseph Theatre. Scarborough is firmly on Britain's theater map, largely thanks to the presence of local resident and noted playwright Alan Ayckbourn, who was for many years the artistic director of this

The ruins of Whitby Abbey rise above the pretty town of Whitby and the River Esk.

theater and premiered most of his acclaimed plays here. His legacy lives on in the theater's commitment to new writing and strong summer repertory season. It has two stages, plus a cinema, restaurant, and bar. ✉ *Westborough* ☎ *01723/370541* 🌐 *www.sjt.uk.com.*

ROBIN HOOD'S BAY

15 miles northwest of Scarborough, 7 miles south of Whitby.

With red-roof cottages and cobbled roads squeezed into a narrow ravine, this tiny fishing village is considered by many to be the prettiest on the Yorkshire coast. Its winding stone staircases eventually bring you to the headland. Despite its name, the village has no connection to the famous medieval outlaw, beyond a historic association with illegal activity. It was once a smuggling center, with contraband passed up the streambed beneath cottages linked to one another by secret passages. The rocks exposed at low tide on the beach are a good hunting ground for Jurassic fossils. ■ **TIP→ Park in the pay lots at the top of the hill. Do not attempt to drive down the hill.**

GETTING HERE AND AROUND

Park in the public lots at the top of the hill. Robin Hood's Bay has no train station, but buses arrive from Scarborough and Whitby throughout the day.

EXPLORING

Robin Hood's Bay Beach. Forget palm trees and white sand—this beach, part of the North York Moors National Park, is all about cliffs, dramatic views, and nature at its most powerful and elemental. It is scenic

All aboard! You can take North Yorkshire Moors Railway steam trains to stations including Goathland.

but deceptive—the tide rushes in quickly, so take care not to get cut off. Provided the tide is out, you can stroll for a couple of hours from the town along a rough stone shore full of rock pools, inlets, and sandy strands (a few are suitable for sunbathers) to the curiously named **Boggle Hole,** three miles to the south, where an old water mill nestles in a ravine. Farther south is **Ravenscar,** a Victorian village that consists of little more than a hotel. It can be reached by walking up the cliff along a hazardous but exhilarating path. **Amenities**: none. **Best for**: walking. ✉ *Robin Hood's Bay* ☎ *01439/772700* 🌐 *www.northyorkmoors.org.uk*.

WHERE TO EAT AND STAY

$ BRITISH

✕ **Bay Hotel.** Perfectly positioned at the bottom of the village atop a seawall, this friendly retreat dating to the Victorian era looks out to dramatic views of the North Sea (if you can get a coveted window table) and a warming open fireplace in winter. The reasonably priced menu leans towards well-prepared traditional pub grub and fresh seafood like Whitby scampi or crab and lemon salad. There are three B&B rooms upstairs (£75–85). [$] *Average main: £10* ✉ *The Dock* ☎ *01947/880278* 🌐 *www.bayhotel.info*.

$$$ RESORT

Raven Hall Hotel. With 100 acres of landscaped grounds, this Georgian country-house hotel dramatically perched 600 feet above sea level on the Ravenscar headlands in North York Moors National Park has lovely views from most rooms. **Pros:** breathtaking coastal views; great for outdoorsy types; relaxing atmosphere. **Cons:** some areas tired; food variable. [$] *Rooms from: £170* ✉ *The Avenue, off Station Rd.,*

Ravenscar ☎ *01723/870353* 🌐 *www.ravenhall.co.uk* 52 *rooms, 8 lodges* 🍽 *Breakfast.*

SPORTS AND THE OUTDOORS

Several superb long-distance walks start at, finish in, or run through Robin Hood's Bay.

Coast-to-Coast Walk. The village marks one end of the 190-mile Coast-to-Coast Walk; the other is at St. Bee's Head on the Irish Sea. Walkers finish at the Bay Hotel, overlooking the harbor. ✉ *Robin Hood's Bay.*

Lyke-Wake Walk. The east-west Lyke-Wake Walk across the moors finishes 3 miles from Robin Hood's Bay at Ravenscar. ✉ *Robin Hood's Bay* 🌐 *www.lykewakewalk.co.uk.*

WHITBY

7 miles northwest of Robin Hood's Bay, 20 miles northeast of Pickering.

Fodor's Choice ★ A fishing port with a Gothic edge (it is host to an annual Goth Weekend), Whitby is also a busy tourist hub, but it handles the crowds so well you might not notice (except at dinnertime, when it's hard to get a seat in a restaurant). Set in a ravine at the mouth of the River Esk, Whitby's narrow streets rise from the curved harbor up cliffs surmounted by the dramatic ruins of a 13th-century abbey. Fine Georgian houses dominate the west side of the river (known as West Cliff). The smaller 17th-century buildings of the old town (known as East Cliff) are found on the other side of an Edwardian swing bridge. Here cobbled Church Street is packed in summer with people exploring the shop-lined alleyways.

Whitby came to prominence as a whaling port in the mid-18th century. Whaling brought wealth, and shipbuilding made it famous: Captain James Cook (1728–79), explorer and navigator, sailed on his first ship from Whitby in 1747, and all four of his subsequent discovery vessels were built here. A scaled-down replica of Cook's ship *Endeavour* runs tours of the Yorkshire coast.

GETTING HERE AND AROUND

A car is a must, as there are no direct buses or trains from London. National Express and Megabus serve the region, but you must change at least once, and the journey can take up to 10 hours. National Express trains from London's King's Cross Station go to Leeds, where you can change to a local train. Alternatively, you can go from King's Cross to Middlesborough and from there take a scenic train ride to Whitby. The entire journey takes around six hours.

Whitby has a small town center and it's easily walkable. The train station is in the town center between its two cliffs. If you're looking for a taxi, they tend to line up outside the station.

ESSENTIALS

Visitor Information Whitby Tourist Information Centre. ✉ *Langborne Rd.* ☎ *01723/383636* 🌐 *www.discoveryorkshirecoast.com.*

EXPLORING

TOP ATTRACTIONS

Church of St. Mary. On top of the East Cliff—reached by climbing 199 stone steps—Whitby's landmark church overlooks the town, while the striking ruins of Whitby Abbey loom above it. Bram Stoker lived in Whitby briefly and later said the image of pallbearers carrying coffins up the church's long stone staircase inspired him to write *Dracula*. The oldest part of the church, primarily the tower and basic structure, are Norman, dating back to 1100, while the distinctive interior, notable for its enclosed box pews and triple-decker pulpit, are Georgian. Almost everything else you see today is the result of 19th- and 20th-century renovations. The churchyard is filled with the weather-beaten gravestones of former mariners and fishermen. **■TIP→ Rather than walking, you can drive to the hilltop and park in the abbey's lot for a small fee. Or take the hourly Esk Valley Bus 97.** ✉ *Abbey Plain, East Cliff* ☎ *01947/603421* 🌐 *www.achurchnearyou.com/whitby-st-mary* 🎫 *Free. £1 suggested donation* ⏲ *Apr.–June., daily 10–4; July–Aug., daily 10–5; Sept.–Mar., daily 10–3* ⏲ *Closed Sun. morning for services.*

Whitby Abbey. Set high on the East Cliff, the strikingly Gothic ruins of this once grand church can be seen from hills on the moors miles away. One of very few founded by a woman, St. Hild in AD 657, the abbey was populated by a mixed community of monks and nuns. Sacked by the Vikings in the 9th century, the abbey was refounded in the 11th century and enlarged in the 13th century, from when it flourished until it was destroyed by Henry VIII. The excellent visitor center has exhibits on St. Hild and *Dracula* author Bram Stoker, Anglo-Saxon artifacts from the site, and interactive displays about the medieval abbey. ✉ *Abbey La.* ☎ *01947/603568* 🌐 *www.english-heritage.org.uk* 🎫 *£6.80* ⏲ *Apr.–Sept., daily 10–6; Oct., daily 10–5; Nov. and late-Feb.–Mar., weekends 10–4; last admission 30 min before closing.*

WORTH NOTING

FAMILY **Bark Endeavour.** This scaled-down replica of Captain Cook's ship was built by local craftspeople using original drawings and specifications, and it includes hardwood decks, detailed rigging, and carved timber mouldings. The ship runs half-hour tours of Whitby harbor and excursions along North Yorkshire's Jurassic coast as far as Sandsend, accompanied by commentary on Cook's life and Whitby sights. ✉ *Fish Quay, Pier Rd.* ☎ *01723/364100* 🌐 *www.endeavourwhitby.com* 🎫 *£3* ⏲ *Apr.–Oct., daily 10:30–dusk, weather permitting.*

Captain Cook Memorial Museum. This museum documenting the life of the famous explorer and those who sailed with him is in the 17th-century house where Cook lodged as an apprentice seaman from 1746 to 1750. Exhibits devoted to Cook's epic expeditions display the legendary explorer's maps, diaries, and drawings. ✉ *Grape La.* ☎ *01947/601900* 🌐 *www.cookmuseumwhitby.co.uk* 🎫 *£4.80* ⏲ *Mid-Feb.–Mar., daily 11–3; Apr.–Oct., daily 9:45–5; Nov.–mid-Feb. by appointment; last admission 30 min before closing.*

OFF THE BEATEN PATH

Goathland. This moorland village, 8 miles southwest of Whitby, has a charming 1865 train station that was the location for Hogsmeade Station, where students bound for Hogwarts disembarked in the film *Harry Potter and the Sorcerer's Stone.* While there, hop on the 18-mile-long **North Yorkshire Moors Railway,** which travels between Grosmont and Pickering, passing through picturesque towns and moorland. The route of the steam-powered trains extends to Whitby twice daily. ✉ *Whitby* 🎫 *Train from £16 round-trip* ⏲ *Train late Mar.–early Nov., daily; early Nov.–Feb., some weekends and holidays.*

Whitby Museum. Exhibits in this quirky museum range from local geology and natural history to archaeology, whaling, and trade routes in Asia, plus an exceptional collection of marine fossils. It's notable for its old-school displays that use handwritten cards. ✉ *Pannett Park* ☎ *01947/602908* 🌐 *www.whitbymuseum.org.uk* 🎫 *£5* ⏲ *Mon.–Sat., 9–5; Sun. 9:30–4:30.*

WHERE TO EAT

$$ BRITISH

✕ **Greens of Whitby.** Specializing in local meat and seafood, Greens is actually two dining venues sharing the same menu but with different atmospheres: downstairs is a buzzy bistro, upstairs a quieter, more intimate restaurant. The selections might include mussels with white wine and herbs, fillet of Whitby turbot in a clam and mussel chowder, or roast rump of Yorkshire lamb, plus a constantly changing catch of the day. There's a two-course set price lunch for £12.50 and dinner for £17.50. The restaurant also rents two stylish boutique apartments. [$] *Average main: £18* ✉ *13 Bridge St.* ☎ *01947/600284* 🌐 *www.greensofwhitby.com.*

$ SEAFOOD Fodor's Choice ★

✕ **Magpie Café.** Seafood is the draw here, and the long menu includes freshly caught salmon, haddock, halibut, and cod—all of which can be grilled or poached. But the crowds come for the outstanding traditional fish-and-chips. The food is good, and fans say it's worth the wait, which can stretch to an hour on busy nights. [$] *Average main: £12* ✉ *14 Pier Rd.* ☎ *01947/602058* 🌐 *www.magpiecafe.co.uk* ⏲ *Closed Jan.*

WHERE TO STAY

$$ B&B/INN

Broom House. In the tiny village of Egton Bridge, about 5 miles outside Whitby, this two-story stone house sits beneath forested hills. **Pros:** gorgeous setting; lovely rooms; friendly staff. **Cons:** far from Whitby; need a car to get around. [$] *Rooms from: £115* ✉ *Broom House La.* ☎ *01947/895279* 🌐 *www.broom-house.co.uk* *6 rooms, 2 suites* *Breakfast.*

$ HOTEL

Dunsley Hall Country House Hotel. Originally a shipping magnate's residence, this Victorian-era country house sits 4 miles west of Whitby on 4 acres of gardens and grounds, with views of the sea in the distance. **Pros:** gardens; attentive staff. **Cons:** modern rooms not as charming; poor Internet signal. [$] *Rooms from: £90* ✉ *Dunsley Rd., Dunsley* ☎ *01947/893437* 🌐 *www.dunsleyhall.com* *26 rooms* *Breakfast.*

$ B&B/INN

Shepherd's Purse. This charming little complex in the cobbled old town consists of shabby-chic guest rooms surrounding a courtyard. **Pros:** quirky, romantic style; comfortable rooms. **Cons:** some rooms are quite small; no breakfast; two-night minimum stay in summer. *Rooms from: £65* *Sanders Yard, 95 Church St.* *01947/820228* *www.theshepherdspurse.com* *7 rooms, 5 with bath* *No meals.*

NIGHTLIFE AND PERFORMING ARTS

Whitby Folk Week. Music, traditional dance, and storytelling fill the town during Whitby Folk Week, usually held the week before the late-August bank holiday. Pubs, halls, and sidewalks become venues for more than 600 traditional folk events by British performers. *Whitby* *01274/833669* *www.whitbyfolk.co.uk.*

SPORTS AND THE OUTDOORS

Whitby Regatta. Held each August, the Whitby Regatta is a three-day jamboree of rowing races, vintage car rallies, naval displays, military fly-bys, fireworks, music, and more. *Whitby* *01947/825896* *www.whitbyregatta.co.uk.*

THE NORTHEAST

WELCOME TO THE NORTHEAST

TOP REASONS TO GO

★ **Hadrian's Wall:** The ancient Roman wall is a wonder for the wild countryside around it as well as its stones and forts, such as Housesteads and Vindolanda.

★ **Castles, castles, castles:** Fought over by the Scots and the English, and prey to Viking raiders, the Northeast was heavily fortified. Durham, Alnwick, and Dunstanburgh castles are spectacular remnants of this history.

★ **Medieval Durham:** A splendid Norman cathedral that dates back to the 11th century is just one of the city's charms. Take a stroll on its ancient winding streets.

★ **Alnwick Castle and Gardens:** The inland seat of the dukes of Northumberland is fascinating with its formidable walls, luxurious interiors, and gardens.

★ **Lindisfarne (Holy Island):** To get to this historic island, you drive across a causeway that floods at high tide. This remote spot includes the ruins of Lindisfarne Priory.

1 Durham and Newcastle. The historic city of Durham, set on a rocky spur, has a stunning castle and cathedral. South and west are scenic towns with castles and industrial heritage sites. Newcastle, to the north, is a sprawling metropolis with a lively regional arts scene.

2 Hadrian's Wall Country. England's wildest countryside is traversed by the remains of the wall that marked the northern border of the Roman Empire. Hexham is a useful base, and Housesteads Roman Fort is a key site. It's stunning country for walking or biking.

3 The Far Northeast Coast. In this dramatic landscape rocky hillsides plunge into the sea. The ruins of castle towers such as Dunstanburgh and Bamburgh stand guard over windswept beaches, and Lindisfarne has a long religious history. Alnwick, inland, has spectacular gardens.

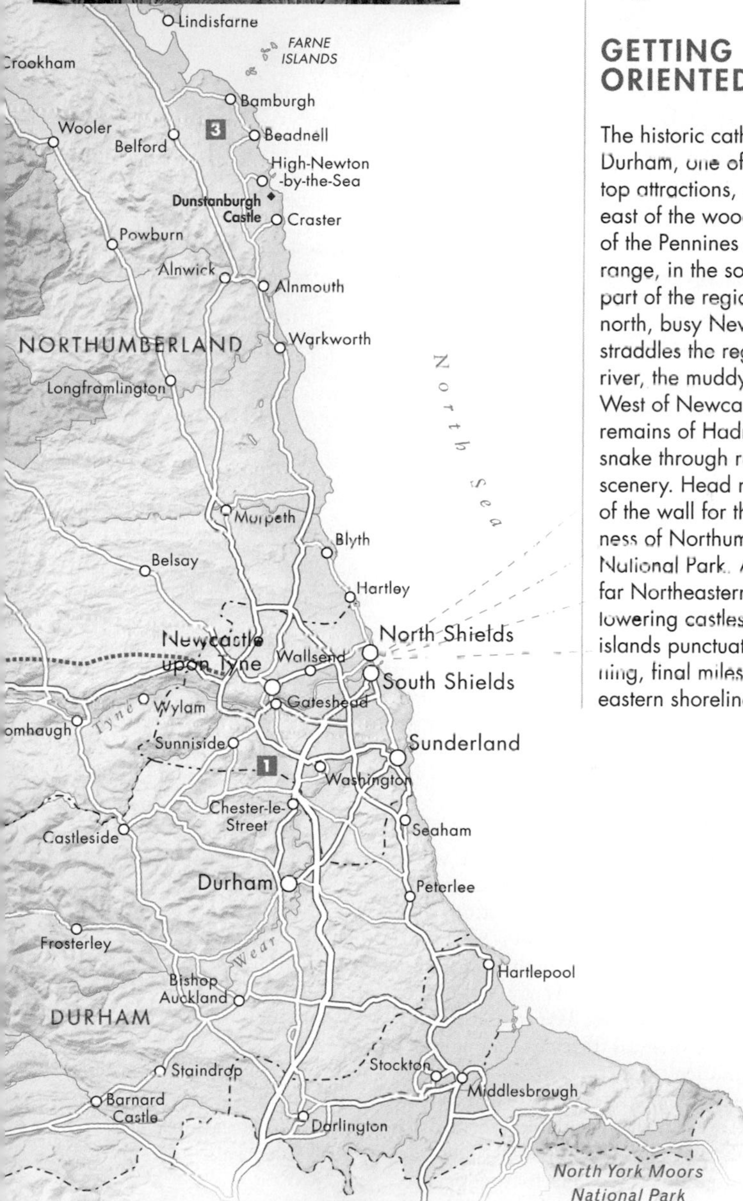

GETTING ORIENTED

The historic cathedral city of Durham, one of the region's top attractions, sits to the east of the wooded foothills of the Pennines mountain range, in the southern part of the region. Farther north, busy Newcastle straddles the region's main river, the muddy Tyne. West of Newcastle, the remains of Hadrian's Wall snake through rugged scenery. Head northwest of the wall for the wilderness of Northumberland National Park. Along the far Northeastern coast, towering castles and misty islands punctuate the stunning, final miles of England's eastern shoreline.

Lindisfarne
FARNE ISLANDS
Crookham
Bamburgh
Wooler
Belford
3
Beadnell
High-Newton -by-the-Sea
Dunstanburgh Castle
Craster
Powburn
Alnwick
Alnmouth
NORTHUMBERLAND
Warkworth
Longframlington
North Sea
Morpeth
Blyth
Belsay
Hartley
North Shields
Newcastle upon Tyne
Wallsend
South Shields
Wylam
Gateshead
Tyne
Sunderland
Sunniside
1
Washington
Chester-le-Street
Seaham
Castleside
Durham
Peterlee
Frosterley
Wear
Hartlepool
Bishop Auckland
DURHAM
Staindrop
Stockton
Middlesbrough
Barnard Castle
Darlington
North York Moors National Park

HADRIAN'S WALL

Winding through the wild and windswept Northumberland countryside, Hadrian's Wall is Britain's most important Roman relic. It once formed the northern frontier of the Roman Empire—its most remote outpost and first line of defense against raiders from the north. Even today, as a ruin, the wall is an awe-inspiring structure.

(above) The wall is a dramatic sight in the countryside; (right, top) Roman writing tablet from Vindolanda; (right, bottom) Remains of a fort near Housesteads

One of the most surprising things about visiting the 73-mile-long wall is its openness and accessibility. Although many of the best-preserved sections are within managed tourist sites, Hadrian's Wall is also part of the landscape, cutting through open countryside. Signposted trails along the entire route allow you to hike or cycle along most of the wall for free. The area around the wall is also rich in archaeological treasures that paint a picture of a thriving, multicultural community. The soldiers and their families who were stationed here came from as far away as Spain and North Africa, and recent discoveries give us an insight into their daily lives. Artifacts displayed at the wall's museums provide fascinating perspective.

POSTCARDS FROM THE PAST

"Oh, how much I want you at my birthday party. You'll make the day so much more fun. Good-bye, sister, my dearest soul."

"I have sent you two pairs of sandals and two pairs of underpants. Greet all your messmates, with whom I pray you live in the greatest good fortune."

—From 1st-century writing tablets unearthed at Vindolanda

SEEING THE WALL'S HIGHLIGHTS

Hadrian's Wall has a handful of Roman-era forts, the best of which are concentrated near Housesteads, Vindolanda, and Chesters. Housesteads is the most complete, although getting there involves a quarter-mile walk up a hill; Chesters and Vindolanda have excellent museums. The separate Roman Army Museum near Greenhead offers a good overview of the wall's history and is near one of the best sections in open countryside, at Walltown Crags.

WHEN TO GO

The best time to visit is midsummer, when the long hours of daylight allow time to see a few of the wall's major attractions and fit in a short hike on the same day. Winter brings icy winds; not all the forts and museums stay open, but those that do can be all but deserted.

GETTING AROUND BY CAR OR BUS

The tiny, winding B6318 road passes within a stone's throw of most of the forts. It's a true back road, so don't expect to get anywhere fast. Public transport is limited; the special AD 122 bus covers the highlights (but only during spring and summer), and several local buses follow parts of the same route.

EXPLORING BY FOOT OR BIKE

Hadrian's Wall Path meanders along the wall's entire length; it's a seven-day hike. Joining it for a mile or so is a great way to see the wall and stunning scenery. Try the section around Walltown, or near Corbridge, where the path goes by the remains of a Roman garrison town. Hadrian's Cycleway, for bicyclists, follows roughly the same route.

SIGHTSEEING RESPONSIBLY

The wall is accessible, but vulnerable. **Do not** climb on it, and **never** break off or remove anything. In muddy weather you're encouraged not to stand directly next to the wall, as over time this can make the soil unstable.

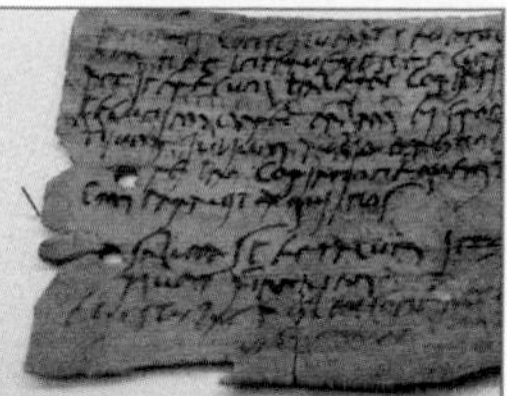

WALL TIMELINE

55 BC Julius Caesar invades what's now southern England, but doesn't stay. He names the island Britannia.

AD 41–50 Full-scale invasion. The Romans establish fortified towns across the south, including Londinium (London).

122 Emperor Hadrian orders the construction of a defensive wall along the territory's northern border.

208 After the Romans make another disastrous attempt to invade Caledonia, Hadrian's Wall is expanded.

410 The Romans leave Britain. Local tribes maintain the wall for at least a century.

1700s Stones from the ruined wall are plundered for road building.

1830s Local philanthropist John Clayton buys land around the wall to save it from further destruction.

1973 First Vindolanda tablets are found. More than 1300 will be excavated over the next 40 years.

1987 Hadrian's Wall becomes a UNESCO World Heritage Site.

Updated by Jack Jewers

For many Britons, the words "the Northeast" provoke a vision of near-Siberian isolation. But although there are wind-hammered, wide-open spaces and empty roads threading the wild high moorland, the Northeast also has simple fishing towns, small villages of remarkable charm, and historic abbeys and castles that are all the more romantic for their often-ruinous state. This is also where you'll find two of England's most iconic sights: the medieval city of Durham and the stark remains of Hadrian's Wall.

Even the remoteness can be relative. Suddenly, around the next bend of a country road, you may come across an imposing church, a tall monastery, or a Victorian country house. The value found in the shops and accommodations, the uncrowded beaches ideal for walking, and the general friendliness of the people add to the appeal. Still, outside of a few key sights, the Northeast is off the well-trodden tourist path.

Mainly composed of the two large counties of Durham and Northumberland, the Northeast includes English villages adjacent to the Scottish border area, renowned in ballads and romantic literature for feuds, raids, and battles. Fittingly, Durham Cathedral, the seat of bishops for nearly 800 years, was once described as "half church of God, half castle 'gainst the Scot." Hadrian's Wall, which marked the northern limit of the Roman Empire, stretches across prehistoric remains and moorland. Not far north of Hadrian's Wall are some of the most interesting parts of Northumberland National Park. Steel, coal, railroads, and shipbuilding created prosperous towns such as Newcastle upon Tyne, which is now remaking itself as a cultural center.

The region's hundred or so miles of largely undeveloped coast is one of the least visited and most dramatic shorelines in all Europe. Several outstanding castles perch on headlands and promontories along here, including Bamburgh, which according to legend was the site of Joyous Garde, the castle of Sir Lancelot of the Round Table.

NORTHEAST PLANNER

WHEN TO GO

The best time to see the Northeast is in summer. This ensures that the museums—and the roads—will be open, and you can take advantage of the countryside walks that are one of the region's greatest pleasures. Rough seas and inclement weather make it dangerous to swim at any of the beaches except in July and August; even then, don't expect warm water. Winter here isn't for the fainthearted. The weather is terrible, but there are few places in England so beautiful and remote.

PLANNING YOUR TIME

If you're interested in exploring Hadrian's Wall and the Roman ruins, you'll probably want to base yourself at a guesthouse in or around Hexham. From there you can easily take in Housesteads and the other local landmarks. Anywhere in this area is within easy reach of Durham, with its lovely ancient buildings, or Newcastle, with its excellent museums. Romantics will want to spend a day or two driving up the coast to take in the incredible views.

GETTING HERE AND AROUND

AIR TRAVEL

Newcastle's airport (a 15-minute drive from the city center) has flights from British and European cities.

Contacts Newcastle Airport. ✉ *Off A696, Woolsington* ☎ *0871/882–1121* 🌐 *www.newcastleairport.com.*

BUS TRAVEL

National Express and Megabus (book online to avoid premium telephone charges) travel to Durham and Newcastle and leave from London's Victoria Coach Station, but the journey takes between six and eight hours, more than twice the time it takes by train. (Though it can be considerably cheaper, especially if you book months in advance.) Connecting services to other parts of the region leave from those cities. Traveline has information. The Explorer Northeast Pass (£9.50) allows unlimited one-day travel on most local bus and Metro train services in the region and is available from the bus driver or local bus or Metro stations.

Contacts Explorer Northeast Pass. ☎ *0191/276–3706* 🌐 *www.networkonetickets.co.uk.* **Megabus.** ☎ *0900/160–0900* 🌐 *www.megabus.com/uk.* **National Express.** ☎ *0871/781–8181* 🌐 *www.nationalexpress.com.* **Traveline.** ☎ *0871/200–2233* 🌐 *www.traveline.org.uk.*

CAR TRAVEL

If you're headed to small villages, remote castles, or Hadrian's Wall, traveling by car is the best alternative. The A1 highway links London and Newcastle (five to six hours). The scenic route is the A697, which branches west off A1 north of Morpeth. For the coast, leave the A1 at Alnwick and follow the minor B1340 and B1339 for Craster, Seahouses, and Bamburgh. Holy Island is reached from the A1.

TRAIN TRAVEL

Within England, the train is still the best way to reach this region. East Coast runs the train service from London to the Northeast. The average travel times from London are three hours to Durham and Newcastle. From Newcastle you can catch local trains to Alnwick, Corbridge, Hexham, and Carlisle; these journeys take about 30 minutes. National Rail Enquiries has information.

Contacts East Coast. ☎ *034/5722–5225* 🌐 *www.eastcoast.co.uk.* **National Rail Enquiries.** ☎ *0845/748–4950* 🌐 *www.nationalrail.co.uk.*

RESTAURANTS

Make sure to sample fine local meats and produce. Look for restaurants that serve game from the Kielder Forest, local lamb from the hillsides, salmon and trout from the rivers, and shellfish, crab, and oysters from the coast. Outside the cities, the region lags somewhat behind other parts of England in terms of good places to eat, although there are special spots to be found. Aside from the ubiquitous chains, the best bets are often small country pubs that serve the traditional, hearty fare associated with the region. Don't wait until 9 pm to have dinner, though, or you may have a hard time finding a place that's still serving.

HOTELS

The large hotel chains don't have much of a presence in the Northeast outside Durham and Newcastle. Instead, you can expect to find country houses converted into welcoming hotels, old coaching inns that still greet guests after 300 years, and cozy bed-and-breakfasts convenient to hiking trails. Many budget accommodations close in winter. ⇨ *Hotel reviews have been shortened. For full information, visit Fodors.com.*

WHAT IT COSTS IN POUNDS

	$	$$	$$$	$$$$
Restaurants	under £15	£15–£19	£20–£25	over £25
Hotels	under £100	£100–£160	£161–£220	over £220

Restaurant prices are the average cost of a main course at dinner, or if dinner is not served, at lunch. Hotels prices are the lowest cost of a standard double room in high season, including 20% V.A.T.

VISITOR INFORMATION

Contacts Hadrian's Wall Country. ☎ *0191/440 5720* 🌐 *www.visithadrianswall.co.uk.*

DURHAM AND NEWCASTLE

Durham—the first major Northeastern town on the main road up from London—is by far the region's most interesting historic city. Its cobblestone streets and towering cathedral make it a charming place to visit. The city is surrounded on all sides by scenic countryside, ruined castles, and isolated villages. Newcastle, though, is the region's biggest, liveliest, and most cosmopolitan city. Most other towns in the area made their fortunes during the Industrial Revolution and have since subsided into slow decline.

DURHAM

250 miles north of London, 15 miles south of Newcastle.

The great medieval city of Durham, seat of County Durham, stands dramatically on a rocky spur, overlooking the countryside. Its cathedral and castle, a World Heritage Site, rise together on a wooded peninsula almost entirely encircled by the River Wear (rhymes with "beer"). For centuries these two ancient structures have dominated Durham—a thriving university town, the Northeast's equivalent of Oxford or Cambridge. Steep, narrow streets overlooked by perilously angled medieval houses and 18th-century town houses make for fun exploring. In the most attractive part of the city, near the Palace Green and along the river, people go boating, anglers cast their lines, and strollers walk along the shaded paths. For great views, take a short stroll along the River Wear and cross the 17th-century Prebends Footbridge. You can return to town via the 12th-century Framwellgate Bridge.

Despite the military advantages of its location, Durham was founded surprisingly late, probably in about the year 1000, growing up around a small Saxon church erected to house the remains of St. Cuthbert. It was the Normans, under William the Conqueror, who put Durham on the map, building the first defensive castle and beginning work on the cathedral. From here Durham's prince-bishops, granted almost dictatorial local powers by William in 1072, kept a tight rein on the county, coining their own money and maintaining their own laws and courts; not until 1836 were these rights finally restored to the English Crown.

GETTING HERE AND AROUND

East Coast trains from London's King's Cross Station arrive at the centrally located Durham Station once an hour during the day. The journey takes about three hours. Trains from York arrive three to four times an hour; that journey takes roughly 50 minutes. A handful of National Express and Megabus buses make the seven-hour trip from London daily. The Durham Cathedral Bus (route 40) links parking lots and the train and bus stations with the cathedral, castle, and university. Between 10 and 4 Monday through Saturday, cars are charged £2 (on top of parking charges) to enter the Palace Green area. You pay the charge at an automatic tollbooth on exiting. **■ TIP→ If you don't have change for the tollbooth, press the button and an attendant will take down your information. Pay later, in person or over the phone, at the Parking Shop. But don't forget to pay by 6 pm the next day (excluding Sundays) or you'll be fined £30.**

ESSENTIALS

Visitor Information Durham Visitor Contact Centre. ✉ *Claypath* ☎ *0300/026–2626* 🌐 *www.thisisdurham.com.* **Parking Shop.** ✉ *Forster House, Finchdale Rd.* ☎ *0191/384–6633* 🌐 *www.durham.gov.uk.*

13

Rounded arches and columns with zigzag patterns are hallmarks of the Romanesque style at Durham Cathedral.

EXPLORING

Durham Castle. Facing the cathedral across Palace Green, Durham's stately, manorlike castle commands a strategic position above the River Wear. For almost 800 years the castle was the home of the enormously powerful prince-bishops; from here they ruled large tracts of the countryside and acted as the main line of defense against Scottish raiders from the north. Henry VIII was the first to curtail the bishops' autonomy, although it wasn't until the 19th century that they finally had their powers annulled. The castle was given over to University College, part of the University of Durham (founded 1832), the oldest in England after Oxford and Cambridge. You can visit the castle only on a 45-minute guided tour. Times can vary, especially on summer afternoons, when the building can be hired out for private events, so it's best to call ahead. ■ **TIP→ During university vacation time, the castle also offers bed-and-breakfast accommodations in the state rooms for around £195 per night; call or check the website for details.** ✉ *Palace Green* ☎ *0191/334–2932* 🌐 *www.dur.ac.uk/durham.castle* 🎫 *£5* ⏲ *Early Oct.–late June, tours daily 2, 3, and 4; late June–early Oct., tours daily 10, 11, 12, 2, 3, and 4.*

QUICK BITES

9 Altars Café. Down a narrow alleyway between the castle and the river, the tiny 9 Altars Café is an excellent spot for coffee and sandwiches. Eat on the river terrace if the weather's good—and you're lucky enough to get a seat. ✉ ***River St.*** ☎ ***0191/374–1120*** 🌐 ***www.9altars.com.***

Fodor's Choice ★ **Durham Cathedral.** A Norman masterpiece in the heart of the city, the cathedral is an amazing vision of solidity and strength, a far cry from

Durham Castle 2
Durham Cathedral 1
Durham University Oriental Museum 3

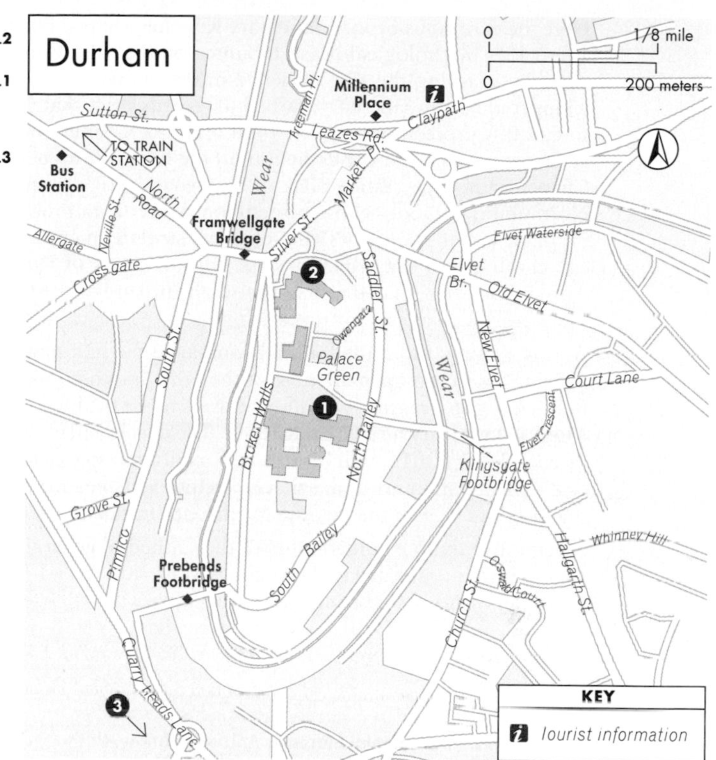

the airy lightness of later Gothic cathedrals. Construction began about 1090, and the main body was finished about 1150. The round arches of the nave and the deep zigzag patterns carved into them typify the heavy, gaunt style of Norman, or Romanesque, building. The technology of Durham, however, was revolutionary. This was the first European cathedral to be given a stone, rather than a wooden, roof. When you consider the means of construction available to its builders—the stones that form the ribs of the roof had to be hoisted by hand and set on a wooden structure, which was then knocked away—the achievement seems staggering.

The story of the Cathedral actually goes back 200 years before the first stones were laid. After a Viking raid on the monastery at Lindisfarne in 875, a group of monks smuggled away the remains of St. Cuthbert, patron saint of Northumbria. The remains were eventually interred in a shrine on this spot, which became a hugely popular destination for pilgrims. The wealth this brought the town was more than enough to pay for the building of the cathedral. Today Cuthbert's shrine is a relatively humble marble slab, although the enormous painting suspended from the ceiling is what the spectacular medieval coffin covering is thought to have looked like.

Note the enormous bronze **Sanctuary Knocker,** shaped like the head of a ferocious mythological beast, mounted on the massive northwestern door. By grasping the ring clenched in the animal's mouth, medieval felons could claim sanctuary; cathedral records show that 331 criminals sought this protection between 1464 and 1524. An unobtrusive tomb at the western end of the cathedral, in the Moorish-influenced **Galilee Chapel,** is the final resting place of the Venerable Bede, an 8th-century Northumbrian monk whose contemporary account of the English people made him the country's first reliable historian. In good weather you can climb the tower, which has spectacular views of Durham. From April to October, guided tours of the cathedral are offered two or three times daily; call ahead for times.

At this writing, the cathedral had completed the first phase of a long-running project to open up more of the cathedral to public view. When finished, **Open Treasure** will allow visitors to see the hitherto closed-off **Monks Dormitory** and **Great Kitchen**. The development, which should be complete by 2016, will include new exhibition spaces for the Cathedral's collection of art and artifacts, including its beautiful illuminated manuscripts. Check the website for the latest updates on progress.

Seventy-five minute guided tours of the Cathedral generally take place two or three times a day. Start times vary; call ahead for the daily schedule. A choral evensong service takes place Tuesday to Saturday at 5:15 and Sunday at 3:30. ✉ *Palace Green* ☎ *0191/386–4266* 🌐 *www.durhamcathedral.co.uk* 🎫 *Free (requested donation £5); tower £5; guided tours £5* ⏲ *Cathedral Mon.–Sat. 9:30–6, Sun. noon–5:30. Tower Mon.–Sat. 10–4, Sun. 1–2:30.*

Durham University Oriental Museum. A 15-minute walk from the cathedral, this museum displays fine art and craftwork from all parts of Asia and the Middle East. Galleries are ordered by culture, including Ancient Egypt, Japan, China, and Korea. Among the highlights are beautiful Qing dynasty jade and laquer ornaments, and a collection of Japanese woodblock prints from the Edo period. A new gallery, focusing on the Himalayas and South Asia, should be open by the end of 2015. ✉ *Elvet Hill, off South Rd.* ☎ *0191/334–5694* 🌐 *www.dur.ac.uk/oriental.museum* 🎫 *£1.50* ⏲ *Weekdays 10–5; weekends and bank holiday Mon. noon–5.*

WHERE TO EAT

$$ FRENCH ✕ **Bistro 21.** This fashionable restaurant, a few miles northwest of the center, is known for its eclectic menu of French classics with a modern twist. Signature dishes include fishcakes with buttered spinach, or confit of duck with Lyonnaise potatoes. Get here by taxi, or take Bus 43 to Durham Hospital and walk five minutes. 💲 *Average main: £17.50* ✉ *Aykley Heads* ☎ *0191/384–4354* 🌐 *www.bistrotwentyone.co.uk* ⏲ *No dinner Sun.*

$$ BRITISH ✕ **Oldfields Noted Eating House.** At this convivial restaurant, cheerful raspberry walls and unfussy walnut furnishings create a nicely laid-back vibe that complements the excellent food. The menu focuses on ultra-traditional flavors made with organic, seasonal, and locally sourced ingredients. Some dishes are likely to baffle anyone from outside the

region; you might find pan haggarty (a classic Northumberland specialty made with cheese, onions, and potatoes), or clapshot (a Scottish favorite made with swede, turnips, potatoes, and beef dripping) alongside mains of cottage (minced beef) pie, cod with spicy sausage, or rib-eye steak with fat chips. There's not much choice for non-carnivores, but let them know in advance and the chef can prepare an extra vegetarian option. *Average main: £17* *18 Clay Path* *0191/370–9595* *www.oldfieldsrealfood.co.uk* *No credit cards.*

$$ THAI **Zen.** This popular restaurant mainly serves Thai food, but the menu is also scattered with Japanese, Chinese, and Indonesian dishes. This rather dizzying trip around Asia can take you from Thai green curry to Mongolian lamb, or perhaps teriyaki beef or cod fillet wrapped in banana leaves served with chili and lime. Make reservations if you're coming on a weekend. *Average main: £15.50* *Court La.* *0191/384–9588* *www.zendurham.co.uk.*

WHERE TO STAY

$ B&B/INN **Georgian Town House.** At the top of a cobbled street overlooking the cathedral and castle, this family-run guesthouse has small, snug bedrooms with pleasant city views. **Pros:** great location; jovial owners; free Wi-Fi. **Cons:** most rooms are small; decor won't please everyone. *Rooms from: £80* *11 Crossgate* *0191/386–8070* *www.thegeorgiantownhousedurham.co.uk* *Closed last wk of Dec.* *8 rooms* *Breakfast.*

$$ HOTEL Fodor's Choice ★ **Lumley Castle Hotel.** This is a real Norman castle, right down to the dungeons and maze of dark flagstone corridors—one room even has a bathroom hidden behind a bookcase. **Pros:** great for antiques lovers; festive meals; good value for such a historic place. **Cons:** it's easy to get lost down the winding corridors. *Rooms from: £114* *B1284, Chester-le-Street* *0191/389–1111* *www.lumleycastle.com* *59 rooms* *Some meals.*

$ HOTEL **Seven Stars Inn.** This early-18th-century coaching inn is cozy and surprisingly affordable. **Pros:** cozy lounge; pleasant staff; dinner and bed-and-breakfast packages are a good value. **Cons:** on a main road; minimum two-night stay at peak times; very strict midnight curfew—guests may be locked out if late. *Rooms from: £68* *High St. N, Shincliffe Village* *0191/384–8454* *www.sevenstarsinn.co.uk* *8 rooms* *Breakfast.*

$ B&B/INN **Victoria Inn.** An authentically Victorian air pervades at this cozy pub near Durham Cathedral that also serves as a B&B. **Pros:** step-back-in-time atmosphere; lovely hosts; free Wi-Fi. **Cons:** few amenities; pub doesn't serve full meals. *Rooms from: £75* *86 Hallgarth St* *0191/386–5269* *www.victoriainn-durhamcity.co.uk* *6 rooms* *Breakfast.*

NIGHTLIFE AND PERFORMING ARTS

Half Moon. This handsome old pub is popular for its excellent range of traditional ales, as well as for its old-school atmosphere that reminds you that pubs like this are a dying breed. *New Elvet* *0191/374–1918* *www.thehalfmooninndurham.co.uk.*

Market Tavern. Fans of real ales are drawn to the Market Tavern, which has been in business since the late 18th century. They also serve decent pub food. ✉ *27 Market Pl.* ☎ *0191/386–2069* 🌐 *www.taylor-walker.co.uk.*

SHOPPING

Bramwells Jewellers. The specialty here is a pendant copy of the gold-and-silver cross of St. Cuthbert. ✉ *24 Elvet Bridge* ☎ *0191/386–8006.*

Durham Indoor Market. The food and bric-a-brac stalls in Durham Indoor Market, a Victorian arcade, are open Monday through Saturday 9–5. An excellent farmers' market is held in Market Place on the third Thursday of every month. ✉ *Market Pl.* ☎ *0191/384–6153* 🌐 *www.durhammarkets.co.uk.*

SPORTS AND THE OUTDOORS

Brown's Boat House. At the downtown Brown's Boat House, you can rent rowboats April through early November. You can also take short cruises from April to October. ✉ *Elvet Bridge* ☎ *0191/386–3779.*

BISHOP AUCKLAND

10 miles southwest of Durham.

For 700 years, between the 12th and 19th century, the powerful prince-bishops of Durham had their country residence in Auckland Castle, in the town of Bishop Auckland. When finally deprived of their powers in 1836, the bishops left Durham and made Bishop Auckland their official home. You can tour the house as well as nearby Raby Castle.

GETTING HERE AND AROUND

Bishop Auckland is just off the A1 motorway from London (260 miles) or Durham (13 miles). There's no direct train service here from London or Durham. However, you can take a train from either city to Darlington and change. The journey takes about three hours from London and one hour from Durham.

ESSENTIALS

Visitor Information Bishop Auckland Tourist Information Centre. ✉ *Town Hall, Market Pl.* ☎ *0300/026–2626* 🌐 *www.thisisdurham.com.*

EXPLORING

Auckland Castle. Arguably the greatest of the prince-bishops of Durham's properties is this episcopal palace, which you enter through an elaborate stone arch. Much of what's on view today dates from the 16th century, although the limestone-and-marble chapel, with its dazzling stained-glass windows, was built in 1665 from the ruins of a 12th-century hall. ■ **TIP→ Don't miss the extraordinary paintings of Jacob and his 12 sons by the 17th-century Spanish artist Francisco de Zurbarán, in the Long Dining Room.** Call ahead to confirm opening times. ✉ *Off Market Pl.* ☎ *01388/743750* 🌐 *www.aucklandcastle.org* 🎫 *£8* ⏲ *Mar.–Oct., Wed.–Mon. 10:30–4; tours 11:30 and 2. Closed Tues.*

FAMILY Fodor's Choice ★ **Head of Steam.** A family-friendly museum in nearby Darlington tells the story of the early days of rail travel. The town gained fame in 1825, when George Stephenson piloted his steam-powered *Locomotion No.*

1 along newly laid tracks the few miles to nearby Stockton, thus kick-starting the railway age. Set in an abandoned 1842 train station, the museum has interactive exhibits and big steam trains that are great for kids; antique engines and scale models help bring history to life. There's also a café and children's activity room. **■ TIP➔ A ticket for families with up to four kids costs £10.** Darlington is 13 miles southeast of Bishop Auckland, on A68. Train connections run roughly every two hours. ✉ *North Road Station, Station Rd., Darlington* ☎ *01325/460532* 🌐 *www.head-of-steam.co.uk* 🎫 *£5.15* ⏲ *Apr.–Sept., Tues.–Sun. 10–4; Oct.–Mar., Wed.–Sun. 11–3:30.*

Fodor's Choice ★ **Raby Castle.** The stone battlements and turrets of moated Raby Castle, once the seat of the powerful Nevills and currently the home of the 11th baron Barnard, stand amid a 200-acre deer park and ornamental gardens. Charles Nevill supported Mary, Queen of Scots in the 1569 uprising against Elizabeth I; when the Rising of the North failed, the estate was confiscated. Dating mostly from the 14th century (using stone plundered from Barnard Castle) and renovated in the 18th and 19th centuries, the luxuriously furnished castle has displays of art and other treasures. Rooms in wonderfully elaborate Gothic Revival, Regency, and Victorian styles are open for viewing. In May, June, and September you can only visit by guided tour, except on Sunday when you're free to wander around (as you can every day except Saturdays in July and August). Raby Castle is 7 miles southwest of Bishop Auckland and 1 mile north of Staindrop. ✉ *A688, Staindrop* ☎ *01833/660202* 🌐 *www.rabycastle.com* 🎫 *£10; park and gardens £6* 🕒 *Castle May–late June and Sept., Sun.–Wed. 1–4:30; late June–Aug., Sun.–Fri. 1–4:30. Grounds May–late June and Sept., Sun.–Wed. 11–5; late June–Aug., Sun.–Fri. 11–5.*

BARNARD CASTLE

14 miles south of Bishop Auckland, 25 miles southwest of Durham.

The handsome market town of Barnard Castle has sights of its own and can also serve as a base for venturing into the Teesdale Valley to the northwest. Its unusual butter-market hall (known locally as Market Cross), surmounted by an old fire-alarm bell, marks the junction of the streets Thorngate, Newgate, and Market Place. Stores, pubs, and cafés line these thoroughfares. In 1838 Charles Dickens stayed at the **King's Head Inn** here while doing research for his novel *Nicholas Nickleby*. The local tourist office has a free "In the Footsteps of Charles Dickens" leaflet.

GETTING HERE AND AROUND

Barnard Castle is about a 20-minute drive from Bishop Auckland on A688. You can make the journey by local buses, but it takes more than an hour and involves a change in Darlington.

ESSENTIALS

Visitor Information Barnard Castle Visitor Information Point. ✉ *The Witham, 3 Horsemarket* ☎ *0300/026–2626* 🌐 *www.thisisdurham.com.*

EXPLORING

Barnard Castle. The substantial ruins of Barnard Castle, which gave the town its name, cling to an aerie overlooking the River Tees. From the outside it looks satisfyingly complete from the right angle; inside it's mostly just a shell. You can see parts of the 14th-century Great Hall and the cylindrical, 13th-century tower. Look for the figure of a carved boar high on the wall of the inner courtyard—it was the family emblem of King Richard III (1452–85), placed there during his reign in honor of the elevated status he bestowed upon the castle. ✉ *Off Galgate* ☎ *01833/638212* 🌐 *www.english-heritage.org.uk* 🎫 *£4.70* 🕒 *Apr.–Oct., daily 10–6; Nov.–Mar., weekends 10–4.*

Fodor's Choice ★ **Bowes Museum.** This vast French-inspired château a mile west of the town center was built between 1862 and 1875. Highlights include paintings by Canaletto, El Greco, Francisco Goya, and François Boucher, in addition to beautiful collections of ceramics and glass, 18th-century French furniture, and 19th- and 20th-century fashion. ■ **TIP→ Don't miss the amazing 18th-century mechanical swan, which catches and swallows an articulated silver fish every day at 2.** The display lasts 40 seconds but it's worth hanging around for. The café serves light meals and afternoon tea. ✉ *Newgate* ☎ *01833/690606* 🌐 *www.thebowesmuseum.org.uk* 🎫 *£9.70* 🕒 *Daily 10–5.*

High Force. The Upper Teesdale Valley's elemental nature shows its most volatile aspect in the sprays of England's highest waterfall, the 72-foot High Force. From the roadside parking lot it's a 10-minute walk through woodland to the massive rocks over which the water tumbles. Access is sometimes closed in bad weather. The waterfall is 15 miles northwest of Barnard Castle. ✉ *Off B6277* ☎ *01833/622209* 🎫 *£1.50; parking £2* ⏲ *Easter–Oct., daily 10–5; Nov.–Easter 10–4; last ticket sold 1 hr before closing.*

WHERE TO EAT

$ BRITISH ✕ **Clarenden's Cafe.** A nicely old-fashioned air pervades this 17th-century building on the main square. Drop in for a tasty light lunch, or just a slice of cake, and tea served from an antique silver pot. They also have a pleasant little homeware and gift shop attached. [$] *Average main: £6* ✉ *29 Market Pl.* ☎ *01833/690110* 🌐 *www.clarendonsofbarnardcastle.co.uk* ▭ *No credit cards* ⏲ *Closed Sun. Nov.–Mar. No dinner.*

NEWCASTLE UPON TYNE

16 miles north of Durham, 42 miles northeast of Barnard Castle.

Durham may have the glories of its castle, cathedral, and university, but the liveliest city of the Northeast is Newcastle, currently reinventing itself (with some success) as a regional center for culture and modern architecture after years of decline. Settled since Roman times on the River Tyne, the city made its fortune twice—first by exporting coal and later by shipbuilding. As a 19th-century industrial center, Newcastle had few equals in Britain, showing off its wealth in grand Victorian buildings lining the broad streets. Some of these remain, particularly on Grey Street. The cluster of bridges (older and newer) crossing the Tyne is a quintessential city sight.

Much of the regeneration since the early 1990s has been based around the Gateshead Quays. Here the Baltic Centre for Contemporary Art and the pedestrian-only Millennium Bridge—the world's first tilting bridge, which opens and shuts like an eyelid—have risen from industrial wasteland.

GETTING HERE AND AROUND

Newcastle Airport, a 15-minute drive from the city center, has flights from British and European cities. Metro trains connect to the center. The A1 highway links London and Newcastle (five to six hours).

East Coast trains from London's King's Cross take about three hours. National Express and Megabus have service from London's Victoria Coach Station several times a day for the six- to seven-and-a-half hour trip.

Newcastle has a good public transportation system. Its Metro light-rail network is easy to use, well signposted, and has stops near most sights. Buses go all the places Metro doesn't reach.

ESSENTIALS

Visitor Information Newcastle upon Tyne Tourist Information Centre. ✉ *8–9 Central Arcade, Market St.* ☎ *0191/277–8000* 🌐 *www.newcastlegateshead.com.*

EXPLORING

TOP ATTRACTIONS

Angel of the North. South of Newcastle, near the junction of A1 and A1(M) at Gateshead, stands England's largest—and one of its most popular—sculptures, the *Angel of the North*. Created by Antony Gormley in 1998, the rust-color steel sculpture is a sturdy, abstract human figure with airplane-like wings rather than arms. It stands 65 feet tall and has a horizontal wingspan of 175 feet. There's parking nearby, signposted on A167. ✉ *A167, Gateshead* 🎫 *Free.*

Baltic Centre for Contemporary Art. Formerly a grain warehouse and now the country's largest national gallery for contemporary art outside London, the Baltic Centre for Contemporary Art presents thought-provoking exhibitions by top names and emerging new talents. The program changes regularly; check the website for details. There's also a café and a rooftop restaurant. ✉ *Gateshead Quays, S. Shore Rd.* ☎ *0191/478–1810* 🌐 *www.balticmill.com* 🎫 *Free* ⏲ *Tues. 10:30–6, Wed.–Mon. 10–6; last admission 15 min before closing.*

FAMILY Fodor's Choice ★ **Beamish Open-Air Museum.** Made up of buildings moved from elsewhere in the region, this sprawling complex explores the way people in the Northeast lived and worked from the early 1800s to the early 1900s. A streetcar takes you around the site and to a reconstructed 1920s shopping street with a dentist's office, pub, and grocery store, staffed by costumed volunteers. Other attractions include a small manor house, a railroad station, and a coal mine. In summer, a steam train makes a short run. ■ **TIP→ There are special events year-round, from weekend-long festivals where you're encouraged to come in old-style fancy dress, to traditional English celebrations such as May Day and Harvest Festival. Allow at least a half day if you come in summer, less in winter.** The museum is about 8 miles south of Newcastle. ✉ *Off A693, Beamis* ☎ *0191/370–4000* 🌐 *www.beamish.org.uk* 🎫 *£18.50; £9.25 Nov.–Mar., Tues.–Thurs.* ⏲ *Apr.–Oct., daily 10–5; Nov.– Mar., Tues.–Thurs. and weekends 10–4; last admission 1 hr before closing.*

Fodor's Choice ★ **Corbridge Roman Town.** The foundations of this important Roman garrison town (the farthest north in the entire Roman Empire) are brought to life with a lively audio commentary, plus occasional reenactments during the summer. The small museum houses the Corbridge Hoard, a surprisingly well-preserved collection of tools and personal possessions left behind by Roman soldiers in the 2nd century. ■ **TIP→ The site is sometimes closed in bad weather, so call ahead.** ✉ *Corchester La., Corbridge* ☎ *01434/632–349* 🌐 *www.english-heritage.org.uk* 🎫 *£5.70* ⏲ *Apr.–Sept., daily 10–5:30; Oct.–early Nov., daily 10–4; early Nov.–Mar., weekends 10–4.*

FAMILY Fodor's Choice ★ **Great North Museum: Hancock and the Hatton Gallery.** An amalgam of several collections belonging to Newcastle University and named for a Victorian founder of the Natural History Society of Northumberland, this beautifully renovated museum contains an impressive array of ancient archaeological finds, plus galleries on natural history and astronomy. Highlights include artifacts left behind by the Roman builders of Hadrian's Wall; ancient Egyptian mummies; and a reconstruction of the 1st-century Temple of Mithras at Carrawburgh. This place isn't designed for kids, but there's plenty here to amuse them, including a planetarium and a life-size model of a T-Rex. A short, signposted walk takes you to the smaller **Hatton Gallery** (*King's Road; 091/208–6059*), which holds artwork by Francis Bacon and Kurt Schwitters. It includes a masterpiece by the latter called *Merz Barn Wall*, a sculpture made of found objects and plaster. Commissioned by New York's Museum of Modern Art in 1948 to replace an earlier version destroyed during World War II, Schwitters died before he completed it. The museum is just off the Great North Road, and five minutes from the Haymarket Metro station. ✉ *Barras Bridge* ☎ *0191/222–6765* 🌐 *www.twmuseums.org.uk/greatnorthmuseum* 🎫 *Free* 🕑 *Mon.–Fri. 10–5, Sat. 10–4, Sun. 11–4. Hatton Gallery Mon.–Sat. 10–5.*

13

QUICK BITES

Tyneside Coffee Rooms. The 70-year-old art-deco Tyneside Coffee Rooms, on the second floor above the Tyneside Cinema, makes an intriguing place to stop for tea, coffee, and a good, unfussy lunch. The popular place is open daily until 10 pm (11 pm on Sunday). ✉ ***10 Pilgrim St.*** ☎ ***0191/227–5520*** 🌐 ***www.tynesidecinema.co.uk.***

Laing Art Gallery. One of the Northeast's finest art museums merits at least an hour's visit for its selection of 19th-century British art. The Pre-Raphaelites are on show, too, as are sculptures by Henry Moore. The new Northern Spirit gallery showcases some of the great artists from the region, including John Martin (1759–1854), who produced dramatic biblical landscapes; and brother-and-sister William and Mary Beilby, whose beautiful creations in enamelled glass creations became highly prized in their 1770s heyday. ✉ *New Bridge St.* ☎ *0191/232–7734* 🌐 *www.twmuseums.org.uk/laing* 🎫 *Free* 🕑 *Mon.–Sat. 10–5, Sun. 2–5.*

WORTH NOTING

FAMILY **Bede's World.** Four miles east of Newcastle, this site holds substantial monastic ruins, the church of St. Paul, and a small museum reflecting the long tradition of religion and learning that began here in AD 681, when the first Saxon church was established on the site. The Venerable Bede (672–735), deemed to be England's earliest historian, moved into the monastery as a child and remained until his death. You can gain a sense of medieval life from the farm buildings, reconstructed by modern historians using traditional methods, and the rare breeds of pigs and cattle that roam the 11-acre Anglo-Saxon farm. There's also a shop and a café. To get here, take Bus 526 or 527, or the Metro to the Bede/Jarrow station (20-minute walk). ✉ *Church Bank, Jarrow* ☎ *0191/489–2106* 🌐 *www.bedesworld.co.uk* 🎫 *£6* 🕑 *Apr.–Sept., daily 10–5; Oct.–Mar., daily 10–4; last admission 1 hr before closing.*

FAMILY **Discovery Museum.** Reconstructed streets and homes lead you from Roman times to the present day in this engaging museum. Kids will like its interactive approach to teaching Newcastle's history, and history buffs will be most thrilled by galleries showing off the town's maritime and industrial achievements, including the *Turbinia*. Built in 1894, it was once the fastest ship in the world and the first to be powered by steam turbines. ✉ *Blandford Sq.* ☎ *0191/232–6789* 🌐 *www.*

Sir Norman Foster designed the Sage Gateshead performance venue, an emblem of Newcastle's revival.

twmuseums.org.uk/discovery *Free* *Weekdays 10–4, weekends 11–4.*

Tyne Bridge. This bridge by the old quayside is the symbol of Newcastle. Built in 1928, it's one of seven bridges spanning the river in the city. *Tyne Bridge.*

WHERE TO EAT

$$ — MODERN BRITISH — Fodor's Choice ★

Café 21. A Newcastle classic, this sleek brasserie is a local favorite for romantic dinners. Warm wood, leather banquettes, and crisp white table linens lend a polished look. The menu focuses on modern versions of classic British food, peppered with European influences; try the slow-cooked beef in red wine sauce, or the fish cakes with buttered spinach and parsley cream. Desserts such as Mandarin soufflé are excellent. *Average main: £18* *Trinity Gardens* *0191/222–0755* *www.cafetwentyone.co.uk.*

$ — SOUTH INDIAN — Fodor's Choice ★

Rasa. The only branch of this super-cool minichain outside London, Rasa serves surprisingly authentic, exceptionally delicious Indian cuisine. The menu is short, focusing entirely on specialties from India's Kerala region; meat is used sparingly, but there are plenty of fish and vegetarian options. Try the *kappayum meenum vevichathu*, which mixes king fish and tamarind in a spicy, fragrant sauce, or the *chemmeen masala*, prawns prepared with a tangy tomato and chili reduction. A shared *dosa* is the ideal way to mop up the last of those heavenly sauces—they're light-as-a-feather flatbreads, stuffed with vegetables or curried potatoes. *Average main: £9* *27 Queen St.* *0191/232–7799* *www.rasarestaurants.com* *No lunch Sun.*

WHERE TO STAY

$ B&B/INN FAMILY **Hedley Hall.** So long as you don't mind the short commute from Newcastle (it's 8 miles south of the city), Hedley Hall makes for a peaceful base. **Pros:** peaceful setting, close to the city; delightful hosts; video games and a playground help keep kids amused. **Cons:** you need a car; self-catering cottages are in a close-knit complex so don't feel very private; no dinner. *Rooms from: £95* *Hedley La., near Sunniside* *0120/723–1835* *www.hedleyhall.com* *4* *Breakfast.*

$$ HOTEL Fodor'sChoice ★ **Jesmond Dene House.** Occupying a sprawling 19th-century mansion in the northeastern part of the city, this hotel is surrounded by lush gardens and filled with polished oak floors, huge windows, and wandering staircases. **Pros:** beautiful light filled rooms; lovely gardens; free Wi-Fi. **Cons:** the restaurant is popular, so you need to book in advance. *Rooms from: £120* *Jesmend Dene Rd.* *0191/212–3000* *www.jesmonddenehouse.co.uk* *40 rooms* *Breakfast.*

$$ HOTEL **Malmaison.** Converted from an old riverside warehouse, this glamorous, design-conscious hotel sits beside the pedestrian Millennium Bridge. **Pros:** spacious and very well soundproofed rooms; relaxing spa; good restaurant. **Cons:** unreliable Wi-Fi. *Rooms from: £105* *Quayside* *0191/245–5000* *www.malmaison.com* *116 rooms* *Breakfast; Some meals.*

$$$$ B&B/INN Fodor'sChoice ★ **Seaham Hall.** Lord Byron married Annabella Milbanke in this four-square mansion on a cliff top overlooking the sea in 1815; today the sumptuous contemporary interior is a haven of luxury. **Pros:** pampering rooms; full of atmosphere. **Cons:** far outside town; high prices; you'll have to dress up for dinner. *Rooms from: £225* *Lord Byron's Walk, Seaham* *0191/516–1400* *www.seaham-hall.co.uk* *No credit cards* *19 suites* *Breakfast.*

NIGHTLIFE AND PERFORMING ARTS

Theatre Royal. The region's most established performing arts center, the Theatre Royal stages high-quality productions and is also a venue for touring musicals and dance. *Grey St.* *0844/811–2121* *www.theatreroyal.co.uk.*

HADRIAN'S WALL COUNTRY

A formidable line of Roman fortifications, Hadrian's Wall was the Romans' most ambitious construction in Britain. The land through which the old wall wanders is wild and inhospitable in places, but that seems only to add to the powerful sense of history it evokes. Museums and information centers along the wall make it possible to learn as much as you want about the Roman era.

HADRIAN'S WALL

73 miles from Wallsend, north of Newcastle, to Bowness-on-Solway, beyond Carlisle.

The most important Roman relic in Britain extends across the countryside and can be accessed in many ways. In Northumberland National Park, about half a mile north of Vindolanda, the Once Brewed National

Park Visitor Centre has informative displays about Hadrian's Wall and can advise about local walks.

GETTING HERE AND AROUND

The A69 roughly follows Hadrian's Wall, although sometimes it's a few miles in either direction. The best sections of the wall are near the narrower B6318, including Vindolanda, Housesteads Roman Fort, and Chesters Roman Fort. There's a small railway station at Hexham, with frequent trains from Newcastle.

The aptly named AD122 public bus runs between Newcastle and Carlisle during the summer months, stopping near all the major destinations along the way. A special Hadrian's Wall Bus offers "rover ticket" passes that give you unlimited travel on the route for one (£12) or three (£24) days. You can extend the tickets to cover any bus operating on the same route for a few extra pounds. Several other local buses depart from Newcastle and other towns in the region to various parts of the wall.

ESSENTIALS

Visitor Information Hadrian's Wall Country Bus. ☎ *0191/4205050* 🌐 *www.simplygo.com/all-services/ad122.*

EXPLORING

Fodor's Choice ★ **Hadrian's Wall.** Dedicated to the Roman god Terminus, the massive span of Hadrian's Wall once marked the northern frontier of the Roman Empire. Today, remnants of the wall wander across pastures and hills, stretching 73 miles from Wallsend in the east to Bowness-on-Solway in the west. The wall is a World Heritage Site, and excavating, interpreting, repairing, and generally managing it remains a Northumbrian growth industry. ■ **TIP→ Chesters, Housesteads, Vindolanda, and the Roman Army Museum near Greenhead give you a good introduction to the life led by Roman soldiers.** In summer there are talks, plays, and festivals; local tourist offices have details.

At Emperor Hadrian's command, three legions of soldiers began building the wall in AD 122 and finished it in four years. It was constructed by soldiers and masons after repeated invasions by troublesome Pictish tribes from what is now Scotland. During the Roman era it was the most heavily fortified wall in the world, with walls 15 feet high and 9 feet thick; behind it lay the vallum, a ditch about 20 feet wide and 10 feet deep. Spaced at 5-mile intervals along the wall were massive forts (such as those at Housesteads and Chesters), which could house up to 1,000 soldiers. Every mile was marked by a thick-walled milecastle (a fort that housed about 30 soldiers), and between each milecastle were two turrets, each lodging four men who kept watch. For more than 250 years the Roman army used the wall to control travel and trade and to fortify Roman Britain against the barbarians to the north.

During the Jacobite Rebellion of 1745, the English army dismantled much of the Roman wall and used the stones to pave what is now the B6318 highway. The most substantial stretches of the remaining wall are between Housesteads and Birdoswald (west of Greenhead). Running through the southern edge of Northumberland National Park and along the sheer escarpment of Whin Sill, this section is also an area of dramatic natural beauty. The ancient ruins, rugged cliffs, dramatic vistas, and spreading pastures make it a great area for hiking. 🌐 *www.visithadrianswall.co.uk.*

SPORTS AND THE OUTDOORS

BIKING

The Bike Place. Here mountain bike rentals start at £25 per day. ✉ *1 King St., Bellingham* ☎ *01434/220210* 🌐 *www.thebikeplace.co.uk.*

Hadrian's Cycleway. Between Tynemouth and Whitehaven, Hadrian's Cycleway follows the River Tyne from the east coast until Newcastle, where it traces the entire length of Hadrian's Wall. It then continues west to the Irish Sea. Maps and guides are available at the Tourist Information Centre in Newcastle. 🌐 *www.cycle-routes.org/hadrianscycleway.*

HIKING

Hadrian's Wall Path. One of Britain's national trails, Hadrian's Wall Path runs the entire 73-mile length of the wall. If you don't have time for it all, take one of the less-challenging circular routes. One of the most scenic but also most difficult sections is the 12-mile western stretch between Sewingshields and Greenhead. 🌐 *www.nationaltrail.co.uk/hadrianswall.*

HEXHAM

22 miles west of Newcastle, 31 miles northwest of Durham.

The area around the busy market town of Hexham is a popular base for visiting Hadrian's Wall. Just a few miles from the most significant remains, it's a bustling working town, but it has enough historic buildings and winding medieval streets to warrant a stop in its own right. First settled in the 7th century, around a Benedictine monastery, Hexham later became a byword for monastic learning, famous for its book painting, sculpture, and singing.

GETTING HERE AND AROUND

The A1 highway links London and the region (five to six hours). No major bus companies travel here, but the AD122 tourist bus from Newcastle and Carlisle does. East Coast trains take about three hours to travel from London's King's Cross to Newcastle. From there, catch a local train.

Hexham is a small, walkable town. It has infrequent local bus service, but you're unlikely to need it. If you're driving, park in the lot by the tourism office and walk into town. The tourism office has free maps and will point you in the right direction.

ESSENTIALS

Visitor Information Hexham Tourism Information Centre. ✉ *Wentworth Car Park, Wentworth Pl.* ☎ *01434/652220* 🌐 *www.visitnorthumberland.com.*

EXPLORING

Birdoswald Roman Fort. Beside the longest unbroken stretch of Hadrian's Wall, Birdoswald Roman Fort reveals the remains of gatehouses, a granary, and a parade ground. You can also see the line of the original turf wall, later rebuilt in stone. Birdoswald has a unique historical footnote: unlike other Roman forts along the wall, it was maintained by local tribes long after being abandoned by the Romans. The small visitor center has artifacts discovered at the site, a full-scale model of the wall, and a good café. ✉ *Wallace Dr., Ravenglass* ☎ *01697/747602* 🌐 *www.hadrians-wall.org* 🎫 *£5.70* ⏲ *Nov.–Mar. and Oct., weekends 10–4; Apr.–Sept., daily 10–5:30.*

Fodor's Choice ★ **Chesters Roman Fort.** In a wooded valley on the banks of the North Tyne River, this cavalry fort was known as Cilurnum in Roman times, when it protected the point where Hadrian's Wall crossed the river. Although the site cannot compete with Housesteads for its setting, the museum holds a fascinating collection of Roman artifacts, including statues of river and water gods, altars, milestones, iron tools, weapons, and jewelry. The military bathhouse by the river is supposedly the best-preserved Roman structure of its kind in the British Isles. The fort is 4 miles north of Hexham. ✉ *B6318, Chollerford* ☎ *01434/681379* 🌐 *www.english-heritage.org.uk* 🎫 *£5.70* ⏲ *Apr.–Oct., daily 10–6; Nov.–Mar., weekends 10–4.*

Fodor's Choice ★ **Hexham Abbey.** A site of Christian worship for more than 1,300 years, ancient Hexham Abbey forms one side of the town's main square. Inside, you can climb the 35 worn stone "night stairs," which once led from the main part of the abbey to the canon's dormitory, to overlook the whole ensemble. Most of the current building dates from the 12th and 13th centuries, and much of the stone, including that of the Anglo-Saxon crypt, was taken from the Roman fort at Corbridge. Note the portraits on the 16th-century wooden rood screen and the four panels from a 15th-century *Dance of Death* in the sanctuary. In September, the abbey hosts the renowned Festival of Music and the Arts, which hosts classical musicians from around the world. ✉ *Beaumont St.* ☎ *01434/602031* 🌐 *www.hexhamabbey.org.uk* 🎫 *Free; requested donation £3* ⏲ *Daily 9:30–5.*

Hexham Market Place. Since 1239, this has been the site of a weekly market, held each Tuesday and Saturday. Crowded stalls are set out across the square under colored awnings, attracting serious shoppers and souvenir hunters year-round. A popular farmers' market takes over on the second and fourth Saturday of the month. ✉ *Market Pl.* ☎ *01670/625577.*

FAMILY **Old Gaol.** Dating from 1330, Hexham's Old Gaol houses fascinating exhibits about the history of the borderlands, including tales of the terrifying "reavers" and their bloodthirsty raids into Northumberland from Scotland during the 16th and 17th centuries. Photographs, weapons, and a reconstructed house interior give a full account of what the region was like in medieval times. A glass elevator takes you to four floors, including the dungeon. ✉ *Hallgate* ☎ *01434/652349* 🌐 *www.hexhamoldgaol.org.uk* 🎫 *£4* ⏲ *Apr.–Sept., Tues.–Sat. and bank holiday Mon. 11–4:30; Oct., Nov., Feb., and Mar., Tues. and Sat. 11–4:30.*

WHERE TO EAT AND STAY

$$$$ BRITISH Fodor's Choice ★ ✕ **Langley Castle.** This lavish 14th-century castle with turrets and battlements offers an elegant fine-dining experience. The baronial dining room is romantic, with little candlelit alcoves draped in rich fabric. Choose from an excellent five-course prix-fixe menu of traditional

English dishes with hints of Asian influence—perhaps the mutton served with miso broth and lobster wonton, or the halibut with samphire and razor clams. There's also a lighter (and cheaper) snack menu, and they do a lavish afternoon tea. If you're really taken with the place, rooms start at around £55 per night. Langley Castle is 6 miles west of Hexham. *Average main: £48 A686, Langley-on-Tyne 01434/688888 www.langleycastle.com.*

$$ B&B/INN **Battlesteads Hotel.** On the outer edge of Hexham, this delightful old inn combines three virtues: good food, cozy rooms, and eco-friendly credentials, with a string of awards to prove it. **Pros:** lovely staff; good food; green ethos. **Cons:** some rooms on the small side; no mobile phone reception. *Rooms from: £115 Wark on Tyne 01434/230209 www.battlesteads.com 17 rooms Breakfast.*

$ B&B/INN **Dene House.** This peaceful stone farmhouse on 9 acres of lovely countryside has beamed ceilings and homey rooms with pine furniture and colorful quilts. **Pros:** tasty breakfasts; warm atmosphere; reasonable rates. **Cons:** no restaurant. *Rooms from: £70 B6303, Juniper 01434/673413 www.denehouse-hexham.co.uk No credit cards 3 rooms, 1 with bath Breakfast.*

SPORTS AND THE OUTDOORS

The Bike Place. This shop in Kielder is the nearest cycle hire shop to Hexham (outside of Newcastle-upon-Tyne itself). Prices start at £25 per day and they can arrange delivery and collection for an extra fee. Kielder is 30 miles north of Hexham; take A6079 from the main A69 road. The shop is clearly signposted on the main road through the village. *Station Garage, Kielder 01434/250457 www.thebikeplace.co.uk.*

NIGHTLIFE AND PERFORMING ARTS

Queen's Hall Arts Centre. Theater, dance, and art exhibitions are on the bill at the Queen's Hall Arts Centre. *Beaumont St. 01434/652477 www.queenshall.co.uk.*

GREENHEAD

18 miles west of Hexham, 49 miles northwest of Durham.

In and around tiny Greenhead you'll find a wealth of historical sites related to Hadrian's Wall, including the fascinating Housesteads Roman Fort, the Roman Army Museum, and the archaeologically rich Vindolanda. In Northumberland National Park, about half a mile north of Vindolanda, the Once Brewed National Park Visitor Centre has informative displays about Hadrian's Wall and can advise about local walks.

GETTING HERE AND AROUND

Greenhead is on the A69 and B6318. The nearest train station is 3 miles east, in Haltwhistle.

ESSENTIALS

Visitor Information Once Brewed National Park Visitor Centre. *Northumberland National Park, Military Rd., Bardon Mill 01434/344396 www.northumberlandnationalpark.org.uk.*

EXPLORING

Fodor's Choice ★ **Housesteads Roman Fort.** If you have time to visit only one Hadrian's Wall site, Housesteads Roman Fort, Britain's most complete example of a Roman fort, is your best bet. It includes long sections of the wall, an excavated fort, and a new visitor center with a collection of artifacts discovered at the site and computer-generated images of what the fort originally looked like. The fort itself is a 10-minute walk uphill from the parking lot (not for those with mobility problems), but the effort is worth it to see the surprisingly extensive ruins, dating from around AD 125. Excavations have revealed the remains of granaries, gateways, barracks, a hospital, and the commandant's house. **■TIP→ The northern tip of the fort, at the crest of the hill, has one of the best views of Hadrian's Wall, passing beside you before disappearing over hills and crags in the distance.** ✉ *B6318, Haydon Bridge* ☎ *01434/344363* 🌐 *www.english-heritage.org.uk* 🎫 *£6.60* ⏲ *Apr.–Oct., daily 10–6; Nov.–Mar., daily 10–4.*

FAMILY Fodor's Choice ★ **Roman Army Museum.** At the garrison fort of Carvoran, this museum makes an excellent introduction to Hadrian's Wall. Full-size models and excavations bring this remote outpost of the empire to life; authentic Roman graffiti adorns the walls of an excavated barracks. There's a well-designed museum with Roman artifacts and a flashy 3D film that puts it all into historical context. Opposite the museum, at Walltown Crags on the Pennine Way (one of Britain's long-distance national hiking trails), are 400 yards of the best-preserved section of the wall. The museum is 1 mile northeast of Greenhead. ✉ *Off B6318* ☎ *01697/747485* 🌐 *www.vindolanda.com* 🎫 *£7; £10.50 with admission to Vindolanda* ⏲ *Mid-Feb–Mar. and Oct., daily 9:30–5; Apr.–Sept., daily 10–6.*

Fodor's Choice ★ **Vindolanda.** About 8 miles east of Greenhead, this archaeological site holds the remains of eight successive Roman forts and civilian settlements, providing an intriguing look into the daily life of a military compound. Most of the visible remains date from the 2nd and 3rd centuries, and new excavations are constantly under way. A reconstructed Roman temple, house, and shop provide context, and the museum displays rare artifacts, such as a handful of extraordinary wooden tablets with messages about everything from household chores to military movements. A full-size reproduction of a section of the wall gives a sense of its massiveness. The site is sometimes closed in bad weather. ✉ *Off B6318, Bardon Mill* ☎ *01434/344277* 🌐 *www.vindolanda.com* 🎫 *£7; £10.50 includes admission to Roman Army Museum* ⏲ *Mid-Feb–Mar. and Oct., daily 9:30–5; Apr.–Sept., daily 10–6.*

WHERE TO EAT AND STAY

$ BRITISH ✕ **Milecastle Inn.** The snug bar and restaurant of this remote, peaceful 17th-century pub make an excellent place to dine. Fine local meat goes into its famous pies; take your pick from wild boar and duckling pie, or maybe a plate of Whitby scampi with chips. The unfussy menu also features such staples as fish-and-chips or lasagna with garlic bread. Two cottages are available for rent. The inn is on the north side of Haltwhistle on B6318. 💲 *Average main: £12* ✉ *Military Rd., Haltwhistle* ☎ *01434/321372* 🌐 *www.milecastle-inn.co.uk.*

The rose displays at Alnwick Garden have a romantic view of nearby Alnwick Castle.

$ B&B/INN **Holmhead Guest House.** Talk about a feel for history—this former farmhouse in open countryside, graced with stone arches and exposed beams, is not only built *on* Hadrian's Wall but also partly *from* it. **Pros:** full of atmosphere; close to Hadrian's Wall; reasonable rates. **Cons:** rooms are a bit of a squeeze; you need a car out here. *Rooms from: £72* *Off A69* *016977/47402* *www.bandbhadrianswall.com* *No credit cards* *4 rooms, 8 beds, 1 apartment* *Breakfast.*

MORPETH

15 miles north of Newcastle, 20 miles south of Alnwick.

Surrounded by idyllic pastures and tiny lanes, the hilly medieval market town of Morpeth is the closest thing this part of Northumberland comes to bustling. It's an ideal stop while visiting some of the region's more hidden-away sights to the north of Newcastle.

GETTING HERE AND AROUND

Just off the A1, Morpeth is easily reached by car. Trains leave Newcastle every hour and take 22 minutes. Buses X14, X15, X18, and 44 connect Newcastle and Morpeth, and the journey takes around 40 minutes.

ESSENTIALS

Visitor Information Morpeth Tourist Information Centre. *The Chantry, Bridge St.* *01670/623455* *www.visitnorthumberland.com.*

EXPLORING

Brinkburn Priory. A fine historical anecdote concerns this idyllic Augustinian priory, founded in the early 12th century. A group of Scottish "reivers" came looking for the place to raid and loot it, but because it was entirely hidden by forest, they were unable to find it and gave up. The monks were so happy that they sounded the bells in celebration, thus revealing the location—and the Scots promptly returned and sacked the place. Most of the beautiful, light-filled building is the result of a Victorian restoration, though elements of the original remain. On the same site is a mill and a 19th-century manor house, which incorporates the undercroft from the former monk's refrectory. Classical music concerts are held here throughout the year. **■TIP➔ The walk from the car park takes 10 minutes, but those with mobility problems can drive all the way down.** ✉ *Off B6344* ☎ *01665/570628* 🌐 *www.english-heritage.org.uk* 🎫 *£3.80* 🕒 *Apr.–Oct., Thurs.–Mon. 11–4.*

FAMILY Fodor's Choice ★ **Cragside.** The turrets and towers of Tudor-style Cragside, a Victorian country house, look out over the edge of a forested hillside. It was built between 1864 and 1895 by Lord Armstrong, an early electrical engineer and inventor, and designed by Richard Norman Shaw, a well-regarded architect. Among Armstrong's contemporaries Cragside was called "the palace of a modern magician" because it contained so many of his inventions. This was the first house in the world to be lighted by hydroelectricity; the grounds also hold an energy center with restored mid-Victorian machinery. There are Pre-Raphaelite paintings and an elaborate mock-Renaissance marble chimneypiece. The gardens, including a huge rock garden and a sculpture trail, are as impressive as the house; in June rhododendrons bloom in the 660-acre park surrounding the mansion. There's also a children's adventure playground. **■TIP➔ Paths around the grounds are steep and distances can be long, so wear comfortable shoes.** ✉ *Off A697 and B6341, Rothbury* ☎ *01669/620333* 🌐 *www.nationaltrust.org.uk* 🎫 *Grounds and house £15; grounds only £9.70, in winter £5.40* 🕒 *House Mar.–mid-July and Sept.–late Oct., Tues.–Fri. 1–5, weekends 11–5; mid-July–Aug., daily 11–5. Grounds Mar.–Oct., Tues.–Sun. 10–7; Nov.–late Dec., Fri.–Sun. 11–4.*

WHERE TO EAT AND STAY

$ DELI ✕ **Central Bean Coffee House.** There's a distinct Pacific Northwest vibe at this funky little independent eatery in central Morpeth. Locals flock to the place for fresh sandwiches, paninis, cakes, or just a fine cup of joe. $ *Average main: £6* ✉ *21 Sandersone Arcade* ☎ *01670/512300* 🌐 *www.centralbean.co.uk* 💳 *No credit cards* 🕒 *No dinner.*

$ HOTEL 🏨 **Macdonald Linden Hall.** Built as a getaway for a wealthy banker in 1812, this secluded country estate is surrounded by 450 acres of private grounds. **Pros:** secluded location; soothing spa; gorgeous original building. **Cons:** can feel dominated by large tour groups; popular wedding venue in summer. $ *Rooms from: £89* ✉ *Off A697, Longhorsley* ☎ *0844/879–9084* 🌐 *www.macdonaldhotels.co.uk* 🛏 *50 rooms* 🍽 *Some meals.*

$ B&B/INN Fodor's Choice ★ 🏨 **Shieldhall Guesthouse.** This lovely 19th-century farmhouse was once home to the family of the legendary landscaper Capability Brown; today it's surrounded by acres of rolling farmland and an ideal base if you want to explore remote stretches of Hadrian's Wall. **Pros:** lots of peace and quiet; discounts for shorter stays; dinners are exceptional. **Cons:** well outside town; need a car to get around. $ *Rooms from: £98* ✉ *Off*

B6342, Wallington ☎ *01830/540387* 🌐 *www.shieldhallguesthouse.co.uk* 🛏 *3 rooms* 🍽 *Breakfast.*

$$ B&B/INN Fodor's Choice ★ **Thistleyhaugh.** This ivy-covered stone farmhouse sits at the center of a 720-acre organic farm. **Pros:** idyllic farmhouse location; wonderful hosts; excellent food. **Cons:** isolated location means you can't get around without a car. $ *Rooms from: £100* ✉ *Off A697, Longframlington* ☎ *01665/570629* 🌐 *www.thistleyhaugh.co.uk* ⏱ *No dinner Sun.* 🛏 *5 rooms* 🍽 *Breakfast.*

13

THE FAR NORTHEAST COAST

Extraordinary medieval fortresses and monasteries line the final 40 miles of the Northeast coast before England gives way to Scotland. Northumbria was an enclave where the flame of learning was kept alive during Europe's Dark Ages, most notably at Lindisfarne, home of saints and scholars. Castles abound, including the spectacularly sited Bamburgh and the desolate Dunstanburgh. The region also has some magnificent beaches, though because of the cold water and rough seas they're far better for walking than swimming. The 3-mile walk from Seahouses to Bamburgh gives splendid views of the Farne Islands, and the 2-mile hike from Craster to Dunstanburgh Castle is unforgettable. A bit inland are a few other pretty towns and castles.

ALNWICK

30 miles north of Newcastle, 46 miles north of Durham.

Dominated by a grand castle, the little market town of Alnwick (pronounced *ahn*-ick) is the best base from which to explore the dramatic coast and countryside of northern Northumberland.

GETTING HERE AND AROUND

If you're driving, Alnwick is just off the A1. Buses X15 and X18 connect Alnwick with Newcastle, Berwick, and Morpeth. The nearest train station is 4 miles away in Alnmouth (pronounced *alun*-mowth); trains travel between here and Newcastle roughly every hour and take 30 minutes.

ESSENTIALS

Visitor Information Visit Alnwick. ✉ *2 The Shambles* ☎ *01670/622152* 🌐 *www.visitalnwick.org.uk.*

EXPLORING

FAMILY Fodor's Choice ★ **Alnwick Castle.** Sometimes called the "Windsor of the North," the imposing Alnwick Castle is more familiar to many as a location in the Harry Potter movies. (The castle grounds appear as the exterior of Hogwarts School.) The building is still home to the dukes of Northumberland, whose family, the Percys, dominated in the Northeast for centuries. Family photos and other knickknacks are scattered around the lavish staterooms, a subtle but pointed reminder that this is a family home rather than a museum. Highlights include the extroardinary gun room, lined with hundreds of antique pistols in swirling patterns; the formal dining room, its table set as if guests are due at any minute; and the

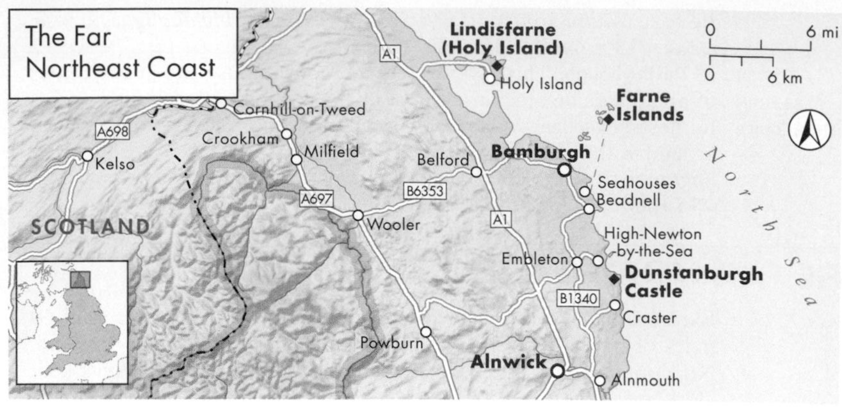

magnificent galleried library, containing 14,000 books in floor-to-ceiling cases.

There's plenty here for younger visitors: **Knights' Quest** lets kids dress up and complete interactive challenges; **Dragon's Quest** is a labyrinth designed to teach a bit of medieval history; and for the very young, there are Harry Potter–style events on certain dates, including **Broomstick Lessons** on the exact spot used in the movie (check website for schedule). Spooky ghost stories are told by costumed actors in the **Lost Cellars.** In addition, the staff hides a toy owl somewhere in each room of the castle, and kids get a certificate if they spot them all. Tickets are valid for one year, so you can come back if you don't see everything in a day. ✉ *Narrowgate* ☎ *01665/511350* 🌐 *www.alnwickcastle.com* 🎫 *£15.50; combined ticket with Alnwick Gardens £27* ⏲ *Late Mar.–late Oct., 10–5:30 (last entry 4:15); Knight's Quest and Dragon Quest 10–5; State Rooms 10:30–4:30 (last entry 4; castle chapel closes 3).*

FAMILY Fodor's Choice ★ **Alnwick Garden.** A marvelous flight of fancy, Alnwick Garden was designed by Capability Brown in 1750. Centering on modern terraced fountains by Belgian designers Jacques and Peter Wirtz, the gardens include traditional features (shaded woodland walks, a rose garden) and funkier, kid-appealing elements such as a Poison Garden and a labyrinth of towering bamboo. ■ **TIP→ You can buy clippings of the unique varieties of roses in the shop.** Opening and closing times are subject to change due to season and weather, so call ahead. This is also the location of one of the area's most unique restaurants, the Treehouse. ✉ *Denwick La.* ☎ *01665/511350* 🌐 *www.alnwickgarden.com* 🎫 *£14; combined ticket with Alnwick Castle £24* ⏲ *Late Mar.–Oct., daily 10–6; Nov.–Jan., daily 11–5; Feb.–late Mar., daily noon–6. Last admission 45 min before closing.*

WHERE TO EAT AND STAY

$$ BRITISH Fodor's Choice ★ ✕ **The Treehouse.** You don't have to visit Alnwick Garden to eat at this extraordinary restaurant set among the treetops. The location may sound gimmicky, but the effect is quite magical, especially when the place is lit up at night. The modern British fare is excellent—Northumbrian lamb

It's worth the scenic coastal walk to see the remote cliff-top ruins of Dunstanburgh Castle.

with smoked cheddar and potato gratin, perhaps, or monkfish wrapped in Parma ham. From July to September, the kitchen only serves prix-fixe menus at night; the rest of the year there's an à la carte selection. You can grab a light lunch or tea and cake at the Potting Shed bar, which is also open for predinner drinks. *Average main: £18 Alnwick Garden, Denwick La. 01665/511852 www.alnwickgarden.com/eat No dinner Mon.–Wed.*

$ B&B/INN Fodor's Choice ★ **Redfoot Lea.** This cozy farmhouse B&B, a couple of miles from Alnwick Castle, is an oasis of contemporary style and homespun charm. **Pros:** beautifully restored farmhouse; truly welcoming hosts. **Cons:** one room has twin beds; located just outside of town (the center is a 2-mile walk away). *Rooms from: £90 Greensfield Moor Farm, off A1 01665/603891 www.redfootlea.co.uk 2 rooms Breakfast.*

DUNSTANBURGH CASTLE

8 miles northeast of Alnwick.

Dunstanburgh is as dramatic an old ruin as they come, and more than worth the effort it takes to get here (this is not the kind of place where you can just drive up to the front gate).

GETTING HERE AND AROUND

The castle is accessible only by footpaths from the villages of Craster or Embleton off the B1339 rural road. The X18 bus from Alnwick is the only practical connection by public transportation; get off in Craster and head to the main public parking lot (the village is small enough that it's easy to find). The coastal path starts here. It's clearly signposted and a beautiful route, but quite a hike at around 1½ miles each way.

EXPLORING

Dunstanburgh Castle. Perched romantically on a cliff 100 feet above the shore, these castle ruins can be reached along a windy, mile-long coastal footpath that heads north from the tiny fishing village of Craster. Built in 1316 as a defense against the Scots, and later enlarged by John of Gaunt, the powerful Duke of Lancaster who virtually ruled England in the late 14th century, the castle is known to many from the popular paintings by 19th-century artist J.M.W. Turner. The castle is a signposted 1.3-mile walk from the nearest parking lot in Craster, on the outskirts of Alnwick. ✉ *Windside Hill, Alnwick* ☎ *01665/576231* 🌐 *www.english-heritage.org.uk* 🎫 *£4.60* 🕐 *Apr.–Sept., daily 10–5; Oct.–Mar., weekends 10–4. Last admission 30 min before closing.*

FARNE ISLANDS

7 miles north of Craster, 13 miles northeast of Alnwick.

Owned by the National Trust, these bleak, wind-tossed islands are home to several seabirds, including puffins and guillemots.

EXPLORING

Farne Islands. Regular boat trips from the little village of Seahouses provide access to the Farne Islands with their impressive colonies of seabirds, including puffins, kittiwakes, terns, shags, and guillemots, and barking groups of gray seals. Inner Farne, where St. Cuthbert, the great abbot of Lindisfarne, died in AD 687, has a tiny chapel. Look out for the ruined lighthouse beacons as you pass Brownsman Island. Four boats are currently licensed to make the trip to Farne and the other islands. Of these, **Glad Tidings** (*01665/720308* 🌐 *www.farne-islands.com*) has the most reliable advertised schedule; they cruise to Inner Farne in April, August, September, and October, daily on the hour from 10 to 3; and in May to July from noon to 3. They also visit the rocky Staple Island May to July, daily at 10, 11, and noon. Cruises to each cost £15 and take 2½ to 3½ hours, including an hour's landfall (in good weather only). The other operators are **Golden Gate** (*01665/721210* 🌐 *www.farneislandsboattrips.co.uk*), **Serenity** (*01665/721667* 🌐 *www.farneislandstours.co.uk*), and **St. Cuthbert** (*01665/720388* 🌐 *www.farneislands.co.uk*); call or check online for their daily schedules. All boat services leave from Seahouses harbor—look for the tiny booth selling tickets or the outlet in the main village parking lot. Each company offers a variety of other cruises, such as seal-spotting expeditions. Visit the individual websites to see what's on offer this season. ✉ *The Harbour, Seahouses* ☎ *01665/721099 National Trust, 01665/720308 for boat trips (Billy Shiel's Boats)* 🌐 *www.farne-islands.com* 🎫 *Landing fees £6* 🕐 *Boat trips Apr.–Oct., daily, weather permitting.*

BAMBURGH

14 miles north of Alnwick.

Tiny Bamburgh has a splendid castle, and several beaches are a few minutes' walk away.

GETTING HERE AND AROUND

Bamburgh can be reached by car on B3140, B3141, or B3142. Buses X18 and 418 run from Alnwick to Bamburgh a few times per day. The nearest train station is in Chathill, about 7 miles away.

EXPLORING

Fodor's Choice ★ **Bamburgh Castle.** You'll see Bamburgh Castle long before you reach it: a solid, weatherbeaten clifftop fortress that dominates the coastal view for miles around. A fortification of some kind has stood here since the 6th century, but the Norman castle was damaged during the 15th century and the central tower is all that remains intact. Much of the structure—the home of the Armstrong family since 1894—was restored during the 18th and 19th centuries. The interior is mostly late Victorian (most impressively, the Great Hall), although a few rooms, such as the small but alarmingly well-stocked armory, have a more authentically medieval feel. The breathtaking view across the North Sea is worth the trip; bring a picnic if the weather's good (or order to-go sandwiches at the café). ✉ *Off B1340* ☎ *01668/214515* 🌐 *www.bamburghcastle.com* 🎫 *£10.50* 🕒 *Early Feb.–Oct., daily 10–5; Nov.–early Feb., weekends 11–4:30; last admission 1 hr before closing.*

WHERE TO EAT AND STAY

$$$$ BRITISH ✕ **Waren House Hotel.** Six acres of woodland surround this Georgian house on a quiet bay between Bamburgh and Holy Island. The crisply elegant restaurant has romantic views of Holy Island when the trees are bare. Three-course fixed-price dinners might include haddock with white crab Hollandaise or local beef fillet with parsley roast vegetables, perhaps followed by apple, rhubarb, and walnut crumble. The public areas are comfortably furnished in period style, and there are 13 guest rooms (£100, including dinner) if you want to linger overnight. [$] *Average main: £42* ✉ *B1342, Waren Mill* ☎ *01668/214581* 🌐 *www.warenhousehotel.co.uk.*

$ HOTEL **Lord Crewe Hotel.** This cozy, stone-walled inn with oak beams sits in the heart of the village, close to Bamburgh Castle. **Pros:** in the center of the village; good restaurant. **Cons:** pub can get quite crowded. [$] *Rooms from: £98* ✉ *Front St.* ☎ *01668/214243* 🌐 *www.lord-crewe.co.uk* *18 rooms* *Breakfast.*

LINDISFARNE (HOLY ISLAND)

6 miles north of Bamburgh off the A1, 22 miles north of Alnwick.

Cradle of northern England's Christianity and home of St. Cuthbert, Lindisfarne (or Holy Island) has a religious history that dates from AD 635, when St. Aidan established a monastery here. Under its greatest abbot, the sainted Cuthbert, Lindisfarne became one of the foremost centers of learning in Christendom. Today you can explore the atmospheric ruined priory and a castle.

GETTING HERE AND AROUND

By car the island is reached from the mainland via a long drive on a causeway that floods at high tide, so check when crossing is safe. The times, which change daily, are displayed at the causeway and printed in local newspapers. Traffic can be heavy; allow at least a half hour for your return trip. The only public transportation to Holy Island is run by Perryman's Buses. Bus 477 has limited service (a few buses per day, and not every day) from Berwick-upon-Tweed railway station to the island.

ESSENTIALS

Bus Contacts **Perryman's Buses.** ☎ *01289/308719* 🌐 *www.perrymansbuses.co.uk.*

EXPLORING

Lindisfarne Castle. Reached during low tide via a causeway from the mainland, this castle appears to grow out of the rocky pinnacle on which it was built 400 years ago, looking for all the world like a fairy-tale illustration. In 1903 architect Sir Edwin Lutyens converted the former Tudor fort into a private home that retains the original's ancient features. Across several fields from the castle is a walled garden designed by Gertrude Jekyll. Opening times are notoriously changeable—especially on Mondays outside of mid-summer—and are always dependant on weather and tides, so it's best to call ahead. ✉ *Marygate, Lindisfarne, Berwick-upon-Tweed* ☎ *01289/389244* 🌐 *www.nationaltrust.org.uk* 🎫 *£7.80* ⏲ *Castle mid-Feb.–Oct., Tues.–Sun. and occasional Mon. (every Mon. in Aug.) 10–3; last admission 30 min before closing.*

Fodor's Choice ★ **Lindisfarne Priory.** In the year 875, Vikings destroyed the Lindisfarne community; only a few monks escaped, carrying with them Cuthbert's bones, which were reburied in Durham Cathedral. The sandstone Norman ruins of Lindisfarne Priory, reestablished in the 11th century, remain impressive and beautiful. A museum here displays Anglo-Saxon carvings. ✉ *Prior La., Lindisfarne* ☎ *01289/389200* 🌐 *www.english-heritage.org.uk* 🎫 *£5.60* ⏲ *Apr.–Sept., daily 9:30–5; Oct., daily 9:30–4; Nov.–Mar., weekends 10–4.*

14

WALES

WELCOME TO WALES

TOP REASONS TO GO

★ **Castle country:** Wales doesn't quite have a castle in each town, but there is a greater concentration than almost anywhere else in Europe—more than 600 in all.

★ **The Gower Peninsula:** This stretch of coastland near Swansea includes some of the region's prettiest beaches, as well as spectacular coastal views and medieval ruins.

★ **Snowdonia:** The biggest of the country's three national parks contains its highest mountain, Snowdon, as well as picture-perfect villages.

★ **Brecon Beacons:** Moorlands, mountains, and valleys make up this rough and wild stretch of the Welsh midlands, as popular with hikers as it is with those who are just happy to take in the stunning views from the road.

★ **Hay-on-Wye:** This pretty village on the Welsh-English border has become world-famous as a book lover's paradise; every street is lined with secondhand bookstores.

GETTING ORIENTED

Wales has three main regions: South, Mid-, and North. South Wales is the most varied, and in just a few miles you can travel from Wales's bustling and cosmopolitan capital city, Cardiff, to the most enchanting old villages and historical sights. Mid-Wales is almost entirely rural (its largest town has a population of just 16,000), and it's fringed on its western shores by the arc of Cardigan Bay. Here you'll find mountain lakes, quiet roads, hillside sheep farms, and traditional market towns. North Wales is a mixture of mountains, popular sandy beaches, and coastal hideaways. Although dominated by rocky Snowdonia National Park, the north has a gentler, greener side along the border with England.

1 South Wales. Cardiff, the lively young capital city, is here, as are two very different national parks: the green, swooping hills of the Brecon Beacons and, in the far west, the sea cliffs, beaches, and estuaries of the Pembrokeshire Coast. Both are excellent for outdoor activities such as walking and mountain biking. Pembrokeshire has some of the region's best beaches.

2 Mid-Wales. The quietest part of Wales is home to scenic countryside, from rolling hills to more rugged mountains. Aberystwyth is a Victorian resort town on the coast, and Hay-on-Wye is a magnet for lovers of antiquarian bookstores.

3 North Wales. Wales's most famous castles are in its northern region. The cream of the crop is Caernarfon, a medieval palace dominating the waterfront on the Menai Strait. Conwy (castle and town) is popular, too. Snowdonia's mountains are a major draw, as is the quirky, faux-Italian village of Portmeirion.

14

CASTLES IN WALES

You can't go far in Wales without seeing a castle: there are more than 600 of them. From crumbling ruins in fields to vast medieval fortresses with rich and violent histories, these castles rank among the most impressive in the world.

(above) The marquess of Bute transformed Cardiff Castle into a Victorian extravaganza; (right, top) Caerphilly Castle's romantic moat; (right, bottom) Raglan Castle's impressive ruins

The first great wave of castle building arrived in England with the Norman Conquest in 1066. When the descendants of those first Anglo-Norman kings invaded Wales 200 years later, they brought with them their awesome skill and expertise. Through deviousness and brutal force, King Edward I (1239–1307) won control over the Welsh lords in the north and wasted no time in building mighty castles, including Caerphilly and Conwy, to consolidate his power. These became known as his "ring of iron." Wars came and went over the next few centuries, until, rendered obsolete by gunpowder and the changing ways of warfare, castles were destroyed or fell into disrepair. Only in the Victorian age, when castles became hugely fashionable, was there widespread acceptance of how important it was to save these historic structures for the nation.

CASTLE GLOSSARY

Bailey: open grounds within a castle's walls.

Battlements: fortified ledge atop castle walls.

Keep: largest, most heavily defended castle building.

Moat: water-filled ditch around castle.

Motte: steep man-made hill on which a castle was often built.

Portcullis: iron drop-gate over entrance.

With such a dizzying array of castles, it can be hard to know where to start. Here are six of the best to help you decide. At the larger sites, buy a guidebook or take an audio or other tour so that you can best appreciate the remains of a distant era.

CAERNARFON CASTLE

Welsh naturalist Thomas Pennant (1726–98) called Caernarfon Castle "that most magnificent badge of our subjection." Built in 1283 on the site of an earlier castle, it's the most significant symbol of Edward I's conquest of Wales. It's also the best preserved of his "ring of iron" and, along with Edward's Beaumaris, Harlech, and Conwy castles in North Wales, is a UNESCO World Heritage Site. *North Wales*

CAERPHILLY CASTLE

Near Cardiff, this is the largest castle in Wales and the second largest in Britain after Windsor Castle. Caerphilly's defenses included a man-made island and two huge lakes. The castle was ruined by centuries of warfare, although modern renovations have recaptured much of its former glory. Kids love it. *South Wales*

CARDIFF CASTLE

Though the capital's titular castle has medieval sections, most of it is, in fact, a Victorian flight of fancy. Its most famous occupant, the third marquess of Bute (1847–1900), was once the richest man in the world, and his love of the exotic led to the bizarre mishmash of styles. *South Wales*

CARREG CENNEN CASTLE

The great views over the countryside are worth the steep hike to this bleak, craggy cliff-top fortress in the Brecon Beacons. This medieval stronghold was partially destroyed during the Wars of the Roses in the 15th century. Some interior rooms, hollowed out from the mountain itself, survive intact. *South Wales*

CONWY CASTLE

Imposing, if partially ruined, Conwy Castle with its eight towers captures like no other the feeling of sheer dominance that Edward I's citadels must have had over the landscape. The approach by foot over the River Conwy, along a 19th-century suspension bridge designed by Thomas Telford, makes for an awesome view. You can walk the ancient walls of Conwy town, which has places to eat and shop. *North Wales*

RAGLAN CASTLE

The boyhood home of Henry VII, the first Tudor king, Raglan is a small but impressive 15th-century castle, surrounded by a steep moat (one of the few in Wales that's still filled with water). Largely a ruin, it's relatively complete from the front, making for some irresistible, fairy-tale photo ops. *South Wales*

14

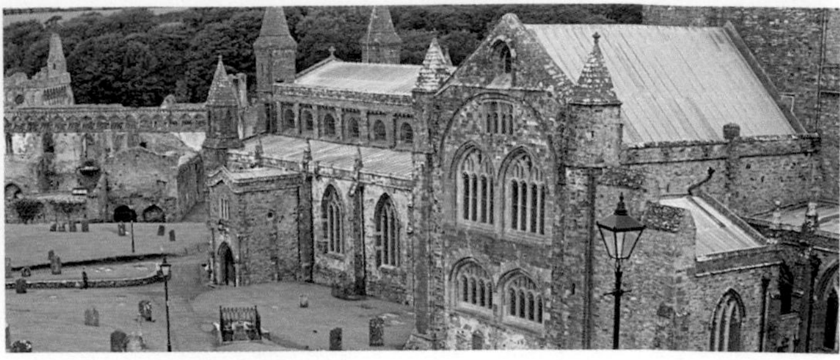

Updated by Jack Jewers

Wales is a land of dramatic national parks, plunging, unspoiled coastlines, and awe-inspiring medieval castles. Its ancient history and deep-rooted Celtic culture make Wales similar in many ways to its more famous neighbors, Scotland and Ireland; and yet it doesn't attract the same hordes of visitors, which is a big part of the appeal.

Vast swaths of Wales were untouched by the industrial boom of the 19th century. Although pockets of the country were given over to industries such as coal mining and manufacturing (both of which have all but disappeared), most of Wales remained unspoiled. The country is largely rural, and there are more than 10 million sheep—but only 3 million people. It has a Britain-as-it-used-to-be feel that can be hugely appealing.

Now is a great time to visit Wales. The country is reveling in a new political autonomy, just a decade-and-a-half old, that's brought with it a flourish of optimism and self-confidence. Welsh culture has undergone something of a renaissance, and its culinary traditions are being embraced and reinvented by an enthusiastic new generation of chefs and artisan foodies. Simply put, Wales loves being Wales, and that enthusiasm is infectious to the visitor. It also means that the tourism industry has grown by leaps and bounds, including some truly unique and special places to stay.

Although Wales is a small country—on average, about 60 miles wide and 170 miles north to south—looking at it on a map is deceptive. It's quite a difficult place to get around, with a distinctly old-fashioned road network and poor public transportation connections. To see it properly, you really need a car. The good news is that along the way you'll experience some beautiful drives. There are rewards to be found in the gentle folds of its valleys and in the shadow of its mountains.

Were some of the more remote attractions in Wales in, say, the west of Ireland, they'd be world famous and overrun with millions of visitors. Here, if you're lucky, you can almost have them to yourself.

WALES PLANNER

WHEN TO GO

The weather in Wales, as in the rest of Britain, is a lottery. It can be hot in summer or never stop raining. Generally it's cool and wet in spring and autumn, but could also be surprisingly warm and sunny. The only surefire rule is that you should be prepared for the unexpected.

Generally speaking, southwest Wales tends to enjoy a milder climate than elsewhere in Britain, thanks in part to the moderating effects of the Gulf Stream. In contrast, mountainous areas like Snowdonia and the Brecon Beacons can be chilly at any time of the year. Book far ahead for major festivals such as the literary Hay Festival, Brecon Jazz, and the Abergavenny Food Festival.

PLANNING YOUR TIME

First-time visitors often try to cover too much ground in too little time. It's not hard to spend half your time traveling between points that look close on the map, but take the better part of a day to reach. From Cardiff, it's easy to visit the Wye Valley, Brecon Beacons, and the Gower Peninsula. Along the North Wales coast, Llandudno and Lake Vyrnwy make good bases for Snowdonia National Park.

The location of Wales lends itself to a border-hopping trip—in both directions. Well-known locations like Bath (near South Wales) and Chester (near North Wales) are no more than an hour from the Welsh border, and you can even take a ferry to Ireland if you want to go farther afield.

GETTING HERE AND AROUND

AIR TRAVEL

If you're arriving from the United States, London's Heathrow and Gatwick airports are generally the best options because of their large number of international flights. Heathrow (2 hours) is slightly closer than Gatwick (2½ hours), but both have excellent motorway links with South Wales. For North Wales, the quickest access is via Manchester Airport, with a travel time of less than an hour to the Welsh border.

Cardiff International Airport, 19 miles from downtown Cardiff, is the only airport in Wales with international flights, but these are mostly from Europe and Canada. A bus service runs from the airport to Cardiff's central train and bus stations.

Airports Cardiff International Airport. ✉ *A4226, Rhoose* ☎ *01446/711111* 🌐 *www.cardiff-airport.com.*

BUS TRAVEL

Most parts of Wales are accessible by bus, but long-distance bus travel takes a long time. National Express travels to all parts of Wales from London's Victoria Coach Station and also direct from London's Heathrow and Gatwick airports. The company also has routes into Wales from many major towns and cities in England and Scotland. Average travel times from London are 3½ hours to Cardiff, 4 hours to Swansea, 7 hours to Aberystwyth, and 4½ hours to Llandudno.

Many of Wales's national parks run summer bus services. In the North, the excellent Snowdon Sherpa runs into and around Snowdonia and links with main rail and bus services. The Pembrokeshire Coastal Bus Service operates in Pembrokeshire Coast National Park. The popular Beacons Bus service, in Brecon Beacons National Park, was put on indefinite hiatus in 2014, leaving the park without its own dedicated general bus service; however, cyclists can take advantage of the Brecon Bike Bus, with its 24-bike trailer, that runs Sundays and holidays from late May to late September.

Bus Contacts Brecon Bike Bus. ☎ *029/2066–6444* 🌐 *www.cardiffbus.com/english/bikebus.* **National Express.** ☎ *0871/781–8178* 🌐 *www.nationalexpress.com.* **Pembrokeshire Coastal Bus.** ☎ *0871/200–2233 Traveline* 🌐 *www.pembrokeshirecoast.org.uk.* **Snowdon Sherpa.** ☎ *0871/200–2233* 🌐 *www.visitsnowdonia.info/snowdon_paths_and_sherpa_bus_service-98.aspx.*

CAR TRAVEL

To explore the Welsh heartland properly, you really need a car. Be prepared to take the scenic route: there are no major highways north of Swansea (which means virtually all of Wales). For the most part it's all back roads, all the way. There are some stunning routes to savor: the A487 road runs along or near most of the coastline, while the A44 and A470 both wind through mountain scenery with magnificent views.

FERRY TRAVEL

Two ferry ports that connect Britain with Ireland are in Wales. Regular daily ferries with Stena Line and Irish Ferries sail from Fishguard, in the southwest, and Holyhead, in the northwest. Stena Line also runs some ferries between Rosslare and Cherbourg in France.

Ferry Contacts Irish Ferries. ☎ *0818/300–400* 🌐 *www.irishferries.com.* **Stena Line.** ☎ *0844/770–7070* 🌐 *www.stenaline.co.uk.*

TRAIN TRAVEL

Travel time on the First Great Western rail service from London's Paddington Station is about two hours to Cardiff and three hours to Swansea. Trains connect London's Euston Station with Mid-Wales and North Wales, often involving changes in cities such as Birmingham. Travel times average between three and five hours. Regional train service covers much of South and North Wales but, frustratingly, there are virtually no direct connections between these regions. For example, to make the 73-mile trip between Cardiff and Aberystwyth you have to make a connection in Shrewsbury, doubling the trip to 147 miles. North Wales has a cluster of steam railways, but these are tourist attractions rather than a practical way of getting around. The mainline long-distance routes can be very scenic indeed, such as the Cambrian Coast Railway, running between Machynlleth and Pwllheli, and the Heart of Wales line, linking Swansea with London, Bristol, and Manchester.

Train Contacts National Rail Enquiries. ☎ *0845/748–4950* 🌐 *www.nationalrail.co.uk.*

DISCOUNTS AND DEALS

For travel within Wales, ask about money-saving unlimited-travel tickets (such as the Freedom of Wales Flexi Pass, the North and Mid-Wales Rover, and the South Wales Flexi Rover), which include the use of bus services. A discount card offering a 20% reduction on each of the steam-driven Great Little Trains of Wales is also available. It costs £10, is valid for 12 months, and can be purchased online.

The Cadw/Welsh Historic Monuments Explorer Pass is good for unlimited admission to most of Wales's historic sites. The seven-day pass costs £22.50 per person, £36.50 per couple, or £44.50 per family; the three-day pass costs £15.20, £23.50, and £32, respectively. Passes are available at any site covered by the Cadw program. All national museums and galleries in Wales are free.

Discount Information Cadw/Welsh Historic Monuments. ✉ *Plas Carew, Unit 5–7 Cefn Coed, Parc Nantgarw* ☎ *01443/336000* 🌐 *cadw.gov.wales.* **Flexi Pass Information.** ☎ *0870/900–0773* 🌐 *www.nationalrail.co.uk.* **Great Little Trains of Wales.** ☎ *0871/200–2233 Traveline* 🌐 *www.greatlittletrainsofwales.co.uk.* **National Museums and Galleries of Wales.** 🌐 *www.museumwales.ac.uk.*

TOURS

In summer there are all-day and half-day tour-bus excursions to most parts of the country. In major resorts and cities, ask for details at a tourist information center or bus station.

Wales Official Tourist Guide Association. The country's official guide organization will set you up only with guides recognized by VisitWales. You can book a driver-guide or someone to accompany you as you drive, or a tailor-made tour. ☎ *01633/774796* 🌐 *www.walestourguides.com.*

RESTAURANTS

Wales has developed a thriving restaurant scene over the last decade or so, and not just in major towns. Some truly outstanding food can be found in rural pubs and hotel restaurants. More and more restaurants are creating dishes using fresh local ingredients—Welsh lamb, Welsh Black beef, Welsh cheeses, and seafood from the Welsh coast—that show off the best of the region's cuisine.

HOTELS

A 19th-century dictum, "I sleeps where I dines," still holds true in Wales, where good hotels and good restaurants often go together. Castles, country mansions, and even disused railway stations are being transformed into interesting hotels and restaurants. Traditional inns with low, beamed ceilings, wood paneling, and fireplaces are often the most appealing places to stay. The best ones tend to be off the beaten track. Cardiff and Swansea have some large chain hotels, and, for luxury, some excellent spas have cropped up in the countryside. An added bonus is that prices are generally lower than they are for equivalent properties in the Cotswolds, Scotland, or southeast England. ⇨ *Hotel reviews have been shortened. For full information, visit Fodors.com.*

WHAT IT COSTS IN POUNDS				
	$	$$	$$$	$$$$
Restaurants	under £15	£15–£19	£20–£25	over £25
Hotels	under £100	£100–£160	£161–£220	over £220

Restaurant prices are the average cost of a main course at dinner, or if dinner is not served, at lunch. Hotels prices are the lowest cost of a standard double room in high season, including 20% V.A.T.

VISITOR INFORMATION

Contacts VisitWales Centre. ☎ *0333/006–3001* 🌐 *www.visitwales.com.* **Wales in Style.** 🌐 *www.walesinstyle.com.*

SOUTH WALES

The most diverse of Wales's three regions, the south covers the area around Cardiff that stretches southwest as far as the rugged coastline of Pembrokeshire. It's the most accessible part of the country, as the roads are relatively good and the rail network is more extensive than it is elsewhere in Wales. Pleasant seaside towns such as Tenby are within a four- to five-hour drive of London; from Cardiff and Swansea you're never more than a half hour away from some gorgeous small villages.

Cardiff has enjoyed a certain success in reinventing itself as a cultured, modern capital, but Swansea and neighboring Newport have struggled to find their place in this postindustrial region. With a few exceptions, it's better to stick to the countryside in South Wales. The heart-stopping Gower Peninsula stretches along 14 miles of sapphire-blue bays and rough-hewn sea cliffs, and Brecon Beacons National Park is an area of grassy mountains and craggy limestone gorges.

CARDIFF CAERDYDD

20 miles southwest of the Second Severn Bridge.

With a population of around 330,000, Cardiff is the largest and most important city in Wales. It's also one of the youngest capitals in Europe: although a settlement has existed here since Roman times, Cardiff wasn't declared a city until 1905, and didn't become the capital until 50 years later. This is an energetic, youthful place, keen to show its new-found cosmopolitanism to the world. Cardiff is experiencing something of a cultural renaissance with the opening of the Wales Millennium Centre in Cardiff Bay.

For all its urban optimism, however, Cardiff is still a rather workaday town, with little to detain you for more than a day. See Cardiff Castle and the National Museum, wander Cardiff Bay, and maybe catch a show. Otherwise, it's a convenient base for exploring the nearby countryside.

Castell Coch looks medieval, but don't be fooled: it's a delightful Victorian-Gothic fantasy.

GETTING HERE AND AROUND

The capital is a major transportation hub with good connections to other parts of South Wales and with England. Getting to Mid-Wales and North Wales is more difficult, as there's no direct north–south train route (you'll have to connect in Bristol or Shrewsbury) and north–south buses are painfully slow. From London, trains from Paddington to Cardiff Central take about two hours; National Express coaches take about three hours. Cardiff is easily accessible by the M4 motorway. You must pay a £6.40 toll to cross the Severn Bridge between England and Wales (though crossing back is free).

TIMING

If you don't like crowds, avoid Cardiff during international rugby tournaments or other major sporting events.

ESSENTIALS

Visitor and Tour Information Cardiff Bay Visitor Centre. ✉ *Wales Millennium Centre, Bute Pl.* ☎ *029/2087–7927* 🌐 *cardiffbay.co.uk/index.php/visitor-centre.* **Cardiff Tourist Information Centre.** ✉ *The Old Library, The Hayes* ☎ *029/2087–3573* 🌐 *www.visitcardiff.com.*

EXPLORING

TOP ATTRACTIONS

FAMILY Fodor'sChoice ★ **Caerphilly Castle.** One of the largest and most impressive fortresses in Wales, and one of the few still to be surrounded by its original moat, Caerphilly must have been awe-inspiring at the time of its construction in the 13th century. Built by an Anglo-Norman lord, the concentric fortification contained powerful inner and outer defenses. It was badly damaged during the English Civil War, although extensive 20th-century

Caerphilly Castle 4
Caerwent Roman Town 8
Cardiff Bay 9
Cardiff Castle 1
Castell Coch 3
Doctor Who Experience 12
Llandaff Cathedral 6
National Museum Cardiff 2
St. Fagans National History Museum 5
Techniquest 10
Tredegar House ..7
Wales Millennium Centre 11

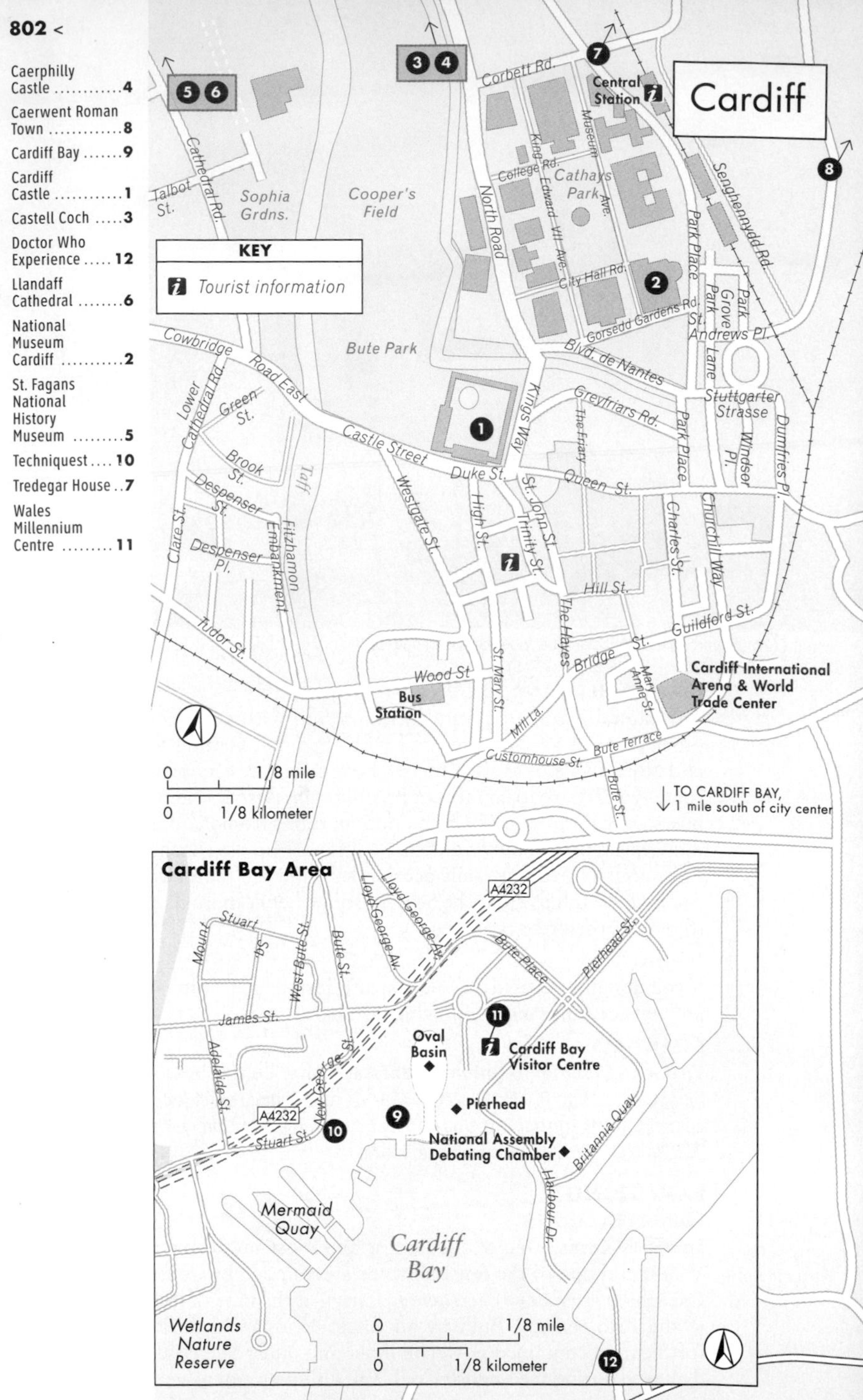

renovations have restored much of its former glory. The original Great Hall is still intact, and near the edge of the inner courtyard there's a replica of a trebuchet—a giant catapult used to launch rocks and other projectiles at the enemy. An interesting collection of modern interpretive sculptures has recently been placed around the castle, inside and outside, effectively turning it into a sculpture park. Caerphilly is 7 miles north of Cardiff. ✉ *Castle St., Caerphilly* ☎ *029/2088–3143* 🌐 *cadw.gov.wales* 🎫 *£5.50* ⏲ *Mar.–June, Sept., and Oct., daily 9:30–5; July and Aug., daily 9:30–6; Nov.–Feb., Mon.–Sat. 10–4, Sun. 11–4; last admission 30 min before closing.*

Cardiff Bay. Perhaps the most potent symbol of Cardiff's 21st-century rebirth, this upscale district is a 10-minute cab ride from Cardiff Central Station. Its museums and other attractions are clustered around the bay itself. The area can seem rather tranquil during the day, but buzzes with activity at night. ✉ *Between Stuart St. and Harbour Dr.*

Fodor's Choice ★ **Cardiff Castle.** A mishmash of styles, from austere Norman keep to over-the-top Victorian mansion, Cardiff Castle is an odd but beguiling place, located right in the middle of the city. Take the tour of the Victorian portion to discover the castle's exuberant side. William Burges (1827–81), an architect obsessed by the Gothic period, transformed the castle into an extravaganza of medieval color for the third marquess of Bute. The result was the Moorish-style ceiling in the Arab Room, the intricately carved shelves lining the Library, and gold leaf murals everywhere. Look for the painting of the Invisible Prince in the Day Nursery; on first glance it's just a tree, but stare long enough and a man takes shape in the branches. Note the not-so-subtle rejection of Darwin's theory of evolution, represented by monkeys tearing up his book around the library's doorway. The vast grounds, which include beautiful rhododendron gardens and a habitat for owls and falcons, are sometimes the setting for jousting in summer. Specialist tours, including tours of the clock tower and evening ghost tours, are held on certain dates year-round; call or check the website for schedule and booking information. ✉ *Castle St.* ☎ *029/2087–8100* 🌐 *www.cardiffcastle.com* 🎫 *£12, with guided tour £15* ⏲ *Mar.–Oct., daily 9–6; Nov.–Feb., daily 9–5. Castle apartments open 9:30, first tour 10 am year-round; last admission 1 hr before closing.*

Fodor's Choice ★ **Castell Coch.** Perched on a hillside is this fairy-tale castle. The turreted Red Castle was built on the site of a medieval stronghold in the 1870s, about the time that the "Fairy-Tale King" Ludwig II of Bavaria was creating his castles in the mountains of Germany. This Victorian fantasy wouldn't look out of place among them. The castle was another collaboration of the third marquess of Bute and William Burges, who transformed Cardiff Castle. Burges created everything, including the whimsical furnishings and murals, in a remarkable exercise of Victorian-Gothic whimsy. ✉ *A470, 4 miles north of Cardiff, Tongwynlais* ☎ *029/2081–0101* 🌐 *cadw.gov.wales* 🎫 *£5.50* ⏲ *Mar.–June, Sept., and Oct., daily 9:30–5; July and Aug., daily 9:30–6; Nov.–Feb., Mon.–Sat. 10–4, Sun. 11–4; last admission 30 min before closing.*

FAMILY **Doctor Who Experience.** The phenomenally popular BBC TV series—which has been made in Wales since 2005—marked its 50th anniversary in 2013, and this suitably high-tech exhibit continues to celebrate its weird and wonderful charms. There are interactive displays, specially re-created sets, and a huge collection of costumes and props from the show, plus an exceedingly well-stocked gift shop. They also run walking tours of local filming locations. Fans will be in heaven. Entry is by timed ticket, and busy dates do sell out in advance, so prebooking is recommended. **■TIP→ Reserve online and save nearly £10 on family tickets.** Kids get a pack of Dr. Who–related goodies, too. ✉ *Discovery Quay, Butetown* ☎ *0844/801–2279 box office, 0844/801–3663 information* 🌐 *www.doctorwhoexperience.com* 🎫 *£16 (£14 prebooked)* ⏲ *Feb.–mid-July and Sept.–Jan., Wed.–Mon. 10–5 (also Tues. during school holidays); mid-July–Aug., daily 10–5. Last admission 90 min before closing.*

National Museum Cardiff. At this splendid museum, you can learn about the story of Wales through its archaeology, art, and industry. The Evolution of Wales gallery uses inventive robotics and audiovisual effects. There's a fine collection of modern European art, including works by Daumier, Renoir, Van Gogh, and Cézanne. Kids, however, will be more interested by the enormous, 9-meter (29-foot) skeleton of a humpback whale that washed ashore near Cardiff in 1982. ✉ *Cathays Park* ☎ *029/2057–3000* 🌐 *www.museumwales.ac.uk* 🎫 *Free* ⏲ *Tues.–Sun. and most holiday Mon. 10–5.*

FAMILY
Fodor's Choice ★
St. Fagans National History Museum. On 100 acres of gardens, this excellent open-air museum celebrates the region's architectural history with a collection of farmhouses, cottages, shops, chapels, a school, and a 16th-century manor house. All but two of the structures were brought here from around Wales. Of special note are the string of ironworkers' cottages, each reflecting a different era from 1805, 1855, 1925, 1955, and 1985, from the decor to the technology to the gardens. Craftspeople work at the museum using traditional methods; most of the work is for sale. Galleries display clothing and other articles from daily life, and special events highlight local customs. ✉ *Off A4232, St. Fagans* ☎ *0300/111–2333* 🌐 *www.museumwales.ac.uk* 🎫 *Free; parking £3.50* ⏲ *Daily 10–5.*

Tredegar House. One of the grandest stately homes in Wales, Tredegar House was bought by the National Trust in 2011 and opened its doors to visitors in 2013. Highlights of the self-guided tour include the grand baroque Jacobean New Hall and the enormous Victorian kitchens, both restored to their former glory. Don't miss the lavish Victorian Side Hall, lined with portraits of the Morgan family, which owned Tredegar until the 1950s. The grounds include immaculately laid-out formal gardens and an orangery. Tredegar is just outside Newport, 12 miles northwest of Cardiff. ✉ *Tradegar House Dr., off A48, Newport* ☎ *01633/815880* 🌐 *www.nationaltrust.org.uk/tredegar-house* 🎫 *£7.50* ⏲ *House and garden: mid-Feb.–late Mar., daily 11–4; late Mar.–Oct., daily 11–5; Nov.–Dec., weekends 11–5. Park: year-round, daily dawn–dusk. Last admission 1 hr before closing.*

WALES: COUNTRY WITHIN A COUNTRY

Is Wales a nation, a state, or a country? The answer—confusingly—is yes, kind of, and yes and no. This requires some untangling.

Wales is a country within the United Kingdom, the same as Scotland and England. It has its own language—which you'll see on every signpost, though everybody also speaks English—its own flag, and sends its own teams to certain international sporting events, like soccer's World Cup.

While Wales has the right to pass some of its own laws, it isn't a sovereign nation. It shares the same head of state and has the same central government as England, Scotland, and Northern Ireland. It uses the same currency, and there are no restrictions for travelers who cross the English border. Practically speaking, it is like an American state—although "state" is a somewhat sensitive term here.

In medieval times Wales was an independent nation, but lacked a single government or ruler. It was slowly annexed by England in a drawn-out series of wars and skirmishes. Although the Welsh retained a strong sense of their own national identity, by the middle of the 16th century their land was effectively part of England.

This was the case until 1997, when Tony Blair was elected prime minister on a platform that included semiautonomous legislatures for Wales and Scotland. Two years later, the Welsh Assembly passed the first laws made solely by and for Wales in more than 400 years.

To avoid offense, you should always refer to Wales as a separate country. Be respectful of the fact that when you cross the border you're entering a place with a rich and proud history of its own.

14

Fodor's Choice ★ **Wales Millennium Centre.** Inviting comparisons to Bilbao's Guggenheim, Cardiff's main arts complex (known locally as "The Armadillo" for its coppery, shingled exterior) is an extraordinary building, inside and out. The materials used in the construction are intended to represent "Welshness." (Slate is for the rocky coastline, for example, while wood is for its ancient forests.) The massive words carved into the curving facade read "In These Stones Horizons Sing" in English and Welsh. Inside there's a maritime feel, from the curving wooden stairs to balconies evoking the bow of a ship. A broad range of cultural programs take place on the various stages, from ballet and opera to major touring shows. Guided tours (£6) depart at 11 and 2:30 daily. ✉ *Bute Pl., Cardiff Bay* ☎ 029/2063–6464 ⊕ *www.wmc.org.uk* ☜ *Free (event tickets vary)* ⊙ *Daily 10–6 (later on show nights).*

WORTH NOTING

Caerwent Roman Town. The Romans founded the little town of Caerwent, just a couple of miles into Wales from the Severn Crossing, in AD 75. The remains of their original settlement lie in a field on the outskirts of the modern town, presented with remarkably little fanfare. The ruins of 5th-century buildings stand almost 17 feet tall in places; the layout of around 15 buildings in total is clear to see, including houses, a forum, and a temple. The ruins are on the west side of Caerwent, signposted from A48, 25 miles northeast of Cardiff. Look out for the parking lot next to a whitewashed building, opposite a large field with a chicken coop. ✉ *Off A48, Caerwent* ☎ *01443/336092 Cadw (off-site phone)* 🌐 *cadw.gov.wales* 🎫 *Free* 🕒 *Daily 10–4.*

Llandaff Cathedral. In a suburb that retains its village feeling, you can visit this cathedral, which was repaired after serious bomb damage in World War II. The cathedral includes the work of a number of Pre-Raphaelites as well as *Christ in Majesty,* a 15-foot-tall aluminum figure by sculptor Jacob Epstein (1880–1959). Guided tours are available by arrangement. From Cardiff, cross the River Taff and follow Cathedral Road for about 2 miles. Buses 25, 62, and 66 from Cardiff Railway Station stop in Llandaff. ✉ *Cathedral Close, Llandaff* ☎ *029/2056–4554* 🌐 *www.llandaffcathedral.org.uk* 🎫 *Free* 🕒 *Mon.–Sat. 9–7:15 (start of final service), Sun. 7–5:15 (start of final service).*

FAMILY **Techniquest.** A large science-discovery center for children, Techniquest has 160 interactive exhibits, a planetarium, and a science theater. ✉ *Stuart St., Cardiff Bay* ☎ *029/2047–5475* 🌐 *www.techniquest.org* 🎫 *£7.50; planetarium £1.50* 🕒 *Jan.–mid-July and Sept.–Dec., Tues.–Fri. 9:30–4:30, weekends 10–5; mid-July–Aug., daily 10–5.*

WHERE TO EAT

$$ FRENCH ✕ **Bayside Brasserie.** With its gorgeous view over Cardiff Bay, this undeniably romantic restaurant is one of the most popular in Cardiff. The classic bistro menu has few surprises, but the kitchen serves up some tasty fare. Start with an appetizer of avocado crab salad, perhaps, before moving on to a juicy rib eye, or salmon fillet glazed with honey and sesame seeds. The extensive wine list includes organic and fair-trade labels. 💲 *Average main: £16* ✉ *Mermaid Quay, Bute Pl.* ☎ *029/2035–8444* 🌐 *www.baysidebrasserie.com.*

$ BRITISH Fodor's Choice ★ ✕ **The Clink.** Well, this is unusual: a trendy restaurant in which all the food is prepared by prisoners. The idea behind the Clink (British slang for jail) is that those serving time for minor crimes are given the chance to turn their lives around by gaining experience as gourmet chefs. The restaurant (just outside the prison grounds) is a bright, modern space, and the Modern British food is genuinely delicious. You might try the breast of roast chicken with sage crust and onion rings, or spring lamb with fondant potatoes and garlic puree. The restaurant is open for lunch all week, plus a single dinner sitting on the last Wednesday of the month. Note: they don't accept credit cards. 💲 *Average main: £11* ✉ *Knox Rd., in front of Cardiff Prison* ☎ *029/2092–3130* 🌐 *www.theclinkcharity.org/the-clink-restaurants/cardiff-wales* 💳 *No credit cards* 🕒 *No dinner* ✍ *Reservations essential.*

$$ BRITISH Fodor's Choice ★ ✕ **The Potted Pig.** Vaulted ceilings and exposed brick walls provide a dramatic backdrop to this restaurant down the block from Cardiff Castle. Formerly a bank vault, the Potted Pig turns out superb Welsh dishes. Starters like pork pâté with toast and pickles and entrées such as five-spiced duck breast keep diners happy. Popular desserts like the jelly roll can run out by the end of the night. Servers are warm and attentive and knowledgeable about wine. The underground atmosphere and candlelight make this a romantic dinner choice. 💲 *Average main: £19*

27 High St. 029/2022–4817 www.thepottedpig.com Closed Mon. No dinner Sun.

$ **Restaurant Minuet.** A longtime favorite with locals, Restaurant Minuet
PIZZA serves simple, fresh Italian lunches at decidedly ungourmet prices. The
FAMILY simple menu won't win any prizes for originality—a simple Capricciosa
Fodor's Choice ★ pizza, perhaps, with pepperoni and artichokes, or pasta with prawns, garlic, and chili—but the cooking is excellent and the atmosphere homey. You might have to wait a little for a table when it's busy (they don't take reservations), but the cheerful atmosphere and extremely reasonable prices certainly make up for that. *Average main: £6 42 Castle Arcade 029/203–41794 www.restaurantminuet.co.uk No dinner. Closed Sun. and holiday Mon. Reservations not accepted.*

$ **Valentino's.** With its nicely understated rustic decor and friendly Italian
ITALIAN staff, this restaurant drips with authenticity. In addition to pizzas and pastas, there is an ever-changing selection of fresh, locally sourced meat and fish dishes. *Average main: £14 5 Windsor Pl. 029/2022–9697 www.valentinocardiff.co.uk Closed Sun.*

14

WHERE TO STAY

$ **Jolyons Boutique Hotel.** This town house, a hop and a skip from the
B&B/INN Wales Millennium Centre in Cardiff Bay, bucks the trend in a city where big, modern hotels are usually a safer bet than boutique places. **Pros:** loads of character; comfortable bar. **Cons:** 10-minute drive from the city center; a bit tired looking in places; no parking. *Rooms from: £95 Bute Crescent 029/2048–8775 www.jolyons.co.uk 6 rooms Breakfast.*

$ **Lincoln House Hotel.** Perhaps the best of the many B&Bs on Cathedral
B&B/INN Road—a handsome enclave of Victorian houses—this place close to the city center is a great find. **Pros:** good service; handy location; free parking. **Cons:** attractive road is spoiled by traffic; no restaurant; breakfast not included in lower rates. *Rooms from: £90 118 Cathedral Rd. 029/2039–5558 www.lincolnhotel.co.uk 24 rooms Breakfast; No meals.*

$ **Park Plaza.** Just off Cardiff's main shopping street, this contemporary
HOTEL hotel is popular with business travelers for its luxurious feel and convenient downtown location. **Pros:** central location; good spa; stainless-steel pool. **Cons:** a bit sterile. *Rooms from: £85 Greyfriars Rd. 029/2011–1111 www.parkplaza.com 129 rooms Breakfast.*

$$ **St. David's Hotel and Spa.** Natural light from a glass atrium floods
HOTEL this starkly modern luxury hotel overlooking Cardiff Bay. The beautifully appointed guest rooms are done in soothing neutral tones, are filled with sleek furnishings, and have private balconies. **Pros:** a bit like staying on a cruise ship; relaxing spa; good deals. **Cons:** out-of-the way location; price fluctuates wildly—under £100 one week, over £200 the next; breakfast is pricey. *Rooms from: £120 Havannah St. 029/2045–4045 www.thestdavidshotel.com 132 rooms Breakfast; No meals.*

NIGHTLIFE AND PERFORMING ARTS

NIGHTLIFE

Café Jazz. With live jazz five nights a week, Café Jazz has video monitors in the bar and restaurant so you can enjoy the on-stage action. ✉ *21 St. Mary St.* ☎ *029/2038–7026* 🌐 *www.cafejazzcardiff.com.*

Clwb Ifor Bach. This hot spot, whose name means "Little Ivor's Club" in Welsh, has three floors of eclectic music from funk to folk to rock. ✉ *11 Womanby St.* ☎ *029/2023–2199* 🌐 *www.clwb.net.*

PERFORMING ARTS

Motorpoint Arena Cardiff. This huge venue is Cardiff's premier location for big-ticket music acts and other touring shows. ✉ *Mary Ann St.* ☎ *029/2022–4488* 🌐 *www.livenation.co.uk/cardiff.*

New Theatre. This refurbished Edwardian playhouse presents big names, including the Royal Shakespeare Company, the National Theatre, and the Northern Ballet. ✉ *Park Pl.* ☎ *029/2087–8889* 🌐 *www.newtheatrecardiff.co.uk.*

SHOPPING

Canopied Victorian and Edwardian shopping arcades lined with specialty stores weave in and out of the city's modern shopping complexes.

Cardiff Antiques Centre. In an 1858 arcade, the Cardiff Antiques Centre is a good place to buy vintage jewelry and accessories. ✉ *Royal Arcade* ☎ *029/2039–8881.*

Cardiff Market. The traditional Cardiff Market sells tempting fresh foods beneath its Victorian glass canopy. ✉ *St. Mary St.* ☎ *029/2087–1214.*

Melin Tregwynt. This elegant shop sells woolen clothing, bags, and cushions woven in an old Pembrokeshire mill. ✉ *26 Royal Arcade* ☎ *029/2022–4997* 🌐 *www.melintregwynt.co.uk.*

ABERGAVENNY Y FENNI

28 miles north of Cardiff.

The market town of Abergavenny, just outside Brecon Beacons National Park, is a popular base for walkers and hikers. It has a ruined castle and is near the industrial history sites at Blaenavon.

GETTING HERE AND AROUND

Abergavenny is on the A40 road, about an hour's drive from Cardiff. Direct trains connect with Cardiff about every half hour and take around 40 minutes.

ESSENTIALS

Visitor Information Abergavenny Tourist Information Centre. ✉ *24 Monmouth Rd.* ☎ *01873/853254* 🌐 *www.visitabergavenny.co.uk.*

EXPLORING

TOP ATTRACTIONS

Abergavenny Castle and Museum. Built early in the 11th century, this castle witnessed a tragic event on Christmas Day, 1176: the Norman knight William de Braose invited the neighboring Welsh chieftains to a feast, and in a crude attempt to gain control of the area, had them

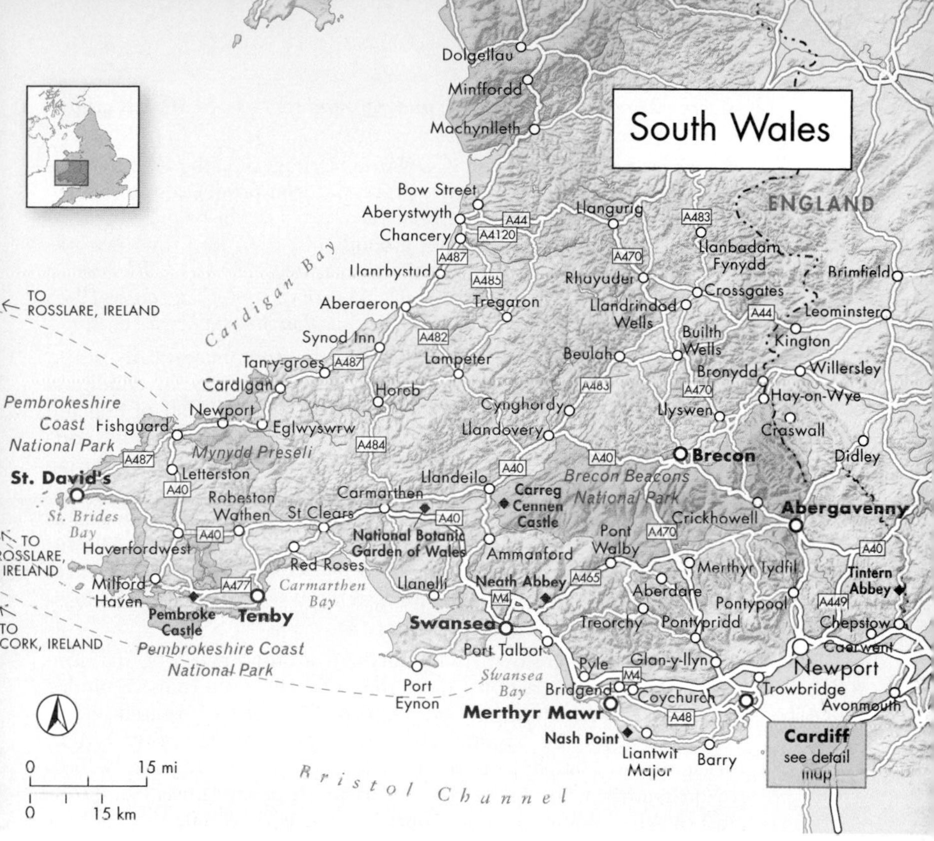

all slaughtered as they sat to dine. The Welsh retaliated and virtually demolished the castle. Most of what now remains dates from the 13th and 14th centuries. The castle's 19th-century hunting lodge houses an excellent museum of regional history. There's a re-created saddler's shop and a World War II air-raid shelter, but the Victorian Welsh farmhouse kitchen, with its old utensils and butter molds, is perhaps the most diverting exhibit. ✉ *Castle St.* ☏ *01873/854282* 🌐 *www.abergavennymuseum.co.uk* 🎫 *Free* 🕐 *Mar.–Oct., Mon.–Sat. 11–1 and 2–5, Sun. 2–5; Nov.–Feb., Mon.–Sat. 11–1 and 2–4.*

FAMILY
Fodor's Choice ★

Big Pit National Coal Museum. For hundreds of years, South Wales has been famous for its mining industry. Decades of decline—particularly during the 1980s—left only a handful of mines in business. The mines around Blaenavon, a small town 7 miles north of Abergavenny, have been designated a UNESCO World Heritage Site, and this fascinating museum is the centerpiece. Ex-miners lead you 300 feet underground into a coal mine. You spend just under an hour examining the old stables, machine rooms, and exposed coalfaces. Afterward you can look around an exhibition housed in the old Pithead Baths, including an extraordinary section on child labor in British mines. ■ **TIP→ Children under 3½ feet tall are not allowed on the underground portion of the tour.** ✉ *Off A4043, Blaenavon* ☏ *029/2057–3650* 🌐 *www.museumwales.*

ac.uk 🎫 *Free* ⏲ *Daily 9:30–5; underground tours 10–3:30; last admission 1 hr before closing.*

Blaenavon Ironworks. A UNESCO World Heritage Site, the 1789 Blaenavon Ironworks traces the entire process of iron production in the late 18th century. Well-preserved blast furnaces, a water-balance lift used to transport materials to higher ground, and a terraced row of workers' cottages show how the business operated. ✉ *A4043, Blaenavon* ☎ *01495/792615* 🌐 *cadw.gov.wales* 🎫 *Free* ⏲ *Apr.–Oct., daily 10–5; Nov.–Mar., Tues.–Thurs. 10–4; last admission 30 min before closing.*

Raglan Castle. Impressively complete from the front, majestically ruined within, Raglan was built in the 15th century and was the childhood home of Henry Tudor (1457–1509), who seized the throne of England in 1485 and became Henry VII. Raglan's heyday was relatively short-lived. The castle was attacked by Parliamentary forces in 1645, during the English Civil War, and has lain in ruins ever since. The hexagonal Great Tower survives in reasonably good condition, as do a handful of rooms on the ground floor. ✉ *A40, Raglan* ☎ *01291/690228* 🌐 *cadw.gov.wales* 🎫 *£4.75* ⏲ *Mar.–June and Sept.–Oct., daily 9:30–5; July–Aug., daily 9:30–6; Nov.–Feb., Mon.–Sat. 10–4, Sun. 11–4; last admission 30 min before closing.*

OFF THE BEATEN PATH

Tintern Abbey. Literally a stone's throw from the English border, Tintern is one of the region's most romantic monastic ruins. Founded in 1131 and dissolved by Henry VIII in 1536, it has inspired its fair share of poets and painters over the years—most famously J.M.W. Turner, who painted the transept covered in moss and ivy, and William Wordsworth, who idolized the setting in his poem "Lines Composed a Few Miles Above Tintern Abbey." Come early or late to avoid the crowds. The abbey, 5 miles north of Chepstow and 19 miles southeast of Abergavenny, is on the banks of the River Wye. ✉ *A466, Tintern* ☎ *01291/689251* 🌐 *cadw.gov.wales* 🎫 *£5.50* ⏲ *Mar.–June and Sept.–Oct., daily 9:30–5; July–Aug., daily 9:30–6; Nov.–Feb., Mon.–Sat. 10–4, Sun. 11–4; last admission 30 min before closing.*

WORTH NOTING

Tretower Court. An extremely rare surviving example of a fortified medieval manor house, Tretower Court was built in the early 1300s and expanded in the 15th century. The atmospheric interior contains a large hall, which was probably used for public business, and a solar, a private space used for working and relaxing. Buildings such as these were huge status symbols in their day, as they combined the security of a castle with the luxury of a manor house. On the grounds are the ruins of an earlier Norman castle. Tretower Court, restored in the 1930s, is singposted from the idyllic village of Crickhowell, which is 5 miles northwest of Abergavenny. ✉ *A479, Crickhowell* ☎ *01874/730279* 🌐 *cadw.gov.wales* 🎫 *£4.75* ⏲ *Apr.–Oct., daily 10–5; Nov.–Mar., Fri. and Sat. 10–4, Sun. 11–4; last admission 30 min before closing.*

WHERE TO EAT AND STAY

$$ BRITISH ✕ **Cripple Creek Inn.** This charming whitewashed inn serves elegant Welsh cuisine in a rustic dining room. Fish is a specialty, underlined with plenty of regional flavors—grilled hake encrusted with Tintern cheese,

for instance—and the beef and lamb are locally sourced. Try the duck breast with kirsch and black cherry sauce; vegetarians may be tempted by the leek-and–Caerphilly cheese puff pastry tart. The inn is about 1½ miles west of Raglan Castle. To get there from the castle, turn left out of the gates onto the one-way road, then backtrack towards Raglan, passing the castle again on your right. At the roundabout, take Clytha Road. *Average main: £16 ✉ Old Abergavenny Rd., Bryngwyn, Raglan ☎ 01291/690256 🌐 www.thecripplecreek.com.*

$$ HOTEL **Bear Hotel.** In the middle of town, this coaching inn is full of character; the low-beamed bar, decorated with memorabilia from the days when stagecoaches stopped here, has a log fire in winter. **Pros:** friendly bar; good food. **Cons:** some rooms overlook the road; rooms vary in size; can get busy on weekends. *Rooms from: £100 ✉ High St., Crickhowell ☎ 01873/810408 🌐 www.bearhotel.co.uk 35 rooms Breakfast.*

$ HOTEL **The Lamb and Flag Inn.** This inn on the outskirts of Abergavenny embodies what the British like to call "cheap and cheerful," meaning good-quality accommodations that cover all the basics. **Pros:** excellent value; good restaurant; free parking. **Cons:** a little way from the town center; few amenities. *Rooms from: £60 ✉ Brecon Rd. ☎ 01873/857611 🌐 www.lambflag.co.uk 5 rooms Breakfast.*

$$ HOTEL Fodor's Choice ★ **Llansantffraed Court Hotel.** Dating from 1400, this grand country house 4 miles southeast of Abergavenny is set on 20 acres of well-tended grounds with lovely views of the Brecon Beacons. **Pros:** excellent food; peaceful setting. **Cons:** out-of-the-way location. *Rooms from: £135 ✉ Old Raglan Rd., Clytha ☎ 01873/840678 🌐 www.llch.co.uk 21 rooms Breakfast.*

NIGHTLIFE AND PERFORMING ARTS

Fodor's Choice ★ **Abergavenny Food Festival.** Held over a weekend in September, the Abergavenny Food Festival is a celebration for foodies and a symbol of the growing interest in Welsh cuisine. It earned a silver award for "Best Event in Wales" from the tourism board in 2014, which if nothing else spoke to the festival's rising profile. There are demonstrations, lectures, special events, and, of course, a food market. Be sure to sample the delicious local cheese called Y Fenni, flavored with a piquant combination of mustard seeds and ale. *✉ Abergavenny ☎ 01873/851643 🌐 www.abergavennyfoodfestival.com.*

BRECON ABERHONDDU

19 miles northwest of Abergavenny, 41 miles north of Cardiff.

The historic market town of Brecon is known for its Georgian buildings, narrow passageways, and pleasant riverside walks. It's also the gateway to Brecon Beacons National Park. The town is particularly appealing on Tuesday and Friday, which are market days. You may want to purchase a hand-carved wooden "love spoon" similar to those on display in the Brecknock Museum.

GETTING HERE AND AROUND

Brecon's nearest railway stations are at Merthyr Tydfil and Abergavenny (both about 19 miles away). Brecon is a handsome town to explore on foot—especially the riverside walk along the Promenade.

One of three national parks in Wales, Brecon Beacons offers some panoramic mountain views, whether you're on foot or in a car.

ESSENTIALS

Visitor Information Brecon Beacons Tourism. ✉ *Market Car Park, Church La.* ☎ *01874/622485* 🌐 *www.breconbeaconstourism.co.uk.*

EXPLORING

TOP ATTRACTIONS

Fodor's Choice ★ **Brecon Beacons National Park.** About 5 miles southwest of Brecon you encounter mountains and wild, windswept uplands that are tipped by shafts of golden light when the weather's fine, or fingers of ghostly mist when it's not. This 519-square-mile park is one of Wales's most breathtaking areas, perfect for a hike or scenic drive. Start at the visitor center on Mynydd Illtyd, a grassy stretch of upland west of the A470. Also known as the Mountain Centre, it's an excellent source of information about the park, including maps and advice on the best routes (guided or self-guided). There's also an excellent tearoom where you can fuel up for the journey or reward yourself with an indulgent slice of cake afterwards. If you want to see it all from your car, any road that crosses the Beacons will offer you with beautiful views, but the most spectacular is the high and undulating A4069, between Brynamman and Llangadog in the park's western end. **■ TIP→ To explore the moorlands on foot, come prepared. Mist and rain descend quickly, and the summits are exposed to high winds.** ✉ *Off A470, Libanus* ☎ *01874/623366* 🌐 *www.breconbeacons.org* 🎫 *Free; parking £1.50 for 2 hrs, £3 all day* ⏲ *Visitor Center: Mar.–June, Sept., and Oct., daily 9:30–5; July–Aug., daily 9:30–5:30; Nov.–Feb., daily 9:30–4.*

Fodor's Choice ★ **Carreg Cennen Castle.** On the edge of Brecon Beacons National Park, about 30 miles west of Brecon, this decaying cliff-top fortress was built

CLOSE UP

Hiking and Biking in Wales

Opened to much fanfare in 2012, the Wales Coast Path is an 870-mile walking path that snakes along the entire coastline. Linking existing routes like the Pembrokeshire Coast Path in southeast Wales with new sections, it passes as close to the coastline as possible. Managed by the Welsh government, the route can be pretty wild in places and there isn't always a guardrail, so keep a close eye on small children. Work is currently underway to link it up with other popular routes, which should create an unbroken system of walking trails extending for more than 1,000 miles within a couple of years.

Other long-distance paths include north–south Offa's Dyke Path, based on the border between England and Wales established by King Offa in the 8th century, and the Glyndr Way, a 128-mile-long highland route that traverses Mid-Wales from the border town of Knighton via Machynlleth to Welshpool. Signposted footpaths in Wales's forested areas are short and easy to follow. Dedicated enthusiasts might prefer the wide-open spaces of Brecon Beacons National Park or the mountains of Snowdonia.

Wales's reputation as both an on-road and off-road cycling mecca is well established. There's an amazing choice of scenic routes and terrain from challenging off-road tracks (🌐 *www.mbwales.com* is for the serious cyclist) to long-distance road rides and gentle family trails; VisitWales has information to get you started.

CONTACTS AND RESOURCES

Cycling Wales. ✉ *Brecon* 🌐 *www.visitwales.com/things-to-do/activities/biking/cycling.*

Offa's Dyke Centre. ✉ *West St., Knighton* ☎ *01547/528753* 🌐 *www.offasdyke.demon.co.uk/odc.htm.*

Pembrokeshire Coast Path. ✉ *Brecon* 🌐 *www.nationaltrail.co.uk.*

Ramblers' Association in Wales. ✉ *Brecon* ☎ *029/2064–4308* 🌐 *www.ramblers.org.uk/wales.*

Wales Coast Path. ✉ *Brecon* 🌐 *www.walescoastpath.gov.uk.*

in the 12th century, and remains of earlier defenses have been found dating back to the Iron Age. The castle, though a ruin, has a partially intact barbican (fortified outer section) and some inner chambers hewn dramatically from the bedrock. The climb to get there is somewhat punishing—you have to trudge up a steep, grassy hill—but the views of the valley, with its patchwork of green fields framed by the peaks of the Black Mountains, are enough to take away whatever breath you have left. ✉ *Off Derwydd Rd., Trapp* ☎ *01443/336000* 🌐 *www.cadw.wales.gov.uk* 🎟 *£4.50* 🕒 *Apr.–Oct., daily 9:30–6:30; Nov.–Mar., daily 9:30–4; last admission 45 min before closing.*

WORTH NOTING

Brecon Cathedral. Modest on the outside but surprisingly cavernous on the inside, this cathedral stands on the hill above the middle of town. The cathedral was built on the site of an 11th-century priory, which was destroyed during Henry VIII's dissolution of the monasteries in the 1530s. It was rebuilt as a parish church fairly soon after and was remodeled in the 1860s. It became an Anglican Cathedral in 1923. The heritage center does a good job of telling the building's history, and there's also a handy café. Local choirs perform concerts here regularly; check the website for event listings. ✉ *Cathedral Close* ☎ *01874/623857* 🌐 *www.breconcathedral.org.uk* 🎟 *Free* ⏲ *Daily 8–6.*

FAMILY **National Show Caves of Wales.** This underground cave system was discovered by two local men in 1912—make that rediscovered, as one of the caves contained 42 human skeletons that had lain undisturbed for around 7,000 years. The main cave system, Dan Yr Ogof (Welsh for "beneath the cave"), is an impressive natural wonder, particularly the Cathedral Cave with natural stone archways and a dramatic waterfall. The whole thing is pitched at kids, with "dramatic" piped music to "enhance" the atmosphere, and a park featuring 200 life-size models of dinosaurs and other prehistoric creatures. There's also a playground, petting zoo, shire horse center, and Victorian farm complete with costumed craftspeople and other "how we lived then" shenanigans. The caves are 17 miles southwest of Brecon. ✉ *Off A48 or B4310, Abercrave* ☎ *01639/730284* 🌐 *www.showcaves.co.uk* 🎟 *£15* ⏲ *Apr.–early Nov., daily 10–3.*

WHERE TO EAT AND STAY

$$ BRITISH Fodor's Choice ★ ✕ **Felin Fach Griffin.** Old and new blend perfectly in this modern country-style inn with old wood floors, comfy leather sofas, and stone walls hung with bright prints. The excellent menu makes use of fresh local produce, much of it coming from the Griffin's own organic garden, in dishes such as local duck with kale and potato gratin and Cornish brill with baby leeks. They also have a B&B costing around £125 per night with dinner packages available. The inn is in Felin Fach, 5 miles northeast of Brecon. $ *Average main: £18.50* ✉ *A470, Felin Fach* ☎ *01874/620111* 🌐 *www.eatdrinksleep.ltd.uk.*

$ HOTEL **Coach House.** This former coach house in the center of Brecon has been converted into a luxurious place to stay, and the friendly hosts—a wealth of information about the local area—can arrange transport to and from the best walking paths in the Beacons. **Pros:** lovely staff; central location; private parking. **Cons:** on a main road. $ *Rooms from: £85* ✉ *Orchard St.* ☎ *01874/640089* 🌐 *www.coachhousebrecon.com* *7 rooms* *Breakfast.*

$ B&B/INN **Felin Glais.** In the 17th century Felin Glais was a barn; enlarged but without losing its ancient character, it provides spacious and comfortable accommodations. **Pros:** beautiful building; spacious rooms; good food; kids stay for nearly half price. **Cons:** dog-friendly environment won't please everyone; cash or check only; 48-hours notice required for dinner. $ *Rooms from: £90* ✉ *Abersycir* ☎ *01874/623107* 🌐 *www.felinglais.co.uk* *No credit cards* *4 rooms* *Breakfast.*

NIGHTLIFE AND PERFORMING ARTS

Brecon Jazz. For a weekend every August, Brecon Jazz, an international music festival, takes over the town. It attracts an increasingly high-profile list of performers and includes a parade through the town on Sunday morning. ✉ *Brecon* ☎ *01874/611622 Box office (Theatr Brycheiniog)* 🌐 *www.breconjazz.com.*

Theatr Brycheiniog. On the canal, Theatr Brycheiniog is the town's main venue for music, plays, and comedy. It also has a waterfront bistro. ✉ *Canal Wharf* ☎ *01874/611622* 🌐 *www.brycheiniog.co.uk.*

SPORTS AND THE OUTDOORS

Biped Cycles. The Brecon Beacons contain some of the best cycling routes in Britain. Biped Cycles will rent you the right bike and equipment. ✉ *10 Ship St.* ☎ *01874/622296* 🌐 *www.bipedcycles.co.uk.*

Crickhowell Adventure Gear. This shop sells outdoor gear and climbing equipment. Crickhowell is on A40, about 14 miles southeast of Brecon. ✉ *21 Ship St.* ☎ *01873/810020.*

MERTHYR MAWR

14

45 miles south of Brecon, 22 miles west of Cardiff.

Fodor's Choice ★ As you cross over an ancient stone bridge into Merthyr Mawr, you feel as if you've entered another world. From stone cottages with beehive-shape thatched roofs to the Victorian-era Church of St. Teilo, with the pieces of its long-gone 5th-century predecessor lined up in its churchyard, it's an idyllic place to wander around. The picturesque ruin of Ogmore Castle is just off the B4524, but the most memorable way to reach it is via the walking path that starts in the car park at the very southern tip of the village. The mile-long route goes through a farm and a Shetland pony stable.

GETTING HERE AND AROUND

Merthyr Mawr is signposted from the A48 and B4524, 7 miles southwest of junction 35 on the M4. The nearest train station is in Bridgend. There's no bus service to the village.

EXPLORING

Fodor's Choice ★ **Nash Point.** Just a few miles south of Merthyr Mawr is this stunning promontory overlooking the Bristol Channel. Twin lighthouses stand guard against the elements; one is still operational, but the other is open for tours. This is also a popular picnic spot, and a small snack kiosk is open during summer months. Nothing beats this place at sunset, when the evening sky ignites in a riot of color. It's one of the most romantic spots in South Wales. ⚠ **There's no guardrail on the cliff, so keep a close eye on children.** ✉ *Marcross* ☎ *01225/245011* 🌐 *www.nashpoint.co.uk* 🎫 *Free; lighthouse £3.50* ⏲ *Lighthouse: Mar.–Oct., weekends and holiday Mon. (also Wed. during school holidays) 12:30–5:30; last admission 30 min before closing.*

Ogmore Castle. Just south of the village are these atmospheric ruins, nestled by a river that can only be crossed via stepping-stones. A number of legends are associated with the castle, one concerning a ghost that supposedly forces passersby to embrace a large rock known as the "Goblin Stone." When you try to draw back, so the story goes, you find that your hands and feet have become part of the rock. ✉ *Ogmore Rd.* 🎫 *Free.*

QUICK BITES

The Pelican in Her Piety. Up a small hill next to Ogmore Castle, The Pelican in Her Piety stands like a mirage. This friendly and fabulously named little pub is a welcome spot for a (rather pricey) snack or restorative pint after the long walk from Merthyr Mawr. ✉ *Ogmore Rd.* ☎ *01656/880049* 🌐 *www.pelicanpub.co.uk.*

WHERE TO EAT

$ BRITISH

✕ **The Plough and Harrow.** A short drive from Nash Point is this friendly local pub, on the edge of the tiny cliff-top village of Monknash. The food is delicious and unfussy; the menu changes daily, but features tasty pub classics like steaks and grilled fish, made with plenty of local ingredients. Everything is served in a cozy dining room with a fireplace. There's a small but decent wine list, and an even better selection of real ales and ciders (they won a prestigious award for "cider pub of the year" in 2014—that's the alcoholic, British kind). This place is popular locally, so call ahead or be prepared to wait. $ *Average main: £13* ✉ *Off Hoel Las, Monknash* ☎ *01656/890209* 🌐 *www.ploughandharrow.org.*

SWANSEA ABERTAWE

22 miles northwest of Merthyr Mawr, 40 miles west of Cardiff.

The birthplace of poet Dylan Thomas (1914–53), Swansea adores its native son. Citywide celebrations in 2014 marked a century since his birth, and every year the poet is honored with his own festival in October and November. But Swansea no longer seems like a place that would inspire poetry. Heavily bombed in World War II, it was clumsily rebuilt. Today it merits a stop primarily for a couple of good museums. However, the surrounding countryside tells a different story. The National Botanic Gardens and Neath Abbey make for interesting diversions, and the stunning Gower Peninsula contains some of the region's best beaches.

GETTING HERE AND AROUND

There's half-hourly rail service from London's Paddington Station. The city has direct National Express bus connections to other parts of Wales, as well as to London and other cities.

ESSENTIALS

Visitor Information Swansea Tourist Information Centre. ✉ *Plymouth St.* ☎ *01792/468321* 🌐 *www.visitswanseabay.com.*

EXPLORING

TOP ATTRACTIONS

Dylan Thomas Centre. Situated on the banks of the Tawe close to the Maritime Quarter, the Dylan Thomas Centre serves as the National Literature Centre for Wales. The center houses a permanent Dylan Thomas exhibition, art gallery, restaurant, and café-bookshop, and hosts the annual Dylan Thomas Festival. **■ TIP→ The poet's fans can buy a booklet that outlines the Dylan Thomas Trail around South Wales. It includes the Boathouse (now a museum), in Laugharne, where the poet lived and wrote for the last four years of his life.** ✉ *Somerset Pl.* ☎ *01792/463980* 🌐 *www.dylanthomas.com* 🎫 *Free* 🕒 *Daily 10–4:30.*

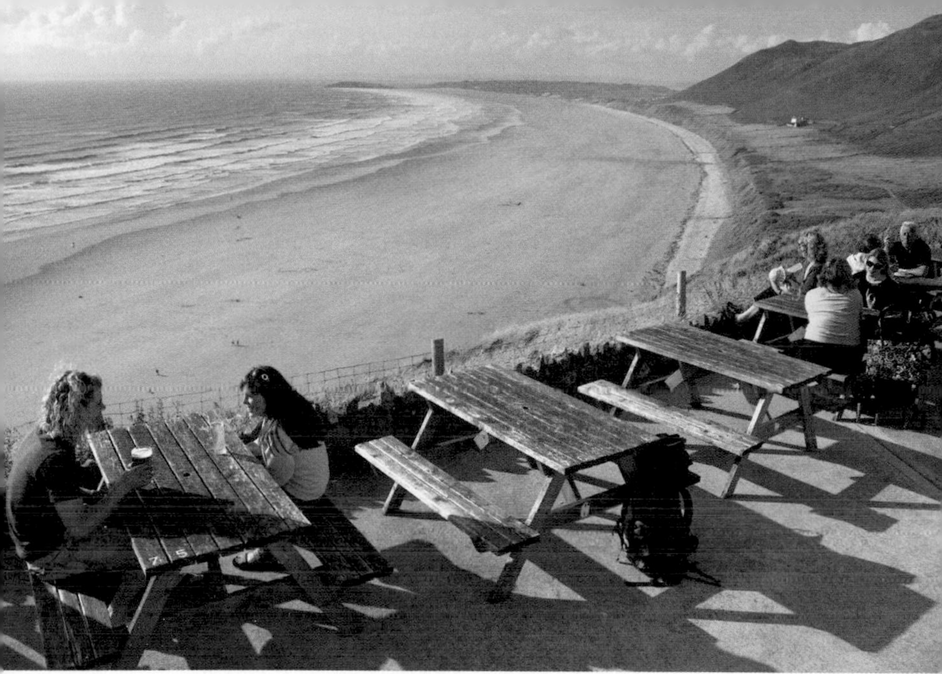

Stretching west of Swansea, the Gower Peninsula has some stunning beaches, including Rhossili.

FAMILY Fodor's Choice ★ **Gower Peninsula.** This peninsula, which stretches westward from Swansea, was the first part of Britain to be designated an Area of Outstanding Natural Beauty. Its shores are a succession of sheltered sandy bays and awesome headlands. The seaside resort of Mumbles, on the outskirts of Swansea, is the most famous town along the route. It's an elegantly faded place to wander on a sunny afternoon, with an amusement pier and seaside promenade. Farther along the peninsula, the secluded Pwlldu Bay can only be reached on foot from nearby villages like Southgate. A few miles westward is the more accessible (and very popular) Three Cliffs Bay, with its sweeping views and wide, sandy beach. At the far western tip of the peninsula, Rhossili has perhaps the best beach of all. Its unusual, snaking causeway—known locally as the Worm's Head—is inaccessible at high tide. ✉ *Swansea* ☎ *01792/361302 Mumbles Tourist Information Centre* 🌐 *www.enjoygower.com.*

Fodor's Choice ★ **National Botanic Garden of Wales.** This 568-acre, 18th-century estate is dotted with lakes, fountains, and a Japanese garden. The centerpiece is the Norman Foster–designed Great Glass House, the largest single-span greenhouse in the world, which blends into the curving landforms of the Tywi Valley. The greenhouse's interior landscape includes a 40-foot-deep ravine and thousands of plants from all over the world. The Ghost Forest is a stunning art installation, made from the carved stumps of ten giant hardwood trees—a powerful statement on how rapidly the world's forests are being destroyed. The grounds have lovely views across the Carmarthenshire countryside, especially from the Paxton's View lookout point. It's marked by Paxton's Tower, a Gothic folly built to honor Horatio Nelson, now owned by the National Trust (it's free to wander, though there's nothing to see inside). The garden, 20 miles northwest of Swansea, is signposted off the main road between Swansea and Carmarthen. ✉ *Off A48 or B4310, Llanarthne* ☎ *01558/667149* 🌐 *www.gardenofwales.org.uk* 🎫 *£8.90* ⏲ *Apr.–Sept., daily 10–6; Oct.–Mar., daily 10–4:30.*

FAMILY **National Waterfront Museum.** Housed in a construction of steel, slate, and glass grafted onto a historic redbrick building, the National Waterfront Museum's galleries have 15 theme areas, presenting Welsh maritime and industrial history through state-of-the-art interactive technology and a host of artifacts. Highlights of the collection include a monoplane built by amateur aviation enthusiasts in the early 1900s, one of the oldest British aircraft in existence. ✉ *Oystermouth Rd., Maritime Quarter* ☎ *0300/111–2333* 🌐 *www.museumwales.ac.uk/swansea* 🎫 *Free* ⏲ *Daily 10–5.*

WORTH NOTING

5 Cwmdonkin Drive. Dylan Thomas was born in this suburban Edwardian house, which remains a place of pilgrimage for the poet's devotees. You can wander the house with no restrictions (they're proud of the fact that nothing is roped off), or prebook tours that are tailored according to how much time you want to spend here. Devoted fans can hang around for hours at 11, 1, and 3. You can also arrange tours of other Thomas-related sites in Swansea and farther afield in the region. The house can be rented as self-catering accommodation for around £150 per night or £580 per week. ✉ *5 Cwmdonkin Dr.* ☎ *01792/472555* 🌐 *www.dylanthomasbirthplace.com* 🎫 *£8* ⏲ *Call ahead for tours.*

Maritime Quarter. Swansea was extensively bombed during World War II, and its old dockland has reemerged as the splendid Maritime Quarter, a modern marina with attractive housing and shops and a seafront that commands views across the sweep of Swansea Bay. ✉ *Swansea.*

Neath Abbey. Built in the 12th century, this abbey was, in its day, one of the largest and most important in the British Isles. Though just a shell, the main church gives an impressive sense of scale, with its tall buttresses and soaring, glassless windows. Here and there small sections of the original building have survived unscathed, including an undercroft with a vaulted stone ceiling. Neath Abbey is 9 miles northeast of Swansea. ✉ *Monastery Rd., Neath Abbey* 🌐 *cadw.gov.wales* 🎫 *Free* ⏲ *Daily 10–4; last admission 30 min before closing.*

Swansea Market. Swansea's covered market, part of Quadrant Shopping Centre, is one of the best fresh-foods markets in Wales. You can buy cockles from the Penclawdd beds on the nearby Gower Peninsula, and laverbread, that unique Welsh delicacy made from seaweed, which is usually served with bacon and eggs. ✉ *Oxford St.* ☎ *01792/654296* 🌐 *www.swanseaindoormarket.co.uk* ⏲ *Weekdays 8–5:30, Sat. 7:30–5:30 (also Sun. 10–4:30 in Dec.).*

Swansea Museum. Founded in 1841, this museum contains a quirky and eclectic collection that includes an Egyptian mummy, local archaeological exhibits, and the intriguing Cabinet of Curiosity, which holds artifacts from Swansea's past. The museum is close to the Maritime

Quarter. ✉ *Victoria Rd.* ☎ *01792/653763* 🌐 *www.swanseaheritage.net* 🎫 *Free* ⏲ *Tues.–Sun. 10–5; last admission 20 min before closing.*

WHERE TO EAT AND STAY

$$ SPANISH ✕ **La Braseria.** Lively and welcoming, this spot resembles a Spanish *bodega* (wine cellar), with its flamenco music, oak barrels, and white-washed walls. Among the house specialties are sea bass in rock salt, roast suckling pig, and pheasant (in season, of course). There's a good choice of 140 Spanish and French wines. $ *Average main: £17* ✉ *28 Wind St.* ☎ *01792/469683* 🌐 *www.labraseria.com* ⏲ *Closed Sun.*

$$ BISTRO ✕ **Pant-y-Gwydr.** This excellent little bistro in the center of Swansea has an air of retro sophistication. The menu is traditionally French; you might start with a half dozen escargots served with garlic butter before moving on to duck leg confit *a l'orange*, or a simple steak *frites*. There are also daily specials and an enormous (entirely French) wine list. $ *Average main: £17* ✉ *Pantygwydr Hotel, Oxford St.* ☎ *01792/455498* 🌐 *www.pantygwydr.co.uk* ⏲ *Closed Sun.–Tues. (also Wed., Nov.–Mar.).*

$$$ HOTEL Fodor'sChoice ★ **Fairyhill.** Luxuriously furnished public rooms, spacious bedrooms, and delicious cooking make this delightfully named 18th-century country house a restful retreat. **Pros:** peaceful surroundings; good restaurant. **Cons:** dinner package required some summer weekends; restaurant always busy. $ *Rooms from: £200* ✉ *Off B4295, 11 miles southwest of Swansea, Reynoldston* ☎ *01792/390139* 🌐 *www.fairyhill.net* *8 rooms* *Breakfast; Some meals.*

$$ HOTEL **Morgans.** Now a hotel, the Victorian-era Port Authority building in the Maritime Quarter has lost none of its period features: moldings, pillars, stained glass, and wood floors. **Pros:** near the marina; short walk to shops; maritime flair. **Cons:** no room service in town house. $ *Rooms from: £125* ✉ *Somerset Pl.* ☎ *01792/484848* 🌐 *www.morganshotel.co.uk* *41 rooms* *No meals.*

TENBY DINBYCH-Y-PYSGOD

53 miles west of Swansea.

Fodor'sChoice ★ Pastel-color Georgian houses cluster around a harbor in this seaside town, which became a fashionable resort in the 19th century and is still popular. Two golden sandy beaches stretch below the hotel-lined cliff top. Medieval Tenby's ancient town walls still stand, enclosing narrow streets and passageways full of shops, inns, and places to eat. From the harbor you can take a short boat trip to Caldey Island, with its active Cistercian community.

GETTING HERE AND AROUND

Tenby is on the southwest Wales rail route from London's Paddington Station. You have to change trains at Swansea or Newport. The center of Tenby, a maze of narrow medieval streets, has parking restrictions. In summer, downtown is closed to traffic, so park in one of the lots and take the shuttle buses.

ESSENTIALS

Visitor Information Tenby Information Centre. ✉ *Upper Park Rd., Unit 2* ☎ *01834/842402* 🌐 *www.pembrokeshire.gov.uk.*

14

EXPLORING

Fodor's Choice ★ **Caldey Island.** This beautiful little island off the coast at Tenby has whitewashed stone buildings that lend it a Mediterranean feel. The island is best known for its Cistercian order, whose black-and-white-robed monks make a famous perfume from the local plants. You can visit tiny St. Illtud's Church to see the Caldey Stone, an early Christian artifact from circa AD 600, engraved in Latin and ancient Celtic. St. David's Church, on a hill above the village, is a simple Norman chapel noted for its art-deco stained glass. The monastery itself isn't open to the public, but its church has a public viewing gallery if you want to observe a service. Boats to Caldey Island leave from Tenby's harbor every 20 minutes or so between Easter and September. ✉ *Caldey Island* ☎ *01834/844453* 🌐 *www.caldey-island.co.uk* 🎫 *Free; boats £12 round-trip* ⏲ *Boats Easter–Oct., weekdays (also Sat. May–Sept) 10–3. Last return usually 5.*

Pembroke Castle. About 10 miles east of Tenby is this remarkably complete Norman fortress dating from 1190. Its walls remain stout, its gatehouse mighty, and the enormous cylindrical keep proved so impregnable to cannon fire in the Civil War that Cromwell's men had to starve out its Royalist defenders. Climb the towers and walk the walls for fine views. A well-stocked gift shop sells faux-medieval knickknacks. ✉ *Westgate Hill, Pembroke* ☎ *01646/684585* 🌐 *www.pembroke-castle.co.uk* 🎫 *£6* ⏲ *Apr.–Aug., daily 9:30–5:30; Sept.–Oct. and Mar., daily 10–5; Nov.–Feb., daily 10–4; last admission 45 min before closing.*

Fodor's Choice ★ **Pembrokeshire Coast National Park.** By far the smallest of the country's three national parks, Pembrokeshire Coast is no less strikingly beautiful than the other two. The park has 13 Blue Flag beaches and a host of spectacular clifftop drives and walks, including some of the most popular stretches of the Wales Coast Path. The park has a smattering of historic sites, including the impossibly picturesque St. David's Cathedral, built in a Viking-proof nook by the Irish Sea. The information center in Tenby is a good place to start. ✉ *Tenby National Park Centre, South Parade* ☎ *01834/845040,* 🌐 *www.pembrokeshirecoast.org.uk* 🎫 *Free* ⏲ *Information Centre: Apr.–Sept., daily 9:30–5; Oct.–Mar., Mon.–Thurs. 10:30–3:30, Fri.–Sat. 10:30–4:30.*

FAMILY **Tenby Museum and Art Gallery.** Close to the castle, this small but informative museum recalls the town's maritime history and its growth as a fashionable resort. Kids will appreciate the section on Tenby's role in the golden age of piracy. Two art galleries feature works by local artists. ✉ *Castle Hill* ☎ *01834/842809* 🌐 *www.tenbymuseum.org.uk* 🎫 *£4* ⏲ *Nov.–Mar., Tues.–Sat. 10–5; Apr.–Oct., daily 10–5; last admission 30 min before closing.*

FAMILY **Tudor Merchant's House.** This late-15th-century home shows how a prosperous trader would have lived in Tudor times. Kids can try on Tudor-style costumes. The gift shop sells handmade pottery based on unique, original designs found at the house. ✉ *Quay Hill* ☎ *01834/842279* 🌐 *www.nationaltrust.org.uk/tudor-merchants-house* 🎫 *£4* ⏲ *Late Mar.–mid-July and early Sept.–Oct., Wed.–Mon. 11–5; mid-July–late Aug., Thurs.–Mon. 11–5, Tues.–Wed. 11–7; late Aug.–early Sept., daily*

11–5; Nov.–late Mar., weekends 11–3; last admission 30 min before closing.

WHERE TO EAT AND STAY

$$ BRITISH Fodor's Choice ★ **Plantagenet House.** Flickering candles, open fireplaces, exposed stone walls, and top-notch locally sourced food are hallmarks of this popular restaurant and bar. The menu contains a selection of Welsh-reared steaks and other meat dishes, but outstanding seafood is the real specialty. The romantic setting is as much of a draw as the food. Check out the huge stone "Flemish chimney," a distinctive style popularized by immigrants during the 16th century. *Average main: £17 Quay Hill 01834/842350 www.plantagenettenby.co.uk Closed Jan.–mid-Feb.*

$ B&B/INN **Ivy Bank Guest House.** This comfortable and immaculate Victorian house sits across from the train station, a five-minute stroll from the sea. **Pros:** cozy and simple; close to beach; senior discounts. **Cons:** you have to park at the train station; first night must be paid in advance (nonrefundable and nonchangeable). *Rooms from: £70 Harding St. 01834/842311 www.ivybanktenby.co.uk 5 rooms Breakfast.*

$$ HOTEL Fodor's Choice ★ **Penally Abbey.** Built on the site of a 6th-century abbey in 5 acres of lush forest overlooking Camarthen Bay, this dignified 18th-century house is awash with period details. **Pros:** informal luxury; great views; friendly hosts. **Cons:** small pool. *Rooms from: £155 Off A4139, 2 miles west of Tenby, Penally 01834/843033 www.penally-abbey.com 17 rooms Breakfast.*

$$ HOTEL Fodor's Choice ★ **St. Brides Spa Hotel.** Between Amroth and Tenby, this luxury hotel has a breathtaking location perched above Camarthen Bay; most of the superbly appointed rooms have stunning sea views. **Pros:** amazing views; wonderful spa; fantastic restaurant; plenty of deals and special offers. **Cons:** steep walk from the beach; minimum stay on weekends. *Rooms from: £160 St. Brides Hill, Saundersfoot 01834/812304 www.stbridesspahotel.com 46 rooms Breakfast.*

SPORTS AND THE OUTDOORS

The town's beaches are hugely popular in summertime. North Beach is the busiest, with shops and a little café along the promenade. The adjoining Harbour Beach is prettier and more secluded. Castle Beach is in a little cove where you can walk out to a small island at low tide. Past that is South Beach, which stretches for more than a mile.

ST. DAVID'S TYDDEWI

35 miles northwest of Tenby.

Despite its minuscule size, this community of fewer than 1,800 people isn't a village or a town—it's actually Britain's smallest city. Historically, little St. David's has punched above its weight due to the presence of St. David's Cathedral, the resting place of the patron saint of Wales and once a major destination for pilgrims. These days, visitors with time on their hands might want to consider approaching the city via the Wales Coast Path, around the St. David's headland from St. Justinian to Caerfai Bay. In May and June the town's hedgerows and coastal paths are ablaze with wildflowers. The visitor center has a small collection of art and artifacts drawn from the collection at the National Museum of Wales.

GETTING HERE AND AROUND

St. David's is on the A487. The nearest train station is 14 miles southeast in Haverfordwest. Bus 411 travels from Haverfordwest to St. David's every hour or so.

ESSENTIALS

Visitor Information Oriel y Parc Gallery and Visitor Centre. ✉ *1 High St.* ☎ *01437/720392* 🌐 *www.orielyparc.co.uk.*

EXPLORING

OFF THE BEATEN PATH

Last Invasion Tapestry. The 100-foot-long Last Invasion Tapestry, on display in the Town Hall in Fishguard, is modeled on the famous Bayeux Tapestry depicting the Norman invasion of 1066. This modern version marks a lesser known and certainly less successful assault on the country. In 1797, a unit of French soldiers, led by an Irish-American general, landed in Fishguard Harbour. They were defeated by a hastily assembled local militia, which included many women. The impressive tapestry, commissioned to mark the event's 200th anniversary, took 70 local women more than 40,000 hours to complete. At 🌐 *www.pembrokeshirevirtualmuseum.co.uk* you can download free walking, driving, and cyclying guides that delve deeper into the history of the failed invasion. Fishguard is 16 miles northeast of St. David's off the A487. ✉ *Fishguard Town Hall, Market Sq., Fishguard* ☎ *01437/776638* 🌐 *www.pembrokeshire.gov.uk* 🎫 *Free* ⏲ *Apr.–Sept., Mon.–Wed. and Fri. 9:30–5, Thurs. 9:30–6:30, Sat. 9:30–5; Oct.–Mar., Mon.–Wed. and Fri. 9:30–5, Thurs. 9:30–6:30, Sat. 9:30–1.*

Fodor's Choice ★

St. David's Cathedral. The idyllic valley location of this cathedral helped protect the church from Viking raiders by hiding it from the view of invaders who came by sea. Originally founded by St. David himself around AD 600, the current building dates from the 12th century, although it has been added to at various times since. You must climb down 39 steps (known locally as the Thirty-Nine Articles) to enter the grounds; then start at the Gatehouse, with its exhibition on the history of the building. In the cathedral itself, the 15th-century choir stalls still have their original floor tiles, while the Holy Trinity Chapel contains an intricate fan-vaulted ceiling and a casket said to contain the patron saint's bones. ■ **TIP→ Don't miss the Treasury and its illuminated gospels, silver chalices, and 700-year-old golden bishop's crosier.** At the rear of the grounds of St. David's Cathedral are the ruins of the 13th-century Bishop's Palace, particularly beautiful at dusk. In August, guided tours costing £4.50 begin Monday at 11:30 and Friday at 2:30, and on other days by arrangement. The cathedral has a good café. ✉ *The Close* ☎ *01437/720202* 🌐 *www.stdavidscathedral.org.uk* 🎫 *Free; £4.50 donation requested* ⏲ *Daily 9–5:30 (Oct.–Mar., closes after prayers at 4 in winter if no evening service).*

WHERE TO STAY

$$ HOTEL

Warpool Court Hotel. Overlooking a stunning stretch of coastline, this hotel sits on a bluff above St. Non's Bay. The building dates from the 1860s, when it housed St. David's Cathedral Choir School. **Pros:**

beautiful sea views; peaceful gardens; good food. **Cons:** few restaurants nearby. $ *Rooms from: £145* ✉ *Off Goat St.* ☎ *01437/720300* 🌐 *www.warpoolcourthotel.com* *25 rooms* *Breakfast.*

MID-WALES

Traditional market towns and country villages, small seaside resorts, quiet roads, and rolling landscapes filled with sheep farms, forests, and lakes make up Mid-Wales, the country's green and rural heart. There are no cities here—the area's largest town is barely more than a big village. Outside of one or two towns, such as Aberystwyth and Llandrindod Wells, accommodations are mainly country inns, small hotels, and rural farmhouses. This area also has some splendid country-house hotels.

There are no motorways through Mid-Wales, and the steam railways that once linked this area with Cardiff are long gone. Getting around requires a bit of advance planning, but it's worth the trouble. The bibliophilic charms of Hay-on-Wye have made the town world-famous, while the countryside around Aberystwyth is peppered with peaceful sandy beaches and dramatic beauty spots.

HAY-ON-WYE Y GELLI GANDRYLL

57 miles north of Cardiff, 25 miles north of Abergavenny.

Fodor's Choice ★ With its crumbling old castle and low-slung buildings framed by lolloping green hills, Hay-on-Wye is a beautiful little place. In 1961 Richard Booth established a small secondhand bookshop here. Other booksellers soon got in on the act, and now there are dozens of shops. It's now the largest secondhand bookselling center in the world, and priceless 14th-century manuscripts rub spines with "job lots" selling for a few pounds.

For 10 days every May and June, Hay-on-Wye is taken over by its Literary Festival, a celebration of literature that attracts famous writers from all over the world. (Bill Clinton, himself an attendee, once called it "the Woodstock of the mind.") Plan ahead if you want to attend, as hotels get booked several months in advance.

GETTING HERE AND AROUND

You'll need a car to get to Hay. Use one of the public lots on the outskirts of town and walk—the whole town is accessible on foot. The nearest train stations are Builth Wells in Wales (19 miles) and Hereford in England (22 miles).

ESSENTIALS

Visitor Information Hay-on-Wye Tourist Information Bureau. ✉ *Oxford Rd.* ☎ *01497/820144* 🌐 *www.hay-on-wye.co.uk/tourism.*

EXPLORING

Hay Castle. On a hilltop are the handsome remains of a 12th-century castle keep, jutting out from behind a 16th-century manor house. ✉ *Castle St.* *Free* *Late Mar.–Oct., daily 9:30–6; Nov.–late Mar., daily 9:30–5:30.*

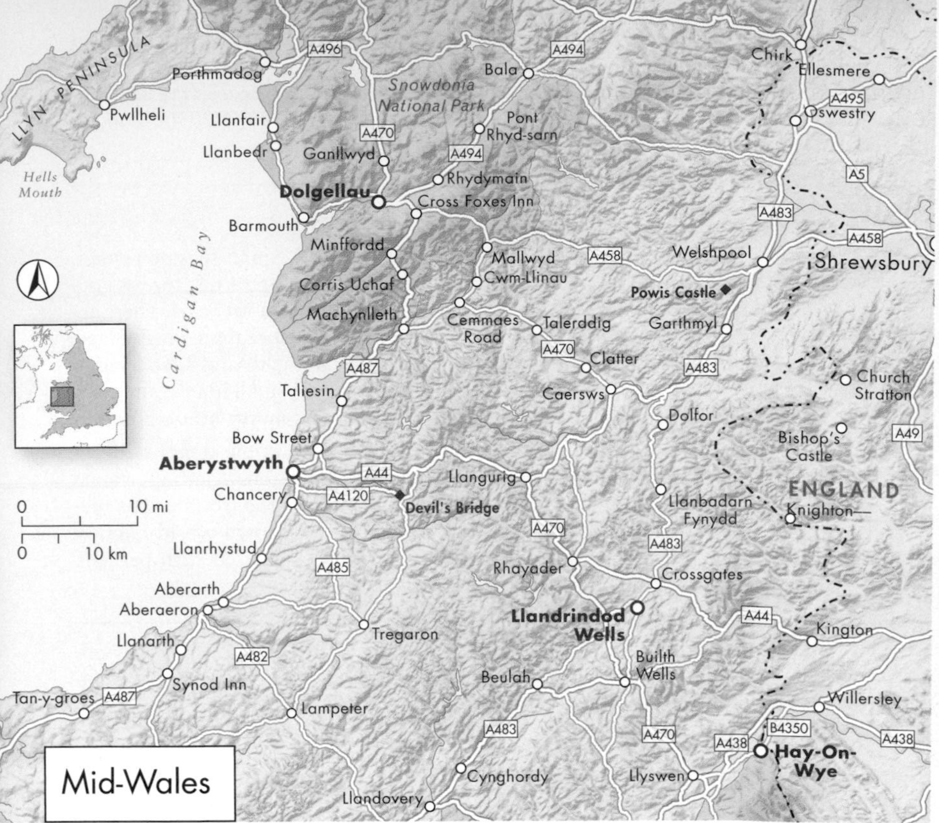

NEED A BREAK?

Shepherd's. The delicious ice cream at Shepherd's is legendary in these parts. Produced at a local farm, its distinct, creamy flavor comes from the fact that it's made from sheep's milk. ✉ ***9 High Town*** ☎ ***01497/821898*** 🌐 ***www.shepherdsicecream.co.uk.***

WHERE TO EAT AND STAY

$$ BRITISH

Old Black Lion. A 17th-century coaching inn close to Hay's center is ideal for a lunch break while you're ransacking the bookshops. The oak-beamed bar serves food, and the breakfasts are especially good. The restaurant's sophisticated cooking emphasizes local meats and produce—in, for example, a pork, apple, and sage burger, or roast salmon in a white wine and cheese sauce. The two-course lunch menu is an excellent value for the money at just £12. You can even opt for an overnight stay in one of the country-style rooms (from about £100 per night). *$ Average main: £15* ✉ *Lion St.* ☎ *01497/820841* 🌐 *www.oldblacklion.co.uk.*

$$$ HOTEL Fodor's Choice ★

Llangoed Hall. This magnificent Jacobean mansion on the banks of the River Wye, about 7 miles west of Hay-on-Wye, has beautiful fabrics and furnishings, open fireplaces, a sweeping carved staircase, and a paneled library dating back to 1632. **Pros:** secluded setting by River Wye; wonderful art collection. **Cons:** often filled with wedding parties; minimum stay sometimes required; no attractions within walking distance. *Rooms from: £175* ✉ *A470, Llyswen* ☎ *01874/754525* 🌐 *www.llangoedhall.co.uk* *23 rooms* *Breakfast.*

$$ HOTEL **The Swan.** Once a coaching inn, this sophisticated lodging on the edge of town retains its sense of history. **Pros:** atmospheric building; friendly staff; good food. **Cons:** wedding parties dominate in summer; two-night minimum on weekends; beds a bit creaky. *Rooms from: £100* ✉ *Church St.* ☎ *01497/821188* 🌐 *www.swanathay.co.uk* *17 rooms* *Breakfast.*

SHOPPING

The Thursday Market takes over much of the town center every Thursday morning. Traders sell everything from antiques to home-baked cakes.

Boz Books. The kind of dusty old bookshop you see in movies, Boz Books has an impressive range of 19th-century first editions, including many by Dickens. ✉ *13A Castle St.* ☎ *01497/821277* 🌐 *www.bozbooks.demon.co.uk.*

Fodor's Choice ★ **Murder and Mayhem.** True to its name, this shop specializes in crime and horror. Head upstairs for a cheaper and more eclectic selection, including old pulp novellas. ✉ *5 Lion St.* ☎ *01497/821613.*

Fodor's Choice ★ **Richard Booth Books.** Shopkeeper Richard Booth once tried to declare Hay an independent kingdom—with himself as king. His bookstore has a huge collection from all over the world, piled haphazardly across two labyrinthine floors. ✉ *44 Lion St.* ☎ *01497/820322* 🌐 *www.boothbooks.co.uk.*

Rose's Books. Easy to spot for its fuchsia-pink front, Rose's Books is devoted entirely to children's books, including rare first editions. ✉ *14 Broad St.* ☎ *01497/820013* 🌐 *www.rosesbooks.com.*

14

LLANDRINDOD WELLS LLANDRINDOD

27 miles north of Hay-on-Wye, 67 miles north of Cardiff.

Also known as Llandod, the old spa town of Llandrindod Wells preserves its Victorian look with turrets, cupolas, loggias, and balustrades everywhere. Cross over to South Crescent, passing the Glen Usk Hotel with its wrought-iron balustrade and the Victorian bandstand in the gardens opposite, and you reach Middleton Street, a Victorian thoroughfare. From there, head to Rock Park and the path that leads to the Pump Room. This historic building is now an alternative health center, but visitors can freely "take the waters."

GETTING HERE AND AROUND

There are about half a dozen trains daily from Cardiff's Craven Arms Station, and the journey takes around three hours. Direct trains from Swansea and Shrewsbury also stop here, but they're less frequent.

ESSENTIALS

Visitor Information Llandrindod Wells Tourist information Centre. ✉ *The Old Town Hall, Temple St.* ☎ *01597/822600* 🌐 *www.llandrindod.co.uk.*

Hay-on-Wye's claims to fame are its many secondhand bookstores and the annual Literary Festival.

EXPLORING

OFF THE BEATEN PATH

Powis Castle. Continuously occupied since the 13th century, Powis Castle rises above the town of Welshpool. One of the most elegant residential castles in Britain, Powis is equally renowned for its magnificent terraced gardens. The interior contains an outstanding art collection, from Greek vases to paintings by Thomas Gainsborough and Joshua Reynolds. The **Clive of India Museum** contains perhaps the most extensive private collection of antique Indian art in Britain. Powis Castle is north of Llandrindod Wells on the A483. ✉ *A483, Welshpool* ☎ *01938/551944* 🌐 *www.nationaltrust.org.uk/powis-castle* 🎫 *Apr.–Oct. £12.50, Nov.–Feb. £6.20; castle only Apr.–Oct. £6.50, Nov.–Feb. £3.40; garden only Apr.–Oct. £9.20, Nov.–Feb. £4.70* ⏲ *Castle Jan.–Feb., weekends noon–3:30 (tours only); Mar. and Oct., daily 11–4; Apr.–Sept., daily 11–5; Nov.–Dec., 11–4 (no tours). Museum Apr.–Sept., daily noon–5; Mar. and Oct.–Dec., daily noon–4. Gardens Apr.–Sept., daily 10–6; Oct.–Mar., 10–4.*

Radnorshire Museum. In Memorial Gardens, this museum tells the story of the town's development from prehistory onwards and includes a small collection of Roman and medieval artifacts. The largest and most interesting section is devoted to the town's Victorian heyday, with some of the "cures" at the spa explained in gruesome detail. ✉ *Temple St.* ☎ *01597/824513* 🌐 *www.powys.gov.uk/radnorshiremuseum* 🎫 *£1* ⏲ *Apr.–Sept., Tues.–Sat. and holiday Mon. 10–4; Oct.–Mar., Tues.–Fri. 10–4, Sat. 10–1.*

Royal Welsh Show. The town of Llanelwedd, 7 miles south of Llandrindod, comes to life in late July for the Royal Welsh Show. The old-school livestock judging, sheepdog competitions, and craft demonstrations are spiced up with events such as vintage air displays and motorbike stunt shows. ✉ *Llanelwedd* ☎ *01982/553683* 🌐 *www.rwas.co.uk/royal-welsh-show* 🎫 *£25.*

Fodor's Choice ★ **Victorian Festival.** The Victorian Festival takes over Llandrindod Wells for a week in late August. Everyone from shopkeepers to hotel clerks dresses up in period costume for events from tea dances to street parades. The main festival is bookended by two mini-festivals where dressing up is also part of the fun: a 1940s Weekend just before and a slightly edgier Steampunk Weekend right afterwards. ✉ *Llandrindod Wells* ☎ *01597/823441* 🌐 *www.victorianfestival.co.uk* 🎫 *Free; special events £8–£25.*

14

WHERE TO EAT AND STAY

$ MEDITERRANEAN ✕ **Sugar and Spice.** This sweet and friendly little bistro looks unassuming from the outside, but its pan-Mediterranean fare has won over legions of local fans. Choose from the selection of tapas (Spanish with a hint of Greek), fresh pasta or pizza, a Mediterranean salad, or just a tasty hamburger. It's all rather haphazard but the cheerful combination works. During the day they serve sandwiches, panini, and light snacks. $ *Average main: £13* ✉ *Park Crescent* ☎ *01597/824442* 🌐 *www.sugarandspicebistro.co.uk.*

$$ HOTEL 🏨 **Lake Country House & Spa.** The place to go for total Victorian country elegance, Lake Country and its 50 acres of sloping lawns contain a trout-filled lake bordered by an impressive spa. **Pros:** superb grounds; good food; luxurious spa. **Cons:** remote location; dress code in evenings. $ *Rooms from: £145* ✉ *Off B4519, Llangammarch Wells* ☎ *01591/620202* 🌐 *www.lakecountryhouse.co.uk* 🛏 *30 rooms* 🍽 *Breakfast.*

$$ HOTEL 🏨 **Metropole.** This grand looking hotel from 1896 is surprisingly contemporary on the inside, with modern furnishings that complement the original architectural flourishes. **Pros:** very central; good service; inexpensive spa. **Cons:** lacks character; can be taken over by conferences. $ *Rooms from: £126* ✉ *Temple St.* ☎ *01597/823700* 🌐 *www.metropole.co.uk* 🛏 *120 rooms* 🍽 *Breakfast.*

ABERYSTWYTH

41 miles northwest of Llandrindod Wells via A44, 118 miles northwest of Cardiff.

A pleasingly eccentric combination of faded Victorian seaside resort and artsy college town, Aberystwyth is the largest community in Mid-Wales, with a population of barely 16,000. When the weather's fine, the beaches along the bay fill up with sunbathers; when it's not, waves crash so ferociously against the sea wall that even the hotels across the street get soaked. To the east of the town are the Cambrian Mountains and the Veil of Rheidol, which can be visited by steam train.

GETTING HERE AND AROUND

All journeys from South Wales are routed through Shrewsbury and take four to five hours. From London, the trip here takes five to six hours. Long-distance buses are infrequent and painfully slow, though the local bus system is good. There are two roads to Aberystwyth, both of them among the most scenic in Wales: the coastal A487 and the mountainous A44.

ESSENTIALS

Visitor Information Aberystwyth Tourist Information Centre. ✉ *Lisburn House, Terrace Rd.* ☎ *01970/612125* 🌐 *www.visitmidwales.co.uk.*

EXPLORING

TOP ATTRACTIONS

FAMILY **Constitution Hill.** At the northern end of the beach promenade, Constitution Hill dominates the skyline. From the top you can see much of the Welsh coastline (and, on *exceptionally* clear days, Ireland). There's a small café at the top and plenty of space for a picnic. If you're feeling hale and hearty, there's a long footpath that zigzags up to the 430-foot summit. From there, a 5-mile-long coastal path stretches to the village of Borth, a smaller, sleepier resort north of Aberystwyth where the remains of a 3,000-year-old petrified forest may be seen on the beach at low tide. ✉ *Aberystwyth.*

Great Aberystwyth Camera Obscura. A modern version of a Victorian amusement, Great Aberystwyth Camera Obscura is a massive 14-inch lens that gives you a bird's-eye view of Cardigan Bay and 26 Welsh mountain peaks. It's reached via the Aberystwyth Cliff Railway. ✉ *Cliff Terr.* ☎ *01970/617642* 🌐 *www.aberystwythcliffrailway.co.uk* 🎫 *Free* 🕒 *Apr.–Oct., daily 10–5.*

FAMILY **Vale of Rheidol Railway.** At Aberystwyth Station you can hop on the steam-powered Vale of Rheidol Railway for an hour-long ride to the **Devil's Bridge** (*Pont y Gwr Drwg*, or, literally, "the Bridge of the Evil One"), where the rivers Rheidol and Mynach meet in a series of spectacular falls. Clamped between two rocky cliffs where a torrent of water pours unceasingly, there are actually three bridges, one built on top of the other. The oldest bridge is about 800 years old. ✉ *Park Ave.* ☎ *01970/625819* 🌐 *www.rheidolrailway.co.uk* 🎫 *£19 round-trip* 🕒 *Easter–Oct. times vary, but departures generally go at 10:30 and 2 daily—call or check website for schedule; Nov., Sun. only.*

WORTH NOTING

Aberystwyth Castle. The British writer Caitlin Moran once wrote fondly of Aberystwyth's "Glitter-glue sea and smashed-cake castle," and these crumbling ruins at the southern end of the bay do have an endearing quality. Built in 1277, the castle was one of the key strongholds captured in the early 15th century by Owain Glyndwr, a Welsh prince who led the country's last serious bid for independence from England. Today it's a romantic, windswept ruin, rather incongruously used as a cut-through walking path by locals for whom it's nothing out of the ordinary at all. To find the ruins, just walk along the bay, away from the town center; they are located just after the small pier. ✉ *New Promenade* 🎫 *Free.*

Aberystwyth Cliff Railway. The Victorian-era Aberystwyth Cliff Railway deposits you at the top of Constitution Hill. Opened in 1896, it's the longest electric cliff railway in Britain. ✉ *Cliff Terr.* ☎ *01970/617642* 🌐 *www.aberystwythcliffrailway.co.uk* 🎫 *£4 round-trip* 🕒 *Apr.–Oct.,* *daily 10–5; Nov.–Mar., timetable varies (generally Wed.–Sun. 10–4, but call for daily times).*

Ceredigion Museum. Housed in a flamboyant 1905 Edwardian theater, the Ceredigion Museum has collections related to folk history and the building's own music hall past. Highlights include a reconstructed mud-walled cottage from 1850 and items illustrating the region's seafaring, lead-mining, and farming history. ✉ *Terrace Rd.* ☎ *01970/633088* 🌐 *museum.ceredigion.gov.uk* 🎟 *Free* ⏲ *Apr.–Sept., Tues.–Sat. 10:30–4, Sun. noon–4; Oct.–Mar., Mon.–Sat. noon–4.*

FAMILY **Llynwenog Silver-Lead Mine.** Outside the village of Ponterwyd, 10 miles east of Aberystwyth, this 200-year-old mine is now a museum where you can tour reproductions of mining buildings and some original machinery, including working waterwheels. Kids over the age of 8 can also enjoy a few harmless scares on the Black Chasm ghost tour, though very young ones will be better off sticking to the Woo Hoo Woods adventure playground. ■ **TIP→ It's cold in the mine, even on hot days, so bring a jacket or sweater.** Times can vary; call to check, especially in off-season. ✉ *Off A44, Ponterwyd* ☎ *01970/890620* 🌐 *www.silvermountainexperience.co.uk* 🎟 *£11; surface attractions only £5* ⏲ *May.–mid-July, Sept., and Oct., daily 10–4; mid-July–Sept., daily 10–5; last tour 1 hr before closing.*

14

WHERE TO EAT

$ BRITISH ✕ **Gannets.** A simple but friendly bistro, Gannets specializes in hearty roasts and traditional Welsh-style dishes that use local meat and fish. Organically grown vegetables and a good wine list are further draws for a university crowd. This place is popular with locals, and you're likely to hear Welsh being spoken at the next table. Ⓢ *Average main: £13* ✉ *7 St. James's Sq.* ☎ *01970/617164* ⏲ *No lunch. Closed Sun.–Tues.*

$$ SPANISH Fodor's Choice ★ ✕ **Ultracomida.** This lively, modern Spanish eatery brings a splash of Mediterranean color to the Mid-Wales coastline. The lunch menu is served tapas style: hake with lentils and Serrano ham, squid fried in garlic with salsa verde, or maybe just some fresh hummus and toast. Or you could just put together an upscale picnic hamper from the in-house deli. Tapas and very reasonably priced sharing plates are available in the evening. Ⓢ *Average main: £15* ✉ *31 Pier St.* ☎ *01970/630686* 🌐 *www.ultracomida.co.uk* ⏲ *No dinner Sun. and Mon.*

WHERE TO STAY

$ HOTEL **Glandyfi Castle.** This fanciful 19th-century folly 12 miles north of Aberystwyth was built to look like the epitome of a fairy-tale castle, complete with battlements and turrets, and the playful pastiche carries through the luxurious, contemporary guest rooms, which incorporate features such as four-poster beds into the otherwise modern design. **Pros:** charming and fanciful building; unique setting; incredible views. **Cons:** style may be a bit twee for some; limited dining options; cheaper rooms inevitably miss out on the views. Ⓢ *Rooms from: £90* ✉ *A487, Glandyfi, Machynlleth* ☎ *01654/781238* 🌐 *www.glandyficastle.co.uk* *8 rooms* 🍽 *Breakfast.*

$ HOTEL Fodor's Choice ★ **Gwesty Cymru.** Converted into one of Aberystwyth's more stylish lodgings, this seafront Edwardian house has public areas decorated with original paintings and illuminated Welsh poetry, and most of the comfortable guest rooms have gorgeous views across the bay. **Pros:** contemporary design; beautiful location. **Cons:** seafront can be noisy at night; limited parking. *Rooms from: £90 ✉ 19 Marine Terr. ☎ 01970/612252 ⊕ www.gwestycymru.com ⇨ 8 rooms ǀ◎ǀ Breakfast.*

$$ HOTEL **Harbourmaster Hotel.** A drive south on the coast road from Aberystwyth brings you to this early 19th-century Georgian-style building right on the harbor among colorfully painted structures. **Pros:** good food; stunning harbor location; friendly hosts. **Cons:** difficult parking; often booked up; minimum stay on weekends. *Rooms from: £135 ✉ Pen Cei, 15 miles south of Aberystwyth, Aberaeron ☎ 01545/570755 ⊕ www.harbour-master.com ⇨ 13 rooms ǀ◎ǀ Breakfast.*

$$$ HOTEL Fodor's Choice ★ **Ynyshir Hall.** This luxurious Georgian mansion is *the* place to stay in this part of Wales if money is no object—as the photos of its world-famous guests on the lobby walls will attest. **Pros:** artsy ambience; unabashed luxury; great food. **Cons:** isolated location; impossible to reach without a car. *Rooms from: £215 ✉ Off A487, southwest of Machynlleth, Eglwysfach ☎ 01654/781209 ⊕ www.ynyshir-hall.co.uk ⇨ 9 rooms ǀ◎ǀ Breakfast.*

NIGHTLIFE AND PERFORMING ARTS

Aberystwyth Arts Centre. In addition to a cinema, the lively Aberystwyth Arts Centre has a theater, a gallery, shops, and a good café and bar. The list of movies is varied, including an international horror movie festival every fall (the rather brilliantly named "Abertoir"). *✉ Aberystwyth University, Penglais Rd. ☎ 01970/623232 ⊕ www.aberystwythartscentre.co.uk.*

DOLGELLAU

34 miles northeast of Aberystwyth.

A solidly Welsh town with dark stone buildings and old coaching inns made of the local gray dolerite and slate, Dolgellau (pronounced dol-*geth*-lee) thrived with the wool trade until the mid-19th century. Prosperity left striking architecture with buildings of different eras side by side on crooked streets that are a legacy from Norman times.

Dolgellau has long been a popular base for people eager to walk the surrounding countryside, which forms the southern tip of Snowdonia National Park. To the south of Dolgellau rises the menacing bulk of 2,927-foot Cadair Idris. The name means "the Chair of Idris," a reference to a giant from ancient Celtic mythology.

GETTING HERE AND AROUND

Dolgellau's nearest railway station is at the town of Barmouth, about 10 miles away. The town is small and full of interesting nooks and crannies easily explored on foot. To discover the surrounding area you'll need a car.

ESSENTIALS

Visitor Information Dolgellau Tourist Information Centre. ✉ *Ty Meirion, Eldon Sq.* ☎ *01341/422888* 🌐 *www.visitmidwales.co.uk.*

EXPLORING

Quaker Heritage Centre. In the town square, this museum commemorates the area's strong links with the Quaker movement and the Quakers' emigration to the American colonies. ✉ *Eldon Sq.* ☎ *01341/424680* 🎫 *Free* 🕙 *Easter–Oct., daily 10–6; Nov.–Easter, Thurs.–Mon. 10–5.*

FAMILY **Ty Siamas.** The National Centre for Welsh Folk Music is in the converted Victorian Market Hall and Assembly Rooms. It has a fascinating interactive folk music exhibition, performance auditorium, and café and bar. ✉ *Neuadd Idris, Eldon Sq.* ☎ *01341/421800* 🌐 *www.tysiamas.com* 🎫 *Free* 🕙 *Easter–Sept., Wed.–Fri. 10–4, Sat. 10–1. Call for off-season hrs.*

NORTH WALES

Wales masses its most dramatic splendor and fierce beauty in the north. Dominating the area is Snowdon, at 3,560 feet the highest peak in England and Wales. The peak gives its name to 840-square-mile Snowdonia National Park, which extends southward all the way to Machynlleth in Mid-Wales. As in other British national parks, much of the land is privately owned, so inside the park are towns, villages, and farms, in addition to some spectacular mountain scenery.

The mock-Italianate village of Portmeirion is an extraordinary architectural flight of fancy, and the seaside resort of Llandudno is as popular today as it was during its Victorian heyday. And scattered across the countryside are a ring of mighty medieval castles, built by King Edward I (1239–1307) at the end of a bloody war to bring the population under English rule.

Although North Wales is more popular with travelers than Mid-Wales, the road network is even more tortuous. In fact, you haven't really experienced North Wales until you've spent a maddening hour snaking along a narrow mountain road, all the while with your destination in plain view.

LLANGOLLEN

23 miles southwest of Chester, 60 miles southwest of Manchester.

Llangollen's setting in a deep valley carved by the River Dee gives it a typically Welsh appearance. The bridge over the Dee, a 14th-century stone structure, is named in a traditional Welsh folk song as one of the "Seven Wonders of Wales." In July the very popular International Musical Eisteddfod brings crowds to town.

For a particularly scenic drive in this area, head for the Horseshoe Pass. For other views, follow the marked footpath from the north end of the canal bridge up a steep hill to see Castell Dinas Bran, the ruins of a 13th-century castle built by a native Welsh ruler. The views of the town and the Vale of Llangollen are worth the 45-minute (one-way) walk.

WELSH: A SHORT PRIMER

The native language of Wales, Welsh (or *Cymraeg*, as it's properly called) is spoken fluently by around a quarter of the population. (The vast majority, however, speaks a little.) Not legally recognized in Britain until the 1960s, it was suppressed beginning in the time of Henry VIII and blamed for poor literacy during the reign of Queen Victoria. Today Welsh children under 17 are required to take classes to learn the language.

Welsh may look daunting, with its complicated words and confusing double consonants, but it's a phonetic language, so pronunciation is actually quite easy once the alphabet is learned. A quick primer to get you started: "dd" is sounded like "th" in they, "f" sounds like "v" in save, and "ff" is the equivalent of the English "f" in forest. The "ll" sound has no English equivalent; the closest match is the "cl" sound in "close."

Terms that crop up frequently in Welsh are *bach* or *fach* (small; also a common term of endearment similar to "dear"), *craig* or *graig* (rock), *cwm* (valley; pronounced coom), *dyffryn* (valley), *eglwys* (church), *glyn* (glen), *llyn* (lake), *mawr* or *fawr* (great, big), *pentre* (village, homestead), *plas* (hall, mansion), and *pont* or *bont* (bridge).

GETTING HERE AND AROUND

You'll need a car to get here, but once you arrive you can take a trip on the Llangollen Railway. Along the Llangollen Canal longboat tours head both west and east. The town itself is easy to explore on foot.

ESSENTIALS

Visitor Information Llangollen Tourist Information Centre. ✉ *Y Capel, Castle St.* ☎ *01978/860828* 🌐 *www.llangollen.org.uk.*

EXPLORING

Castell Dinas Brân. This romantic hilltop ruin looks out over a breathtaking patchwork of green fields and mountains. The fortress was built in the 1260s on the site of an earlier castle, which was an Iron Age fort before that. Its heyday was incredibly short lived; by the end of the 13th century it had been captured and abandoned by English forces after which it gradually fell into ruin. The castle is located on top of a hill just north of Llangollen town center. There are no roads to the summit; the best walking path starts at Canal Bridge in Llangollen and zigzags up the side of the hill. The rather punishing hike is a little over a mile long. ✉ *Llangollen* 🎫 *Free* ⏲ *Daily dawn–dusk (open site).*

Fodor's Choice ★ **Chirk Castle.** This impressive medieval fortress has evolved from its 14th-century origins into a grand home complete with an 18th-century servants' hall and interiors furnished in 16th- to 19th-century styles. However, it still looks satisfyingly medieval from the outside—and also below ground, where you tour the original dungeons. Surrounding the castle are beautiful formal gardens and parkland. Chirk Castle is 5 miles southeast of Llangollen. ✉ *Off B4500, Chirk* ☎ *01691/777701* 🌐 *www.nationaltrust.org.uk/chirk-castle* 🎫 *£11* ⏲ *State Rooms: Mar. and Oct., daily 11–4 (tours only 11–noon); Apr.–Sept., daily 10–5 (tours only*

Llangollen's yearly International Musical Eisteddfod, a gathering of international choirs and dancers, shows that Wales is truly a land of song.

11–noon). Gardens and Tower: Feb.–Mar. and Oct., daily 10–4; Apr.–Sept., daily 10–5; Nov. weekends 11–4.

FAMILY **Llangollen Railway.** This restored standard-gauge steam line runs for 7 miles along the scenic Dee Valley. The terminus is near the town's bridge. ✉ *Abbey Rd.* ☎ *01978/860979* 🌐 *www.llangollen-railway.co.uk* 🎫 *£15 round-trip* ⏲ *Departure times vary by day; call or check website for schedule—generally 3 trips daily, Apr.–Oct.; weekends only Nov.–Mar.*

Fodor's Choice ★ **Plas Newydd.** From 1778 to 1828 Plas Newydd (not to be confused with the similarly named Isle of Anglesey estate) was the home of Lady Eleanor Butler and Sarah Ponsonby, the eccentric Ladies of Llangollen, who set up a then-scandalous single-sex household, collected curios and magnificent carvings, and made it into a tourist attraction even during their lifetimes. You can take tea there, as did Wordsworth and the Duke of Wellington, and stroll in the attractively terraced gardens. ✉ *Hill St.* ☎ *01978/862834* 🌐 *www.denbighshire.gov.uk* 🎫 *£6* ⏲ *Apr.–Sept., Wed.–Mon. 10:30–5; last admission 1 hr before closing.*

Pontcysyllte. From the Llangollen Canal Wharf you can take a 45-minute or two-hour trip on a horse-drawn boat or a narrow boat (a slender barge) along the canal to the world's longest and highest navigable cast-iron aqueduct: Pontcysyllte (Welsh for "the bridge that connects"), a UNESCO World Heritage Site. The aqueduct is more than 1,000 feet long. Pontcysyllte is 3 miles east of Llangollen. ✉ *Llangollen Canal Wharf, Wharf Hill* ☎ *01978/860702 Llangollen Wharf* 🌐 *www.horsedrawnboats.co.uk* 🎫 *£6.50 (45 min), £12 (2 hrs).*

Vale of Ceiriog. Near Llangollen is this verdant valley, known locally as "Little Switzerland." The B4500 road, running between Chirk and the village of Glyn Ceiriog, at the foothills of the Berwyn Mountains, is one of the region's great drives. It's just remote enough that you can often have the road to yourself. ✉ *Llangollen.*

Fodor's Choice ★ **Valle Crucis Abbey.** The last abbey of the Cistercian order to be founded in Wales, Valle Crucis was built in 1201 and abandoned in 1537—a victim of Henry VIII's violent dissolution of the monastaries. Today it's a highly picturesque ruin beside a glassy lake. Surprisingly large sections survive relatively intact—particularly the sacristy and more or less complete chapter house, with its intricate vaulted ceiling. In its day Valle Crucis was one of the richest and most powerful abbeys in Wales; despite half a millennium of decay, this is still an impressive site to wander. ✉ *Off A542* ☎ *01639/651931* 🌐 *cadw.gov.wales* 🎫 *£3.50; free Nov.–Mar.* ⏲ *Apr.–Oct., daily 10–5; Nov.–Mar., daily 10–4; last admission 30 min before closing.*

WHERE TO EAT AND STAY

$ BRITISH ✕ **The Corn Mill.** In a converted mill on the River Dee, this pub and restaurant has an old water wheel that turns behind the bar. Dine on the open-air deck or in the cozy dining room, sampling stylishly updated pub fare, such as steak-and-ale pie with strong mustard mash and Isle of Anglesey sea bass with crab croquettes. There are light bites, too, and dessert classics such as hot waffles with chocolate sauce and bananas. Several of the ales are from Welsh microbreweries. $ *Average main: £13* ✉ *Dee La.* ☎ *01978/869555* 🌐 *www.brunningandprice.co.uk/cornmill.*

$$ B&B/INN 🏨 **Cornerstones Guesthouse.** Made up of three 16th-century cottages with views over the River Dee, this little B&B mixes period charm with modern comfort. **Pros:** spacious bedrooms; free passes for town parking lots. **Cons:** directly on the street. $ *Rooms from: £100* ✉ *15 Bridge St.* ☎ *01978/861569* 🌐 *www.cornerstones-guesthouse.co.uk* 🛏 *3 rooms, 2 suites* 🍽 *Breakfast.*

NIGHTLIFE AND PERFORMING ARTS

International Musical Eisteddfod. The six-day International Musical Eisteddfod, held in early July, brings together amateur choirs and dancers—more than 12,000 participants in all—from all corners of the globe for a colorful folk festival. The tradition of the eisteddfod, held throughout Wales, goes back to the 12th century. Originally gatherings of bards, the *eisteddfodau* of today are more like national festivals. ✉ *Llangollen* ☎ *01978/862001* 🌐 *www.international-eisteddfod.co.uk.*

LAKE VYRNWY LLYN EFYRNWY

27 miles southwest of Llangollen.

This beautiful lake has a sense of tranquillity that doesn't entirely befit its history. Lake Vyrnwy was created in the 1880s to provide water for the people of Liverpool, 80 miles north. Unfortunately, this meant forcibly evicting the residents of a small town—an act that's still controversial in Wales. Today it's a peaceful spot surrounded by a thriving nature

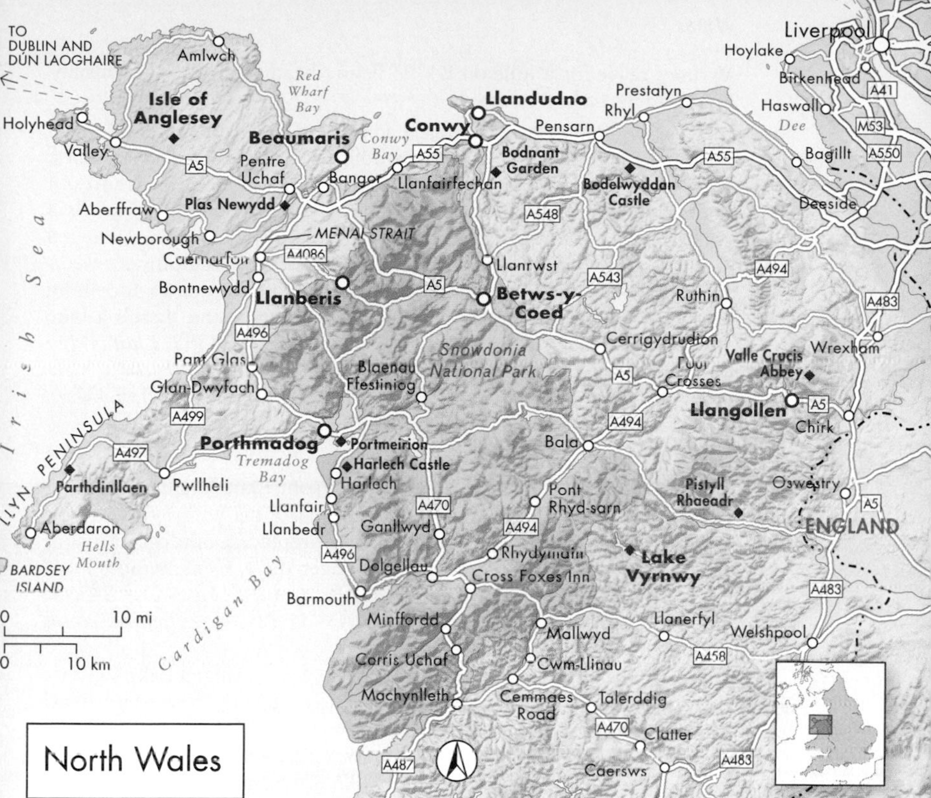

reserve. The closest settlement is tiny Llanwddyn, and a bit farther away is Bala, a pretty town with an almost-as-lovely natural lake of its own.

GETTING HERE AND AROUND

Rural bus service is infrequent, so you need a car to explore the area. The B4393 circles Lake Vyrnwy itself; from here, Bala is a 14-mile drive over hair-raising Bwlch y Groes pass or a circuitous drive along the B4391. Llangollen is 27 miles northeast of Lake Vyrnwy on the B4396.

EXPLORING

FAMILY **Bala Lake Railway.** The steam-powered train runs along the southern shores of Bala Lake (Llyn Tegid, or "Lake of Beauty"), a large natural reservoir just northeast of Lake Vyrnwy. Bala Lake is also popular for kayaking and other water sports. Call to check daily departure times. ✉ *Off B4403, Llanuwchllyn* ☎ *01678/540666* 🌐 *www.bala-lake-railway.co.uk* 🎟 *£9.80 round-trip* 🕒 *Apr.–Sept., most days, times vary; check website or call for schedule (but generally Llanuwchllyn departures daily, 11, 12:45, 2:15, and 3:45; Bala departures daily, 11:35, 1:20, 2:50, and 4:20).*

Bwlch y Groes. One of the great drives of North Wales, the sweeping, vertiginous panoramas of Bwlch y Groes (Pass of the Cross) form the highest mountain pass accessible by road in the country. From Lake

Vyrnwy, drive for a mile on B4393 before heading west on the mountain road. ✉ *Lake Vyrnwy.*

FAMILY Fodor's Choice ★ **Lake Vyrnwy Nature Reserve.** Bordered by lush forest and emerald green hills, Lake Vyrnwy is a haven for wildlife. It's rich in rare bird species, from falcons to siskins and curlews. Stretching out along the shores of the lake near the visitor center, the Lake Vyrnwy Sculpture Park is a collection of pieces by talented local artist Andy Hancock. Arranged along a paved walking trail, many of the wooden sculptures resemble oversize versions of the lake's wildlife, including a 15-foot-long dragonfly. It's an extremely popular cycling route, and there's a bike shop and coffee shop near the visitor center. ✉ *Off B4393, Llanwddyn* ☎ *01691/870278* 🌐 *www.lake-vyrnwy.com* *Free* *Visitor Center Apr.–Oct., daily 10:30–5:20; Nov.–Dec., daily 10:30–4:30; Jan.–Mar., weekdays 10:30–4, weekends 10:30–5. Park daily year-round.*

WHERE TO STAY

$$ B&B/INN **Cyfie Farm.** In a tranquil area 5 miles from Lake Vyrnwy, this ivy-clad 17th-century farmhouse has huge bedrooms with exposed oak beams and log fireplaces. **Pros:** in-room fireplaces; outdoor hot tub; hosts are trained chefs; discounts for longer stays. **Cons:** remote location; need a car to get around. *Rooms from: £118* ✉ *Off B4393, Llanfihangel-yng-Ngwynfa* ☎ *01691/648451* 🌐 *www.cyfiefarm.co.uk* *4 suites* *Breakfast.*

$$ B&B/INN Fodor's Choice ★ **Lake Vyrnwy Hotel.** Awesome views of mountain-ringed Lake Vyrnwy are just one asset of this country mansion on a 24,000-acre estate. **Pros:** perfect for outdoor pursuits; luxurious spa; excellent package deals. **Cons:** too remote for some; minimum stay on some summer weekends. *Rooms from: £145* ✉ *Off B4393, Llanwddyn* ☎ *01691/870692* 🌐 *www.lakevyrnwy.com* *52 rooms* *Breakfast.*

PORTHMADOG

35 miles southeast of Lake Vyrnwy, 16 miles southeast of Caernarfon.

The little seaside town of Porthmadog, built as a harbor to export slate from nearby Blaenau Ffestiniog, stands at the gateway to the Llŷn Peninsula (pronounced like "lean," with your tongue touching your palate), with its virtually unspoiled coastline and undulating wildflower-covered hills. It's also near the town of Harlech, which contains one of the great castles of Wales, and the weird and wonderful Portmeirion.

GETTING HERE AND AROUND

The picturesque Cambrian Coast Railway runs from Machynlleth, near Aberystwyth, up the coast to Porthmadog. When you arrive you can take a scenic trip on the town's "little railways." Porthmadog is a stop on the excellent Snowdon Sherpa bus service. The town itself is totally walkable and has good access to coastal trails.

ESSENTIALS

Visitor Information Porthmadog Tourist Information Centre. ✉ *High St.* ☎ *01766/512981* 🌐 *www.visitsnowdonia.info.*

EXPLORING

TOP ATTRACTIONS

FAMILY **Ffestiniog Railway.** Founded in the early 19th century to carry slate, the Ffestiniog Railway starts at the quayside and climbs up 700 feet through a wooded vale, past a waterfall, and across the mountains. The northern terminus is in Blaenau Ffestiniog, where you can visit an old slate mine. The Ffestiniog Railway is perhaps the best of several small steam lines in this part of the country. Porthmadog gets very crowded in summer, and parking is limited, so you might want to make this journey from Blaenau Ffestiniog to Porthmadog instead. Call to check the daily timetable. ✉ *Harbour Station, High St.* ☎ *01766/516000* 🌐 *www.festrail.co.uk* 🎫 *£22 round-trip* ⏲ *Apr.–Oct., daily; call for times (also occasional days off-season).*

14

Fodor's Choice ★ **Harlech Castle.** A wealth of legend, poetry, and song is conjured up by the 13th-century Harlech Castle, built by Edward I to help subdue the Welsh. Its mighty ruins, visible for miles, are as dramatic as its history (though you have to imagine the sea, which used to crash against the rocks below but receded in the 19th century). Harlech was occupied by the Welsh Prince Owain Glyndwr from 1404 to 1408 during his revolt against the English. The music of the traditional folk song "Men of Harlech" refers to the heroic defense of this castle in 1468 by Dafydd ap Eynion, who, summoned to surrender, is alleged to have replied: "I held a castle in France until every old woman in Wales heard of it, and I will hold a castle in Wales until every old woman in France hears of it." On a clear day you can climb the battlements for a spectacular view of the surrounding countryside. The castle dominates the coastal town of Harlech, 12 miles south of Porthmadog. ✉ *Off B4573, Harlech* ☎ *01766/780552* 🌐 *www.cadw.wales.gov.uk* 🎫 *£4.50* ⏲ *Mar.–June, Sept., and Oct., daily 9:30–5; July and Aug., daily 9:30–6; Nov.–Feb., Mon.–Sat. 10–4, Sun. 11–4; last admission 30 min before closing.*

Fodor's Choice ★ **Portmeirion.** One of the true highlights of North Wales is Portmeirion, a tiny fantasy-Italianate village on a private peninsula surrounded by hills; it's said to be loosely modeled after Portofino in Italy. Designed in the 1920s by architect Clough Williams-Ellis (1883–1978), the village has a hotel and restaurant among its multicolored buildings, and gift shops sell a distinctive local pottery. On the edge of town is a peaceful woodland trail punctuated here and there by such flourishes as a red iron bridge and a miniature pagoda. Williams-Ellis called it his "light-opera approach to architecture," and the result is magical, though distinctly un-Welsh. Portmeirion is about 2 miles east of Porthmadog. ✉ *Off A487, Portmeirion* ☎ *01766/772311* 🌐 *www.portmeirion-village.com* 🎫 *£10* ⏲ *Daily 9:30–7:30.*

Fodor's Choice ★ **Tre'r Ceiri.** Remote, atmospheric, and astoundingly little known, Tre'r Ceiri is one of the most impressive ancient monuments in Wales. Today parts of the 4th-century fort's outer walls are still intact (rising more than 18 feet in places), and within are the ruins of 150 stone huts. They were inhabited by a Celtic tribe known as the Ordovices, and may have survived as a settlement for up to 700 years. From Porthmadog, take the A497 west, then turn left onto the A499 just before Pwllheli. At the village of Llanaelhaearn, turn left onto the B4417. Less than a mile down this road is an unmarked footpath on the right leading straight up a hill to Tre'r Ceiri. ✉ *B4417, Llanaelhaearn* 🎫 *Free.*

WORTH NOTING

FAMILY **Llechwedd Slate Caverns.** At these caverns you can descend 500 feet on Britain's deepest underground railway to a mine where you walk by an eerie underground lake. Here Victorian working conditions have been re-created, and the tour gives a good idea of the difficult lives the miners had to endure. Above are a re-created Victorian village and slate-splitting demonstrations. Thrill-seekers will enjoy the hair-raising 5-mile zip line, where you can reach speeds of up to 70 mph; visit 🌐 *www.zipworld.co.uk* for more information. There's also a new underground trampoline playground for young children. Wear sturdy footwear when visiting the mine—during busy times you may have to climb 70 steps as part of the tour. ✉ *Off A470, Blaenau Ffestiniog* ☎ *01766/830306* 🌐 *www.llechwedd-slate-caverns.co.uk* 🎫 *£16; zip line £50; Bounce Below playground £20* 🕒 *Mid-Mar.–Sept., daily 9–5:30; Oct.–mid-Mar., daily 10–5. Last tours: Sat.–Thurs. 4:30, Fri. 4.*

Porthdinllaen. On the very tip of a thumb-shape bay jutting out into the Irish Sea, this miniscule but gorgeous little harbor community is 20 miles from Porthmadog. There's a wide, sheltered beach where the sand is so fine that it squeaks underfoot, and whitewashed cottages line the curving seafront. Park at the nearby visitor center. ✉ *Porthdinllaen.*

WHERE TO EAT AND STAY

$$$$ BRITISH ✕ **Castle Cottage.** Close to Harlech's mighty castle, this friendly "restaurant with rooms" is a wonderful find, with an emphasis on the exceptional cuisine of chef-proprietor Glyn Roberts, who uses locally sourced ingredients from lobster to lamb to create imaginative, beautifully presented contemporary dishes. The fixed-price dinner menu starts at £35 for two courses. There are three spacious, modern rooms (from £130) in the main house and four more in the annex, a 16th-century coaching inn. Those staying the night receive a discount on dinner. [$] *Average main: £35* ✉ *Near B4573, Harlech* ☎ *01766/780479* 🌐 *www.castlecottageharlech.co.uk* 🕒 *No lunch.*

$ BRITISH ✕ **Ty Coch Inn.** In a seafront building in picture-postcard Porthdinllaen, this pub has what is undoubtedly one of the best locations in Wales. The lunches are honest and unpretentious: pies, sandwiches, bangers and mash, or perhaps a plate of local mussels in garlic butter. Everything is delicious and reasonably priced. The atmosphere is friendly and slightly bohemian; this is the kind of place where they're pleasantly surprised you've managed to find it. [$] *Average main: £8* ✉ *Off B4417, Porthdinllaen* ☎ *01758/720498* 🌐 *www.tycoch.co.uk* 🕒 *No dinner.*

$$$ HOTEL Fodor's Choice ★ 🏨 **Hotel Portmeirion.** One of the most elegant and unusual places to stay in Wales, this waterfront mansion is located at the heart of Portmeirion. **Pros:** unique location; beautiful building; woodland walks. **Cons:** gets crowded with day-trippers; minimum stay on weekends. [$] *Rooms from: £179* ✉ *Off A487, Portmeirion* ☎ *01766/770000* 🌐 *www.portmeirion-village.com* 🛏 *42 rooms, 11 suites* 🍽 *Breakfast; Some meals.*

$ B&B/INN 🏨 **Y Branwen Hotel.** A pleasant, no-frills lodging just down the hill from Harlech Castle, Y Branwen is a popular local pub and a friendly place for an overnight stay. **Pros:** pleasant and comfortable; welcoming hosts; good food. **Cons:** few frills; inevitably there can be noise from the bar. $ *Rooms from: £95* ✉ *Fford Newydd* ☎ *01766/780477* 🌐 *www.branwenhotel.co.uk* 8 *rooms* 🍽 *Breakfast.*

BETWS-Y-COED

25 miles northeast of Porthmadog, 19 miles south of Llandudno.

The rivers Llugwy and Conwy meet at Betws-y-Coed, a popular village surrounded by woodland with excellent views of Snowdonia. It can be used as a base to explore the national park, although its diminutive size means that it can get overcrowded in summer. The most famous landmark in the village is the ornate iron Waterloo Bridge over the River Conwy, designed in 1815 by Thomas Telford.

14

GETTING HERE AND AROUND

The town is easy to reach on the Conwy Valley Railway that runs from Llandudno to Blaenau Ffestiniog. Betws-y-Coed is also a hub for the excellent Snowdon Sherpa bus service that covers most of Snowdonia's beauty spots, so it's feasible to explore this part of Wales without a car.

ESSENTIALS

Visitor Information Betws-y-Coed Tourist Information Centre. ✉ *Royal Oak Stables, Station Rd.* ☎ *01690/710426* 🌐 *www.betws-y-coed.co.uk.*

EXPLORING

Gwydyr Forest and Swallow Falls. Betws-y-Coed is bordered by Gwydyr Forest, which has several well-marked walking trails. The forest also contains a half dozen or so mines, the last of which was abandoned in the 1940s. On the western approach to the village you'll find Swallow Falls, where the River Llugwy tumbles down through a wooded chasm. **■ TIP→ Be careful on the footpath: there's no guardrail.** ✉ *Off A5.*

FAMILY Fodor's Choice ★ **Snowdonia National Park.** Stretching from the Welsh midlands almost to its northern coast, Snowdonia National Park covers a vast swath of North Wales. The park consists of 840 square miles of rocky mountains, valleys clothed in oak woods, moorlands, lakes, and rivers, all guaranteeing natural beauty and, to a varying extent, solitude. Its most famous attraction, by far, is the towering peak of Mt. Snowdon. The view from the top is jaw-dropping: to the northwest you can see the Menai Strait and Anglesey; to the south, Harlech Castle and the Cadair Idris mountain range. To the southwest, on an exceedingly clear day, you can make out the distant peaks of Ireland's Wicklow Mountains. There are six different walking paths to the top, but a far less punishing way is via the Snowdon Mountain Railway in nearby Llanberis.

Perched at the top of Snowdon is Hafod Eryri, an eco-friendly replacement for the previous visitor center (once described by Prince Charles as "the highest slum in Wales"). The granite-roof building, which blends beautifully into the rocky landscape, has a café and exhibitions about the mountain, its ecology, and its history. If you're planning to make the ascent, the visitor center in Betws-y-Coed is the best place to stop for information. ✉ *Royal Oak Stables, Station Rd.* ☎ *01690/710426* 🌐 *www.eryri-npa.gov.uk/home.*

The Llanberis Path is one route to the top of Snowdon, the highest peak in Wales, in Snowdonia National Park.

WHERE TO EAT AND STAY

$$ BRITISH — **Ty Gwyn.** This coaching inn, built in 1636, is one of the best places to eat in Snowdonia. The food is traditional Welsh fare, beautifully prepared with local ingredients. Standouts include halibut with creamed leeks, and South Wales lamb with peppercorn and onion marmalade. Vegetarians are well cared for with such dishes as mushroom and pine nut stroganoff. The inn also has simple, cozy bedrooms starting at £60 per night. *Average main: £16 A5 01690/710383 www.tygwynhotel.co.uk.*

$ B&B/INN — **Aberconwy House.** This luxurious Victorian house has panoramic views over Betws-y-Coed. **Pros:** breathtaking countryside views; great breakfasts; charge for kids under three only £5 per night. **Cons:** no bar or evening meal. *Rooms from: £75 Lôn Muriau, off A470 01690/710202 www.aberconwy-house.co.uk 8 rooms Breakfast.*

$ B&B/INN Fodor's Choice ★ — **Pengwern Country House.** Hosts Ian and Gwawr Mowatt are charmingly adept at making their guests feel at home in this former Victorian artists' colony. **Pros:** woodland location; wealth of Victorian details; lovely hosts. **Cons:** close to main road; car is essential. *Rooms from: £75 On A5, Allt Dinas 01690/710480 www.snowdoniaaccommodation.co.uk 3 rooms Breakfast.*

$$ B&B/INN — **Tan-y-Foel Country House.** Hidden away on a wooded hillside outside Betws-y-Coed, this quiet, contemporary hideaway has views over the Conwy Valley. **Pros:** striking decor; inventive cuisine. **Cons:** meals must be arranged in advance; too far to walk into town. *Rooms from: £130 Off A5, Capel Garmon 01690/710507 www.tyfhotel.co.uk 6 rooms Breakfast.*

LLANBERIS

17 miles west of Betws-y-Coed.

Like Betws-y-Coed, Llanberis is a focal point for people visiting Snowdonia National Park.

GETTING HERE AND AROUND

Llanberis is accessible by bus. The most convenient service, targeted at visitors, is the Snowdon Sherpa bus route.

ESSENTIALS

Visitor Information Llanberis Tourist Information Centre. ✉ *Electric Mountain, Off A4086* ☎ *01286/870765* 🌐 *www.visitsnowdonia.info.*

EXPLORING

Fodor's Choice ★ **Caernarfon Castle.** The grim, majestic mass of Caernarfon Castle, a UNESCO World Heritage Site, looms over the waters of the River Seiont. Numerous bloody encounters were witnessed by these sullen walls, erected by Edward I in 1283 as a symbol of his determination to subdue the Welsh. The castle's towers, unlike those of Edward I's other castles, are polygonal and patterned with bands of different-color stone. In 1284 the monarch thought of a scheme to steal the Welsh throne. Knowing that the Welsh chieftains would accept no foreign prince, Edward promised to designate a ruler who could speak no word of English. Edward presented his infant son to the assembled chieftains as their prince "who spoke no English, had been born on Welsh soil, and whose first words would be spoken in Welsh." The ruse worked, and on that day was created the first prince of Wales of English lineage. In the Queen's Tower, a museum charts the history of the local regiment, the Royal Welsh Fusiliers. The castle is in the town of Caernarfon, 7 miles west of Llanberis. ✉ *Castle Hill, Caernarfon* ☎ *01286/677617* 🌐 *cadw.gov.wales* 🎫 *£7* 🕒 *Mar.–June, Sept., and Oct., daily 9:30–5; July and Aug., daily 9:30–6; Nov.–Feb., Mon.–Sat. 10–4, Sun. 11–4; last admission 30 min before closing.*

National Slate Museum. In Padarn Country Park, this museum in the old Dinorwig Slate Quarry is dedicated to what was once an important industry for the area. The museum has quarry workshops and slate-splitting demonstrations, as well as restored worker housing, all of which convey the development of the industry and the challenges faced by those who worked in it. The narrow-gauge Llanberis Lake Railway departs from here. ✉ *Padarn Country Park, A4086* ☎ *029/2057–3700* 🌐 *www.museumwales.ac.uk/slate* 🎫 *Free* 🕒 *Easter–Oct., daily 10–5; Nov.–Easter, Sun.–Fri. 10–4.*

FAMILY Fodor's Choice ★ **Snowdon Mountain Railway.** One of the region's most famous attractions is the rack-and-pinion Snowdon Mountain Railway, with some of its track at a thrillingly steep grade. The 3,560-foot-high Snowdon—*Yr Wyddfa* in Welsh—is the highest peak south of Scotland and lies within the 840-square-mile national park. Weather permitting, trains go all the way to the summit; on a clear day you can see as far as the Wicklow Mountains in Ireland, about 90 miles away. You can take two types of train: a modern diesel-driven version, or the brand-new "heritage" version, complete with restored carriages and working steam engine. From mid-March to May, or in times of high winds, the journey is truncated so you don't get all the way up to the summit; if so, tickets are a few pounds cheaper. ■ **TIP→ Tickets can sell out early on busy days, so try to book in advance.** ✉ *A4086* ☎ *0844/493–8120* 🌐 *www.snowdonrailway.co.uk* *Diesel service: £27 round-trip; Heritage service: £35 round-trip* ⏲ *Mid-Mar.–Oct., daily; call for schedule.*

WHERE TO EAT AND STAY

$ PIZZA ✕ **Gallt y Glyn.** This laid-back restaurant is popular with locals, drawn by the delicious, fresh pizza (though the free drinks also help). Pizzas are made entirely to order, so there's no menu for them as such—you just create your own from a list of toppings. They also serve salads, steaks, and other comfort food. In an unashamedly crowd-pleasing move, all (adult) diners get a free pint of beer with their main. They also do basic B&B accommodations from £60 per night. Gallt y Glyn is just under 1 mile northeast of Llanberis. $ *Average main: £11* ✉ *A4086* ☎ *01286/870370* 🌐 *www.gallt-y-glyn.co.uk* ⏲ *No lunch.*

$ B&B/INN **Dolafon Guest House.** This cozy, traditional B&B in the center of Llanberis makes no pretense to contemporary style, and that's precisely the appeal. **Pros:** characterful house; charming owner; central location. **Cons:** style may be a bit fussy for some; one room has a bathroom down the hall; full cooked breakfast (as opposed to "Continental" style) is £5 extra. $ *Rooms from: £75* ✉ *High St.* ☎ *01286/870993* 🌐 *www.dolafon.com* *7 rooms* *Breakfast.*

BEAUMARIS (BIWMARES) AND ANGLESEY (YNYS MÔN)

14 miles north of Llanberis.

Elegant Beaumaris is on the Isle of Anglesey, the largest island directly off the shore of Wales. It's linked to the mainland by the Britannia road and rail bridge and by Thomas Telford's remarkable chain suspension bridge, built in 1826 over the Menai Strait. Though its name means "beautiful marsh," Beaumaris has become a town of pretty cottages, Georgian houses, and bright shops; it also has Plas Newydd, one of the grandest stately homes in Wales.

Around 70% of Anglesey's 60,000 or so inhabitants speak Welsh, so you'll probably hear it more than English.

GETTING HERE AND AROUND

Anglesey is linked to the mainland by the A55 and A5. The roads on the island are in good condition, and there's a relatively extensive bus network. Ferries and catamarans to Ireland leave from Holyhead, on the island's western side.

EXPLORING

Fodor's Choice ★ **Beaumaris Castle.** The town of Beaumaris dates from 1295, when Edward I commenced work on this impressive castle, the last and largest link in an "iron ring" of fortifications around North Wales built to contain the Welsh. Guarding the western approach to the Menai Strait, the unfinished castle (a World Heritage Site) is solid and symmetrical, with concentric lines of fortification, arrow slits, and a moat: a superb example of medieval defensive planning. ✉ *Castle St., Beaumaris*

01248/810361 cadw.gov.wales £5.50 Mar.–June, Sept., and Oct., daily 9:30–5; July and Aug., daily 9:30–6; Nov.–Feb., Mon.–Sat. 10–4, Sun. 11–4; last admission 30 min before closing.

Fodor's Choice ★ **Bryn Celli Ddu.** Dating from around 3000 BC, this megalithic passage tomb is the most complete site of its kind in Wales. You enter via a narrow opening built into a burial mound. The passage extends for around 25 feet before opening out into a wider burial chamber. The far wall, made of quartz, is illuminated at dawn on the summer solstice. Bring a flashlight, as the tomb has no artificial lighting. Next to the entrance is a replica of a stone pillar carved with Celtic spirals, found here in 1928. The original is in the National Museum in Cardiff. The site is 7 miles southwest of Beaumaris. *Off A4080, Llanddaniel Fab Free Daily, dawn–dusk.*

Fodor's Choice ★ **Plas Newydd.** Some historians consider Plas Newydd to be the finest mansion in Wales. Remodeled in the 18th century by James Wyatt (1747–1813) for the marquesses of Anglesey (whose descendants still live here), it stands on the Menai Strait about 7 miles southwest of Beaumaris. The interior has some fine 18th-century Gothic Revival decorations. Between 1936 and 1940 the society artist Rex Whistler (1905–44) painted the mural in the dining room. A museum commemorates the Battle of Waterloo, where the first marquess led the cavalry. The woodland walk and rhododendron gardens are worth exploring, and it's sometimes possible to take boat trips on the strait. Plas Newydd is not to be confused with the Gothic mansion of the same name in Llangollen. *Off A4080, southwest of Britannia Bridge, Llanfairpwll 01248/714795 www.nationaltrust.org.uk/plas-newydd House and garden £9.80; garden only £7.80 House Feb.–mid-Mar., weekends 11–3; mid-Mar.–early Nov., Sat.–Wed. 11–4:30 (tours only 11–noon). Garden Jan. and Feb., weekends 11–3; Mar.–June and Sept.–early Nov., Sat.–Thurs. 10:30–5:30; July and Aug., daily 10:30–5:30; mid-Nov.–Dec., Sat.–Thurs. 11–3.*

WHERE TO STAY

$$ B&B/INN **Cleifiog.** This cozy manor house, mostly Georgian in style, is on the banks of the Menai Strait a short stroll from Beaumaris Castle. **Pros:** seafront location; close to town; interesting history. **Cons:** minimum stay on weekends. *Rooms from: £100 A454, Beaumaris 01248/811507 www.cleifiogbandb.co.uk 3 rooms Breakfast.*

$ B&B/INN **Ye Olde Bull's Head and Townhouse.** These twin hotels, a stone's throw away from each other, could hardly be more different: one is a restored 15th-century coaching inn, the other a contemporary lodging. **Pros:** lovely blend of historic and contemporary; good food. **Cons:** Bull's Head has low ceilings. *Rooms from: £95 Castle St., Beaumaris 01248/810329 www.bullsheadinn.co.uk 13 rooms Breakfast.*

SPORTS AND THE OUTDOORS

Anglesey is a great place to get outdoors.

Isle of Anglesey Coastal Path. Extending 125 miles around the island, this path leads past cliffs, sandy coves, and plenty of scenic variety. Pick up information at any of the regional tourist offices and choose a section;

the west coast has the most dramatic scenery. ✉ *Beaumaris* 🌐 *www.loveanglesey.co.uk*.

CONWY

23 miles east of Beaumaris, 48 miles northwest of Chester.

The still-authentic medieval town of Conwy grew up around its castle on the west bank of the River Conwy. A ring of ancient but well-preserved walls, built in the 13th century to protect the English merchants who lived here, enclose the old town and add to the pervading sense of history. Sections of the walls, with their 21 towers, can still be walked. The impressive views from the top take in the castle and the estuary, with mountains in the distance.

GETTING HERE AND AROUND

The A55 expressway links Conwy into the central U.K. motorway system via the M56. The town is also on the North Wales coast rail route, which ends at Holyhead on Anglesey. The town itself—surrounded by its wonderfully preserved walls—is perfect for pedestrians.

ESSENTIALS

Visitor Information Conwy Tourist Information Centre. ✉ *Muriau Buildings, Rosehill St.* ☎ *01492/577566* 🌐 *www.visitconwytown.co.uk.*

EXPLORING

Aberconwy House. Thought to be the oldest complete medieval house in Wales, Aberconwy House's rooms have been restored to reflect three distinct periods in its history: medieval, Jacobean, and Victorian. It's a diverting and atmsopheric little place, which also holds the distinction of (supposedly) being one of the most haunted buildings in North Wales. ✉ *Castle St.* ☎ *01492/592246* 🌐 *www.nationaltrust.org.uk/aberconwy-house* 🎫 *£3.50* ⏲ *Mid-Mar.–Oct., daily 11–5; Nov. and Dec., weekends 10–4.*

Fodor's Choice ★ **Bodnant Garden.** Undoubtedly one of the best gardens in Wales, Bodnant Garden is something of a pilgrimage spot for horticulturists from around the world. Laid out in 1875, the 87 acres are particularly famed for rhododendrons, camellias, and magnolias. **■TIP→ Visit in May to see the laburnum arch that forms a huge tunnel of golden blooms.** The mountains of Snowdonia form a magnificent backdrop to the Italianate terraces, rock and rose gardens, and pinetum. The gardens are about 5 miles south of Conwy. ✉ *Off A470, Tal-y-Cafn* ☎ *01492/650460* 🌐 *www.nationaltrust.org.uk/bodnant-garden* 🎫 *£10.50 (£5.25 winter)* ⏲ *Mar.–Oct., daily 10–5; Nov.–Feb., daily 10–4.*

Fodor's Choice ★ **Conwy Castle.** Of all Edward I's Welsh strongholds, it is perhaps Conwy Castle that best preserves a sheer sense of power and dominance. The eight large round towers and tall curtain wall, set on a rocky promontory, provide sweeping views of the area and the town walls. Although the castle is roofless (and floorless in places), the signage does a pretty good job of helping you visualize how rooms such as the Great Hall must once have looked. Conwy Castle can be approached on foot by a dramatic suspension bridge completed in 1828; engineer Thomas Telford designed the bridge with turrets to blend in with the fortress's presence. ✉ *Rose Hill St.* ☎ *01492/592358* 🌐 *cadw.gov.wales* 🎟 *£7* ⏲ *Mar.–June, Sept., and Oct., daily 9:30–5; July and Aug., daily 9:30–7; Nov.–Feb., Mon.–Sat. 10–4, Sun. 11–4; last admission 30 min before closing.*

QUICK BITES

Popty Conwy Bakery. This excellent bakery in the shadow of Conwy Castle sells delicious, generously proportioned sandwiches, cakes, and other treats to take out. The enormous vanilla slices are somewhat legendary among locals. Popty is Welsh for "oven." ✉ ***4 Castle St.*** ☎ ***01492/581004.***

Plas Mawr. Dating from 1576, Plas Mawr is one of the best-preserved Elizabethan town houses in Britain. Richly decorated with ornamental plasterwork, it gives a unique insight into the lives of the Tudor gentry and their servants. ✉ *High St.* ☎ *01492/580167* 🌐 *cadw.gov.wales* 🎟 *£6* ⏲ *Apr.–Sept., daily 9:30–5 (last admission 45 min before closing); Oct., daily 9:30–4 (last admission 30 min before closing).*

14

Smallest House in Britain. What is said to be Britain's smallest house is furnished in mid-Victorian Welsh style. The house, which is 6 feet wide and 10 feet high, was reputedly last occupied in 1900 by a fisherman who was more than 6 feet tall. ✉ *Lower Gate St.* ☎ *01492/593484* 🌐 *www.thesmallesthouseingreatbritain.co.uk* 🎟 *£1* ⏲ *Apr.–Oct., Mon.–Sat. 10–5:30, Sun. 11–4. Hrs sometimes extended in summer.*

WHERE TO EAT

$ BRITISH Fodor's Choice ★

✕ **Bodnant Welsh Food Centre.** Wales has undergone something of a culinary renaissance in the last decade and a half, and this fantastic center is a great place to explore why. Traditional cheeses, homemade ice creams, and other artisanal food products are for sale in the farm shop and deli; there's also a bakery and a wine shop where you can pick up Welsh malt whisky. The excellent Hayloft Restaurant serves delicious meals made with local produce (of course), so you might find Snowdonia beef served with Aberwen cheese-glazed potatoes, or cod with Conwy mussel cream. ■ **TIP→ The two-course, £15 menu—available at lunchtime and until 9 pm Monday and Tuesday and until 6 pm Friday and Saturday—is an excellent value.** Bodnant is on A470, 12 miles north of Conwy. 💲 *Average main: £14* ✉ *Furnace Farm, Tal-y-Cafn* ☎ *01492/651102* 🌐 *www.bodnant-welshfood.co.uk.*

$$ MODERN BRITISH

✕ **Groes Inn.** Beamed ceilings, log fires, and rambling rooms abound at this old inn dating back to the 15th century. Eat in the restaurant or the more casual bar. The menu consists of pub classics done well—Welsh beef burger with local Bodnant cheese, perhaps, or sea bass with scallops and pureed cauliflower. Bedrooms are also available upstairs, starting at £125. The name, which rhymes with "choice," means "cross" in Welsh. The inn is 2 miles south of Conwy. 💲 *Average main: £15* ✉ *B5106, Ty'n-y-Groes* ☎ *01492/650545* 🌐 *www.groesinn.com.*

$$ MODERN BRITISH

✕ **Le Gallois.** Just off the coast road 4 miles west of Conwy, this small and unpretentious restaurant is a culinary oasis. The chef-proprietor offers a daily menu using the best local produce. Dishes may include juicy scallops with a beurre blanc, Conwy crab au gratin, or local lamb cooked with a mint-and-Madeira sauce. 💲 *Average main: £18* ✉ *Pant yr Afon, Penmaenmawr* ☎ *01492/623820* ⏲ *Closed Mon.–Wed. No lunch.*

With plants and trees from around the world, Bodnant Garden, south of Conwy, is colorful in fall.

$$ BRITISH Fodor's Choice ★ **Watson's Bistro.** This popular bistro in central Conwy combines traditional Welsh flavors with accents of the Mediterranean. You may start with salt-and-pepper squid with a salad of watercress and pink grapefruit, before moving on to a fricasse of prawns, haddock, and salmon, or roast lamb with leeks and port jus. **TIP→ The £11 two-course lunch menu is an exceptional value.** *Average main: £17 ✉ Chapel St. ☎ 01492/596326 🌐 www.watsonsbistroconwy.co.uk ⏲ Closed Mon.*

WHERE TO STAY

$$$ HOTEL **Castle Hotel.** Nestled within Conwy's medieval walls, this former coaching inn has wood beams, stone fireplaces, and plenty of antiques. **Pros:** oozes history; in the heart of Conwy; good food. **Cons:** small rooms; noisy seagulls; lower rates do not include breakfast. *Rooms from: £164 ✉ High St. ☎ 01492/582800 🌐 www.castlewales.co.uk 28 rooms No meals.*

$$ HOTEL **Sychnant Pass House.** On a peaceful wooded hillside 2 miles west of Conwy, this country-house hotel has a laid-back atmosphere. **Pros:** great indoor pool and hot tub; beautiful grounds; unforced hospitality. **Cons:** far outside Conwy. *Rooms from: £135 ✉ Sychnant Pass Rd. ☎ 01492/596868 🌐 www.sychnant-pass-house.co.uk 12 rooms Breakfast.*

LLANDUDNO

3 miles north of Conwy, 50 miles northwest of Chester.

This engagingly old-fashioned North Wales seaside resort has a wealth of well-preserved Victorian architecture and an ornate amusement pier with entertainments, shops, and places to eat. Grand-looking small hotels line the wide promenade with a view of the deep-blue waters of the bay. The shopping district beyond retains its original canopied walkways.

GETTING HERE AND AROUND

Llandudno is on the North Wales railway line with fast access from London and other major cities. By road, it's connected to the motorway system via the A55 expressway. The scenic Conwy Valley rail line runs to Blaenau Ffestiniog, and the town is also on the network covered by the Snowdon Sherpa bus service.

ESSENTIALS

Visitor Information Llandudno Tourist Information Centre. ✉ *Library Building, Mostyn St.* ☎ *01492/577577* 🌐 *www.visitllandudno.org.uk.*

EXPLORING

OFF THE BEATEN PATH

Bodelwyddan Castle. Between Abergele and St. Asaph, this castle is the Welsh home of London's National Portrait Gallery. Paintings on display include works by John Singer Sargent, Dante Gabriel Rossetti, and Edwin Landseer. The castle grounds contain a fascinating, if somber historical footnote: a network of overgrown World War I trenches, used by the army to train new recruits. A series of interactive displays help bring the history to life. Also on the grounds are a maze, an aviary, and pretty woodland walks. The castle is 16 miles east of Llandudno. ✉ *Off A55, Bodelwyddan* ☎ *01745/584060* 🌐 *www.bodelwyddan-castle.co.uk* 🎫 *£7.50; park only £4.50* 🕒 *Mid-Apr. and late July–Aug., daily 10:30–5; May–late July and Sept.–Oct., Tues.–Thurs. and weekends 10:30–5; Nov.–Mar., weekends 10:30–4.*

Great Orme. Named for the Norse word meaning "sea monster," the 679-foot headland called Great Orme towers over Llandudno, affording extraordinary views over the bay. The **Llandudno Cable Car** (North Parade) zips you one mile to the top of Great Orme. At the summit there's an artificial ski slope and a toboggan run, both usable all year. The most picturesque way to reach the summit is the **Great Orme Tramway** (Victoria Station, Church Walks). Trips depart about every 20 minutes. The summit is a sylvan spot, with open grassland, fields of wildflowers, and rare butterflies. ✉ *Llandudno* ☎ *01492/879306 Cable car, 01492/577877 Tramway* 🌐 *www.greatormetramway.co.uk* 🎫 *Cable car £8 round-trip; tramway £6.50 round-trip* 🕒 *Cable car mid-Mar.–Oct., daily 10–4:30; tramway late Mar. and Oct., daily 10–5, Apr.–Sept., daily 10–6.*

FAMILY **Great Orme Mines.** Discovered in 1987, these mines date back 4,000 years to when copper was first mined in the area. You can take a tour and learn about the technology that ancient people used to dig the tunnels, which are thought to be the largest surviving prehistoric mines in the world. ✉ *Pyllau Rd.* ☎ *01492/870447* 🌐 *www.greatormemines.info* 🎫 *£7* 🕒 *Mid-Mar.–Oct., daily 10–4:30; last admission 1 hr before closing.*

WHERE TO STAY

$$$ HOTEL Fodor's Choice ★ **Bodysgallen Hall.** Tasteful antiques, polished wood, and comfortable chairs by cheery fires distinguish one of Wales's most luxurious country-house hotels. **Pros:** superb spa and pool; rare 17th-century knot garden; elegant dining. **Cons:** too formal for some; hard to get to without a car. *Rooms from: £179 Off A470 01492/584466 www.bodysgallen.com 15 rooms, 16 cottage suites Breakfast.*

$ HOTEL **Bryn Derwen Hotel.** This immaculate, impeccably run Victorian hotel is traditional in style, but has a contemporary edge. **Pros:** historic building; free Wi-Fi; close to the beach. **Cons:** no sea views. *Rooms from: £80 34 Abbey Rd. 01492/876804 www.bryn-derwen.co.uk 9 rooms Breakfast.*

$$ HOTEL **St. Tudno Hotel.** Perfectly situated on the seafront promenade overlooking the beach and pier, this hotel has been run by the same family for nearly 40 years. **Pros:** ocean views; swimming pool; good food. **Cons:** some rooms are snug; overly fussy decor. *Rooms from: £114 Promenade 01492/874411 www.st-tudno.co.uk 18 rooms Breakfast.*

TRAVEL SMART ENGLAND

GETTING HERE AND AROUND

AIR TRAVEL

The least expensive airfares to England are often priced for round-trip travel and must usually be purchased in advance. Airlines generally allow you to change your return date for a fee; most low-fare tickets, however, are nonrefundable.

Flying time to London is about 6½ hours from New York, 7½ hours from Chicago, 9 hours from Dallas, 10½ hours from Los Angeles, and 21 hours from Sydney. From London, flights take an hour to Paris or Amsterdam, 1½ hours to cities in Switzerland or Luxembourg, and 2 hours to Rome.

If you're flying from England, plan to arrive at the airport 90 minutes in advance for flights to Europe, 2 hours for the United States. Security at Gatwick and Heathrow airports is always fairly intense. Most people can expect to be patted down after they pass through metal detectors. Travelers are randomly searched again at the gate before transatlantic flights.

Airline Security Issues Transportation Security Administration. ☎ *866/289–9673 in U.S.* 🌐 *www.tsa.gov.*

AIRPORTS

Most international flights to London arrive at either Heathrow Airport (LHR), 15 miles west of London, or at Gatwick Airport (LGW), 27 miles south of the capital. Most flights from the United States go to Heathrow, with Terminals 3, 4, and 5 handling transatlantic flights (British Airways uses Terminal 5). Gatwick is London's second gateway, serving many U.S. destinations. A third, much smaller airport, Stansted (STN), is 40 miles northeast of the city. It handles mainly European and domestic traffic.

London City Airport (LCY), a small airport inside the city near Canary Wharf, has twice-daily business-class flights to New York on British Airways, as well as flights to European destinations. Luton Airport (LLA), 32 miles north of the city, is also quite small, and serves British and European destinations. Luton is the hub for low-cost easyJet. Manchester (MAN) in northwest England handles some flights from the United States, as does Birmingham (BHX).

Heathrow and Gatwick are enormous and can seem like shopping malls (Heathrow even offers a personal shopping service). Both airports have bars and pubs and dining options. Several hotels are connected to each airport, and both Gatwick and Heathrow are near dozens of hotels that run free shuttles to the airports. Heathrow has a Hotel Hoppa service that runs shuttles between the airport and around 25 nearby hotels for £4 each way. A free, subsidized local bus service operates between the Central Bus Station serving Terminals 1, 2, and 3 and nearby hotels. You can find out more at the Central Bus Station or at the Transport for London (TfL) Information Centre in the Underground station serving Terminals 1, 2, and 3. Yotel has budget pod hotels in both Heathrow and Gatwick with cabin-size rooms to be booked in advance in four-hour blocks or overnight. Prices begin at about £50, depending on how long you stay and the time of day.

In comparison, other British airports have much more limited shopping, hotel, and dining options; a delay of a few hours can seem like years.

Airport Information Birmingham Airport. ☎ *0871/222–0072* 🌐 *www.birminghamairport.co.uk.* **Gatwick Airport.** ☎ *0844/892–0322* 🌐 *www.gatwickairport.com.* **Heathrow Airport.** ☎ *0844/335–1801* 🌐 *www.heathrowairport.com.* **London City Airport.** ☎ *0207/646–0000* 🌐 *www.londoncityairport.com.* **Luton Airport.** ☎ *01582/405100* 🌐 *www.london-luton.co.uk.* **Manchester Airport.** ☎ *0871/271–0711* 🌐 *www.manchesterairport.*

co.uk. **Stansted Airport.** ☎ *0844/355–1803* 🌐 *www.stanstedairport.com.*

GROUND TRANSPORTATION

London has excellent bus and train connections between its airports and downtown. Train service can be the fastest, but the downside is that you must get yourself and your luggage to the terminal, often via a series of escalators and connecting trams. Airport buses (generally run by National Express) may be located nearer to the terminals and drop you closer to central hotels, but they're subject to London traffic, which can be horrendous. Taxis can be more convenient than buses, but prices can go through the roof. Minicabs are more economical, but go with recommended companies.

The Transport for London website has helpful information, as does Airport Travel Line. The official sites for Gatwick, Heathrow, and Stansted are useful resources for transportation options.

FROM HEATHROW TO CENTRAL LONDON

Travel Mode	Time	Cost
Taxi	40–80 minutes	£50–£80
Heathrow Express Train	15 minutes	£20 one way
Underground	50 minutes	£5.70 one-way
National Express Bus	45–80 minutes	£6 one-way

Heathrow by Bus: National Express buses take around one hour (longer at peak time) to reach the city center (Victoria Coach Station) and cost £6 one-way and £11.20 round-trip. Buses leave every 5 to 75 minutes from 4:20 am to 10 pm. The National Express Hotel Hoppa service runs from all terminals to around 25 hotels near the airport (£4). Alternatively, nearly every hotel in London is served by the Hotel By Bus service. Fares to Central London begin at £22.50. SkyShuttle also offers a minibus service between Heathrow and any London hotel. The N9 night bus runs every 20 minutes from 11:35 pm to 5 am to Kensington, Hyde Park Corner, Trafalgar Square, and Aldwych; it takes about 75 minutes and costs £2.20.

Heathrow by Train: The cheap, direct route into London is via the Piccadilly line of the Underground (London's extensive subway system, or "Tube"). Trains normally run every three to seven minutes from all terminals from around 5 am until just before midnight. The 50-minute trip into central London costs £5.70 (cash), £5 (Oystercard peak times) or £3 (Oystercard off-peak). The Heathrow Express train is comfortable and very convenient, if costly, speeding into London's Paddington Station in 15 minutes. Standard one-way tickets cost £26 (£21 in advance), or £29 for first class. Book online for the lowest fares. If you arrive without tickets you should purchase them at a kiosk before you board, as they're more expensive on the train. There's daily service from 5:10 am (5:03 am on Sunday) to 11:25 pm (11:53 pm on Sunday), with departures every 15 minutes. A less expensive option is the Heathrow Connect train, which stops at local stations between the airport and Paddington. Daily service is every half hour from 5:23 am (6:07 am on Sunday) to 12:01 am. The journey takes about 30 minutes and costs £9.90 one-way.

Gatwick by Bus: Hourly bus service runs from Gatwick's north and south terminals to Victoria Coach Station with 14 stops along the way. The journey takes 70–120 minutes and costs from £8 one-way. Make sure you get on a direct bus not requiring a change; otherwise the journey could take much longer. The easyBus service runs a service to Earls Court in west London from as little as £2; the later the ticket is booked online, the higher the price (up to £10 on board).

Gatwick by Train: The fast, nonstop Gatwick Express leaves for Victoria Station every 15 minutes 4:35 am–1:35 am. The 30-minute trip costs £18.70 one-way online. Tickets cost more on board. The

First Capital Connect rail company's nonexpress services are cheaper. Trains run regularly throughout the day until midnight to St. Pancras International, London Bridge, and Blackfriars stations; daytime departures are every 10–25 minutes (hourly between 1:30 am and 5 am), and the journey to St. Pancras takes 30 to 60 minutes. Tickets are from £10 one-way. You can also reach Gatwick by First Capital Connect coming from Brighton in the opposite direction. First Capital Connect service is on commuter trains, and during rush hour trains can be crowded, with little room for baggage and seats at a premium.

Stansted by Bus: National Express Airport bus A6 (24 hours a day) to Victoria Coach Station costs from £10 one-way, leaves every 15 minutes, and takes 90–120 minutes. Stops include Golders Green, Finchley Road, St. John's Wood, Baker Street, Marble Arch, and Hyde Park Corner. The easyBus service to Victoria via Baker Street costs from £2. The Terravision bus goes to Liverpool Street station every half-hour and costs £8. Travel is extended to Victoria Coach Station between 8 pm and 6 am, and the fare is £9. Travel time is 60 minutes (Liverpool St.) or 75 minutes (Victoria).

Stansted by Train: The Stansted Express to Liverpool Street Station (with a stop at Tottenham Hale) runs every 15 minutes 5:30 am–12:30 am daily (until 1:30 am Friday and Saturday). The 45-minute trip costs £18 each way if booked online. Tickets cost more on board.

Luton by Bus and Train: A free airport shuttle runs from Luton Airport to the nearby Luton Airport Parkway Station, where you can take a train or bus into London. From there, the First Capital Connect train service runs to St. Pancras, Farringdon, Blackfriars, and London Bridge. The journey takes about 40 minutes. Trains leave every 10 minutes or so from 5 am until midnight, hourly at other times. One-way tickets begin at £15.50. The Terravision Shuttle bus runs from Luton to Victoria Coach Station, with departures every 20 to 30 minutes during peak hours. The journey takes around an hour, and the one-way fare is £10. The Green Line 757 bus service from Luton to Victoria Station runs every 15 minutes between 7 am and midnight, takes 85 to 100 minutes, and costs from £10, while an easyBus shuttle has tickets starting from £2. National Express runs coaches from Victoria Coach Station to Luton from £5 one-way.

Heathrow, Gatwick, Stansted, and Luton by Taxi: This is an expensive and time-consuming option. If your destination is within the city's congestion zone, £10 will be added to the bill during charging hours. If you get stuck in traffic, a taxi from the stand will be even more expensive; a cab booked ahead is a set price. A taxi trip from Heathrow to Victoria, for example, can take more than an hour and cost more than £58. Private hire cars may be the same price or even less—at this writing, the fee to Victoria Station is about £50 from Heathrow and £100 from Gatwick and Stansted, not including the congestion charge. Another option, if you have friends in the London area, is to have them book a reputable minicab firm to pick you up. The cost of a minicab from Heathrow to central London is approximately £47. Your hotel may also be able to recommend a car service.

TRANSFERS BETWEEN AIRPORTS

Allow at least two to three hours for transferring between airports. The National Express Airport bus is the most direct option between Gatwick and Heathrow. Buses depart from Gatwick every 5–35 minutes between 5:35 am and 11:35 am (every hour from 1:50 am to 5:35 am) and from Heathrow every 5–35 minutes from 2:35 am to 12:35 am. The trip takes 80 to 100 minutes, and the fare is £25 each way. Book tickets in advance. National Express buses between Stansted and Gatwick depart every 40 to 80 minutes and take between 3 and 4½ hours. The one-way fare is from £18 to £31.80. The

National Express bus between Stansted and Heathrow takes about an hour, runs every 60–100 minutes, and costs from £24.60. Some airlines may offer shuttle services as well—check with your airline before your journey.

The cheapest option—but most complicated—is public transportation: from Gatwick to Stansted, for instance, catch the Gatwick Express train from Gatwick to Victoria Station, take the Tube to Liverpool Street Station, then hop on the train to Stansted. Alternatively, take the Thameslink train to Farringdon and transfer to the Tube bound for Liverpool Street. From Heathrow to Gatwick, take the Tube to King's Cross/St. Pancras, then take the Thameslink train to Gatwick, or else transfer from the Piccadilly Line to the District/Circle Line at Hammersmith, head to Victoria Station, and take the Gatwick Express.

All this should get much easier when the new Crossrail service debuts in 2018. It will travel directly from Heathrow to Liverpool Street Station for Stansted connections and directly to Farringdon for the Thameslink to Gatwick.

TIP→ Check the Transport for London website (www.tfl.gov.uk) to make sure trains and Tube lines are running, especially on weekends when they may be suspended for engineering works.

Contacts Crossrail. ☎ *0345/602–3813* 🌐 *www.crossrail.co.uk.* **easyBus.** 🌐 *www.easybus.co.uk.* **Gatwick Express.** ☎ *0845/850–1530, 0208/528–2900 from U.S.* 🌐 *www.gatwickexpress.com.* **Green Line.** ☎ *0844/800–4411* 🌐 *www.greenline.co.uk.* **Heathrow Connect.** ☎ *0345/604–1515* 🌐 *www.heathrowconnect.com.* **Heathrow Express.** ☎ *0845/600–1515* 🌐 *www.heathrowexpress.com.* **National Express.** ☎ *0871/781–8178* 🌐 *www.nationalexpress.com.* **Stansted Express.** ☎ *0345/600–7245* 🌐 *www.stanstedexpress.com.* **Terravision.** ☎ *01279/662931* 🌐 *www.terravision.eu.* **Transport for London.** ☎ *0343/222–1234* 🌐 *www.tfl.gov.uk.* **Traveline.** ☎ *0871/200–2233* 🌐 *www.traveline.info.*

FLIGHTS

British Airways offers mostly nonstop flights from 20 U.S. cities to Heathrow, along with flights to Manchester, Leeds, Newcastle, Edinburgh, Aberdeen, and Glasgow and a vast program of discount airfare–hotel packages. Britain-based Virgin Atlantic is a strong competitor in terms of packages. London is a very popular destination, so many U.S. carriers have flights and packages, too.

Because England is such a small country, internal air travel is much less important than it is in the United States. For trips of less than 200 miles, trains are often quicker because rail stations are more centrally located. Flying tends to cost more, but for longer trips air travel has a considerable time advantage (you need to factor in time to get to and from the airport, though).

British Airways operates shuttle services between Heathrow or Gatwick and Manchester, while Virgin's Little Red takes you from London to Manchester, Edinburgh, and Aberdeen. Low-cost airlines such as easyJet and Ryanair offer flights within the United Kingdom as well as to cities in Ireland and continental Europe. Prices are low, but these airlines usually fly out of smaller British airports such as Stansted and Luton, both near London. Check 🌐 *www.cheapflights.com* for price comparisons.

BOAT TRAVEL

Ferries and other boats travel regular routes to France, Spain, Ireland, and Scandinavia. P&O runs ferries to Belgium, France, Ireland, and the Netherlands. DFDS Seaways serves France, Denmark, Belgium, and the Netherlands, and Stena Line serves Ireland, Northern Ireland, and the Netherlands.

Low-cost airlines and Eurotunnel (which lets you take a car to France on the train) have cut into ferry travel, but companies have responded by cutting fares and upgrading equipment.

Prices vary; booking early ensures cheaper fares, but also ask about special deals. Seaview is a comprehensive online ferry- and cruise-booking portal for Britain and continental Europe. Ferry Cheap is a discount website.

Information DFDS Seaways. ☎ *0871/574–7235, 208/127–8303 in U.S.* 🌐 *www.dfdsseaways.co.uk.* **Ferry Cheap.** ☎ *0844/493–1474* 🌐 *www.ferrycheap.com.* **P&O.** ☎ *0871/664–6464* 🌐 *www.poferries.com.* **Seaview.** ☎ *01442/843–050* 🌐 *www.seaviewferries.co.uk.* **Stena Line.** ☎ *0844/770–7070* 🌐 *www.stenaline.co.uk.*

TRANSATLANTIC AND OTHER CRUISES

Most cruise ships leave from southern England—particularly Southampton and Portsmouth. Some ships leave from Liverpool and Dover as well, or from Harwich, near Cambridge.

Cruise Lines Cunard Line. ☎ *800/728–6273 in U.S., 0843/374–2224 in U.K* 🌐 *www.cunard.co.uk.* **Holland America Line.** ☎ *020/7940–4470 in U.K.* 🌐 *www.hollandamerica.com.* **Norwegian Cruise Line.** ☎ *0845/201–8900 in U.K, 866/234–7350 in U.S.* 🌐 *www.ncl.com.* **Princess Cruises.** ☎ *800/774–6237 in U.S., 0843/374–4444 in U.K.* 🌐 *www.princess.com.* **Royal Caribbean International.** ☎ *800/398–9819 in U.S., 0844/493–4005 in U.K.* 🌐 *www.royalcaribbean.com.*

BUS TRAVEL

Britain has a comprehensive bus (short-haul, multi-stop public transportation) and coach (more direct, plusher long-distance buses) network that offers an inexpensive way of seeing England. National Express is the major coach operator, and Victoria Coach Station, near Victoria Station in central London, is its hub in the region. The company serves more than 1,000 destinations within Britain (and, via Eurolines, 500 more in continental Europe). There are 2,000 ticket agents nationwide, including offices at London's Heathrow and Gatwick airport coach stations.

Green Line is the second-largest national service, serving airports and major tourist towns. A budget option for long-distance travel, Megabus has double-decker buses that serve cities across Britain, with seats that turn into bunk beds on routes to Scotland. Greyhound has low-cost, long-distance bus service to five destinations in Wales. In London, the latter two companies depart from Victoria Coach Station as well as other stops, while Green Line buses also stop at Baker Street and Hyde Park Corner.

Bus tickets can be much less than the price of a train ticket (even lower if you take advantage of special deals). For example, an Oxford Tube bus ticket from London to Oxford is £14, whereas a train ticket may be £22. Buses are also just as comfortable as trains. However, buses often take twice as long to reach their destinations. Greyhound and Oxford Tube have onboard Wi-Fi. All bus services forbid smoking.

Double-decker buses, run by private companies, offer local bus service in cities and regions. Check with the local bus station or tourist information center for routes and schedules. Most companies offer day-long or weeklong unlimited-travel tickets, and those in popular tourist areas operate special scenic tours in summer. The top deck of a double-decker bus is a great place from which to view the countryside.

DISCOUNTS AND DEALS

National Express's Young Persons' CoachCard for students age 16 to 26 costs £10 annually and gets 20% to 30% discounts off many fares. Most companies also offer a discount for children under 15. A Senior CoachCard for the over-60s cuts many fares by a third. Apex tickets (advance-purchase tickets) save money on standard fares, and traveling midweek is cheaper than over weekends and holidays.

FARES AND SCHEDULES

You can find schedules online, pick them up from tourist information offices, or get them by phone from the bus companies. Fares vary based on how close to the time of travel you book—Megabus tickets, for example, are cheaper if ordered in advance online.

PAYING

Tickets for National Express can be bought from the Victoria, Heathrow, or Gatwick coach stations, by phone, online, or from most British travel agencies. Reservations are advised. Tickets for Megabus must be purchased online or by phone (avoid calling, as there's a surcharge).

Most companies accept credit cards for advance purchases, but some companies require cash for onboard transactions.

RESERVATIONS

Book in advance, as buses on busy routes fill up quickly. With most bus companies (National Express, Megabus, Green Line), advance payment means you receive an email receipt and your name is placed on a list given to the bus driver.

Bus Contacts Green Line. ☎ *0844/800–4411* 🌐 *www.greenline.co.uk.* **Greyhound.** ☎ *01792/341120* 🌐 *www.greyhounduk.com.* **Megabus.** ☎ *0141/352–4444* 🌐 *uk.megabus.com.* **National Express.** ☎ *0871/781–8178* 🌐 *www.nationalexpress.com.* **Oxford Tube.** ☎ *01865/772250* 🌐 *www.oxfordtube.com.* **Traveline.** ☎ *0871/200–2233* 🌐 *www.traveline.info.* **Victoria Coach Station.** ✉ *164 Buckingham Palace Rd.,* ☎ *No phone* 🌐 *www.tfl.gov.uk.*

CAR TRAVEL

Britain can be a challenging place for most foreigners to drive, considering that people drive on the left side of the often disconcertingly narrow roads, many rental cars have standard transmissions, and the gearshift is on the wrong side entirely.

There's no reason to rent a car for a stay in London because the city and its suburbs are well served by public transportation and traffic is desperately congested. Here and in other major cities it's best to rely on public transportation.

Outside the cities, a car can be very handy. Many sights aren't easily reached without one—castles, for example, are rarely connected to any public transportation system. Small villages might have only one or two buses a day pass through them. If you're comfortable on the road, the experience of driving between the tall hedgerows or on country roads is a truly English experience.

In England and Wales your own driver's license is acceptable. However, you may choose to get an International Driving Permit (IDP), which can be used only in conjunction with a valid driver's license and which translates your license into 10 languages. Check the Automobile Association of America website for more info as well as for IDPs ($15) themselves. These permits are universally recognized, and having one in your wallet may save you a problem with the local authorities.

GASOLINE

Gasoline is called petrol in England and is sold by the liter. The price you see posted at a petrol station is the price of a liter, and there are about 4 liters in a U.S. gallon. Petrol is expensive; it was around £1.35 per liter, or $2.10 per liter, at the time of this writing. Supermarket pumps just outside city centers frequently offer the best prices. Premium and superpremium are the two varieties, and most cars run on premium. Diesel is widely used; be sure not to use it by mistake. Along busy motorways, most large stations are open 24 hours a day, 7 days a week. In rural areas, hours can vary. Most service stations accept major credit cards, and most are self-service.

PARKING

Parking regulations are strictly enforced, and fines are high. If there are no signs on a street, you can park there. Many streets have centralized "pay and display" machines, in which you deposit the required money and get a ticket allowing you to park for a set period of time. In London's City of Westminster (🌐 *www.westminster.gov.uk*) and some other boroughs, parking machines have been replaced by a pay-by-phone plan, enabling you to pay by cell phone if you've preregistered. In town centers your best bet is to park in a public lot marked with a square blue sign with a white "P" in the center.

If you park on the street, follow these basic rules: Do not park within 15 yards of an intersection. Never park in bus lanes or on double yellow lines, and do not park on single yellow lines when parking meters are in effect. On busy roads with red lines painted on the street you cannot park or stop to let a passenger out of the car.

RENTALS

Rental rates are generally reasonable, and insurance costs are lower than in the United States. If you want the car only for country trips, consider renting outside London. Rates are cheaper, and you avoid traversing London's notoriously complex road system. Rental rates vary widely, beginning at £30 a day and £117 a week for a midsize car, usually with manual transmission. As in the United States, prices rise in summer and during holidays. Car seats for children cost £5–£20, and GPS is usually around £10. You can also arrange for cell phone hire or a portable Wi-Fi hot spot with your rental.

Major car-rental agencies are much the same in Britain as in the United States: Alamo, Avis, Budget, Enterprise, Hertz, Thrifty, and National all have offices in Britain. Europcar is another large company. Companies may not rent cars to people who are under 23. Some have an upper age limit of 75.

ROAD CONDITIONS

There's a good network of major highways (motorways) and divided highways (dual carriageways) throughout most of England and Wales. Motorways (with the prefix "M"), shown in blue on most maps, are mainly two or three lanes in each direction. Other major roads (with the prefix "A") are shown on maps in green and red. Sections of fast dual carriageways (with black-edged, thick outlines on maps) have both traffic lights and traffic circles. Turnoffs are often marked by highway numbers, rather than place names. An exit is called a junction in Britain.

The vast network of lesser roads, for the most part old coach and turnpike roads, might make your trip twice as long but show you twice as much. Minor roads are drawn in yellow or white on maps, the former prefixed by "B," the latter unlettered and unnumbered. Should you take one of these, be prepared to back up into a passing place if you meet an oncoming car.

ROADSIDE EMERGENCIES

On major highways emergency roadside telephone booths are positioned at regular intervals. Contact your car-rental company or call the police. You can also call the British Automobile Association (AA) toll-free. You can join and receive assistance from the AA or the RAC on the spot, but the charge is higher than a simple membership fee. If you're a member of the American Automobile Association, check before you travel; reciprocal agreements may give you free roadside aid.

Emergency Services Ambulance, fire, police. ☎ *999 emergency, 101 police nonemergency.* **Automobile Association.** ☎ *0800/887–766 emergency service, 0800/068–2912 general calls* 🌐 *www.theaa.com.* **RAC.** ☎ *0800/197–7815 emergency service, 0800/015–6000 general inquiries* 🌐 *www.rac.co.uk.*

RULES OF THE ROAD

Driving on the left side of the road might be easier than you expected, as the steering and mirrors on British cars are designed for driving on the left. If you have a standard transmission car, you have to shift gears with your left hand. Give yourself time to adjust before leaving the rental-car lot. Seat belts are obligatory in the front and back seats. It's illegal to talk on a handheld cell phone while driving.

Pick up a copy of the official Highway Code (£2.50) at a service station, newsstand, or bookstore, or check it out online by going to *www.gov.uk* and putting "Highway Code" in the search bar. Besides driving rules and illustrations of signs and road markings, this booklet contains information for motorcyclists, cyclists, and pedestrians.

Speed limits are complicated, and there are speed cameras everywhere. The speed limit (shown on circular red signs) is generally 20 or 30 mph in towns and cities, 40 to 60 mph on two-lane highways, and 70 mph on motorways. At traffic circles (called roundabouts), you turn clockwise. As cars enter the circle, they must yield to those already in the circle or entering from the right. If you're taking an exit all the way around the circle, signal right as you enter, stay to the center, and then signal and move left just before your own exit.

Pedestrians have the right-of-way on "zebra" crossings (black-and-white-stripe crosswalks between two orange-flashing globe lights). At other crossings, pedestrians must yield to traffic, but they do have the right-of-way over traffic turning left.

Drunk-driving laws are strictly enforced. The legal limit is 80 milligrams of alcohol per 100 milliliters of blood, which means two units of alcohol—approximately one glass of wine, 1–1.5 pints of beer, or two shots of whisky. However, these figures will vary according to the alcohol's strength, your size and weight (so women tend to reach the limit on less), and how much you've eaten that day.

TRAIN TRAVEL

Operated by several different private companies, the train system in Britain is extensive and useful, though less than perfect. Some regional trains are old, and virtually all lines suffer from occasional delays, schedule changes, and periodic repair work that runs over schedule. All major cities and many small towns are served by trains, and despite the difficulties, rail travel is the most pleasant way to cover long distances.

On long-distance runs some rail lines have buffet cars; on others you can purchase snacks from a mobile snack cart. Most train companies now have "quiet cars" where mobile-phone use is forbidden (in theory if not always in practice).

CLASSES

Most rail lines have first-class and second-class cars. In virtually all cases, second class is perfectly comfortable. First class is quieter and less crowded, has better furnishings, and marginally larger seats. It also usually costs two to three times the price of second class, but not always, so it's worth comparing prices. Most train operators offer a Weekend First ticket. Available on weekends and holidays, these tickets allow you to upgrade for as little as £5.

FARES AND SCHEDULES

National Rail Enquiries is a helpful, comprehensive, and free service that covers all the country's rail lines. National Rail will help you choose the best train, and then connect you with the right ticket office. You can also book tickets online. A similar service is offered by the Trainline, which provides online train information and ticket booking for all rail services. The Man in Seat 61, a website, offers objective information along with booking facilities.

Ticket prices are more expensive during rush hour, so plan accordingly. For long-distance travel, tickets cost more the longer you wait. Book in advance and tickets can be half of what you'd pay on the day of departure. A journey from London to Cardiff costs £18 if you buy a ticket two weeks in advance, but the fare rises to £42 if you wait until the day of your trip.

TIP→ Ask the local tourist board about hotel and local transportation packages that include tickets to major events.

Travel Times by Train

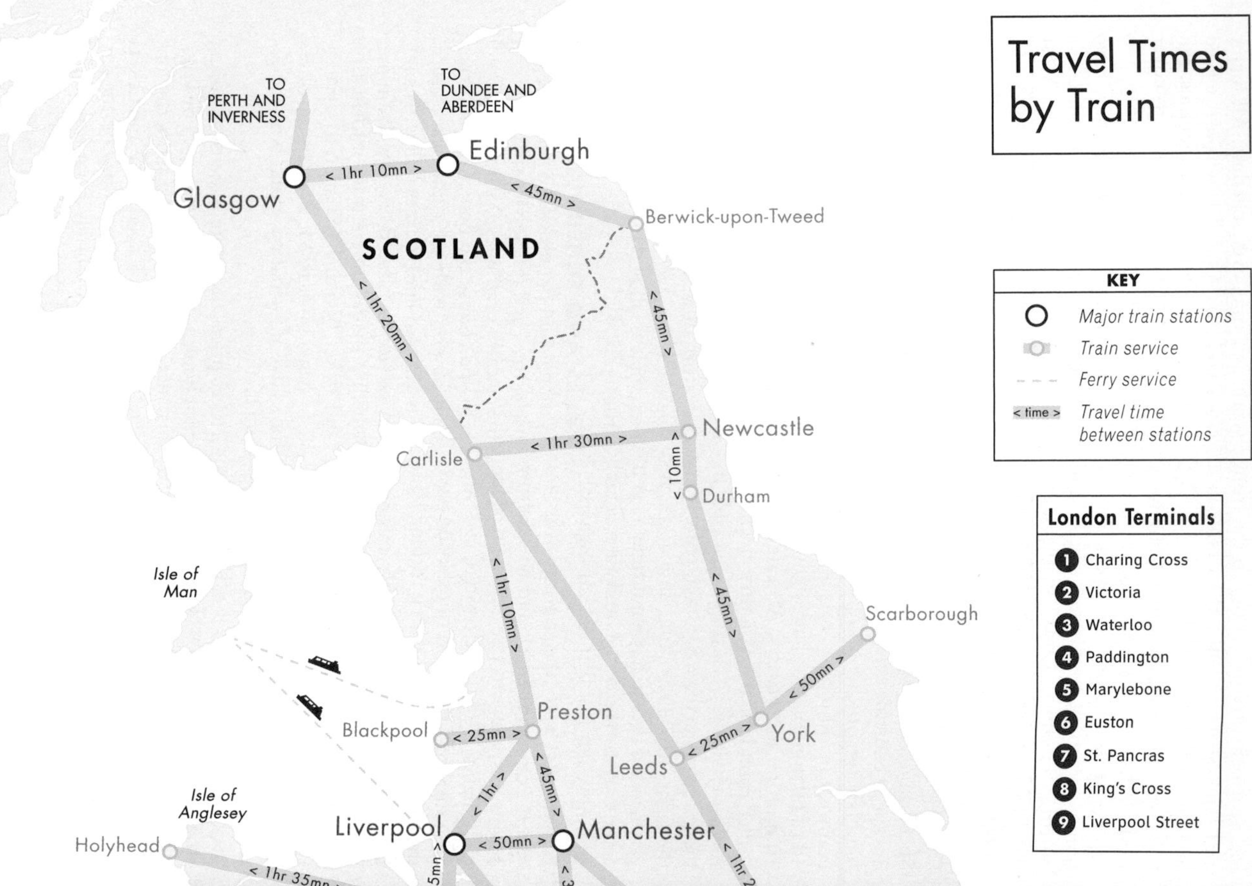

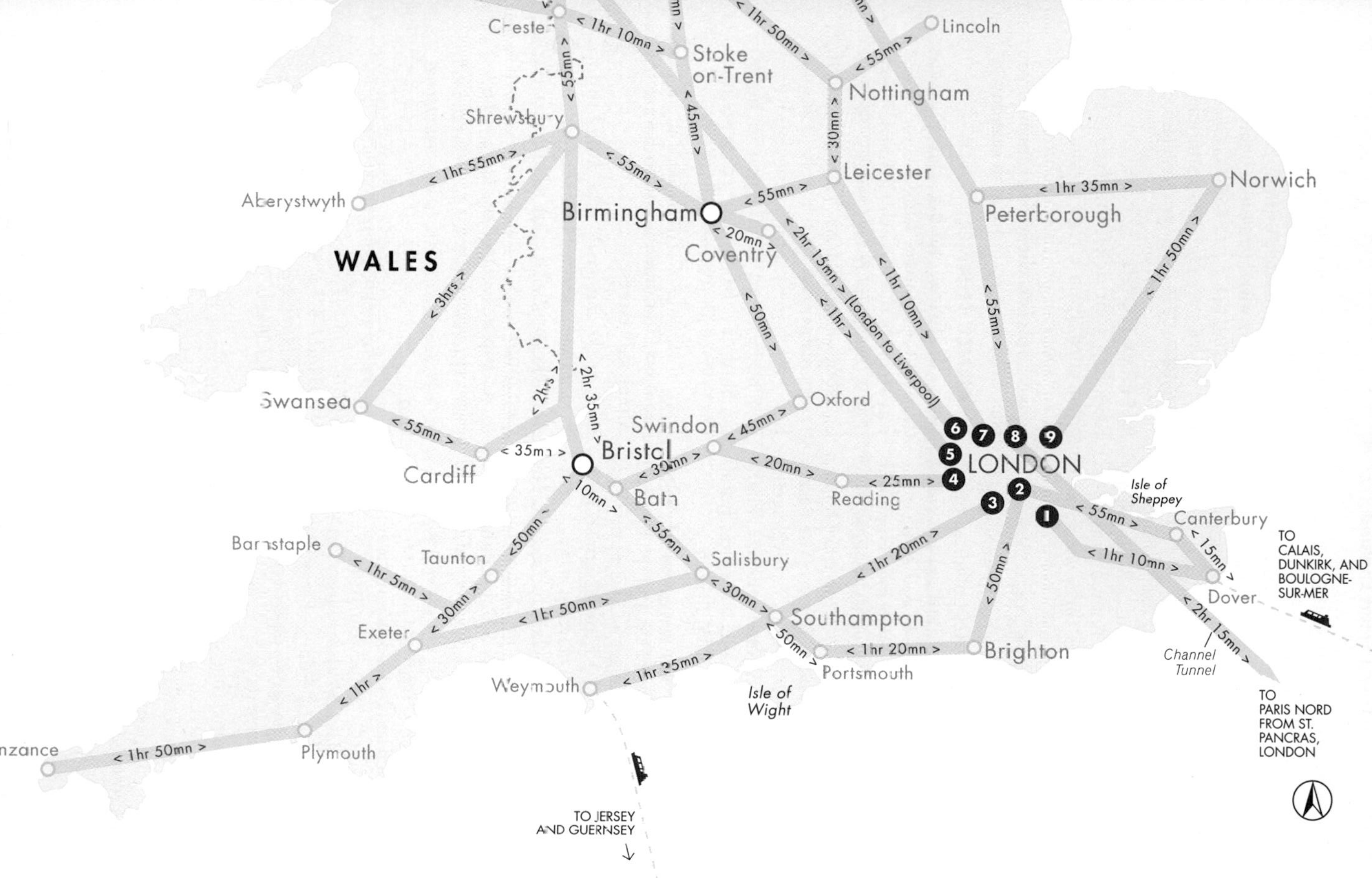
Lincoln
Stoke on-Trent
Nottingham
Shrewsbury
Leicester
Norwich
Aberystwyth
Birmingham
Peterborough
Coventry
WALES
Oxford
Swansea
Swindon
LONDON
Bristol
Cardiff
Bath
Reading
Isle of Sheppey
Canterbury
Barnstaple
Taunton
Salisbury
TO CALAIS, DUNKIRK, AND BOULOGNE-SUR-MER
Dover
Exeter
Southampton
Brighton
Channel Tunnel
Weymouth
Portsmouth
Isle of Wight
TO PARIS NORD FROM ST. PANCRAS, LONDON
Penzance
Plymouth
TO JERSEY AND GUERNSEY
< 1hr 10mn >
< 55mn >
< 1hr 50mn >
< 45mn >
< 30mn >
< 1hr 55mn >
< 1hr 35mn >
< 20mn >
< 2hr 15mn > (London to Liverpool)
< 1hr 10mn >
< 3hrs >
< 50mn >
< 1hr >
< 2hr 35mn >
< 2hrs >
< 45mn >
< 35mn >
< 30mn >
< 20mn >
< 25mn >
< 10mn >
< 15mn >
< 1hr 5mn >
< 1hr 20mn >
< 2hr 15mn >
< 1hr 25mn >
< 1hr >
< 1hr 50mn >

Information The Man in Seat 61. *www.seat61.com.* **National Rail Enquiries.** *0845/748–4950, 020/7278–5240 outside U.K.* *www.nationalrail.co.uk.* **Trainline.** *0871/244–1545* *www.thetrainline.com.*

PASSES

National Rail Enquiries has information about rail passes such as All Line Rovers, which offers unlimited travel on National Rail services for a week, with some restrictions, for £478.

If you plan to travel a lot by train in England and Wales, consider purchasing a BritRail Pass, which gives unlimited travel over the entire British rail network and can save you money. If you don't plan to cover many miles, you may come out ahead by buying individual tickets. Buy your BritRail Pass before you leave home, as they are not sold in Britain. The passes are available from most U.S. travel agents or from ACP Rail International, Flight Centre, or VisitBritain. Note that Eurail Passes aren't honored in Britain.

BritRail passes come in two basic varieties: the Consecutive Pass and the England FlexiPass. You can get a Consecutive Pass good for 3, 4, 8, 15, or 22 consecutive days or one month starting at $179 standard and $269 first-class for 3 days. The FlexiPass for 3, 4, 8, or 15 days of travel in two months costs $229 standard and $335 first class for 3 days. If you're based in London, the BritRail London Plus pass offers access to southern England destinations such as Oxford, Cambridge, Bath, or Stratford-upon-Avon from $126 for standard class, $191 for First. Tickets can be used for 2 or 4 days of travel within 8 consecutive days or 7 days of travel within 15 consecutive days.

Don't assume that a rail pass guarantees you a seat on a particular train. You need to book seats even if you're using a rail pass, especially on trains that may be crowded, particularly in summer on popular routes.

Discount Passes ACP Rail International. *866/938–7245 in U.S., 0207/953–4062 in U.K.* *www.acprail.com.* **BritRail.** *866/938–7245 in U.S.* *www.britrail.net.* **Flight Centre.** *0800/678–1134 in U.K., 866/743–3648 in U.S.* *www.flightcentre.co.uk.* **VisitBritain.** *020/8846–9000* *www.visitbritainshop.com.*

RESERVATIONS

Reserving your ticket in advance is recommended. Even a reservation 24 hours in advance can provide a substantial discount. Look into cheap day returns if you plan to travel a round-trip in one day.

CHANNEL TUNNEL

Short of flying, taking the Eurostar through the Channel Tunnel is the fastest way to cross the English Channel. Travel time is 2¼ hours from London's St. Pancras Station to Paris's Gare du Nord. Trains also travel to Brussels (2 hours), Lille (1¼ hours), and Disneyland Paris (2¾ hours), and to Avignon (6 hours) on Saturday from July to September. On Fridays and Saturdays between mid-December and mid-April, ski trains go to Moûtiers (7 hours) and four other nearby Alpine ski resorts.

Early risers can easily take a day trip to Paris if time is short. Book ahead, as Eurostar ticket prices increase as the departure date approaches. If purchased in advance, round-trip tickets to Paris start at £69.

Channel Tunnel Car Transport Eurotunnel. *0844/335–3535 in U.K.,* *www.eurotunnel.com.*

Channel Tunnel Passenger Service Eurostar. *0843/218–6186 in U.K., 44-1233/617–575 in U.S.* *www.eurostar.com.* **Rail Europe.** *800/622–8600 in U.S., 0844/848–5848 in U.K.* *www.raileurope.com.*

ESSENTIALS

ACCOMMODATIONS

Hotels, bed-and-breakfasts, rural inns, or luxurious country houses—there's a style and price to suit most travelers. Wherever you stay, make reservations well in advance. (⇨ *For additional descriptions of kinds of lodgings, see the England Lodging Primer in Chapter 1.*)

Our local writers vet every hotel to recommend the best overnights in each price category, from budget to expensive. Unless otherwise specified, you can expect private bath, phone, and TV in your room. ⇨ *For expanded reviews, facilities, and current deals, visit Fodors.com.*

Lodgings are indicated in the text by. Throughout Britain, lodging prices often include breakfast of some kind, but this is generally not the case in London. ⇨ *Prices in the reviews are the lowest cost of a standard double room in high season, including 20% V.A.T.*

APARTMENT AND HOUSE RENTALS

If you deal directly with local agents, get a recommendation from someone who's used the company. Unlike with hotels, there's no accredited system for apartment-rental standards. ⇨ *Also see Chapter 2 for London rental resources.*

BED-AND-BREAKFASTS

B&Bs can be a good budget option, and will also help you meet the locals. Cottages, unlike B&Bs, usually do not provide breakfast.

Reservation Services Bed & Breakfast.com. ☎ *512/322–2710* 🌐 *www.bedandbreakfast.com.* **The Bed and Breakfast Club.** ☎ *01243/370692* 🌐 *www.thebedandbreakfastclub.co.uk.* **Wolsey Lodges.** ☎ *01473/822058* 🌐 *www.wolseylodges.com.*

Online Booking Resources		
CONTACTS		
The Apartment Service	0208/944–1444	www.apartmentservice.com
At Home Abroad	212/421–9165	www.athomeabroadinc.com
Barclay International Group	516/364–0064 or 800/845–6636	www.barclayweb.com
English Country Cottages	0845/268–0785	www.english-country-cottages.co.uk
Housetrip	0203/463–0087	www.housetrip.com
In the English Manner	01559/371600 or 800/422–0799	www.english-manner.com
Living Architecture	07734/323464	www.living-architecture.co.uk
National Trust	0844/800–2070	www.nationaltrustcottages.co.uk
One Fine Stay	0203/468–2625	www.onefinestay.com
Suzanne B. Cohen & Associates	207/622–0743	www.villaeurope.com
Vacation Rentals By Owner	877/228–3145	www.vrbo.com
Villas International	415/499–9490 or 800/221–2260	www.villasintl.com

COTTAGES

Contacts Classic Cottages. ☎ *01326/555555* 🌐 *www.classic.co.uk.* **National Trust Cottages.** ☎ *344/335–1287, 870/458–4422 booking* 🌐 *www.nationaltrustholidays.org.uk.* **Rural Retreats.** ☎ *01386/897262* 🌐 *www.ruralretreats.co.uk.* **VisitBritain.** ☎ *0207/578–1000* 🌐 *www.visitbritain.com.*

FARMHOUSES

Contacts Farm & Cottage Holidays UK. ☎ *01237/459–888* 🌐 *www.holidaycottages.co.uk.* **Farm Stay UK.** ☎ *024/7669–6909* 🌐 *www.farmstayuk.co.uk.*

HISTORIC BUILDINGS

Contacts Celtic Castles. ☎ *01422/323200* 🌐 *www.celticcastles.com.* **English Heritage.** ☎ *0370/333–1181* 🌐 *www.english-heritage.org.uk.* **Landmark Trust.** ☎ *01628/825920* 🌐 *www.landmarktrust.org.uk.* **National Trust.** ☎ *0870/458–4422, 800/913–6565 in U.S.* 🌐 *www.nationaltrustcottages.co.uk.* **Portmeirion Cottages.** ☎ *01766/770000* 🌐 *www.portmeirion-village.com.* **Rural Retreats.** ☎ *01386/897198* 🌐 *www.ruralretreats.co.uk.* **Stately Holiday Cottages.** ☎ *01638/660066* 🌐 *www.statelyholidaycottages.co.uk.* **Unique Home Stays.** ☎ *01637/881183* 🌐 *www.uniquehomestays.com.* **Vivat Trust.** ☎ *01981/550753 in U.K.* 🌐 *www.vivat-trust.org.*

HOME EXCHANGES

With a direct home exchange you stay in someone else's home while they stay in yours. Some outfits handle vacation homes, so you're staying in someone's vacant weekend place. Home Exchange.com offers a one-year membership for $101; HomeLink International costs $89 for an annual online membership, which includes a directory listing; and Intervac U.S. offers international membership for $99.

Exchange Clubs Home Exchange.com. ☎ *800/877–8723 in U.S.* 🌐 *www.homeexchange.com.* **HomeLink International.** ☎ *800/638–3841 in U.S.* 🌐 *www.homelink-usa.org.* **Intervac.** ☎ *866/884–7567 in U.S.* 🌐 *www.intervac-homeexchange.com.*

HOTELS

Most hotels have rooms with "ensuite" bathrooms—as private bathrooms are called—although some B&Bs may have only washbasins; in this case, showers and toilets are usually down the hall. Especially in London, rooms and bathrooms may be smaller than those you find in the United States.

Besides familiar international chains, England has some local chains that are worth a look; they provide rooms from the less expensive (the basic but bargain Travelodge and the slightly more upscale Premier Inn are the most widespread, with the latter and Jurys Inns offering good value in city centers) to the trendy (ABode, Hotel du Vin, Malmaison).

Local Chains ABode. 🌐 *www.abodehotels.co.uk.* **Hotel du Vin.** ☎ *0871/943–0345* 🌐 *www.hotelduvin.com.* **Jurys Inn.** ☎ *0870/410–0800* 🌐 *www.jurysinn.com.* **Malmaison.** ☎ *0871/941–0350* 🌐 *www.malmaison.com.* **Premier Inn.** ☎ *0333/003–0025* 🌐 *www.premierinn.com.* **Travelodge.** ☎ *0871/984–8484 in U.K., 800/525–4055 in U.S.* 🌐 *www.travelodge.co.uk.*

HOTEL GRADING SYSTEM

Hotels, guesthouses, inns, and B&Bs in the United Kingdom are all graded from one to five stars by the tourism board, VisitBritain. Basically, the more stars a property has, the more amenities it has, and the facilities will be of a higher standard. It's a fairly good reflection of lodging from small B&Bs up to palatial hotels. The most luxurious hotels will have five stars; a simple, clean, acceptable hostelry will have one star.

DISCOUNTS AND DEALS

Hotel rates in major cities tend to be cheapest on weekends, whereas rural hotels are cheapest on weeknights. The lowest occupancy is between November and April, so hotels lower their prices substantially during these months.

Lastminute.com offers deals on hotel rooms all over the United Kingdom.

LOCAL DOS AND TABOOS

CUSTOMS OF THE COUNTRY

In general, British and American rules of etiquette are much the same. Differences are subtle. British people find Americans' bluntness somewhat startling from time to time, but are charmed by their friendliness.

Many of the English still tend to take politeness extremely seriously, but younger people and urbanites have a more casual approach. Self-deprecating humor, however, always goes down well. The famous British reserve is still in place, but on social occasions it's best to observe what the others do, and go with the flow. If you're visiting a family home, a gift of flowers is welcome, as is a bottle of wine.

GREETINGS

Older British people will shake hands on greeting old friends or acquaintances; female friends may greet each other with a kiss on the cheek. In Britain, you can never say "please," "thank you," or "sorry" too often; to thank your host, a phone call or thank-you card does nicely. Email and other electronic messages are fine for younger hosts.

SIGHTSEEING

As in the United States, in public places it's considered polite to give up your seat to an elderly person, to a pregnant woman, or to a parent struggling with children and bags. Jaywalking isn't illegal in England and everybody does it. However, since driving is on the left in England, the traffic flow may be confusing; use caution.

British people used to take waiting in line (called queuing) incredibly seriously, but, especially in London bus queues, line discipline is breaking down. Nevertheless, many still highly value patience, and will turn on "queue jumpers" who try to cut in line. Complaining while waiting in line is considered wimpy. Enduring the wait with good humor is considered a sign of strong moral character.

The single thing you can do that will most mark you as a tourist—and an impolite one—is fail to observe the written and spoken rule that, on virtually all escalators but especially those in Tube stations, you stand on the right side of the escalator and leave room for people to walk past you on the left.

OUT ON THE TOWN

Etiquette in restaurants is much the same as in any major U.S. city. In restaurants you hail a waiter by saying, "Excuse me…" as one passes by, or by politely signaling with subtle hand signals (but no snapping fingers). It's common to have drinks before dinner, and wine with dinner. Friends and co-workers frequently gather in pubs, but you don't have to drink alcohol—some people in the pub drink juice or sodas. Nonetheless, drunkenness can be common in major cities after 10 pm.

"Smart casual" is fine for the theater, and those going to nightclubs will dress just the same here as they would in New York or Chicago—the flashier the better. Pubs are very casual places, however.

Smoking is forbidden in all public places, including bars and restaurants.

DOING BUSINESS

Punctuality is of prime importance; if you anticipate a late arrival, call ahead. For business dinners, if you proffered the invitation, it's usually assumed that you'll pick up the tab. If you're the visitor, however, it's good form for the host to pay the bill. Alternatively, play it safe and offer to split the check.

VisitLondon.com, London's official website, has some good deals.

Local Resources Lastminute.com. ☎ *0800/083–4000* 🌐 *www.lastminute.com.*

COMMUNICATIONS

INTERNET

If you're traveling with a laptop or tablet, carry a spare power cord and adapter. If your hotel has dial-up (a rarity these days), get a telephone cord that's compatible with a British phone jack; these are available in Britain at airports and electronics stores. Wi-Fi is increasingly available in hotels, and broadband coverage is widespread in cities. You can also buy a dongle or MiFi device from a cell-phone network's retail outlet to create a personal Wi-Fi hot spot. Many London Underground stations now have Wi-Fi (for a fee). Outside big cities, wireless access is relatively rare in cafés and coffee shops, but its popularity there is growing.

Contacts Wi-Fi Freespot. 🌐 *www.wififreespot.com.*

PHONES

All calls (including local calls) made within the United Kingdom are charged according to the time of day. The standard landline rate applies weekdays 7 am to 7 pm; a cheaper rate is in effect weekdays 7 pm to 7 am and all day on weekends, when it's even cheaper.

A word of warning: 0870 numbers are *not* toll-free numbers in Britain; in fact, numbers beginning with this or the 0871, 0844, or 0845 prefixes cost extra to call. The amount varies and is usually relatively small—except for numbers with the premium-rate 090 prefix, which cost an eye-watering £1 per minute when dialed from within the country—but can be excessive when dialed from outside Britain.

CALLING ENGLAND

The country code for Great Britain (and thus England) is 44. When dialing an English number from abroad, drop the initial 0 from before the local area code. For example, let's say you're calling Buckingham Palace—0207/7930–4832—from the United States. First, dial 011 (the international access code), then 44 (Great Britain's country code), then 207 (London's center-city code—without its initial 0), then the remainder of the number.

CALLING WITHIN ENGLAND

For all calls within England (and Britain), dial the area code (which usually begins with 01, except in London), followed by the telephone number.

There are two types of pay phones: those that make calls to landlines or mobiles and those that also let you send texts or email. Most coin-operated phones take 10p, 20p, 50p, and £1 coins. There are very few of either type left except at air and rail terminals. SIM cards for your own cell phone and inexpensive pay-as-you-go cell phones are widely available from mobile network retailers such as 3, O2, T-Mobile, Vodaphone, and Virgin, as well as the Carphone Warehouse chain.

For pay and other phones, if you hear a repeated single tone after dialing, the line is busy; a continuous tone means the number didn't work.

There are several different directory-assistance providers, all beginning with the prefix 118, such as 118–888 or 118–429; you'll need to know the town and the street (or at least the neighborhood) of the person you're trying to reach. Charges range from 75 cents (118–811) to $3.70 per minute from a landline. Cell phone networks may charge even more. For the operator, dial 100. For genuine emergencies, dial 999. For nonurgent police matters, dial 101.

CALLING OUTSIDE ENGLAND

For direct overseas dialing from England (and Britain), dial 00, then the country code, area code, and number. For the international operator, credit card, or collect calls, dial 155; for international directory assistance, dial 118505. The country code for the United States is 1.

Access Codes AT&T Direct. ☎ *0800/890–011.* **MCI WorldPhone.** ☎ *0800/279–5088.*

CALLING CARDS

You can buy international cards similar to U.S. calling cards for making calls to specific countries from post offices, some supermarkets, cell phone network retail outlets, or on the Internet. Rates vary, but the O2 network charges as little as two cents per minute to call the U.S. Where credit cards are taken, slide the card in as indicated.

MOBILE PHONES

Any cell phone can be used in Europe if it's tri-band, quad-band, or GSM. Travelers should ask their cell-phone company if their phone fits in this category and make sure it's activated for international calling before leaving their home country. Roaming fees can be steep, however: $1 a minute is considered reasonable. And overseas you normally pay the toll charges for incoming calls. It's almost always cheaper to send a text message than to make a call, since text messages have a low set fee (often less than 25¢).

If you just want to make local calls, consider buying a new SIM card (your provider may have to unlock your phone for you) and a prepaid local service plan. You'll then have a local number and can make local calls at local rates. You can also rent a cell phone from most major car-rental agencies in England. Some upscale hotels now provide loaner cell phones to their guests. Beware, however, of the per-minute rates charged. Alternatively, you may want to buy a basic pay-as-you-go phone for around £15.

Contacts Carphone Warehouse. ☎ *0800/049–6250* 🌐 *www.carphonewarehouse.com.* **Cellular Abroad.** ☎ *800/287–5072* 🌐 *www.cellularabroad.com.* **Mobal.** ☎ *888/888–9162* 🌐 *www.mobal.com.* **Planet Fone.** ☎ *888/988–4777* 🌐 *www.planetfone.com.*

CUSTOMS AND DUTIES

You're always allowed to bring goods of a certain value back home without having to pay any duty or import tax. But there's a limit on the amount of tobacco and liquor you can bring back duty-free, and some countries have separate limits for perfumes; for exact figures, check with your customs department. The values of so-called duty-free goods are included in these amounts. When you shop abroad, save all your receipts, as customs inspectors may ask to see them as well as the items you purchased. If the total value of your goods is more than the duty-free limit, you'll have to pay a tax (most often a flat percentage) on the value of everything beyond that limit.

Fresh meats, plants and vegetables, controlled drugs, and firearms (including replicas) and ammunition may not be brought into the United Kingdom, nor can dairy products from non-EU countries. Pets from the United States with the proper documentation may be brought into the country without quarantine under the U.K. Pet Travel Scheme (PETS). The process takes about four months to complete and involves detailed steps.

You'll face no customs formalities if you enter Scotland or Wales from any other part of the United Kingdom.

Information in England HM Revenue and Customs. ☎ *0800/595–000 in U.K.* 🌐 *www.gov.uk.* **Pet Travel Scheme.** ☎ *0370/241–1710 in U.K.* 🌐 *www.gov.uk.*

U.S. Information U.S. Customs and Border Protection. ☎ *877/228–5511 in U.S.* 🌐 *www.cbp.gov.*

EATING OUT

The stereotypical notion of English meals as parades of roast beef, overcooked vegetables, and stodgy puddings has largely been replaced—particularly in London, other major cities, and some country hot spots—with an evolving picture of the country as foodie territory. From trendy gastro-pubs to interesting ethnic-fusion restaurants to see-and-be-seen dining shrines, English food is now known for an innovative take on traditional dishes, with an emphasis on the local and seasonal. In less cosmopolitan areas, though, you're still looking at lots of offerings that are either stodgy, fried, sausages, or Indian.

In general, restaurant prices are high. If you're watching your budget, seek out pubs and ethnic restaurants.

DISCOUNTS AND DEALS

Eating out in England's big cities in particular can be expensive, but you can do it cheaply. Try local cafés, more popularly known as "caffs," where heaping plates of English comfort food (bacon sandwiches and stuffed baked potatoes, for example) are served. England has plenty of the big names in fast food, as well as smaller places selling sandwiches, fish-and-chips, burgers, falafels, kebabs, and the like. For a local touch, check out Indian restaurants, which are found almost everywhere. Marks & Spencer, Sainsbury's, Morrison's, Tesco, and Waitrose are chain supermarkets with outlets throughout the country. They're good choices for groceries, premade sandwiches, or picnic fixings.

MEALS AND MEALTIMES

Cafés serving the traditional English breakfast (called a "fry-up") of eggs, bacon, sausage, beans, mushrooms, half a grilled tomato, toast, and strong tea are often the cheapest—and most authentic—places for breakfast. For lighter morning fare (or for real brewed coffee), try the Continental-style sandwich bars and coffee shops—the Pret-a-Manger chain being one of the largest—offering croissants and other pastries.

At lunch you can grab a sandwich between sights, pop into the local pub, or sit down in a restaurant. Dinner, too, has no set rules, but a three-course meal is standard in most mid-range or high-end restaurants. Pre- or post-theater menus, offering two or three courses for a set price, are usually a good value.

Note that most traditional pubs don't have any waitstaff and you're expected to go to the bar to order a beverage and your meal. Also, in cities many pubs don't serve food after 3 pm, so they're usually a better lunch option than dinner. In rural areas it's not uncommon for pubs to stop serving lunch after 2:30 and dinner after 9 pm.

Breakfast is generally served between 7:30 and 9, lunch between noon and 2, and dinner or supper between 7:30 and 9:30—sometimes earlier and seldom later except in large cities. These days high tea is rarely a proper meal anymore (it was once served between 4:30 and 6), and tearooms are often open all day in touristy areas (they're not found at all in non-touristy places). So you can have a cup and pastry or sandwich whenever you feel you need it. Sunday roasts at pubs last from 11 am or noon to 3 pm.

Smoking is banned in pubs, clubs, and restaurants throughout Britain.

PAYING

Credit cards are widely accepted in restaurants and pubs, though some require a minimum charge of around £10. Be sure that you don't double-pay a service charge. Many restaurants exclude service charges from the printed menu (which the law obliges them to display outside), and then add 10% to 15% to the check. Others will stamp "Service not included" along the bottom of the bill, in which case you should add 10% to 15%. Cash is always appreciated, as it's more likely to go to the specific waiter.

PUBS

A common misconception among visitors to England is that pubs are simply bars. Pubs are also community gathering places and even restaurants. In many pubs the social interaction is as important as the alcohol. Pubs are, generally speaking, where people go to meet their friends and catch up on one another's lives. In small towns pubs act almost as town halls. Traditionally pub hours are 11–11, with last orders called about 20 minutes before closing time, but pubs can choose to stay open until midnight or 1 am, or later.

Though to travelers it may appear that there's a pub on almost every corner, in fact pubs are something of an endangered species, closing at a rate of 14 a week (as of 2013), with independent, non-chain pubs at particular risk.

Most pubs tend to be child-friendly, but others have restricted hours for children. If a pub serves food, it'll generally allow children in during the day with adults. Some pubs are stricter than others, though, and won't admit anyone younger than 18. Some will allow children in during the day, but only until 6 pm. Family-friendly pubs tend to be packed with kids, parents, and all of their accoutrements.

RESERVATIONS AND DRESS

Regardless of where you are, it's a good idea to make a reservation if you can. We mention them specifically only when reservations are essential or when they're not accepted. For popular restaurants, book as far ahead as you can (often 30 days), and reconfirm as soon as you arrive. (Large parties should always call ahead to check the reservations policy.) We mention dress only when men are required to wear a jacket or a jacket and tie.

Online reservation services aren't as popular in England as in the United States, but Open Table and Square Meal have a fair number of listings in England.

Contacts Open Table. ☏ *0207/299–2949* 🌐 *www.opentable.co.uk.* **Square Meal.** ☏ *0207/582–0222* 🌐 *www.squaremeal.co.uk.*

WINES, BEER, AND SPIRITS

Although hundreds of varieties of beer are brewed around the country, the traditional brew is known as bitter and isn't carbonated; it's usually served at room temperature. Fizzy American-style beer is called lager. There are also plenty of other alternatives: stouts like Guinness and Murphy's are thick, pitch-black brews you'll either love or hate; ciders, made from apples, are alcoholic in Britain (Bulmer's and Strongbow are the big names, but look out for local microbrews); shandies are a low-alcohol mix of lager and lemon soda. Real ales, which have a natural second fermentation in the cask, have a shorter shelf life (so many are brewed locally) but special flavor; these are worth seeking out. Generally the selection and quality of cocktails is higher in a wine bar or café than in a pub. The legal drinking age is 18.

ECOTOURISM

Ecotourism is an emerging trend in the United Kingdom. The Shetland Environmental Agency Ltd. runs the Green Tourism Business Scheme, a program that evaluates lodgings in England, Scotland, and Wales and gives them gold, silver, or bronze ratings. You can find a list of green hotels, B&Bs, and apartments on the GTBS website. Also check out the VisitBritain website, which has information and tips about green travel in Britain.

Contacts Green Tourism Business Scheme. ☏ *01738/632162* 🌐 *www.green-tourism.com.*

ELECTRICITY

The electrical current in Great Britain is 220–240 volts (in line with the rest of Europe), 50 cycles alternating current (AC); wall outlets take three-pin plugs, and shaver sockets take two round, oversize prongs. British bathrooms aren't permitted to have 220–240 volt outlets in them. Consider making a small investment in a universal adapter, which has several types of plugs in one lightweight, compact unit. Most laptops and mobile phone chargers are dual voltage (i.e., they operate equally well on 110 and 220 volts), so require only an adapter. These days the same is true of small appliances such as hair dryers. Always check labels and manufacturer instructions. Don't use 110-volt outlets marked "For shavers only" for high-wattage appliances such as hair dryers.

Contacts **Walkabout Travel Gear.** ☎ *888/807–4997* 🌐 *www.walkabouttravelgear.com.*

EMERGENCIES

If you need to report an emergency, dial 999 for police, fire, or ambulance. Be prepared to give the telephone number you're calling from. 101 is the number for nonurgent police calls, such as reporting a stolen car. You can get 24-hour treatment in Accident and Emergency at British hospitals, although you may have to wait hours for treatment. Prescriptions are valid only if made out by doctors registered in the United Kingdom.

Although England has a subsidized National Health Service, free at the point of service for British residents, foreign visitors are expected to pay for any treatment they receive. Expect to receive a bill after you return home. Check with your health-insurance company to make sure you're covered. Some British hospitals now require a credit card or other payment before they'll offer treatment.

U.S. Embassies **American Embassy.** ✉ *24 Grosvenor Sq.,* ☎ *0207/499–9000* 🌐 *london.usembassy.gov.* **U.S. Passport Unit.** ✉ *24 Grosvenor Sq.,* ☎ *0207/499–9000* 🌐 *london.usembassy.gov.*

HEALTH

SPECIFIC ISSUES IN ENGLAND

If you take prescription drugs, keep a supply in your carry-on luggage and make a list of all your prescriptions to keep on file at home while you're abroad. You won't be able to renew a U.S. prescription at a pharmacy in Britain. Prescriptions are accepted only if issued by a U.K.-registered physician.

OVER-THE-COUNTER REMEDIES

Over-the-counter medications in England are similar to those in the United States, with a few significant differences. Medications are sold in boxes rather than bottles, and are sold in small amounts—usually no more than 24 pills. There may also be fewer brands. All headache medicine is usually filed under "painkillers." You can buy generic ibuprofen or a popular European brand of ibuprofen, Nurofen. Tylenol isn't sold in the United Kingdom, although its main ingredient, acetaminophen, is found in brands like Panadol.

Among sinus and allergy medicines, Clarityn is the main option here; it's spelled slightly differently but is the same brand sold in the United States. Some medicines are pretty much the same as brands sold in the United States—instead of Nyquil cold medicine, there's Sudafed or Lemsip. The most popular over-the-counter cough medicine is Benylin.

Drugstores are generally called pharmacies, but sometimes referred to as chemists' shops. The biggest drugstore chain in the country is Boots, which has outlets everywhere, except for the smallest towns. If you're in a rural area, look for shops marked with a sign of a green cross.

If you can't find what you want, ask at the counter; many over-the-counter medicines are kept behind the register.

SHOTS AND MEDICATIONS

No special shots are required or suggested for England.

Health Warnings **National Centers for Disease Control & Prevention** *(CDC).* ☎ *800/232–4636 travelers' health line* 🌐 *www.cdc.gov/travel.* **World Health Organization** *(WHO).* 🌐 *www.who.int.*

HOURS OF OPERATION

In big cities, most banks are open weekdays from 9 until 5 or 6. Some are open until 7, and many are open Saturday morning until 1 and some until 4. In smaller towns, hours are 9:30 to 3:30.

Saturday hours are 10 to 2, if they're open at all. Normal office hours for most businesses are weekdays 9 to 5.

The major national museums and galleries are open daily 9–6, including lunchtime, but have shorter hours on Sunday. Regional museums are usually closed Monday and have shorter hours in winter. In London many museums are open late one evening a week.

Independently owned pharmacies are generally open Monday through Saturday 9:30–5:30, although in larger cities some stay open until 10 pm; local newspapers list which pharmacies are open late.

Usual retail business hours are Monday through Saturday 9–5:30 or 10–6:30, Sunday noon–4. In some small villages shops may close at 1 pm once a week, often Wednesday or Thursday. They may also close for lunch and not open on Sunday at all. In large cities—especially London—department stores stay open late (usually until 7:30 or 8) one night a week, usually Thursday. On national holidays most stores are closed, and over the Christmas holidays most restaurants are closed as well.

HOLIDAYS

Holidays are January 1, New Year's Day; Good Friday and Easter Monday; May Day (first Monday in May); spring and summer bank holidays (last Monday in May and August, respectively); December 25, Christmas Day; and December 26, Boxing Day (day after Christmas). If these holidays fall on a weekend, the holiday is observed on the following Monday. During the Christmas holidays many restaurants, as well as museums and other attractions, may close for at least a week—call to verify hours. Book hotels for Christmas travel well in advance, and check whether the hotel restaurant will be open.

MAIL

Stamps can be bought from post offices (hours vary according to branch, but usual opening hours are weekdays 9–5:30, with some closing early one day a week, especially in smaller towns, and Saturday 9–noon), from stamp machines outside post offices, and from newsagents. Some post offices are located within supermarkets or general stores. Specialized shipping shops like Mail Boxes Etc. also sell stamps. Mailboxes, known as post or letter boxes, are painted bright red. Allow 7 days for a letter to reach the United States and about 10 days to two weeks to Australia or New Zealand. The useful Royal Mail website has information on everything from buying stamps to finding a post office.

As of this writing, airmail letters up to 20 grams (0.75 ounce) to North America cost 97p. Letters within Britain weighing up to 100 grams (3.5 ounces) are 62p for first class, 53p for second class. Rates for envelopes larger than 353 mm (13.9 inches) long, 250 mm (9.84 inches) wide, and 25 mm (1 inch) deep are higher. You can find prices and print postage on the Royal Mail website.

Contact Royal Mail. ☎ *03457/740740* 🌐 *www.royalmail.com.*

SHIPPING PACKAGES

Most department stores and retail outlets can ship your goods home. You should check your insurance for coverage of possible damage. Private delivery companies such as Federal Express and DHL offer two-day delivery service to the United States, but you'll pay a considerable amount for the privilege.

Express Services DHL. ☎ *0844/248-0844* 🌐 *www.dhl.co.uk.* **Federal Express.** ☎ *0845/600-0068* 🌐 *www.fedex.com/gb.* **Mail Boxes Etc.** ☎ *0800/623123* 🌐 *www.mbe.co.uk.* **Parcelforce.** ☎ *0344/800-4466* 🌐 *www.parcelforce.com.* **UPS.** ☎ *0345/787-7877 in U.K.* 🌐 *www.ups.com.*

MONEY

Prices in England can seem high because of the exchange rate. London remains one of the most expensive cities in the world. But for every yin there's a yang, and travelers can get breaks: staying in bed-and-breakfasts or renting a city apartment brings down lodging costs, and national museums are free. *The chart below gives some ideas of the prices you can expect to pay for day-to-day life.*

ITEM	AVERAGE COST
Cup of Coffee	£1.50–£3
Glass of Wine	£3.50 in a pub or wine bar, £5.50 or more in a restaurant
Glass of Beer	£2.70 or more
Sandwich	£3.50
One-Mile Taxi Ride in London	£5.50–£8.60
Museum Admission	National museums free; others £5–£10

Prices throughout this guide are given for adults. Substantially reduced fees—generally referred to as "concessions" throughout Great Britain—are almost always available for children, students, and senior citizens.

TIP→ Banks have limited amounts of foreign currencies on hand, and it may take as long as a week to order. If you're planning to exchange funds before leaving home, don't wait until the last minute.

ATMS AND BANKS

Make sure before leaving home that your credit and debit cards have been programmed for ATM use abroad—ATMs in England and Wales accept PINs of four or fewer digits only. If you know your PIN as a word, learn the numerical equivalent, since most keypads in England show numbers only, not letters. Most ATMs are on both the Cirrus and Plus networks. ATMs are available at most main-street banks, large supermarkets such as Sainsbury's and Tesco, some Tube stops in London, and many rail stations. Major banks include Barclays, HSBC, and NatWest.

Your own bank will probably charge a fee for using ATMs abroad (unless you use your bank's British partner); the foreign bank you use may also charge a fee. Nevertheless, you'll usually get a better rate of exchange at an ATM than you will at a currency-exchange office or even when changing money in a bank. And extracting funds as you need them is a safer option than carrying around a large amount of cash.

CREDIT CARDS

The Discover card isn't accepted throughout Britain. Other major credit cards, except Diners Club and American Express, are accepted virtually everywhere in Britain; however, you're expected to know and use your pin number for all transactions—even for credit cards. So it's a good idea to do some quick memorization for whichever card you intend to use in England.

Keep in mind that most European credit cards store information in microchips, rather than magnetic strips. Although some banks in the United States, such as Chase and Wells Fargo, are starting to adopt this system, you may find some places in England that can't process your credit card. It's a good idea to carry enough cash to cover small purchases.

Inform your credit-card company before you travel, especially if you're going abroad and don't travel internationally very often. Otherwise, the credit-card company might put a hold on your card owing to unusual activity. Record all your credit-card numbers in a safe place. Both MasterCard and Visa have general numbers you can call (collect if you're abroad) if your card is lost, but you're better off calling the number of your issuing bank, since MasterCard and Visa usually just transfer you to your bank; your bank's number is usually printed on your card.

If you plan to use your credit card for cash advances, you'll need to apply for a

PIN at least two weeks before your trip. Although it's usually cheaper (and safer) to use a credit card abroad for large purchases (so you can cancel payments or be reimbursed if there's a problem), note that some credit-card companies *and* the banks that issue them add substantial percentages to all foreign transactions, whether they're in a foreign currency or not. Check on these fees before traveling.

Reporting Lost Cards American Express. ☎ *336/393–1111 lost or stolen cards collect from abroad, 800/528–4800 in U.S.* 🌐 *www.americanexpress.com.* **Diners Club.** ☎ *514/877–1577 lost or stolen card collect from abroad* 🌐 *www.dinersclubus.com.* **MasterCard.** ☎ *636/722–7111 lost or stolen card collect from abroad* 🌐 *www.mastercard.us.* **Visa.** ☎ *0800/891725 lost or stolen card in UK* 🌐 *usa.visa.com.*

CURRENCY AND EXCHANGE

The unit of currency in Great Britain is the pound sterling (£), divided into 100 pence (p). The bills (called notes in Britain) are 50, 20, 10, and 5 pounds. Coins are £2, £1, 50p, 20p, 10p, 5p, 2p, and 1p. If you're traveling beyond England and Wales, note that Scotland and the Channel Islands have their own bills, and the Channel Islands their own coins, too. Scottish bills are accepted (often reluctantly) in the rest of Britain, but you can't use Channel Islands currency outside the islands.

At the time of this writing, the exchange rate was about U.S. $1.68 to £1.

British post offices exchange currency with no fee, and at decent rates.

■ TIP→ Even if a currency-exchange booth has a sign promising no commission, rest assured that there's some kind of huge, hidden fee. And as for rates, you're almost always better off getting foreign currency at an ATM or exchanging money at a bank. XE.com, Oanda.com, and Currency have popular conversion apps that are available for both Android and iPhone.

Currency Conversion Google. 🌐 *www.google.com.* **Oanda.com.** 🌐 *www.oanda.com.* **XE.com.** 🌐 *www.xe.com.*

PACKING

England can be cool, damp, and overcast, even in summer. You'll want a heavy coat for winter and a lightweight coat or warm jacket for summer. There's no time of year when a raincoat or umbrella won't come in handy. For the cities, pack as you would for an American city: coats and ties for expensive restaurants and nightspots, casual clothes elsewhere. If you plan to stay in budget hotels, take your own soap. It's also a good idea to take a washcloth. Pack insect repellent if you plan to hike.

PASSPORTS

U.S. citizens need only a valid passport to enter Great Britain for stays of up to six months. Travelers should be prepared to show sufficient funds to support and accommodate themselves while in Britain (credit cards will usually suffice for this) and to show a return or onward ticket. If you're within six months of your passport's expiration date, renew it before you leave—nearly expired passports aren't strictly banned, but they make immigration officials anxious, and may cause you problems. Health certificates aren't required.

RESTROOMS

Public restrooms are sparse in England, although most big cities maintain public facilities that are clean and modern. Train stations and department stores have public restrooms that occasionally charge a small fee, usually 30p. Most pubs, restaurants, and even fast-food chains reserve their bathrooms for customers. Hotels and museums are usually a good place to find clean, free facilities. On the road, gas-station facilities are usually clean and free. Toiletocity and Find Toilets both offer helpful iPhone apps, while ToDaLoo for

Android provides guidance about public toilets in London.

Find a Loo The Bathroom Diaries. *www.thebathroomdiaries.com.*

SAFETY

England has a low incidence of violent crime. However, petty crime, mostly in urban areas, is on the rise, and tourists can be the targets. Use common sense: when in a city center, if you're paying at a shop or a restaurant, never put your wallet down or let your bag out of your hand. When sitting on a chair in a public place, keep your purse on your lap or between your feet. Don't wear expensive jewelry or watches, and don't flash fancy smartphones outside Tube stations, where there have been some thefts. Store your passport in the hotel safe, and keep a copy with you. Don't leave anything in your car.

Although scams do occur in Britain, they aren't pervasive. If you're getting money out of an ATM, beware of someone bumping into you to distract you. You may want to use ATMs inside banks rather than those outside them. In London scams are most common at ATMs on Oxford Street and around Piccadilly Circus. Watch out for pickpockets, particularly in London. They often work in pairs, one distracting you in some way.

Always take a licensed black taxi or call a car service (sometimes called minicabs) recommended by your hotel. Avoid drivers who approach you on the street, as in most cases they'll overcharge you. Always buy theater tickets from a reputable dealer. If you're driving in from a British port, beware of thieves posing as customs officials who try to "confiscate illegal goods."

While traveling, don't leave any bags unattended, as they may be viewed as a security risk and destroyed by the authorities. If you see an unattended bag on the train, bus, or Tube, find a worker and report it. Never hesitate to get off a Tube, train, or bus if you feel unsafe.

TIP→ Distribute your cash, credit cards, IDs, and other valuables between a deep front pocket, an inside jacket or vest pocket, and a hidden money pouch. Don't reach for the money pouch once you're in public.

General Information and Warnings Transportation Security Administration (*TSA*). *866/289–9673* *www.tsa.gov.* **U.K. Foreign & Commonwealth Office.** *0207/008–1500* *www.gov.uk/foreign-travel-advice.* **U.S. Department of State.** *888/407–4747 traveler hotline* *www.state.gov/travel.*

SIGHTSEEING PASSES

DISCOUNT PASSES

If you plan to visit castles, gardens, and historic houses during your stay in England and Wales, look into discount passes or memberships that offer significant savings. Just be sure to match what the pass or membership offers against your itinerary to see if it's worthwhile.

The National Trust, English Heritage, and the Historic Houses Association each encompass hundreds of properties. English Heritage's Overseas Visitors Pass costs £24 for a nine-day pass and £28 for a 16-day pass for one adult. You can order it in advance by phone or online, or purchase it at a participating property in England. The National Trust Touring Pass, for overseas visitors, must be purchased in advance, either by phone or online. A seven-day pass is £25; a 14-day pass is £30.

The London Pass gets you into more than 60 attractions and tours in the capital, and can help you bypass some queues. Packages range from one day (£49) to six days (£108). Annual membership in the National Trust (through the Royal Oak Foundation, the U.S. affiliate) is $65 a year. English Heritage membership is £48, and the Historic Houses Association is £45. Memberships entitle you to free entry to properties.

⇨ *For passes specifically for Wales, see Chapter 14.*

Information English Heritage. ☎ *0370/333–1181* 🌐 *www.english-heritage.org.uk.* **Historic Houses Association.** ☎ *0207/259–5688* 🌐 *www.hha.org.uk.* **London Pass.** ☎ *0207/293–0972* 🌐 *www.londonpass.com.* **National Trust.** ☎ *0844/800–1895* 🌐 *www.nationaltrust.org.uk.* **Royal Oak Foundation.** ☎ *212/480–2889 in U.S, 800/913–6565* 🌐 *www.royal-oak.org.*

SPORTS AND THE OUTDOORS

VisitBritain and local Tourist Information Centres can recommend places to enjoy your favorite sport.

BIKING

The national body promoting cycle touring is the Cyclists' Touring Club (£39 a year). Members get free advice and route information and a magazine. Transport for London publishes maps of recommended routes across the capital, and British Cycling has online route maps of the United Kingdom. The CTC organizes cycling vacations.

Contacts British Cycling. ☎ *0161/274–2000* 🌐 *www.britishcycling.org.uk.* **Cyclists' Touring Club.** ☎ *0844/736–8451* 🌐 *www.ctc.org.uk.*

BOATING

Boating—whether on bucolic rivers or industrial canals—can be a leisurely way to explore the English landscape. For boat-rental operators along Britain's several hundred miles of historic canals and waterways, from the Norfolk Broads to the Lake District, contact the Association of Pleasure Craft Operators or Waterways Holidays. The Canal and River Trust has maps and other information. Waterways Holidays arranges boat accommodations from traditional narrow boats to wide-beam canal boats, motorboats, and sailboats.

Contacts Association of Pleasure Craft Operators. ☎ *01784/473377* 🌐 *www.britishmarine.co.uk.* **Canal and River Trust.** ☎ *0303/040–4040* 🌐 *www.canalrivertrust.org.uk.* **Waterways Holidays.** ☎ *01252/796400* 🌐 *www.waterwaysholidays.com.*

GOLF

Invented in Scotland, golf is a beloved pastime all over England. Some courses take advantage of spectacular natural settings, from the ocean to mountain backdrops. Most courses are reserved for club members and adhere to strict rules of protocol and dress. However, many famous courses can be used by visiting golfers reserving well in advance. In addition, numerous public courses are open to anyone, though advance reservations are advised. Package tours with companies such as Golf International and Owenoak International Golf Travel allow you into exclusive clubs. For further information on courses, fees, and locations, try the website English Golf Courses.

Contacts English Golf Courses. ☎ *0141/353–2222* 🌐 *www.englishgolf-courses.co.uk.* **Golf International.** ☎ *212/986–9176, 800/833–1389* 🌐 *www.golfinternational.com.* **Owenoak International Golf Travel.** ☎ *203/054–9000, 800/426–4498* 🌐 *www.owenoak.com.* **UK Golf Guide.** 🌐 *www.ukgolfguide.com.*

WALKING

Walking and hiking, from the slowest ramble to a challenging mountainside climb, are enormously popular in England. National Trails, funded by Natural England and the Countryside Counsel for Wales, has great resources online. The Ramblers, a well-known charitable organization promoting walking and care of footpaths, has helpful information, including a list of B&Bs close to selected long-distance footpaths. Some of the best maps for walking are the Explorer Maps, published by the Ordnance Survey; check out 🌐 *www.ordnancesurvey.co.uk.*

Contacts National Trails. *www.nationaltrail.co.uk.* **The Ramblers.** *0207/339–8500 www.ramblers.org.uk.*

TAXES

Air Passenger Duty (APD) is a tax included in the price of your ticket. The U.K.'s APD fees, currently the highest in the world, are divided into four bands: short-haul destinations under 2,000 miles, £13 per person in economy, £26 and £52 in all first and business class; medium-haul destinations under 4,000 miles (including the United States), £69 economy, £138 and £276 first and business class; long-haul destinations under 6,000 miles, £85 economy, £170 and £340 first and business class; ultra-long-haul destinations over 6,000 miles, £97 economy, £194 and £388 first and business class.

The British sales tax (Value Added Tax, or V.A.T.) is 20%. The tax is almost always included in quoted prices in shops, hotels, and restaurants. The most common exception is at high-end hotels, where prices often exclude V.A.T. Outside of hotels and rental-car agencies, which have specific additional taxes, there's no other sales tax in England.

Refunds apply for V.A.T. only on goods being taken out of Britain. Many large stores provide a V.A.T.–refund service, but only if you request it. You must ask the store to complete Form V.A.T. 407, to be given to customs at departure along with a V.A.T. Tax Free Shopping scheme invoice. Fill in the form at the shop, have the salesperson sign it, have it stamped by customs when you leave the country, then mail the stamped form to the shop or to a commercial refund company. Alternatively, you may be able to take the form to an airport refund-service counter after you're through passport control for an on-the-spot refund. There is an extra fee for this service, and lines tend to be long.

Global Blue is a Europe-wide service with 270,000 affiliated stores. It has refund counters in the U.K. at Heathrow and Gatwick, as well as on Oxford Street and in the Westfield Shopping Centre. Its refund form, called a Tax Free Check, is the most common across the European continent. The service issues refunds in the form of cash, check, or credit-card adjustment. The latter is useful for small purchases as the cost of cashing a foreign-currency check may exceed the amount of the refund.

V.A.T. Refunds Global Blue. *866/706–6090 in U.S., 800/3211–1111 in U.K. www.globalblue.com.* **HM Revenue and Customs.** *0292/501261 from U.S., 0300/200–3700 from U.K. www.gov.uk/tax-on-shopping.*

TIME

England sets its clocks by Greenwich Mean Time, five hours ahead of the U.S. East Coast. British summer time (GMT plus one hour) generally coincides with American daylight saving time adjustments.

Time Zones Timeanddate.com. *www.timeanddate.com.*

TIPPING

Tipping is done in Britain just as in the United States, but at a lower level than you would back home, generally 12.5% to 15%. Tipping more can look like you're showing off. Don't tip bar staff in pubs—although you can always offer to buy them a drink. There's no need to tip at clubs (it's acceptable at posher establishments, though) unless you're being served at your table. Rounding up to the nearest pound or 50p is appreciated.

TIPPING GUIDELINES FOR ENGLAND	
Bartender	£1–£2 per round of drinks, depending on the number of drinks, except in pubs, where tipping isn't the custom
Bellhop	£1 per bag, depending on the level of the hotel
Hotel Concierge	£5 or more, if he or she performs a service for you
Hotel Doorman	£1 if he helps you get a cab
Hotel Maid/ Housekeeping	£1 or £2 per day
Hotel Room-Service Waiter	Same as a waiter, unless a service charge has been added to the bill
Porter at Airport or Train Station	£1 per bag
Skycap at Airport	£1 per bag checked
Taxi Driver	10p per pound of the fare, then round up to nearest pound
Tour Guide	Tipping optional: £1 or £2 is generous
Waiter	12.5%–15%, with 15% being the norm at high-end London restaurants; nothing additional if a service charge is added to the bill, unless you want to reward particularly good service. Tips in cash preferred
Other	Restroom attendants in more expensive restaurants expect some small change or £1. Tip coat-check personnel £1 unless there's a fee, then nothing. Hairdressers and barbers get 10%–15%

TOURS

Visiting London on a fully escorted tour is unnecessary because of its extensive public transport and wide network of taxicabs. Many tour companies offer day tours to the main sights, and getting around is fairly easy.

FODORS.COM CONNECTION

Before your trip, be sure to check out what other travelers are saying in Talk on *www.fodors.com.*

If you're traveling beyond London, packaged tours can be very useful, particularly if you don't want to rent a car. Because many sights are off the beaten track and not accessible by public transportation—particularly castles, great houses, and small villages—tour groups make the country accessible to all. There are a few downsides to escorted tours: rooms in castles and medieval houses tend to be small and can feel overrun when tour groups roll in. And as on a cruise, your traveling companions are inescapable.

Dozens of companies offer fully guided tours in Britain. Most of these are full packages including lodging, food, and transportation costs in one flat fee. Do a bit of research before booking. You'll want to know about the hotels you'll be staying in, how big your group is likely to be, how your days will be structured, and who the other people are likely to be.

SPECIAL-INTEREST TOURS

CULINARY

Contact Gourmet on Tour. *646/461–6088 in U.S., 0207/558–8796 in U.K. www.gourmetontour.com.*

GARDENS

Contacts Adderley Travel Ltd. *01953/606706 www.adderleytravel.com.* **Coopersmith's.** *415/669–1914 in U.S. www.coopersmiths.com.* **Flora Garden Tours.** *01366/328946 www.flora-garden-tours.co.uk.* **Lynott Tours.** *800/221–2474 in U.S. www.lynotttours.com.*

HIKING AND WALKING

Contacts Adventureline. *01209/820847 www.adventureline.co.uk.* **CW Adventures.** *800/234–6900 in U.S. www.cwadventures.com.* **English Lakeland Ramblers.** *800/724–8801 in U.S. www.ramblers.com.*

The Wayfarers. ☎ *800/249–4620 in U.S.* 🌐 *www.thewayfarers.com.*

HISTORY

Contacts **Classic England.** ☎ *01277/841651 in U.K., 866/464–7389 toll-free in U.S.* 🌐 *www.classic-england.com.*

VISITOR INFORMATION

ONLINE TRAVEL TOOLS

ALL ABOUT ENGLAND

All of England's regions, along with most major towns and cities, have their own dedicated tourism websites providing information. VisitBritain (🌐 *www.visitbritain.com*), the official visitor website, focuses on information most helpful to England-bound U.S. travelers, from practical information to money-saving deals; you can even find out about movie locations. The London visitor website (🌐 *www.visitlondon.com*) can help you book your accommodations.

GARDENS

The National Gardens Scheme opens exceptional gardens attached to private houses and private garden squares to the public on selected weekends.

Contact **National Gardens Scheme.** ☎ *01483/211535* 🌐 *www.ngs.org.uk.*

HISTORIC SITES

The British monarchy has an official website with information about visiting royal homes and more. English Heritage, the National Trust, and VisitBritain all offer discount passes.

Contacts **The British Monarchy.** ☎ *0207/930–4832* 🌐 *www.royal.gov.uk.* **English Heritage.** ☎ *0870/333–1181* 🌐 *www.english-heritage.org.uk.* **National Trust.** ☎ *0844/800–1895* 🌐 *www.nationaltrust.org.uk.*

MUSEUMS AND THE ARTS

The London Theatre Guide, created by the Society of London Theatre, presents what's on and sells tickets. Their half-price ticket booths, tkts, located in London's Leicester Square and Brent Cross Shopping Centre, offer same-day bargains. Culture 24 is a nonprofit site with information about publicly funded museums, art galleries, and historic sights. Theatre Tokens sells gift vouchers for theater tickets.

Contacts **Culture 24.** ☎ *01273/623266* 🌐 *www.culture24.org.uk.* **London Theatre Guide.** ☎ *0207/557–6700* 🌐 *www.officiallondontheatre.co.uk.* **Theatre Tokens.** ☎ *0203/011–0755* 🌐 *www.theatretokens.com.* **tkts.** ☎ *0207/557–6700* 🌐 *www.tkts.co.uk.*

VISITOR INFORMATION OFFICES

In some towns there are local and regional tourist information centers; many have websites. Offices offer services from discounts for local attractions to visitor guides, maps, parking information, and accommodation advice.

London Travel Information Centres. Eight visitor information centers in London can be found at travel hubs like King's Cross-St. Pancras International, Victoria station, Euston, Heathrow, Liverpool Street station, and Piccadilly Circus, plus Greenwich and the City of London. They offer guides, advice, and tickets for tours and attractions, as well as Oyster cards and other public transportation passes. ✉ *London* ☎ *0207/234–5800* 🌐 *www.visitlondon.com.*

In the U.S. **VisitBritain.** ☎ *212/850–0336 in U.S.* 🌐 *www.visitbritain.com.*

INDEX

C

D

E

I

J

K

L

M

S

T

Z

PHOTO CREDITS

Front cover: Funkystock/age fotostock [Description: Blenheim Palace Italian Garden, Oxfordshire, England]. 1, Adam Woolfitt/age fotostock. 2, Joe Cornish/Britain on View/photolibrary.com 5, Martin Pettitt/Flickr, [CC BY 2.0]. Chapter 1: Experience England: 10-11, Heeb Christian/age fotostock. 12, David Peta/Shutterstock. 13, Jim Champion/Flickr, [CC BY-SA 2.0]. 14, Monkey Business Images/Shutterstock. 15 (left), ChrisAngove/Wikimedia Commons. 15 (right), redlentil/Wikimedia Commons. 16, Gail Johnson/Shutterstock. 17 (left), Gail Johnson/Shutterstock. 17 (right), Stewart Smith Photography/Shutterstock. 20 (left), StraH/Shutterstock. 20 (top center), Davidmartyn | Dreamstime.com. 20 (bottom center), Matthew Jacques/Shutterstock. 20 (bottom right), Pecold/Shutterstock. 20 (top right), Khrizmo | Dreamstime.com. 21 (left), Bill Gats/Wikimedia Commons. 21 (top center), Adrian Zenz/Shutterstock. 21 (bottom center), Ian Woolcock/Shutterstock. 21 (top right), David Hughes/Shutterstock. 21 (bottom right), Kevin Eaves/Shutterstock. 22, Crystian Cruz/Flickr, [CC BY-SA 2.0]. 23, Nikki Bidgood/Hemera/Thinkstock. 24, David Hughes/Shutterstock. 25 (left), William Warby/Flickr, [CC BY 2.0]. 25 (right), thinboyfatter/Flickr, [CC BY 2.0]. 26, Firmdale Hotels. 27 (left) Caitlin/Flickr, [CC BY 2.0]. 27 (right), Kevin Eaves/Shutterstock. 28, Leon Brocard/Flickr, [CC BY 2.0]. 29 (left), Simon Doggett/Flickr, [CC BY 2.0]. 29 (right), Elzbieta Sekowska/Shutterstock. 30, Roberto Arias/Flickr, [CC BY 2.0]. 32, David Woods/Shutterstock. 33 (left), JCElv/Shutterstock. 33 (right), Debu55y/Shutterstock. 34, Herbert Ortner/Wikimedia Commons. 36, Peekaboopink/Wikimedia Commons. Chapter 2: London: 37, Doug Pearson/age fotostock. 38, Angelina Dimitrova/Shutterstock. 39, Christopher Steer/iStockphoto. 40, Tan, Kim Pin/Shutterstock. 45, ktylerconk/Flickr. 52, Britain on View/photolibrary.com. 63, Jarno Gonzalez Zarraonandia/Shutterstock. 71, iStockphoto. 73 (left), Walter Bibikow/viestiphoto.com. 73 (right), Tom Hanley/Alamy. 74, News Team International Ltd. 75, Peter Phipp/age fotostock. 76 (left), Mary Evans Picture Library/Alamy. 76 (center), Reflex Picture Library/Alamy. 76 (right), Classic Image/Alamy. 77, Jan Kranendonk/iStockphoto. 87, Londonstills.com/Alamy. 96, Danilo Donadoni/Marka/age fotostock. 146, Bettina Strenske/age fotostock. 154, Britain on View/photolibrary.com. 159, Jess Moss. Chapter 3: The Southeast: 165, Daiviet | Dreamstime.com. 166, Harvey Barrison/Flickr, [CC BY-SA 2.0]. 167 (top), Jake Keup/Wikimedia Commons. 168, Adam Burt/Flickr, [CC BY-SA 2.0]. 169 (bottom), David Ooms/Flickr, [CC BY 2.0] 169 (top), shtukicrew/Shutterstock. 170, Alan Smithers/iStockphoto. 177, Hans Musil/Wikimedia Commons. 184, David Sellman/Britain on View/photolibrary.com. 194, Dave Porter/Britain on View/photolibrary.com. 200, Britain on View/photolibrary.com. 220, SuzanneKn/Wikimedia Commons. 221 (top), C Zaduck/Wikimedia Commons. 221 (bottom), Charlesdrakew/Wikimedia Commons. 222, 6mat1/Wikimedia Commons. 223, Chris Parfitt/Flickr, [CC BY 2.0]. 224, David Strydom/iStockphoto/Thinkstock. Chapter 4: The South: 229, Guy Edwardes/Britain on View/photolibrary.com. 230, Joe Gough/Shutterstock. 231, Sweet/Shutterstock. 232, Kevin Walsh/Flickr, [CC BY 2.0]. 233 (top), csp/Shutterstock. 233 (bottom), David Hughes/Shutterstock. 234, Britain on View/photolibrary.com. 241, Lukyslukys | Dreamstime.com. 250, Rod Edwards/Britain on View/photolibrary.com. 261, Graham Taylor/Shutterstock. 262, H & D Zielske/age fotostock. 268, David Nunuk/age fotostock. 269, DEA PUBBLI AER FOTO/age fotostock. 271 (left), Auz/Flickr, [CC BY-SA 2.0]. 271 (right), tpholland/Flickr, [CC BY 2.0]. 272, Martin Beddall/Alamy. 273, Blueskyimages Ltd/Britain On View/photolibrary.com. 274, Martin Brent/Britain On View/photolibrary.com. 287, Guy Edwardes/Britain on View/photolibrary.com. 294, Adam Burton/Britain on View/photolibrary.com. Chapter 5: The West Country: 297, Lee Pengelly/Silverscene Photography/Britain on View/photolibrary.com. 298, Kay-Uwe Gätz/Flickr, [CC BY-SA 2.0]. 299 (top), Tim Lewy/Wikimedia Commons. 299 (bottom), Caro11ne/Flickr, [CC BY-SA 2.0]. 300, Kevin O'Hara/age fotostock. 301 (top), Hicki/Shutterstock. 301 (bottom), Rachelle Burnside/Shutterstock. 302, Ant Clausen/Shutterstock. 313, Guy Edwardes/Britain on View/photolibrary.com. 316, Craig Joiner/age fotostock. 318, Toby Adamson/age fotostock. 322, David Jerome Ball/age fotostock. 327, Hicki/Shutterstock. 337, Markus Keller/age fotostock. 345, WJournalist/Wikimedia Commons. 349, Britain on View/photolibrary.com. 355, National Trust Photo Library/Britain on View/photolibrary.com. Chapter 6: The Thames Valley: 369, Adam Woolfitt/age fotostock. 370, Andrew Rivett/Flickr, [CC BY 2.0]. 371 (top), Cody/Flickr, [CC BY 2.0]. 371 (bottom), Skoll World Forum/Flickr, [CC BY 2.0]. 372, Jevgenija Pigozne/age fotostock. 373 (top), Carlton Browne/Flickr, [CC BY 2.0]. 373 (bottom), Dan Taylor/Flickr, [CC BY 2.0]. 374, Jun/Flickr, [CC BY-SA 2.0]. 382, Travel Pix Collection/age fotostock. 385, Neil Tingle/age fotostock. 389, Howard Sayer/Britain on View/photolibrary.com. 401 (top), Michael Kemp/Alamy. 401 (bottom), Fuller, Smith & Turner. 402 (left), Britain On View/photolibrary.com. 403, Phil Whitehouse/Flickr, [CC BY 2.0]. 404 (top left), Simon Frost/Flickr, [CC BY 2.0]. 404 (bottom left), Fuller, Smith & Turner. 404 (top right), Wapster/Flickr, [CC BY 2.0]. 404 (center), Fuller, Smith & Turner. 404 (bottom right), Zach Heller/Flickr, [CC BY 2.0]. 405 (left), Kelly Cline/iStockphoto. 405 (right), Elzbieta Sekowska/Shutterstock. 409, Fotoseach RM/age fotostock. Chapter 7: Bath and the Cotswolds: 417, Atlantide SNC/age fotostock. 418, Patricia Hofmeester/Shutterstock. 419 (top), profernity/Flickr, [CC BY 2.0]. 419 (bottom), VashiDonsk/Wikimedia Commons. 420, David Hughes/age fotostock. 421 (top), Jo Ann Snover/Shutterstock. 421 (bottom), Ballista/Wikimedia Commons. 422, Britain on View/photolibrary.com. 428, André Viegas/Shutterstock. 440, Adam Burton/age fotostock. 446, Britain on View/photolibrary.com. 450, H & D Zielske/age fotostock. 454-455, Arcaid Images/Alamy. 456 (top left), Martin Pettitt. 456 (top right), Britain On View/photolibrary.com. 456 (center), LOOK Die Bildagentur der Fotografen GmbH/Alamy. 456 (bottom), Andreas Tille/Wikimedia Commons. 457, John Glover/age fotostock. 458, National Trust Photo Library/Britain On View/photolibrary.com. 459 (top), North Light Images/age fotostock. 459 (bottom), David Sellman/Britain On View/photolibrary.com. 460, Paul Felix/Britain On View/photolibrary.com. 461 (left), Targeman/Wikimedia Commons. 461 (right), Wendy Cutler/Flickr, [CC BY 2.0]. 462, Peter Packer/Britain On View/photolibrary.com. 473, Andy Williams/age fotostock. 478, Simon Tranter/age fotostock. Chapter 8: Stratford-Upon-Avon and the Heart of England: 481, John Martin/Alamy. 483 (top) David Benton/Shutterstock. 483 (bottom), Allan Harris/Flickr, [CC BY-SA 2.0]. 484, Simon Reddy/Alamy. 485 (top), Monkey Business Images/Shutterstock. 485 (bottom), Foodpics/Shutterstock. 486, Ironbridge Gorge Museum Trust. 490, Cotswolds Photo Library/Britain on View/photolibrary.com. 497, Travel Pix Collection/age fotostock. 506, Britain on View/photolibrary.com. 520, kodachrome25/iStockphoto. 528, Ironbridge Gorge Museum Trust. 534, Nadia/Flickr, [CC BY-SA 2.0]. Chapter 9: Manchester, Liverpool, and the Peak District: 537, James Osmond/Britain on View/photolibrary.com. 539 (top), Paul Collins/Wikimedia Commons. 539 (bottom), Sue Hasker/Flickr, [CC BY-SA 2.0]. 540, Land of Lost Content/age fotostock. 541 (top), Havaska/Wikimedia Commons. 541 (bottom), Jennifer Boyer/Flickr, [CC BY 2.0]. 542, Maisant Ludovic/age fotostock. 547, Pawel Libera/Britain on View/photolibrary.com. 556, Chris Brink/age fotostock. 564, Britain on View/photolibrary.com. 578, Alan Novelli/Britain on View/photolibrary.com. Chapter 10: The Lake District: 585, Rob Carter/Alamy. 586, Kevin Eaves/Shutterstock. 587 (top), Kevin Eaves/Shutterstock. 587 (bottom), Alan Cleaver/Flickr, [CC BY 2.0]. 588, Douglas Freer/Shutterstock. 589 (top), sarsmis/Shutterstock. 589 (bottom), Monkey Business Images/Shutterstock. 590, Alex Southward/Flickr, [CC BY-SA 2.0]. 595, Val Corbett. 599, Simon Balson/Alamy. 606, Val Corbett/Britain on View/photolibrary.com. 612, Alan Novelli/Britain On View/photolibrary.com. 613, Roy Shakespeare/age fotostock. 614, Stewart Smith Photography/Shutterstock. 615 (top left), Julius Honnor. 615 (top right), Stewart Smith Photography/Shutterstock. 615 (bottom), Julius Honnor. 616, Britain on View/photolibrary.com. 617 (left), Larra Jungle Princess/Flickr, [CC BY-SA 2.0]. 617 (right), Mike D Williams/Shutterstock. 621, National Trust Photo Library/Britain on View/photolibrary.com. 629, Ashley Cooper/age fotostock. 632, D & S Tollerton/age fotostock. Chapter 11: East Anglia: 637, Alistair Laming/age fotostock. 638, Burghley House Preservation Trust. 639 (top), Binns Motor Inn/Flickr, [CC BY 2.0]. 639 (bottom), Jared and Corin/Flickr, [CC BY-SA 2.0]. 640, Shane W Thompson/Shutterstock. 641 (top), Monkey Business Images/Shutterstock. 641 (bottom), Roddy Paine/age fotostock. 642, Kelbv/Flickr, [CC BY 2.0]. 647, Quentin Bargate/age fotostock. 650, Mark Sunderland/age fotostock. 664, Vidler/age fotostock. 671, Duncan Soar/Alamy. 672 (left), Matthew Collingwood/Shutterstock. 672 (top center), JustAnotherGuyInCardiff/Flickr, [CC BY-SA 2.0]. 672 (bottom), Portable Antiquities Scheme/Flickr, [CC BY 2.0]. 672 (right), public domain. 673 (left), Jan Kranendonk/iStockphoto. 673 (top right), Public Domain. 673 (bottom center), Marie-Lan Nguyen/Wikimedia Commons. 673 (bottom right), Public Domain. 674 (top left), Rachelle Burnside/Shutterstock. 674 (bottom left, bottom center, top right, and bottom right), Public Domain. 675 (top left), Art Renewal Center. 675 (bottom left), SuperStock/age fotostock. 675 (bottom center and top right), Public domain. 675 (bottom right), jeff gynane/iStockphoto. 676 (top left), Public domain. 676 (bottom left), The Print Collector/age fotostock. 676 (center), The National Archives/age fotostock. 676 (right), NinaZed/Flickr, [CC BY 2.0]. 677 (top left), Zaha Hadid/2012 Olympics. 677 (bottom left), Library of Congress Prints and Photographs division. 677 (top right), United Press International (UPI Telephoto)/LOC. 677 (bottom right), Trinity Mirror/Mirrorpix/Alamy. 692, Burghley House Preservation Trust. Chapter 12: Yorkshire: 695, Jason Friend/age fotostock. 696, subberculture/Flickr, [CC BY-SA 2.0]. 697 (top), Kevin Eaves/Shutterstock. 697 (bottom), Matthew Hillier/Flickr, [CC BY 2.0]. 698, Britain on View/photolibrary.com. 699 (top), Haydn Blackey/Flickr, [CC BY-SA 2.0]. 699 (bottom), adora/Flickr, [CC BY-SA 2.0]. 700, Allan Harris. 707, Peter Baker/age fotostock. 710, Charlie Edward/Shutterstock. 711 (left), David Joyce/Flickr, [CC BY-SA 2.0]. 711 (top right), Lee Beel/Britain On View/photolibrary.com. 711 (bottom right), Convit/Shutterstock. 712 (left), Derek Croucher/Britain On View/photolibrary.com. 712 (center), Mattana/Wikimedia Commons. 712, (right), Joevare/Flickr, [CC BY-SA 2.0]. 713 (left), Charlie Edward/Shutterstock. 713 (right), Lee Beel/Britain On View/photolibrary.com. 714 (top), Martin Brent/Britain On View/photolibrary.com. 714 (bottom), Richard Croft/Wikimedia Commons. 718, Britain on View/photolibrary.com. 723, Richard Watson/Britain on View/

photolibrary.com. 726, Xavier Subias/age fotostock. 734, Wojtek Buss/age fotostock. 737, Dave Porter/Britain on View/photolibrary.com. 746, Robert Westwood/Britain on View/photolibrary.com. 748, Alan Copson/age fotostock. 751, Kevin Eaves/Shutterstock. 752, SuperStock/age fotostock. Chapter 13: The Northeast: 757, Lee Frost/age fotostock. 758, Dave Ellis/Flickr, [CC BY 2.0]. 759 (top), Gordon Cable/Shutterstock. 760, Ian McDonald/Shutterstock. 761 (top), Michel wal/Wikimedia Commons. 761 (bottom), Mark A. Wilson (Department of Geology, The College of Wooster)/Wikimedia Commons. 762, David Wilson Clarke/Wikimedia Commons. 766, Rod Edwards/Britain on View/photolibrary.com. 776, Alan Dawson/age fotostock. 783, Jerry Harpur/age fotostock. 787, Andrew Michael/age fotostock. Chapter 14: Wales: 791, FLPAWayne Hutchinson/age fotostock. 792, Marina Kryukova/Shutterstock. 793 (top), Gail Johnson/Shutterstock. 793 (bottom), Allan Harris/Flickr, [CC BY-SA 2.0]. 794, Britain on View/photolibrary.com. 795 (top), eldo/Shutterstock. 795 (bottom), Lukáš Hejtman/Shutterstock. 796, Colin Hutchings/Shutterstock. 801, Peter Thompson/age fotostock. 812, David Hughes/Shutterstock. 817, Bernd Tschakert/age fotostock. 826, Michael Hilgert/age fotostock. 833, Britain on View/photolibrary.com. 840, Sebastian Wasek/age fotostock. 846, Gail Johnson/Shutterstock. Back cover, from left to right: Nikada/iStockphoto; James D. Hay/Shutterstock; witchcraft/Shutterstock. Spine: Pecold/Shutterstock. About Our Writers: All photos are courtesy of the writers except for the following: Julius Honnor, courtesy of Clair Honnor; Kate Hughes, courtesy of Ellen Hughes.

NOTES

NOTES